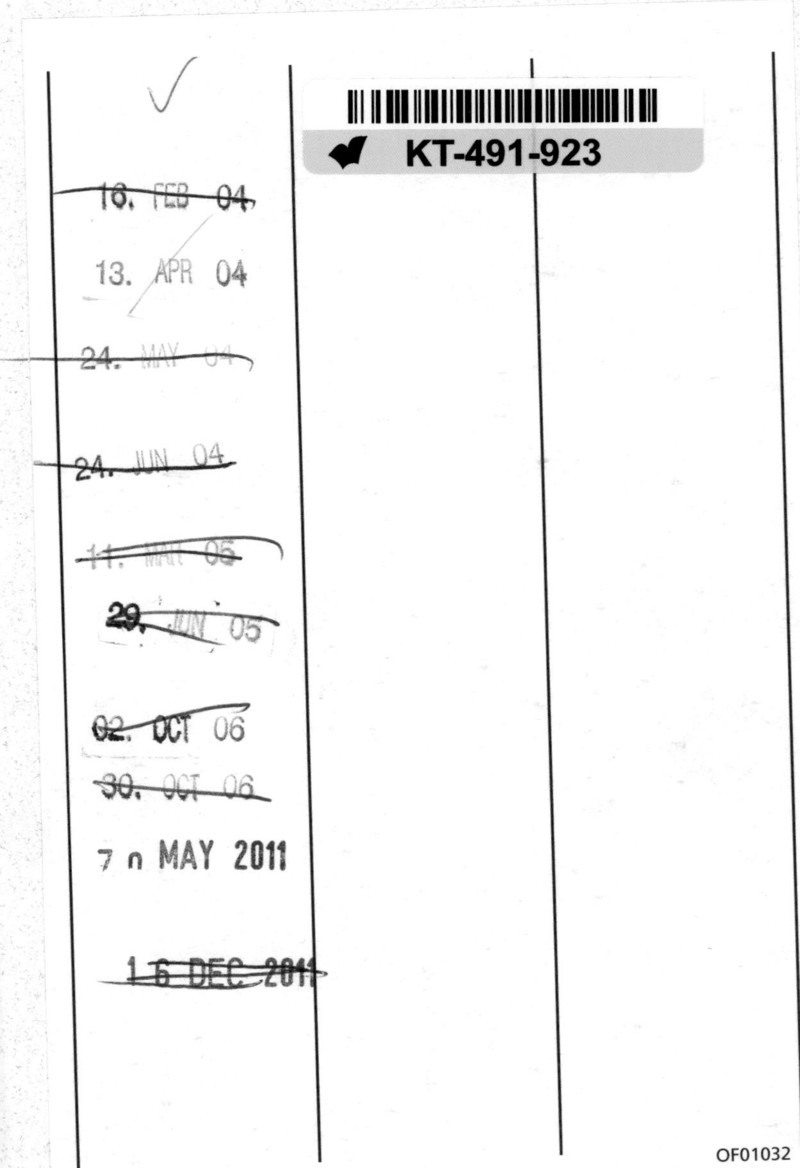

social psychology

TENTH EDITION

ROBERT A. BARON
Rensselaer Polytechnic Institute

DONN BYRNE
The University at Albany/State University of New York

Boston New York San Francisco
Mexico City Montreal Toronto London Madrid Munich Paris
Hong Kong Singapore Tokyo Cape Town Sydney

Executive Editor: Carolyn Merrill
Editorial Assistant: Jonathan Bender
Senior Marketing Manager: Wendy Gordon
Editorial-Production Administrator: Annette Joseph
Editorial-Production Service: Colophon
Text Designer: Seventeenth Street Studios
Photo Researcher: Helane Prottas
Electronic Composition: Omegatype Typography, Inc.
Composition and Prepress Buyer: Linda Cox
Manufacturing Buyer: Megan Cochran
Cover Administrator: Linda Knowles
Cover Designer: Susan Paradise

For related titles and support materials, visit our online catalog at *www.ablongman.com.*

Library of Congress Cataloging-in-Publication Data

Baron, Robert A.
Social psychology / Robert A. Baron, Donn Byrne.—10th ed.
p. cm.
Includes bibliographical references and index.
ISBN 0-205-34977-3 (alk. paper)
1. Social psychology. I. Byrne, Donn Erwin. II. Title.

HM1033.B35 2002
302—dc21

2002016459

Printed in the United States of America

10 9 8 7 6 5 4 3 2 1 VHP 07 06 05 04 03 02

Photo credits appear on page 671, which constitutes a continuation of the copyright page.

Dedication

To my daughter Jessica who is truly one of the lights of my life, and to her husband Ted, who has greatly enriched our small family by joining it! And to my parents, Ruth and Bernard, whose confidence in me has always been a major "plus" in my life.

—RAB

To Karen who taught me that love is lovelier with both feet on the ground.

—DB

Brief Contents

Contents

CLOSE RELATIONSHIPS:

9 SOCIAL INFLUENCE:

Special Features

Foreword

Social psychology has moved to the very central core of modern psychology from its once remote peripheral position, because it now illuminates the mind of individual functioning and enriches the soul of our society. Through rigorous laboratory and field research, social psychologists have demonstrated that to fully understand behavior it is necessary to recognize how context, content, and culture matter. We have demonstrated the power of situational variables in transforming behavior in ways not predictable from simply understanding what is "inside" the individual, such as inherited and learned dispositions. Those social situations are not the external stimulus variables of the radical behaviorists but shared construals of reality, subjective constructions that we create and pass along to others. At times people are less rational and more rationalizing than they believe they are, and human intuition is often quite fallible, as social psychological theorists and researchers have also shown. Unlike other domains of psychology that focus solely on the individual as the unit of analysis, social psychologists explore behavior in its social context, in patterns of interpersonal relationships and group dynamics. By searching for how people and situations interact to generate significant thoughts, feelings, and actions, social psychologists help weave the richest tapestry of human nature. But we go further in both stretching the boundaries of psychology—from brain processes to cultural mechanisms—as well as in translating the wisdom of our research into practical applications. Social psychologists virtually run Psychology's Store, the one that "gives psychology away to the public," for free and in ways ordinary people can best appreciate and use in their lives.

In celebrating the 30th anniversary of this remarkable text by Robert Baron and Donn Byrne, I, and my social psychological colleagues, congratulate them both for enriching our field through their original research and inspiring writing. Their collective body of research has informed us about some of the most basic aspects of interpersonal behavior—sex and aggression—why people are attracted to each other and why they hurt one another. They have made vital contributions to theory, as in Byrne's ideas on attachment theory and style, and to applying social psychology, as in Baron's field work on reducing conflict in organizations and building cooperation in work settings. They are also in the "export business" by bringing social psychological perspectives and methodology to other fields, notably Baron's bridge-building with the business domain of entrepreneurship. In these and other ways, Robert Baron and Donn Byrne typify what is best in social psychological research, its adventurous curiosity, its openness to new vistas, its asking big questions and answering with creative methods, and all the while with an eye toward making a difference in the "real world."

They have also made a major contribution to education by collaborating in the creation and systematic renewal of this successful text over the past three decades. I think the secret of their success is their ability to entertain readers while they educate them, to tell gripping stories with meaningful messages, and to constantly add new songs and dance steps to their inviting repertoire.

What comes through to student readers is the clear, personal voice of master teachers sharing their passion for this domain of knowledge. Baron and Byrne talk directly to their readers, never down to them or over their heads. Their personalities and unique styles are evident in the examples that abundantly extend principles and abstract concepts. Unlike some text authors whose audience-vision is other experts they want to impress, Baron and Byrne always have in perfect sight the target audience of young scholars embarking on a psychological journey.

Another ingredient to their success is the synergy between the authors' teaching and writing. Both are gifted teachers who are constantly learning from their class interactions, trying out examples, demonstrations, and new explanations that, if they work in class, find a home in their text. Similarly, the classroom provides a testing ground for sampling ideas and modes of story telling developed in early drafts of the text. It is the Yin and Yang of teacher–author who blend both tasks into a holistic way of being an educator and professional writer. And, because good teachers constantly reinvent their courses, these authors pursue perfection in their trade by constantly changing much in each new revision. Keep the best, jettison the rest, seems to be the motto as they sail on to ever new waters.

The greatest difficulty most text authors face with each revision is how to balance adding the stream of new information while presenting the basic foundation of their field which demands retaining the oldies but goodies classics. Baron and Byrne have become the class balancing act among all psychology textbook authors by seamlessly incorporating the best of the new with the tested and true of the past. Every edition has been distinguished by new features, such as Beyond the Headlines, that enable students to discover how social psychology helps understand current topics reported in the media. This new 10th edition features an overview of "Thirty Years of Progress" that promises to delight the authors' colleagues as much as their student readers.

So, bravo, Bob and Donn, for a masterful job so well done over all these years of making our field of social psychology so appetizing to the next generation of our students. May you continue to feed them with the abundance and elegance we have come to expect of your magical collaboration.

—Philip G. Zimbardo, Ph.D.
STANFORD UNIVERSITY

Preface

REFLECTIONS ON THE 10TH EDITION: OBSERVING—AND PARTICIPATING IN—THIRTY YEARS OF PROGRESS

Thirty years—that's a long, long time. But it is precisely how long we have been writing this book. When we began, in 1972, the world was a very different place. Nixon was president but "Watergate" was still an unknown word to most Americans. Personal computers were twelve years or so in the future, and cellular phones, CDs, and Palm Pilots—electronic marvels we now take for granted—existed largely in the realm of science fiction. Fashions, too, were very different: mini-skirts and "hot pants" were all the rage for women, while long sideburns, extra-wide ties, and widely flaring bell-bottoms were definitely "in" for men.

Social psychology, too, was very different. Some of the topics included in the table of contents for the first edition are still present in this, the 10th edition: topics such as aggression, attraction, and attitudes. But many other topics now central to social psychology were not included: for example, social cognition, the role of gender and cultural diversity, long-term relationships, and the self. Further, the methods used by social psychologists in their research have changed too, so that today, they are more sophisticated and effective than ever before.

One thing that has not changed, though, is our concept of what this book should be. When we began working on the first edition we felt very strongly that it should reflect modern social psychology as it exists today. We have never altered this belief, so over the years, and through succeeding editions, this book has also changed to keep pace with the rapid progress of our field. Very few books survive into a tenth edition, and fewer still remain popular through this long period. Yet, we are proud to say that this text has remained the most widely read throughout these years. In fact, it has been used by almost 2 million students to date.

We attribute this longevity to three major factors. First, we do indeed make strong efforts to keep up, to reflect the latest findings and theories in social psychology. Second, we *listen to our colleagues.* When they send us their comments about an existing edition and make recommendations for improving it, we pay careful attention and often make the changes they suggest. Third, and equally important, we are not simply observers and recorders of progress in social psychology—we have both continued to participate in it. True, the specific topics we study in our own research have changed. For instance, Robert Baron now investigates the causes and effects of workplace aggression rather than aggression generally, and he also focuses on identifying the cognitive and social factors that influence entrepreneurs' success. Donn Byrne is now concentrating on the effects of adult attachment patterns on interpersonal interactions rather than initial reactions to strangers and also he focuses on the factors determining coercive sexuality. But although the specific content of our research has changed, the research itself remains firmly tied to the mainstream of social psychology. This, in turn, helps us to understand the research of other social psychologists and assists us in reaching our primary goal: making this book a very broad, readable, and (we hope!) thought-provoking overview of social psychology as it exists today.

Changes Designed to Keep the 10th Edition Truly Fresh

So what have we done to make the new 10th edition fresh in content and a true reflection of recent developments in our field? Several things. First, as always, we have thoroughly updated each chapter. As a result, you will find literally hundreds of new references from 2000 and 2001 in its pages. Further, within chapters, we have included dozens of new topics to take account of emerging lines of research and important advances. Here are just a few of these new topics:

Chapter 1: Increased coverage of evolutionary psychology, including evolved psychological mechanisms.

Chapter 2: Using nonverbal cues to recognize deception; regulatory focus theory.

Chapter 3: The negativity bias; the bracing for loss phenomenon.

Chapter 4: Attitude ambivalence; dissonance as a source of negative affect.

Chapter 5: New findings on the sexual self-schema; new observational data about how parents talk differently to their sons and daughters about a "male" topic such as science.

Chapter 6: Implicit prejudice and stereotypes; hostile versus benevolent sexism.

Chapter 7: Increased coverage of the biological aspects of interpersonal attraction; new findings dealing with the attractiveness of composite faces.

Chapter 8: New evidence supporting the evolutionary underpinnings of the need to form relationships; data indicating that secure attachment is associated with relationship satisfaction.

Chapter 9: The persistence of social norms; extreme forms of social influence, including intense indoctrination.

Chapter 10: Information on the biological underpinnings of empathy; new conceptualization of the six basic functions served by volunteer work.

Chapter 11: Displaced aggression and trivial triggering provocations; bullying.

Chapter 12: The discontinuity effect; the status quo bias.

Chapter 13: Effects of verbal misconduct by prosecutors on juror decisions; the evolutionary basis of overeating; self-evaluations in job satisfaction; the role of the Big Five Dimensions of personality in leadership.

Second, to call attention to major advances in social psychology during the past three decades, we have included a new special feature entitled **Social Psychology: Thirty Years of Progress.** This feature compares research being conducted thirty years ago, when we were writing the first edition of this text, to modern research on the same or similar topics being conducted today. In this way, we can highlight the ways in which social psychological research has added to our understanding of important aspects of social behavior and social thought. Here is a list of these features:

Chapter 2: From Cognitive Algebra to Motivated Processing

Chapter 3: The Effects of Being in a Good Mood on Social Behavior and Social Cognition: From "The Warm Glow of Success" to the Effects of Mood on Heuristic Thinking

Chapter 4: Studying the Attitude–Behavior Link

SOCIAL PSYCHOLOGY: THIRTY YEARS OF PROGRESS

THE EFFECTS OF BEING IN A GOOD MOOD ON SOCIAL BEHAVIOR AND SOCIAL COGNITION: FROM "THE WARM GLOW OF SUCCESS" TO THE EFFECTS OF MOOD ON HEURISTIC THINKING

When research on the effects of our current moods began, the "cognitive revolution" had not yet occurred in social psychology. Social psychologists were certainly interested in social cognition, but they did not yet view it as central to all the topics they studied. For this reason, the earliest studies on the effects of affective states focused on their impact on social behavior rather than social thought. Among this work, the most influential was that conducted by Alice Isen. She was interested in a question that has intrigued social psychologists ever since: Does being in a good mood increase our willingness to help others? Isen reasoned that this would be the case because helping others is a positive behavior that "fits" with being in a good mood. Also, when we are in a good mood, we want to maintain it, and one way of doing that is by helping others: this boosts our self-image and makes us feel good about ourselves.

To see if being in a good mood actually did increase helping, Isen conducted several studies in which she used ingenious techniques to put people into a good mood. In the first (Isen, 1970), she told participants (school teachers) that they had done very well or very poorly on a series of tasks. Those told they had done very well would, she reasoned, experience "the warm glow of success," and would be in a better mood. The measure of helping was the amount of money participants donated to a fund to purchase air conditioning for a local school. Results indicated that those in a good mood did in fact donate more—an average of forty-six cents versus an average of only seven cents for those told they had done poorly on the tasks and who, presumably, were in a less happy mood.

In follow-up studies, Isen varied the participants' moods by such techniques as giving them cookies (Isen & Levin, 1972) and even placing a coin in a phone booth, so that people who entered found it there (Isen & Levin, 1972). No matter how she varied mood, Isen found the same result: Persons in a good mood were more helpful to others than were those not in a good mood. Subsequent research has verified this finding; for instance, even pleasant odors in a shopping mall increase the willingness of passersby to help a stranger (Baron, 1997a). However, additional research indicates that being in a good mood does not always increase helpfulness. If, for example, the costs of helping are high, or if helping might tend to spoil a person's good mood, persons in a good mood are *not* always more helpful (e.g., Isen, 1984).

Although research on the effects of mood on social behavior has continued (we'll describe it in Chapter 10), many social psychologists have focused, instead, on the question we have been discussing in this chapter: How do affective states influence social cognition? And here, growing evidence suggests that one effect of being in a good mood is that we tend to shift our social thought toward the use of heuristics—mental shortcuts that reduce effort. A clear illustration of such effects is provided by research conducted by Park and Banaji (2000).

On the basis of previous studies, Park and Banaji predicted that being in a good mood would lead individuals to rely more heavily on stereotypes, because these mental frameworks do indeed reduce mental effort, and when people are in a good mood, they do not want to do anything to disrupt it. Because careful, systematic thinking is hard work, people in a good mood tend to avoid such effort. To test this idea, these researchers asked participants to indicate whether various names—some African American and some European American in nature—belonged to the category "criminal" or to the category "politician." Half of the participants were placed in a good mood by watching a funny segment of a TV show and half were placed in a more neutral mood by viewing scenes of mountains, rivers, and so on. Park and Banaji (2000) predicted that being in a good mood would increase the use of stereotypes. Thus, participants in a good mood would show an enhanced tendency to place African American names in the "criminal" category and an increased tendency to place European American names in the "politician" category. This is precisely what happened: Persons in a good mood were indeed more likely to show this pattern than were persons in a neutral mood.

In follow-up studies, Park and Banaji (2000) found that this increased reliance on stereotyping by persons in a good mood stems from two sources: reduced sensitivity to names (lowered ability to distinguish between them; see Figure 3.15) and a lowered decision criterion for assigning names to a specific category (*i.e., criminal or politician*). Interestingly, being in a negative mood (as a result of watching a sad movie) did *not* produce such effects; if anything, it seemed to reduce reliance on stereotypes by raising the decision criterion

106 CHAPTER 3 / SOCIAL COGNITION

Chapter 5: *The Gender Revolution in Social Psychology*

Chapter 6: *Hard Economic Times and Violence against Minority Groups: From Lynchings in the South to Hate Crimes in New York*

Chapter 7: *Similarity, Dissimilarity, or Both?*

Chapter 8: *The Importance of Adult Attachment Style in Interpersonal Behavior*

Chapter 9: *The Persistence of Social Norms: From the Autokinetic Phenomenon to the "Culture of Honor"*

Chapter 10: *The Study of Prosocial Behavior Began with a Murder*

Chapter 11: *Studying Heat and Aggression: From the Laboratory to Police Records of Assaults*

Chapter 12: *From Drive to Attentional Focus: How Does the Presence of Others Influence Task Performance?*

Chapter 13: *Understanding the Dimensions—and Limits—of Leadership Style: From Autocratic and Democratic Leaders to Charisma*

BEYOND THE HEADLINES: AS SOCIAL PSYCHOLOGISTS SEE IT

WHEN A PHYSICAL ADDICTION AND DISSONANCE COLLIDE, GUESS WHICH WINS?

99 Percent Call Smoking Harmful: Poll Discovers Conflict Between Views and Usage

Washington (November 10, 2000)—Although the nation can't agree on who should be president, it appears to be united on the health risks of smoking: 99 percent of Americans say smoking is harmful, according to research released here Tuesday. Nevertheless, two in 10 Americans regularly light up according to the survey sponsored by Mississippi State University. . . . When asked about smoking Americans tend to say one thing and do the other, said Arthur Cosby, director of the University's Social Science Research Center.

Americans are quite conflicted about tobacco control and use, Cosby said. For example, they puff with one breath but acknowledge the danger with the next. Likewise, many adults say teenagers shouldn't smoke, even while lighting up in front of them. . . . The apparent contradiction between belief and behavior could be "a reflection of the power of addiction," Cosby said. Many smokers might not be able to quit even though they are "people who intelligently decide that tobacco-control notions are good things." About 9 of every 10 Americans said parents shouldn't allow underage children to smoke and 93 percent said stores that sell tobacco to minors should be punished . . .

Any poll that yields 99 percent agreement among the people responding to it deserves to be taken seriously, and this one appears to have been conducted quite carefully. The key finding—that virtually everyone agrees that smoking is harmful, yet many people continue to smoke—is definitely food for thought. Cognitive dissonance should be very strong among smokers; after all, if they believe that smoking is harmful to their health, how can they continue to engage in this behavior? This is akin to saying, "Oh well, so I'll do something that will destroy my health and possibly kill me . . . so what?"

As we noted above, smokers have many ways of reducing such dissonance—for instance, convincing themselves that only a few smokers get ill, that such effects occur only for very heavy smokers, or that if smoking doesn't get them, something else will! So this may well be part of the answer. Another possibility, though, is that the physical addiction of smoking is very powerful. Thus, if smokers try to quit their habit, the negative feelings they experience are far stronger than those produced by cognitive dissonance. I have a friend who quit smoking more than thirty years ago, yet, as he often tells me, he *still* craves a cigarette while drinking a cup of coffee after a meal. Experiences like this suggest that smoking is indeed a powerful addiction.

Yet despite this fact, some people (like my friend) do manage to quit. Perhaps for such persons the addiction is not as strong to begin with, or perhaps they are especially disturbed by the inconsistency between their attitudes and their behavior. Whatever the reason, it seems clear that the best technique for avoiding both an addiction to tobacco *and* the dissonance that can result from smoking while recognizing the harmful effects of this behavior is simple: Never start in the first place!

To eliminate this problem, Harmon-Jones (2000) conducted research in which participants wrote counterattitudinal statements under conditions in which expressing views contrary to their real ones could *not* produce aversive consequences. In fact, they were told to throw their statements away after writing them. The issue on which they wrote the essays, too, was fairly trivial: they were to

Cognitive Dissonance: Why Our Behavior Can Sometimes Influence Our Attitudes 147

What Remains the Same?

While we have made many changes, our basic approach to writing the book remains the same: we have tried very hard to produce a text that accurately reflects the nature and content of modern social psychology but at the same time is highly readable and useful for students. To attain this goal, we have retained several special features of previous editions:

- **Beyond the Headlines,** which appears in every chapter, takes an actual newspaper headline and examines it from the perspective of social psychology. This feature illustrates how social psychologists think and how the principles of our field can be applied to virtually any aspect of human social behavior. While the idea behind this feature remains much the same, the content is all *new* to this edition.

- **Ideas to Take with You—And Use!** appears at the end of each chapter and is designed to highlight important concepts you should remember—and use—long after this course is over. In our view, you will definitely find these principles helpful in many contexts in the years ahead.

IDEAS TO TAKE WITH YOU—AND USE!

IMPROVING THE NEGATIVE SELF-PERCEPTIONS OF WOMEN

A consistent and pervasive difference between men and women—especially in Western societies—involves the way they perceive and evaluate their appearance. Beginning in adolescence, women are much more concerned about body image than are men. What could be done to decrease such concern?

Be Realistic about the Meaningfulness of Appearance.

"Be realistic" is obviously easier to say than to do. Nevertheless, as you will discover in Chapter 7, the adage that "you can't judge a book by its cover" is true. The most attractive individuals in the world do not differ from the rest of us in intelligence, creativity, character, kindness, or anything else that matters—except in the fact that they are liked on the basis of their looks. Think of the most unkind, dishonest, and totally detestable human being you know. Would you find that person more acceptable if he or she suddenly acquired a stunningly attractive face and body? And, if you meet an attractive person for the first time, try to remember that appearance gives you no information at all about this individual.

Eleanor Roosevelt

Ask Yourself How Important Your Weight Is to Others.

Women in the United States and other Western nations are often obsessed with their weight. Most men are not nearly as weight-conscious as women with respect to themselves or with respect to the opposite sex. Most people won't even notice if you gain a few pounds or lose a few. And very few people of either sex are really that concerned about how many pounds you weigh.

Rest Assured That Men Are Not That Aware of Every Detail of a Woman's Appearance.

Humorist Dave Barry (1998) said it very well: "Men don't even notice 97 percent of the beauty efforts you make anyway. Take fingernails. The average women spends 5,000 hours per year worrying about her fingernails; I have never once, in more than 40 years of listening to men talk about women, heard a man say, 'She has a nice set of fingernails!' Many men would not notice if a woman had upward of four hands." To the extent that some men believe that appearance is the only meaningful characteristic to consider with respect to women, it might be helpful to read Chapter 7, including the opening story.

Select an Appropriate Group for Social Comparison.

When you look through magazines showing page after page of ultrathin models and movie stars, you can easily assume that because you don't measure up to these unrealistic standards, you must be inadequate. You're not. For whatever reason, most men do not feel depressed that they are not as tall as the average NBA star, don't run as

(continued)

Ideas to Take with You—And Use! 203

- **Special Icons in the Margin to mark sections of the text dealing with Diversity and the Evolutionary Perspective.** Interest in these topics is strong in social psychology, so we want to call discussions of them to your attention.

- **Other Features Designed to Make the Book More Useful:** Each chapter begins with an outline that provides you with a "road map" that points out the major sections within the chapter. Within the text itself, key terms are printed in dark type like **this** and are followed by a definition. These key terms are also defined in a running glossary in the margins, as well as in a glossary at the end of the book. To help you understand what you have read, each major section is followed by a list of Key Points, a brief summary of major concepts and findings. We believe that reviewing this section carefully will be an important aid to your studying.

All figures and tables are designed to be clear and simple, and most contain special labels and notes the purpose of which is to help you understand their meaning.

Supplementary Materials

All good texts should be supported by a complete package of supplementary material, both for the students and for the instructor. This book provides ample aid for both.

■ FOR THE INSTRUCTOR:

Instructor's Resource Manual (IRM)

George E. Schreer of Manhattanville College has once again crafted a rich collection of material that will aid any instructor, seasoned or new, in creating a vibrant classroom experience. Each chapter begins with a valuable grid correlating the text to every print and media supplement available. In addition, the Instructor's Resource Manual contains a wealth of activities, handouts, and numerous teaching aids.

Test Bank and Computerized Test Bank

Eric Miller of Kent State University–East Liverpool Campus has developed a lengthy Test Bank, which is also available on a dual platform CD-ROM. Many of the items have been classroom tested. More than 1,500 multiple-choice questions are available on the Test Bank, in addition to numerous true/false, short-answer, and longer essay questions.

Transparency Package

Over 70 full-color transparencies taken from the text are available from your Allyn & Bacon sales representative upon adoption of the book.

Video

A custom videotape, featuring interviews with leaders in the field, is available upon adoption of the text.

PowerPoint Presentation

Created by the author of the Instructor's Resource Manual, this dynamic presentation includes highlights and figures from the text. As a bonus, an electronic copy of the Instructor's Resource Manual has been added to the CD-ROM (for Windows users only). It is available free to adopters of the book.

CourseCompass

Allyn & Bacon's Course Management Systems combine premium online content with enhanced class management tools such as quizzing and grading, syllabus building, and results reporting. To learn more, visit www.abinteractive.com.

■ FOR THE STUDENT:

GradeAid Study Manual

This pedagogically advanced study guide asks students to create a valuable review manual as they read. Each chapter features brief exercises, the answers to which can be found directly in the text and should be filled in as the student is absorbing the material. Several practice tests accompany each chapter; to prepare for them, the student must simply review the exercises they have completed. Written by Test Bank author Eric Miller, this guide aids students in synthesizing the material they are learning, in addition to helping them prepare for their exams.

Companion Website

A Companion Website was designed to accompany this 10th edition. Available on this free site is an online study guide which includes learning objectives, summaries, and web links. Interactive activities and multiple-choice questions help students test their mastery of each chapter's content. Visit www.ablongman.com/baronbyrne for a preview.

Some Concluding Comments

In closing, we would like to ask, once again, for your help. As was true of past editions, we have spared no effort to make this new one the best ever. While human beings can imagine perfection, however, they always fall far short of it. So, we realize that there is always room for improvement. In this respect, we sincerely request your input. If there is something you feel can be improved, please let us know. Write, call, fax, or e-mail us at the addresses below. We will be genuinely glad to receive your input and—even more important—we will definitely listen! Thanks in advance for your help.

Robert A. Baron
Pittsburgh Building
Rensselaer Polytechnic Institute
Troy, NY 12180–3590
Phone: (518) 276–2864
Fax: (518) 276–8661
E-mail: *baronr@rpi.edu*

Donn Byrne
Department of Psychology
University at Albany, SUNY
Albany, NY 12222
Phone: (518) 768–2643
Fax: (518) 442–4867
E-mail: *vyaduckdb@aol.com*

Acknowledgments

WORDS OF THANKS

Each time we write this book, we gain a stronger appreciation of the following fact: we couldn't do it without the help of many talented, dedicated people. While we can't possibly thank all of them here, we do wish to express our appreciation to those whose help has been most valuable.

First, our sincere thanks to the colleagues listed below who responded to our survey regarding how the 10th edition could be improved. Their input was invaluable to us in planning this new edition.

Charles A. Alexander, *Rock Valley College*
Linda J. Allred, *East Carolina University*
Lisa M. Bohon-Hock, *California State University, Sacramento*
Robert F. Bornstein, *Gettysburg College*
David M. Bush, *Utah State University*
Winona Cochran, *Bloomsburg University*
Diana I. Cordova, *Yale University*
Curt Dunkel, *Illinois Central College*
Edward Fernandez, *East Carolina University*
Susan E. O. Field, *Georgian Court College*
Lisa Finkelstein, *Northern Illinois University*
Phillip Finney, *Southeast Missouri State University*
Stella D. Garcia-Lopez, *University of Texas at San Antonio*
Barry Gillen, *Old Dominion University*
Drusilla D. Glascoe, *Salt Lake Community College*
Nicole Goulet, *University of Albany, SUNY*
Lana Hamilton, *Kent State University*
Jay Hewitt, *University of Missouri at Kansas City*
Matthew Hogben, *Centers for Disease Control and Prevention*
Tony Johnson, *LaGrange College*
Paul Kwon, *Washington State University*
Jeffrey Scott Mio, *California Polytechnic Institute at Pomona*
Mitchell S. Nesler, *Excelsior College*
Darren Newtson, *University of Virginia*
Virginia Norris, *South Dakota State University*
Robert J. Pellegrini, *San Jose State University*
Jacqueline Pope, *Western Kentucky University*
Brad Redburn, *Johnson County Community College*
Debra Steele-Johnson, *Wright State University*
Michael Strube, *Washington University*
Ann L. Weber, *University of North Carolina at Asheville*

We also wish to thank the reviewers who read chapters of the 9th edition and provided helpful comments to aid in our work on the 10th edition.

Julie A. Allison, *Pittsburg State University*
David Barkmeier, *Northeastern University*
Bruce D. Bartholow, *University of North Carolina at Chapel Hill*
Thomas W. Britt, *Clemson University*
Brad J. Bushman, *Iowa State University*
Stella Garcia-Lopez, *University of Texas at San Antonio*
Scott Geller, *Virginia Polytechnic and State University*
Jeff L. Greenberg, *University of Arizona*
Lauri Hyers, *University of Tennessee, Chattanooga*
Craig Johnson, *Hofstra University*
Cheryl Kaiser, *University of Vermont*
Darren L. Newtson, *University of Virginia*
Carol K. Oyster, *University of Wisconsin–La Crosse*
Derrick Proctor, *Andrews University*
George Schreer, *Manhattanville College*
Charles Stangor, *University of Maryland*
Yvonne Wells, *Suffolk University*

Second, we wish to offer our personal thanks to Carolyn Merrill, our editor at Allyn & Bacon. She was immensely helpful throughout the project, and we continue to view her as a good friend rather than simply as an editor.

Third, our sincere thanks to Anne Weaver, our Developmental Editor. Her insightful comments helped to improve the book in more ways than we can possibly describe here, and we are grateful for her assistance.

Fourth, our thanks to Kris Smead for very careful and constructive copy-editing. Her comments were insightful and thought-provoking, providing valuable help in improving and clarifying our words.

Fifth, our thanks to all of those others who contributed to various aspects of the production process: to Helane Prottas for photo research, to Seventeenth Street Studios for design work, and to Susan Paradise for the cover design.

We also wish to offer our thanks to the many colleagues who provided reprints and preprints of their work. These individuals are too numerous to list here, but their input is gratefully acknowledged.

Our sincere thanks to George Schreer of Manhattanville College for outstanding work on the Instructor's Resource Manual and PowerPoint Presentation, and to Eric Miller for his help in preparing the GradeAid and his work on the Test Bank.

To all of these truly outstanding people, and to many others, too, our warmest personal regards and thanks.

About the Authors

Robert A. Baron is Professor of Psychology and Wellington Professor of Management at Rensselaer Polytechnic Institute. He received his Ph.D. degree from the University of Iowa in 1968. Professor Baron has held faculty appointments at Purdue University, the University of Minnesota, University of Texas, University of South Carolina, and Princeton University. In 1982 he was a Visiting Fellow at Oxford University. From 1979 to 1981 he served as a Program Director at the National Science Foundation in Washington, D.C. He has been a Fellow of the American Psychological Association and is also a Fellow of the American Psychological Society. In 2001, he was appointed an Invited Senior Research Fellow by the French government and held this post at the Université des Sciences Sociales at Toulouse, France.

Professor Baron has published more than ninety-five articles in professional journals and twenty-seven chapters in edited volumes. He is the author or co-author of thirty-eight books, including *Behavior in Organizations* (8th ed.), *Human Aggression* (2nd ed.), *Understanding Human Relations* (4th ed.), and *Psychology* (5th ed.). Textbooks by Professor Baron have been used by more than 3 million students in colleges and universities throughout the world.

Robert A. Baron ***(left)*** and Donn Byrne

Professor Baron served as a member of the Board of Directors of the Albany Symphony Orchestra (1993–1996) and as President of Innovative Environmental Products, Inc., a company engaged in the design of equipment for enhancing the physical environment of work settings and living spaces (e.g., air filtration, noise control, etc.). He holds three U.S. patents.

Professor Baron's research currently focuses primarily on social and cognitive factors in entrepreneurship, workplace aggression and violence, and impact of the physical environment (e.g., lighting, air quality, temperature) on social behavior and task performance.

Donn Byrne holds the rank of Distinguished Professor of Psychology at the University at Albany, State University of New York, and also heads the Social-Personality program there. He received his Ph.D. degree in 1958 from Stanford University and has held academic positions at the California State University at San Francisco, the University of Texas, and Purdue University as well as visiting professorships at the University of Hawaii and Stanford University. He has been President of the Midwestern Psychological Association and of the Society for the Scientific Study of Sexuality, as well as the Chair of the Department of Psychology at Albany. Professor Byrne is a Fellow of the American Psychological Association, the Society for Personality and Social Psychology, and the Society for the Scientific Study of Sexuality. He is also a Charter Fellow of the American Psychological Society.

Professor Byrne has published over 150 articles in professional journals, and twenty-seven of those have been republished in books of readings. He has authored or co-authored thirty-three chapters in edited volumes and fourteen books, including *Psychology: An Introduction to Behavioral Sciences* (four editions plus translations in Spanish, Portuguese, and Chinese), *An Introduction to Personality* (three editions), *The Attraction Paradigm,* and *Exploring Human Sexuality.*

He has served on the Editorial Boards of numerous professional journals, and has directed the doctoral work of forty-five Ph.D.'s as well as that of six current graduate students at Albany. He was invited to deliver a G. Stanley Hall lecture at the 1981 meeting of the American Psychological Association in Los Angeles and a State of the Science Address at the 1981 meeting of the Society for the Scientific Study of Sexuality in New York City. He was invited to testify at Attorney General Meese's Commission on Obscenity and Pornography in Houston in 1986 and to participate in Surgeon General Koop's Workshop on Pornography and Health in 1986. Professor Byrne received the Excellence in Research Award from the University at Albany in 1987 and the Distinguished Scientific Achievement Award from the Society for the Scientific Study of Sexuality in 1989.

Professor Byrne's current research focuses on the effects of adult attachment style on interpersonal behavior, the effects of proclivity for legitimized aggression on sexual coercion and other aggressive acts, and the determinants of interpersonal attraction and sexual attraction.

social psychology

Romare Bearden, *Bopping at Birdland (Stomp Time)*. 1979. From the Jazz Series. Color lithograph on paper, 24 × 33 ¼ in. © Romare Bearden Foundation/Licensed by VAGA, New York, NY. © Copyright Smithsonian American Art Museum, Washington, D.C./Art Resource, NY.

1 THE FIELD OF SOCIAL PSYCHOLOGY: HOW WE THINK ABOUT AND INTERACT WITH OTHERS

CHAPTER OUTLINE

Every so often, a student in my class asks, "Professor Baron, did you always want to be a social psychologist?" If truth be told, the answer is "No." When I entered graduate school, I planned to become an experimental psychologist and wanted to study topics like learning and motivation. But fate had another life in store for me, even though I didn't know it at the time. In the spring of my first year as a graduate student, I took a course in social psychology—one we were all required to take. I didn't think I would find it interesting, but much to my surprise, it quickly became my favorite course. As we discussed questions such as "How do people try to influence each other?", "Do groups make riskier or more cautious decisions than individuals?", and "Why are we attracted to some people but not others?", I gradually came to realize that these were the kind of things I really wanted to study in my future career. By the end of the semester, I had made up my mind, and went to my adviser to change fields. I can honestly say that I have never regretted that decision. Social psychology has taken me on a journey I didn't initially plan, but—wow!—has it been interesting! And truly, how could it be otherwise? How could a field that focuses on the social side of life—how we think about and interact with other people—be anything *but* interesting and important? If you need more convincing, just take a look at the questions in Table 1.1, which presents a very small sampling of the topics currently being studied by social psychologists. I am certain you will find them both intriguing *and* highly relevant to your own life.

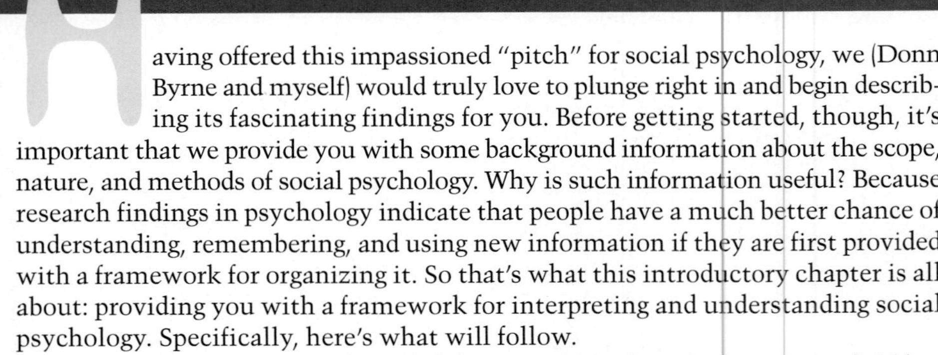

Having offered this impassioned "pitch" for social psychology, we (Donn Byrne and myself) would truly love to plunge right in and begin describing its fascinating findings for you. Before getting started, though, it's important that we provide you with some background information about the scope, nature, and methods of social psychology. Why is such information useful? Because research findings in psychology indicate that people have a much better chance of understanding, remembering, and using new information if they are first provided with a framework for organizing it. So that's what this introductory chapter is all about: providing you with a framework for interpreting and understanding social psychology. Specifically, here's what will follow.

First, we'll present a more formal *definition* of social psychology. Every field has its basic assumptions, and understanding these will help you understand why social psychologists study the topics they do and why they approach them in certain ways. Second, we'll describe some of the major characteristics of social psychology as it exists right now: where it is and where it seems to be going in this new millennium. Third, we will examine some of the methods used by social psychologists to answer questions about the social side of life. A working knowledge of these basic methods will help you to understand how social psychologists add to our understanding of social thought and social behavior—how, in short, the knowledge presented in this text was obtained.

TABLE 1.1

Questions Currently Being Investigated by Social Psychologists. As shown here, social psychologists ask—and attempt to answer—many intriguing questions about the social side of life: how we think about and interact with others.

QUESTION	CHAPTER IN WHICH IT IS COVERED
Do people with firm handshakes really make better first impressions on others?	Chapter 2
What happens when we imagine "what might have been" in various situations?	Chapter 3
Can our attitudes be changed by information we don't even notice?	Chapter 4
If we are confident that we can perform a task successfully, does this increase the chances that we really can?	Chapter 5
Have gender stereotypes changed in recent years? Will they go on changing?	Chapter 5
It there an "antifat" prejudice? Does it exist in all countries?	Chapter 6
Do we prefer as romantic partners people who view us favorably or people who see us as we see ourselves?	Chapter 7
What is jealousy? What are its major causes?	Chapter 8
How can we get other people to say "yes" to our requests?	Chapter 9
Is there such a thing as "pure altruism"—helping others without expecting *anything* in return?	Chapter 10
Does heat really increase aggression? Are there any limits to this relationship, so that when it is very hot, people actually become *less* aggressive?	Chapter 11
When people work together, do they actually accomplish more than each would accomplish by working alone?	Chapter 12
Is justice really "blind"? Are jurors influenced by the appearance, race, and gender of persons on trial?	Chapter 13

Social Psychology: A Working Definition

Providing a formal definition of almost any field is a complex task. In the case of social psychology, this difficulty is increased by two factors: the field's broad scope and its rapid rate of change. As suggested by Table 1.1, social psychologists have a very broad range of interests. Yet, despite this fact, most social psychologists focus mainly on the following task: understanding how and why individuals behave, think, and feel as they do in social situations—ones involving the actual or imagined presence of other persons. Reflecting this fact, we define **social psychology** as *the scientific field that seeks to understand the nature and causes of individual behavior and thought in social situations.* Let's now take a closer look at several aspects of this definition.

Social Psychology Is Scientific in Nature

What is *science?* Many people seem to believe that this term refers only to fields such as chemistry, physics, and biology—ones that use the kind of equipment shown in Figure 1.1 on page 6. If you share that view, you may find our

social psychology: The scientific field that seeks to understand the nature and causes of individual behavior and thought in social situations.

FIGURE 1.1

Does Impressive Equipment Equal Science?
Many people seem to believe that only fields that use equipment like this can be described as "scientific." In fact, however, this is not really so.

suggestion that social psychology is a scientific discipline somewhat puzzling. How can a field that seeks to study the nature of love, the causes of aggression, and everything in between be scientific in the same sense as physics, biochemistry, and computer science? The answer is surprisingly simple.

In reality, the term *science* does not refer to a special group of highly advanced fields. Rather, it refers to two things: (1) a set of values, and (2) several methods that can be used to study a wide range of topics. In deciding whether a given field is or is not scientific, therefore, the critical question is: *Does it adopt these values and methods?* To the extent that it does, it is scientific in nature. To the extent that it does not, it falls outside the realm of science. We'll examine the procedures used by social psychologists in their research in detail in a later section; here, we'll focus on the core values that all fields must adopt to be considered scientific in nature. Four of these are most important:

Accuracy: A commitment to gathering and evaluating information about the world (including social behavior and thought) in as careful, precise, and error-free a manner as possible.

Objectivity: A commitment to obtaining and evaluating such information in a manner that is as free from bias as humanly possible.

Skepticism: A commitment to accepting findings as accurate only to the extent that they have been verified over and over again.

Open-Mindedness: A commitment to changing one's views—even views that are strongly held—if existing evidence suggests that these views are inaccurate.

Social psychology, as a field, is deeply committed to these values and applies them in its efforts to understand the nature of social behavior and social thought. For this reason, it makes sense to describe the field as scientific in orientation. In contrast, fields that are *not* scientific make assertions about the world, and about people, that are not subjected to the careful testing and analysis required by the values listed above. In such fields—ones like astrology and aromatherapy—intuition, faith, and unobservable forces are considered to be sufficient (see Figure 1.2).

"But why adopt the scientific approach? Isn't social psychology just common sense?" Having taught for many years (more than seventy-five between us!), we can almost hear you asking this question. And we understand why you might feel this way; after all, each of us has spent our entire life interacting with others. As a result of such experience, we are all amateur social psychologists. So why not rely on our own experience—or even on folklore and "the wisdom of the ages"—in order to understand the social side of life? Our answer is straightforward: because such sources provide an inconsistent and unreliable guide to social behavior.

For instance, consider the following statement, suggested by common sense: "Absence makes the heart grow fonder." Do you agree? Is it true that when people are separated from those they love, they miss them and so experience increased longing for them? Many people would agree. They would answer, "Yes, that's right. Let me tell you about the time I was separated from . . . ." But now consider the following statement: "Out of sight, out of mind." (Variation: "When I'm not near the one I love, I love the one I'm near.") How about this statement? Is it true? When people are separated from those they love, do they quickly find another romantic interest? As you can see, these two views—both suggested by common

FIGURE 1.2

Science versus Nonscience: Different Values, Different Methods. Fields such as the one shown here are definitely *not* scientific; they do not accept the core values of science (accuracy, objectivity, skepticism, open-mindedness) and do not use scientific methods to test specific hypotheses.

sense—are contradictory. The same is true for many other informal observations about human behavior (e.g., "Birds of a feather flock together"—similarity leads to attraction; "Opposites attract"—*dis*similarity attracts). We could go on to list others, but by now the main point should be clear: Common sense often suggests a confusing and inconsistent picture of human behavior. This is one important reason why social psychologists put their faith in the scientific method: it yields much more conclusive evidence.

But this is not the only reason for being suspicious of common sense. Another one relates to the fact that unlike Mr. Spock of *Star Trek* fame, we are *not* perfect information-processing machines. On the contrary, as we'll note over and over again (e.g., Chapters 2, 3, and 4), our thinking is subject to several forms of error that can lead us badly astray. Here's one example. Suppose that while at the shopping mall, you encounter people soliciting donations for a very worthy cause (e.g., donations to help the victims of a recent tragic disaster). What is the probability that you will make a contribution—10 percent? 50 percent? 80 percent? Now, what about other shoppers at the mall—how likely is it that *they* will make a donation? If you are like most people, you probably estimated your own probability of donating as higher than that of other people—something social psychologists describe as the *holier than thou effect* (e.g., Epley & Dunning, 2000). In other words, we tend to believe that we are more likely to engage in kind, generous acts than are other people, and to think that we are better than "average" in many ways (another term for this is the *self-serving bias;* see Chapter 3). Why do we do this? Perhaps because in estimating the likelihood that we will act in a kind manner, we think about our own character: "What a fine, generous person I am!" But in estimating others' behavior, we think about how we have seen them act in similar situations in the past (e.g., ignoring requests for donations), and then we use this information as a basis for our predictions. In any case, this is just one of the many ways in which we can—and often do—make errors in thinking about other people (and ourselves); we'll consider many others in Chapter 3. Because we are prone to such errors in our informal thinking about the social world, we cannot rely on it—or on common sense—to solve the mysteries of social behavior. Rather, we need scientific evidence, and that, in essence, is what social psychology is all about.

Social Psychology Focuses on the Behavior of Individuals

Societies differ greatly in terms of their views concerning courtship and marriage; yet, it is still individuals who fall in love. Similarly, societies vary greatly in terms of their overall levels of violence; yet, it is still individuals who perform aggressive actions or refrain from doing so. The same argument applies to virtually all other aspects of social behavior, from prejudice to helping: the actions are performed by, and the thoughts occur in, the minds of individuals. Because of this basic fact, the focus in social psychology is squarely on individuals. Social psychologists realize, of course, that we do not exist in isolation from social and cultural influences—far from it. But the field's major interest lies in understanding the factors that shape the actions and thoughts of individual human beings in social settings. This contrasts sharply with the field of *sociology,* which you may have studied in other courses. Sociology studies some of the same topics as social psychology, but it is concerned not with the behavior and thoughts of individuals; rather, it focuses on large groups of persons or society as a whole. For instance, both social psychology and sociology study the topic of violent crime. While social psychologists focus on the factors that cause specific persons to engage in such behavior, sociologists are interested in comparing rates of violent crime in different segments of one society (e.g., high- and low-income groups), or in comparing such rates in several different societies.

Social Psychology Seeks to Understand the Causes of Social Behavior and Thought

In a key sense, the heading of this section states the most central aspect of our definition. What it means is that social psychologists are primarily interested in understanding the many factors and conditions that shape the social behavior and thought of individuals—their actions, feelings, beliefs, memories, and inferences—concerning other persons. Obviously, a huge number of variables play a role in this regard. Most, though, fall under the five major headings described below.

■ THE ACTIONS AND CHARACTERISTICS OF OTHER PERSONS. Imagine the following events:

> You are standing on line outside a move theater; suddenly, another person walks up and cuts in line in front of you.
>
> The person you've been dating exclusively for six months suddenly says, "I think we should date other people."
>
> You are playing a computer game when two attractive strangers walk up and begin to watch your performance with great interest.

Will these actions by other persons have any effect on your behavior and thoughts? Absolutely. So, it's clear that we are often strongly affected by the actions of other persons (see Figure 1.3).

In addition, we are also often affected by the physical appearance of others. Be honest: Have you ever felt uneasy in the presence of a person with a physical disability? Do you ever behave differently toward highly attractive persons than toward less attractive ones? Toward elderly persons than toward young ones? Toward persons belonging to racial and ethnic groups different from your own? Your answer to some of these questions is probably *yes,* because we do often react to the others' visible characteristics, such as their appearance (e.g., McCall, 1997; Twenge & Manis, 1998). In fact, findings reported by Hassin and Trope (2000) indicate that we cannot ignore others' appearance, even when we consciously try to do so. These researchers showed participants in their studies photos of people who were supposedly candidates for various jobs (e.g., clerk, optometrist, electrician).

"I don't know why. I just suddenly felt like calling."

FIGURE 1.3
Others' Behavior: An Important Factor in Our Social Behavior and Thought. As shown here, we are often strongly affected by the actions of other persons, even when we are not aware of this fact.
[SOURCE: © THE NEW YORKER COLLECTION 2000 MICK STEVENS FROM CARTOONBANK.COM. ALL RIGHTS RESERVED.]

Background information about the persons was also provided, and the participants' task was to rate the suitability of these persons for a specific job. Half were told to ignore the photos when making their decisions, while the others were not given such instructions. The photos were chosen to show people who either looked like or did not look like the "typical" holder of the job in question. (Previous research had revealed what the "typical" holder of various jobs looks like.) Results indicated that persons in the photos who looked like the "typical" holder of each job received higher ratings than those who did not. Moreover, this was true even when participants were specifically told to ignore the photos in making their ratings (see Figure 1.4). Findings like these suggest that our reactions to others are indeed strongly affected by their outward appearance.

■ COGNITIVE PROCESSES. Suppose that you have arranged to meet a friend, and this person is late. In fact, after thirty minutes you begin to suspect that your friend will never arrive. Finally, this person does appear and says, "Sorry . . . I forgot all about meeting you until a few minutes ago." How will you react? Probably with considerable annoyance. Imagine that instead, however, your friend says, "I'm so sorry to be late. . . . There was a big accident, and the traffic was tied up for miles." Now how will you react? Probably with less annoyance—but not necessarily. If your friend is often late and has used this excuse before, you may be suspicious about whether this explanation is true. In contrast, if this is the first time your friend has been late, or if your friend has never used such an excuse in the past, you may accept it as true. In other words, your reactions in this situation will depend strongly upon your *memories* of your friend's past behavior and your *inferences* about whether her or his explanation is really true. Situations like this one call attention to the fact that *cognitive processes* play a crucial role in social behavior and social thought. Social psychologists are well aware of the importance of such processes and realize that in order to understand people's behavior in social situations, we must under-

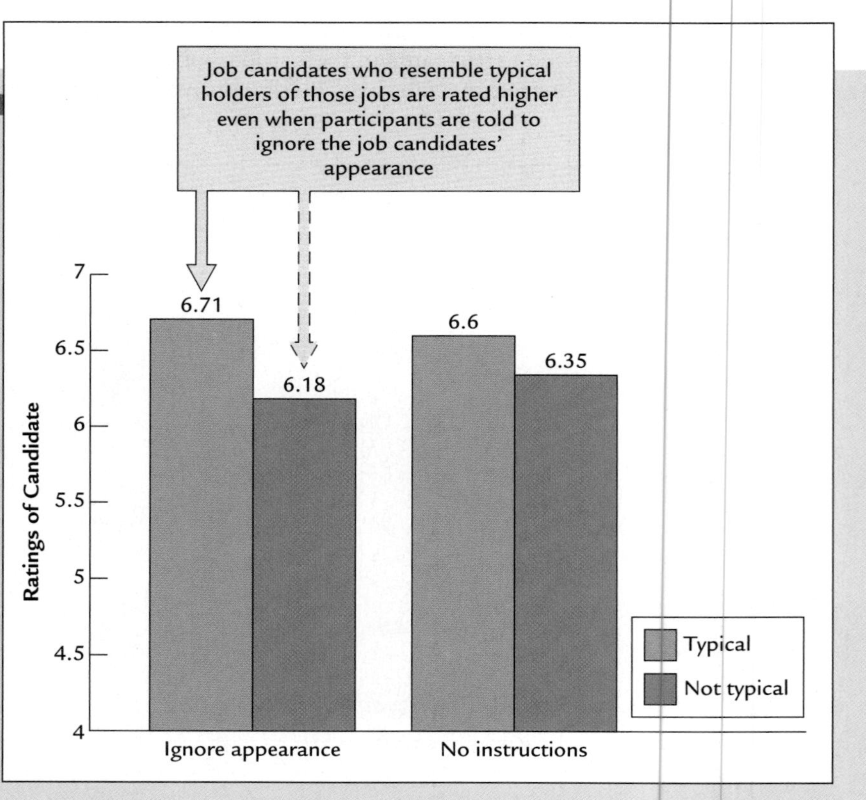

FIGURE 1.4

Evidence That We Can't Ignore Others' Appearance, Even if We Try. Research participants assigned higher ratings to job candidates who looked like the "typical" holder of that job than to ones who did not, even if participants were specifically told to ignore the job candidates' appearance.

[SOURCE: BASED ON DATA FROM HASSIN & TROPE, 2000.] ■

stand their thinking about such situations—*construals,* as they are often termed by social psychologists (e.g., Killeya & Johnson, 1998; Swann & Gill, 1997).

■ ENVIRONMENTAL VARIABLES: IMPACT OF THE PHYSICAL WORLD. Are people more prone to wild impulsive behavior during the full moon than at other times (Rotton & Kelley, 1985)? Do we become more irritable and aggressive when the weather is hot and steamy than when it is cool and comfortable (Anderson, Bushman, & Groom, 1997; Rotton & Cohn, 2000)? Does exposure to a pleasant smell in the air make people more helpful to others (Baron, 1997a)? Research findings indicate that the physical environment does indeed influence our feelings, thoughts, and behavior; so ecological variables certainly fall within the realm of modern social psychology.

■ CULTURAL CONTEXT. When I (RAB) was in high school, most of the female movie stars and all of the models in advertisements and on television were, to put it simply, *curvy.* And all of the young women I knew wanted to have a figure like Marilyn Monroe's. Now, things are very different. Movie stars and models look, at least to me, to be dangerously thin. And recent findings indicate that they really *are* too thin. One recent study of *Playboy* centerfold models and fashion models (Owen & Laurel-Seller, 2000) found that almost 33 percent of the *Playboy* centerfold models and about 20 percent of all fashion models can be classified as being anorexic (i.e., as showing signs of a serious eating disorder; see Figure 1.5). Not surprisingly, many young women express the desire to be as thin as these models of feminine beauty. In fact, even girls as young as eight or nine express concern that they are too fat to be attractive!

How did this tremendous change come about? The answer involves shifting cultural values, which, for many complex reasons, have come to view being thin as highly desirable (e.g., a growing emphasis on being fit). Whatever the reason, these dramatic changes in what is considered to be attractive or sexy illustrate yet another important point about social behavior: it does not occur in a cultural vacuum. On the contrary, it is often strongly affected by cultural norms (social rules concerning how people should behave in specific situations; see Chapter 9), membership in various groups, and changing societal values. Whom should people marry? How many children should they have? Should they keep their emotional reactions to themselves or demonstrate them openly? How close should they stand to others when talking to them? Is it appropriate to give gifts to professors or government

FIGURE 1.5
Changing Cultural Standards of Beauty.
Up until the 1960s, cultural standards of feminine beauty indicated that a rounded or curvy figure was most attractive. In recent years, however, these cultural definitions of what is attractive have swung greatly toward a much thinner figure. In fact, recent findings indicate that many models are so thin that they can be classified as being anorexic.

officials? These are only a small sampling of the aspects of social behavior that can be—and are—influenced by cultural factors. (The term *culture* refers to the system of shared meanings, perceptions, and beliefs held by persons belonging to some group; Smith & Bond, 1993.)

As we'll note below, attention to the effects of cultural factors is an increasingly important trend in social psychology as our field attempts to take account of the growing cultural diversity in many different countries.

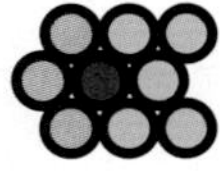

■ BIOLOGICAL FACTORS. Is social behavior influenced by biological processes and genetic factors? Ten years ago, most social psychologists would have answered *no,* at least to the genetic part of this question. Now, however, many have come to believe that our preferences, behaviors, emotional reactions, and even attitudes are affected, to some extent, by our biological inheritance (Buss, 1999; Nisbett, 1990).

The view that biological factors play an important role in social behavior comes from the field of **evolutionary psychology** (e.g., Buss, 1995; Buss & Shackelford, 1997). This new branch of psychology suggests that our species, like all others on the planet, has been subject to the process of biological evolution throughout its history, and that as a result of this process, we now possess a large number of *evolved psychological mechanisms* that help (or once helped) us to deal with important problems relating to survival. How do these become part of our biological inheritance? Through the process of evolution, which, in turn, involves three basic components: *variation, inheritance,* and *selection. Variation* refers to the fact that organisms belonging to a given species vary in many different ways; indeed, such variation is a basic part of life on our planet. Human beings, as you already know, come in a wide variety of shapes and sizes, and vary on what sometimes seems to be an almost countless number of dimensions.

Inheritance refers to the fact that some of these variations can be passed from one generation to the next through complex mechanisms that we are only now beginning to fully understand. *Selection* refers to the fact that some variations give the individuals who possess them an "edge" in terms of reproduction: they are more likely to survive, find mates, and pass these variations on to succeeding generations. The result is that over time, more and more members of the species possess these variations. This change in the characteristics of a species over time—often immensely long periods of time—is the concrete outcome of evolution. (See Figure 1.6 for a summary of this process.)

evolutionary psychology: A new branch of psychology that seeks to investigate the potential role of genetic factors in various aspects of human behavior.

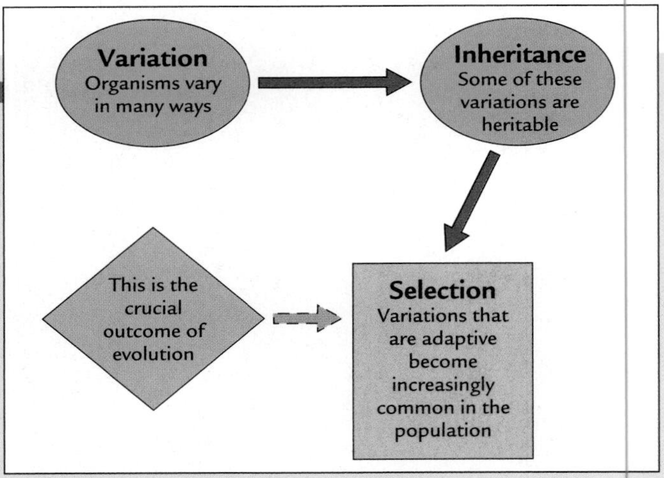

Social psychologists who adopt the evolutionary perspective suggest that this process applies to at least some aspects of social behavior. For instance, consider

FIGURE 1.6

Evolution: An Overview. As shown here, evolution involves three major components: variation, inheritance, and selection.

the question of mate preference. Why do we find some people attractive? According to the evolutionary perspective, it is because the characteristics they show—symmetrical facial features, well-toned and shapely bodies (e.g., a relatively large waist-to-hip ratio in females; Tesser & Martin, 1996), clear skin, lustrous hair—are associated with reproductive capacity. In other words, these are outward signs of inner health and vigor. Thus, a preference for these characteristics in mates among our ancestors increased the chances that they would reproduce successfully; this, in turn, contributed to our preference for these aspects of appearance. (Interestingly, reasonable as these suggestions seem to be, they have not been uniformly confirmed in research findings; e.g., Tassinary & Hansen, 1998.)

Because the evolutionary perspective makes many intriguing predictions about social behavior and thought, it has gained increasing recognition in social psychology. Thus, we'll have reason to refer to it at several points in this book. But please don't misunderstand: the evolutionary perspective does *not* suggest that we inherit specific patterns of social behavior; rather, it contends that we inherit tendencies or predispositions that may or may not be translated into reality, depending on the environments in which we live. For instance, consider an individual who has inherited the tendency to show a very strong sexual drive. Will this person have multiple sexual partners or only one? Clearly, this depends on where he or she lives. If the person lives in a culture where having many multiple partners is considered appropriate, she or he may indeed have many lovers; but if this individual lives in a culture where such behavior is strongly disapproved, she or he may have only one—or at least a smaller number than would be true in a more permissive cultural setting.

Social Psychology: Summing Up

In sum, social psychology focuses mainly on understanding the causes of social behavior and social thought—on identifying factors that shape our feelings, behavior, and thought in social situations. It seeks to accomplish this goal through the use of scientific methods, and it takes careful note of the fact that social behavior and thought are influenced by a wide range of social, cognitive, environmental, cultural, and biological factors.

The remainder of this text is devoted to describing some of the key findings of social psychology. This information is truly fascinating, so we're certain that you will find it of interest. We're equally sure, however, that you will also find some of it surprising, and that it will challenge many of your ideas about people and social relations. So please get ready for some new insights. We predict that after reading this book, you'll never think about social behavior in quite the same way as before.

KEY POINTS

- *Social Psychology* is the scientific field that seeks to understand the nature and causes of individual behavior and thought in social situations.
- Social psychology is scientific in nature because it adopts the values and methods used in other fields of science.
- Social psychologists adopt the scientific method because "common sense" provides an unreliable guide to social behavior, and because our thought is influenced by many potential sources of bias.
- Social psychology focuses on the behavior of individuals and seeks to understand the causes of social behavior and thought.
- Important causes of social behavior and thought include the behavior and characteristics of other persons, cognitive processes, aspects of the physical environment, culture, and biological and genetic factors.

Social Psychology in the New Millennium: New Perspectives, New Methods

Earlier, we noted that the major purpose of this chapter is providing you with a framework for understanding the "big picture"—what social psychology is all about and how it seeks new knowledge about social behavior and social thought. Continuing with this theme, we'll now comment briefly on several major aspects of social psychology as it exists today. Knowing about these is helpful because they play an important role in shaping the questions and topics social psychologists study and the methods they choose for their research. Here are some issues worthy of your attention.

Influence of a Cognitive Perspective

We have defined *social psychology* as the field that studies both social behavior and social thought. This definition reflects the fact that social psychologists have always been interested in how individuals think about other persons and about social situations. In recent decades, however, the cognitive side of social psychology has grown dramatically in importance. At present, most social psychologists believe that how people act in various social situations is strongly determined by their thoughts about these situations. Thus, understanding social thought is, in a real sense, a powerful key for unraveling the complex patterns of our social relations with other persons. But please don't misunderstand: this emphasis on cognitive processes does *not* mean that social psychologists ignore social behavior. On the contrary, current research often seeks to understand the links between social thought and overt social behavior. For instance, research focused on the effects of affirmative action has investigated the possibility that if students conclude that they were admitted to their university partly because of their gender, race, or ethnic identity, this will cause them to feel stigmatized (singled out in a negative way), and to experience doubt about their own abilities (e.g., Steele, 1997). As a result, their actual performance will be reduced. Discouragingly, research findings suggest that such effects actually do occur: the stronger minority students' suspicions are that they were admitted because of their race, the poorer their academic performance tends to be (Brown et al., 2000).

The cognitive perspective is reflected in social psychological research in many ways, but two are perhaps most important. First, social psychologists have attempted to apply basic knowledge about *memory, reasoning,* and *decision making* to various aspects of social thought and behavior (e.g., Albarracin & Wyer, 2000). For instance, within this context, researchers have sought to determine whether prejudice stems, at least in part, from our tendency to remember only information consistent with stereotypes of various groups, or tendencies to process information about one's own social group differently from information about other social groups (e.g., Forgas & Fiedler, 1996).

Second, there has been growing interest in the question of how we process social information—in a "quick-and-dirty" manner designed to reduce effort (*heuristically*), or in a more careful, effortful manner (*systematically*; e.g., Eagly & Chaiken, 1998; Killeya & Johnson, 1998). As we'll see in several later chapters (Chapters 2, 3, 6, and 12), these differences in processing can strongly shape our inferences, conclusions, decisions, and judgments about others, so they are a key aspect of social cognition.

In sum, insights provided by a cognitive perspective have added greatly to our understanding of many aspects of social behavior, and this approach is definitely a major theme of social psychology as we move into the twenty-first century.

Growing Emphasis on Application: Exporting Social Psychology

A second major theme in social psychology today is growing concern with the *application* of the knowledge gathered by social psychology. An increasing number of social psychologists have turned their attention to questions concerning *personal health, the legal process, social behavior in work settings, environmental issues,* and even the study of *entrepreneurship* (e.g., recent studies have examined the impact of entrepreneurs' social skills on their success; Baron & Markman, in press). In short, there has been growing interest in applying the findings and principles of social psychology to the solution of practical problems. This theme is certainly not new in the field: Kurt Lewin, one of the founders of social psychology, once remarked, "There's nothing as practical as a good theory," by which he meant that theories of social behavior and thought developed through systematic research often turn out to be extremely useful in solving practical problems. There seems little doubt, however, that interest in applying the knowledge of social psychology to practical issues has increased in recent years, with many beneficial results. We'll examine this work in Chapter 13.

Adoption of a Multicultural Perspective: Taking Full Account of Social Diversity

When I entered graduate school in 1964, social psychology was largely a North American field: a large majority of social psychologists lived and worked in the United States or Canada. Moreover, most research in the field was conducted in the United States with Americans as research participants. The result? There was little appreciation of the importance of *diversity*—differences in the behavior or characteristics of individuals from different cultures or ethnic groups. Indeed, there was even little interest in possible differences between males and females! The prevailing point of view was that if such cultural or gender differences exist, they are relatively unimportant. After all, if social psychology is a science, the principles and laws it establishes should apply to *all* human beings, regardless of where they live, their personal background, or their cultural identity.

This point of view is no longer dominant. While social psychologists have not abandoned the goal of developing a body of knowledge that applies to all human beings, they have become far more aware of the importance of cultural and ethnic diversity, and now recognize that such differences *must* be included in our efforts to understand social behavior. For instance, consider the topic of romantic love. "Surely," you might be tempted to think, "love is much the same all over the globe." But think again: some cultures do not seem to possess the notion of *romantic love* so well known in Western cultures (see Figure 1.7 on page 16). Do people in these cultures experience love in the same way, and fall in and out of love for the same reasons, as people in cultures where the idea of romantic love is popular? Perhaps; but perhaps not.

As recognition of the importance of cultural, ethnic, and gender differences has grown, the field of social psychology has adopted an increasingly **multicultural perspective**—an approach that pays careful attention to the role of culture and human diversity as factors that influence social behavior and social thought (e.g., Choi & Nisbett, 1998; Crandall et al., 2000).

In addition, social psychologists have shown increasing recognition of the fact that findings obtained with one gender may not necessarily apply to the other gender. Although differences in the behavior of females and males have often been exaggerated by gender stereotypes concerning the supposed traits of women and men

multicultural perspective: A focus on understanding the cultural and ethnic factors that influence social behavior.

FIGURE 1.7

Cultural Diversity: An Important Consideration for Social Psychology. Social psychologists now take full account of the fact that ethnic and cultural diversity can strongly influence social thought and social behavior. For instance, while the idea of romantic love is well known in many Western cultures and plays an important role in courtship and marriage, it is given much less emphasis in other cultures where, for instance, marriages are arranged and couples are *not* expected to be romantically in love when they marry.

(e.g., Diekman & Eagly, 2000), some differences in social behavior do exist (Feingold, 1994; Oliver & Hyde, 1993). For instance, recent results indicate that women show greater appreciation of and insight into their own emotions (and the emotions of others) than do men (e.g., Barrett et al., 2000). They describe their own and others' emotions in richer and more complex terms, are better at remembering emotional events (Davis, 1999), and are also more successful at both "reading" and sending emotional messages (through, e.g., facial expressions; Brody & Hall, 1993).

We will highlight social psychology's growing attention to diversity at many points throughout the text. Specifically, we will describe research that focused on the effects of cultural and ethnic factors or of gender. In describing such research, we will point out how the findings are related to other topics in social psychology. Sections in which we discuss social diversity will be marked, in the margins, by means of the following special symbol.

Increasing Attention to the Potential Role of Biological Factors and the Evolutionary Perspective

Another important trend in modern social psychology—one we mentioned before—is the increasing influence of a biological or evolutionary perspective (e.g., Buss, 1999). Growing evidence suggests that biological and genetic factors play at least some role in many forms of social behavior—everything from physical attraction and mate selection on one side through aggression on the other (see Chapters 7, 10, and 11). As an illustration of such research, consider an intriguing study by Mueller and Mazur (1996). These researchers showed photos of 434 West Point cadets to raters and had these persons assess the extent to which the cadets' faces showed dominance. The evolutionary perspective suggests that, for men, dominance will be a positive attribute—it will give them access to a large number of mates, and in this way, will help increase their potential number of offspring. For women, in contrast, dominance will not be as desirable a characteristic, because no

FIGURE 1.8

Facial Dominance and Career Success: Evidence for the Role of Genetic Factors in Social Behavior.

West Point cadets who had dominant-looking faces *(left photo)* rose to higher military rank than did cadets who had non-dominant-looking faces *(right photo).* Findings such as these indicate that dominance—or even the mere appearance of dominance—is linked to positive outcomes, at least for males. These findings are consistent with predictions from an evolutionary perspective—one whose influence has increased in social psychology in recent years.

matter how many mates a woman has, she can still produce only a limited number of children. On the basis of such reasoning, Mueller and Mazur (1996) predicted that men who looked dominant (i.e., those who had inherited certain facial characteristics) would attain higher military rank in their careers than would men who did not look dominant (see Figure 1.8). The results of their study offered support for this hypothesis. Of course, we cannot tell from such research precisely *why* looking dominant leads to career success in the military. But this and many other studies conducted from the evolutionary perspective do suggest that biological and genetic factors play some role in many aspects of social behavior (see, e.g., Buss, 1999).

KEY POINTS

- A major theme in modern social psychology is the growing influence of a cognitive perspective. This perspective suggests that how people act in various social situations is strongly determined by their thoughts about these situations and other persons.
- Another major theme of social psychology is the growing interest in application—applying the knowledge and findings of social psychology to many practical problems.
- Social psychology currently adopts a *multicultural perspective.* This perspective recognizes the importance of cultural factors in social behavior and social thought, and notes that research findings obtained in one culture do not necessarily generalize to other cultures.
- There is growing recognition, in modern social psychology, of the potential role of biological and genetic factors in social behavior and social thought.

Answering Questions about Social Behavior and Social Thought: Research Methods in Social Psychology

Now that we've described the current state of social psychology, we can turn to the third major task mentioned at the start of this chapter: explaining how social psychologists attempt to answer questions about social behavior and social thought—how, in short, they conduct their research. To provide you with basic information about this important issue, we'll examine three related topics. First, we will describe several *methods of research* in social psychology. Next, we will consider the role of *theory* in such research. Finally, we'll touch on some of the complex *ethical issues* relating to social psychological research.

Systematic Observation: Describing the World around Us

One basic technique for studying social behavior involves **systematic observation**—carefully observing behavior as it occurs. Such observation is not the kind of informal observation we all practice from childhood on; rather, in a scientific field such as social psychology, it is observation accompanied by careful, accurate measurement. For example, suppose that a social psychologist wanted to find out how frequently people touch each other in different settings. The researcher could study this topic by going to shopping malls, airports, college campuses, and many other locations and observing, in those settings, who touches whom, how they touch, and with what frequency. Such research (which has actually been conducted—see Chapter 2) would be employing what is known as *naturalistic observation*—observation of behavior in natural settings (Linden, 1992). Note that in such observation, the researcher would simply notice what is happening in various contexts; she or he would make no attempt to change the behavior of the persons being observed. In fact, such observation requires that the researcher take great pains to *avoid* influencing the persons observed. Thus, the psychologist would try to remain as inconspicuous as possible, and might even try to hide behind barriers such as telephone polls, walls, or even bushes! This is what I (RAB) did more than twenty years ago in a study I conducted on the effects of temperature on motorists' horn honking (Baron, 1976). I arranged for an assistant to drive up to a red light and then to remain motionless after the light turned green. Another assistant hid behind some bushes and recorded the number of seconds that passed before drivers honked their horns. As we expected, they honked sooner on hot days than on cooler ones (see Figure 1.9).

Another technique that is often included under the heading of systematic observation is known as the **survey method.** Here, researchers ask large numbers of persons to respond to questions about their attitudes or behavior. Surveys are used for many purposes—to measure attitudes toward specific issues. Social psychologists sometimes use this method to measure attitudes concerning social issues—for instance, national health care or affirmative action programs. Scientists and practitioners in other fields use the survey method to measure voting preference prior to elections and to assess consumer reactions to new products.

Surveys offer several advantages. Information can be gathered about thousands or even hundreds of thousands of persons with relative ease. Further, because surveys can be readily created, public opinion on new issues can be obtained quickly—very soon after the issues arise. In order to be useful as a research tool, though, surveys must meet certain requirements. First, the persons who participate must be *representative* of the larger population about which conclusions are to be

systematic observation: A method of research in which behavior is systematically observed and recorded.

survey method: A method of research in which a large number of persons answer questions about their attitudes or behavior.

FIGURE 1.9

Naturalistic Observation in Social Psychological Research.
In a study that employed naturalistic observation, one of the authors (RAB) arranged for an accomplice to drive up to a red light and then to remain motionless after the light turned green. An assistant, hidden behind some bushes, recorded the number of seconds that passed before drivers honked at the accomplice. Results indicated that, as expected, drivers honked sooner on hot days than on cooler ones.

drawn—the issue of *sampling.* If this condition is not met, serious errors can result. For instance, every day, CNN conducts a poll on some current issue; the next day, it presents the results. One recent topic, for instance, was "Do you think there will soon be a lasting peace in the Middle East?" Results, shown the next day, indicated that fully 92 percent of the people who responded thought this would not happen. Can we have confidence in these findings? Probably not, because they simply reflect the views of the people who bothered to call CNN and express their views. There is no guarantee that these persons constitute a representative sample of the entire population. In fact, in all likelihood, they do not.

Yet another issue that must be carefully addressed with respect to surveys is this: The way in which the items are worded can exert strong effects on the outcomes obtained. For example, suppose a survey asked, "Do you think that persons convicted of multiple murders should be executed?" Many people might agree; after all, the convicted criminals have murdered several victims. But if, instead, the survey asked, "Are you in favor of the death penalty?" a smaller percent might agree. So, the way in which questions are posed can strongly affect the results.

In sum, the survey method can be a useful approach for studying some aspects of social behavior, but the results obtained are accurate only to the extent that issues relating to sampling and wording are carefully addressed.

Correlation: The Search for Relationships

At various times, you have probably noticed that some events appear to be related to each other: as one changes, the other changes, too. For example, perhaps you've noticed that people who drive new, expensive cars tend to be older than people who drive old, inexpensive ones, or that when interest rates rise, the stock market often falls. When two events are related in this way, they are said to be *correlated* or that a correlation exists between them. The term *correlation* refers to a tendency for one event to change as the other changes. Social psychologists refer to such changeable aspects of the natural world as *variables,* because they can take different values.

From the point of view of science, the existence of a correlation between two variables can be very useful. This is so because when a correlation exists, it is possible to predict one variable from information about one or more other variables. The ability to make such *predictions* is one important goal of all branches of science, including social psychology. Being able to make accurate predictions can be very useful. For instance, imagine that a correlation is observed between certain attitudes on the part of individuals (one variable) and the likelihood that they will later commit serious crimes, such as rape (another variable). This correlation could be very useful in identifying potentially dangerous persons so that they can receive treatment designed to prevent them from engaging in such harmful behavior. Similarly, suppose that a correlation is observed between certain patterns of behavior in married couples (e.g., the tendency to criticize each other harshly) and the likelihood that they will later divorce. Again, this information might be helpful in counseling the persons involved and perhaps, if this is what they desire, in saving their relationship. (See Chapter 8 for a discussion of why long-term relationships sometimes fail.)

How accurately can such predictions be made? The stronger the correlation between the variables in question, the more accurate the predictions. Correlations can range from 0 to –1.00 or +1.00; the greater the departure from 0, the stronger the correlation. Positive numbers mean that as one variable increases, the other increases, too. Negative numbers indicate that as one variable increases, the other decreases. For instance, there is a negative correlation between age and the amount of hair on the heads of males: the older they grow, the less hair they have.

These basic facts underlie an important method of research sometimes used by social psychologists: the **correlational method.** In this approach, social psychologists attempt to determine whether, and to what extent, different variables are related to each other. This involves making careful observations of each variable, and then performing appropriate statistical tests to determine whether and to what degree the variables are correlated. Perhaps a concrete example will help.

Imagine that a social psychologist wants to find out whether one piece of "folk wisdom" is true—the belief that firm handshakes produce better first impressions than weak ones. (This relationship has long been suggested by books on etiquette and gaining success in business, but had never been studied in a scientific manner until one group of social psychologists did so recently; Chaplin et al., 2000.) How could research on this **hypothesis**—an as yet unverified prediction—be conducted? One very basic approach would go something like this. The researcher might arrange for several pairs of strangers to shake hands with each other. They would then rate each others' handshakes (e.g., in terms of strength, vigor, duration, and completeness of grip) and their first impressions of each other (e.g., how much they like the other person, how friendly he or she seemed to be, etc.). If positive correlations are obtained between various aspects of the handshakes (e.g., their strength) and these first impressions, this would provide some evidence for the hypothesis that handshakes do indeed influence our reactions to strangers when we meet them for the first time.

Suppose that the researcher did find such a correlation (e.g., a correlation of +.58 between strength of handshakes and the favorableness of first impression); what could she or he conclude? That firm handshakes lead to (i.e., produce, cause) positive first impressions? Perhaps; but this conclusion, reasonable as it may seem, may be totally false. Here's why: It may well be the case that persons who give firm

correlational method: A method of research in which a scientist systematically observes two or more variables to determine whether changes in one are accompanied by changes in the other.

hypothesis: An as yet unverified prediction based on a theory.

FIGURE 1.10

An Illustration of the Fact That Correlation Does *Not* Equal Causation. When one event precedes another, it is sometimes tempting to assume that the first event caused the second. As you can see from this cartoon, however, such assumptions are often on shaky ground! [SOURCE: REPRINTED WITH SPECIAL PERMISSION OF KING FEATURES SYNDICATE.]

handshakes are friendlier, more confident, and more outgoing than those who give weak ones. Thus, it may be *these* factors—not the strength of the handshakes themselves—that generate positive first impressions. In other words, if you meet someone who is friendly and confident, she or he is more likely to give you a firm handshake than is someone who is not friendly or confident, and you might like this person because she or he is friendly and confident, *not* because this stranger gave you a firm handshake. There is an important principle in this example, light-hearted as it may be: *The fact that two variables are correlated, even highly correlated, does not guarantee that there is a causal link between them—that changes in one cause changes in the other.* In fact, any correlation between them may be due to chance or random factors or to the fact that changes in both variables are related to a third variable (see Figure 1.10). Additional illustrations of the fact that even strong correlations between two variables do not necessarily mean that one causes the other are presented in the **Ideas to Take with You—And Use!** feature on page 33.

Despite this major drawback, the correlational method of research is sometimes very useful to social psychologists. It can be used in natural settings, and it is often highly efficient: a large amount of information can be obtained in a relatively short period of time. However, the fact that it is generally not conclusive with respect to cause-and-effect relationships is a serious flaw—one that leads social psychologists to prefer a different method. It is to this approach that we turn next.

KEY POINTS

- In *systematic observation,* behavior is carefully observed and recorded. In naturalistic observation, such observations are made in settings where the behavior naturally occurs.
- In the *survey method,* large numbers of persons respond to questions about their attitudes or behavior.
- In the *correlational method* of research, two or more variables are measured to determine whether they are related to one another in any way.
- The existence of even strong correlations between variables does not indicate that they are causally related to each other.

The Experimental Method: Knowledge through Systematic Intervention

As we have just seen, the correlational method of research is very useful from the point of view of one important goal of science: being able to make accurate predictions. It is less useful, though, from the point of view of reaching yet another goal: *explanation.* This is sometimes known as the "why" question because scientists do not merely wish to describe the world and relationships between variables in it: they want to be able to *explain* these relationships, too. For instance, continuing with the handshaking example used above, if a link between firmness of handshakes and first impressions exists, social psychologists would want to know *why* this is so. Do firm handshakes suggest that the persons who give them are friendly or interested in the recipient? Or, perhaps, do firm handshakes increase activation or arousal among persons who receive them, and so make them more interested in the hand-shaker?

In order to attain the goal of explanation, social psychologists employ a method of research known as **experimentation** or the **experimental method.** As the heading of this section suggests, experimentation involves the following strategy: One variable is changed systematically, and the effects of these changes on one or more other variables are carefully measured. If systematic changes in one variable produce changes in another variable (and if two additional conditions we'll describe below are also met), it is possible to conclude with reasonable certainty that there is indeed a causal relationship between these variables: that changes in one do indeed *cause* changes in the other. Because the experimental method is so valuable in answering this kind of question, it is frequently the method of choice in social psychology. But please bear in mind that there is no single "best" method of research. Rather, social psychologists, like all other scientists, choose the method that is most appropriate for studying a particular topic.

■ EXPERIMENTATION: ITS BASIC NATURE. In its most basic form, the experimental method involves two key steps: (1) The presence or strength of some variable believed to affect an aspect of social behavior or thought is systematically altered, and (2) the effects of such alterations (if any) are carefully measured. The factor systematically varied by the researcher is termed the **independent variable,** while the aspect of behavior studied is termed the **dependent variable.** In a simple experiment, then, different groups of participants are exposed to contrasting levels of the independent variable (such as low, moderate, and high). The researcher then carefully measures the participants' behavior to determine whether it does in fact vary with these changes in the independent variable. If it does—and if two other conditions are also met—the researcher can tentatively conclude that the independent variable does indeed cause changes in the aspect of behavior being studied.

To illustrate the basic nature of experimentation in social psychology, let's return again to the handshaking example. How could a social psychologist study this topic through experimentation? One possibility is as follows. The researcher would arrange for participants to come to a laboratory or other setting, where they meet assistants who shake their hands. (The participants would not know that the persons they meet are assistants of the experimenter.) The assistants would have been trained, in advance, to be able to give weak handshakes, moderate handshakes, or firm handshakes, and depending on experimental condition, they would deliver a handshake of the required type to each participant. Then, perhaps, the assistant and the participants would perform some tasks together or have a brief conversation (the assistant's behavior would be held as con-

experimentation (experimental method): A method of research in which one or more factors (the independent variables) are systematically changed to determine whether such variations affect one or more other factors (dependent variables).

independent variable: The variable that is systematically changed (i.e., varied) in an experiment.

dependent variable: The variable that is measured in an experiment.

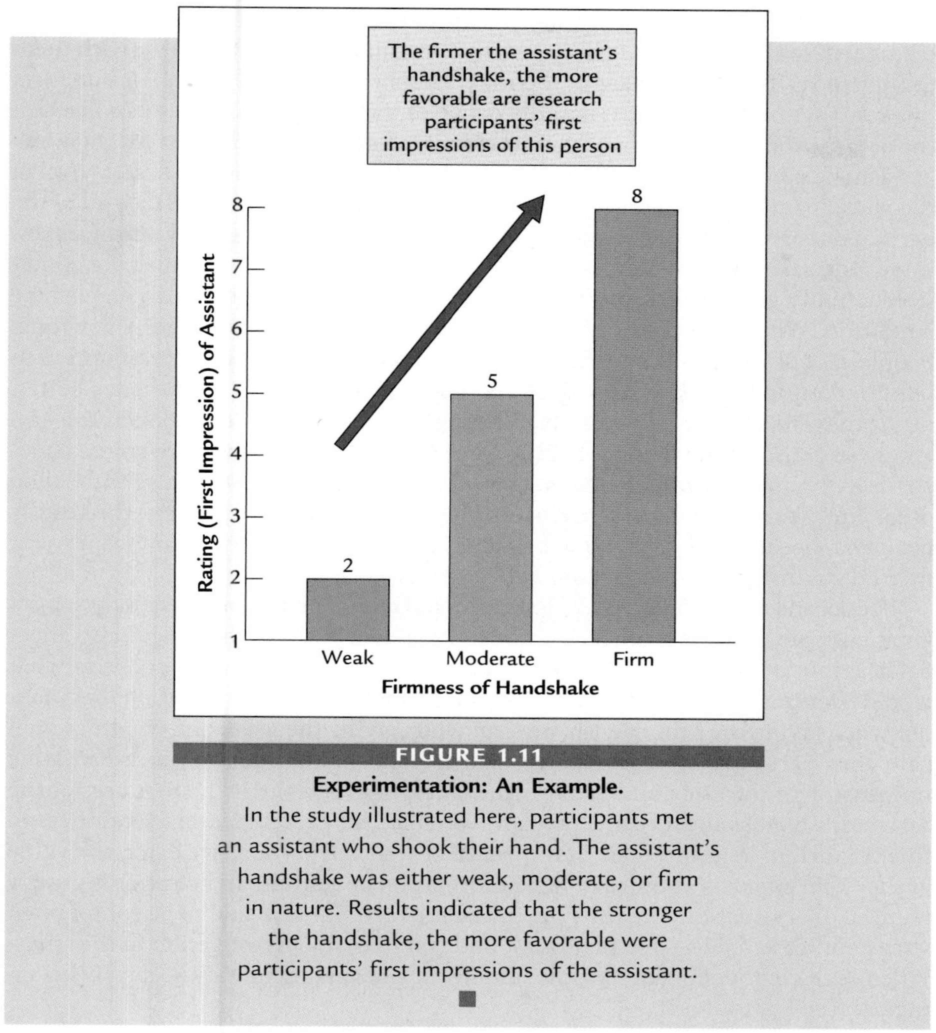

FIGURE 1.11

Experimentation: An Example.
In the study illustrated here, participants met an assistant who shook their hand. The assistant's handshake was either weak, moderate, or firm in nature. Results indicated that the stronger the handshake, the more favorable were participants' first impressions of the assistant.

stant as possible in these situations). Finally, the participants would rate their first impression of the assistant.

If the results now look like those in Figure 1.11, the researcher could conclude, at least tentatively, that firm handshakes do indeed produce more positive first impressions than do weak ones. It's important to note that in experimentation, such knowledge is obtained through direct intervention: Firmness of handshakes—the independent variable—is systematically changed by the researcher. In the correlational method, in contrast, variables are *not* altered in this manner; rather, naturally occurring changes in them are simply observed and recorded.

random assignment of participants to experimental conditions: A basic requirement for conducting valid experiments. According to this principle, research participants must have an equal chance of being exposed to each level of the independent variable.

■ EXPERIMENTATION: TWO REQUIREMENTS FOR ITS SUCCESS. Earlier, we referred to two conditions that must be met before a researcher can conclude that changes in an independent variable have caused changes in a dependent variable. Let's consider these conditions now. The first involves what is termed **random assignment of participants to experimental conditions.** This requirement means that all participants in an experiment must have an equal chance of being exposed to each level of the independent variable. The reason for this rule is simple: If participants are *not* randomly assigned to each condition, it may later be impossible to determine whether differences in their behavior stem from differences they brought with them to the study, from the impact of the independent variable, or both. For instance, imagine that in the study just described, one of the assistants decides to collect all the data for the firm handshake condition on one day, and all the data for the weak handshake condition on the next day. It just so happens that on the first day, all of the participants are students from a music class, while on the second day, all of the participants are members of a weight-lifting club (they volunteered for the experiment together). Results indicate that participants in the firm handshake condition actually give the assistant *lower* ratings than those in the weak handshake condition. Why? One possibility is that the experimenter's hypothesis is wrong: People do not form more positive impressions of strangers who give them firm handshakes; in fact, they like strangers who give them weak handshakes better. But it may also be the case that the findings reflect differences between the two groups of participants: the weightlifters are so strong that they view even the handshake as "wimpy," while the musicians like weak handshakes because these mild grips don't harm their delicate fingers. So in fact, we can't tell *why* the results occurred, because the principle of random assignment of participants to experimental conditions has been violated.

The second condition essential for successful experimentation is as follows: Insofar as possible, all factors other than the independent variable that might also affect participants' behavior must be held constant. To see why this is so, consider what would happen if, in the study on handshaking, the assistant acts in a friendlier manner when giving the firm handshake than when giving the weak one. Findings indicate that participants who receive a firm handshake report a more favorable impression of the assistant. What is the cause of this result? The firmness of the assistant's handshake (the independent variable), his or her greater friendliness in this condition, or both? Once again, we can't tell; and because we can't, the value of the experiment as a source of new information about human behavior is greatly reduced. In a situation like this, the independent variable is said to be *confounded* with another variable—one that is *not* under systematic investigation in the study. When such confounding occurs, the findings of an experiment may be largely meaningless (see Figure 1.12).

But why, you may now be wondering, would a psychologist make such a muddle of a research project? Why would the researcher allow the assistant to be friendlier in the firm handshake condition than in the weak handshake condition? The answer is that the researcher certainly wouldn't do this on purpose. But suppose that the assistant knows the hypothesis of the study—that firm handshakes produce better first impressions. This knowledge might then lead the assistant to act differently in the various handshake conditions either consciously (she or he wants to "help" the results turn out right!) or unconsciously (the assistant changes her or his behavior without intending to do so). To avoid such **experimenter effects**—unintended effects on participants' behavior produced by researchers—social psychologists often use a *double-blind procedure,* in which the researchers who have contact with participants do *not* know the hypothesis under investigation. Because they don't, the likelihood that they will influence results in subtle ways is reduced.

experimenter effects: Unintended effects on participants' behavior produced by researchers.

external validity: The extent to which findings of an experiment can be generalized to real-life social situations and perhaps to persons different from those who participated in the research.

In sum, experimentation is, in several respects, the crown jewel among social psychology's methods. It certainly isn't perfect; for example, because experimentation is often conducted in laboratory settings quite different from the locations in which social behavior actually occurs, the question of **external validity** often arises—to what extent can the findings of experiments be generalized to real-life social situations and perhaps persons different from those who participated in the

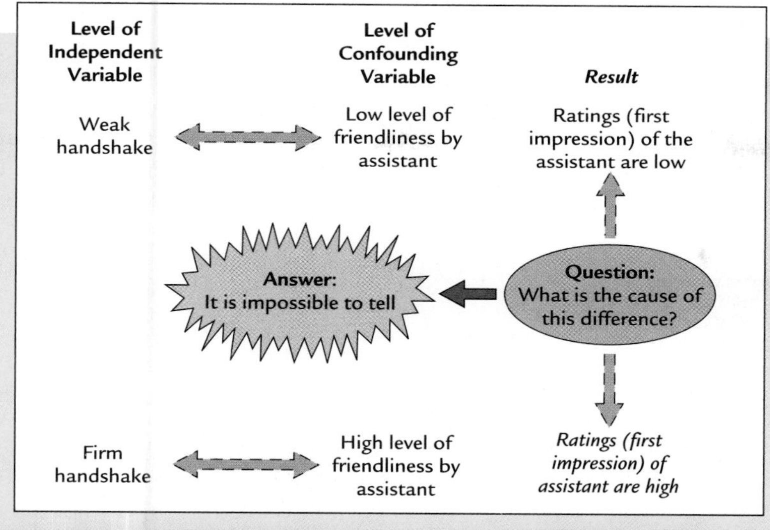

FIGURE 1.12

Confounding of Variables: A Fatal Flaw in Experimentation. In a hypothetical experiment designed to investigate the effects of handshakes on first impressions, firmness of handshake—the independent variable—is confounded with another variable—level of friendliness by the assistant. The assistant acts in a friendlier manner toward participants in the study when giving firm handshakes than when giving weak ones. As a result of this confounding, it is impossible to tell whether any differences between the behavior of participants in these two conditions stemmed from the independent variable, the confounding variable, or both.

research? When experimentation is used with skill and care, however, it can yield results that help us to answer complex questions about social behavior and social thought. Why, if this is so, don't social psychologists use it all the time? (Why, for instance, do they sometimes use the correlational method?) The answer is this: in some situations, experimentation simply cannot be used because of practical or ethical considerations. For example, imagine that a social psychologist formulates the following hypothesis: The more sincere politicians appear to be when giving their speeches, the more likely they are to win election. Could the psychologist convince two groups of politicians to vary their speeches in this respect, so that one group comes across as sincere but the other as phony? Almost certainly not! So although this research could, in principle, be conducted, there are *practical barriers* that prevent it from actually taking place.

Second, ethical constraints may prevent a researcher from conducting a study that is, in fact, feasible. In other words, the study could be conducted, but doing so would violate ethical standards accepted by scientists or society. Suppose, for example, that a researcher has good reason to believe that exposure to certain kinds of programs on television encourages teenagers to engage in unprotected sex. Could the researcher ethically conduct an experiment on this topic, exposing some teenagers to lots of these programs and others to none and then comparing their rates of unprotected sex? In principle, such research is possible, but no ethical social psychologist would perform it, because it might harm some of the participants in serious ways.

It is partly because of these and related problems that social psychologists often turn to systematic observation and the correlational method in their research. So, to repeat: All research methods offer a mixed bag of advantages and disadvantages, and social psychologists simply choose the method that seems best for studying a particular topic or question.

KEY POINTS

- *Experimentation* involves systematically altering one or more variables (independent variables) in order to determine whether changes in these variables affect some aspect of behavior (dependent variable).
- Successful use of the experimental method requires *random assignment of participants to experimental conditions,* holding all other factors that might also influence behavior constant so as to avoid confounding of variables.
- *Experimenter effects* occur when researchers unintentionally influence the behavior of participants. Such effects can be eliminated or minimized by double-blind procedures.
- Although it is a very powerful research tool, the experimental method is not perfect—questions concerning its *external validity* often arise. Further, it cannot be used in some situations because of practical or ethical considerations.

Interpreting Research Results: The Use of Statistics and Social Psychologists as Perennial Skeptics

Once a research project has been completed, social psychologists must turn their attention to another crucial task: interpreting the results. The key question is this: How much confidence can we place in the findings? Are correlations between variables, or observed differences between experimental conditions, real ones we can accept with confidence as being accurate? In order to answer this question, social psychologists generally employ **inferential statistics**—a special form of mathematics that allows us to evaluate the likelihood that a given pattern of research results occurred by chance alone. To determine whether the findings of a study are indeed real—unlikely to be a chance event—psychologists perform appropriate statistical analyses on the data they collect. If these analyses suggest that the likelihood of obtaining the observed findings by chance is low (usually, fewer than 5 times in 100), the results are described as *significant.* Only then are they interpreted as being of value in helping us understand some aspect of social behavior or social thought. All of the findings reported in this book have passed this basic test, so you can be confident that they refer to real (i.e., significant) results.

inferential statistics: A special form of mathematics that allows us to evaluate the likelihood that a given pattern of research results occurred by chance alone.

It's important to realize, however, that the likelihood that a given pattern of findings is a chance event is *never* zero. It can be very low—1 chance in 10,000, for instance—but it can never be zero. For this reason, a specific finding is always viewed as tentative in nature until it is replicated—reported again by different researchers in different laboratories. Only when findings have passed this additional test are they viewed with confidence by social psychologists. But here is where a serious problem arises: Only rarely do the results of social psychological research yield consistent findings. A more common pattern is for some studies to offer support for a given hypothesis while others fail to offer such support. For instance, some research on the effects of heat on aggression suggests that this relationship has limits: when it gets extremely hot, people become too exhausted or tired to engage in aggression, so such behavior actually decreases in frequency (e.g., Cohn & Rotton, 1997; Rotton & Cohn, 2000). In contrast, other research suggests that aggression continues to increase as temperatures rise, even at extreme levels of heat (e.g., Anderson et al., 1997). Why do such discrepancies arise? In part because different researchers may use different methods. For instance, in heat-and-aggression research, they may use somewhat different measures of aggression (e.g., murders versus less deadly assaults), or different researchers may conduct their research in regions with different climates. What is defined as "hot" by local residents, for instance, may be very different in Dallas or Bombay than it is in Boston or London. Whatever the cause, contrasting results in different studies pose a serious issue that must be carefully addressed.

■ INTERPRETING DIVERSE RESULTS: THE ROLE OF META-ANALYSIS. What do social psychologists do when confronted with contrasting results from different studies? One answer involves the use of a technique known as **meta-analysis** (e.g., Bond & Smith, 1996). This procedure allows us to combine the results of many different studies in order to estimate both the direction and the magnitude of the effects of independent variables. Meta-analytic procedures are mathematical in nature, so they eliminate potential sources of errors that might arise if we attempted to examine the findings of several studies in a more informal manner, such as through a simple count to see how many studies offered support for the hypothesis and how many did not. Overall, it is an important tool for interpreting the results of social psychological research, and we'll describe many studies that use this tool in later chapters.

The Role of Theory in Social Psychology

There is one more aspect of social psychological research we should consider before concluding. As we noted earlier, in their research social psychologists seek to do more than simply describe the world; they want to be able to *explain* it, too. For instance, social psychologists don't want to merely state that racial prejudice is common in the United States; they want to be able to explain *why* some persons hold these negative views. In social psychology, as in all branches of science, explanation involves the construction of **theories**—frameworks for explaining various events or processes. The procedure involved in building a theory goes something like this:

1. On the basis of existing evidence, a theory that reflects this evidence is proposed.
2. This theory, which consists of basic concepts and statements about how these concepts are related, helps to organize existing information and makes predictions about observable events. For instance, the theory might predict the conditions under which individuals acquire racial prejudice.
3. These predictions, known as *hypotheses,* are then tested by actual research.

meta-analysis: A statistical technique for combining data from independent studies in order to determine whether specific variables (or interactions between variables) have significant effects across these studies.

theories: Frameworks constructed by scientists in any field to explain why certain events or processes occur as they do.

4. If results are consistent with the theory, confidence in its accuracy is increased. If they are not, the theory is modified and further tests are conducted.

5. Ultimately, the theory is either accepted as accurate or rejected as inaccurate. Even if it is accepted as accurate, however, the theory remains open to further refinement as improved methods of research are developed and additional evidence relevant to the theory's predictions is obtained.

This may sound a bit abstract, so let's turn to a concrete example. Suppose that a social psychologist formulates the following theory: People are prejudiced against specific social groups (e.g., ethnic or racial minorities) when they conclude that (1) these groups have negative attributes, and (2) these groups are responsible for such attributes. This theory leads logically to various predictions, including these: (1) The more negative attributes a group is perceived as having, and the more it is seen as being responsible for these faults, the greater will be the prejudice against it; and (2) if a group is perceived as having negative attributes but these are *not* seen as being ones for which the group itself is responsible, then prejudice against that group will not occur, or will be minimal. So, for example, this reasoning would lead us to predict that Americans of European descent who view African Americans as having negative attributes but who do not hold them responsible for these attributes (e.g., they were, after all, the unwilling victims of slavery) will be less prejudiced against African Americans than will persons who view them as responsible for these supposed attributes. If research findings are consistent with these predictions and with others derived from the theory, confidence in the theory is increased. If findings are *not* consistent with the theory, it will be modified or perhaps rejected, as noted above. (See Chapter 6 for a discussion of the causes of racial prejudice, and of research designed to test this specific theory; Crandall et al., 2001.)

This process of formulating a theory, testing it, modifying the theory, testing it again, and so on, lies close to the core of the scientific method, so it is an important aspect of social psychological research (see Figure 1.13). Thus, many different theories relating to important aspects of social behavior and social thought will be presented in this book.

Two final points: First, theories are never *proven* in any final, ultimate sense. Rather, they are always open to test and are accepted with more or less confidence, depending on the weight of available evidence. Second, research is *not* undertaken to prove or verify a theory; it is performed to gather evidence relevant to the theory. If a researcher sets out to "prove" her or his pet theory, this is a serious violation of the principles of scientific skepticism, objectivity, and open-mindedness described on p. 6.

KEY POINTS

- In order to determine whether the results of a research project are real or due to chance, social psychologists use *inferential statistics.*
- If the chances are small that research results occurred by chance (less than 5 times in 100), results are described as significant.
- In order to assess the direction and magnitude of the effects of independent variables across different studies, social psychologists use a statistical technique known as *meta-analysis.*
- *Theories* are frameworks for explaining various events or processes. They play a key role in social psychological research.

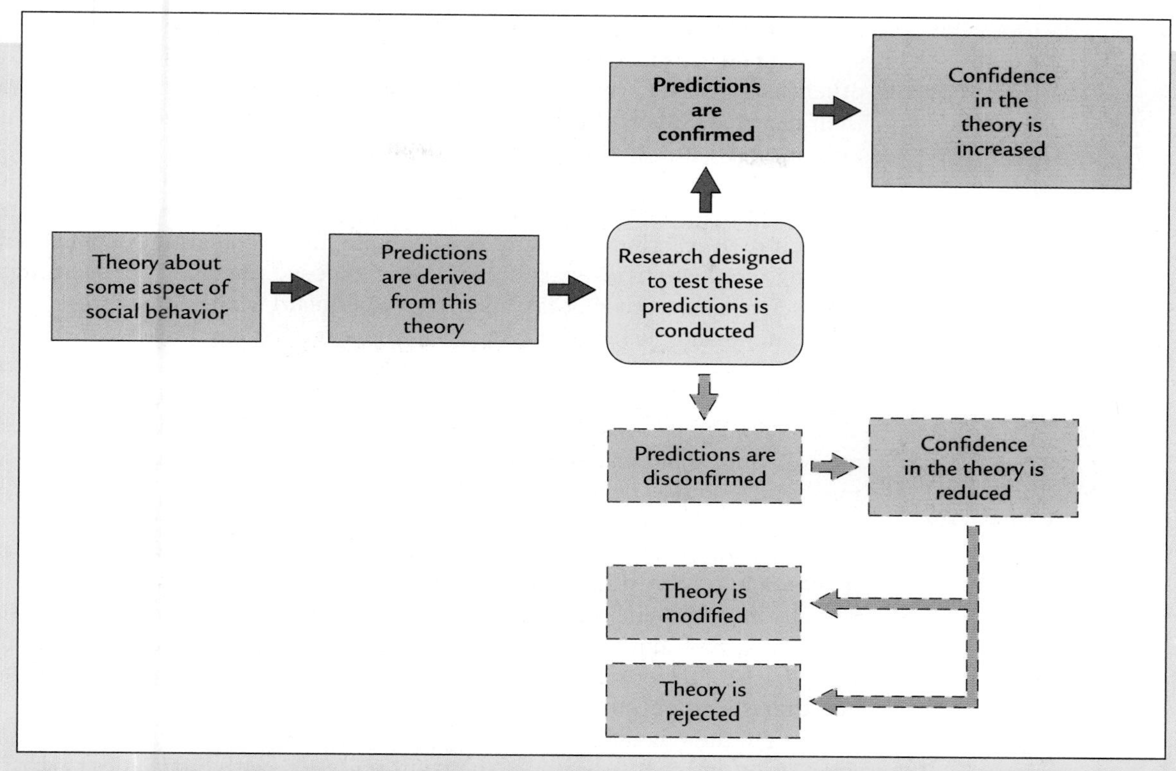

FIGURE 1.13

The Role of Theory in Social Psychological Research.
Theories both organize existing knowledge and make predictions about how various events or processes will occur. Once a theory is formulated, *hypotheses* derived logically from it are tested through careful research. If results agree with the predictions, confidence in the theory is increased. If results disagree with such predictions, the theory may be modified—or, ultimately, rejected as false.

The Quest for Knowledge and Rights of Individuals: Seeking an Appropriate Balance

In their use of experimentation, correlation, and systematic observation, social psychologists do not differ from researchers in many other fields. One technique, however, does seem to be unique to research in social psychology: **deception.** This technique involves efforts by researchers to withhold or conceal information about the purposes of a study from participants. The reason for using this procedure is simple: Many social psychologists believe that if participants know the true purposes of a study, their behavior in it will be changed by that knowledge. Thus, the research will *not* yield valid information about social behavior or social thought.

Some kinds of research do seem to require the use of temporary deception. For example, imagine that in a study designed to examine the effects of heat on aggression, participants are informed of this purpose. Will they now react differently than they would in the absence of this information? Perhaps, for instance, they might lean over backwards to avoid being irritable or aggressive in order to show the experimenter that they—not environmental factors—are in control of their own behavior.

deception: A technique whereby researchers withhold information about the purposes or procedures of a study from persons participating in it.

Alternatively, they might use this information as an excuse for being highly aggressive; after all, this is what the experimenter expects—and wants! In this and many other cases, social psychologists feel compelled to employ temporary deception in their research (Suls & Rosnow, 1988). However, the use of deception raises important ethical issues that cannot be ignored.

First, there is the chance, however slim, that deception may result in some kind of harm to the persons exposed to it. They may be upset by the procedures used or by their own reactions to them. For example, in several studies concerned with helping in emergencies, participants were exposed to staged but seemingly real emergency situations. For instance, they overheard what seemed to be a medical emergency—another person having an apparent seizure (e.g., Darley & Latané, 1968). Many participants were strongly upset by these staged events, and others were disturbed by the fact that although they recognized the need to help, they failed to do so. Clearly, the fact that participants experienced emotional upset raises complex ethical issues about just how far researchers can go when studying even very important topics such as this one.

We should hasten to emphasize that such research represents an extreme use of deception: generally, deception takes much milder forms. For example, participants may receive a request for help—or a handshake!—from a stranger who is actually an accomplice of the researchers; or they may be informed that most other students in their university hold certain views when in fact they do not. Still, even in such cases, the potential for some kind of harmful effects to participants exists, and this is a potentially serious drawback to the use of deception.

Second, there is the possibility that participants will resent being "fooled" during a study and that, as a result, they will acquire negative attitudes toward social psychology and psychological research in general; for instance, they may become suspicious about information presented by researchers (Kelman, 1967). To the extent such reactions occur—and findings indicate that they do, at least to a degree (Epley & Huff, 1998)—they have disturbing implications for the future of social psychology, which places so much emphasis on scientific research.

Because of such possibilities, the use of deception poses something of a dilemma to social psychologists. On the one hand, it seems essential to their research. On the other, its use raises serious problems. How can this issue be resolved? Although opinion remains somewhat divided, most social psychologists agree on the following points: First, deception should *never* be used to persuade people to take part in a study; withholding information about what will happen in an experiment or providing misleading information in order to induce people to take part in it is definitely *not* acceptable (Sigall, 1997). Second, most social psychologists agree that temporary deception may sometimes be acceptable provided two basic safeguards are employed. One of these is **informed consent**—giving participants as much information as possible about the procedures to be followed before they make their decision to participate. In short, this is the opposite of withholding information in order to persuade people to participate. The second is careful **debriefing**—providing participants with a full description of the purposes of a study after they have participated in it (see Figure 1.14). Such information should also include an explanation of deception and of why it was necessary to employ it.

informed consent: A procedure in which research participants are provided with as much information as possible about a research project before deciding whether to participate in it.

debriefing: Procedures at the conclusion of a research session in which participants are given full information about the nature of the research and the hypothesis or hypotheses under investigation.

Fortunately, a growing body of evidence indicates that, together, informed consent and thorough debriefing can substantially reduce the potential dangers of deception (Smith & Richardson, 1985). For example, most participants report that they view temporary deception as acceptable, provided that potential benefits outweigh potential costs and if there is no other means of obtaining the information sought (Rogers, 1980; Sharpe, Adair, & Roese, 1992). Further, persons who have participated in research employing deception report generally favorable attitudes about psychological research—attitudes just as favorable as those of persons who have

FIGURE 1.14
Careful Debriefing:
A Requirement in Studies That Use Deception.
After an experiment is completed, participants should be provided with *debriefing*—full information about the experiment's goals and the reasons why temporary deception was used.

not participated in such research (Sharp et al., 1992). However, as we noted above, there is some indication that they do become somewhat more suspicious about what researchers tell them during an experiment; even worse, such increased suspiciousness seems to last over several months (Epley & Huff, 1998).

Overall, then, existing evidence seems to suggest that most research participants do not react negatively to temporary deception as long as its purpose and necessity are clear. Indeed, they may be more upset by what happens during an experiment—for instance, receiving negative feedback on their work—than by the fact that such information was false and that they were deceived by the researcher. However, these findings do *not* mean that the safety or appropriateness of deception should be taken for granted (Rubin, 1985). On the contrary, the guiding principles for all researchers planning to use this procedure should be: (1) Use deception only when it is absolutely essential to do so—when no other means for conducting the research exists; (2) always proceed with caution; and (3) make certain that every possible precaution is taken to protect the rights, safety, and well-being of research participants.

KEY POINTS

- *Deception* involves efforts by social psychologists to withhold or conceal information about the purposes of a study from participants.
- Most social psychologists believe that temporary deception is often necessary in order to obtain valid research results.
- However, they view deception as acceptable only when important safeguards are employed: *informed consent* and thorough *debriefing*.

Using This Book: A Road Map for Readers

Although it was many years ago, both of us can remember our own first course in social psychology—and can also recall struggling very hard to understand many sections of the textbooks we used! Because we don't want you to experience the same difficulties, we have tried our best to make this book easy to read, and have also included a number of features designed to make it more enjoyable—and useful. Here is an overview of the steps we've taken to make reading this book a pleasant and informative experience.

First, each chapter begins with an outline and ends with a summary. Within the text itself, key terms are printed in **dark type like this** and are followed by a definition. These terms are also defined in a running glossary in the margins, as well as listed in a glossary at the end of the book. To help you understand and remember what you have read, each major section is followed by a list of **Key Points**—a brief summary of major points. All figures and tables are clear and simple, and most contain special labels and notes designed to help you understand them (see Figure 1.11 on page 23 for an example). Finally, each chapter ends with a *summary and review* of the Key Points. Reviewing this section can be an important aid to your studying.

Second, this book has an underlying theme, which can be stated as follows: Social psychology is much more than just a collection of interesting findings to be enjoyed for the moment, recalled on tests, and then quickly forgotten. On the contrary, we believe that it provides a new way of looking at the social world that everyone should take with them and use long after this course is over. To emphasize this theme of "taking social psychology with you," we've included several special features, which appear in each chapter. One of these is labeled **Beyond the Headlines: As Social Psychologists See It.** These sections take an actual newspaper headline and examine it from the perspective of social psychology. They illustrate how social psychologists think, and how the principles of our field can be applied to virtually *any* aspect of human social behavior.

Another feature relating to the theme of "taking social psychology with you" is labeled **Ideas to Take with You—And Use!** One of these special pages occurs in each chapter (see p. 33 for an example), and each is designed to highlight important concepts you should remember—and use—long after this course is over. In our view, you may well find them useful in your own life in the years ahead.

Although you may not have noticed it, this is the *tenth edition* of this book. That means that we have been writing it for thirty years! During these decades, social psychology has changed tremendously. To highlight these changes, we include special sections titled **Social Psychology: Thirty Years of Progress.** In these sections, we describe research that was occurring when this book was first being written (1971 to 1972), and then contrast this work with research on the same or similar topics occurring today. These sections will help you appreciate just how interesting, important, and timeless the topics studied by social psychologists are. In addition, these sections also illustrate the tremendous amount of progress our field has made in understanding these topics through use of the scientific method.

As we noted earlier, modern social psychology is distinguished by growing interest in social diversity and in the potential role of biological and genetic factors in human social behavior. These important themes are discussed at numerous points throughout the text. To help you identify them, the symbols (evolutionary perspective) and (diversity) are inserted in the margin next to these discussions.

Finally, to help you understand how research in each area of social psychology is related to research in other areas, we've included special **Connections** tables at the end of each chapter. These tables provide a kind of global review, reminding you of related topics discussed elsewhere in the book. In addition, they emphasize the fact that many aspects of social behavior and thought are closely linked: they do not occur in isolation from one another.

All of these features are designed to help you get the most out of your first encounter with social psychology. But, in a key sense, only *you* can transfer the information on the pages of this book into your own memory—and into your own life. So please do *use* this book. Read the summaries and chapter outlines, review the Key Points, and pay special attention to the Ideas to Take with You—And Use! pages. Doing so, we believe, will improve your understanding of social psychology—and your grade, too! We'll close this introductory chapter with our best wishes for a happy and successful life—one enriched by what you learn from the pages of this book and from your first encounter with the field of social psychology.

IDEAS TO TAKE WITH YOU—AND USE!

WHY CORRELATION DOES NOT NECESSARILY EQUAL CAUSATION

The fact that two variables are correlated—even strongly correlated—does not necessarily mean that changes in one cause changes in the other. This is true because changes in both variables may actually be related to—or caused by—a third variable. Two examples:

Observation: As Weight Increases, Income Increases.

Possible interpretations:

1. Weight gain causes increased income

Weight gain —Causes→ Increased income

2. As people grow older, they tend to gain weight *and* earn higher incomes; both variables are actually related to *age*.

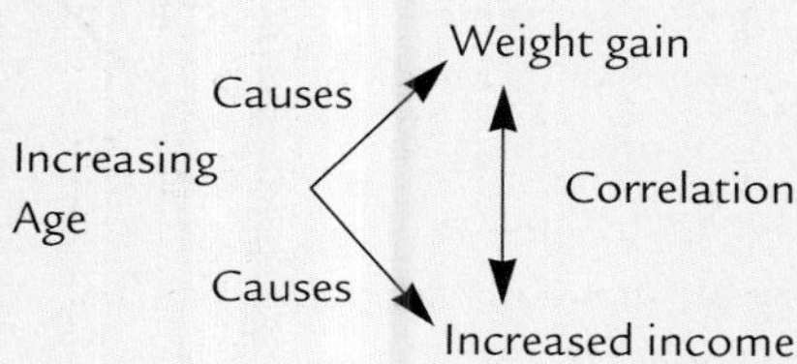

Observation: The More Violent Television and Movies People Watch, the More Likely They Are to Engage in Dangerous Acts of Aggression.

Possible interpretations:

1. Exposure to media violence is one factor that increases aggression.

Exposure to media violence —Causes→ Increased aggression

2. People who prefer a high level of stimulation have little control over their impulses; thus, they choose to watch displays of violence and also act aggressively more often than other people. Both variables are related to a need for certain kinds of stimulation.

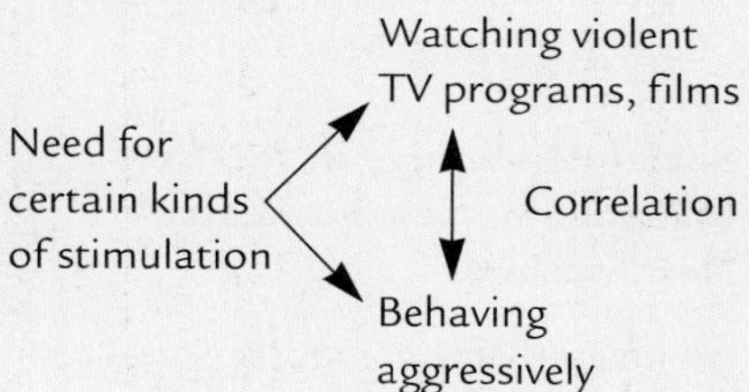

Key Conclusion: Even If Two Variables Are Strongly Correlated, This Does Not Necessarily Mean That Changes in One Cause Changes in the Other.

SUMMARY AND REVIEW OF KEY POINTS

Social Psychology: A Working Definition

- *Social psychology* is the scientific field that seeks to understand the nature and causes of individual behavior and thought in social situations.
- It is scientific in nature because it adopts the values and methods used in other fields of science.
- Social psychologists adopt the scientific method because "common sense" provides an unreliable guide to social behavior, and because human thought is influenced by many potential sources of bias.
- Social psychology focuses on the behavior of individuals and seeks to understand the causes of social behavior and thought.
- Important causes of social behavior and thought include the behavior and characteristics of other persons, cognitive processes, aspects of the physical environment, culture, and biological and genetic factors.

Social Psychology in the New Millennium: New Interests, New Methods

- A major theme in modern social psychology is the growing influence of a cognitive perspective. This perspective suggests that how people act in various social situations is strongly determined by their thoughts about these situations and other persons.
- Another major theme of social psychology is the growing interest in application—applying the knowledge and findings of social psychology to many practical problems.
- Social psychology currently adopts a *multicultural perspective.* This perspective recognizes the importance of cultural factors in social behavior and social thought, and notes that research findings obtained in one culture do not necessarily generalize to other cultures.
- There is growing recognition, in modern social psychology, of the potential role of biological and genetic factors in social behavior and social thought.

Answering Questions about Social Behavior and Social Thought: Research Methods in Social Psychology

- In *systematic observation,* behavior is carefully observed and recorded. In naturalistic observation, such observations are made in settings where the behavior naturally occurs.
- In the *survey method,* large numbers of persons respond to questions about their attitudes or behavior.
- In the *correlational method* of research, two or more variables are measured to determine whether they are related to one another in any way.
- The existence of even strong correlations between variables does not indicate that they are causally related to one another.
- In order to determine whether the results of a research project are real or due to chance, social psychologists use *inferential statistics.*
- If the likelihood is small that research results occurred by chance (less than 5 times in 100), results are described as significant.
- In order to assess the direction and magnitude of the effects of independent variables across different studies, social psychologists use a statistical technique known as *meta-analysis.*
- *Theories* are frameworks for explaining various events or processes. They play a key role in social psychological research.

The Quest for Knowledge and Rights of Individuals: Seeking an Appropriate Balance

- *Deception* involves efforts by social psychologists to withhold or conceal information about the purposes of a study from participants.
- Most social psychologists believe that temporary deception is often necessary in order to obtain valid research results.
- However, they view deception as acceptable only when important safeguards are employed: *informed consent* and thorough *debriefing.*

KEY TERMS

correlational method (p. 20)
debriefing (p. 30)
deception (p. 29)
dependent variable (p. 22)
evolutionary psychology (p. 12)
experimentation (experimental method) (p. 22)
experimenter effects (p. 24)
external validity (p. 24)
hypothesis (p. 20)
independent variable (p. 22)
inferential statistics (p. 26)
informed consent (p. 30)
meta-analysis (p. 27)
multicultural perspective (p. 15)
random assignment of participants to experimental conditions (p. 23)
social psychology (p. 5)
survey method (p. 18)
systematic observation (p. 18)
theories (p. 27)

FOR MORE INFORMATION

Buss, D. M. (1999). *Evolutionary psychology: The new science of the mind.* Boston: Allyn and Bacon.

- If you'd like to learn more about psychologists' efforts to understand the possible role of genetic and biological factors in our social behavior, this book is an excellent place to begin. The chapters on mating strategies, kinship, and aggression and warfare are truly fascinating.

Jackson, J. M. (1993). *Social psychology, past and present.* Hillsdale, NJ: Erlbaum.

- A thoughtful overview of the roots and development of social psychology. Organized around major themes in social psychological research, the book emphasizes the multidisciplinary roots of social psychology. The chapter on current trends is especially valuable.

Jean François Debord, *Café Les Deux-Magots.* 1967. © Copyright Giraudon/Art Resource, NY. Used with kind permission of the artist.

SOCIAL PERCEPTION: UNDERSTANDING OTHERS

CHAPTER OUTLINE

When I (RAB) was in college, I had a friend named Steve. Steve was short and on the plump side, and he was not, by any stretch of the imagination, handsome. But Steve dated one attractive woman after another, and whenever you saw him, he usually had one clinging affectionately to his arm. My other friends and I often wondered, "What has this guy *got?*" One day, after I had done Steve a big favor, I asked him to tell me the secret of his success with the opposite sex. His answer really surprised me. Here's what he said: "My secret? It's that I only go after women I know will like me." When I asked him to explain how he could tell, he added: "By the way they look at me . . . it's kind of a wide-eyed look that says, 'I could be interested'. . . ." I still didn't get it, so Steve promised to give me a lesson at a party we were going to that night. When we came in, he stood by the door and looked around the room. Then he said, "See that one—the blonde in the corner? She could be interested. And that one, too, over there. The others—I won't waste my time." And then Steve went into action. I watched as he gazed at the first woman and then smiled at her. She smiled back, and he immediately walked over and started talking with her. Long before the end of the party, they had left together. I was still not sure exactly what Steve had done, but I was beginning to figure it out; somehow, he was better than the rest of us at "reading" people—especially women. And he put this skill to good use in building a love life the rest of us envied.

Stated in other terms, Steve was very good at certain aspects of what social psychologists term **social perception**—the process (or, really, processes) through which we seek to understand other persons (see Figure 2.1). Because other people play such important roles in our lives, we engage in this process very often and devote a lot of effort to trying to figure out what makes other people tick—what they are like as individuals, why they act (or don't act) in certain ways, how they will behave in the future or in other situations. Sometimes these efforts succeed, but as we'll see in later sections of this chapter, this is not always so, and we often make errors in our efforts to understand others.

Social perception has long been a topic of interest to social psychologists. To acquaint you with what research on this topic has revealed, we'll focus on four aspects of it. First, we'll examine the process of **nonverbal communication**—communication between individuals involving an unspoken language of facial expressions, eye contact, body movements, and postures (e.g., Zebrowitz, 1997). This was the facet of social perception at which my friend Steve excelled: he could recognize romantic interest from across the room, and without ever having said a word to the woman in question.

Next, we'll examine *attribution,* the complex process through which we attempt to understand the reasons behind others' behavior—*why* they have acted as they have in a given situation. Third, we'll examine the nature of *impression formation*—how we form first impressions of others, and *impression management* (or *self-presentation*)—efforts to assure that these impressions are favorable ones.

social perception: The process through which we seek to know and understand other persons.

FIGURE 2.1

Social Perception: Efforts to Understand Others Are a Key Part of Everyday Life. As shown here, we often try to understand others—but we aren't always successful!

[SOURCE: DILBERT REPRINTED BY PERMISSION OF UNITED FEATURE SYNDICATE, INC.]

Finally, we'll turn to the question of how *accurate,* in general, social perception really is. Research suggests that although our perceptions of others are subject to many potential errors, we often *are* quite accurate in this respect, so we'll be able to end on an optimistic note.

Nonverbal Communication: The Language of Expressions, Gazes, and Gestures

Often, social behavior is strongly affected by temporary factors or causes. Changing moods, shifting emotions, fatigue, illness, drugs—all can influence the ways in which we think and behave. For example, most people are more willing to do favors for others when in a good mood than when in a bad mood (e.g., Baron, 1997a). Similarly, most people are more likely to lose their tempers and lash out at others in some manner when feeling irritable than when feeling pleasant (Berkowitz, in press).

Because such temporary factors exert important effects on social behavior and thought, we are often interested in them: we try to find out how others are feeling right now. How do we go about this process? Sometimes, in a very straightforward way—we ask other persons directly. Unfortunately, this strategy often fails, because others are unwilling to reveal their inner feelings to us. On the contrary, they may actively seek to conceal such information or even lie to us about their current emotions (e.g., DePaulo et al., 1996; Forrest & Feldman, 2000). For example, negotiators often hide their reactions from their opponents; salespersons frequently show more liking and friendliness toward potential customers than they really feel.

In situations like these, we often fall back upon another, less direct method for gaining information about others' reactions: we pay careful attention to *nonverbal cues* provided by changes in their facial expressions, eye contact, posture, body movements, and other expressive actions. As noted by DePaulo (1992), such behavior is relatively *irrepressible*—difficult to control—so that even when others try to conceal their inner feelings from us, these often leak out in many ways through nonverbal cues. The information conveyed by such cues, and our efforts to interpret this input, are often described by the term *nonverbal communication.* In this section, we'll first examine the basic channels through which nonverbal communication takes place. Then we'll turn to some interesting findings concerning how we use nonverbal cues to cut through *deception*—efforts by other persons to mislead us about their true feelings or beliefs (e.g., DePaulo, 1994). Before beginning,

nonverbal communication: Communication between individuals that does not involve the content of spoken language. It relies instead on an unspoken language of facial expressions, eye contact, and body language.

though, we should make one more point: Nonverbal cues emitted by other persons can affect our own feelings even if we are *not* consciously paying attention to these cues or trying to figure out how these persons feel. For instance, Neumann and Strack (2000) found that when individuals listen to another person read a speech, the tone of this person's voice (happy, neutral, or sad) can influence the listeners' moods even though they are concentrating on the content of the speech and not on the reader's emotional state. Neumann and Strack refer to such effects as *emotional contagion*—a mechanism through which feelings are transferred in a seemingly automatic way from one person to another. Now, on to the basic channels of nonverbal communication.

Nonverbal Communication: The Basic Channels

Think for a moment: Do you act differently when you are feeling happy than when you are feeling really sad? Most likely, you do. People tend to behave differently when experiencing different emotional states. But precisely how do differences in your inner states—your emotions, feelings, and moods—show up in your behavior? This question relates to the *basic channels* through which such communication takes place. Research findings indicate that, in fact, information about our inner states is often revealed through five basic channels: *facial expressions, eye contact, body movements, posture,* and *touching.*

■ UNMASKING THE FACE: FACIAL EXPRESSIONS AS CLUES TO OTHERS' EMOTIONS. More than two thousand years ago, the Roman orator Cicero stated: "The face is the image of the soul." By this he meant that human feelings and emotions are often reflected in the face and can be read there in specific expressions. Modern research suggests that Cicero—and many other observers of human behavior—were correct: it *is* possible to learn much about others' current moods and feelings from their facial expressions. In fact, it appears that six different basic emotions are represented clearly, and from a very early age, on the human face: anger, fear, happiness, sadness, surprise, and disgust (Izard, 1991; Rozin, Lowery, & Ebert, 1994). Additional findings suggest that another expression—contempt—may also be quite basic (e.g., Ekman & Heider, 1988, 1992). However, agreement on what specific facial expression represents this emotion is less consistent than that for the other six emotions just mentioned.

It's important to realize that these findings concerning a relatively small number of basic facial expressions in no way imply that human beings can show only a small number of facial expressions. On the contrary, emotions occur in many combinations (for example, joy tinged with sorrow, surprise combined with fear), and each of these reactions can vary greatly in strength. Thus, while there may be only a small number of basic themes in facial expression, the number of variations on these themes is immense (see Figure 2.2).

Now for another important question: Are facial expressions universal? In other words, if you traveled to a remote part of the world and visited a group of people who had never before met an outsider, would their facial expressions in various situations resemble your own? Would they smile in reaction to events that made them happy, frown when exposed to conditions that made them angry, and so on? Further, would you be able to recognize these distinct expressions as readily as the ones shown by persons belonging to your own culture? Early research on this question seemed to suggest that facial expressions *are* universal in both respects (e.g., Ekman & Friesen, 1975). However, some findings have called this conclusion into question (Russell, 1994). The results of more recent studies (e.g., Russell, 1994; Carroll & Russell, 1996) indicate that while facial expressions may indeed reveal much about others' emotions, our judgments in this respect are also affected by the context in which the facial expressions occur and various situational cues. For instance,

FIGURE 2.2

Facial Expressions: The Range Is Immense.
Although there is general agreement among researchers that only a small number of emotions are represented by distinct facial expressions, emotions can occur in many combinations, so people actually show an enormous number of different expressions.

if individuals view a photo of a face showing what would normally be judged as *fear* but also read a story suggesting that this person is actually showing *anger,* many describe the face as showing anger, not fear (Carroll & Russell, 1996). Findings such as these suggest that facial expressions may not be as universal in terms of providing clear signals about underlying emotions as was previously assumed. However, additional evidence (e.g., Rosenberg & Ekman, 1995) provides support for the view that when situational cues and facial expressions are *not* inconsistent, others' facial expressions do provide an accurate guide to their underlying emotions. Overall then, it seems safest to conclude that while facial expressions are not totally universal around the world—cultural and contextual differences do exist with respect to their precise meaning—they generally need very little "translation" as compared to spoken languages.

■ GAZES AND STARES: EYE CONTACT AS A NONVERBAL CUE. Have you ever had a conversation with someone wearing very dark or mirrored sunglasses? If so, you realize that this can be an uncomfortable situation. Because you can't see the other person's eyes, you are uncertain about how she or he is reacting. Taking note of the importance of cues provided by others' eyes, ancient poets often described the eyes as "windows to the soul." In one important sense, they were correct: we do often learn much about others' feelings from their eyes. For example, we interpret a high level of gazing from another as a sign of liking or friendliness (Kleinke, 1986). In contrast, if others avoid eye contact with us, we may conclude that they are unfriendly, don't like us, or are simply shy (Zimbardo, 1977).

While a high level of eye contact with others is usually interpreted as a sign of liking or positive feelings, there is one exception to this general rule. If another person gazes at us continuously and maintains such contact regardless of what we do, she or he can be said to be **staring.** A stare is often interpreted as a sign of anger or hostility—as in *cold stare*—and most people find this particular nonverbal cue disturbing (Ellsworth & Carlsmith, 1973). In fact, we may quickly terminate social interaction with someone who stares at us and may even leave the scene (Greenbaum & Rosenfield, 1978). This is one reason why experts on road rage—highly aggressive driving by motorists, sometimes followed by actual assaults—recommend that drivers avoid eye contact with people who are disobeying traffic laws and rules of the road (e.g., Bushman, 1998). Apparently, such persons, who are already in a highly excitable state, interpret anything approaching a stare from another driver as an aggressive act and may react accordingly.

staring: A form of eye contact in which one person continues to gaze steadily at another regardless of what the recipient does.

■ BODY LANGUAGE: GESTURES, POSTURE, AND MOVEMENTS. Try this simple demonstration for yourself:

First, remember some incident that made you angry—the angrier the better. Think about it for a minute.

Now, try to remember another incident, one that made you feel sad—again, the sadder the better.

Compare your behavior in the two contexts. Did you change your posture or move your hands, arms, or legs as your thoughts shifted from the first event to the second? There is a good chance that you did, for our current moods or emotions are often reflected in the position, posture, and movement of our bodies. Together, such nonverbal behaviors are termed **body language,** and they, too, can provide us with useful information about others.

First, body language often reveals others' emotional states. Large numbers of movements—especially ones in which one part of the body does something to another part (touching, rubbing, scratching)—suggest emotional arousal. The greater the frequency of such behavior, the higher the level of arousal or nervousness.

Larger patterns of movements, involving the whole body, can also be informative. Such phrases as "she adopted a *threatening posture*" and "he greeted her with *open arms*" suggest that different body orientations or postures indicate contrasting emotional states. In fact, research by Aronoff, Woike, and Hyman (1992) confirms this possibility. These researchers first identified two groups of characters in classical ballet: ones who played a dangerous or threatening role (e.g., Macbeth, the Angel of Death, Lizzie Borden) and ones who played warm, sympathetic roles (Juliet, Romeo). Then, they examined examples of dancing by these characters in actual ballets to see if they adopted different kinds of postures. Aronoff and his colleagues predicted that the dangerous, threatening characters would show more diagonal or angular postures, while the warm sympathetic characters would show more rounded postures; and results strongly confirmed this hypothesis. These and related findings indicate that large-scale body movements or postures can sometimes provide important information about others' emotions, and even about their apparent traits.

body language: Cues provided by the position, posture, and movement of others' bodies or body parts.

Finally, we should add that more specific information about others' feelings is often provided by gestures. Gestures fall into several categories, but perhaps the most important are *emblems*—body movements carrying specific meanings in a given culture. Do you recognize the gestures shown in Figure 2.3? In the United

FIGURE 2.3

Gestures: A Basic Channel of Nonverbal Communication.

Do you recognize the gestures shown here? Can you tell what they mean? In the United States and other Western cultures, each of these gestures has a specific meaning. However, they might well have no meaning, or entirely different meanings, in other cultures.

States and several other countries, these movements have clear and definite meanings. However, in other cultures, they might have no meaning, or even a different meaning. For this reason, it is wise to be careful about using gestures while traveling in cultures different from your own: you may offend the people around you without meaning to do so!

■ TOUCHING: IS A FIRM HANDSHAKE REALLY A "PLUS"? Suppose that during a brief conversation with another person, she or he touched you briefly. How would you react? What information would this behavior convey? The answer to both questions is, *it depends.* And what it depends upon is several factors relating to who does the touching (a friend, or a stranger, a member of your own or the other gender); the nature of this physical contact (brief or prolonged, gentle or rough, what part of the body is touched); and the context in which the touching takes place (a business or social setting, a doctor's office). Depending on such factors, touch can suggest affection, sexual interest, dominance, caring, or even aggression. Despite such complexities, existing evidence indicates that when touching is considered appropriate, it often produces positive reactions in the person being touched (e.g., Alagna, Whitcher, & Fisher, 1979; Smith, Gier, & Willis, 1982). But remember: It must be viewed as appropriate to produce such reactions.

One acceptable way in which people in many different cultures touch strangers is through handshaking (see Figure 2.4). Pop psychology and even books on etiquette (e.g., Vanderbilt, 1957) suggest that handshakes reveal much about other persons—for instance, their personalities—and that a firm handshake is a good way to make a favorable first impression on others. Are such observations true? Is this form of nonverbal communication actually revealing? Ingenious research by Chaplin and his colleagues (Chaplin et al., 2000) suggests that it is. (As you may recall, we used handshaking as a means of illustrating methods of research in social psychology in Chapter 1.)

To study handshaking as a nonverbal cue to others' personalities, Chaplin and his colleagues (2000) first trained four advanced psychology students to rate handshakes along several basic dimensions (strength, grip, dryness, temperature, vigor, duration, etc.). Then, they had these raters shake hands with undergraduate students

FIGURE 2.4

Handshakes: How Much Information Do They Convey? Handshaking is a common form of greeting in many cultures around the world. Folk wisdom has long suggested that we can learn much from the way in which others shake our hands. Do you think this is true? ■

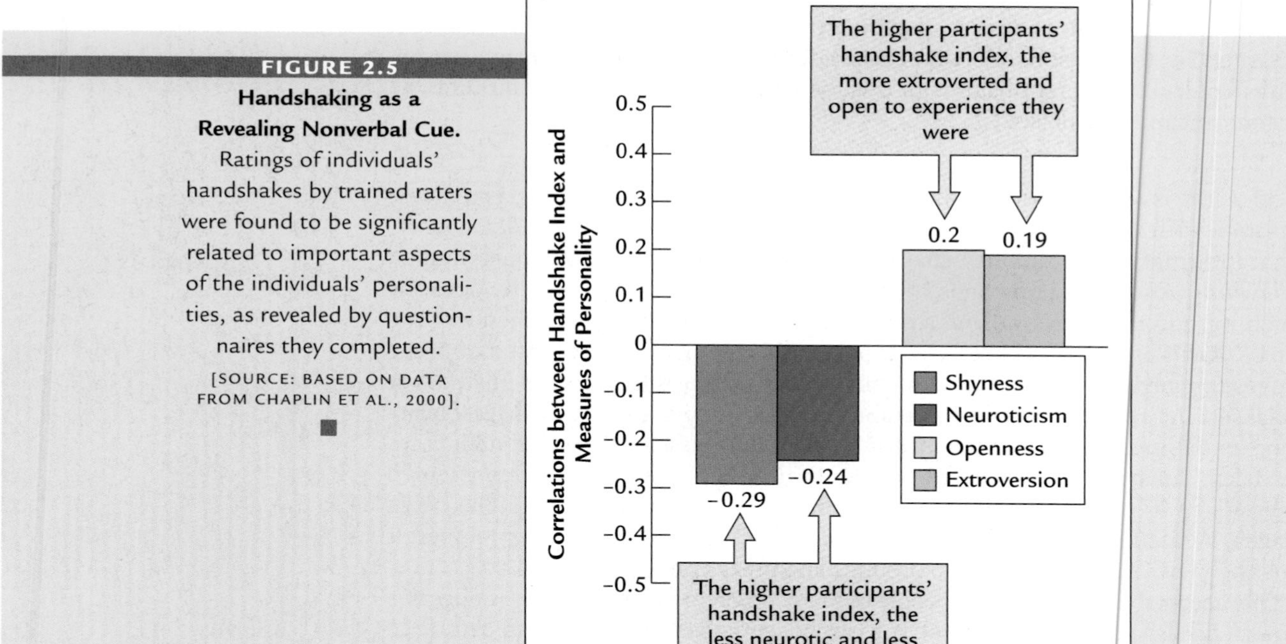

FIGURE 2.5

Handshaking as a Revealing Nonverbal Cue. Ratings of individuals' handshakes by trained raters were found to be significantly related to important aspects of the individuals' personalities, as revealed by questionnaires they completed.

[SOURCE: BASED ON DATA FROM CHAPLIN ET AL., 2000].

(both men and women) twice: when they first came to the laboratory for appointments and again just before they left. In between these two handshakes, the research participants completed questionnaires designed to measure several key aspects of personality (e.g., extroversion, agreeableness, conscientiousness, openness to experience, expressiveness). In addition, the raters indicated their first impressions of each participant.

Several aspects of handshaking (e.g., duration, completeness of grip, strength, vigor) were closely related, so these were combined into a single index of handshakes. Results indicated that this index, in turn, was strongly related to several aspects of participants' personality, as revealed by the questionnaire they completed. Specifically, the higher the participants' handshake index, the more extroverted and open to experience and less shy they were (see Figure 2.5). In addition, for women, but not for men, the higher the participants' handshake index, the more agreeable they were. First impressions, too, were related to handshaking: the higher the participants' handshake index, the more favorable were raters' impressions of them.

In sum, this particular kind of touching was in fact quite revealing about the persons who engaged in it. As the authors of etiquette books and guides to success have long suggested, a firm handshake *is* a valuable asset, at least in cultures where handshakes are used for greetings and departures.

Recognizing Deception: The Role of Nonverbal Cues

A little inaccuracy sometimes saves tons of explanation. *(Saki, 1924)*

While this quotation may ring true, it is also the case that people often lie for other, less socially desirable reasons—to advance their own interests, to influence others, to conceal their true motives or goals. In short, lying is an all-too-common part of social life. This sad fact raises an important question: How can we tell when others are lying? Part of the answer seems to involve nonverbal cues. When people lie, subtle changes often occur in their facial expressions, body posture or movements, and certain nonverbal aspects of speech (aspects that are not related to the meaning of the words they speak—for instance, the tone of their voices). Let's take a look at these and several other facets of our ability to detect deception by other persons.

■ NONVERBAL CUES TO DECEPTION. One useful cue that others are lying is revealed by **microexpressions**—fleeting facial expressions lasting only a few tenths of a second. Such reactions appear on the face very quickly after an emotion-provoking event and are difficult to suppress (Ekman, 1985). As result, they can be very revealing about others' true feelings or emotions. For instance, if you ask another person whether they like something (you, an idea you have expressed, or anything else), watch their faces closely as they respond. If you see one expression (e.g., a frown), which is followed very quickly by another (e.g., a smile), this can be a useful sign that they are lying—they are stating one opinion or reaction when, in fact, they really have another.

A second nonverbal cue that is revealing of deception is known as *interchannel discrepancies.* These are inconsistencies between nonverbal cues from different basic channels, and they result from the fact that persons who are lying often find it difficult to control all of these channels at once. For instance, they may manage their facial expressions well but may have difficulty looking you in the eye as they tell their lie.

A third nonverbal cue involves *nonverbal* aspects of speech. When people lie, the pitch of their voices often rises and they tend to speak in a more hesitating manner and to make more errors (e.g., DePaulo, Stone, & Lassiter, 1985; Stiff et al., 1989). If you detect these kinds of changes in another person's voice, this, too, can be a sign that they are lying.

Fourth, deception is frequently revealed by certain aspects of *eye contact.* Persons who are lying often blink more often and show pupils that are more dilated than do persons who are telling the truth. They may also show an unusually low level of eye contact or—surprisingly—an unusually high one, as they attempt to fake being honest by looking others right in the eye (Kleinke, 1986).

Finally, persons who are lying sometimes show *exaggerated facial expressions.* They may smile more—or more broadly—than usual or may show greater sorrow than is typical in a given situation. A prime example: Someone says "no" to a request you've made and then shows exaggerated regret. This is a good sign that the reasons the person has supplied for saying "no" may not be true.

Through careful attention to these nonverbal cues, we can often tell when others are lying—or merely trying to hide their own feelings from us. Success in detecting deception is far from certain; some persons are very skillful liars. But if you pay careful attention to the cues described above, you will make their task of pulling the wool over your eyes much more difficult.

■ COGNITIVE FACTORS IN THE DETECTION OF DECEPTION. Our comments so far might seem to suggest that the harder we try to detect deception, the more successful we will be at this task. Surprisingly, though, this is not always the case. Here's why: When others try to deceive us, we can pay careful attention either to their words *or* to their nonverbal cues—because we have limited cognitive capacity, it is difficult to do both at once. Further, the more strongly motivated we are to detect deception, the more likely we are to pay careful attention to their words—to listen carefully to what they say. In fact, though, the most revealing cues to

microexpressions: Fleeting facial expressions lasting only a few tenths of a second.

deception are often nonverbal ones. So, paradoxically, the more motivated we are to detect deception, the less effective we may be at this task.

Direct evidence for this conclusion is provided by research conducted by Forrest and Feldman (2000). These researchers had undergraduate students either present their real views on various issues (e.g., the death penalty, restrictions on immigration) or lie about their views and present ones opposite to those they really held. Their presentations were taped and then shown to another group of participants in the study, who were asked to judge whether the persons shown in the tape were telling the truth or were lying. To vary the judges' motivation for detecting deception, half (the high-involvement group) were told that they would later be asked questions about the messages on the tape and that success in answering these questions would provide a good measure of their intelligence and social skills. The other half (the low-involvement group) was told that they would be asked questions about issues not discussed on the tape and were not told that their success at this task would constitute a good measure of their intelligence or social skills.

Forrest and Feldman (2000) predicted that judges in the low-involvement group would actually do better than those in the high-involvement group in determining whether the persons they saw were lying or telling the truth, and as you can see from Figure 2.6, this is precisely what was found. The authors interpreted this finding as stemming from the fact that participants in the high-involvement condition directed most of their attention to the words spoken by the persons on the tape, while those in the low-involvement group paid more attention to nonverbal cues. Whatever the precise mechanism involved, the findings of this study and

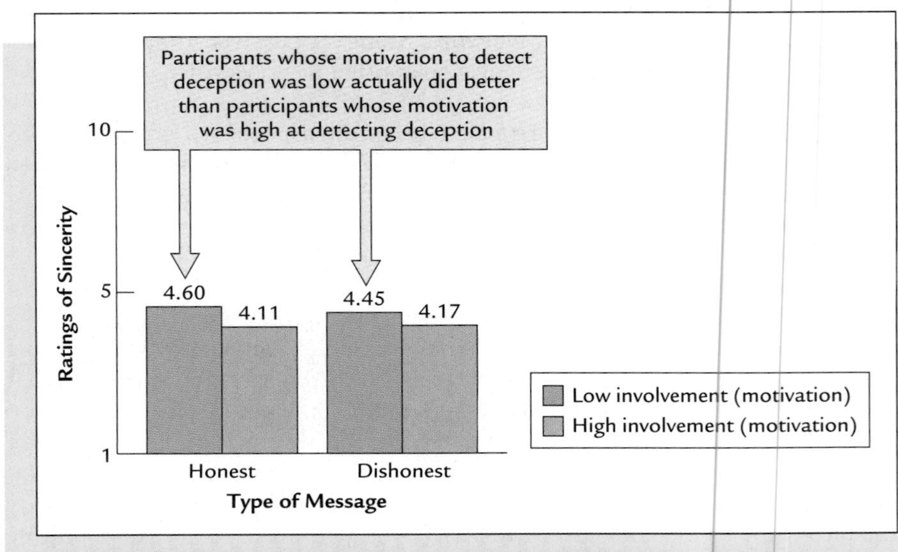

FIGURE 2.6

Motivation to Detect Deception: Evidence That It Can Backfire. Individuals who were highly motivated to detect others' deception actually did worse at this task than did individuals who were not as highly motivated to detect deception. This may occur because when we are highly motivated to recognize others' deception, we tend to pay close attention to their words—and so overlook important nonverbal cues to deception. [SOURCE: BASED ON DATA FROM FORREST & FELDMAN, 2000.]

those of several others suggest that as is true with respect to many other tasks, trying too hard to detect others' deception can sometimes be counterproductive and actually reduce our success in this respect.

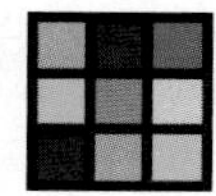

Before concluding this discussion of deception, we should address one final question: Can lies be detected across cultures? In other words, does someone have to be from our own culture in order for us to be able to tell when she or he is lying, or can we recognize deception even if the person engaging in such behavior is from another culture and doesn't even speak our language? Research by Bond and Atoum (2000) indicates that we can indeed tell when people from cultures other than our own are lying. In their research, Bond and Atoum (2000) had persons from widely different cultures (the United States, Jordan, India) view videotapes of persons from their own and other cultures who were either lying or telling the truth. As you might expect, participants were more accurate at recognizing lies by persons in their own culture than by persons from another culture. But they were able to recognize lies with greater than chance success, even when the lies were told by persons from a different culture. Findings such as these suggest that, in contrast to spoken language, the language of nonverbal cues requires no interpreter. (For information about another nonverbal cue people send to one another, see the **Beyond the Headlines** section below.)

BEYOND THE HEADLINES: AS SOCIAL PSYCHOLOGISTS SEE IT

FRAGRANCE: A FADING NONVERBAL CUE?

It Isn't a Nose Dive, but Perfume Sales Are Steadily Dropping

Wall Street Journal, December 27, 1998—Ari Kopelman, the president of Chanel, Inc. often finds a way to see the master bedroom when he visits friends. On vanity after vanity, he often sees dozens of half-used perfume bottles gathering dust. "Every woman must have 157 years' supply of fragrance," Mr. Kopelman says.

Call it an olfactory shift. Women are walking down the aisle, into offices and out to dinner these days with a lot less on in terms of scents. Mary Collins, a 31-year-old marketing manager in Atlanta puts it: "I don't like perfume enough to spend a lot on it anymore."

The perfume industry first took off after World War II when returning GIs brought the classic Chanel No. 5 ashore for sweethearts. Pricey fragrances became fixtures on dressing tables. The perfume industry blossomed into a $6 billion industry in the 1980s. But growth slowed in the early 1990s and has actually dropped 2% to 4% annually for the past three years.

Upwardly mobile women began shunning fragrances at work. . . . Fashion designers caught the mood and came out with their own, toned-down fragrances. Light perfume gave the industry a lift, but it also continued the process of weaning consumers away from traditional, big-name fragrances. . . . "I used to buy Chanel and Joy," says 60-year-old Dorothy Liadakis of Baltimore, but now she snaps up drugstore bath gels instead. "I don't know if it's me or the fragrances that have changed. . . ."

Facial expressions, eye contact, gestures, body movements—these are the basic channels of nonverbal communication. But, in a sense, fragrance, too, can be classified as a nonverbal cue. After all, ads such as the one in Figure 2.7 on page 48 suggest that by using a specific fragrance, we can send subtle—or not so subtle!—messages to other people. "I'm romantic," "I'm sensitive," "I'm mysterious"—the list is limited only by advertisers' imaginations!

(continued)

FIGURE 2.7
Fragrance: Another Type of Nonverbal Cue.
People often use artificial fragrances to send each other nonverbal cues. In any case, this is what the fragrance industry—and advertisers—would like us to believe.

So why have people of all ages reduced their use of fragrance—or, at least, their willingness to pay high prices for famous brands that advertise lavishly? Many factors probably contribute to this trend. First, people all over the world—but especially in the United States, one of the largest markets for fragrances—now dress down with increasing frequency. And if one is wearing jeans and a sweatshirt, it makes little sense to put on a $50-per ounce perfume. Second, as suggested by the article above, working women do not want to wear strong perfumes to the office; they feel this will send bosses and coworkers the wrong message about their career commitment. Finally, the shift toward *light* (as in "light beer" and "light foods") seems to call for subtler fragrances, too. And these can be purchased much more cheaply in a local pharmacy than at the perfume counter of an up-scale department store.

In short, many trends have combined to reduce the use of fragrance by both women and men. This is bad news for the fragrance industry but pleases many persons who find strong fragrances intrusive or even annoying. In any case, it is clear that growing numbers of persons have concluded that they can do their nonverbal communicating through channels other than the one connected to our noses.

KEY POINTS

- *Social perception* involves the processes through which we seek to understand other persons. It plays a key role in social behavior and social thought.
- In order to understand others' emotional states, we often rely on *nonverbal communication*—an unspoken language of facial expressions, eye contact, and body movements and postures.
- Although facial expressions may not be as universal as once believed, they do often provide useful information about others' emotional states. Useful information is also provided by eye contact, body language, and touching.
- Research findings indicate that handshaking provides useful nonverbal cues about others' personality, and can influence first impressions of strangers.
- If we pay careful attention to certain nonverbal cues, we can recognize efforts at deception by others—even if these persons are from cultures other than our own.
- Fragrance can be viewed as another type of nonverbal cue. The use of such communication seems to be decreasing, as indicated by declining perfume sales.

Attribution: Understanding the Causes of Others' Behavior

Accurate knowledge of others' current moods or feelings can be useful in many ways. Yet, where social perception is concerned, this knowledge is often only the first step. In addition, we usually want to know more—to understand others' lasting traits and to know the causes behind their behavior. Social psychologists believe that our interest in such questions stems, in large measure, from our basic desire to understand cause-and-effect relationships in the social world (Pittman, 1993; Van Overwalle, 1998). In other words, we don't simply want to know *how* others have acted; we want to understand *why* they have done so, too. The process through which we seek such information is known as **attribution.** More formally, *attribution* refers to our efforts to understand the causes behind others' behavior and, on some occasions, the causes behind *our* behavior, too (see Figure 2.8 on page 50). Social psychologists have studied attribution for several decades, and their research has yielded many intriguing insights into this important process (e.g., Graham & Folkes, 1990; Heider, 1958; Read & Miller, 1998).

Theories of Attribution: Frameworks for Understanding How We Attempt to Make Sense of the Social World

Because attribution is complex, many theories have been proposed to explain its operation. Here, we will focus on two classic views that have been especially influential.

attribution: The process through which we seek to identify the causes of others' behavior and so gain knowledge of their stable traits and dispositions.

"It's so silly. Now I can't even remember why I killed him."

FIGURE 2.8
Attribution: Efforts to Understand the Causes behind Others' Behavior—and Our Own. We often try to understand *why* other people have acted in certain ways, and sometimes (as shown here), we turn this process inward and ask ourselves, "Why did *I* do what I did?"

■ FROM ACTS TO DISPOSITIONS: USING OTHERS' BEHAVIOR AS A GUIDE TO THEIR LASTING TRAITS. The first of these classic theories—Jones and Davis's (1965) theory of **correspondent inference**—asks how we use information about others' behavior as a basis for inferring that they possess various traits. In other words, the theory is concerned with how we decide, on the basis of observing others' behavior, that they possess specific traits or dispositions that will remain fairly stable over time.

At first glance, this might seem to be a simple task. Others' behavior provides us with a rich source on which to draw, so if we observe it carefully, we should be able to learn a lot about them. Up to a point, this is true. The task is complicated, however, by the following fact: Often, individuals act in certain ways not because doing so reflects their own preferences or traits, but because external factors leave them little choice. For example, suppose you observe a woman rushing through an airport, pushing people out of the way in her haste. Does this mean that she is impatient and rude? Not necessarily; she may simply be responding to the fact that her plane is about to leave without her. This traveler may actually be shy and polite most of the time; her behavior now may be the exception, not the rule. Situations like this are quite common, and in them, using others' behavior as a guide to their lasting traits or motives can be very misleading. How do we cope with such complications? According to Jones and Davis's theory (Jones & Davis, 1965; Jones & McGillis, 1976), we accomplish this task by focusing our attention on certain types of actions—those most likely to prove informative.

First, we consider only behaviors that seem to have been freely chosen, while largely ignoring ones that were somehow forced on the person in question. Second, we pay careful attention to actions that show what Jones and Davis term **noncommon effects**—effects that can be caused by one specific factor but not by others. (Don't confuse this word with *uncommon,* which simply means infrequent.) Why are actions that produce noncommon effects informative? Because they allow us to zero in on the causes of others' behavior. Perhaps a concrete example will help.

Imagine that one of your casual friends has just gotten engaged. Her future spouse is very handsome, has a great personality, is wildly in love with your friend, and

correspondent inference (theory of): A theory describing how we use others' behavior as a basis for inferring their stable dispositions.

noncommon effects: Effects produced by a particular cause that could not be produced by any other apparent cause.

is very rich. What can you learn about her from her decision to marry this man? Not much. There are so many good reasons that you can't choose among them. In contrast, imagine that your friend's fiancé is very handsome but that he treats her with indifference and is known to be extremely boring; also, he has no visible means of support and intends to live on your friend's salary. Does the fact that she is marrying him tell you anything about her personal characteristics? Definitely. You can probably conclude that she places more importance on physical attractiveness in a husband than on personality or wealth. As you can see from this example, then, we can usually learn more about others from actions on their part that yield noncommon effects than from ones that do not.

Finally, Jones and Davis (1965) suggest that we also pay greater attention to actions by others that are low in *social desirability* than to actions that are high on this dimension. In other words, we learn more about others' traits from actions they perform that are somehow out of the ordinary than from actions that are very much like those performed by most other persons. For instance, I once had a neighbor who owned a huge St. Bernard dog. For some reason unknown to me, this dog selected my front lawn as the place where he left his daily "calling card." I mentioned this to my neighbor several times, but instead of expressing dismay and regret, he stared at me as if to say, "Why would that bother you?" To me, this was definitely behavior low in social desirability, and it told me quite a bit about my neighbor and his view of the world. Fortunately for me, he was suddenly transferred to a distant branch of his company, so the situation had a happy ending.

In sum, according to the theory proposed by Jones and Davis, we are most likely to conclude that others' behavior reflects their stable traits (that is, we are likely to reach *correspondent* inferences about them) when that behavior (1) is freely chosen; (2) yields distinctive, noncommon effects; and (3) is low in social desirability.

■ KELLEY'S THEORY OF CAUSAL ATTRIBUTIONS: HOW WE ANSWER THE QUESTION "WHY?"

Consider the following events:

> You arrange to meet someone for lunch, but he doesn't show up.
>
> You leave several messages for a friend, but she doesn't call back.
>
> You expect a promotion in your job, but don't receive it.

What question would arise in your mind in each of these situations? Probably, the question "Why?" You'd want to know *why* your lunch date didn't show up—did he forget? Did he do it on purpose? You'd want to know *why* your friend hasn't returned your calls—is she angry at you? Is her answering machine broken? And you'd want to know *why* you didn't get the promotion—is your boss disappointed in your performance? Were you the victim of some kind of discrimination? In many situations, this is the central attributional task we face: We want to know why other people have acted as they have or why events have turned out in a specific way. Such knowledge is crucial, for only if we understand the causes behind others' actions or events that occur can we hope to make sense out of the social world. Obviously, the number of specific causes behind others' behavior is very large. To make the task more manageable, therefore, we often begin with a preliminary question: Did others' behavior stem mainly from *internal* causes (their own traits, motives, intentions), mainly from *external* causes (some aspect of the social or physical world); or from a combination of the two? For example, you might wonder whether you didn't receive the promotion because you didn't work hard enough on a major project paper (an internal cause), because your boss is unfair and biased against you (an external cause), or perhaps because of both factors. How do we attempt to answer this question? A theory proposed by Kelley (Kelley, 1972; Kelley & Michela, 1980) provides important insights into this process.

According to Kelley, in our attempts to answer the question *why* about others' behavior, we focus on information relating to three major sources of information. First, we consider **consensus**—the extent to which other persons react to a given stimulus or event in the same manner as the person we are considering. The higher the proportion of people who react in the same way, the higher the consensus. Second, we consider **consistency**—the extent to which the person in question reacts to the stimulus or event in the same way on other occasions, over time. And third, we examine **distinctiveness**—the extent to which this person reacts in the same manner to other, different stimuli or events.

According to Kelley's theory, we are most likely to attribute another's behavior to *internal* causes under conditions in which consensus and distinctiveness are low but consistency is high. In contrast, we are most likely to attribute another's behavior to *external* causes when consensus, consistency, and distinctiveness are all high. Finally, we usually attribute another's behavior to a combination of internal and external factors when consensus is low but consistency and distinctiveness are high. Perhaps a concrete example will help illustrate the very reasonable nature of these ideas.

Imagine that you see a server in a restaurant flirt with a customer. This behavior might be fun to observe, but it also raises an interesting question: Why does the server act this way? Because of internal causes or external causes? Is he simply someone who likes to flirt (an internal cause)? Or is the customer extremely attractive (an external cause)? According to Kelley's theory, your decision (as an observer of this scene) would depend on information relating to the three factors mentioned above. First, assume that the following conditions prevail: (1) You observe other servers flirting with this customer (consensus is high); (2) you have seen this server flirt with the same customer on other occasions (consistency is high); and (3) you have *not* seen this server flirt with other customers (distinctiveness is high). Under these conditions—high consensus, consistency, and distinctiveness—you would probably attribute the clerk's behavior to external causes: this customer is really attractive and that's why the server flirts with her.

Now, in contrast, assume these conditions exist: (1) No other servers flirt with the customer (consensus is low); (2) you have seen this server flirt with the same customer on other occasions (consistency is high); and (3) you have seen this server flirt with many other customers, too (distinctiveness is low). In this case, Kelley's theory suggests that you would attribute the server's behavior to internal causes: the server is simply a person who likes to flirt (see Figure 2.9).

The basic assumptions of Kelley's theory have been confirmed in a wide range of social situations, so the theory seems to provide important insights into the nature of causal attributions. However, research on the theory also suggests the need for certain modifications or extensions, as described below.

consensus: The extent to which other persons react to some stimulus or even in the same manner as the person we are considering.

consistency: The extent to which an individual responds to a given stimulus or situation in the same way on different occasions (i.e., across time).

distinctiveness: The extent to which an individual responds in the same manner to different stimuli or events.

■ OTHER DIMENSIONS OF CAUSAL ATTRIBUTION. While we are often very interested in knowing whether others' behavior stemmed mainly from internal or external causes, this is not the entire story. In addition, we are also concerned with two other questions: (1) Are the causal factors that influenced their behavior likely to be *stable* over time or to change? And (2) are these factors *controllable*—can the individual change or influence them if she or he wishes to do so (Weiner, 1993, 1995)? These dimensions are independent of the internal–external dimension we have just considered. For instance, some internal causes of behavior, such as personality traits and temperament, tend to be quite stable over time (e.g., Miles & Carey, 1997). In contrast, other internal causes can, and often do, change greatly—for instance, motives, health, and fatigue. Similarly, some internal causes are controllable; individuals can, if they wish, learn to hold their tempers in check. Other internal causes, such as chronic illnesses or disabilities, are not. I (RAB) am nearsighted, so no matter how

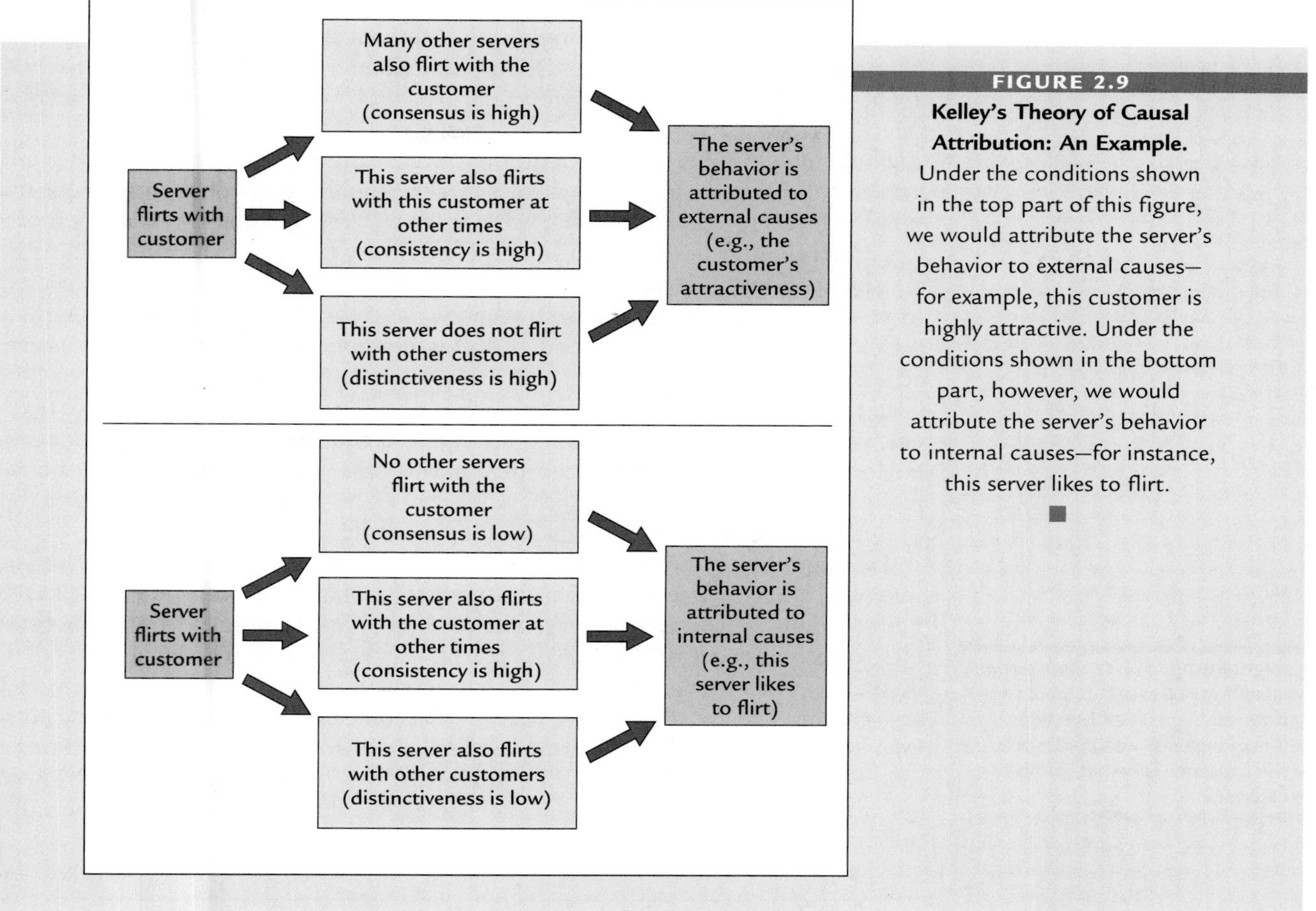

FIGURE 2.9

Kelley's Theory of Causal Attribution: An Example. Under the conditions shown in the top part of this figure, we would attribute the server's behavior to external causes—for example, this customer is highly attractive. Under the conditions shown in the bottom part, however, we would attribute the server's behavior to internal causes—for instance, this server likes to flirt.

hard I try, I can't see distant objects clearly without my glasses—this causal factor is not under my personal control. A large body of evidence indicates that in trying to understand the causes behind others' behavior, we do take note of all three of these dimensions—internal–external, stable–unstable, controllable–uncontrollable (Weiner, 1985, 1995). Moreover, our thinking in this respect strongly influences our conclusions concerning important matters, such as whether others are *personally responsible* for their own actions (e.g., Graham, Weiner, & Zucker, 1997).

AUGMENTING AND DISCOUNTING: HOW WE HANDLE MULTIPLE POTENTIAL CAUSES. Suppose that one day your boss stops by your desk and praises your work, telling you that you are doing a wonderful job and that she is glad to have you working with her. She does this in front of several other employees, who all congratulate you after she leaves. For the rest of the morning you feel great. But then, after lunch, she calls you into her office and asks if you would be willing to take on an extra, difficult work assignment. Now you begin to wonder: Why did she praise your work? Because she really wanted to thank you for doing such a good job *or* because she knew all along that she was going to ask you to take on extra work? There are two possible causes behind her behavior, and because there are, you may well engage in what social psychologists term **discounting**—you will view the first possible cause (her genuine desire to give you positive feedback) as less important or likely because another possible cause for this action exists, too (i.e., she wanted to

discounting: The tendency to attach less importance to one potential cause of some behavior when other potential causes are also present.

"set you up" to agree with her request to do extra work). Many studies indicate that discounting is a common occurrence and exerts a strong impact upon our attributions in many situations (e.g., Gilbert & Malone, 1995; Morris & Larrick, 1995; Trope & Liberman, 1996). However, as we'll soon see, it is far from universal (McClure, 1998).

Now, imagine the same situation with one difference: Your boss has a well-known policy against giving employees feedback publicly, in front of other persons. What will you conclude about her behavior now? Probably that it was really motivated by a genuine desire to tell you that she is very pleased with your work. After all, she has done so despite the presence of another factor that would be expected to *prevent* her from doing so (her own policy against public feedback). This illustrates what social psychologists describe as **augmenting**—the tendency to assign added weight or importance to a factor that might facilitate a given behavior when both this factor and another factor that might *inhibit* such behavior are both present, *yet the behavior still occurs.* (See Figure 2.10 for an overview of both attributional discounting and augmenting.) In this case, you conclude that your boss really is very pleased with your behavior because she praised it publicly despite the presence of a strong inhibitory factor (her policy against public feedback).

augmenting: The tendency to attach greater importance to potential causes of behavior if the behavior occurs despite the presence of other, inhibitory causes.

Do augmenting and discounting have any practical effects? Absolutely. For instance, consider a recent research study by Baron, Markman, and Hirsa (2001). Baron and his colleagues (2001) hypothesized that because women face larger obstacles to becoming entrepreneurs (i.e., persons who start their own businesses) than do men, women who actually become entrepreneurs will benefit from attributional augmenting. Specifically, because they have become entrepreneurs despite the presence of major obstacles (inhibitory factors), such women will be perceived more favorably than will women in other fields (e.g., women who are managers). These researchers also hypothesized that such effects would be weaker for men, because

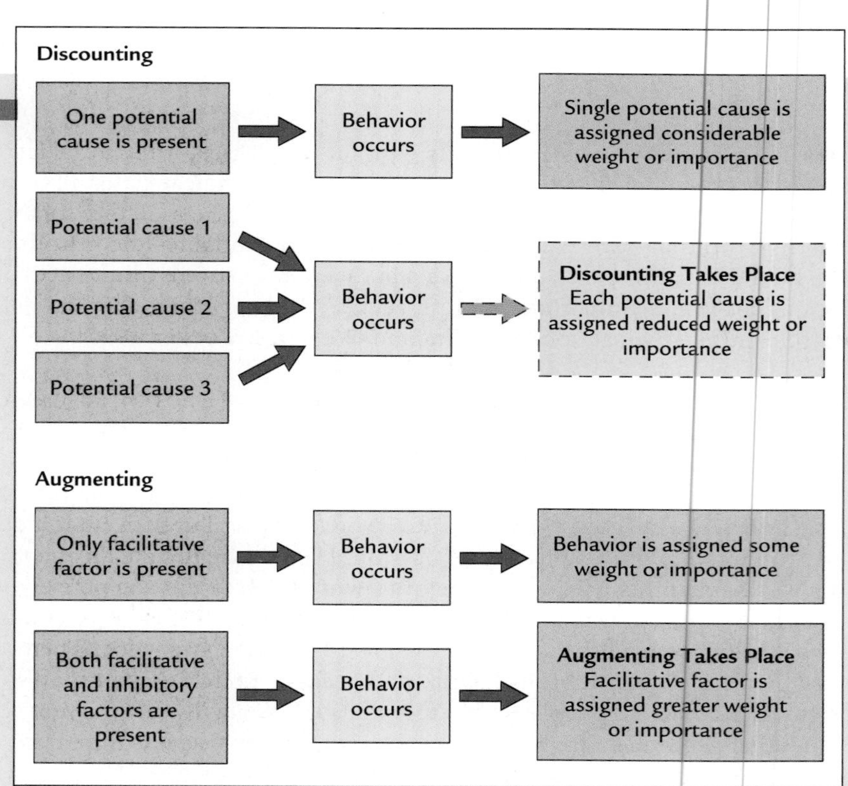

FIGURE 2.10

Augmenting and Discounting in Causal Attribution. According to the *discounting* principle *(upper diagram),* we attach less weight or importance to a given cause of some behavior when other potential causes of that behavior are also present. According to the *augmenting* principle *(lower diagram),* we attach greater weight to a potential cause of some behavior if the behavior occurs despite the presence of another factor that would tend to inhibit its occurrence.

they face smaller obstacles to becoming entrepreneurs, and so would benefit less from attributional augmenting.

To test these hypotheses, Baron and his colleagues (2001) showed photos of actual entrepreneurs to a large number of employed persons, asking them to rate the persons in the photos in terms of a number of traits (e.g., assertiveness, decisiveness, seriousness about their careers, etc.). Half of the photos showed women entrepreneurs, while the other half showed men. Raters in two groups were told either that the persons shown were entrepreneurs or that they were managers. Results offered clear support for the hypothesis that women would benefit from attributional augmenting to a greater degree than would men. As you can see from Figure 2.11, women described as being entrepreneurs were rated significantly more favorably than were those described as being managers. For men, however, ratings were not significantly affected by whether they were described as being entrepreneurs or managers. Because positive perceptions of women entrepreneurs may help them to overcome the daunting obstacles they continue to face, even after "taking the plunge" and starting their own businesses (e.g., Cooper, Gimeno-Gascon, & Woo, 1994; Cliff, 1998), these findings appear to have practical—and encouraging—implications.

■ REGULATORY FOCUS THEORY: DO AUGMENTING AND DISCOUNTING ALWAYS OCCUR? Earlier, we noted that discounting does not occur in all situations in which multiple potential causes of others' behavior are present (see McClure, 1998). Perhaps

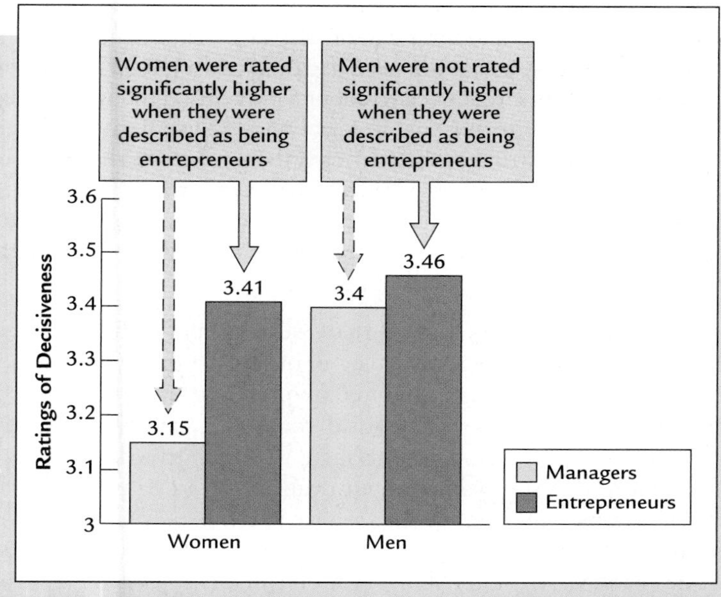

FIGURE 2.11

Attributional Augmenting: Evidence That It Can Benefit Women Entrepreneurs.

Women were rated significantly more favorably by research participants when the women were described as being entrepreneurs than when they were described as being managers. Similar effects did not occur for men. These findings may stem from attributional augmenting: Because women face greater obstacles to becoming entrepreneurs than do men, women who actually adopt this role are perceived more favorably—ratings of them are boosted by attributional augmenting.

[SOURCE: BASED ON DATA FROM BARON, MARKMAN, & HIRSA, 2001.]

the most intriguing evidence on this issue is provided by Liberman and her colleagues (Liberman et al., 2001), who relate discounting to a perspective known as **regulatory focus theory** (e.g., Higgins, 1998). This theory suggests that in regulating their own behavior in order to attain desired goals, individuals can adopt one of two different perspectives: a *promotion focus,* in which they emphasize the presence and absence of positive outcomes, or a *prevention focus,* in which they emphasize negative outcomes. A promotion focus leads individuals to be concerned with identifying correct hypotheses about the social world (hits) and also with avoiding misses (failures to notice a correct hypothesis that exists), while a prevention focus leads individuals to be concerned primarily with correctly rejecting hypotheses that are false (correct rejections) and avoiding the acceptance of hypotheses that are, in fact, false (false alarms). This reasoning, in turn, suggests that when individuals adopt a promotion focus, they will be less likely to discount potential causes of others' behavior than is true when they adopt a prevention focus. Why? Because persons with a promotion focus are eager to generate, and test, as many hypotheses as possible, so why reject or discount one potential causal factor just because another is also present? In contrast, persons with a prevention focus are concerned about the possibility of accepting a false hypothesis, so they are quite ready to eliminate (discount) potential causes of others' behavior.

To test this hypothesis, Liberman and her colleagues (2001) measured individuals' tendency to adopt a promotion or prevention focus. Participants then read about an incident in which a character named Bill helps a woman to move a large package. The story was written so as to be ambiguous as to the reasons why Bill offered his help—because he is a helpful person (a personal cause), because the woman he helped was obviously in need of help (an entity cause), or because he knew her and could readily assist her (a situational cause). Results indicated that the stronger the participants' tendency to adopt a prevention focus, the greater their tendency to engage in discounting (i.e., to reject one of the potential causes of Bill's behavior). In contrast, the stronger the participants' tendency to adopt a promotion tendency, the weaker their tendency to engage in discounting. These findings indicate that the tendency to engage in discounting is neither universal nor invariant; rather, it may be strengthened—or weakened—by other cognitive factors that influence our understanding of the social world.

■ BEYOND THE PERSON-SITUATION DISTINCTION: HOW PEOPLE ACTUALLY THINK ABOUT CAUSAL EXPLANATIONS. Dividing the causes of others' behavior into person (internal) factors (something about the individual in question) and situational (external) factors (something about the external world) makes a great deal of sense in many situations. There are many situations, though, in which this distinction does not seem to fully capture the complexity of our thinking about causality. For instance, in trying to understand why other people behave as they do, we often consider their desires, values, or beliefs—factors one social psychologist (Malle, 1999) describes as *reasons.* For instance, why did Hillary Clinton run for senator in New York State? Possible explanations include: she wanted power; she wanted to remain in government; she genuinely wanted to serve the people of New York—and many others. All of these refer to internal states of which she was aware, so they can be described as reasons. In addition, though, we often consider other factors that can shape people's behavior, *even though the persons involved are not aware of them* at the time of their behavior. Malle (1999) refers to these as *causal history of reason* explanations. For instance, why does Yasser Arafat, leader of the Palestine people, often appear to be unyielding and belligerent? Possibilities include: he is truly a confrontational kind of person; he has practiced this role so long that it has become second nature, and so on. Note that although these factors refer to something about Arafat, they are not necessarily ones he would think about while acting belligerently (e.g., he probably wouldn't say to himself, "I'm a confrontational person, so I'll refuse the latest offer and show a lot of anger").

regulatory focus theory: A theory suggesting that in regulating their own behavior in order to attain desired goals, individuals adopt one of two different perspectives: a promotion focus, in which they emphasize the presence and absence of positive outcomes; or a prevention focus, in which they emphasize negative outcomes.

Recent research by Malle and his colleagues (Malle et al., 2000) indicates that people do often think in these complex ways when trying to understand others' behavior. So although the person–situation distinction is a useful one in many contexts, it seems clear that it does not capture all aspects of our thinking when we try to answer the question "Why?"

KEY POINTS

- In order to obtain information about others' lasting traits, motives, and intentions, we often engage in *attribution*—efforts to understand why others have acted as they have.
- According to Jones and Davis's theory of *correspondent inference,* we attempt to infer others' traits from observing certain aspects of their behavior—especially behavior that is freely chosen, produces *noncommon effects,* and is low in social desirability.
- Another theory, Kelley's theory of causal attribution, focuses on the question of whether others' behavior stemmed from internal or external causes. To answer this question, we focus on information relating to *consensus, consistency,* and *distinctiveness.*
- When two or more potential causes of another person's behavior exist, we tend to downplay the importance of each—an effect known as *discounting.* When a cause that facilitates a behavior and a cause that inhibits both exist but the behavior still occurs, we assign added weight to the facilitative factors—an effect known as *augmenting.*
- Augmenting occurs in many situations. For instance, it can boost perceptions of women who become entrepreneurs.
- Discounting does not occur in all instances; it is more likely when individuals adopt a prevention focus than when they adopt a promotion focus.
- Recent findings indicate that the internal (person)-external (situation) distinction given much importance in Kelley's theory does not capture all aspects of our thinking about the causes of others' behavior. Rather, we often consider others' reasons (their conscious motives, desires, intentions) and other factors, too.

Attribution: Some Basic Sources of Error

A basic theme we'll develop throughout this book is that although we generally do a good job in terms of thinking about the social world, we are far from perfect in this respect. In fact, our efforts to understand other persons—and ourselves—are subject to several types of errors that can lead us to false conclusions about why others have acted as they have and how they will behave in the future. Let's take a look at several of these errors now.

THE CORRESPONDENCE BIAS: OVERESTIMATING THE ROLE OF DISPOSITIONAL CAUSES. Imagine that you witness the following scene. A man arrives at a meeting one hour late. On entering, he drops his notes on the floor. While trying to pick them up, his glasses fall off and break. Later, he spills coffee all over his tie. How would you explain these events? The chances are good that you would reach conclusions such as "This person is disorganized and clumsy." Are such attributions accurate? Perhaps; but it is also possible that the man was late because of unavoidable delays at the airport, dropped his notes because they were printed on slick paper, and spilled his coffee because the cup was too hot to hold. The fact that you would be less likely to consider such potential external causes illustrates what Jones (1979) labeled the

correspondence bias—the tendency to explain others' actions as stemming from (corresponding to) dispositions even in the presence of clear situational causes (e.g., Gilbert & Malone, 1995). This bias seems to be so general in scope that many social psychologists refer to it as the **fundamental attribution error.** In short, we tend to perceive others as acting as they do because they are "that kind of person," rather than because of the many external factors that may influence their behavior. We should add that while the fundamental attribution error does seem to be very widespread in occurrence, research findings (e.g., Van Overwalle, 1997) indicate that the tendency to attribute others' actions to dispositional (internal) causes seems to occur most strongly in situations in which both consensus and distinctiveness are low, as predicted by Kelley's theory.

Social psychologists have conducted many studies in order to find out why this bias occurs (e.g., Robins, Spranca, & Mendelsohn, 1996), but the issue is still somewhat in doubt. One possibility is that when we observe another person's behavior, we tend to focus on his or her actions; the context in which the person behaves, and hence potential situational causes of his or her behavior, often fade into the background. As a result, dispositional causes (internal causes) are easier to notice (they are more *salient*) than situational ones. In other words, from our perspective, the person we are observing is high in *perceptual salience* and is the focus of our attention, while situational factors that might also have influenced this person's behavior are less salient and so seem less important to us. Another explanation is that we notice such situational causes but give them insufficient weight in our attributions. Still another explanation is when we focus on others' behavior, we tend to begin by assuming that their actions reflect their underlying characteristics. Then, we attempt to correct for any possible effects of the external world—the current situation—by taking these into account. (This involves a kind of mental shortcut. This correction, however, is often insufficient—we don't make enough allowance for the impact of external factors. We don't give enough weight to the possibility of delays at the airport or a slippery floor, when reaching our conclusions (Gilbert & Malone, 1995).

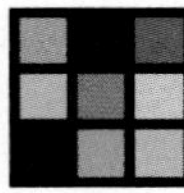

Is this tendency to emphasize dispositional causes truly universal, or is it influenced, like many other aspects of social behavior and thought, by cultural factors? Research findings indicate that, in fact, culture does play a role. Specifically, the fundamental attribution error appears to be more common or stronger in cultures that emphasize individual freedom—*individualistic* cultures such as those in Western Europe or the United States and Canada—than in *collectivistic* cultures that emphasize group membership, conformity, and interdependence (e.g., Triandis, 1990; see Figure 2.12). For example, in one study, Morris and Pang (1994) analyzed newspaper articles about two mass murders in the United States—one committed by a Chinese graduate student and one committed by a Caucasian postal worker. The articles were published in English in the *New York Times* and in Chinese in the *World Journal,* a Chinese-language newspaper published in the United States. Results were clear: The articles in English attributed both murderers' actions to dispositional factors to a greater extent than did the articles written in Chinese.

correspondence bias (fundamental attribution error): The tendency to explain others' actions as stemming from dispositions, even in the presence of clear situational causes.

fundamental attribution error (correspondence bias): The tendency to overestimate the impact of dispositional cues on others' behavior.

Results confirming the fact that the correspondence bias is stronger in Western cultures than in Asian ones has also been reported by Choi and Nisbett (1998). These researchers asked students in the United States and Korea to read essays supposedly written by another person; the essays were either in favor of or against capital punishment, and participants were led to believe that the person who wrote them either did so of his or her own free choice, or did so because he or she was told to write an essay favoring one point of view or the other. When asked questions about the writer's actual attitude toward capital punishment, U.S. students showed the correspondence bias quite strongly: they acted as if the essay reflected this person's true attitudes even if the writer had been *told* to write the essay they read. In contrast, Korean students showed this bias to a much weaker degree; indeed, in

FIGURE 2.12

Cultural Differences and the Fundamental Attributional Error. Research findings indicate that the fundamental attributional error—the tendency to overattribute others' actions to dispositional causes—is stronger in individualistic societies than in collectivistic ones.

one condition, when it was made clear that the essay writer had simply repeated arguments given to him by the researchers, they showed no correspondence bias at all! Clearly, then, cultural factors play a role even in this very basic aspect of attribution.

■ THE ACTOR–OBSERVER EFFECT: YOU FELL; I WAS PUSHED. Another and closely related type of attributional error involves our tendency to attribute our own behavior to situational (external) causes, but that of others to dispositional (internal) ones. Thus, when we see another person trip and fall, we tend to attribute this event to his or her clumsiness. If *we* trip, however, we are more likely to attribute this event to situational causes, such as ice on the sidewalk. This "tilt" in our attributions is known as the **actor–observer effect** (Jones & Nisbett, 1971) and has been observed in many different contexts.

Why does the actor–observer effect occur? In part, because we are quite aware of the many external factors affecting our own actions but are less aware of such factors when we turn our attention to the actions of other persons. Thus, we tend to perceive our own behavior as arising largely from situational causes, but that of others as deriving mainly from their traits or dispositions.

■ THE SELF-SERVING BIAS: "I'M GOOD; YOU'RE LUCKY." Suppose that you write a term paper and when you get it back, you find the following comment on the first page: "An outstanding paper—one of the best I've see in years. A+." To what will you attribute this success? Probably, you will explain it in terms of internal causes—your high level of talent, the effort you invested in writing the paper, and so on.

Now, in contrast, imagine that when you get the paper back, *these* comments are written on it. "Horrible paper—one of the worst I've seen in years. D–." How will you interpret this outcome? The chances are good that you will be tempted to focus mainly on external (situational factors)—the difficulty of the task, your professor's unfairly harsh grading standards, the fact that you didn't have enough time to do a good job, and so on.

This tendency to attribute our own positive outcomes to internal causes but negative ones to external factors is known as the **self-serving bias,** and it appears to be both general in scope and powerful in its effects (Brown & Rogers, 1991; Miller & Ross, 1975).

actor–observer effect: The tendency to attribute our own behavior mainly to situational causes but the behavior of others mainly to internal (dispositional) causes.

self-serving bias: The tendency to attribute positive outcomes to internal causes (e.g., one's own traits or characteristics) but negative outcomes or events to external causes (e.g., chance, task difficulty).

Why does this tilt in our attributions occur? Several possibilities have been suggested, but most of these fall into two categories: cognitive and motivational explanations. The cognitive model suggests that the self-serving bias stems mainly from certain tendencies in the way we process social information (see Chapter 3; Ross, 1977). Specifically, it suggests that we attribute positive outcomes to internal causes but negative ones to external causes because we *expect* to succeed and have a tendency to attribute expected outcomes to internal causes more than to external causes. In contrast, the motivational explanation suggests that the self-serving bias stems from our need to protect and enhance our self-esteem or from the related desire to look good to others (Greenberg, Pyszczynsik, & Solomon, 1982). While both cognitive and motivational factors may well play a role in this kind of attributional error, research evidence seems to offer more support for the motivational view (e.g., Brown & Rogers, 1991).

Whatever the origins of the self-serving bias, it can be the cause of much interpersonal friction. It often leads persons who work with others on a joint task to perceive that *they*, not their partners, have made the major contributions. I see this effect in my own classes every semester when students rate their own contribution and that of the other members of their team in a term project that I require. The result? Most students take lots of credit for themselves when the project has gone well, but tend to blame (and downrate) their partners if it has not.

Interestingly, the results of several studies indicate that the strength of the self-serving bias varies across different cultures (e.g., Oettingen, 1995; Oettingen & Seligman, 1990). In particular, it is weaker in cultures, such as those in Asia, that place a greater emphasis on group outcomes and group harmony than it is in Western cultures, where individual accomplishments are emphasized and it is considered appropriate for winners to gloat (at least a little!) over their victories (see Figure 2.13). For example, Lee and Seligman (1997) found that Americans of European descent showed a larger self-serving bias than either Chinese Americans or mainland Chinese. Once again, therefore, we see that cultural factors often play an important role even in very basic aspects of social behavior and social thought.

Before concluding this discussion, we should note that despite all the errors described here, growing evidence suggests that social perception *can* be quite accurate: we do, in many cases, reach accurate conclusions about others' traits

FIGURE 2.13

The Self-Serving Bias: Stronger in Some Cultures than in Others. The self-serving bias, another important attributional error, is stronger in Western cultures (which are individualistic in orientation) than in Asian ones (which are collectivistic in orientation.)

and motives from observing their behavior. We'll examine some of the evidence pointing to this conclusion as part of our discussion of the process of impression formation later in the chapter. (See the *Ideas to Take with You—And Use!* feature at the end of this chapter for some tips on how to avoid various attributional errors.)

KEY POINTS

- Attribution is subject to many potential sources of error. One of the most important of these is the *correspondence bias*—the tendency to explain others' actions as stemming from dispositions even in the presence of situational causes. This tendency seems to be stronger in Western cultures than in Asian cultures.
- Two other attributional errors are the *actor–observer effect*—the tendency to attribute our own behavior to external (situational causes) but that of others to internal causes—and the *self-serving bias*—the tendency to attribute our own positive outcomes to internal causes but negative ones to external causes.
- The strength of the self-serving bias differs across various cultures, being stronger in Western societies such as the United States than in Asian cultures such as China.

Applications of Attribution Theory: Insights and Interventions

Kurt Lewin, one of the founders of modern social psychology (see Chapter 1), often remarked, "There's nothing as practical as a good theory." By this he meant that once we obtain scientific understanding of some aspect of social behavior or social thought, we can, potentially, put this knowledge to practical use. Where attribution theory is concerned, this has definitely been the case. As basic knowledge about attribution has grown, so, too, has the range of practical problems to which such information has been applied (Graham & Folkes, 1990). Here, we'll examine two important, and especially timely, applications of attribution theory.

■ ATTRIBUTION AND DEPRESSION. Depression is the most common psychological disorder. In fact, it has been estimated that almost half of all human beings experience such problems at some time during their lives (e.g., Blazer et al., 1994). Although many factors play a role in depression, one that has received increasing attention is what might be termed a *self-defeating* pattern of attributions. In contrast to most people, who show the self-serving bias described above, depressed individuals tend to adopt an opposite pattern. They attribute *negative* outcomes to lasting, internal causes such as their own traits or lack of ability, but attribute *positive* outcomes to temporary, external causes such as good luck or special favors from others (see Figure 2.14 on page 62). As a result, such persons perceive that they have little or no control over what happens to them—they are mere chips in the winds of unpredictable fate. Little wonder that they become depressed and tend to give up on life.

Fortunately, several forms of therapy that focus on changing such attributions have been developed, and these appear to be quite successful (e.g., Bruder et al., 1997; Robinson, Berman, & Neimeyer, 1990). These new forms of therapy focus on getting depressed persons to change their attributions—to take personal credit

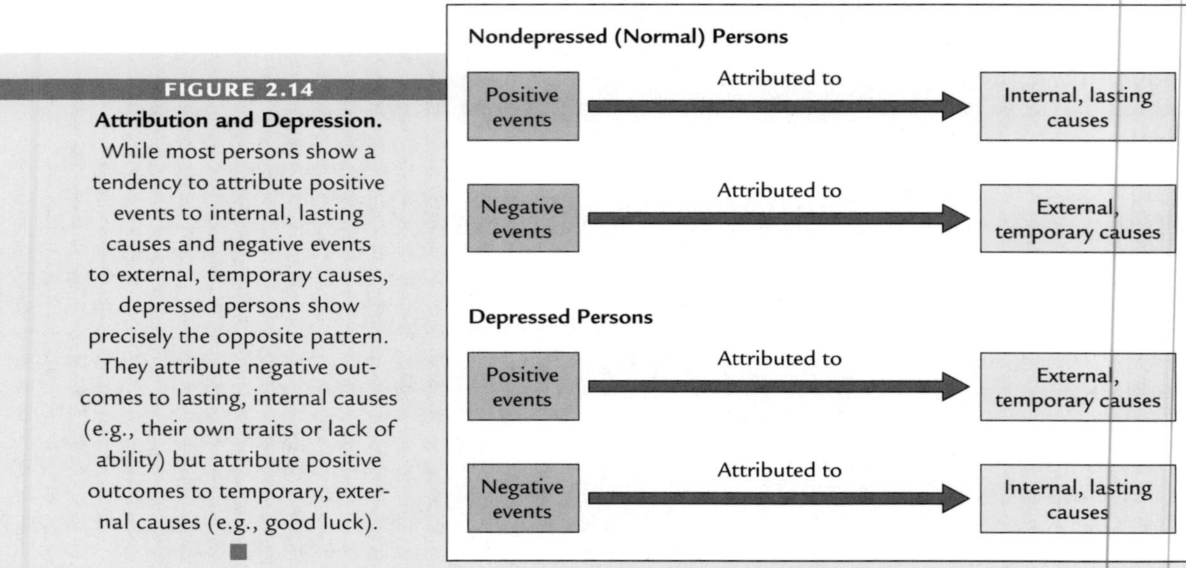

FIGURE 2.14

Attribution and Depression. While most persons show a tendency to attribute positive events to internal, lasting causes and negative events to external, temporary causes, depressed persons show precisely the opposite pattern. They attribute negative outcomes to lasting, internal causes (e.g., their own traits or lack of ability) but attribute positive outcomes to temporary, external causes (e.g., good luck).

for successful outcomes, to stop blaming themselves for negative outcomes (especially ones that can't be avoided), and to view at least some failures as the result of external factors beyond their control. These new forms of therapy do not explore repressed urges, inner conflicts, or traumatic events during childhood, but they *do* seem to be successful. Attribution theory provides the basis for these new forms of treatment, so it has certainly proved very useful in this respect.

ATTRIBUTION AND PREJUDICE: THE SOCIAL COSTS OF COMPLAINING ABOUT DISCRIMINATION. Imagine the following situation: You meet a person belonging to a minority group and soon afterward, this individual tells you about a recent experience in which she was rejected for a job on the basis of prejudice—simply because of her membership in a racial or ethnic group. What kind of impression would you form of this person? Principles of fairness strongly suggest that you should be sympathetic, because prejudice is clearly an evil contrary to the best values of most societies. But another possibility exists, too: perhaps, you might think, this person is wrong—she was actually rejected because of a lack of qualifications. To the extent you reach that conclusion, you might form a negative impression of her, viewing her as a chronic complainer who wants to blame all negative outcomes on prejudice and discrimination.

In fact, attribution theory suggests that the latter, disturbing outcome is quite possible. In many situations, it is difficult to know whether negative outcomes experienced by minority persons are the result of prejudice or other factors. Because of this uncertainty, when such persons attribute these outcomes to prejudice, some bystanders conclude that they are wrong and so—in a cruel twist of cognitive processes—think less highly of them.

Evidence for precisely such effects has been obtained in several recent studies (e.g., Ruggiero et al., 2000). Perhaps these effects are most directly illustrated, though, in findings reported by Kaiser and Miller (2001). These researchers asked participants in their studies to rate an African American student who, upon learning that he had failed a test, attributed this failure either to discrimination on the part of the test scorers (a panel of eight white persons) or to the quality of his answers. Participants rated the African American student on a scale of complaining (the extent to which he was hypersensitive, a complainer, a troublemaker, argumentative, etc.) and in terms of their overall impressions of him (how likable, friendly, honest, intelligent, and easy to get along with he was). Before rating the student, participants learned that the chance that discrimination had actually played a role in his failure on the test was low, moderate, or high (none, half, or all of the judges had previously shown signs of being prejudiced against African Americans).

Results were quite unsettling: Regardless of the likelihood that discrimination had actually contributed to the failing score, participants rated the African American student as more of a complainer and formed a less favorable impression of him when he attributed his failure to discrimination than when he attributed it to his own answers (see Figure 2.15). In other words, *even when all the test scorers were known to be prejudiced, participants downrated the minority student for attributing his failure to this factor!*

As noted by Kaiser and Miller (2001), these findings have distressing implications. They indicate that the fear of being negatively evaluated by others may prevent minority persons from challenging discrimination when they encounter it: they are afraid that if they do, they will be seen by others as chronic complainers. We'll return to this and other disturbing aspects of prejudice in Chapter 6. For now, though, we simply want to note that an attributional perspective can shed much light on this important topic, and perhaps suggest ways of countering the harmful effects of prejudice.

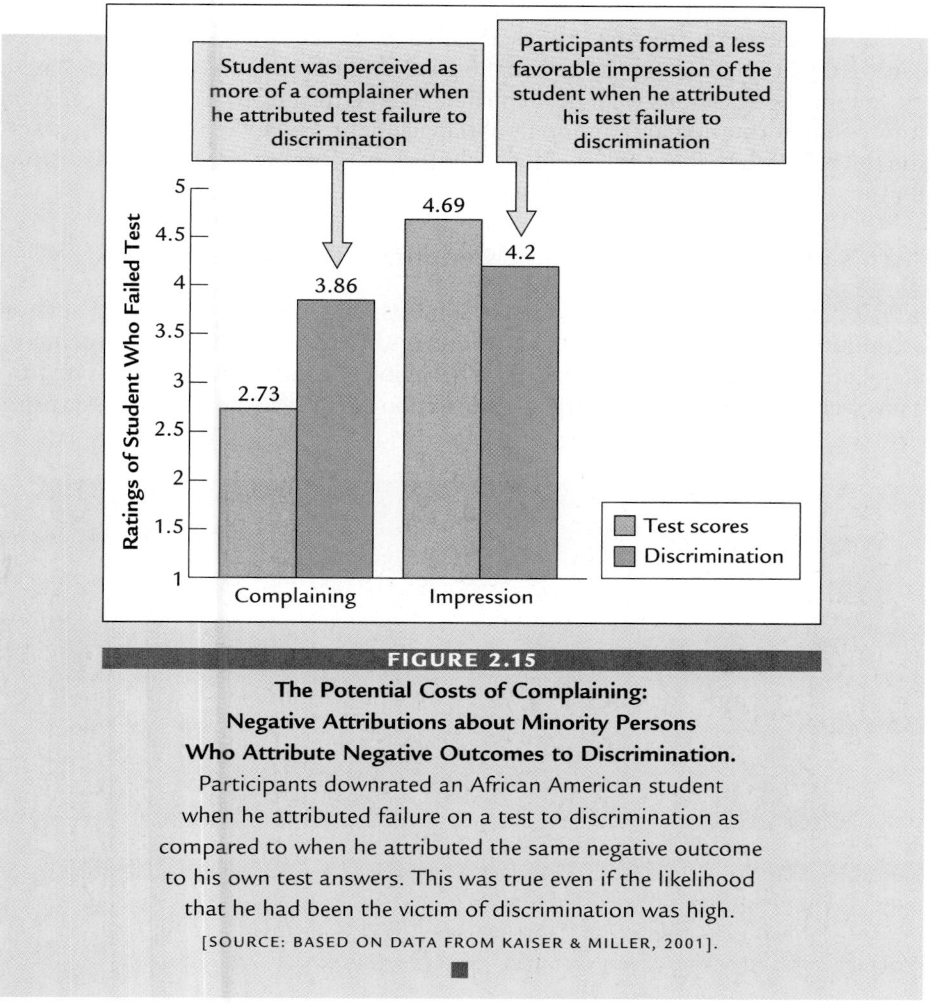

FIGURE 2.15

The Potential Costs of Complaining: Negative Attributions about Minority Persons Who Attribute Negative Outcomes to Discrimination. Participants downrated an African American student when he attributed failure on a test to discrimination as compared to when he attributed the same negative outcome to his own test answers. This was true even if the likelihood that he had been the victim of discrimination was high. [SOURCE: BASED ON DATA FROM KAISER & MILLER, 2001].

KEY POINTS

- *Attribution* has been applied to many practical problems, often with great success. Depressed persons often show a pattern of attributions opposite to that of the *self-serving bias:* they attribute positive events to external causes and negative ones to internal causes. Therapy designed to change this pattern has proved highly effective.
- Attribution theory helps explain why minority persons who are the victims of discrimination are often reluctant to challenge it: they fear that if they attribute negative outcomes to prejudice, they will be perceived negatively by others (e.g., as chronic complainers).

Impression Formation and Impression Management: How We Combine—and Use—Social Information

Do you care about making a good first impression on others (see Figure 2.16)? Research findings indicate that you should, because such impressions *do* seem to exert strong and lasting effects on other persons' perceptions of us; and as we've seen throughout this chapter, the way other persons perceive us can strongly influence their behavior toward us (e.g., Fiske, Lin, & Neuberg, 1999; Swann & Gill, 1997).

But what, exactly, *are* first impressions? How are they formed? And what steps can we take to make sure that we make good first impressions on others? These are among the questions we'll now consider. Before turning to modern research on impression formation and impression management, however, let's briefly examine the research that started social psychologists thinking about impression formation—a series of influential studies by Solomon Asch.

Asch's Research on Central and Peripheral Traits

As we have already seen, some aspects of social perception, such as attribution, require lots of hard mental work: it's not always easy to draw inferences about others' motives or traits from their behavior. In contrast, forming first impressions seems to be relatively effortless. As Solomon Asch (1946) put it in a classic paper

FIGURE 2.16

First Impressions Really Do Matter.

A large body of research findings indicates that first impressions really do matter: they exert important and lasting effects on others' perceptions of us.

on this topic: "We look at a person and immediately a certain impression of his character forms itself in us. A glance, a few spoken words are sufficient to tell us a story about a highly complex matter . . . " (1946, p. 258; see Figure 2.17). How do we manage this feat? How, in short, do we form unified impressions of others in the quick and seemingly effortless way that we often do? This is the question Asch set out to study.

At the time Asch conducted his research, social psychologists were heavily influenced by the work of *Gestalt psychologists,* specialists in the field of perception. A basic principle of Gestalt psychology was this: "The whole is often greater than the sum of its parts." This means that what we perceive is often more than the sum of individual sensations. To illustrate this point for yourself, simply look at any painting (except a very modern one!). What you see is *not* individual splotches of paint on the canvas; rather, you perceive an integrated whole—a portrait, a landscape, a bowl of fruit, whatever the artist intended. So, as Gestalt psychologists suggested, each part of the world around us is interpreted, and understood, only in terms of its relationships to other parts or stimuli.

FIGURE 2.17
Solomon Asch: A Pioneer in the Study of Impression Formation. Asch conducted some of the first research on impression formation. His methods and findings captured the attention of social psychologists and paved the way for many other studies on impression formation.

Asch applied these ideas to understanding impression formation, suggesting that we do *not* form impressions simply by adding together all of the traits we observe in other persons. Rather, we perceive these traits *in relation to one another* so that the traits cease to exist individually and become, instead, part of an integrated, dynamic whole. How could these ideas be tested? Asch came up with an ingenious answer. He gave individuals lists of traits supposedly possessed by a stranger, then asked them to indicate their impressions of this person by putting check marks next to traits (on a much longer list) that they felt fit their overall impression of the stranger.

For example, in one study, participants read one of the following two lists:

intelligent—skillful—industrious—warm—determined—practical—cautious

intelligent—skillful—industrious—cold—determined—practical—cautious

As you can see, the lists differ only with respect to two words: *warm* and *cold.* Thus, if people form impressions merely by adding together individual traits, the impressions formed by persons exposed to these two lists shouldn't differ very much. However, this was not the case. Persons who read the list containing *warm* were much more likely to view the stranger as generous, happy, good-natured, sociable, popular, and altruistic than were people who read the list containing *cold.* The words *warm* and *cold,* Asch concluded, described *central traits*—ones that strongly shaped overall impressions of the stranger and colored the other adjectives in the lists. Asch obtained additional support for this view by substituting the words *polite* and *blunt* for *warm* and *cold.* When he did this, the two lists yielded highly similar impressions of the stranger. So, *polite* and *blunt,* it appeared, were *not* central traits that colored the entire impressions of the stranger.

On the basis of many studies such as this one, Asch concluded that forming impressions of others involves more than simply adding together individual traits. As he put it: "There is an attempt to form an impression of the *entire* person. . . . As soon as two or more traits are understood to belong to one person they cease to exist as isolated traits, and come into immediate . . . interaction. . . . The subject perceives not this *and* that quality, but the two entering into a particular relation . . . " (1946, p. 284). While research on impression formation has become far more sophisticated since Asch's early work, many of his basic ideas about impression formation have withstood the test of time. Thus, his research exerted a lasting impact on the field and is still worthy of careful attention even today.

Impression Formation: A Cognitive Perspective

Creative as it was, Asch's research was only the beginning where the study of **impression formation**—the process through which we form impressions of others—is concerned. Social psychologists have made a great deal of

impression formation: The process through which we form impressions of others.

progress in this respect and now understand much about how first impressions are formed and how they influence our judgments and decisions about other persons (e.g., Fiske, Lin, & Neuberg, 1999). A major reason for this progress has been adoption of a cognitive perspective on this topic. Briefly, social psychologists have found it very useful to examine impression formation in terms of basic cognitive processes. For instance, when we meet others for the first time, we don't pay equal attention to all kinds of information about them; rather, we focus on certain kinds—the kinds of input we view as being most useful (e.g., DeBruin & Van Lange, 2000). Further, in order to form lasting first impressions, we must enter var-

SOCIAL PSYCHOLOGY: THIRTY YEARS OF PROGRESS

FROM COGNITIVE ALGEBRA TO MOTIVATED PROCESSING

In the first edition of this text, we noted that when we meet another person for the first time, we usually receive a considerable amount of information about him or her. This fact led us to pose the following question, which, in the early 1970s, was a very central one in the study of impression formation: How do we manage to combine diverse information about other persons into unified impressions of them? Many studies at that time were designed to test two possibilities: We form unified impressions of others by *adding* discrete pieces of information about them or, alternatively, we form our impressions by *averaging* available information in some way. The research that was then being conducted to compare these two possibilities went something like this (e.g., Anderson, 1965, 1968).

Research participants were asked to indicate their degree of liking for a stranger (whom they did not actually meet). This stranger was described as possessing either two highly favorable traits (e.g., truthful, reasonable) or two highly favorable traits *and* two moderately favorable ones (e.g., truthful, reasonable, painstaking, persuasive). Researchers at the time reasoned that if people combined the information they received simply by adding it together, they would like the second person more than first one because he was described as possessing a greater number of positive characteristics. If they combined the information through averaging, however, they would like the first one better, because the average of two highly favorable traits is higher than the average of two highly favorable *and* two moderately favorable traits. Results generally offered support for this hypothesis. The nature of such averaging was soon studied in further experiments (e.g., Anderson, 1973), but the basic conclusion remained largely unchanged: We form our impressions of others on the basis of a relatively simple kind of "cognitive algebra."

Now, let's contrast this early work with the kind of studies being conducted by social psychologists today. One basic question not addressed by the studies described above is this: What kind of information, exactly, do people focus on when meeting others for the first time? This question has many answers, depending, to some extent, on the precise context in which we encounter strangers. For instance, we might want different kinds of information about a physician we visit than we would want about someone we meet at a party or in a bar. The findings of many studies, however, indicate that across a wide range of contexts, we focus first on information concerning others' traits, values, and principles and only then turn to information about their competence—how well they can do various tasks. For instance, wouldn't you find information about whether another person is considerate and interested in people more revealing than information about this person's ability to master various tasks quickly? A clear illustration of this point, and of the nature of modern investigations of impression formation, is provided by research conducted by DeBruin and Van Lange (2000).

To study the question of what kind of information people look for when meeting others, they arranged for participants to play a mixed-motive game with a stranger. (Mixed-motive games are ones in which there are pressures both to cooperate and to compete with one's opponent—just as there are in many real-life situations.) Before beginning, participants were told that they were going to receive information about the opponent, and they actually did. The first information they received focused on the opponent's values and traits and was either positive (e.g., it indicated that this person is considerate and helpful) or negative (e.g., it suggested that this person is inconsiderate and not at all ious kinds of information into memory so that we can recall it at later times. And, of course, our first impressions of others will depend, to a degree, on our own characteristics. In fact, we can't help but see others through the lens of our own traits, motives, and desires (Schul & Vinokur, 2000). We think that a very useful way of illustrating the kind of progress generated by this cognitive perspective is through a comparison of the kind of research on impression formation that was being conducted thirty years ago with the much more sophisticated work being conducted today. This comparison is made in the special **Social Psychology: Thirty Years of Progress** section below.

helpful). Next, they received information about the opponent's competence, which, again, was either positive or negative (this person was described as being competent or incompetent in many situations). To determine which type of information was of greater interest to participants, the amount of time they spent reading it was recorded. As you can see from Figure 2.18, participants in the study did indeed spend considerably more time reading information about the opponent's values than about this person's competence. In addition, and also as predicted, they spent more time reading information about their opponent's values when it was negative than when it was positive; this is known as the *negativity effect*—a tendency to pay more attention to negative than positive information about others—and it has been observed in many different studies. Finally, results also indicated that after receiving negative information about the opponent's values, participants spent less time reading information about this person's competence. It was as if once they learned that the opponent was not a nice person, they lost interest in processing any further information about him or her.

As you can see, modern research on impression formation has gone a long way beyond the idea that we form impressions by averaging information about persons we meet, both in terms of the methods it uses and the theoretical frameworks it seeks to investigate. The result? We are now much closer to understanding this complex aspect of person perception than was true thirty years ago, when we wrote the first edition of this text.

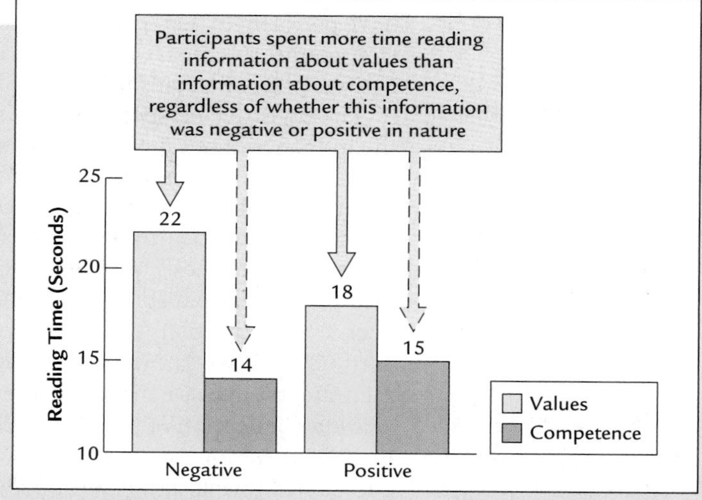

FIGURE 2.18

Forming Impressions of Others: What Kind of Information Do We Find Most Useful?

Research participants spent more time reading information about a stranger's values than information about this person's competence in performing tasks. They also spent more time reading such information when it was negative in nature than when it was positive. These findings indicate that we do indeed focus first on certain kinds of information when forming impressions of others.

[SOURCE: BASED ON DATA FROM DEBRUIN & VAN LANGE, 2000.]

Other Aspects of Impression Formation: The Nature of First Impressions and Our Motives for Forming Them

Earlier, we noted that a cognitive perspective has proved very useful in the study of impression formation. In fact, this perspective has provided important insights into the basic nature of first impressions (e.g., Wyer et al., 1994; Ruscher & Hammer, 1994). For instance, most social psychologists now agree that impressions of others involve two major components: concrete examples of behaviors they have performed that are consistent with a given trait (*exemplars* of this trait) and mental summaries that are abstracted from repeated observations of others' behavior (*abstractions,* as they are usually termed) (e.g., Klein, Loftus, & Plog, 1992; Smith & Zarate, 1992). Some models of impression formation stress the role of behavioral exemplars. These models suggest that when we make judgments about others, we recall examples of their behavior and base our judgments—and our impressions—on these. In contrast, other models stress the role of abstractions (sometimes referred to as *categorical judgments*). Such views suggest that when we make judgments about others, we simply bring our previously formed abstractions to mind and then use these as the basis for our impressions and our decisions. For instance, we recall that we have previously judged a person to be kind or unkind, friendly or hostile, optimistic or pessimistic, and then combine these traits into an impression of this individual.

Existing evidence suggests that both exemplars and mental abstractions play a role in impression formation (e.g., Budesheim & Bonnelle, 1998; Klein & Loftus, 1993; Klein et al., 1992). In fact, it appears that the nature of impressions may shift as we gain increasing experience with others. At first, our impression of someone we have just met consists largely of exemplars (concrete examples of behaviors they have performed). Later, as our experience with this person increases, our impression comes to consist mainly of mental abstractions derived from many observations of the person's behavior (Sherman & Klein, 1994).

The cognitive perspective has also shed new light on another important issue—the influence of our motives (what we are trying to accomplish in a given situation) on the kind of impressions we form, and even the processes through which we form them. As we'll see in Chapter 3, people generally do the least amount of cognitive work they can, and impression formation is no exception to this rule. So, usually, we form impressions in the simplest and easiest way possible—by placing people into large social categories with which we are already familiar (e.g., "she is an engineer," "he is an Irish American," etc.). Then, we base our impressions, at least in part, on what we know about these social groups. If we are motivated to be more accurate, though, we may focus on people we meet more as individuals possessing a unique collection of traits (e.g., Fiske, Lin, & Neuberg, 1999). Clear evidence for the role of our motives in the way we form impressions is provided by research conducted by Stevens and Fiske (2000). They found that when individuals find themselves in a situation in which they have less power than another person, they spend extra effort to form accurate impressions of this powerful person.

In sum, a cognitive perspective on impression formation has provided many valuable insights into the nature of this process. Such research suggests that although we seem to form impressions of others in a rapid and seemingly effortless manner, these impressions actually emerge out of the operation of cognitive processes relating to the storage, recall, and integration of social information. In short, there is a lot more going on beneath the surface than you might at first suspect.

KEY POINTS 

- Most people are concerned with making good first impressions on others because they believe that these impressions will exert lasting effects.

- Research on *impression formation*—the process through which we form impressions of others—suggests that first impressions are indeed important. Asch's classic research on impression formation indicated that our impressions of others involve more than simple summaries of their traits.
- Modern research, conducted from a cognitive perspective, has confirmed and extended this view, suggesting that in forming impressions of others we emphasize certain kinds of information (e.g., information about their traits and values rather than information about their competence.)
- Additional research indicates that impressions of others consist of examples of both behavior relating to specific traits (exemplars) and mental abstractions based on observations of many instances of behavior.
- In general, we form impressions of others in the least effortful manner possible (e.g., by categorizing them in various social groups). When motivated to do so, however, we strive for greater accuracy. This happens, for instance, in situations in which we have less power than the person about whom we are forming an impression.

Impression Management: The Fine Art of Looking Good

The desire to make a favorable impression on others is a strong one, so most of us do our best to look good to others when we meet them for the first time. Social psychologists use the term **impression management** (or **self-presentation**) to describe these efforts to make a good impression on others, and the results of their research on such efforts suggest that they are worthwhile: Persons who perform impression management successfully *do* often gain important advantages in many situations (e.g., Sharp & Getz, 1996; Wayne & Liden, 1995). What tactics do individuals use to make favorable impressions on others? Which work best? Let's see what research findings indicate about these intriguing questions.

TACTICS OF IMPRESSION MANAGEMENT AND THEIR RELATIVE SUCCESS. While individuals use many different techniques for boosting their image, most of these fall into two major categories: *self-enhancement,* efforts to increase their appeal to others, and *other-enhancement,* efforts to make the target person feel good in various ways.

With respect to self-enhancement, specific strategies include efforts to boost one's physical appearance through style of dress, personal grooming, and the use of various props (e.g., eyeglasses, which have been found to encourage impressions of intelligence; Terry & Krantz, 1993). Additional tactics of self-enhancement involve efforts to describe oneself in positive terms, explaining, for instance, how they (the person engaging in impression management) overcame daunting obstacles or rose to meet a challenge (Stevens & Kristof, 1995). Other findings (e.g., Rowatt, Cunningham, & Druen, 1998) indicate that many persons use this tactic to increase their appeal to potential dating partners; they describe themselves in very favorable terms (more favorable than they really deserve!) in order to impress persons they want to date. In short, they bend the truth to enhance their own appeal (see Figure 2.19 on page 70).

Turning to *other-enhancement,* individuals use many different tactics to induce positive moods and reactions in others. A large body of research findings suggests that such reactions, in turn, play an important role in generating liking for the person responsible for them (Byrne, 1992). The most commonly used tactic of other-enhancement is *flattery*—making statements that praise the target person, his or her traits or accomplishments, or the organization with which the target person is associated (Kilduff & Day, 1994). Such tactics are often highly successful, provided they are not overdone. Additional tactics of other-enhancement involve expressing agreement with the target person's views, showing a high degree of interest in this

impression management (self-presentation): Efforts by individuals to produce favorable first impressions on others.

FIGURE 2.19

Pretending to Have Special Skills or Knowledge: One Tactic of Impression Management. Individuals engaging in impression management often try to dazzle others with their special skills or knowledge—even if they don't really have them!

[SOURCE: DILBERT REPRINTED BY PERMISSION OF UNITED FEATURE SYNDICATE, INC.]

person, doing small favors for them, asking for their advice and feedback in some manner (Morrison & Bies, 1991), or expressing liking for them nonverbally (e.g., through high levels of eye contact, nodding in agreement, and smiling; Wayne & Ferris, 1990).

That individuals often employ such tactics is obvious: you can probably recall many instances in which you either used or were the target of such strategies. A key question, however, is this: Do they work? Do these tactics of impression management succeed in generating positive feelings and reactions on the part of the persons toward whom they are directed? The answer provided by a growing body of literature is clear: *Yes,* provided they are used with skill and care. For example, in one large-scale study involving more than 1,400 employees, Wayne and his associates (1997) found that social skills (including impression management) were the single best predictor of job performance ratings and assessments of potential for promotion for employees in a wide range of jobs. These findings, and those of many related studies (e.g., Wayne & Kacmar, 1991; Paulhus, Bruce, & Trapnell, 1995), indicate that impression management tactics often do succeed in enhancing the appeal of persons who use them effectively. However, we should hasten to add that the use of these tactics involves potential pitfalls: if they are overused or used ineffectively, they can backfire and produce negative rather than positive reactions from others. For instance, in a thought-provoking study, Vonk (1998) found strong evidence for what he terms the **slime effect**—a tendency to form very negative impressions of others who "lick upward but kick downward"; that is, persons in a work setting who play up to their superiors but treat subordinates with disdain and contempt. The moral of these findings is clear: While tactics of impression management often succeed, this is not always the case; sometimes they can boomerang, adversely affecting reactions to the persons who use them.

slime effect: A tendency to form very negative impressions of others who "lick upward but kick downward"; that is, persons in a work setting who play up to their superiors but treat subordinates with disdain and contempt.

■ IMPRESSION MANAGEMENT: THE ROLE OF COGNITIVE LOAD. That we try to make a favorable impression on others in many situation is obvious; and this makes a great deal of common sense. We have strong reasons for wanting to "look good" in job interviews, on first dates, and in many other contexts. Generally, we can do quite a good job in this respect because we have practiced impression management skills for many years. As a result, we can engage in positive self-presentation in a relatively automatic and effortless manner—we are just following well-practiced scripts (see Schlenker & Pontari, in press). Some situations in which we try to make a good first impression on others, however, are very demanding ones: a lot is going on, so we don't have the luxury of concentrating solely or entirely on making a good first impression. For instance, when professors interview for jobs at universities, they are usually required to give a formal presentation about their research. Such talks require lots of cognitive effort, so while giving them, the task of impression management may recede into the background, with the result that the person giving the talk does a less effective job at presenting himself or herself favorably. For instance, they may make a comment that is unflattering to the research of one of the people in the audience. Similarly, a first date may put people in a situation in which they have to concentrate on other tasks (e.g., finding their way to a new restaurant, choosing what to order) aside from making a good impression. What effect does such extra *cognitive load* have on the ability to present oneself in a favorable light?

At first, you might guess that it would always be detrimental: when we are busy performing other tasks, we can't do as good a job at presenting ourselves, and in general, this appears to be true (e.g., Tice et al., 1995). But consider this: Some persons are very uncomfortable in social situations, because they feel anxious and tend to worry about how others will perceive them. For such persons, being busy with other tasks may distract them from such feelings and thoughts and so actually *enhance* their ability to present themselves favorably. In fact, research by Pontari and Schlenker (2000) indicates that this is true. They had persons who were extroverts (outgoing, friendly, sociable) and persons who were introverts (reserved, shy, withdrawn) take part in a mock job interview in which they tried to present themselves either as they were (extroverted or introverted) or as the opposite kind of person. During the interview, participants either were busy performing another task (trying to remember an eight-digit number) or were not busy. Results indicated that for the extroverts, cognitive busyness interfered with their ability to present themselves as introverts (i.e., to appear shy, withdrawn, etc.) For introverts, however, the opposite was true: trying to remember the eight-digit number actually improved their ability to appear to be extroverts. Pontari and Schlenker (2000) interpret these findings as indicating that being busy with other tasks prevented introverts from feeling anxious and focusing on their fear of doing poorly. Thus, for such persons, cognitive distraction was actually a plus—it helped them to do a better job at self-presentation. Once again, therefore, a cognitive perspective helps us to understand the complex processes at work when people meet for the first time and try—often while doing several other things—to present themselves in a favorable light.

KEY POINTS

- In order to make a good impression on others, individuals often engage in *impression management* (*self-presentation*).
- Many techniques are used for this purpose, but most fall under two major headings: self-enhancement—efforts to boost one's appeal to others—and other-enhancement—efforts to induce positive moods or reactions in others.
- Impression management is something we practice throughout life, so we can usually engage it in a fairly effortless manner. When other tasks require our cognitive resources, however, impression management can sometimes suffer—unless such tasks distract us from anxiety and fears about performing poorly.

The Accuracy of Social Perception: Evidence That It's Higher than You May Think

Conflicting nonverbal cues, attributional errors, impression management—having read our discussions of these topics, you may now be feeling less than confident about your ability to form accurate perceptions of others (Swann & Gill, 1997). But don't be discouraged: a growing body of evidence gathered by social psychologists suggests that there is actually considerable room for optimism on this score. Despite the complexity of this task and the many potential pitfalls that can lead us into error, we *do* seem capable of forming accurate perceptions and impressions of others (e.g., Berry, 1991; Kenney et al., 1994; Gifford, 1994). Indeed, we are quite successful at this task, even if we have very little information to go by, for instance, after a very brief meeting with them, if we spend a few minutes speaking to them, or even if we merely see videotapes of their behavior or photos of their faces. On the basis of such fragmentary information, we seem capable of forming accurate impressions of where other persons stand on several basic dimensions of personality—dimensions such as submissive–dominant, agreeable–quarrelsome, and responsible–irresponsible (e.g., Kenny et al., 1994). How do we know that these first impressions are accurate? Because they correlate quite highly with ratings of the same persons provided by people who know them very well—family members, spouses, best friends (e.g., Ambady & Rosenthal, 1992; Baron & Markman, 2001; Zebrowitz & Collins, 1997)—and also with the individuals' overt behavior (e.g., Moskowitz, 1990). Several complex mechanisms may contribute to our apparent skill in this respect—for instance, certain physical characteristics can lead the persons who possess them to develop certain traits. One example: Highly attractive persons are treated in a friendly way by many other persons and, as a result, may develop greater confidence and better social skills than less attractive persons. Whatever the precise mechanisms involved, however, one fact seems clear: We are often quite successful in forming accurate perceptions of others. So in a sense, Henry David Thoreau was correct when he said, "You know about a person who deeply interests you more than you can be told."

CONNECTIONS: INTEGRATING SOCIAL PSYCHOLOGY

IN THIS CHAPTER, YOU READ ABOUT . . .	IN OTHER CHAPTERS, YOU WILL FIND RELATED DISCUSSIONS OF . . .
basic channels of nonverbal communication	the role of nonverbal cues in interpersonal attraction (Chapter 7), persuasion (Chapter 4), prejudice (Chapter 6), and charismatic leadership (Chapter 12)
theories of attribution	the role of attribution in persuasion (Chapter 4), social identity and self-perception (Chapter 5), prejudice (Chapter 6), long-term relationships (Chapter 8), prosocial behavior (Chapter 10), and aggression (Chapter 11)
first impressions and impression management	the role of first impressions in interpersonal attraction (Chapter 7), and the role of impression management in job interviews (Chapter 13)

THINKING ABOUT CONNECTIONS

1. As we'll point out in Chapters 4 (Attitudes) and 9 (Social Influence), influence is an important fact of social life: each day, we attempt to change others' attitudes or behavior and they attempt to change ours. Having read about attribution in this chapter, do you think that influence attempts that conceal their true goal will be more successful than ones that do not? If so, why? If not, why?
2. In Chapter 11 (Aggression), we'll see that some persons experience much more than their fair share of aggressive encounters. Such persons, it appears, are lacking in basic social skills, such as the ability to accurately read nonverbal cues. On the basis of the discussion of nonverbal cues in this chapter, can you explain how this lack could contribute to these persons' problems with respect to aggression?
3. Suppose you were preparing for an important job interview (see Chapter 13). On the basis of information presented in this chapter, what steps could you take to improve your chances of actually getting the job?
4. Suppose you compared happy couples with ones that were unhappy and likely to break up. Do you think that the members of these couples would differ in their attributions concerning their partners' behavior? For instance, would the happy couples attribute their partners' behavior to more positive causes than the unhappy couples?

IDEAS TO TAKE WITH YOU—AND USE!

MINIMIZING THE IMPACT OF ATTRIBUTIONAL ERRORS

Attribution is subject to many errors, and these can prove costly both to you and to the people with whom you interact, so it's well worth the effort to avoid such pitfalls. Here are our suggestions for recognizing—and minimizing—several important attributional errors.

The Correspondence Bias: The Fundamental Attribution Error.

We have a strong tendency to attribute others' behavior to internal (dispositional) causes even when strong external (situational) factors that might have influenced their behavior are present. To reduce this error, always try to put yourself in the shoes of the person whose behavior you are trying to explain. In other words, try to see the world through their eyes. If you do, you will probably realize that, from their perspective, there are many external factors that played a role in their behavior.

The Actor–Observer Effect: "I Behave as I Do because of Situational Causes; You Behave as *You* Do because You Are That Kind of Person."

Consistent with the fundamental attribution error, we have a strong tendency to attribute our own behavior to external causes, but that of others to internal causes. This can lead us to false generalizations about others and the traits they possess. To minimize this error, try to imagine yourself in their place and ask yourself, "Why would *I* have acted in that way?" If you do, you'll quickly realize that external factors might have influenced your behavior. Similarly, ask yourself, "Did I behave that way because doing so reflected traits or motives of which I'm not very aware?" This may help you to appreciate the *internal* causes of your own behavior.

The Self-Serving Bias: "I'm Good; You're Lucky."

Perhaps the strongest attributional error we make is that of attributing positive outcomes to internal causes such as our own abilities or effort, but negative outcomes to external factors such as luck or forces beyond our control. This can lead us to overestimate our own contributions to group projects, thus producing unnecessary friction with others. It can also reduce the chances that we will learn something valuable from negative outcomes—for instance, how we might do better the next time! You can help minimize this error simply by being aware of it; once you know it exists, you may realize that all your positive outcomes don't stem from internal causes, and that you may have played a role in producing negative ones. In addition, try to remember that other people are subject to the same bias; doing so can help remind you that they, too, want to take as much credit for positive outcomes but shift the blame for negative ones to external causes—such as you!

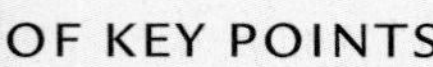

SUMMARY AND REVIEW OF KEY POINTS

Nonverbal Communication: The Language of Expressions, Gazes, and Gestures

- *Social perception* involves the processes through which seek to understand other persons. It plays a key role in social behavior and social thought.
- In order to understand others' emotional states, we often rely on *nonverbal communication*—an unspoken language of facial expressions, eye contact, and body movements and postures.
- While facial expressions may not be as universal as once believed, they do often provide useful information about others' emotional states. Useful information on this issue is also provided by eye contact, *body language,* and touching.
- Recent findings indicate that handshaking provides useful, important nonverbal cues about others' personalities and can influence the first impressions of strangers.
- If we pay careful attention to certain nonverbal cues, we can recognize efforts at deception by others—even if these persons are from a culture other than our own.
- Fragrance can be viewed as another type of nonverbal cue. The use of such communication seems to be decreasing, as indicated by declining perfume sales.

Attribution: Understanding the Causes of Others' Behavior

- In order to obtain information about others' lasting traits, motives, and intentions, we often engage in *attribution*—efforts to understand why others have acted as they have. According to Jones and Davis's theory of *correspondent inference,* we attempt to infer others' traits from observing certain aspects of their behavior—especially behavior that is freely chosen, produces *noncommon effects,* and is low in social desirability.
- Another theory, Kelley's theory of causal attribution, focuses on the question of whether others' behavior stems from internal or external causes. To answer this question, we focus on information relating to *consensus, consistency,* and *distinctiveness.*
- When two or more potential causes of another person's behavior exist, we tend to downplay the importance of each—an effect known as *discounting.* When a cause that facilitates a behavior and a cause that inhibits it both exist but the behavior still occurs, we assign added weight to the facilitative factors—an effect known as *augmenting.*
- Augmenting occurs in many situations. For instance, it can boost perceptions of women who become entrepreneurs.
- *Discounting* does not occur in all instances; it is more likely to occur when individuals adopt a prevention focus than when they adopt a promotion focus.
- Recent findings indicate that the internal (person)–external (situation) distinction given much importance in Kelley's theory does not capture all aspects of our thinking about the causes of others' behavior. Rather, we often consider others' reasons (their conscious motives, desires, intentions) as well as other factors.
- Attribution is subject to many potential sources of error. One of the most important of these is the *correspondence bias*—the tendency to explain others' actions as stemming from dispositions even in the presence of situational causes. This tendency seems to be stronger in Western cultures than in Asian cultures.
- Two other attributional errors are the *actor–observer effect*—the tendency to attribute our own behavior to external (situational causes) but that of others to internal causes—and the *self-serving bias*—the tendency to attribute our own positive outcomes to internal causes but negative ones to external causes.
- The strength of the self-serving bias differs across various cultures, being stronger in Western societies such as the United States than in Asian cultures such as China.
- Attribution has been applied to many practical problems, often with great success.
- Depressed persons often show a pattern of attributions opposite to that of the self-serving bias: they attribute positive events to external causes and negative ones to internal causes. Therapy designed to change this pattern has proved highly effective.
- Attribution theory helps explain why minority persons who are the victims of discrimination are often reluctant to challenge it: they fear that if they attribute negative outcomes to prejudice, they will be perceived negatively by others (e.g., as chronic complainers).

Impression Formation and Impression Management: How We Combine—and Use—Social Information

- Most people are concerned with making good first impressions on others, because they believe that these impressions will exert lasting effects.
- Research on *impression formation*—the process through which we form impressions of others—suggests that this is true. Asch's classic research on impression formation indicated that

our impressions of others involve more than simple summaries of their traits.

- Modern research, conducted from a cognitive perspective, has confirmed and extended this view, suggesting that in forming impressions of others we emphasize certain kinds of information (e.g., information about their traits and values rather than information about their competence.)
- Additional research indicates impressions of others consists of examples of both behavior relating to specific traits (exemplars) and mental abstractions based on observations of many instances of behavior.
- In general, we form impressions of others in the least effortful manner possible (e.g., by categorizing them in various social groups). When motivated to do so, however, we strive for greater accuracy. This happens, for instance, in situations in which we have less power than the person about whom we are forming an impression.
- In order to make a good impression on others, individuals often engage in *impression management* (*self-presentation*).
- Many techniques are used for this purpose, but most fall under two major headings: self-enhancement, or efforts to boost one's appeal to others, and other-enhancement, or efforts to induce positive moods or reactions in others.
- Impression management is something we practice throughout life, so we can usually engage it in a fairly effortless manner. When other tasks require our cognitive resources, however, impression management can sometimes suffer—unless such tasks distract us from anxiety and fears about performing poorly.

KEY TERMS

actor–observer effect (p. 59)
attribution (p. 49)
augmenting (p. 54)
body language (p. 42)
consensus (p. 52)
consistency (p. 52)
correspondence bias (p. 58)
correspondent inference (theory of) (p. 50)
discounting (p. 53)
distinctiveness (p. 52)
fundamental attribution error (p. 58)
impression formation (p. 65)
impression management (self-presentation) (p. 69)
microexpressions (p. 45)
noncommon effects (p. 50)
nonverbal communication (p. 39)
regulatory focus theory (p. 56)
self-serving bias (p. 59)
slime effect (p. 70)
social perception (p. 38)
staring (p. 41)

FOR MORE INFORMATION

Darley, J. M. & Cooper, J. (1998). *Attribution and social interaction: The legacy of Edward E. Jones.*

- In this book, experts on attribution theory review evidence concerning the role of attribution in social behavior. Many of the ideas considered were proposed by Edward E. Jones, a pioneer in the study of attribution. (We considered some of his work in this chapter.)

Malandro, L. A., Barker, L., & Barker, D. A. (1994). *Nonverbal communication* (3rd ed.). New York: Random House.

- This is a basic and very readable text that examines all aspects of nonverbal communication. Body movements and gestures, facial expressions, eye-contact, touching, smell, and voice characteristics are among the topics considered.

Zebrowitz, L. A. (1997). *Reading faces.* Boulder, CO: Westview Press.

- In this book, a well-known researcher provides an overview of the influence of facial features and expressions on social perception. Especially revealing are the discussions of the ways in which how people look can actually be linked to their psychological traits.

Pierre Bonnard, *Morning in Paris.* 1911. © Copyright 2002 Artists Rights Society (ARS), New York/ ADAGP, Paris. © Copyright Giraudon/Art Resource, NY.

3

SOCIAL COGNITION: THINKING ABOUT THE SOCIAL WORLD

CHAPTER OUTLINE

A few months ago, I (RAB) was driving to my office. On the way, I stopped for a red light at a very busy intersection. The driver of the car in front of me was talking on her cell phone, and I could see from the way she shook her head and waved her arms that it was an important conversation. Then, suddenly, although the light was still red, she began to roll forward, straight into the intersection. I braced for the worst and watched in horror as cars from both directions honked their horns, swerved, and hit their brakes to avoid colliding with her. Fortunately, she made it through without an accident, but I could tell that she was very shaken by the experience; she pulled over and got out of her car. As I drove past her (after the light turned green, of course!), I could see her standing there, still trying to catch her breath.

Why do I begin with this incident? Because it illustrates several important points about human cognition—how, in essence, our minds work as we try to understand the world around us and function in it in adaptive ways. And such cognition, of course, is the basis of **social cognition,** the central topic of this chapter. Social psychologists use this term to refer to the ways in which we interpret, analyze, remember, and use information about the social world—in other words, how we think about other people.

But what, precisely, does the traffic incident described above tell us about cognition? First, that it often occurs on "automatic." In many situations, we can process information from the world around us (information brought to us by our senses) in a seemingly automatic, effortless, and unintentional manner. This is why we can often do two things at once—drive and listen to the radio, tie our shoelaces while talking to a friend, brush our teeth while thinking about our plans for the weekend. As we'll see later in this chapter, social cognition, too, can often proceed on automatic. For instance, once we know that someone belongs to a specific social group (e.g., African Americans, Irish Americans, Arabs), we tend to assume, often in an automatic and unintentional manner, that they possess certain traits (e.g., Bargh, Chen, & Burrows, 1996; Greenwald, McGhee, & Schwartz, 1998).

Second, and on the other side of the cognitive coin, this traffic incident also illustrates the fact that our cognitive capacities are definitely limited. Yes, the driver in question could sometimes talk on the phone and drive at the same time (although whether she could drive *safely* is an open question currently being debated around the world). On this day, however, the conversation was so absorbing or complex that she "lost it" where driving was concerned and put herself and many other motorists in danger. This is another important theme of research on social cognition: There are definite limits on our capacity to think about other people. For this reason, we often adopt shortcuts designed to save mental effort and preserve our precious cognitive capacity (e.g., Jonas et al., 2001). While these succeed in reducing such effort, they do so at a cost: sometimes, they lead us into serious errors in our thinking about others.

social cognition: The manner in which we interpret, analyze, remember, and use information about the social world.

"I've done the numbers, and I will marry you."

FIGURE 3.1
Social Cognition: Thinking about Other Persons.
As this cartoon suggests, thinking about other persons is an important part of daily life. In contrast to the character shown here, though, for most of us, our thoughts are strongly influenced by our emotions or feelings!
[SOURCE: © THE NEW YORKER COLLECTION 2000 WILLIAM HAMILTON FROM CARTOONBANK.COM. ALL RIGHTS RESERVED.]

Finally, this incident also illustrates the important links between cognition and affect—how we think and how we feel. After rolling slowly through the intersection, the driver suddenly realized what she had done. As she thought about what might have occurred—a devastating or even fatal accident—she experienced a powerful emotional reaction. As we'll soon see, the link between cognition and affect works both ways: our thinking can influence our emotions and feelings, and our feelings, in turn, can shape our thoughts (see Figure 3.1)

Social cognition is a very important area of research in social psychology; in fact, as we noted in Chapter 1, it has become a guiding framework for most, if not all, research in the field. To acquaint you with some of the truly fascinating aspects of social thought uncovered by social psychologists, we'll focus on the following topics. First, we'll examine a basic component of social thought—*schemas.* These are mental frameworks that allow us to organize large amounts of information in an efficient manner. Once formed, however, these frameworks exert strong effects on social thought—effects that are not always beneficial from the point of view of accuracy. Second, we'll consider several of the mental shortcuts mentioned above—techniques people use to reduce the cognitive effort involved in making sense of the social world (e.g., Kunda, 1999). Third, we'll examine several specific tendencies or "tilts" in social thought—tendencies that can lead us to false conclusions about others or to other kinds of errors in our efforts to understand the social world. Many of these errors exist, so here we'll focus on several that appear to exert strong effects on social thought (Jonas et al., 2001). Finally, we'll focus on the complex interplay between **affect**—our current feelings or moods—and various aspects of social cognition (e.g., Forgas, 1995a). Please note that we have already examined another important aspect of social cognition in Chapter 2, where we focused on *attributions*—our efforts to understand the causes of others' or our own behavior—and will consider several others in Chapter 5, where we'll focus on efforts to understand *ourselves.*

affect: Our current feelings and moods.

Schemas: Mental Frameworks for Organizing—and Using—Social Information

Several years ago, I visited the African nation of Morocco. I had many wonderful experiences there, but perhaps one of the most interesting occurred at a very popular restaurant in the city of Marrakech the first day I arrived. When we entered, my traveling companion and I passed a group of musicians. As we passed, they began to play, and they continued playing until we had been seated. Then, they stopped. At first I was a little puzzled. But when they began playing again as another couple entered, I understood what was going on: they played to greet new customers, and then remained silent until the next couple or group entered. After we were seated (on cushions, on the floor), a young man approached with what looked like a huge teapot. He held it out, motioning toward a metal bowl in the middle of the table. In a flash, I understood: he wanted us to hold our hands over the bowl so he could pour water over them. That was a good thing, I discovered, because there were no knives or forks: we ate using the delicious bread provided. And I quickly noticed that the bread was cut into just the right size and shape to serve as a spoon. The food was wonderful, and the evening was very pleasant. On the way out, the musicians began to play, and I noticed a large plate filled with coins placed strategically nearby. I tossed some coins into it, and the leader nodded in thanks—I had done the right thing.

Now for a key question: I had never been to Morocco before and had never had these experiences (eating on the floor, holding out my hands to be washed, etc.), so how was I able to figure out what was going on so quickly and easily? Part of the answer involves the fact that I have been in many similar situations in the past: I have eaten in hundreds of restaurants all over the world. In some, waiters gave me a hot towel for washing my hands; in others, a small finger bowl was provided for the same task. And I have certainly given tips to many persons—waitpersons, parking lot attendants, and so on. As a result of these experiences, I have acquired a kind of mental framework for understanding such situations and others' behavior in them. Such frameworks are known as **schemas**—mental structures that help us to organize social information, and that guide the processing of it. Schemas generally center around a particular subject or theme. For instance, in the situation here, the schema that was activated might be described as my "restaurant schema"; it is a mental framework, built up through experience in many previous restaurants, that helped me to make sense of the new social information I was encountering—a waiter who wanted to pour water over my hands, musicians who play only when customers enter or leave, and so on (see Figure 3.2). Clearly, such schemas are shaped by the culture in which we live: my schema for "restaurant dining" is somewhat different from that of people living in Morocco. But in this case, it was close enough to help me interpret and understand the evening's events.

Once schemas are formed, they exert powerful effects on several aspects of social cognition, and therefore on our social behavior. Let's take a closer look at these efforts to make sense out of the complex social world around us.

The Impact of Schemas on Social Cognition: Attention, Encoding, Retrieval

schemas: Mental frameworks centering around a specific theme that help us to organize social information.

How do schemas influence social thought? Research findings suggest that they exert strong effects on three basic processes: attention, encoding, and retrieval. *Attention* refers to what information we notice. *Encoding* refers to the processes through which information we notice gets stored in memory. Finally,

FIGURE 3.2
Cognitive Frameworks for Understanding the Social World.
Although you may never have eaten in a restaurant like this one in Ethiopia, you probably have a well-developed *schema* for eating in restaurants. This schema helped me to understand what was happening and what I was supposed to do when I ate in a Moroccan restaurant for the first time.

retrieval refers to the processes through which we recover information from memory in order to use it in some manner—for example, in making judgments about other people.

Schemas have been found to influence all of these basic aspects of social cognition (Wyer & Srull, 1994). With respect to attention, schemas often act as a kind of filter: information consistent with them is more likely to be noticed and to enter our consciousness. Information that does not fit with our schemas is often ignored (Fiske, 1993), unless it is so extreme that we can't help but notice it. And even then, it is often discounted as "the exception that proves the rule."

Turning to encoding—what information is entered into memory—it is a basic fact that information that becomes the focus of our attention is much more likely to be stored in long-term memory. So again, in general, it is information that is consistent with our schemas that is encoded. However, information that is sharply inconsistent with our schemas—information that does *not* agree with our expectations in a given situation—may sometimes be encoded into a separate memory location and marked with a unique "tag." After all, it is so unexpected that it literally seizes our attention and almost forces us to place it in long-term memory (Stangor & McMillan, 1992).

That leads us to the third process: retrieval from memory. What information is most readily remembered—information that is consistent with our schemas or information that is inconsistent with these mental frameworks? This is a complex question that has been investigated in many different studies (e.g., Stangor & McMillan, 1992). Overall, this research suggests that people tend to report remembering and using information that is consistent with schemas to a greater extent than information that is inconsistent. However, this action could potentially stem from differences in actual memory or, alternatively, from simple response tendencies. In other words, information inconsistent with schemas might be present as strongly or even more strongly in memory than information consistent with schemas, but people simply have a tendency to report (describe) information consistent with their schemas. In fact, this appears to be the case. When measures of memory are corrected for this response tendency, or when individuals are asked to actually *recall* information rather than simply use it or indicate whether they recognize it, a strong tendency to remember schema-incongruent information appears. So, there is no simple answer to the question, "Which do we remember better—information consistent or inconsistent with our schemas or expectations?" Rather, this depends on the measure of memory employed. In general, people *report* information consistent with their schemas, but, in fact, information inconsistent with schemas may be strongly present in memory, too.

At this point, it's important to note that the effects of schemas on social cognition (e.g., what we remember, how we use this information to make decisions or judgments) are strongly influenced by several other factors. For instance, such effects are stronger when schemas are themselves strong and well developed (e.g., Stangor & McMillan, 1992; Tice, Bratslavky, & Baumeister, 2000), and stronger when *cognitive load*—how much mental effort we are expending at a given time—is high rather than low (e.g., Kunda, 1999). In other words, when we are trying to handle a lot of social information at one time, we fall back upon schemas because these frameworks allow us to process this information with less effort.

Before concluding, we should call attention to the fact that although schemas are based on our past experience (they reflect knowledge we have extracted from our experiences in the social world) and are often helpful to us, they have a serious downside, too. By influencing what we notice, entering into memory, and later remembering, schemas can produce distortions in our understanding of the social world. For example, as we'll see in Chapter 6, schemas play an important role in prejudice, forming one basic component of stereotypes about specific social groups. And, unfortunately, once they are formed, schemas are often very resistant to change—they show a strong **perseverance effect,** remaining unchanged even in the face of contradictory information (e.g., Kunda & Oleson, 1995). For instance, when we encounter information inconsistent with our schemas, such as a highly intelligent and cultivated person who is also a member of a minority group, we do not necessarily alter our schema. Rather, we may place such persons into a special category or *subtype* consisting of persons who do not confirm to the schema or stereotype (e.g., Richards & Hewstone, 2001). Perhaps even worse, schemas can sometimes be *self-fulfilling:* they influence the social world in ways that *make* it consistent with the schema! Let's take a closer look at this process, known in social psychology as the *self-fulfilling prophecy* or the *self-confirming nature* of schemas.

Evidence for the Self-Confirming Nature of Schemas: When—and Why—Beliefs Shape Reality

During the depression of 1929, many banks faced the following situation: they were quite solvent, but rumors circulated indicating that they were not. As a result, so many depositors lined up to withdraw their funds that, ultimately, the banks really did fail: they didn't have enough money on hand to meet all of their customers' demands (see Figure 3.3). In a sense, depositors in the banks actually caused their own worst fears to be confirmed.

Interestingly, schemas, too, can produce such effects, which are sometimes described as a **self-fulfilling prophecy**—predictions that, in a sense, make themselves come true. Classic evidence for such effects was provided by Robert Rosenthal and Lenore Jacobson (1968) during the turbulent 1960s. During that period, there was growing concern over the possibility that teachers' beliefs about minority students—their schemas for such youngsters—were causing them to treat such children differently (less favorably) than majority-group students and that, as a result, the minority-group students were falling further and further behind. No, the teachers weren't overtly prejudiced; rather, their behavior was shaped by their expectations and beliefs—their schemas for different racial or ethnic groups.

perseverance effect: The tendency for beliefs and schemas to remain unchanged even in the face of contradictory information.

self-fulfilling prophecies: Predictions that, in a sense, make themselves come true.

FIGURE 3.3

The Self-Confirming Nature of Beliefs. During the depression of 1929, many people believed rumors indicating that their banks would fail. As a result, large numbers rushed to withdraw their deposits, and this actually *caused* perfectly sound banks to fail. The same kind of self-confirming effects are often produced by schemas concerning social groups (e.g., racial or ethnic minorities). ■

To gather evidence on the possible occurrence of such effects, Rosenthal and Jacobson conducted an ingenious study that exerted a powerful effect on subsequent research in social psychology. They went to an elementary school in San Francisco and administered an IQ test to all students. They then told the teachers that some of the students had scored very high and were about to bloom academically. In fact, this was not true: the researchers chose the names of these students randomly. But Rosenthal and Jacobson predicted that this information might change teachers' expectations (and schemas) about these children, and hence their behavior toward them. Teachers were not given such information about other students, who constituted a control group.

To find out whether this were true, Rosenthal and Jacobson returned eight months later and tested both groups of children once again. Results were clear—and dramatic: Those who had been described as "bloomers" to their teachers showed significantly larger gains on the IQ test than those in the control group. In short, teachers' beliefs about the students had operated in a self-fulfilling manner: the students that teachers believed would bloom academically actually did.

How did such effects occur? In part, through the impact of schemas on the teachers' behavior. Further research (Rosenthal, 1994) indicated that teachers gave the bloomers more attention, more challenging tasks, more and better feedback, and more opportunities to respond in class. In short, the teachers acted in ways that benefited the students they expected to bloom, and, as a result, these youngsters really did.

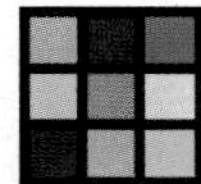

As a result of this early research, social psychologists began to search for other self-confirming effects of schemas in many settings—in education, therapy, and business, to name just a few. They soon uncovered much evidence that schemas do often shape behavior in ways that lead to their confirmation. For example, they found that teachers' lower expectancies for success by minority students or females often undermined the confidence of these groups and actually contributed to poorer performance by them (e.g., Sadker & Sadker, 1994). In view of these and many related findings, we now know that stereotypes not only may influence—they may, through their self-confirming effects, shape social reality as well.

KEY POINTS

- Because we have limited cognitive capacity, we often attempt to reduce the effort we expend on *social cognition*—how we think about other persons. This can increase efficiency but reduce our accuracy with respect to this important task.
- One basic component of social cognition is *schemas*—mental frameworks centering around a specific theme that help us to organize social information.
- Once formed, schemas exert powerful effects on what we notice (attention), enter into memory (encoding), and later remember (retrieval). Individuals report remembering more information consistent with their schemas than information inconsistent with them, but in fact, inconsistent information, too, is strongly represented in memory.
- Schemas help us to process information, but they often persist, even in the face of disconfirming information, thus distorting our understanding of the social world.
- Schemas can also exert self-confirming effects, causing us to behave in ways that confirm them.

Heuristics and Automatic Processing: How We Reduce Our Effort in Social Cognition

At the start of this chapter, we described an incident in which a driver talking on a cell phone rolled slowly through a busy intersection. One reason why this may have happened is that she had overloaded her cognitive capacity: the conversation she was having was so absorbing that it did not leave even enough cognitive resources for her to drive safely, even though driving was, for her, a highly practiced activity that she could usually perform with little or no conscious attention. In short, she may have entered a state of **information overload:** the demands on her cognitive system were greater than it could handle. Because we encounter situations like this quite often, we adopt various strategies designed to stretch our cognitive resources—to let us do more, with less effort, than would otherwise be the case. To be successful, such strategies must meet two requirements: They must provide a quick and simple way of dealing with large amounts of social information, and they must work—they must be reasonably accurate much of the time. Many potential shortcuts for reducing mental effort exist, but among these perhaps the most useful are **heuristics**—simple rules for making complex decisions or drawing inferences in a rapid and seemingly effortless manner.

information overload: Instances in which our ability to process information is exceeded.

heuristics: Simple rules for making complex decisions or drawing inferences in a rapid and seemingly effortless manner.

Another means of dealing with the fact that the social world is complex yet our information-processing capacity is limited is to put many activities—including some aspects of social thought and social behavior—on *automatic* (or *automatic processing,* as psychologists term it; e.g., Ohman, Lundqvist, & Esteves, 2001). After discussing several heuristics, therefore, we'll consider this process and its effects.

Representativeness: Judging by Resemblance

Suppose that you have just met your next-door neighbor for the first time. While chatting with her, you notice that she is dressed in a conservative manner, is very neat in her personal habits, has a very large library in her home, and seems to be very gentle and a little shy. Later you realize that she never mentioned what she does for a living. Is she a business manager, a physician, a waitress, an attorney, a dancer, or a librarian? One quick way of making a guess is to compare her with other members of each of these occupations. How well does she resemble persons you have met in each of these fields or, perhaps, the typical member of these fields? If you proceed in this manner, you may quickly conclude that she is probably a librarian; her traits seem closer to those associated with this profession than they do to the traits associated with being a physician, dancer, or executive. If you made your judgment about your neighbor's occupation in this manner, you would be using the **representativeness heuristic.** In other words, you would make your judgment on the basis of a relatively simple rule: *The more similar an individual is to typical members of a given group, the more likely she or he is to belong to that group.*

Are such judgments accurate? Often they are, because belonging to certain groups does affect the behavior and style of persons in them, and because people with certain traits are attracted to particular groups in the first place. But sometimes, judgments based on representativeness are wrong, mainly for the following reason: Decisions or judgments made on the basis of this rule tend to ignore *base rates*—the frequency with which given events or patterns (e.g., occupations) occur in the total population (Tversky & Kahneman, 1973; Koehler, 1993). In fact, there are many more business managers than librarians—perhaps fifty times as many! Thus, even though your neighbor seemed more similar to librarians than to managers in her personal traits, the chances are actually higher that she is in business than that she is a librarian. In this and related ways, the representativeness heuristic can lead to errors in our thinking about other persons.

Availability: "If I Can Think of It, It Must Be Important"

Which are more common: words that start with the letter *k* (e.g., *king*) or words with *k* as the third letter (e.g., *awkward*)? In English there are more than twice as many words with *k* in the third position as there are with *k* in the first position. Yet, despite this fact, when asked this question most people guess incorrectly (Tversky & Kahneman, 1982). Why? In part because of the operation of another heuristic—the **availability heuristic,** which suggests that the easier it is to bring information to mind, the greater its impact on subsequent judgments or decisions. This heuristic, too, makes good sense: after all, the fact that we can bring some information to mind quite easily suggests that it must be important and *should* influence our judgments and decisions. But relying on availability in making social judgments can also lead to errors. For instance, it can lead us to overestimate the likelihood of events that are dramatic but rare, because they are easy to bring to mind. Consistent with this principle, many people fear travel in airplanes

representativeness heuristic: A strategy for making judgments based on the extent to which current stimuli or events resemble other stimuli or categories.

availability heuristic: A strategy for making judgments on the basis of how easily specific kinds of information can be brought to mind.

FIGURE 3.4

The Availability Heuristic: Sometimes, It Leads to Errors.

Many people express stronger fears about being hurt or killed in airplane crashes than they do about being hurt or killed in automobile accidents. Yet, in fact, the odds of injury or death are much higher for automobiles. This difference may stem from the fact that airplane crashes are much more dramatic and receive much more attention from the media than do automobile accidents. As a result, airplane crashes are brought to mind more easily and so have a stronger impact on individuals' judgments and thoughts.

more than travel in automobiles, even though the chance of dying in an auto accident is hundreds of times higher (see Figure 3.4). Here's another example: Suppose that at some time in the future, you are a manager and are asked to evaluate the performance of one of your employees. When you think about his performance, what do you tend to remember? Unless you have kept careful records to help you in this task, you are likely to remember instances in which his behavior was extreme or unusual—the time he lost his temper and shouted angrily at you, the day he called in sick just when two other key employees were also absent, and so on. While these extreme or unusual events come to mind easily, they may not be indicative of his actual overall performance; yet they may well exert a strong effect on your evaluations of him.

Interestingly, research suggests that there is more to the availability heuristic than merely the subjective ease with which relevant information comes to mind. In addition, the *amount* of information we can bring to mind seems to matter, too (e.g., Schwarz et al., 1991b). The more information we can think of, the greater its impact on our judgments. Which of these two factors is more important? The answer appears to involve the kind of judgment we are making. If it is one involving emotions or feelings, we tend to rely on the "ease" rule, while if it is one involving facts or information, we tend to rely more on the "amount" rule (e.g., Rothman and Hardin, 1997).

PRIMING: SOME EFFECTS OF INCREASED AVAILABILITY. The availability heuristic has been found to play a role in many aspects of social thought, including the self-serving bias (see Chapter 2) and also in several topics we'll examine in later chapters (e.g., stereotyping; see Chapter 6). In addition, it is related to another especially important process: **priming**—increased availability of information resulting from exposure to specific stimuli or events.

priming: Increased availability of information in memory or consciousness, resulting from exposure to specific stimuli or events.

Here's a good example of such priming: During the first year of medical school, many students experience the "medical student syndrome": they begin to suspect that they or others have many serious illnesses. An ordinary headache may lead them to wonder if they have a brain tumor, while a mild sore throat may lead to anxiety over the possibility of some rare but fatal type of infection. What accounts for such effects? The explanation favored by social psychologists is as follows. The students are exposed to descriptions of diseases day after day in their classes and assigned readings. As a result, such information increases in availability. This, in turn, leads them to imagine the worst when confronted with mild symptoms.

Priming effects also occur in many other contexts—for example, our magnified fears after watching a horror film, or increased romantic feelings after watching love scenes. Thus, they appear to be an important aspect of social thought (e.g., Higgins & King, 1981; Higgins, Rohles, & Jones, 1977). In fact, research evidence indicates that priming may occur even when individuals are unaware of the priming stimuli—an effect known as *automatic priming* (e.g., Bargh & Pietromonaco, 1982). In other words, the availability of certain kinds of information can be increased by priming stimuli even though we are not aware of having been exposed to these stimuli. For instance, suppose that while waiting for a movie to start, you are thinking about some important matter. As a result, you do not even notice that a message urging you to eat popcorn has appeared on the screen. A few minutes later, you see a person in the row in front of you returning to his seat with a box of popcorn. Suddenly, you have a strong urge to buy some yourself. Why? Perhaps because you are hungry and like popcorn; but it is also possible that your urge to buy popcorn stems, at least in part, from the fact that you were primed to do so by the message you did not consciously notice.

In sum, it appears that priming is a basic fact of social thought. External events and conditions—or even our own thoughts—can increase the availability of specific types of information. And increased availability, in turn, influences our judgments with respect to such information. "If I can think of it," we seem to reason, "then it must be important, frequent, or true," and we often reach such conclusions even if they are not supported by social reality.

Automatic Processing in Social Thought: How We Manage to Do Two Things at Once

As we've noted repeatedly, a central dilemma we face with respect to social cognition is this: Our capacity to process information (including social information) is limited, yet daily life floods us with large amounts of information and requires us to deal with it both effectively and efficiently. As we've already seen, heuristics is one means of solving this problem. Another involves **automatic processing.** This occurs when, after extensive experience with a task or type of information, we reach the stage where we can perform the task or process the information in a seemingly effortless, automatic, and nonconscious manner. Do you remember your efforts to learn to ride a bicycle? At first, you had to devote a lot of attention to this task; if you didn't, you would fall down! But as you mastered it, riding required less and less attention until, finally, you could do it while thinking of entirely different topics, or even while engaging in other tasks, such as talking to a friend. So, in many cases, the shift from *controlled processing* (which is effortful and conscious) to automatic processing is something we *want* to happen: it saves us a great deal of effort.

To an extent, this is true with respect to social thought as well. For instance, once we have a well-developed schemas for a social group (e.g., for doctors or any other profession), we can think in short-hand ways about members of that group. We can, for instance, assume that all doctors will be busy, so it's necessary to get right to the point with them; that they are intelligent but not always very considerate; and so on. But as is usually the case, these gains in efficiency or ease are offset by potential losses in accuracy. For instance, growing evidence indicates that

automatic processing: This occurs when, after extensive experience with a task or type of information, we reach the stage where we can perform the task or process the information in a seemingly effortless, automatic, and nonconscious manner.

one type of schema—stereotypes—can be activated in an automatic and nonconscious manner by the physical features associated with the stereotyped group (e.g., Pratto & Bargh, 1991). Thus, dark skin may automatically trigger a negative stereotype about African Americans, even if the person in question has no intention of thinking in terms of this stereotype. Similarly, attitudes (beliefs and evaluations of some aspect of the social world) may be automatically triggered by the mere presence of the attitude object (e.g., Wegner & Bargh, 1998). Such automatic processing of social information can, of course, lead to serious errors.

Perhaps even more surprising, research findings indicate that schemas, once activated, may even exert seemingly automatic effects on behavior. In others words, people may act in ways consistent with these schemas, even though they do not intend to do so, and are unaware that they are acting in this manner. A clear illustration of such effects is provided by research conducted by Bargh, Chen, and Burrows (1996).

In one study, these researchers first activated either the schema for the trait of *rudeness* or the schema for the trait of *politeness* through priming. Participants worked on unscrambling scrambled sentences containing words related either to rudeness (e.g., *bold, rude, impolitely, bluntly*) or words related to politeness (*cordially, patiently, polite, courteous, discreetly*). Exposure to words related to schemas has been found, in past research, to prime or activate these mental frameworks. Persons in a third (control) group unscrambled sentences containing words unrelated to either trait (e.g., *exercising, flawlessly, occasionally, rapidly, normally*). After completing these tasks, participants in the study were asked to report back to the experimenter, who would give them additional tasks. When they approached the experimenter, he or she was engaged in a conversation with another person (an accomplice). The experimenter continued this conversation, ignoring the participant. The major dependent measure was whether the participant interrupted the conversation in order to receive further instructions. The researchers predicted that persons for whom the trait *rudeness* had been primed would be more likely to interrupt than would those for whom the trait *politeness* had been primed. As you can see from Figure 3.5, this is precisely what happened. Further findings indicated that these effects occurred despite the fact that participants' ratings of the experimenter in terms of politeness did not differ

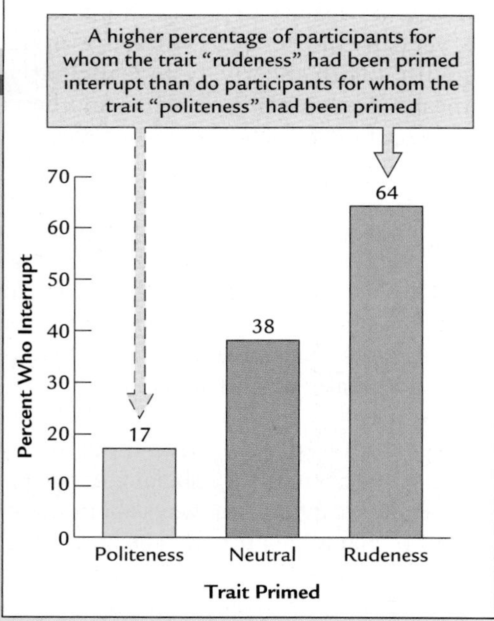

FIGURE 3.5

Automatic Processing and Social Behavior. Individuals for whom the schema for "rudeness" had been primed were much more likely to interrupt an experimenter's conversation than were individuals for whom the schema for "politeness" had been primed. This was true despite the fact that both groups rated the experimenter the same in terms of politeness.

[SOURCE: BASED ON DATA FROM BARGH, CHEN, AND BURROWS, 1996.]

across the three experimental conditions. Thus, these differences in behavior seemed to occur in a nonconscious, automatic manner.

In a second study, Bargh, Chen, and Burrows (1996) either primed the stereotype for *elderly* (again through exposure to words related to this schema) or did not prime it. Then they timed the number of seconds it took participants to walk down a hallway at the end of the study. As predicted, those for whom the stereotype *elderly* had been primed actually walked slower! Together, the results of these studies indicate that activating stereotypes or schemas can exert seemingly automatic effects on behavior—effects that occur in the absence of intention or conscious awareness. These findings have important implications. For instance, they suggest that once stereotypes are activated, individuals not only think in terms of these mental frameworks—they may actually behave in ways consistent with them as well. Thus, negative stereotypes of minority groups may lead the persons possessing them to act in hostile ways toward members of these groups, even if they do not intend to do so. Clearly, then, automatic processing is an important aspect of social thought—one that may often become visible in outward, overt behavior.

KEY POINTS

- Because our capacity to process information is limited, we often experience *information overload.* To avoid this, we make use of *heuristics*—rules for making decisions in a quick and relatively effortless manner.
- One such heuristic is *representativeness,* which suggests that the more similar an individual is to typical members of a given group, the more likely she or he is to belong to that group.
- Another heuristic is *availability,* which suggests that the easier it is to bring information to mind, the greater its impact on subsequent decisions or judgments. In some cases, availability may also involve the amount of information we bring to mind.
- *Priming* refers to increased availability of information resulting from exposure to specific stimuli or events.
- Another means of reducing mental effort involves *automatic processing* of social information—processing that occurs in a seemingly automatic, effortless, and nonconscious manner. Research findings indicate that, once activated, schemas and other mental frameworks may influence not only social thought, but social behavior as well.

Potential Sources of Error in Social Cognition: Why Total Rationality Is Rarer Than You Think

Human beings are definitely not computers. Although we can *imagine* being able to reason in a perfectly logical way, we know from our own experience that we often fall short of this goal. This is definitely true with respect to many aspects of social thought. In our efforts to understand others and make sense out of the social world, we are subject to a wide range of tendencies that, together, can lead us into serious error. In this section, we'll consider several of these "tilts" in social cognition. Before doing so, however, we should emphasize the following point: While these aspects of social thought do sometimes result in errors, they are also quite adaptive. They often help us to focus on the kinds of information that are most informative, and they reduce the effort required for understanding the social world. So they are definitely something of a mixed bag, supplying us with tangible benefits as well as exacting important costs.

Negativity Bias: The Tendency to Pay Extra Attention to Negative Information

Imagine that in describing someone you haven't met, one of your friends mentions many positive things about this person—he or she is pleasant, intelligent, good-looking, friendly, and so on. Then, your friend mentions one negative piece of information: this person is also somewhat conceited. What are you likely to remember? Research findings indicate that, probably, the negative information will stand out in your memory (e.g., Kunda, 1999). Moreover, because of this, the negative information will have a stronger influence on your desire to meet this person than will any one equivalent piece of positive information. Such findings suggest that we show a strong **negativity bias**—greater sensitivity to negative information than to positive information. This is also true of both social information and information about other aspects of the world see (Figure 3.6).

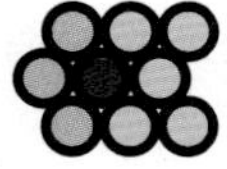

Why do we have this tendency? From an evolutionary perspective, it makes a great deal of sense. Negative information reflects features of the external world that may be threatening to our safety or well-being. For this reason, it is especially important that we be sensitive to such stimuli and thus able to respond to them quickly. Several research findings offer support for this reasoning. For instance, consider our ability to recognize facial expressions in others. The results of many studies indicate that we are faster and more accurate in detecting negative facial expressions (e.g., ones showing anger or hostility) than positive facial expressions (e.g., ones showing friendliness).

negativity bias: Refers to the fact that we show greater sensitivity to negative information than to positive information.

A clear illustration of such effects is provided by studies conducted by Ohman, Lundqvist, and Esteves (2001). These researchers asked participants to search for neutral, friendly, or threatening faces present among other faces with discrepant expressions (e.g., the friendly face was shown among neutral or threatening faces;

FIGURE 3.6

The Negativity Bias in Operation.

As suggested by this cartoon, we tend to be more sensitive to negative information than positive information.

[SOURCE: © LYNN JOHNSTON PRODUCTIONS, INC./DIST. BY UNITED FEATURE SYNDICATE, INC.]

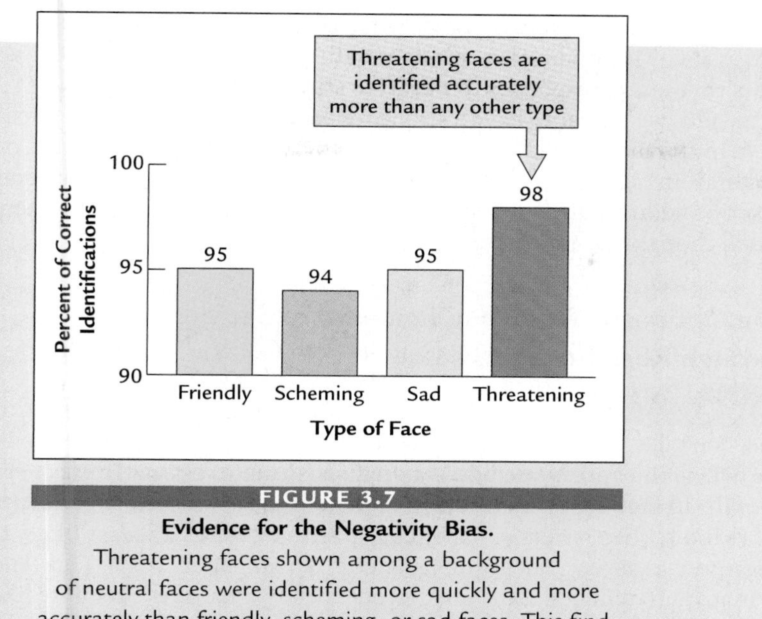

FIGURE 3.7

Evidence for the Negativity Bias.

Threatening faces shown among a background of neutral faces were identified more quickly and more accurately than friendly, scheming, or sad faces. This finding provides evidence for the existence of the *negativity bias*—enhanced sensitivity to negative stimuli or information.

[SOURCE: BASED ON DATA FROM OHMAN, LUNDQVIST, AND ESTEVES, 2001.]

the threatening face was shown among friendly or neutral faces; and so on). Results indicated that regardless of the background faces, participants were faster and more accurate in identifying threatening faces. In an additional study, participants were asked to search for several kinds of faces—threatening, friendly, scheming, or sad—among an array of neutral faces. Again, the threatening faces were identified faster and more accurately than any of the others (see Figure 3.7).

■ SOCIAL COGNITIVE AND NEUROSCIENCE: THE NEURAL BASIS OF THE NEGATIVITY BIAS. In recent years, a growing number of social psychologists have begun to use modern techniques for studying the brain to uncover the neural bases of social thought (e.g., Cacioppo, Gardner, & Berntson, 1999; Crites et al., 1995). Some of this research has focused on the negativity bias, and it provides evidence that this bias may, in fact, be built into the basic functioning of our brains. For instance, in one informative study, Ito and his colleagues (1998) showed participants neutral, positive, or negative stimuli in the context of other, neutral stimuli. The neutral stimuli were photos of a plate, a hair dryer, or an electrical outlet. Positive stimuli were photos of a red Ferrari or people enjoying a roller coaster ride. Negative stimuli included photos of a mutilated face or a handgun aimed at the camera. Participants were asked to look at each picture and to think about whether it showed something they found to be positive, negative, or neutral, and then to indicate their evaluation by pressing keys on a computer keyboard. Electrical activity in their brains was recorded as they watched and responded to the photos. This activity (known as *late positive potentials,* or LPPs for short) had previously been shown to reflect the *evaluative-categorization* stage of social cognition—our initial decision about whether a stimulus is something we like or dislike. Results indicated that negative stimuli produced larger LPPs than did positive stimuli. These findings suggest that the negativity bias operates during very early stages of social cognition—the stage at which we are first evaluating a stimulus on a simple positive–negative dimension. This finding is consistent with the evolutionary perspective, which suggests that quick responses to negative stimuli are often important for survival.

In sum, we appear to have a strong tendency to show enhanced sensitivity to negative information. This tendency seems to be a very basic aspect of social thought, and may, in fact, be built into the structure and functioning of our brains. (We will describe additional efforts by social psychologists to identify the neutral bases of social thought in our discussion of attitudes in Chapter 4.)

The Optimistic Bias: Our Tendency to See the World through Rose-Colored Glasses

Although the tendency to notice negative information is a strong one, don't despair: despite its existence, we also have a seemingly opposite tendency known as the **optimistic bias**—a predisposition to expect things to turn out well overall. In fact, research findings indicate that most people believe that they are *more* likely than others to experience positive events, and *less* likely to experience negative events (e.g., Shepperd, Ouellette, & Fernandez, 1996). This tendency is seen in many different contexts: most people believe that they are more likely than others to get a good job, have a happy marriage, and live to a ripe old age, but less likely to experience negative outcomes such as being fired, getting seriously ill, or being divorced (e.g., Schwarzer, 1994).

Yet another illustration is with respect to the **planning fallacy**—our tendency to believe that we can get more done in a given period of time than we actually can. Because of this aspect of the optimistic bias, governments frequently announce overly optimistic schedules for public works (e.g., new roads, new airports, new bridges; see Figure 3.8), and individuals adopt unrealistically optimistic schedules for their own work. If you have ever estimated that a project would take you a certain amount of time but then found that it took much longer, you are already familiar with this effect and with the planning fallacy.

optimistic bias: Our predisposition to expect things to turn out well overall.

planning fallacy: The tendency to make optimistic predictions concerning how long a given task will take for completion.

Why do we fall prey to this particular kind of optimism? According to Buehler, Griffin, and Ross (1994), social psychologists who have studied this tendency in

FIGURE 3.8

The Planning Fallacy in Action. Governments often announce overly optimistic schedules for completion of major projects—roads, bridges, airports. This may reflect operation of the *planning fallacy*—the tendency to believe that we can accomplish more than we actually can in a given period of time.

detail, several factors play a role. One is that when individuals make predictions about how long it will take them to complete a given task, they enter a *planning* or *narrative* mode of thought in which they focus primarily on the future and how they will perform the task. This, in turn, prevents them from looking backward in time and remembering how long similar tasks took them in the past. As a result, one important reality check that might help them avoid being overly optimistic is removed. In addition, when individuals *do* consider past experiences in which tasks took longer than expected, they tend to attribute such outcomes to factors outside their control. The result: They tend to overlook important potential obstacles when predicting how long a task will take, and fall prey to the planning fallacy. These predictions have been confirmed in several studies (e.g., Buehler, Griffin, & Ross, 1994), so they do seem to provide important insights into the origins of the tendency to make optimistic predictions about task completion.

This is not the entire story, though. Research suggests that another factor, too, may play an important role in the planning fallacy: *motivation* to complete a task. When predicting what will happen, individuals often guess that what will happen is what they *want* to happen (e.g., Johnson & Sherman, 1990). In cases in which they are strongly motivated to complete a task, therefore, they make overoptimistic predictions concerning when this desired state of affairs will occur. Research findings offer support for this reasoning, too (e.g., Buehler, Griffin, & MacDonald, 1997), so it appears that our estimates of when we will complete a task are indeed influenced by our hopes and desires: we want to finish early or on time, so we predict that we will. The result? Unfounded optimism strikes again!

■ BRACING FOR LOSS: AN EXCEPTION TO THE OPTIMISTIC RULE. Although optimism seems to be the general rule where our social thought is concerned, there is one important exception to this pattern. When individuals expect to receive feedback or information that may be negative in nature and that has important consequences for them, they seem to *brace for loss* (or for the worst) and show a reversal of the usual optimistic pattern: in fact, they tend to be *pessimistic,* showing an enhanced tendency to anticipate *negative* outcomes (e.g., Taylor & Shepperd, 1998).

Why does this occur? Recent research by Shepperd and his colleagues (Shepperd et al., 2000) suggests that it is in fact due to the desire to be ready—braced—for the worst. In several related studies, Shepperd and his colleagues (2000) asked students to estimate the likelihood that they would receive an additional bill (a negative outcome) or a refund (a positive outcome) from the registrar at their college. (Supposedly, the registrar had made a number of errors, resulting in fully 25 percent of the students receiving incorrect bills for tuition and fees). The researchers predicted that students who were financially needy—for whom the additional bill would be a major problem—would show a stronger brace-for-loss effect than would those who were not financially needy, because an extra bill would have more serious consequences for the poorer students. Results confirmed this prediction. In several studies, such students estimated the likelihood that they would receive an additional bill at between 40 percent and 67 percent—much higher than the 25 percent chance figure, and higher than that estimated by students who were not financially needy. Further, they showed such pessimism only for themselves, not for a friend, and regardless of whether they were primed to think about past financial losses.

Together, these findings suggest that people do indeed brace for the worst and turn pessimistic under conditions where they anticipate possible bad news that will have strong negative effects upon them. But again, we should emphasize that this is the exception to a general rule of optimism. In most situations, we tend to be overly optimistic about our lives and social outcome, but we can switch to pessimism when this helps us protect ourselves from the crushing blows of unexpected bad news.

KEY POINTS 

- We show a strong *negativity bias*—a tendency to be highly sensitive to negative stimuli or information. This tendency appears to be very basic and may be built into the functioning of our brains. Thus, it may be the result of evolutionary factors.
- We also show a strong *optimistic bias,* expecting positive events and outcomes in many contexts. In addition, we tend to make overly optimistic predictions about how long it will take to complete a given task, an effect known as the *planning fallacy.*
- The optimistic bias also shows up in our tendency to assume that we are more likely than other persons to experience positive outcomes, but less likely than others to experience negative ones.
- The optimistic bias may be reversed and turn to pessimism, however, when we anticipate receiving bad news with important consequences for us; in such cases, we brace for loss and show an enhanced tendency to predict negative outcomes.

The Potential Costs of Thinking Too Much: Why, Sometimes, Our Tendency to Do as Little Cognitive Work as Possible May Be Justified

As we have already seen, there are many instances in which we adopt an intuitive approach to thinking about the social world. Yet there are other instances in which we *do* try to be as rational and systematic as possible in our thought, despite the extra effort this involves. At first glance, such deliberate, rational thought would seem to be uniformly beneficial: after all, it should be less prone to errors or bias. But on close examination, it appears that perhaps this is not always so. Have you ever had the experience of thinking about some problem or decision so long and so hard that ultimately, you found yourself becoming more and more confused? If so, you are aware of the fact that even where rational thought is concerned, there can sometimes be too much of a good thing.

Surprising as this conclusion may be, it has been confirmed by many studies (e.g., Schooler & Engstler-Schooler, 1990; Wilson, 1990). Perhaps the most dramatic evidence for the potential downside of thinking too much is that provided by Wilson and Schooler (1991). These researchers asked college students to sample and rate several strawberry jams. Half of the participants were simply asked to taste the jams and rate them; the others were asked to analyze their reactions to the jams—to indicate why they felt the way they did about each product. Wilson and Schooler (1991) reasoned that when individuals engage in such careful introspection, the reasons they bring to mind may simply be the ones that are most prominent and accessible—the easiest to remember or put into words. However, they may not be the most important factors in their judgments. As a result, people may actually be misled by the reasons they report, and this can cause them to make less accurate judgments.

To determine if this actually happens, Wilson and Schooler (1991) compared the judgments made by the participants who analyzed the reasons behind their ratings, and the judgments made by those who did not, with ratings by a panel of experts—persons who make their living comparing various products. As expected, participants who simply rated the jams agreed much more closely with the experts than did participants who tried to report the reasons behind their reactions to the various jams.

Similar findings have been obtained in several related studies, so there appear to be strong grounds for concluding that, sometimes, thinking too much can get us into serious cognitive trouble. Yes, trying to think systematically and rationally about important matters is important; such high-effort activities do often yield better decisions and more accurate judgments than shoot-from-the-hip modes of thought. But careful thought, like anything else, can be overdone; and when it is, the result may be increased confusion and frustration rather than better and more accurate decisions or conclusions.

Counterfactual Thinking: The Effects of Considering "What Might Have Been"

Suppose that you take an important exam; when you receive your score, it is a C– —much lower than you hoped. What thoughts will enter you mind as you consider your grade? If you are like most people, you may quickly begin to imagine "what might have been"—receiving a higher grade—along with thoughts about how you could have obtained that better outcome. "If only I had studied more, or come to class more often," you may think to yourself. Then, perhaps, you may begin to formulate plans for actually *doing* better on the next test.

Such thoughts about what might have been—known in social psychology as **counterfactual thinking**—occur in a wide range of situations, not just ones in which we experience disappointments. Remember the driver who drifted across a busy intersection while talking on her cell phone? She imagined what might have happened if she hadn't been so lucky. She imagined *worse* outcomes than she experienced, not better ones. So, counterfactual thinking can involve imagining either better outcomes (*upward* counterfactuals) or worse ones (*downward* counterfactuals) than we actually experience.

When counterfactual thinking involves imagining better outcomes than actually occurred, it is closely related to the experience of regret. And such regrets seem to be more intense when they involve things we *did not do* but wish we had, rather than things we did do that turned out poorly (Gilovich & Medvec, 1994). Why is this the case? In part, because when we think about things we *did* do that turned out badly, we know what happened and can rationalize away our decisions or actions, finding good reasons for them. When we think about missed opportunities, however, the situation is very different. As time passes, we gradually downplay or lose sight of the factors that prevented us from acting at the time—these seem less and less important. Even worse, we tend to imagine in vivid detail the wonderful benefits that would have resulted if we *had* acted. The result: Our regrets intensify over time and can haunt us for an entire lifetime (Medvec, Madey, & Gilovich, 1995).

Interestingly, recent findings indicate that people who start their own businesses—entrepreneurs—are less likely to engage in counterfactual thinking and less likely to experience regret over missed opportunities than are other persons (Baron, 2000). Apparently, they believe that missed opportunities don't matter: there's always a new one around the next corner. Accordingly, they don't spend much time thinking about what might have been: they are too busy thinking about what may *yet* be!

These are not the only effects of counterfactual thinking, however. As noted by Neal Roese (1997), a social psychologist who has conducted many studies on counterfactual thinking, engaging in such thought can yield a wide range of results, some of which are beneficial and some of which are costly to the persons involved. For instance, counterfactual thinking can, depending on its focus, yield either boosts to or reductions in our current moods. If individuals imagine *upward counterfactuals,* comparing their current outcomes with more favorable ones than they experienced, the result may be strong feelings of dissatisfaction or envy, especially if they do not feel capable of obtaining better outcomes in the future (Sanna, 1997). Olympic athletes who win a silver medal but imagine winning a gold one experience such reactions (see Figure 3.9 on page 96; e.g., Medvec, Madey, & Gilovich,

counterfactual thinking: The tendency to imagine other outcomes in a situation than the ones that actually occurred—to think about "what might have been."

FIGURE 3.9

Counterfactual Thinking at the Olympics. Research findings indicate that Olympic athletes who win bronze medals are actually happier than those who win silver medals. Why? Because they imagine not winning any medal at all (downward counterfactuals) and so are glad to have received any medal at all. In contrast, those who win a silver medal imagine winning a gold medal (upward counterfactuals) and so are relatively dissatisfied with the medal they actually received.

1995). Alternatively, if individuals compare their current outcomes with less favorable ones, or if they contemplate various ways in which disappointing results could have been avoided and positive ones attained, they may experience positive feelings of satisfaction or hopefulness. Such reactions have been found among Olympic athletes who win bronze medals, and who therefore imagine what it would be like to have won no medal whatsoever (e.g., Gleicher et al., 1995). In sum, engaging in counterfactual thought can strongly influence affective states (Medvec & Savitsky, 1997).

In addition, it appears that we often use counterfactual thinking to mitigate the bitterness of disappointments. After tragic events such as the death of a loved one, people often find solace in thinking, "Nothing more could be done; the death was inevitable." In other words, they adjust their view concerning the inevitability of the death so as to make it seem more certain and therefore unavoidable. In contrast, if they have different counterfactual thoughts—"If only the illness had been diagnosed sooner . . . " or "If only we had gotten him to the hospital quicker . . . "—their suffering may be increased. So, by assuming that negative events or disappointments were inevitable, we tend to make these events more bearable (Tykocinski, 2001). We'll have more to say about such effects in a later section.

Still another effect of counterfactual thinking—or, in this case, of anticipating that we will engage in it—is known as *inaction inertia.* This occurs when an individual has decided *not* to take some action and so loses the opportunity to gain a positive outcome. As a result, he or she becomes less likely to take similar actions in the future, especially if these actions will yield smaller gains. For instance, imagine that you meant to buy a stereo when it was on sale at 50 percent off the regular price, but didn't get down to the store in time. Now, the stereo is on sale at 25 percent off. Will you buy it? Research findings indicate that you may actually be less likely to do so than if you hadn't missed the original sale (e.g., Tykocinski, Pittman, & Tuttle, 1995). Why? Apparently, because we realize that if we buy the stereo now, we'll remind ourselves about the fact that we could have bought it for less; we want to avoid that, because such counterfactual thinking will result in unpleasant feelings of regret. Findings reported by Tykocinski and Pittman (1998) offer clear support for this reasoning: Individuals in these studies were most likely to show inaction inertia when such inertia could indeed protect them from thinking about past missed opportunities. When they couldn't avoid thinking about these missed opportunities (e.g., every day they had to walk past a very desirable apartment they had failed to rent), inaction inertia decreased.

In sum, imagining what might have been in a given situation can yield many effects, ranging from despair and intense regret on the one hand, through hopefulness and increased determination to do better on the other. Our tendency to think not only about what is but also about what *might* be, therefore, can have far-reaching effects on many aspects of our social thought and social behavior.

KEY POINTS

- When individuals think too deeply about some topic, they may become confused about the factors that actually play a role their behavior, with the result that they make less accurate judgments or decisions.
- In many situations, individuals imagine "what might have been"—they engage in *counterfactual thinking.* Such thinking can affect our sympathy for persons who have experienced negative outcomes and can cause us to experience strong regret over missed opportunities.
- By assuming that disappointing or tragic events are unavoidable, individuals can make them more bearable; this is a very adaptive function of counterfactual thought.
- Counterfactual thinking can also strongly influence our affective states and can lead to inaction inertia, which occurs when individuals fail to perform an action that would yield positive outcomes and then become reluctant to take it in the future to avoid thinking about the initial missed opportunity.

Magical Thinking: Would You Eat a Chocolate Shaped Like a Spider?

Answer truthfully:

If you are in class and don't want the professor to call on you, if you think about her calling on you, does this increase the chances that she really will?

Suppose someone who had died of cancer had bought a sweater sealed in a plastic bag and put it away in a drawer; if someone gave the sweater to you a year after the person's death, would you wear it?

Imagine that someone offered you a piece of chocolate shaped like a spider—would you eat it? How about a chocolate shaped like some human body part? (see Figure 3.10 on page 98).

On the basis of purely rational considerations, you know what your answers should be to these questions: No, yes, and yes. But are those the answer you actually gave? If you are like most persons, perhaps not. In fact, research findings indicate that, as human beings, we are quite susceptible to what has been termed **magical thinking** (Rozin & Nemeroff, 1990). Such thinking makes assumptions that don't hold up to rational scrutiny but that are compelling nonetheless. One principle of such magical thinking is the *law of contagion:* it holds that when two objects touch, they pass properties to one another, and the effects of that contact may last well beyond the end of the contact between them (Zusne & Jones, 1989). Another is the *law of similarity,* which suggests that things that resemble one another share basic properties. Still a third assumes that one's thoughts can influence the physical world

magical thinking: Thinking involving assumptions that don't hold up to rational scrutiny—for example, the belief that things that resemble one another share fundamental properties.

FIGURE 3.10

Magical Thinking in Action. Would you eat the object shown here if you knew that it was made out of pure chocolate and was 100 percent safe to consume? Many persons would not because of the influence of what social psychologists term *magical thinking.*

in a manner not governed by the laws of physics. Can you see how these assumptions relate to the questions above? The law of contagion is linked to the question about the sweater; the law of similarity has to do with the chocolate; and the third principle relates to the possibility that thinking about some event can make it happen.

Surprising as it may seem, our thinking about many situations—including social ones—is often influenced by such magical thinking. For example, in one study on this topic, Rozin, Markwith, and Nemeroff (1992) asked individuals to rate a sweater owned either by a person with AIDS or by a healthy person, which had been left in a sealed plastic bag and never touched by the owner. Consistent with the law of contagion, participants rated the sweater less favorably when it had been owned by the person with AIDs, even though they knew that there was no chance they could catch the disease from the sweater.

So, the next time you are tempted to make fun of someone's superstitious belief (e.g., fear of the number thirteen or of black cats crossing one's path), think again: although you may not accept these superstitions yourself, this does not suggest that your own thinking is totally free from the kind of "magical" assumptions considered here.

Thought Suppression: Why Efforts to Avoid Thinking Certain Thoughts Sometimes Backfire

At some time or other, everyone has tried to suppress certain thoughts—to keep ideas and images from coming into consciousness. For example, a person on a diet may try to avoid thinking about delicious desserts, someone who is trying to quit smoking might try to avoid thoughts about the pleasures of lighting up, and someone who is nervous about giving a speech might try to avoid thinking about all the ways in which he or she risks looking foolish while speaking to a large audience.

How do we accomplish such **thought suppression,** and what are the effects of this process? According to Daniel Wegner (1992b, 1994), a social psychologist who has studied thought suppression in detail, efforts to keep certain thoughts out of consciousness involve two components. First, there is an automatic *monitoring process,* which searches for evidence that unwanted thoughts are about to intrude. When such thoughts are detected by the first process, a second one, which is more effortful and less automatic (i.e., more controlled), swings into operation. This *operating process* involves effortful, conscious attempts to distract oneself by finding something else to think about. In a sense, the monitoring process is an "early warn-

thought suppression: Efforts to prevent certain thoughts from entering consciousness.

ing" system that tells the person unwanted thoughts are present, and the second one is an active prevention system that keeps such thoughts out of consciousness through distraction.

Under normal circumstances, the two processes do a good job of suppressing unwanted thoughts. When information overload occurs or when individuals are fatigued, however, the monitoring process continues to identify unwanted thoughts but the operating process no longer has the resources to keep them from entering consciousness. The result: The individual actually experiences a pronounced *rebound* effect in which the unwanted thoughts occur at an even higher rate than was true before efforts to suppress them began. As we'll soon see, this can have serious consequences for the persons involved.

The operation of the two processes described by Wegner (1992a, 1994) has been confirmed in many different studies (e.g., Wegner & Zanakos, 1994) and with respect to thoughts ranging from strange or unusual images (e.g., a white elephant) to thoughts about former lovers (Wegner & Gold, 1995). So this model of thought suppression appears to be an accurate one.

Now for the second question we posed above: What are the effects of engaging in thought suppression—and of failing to accomplish this task? Generally, people engage in thought suppression as a means of influencing their own feelings and behavior. For example, if you want to avoid feeling angry, it's best not to think about incidents that cause you to feel resentment toward others. Similarly, if you want to avoid feeling depressed, it's useful to avoid thinking about events or experiences that make you feel sad. But sometimes, people engage in thought suppression because they are told to do so by someone else—such as a therapist who is trying to help them cope with a personal problem. Imagine that someone is trying to suppress thoughts of alcohol in order to deal with a drinking problem. For example, a therapist may tell an individual who is trying to reduce her or his alcohol consumption to avoid thinking about the pleasures of drinking. If the individual succeeds in suppressing such thoughts, this may be a plus for this person's treatment. But consider what happens if the individual fails in these efforts at thought suppression. This may lead the patient to think: "What a failure I am—I can't even control my thoughts!" As a result, the person's motivation to continue these efforts—or even to continue therapy—may drop, with predictable, negative outcomes (e.g., Kelly & Kahn, 1994).

Unfortunately, some people, because they possess certain personal characteristics, seem especially likely to experience such failures. Individuals high in *reactance*—ones who react very negatively to perceived threats to their personal freedom—may be especially at risk for such effects. Such persons often reject advice or suggestions from others because they want to do their own thing, so they may find instructions to suppress certain thoughts hard to follow. That this is actually so is indicated by research carried out by Kelly and Nauta (1997).

These researchers asked individuals previously found to be high or low in reactance to generate their own most frequently occurring intrusive thought and then to either suppress or express that thought in writing. Later, participants were asked to rate the extent to which they felt out of control and distressed by their intrusive thoughts. Kelly and Nauta (1997) predicted that persons high in reactance would have more difficulty in following instructions to suppress intrusive thoughts and would later report being more disturbed by these thoughts when they occurred. As shown in Figure 3.11 on page 100, this is precisely what happened: Persons high in reactance did not differ from those low in reactance when told to express their intrusive thoughts. This was predicted, because reactance should *not* influence their behavior under these conditions. When told to suppress these thoughts, however, persons high in reactance reported a significantly higher incidence of the thoughts they were told to suppress. Apparently, they either acted in a manner opposite to the experimenters' instructions (this is what persons high in reactance often do!) or tried to suppress their thoughts more completely—with the result that they experienced

FIGURE 3.11

Reactance and Thought Suppression. When told to suppress intrusive thoughts, persons high in reactance reported more instances of such thoughts and great disturbance over them than did persons low in reactance. No differences between these groups occurred when they were told to express their intrusive thoughts rather than suppress them.

[SOURCE: BASED ON DATA FROM KELLY & NAUTA, 1997.]

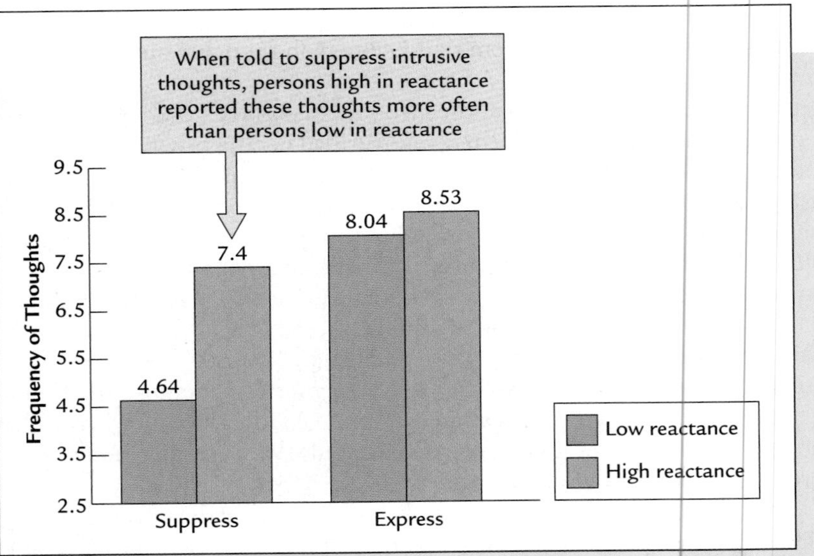

a greater rebound effect. Whatever the precise explanation, it seems clear that personal characteristics can indeed play a role in thought suppression, and that persons high in reactance may not be very good candidates for forms of therapy that include suppressing unwanted thoughts as part of their procedures. (See the **Ideas to Take with You—And Use!** feature on page 111 for an overview of the many sources of error that can influence social cognition. For an example of such effects in one important real-life context, see the **Beyond the Headlines** feature below.)

BEYOND THE HEADLINES: AS SOCIAL PSYCHOLOGISTS SEE IT

HOW THE CRIMINAL JUSTICE SYSTEM COULD BE IMPROVED—BUT ISN'T: THE POTENTIAL ROLE OF COGNITIVE BIASES

Under Suspicion: The Fugitive Science of Criminal Justice

The New Yorker, January 8, 2001—Each year in the United States, more than seventy-five thousand people become criminal suspects based on eyewitness identification, with lineups used as a standard technique. Studies of wrongful convictions—cases where a defendant was later exonerated by DNA testing—have shown the most common cause to be eyewitness error. Yet, the law has balked at submitting its methods to scientific inquiry. Researchers working outside the legal system have discovered that surprisingly simple changes in legal procedures could substantially reduce misidentifications. They suggest how scientific experimentation, which transformed medicine in the last century, could transform the justice system in the next. For example, social psychologist Gary Wells has found that eyewitnesses are more likely to make a false identification when they are presented with the standard lineup and choose one of the people in it as the perpetrator. If, instead, witnesses are shown only one person at a time and asked to decide whether this person was the culprit before moving on, false identifications are reduced by well over fifty percent—without sacrificing correct identifications. These results have been replicated by other researchers. . . . The technique is beautifully simple and it wouldn't cost a dime to adopt it. But fifteen years after he published these results, the procedure is not being followed. "In general," Wells reports, "the reaction of criminal law audiences to my findings was 'Well that's very interesting, but . . .' " A Department of Justice report released in 1999 acknowledged that scientific evidence had established the superiority of sequential-lineup procedures. Yet the report goes on to emphasize that the department still has no preference between the two methods. . . ."

What's going on here? A simple change in the way lineups (see Figure 3.12) are used could reduce false identification by eyewitnesses to crimes by more than 50 percent, yet the criminal justice system has *not* adopted this change. How can this be? One answer, we believe, lies in the kind of "tilts," or biases, in social cognition we have been discussing in this chapter.

Consider this fact: Lawyers, police, and other persons working in the criminal justice system often have no training in the methods of science. Thus, they have no schema for processing information relating to scientific experiments (e.g., for interpreting the findings). As a result, they often have a great deal of trouble understanding these results or why they are valuable. Lawyers and others in the criminal justice system live in a culture based on precedent and convention. The answer to complex questions, they believe, lies not in scientific research but in what was done before (precedent, convention) and in common sense. As Wells puts it, "The legal system doesn't understand science. I taught in law school for a year. Believe me, there's no science there at all." When Wells speaks to people in the justice system about his work, he finds that most of his time is spent educating them about basic scientific methods. "To them, it seems like magic handwaving and—boom—here's the result. So then all they want to know is who's side you're on—the prosecutor's or the defendant's."

This in no way implies that lawyers and police officers are lacking in intelligence—far from it. Rather, we are suggesting that because they do not have basic training in the scientific method and because they work in an environment in which taking sides (an adversarial approach) is an ingrained part of the culture, they tend to judge "truth" in terms other than the findings of careful scientific research.

FIGURE 3.12

Lineups: A Source of Error for Eyewitnesses?
Lineups that show a number of suspects at once result in a high level of false identifications by eyewitnesses (they often identify one of the persons shown as the criminal even though he or she is not really present). Research findings indicate that such errors can be greatly reduced by using procedures in which eyewitnesses look at one suspect at a time. Yet the criminal justice system has *not* adopted this simple change. Aspects of social cognition may help explain why this is so.

(continued)

BEYOND THE HEADLINES: AS SOCIAL PSYCHOLOGISTS SEE IT (CONTINUED)

Further, being unaware of the kind of cognitive pitfalls discussed in this chapter, they place great faith in our ability to do such things as (1) ignore information we have heard and processed if later instructed to do so; (2) refrain from letting the appearance, gender, race, or ethnic background of defendants influence our judgments about their guilt or innocence; and (3) prevent our feelings and moods from affecting our decisions. As we've already seen in this chapter, and as we'll note in Chapter 13 (in which we discuss the implications of social psychology for the legal system), the limits of our own cognitive system may make it all but impossible for us to accomplish these tasks.

Will this situation change in the future? Will the criminal justice system adopt procedures shown to be effective, by scientific research, in increasing eyewitness accuracy? Being subject to the optimistic bias, we are hopeful, and agree with Gary Wells, who states: "This may be my American optimism talking, but don't you think in the long run, the better idea will prevail?" We certainly hope so!

Social Cognition: A Word of Optimism

The negativity bias, the optimistic bias, the costs of thinking too much, counterfactual thinking, magical thinking, thought suppression—having discussed these sources of error in social thought, you may be ready to despair: can we ever get it right? The answer, we believe, is *absolutely.* No, we're not perfect information-processing machines. We have limited cognitive capacities and we can't increase these by buying pop-in memory chips. And yes, we are somewhat lazy: we generally do the least amount of cognitive work possible in any situation. Despite these limitations, though, we frequently do an impressive job in thinking about others. Despite being flooded by truly enormous amounts of social information, we manage to sort, store, remember, and use a large portion of this input in an intelligent and highly efficient manner. Our thinking is indeed subject to many potential sources of bias, and we do make errors. But by and large, we do a very good job of processing social information and making sense out of the social worlds in which we live. So, while we can imagine being even better at these tasks than we actually are, there's no reason to be discouraged. On the contrary, we can take pride in the fact that we accomplish so much with the limited tools at our disposal.

KEY POINTS

- We often engage in *magical thinking*—thinking based on assumptions that don't hold up to rational scrutiny. For instance, we may believe that if two objects are in contact, properties can pass from one to the other.
- Individuals often engage in *thought suppression,* trying to prevent themselves from thinking about certain topics (e.g., delicious desserts, alcohol, cigarettes).
- These efforts are often successful, but sometimes they result in a rebound effect, in which such thoughts actually increase in frequency. Persons high in reactance are more likely than those low in reactance to experience such effects.
- The criminal justice system has failed to adopt simple changes in procedure that could reduce false identifications by eyewitnesses. This reluctance can be explained, in part, by aspects of social cognition.
- Although social cognition is subject to many sources of error, we generally do an excellent job of understanding the social world.

Affect and Cognition: How Feelings Shape Thought and Thought Shapes Feelings

In our earlier discussion of the optimistic bias, we used the phrase "seeing the world through rose-colored glasses" to reflect our tendency to expect positive outcomes in many situations. But there's another way in which these words apply to social cognition: they also illustrate the effects that being in a good mood has on our thoughts and perceptions (see Figure 3.13). Think of a time in your own life when you were in a very good mood; didn't the world seem to be a happier place? And didn't you see everything and everyone with whom you came into contact more favorably than you would when in a less pleasant mood? Experiences such as this illustrate the fact that there is often a complex interplay between *affect*—our current moods—and *cognition*—the ways in which we process, store, remember, and use social information (Forgas, 1995a; Isen & Baron, 1991). We say *interplay* because research on this topic indicates that, in fact, the relationship is very much a two-way street: our feelings and moods strongly influence several aspects of cognition, and cognition, in turn, exerts strong effects on our feelings and moods (e.g., McDonald & Hirt, 1997; Seta, Hayes, & Seta, 1994). What are these effects like? Let's see what research findings tell us.

The Influence of Affect on Cognition

We have already mentioned the impact of moods on our perceptions of the world around us. Such effects apply to people as well as objects. Imagine, for instance, that you have just received some very good news—you did much better on an important exam than you expected. As a result, you are feeling great. Now, you run into one of your friends and she introduces you to someone you don't know. You chat with this person for a while and then leave for another class. Will your first impression of the stranger be influenced by the fact that you are feeling so good? The findings of many different studies suggest strongly that it will (Bower, 1991; Mayer & Hanson, 1995; Clore, Schwarz, & Conway, 1993). In other words, our current moods can strongly affect our reactions to new stimuli we encounter for the first time, whether these are people, foods, or even geographic locations we've never visited before, causing us to perceive them more favorably than would otherwise be the case.

FIGURE 3.13

Impact of Affect on Cognition: When We Are in a Good Mood, the World Is a Happier Place. When we are in a good mood, we tend to perceive everything and everyone around us more favorably. Experiences such as these illustrate the important effects of affect on cognition.

Such effects have important practical implications. For instance, consider their impact on job interviews—a context in which interviewers meet many people for the first time. A growing body of evidence indicates that even experienced interviewers can't avoid being influenced by their current moods: they assign higher ratings to the persons they interview when they are in a good mood than to those they interview when they are in a bad mood (e.g., Baron, 1993a; Robbins & DeNisi, 1994).

Another way in which affect influences cognition involves its impact on memory. Here, two different, but related, kinds of effects seem to occur. One is known as **mood-dependent memory.** This refers to the fact that what we remember while in a given mood may be determined, in part, by what we learned when previously in that mood. For instance, if you stored some information into long-term memory when in a good mood, you are more likely to remember this information when in a similar mood. A second kind of effect is known as **mood congruence effects.** This refers to the fact that we are more likely to store or remember positive information when in a positive mood and negative information when in a negative mood; in other words, we notice or remember information that is congruent with our current moods (Blaney, 1986). A simple way to think about the difference between mood-dependent memory and mood congruence effects is this: In mood-dependent memory, the nature of the information doesn't matter—only your mood at the time you learned it and your mood when you try to recall it are relevant. In mood congruence effects, in contrast, the affective nature of the information—whether it is positive or negative—is crucial. When we are in a positive mood, we tend to remember positive information, and when in a negative mood, we tend to remember negative information (see Figure 3.14).

mood-dependent memory: The fact that what we remember while in a given mood may be determined, in part, by what we learned when previously in that mood.

mood congruence effects: Our tendency to store or remember positive information when in a positive mood and negative information when in a negative mood.

Research confirms the existence of mood-dependent memory (Eich, 1995) and also suggests that such effects may be quite important. For instance, mood-dependent memory helps explain why depressed persons have difficulty in remembering times when they felt better (Schachter & Kihlstrom, 1989): being in a very negative mood

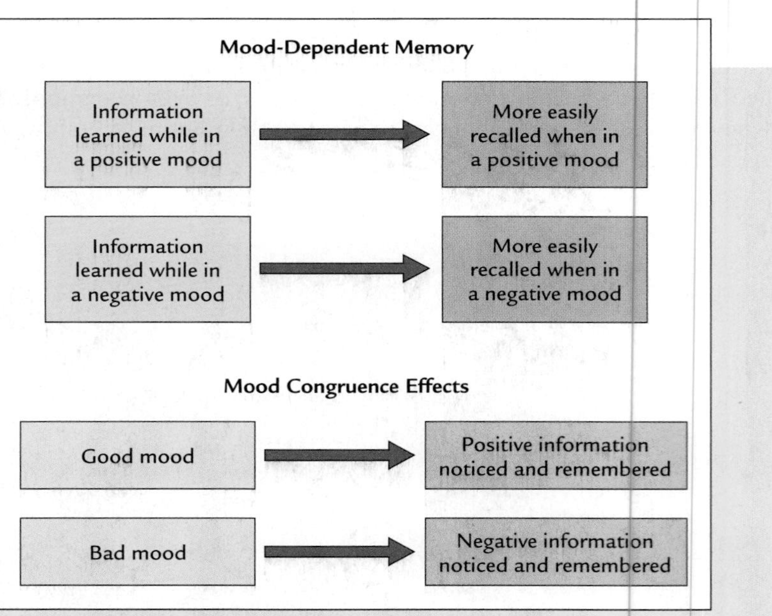

FIGURE 3.14

The Effects of Mood on Memory.

Our moods influence what we remember through two mechanisms: *mood-dependent memory,* which refers to the fact that what we remember while in a given mood is determined, in part, by what we learned when previously in that mood; and *mood congruence effects,* which refer to the fact that we are more likely to store or remember positive information consistent with our current mood.

now, they tend to remember information they entered into memory when in the same mood—and this information relates to feeling depressed. This is important because being able to remember what it felt like to *not* be depressed can play an important part in successful treatment of this problem. (We'll discuss other aspects of personal health in Chapter 13.)

Our current moods also influence another important component of cognition—creativity. The results of several studies suggest that being in a happy mood can increase creativity—perhaps because being in a happy mood activates a wider range of ideas and associations than being in a negative mood, and creativity consists, in part, of combining such associations into new patterns (e.g., Estrada, Isen, & Young, 1995).

Finally, findings indicate that information that evokes affective reactions may be processed differently than other kinds of information, and that, as a result, this information may be almost impossible to ignore or disregard (e.g., Edwards, Heindel, & Louis-Dreyfus, 1996; Wegner & Gold, 1995). Clear evidence pointing to such conclusions has been reported by Edwards and Bryan (1997).

These researchers reasoned that emotional information may be a potent source of **mental contamination**—a process in which our judgments, emotions, or behaviors are influenced by mental processing that is unconscious and uncontrollable (Wilson & Brekke, 1994). Specifically, Edwards and Bryan suggested that information that evokes emotional reactions may be especially likely to produce such effects because individuals often have little control over emotional reactions, and because such reactions are diffuse in nature and foster integrative rather than analytic processing. The result: Once we are exposed to emotion-generating information, we can't ignore it, no matter how hard we try.

To test this reasoning, these researchers conducted an experiment in which participants played the role of jurors. They read a transcript of a murder trial that contained information about the defendant's previous criminal record. In one experimental condition, this information was presented in an emotion-generating manner (it described a vicious attack the man had made on a woman); in another condition, it was presented in a more neutral manner (the transcript simply mentioned that the man was accused of a prior assault). For half the participants, the transcript indicated that this information about the defendant was admissible and should be considered; for the other half, the transcript described the information as inadmissible, and "jurors" were told to ignore it in reaching their verdict.

After reading the transcript, participants were asked to rate the guilt of the defendant and to recommend a sentence for him. Edwards and Bryan (1997) predicted that because of the factors described above, individuals would *not* be able to ignore the emotion-generating information. In fact, when told to do so, they might find themselves thinking about it more often than when *not* told to do this—the kind of *rebound* effect we described in connection with our discussion of thought suppression. Thus, they would view the defendant as more guilty and recommend a harsher sentence for him under these conditions (when exposed to emotion-generating information and told to ignore it). Results confirmed these predictions. These findings have important implications for the legal system, where jurors are often told to ignore emotion-provoking information. The results obtained by Edwards and Bryan (1997) and other researchers suggest that this may be an impossible task. We'll return to this and related topics in Chapter 13.

Research on the influence of affect on cognition has continued in social psychology for many years, and has become increasingly sophisticated. To see how our understanding of this topic has advanced, please see the **Social Psychology: Thirty Years of Progress** section on page 106.

mental contamination: A process in which our judgments, emotions, or behaviors are influenced by mental processing that is unconscious and uncontrollable.

SOCIAL PSYCHOLOGY: THIRTY YEARS OF PROGRESS

THE EFFECTS OF BEING IN A GOOD MOOD ON SOCIAL BEHAVIOR AND SOCIAL COGNITION: FROM "THE WARM GLOW OF SUCCESS" TO THE EFFECTS OF MOOD ON HEURISTIC THINKING

When research on the effects of our current moods began, the "cognitive revolution" had not yet occurred in social psychology. Social psychologists were certainly interested in social cognition, but they did not yet view it as central to all the topics they studied. For this reason, the earliest studies on the effects of affective states focused on their impact on social behavior rather than social thought. Among this work, the most influential was that conducted by Alice Isen. She was interested in a question that has intrigued social psychologists ever since: Does being in a good mood increase our willingness to help others? Isen reasoned that this would be the case because helping others is a positive behavior that "fits" with being in a good mood. Also, when we are in a good mood, we want to maintain it, and one way of doing that is by helping others: this boosts our self-image and makes us feel good about ourselves.

To see if being in a good mood actually did increase helping, Isen conducted several studies in which she used ingenious techniques to put people into a good mood. In the first (Isen, 1970), she told participants (school teachers) that they had done very well or very poorly on a series of tasks. Those told they had done very well would, she reasoned, experience "the warm glow of success," and would be in a better mood. The measure of helping was the amount of money participants donated to a fund to purchase air conditioning for a local school. Results indicated that those in a good mood did in fact donate more—an average of forty-six cents versus an average of only seven cents for those told they had done poorly on the tasks and who, presumably, were in a less happy mood.

In follow-up studies, Isen varied the participants' moods by such techniques as giving them cookies (Isen & Levin, 1972) and even placing a coin in a phone booth, so that people who entered found it there (Isen & Levin, 1972). No matter how she varied mood, Isen found the same result: Persons in a good mood were more helpful to others than were those not in a good mood. Subsequent research has verified this finding; for instance, even pleasant odors in a shopping mall increase the willingness of passersby to help a stranger (Baron, 1997a). However, additional research indicates that being in a good mood does not always increase helpfulness. If, for example, the costs of helping are high, or if helping might tend to spoil a person's good mood, persons in a good mood are *not* always more helpful (e.g., Isen, 1984).

Although research on the effects of mood on social behavior has continued (we'll describe it in Chapter 10), many social psychologists have focused, instead, on the question we have been discussing in this chapter: How do affective states influence social cognition? And here, growing evidence suggests that one effect of being in a good mood is that we tend to shift our social thought toward the use of heuristics—mental shortcuts that reduce effort. A clear illustration of such effects is provided by research conducted by Park and Banaji (2000).

On the basis of previous studies, Park and Banaji predicted that being in a good mood would lead individuals to rely more heavily on stereotypes, because these mental frameworks do indeed reduce mental effort, and when people are in a good mood, they do not want to do anything to disrupt it. Because careful, systematic thinking is hard work, people in a good mood tend to avoid such effort. To test this idea, these researchers asked participants to indicate whether various names—some African American and some European American in nature—belonged to the category "criminal" or to the category "politician." Half of the participants were placed in a good mood by watching a funny segment of a TV show and half were placed in a more neutral mood by viewing scenes of mountains, rivers, and so on. Park and Banaji (2000) predicted that being in a good mood would increase the use of stereotypes. Thus, participants in a good mood would show an enhanced tendency to place African American names in the "criminal" category and an increased tendency to place European American names in the "politician" category. This is precisely what happened: Persons in a good mood were indeed more likely to show this pattern than were persons in a neutral mood.

In follow-up studies, Park and Banaji (2000) found that this increased reliance on stereotyping by persons in a good mood stems from two sources: reduced sensitivity to names (lowered ability to distinguish between them; see Figure 3.15) and a lowered decision criterion for assigning names to a specific category (i.e., criminal or politician). Interestingly, being in a negative mood (as a result of watching a sad movie) did *not* produce such effects; if anything, it seemed to reduce reliance on stereotypes by raising the decision criterion

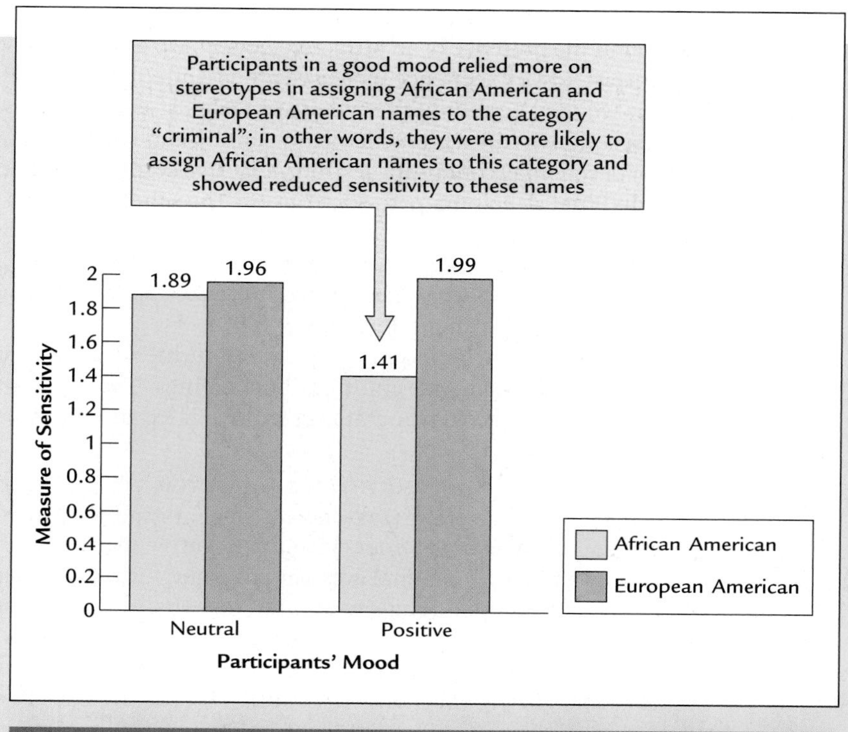

FIGURE 3.15

Effects of Being in a Good Mood on Heuristic Thinking. Participants in a good mood showed stronger tendencies to rely on stereotypes—one form of mental shortcut in social thought. Thus, they were more likely to classify African American names as belonging to the category "criminal" and more likely to classify European American names as belonging to the category "politician." These effects stemmed from the fact that persons in a good mood showed reduced sensitivity to stimuli—reduced ability to distinguish between the two groups of names.

[SOURCE: BASED ON DATA FROM PARK AND BANAJI, 2000.]

for assigning names to specific categories. This has been a general finding of research on the effects of mood on cognition: Positive moods increase our tendency to use mental shortcuts such as stereotypes or heuristics, while negative moods do not generate such effects.

As you can see, research on the effects of positive affect has made impressive progress. We now know not only that positive moods influence overt forms of social behavior such as helping (Isen, 1984; Baron, 1997a), but also when and how such moods (and affective states generally) influence social thought. Further, we have gained a great deal of insight into the mechanisms through which such effects occur. We don't believe we are thinking heuristically (!) when we state that, in our opinion, this is indeed major progress.

The Influence of Cognition on Affect

Most research on the relationship between affect and cognition has focused on how feelings influence thought. However, there is also strong evidence for the reverse—the impact of cognition on affect. One aspect of this relationship is described in what is known as the *two-factor theory* of emotion (Schachter, 1964). This theory suggests that, often, we don't know our own feelings or attitudes directly. Rather, because these internal reactions are often somewhat ambiguous, we infer their nature from the external world—from the kinds of situations in which we experience these reactions. For example, if we experience increased arousal in the presence of an attractive person, we may conclude that we are in love. In contrast, if we experience increased arousal after being cut off in traffic by another driver, we may conclude that what we feel is anger.

A second way in which cognition can influence emotions is through the activation of schemas containing a strong affective component. For example, if we label an individual as belonging to some group, the schema for this social category may suggest what traits he or she probably possesses. In addition, it may tell us how we *feel* about such persons. Thus, activation of a strong racial, ethnic, or religious schema or stereotype may exert powerful effects upon our current feelings or mood. (We'll return to this topic in Chapter 6.)

A third way in which our thoughts can influence our affective states involves our efforts to regulate our emotions and feelings. This topic is so important and is receiving so much attention at present, we'll examine it more closely.

■ COGNITION AND THE REGULATION OF AFFECTIVE STATES. Learning to regulate our emotions is an important task; negative events and outcomes are an unavoidable part of life, so learning to cope with the negative feelings these events generate is crucial for effective personal adjustment—and for good social relations with others. For example, individuals who often lose their tempers usually find it difficult to get along with others and may, in fact, be avoided by others. Among the most important techniques we use for regulating our moods and emotions are ones involving cognitive mechanisms. In other words, we use our thoughts to regulate our feelings. Many techniques for accomplishing this goal exist, but here, we'll consider two that are especially interesting: a tactic that could be termed the "I never had a chance effect," and another involving yielding to temptation.

Do you remember our discussion of how people often attempt to soften the blow of negative or tragic events by assuming that these events were inevitable? In other words, they use counterfactual thinking—adjusting their thoughts about the probability of negative events—to make these seem unavoidable and therefore less distressing. Direct evidence for such effects has been reported by Tykocinski (2001). He asked participants in the study to read a scenario in which they rushed to a store in order to obtain an item on sale. Participants in one condition learned that they had succeeded—they reached the store on time; others read that they failed—the store was closed when they arrived. Still others read a scenario indicating that they were still on the way to the store and did not know whether it would be open when they arrived. The price reduction on the item they wanted to buy (a Swatch wristwatch) was either very large or small, so that participants' motivation for reaching the store on time was also varied. After reading about one of these possible situations, participants in the success (arrived-on-time) and failure (arrived-too-late) conditions rated the likelihood, in retrospect, that they would have reached the store on time; those in the prior-to-outcomes condition rated the future chances that they would reach the store on time. Tykocinski (2001) predicted that those who had failed to reach the store on time would adjust the probability of getting there on time downward, especially in the large price reduction condition; they would do this to soften the blow of their disappointment. In contrast, those in the success and prior-to-outcomes conditions would not show this pattern. That is just what the results showed. These findings indicate that we do indeed sometimes use counterfactual thinking to reduce the bitterness of disappointments: by mentally reducing the odds of success—that is, by convincing ourselves that "we never had a chance"—we reduce our disappointment, and so regulate our affective states.

Another cognitive mechanism we use to regulate our affective states—and especially to reduce or eliminate negative feelings—involves giving in to temptation. When they are feeling "down" or distressed, many persons engage in activities that they know are bad for them but which make them feel better, at least temporarily (e.g., eating fattening snacks, wasting time by watching television). These actions make them feel better, but only temporarily. Why do people do this? In the past, it was assumed that they did so because emotional distress reduces either our capacity or our motivation to control our impulses to do things that are enjoyable but potentially bad for us. However, Tice, Bratslavky, and Baumeister (2000) argue that, in fact, cognitive factors play a role in such behavior. They argue that people consciously choose to yield to temptations at times when they experience strong negative affect. In other words, this is not an automatic behavior or a sign of weakness; rather, it is a strategic choice. People yield to temptation because, in the face of intense negative affect, they shift their priorities. Reducing their negative affect becomes their primary goal, so they do whatever it takes to achieve this objective.

To test this prediction, Tice, Bratslavsky, and Baumeister (2000) conducted a study in which participants were first put into a good or bad mood (by reading stories in which they either saved a child's life or ran a red light and so caused the death of a child). Then, they were either told that their moods could change over time or that, because of an aromatherapy candle the experimenter lit, their moods were "frozen" and could not change much. Participants were then told that they would work on an intelligence test and would receive feedback on their performance. Before doing the test, though, they would have a fifteen-minute practice session to prepare for it. The experimenter then left them in a room containing materials for practicing the test *and* distractors—other tasks on which they could work. For half the participants, these tasks were attractive and tempting (e.g., a challenging puzzle, a video game, popular magazines). For the others, the tasks were less attractive (a preschool-level plastic puzzle, out-of-date technical journals). The main question was this: Would persons in a bad mood spend more of the practice time playing with the distractors (procrastinating) than would persons in a good mood? More importantly, would this occur only in the condition in which participants believed they could change their own moods? After all, there would be no use in playing with the distractors if participants believed that their moods were frozen and could not be altered. The researchers predicted that this would be the case: Persons in a bad mood would procrastinate more, but only when they believed doing so would enhance their moods.

As you can see from Figure 3.16 on page 110, results offered clear support for the prediction. These findings indicate that the tendency to yield to temptation and engage in forbidden pleasures is one technique we use to reduce negative feelings of distress. Further, it appears that such actions may represent a strategic and conscious choice, not a simple lapse in motivation or ability to restrain our own impulses. It is important to note, however, that while this technique may succeed, it may involve high costs—the actions we take to counter our negative feelings may be damaging to our health or well-being. Clearly, then, this is one tactic we should use with care!

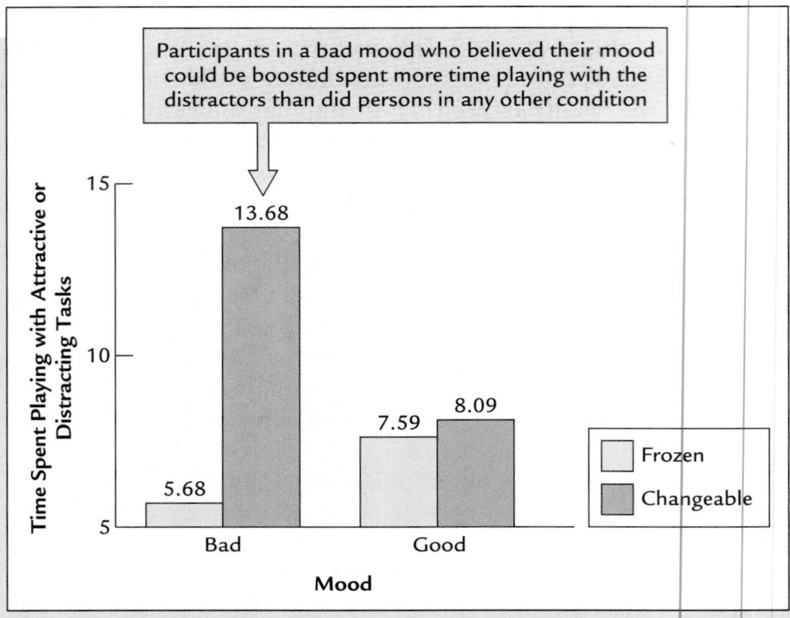

FIGURE 3.16

Yielding to Temptation as a Cognitive Strategy for Reducing Emotional Distress. Individuals experiencing strong negative affect spent more time playing with attractive distracting tasks (procrastinating) than did individuals in a good mood or individuals who had only unattractive distracting tasks available to them. These findings provide evidence that yielding to temptation may sometimes be a conscious cognitive strategy for reducing emotional distress. (Note: Only data for attractive distracting tasks are presented here.) [SOURCE: BASED ON DATA FROM TICE, BRATSLAVSKY, & BAUMEISTER, 2000].

KEY POINTS

- Affect influences cognition in several ways. Our current moods can cause us to react positively or negatively to new stimuli, including other persons, the extent to which we think systematically or heuristically, and can influence memory through *mood-dependent memory* and *mood congruence effects*.
- Affect can also influence creativity. Findings indicate that emotion-provoking information can strongly influence judgments and decisions even if we try to ignore it.
- When we are in a positive mood, we tend to think heuristically to a greater extent than when we are a negative mood. Specifically, we show increased reliance on stereotypes and other mental shortcuts.
- Cognition influences affect through our interpretation of emotion-provoking events and through the activation of schemas containing a strong affective component.
- We employ several cognitive techniques to regulate our emotions or feelings; through counterfactual thinking, we can make negative outcomes seem inevitable and so less distressing; when distressed, we can consciously choose to engage in activities that, while damaging in the long run, make us feel better in the short run.

CONNECTIONS: INTEGRATING SOCIAL PSYCHOLOGY

IN THIS CHAPTER YOU READ ABOUT . . .	IN OTHER CHAPTERS, YOU WILL FIND RELATED DISCUSSIONS OF . . .
schemas	the effects of schemas on other aspects of social behavior, such as attitudes (Chapter 4) and prejudice (Chapter 6)
potential sources of error in social cognition	the role of these errors in first impressions (Chapter 2), persuasion (Chapter 4), and the legal system (Chapter 13)
the interplay between affect and cognition	the roles of these links in many forms of social behavior, including prejudice (Chapter 6), attraction (Chapter 7), helping (Chapter 10), aggression (Chapter 11), and behavior in work settings (Chapter 13)

THINKING ABOUT CONNECTIONS

1. Schemas help us understand and interpret many social situations. Do you think they play a role in long-term relationships (see Chapter 8)? For instance, do you think we possess relatively clear schemas suggesting, for instance, that relationships should develop in various ways over time, and even *when* such changes should occur?

2. Have you ever tried to suppress certain thoughts in order to make a beneficial change in your own behavior—for instance, lose weight or change a bad habit? If so, were you successful? Do you think that after reading the information in this chapter, you might be able to do a better job in this respect? Could you, for instance, do a better job of keeping your temper in check (see Chapter 11) or avoiding negative feelings toward members of various minority groups (Chapter 6)?

3. Have you ever tried to reduce feelings of distress by concluding that the negative events that caused this distress were unavoidable? If so, did this strategy work—did you feel better after reaching the conclusion that the disappointment or negative outcome you experienced was inevitable?

IDEAS TO TAKE WITH YOU—AND USE!

COMBATING ERRORS IN SOCIAL COGNITION

Social cognition—our efforts to interpret, analyze, remember, and use information about the social world—is subject to many sources of error. Here are some of the most important ones—errors of which you should be aware and try to guard against in the future.

The Self-Confirming Effects of Schemas

Once they are formed, schemas—mental frameworks for organizing and interpreting social information—tend to become self-confirming: they lead us to notice only information that is consistent with them, and they cause us to act in ways that confirm their validity.

(continued)

IDEAS TO TAKE WITH YOU—AND USE! *(CONTINUED)*

The Negativity Bias

We tend to be highly sensitive to negative information, devoting more attention to it and assigning it more importance than we do for positive information.

The Optimistic Bias

We generally expect things to turn out well, even when such expectations are somewhat unrealistic. However, if we anticipate feedback that may be negative and have important consequences for us, we may brace for the worst and show a reversal of our usual optimism.

Counterfactual Thinking: Imagining What Might Have Been

When we imagine outcomes different from those that actually occurred, we are engaging in counterfactual thinking. Such thought can increase our satisfaction if we imagine worse outcomes than actually occurred; but it can lead to strong feelings of regret and envy if we imagine better outcomes than actually occurred.

Thought Suppression: Trying To Keep Certain Thoughts Out of Consciousness

In many situations, we try to suppress thoughts that we believe will get us into trouble. For example, dieters try to suppress thoughts of delicious foods, and people trying to quit smoking try to avoid thinking about the pleasure of lighting up. Unfortunately, trying to suppress such thoughts often leads us to have them *more* often than would otherwise be the case.

The Role of Affective States

When we are in a good mood, we evaluate almost everything more positively than would otherwise be the case. The opposite is true when we are in a bad mood. Unfortunately, such effects can lead to serious errors in our efforts to make judgments about other persons.

SUMMARY AND REVIEW OF KEY POINTS

Schemas: Mental Frameworks for Organizing—and Using—Social Information

- Because we have limited cognitive capacity, we often attempt to reduce the effort we expend on *social cognition*—how we think about other persons. This can increase efficiency but reduce our accuracy with respect to this important task.
- One basic component of social cognition is *schemas*—mental frameworks centering around a specific theme that help us to organize social information.

- Once formed, schemas exert powerful effects on what we notice (attention), enter into memory (encoding), and later remember (retrieval). Individuals report remembering more information consistent with their schemas than information inconsistent with them, but, in fact, inconsistent information, too, is strongly represented in memory.

- Schemas help us to process information, but they often persist in the face of disconfirming information, thus distorting our understanding of the social world.

- Schemas can also exert self-confirming effects, causing us to behave in ways that confirm them.

Heuristics and Automatic Processing: How We Reduce Our Effort in Social Cognition

- Because our capacity to process information is limited, we often experience *information overload.* To avoid this, we make use of *heuristics*—rules for making decisions in a quick and relatively effortless manner.

- One such heuristic is *representativeness,* which suggests that the more similar an individual is to typical members of a given group, the more likely she or he is to belong to that group.

- Another heuristic is *availability,* which suggests that the easier it is to bring information to mind, the greater its impact on subsequent decisions or judgments. In some cases, availability may also involve the amount of information we bring to mind.

- *Priming* refers to increased availability of information resulting from exposure to specific stimuli or events.

- Another means of reducing mental effort involves *automatic processing* of social information—processing that occurs in a seemingly automatic, effortless, and nonconscious manner. Research findings indicate that once activated, schemas and other mental frameworks may influence not only social thought, but social behavior as well.

Potential Sources of Error in Social Cognition: Why Total Rationality Is Rarer Than You Think

- We show a strong *negativity* bias—a tendency to be highly sensitive to negative stimuli or information. This tendency appears to be very basic and may be built into the functioning of our brains. Thus, it may be the result of evolutionary factors.

- We also show a strong *optimistic bias,* expecting positive events and outcomes in many contexts. In addition, we tend to make overly optimistic predictions about how long it will take us to complete a given task, an effect known as the *planning fallacy.*

- The optimistic bias also shows up in our tendency to assume that we are more likely than other persons to experience positive outcomes, but less likely than others to experience negative ones.

- The optimistic bias may be reversed and turn into pessimism, however, when we anticipate receiving bad news with important consequences for us; in such cases, we brace for the worst and show an enhanced tendency to predict negative outcomes.

- When individuals think too deeply about some topic, they may become confused about the factors that actually play a role their behavior, with the result that they make less accurate judgments or decisions.

- In many situations, individuals imagine "what might have been"—they engage in *counterfactual thinking.* Such thoughts can affect our sympathy for persons who have experienced negative outcomes, and can cause us to experience strong regret over missed opportunities.

- By assuming that disappointing or tragic events are unavoidable, individuals can make them more bearable; this is a very adaptive function of counterfactual thought.

- Counterfactual thinking can also strongly influence our affective states and can lead to inaction inertia, which occurs when individuals fail to perform an action that would yield positive outcomes and then become reluctant to take it in the future to avoid thinking about the initial missed opportunity.

- We often engage in *magical thinking*—thinking based on assumptions that don't hold up to rational scrutiny. For instance, we may believe that if two objects are in contact, properties can pass from one to the other.

- Individuals often engage in *thought suppression,* trying to prevent themselves from thinking about certain topics (e.g., delicious desserts, alcohol, cigarettes).

- These efforts are often successful, but sometimes they result in a rebound effect, in which such thoughts actually increase in frequency. Persons high in reactance are more likely than those low in reactance to experience such effects.

- The criminal justice system has failed to adopt simple changes in procedure that could reduce false identifications by eyewitnesses. This reluctance can be explained, in part, by aspects of social cognition.

- Although social cognition is subject to many sources of error, we generally do an excellent job of understanding the social world.

Affect and Cognition: How Feelings Shape Thought and Thought Shapes Feelings

- Affect influences cognition in several ways. Our current moods can cause us to react positively or negatively to new stimuli, including other persons, the extent to which we think systematically or heuristically, and can influence memory through *mood-dependent memory* and *mood congruence effects.*

- Affect can also influence creativity. Findings indicate that emotion-provoking information can strongly influence judgments and decisions even if we try to ignore it.

- When we are in a positive mood, we tend to think heuristically to a greater extent than when we are a negative mood. Specifically, we show increased reliance on stereotypes and other mental shortcuts.

- Cognition influences affect through our interpretation of emotion-provoking events and through the activation of schemas containing a strong affective component.

- We employ several cognitive techniques to regulate our emotions or feelings; through *counterfactual thinking,* we can make negative outcomes seem inevitable and so less distressing; when distressed, we can consciously choose to engage in activities that, while damaging in the long run, make us feel better in the short run.

KEY TERMS

affect (p. 79)

automatic processing (p. 87)

availability heuristic (p. 85)

counterfactual thinking (p. 95)

heuristics (p. 84)

information overload (p. 84)

magical thinking (p. 97)

mental contamination (p. 105)

mood congruence effects (p. 104)

mood-dependent memory (p. 104)

negativity bias (p. 90)

optimistic bias (p. 92)

perseverance effect (p. 82)

planning fallacy (p. 92)

priming (p. 86)

representativeness heuristic (p. 85)

schemas (p. 80)

self-fulfilling prophecies (p. 82)

social cognition (p. 78)

thought suppression (p. 98)

FOR MORE INFORMATION

Kunda, Z. (1999). *Social cognition: Making sense of people.* Cambridge, MA: MIT Press.

- This text describes our current knowledge about many aspects of social cognition. It is well written and discusses many of the topics covered in this chapter (e.g., schemas, errors in social cognition) in detail. This is an excellent book to read if you want to know more about social thought and how we try to understand other people.

Roese, N. J., & Olson, J. M. (Eds.). (1997). *What might have been: The social psychology of counterfactual thinking.* Mahwah, NJ: Erlbaum.

- This book focuses on counterfactual thinking—imagining "what might have been" in a specific situation. The nature of such thought and its effects are examined from many different perspectives by social psychologists who have studied this fascinating topic. If you want to know more about counterfactual thinking, this is an excellent source.

Wyer, R. S., Jr., & Bargh, J. A. (Eds.). (1997). *The automaticity of everyday life. Advances in Social Cognition, 10.*

- To what extent is our social thought and social behavior "automatic"—occurring without conscious thought? The papers in this excellent volume present data suggesting that, in fact, our thoughts and behaviors are often triggered in an automatic manner by external conditions.

Massimo Campigli, *Women by the Sea* © Copyright Alinari/Art Resource, NY. © 2002 Artists Rights Society (ARS), New York/SIAE, Rome.

ATTITUDES: EVALUATING THE SOCIAL WORLD

CHAPTER OUTLINE

A few months ago, while at a convention in San Diego, I (RAB) witnessed the following scene. I was at dinner with several other professors, and after we had eaten, the waiter brought the dessert tray to our table. One of the women present literally turned glassy-eyed as she gazed at one item on the tray—a rich blend of several kinds of chocolate. But she declined to order it when the waiter asked if he should bring it to her. Several of the other people urged her to indulge: "Oh, go ahead," one said, "live a little." "Right," added another, "enjoy yourself! Life is too short to skip dessert!" But although she looked wistfully at the dessert, she stuck to her guns and refused to order it, explaining: "I'd love to, but if I do, I'll only hate myself in the morning!" Everyone laughed, and the conversation soon turned to other topics.

Why do I begin with this incident? Because it illustrates several important points about the nature of **attitudes,** a central topic in social psychology and the focus of this chapter. Social psychologists generally use the term *attitudes* to refer to our evaluations of virtually any aspect of the social world (e.g., Fazio & Roskos-Ewoldson, 1994; Tesser & Martin, 1996)—the extent to which we have favorable or unfavorable reactions to issues, ideas, persons, social groups, objects—including desserts. In the incident above, it was clear that the woman liked the chocolate dessert very much. The fact that she didn't order it, though, illustrates another important aspect of attitudes: Often, they are reflected in our behavior, but sometimes, this is not the case. Although the woman in question had a very positive attitude toward the dessert, this wasn't reflected in her actions: she didn't order it. Why not? Perhaps because of a third important aspect of attitudes—the fact that they are often *ambivalent.* **Attitude ambivalence** refers to the fact that our evaluations of objects, issues, people, or events are not always uniformly positive or negative; on the contrary, these evaluations are often mixed, consisting of both positive and negative reactions (e.g., Priester & Petty, 2001; Thompson, Zanna, & Griffin, 1995). My friend certainly liked the chocolate dessert (a positive evaluation), but she also viewed it as too rich and too fattening (negative evaluations). In this case, the negative evaluations won out and she decided not to order the dessert. So, in a sense, her attitudes *were* reflected in her behavior; it's just that these reactions were ambivalent in nature, and the negative component was dominant (see Figure 4.1).

Finally, this incident illustrates the fact that once attitudes are formed, they are often difficult to change. Several members of our group urged my friend to forget about the calories and have the dessert, yet she resisted all of these suggestions. Of course, because her attitude toward the dessert was ambivalent (she liked it *and* objected to the number of calories it contained), it is possible that, on other occasions, she might yield to persuasion (and temptation) and order the dessert. When attitudes are uniformly positive or negative, however, they are even more

attitudes: Evaluations of various aspects of the social world.

attitude ambivalence: Refers to the fact that we often have positive and negative evaluations of the same attitude object; thus, our attitude toward it is ambivalent.

FIGURE 4.1
Attitudes: Often, They Are Ambivalent. Our attitudes are often ambivalent: we evaluate various issues, people, groups, or objects both positively *and* negatively. As shown here, this is often true with respect to rich desserts. Many people love them, but also react negatively to the number of calories they contain.

difficult to change; indeed, they often remain unchanged for long periods of time. If you have ever seen a political debate between people holding opposing views, you already know that this is true: neither person usually manages to budge the other at all, because strong attitudes that are not ambivalent are indeed difficult to change.

Social psychologists don't view attitudes as important only because they are hard to change, however. On the contrary, they have made the study of attitudes central to their field for the following reasons. First, attitudes strongly influence our social thought, even if they are not always reflected in our overt behavior. In fact, growing evidence suggests that attitudes, as evaluations of the world around us, represent a very basic aspect of social cognition. As we saw in Chapter 3, the tendency to evaluate stimuli as positive or negative—something we like or dislike—appears to be an initial step in our efforts to make sense out of the social world. In fact, it occurs almost immediately, and certainly before we attempt to understand the meaning of stimuli or integrate them with our previous experience (Ito et al., 1998). So, in a sense, attitudes truly reflect an essential, and early, building block of social thought (e.g., Eagly & Chaiken, 1998).

Second, social psychologists view attitudes as important because, as noted earlier, they often *do* affect our behavior. As you might guess, this is especially likely to be true when attitudes are strong and well established (e.g., Petty & Krosnick, 1995). Do you hold a negative attitude toward the current president? If so, you are unlikely to vote for him if he runs for reelection. Do you like pizza? If so, you will probably choose to eat it on many occasions. If attitudes influence behavior, then knowing something about them can help us to predict people's behavior in a wide range of contexts. As we'll see in Chapter 7, we also hold attitudes toward specific persons—for example, we like them or dislike them. Clearly, such attitudes can play a crucial role in our relations with these persons.

For these and related reasons, attitudes have been a central concept in social psychology since its earliest days (e.g., Allport, 1924). In this chapter, we'll provide you with an overview of what social psychologists have discovered about these evaluations of the social world. First, we'll consider the ways in which attitudes are *formed,* and why we construct them in the first place—in other words, what functions do they serve? Next, we'll consider a question we have already mentioned several times: When do attitudes influence behavior? Clearly, attitudes sometimes exert such effects, but just as clearly, this is not always so. Why? The findings of recent research shed important light on this complex puzzle. Third, we'll turn to the related question of how, sometimes, attitudes are changed—the process of *persuasion.* We emphasize the word *sometimes* because, as noted above, changing attitudes is a difficult business—far more difficult than advertisers, politicians, salespersons, and many other would-be persuaders seem to assume. Still, as suggested by Figure 4.2, such persons have many tricks up their sleeve, and use all of them in their efforts to change our views! Fourth, we'll examine some of the reasons *why* attitudes are often so difficult to change. Finally, we'll consider the intriguing fact that, on some occasions, our actions shape our attitudes rather than vice versa. The process that underlies such effects is known as *cognitive dissonance,* and it has fascinating implications, not just for attitude change, but for many aspects of social behavior as well.

FIGURE 4.2
Techniques for Changing Attitudes: The Range Is Immense.
As suggested by this cartoon, people wishing to change our attitudes have many techniques for attaining this goal.
[SOURCE: © 1997 JOHN MCPHERSON / DIST. BY UNIVERSAL PRESS SYNDICATE.]

Attitude Formation: How—and Why—Attitudes Develop

What are your views about President Bush? Using the drug *ecstasy*? The film *Harry Potter*? Talking on a cell phone while driving? Almost certainly, you have attitudes about all of these. But where, precisely, did these views come from? Were you born with them? Or did you acquire them as a result of various life experiences? And why did you form them in the first place—in other words, what functions do they serve? With respect to the first question, most people—and almost all social psychologists—believe that attitudes are *learned,* and most of our discussion of this issue will focus on the processes through which attitudes are acquired. But please take note: We would be remiss if we did not mention that a small but growing body of evidence suggests that attitudes may be influenced by genetic factors, too. We'll describe some of the evidence for this surprising idea below.

Turning to the first question—*why* do we form attitudes (i.e., what functions do they serve?)—we'll soon see that, in fact, attitudes serve several different functions and are useful to us in many different respects.

Social Learning: Acquiring Attitudes from Others

One important source of our attitudes is obvious: We acquire them from other persons through the process of **social learning.** In other words, many of our views are acquired in situations in which we interact with others or merely observe their behavior. Such learning occurs through several processes.

CLASSICAL CONDITIONING: LEARNING BASED ON ASSOCIATION.

It is a basic principle of psychology that when one stimulus regularly precedes another, the one that occurs first may soon become a signal for the one that occurs second. In other words, when the first stimulus occurs, individuals expect that the second will soon follow. As a result, they gradually acquire the same kind of reactions to the first stimulus as they show to the second stimulus, especially if the second is one that induces fairly strong and automatic reactions. For instance, my clock radio emits a loud "click" just before the alarm comes on. At first, I showed little or no reaction to the click. But now, because it has been paired many times with what follows (loud music), I usually wake up when I hear the click, even before the music starts.

What does this process—known as **classical conditioning**—have to do with attitude formation? Potentially, quite a lot. To see how this process might influence attitudes under real-life conditions, imagine the following scene. A young child sees her mother frown and show other signs of displeasure each time the mother encounters a member of a particular ethnic group. At first, the child is neutral toward members of this group and their visible characteristics (e.g., skin color, style of dress, accent). After these cues are paired with the mother's negative emotional reactions many times, however, classical conditioning occurs, and the child comes to react negatively to these stimuli—and to members of this ethnic group (see Figure 4.3 on page 122). The result: The child acquires a negative attitude toward such persons—an attitude that may form the core of a full-blown ethnic prejudice. (We'll examine prejudice in detail in Chapter 6.)

Interestingly, studies indicate that classical conditioning can occur below the level of conscious awareness—even when people are not aware of the stimuli that serve as the basis for this kind of conditioning. For instance, in one experiment on this topic (Krosnick et al., 1992), students saw photos of a stranger engaged in routine

social learning: The process through which we acquire new information, forms of behavior, or attitudes from other persons.

classical conditioning: A basic form of learning in which one stimulus, initially neutral, acquires the capacity to evoke reactions through repeated pairing with another stimulus. In a sense, one stimulus becomes a signal for the presentation or occurrence of the other.

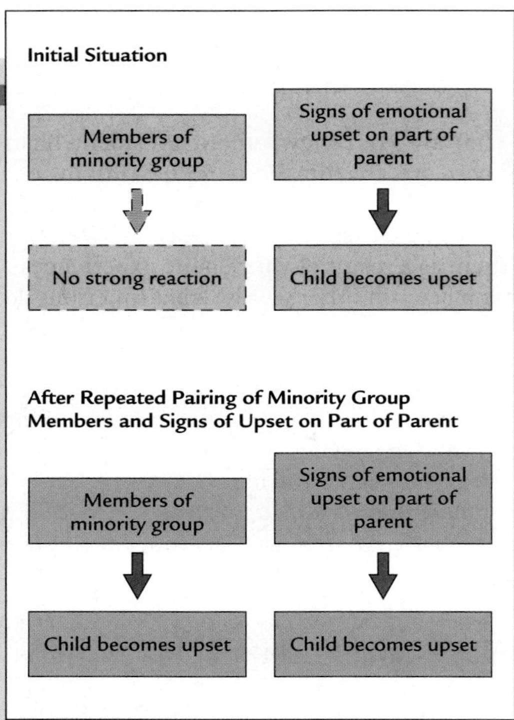

FIGURE 4.3
Classical Conditioning of Attitudes.
Initially, a young child has little or no emotional reaction to the visible characteristics of members of some minority group. If she sees her mother showing signs of negative reactions when in the presence of these persons, however, she too may gradually acquire negative reactions to them, through the process of *classical conditioning.*

daily activities such as shopping in a grocery store or walking into her apartment. While these photos were shown, other photos known to induce either positive or negative feelings were presented very briefly—so briefly that participants were not aware of their presence. One group of research participants was exposed to photos that induced positive feelings (e.g., a bridal couple, people playing cards and laughing), while another was exposed to photos that induced negative feelings (e.g., open-heart surgery, a werewolf). Later, both groups expressed their attitudes toward the stranger. Results indicated that even though participants were unaware of the second group of photos (the ones presented very briefly), these stimuli significantly influenced their attitudes toward the stranger. Those exposed to the positive photos reported more favorable attitudes toward this person than did those exposed to the negative photos. These findings suggest that attitudes can be influenced by **subliminal conditioning**—classical conditioning that occurs in the absence of conscious awareness of the stimuli involved.

subliminal conditioning (of attitudes): Classical conditioning that occurs through exposure to stimuli that are below individuals' thresholds of conscious awareness.

instrumental conditioning: A basic form of learning in which responses that lead to positive outcomes or that permit avoidance of negative outcomes are strengthened.

INSTRUMENTAL CONDITIONING: LEARNING TO HOLD THE "RIGHT" VIEWS. Have you ever heard a three-year-old state, with great conviction, that she is a Republican or a Democrat? Or that Fords (or Hondas) are better than Chevrolets (or Toyotas)? Children of this age have little understanding of what these statements mean. Yet they make them all the same. Why? The answer is obvious: They have been praised or rewarded in various ways by their parents for stating such views. As we're sure you know, behaviors that are followed by positive outcomes are strengthened and tend to be repeated. In contrast, behaviors that are followed by negative outcomes are weakened, or at least suppressed. Thus, another way in which attitudes are acquired from others is through the process of **instrumental conditioning.** By rewarding children with smiles, approval, or hugs for stating the "right" views—the ones parents themselves favor—parents (and other adults) play an active role in shaping youngsters' attitudes. It is for this reason that until children reach their teen years, most express political, religious, and social views highly similar to those of their families. Given the powerful effect of reinforcement on behavior, it would be surprising if they did not.

■ OBSERVATIONAL LEARNING: LEARNING BY EXAMPLE. A third process through which attitudes are formed can operate even when parents have no desire to transmit specific views to their children. This process is **observational learning,** and it occurs when individuals acquire new forms of behavior or thought simply by observing the actions of others (e.g., Bandura, 1997). Where attitude formation is concerned, observational learning appears to play an important role. In many cases, children hear their parents say things not intended for their ears, or observe their parents engaging in actions the parents tell them not to perform. For example, parents who smoke often warn their children against this habit, even as they light up (see Figure 4.4). What message do children acquire from such instances? The evidence is clear: They often learn to do as their parents *do,* not as they *say.*

In addition, of course, both children and adults often acquire attitudes from exposure to the mass media—television, magazines, films, and so on. For instance, the characters in most American films now make liberal use of four-letter words that, in the past, were considered unacceptable in most situations. The result: Persons under the age of thirty, who have grown up watching such films, don't find them as objectionable as older persons sometimes do.

observational learning: A basic form of learning in which individuals acquire new forms of behavior or thought through observing others.

social comparison: The process through which we compare ourselves to others in order to determine whether our view of social reality is or is not correct.

■ SOCIAL COMPARISON AND ATTITUDE FORMATION: ONE BASIS FOR OBSERVATIONAL LEARNING. Why, you may be wondering, do children—and even adults—adopt the attitudes that others express or the behaviors shown by these persons? One answer involves the mechanism of **social comparison**—our tendency to compare ourselves with others in order to determine whether our view of social reality is or is not correct (Festinger, 1954). To the extent that our views agree with those of others, we conclude that our ideas and attitudes are accurate; after all, if others hold the same

FIGURE 4.4
Observational Learning in Action.
Children learn many things, including attitudes their parents may not want the children to acquire, such as a positive view of smoking.

views, these views *must* be right. Because of this process, we often change our attitudes so as to hold views closer to those of others. And on some occasions, social comparison may contribute to the formation of new attitudes. For instance, imagine that you heard persons you like and respect expressing negative views toward a group with whom you've had no contact. Would this influence your attitudes? It's tempting to say, "Absolutely not!" However, research findings indicate that hearing others state negative views about this group might actually lead you to adopt similar attitudes—without ever meeting a member of the group in question (e.g., Maio, Esses, & Bell, 1994; Shaver, 1993). In such cases, attitudes are shaped by social information from others (what we see them saying or doing), coupled with our own desire to be similar to people we like or respect.

Genetic Factors: Some Surprising Findings

Can we inherit our attitudes, or at least a tendency to develop certain views about various topics or issues? Your first reply is likely to be "No!" While we readily accept the fact that genetic factors can influence our height, eye color, and other physical traits, the idea that they might also play a role in our thinking seems strange, to say the least. Yet if we remember that thought occurs within the brain and that brain structure, like every other part of our bodies, is affected by genetic factors, the idea of genetic influences on attitudes becomes, perhaps, a little easier to imagine. In fact, a small but growing body of evidence indicates that genetic factors may actually play some role, although a small one, in attitudes (e.g., Arvey et al., 1989; Keller et al., 1992).

Most of this evidence involves comparisons between identical (monozygotic) and nonidentical (dizygotic) twins. Because identical twins share the same genetic inheritance, while nonidentical twins do not, higher correlations between the attitudes of identical twins than between those of nonidentical twins would suggest that genetic factors play a role in shaping such attitudes. This is precisely what has been found: the attitudes of identical twins *do* correlate more highly than those of nonidentical twins (e.g., Waller et al., 1990). Moreover, this is the case even if the twins have been separated early in life and raised in sharply contrasting environments from then on (see Figure 4.5; Bouchard et al., 1992; Hershberger, Lichtenstein, & Knox, 1994). Under these conditions, greater similarity between the

FIGURE 4.5

Evidence for the Role of Genetic Factors in Attitudes. The attitudes of identical twins separated very early in life correlate more highly than those of nonidentical twins or unrelated persons. This finding provides evidence for the view that attitudes are influenced by genetic factors, at least to some extent.

attitudes of identical twins than in the attitudes of other persons can't be attributed to the fact that environmental factors are more similar for identical twins.

Additional results suggest, not surprisingly, that genetic factors play a stronger role in shaping some attitudes than others—in other words, some attitudes are more *heritable* than others. Although it is too early to reach definite conclusions, some findings suggest that attitudes involving gut-level preferences (e.g., a preference for certain kinds of music or specific kinds of foods) may be more strongly influenced by genetic factors than attitudes that are more cognitive in nature (e.g., attitudes about complex issues such as capital punishment or about situations and objects with which individuals have had little direct experience—such as social groups with whom they have little or no contact; Tesser, 1993). In addition, it appears that attitudes that are highly heritable may be more difficult to change than ones that are not, and that highly heritable attitudes may exert stronger effects on behavior (e.g., Crelia & Tesser, 1998). For instance, we seem to like strangers who express attitudes similar to ours more when these attitudes are highly heritable than when they are less heritable (Tesser, 1993). We'll return to these points in a later discussion of the effects of attitudes on behavior.

But how can such effects occur—how can genetic factors influence our attitudes? One possibility is that genetic factors influence more general dispositions, such as the tendency to experience mainly positive or negative affect—to be in a positive or negative mood most of the time (George, 1990). Such tendencies, in turn, could then influence evaluations of many aspects of the social world. For instance, an individual who tends to be in a positive mood much of the time might tend to express a high level of job satisfaction, no matter where he or she works; in contrast, someone who tends to be in a negative mood much of the time might tend to express more negative attitudes in virtually any work setting. Only time, and further research, will allow us to determine whether, and how, genetic factors influence attitudes. But given that such factors appear to influence many other aspects of social behavior and social thought, ranging from our choice of romantic partners through aggression (e.g., Buss, 1999), the idea that attitudes, too, may be subject to such influences is no longer viewed as weird or improbable by most social psychologists.

KEY POINTS

- *Attitudes* are evaluations of any aspect of the social world. Often, attitudes are *ambivalent*—we evaluate the attitude object both positively and negatively.
- Attitudes are often acquired from other persons through *social learning.* Such learning can involve *classical conditioning, instrumental conditioning,* or *observational learning.*
- Attitudes are also formed on the basis of *social comparison*—our tendency to compare ourselves with others to determine whether our view of social reality is or is not correct. In order to be similar to others we like or respect, we often accept the attitudes that they hold.
- Studies conducted with identical twins suggest that attitudes may also be influenced by genetic factors, although the magnitude of such effects varies greatly for different attitudes.

Attitude Functions: Why We Form Attitudes in the First Place

That we hold many attitudes is obvious; in fact, it is safe to say that we are rarely completely neutral to almost *any* aspect of the world around us. But why do we bother to form the many attitudes each of us has? In one sense, attitudes can be viewed as almost automatic reactions to the world around us; as we noted earlier, research employing sophisticated techniques for observing activity in the human brain suggests that we seem to classify stimuli we encounter as either positive or negative almost immediately (e.g., Ito et al., 1998). But apart from this, attitudes serve a number of useful functions.

First, they seem to operate as *schemas*—mental frameworks that help us to interpret and process many kinds of information. Moreover, they strongly color our perceptions and thoughts about the issues, persons, objects, or groups to which they refer. For instance, research findings indicate that we view information that offers support for our attitudes as more convincing and accurate than information that refutes them (e.g., Munro & Ditto, 1997), although, surprisingly, we do *not* remember information that supports our views better than information that does not (Eagly et al., 2000). (We'll have more to say about such effects in a later section). Similarly, we view sources that provide evidence contrary to our views as highly suspect—biased and unreliable (e.g., Giner-Sorolla & Chaiken, 1994, 1997). In sum, attitudes are useful in terms of our efforts to make sense out of the social world—although, like other cognitive frameworks and shortcuts, they can sometimes lead us astray.

In addition to this *knowledge function* (the usefulness of attitudes in organizing and interpreting social information), attitudes play several other roles as well (e.g., Shavitt, 1989, 1990). First, they permit us to express our central values or beliefs—a *self-expression* or *self-identity function.* For instance, if being politically liberal is crucial to your self-identity, you may find it important to hold proenvironmental attitudes, because these allow you to express your central beliefs.

Second, attitudes often serve a *self-esteem function,* helping us to maintain or enhance our feelings of self-worth. For example, many people get a boost out of believing that the attitudes they hold are the "right" ones—the ones that intelligent, cultivated, sensitive people should hold. Expressing these views sometimes helps these people to feel superior to others.

And speaking of egos, attitudes also sometimes serve an *ego-defensive function* (Katz, 1960), helping people to protect themselves from unwanted information about themselves. For instance, many persons who are quite bigoted express the view that they are against prejudice and discrimination. By stating such attitudes, they protect themselves from seeing that, in fact, they *are* actually highly prejudiced against others.

Finally, attitudes also often serve an *impression motivation function.* As you may recall from our discussion of this topic in Chapter 2, we often wish to make a good impression on others, and expressing the "right" views is one way of doing so (e.g., Chaiken, Giner-Sorolla, & Chen, 1996). Interestingly, recent findings indicate that the extent to which attitudes serve this function can strongly affect their impact on the processing of social information. Such effects are clearly demonstrated in a study by Nienhuis, Manstead, and Spears (2001).

These researchers reasoned that when attitudes serve an impression motivation function, individuals will tend to generate arguments that support them, and that the stronger this function of the attitudes, the more arguments they will generate. To test this prediction, they asked participants to read a message arguing in favor of legalizing hard drugs. Then, participants were told that they would be asked to defend this view later to another person. To vary the level of participants' impression motivation, some were told that their performance in this role would not be evaluated (low motivation), others were told that it would be evaluated by one other person (the person they tried to convince; this was the moderate motivation condition), and still others were informed that it would be evaluated by the recipient plus two other people (high motivation). After receiving this information and reading the message, participants reported their attitudes and also indicated to what extent they had generated new arguments in favor of this position. As predicted, those in the high-motivation condition generated more new arguments and also reported that they would be more likely to use them in convincing the other person (see Figure 4.6).

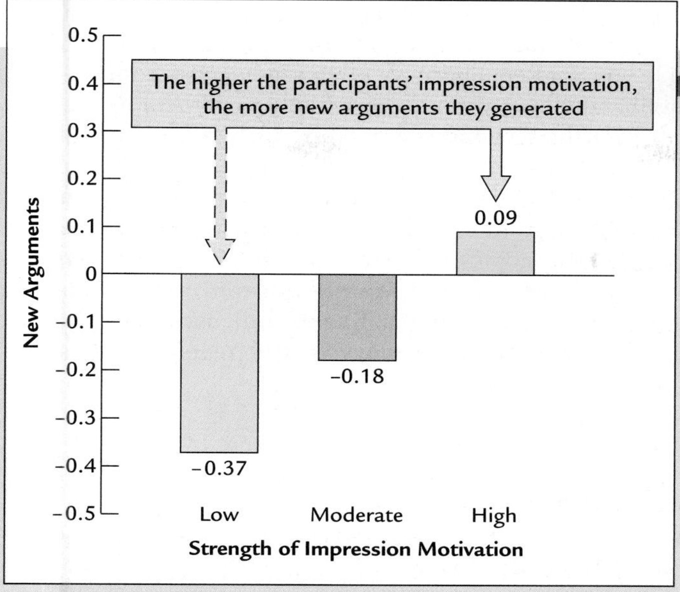

FIGURE 4.6

Attitudes: Their Impression Motivation Function. We sometimes use attitudes to make a good impression on others. In the study presented here, participants whose impression motivation was high generated more new arguments in support of their attitudes than did participants whose impression motivation was moderate or low.

[SOURCE: BASED ON DATA FROM NIENHUIS, MANSTEAD, & SPEARS, 2001.]

The findings of this study indicate that the greater the extent to which attitudes serve an impression motivation function, the more they lead individuals to formulate arguments favoring these views. As we'll see in a later section, this, in turn, may make it more difficult to change such attitudes; after all, the persons who hold them can offer many arguments for doing so! In short, our attitudes serve many functions for us, and these functions, in turn, can strongly shape the impact of our attitudes' influence on our processing of social information.

The Attitude-Behavior Link: When—and How—Attitudes Influence Behavior

When I was a new assistant professor, back in the late 1960s, social psychology was experiencing a serious crisis. For decades, attitudes had been one of the central concepts of the field, and much research had been conducted to study how attitudes are formed and how they can be changed. Implicit in all of this work was the common-sense belief that attitudes are an important determinant of behavior. Yet, by the late 1960s, many studies seemed to point to a very different conclusion: The link between attitudes and behavior is actually quite weak. Thus, knowing someone's attitude was *not* very useful in predicting their overt behavior. You have probably experienced a gap between your own attitudes and behavior on many occasions. For instance, what do you say when one of your friends shows you a new possession of which she or he is proud (a new car, pair of jeans, whatever) and asks for your opinion? Suppose you think it is really ugly; do you state that view? Perhaps. But the chances are good that you will try to avoid hurting your friend's feelings by saying that you like her or his new possession. In such cases—and in many other situations—there is a sizable gap between our attitudes and our behavior.

It is equally clear, however, that our attitudes often *do* exert important effects on our behavior; after all, think of the many times when your reactions to people, ideas, or issues *do* shape your actions concerning these aspects of the social world.

For instance, if you like pepperoni pizza but dislike pizza with anchovies, guess which one you will order? Similarly, if you hold conservative political views, you will probably vote for Republicans or other candidates who share your views, while if you hold liberal views, you are more likely to vote for Democrats or other liberals. Recognizing this fact, more recent research by social psychologists has focused on the question "*When* and *how* do attitudes influence behavior?" rather than on the question "*Do* they exert such effects?" The findings of such research are very informative and also paint a much more encouraging picture concerning the possibility of predicting people's behavior from their attitudes. Before turning to the details of such research, however, we will illustrate the important progress made by social psychologists in understanding the link between attitudes and behavior in one of our special **Social Psychology: Thirty Years of Progress** sections.

SOCIAL PSYCHOLOGY: THIRTY YEARS OF PROGRESS

STUDYING THE ATTITUDE–BEHAVIOR LINK

Actually, in this case, we will start with a study performed much more than thirty years ago because it is a true "classic" in social psychologists' efforts to understand the attitude–behavior link. This study was conducted by LaPiere (1934) during the great economic depression of the 1930s.

At that time, social psychologists generally defined attitudes largely in terms of behavior—as tendencies or predispositions to behave in certain ways in social situations (Allport, 1924). Thus, they assumed that attitudes were usually reflected in overt behavior. LaPiere, however, was not so certain. He wondered whether persons holding various prejudices—negative attitudes toward the members of specific social groups (see Chapter 6)—would demonstrate these attitudes in their overt behaviors as well as in their verbal statements. To find out, he spent two years traveling around the United States with a young Chinese couple. During these travels, they stopped at 184 restaurants and 66 hotels and "tourist camps" (predecessors of the modern motel). In the overwhelming majority of the cases, they were treated courteously. In fact, they were refused service only once; and in most cases, LaPiere reported, they received what he considered to be average to above-average service.

Now, however, the study gets really interesting. After the travels were complete, LaPiere wrote to all the businesses where he and the Chinese couple had stayed or dined, and asked whether they would offer service to Chinese visitors. The results were startling: Of the 128 businesses that responded, 92 percent of the restaurants and 91 percent of the hotels said "No!" In short, there was a tremendous gap between the attitudes expressed by these businesses (generally by the owners or managers) and what they had done when confronted with live, in-the-flesh Chinese customers (see Figure 4.7). Similar attitudes were expressed by hotels and restaurants LaPiere did not visit, so the sample appears to have been a representative one.

LaPiere (1934) interpreted his results as indicating that there is often a sizable gap between attitudes and behavior—between what people say and what they actually do. This classic study, and related findings reported in later decades, led some social psychologists (e.g., Wicker, 1969) to conclude that the field had been largely wasting its time studying attitudes, because they didn't strongly influence overt behavior. Was this true? Absolutely not! More sophisticated research soon indicated that, under certain conditions, attitudes do indeed influence behavior. The key task, then, was determining what these conditions were—when and how attitudes shape overt actions. As an example of modern research on this issue, let's consider a study by Armitage and Conner (2000), concerned with the role of attitudinal ambivalence in the attitude–behavior link.

Do you remember the chocolate dessert example at the start of this chapter? The woman in that example held an ambivalent attitude toward this particular object: she loved the way the dessert tasted, but felt it was too fattening. Because of this ambivalence, she might reject the dessert on some occasions but decide to eat it on others, depending on whether her positive or negative reactions won out. Recognizing the importance of attitude ambivalence in the attitude–behavior link, Armitage and Conner (2000) attempted to determine whether, as we might well expect, ambivalent attitudes are weaker predictors of behavior than attitudes that

When Do Attitudes Influence Behavior? Specificity, Strength, Accessibility, and Other Factors

Continuing with our major question, we'll now focus on several factors that determine the extent to which attitudes influence behavior. As we'll soon see, these involve aspects of the situations in which attitudes are expressed and aspects of the attitudes themselves. After considering these factors, we'll examine the question of *how* attitudes influence behavior—the underlying mechanisms involved in this important link.

■ ASPECTS OF THE SITUATION: FACTORS THAT PREVENT US FROM EXPRESSING OUR ATTITUDES. Have you ever been in the following situation? You are in a restaurant eating

FIGURE 4.7

Evidence That Attitudes Don't Always Predict Behavior. Virtually all restaurants, hotels, and motels visited by LaPiere and a young Chinese couple offered courteous service. When asked by mail whether they would serve Chinese customers, however, more than 90 percent said no. These findings suggests that a sizable gap sometimes exists between attitudes and behavior.

[SOURCE: BASED ON DATA FROM LAPIERE, 1934.]

are not ambivalent. To find out, they asked more than five hundred hospital employees to express their attitudes toward eating a low-fat diet (both positive and negative feelings about this action) and their intentions to do so. Five months later, these persons completed the same measures and also indicated whether they had actually eaten a low-fat diet during the intervening months. Finally, three months after the second session, participants once again reported their attitudes, intentions, and behavior. On the basis of their reported attitudes toward a low-fat diet, participants were divided into those with ambivalent and nonambivalent attitudes (i.e., those who had both positive and negative feelings about such a diet, and those who had only positive or only negative feelings about it). The researchers predicted that ambivalent attitudes would be a weaker predictor of actual behavior (following or not following such a diet) than nonambivalent attitudes, and this is precisely what happened.

In short, the somewhat discouraging results reported by LaPiere (1934) have been overturned by later, more sophisticated research. Under some conditions—for instance, when they are *not* ambivalent—attitudes do indeed predict behavior. We'll now take a closer look at just what these conditions are (i.e., at other factors that determine whether, and to what extent, attitudes influence behavior). But the main point of our discussion so far should be clear: Social psychologists have made a great deal of progress toward the goal of understanding the link between attitudes and behavior; this, in turn, is one of the central questions concerning attitudes and their role in our lives.

with a groups of friends, and when the food arrives, there's something wrong—for instance, it's not what you ordered or it's cold. Yet when the waitperson asks, "How is everything?" you and everyone else in your group answer, "Fine." Why don't you express your true reactions? In other words, why doesn't your behavior in this situation reflect your underlying attitudes? Mainly because, in the United States, most people are reluctant to complain about such matters, especially when dining with their friends. After all, complaining will put a damper on what should be an enjoyable situation; and besides, if you do complain, you may have to wait a long time for the kitchen to correct the mistake, and may end up sitting there watching your friends eat while you have no food. In this and many other contexts, *situational constraints* moderate the relationship between attitudes and behavior: they prevent attitudes from being expressed in overt behavior (e.g., Ajzen & Fishbein, 1980; Fazio & Roskos-Ewoldsen, 1994).

Situational factors can influence the link between attitudes and behavior in one additional way worth noting. Think for a moment: Whom are you likely to find at a rally against affirmative action? The answer is clear: Except perhaps for a few hecklers, most people present at such meetings will be fervent opponents of affirmative action. The same principle holds for many other situations, and this points to an important fact: In general, we tend to prefer situations that allow us to express our attitudes in our behavior. In other words, we often choose to enter and spend time in situations in which what we say and what we do can coincide (Snyder & Ickes, 1985). Indeed, because individuals tend to choose situations in which they can engage in behaviors consistent with their attitudes, the attitudes themselves may be strengthened by this overt expression and so become even better predictors of behavior (DeBono & Snyder, 1995). In sum, the relationship between attitudes and situations may be a two-way street. Situational pressures shape the extent to which attitudes can be expressed in overt actions, but, in addition, attitudes determine whether individuals enter various situations. In order to understand the link between attitudes and behavior, then, we must carefully consider both sets of factors.

■ ASPECTS OF ATTITUDES THEMSELVES. Years ago, I witnessed a very dramatic scene. A large timber company had signed a contract with the government, allowing the company to cut trees in a national forest. Some of the trees scheduled to become backyard fences were ancient giants, hundreds of feet tall. A group of conservationists objected strongly to cutting these magnificent trees and quickly moved to block this action. They joined hands and formed a human ring around each of the largest trees, thus preventing the loggers from cutting them down (see Figure 4.8). The tactic worked: so much publicity occurred that the contract was revoked and the trees were saved—at least temporarily.

Why did these people take such drastic action? The answer is clear: They were passionately committed to saving the trees. In other words, they held powerful attitudes that strongly affected their behavior. Incidents like this one are far from rare. For example, residents of my neighborhood held a rally two years ago to prevent construction of a locomotive factory less than half a mile from our homes; tempers grew heated, and for a while I thought that pro-factory and anti-factory people would come to blows! Incidents like these call attention to the fact that the link between attitudes and behavior is strongly determined (moderated) by several aspects of attitudes themselves. Let's consider several of the most important of these.

Attitude Origins. One such factor has to do with how attitudes are formed in the first place. Considerable evidence indicates that attitudes formed on the basis of direct experience often exert stronger effects on behavior than ones formed indirectly, through hearsay. Apparently, attitudes formed on the basis of direct experience are easier to bring to mind, and this increases their impact on behavior.

FIGURE 4.8
Strong Attitudes *Do* Predict Behavior. When individuals hold strong attitudes about some issue, they often act in ways that are consistent with such views, like the person shown here.

Attitude Strength. Another factor—clearly one of the most important—involves what is typically termed the *strength* of the attitudes in question. The stronger attitudes are, the greater their impact on behavior (Petkova, Ajzen, & Driver, 1995). The term *strength,* however, includes several factors: the extremity or *intensity* of an attitude (how strong is the emotional reaction provoked by the attitude object); its *importance* (the extent to which an individual cares deeply about and is personally affected by the attitude); *knowledge* (how much an individual knows about the attitude object); and *accessibility* (how easily the attitude comes to mind in various situations; Petty & Krosnick, 1995). Research indicates that all of these components play a role in attitude strength and that all are related (Krosnick et al., 1993). So important is attitude strength in determining the extent to which attitudes are related to overt behavior that it is worth taking a closer look at some of the components that influence it (Kraus, 1995).

Let's focus first on attitude *importance*—the extent to which an individual cares about the attitude (Krosnick, 1988). One of the key determinants of such importance is what social psychologists term *vested interest*—the extent to which the attitude is personally relevant to the individual who holds it, in that the object or issue to which it refers has important consequences for this person. The results of many studies indicate that the greater such vested interest, the stronger the impact of the attitude on behavior (e.g., Crano, 1995; Crano & Prislin, 1995). For instance, in one well-known study on this issue (Sivacek & Crano, 1982), students at a large university were telephoned and asked if they would participate in a campaign against increasing the legal age for drinking alcohol from eighteen to twenty-one. It was reasoned that students who would be affected by this new law—those

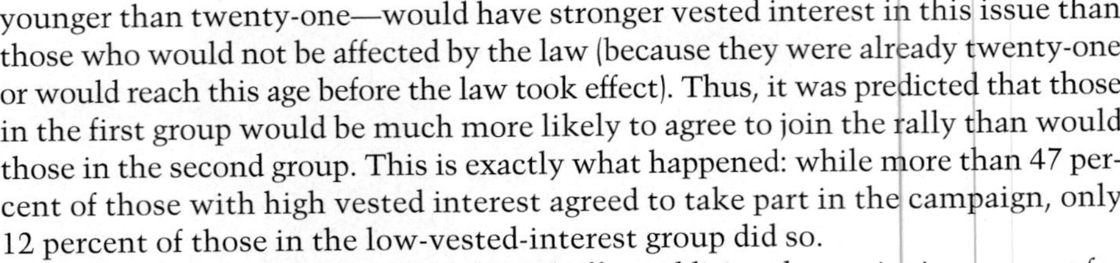

younger than twenty-one—would have stronger vested interest in this issue than those who would not be affected by the law (because they were already twenty-one or would reach this age before the law took effect). Thus, it was predicted that those in the first group would be much more likely to agree to join the rally than would those in the second group. This is exactly what happened: while more than 47 percent of those with high vested interest agreed to take part in the campaign, only 12 percent of those in the low-vested-interest group did so.

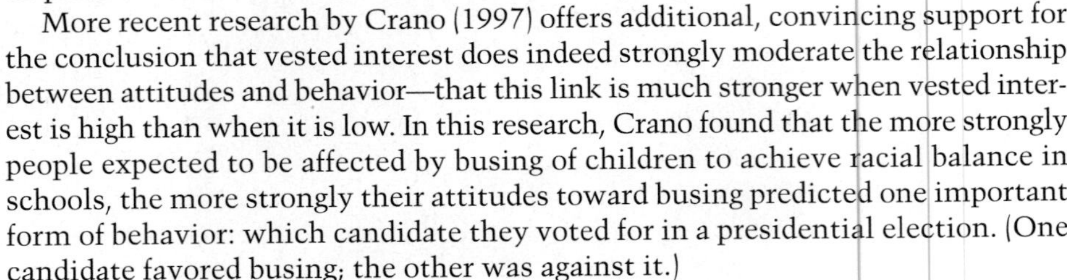

More recent research by Crano (1997) offers additional, convincing support for the conclusion that vested interest does indeed strongly moderate the relationship between attitudes and behavior—that this link is much stronger when vested interest is high than when it is low. In this research, Crano found that the more strongly people expected to be affected by busing of children to achieve racial balance in schools, the more strongly their attitudes toward busing predicted one important form of behavior: which candidate they voted for in a presidential election. (One candidate favored busing; the other was against it.)

Attitude Specificity. A third aspect of attitudes that influences their relationship to behavior is *attitude specificity*—the extent to which attitudes are focused on specific objects or situations rather than on general ones. For example, you may have a general attitude toward religion (e.g., you believe that it is important for everyone to have religious convictions versus not having them); in addition to this general attitude, you may have several more specific attitudes about various aspects of religion—for instance, the importance of going to church every week (this is important or unimportant). Research findings indicate that the attitude–behavior link is stronger when attitudes and behaviors are measured at the same level of specificity. Thus, we'd probably be more accurate in predicting whether you'll go to services *this* week from your attitude about the importance of attending such services than from your attitude about religion generally. On the other hand, we'd probably be more accurate in predicting your willingness to take action to protect religious freedoms from your general attitude toward religion than from your attitude about wearing religious jewelry (Fazio & Roskos-Ewoldsen, 1994). So, attitude specificity, too, is an important factor in the attitude–behavior link.

In sum, as we noted earlier, existing evidence suggests that attitudes really *do* affect behavior (e.g., Petty & Krosnick, 1995). However, the strength of this link is strongly determined by a number of different factors—situational constraints that permit or do not permit us to give overt expressions to our attitudes, as well as several aspects of attitudes themselves (e.g., their origins, strength, and specificity, among others).

How Do Attitudes Influence Behavior? Intentions, Willingness, and Action

Understanding *when* attitudes influence behavior is an important topic. But as we noted in Chapter 1, social psychologists are interested not only in the *when* of social thought and behavior but in the *why* and *how* as well. So it should come as no surprise that researchers have also tried to understand *how* attitudes influence behavior. Work on this issue points to the conclusion that, in fact, there are several basic mechanisms through which attitudes shape behavior.

theory of reasoned action: A theory suggesting that the decision to engage in a particular behavior is the result of a rational process in which behavioral options are considered, consequences or outcomes of each are evaluated, and a decision is reached to act or not to act. That decision is then reflected in behavioral intentions, which strongly influence overt behavior.

■ ATTITUDES, REASONED THOUGHT, AND BEHAVIOR. The first of these mechanisms operates in situations in which we give careful, deliberate thought to our attitudes and their implications for our behavior. Insights into the nature of this process are provided by the **theory of reasoned action** (and a later version of this framework, known as the **theory of planned behavior**), proposed by Ajzen and Fishbein (1980; Ajzen, 1991). This theory suggests that the decision to engage in a particular behavior is the result of a rational process that is goal-oriented and that follows a logical sequence. Behavioral options are considered, consequences or outcomes of each are evaluated, and a decision is reached to act or not to act. That decision is then reflected in *behavioral intentions,* which, according to Fishbein, Ajzen, and many other researchers, are often strong predictors of how we will act in a given situation (Ajzen, 1987). According to the theory, intentions, in turn, are determined by two factors: *attitudes toward a behavior*—people's positive or negative evaluations of performing the behavior (whether they think it will yield positive or negative consequences)—and *subjective norms*—people's perceptions of whether others will approve or disapprove of this behavior. The theory of planned behavior (which is primarily an extension or refinement of the theory of reasoned action), adds a third factor: *perceived behavioral control*—people's appraisals of their ability to perform the behavior. Perhaps a specific example will help illustrate the very reasonable nature of these ideas (see Figure 4.9).

Suppose a student is considering body piercing—for instance, wearing a nose ornament. Will she actually take this action? According to Ajzen and Fishbein, the answer depends on her intentions, and these, in turn, are strongly influenced by the factors noted above. If the student believes that body piercing will be relatively painless and will make her look really attractive (she has positive attitudes toward the behavior), that people whose opinions she values will approve of this action (subjective norms), and that she can readily do it (she knows an expert body-piercer), her intentions to carry out this action will be strong. On the other hand, if she believes that piercing will be painful and will not improve her appearance

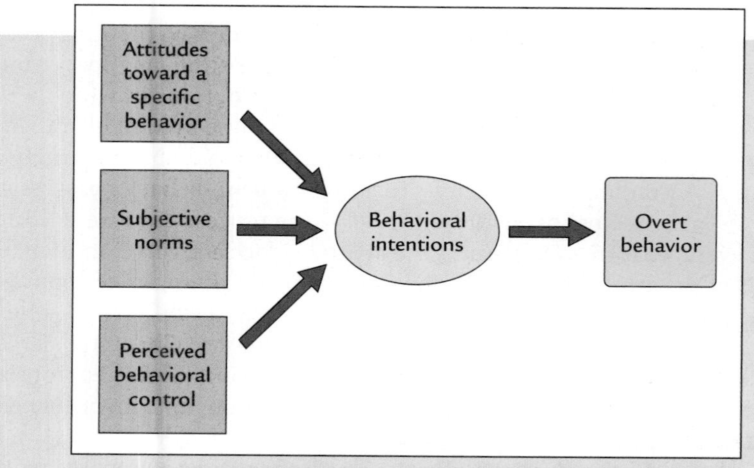

FIGURE 4.9

The Theories of Reasoned Action and Planned Behavior.
The two theories summarized here suggest that several factors (attitudes toward a given behavior, subjective norms concerning that behavior, and perceived ability to perform it) determine behavioral intentions concerning the behavior. Such intentions, in turn, are a strong determinant of whether the behavior is actually performed.

[SOURCE: BASED ON SUGGESTIONS BY AJZEN & FISHBEIN, 1980; AJZEN, 1991.]

theory of planned behavior: An extension of the *theory of reasoned action,* suggesting that in addition to attitudes toward a given behavior and subjective norms about it, individuals also consider perceived behavioral control—their ability to perform the behavior.

much, that her friends will disapprove of this behavior, and that she will have trouble finding an expert to do it safely, her intentions to get the nose ornament will be weak.

These two theories (reasoned action and planned behavior) have been applied to predicting behavior in many settings, with considerable success. For instance, they have been used to predict people's intentions to use various drugs, such as marijuana, alcohol, and tobacco (e.g., Morojele & Stephenson, 1994; Conner & McMillan, 1999). And more recent work suggests that these theories are useful for predicting whether individuals will use *ecstasy,* a highly dangerous drug that is now used by a growing number of young persons between the ages of fifteen and twenty-five.

For instance, consider a study by Orbell and her colleagues (2001). They approached young people in various locations and asked them to complete a questionnaire designed to measure (1) their attitude toward ecstasy (e.g., is this drug enjoyable or unenjoyable, pleasant or unpleasant, beneficial or harmful, etc.), (2) their intention to use it in the next two months, (3) subjective norms (whether their friends would approve of their using it), and (4) two aspects of perceived control over using this drug—whether they could obtain it and whether they could resist taking it if they had some. Two months later, the same persons were contacted and asked whether they had actually used ecstasy ("How many pills of ecstasy have you taken in the last two months?"). Results indicated that attitudes toward ecstasy, subjective norms, and control over using it were all significant predictors of intention to use this drug. Further, attitudes, subjective norms, and intentions were significant predictors of actual use of ecstasy. Thus, overall, results were consistent with the theories of reasoned action and planned behavior and indicated that the variables identified by these theories are very useful in predicting whether specific persons will or will not use this dangerous drug.

■ ATTITUDES AND IMMEDIATE BEHAVIORAL REACTIONS. The two theories described above are accurate in situations in which we have the time and opportunity to reflect carefully on various actions. But what about situations in which we have to act quickly—for example, if another person cuts into line in front of you. In such cases, attitudes seem to influence behavior in a more direct and seemingly automatic manner. According to one theory—Fazio's **attitude-to-behavior process model** (Fazio, 1989; Fazio & Roskos-Ewoldsen, 1994)—the process goes something like this. Some event activates an attitude; the attitude, once activated, influences our perceptions of the attitude object. At the same time, our knowledge about what's appropriate in a given situation (our knowledge of various *social norms*—rules governing behavior in a particular context) is also activated (see Chapter 9). Together, the attitude and this previously stored information about what's appropriate or expected shape our definition of the event. This perception, in turn, influences our behavior. Let's consider a concrete example.

Imagine that someone does actually cut into line in front of you in a store (see Figure 4.10). This event triggers your attitude toward people who engage in such behavior and, at the same time, your understanding of how people are expected to behave in stores. Together, these factors influence your definition (perception) of the event, which might be "Who does this person think he is? What nerve!" or, perhaps, "Gee, this person must be in a big hurry; or maybe he is a foreigner who doesn't know that people are supposed to wait in line." Your definition of the event then shapes your behavior. Several studies provide support for this model, so it seems to offer a useful explanation of how attitudes influence behavior in some situations.

attitude-to-behavior process model: A model of how attitudes guide behavior that emphasizes the influence of both attitudes and stored knowledge of what is appropriate in a given situation on an individual's definition of the present situation. This definition, in turn, influences overt behavior.

In short, it appears that attitudes affect our behavior through at least two mechanisms, and that these operate under somewhat contrasting conditions. When we have time to engage in careful, reasoned thought, we can weigh all the alternatives

FIGURE 4.10

The Attitude-to-Behavior Process Model.

According to one model of how attitudes influence behavior (the *attitude-to-behavior process model*), events such as someone cutting into line in front of you trigger our attitudes and, simultaneously, our understanding of how people are expected to behave in a specific situation. Together, these factors influence our definition (perception) of the event and this, in turn, determines how we behave. Thus, attitudes are an important factor in shaping our overt behavior.

and decide, quite deliberately, how to act. Under the hectic conditions of everyday life, however, we often don't have time for this kind of deliberate weighing of alternatives; in such cases, our attitudes seem to spontaneously shape our perceptions of various events and thus our immediate behavioral reactions to them (e.g., Bargh, 1997; Dovidio et al., 1996).

KEY POINTS

- Several factors affect the strength of the relationship between attitudes and behavior; some of these relate to the situation in which the attitudes are activated, and some relate to aspects of the attitudes themselves.
- Situational constraints may prevent us from expressing our attitudes overtly. In addition, we tend to prefer situations that allow us to express our attitudes, and this may further strengthen these views.
- Several aspects of attitudes themselves also moderate the attitude–behavior link. These include attitude origins (how attitudes were formed), attitude strength (which includes attitude accessibility, knowledge, importance, and vested interest), and attitude specificity.
- Attitudes seem to influence behavior through two different mechanisms. When we can give careful thought to our attitudes, intentions derived from our attitudes strongly predict behavior. In situations in which we can't engage in such deliberate thought, attitudes influence behavior by shaping our perceptions of the situation.

FIGURE 4.11

Persuasion: A Part of Daily Life. Each day, we are literally bombarded with dozens of messages designed to change our attitudes and our behavior.

The Fine Art of Persuasion: Using Messages to Change Attitudes

How many times during the past day has someone tried to change your attitudes? If you stop and think for a moment, you may be surprised at the answer, for it is clear that each day, we are literally bombarded with many efforts of this type (see Figure 4.11). Billboards, radio and television commercials, newspaper and magazine ads, political speeches, appeals from charities—the list seems almost endless. To what extent are such attempts at **persuasion**—efforts to change our attitudes through the use of various kinds of messages—successful? And what factors determine whether they succeed or fail? Social psychologists have studied these issues for decades, and as we'll soon see, their efforts have yielded important insights into the cognitive processes that play a role in persuasion (e.g., Eagly, Wood, & Chaiken, 1996; Lavine, Thomsen, & Gonzales, 1997; Munro & Ditto, 1997).

Persuasion: The Early Approach

In most cases, efforts at persuasion involve the following elements: some *source* directs some type of *message* (the *communication*) to some person or group of persons (the *audience*). Taking note of this fact, early research on persuasion (e.g., Hovland, Janis, & Kelley, 1953) focused on these key elements, asking "*Who* says *what* to *whom* with what effect?" This approach yielded many interesting findings, among which the following were the most consistent:

- Communicators who are *credible*—who seem to know what they are talking about or are expert with respect to the topics or issues they are presenting—are more persuasive than nonexperts. For instance, in a famous study on this topic, Hovland and Weiss (1951) asked participants to read communications dealing with various issues (e.g., atomic submarines, the future of movie theaters—remember, this was back in 1950!). The supposed source of these messages was varied so as to be high or low; for instance, for atomic submarines, a high-credibility source was the famous scientist Robert J. Oppenheimer, while the low-credibility source was *Pravda*, the newspaper

persuasion: Efforts to change others' attitudes through the use of various kinds of messages.

"A word to the wise, Benton. Don't squander your credibility."

FIGURE 4.12
Credibility: An Important Factor in Persuasion. Research findings suggest that the character in this cartoon is correct: Credibility—the extent to which persons trying to change our attitudes are viewed as believable—is indeed an important factor in persuasion.

of the Communist party in the Soviet Union. Participants expressed their attitudes toward these issues a week before the experiment and then immediately after receiving the communications. As you can guess, those who were told that the source of the messages they read were high in credibility showed significantly greater attitude change. So, as the cartoon in Figure 4.12 suggests, source credibility is indeed an important factor in persuasion.

- Communicators who are attractive in some way (e.g., physically) are more persuasive than communicators who are low in attractiveness and expertise (Hovland & Weiss, 1951). This is one reason why advertisements often include attractive models.
- Messages that do not appear to be designed to change our attitudes are often more successful in this respect than ones that seem intended to reach this goal (Walster & Festinger, 1962).
- People are sometimes more susceptible to persuasion when they are distracted by some extraneous event than when they are paying full attention to what is being said (Allyn & Festinger, 1961). This is one reason why political candidates often arrange for spontaneous demonstrations during their speeches. The distraction generated among audience members may enhance their acceptance of the speaker's points.
- When an audience holds attitudes contrary to those of a would-be persuader, it is often more effective for the communicator to adopt a *two-sided* approach, in which both sides of the argument are presented, than to take a *one-sided* approach.

- People who speak rapidly are often more persuasive than persons who speak more slowly (e.g., Miller et al., 1976).
- Persuasion can be enhanced by messages that arouse strong emotions (especially fear) in the audience, particularly when the communication provides specific recommendations about how to prevent or avoid the fear-producing events described (e.g., Leventhal, Singer, & Jones, 1965; Robberson & Rogers, 1988).

We're confident that you find all of these points to be reasonable ones that probably fit with your own experience, so early research on persuasion certainly provided important insights into the factors that influence persuasion. What such work *didn't* do, however, was offer a comprehensive account of *how* persuasion occurs. For instance, why, precisely, are highly credible or attractive communicators more effective in changing attitudes than less credible or attractive ones? Why does distraction increase attitude change? Why are fast speakers more effective in changing attitudes than slower ones? In recent years, social psychologists have recognized that to answer such questions, it is necessary to carefully examine the cognitive factors and processes that underlie persuasion—in other words, what goes on in people's minds while they listen to a persuasive message and why they are influenced or not influenced by it. It is to this highly sophisticated work that we turn next.

The Cognitive Approach to Persuasion: Systematic versus Heuristic Processing

What happens when you are exposed to a persuasive message—for instance, when you watch a television commercial or listen to a political speech? Your first answer might be something like "I think about what's happening or what's being said"; and, in a sense, that's correct. But as we saw in Chapter 3, social psychologists know that, in general, we do the least amount of cognitive work that we can in a given situation. So, the central issue—the one that seems to provide the key to understanding the entire process of persuasion—is really a cognitive one: "How do we process (absorb, interpret, evaluate) the information contained in such messages?" The answer that has emerged from hundreds of separate studies is that, basically, we process persuasive messages in two distinct ways.

The first of these is known as **systematic processing** or the **central route,** and it involves careful consideration of message content and the ideas it contains. Such processing is quite effortful, and absorbs much of our information-processing capacity. The second approach, known as **heuristic processing** or the **peripheral route,** involves the use of simple rules of thumb or mental shortcuts—such as the belief that "experts' statements can be trusted" or the idea that "if it makes me feel good, I'm in favor of it." This kind of processing is much less effortful and allows us to react to persuasive messages in an automatic manner. It occurs in response to cues in the message or situation that evoke various mental shortcuts (e.g., beautiful models evoke the "What's beautiful is good and worth listening to" heuristic).

When do we engage in each of these two distinct modes of thought? Modern theories of persuasion such as the **elaboration likelihood model** (ELM for short; e.g., Petty & Cacioppo, 1986; Petty et al., 1994) and the heuristic–systematic model (e.g., Chaiken, Liberman, & Eagly, 1989; Eagly & Chaiken, 1998) provide the following answer. We engage in the effortful type of processing (systematic processing) when our capacity to process information relating to the persuasive message is high (e.g., we have lots of knowledge about it or lots of time to engage in such thought) or when we are *motivated* to do so—the issue is important to us and we believe it is essential to form an accurate view (e.g., Maheswaran & Chaiken, 1991; Petty & Cacioppo, 1990). In contrast, we engage in the less effortful type of processing

systematic processing: Processing of information in a persuasive message that involves careful consideration of message content and ideas.

central route (to persuasion): Attitude change resulting from systematic processing of information presented in persuasive messages.

heuristic processing: Processing of information in a persuasive message that involves the use of simple rules of thumb or mental shortcuts.

peripheral route (to persuasion): Attitude change that occurs in response to persuasion cues—information concerning the expertise or status of would-be persuaders.

elaboration likelihood model (of persuasion): A theory suggesting that persuasion can occur in either of two distinct ways, which differ in the amount of cognitive effort or elaboration they require.

(heuristic processing) when we lack the ability or capacity to process more carefully (we must make up our minds very quickly or we have little knowledge about the issue) or when our motivation to perform such cognitive work is low (the issue is unimportant to us or has little potential effect on us). Advertisers, politicians, salespersons, and others wishing to change our attitudes prefer to push us into the heuristic mode of processing because, for reasons we'll describe below, it is often easier to change our attitudes when we think in this mode than when we engage in more careful and systematic processing. (See Figure 4.13 for an overview of one cognitive theory of persuasion, the ELM model.)

Earlier, we noted that the discovery of these two contrasting modes of processing provided an important key to understanding the process of persuasion. The existence of these two modes of thought help us to solve many intriguing puzzles. For instance, it has been found that when persuasive messages are not interesting or relevant to individuals, the amount of persuasion they produce is *not* strongly influenced by the strength of the arguments they contain. When such messages are highly relevant to individuals, they are much more successful in inducing persuasion if the arguments they contain *are* strong and convincing. Can you see why this is so? According to modern theories such as the ELM and heuristic–systematic model, when relevance is low, individuals tend to process messages through the heuristic mode by means of cognitive shortcuts. Thus, argument strength has little impact on them. In contrast, when relevance is high, they process persuasive messages more systematically, and in this mode, argument strength *is* important (e.g., Petty & Cacioppo, 1990).

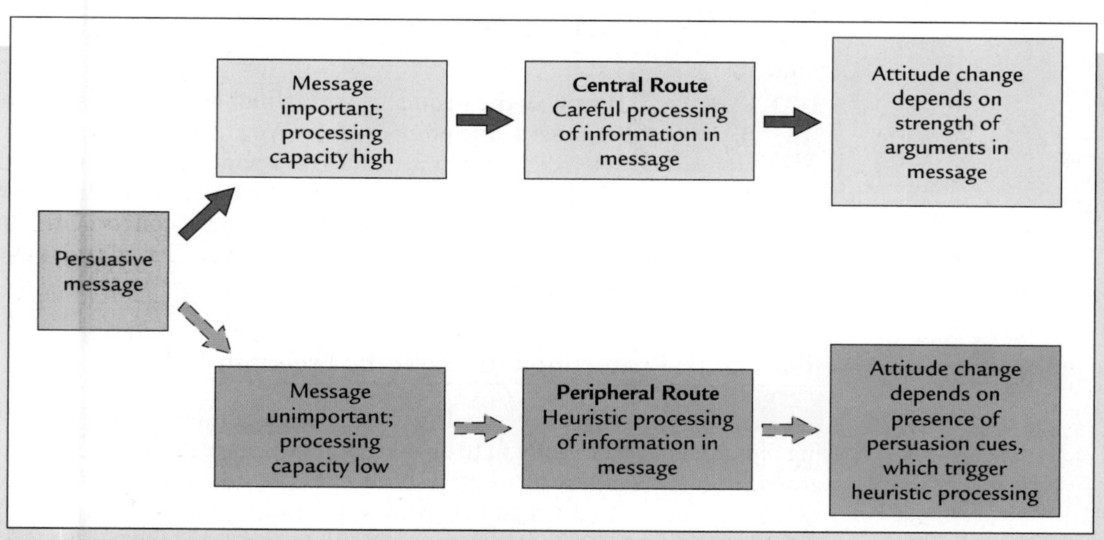

FIGURE 4.13

The ELM Model: One Cognitive Theory of Persuasion.

According to the *elaboration likelihood model* (ELM), persuasion can occur in either of two distinct ways: through careful, systematic processing of the information contained in the persuasive messages (the *central route*) or through less systematic processing based on heuristics or mental shortcuts. We engage in *systematic processing* when the message is important to us and we have the cognitive resources (and time) to think about it carefully. We engage in *heuristic processing* when the message is not important to us or we do not have the cognitive resources (or time) to engage in careful thought.

[SOURCE: BASED ON SUGGESTIONS BY PETTY & CACIOPPO, 1986.]

Similarly, the systematic versus heuristic distinction helps explain why people are more easily persuaded when they are somehow distracted—in a sense, asked to do two things at once—than when they are not. Under these conditions, the capacity to process the information in a persuasive message is limited, so people adopt the heuristic mode of thought. If the message contains the "right" cues (e.g., communicators who are attractive or seemingly expert), persuasion may occur because people respond to these cues and not to the arguments being presented. In sum, this modern cognitive approach really does seem to provide a crucial key to understanding many aspects of persuasion.

KEY POINTS

- Early research on *persuasion*—efforts to change attitudes through the use of messages—focused primarily on characteristics of the communicator (e.g., expertise, attractiveness), message (e.g., one-sidedness versus two-sidedness), and audience.
- More recent research has sought to understand the cognitive processes that play a role in persuasion. Such research suggests that we process persuasive messages in two distinct ways: through *systematic processing*, which involves careful attention to message content, or through *heuristic processing*, which involves the use of mental shortcuts (e.g., "experts are usually right").

When Attitude Change Fails: Resistance to Persuasion

In view of the frequency with which we are exposed to persuasive messages, one point is clear: We are highly resistant to them. If we were not, our attitudes on a wide range of issues would be in a constant state of change. This raises an intriguing question: Why are we such a "tough sell" where efforts to change our attitudes are concerned? The answer involves several factors that, together, enhance our ability to resist even highly skilled efforts at persuasion.

Reactance: Protecting Our Personal Freedom

Have you ever had an experience like this? Someone exerts mounting pressure on you to get you to change your attitudes. As they do, you experience growing levels of annoyance and resentment. The final outcome: Not only do you resist; you may actually lean over backwards to adopt views *opposite* to those the would-be persuader wants you to adopt. Such behavior is an example of what social psychologists call **reactance**—a negative reaction to efforts by others to reduce our freedom by getting us to do what they want us to do. Research findings indicate that in such situations, we often really do change our attitudes (or behavior) in a direction exactly opposite to that being urged on us—an effect known as *negative attitude change* (Brehm, 1966; Rhodewalt & Davison, 1983).

The existence of reactance is one reason why hard-sell attempts at persuasion often fail. When individuals perceive such appeals as direct threats to their personal freedom (or their image of being an independent person), they are strongly motivated to resist. Such resistance, in turn, virtually assures that would-be persuaders will fail.

reactance: Negative reaction to threats to one's personal freedom. Reactance often increases resistance to persuasion.

Forewarning: Prior Knowledge of Persuasive Intent

When we watch television, we expect commercials to interrupt most programs (except on public television). We know full well that these messages are designed to change our views—to get us to buy various products. Similarly, we know, when we listen to a political speech, that the person delivering it has an ulterior motive: she or he wants our vote. Does the fact that we know in advance about the persuasive intent behind such messages help us to resist them? Research on the effects of such advance knowledge—known as **forewarning**—indicates that it does (e.g., Cialdini & Petty, 1979; Johnson, 1994). When we know that a speech, taped message, or written appeal is designed to alter our views, we are often less likely to be affected by it than when we do not possess such knowledge. Why is this the case? Because forewarning influences several cognitive processes that play a role in persuasion.

First, forewarning provides us with more opportunity to formulate *counterarguments* that can lessen the message's impact. In addition, forewarning also provides us with more time in which to recall relevant facts and information that may prove useful in refuting a persuasive message (Wood, 1982). The benefits of forewarning are more likely to occur with respect to attitudes we consider important (Krosnick, 1989), but they seem to occur to a smaller degree even for attitudes we view as fairly trivial. In many cases, then, it appears that to be forewarned is indeed to be forearmed where persuasion is concerned.

Selective Avoidance

Still another way in which we resist attempts at persuasion is through **selective avoidance,** a tendency to direct our attention away from information that challenges our existing attitudes. As we explained in Chapter 3, selective avoidance is one of the ways in which schemas guide the processing of social information, and attitudes often operate as schemas. A clear illustration of the effects of selective avoidance is provided by television viewing. People do not simply sit in front of the tube passively absorbing whatever the media decides to dish out. Instead, they channel surf, mute the commercials, or simply cognitively tune out when confronted with information contrary to their views. The opposite effect occurs as well. When we encounter information that *supports* our views, we tend to give it our full attention. These tendencies to ignore or avoid information that contradicts our attitudes while actively seeking information consistent with them constitute two sides of what social psychologists term *selective exposure,* and such selectivity in what we make the focus of our attention helps ensure that our attitudes remain largely intact for long periods of time.

Active Defense of Our Existing Attitudes: Counterarguing against Competing Views

Ignoring or screening out information incongruent with our current views is certainly one way of resisting persuasion. But growing evidence suggests that, in addition to this kind of passive defense of our attitudes, we also use a more active strategy: We actively counterargue against views contrary to our own (e.g., Eagly et al., 1999). Doing so makes these opposing views more memorable but reduces their impact on our attitudes. Clear evidence for such effects has been reported recently by Eagly and her colleagues (2000).

These researchers exposed students previously identified as either for (pro-choice) or against (pro-life) abortion on demand to persuasive messages delivered by a female communicator; these messages were either consistent with their attitudes

forewarning: Advance knowledge that one is about to become the target of an attempt at persuasion. Forewarning often increases resistance to the persuasion that follows.

selective avoidance: A tendency to direct attention away from information that challenges existing attitudes. Such avoidance increases resistance to persuasion.

or contrary to their views. After hearing the messages, participants reported their attitudes toward abortion, how sure they were of their views (a measure of attitude strength), and all of the arguments in the message they could recall (a measure of memory). In addition, they listed the thoughts they had while listening to the message; this provided information on the extent to which they counterargued internally against the message that was contrary to their own views.

Results indicated that, as expected, the counterattitudinal message and the proattitudinal message were equally memorable. However, participants reported thinking more systematically about the counterattitudinal message, and reported having more oppositional thoughts about it—a clear sign that they were indeed counterarguing against this message. In contrast, they reported more supportive thoughts in response to the proattitudinal message (see Figure 4.14).

So it appears that one reason we are so good at resisting persuasion is that we not only ignore information inconsistent with our current views—we also carefully process such counterattitudinal input and argue actively against it. In a sense, we provide our own strong defense against efforts to change our attitudes.

■ INOCULATION AGAINST "BAD IDEAS": WHEN OTHERS DO OUR COUNTERARGUING FOR US. Actually, the idea that resistance to persuasion stems, at least in part, from gen-

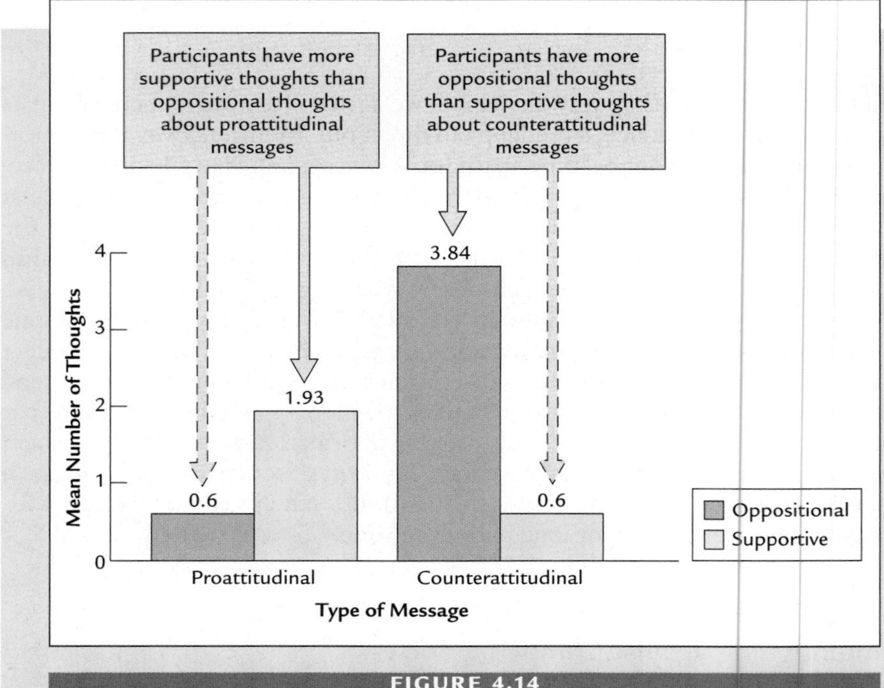

FIGURE 4.14

Counterarguing against Counterattitudinal Messages. Participants reported having more oppositional thoughts about a counterattitudinal message than about a proattitudinal message. In contrast, they reported having more supportive thoughts about a proattitudinal message than about a counterattitudinal message. These findings are consistent with the view that one reason we are so good at resisting persuasion is that we actively defend our attitudes against opposing views by counterarguing against them.

[SOURCE: BASED ON DATA FROM EAGLY ET AL., 2000.]

erating arguments against the views presented in persuasive messages is far from new in social psychology. In fact, more than forty years ago McGuire (1961) suggested that people could be "inoculated" against persuasion by presenting them with views opposed to their own, along with arguments that refuted these counterattitudinal positions. He reasoned that when they were presented with counterarguments against the opposing view, people would be stimulated to generate additional counterarguments of their own, and that this would make it more difficult to change their attitudes.

To test this prediction, he conducted several studies (e.g., McGuire & Papageorgis, 1961) in which individuals received attitude statements (e.g., truisms such as "everyone should brush his or her teeth after every meal") along with one of two sets of arguments: arguments supporting this truism (the *supportive defense* condition) or arguments against the truism, which were then refuted (the *refutational defense* condition). Two days later, participants received additional messages that attacked the original truisms with new arguments. Finally, they reported their attitudes toward these views. As predicted, the refutational defense was more effective in preventing persuasion. In other words, exposure to relatively weak doses of arguments opposed to our attitudes can serve to strengthen the views we already hold, and our resistance to subsequent efforts to change them. In a sense, we can indeed be inoculated against "bad ideas"—ones contrary to our own!

Biased Assimilation and Attitude Polarization: "If It's Contrary to What I Believe, Then It Must Be Unreliable—or Worse!"

Before concluding, we should briefly mention two additional processes that play a role in our ability to resist efforts at persuasion. These are known, respectively, as **biased assimilation**—a tendency to evaluate information contrary to our existing views as less convincing and less reliable than information consistent with these views (e.g., Lord, Ross, & Lepper, 1979; Miller et al., 1993)—and **attitude polarization**—a tendency to evaluate mixed evidence or information in such a way that it strengthens our initial views and makes them more extreme (e.g., Pomerantz, Chaiken, & Tordesilla, 1995).

As a result of these two processes, our attitudes really *do* seem to be beyond the reach of many efforts to change them, and they tend to persist even when we are confronted with new information that strongly challenges them (e.g., Munro & Ditto, 1997). To put the icing on the cake, additional research (e.g., Duck, Terry, & Hogg, 1998; Vallone, Ross, & Lepper, 1985) indicates that we also tend to perceive the *source* of information contrary to our views—not just the information itself—as biased, an effect known as the *hostile media bias,* as in "Media coverage that disagrees with *my* views is biased!" (e.g., Duck, Terry, & Hogg, 1997). To the extent such effects occur, even strong arguments are rejected, and there is little chance that attitude change will occur. (See the **Ideas To Take With You—And Use!** feature on page 154 for our advice on how to resist persuasion.)

biased assimilation: The tendency to evaluate information that disconfirms our existing views as less convincing or reliable than information that confirms these views.

attitude polarization: The tendency to evaluate mixed evidence or information in such a way that it strengthens our initial views and makes them more extreme.

KEY POINTS

- Our attitudes tend to remain quite stable despite many efforts to change them. Several factors contribute to such *resistance to persuasion.*
- One such factor is *reactance*—negative reactions to efforts by others to reduce or limit our personal freedom.

(continued)

KEY POINTS *(CONTINUED)*

- Resistance to persuasion is often increased by *forewarning*—the knowledge that someone is trying to change our attitudes—and by *selective avoidance*—the tendency to avoid exposure to information that contradicts our views.
- In addition, when we are exposed to persuasive messages contrary to our existing views, we actively counterargue against the information they contain. This, too increases our resistance to persuasion.
- If we receive arguments against our views along with arguments that refute these counterattitudinal positions, our resistance to subsequent persuasion increases; this is sometimes known as inoculation against counterattitudinal views.
- Two additional processes—*biased assimilation* and *attitude polarization*—also play a role in resistance to persuasion. Biased assimilation refers to our tendency to evaluate information inconsistent with our attitudes as less reliable or convincing than information consistent with our views. Attitude polarization refers to the tendency to interpret mixed evidence in ways that strengthen our existing views and make them more extreme.

Cognitive Dissonance: Why Our Behavior Can Sometimes Influence Our Attitudes

When we first introduced the questions of whether, and to what extent, attitudes and behavior are linked, we noted that, in many situations, there is a sizable gap between what we feel on the inside (positive or negative reactions to some object or issue) and what we show on the outside. For instance, I have a neighbor who recently purchased a huge SUV. I have very strong, negative attitudes toward such giant vehicles because they get very low gas mileage, add to pollution, block my view while driving, and are generally just plain wasteful (almost no one who owns one really drives it off-road). But when my neighbor asked how I liked his new vehicle, I swallowed hard and said, "Nice, very nice" with as much enthusiasm as I could muster. He is a very good neighbor who looks after my house when I'm away, and I did not want to offend or upset him. But I certainly felt very uncomfortable when I uttered these words. Why? Because in this situation my behavior was *not* consistent with my attitudes, and this is an uncomfortable state for most of us. Social psychologists term the negative reaction I experienced **cognitive dissonance**—an unpleasant state that occurs when we notice that various attitudes we hold, or our attitudes and our behavior, are somehow inconsistent.

As you probably know from your own experience, cognitive dissonance is a frequent occurrence in everyday life. Any time you say things you don't really believe (e.g., praise something you don't actually like just to be polite), make a difficult decision that requires you to reject an alternative you find attractive, or discover that something you've invested effort or money to obtain is not as good as you expected, you may well experience dissonance. In all of these situations, there is a gap between your attitudes and your actions, and such gaps tend to make us quite uncomfortable. Most important from the present perspective, cognitive dissonance can sometimes lead us to change our attitudes—to shift them so that they *are* consistent with other attitudes we hold or with our overt behavior. Put another way, because of cognitive dissonance and its effects, *we sometimes change our own attitudes,* even in

cognitive dissonance: An unpleasant internal state that results when individuals notice inconsistency between two or more of their attitudes or between their attitudes and their behavior.

the absence of any strong external pressure to do so. Let's take a closer look at cognitive dissonance and its intriguing implications for attitude change.

Cognitive Dissonance: What It Is and Various Ways (Direct and Indirect) to Reduce It

Dissonance theory, we've already noted, begins with a very reasonable idea: People don't like inconsistency and are uncomfortable when it occurs. In other words, when we notice that our attitudes and our behavior don't match, or that two attitudes we hold are inconsistent, we are motivated to do something about this situation—to reduce the dissonance. How can we accomplish this goal?

In its early forms (e.g., Aronson, 1968; Festinger, 1957), dissonance focused on three basic mechanisms. First, we can change our attitudes or our behavior so that these are more consistent with each other. For instance, consider the character in Figure 4.15. He believes that his plan is a good one, but the numbers provided by Dilbert suggest that it is not. The result? He changes his attitude toward the numbers, concluding that they must be faulty! Changes like this are a common result of cognitive dissonance. Second, we can reduce cognitive dissonance by acquiring new information that supports our attitudes or our behavior. Many persons who smoke, for instance, search for evidence suggesting that the harmful effects of this habit are minimal or only occur for very heavy smokers, or that the benefits (e.g., reduced tension, improved weight control) more than outweigh the costs (Lipkus et al., 2001). Finally, we can decide that the inconsistency actually doesn't matter; in other words, we can engage in **trivialization**—concluding that the attitudes or behaviors in question are not important ones, so any inconsistency between them is insignificant (Simon, Greenberg, & Brehm, 1995).

All of these strategies can be viewed as *direct* approaches to dissonance reduction: they focus on the attitude–behavior discrepancies that are causing the dissonance. Research by Steele and his colleagues (e.g., Steele & Lui, 1983; Steele, 1988), however, indicates that dissonance can also be reduced through *indirect* tactics—ones that leave the basic discrepancy between attitudes and behavior intact but reduce the unpleasant negative feelings generated by dissonance. According to Steele (1988), adoption of such indirect routes to dissonance reduction is most likely to occur when an attitude–behavior discrepancy involves important attitudes or self-beliefs.

FIGURE 4.15

Cognitive Dissonance in Action.

The character in this cartoon illustrates how cognitive dissonance can affect our attitudes—and our thinking!

[SOURCE: DILBERT REPRINTED BY PERMISSION OF UNITED FEATURE SYNDICATE, INC.]

trivialization: A technique for reducing dissonance in which the importance of attitudes and behaviors that are inconsistent with each other is cognitively reduced.

Under these conditions, Steele suggests (e.g., Steele, Spencer, & Lynch, 1993), individuals experiencing dissonance may focus not so much on reducing the gap between their attitudes and behavior as on *self-affirmation*—restoring positive self-evaluations that are threatened by the dissonance (e.g., Elliot & Devine, 1994; Tesser, Martin, & Cornell, 1996). How can they accomplish this goal? By focusing on their positive self-attributes—good things about themselves (e.g., Steele, 1988). For instance, when I experienced dissonance as a result of saying nice things about my neighbor's giant new SUV even though I am strongly against such vehicles, I could have reminded myself that I had recently spoken out against SUVs at a party or that I had served as a volunteer for our local public television station the previous week. Contemplating these positive actions would help reduce the discomfort produced by my failure to act in a way consistent with my proenvironmental attitudes.

Other research suggests, however, that engaging in self-affirmation may not be necessary for dissonance reduction via the indirect route. In fact, almost anything we do that reduces the discomfort and negative affect generated by dissonance can sometimes succeed in this respect—everything from consuming alcohol (e.g., Steele, Southwick, & Critchlow, 1981) to engaging in distracting activities that take one's mind off the dissonance (e.g., Zanna & Aziza, 1976) to simple expressions of positive affect (Cooper, Fazio, & Rhodewalt, 1978).

In sum, dissonance can be reduced in many different ways—through indirect tactics as well as direct ones focused on reducing the attitude–behavior discrepancy. And as we'll soon see, the choice among these various alternatives may be a function of what's available and the specific context in which dissonance occurs (e.g., Fried & Aronson, 1995).

While the tendency to reduce dissonance appears to be quite strong, it can sometimes be overridden by other factors, with the result that people manage to live with even huge gaps between their attitudes and their behavior. For a chilling illustration of this fact, please see the **Beyond the Headlines** section on page 147.

■ IS DISSONANCE REALLY UNPLEASANT? In our comments so far, we've suggested that dissonance is an unpleasant state. This idea certainly fits with our everyday experience: when we say or do things contrary to our true beliefs we often *do* feel uncomfortable as a result of doing so. Until recently, however, there was little direct scientific evidence relating to this issue.

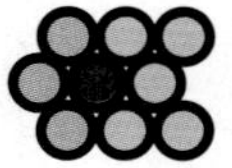

That dissonance is arousing in a physiological sense had been well documented (e.g., Elkin & Leippe, 1986; Losch & Cacioppo, 1990; Steele, Southwick, & Critchlow, 1981). But there was little direct evidence that dissonance is also unpleasant—a central assumption of dissonance theory. (After all, it is this unpleasantness, supposedly, that motivates efforts to reduce dissonance when it occurs). Fortunately, this gap in our knowledge has been closed by more recent research. For example, Elliot and Devine (1994) found that students who wrote an essay arguing against their own views (the students wrote in favor of a large tuition increase) reported high levels of emotional discomfort immediately after writing these essays. In contrast, those who wrote the same kind of essay, then reported on their attitudes toward the tuition hike, and only *then* rated their feelings, reported lower levels of discomfort. This is what dissonance theory would predict, because persons in this latter condition had an opportunity to reduce dissonance by changing their attitudes after writing the essay (making them more favorable to the tuition hike); this would reduce the discomfort they experienced.

There is one serious problem in interpreting these findings, however: the students were told that the essays they wrote (in favor of a tuition increase) would be sent to a university committee that would take their essay into account in recommending for or against the tuition hike to the administration. Thus, it may have been concern over such consequences rather than dissonance itself that generated participants' negative feelings after writing their counterattitudinal essays.

BEYOND THE HEADLINES: AS SOCIAL PSYCHOLOGISTS SEE IT

WHEN A PHYSICAL ADDICTION AND DISSONANCE COLLIDE, GUESS WHICH WINS?

99 Percent Call Smoking Harmful: Poll Discovers Conflict Between Views and Usage

Washington (November 10, 2000)—Although the nation can't agree on who should be president, it appears to be united on the health risks of smoking; 99 percent of Americans say smoking is harmful, according to research released here Tuesday. Nevertheless, two in 10 Americans regularly light up according to the survey sponsored by Mississippi State University. . . . When asked about smoking Americans tend to say one thing and do the other, said Arthur Cosby, director of the University's Social Science Research Center.

Americans are quite conflicted about tobacco control and use, Cosby said. For example, they puff with one breath but acknowledge the danger with the next. Likewise, many adults say teenagers shouldn't smoke, even while lighting up in front of them. . . . The apparent contradiction between belief and behavior could be "a reflection of the power of addiction," Cosby said. Many smokers might not be able to quit even though they are "people who intelligently decide that tobacco-control notions are good things." About 9 of every 10 Americans said parents shouldn't allow underage children to smoke and 93 percent said stores that sell tobacco to minors should be punished . . .

Any poll that yields 99 percent agreement among the people responding to it deserves to be taken seriously, and this one appears to have been conducted quite carefully. The key finding—that virtually everyone agrees that smoking is harmful, yet many people continue to smoke—is definitely food for thought. Cognitive dissonance should be very strong among smokers; after all, if they believe that smoking is harmful to their health, how can they continue to engage in this behavior? This is akin to saying, "Oh well, so I'll do something that will destroy my health and possibly kill me . . . so what?"

As we noted above, smokers have many ways of reducing such dissonance—for instance, convincing themselves that only a few smokers get ill, that such effects occur only for very heavy smokers, or that if smoking doesn't get them, something else will! So this may well be part of the answer. Another possibility, though, is that the physical addiction of smoking is very powerful. Thus, if smokers try to quit their habit, the negative feelings they experience are far stronger than those produced by cognitive dissonance. I have a friend who quit smoking more than thirty years ago, yet, as he often tells me, he *still* craves a cigarette while drinking a cup of coffee after a meal. Experiences like this suggest that smoking is indeed a powerful addiction.

Yet despite this fact, some people (like my friend) do manage to quit. Perhaps for such persons the addiction is not as strong to begin with, or perhaps they are especially disturbed by the inconsistency between their attitudes and their behavior. Whatever the reason, it seems clear that the best technique for avoiding both an addiction to tobacco *and* the dissonance that can result from smoking while recognizing the harmful effects of this behavior is simple: Never start in the first place!

To eliminate this problem, Harmon-Jones (2000) conducted research in which participants wrote counterattitudinal statements under conditions in which expressing views contrary to their real ones could *not* produce aversive consequences. In fact, they were told to throw their statements away after writing them. The issue on which they wrote the essays, too, was fairly trivial: they were to describe a boring paragraph as interesting. Participants were asked to write these statements under one of two conditions: low choice (they were simply told to describe the boring paragraph as interesting) or high choice (they were told that they could describe it any way they wished, but that the experimenter would really appreciate it if they wrote that the dull paragraph was interesting). Only in the high-choice condition, of course, would they be expected to experience dissonance.

After completing their statements, participants indicated their attitude toward the paragraph they read and their affective state—the discomfort they felt (e.g., how uneasy or bothered they were) and general negative affect (e.g., how tense, distressed, and irritable they felt). Results indicated that, as expected, those in the high-choice condition rated the dull paragraph as more interesting. More importantly, persons in this group also reported feeling more discomfort and more general negative affect than those in the low-choice condition (see Figure 4.16). Because the statements they wrote could not have any aversive consequences, these findings suggest that dissonance does indeed produce negative affect, as Festinger (1957) originally proposed.

IS DISSONANCE A UNIVERSAL HUMAN EXPERIENCE? According to dissonance theory, human beings dislike inconsistency. They feel uncomfortable when they perceive it in their attitudes or behavior, and this often leads them to engage in active efforts to reduce it. As we have already seen, a large body of evidence offers support for these ideas, so dissonance theory appears to be a source of important insights into several aspects of social thought. It's important to note, though, that a vast majority of studies on dissonance has been conducted in North America and Western Europe. This raises an important question: Does cognitive dissonance occur in other cultures, too? Although initial studies on this topic yielded mixed results (e.g., Takata & Hashimoto, 1973; Yoshida, 1977), more recent findings reported by Heine and Lehman (1997a) point to the conclusion that dissonance is indeed a universal aspect of human thought—although the factors that produce dissonance and even its magnitude can be influenced by cultural factors. For instance, consider the study by Heine and Lehman (1997a).

These researchers reasoned that although dissonance might well occur all around the world, it could be less likely to influence attitudes in some cultures than in others. Specifically, they suggested that after making a choice between closely ranked alternatives, persons from cultures such as those in the United States and Canada

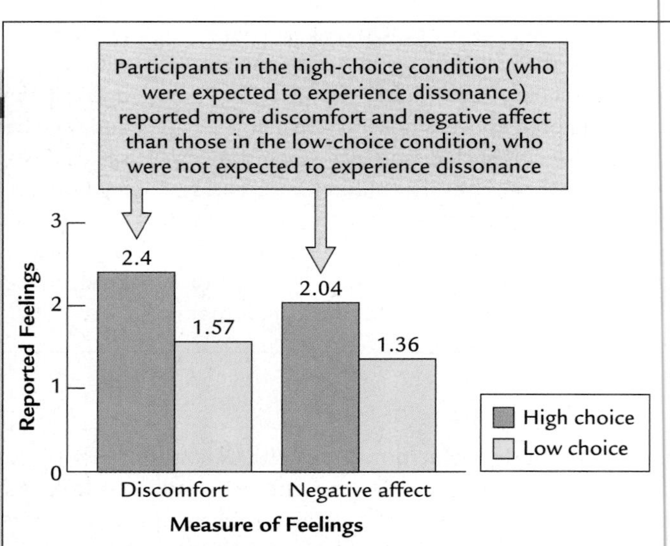

FIGURE 4.16

Evidence That Dissonance Generates Negative Affect. Persons who wrote statements counter to their own attitudes under conditions in which they freely chose to do so reported higher levels of discomfort and general negative affect than did persons who wrote such statements because they were told to do so (low choice).

[SOURCE: BASED ON DATA FROM HARMON-JONES, 2000.]

would be more likely to experience post-decision dissonance than would persons from cultures such as those in Japan and other Asian countries. Why? Because in Western cultures, the *self* is linked to individual actions, such as making correct decisions. After making a choice between alternatives (different courses of action, different objects), individuals in such cultures experience considerable dissonance because the possibility of having made an incorrect choice poses a threat to their self-esteem. After all, in such cultures, making correct choices as individuals is highly valued. In many Asian cultures, in contrast, the self is not as closely linked to individual actions or choices. Rather, it is more strongly tied to roles and status—to an individual's place in society and the obligations this involves (see Figure 4.17). Thus, persons in such cultures should be less likely to perceive the possibility of making an incorrect decision as a threat to their self. As a result, they would also be less likely to experience dissonance.

To test this reasoning, Heine and Lehman (1997a) had both Canadian students and Japanese students temporarily living in Canada choose the ten CDs from a group of 40 CDs that they would most like to own. The participants also evaluated how much they would like each of these ten CDs. At this point, participants were told that they could actually have *either* the CD they ranked fifth or the one they ranked sixth. After making their choices, participants rated the two CDs once again. Previous research suggests that in order to reduce dissonance, individuals who make such decisions often downrate the item they didn't choose while raising their ratings of the item they did choose—an effect known as *spreading of alternatives* (e.g., Steele, Spencer, & Lynch, 1993). The researchers predicted that such effects would be stronger for Canadians than for Japanese participants, and this is precisely what happened. The Canadian students showed the spreading of alternatives effect which results from dissonance reduction to a significant degree; the Japanese students did not.

These findings suggest that cultural factors do indeed influence the operation of dissonance. While all human beings are made somewhat uneasy by inconsistencies between their attitudes or inconsistencies between their attitudes and their behavior, the intensity of such reactions, the precise conditions under which they occur, and the strategies used to reduce them may all be influenced by cultural factors.

FIGURE 4.17

Cultural Factors in the Occurrence of Dissonance.

In Western cultures, the self is linked closely to individual actions or choices. In many Asian cultures, however, the self is more strongly tied to roles and status—to an individual's place in society and the obligations this involves. For these reasons, post-decision dissonance may be stronger for persons from Western cultures than for persons from several Asian cultures. Support for this prediction has been obtained in several studies (e.g., Heine & Lehman, 1997b.)

Even with respect to very basic aspects of social thought, then, it is essential to take careful account of cultural diversity.

Dissonance and Attitude Change: The Effects of Induced Compliance

As we've noted repeatedly, there are many occasions in everyday life when we must say or do things inconsistent with our real attitudes. Social psychologists refer to such situations as ones involving **induced compliance** (or **forced compliance**)—we are induced, somehow, to say or do something contrary to our real views. And, by now, you can probably guess what may happen in such situations: dissonance will be aroused, and when it is, we may feel pressure to change our attitudes so that they are more consistent with our words or other actions. Moreover, we are especially likely to make such changes when other techniques for reducing dissonance are unavailable or require greater effort. (This is a general rule about various techniques for reducing dissonance: All other things being equal, we prefer the technique that requires the least effort.)

■ DISSONANCE AND THE LESS-LEADS-TO-MORE EFFECT. So far, so good. Predictions derived from dissonance theory seem to make good sense. But now consider this question: Will the reasons why you engaged in behavior inconsistent with your attitudes matter? Obviously, we can engage in attitude-discrepant behavior for many reasons, and some of these are stronger or more compelling than others. For instance, remember my friend with the new SUV? If he has recently done several favors for me and I feel very much in his debt, I would have fairly strong reasons for concealing my real views about his new vehicle, and for telling him that I like it. But if, instead, he is about to move to another state and I don't expect to see him again in the future, I would have weaker reasons for saying that I like this giant gas-guzzler. Now for the key question: When will dissonance be stronger—when we have many good reasons for engaging in attitude-discrepant behavior or when we have few such reasons? Dissonance theory offers an unexpected answer: Dissonance will be stronger when we have *few* reasons for engaging in attitude-discrepant behavior. This is so because, under these conditions, we can't explain away our actions to ourselves; we performed them even though there was no strong reason for doing so. The result: Dissonance is quite intense.

In other words, as shown in Figure 4.18, dissonance theory predicts that it may be easier to change individuals' attitudes by offering them *just barely enough* to get them to engage in attitude-discrepant behavior. Additional reasons or rewards beyond this level will reduce dissonance—and subsequent attitude change. Social psychologists sometimes refer to this surprising prediction as the **less-leads-to-more effect**—fewer reasons or rewards lead to more attitude change—and it has been confirmed in many studies (e.g., Riess & Schlenker, 1977). For example, in the first and most famous of these experiments (Festinger & Carlsmith, 1959), participants were offered either a small reward ($1) or a large one ($20) for telling another person that some dull tasks they had just performed were very interesting. One of these tasks involved placing spools on a tray, dumping them out, and repeating the process over and over again. After engaging in the attitude-discrepant behavior—telling another person the dull tasks were interesting—participants were asked to indicate their own liking for these tasks. As predicted by the less-leads-to-more effect, those given the small reward for misleading a stranger actually reported liking the tasks more than those given the large reward.

While this effect has been confirmed many times, we should note that it does not occur under all conditions. Rather, it seems to happen only when several conditions exist (Cooper & Scher, 1994). First, the less-leads-to-more effect occurs only in situations in which people believe that they have a choice as to whether or not to perform the attitude-discrepant behavior. Second, small rewards lead to greater

induced or forced compliance: Situations in which individuals are somehow induced to say or do things inconsistent with their true attitudes.

less-leads-to-more effect: The fact that offering individuals small rewards for engaging in counterattitudinal behavior often produces more dissonance, and so more attitude change, than offering them larger rewards.

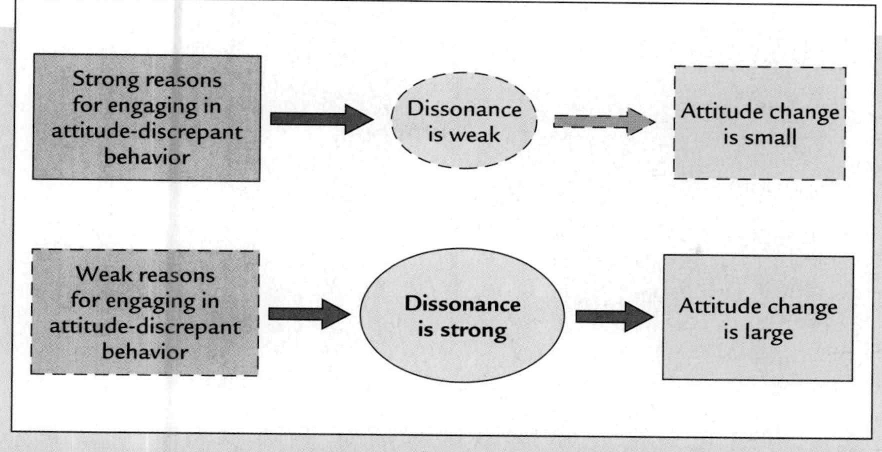

FIGURE 4.18

Why Less (Smaller Inducements) Often Leads to More (Greater Attitude Change) after Attitude-Discrepant Behavior. When individuals have strong reasons for engaging in attitude-discrepant behavior, they experience relatively weak dissonance and weak pressure to change their attitudes. When they have weak reasons for engaging in attitude-discrepant behavior, in contrast, they experience stronger dissonance and stronger pressure to change their attitudes. The result: Less leads to more.

attitude change only when people believe that they were personally responsible for both the chosen course of action and any negative effects it produced. And third, the less-leads-to-more effect does not occur when people view the payment they receive as a bribe rather than as a well-deserved payment for services rendered. Because these conditions do often exist, however, the strategy of offering others just barely enough to induce them to say or do things contrary to their true attitudes can often be an effective technique for inducing attitude change.

Dissonance as a Tool for Beneficial Changes in Behavior: When Hypocrisy Can Be a Force for Good

People who don't wear safety belts are much more likely to die in accidents than those who do. People who smoke heavily are much more likely to suffer from lung cancer and heart disease than those who don't. People who are extremely overweight are much more likely to suffer from diabetes, heart attacks, and many other health problems than persons of normal weight. And people who engage in unprotected sex are much more likely than those who engage in safe sex to contract dangerous diseases, including AIDS.

As we move into the twenty-first century, most persons know these statements are true (e.g., Carey, Morrison-Beedy, & Johnson, 1997), so their attitudes are generally favorable toward using seat belts, quitting smoking, losing weight, and engaging in safe sex. Yet, as you well know, these attitudes are often *not* translated into overt actions: people continue to drive without seat belts, to smoke, and so on (see Figure 4.19 on page 152). What's needed, in other words, is not so much changes in attitudes as shifts in overt behavior. Can dissonance be useful in promoting such beneficial changes? A growing body of evidence suggests that it can (e.g., Gibbons, Eggleston, & Benthin, 1997; Stone et al., 1994), especially when it is used to generate feelings of **hypocrisy**—awareness that one is publicly advocating

hypocrisy: Publicly advocating some attitudes or behavior but then acting in a way that is inconsistent with these attitudes or behavior.

FIGURE 4.19

Health-Related Attitudes and Health-Related Behavior: The Gap Is Often Large. Almost everyone knows the risks involved in failing to wear safety belts, smoking, being much overweight, and engaging in unprotected sex. Yet these attitudes often fail to influence behavior. Techniques based on dissonance theory may be effective in closing this important kind of gap.

some attitude or behavior but then acting in a way that is inconsistent with the attitude or behavior. Under these conditions, several researchers have reasoned (e.g., Aronson, Fried, & Stone, 1991), the individuals involved should experience strong dissonance. Moreover, such feelings would be so intense that adopting indirect modes of dissonance reduction (e.g., distracting oneself, bolstering one's ego by thinking about or engaging in other positively evaluated behaviors) would not do the trick: only actions that reduce dissonance directly, removing the discrepancy between one's words and deeds, would be effective.

These predictions have been tested in several studies. For instance, in one interesting study, Stone and his colleagues (1997) asked participants to prepare a videotape advocating the use of condoms (safe sex) to prevent transmission of HIV. Next, participants were asked to think about reasons why they themselves hadn't used condoms in the past (personal reasons) or reasons why people in general sometimes fail to use condoms (normative reasons that didn't center on their own behavior). The researchers predicted that hypocrisy would be maximized in the personal reasons condition, in which participants had to come face to face with their own hypocrisy. Finally, all persons in the study were given a choice between a direct means of reducing dissonance (purchasing condoms at a reduced price) and an indirect means of reducing dissonance (making a donation to a program designed to aid homeless persons).

Results indicated that when participants had been asked to focus on the reasons why they hadn't engaged in safe sex in the past, an overwhelming majority chose to purchase condoms—the direct route to dissonance reduction. In contrast, when asked to think about reasons why people in general didn't engage in safe sex, more actually chose the indirect route to dissonance reduction—a donation to the aid-the-homeless project (see Figure 4.20).

These findings suggest that using dissonance to generate hypocrisy can indeed be a powerful tool for changing people's behavior in desirable ways—ones that protect their health and safety. To be maximally effective, however, such procedures must involve several elements: The persons in question must publicly advocate the desired behaviors (e.g., using condoms, wearing safety belts), must be induced to think about their own failures to show these behaviors in the past, and must be given access to direct means for reducing their dissonance. When these conditions are met, beneficial changes in behavior can definitely follow.

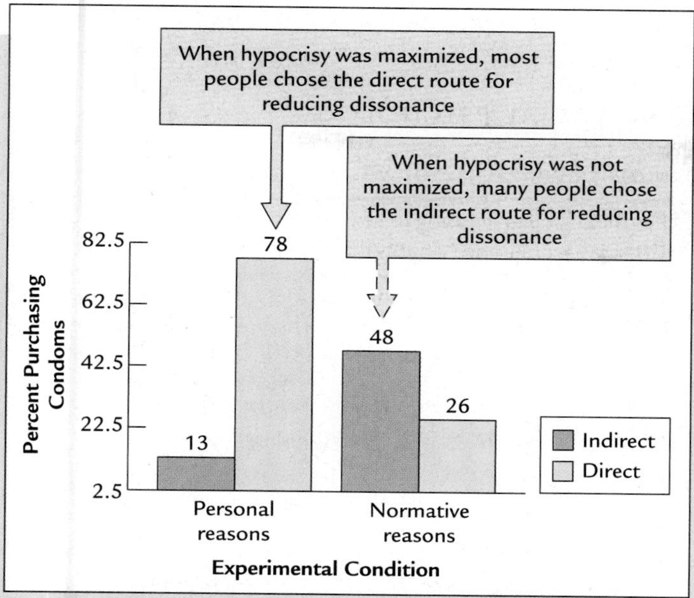

FIGURE 4.20

Using Hypocrisy to Change Behavior.
When individuals were made to confront their own hypocrisy—by being asked to list reasons why they hadn't engaged in safe sex in the past—most chose to reduce such dissonance through direct means (by purchasing condoms). In contrast, when individuals were asked to think about reasons why people in general didn't engage in safe sex, many chose to reduce dissonance via an indirect route (making a donation to an aid-the-homeless project).
[SOURCE: BASED ON DATA FROM STONE ET AL., 1997.]

KEY POINTS

- *Cognitive dissonance* is an unpleasant state that occurs when we notice discrepancies between our attitudes or between our attitudes and behavior. Research indicates that it does indeed produce negative affect.
- Dissonance often occurs in situations involving *induced (forced) compliance*—ones in which we are induced by external factors to say or do things that are inconsistent with our true attitudes.
- In such situations, attitude change is maximum when we have reasons that are barely sufficient to get us to engage in attitude-discrepant behavior. Stronger reasons (or larger rewards) produce less attitude change—the *less-leads-to-more effect.*
- Dissonance induced through *hypocrisy*—inducing individuals to advocate certain attitudes or behaviors and then reminding them that they haven't always behaved in ways consistent with these—can be a powerful tool for inducing beneficial changes in behavior.
- Dissonance appears to be a universal aspect of social thought, but the conditions under which it occurs and the tactics individuals choose to reduce it appear to be influenced by cultural factors.

CONNECTIONS: INTEGRATING SOCIAL PSYCHOLOGY

IN THIS CHAPTER, YOU READ ABOUT . . .	IN OTHER CHAPTERS, YOU WILL FIND RELATED DISCUSSIONS OF . . .
the role of social learning in attitude formation	the role of social learning in several forms of social behavior—attraction (Chapter 5), helping (Chapter 10), and aggression (Chapter 11)
persuasion and resistance to persuasion	other techniques for changing attitudes and behavior and why they are effective or ineffective (Chapter 9), the use of persuasive techniques in health-related messages (Chapter 13), and leadership (Chapter 12)
cognitive dissonance	the role of cognitive dissonance in various attitudes and forms of social behavior; for example, job satisfaction (Chapter 13)

THINKING ABOUT CONNECTIONS

1. Suppose you wanted to launch a campaign to persuade adults of all ages to engage in safe sex (e.g., use condoms). What specific features would you include in this program in order to maximize its effectiveness and so improve the health of large numbers of persons (see Chapter 13)?
2. If we are so resistant to persuasion, why does advertising work? Or does it?
3. If attitudes are learned, it is reasonable to suggest that the mass media (television, films, magazines) are important factors in attitude formation. What do you think the media are currently teaching children about key aspects of social behavior—love and sexual relations (Chapters 7 and 8), aggression (Chapter 11), honesty and integrity (Chapters 5 and 12)? Would you change any of this if you could?

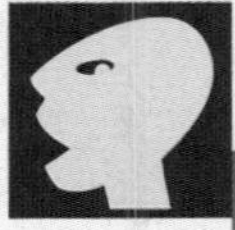

IDEAS TO TAKE WITH YOU—AND USE!

RESISTING PERSUASION: SOME USEFUL STEPS

Each day, we are exposed to many attempts to change our attitudes. Advertisers, politicians, charities—all seek to exert this kind of influence upon us. How can you resist such efforts, which are often highly skilled? Here are some suggestions, based on the research findings of social psychology.

View Attempts at Persuasion as Assaults on Your Personal Freedom.

No one likes being told what to do; but, in a sense, this is precisely what advertisers, politicians, and the like are *trying* to do when they attempt to change your attitudes. So, when you are on the receiving end of such appeals, remind yourself that *you* are in charge of your own life and that there's no reason to listen to or accept what these would-be persuaders tell you.

Recognize Attempts at Persuasion When You See Them.

As we noted earlier, knowing that someone is trying to persuade you—being forewarned—is often useful from the point of view of resisting efforts at persuasion. So, whenever you encounter someone or some organization that seeks to influence your views, remind yourself that no matter how charming or friendly they

are, *persuasion* is their goal. This will help you resist.

Remind Yourself of Your Own Views and How These Differ from the Ones Being Urged upon You.

While biased assimilation—the tendency to perceive views different from our own as unconvincing and unreliable—can prevent us from absorbing potentially useful information, it is also an effective means for resisting persuasion. When others offer views different from your own as part of a persuasive appeal, focus on how different these ideas are from those you hold. The rest will often take care of itself!

Actively Counterargue in Your Own Mind against the Views Being "Pushed" on You by Others.

The more arguments against such views that you can generate, the less likely these views are to influence you.

SUMMARY AND REVIEW OF KEY POINTS

Attitude Formation: How—and Why—Attitudes Develop

- *Attitudes* are evaluations of any aspect of the social world. Often, attitudes are *ambivalent*—we evaluate the attitude object both positively and negatively.
- Attitudes are often acquired from other persons through *social learning*. Such learning can involve *classical conditioning, instrumental conditioning,* or *observational learning*.
- Attitudes are also formed on the basis of *social comparison*—our tendency to compare ourselves with others to determine whether our view of social reality is or is not correct. In order to be similar to others we like or respect, we accept the attitudes that they hold.
- Studies conducted with identical twins suggest that attitudes may also be influenced by genetic factors, although the magnitude of such effects varies greatly across different attitudes.

The Attitude–Behavior Link: When—and How—Attitudes Influence Behavior

- Several factors affect the strength of the relationship between attitudes and behavior; some of these relate to the situation in which the attitudes are activated, and some relate to aspects of the attitudes themselves.
- Situational constraints may prevent us from expressing our attitudes overtly. In addition, we tend to prefer situations that allow us to express our attitudes, and this may further strengthen these views.
- Several aspects of attitudes themselves also moderate the attitude-behavior link. These include attitude origins (how attitudes were formed), attitude strength (which includes *attitude accessibility,* knowledge, importance, and vested interest), and attitude specificity.
- Attitudes seem to influence behavior through two different mechanisms. When we can give careful thought to our attitudes, intentions derived from our attitudes strongly predict behavior. In situations in which we can't engage in such deliberate thought, attitudes influence behavior by shaping our perceptions of the situation.

The Fine Art of Persuasion: Using Messages to Change Attitudes

- Early research on *persuasion*—efforts to change attitudes through the use of messages—focused primarily on characteristics of the communicator (e.g., expertise, attractiveness), message (e.g., one-sidedness versus two-sidedness), and audience.

- More recent research has sought to understand the cognitive processes that play a role in persuasion. Such research suggests that we process persuasive messages in two distinct ways: through *systematic processing,* which involves careful attention to message content, or through *heuristic processing,* which involves the use of mental shortcuts (e.g., "experts are usually right").

When Attitude Change Fails: Resistance to Persuasion

- Our attitudes tend to remain quite stable despite many efforts to change them. Several factors contribute to such resistance to persuasion.

- One such factor is *reactance*—negative reactions to efforts by others to reduce or limit our personal freedom.

- Resistance to persuasion is often increased by *forewarning*—the knowledge that someone is trying to change our attitudes—and by *selective avoidance*—the tendency to avoid exposure to information that contradicts our views.

- In addition, when we are exposed to persuasive messages contrary to our existing views, we actively counterargue against the information they contain. This, too, increases our resistance to persuasion.

- If we receive arguments against our views along with arguments that refute these counterattitudinal positions, our resistance to subsequent persuasion increases; this is sometimes known as inoculation against counterattitudinal views.

- Two additional processes—*biased assimilation* and *attitude polarization*—also play a role in resistance to persuasion. Biased assimilation refers to our tendency to evaluate information inconsistent with our attitudes as less reliable or convincing than information consistent with our views. Attitude polarization refers to the tendency to interpret mixed evidence in ways that strengthen our existing views and make them more extreme.

Cognitive Dissonance: Why Our Behavior Can Sometimes Influence Our Attitudes

- *Cognitive dissonance* is an unpleasant state that occurs when we notice discrepancies between our attitudes or our attitudes and behavior. Research indicates that it does indeed produce negative affect.

- Dissonance often occurs in situations involving *induced (forced) compliance*—ones in which we are induced by external factors to say or do things that are inconsistent with our true attitudes.

- In such situations, attitude change is maximum when we have reasons that are barely sufficient to get us to engage in attitude-discrepant behavior. Stronger reasons (or larger rewards) produce *less* attitude change—the *less-leads-to-more effect.*

- Dissonance induced through *hypocrisy*—inducing individuals to advocate certain attitudes or behaviors and then reminding them that they haven't always behaved in ways consistent with these—can be a powerful tool for inducing beneficial changes in behavior.

- Dissonance appears to be a universal aspect of social thought, but the conditions under which it occurs and the tactics individuals choose to reduce it appear to be influenced by cultural factors.

KEY TERMS

attitude ambivalence (p. 118)
attitude polarization (p. 143)
attitude-to-behavior process model (p. 134)
attitudes (p. 118)
biased assimilation (p. 143)
central route (to persuasion) (p. 138)
classical conditioning (p. 121)
cognitive dissonance (p. 144)
elaboration likelihood model (of persuasion) (p. 138)
forewarning (p. 141)
heuristic processing (p. 138)
hypocrisy (p. 151)
induced or forced compliance (p. 150)
instrumental conditioning (p. 122)
less-leads-to-more effect (p. 150)
observational learning (p. 123)
peripheral route (to persuasion) (p. 138)
persuasion (p. 136)
reactance (p. 140)
selective avoidance (p. 141)
social comparison (p. 123)
social learning (p. 121)
subliminal conditioning (of attitudes) (p. 122)
systematic processing (p. 138)
theory of planned behavior (p. 133)
theory of reasoned action (p. 132)
trivialization (p. 145)

FOR MORE INFORMATION

Gollwitzer, P. M., & Barth, J. A. (1996). *The psychology of action: Linking motivation and cognition in behavior.* New York: Guilford.

- A collection of insightful chapters focused on efforts by social psychologists to understand one of the essential puzzles of life: Why other people behave in the way that they do.

Harmon-Jones, E., & Mills, J. (Eds.). (1999). *Cognitive dissonance: Progress on a pivotal theory in social psychology.* Washington, DC: American Psychological Association.

- This interesting book describes recent studies and findings concerning cognitive dissonance—one of the most influential theories in the history of social psychology.

Shavitt, S., & Brock, T. C. (1994). *Persuasion: Psychological insights and perspectives.* Boston: Allyn and Bacon.

- This book explores all aspects of persuasion. The chapters on when and how attitudes influence behavior, cognitive dissonance, and the cognitive perspective on persuasion are all excellent.

Alexandra Rozenman, *Early Fall.* 16 × 20", oil on canvas. © Alexandra Rozenman. Used with kind permission of the artist.

5 ASPECTS OF SOCIAL IDENTITY: SELF AND GENDER

CHAPTER OUTLINE

For a great many years, much of whatever leisure time I (DB) can find has been spent reading fiction. There is more than enough factual stuff in my real life. In any event, much of my reading involves crime, detectives, and the courtroom—far away from life in a University. Beyond old and new favorites, from Dashiell Hammett and Agatha Christie to Kathy Reichs and John Grisham, I am always looking for new authors to add to my list. A few years ago, I stumbled onto Ellis Peters whose "detective" is an unusual character. Brother Cadfael is a Benedictine monk in twelfth-century England. In his younger days, Brother Cadfael was a soldier in the Crusades, and he did not enter a religious order until fairly late in his life. I thought that Peters captured very well the way in which this tough fighting man had become a gentle monk whose worldly knowledge was applied to creating medicines and solving mysteries. One wonders how much of the author's life experiences might be reflected in his creations. Had Peters once been a soldier? Had he ever contemplated joining a religious order?

Then, quite recently, I read the dust jacket on one of the twenty-one books for the first time. To my surprise, I discovered that Ellis Peters is the pen name used by the late Edith Pargeter. Though I had until then assumed that I had been reading the work of a male author, I suddenly realized that he was a she. I wondered why an accomplished female writer decided to write this series using a male name. Did she assume that it would make a difference in her writing or in her readership? Why should gender matter at all? The books, the printed words, and the characters are the same regardless of the maleness or femaleness of the author. Nevertheless, knowing that "Ellis Peters" was a woman led me to rethink what I had read. The author was not a male who was reflected in the character of Brother Cadfael but a female who had done something much more difficult in creating a very believable member of the other gender. I was impressed by her work, and I wanted to explore further my own possibly sexist reactions to it, so I am now rereading the books with a totally different mental set.

The fact that the Brother Cadfael novels seem different (more creative in fact) because they were written by a woman rather than a man does not sound at all reasonable to me. We tend to assume far too much about other people and the work they do on the basis of assumptions and beliefs about what it means to be a man or a woman. We have stereotypes about gender just as we do about race, ethnicity, and sexual orientation. As with other stereotypes, we are sometimes right and often wrong (see Chapter 6).

But we don't simply make assumptions about others on the basis of broad categories; we also make assumptions about ourselves on the basis of whatever categories we perceive as relevant. What effects do these self-categorizations have on our attitudes, beliefs, and behavior?

In this chapter, we will examine such effects. First, we will provide an overview of the concept of *social identity* and then turn our attention to two of the major components of social identity: *self* and *gender.* We will describe many of the crucial elements that make up the self, including self-concept, self-esteem, self-focusing, self-monitoring, and self-efficacy. Then, we will examine gender, especially the social determinants of gender identity, gender roles, and the way behavior is influenced by these attributes.

Social Identity: An Overview

Very early in life, each of us begins acquiring a view of who he is or who she is, including whether we should be labeled "girl" or "boy." That is, we each develop a **social identity,** a self-definition that guides precisely how we conceptualize and evaluate ourselves (Deaux, 1993). Social identity includes many unique characteristics, such as one's name and *self-concept* as well as many other characteristics that we share with others (Sherman, 1994). Among the latter are gender, our interpersonal relationships (daughter, son, spouse, parent, etc.); our vocations or avocations (student, musician, psychologist, surfer, jock, bird-watcher, etc.); political or ideological affiliations (feminist, environmentalist, Democrat, Republican, vegetarian, etc.); specific attributes (homosexual, bright, disabled, short, handsome, etc.); and ethnicity or religious affiliation (Catholic, Southerner, Hispanic, Jew, African American, Muslim, atheist, hick, etc.) (Deaux et al., 1995).

When we interact with strangers and are totally anonymous (as on the Internet) in contrast to interacting with strangers we can see (as on video), we increasingly tend to categorize ourselves in terms of such groups, to feel positively about the groups, and to stereotype others on the basis of the groups to which they belong (Lea, Spears, & de Groot, 2001).

According to Jackson and Smith (1999), social identity can best be conceptualized along four dimensions: perception of the intergroup context, in-group attraction, interdependency of beliefs, and depersonalization, as outlined in Figure 5.1. The role that social identity plays in intergroup relationships depends on which dimensions are operating. Jackson and Smith (1999) suggest that underlying the four dimensions are two basic types of social identity: secure and insecure. When there is a

social identity: A person's definition of who he or she is, including personal attributes and attributes shared with others, such as gender and race.

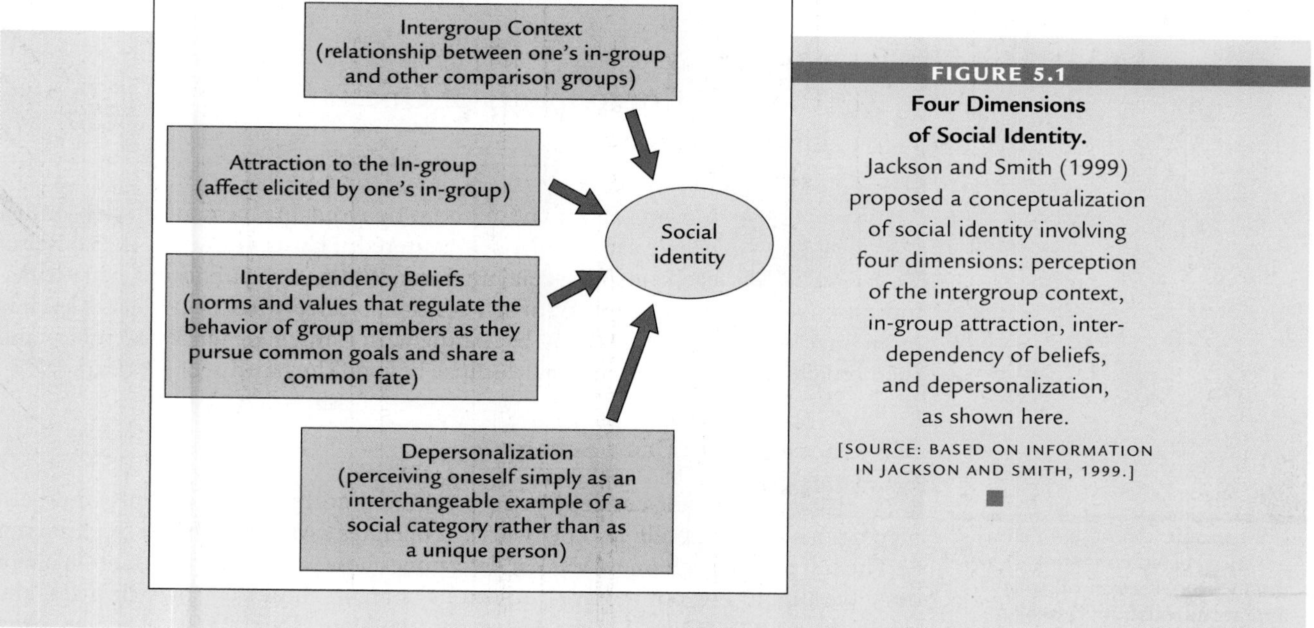

FIGURE 5.1
Four Dimensions of Social Identity.
Jackson and Smith (1999) proposed a conceptualization of social identity involving four dimensions: perception of the intergroup context, in-group attraction, interdependency of beliefs, and depersonalization, as shown here.
[SOURCE: BASED ON INFORMATION IN JACKSON AND SMITH, 1999.]

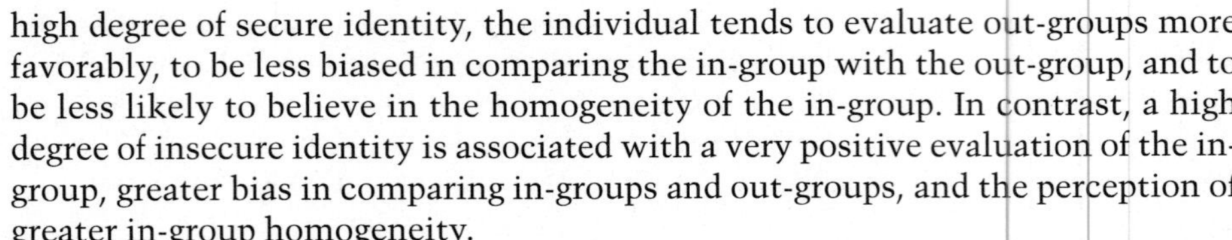

high degree of secure identity, the individual tends to evaluate out-groups more favorably, to be less biased in comparing the in-group with the out-group, and to be less likely to believe in the homogeneity of the in-group. In contrast, a high degree of insecure identity is associated with a very positive evaluation of the in-group, greater bias in comparing in-groups and out-groups, and the perception of greater in-group homogeneity.

Despite the obvious fact that we acquire many aspects of our identity from other people, who we are is in part determined by heredity. Physical characteristics such as sex, race, and hair color are obvious examples, but there are other genetic influences as well. One approach to determining such influences is to compare identical twins with fraternal twins; a genetic factor is indicated when identical twins are more similar with respect to a given characteristic than are fraternal twins. Hur, McGue, and Iacono (1998) compared several hundred pairs of the two types of twin girls (aged eleven and twelve) with respect to how similar they were in various aspects of social identity. About a third of the variation in the girls' self-concepts was attributable to genetic differences. The greatest genetic effects were on self-perceived popularity and physical appearance, but there were significant, though smaller, effects on perceptions of anxiety, happiness, and academic ability. Part of who we are and how we perceive ourselves is based on inborn factors.

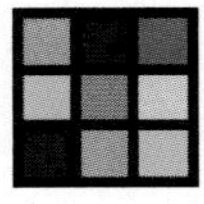

The many categories that make up social identity are tied to the interpersonal world. They indicate the extent to which we are like and unlike those around us. When a person's social context changes, developing a new social identity can be a major source of stress (Sussman, 2000). Individuals cope with such stress in a variety of ways (see Chapter 13). For example, when Hispanic students in the United States leave a subculture in which they are the majority and enter a primarily Anglo subculture—as when they enter college or become employees in an organization—the resulting stress often leads to one of two common reactions. One alternative is to become increasingly *more* identified with and involved in Hispanic activities, Spanish-speaking groups, Hispanic music and clothing styles, and so forth. The result is a stronger identification with the ethnic aspects of social identity. This kind of collective identity can become politicized as a struggle for power and influence in the surrounding culture (Simon & Klandermans, 2001). The opposite reaction is to become *less* identified with Hispanic matters, perhaps even adopting an Anglo version of one's name, learning to speak without an accent, and generally becoming *assimilated* and indistinguishable from others in the majority culture (Ethier & Deaux, 1994).

The Self: Components of One's Unique Identity

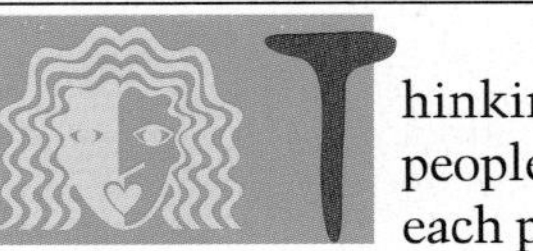

Thinking about oneself is an unavoidable human activity—most people are literally self-centered. That is, the self is the center of each person's social universe. While, as we indicated, genetic factors play a role, one's self-identity, or self-concept, is largely based on what is learned in interactions with other people—beginning with immediate family members and then broadening to interactions with those beyond the family (Lau & Pun, 1999).

Self-Concept: The Basic Schema

The **self-concept** is an organized collection of beliefs and self-perceptions about oneself. In other words, it operates as a basic schema (see Chapter 3). The self provides a framework that determines how we process information about ourselves, including our motives, emotional states, self-evaluations, abilities, and much else besides (Klein, Loftus, & Burton, 1989; Van Hook & Higgins, 1988). And

self-concept: One's self-identity, a basic schema consisting of an organized collection of beliefs and attitudes about oneself.

we work very hard to protect our self-image from threatening information (Sedikides & Green, 2000), to maintain self-consistency (Tschanz & Rhodewalt, 2001), and to find excuses for any inconsistencies (Schlenker, Pontari, & Christopher, 2001).

Thus, people tend to resist change and to misconstrue or explain away information that is inconsistent with their self-concepts. Such defensive reactions are reduced when an individual has an unrelated, self-affirming experience. For example, assume that a person places a high value on his or her sense of humor and is asked to write about or think about a situation in which being humorous had a positive effect. Afterward, that individual is more open to new information and less defensive about potentially threatening information about the self (Cohen, Aronson, & Steele, 2000). In general, when attention is focused on some unrelated aspect of one's identity (in this example, being humorous), the result is more openness to information and less defensiveness. In a similar way, discovering that other people like you reduces defensiveness (Schimel et al., 2001).

Sedikides and Skowronski (1997) propose that the self evolved as an adaptive characteristic. The first aspect to emerge was **subjective self-awareness;** this involves the ability of the organism to differentiate itself to some degree from its physical and social environment. It seems obvious that plants don't have subjective self-awareness, but most animals *do* share this characteristic, and it increases the odds of survival (Damasio, 1994; Lewis, 1992). A few animals (the primates) eventually developed **objective self-awareness**—the organism's capacity to be the object of its own attention (Gallup, 1994), to be aware of its own state of mind (Cheney & Seyfarth, 1992), and "to know it knows, to remember it remembers" (Lewis, 1992, p. 124). See Figure 5.2 for an example of research on objective self-awareness

FIGURE 5.2

Objective Self-Awareness: Recognizing Oneself.

Only among primates, such as the chimp shown here and humans, does there appear to be *objective self-awareness*—including the capacity to be aware of oneself. When a red spot is placed on the forehead of a chimpanzee, it can't be seen by the animal except in a mirror. The fact that seeing this image in the mirror leads a chimp to touch its own forehead is powerful evidence that there is some recognition that the reflected image is himself.

subjective self-awareness: The ability of an organism to differentiate itself, however crudely, from its physical and social environment.

objective self-awareness: An organism's capacity to be the object of its own attention, to be aware of its own state of mind, and to know that it knows and remember that it remembers.

in chimpanzees. Only humans seem to have reached a third level of self-functioning—**symbolic self-awareness**—the ability to form an abstract cognitive representation of self through language. This representation, in turn, makes it possible for us to communicate, form relationships, set goals, evaluate outcomes, develop self-related attitudes, and defend ourselves against threatening communications. Throughout each person's life, interactions with others in many different contexts continue to influence and to modify the specific contents of that person's self-identity.

■ WHAT MAKES UP THE SELF-CONCEPT AND HOW DOES IT FUNCTION? Who are you? Before you read further, try to give twenty different answers to that question.

Questions such as "Who are you?" and "Who am I?" have been asked for more than a hundred years as psychologists, beginning with William James (1890), have endeavored to determine the specific content of the individual self-concept (Ziller, 1990). This technique was used by Rentsch and Heffner (1994) when they asked over two hundred college students to give repeated answers to the question "Who are you?" The basic content of the self, as perceived by these students, consisted of eight categories. Some of these refer to aspects of social identity (nationality, race, etc.) and others refer to personal attributes (relationships, hobbies, etc.).

Self-schemas are probably much more complex and detailed than can be determined by questions about who you are. Consider some of the possibilities. Beyond an overall framework, a self-schema would include your past experiences, your detailed knowledge about what you are like now as opposed to in the past, and your expectancies about the changes you will undergo in the future. In other words, a self-schema is the sum of everything a person remembers, knows, and can imagine about herself or himself. A self-schema also plays a role in guiding behavior (Kendzierski & Whitaker, 1997). For example, the intention to lose weight is quite common, but the ability to link that intention to mildly unpleasant behaviors (dieting, exercising on a very hot day) requires a consistent guiding force. It helps to have a clear conceptualization of who you are now and who you want to be in the future. Otherwise, it is much easier simply to eat and drink whatever you want and avoid working up a sweat.

Because the self is the center of each person's social world and because self-schemas are very well developed, it follows that we are able to do a better job of processing self-relevant information than anything else. This phenomenon is known as the **self-reference effect.** For example, because my last name is Byrne, I tend to pay attention to, remember, and retrieve information involving that name more efficiently than any other name—and more so than would be likely for a non-Byrne. That is, I am well aware of Gabriel Byrne, the Irish actor; Jane Byrne, the former mayor of Chicago; David Byrne, the lead singer of the Talking Heads; Brendan Byrne, the former governor of New Jersey; and Barbara Byrne, whose work on social self-concept is discussed later in this chapter—even though I have never met or even seen any of these individuals in person. Similarly, you would expect that the co-author of this book would do much better at supplying a list of people named Baron.

The self-reference effect is much broader than simply one's name, however. We are even biased toward those letters of the alphabet that are in our names and the numbers that make up our birth dates (Koole, Dijksterhuis, & van Knippenberg, 2001).

Imagine that you participate in an experiment in which you are shown a series of words and asked about each one, "Does this word describe you?" Compare that with a different experimental condition involving the same series of words, but the question about each is, "Is this word printed in big letters?" In which condition do you think you would remember more of the words afterward? Research participants remember many more of the words in the condition in which they are asked about self-description. That question made the words self-relevant, and thus more likely to receive attention, to be retained in memory, and to be recalled easily (Higgins & Bargh, 1987). The basic reason for this effect is that self-relevant material is

symbolic self-awareness: An organism's ability to form an abstract concept of self through language. This ability enables the organism to communicate, form relationships, set goals, evaluate outcomes, develop self-related attitudes, and defend itself against threatening communications.

self-reference effect: The effect on attention and memory that occurs because the cognitive processing of information relevant to the self is more efficient than the processing of other types of information.

processed more efficiently (Klein & Loftus, 1988). That is, we spend more time thinking about words or events that are relevant to ourselves (*elaborative processing*), and we organize self-relevant information in categories that are already present (*categorical processing*). There is even evidence from studies of brain activation that while memory encoding processes involve the left frontal regions of the brain, self-related information is encoded there *and* in the right frontal lobe (Craik et al., 1999). Thus, the self-reference effect has a neurological as well as a psychological basis.

■ HOW IS THE SELF-CONCEPT STRUCTURED? Though we each possess a self-concept, the content of this schema can be organized in various ways. For example, self-conceptions can be relatively *central* or relatively *peripheral* (Sedikides, 1995). Central self-conceptions are more extreme (positive or negative) than peripheral self-conceptions. You might think of yourself as extremely bright and extremely attractive (central) but only moderately good at math and moderately strong (peripheral). Would these self-assessments be affected by your mood? When research participants are induced to feel sad, neutral, or happy, peripheral self-conceptions are influenced by the mood manipulation, but central self-conceptions are not. In the example just given, even when you are very sad you should continue to perceive yourself as bright and attractive, but you may devalue your math ability and your strength. It is more difficult to bring about change in central self-conceptions than in peripheral ones because central self-concepts are elaborated in greater detail, more strongly consolidated, and held with greater certainty.

■ SEXUAL SELF-CONCEPT. Self-concept can also be divided into specific *content areas.* For example, Andersen and Cyranowski (1994) have conducted research on **sexual self-schema**—the cognitive representations of the sexual aspects of self. These investigators first studied women and were able to identify three distinct types of sexual schemas. The research participants described themselves in terms of being passionate and romantic (warm, loving, sympathetic), open and direct (frank, outspoken, uninhibited), or embarrassed and conservative (cautious, self-conscious, timid). Further, the women's sexual attitudes, emotional reactions, and behavior were based on the one specific schema that was most characteristic of them. For example, women with relatively positive sexual self-schemas (romantic/passionate or open/direct) report being more sexually active, engaging in more varied sexual activity and having more sexual partners than women with negative sexual self-schema (embarrassed/conservative). Such schemas also determine the way they remember personal sexual–romantic experiences, predict future behavior in sexual–romantic situations, and make sexually relevant judgments about themselves (Cyranowski & Andersen, 2000).

In research with male participants, Andersen, Cyranowski, and Espindle (1999) also found three dimensions of sexual self-schemas, but these were somewhat different from those of females. Men also express a passionate/loving dimension (sensitive and sensual) and one that is closed-minded and conservative. Unique among men, however, is a powerful/aggressive schema (exciting, domineering, spontaneous). As with women, these schemas are associated with sexual behavior. Men high on the passionate/loving dimension report greater arousal during sexual activities, more love toward their partners, and a tendency to form long-term relationships. The powerful/aggressive dimension is associated with number of sexual activities, number of one-night stands, number of sexual partners, sexually coercive behavior, and sex without commitment.

In many respects, men and women have similar sexual schemas. Both males and females reveal a primary dimension involving passion and romance, and both describe themselves on a dimension that involves such concepts as open-minded and broad-minded. Two major gender differences were obvious. First, many women

sexual self-schema: Cognitive representations of the sexual aspects of oneself.

have the quite negative schema of embarrassed/conservative that suggests anxiety and guilt in response to sex—men do not ordinarily respond in this way. Men have a schema based on behavioral traits involving aggression and power—this is not characteristic of women.

These findings can be summarized as suggesting that a major source of conflict in female sexuality centers on positive and negative reactions to sexuality. For males, the conflict is between being passionate and loving on the one hand and aggressive and domineering on the other.

■ SOCIAL SELF-CONCEPT. In addition to the unique identity that is sometimes labeled the personal self-concept, there are also social aspects of the self that we share with others (Brewer & Gardner, 1996). It is not simply that we form associations, for example, with a given ethnic group. Rather, the self is actually defined differently, depending on our ethnic affiliation. Part of who we are and how we think of ourselves is determined by a collective identity that is the **social self** (as opposed to the personal self). The social self, in turn, consists of two components: (1) that derived from interpersonal relationships and (2) that derived from belonging to larger, less personal groupings such as race, ethnicity, or culture. Such relationships and categories become part of the self (Smith & Henry, 1996). Baumeister and Leary (1995) argue that the social self is based on a fundamental "need to belong" that is a genetically based characteristic of humans. In Chapter 7, we describe relevant work on the biological basis of the need for affiliation.

When interactions are considered with respect to self, it becomes necessary to take the context into account. Instead of the question we asked earlier—"Who are you?"—consider a slightly different question: "Who are you . . . when . . . ?" Mendoza-Denton and his colleagues (2001) gave research participants one of two different types of a sentence-completion task. The sentence structure "I am a (an) ________" prompted global, traitlike self-descriptions of the kind we noted earlier (e.g., "I am an ambitious person."). The other kind of sentence structure was "I am a (an) ________ when ________." This situational context prompted responses such as "I am an ambitious person when a professor provides me with a challenge." With these conditional, situation-based prompts, the responses were less extreme and less bound by stereotypes.

When we examine the role of interpersonal relationships in the self-concept, we necessarily consider a situational context in that a relationship includes someone else. For example, Byrne and Shavelson (1996) categorized the social interactions of young people into those involving school and those involving family, and these can be further categorized in terms of teachers and classmates, siblings and parents, and so on, as outlined in Figure 5.3. These investigators studied three age groups (preadolescents, early adolescents, and late adolescents) and found that the social self-concept becomes increasingly differentiated and better defined with age.

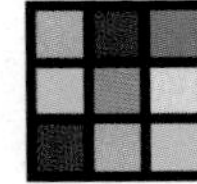

Because self-concepts develop in a cultural context, one would expect differences across cultures. Specific factors influence developmental differences, such as the relatively less positive self-concepts of young Palestinians living in Jordanian refugee camps (Al-Simadi & Atoum, 2000) and the lack of independence and responsibility among children raised in the autocratic setting of traditional Arab families and schools (Abu-Hilal & Bahri, 2000). Among Chinese secondary school students in Hong Kong, a cohesive, achieving family environment is found to be associated with a more positive self-concept and less depression (Lau & Kwok, 2000).

social self: A collective identity that includes interpersonal relationships plus those aspects of identity that are derived from membership in larger, less personal groups based on race, ethnicity, and culture.

Much of the research interest in cultural differences has centered on the effects of individualism versus collectivism on the self-concept. Apparently unique to the Western world is the norm prescribing that self-interest is and *ought to be* a central determinant of one's behavior (Miller, 1999). In much of the rest of the world, the emphasis is more on the welfare of the group than of the individual. As one

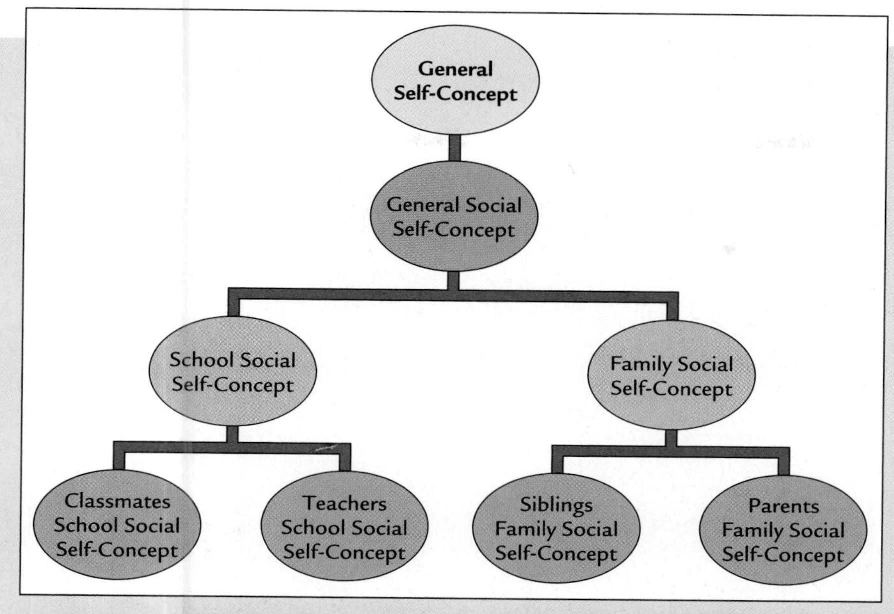

FIGURE 5.3

Social Self-Concept.

Each person's overall self-concept is composed of many distinct components that provide schemas for specific aspects of one's life. One such component, social interaction, is shown here. For young people, this social self-concept can be further divided into more specific categories such as social interactions at school and social interactions within the family. Within each, a further specification is interactions with classmates versus teachers and with parents versus siblings.

[SOURCE: BASED ON INFORMATION IN BYRNE & SHAVELSON, 1996.]

example, Kitayama and his colleagues (1997) proposed that people raised in Western, individualistic cultures learn that everyday life involves opportunities for self-enhancement. In effect, the individual self-concept is more important than the social or collective self-concept (Gaertner, Sedikides, & Graetz, 1999). In Eastern, collectivist cultures, however, everyday life provides opportunities for self-criticism and self-improvement. Such improvement makes one a better member of the family and of other groups. For example, Japanese college students are more self-critical than are either European or Asian Canadians, but they are not as unhappy about discovering their deficiencies (Heine & Lehman, 1999).

Studies of students in Japan and the United States found not only the self-enhancing versus the self-criticizing differences, but also a general tendency for Americans to emphasize the individual and Japanese to emphasize the group. Analogous results are found in other research comparing Japanese and American students (Regan, Snyder, & Kassin, 1995), Chinese students in Hong Kong with their North American counterparts (Yik, Bond, & Paulhus, 1998), and Japanese and Canadian students (Heine & Lehman, 1997b).

In addition to comparing Japanese and American students in this respect, Kanagawa, Cross, and Markus (2001) also examined the specific situational arrangement in which the participants were asked to describe themselves: in a group, with a faculty member, with a peer, and alone. The investigators found self-concept variations as a function of the culture, of the situation, and of the interaction of the two.

FIGURE 5.4
Cultural Differences in the Self-Concept.
When Japanese and American students are asked to describe themselves, they tend to be similar in some respects and different in others. Representatives from a collectivist culture such as Japan tend to express a self-critical orientation that motivates self-improvement aimed at adapting to the needs of a group. In an individualistic culture such as the United States, the self tends to reflect each person's unique, positive attributes that are stable over time and across situations.
[SOURCE: BASED ON INFORMATION IN KANAGAWA, CROSS, & MARKUS, 2001.]

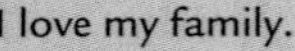

Figure 5.4 depicts some of the ways in which Japanese and American students differ. The Japanese students were not only more self-critical, but also more affected by the situation than was true for the Americans. In terms of content, Americans were more likely than the Japanese respondents to provide self-descriptions in terms of abstract, internal attributes, and they also made more references to friends and family. The Japanese students, more than the Americans, described themselves in terms of physical attributes and appearance, activities, the immediate situations, and possessions. In each of the categories, Americans generated more positive self-descriptions than did the Japanese.

The most general conclusion of these various cross-cultural findings is that a statement such as "just be yourself" has different meanings in different cultures (Kanagawa, Cross, & Markus, 2001). A person raised in an individualistic culture assumes the request to mean that you should behave on the basis of a central set of characteristics, regardless of the situation, in a way that reflects one's unique, positive attributes. For someone raised in a collectivist culture, the statement implies a self defined by relationships within the situation and a self-critical orientation that helps one adapt to the situation. The difference is between a fixed and stable self-concept versus a changeable and evolving self-concept.

■ ONE SELF-CONCEPT OR MANY? Though people in individualistic cultures generally assume that the self remains constant, it is nevertheless true that people can and do change over time. In fact, comparing oneself now with oneself in the past is often gratifying because it is possible to see improvement over time (Wilson & Ross, 2000, 2001).

You also are not likely to be the same person ten years from now that you are today; there is the possibility of even more improvement. In thinking about the future, you can envision not only your present self-concept, but other **possible selves** that you may become. Role models can inspire individuals to generate spectacular hopes and achievements with respect to their future selves (Lockwood & Kunda, 1999).

A person's self-concept at any given time is actually just a *working self-concept,* something open to change in response to new experiences, new feedback, and new self-relevant information (Markus & Nurius, 1986). The image of a possible future self can influence your *motivation;* you may be able to study harder or to give up cigarettes if you imagine the new and improved you that will result. The custom of making New Year's resolutions seems to be based on such images. Nevertheless, the failure to keep such resolutions is a common experience. Polivy and Herman (2000) suggest that embarking on self-change induces feelings of control and optimism. Such confidence is good, but overconfidence in one's ability to change leads to false hope, unrealistic expectations of success, and, eventually, the unhappy realization of failure.

Though you may have a clear image of your future self, other people tend to perceive only your present self, and the difference between the two can cause misunderstandings. For example, my two younger daughters perceive me as someone who will be sitting at a computer, writing a text for the rest of my life. I see myself as someone involved in a book for the next few months, but then as someone involved in very different activities.

Optimistic individuals have more confidence than pessimistic ones that they will be able to achieve positive self changes (Carver, Reynolds, & Scheier, 1994). People differ with respect to the number of possible selves they can imagine. If you can envision only a relatively limited number of alternatives, you are especially vulnerable to negative feedback (Niedenthal, Setterlund, & Wherry, 1992). For example, a person who is considering twenty different possible careers is not overwhelmed by discovering that he or she lacks the necessary ability to succeed in one of them; after all, there are nineteen other attractive possibilities. If a person is set on a single career goal, however, the discovery of an obstacle is devastating. More broadly, those who can envision many different selves adjust better to setbacks than do those who envision only one (Morgan & Janoff-Bulman, 1994).

It would seem that attempts to persuade people to consider multiple possible selves (so long as these are realistic) would be beneficial. Among white students, research indicates that the best approach is to stress achievement-related possible selves by emphasizing individualism, the work ethic, and the fact that some possible selves are more positive than others. Among African American students, however, a more effective strategy is to stress collectivism and an emphasis on racial identity (Oyserman, Gant, & Ager, 1995). Though the focus on race may appear to be counterproductive, individuals who are the object of prejudice and discrimination tend to react with greater self-esteem and self-enhancement when racial images are paramount (Rubin & Hewstone, 1998). Positive concepts such as black pride, black power, and "black is beautiful" develop in part as a response to negative interracial experiences, but they can provide positive motivation.

■ EXTERNAL FACTORS AFFECTING THE SELF-CONCEPT. Though people often make an effort to change their self-concepts, most changes occur as the result of factors other than the desire for self-improvement. Change is likely to occur as one ages, for example, because different demands are made on us at different ages. In addition, change is very likely to occur in response to feedback that is inconsistent with one's current self-schema (Bober & Grolnick, 1995) or in response to relocating in a different community (Kling, Ryff, & Essex, 1997).

possible selves: Mental representations of what we might become, or should become, in the future.

FIGURE 5.5

Self-Concepts Change as Situations Change. Among the many factors that bring about changes in the self-concept are those associated with one's job. For example, a person's self-perception is strongly affected by occupation.

Entering a new occupation also tends to bring about changes in one's self-concept, as suggested in Figure 5.5. Research indicates that becoming a police officer results in new and different self-perceptions (Stradling, Crowe, & Tuohy, 1993). Visualize the probable changes in a late adolescent who is working at a fast-food outlet, then passes an entrance exam and becomes an officer of the law. Instead of the outfit required by the food chain, he or she now wears a uniform, carries weapons, and is given responsibilities more demanding and serious than asking if a customer would "like fries with that." An equally dramatic example of change is the transformation from being a civilian to being in the armed forces and facing combat, which usually leads to a new and very different self-identity (Silverstein, 1994). Analogous changes result when a college student becomes a stockbroker, a bank officer, or a professor. In addition to such shifts in self-image, very negative effects on one's self-concept occur as the result of major life changes, such as losing a job (Sheeran & Abraham, 1994). Thinking of oneself as an electrical engineer is very different from thinking of oneself as someone who is unemployed.

Less impactful events can also bring about changes in self-concept. For example, changes in the self occur during interpersonal interactions. Just thinking about a significant other leads to a shift in self-descriptions that reflects the way one is with that other person (Hinkley & Andersen, 1996). Even same-sex college roommates change as they interact over time (McNulty & Swann, 1994). Research participants rated themselves and their roommates over several weeks with respect to such characteristics as social skills, attractiveness, and agreeableness. The findings indicated a reciprocal process in which self-perceptions influence the other person's perceptions, and those perceptions in turn affect self-perceptions. It can be argued that relationships occur "in the heads of individuals" and that each participant has his or her own idiosyncratic views of the relationship as well as the shared view of the two participants (Hinde, Finkenauer, & Auhagen, 2001). McNulty and Swann (1994) propose that the self acts as an "architect" in shaping and determining the reactions of others, but that the self is also altered by how others react.

Given the fact that mutual influences occur in pairs of roommates, it seems very likely that this process is even stronger in close relationships such as friendship and marriage. A close partner's support and affirmation can cause an individual to move closer to his or her ideal self. Drigotas and his colleagues (1999) describe such a partner as a sculptor, and the resulting change in the other individual as the *Michelangelo phenomenon.*

Self-Esteem: Attitudes about Oneself

Probably the most important attitude a person develops is the attitude about self. This evaluation of oneself is known as **self-esteem** (James, 1890). Figure 5.6 portrays someone at the negative end of this dimension. Though there are a variety of measuring devices to assess self-esteem (e.g., Greenwald & Farnham, 2000), the simplest involves just one item (Robins, Hendin, & Trzesniewski, 2001): "I have high self-esteem." You can respond to that statement on a five-point scale ranging from 1 (not very true of me) to 5 (very true of me). Keep in mind the number that you think best describes your own evaluation as you read the following section. Think about the extent to which the research results apply to you.

Sedikides (1993) suggests three possible motives for self-evaluation. People may seek *self-assessment* (to obtain accurate knowledge about themselves), *self-enhancement* (to provide positive information about themselves), or *self-verification* (to confirm what they already know about themselves).

Which of these motives is most likely to be activated is a matter of one's culture and personality as well as the situation (Bosson & Swann, 1999; Rudich & Vallacher, 1999; Taylor, Neter, & Wayment, 1995). We have already discussed the role of self-enhancement in Western societies and self-assessment in collectivist societies. A search for self-verification is common among those with negative self-views who don't want to change. To maintain their negative self-evaluation, they seek partners who view them negatively, behave so as to elicit negative perceptions, and perceive the reactions of others as negative whether they are or not (Swann, 1997).

■ EVALUATING ONESELF. Having high self-esteem means that an individual likes himself or herself. This positive evaluation is based in part on the opinions of others and in part on specific experiences. As we will discuss in Chapter 8, attitudes about oneself probably begin with the earliest interactions between an infant and its mother or other caregiver.

Cultural differences also influence what is important to one's self-esteem. For example, harmony in interpersonal relationships is an essential element in collectivist

self-esteem: The self-evaluation made by each individual; one's attitude toward oneself along a positive–negative dimension.

FIGURE 5.6
Self-Esteem: Evaluating Oneself.
Self-esteem refers to the attitude one has about oneself, ranging from very negative to very positive. The individual shown here presumably holds a negative attitude about himself.
[SOURCE: © THE NEW YORKER COLLECTION 1996 MIKE TWOHY FROM CARTOONBANK.COM. ALL RIGHTS RESERVED.]

cultures, whereas self-worth is all-important in individualistic cultures (Kwan, Bond, & Singelis, 1997).

The behavior of individuals with relatively low self-esteem is easier to predict than that of those with relatively high self-esteem. Why? It seems that negative self-schemas are more tightly organized than positive ones (Malle & Horowitz, 1995). For example, if you view yourself negatively, you can easily explain any failure or rejection in terms of your own shortcomings (Brown & Dutton, 1995; Nezlek et al., 1997).

Though we often speak of self-esteem as a single, global entity, it is common for individuals to evaluate themselves along multiple dimensions such as sports, academics, interpersonal relations, and so on. Overall self-esteem represents a summary of these specific evaluations (Marsh, 1995; Pelham, 1995a, 1995b).

Self-esteem is often measured as a rating along a dimension that ranges from negative to positive or low to high. A different approach is to ask respondents to indicate what their ideal self would be, what their actual self is, and then examine the discrepancy between the two. The greater the discrepancy between self and ideal, the lower the self-esteem. Even though the specific content may vary over time, self-ideal discrepancy tends to remain stable (Strauman, 1996). It is pleasant to receive feedback that indicates we are functioning at the ideal level in some aspect of our lives, and unpleasant to confront evidence that we are falling short of the ideal (Eisenstadt & Leippe, 1994).

A major source of information relevant to self-evaluation is other people—we judge ourselves on the basis of *social comparisons* (Browne, 1992; Wayment & Taylor, 1995). Depending on your particular comparison group, specific behavior on your part may seem inadequate, average, or extremely good. Two individuals whose actions are identical may have very different self-evaluations because they are comparing themselves to quite different groups. We'll use academic performance as an example.

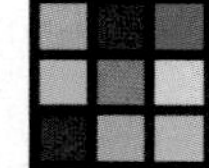

A general finding in U.S. schools is that African American students perform less well academically than whites; nevertheless, their global self-esteem is higher (Osborne, 1995). Why? In the earliest grades, students of both races base self-evaluation in part on academic success and failure. By the tenth grade, however, the relationship between grades and self-esteem drops dramatically for black students, especially males (Steele, 1992). For them, social comparison shifts from classmates engaged in schoolwork to friends and neighbors engaged in nonacademic activities.

Altogether, the selection of comparison groups is crucial. The effect of perceiving that someone is worse off that you—known as **downward social comparison**—can be positive or negative, depending on the group. That is, when you compare yourself to strangers, finding someone who is inadequate compared to yourself creates positive affect and raises your self-esteem (Crocker, 1993). For example, you might pass someone on the sidewalk and note that she is more overweight than you, and this contrast makes you feel better about yourself (Reis, Gerrard, & Gibbons, 1993). An inadequacy in members of your in-group is also positive as a contrast effect. If your artistic ability exceeds that of those in your group, you feel good—you're a big frog in a little pond (McFarland & Buehler, 1995). On the other hand, when someone *very close* to you is perceived as inferior in some respect, this is a negative event that lowers self-esteem. Downward social comparison in this instance means that you are associated with the inferiority—an *assimilation effect.* If your best friend (or your sibling or your spouse) is emotionally disturbed, it somehow reflects badly on you.

An additional aspect of the effect of downward social comparison involves individual differences in the amount of control individuals feel over the dimension in question (Michinov, 2001). In research with college students, *sense of control* was measured by the extent of agreement–disagreement with the following four statements: "I can do just about anything I really set my mind to." "When I want to do something, I usually find a way to succeed at it." "Whether or not I am able to get what I want is in my own hands." "What happens to me in the future mostly

downward social comparison: Comparing yourself to someone who is worse off than you with respect to a particular attribute.

depends on me." When given information about another student's academic performance, downward social comparison resulted in more negative affect for participants low in the sense of control. This negative affect was in part attributable to identification with the comparison other who was performing badly. In effect, the students seemed to respond unhappily to the possibility that "she and I are similar, I have little control over what happens to me, and so my academic performance may become equally bad."

The comparison group is also crucial when you observe someone who is better off than you—an **upward social comparison.** With respect to comparing yourself with a stranger, the fact that he or she is better than you usually doesn't matter. It's not likely to make you feel inferior to discover that you don't play basketball as well as Michael Jordan. If, however, the upward social comparison is with a member of your in-group, that person's superiority makes you feel depressed, resulting in lowered self-esteem (Major, Sciacchitano, & Crocker, 1993). There is a negative contrast effect when you decide that you do less well in math than your classmates. One solution is to shift your social identity, emphasizing your differences from the comparison group, and thus protecting yourself from threat; such a strategy is used most often by those high in self-esteem (Mussweiler, Gabriel, & Bodenhausen, 2000). In comparing yourself with someone close to you, upward social comparison can be a positive experience that raises your self-esteem—again, an assimilation effect (Pelham & Wachsmuth, 1995). The effects on self-esteem of downward and upward social comparisons with different groups is outlined in Figure 5.7.

upward social comparison: Comparing yourself to someone who is better off than you with respect to a particular attribute.

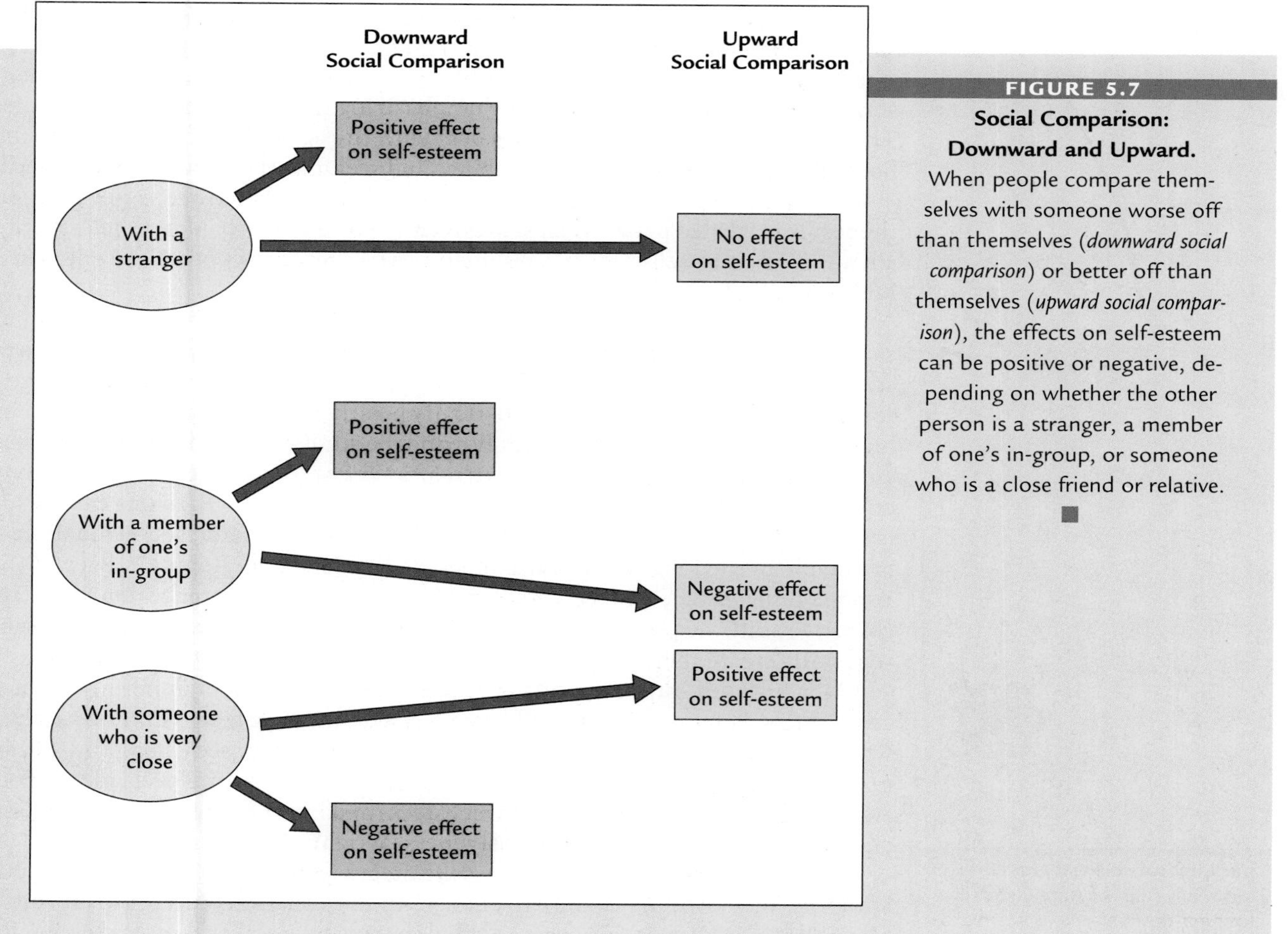

FIGURE 5.7

Social Comparison: Downward and Upward. When people compare themselves with someone worse off than themselves (*downward social comparison*) or better off than themselves (*upward social comparison*), the effects on self-esteem can be positive or negative, depending on whether the other person is a stranger, a member of one's in-group, or someone who is a close friend or relative.

EFFECTS OF HIGH VERSUS LOW SELF-ESTEEM. In most instances, high self-esteem has positive consequences, while low self-esteem has the opposite effect (Leary, Schreindorfer, & Haupt, 1995). For example, negative self-evaluations are associated with inadequate social skills (Olmstead et al., 1991), loneliness (McWhirter, 1997), depression (Jex, Cvetanovski, & Allen, 1994), and poorer performance following a failure experience (Taforodi & Vu, 1997).

Males with low self-esteem expressed their anger outwardly after being provoked by an experimental assistant (Nunn & Thomas, 1999), and it might seem obvious that bullying and other aggressive behavior is caused by low self-esteem. It is found, however, that aggressive people typically have *high* self-esteem. Very violent men, for example, tend to have a strong sense of superiority; they engage in violence when someone disputes their favorable self-view and thus wounds their pride (Baumeister, Smart, & Boden, 1996). Of course, many nonaggressive people also have high self-esteem, so it is necessary to consider additional factors such as being self-centered, unstable, and defensive in order to be able to predict aggression and bullying (Baumeister, Bushman, & Campbell, 2000; Salmivalli et al., 1999).

Decades of research provide evidence that we should not assume that high self-esteem is good and low self-esteem is bad, or assume that self-esteem is irrelevant—the effects are much more complicated than either alternative and not yet fully understood (Dubois & Tevendale, 1999).

One's body can be a source of self-esteem, and being reminded of one's mortality increases self-esteem striving (Goldenberg et al., 2000). Mortality salience is created by asking research participants various questions, including "What do you think happens to you as you physically die and once you are physically dead?" Those who evaluate their bodies positively respond to such reminders of death by showing increased identification with their bodies and increased interest in sex. The investigators suggest that those who are pleased with their bodies defend themselves against mortality concerns by emphasizing the importance of their bodies. Those not pleased with their bodies deal with the issue of mortality by reducing how much they monitor their appearance and seeking other sources of self-worth.

When a person's actual competence does not match his or her self-evaluation, the result is labeled **paradoxical self-esteem** (Taforodi, 1998). Nevertheless, unrealistically positive self-esteem can sometimes be a temporary benefit to one's mental health (Taylor & Brown, 1988).

Can such inaccuracy about your ability actually be helpful? To answer that question, Wright (2000) asked introductory psychology students to rate themselves on academic ability, and these self-ratings were compared with their actual academic records. Students who were unrealistically positive about their abilities received higher grades during the semester following the study than did students who were either realistic or unrealistically negative! As Wright (2000) suggests, it can be beneficial to look at oneself in a rose-colored mirror—positive illusions can be surprisingly helpful. Despite such effects, however, accurate self-evaluation is preferable in the long run (Colvin, Block, & Funder, 1995; Robins & Beer, 2001). For one thing, people who can't recognize their own incompetence don't have the cognitive skills necessary to recognize their own limitations, and limited cognitive skills create their own problems (Kruger & Dunning, 1999).

While high self-esteem usually is beneficial, low self-esteem uniformly has negative effects. For example, low self-esteem can weaken the body's immune system, while high self-esteem helps ward off infections and illness (see Chapter 13) (Strauman, Lemieux, & Coe, 1993). There is evidence that *serotonin* levels in the blood are associated with self-esteem—lower esteem and lower serotonin levels are associated with impulsivity and aggressiveness (Wright, 1995).

paradoxical self-esteem: Unrealistically high or unrealistically low self-esteem.

Even worse emotionally than low self-esteem is *variable self-esteem*—fluctuations up and down in response to changes in the situation (Butler, Hokanson, & Flynn, 1994). Why does this occur? Perhaps because the ability to resist being influenced by the demands of the situation requires a stable base of self-worth (Kernis et al., 1998). Stable self-esteem acts as a buffer against the effects of negative events (Wiener, Muczyk, & Martin, 1992). Unstable self-esteem is associated with low self-determination, a less clear self-concept, and tenseness about reaching one's goal (Kernis et al., 2000; Nezlek & Plesko, 2001).

■ CHANGES IN SELF-ESTEEM. Negative life events have negative effects on self-esteem. For example, when problems arise in school, at work, within the family, or among friends, self-esteem decreases, anxiety increases, and the beleaguered individual seeks reassurance in a variety of ways (Joiner, Katz, & Lew, 1999).

Ordinarily, however, our level of self-esteem remains fairly constant because we use multiple mechanisms to maintain that level (Tesser, 2001). As one example, consider the reaction to favorable or unfavorable experiences. Those with high self-esteem recall the favorable events more accurately, which helps to maintain a positive self-evaluation. Those with low self-esteem do the opposite, recalling unfavorable events more accurately, thus maintaining a negative self-evaluation (Story, 1998). In a similar way, a failure experience leads those with low self-esteem to focus on their weaknesses, but those with high self-esteem focus on their strengths (Dodgson & Wood, 1998).

Because high self-esteem is generally preferable to low self-esteem, most attempts to change self-esteem have been directed at bringing about more positive self-evaluations. Many forms of psychotherapy, such as that of Rogers (1951), were developed with the goal of raising self-esteem and decreasing the discrepancy between self and ideal-self. A major component of such therapy is providing *unconditional positive regard* for the client. The person's *behavior* may be unacceptable, but the *individual* is nevertheless evaluated positively. The beneficial effects of such therapy have been demonstrated repeatedly (Shechtman, 1993).

Short-term increases in self-esteem can be brought about fairly easily in the laboratory. For example, false feedback about doing well on a personality test raises self-esteem (Greenberg et al., 1992). Positive feedback about interpersonal acceptance has a similar effect (Leary, 1999; Leary et al., 1998). Self-esteem is even enhanced by wearing clothing that you like (Kwon, 1994) or directing your thoughts toward desirable aspects of yourself (McGuire & McGuire, 1996).

Obviously, the opposite effects can be brought about when parents and others reject the individual as well as the behavior, when the individual performs poorly, when interpersonal rejection occurs, when one's clothing is disliked, or when thoughts are directed at undesirable aspects of oneself. It is especially negative to be teased frequently in childhood; such experiences lead to lower self-esteem and poorer body image in adolescence for both males and females (Gleason, Alexander, & Somers, 2000). To the extent that it is possible, parents, teachers, supervisors, and others can strive to maximize self-enhancing experiences and to minimize self-denigrating experiences—the results are well worth it.

Other Aspects of Self-Functioning: Focusing, Monitoring, and Efficacy

Self-concept and self-esteem are the basic components of research and theory dealing with the self, but other aspects of self-functioning are also of considerable importance. We will examine three of these: *self-focusing, self-monitoring,* and *self-efficacy.*

■ FOCUSING ATTENTION ON SELF OR ON THE EXTERNAL WORLD. At any given moment, one's attention may be directed inward toward oneself or outward toward the external world (Fiske & Taylor, 1991). **Self-focusing** is defined as the extent to which attention is directed toward oneself.

self-focusing: The act of directing one's attention toward oneself as opposed to toward one's surroundings.

It is fairly easy to shift your focus of attention. For example, would you please look at and think about the front cover of this book? If you did as requested, your focus was shifted away from yourself and toward the book cover. Now, please think about the most embarrassing moment in your life. If you did that, you just engaged in self-focusing. Besides following instructions or simply deciding to focus on something specific about yourself, external cues such as the presence of a mirror or a video camera can also lead to self-focusing (Fenigstein & Abrams, 1993).

A question such as "Where were you born?" directs you to retrieve factual information about yourself. A more complicated question such as "How would you describe your relationship with your parents?" can potentially involve not only retrieval, but also some relatively complex judgments about yourself. Very small children focus primarily on the external world, but self-focusing increases between childhood and adolescence (Ullman, 1987). In adulthood, individuals differ considerably in the extent to which they engage in self-focusing (Dana, Lalwani, & Duvall, 1997).

Continual and consistent self-focusing can create difficulties. For example, in response to an unpleasant social interaction, individuals with a self-focusing style experience more negative feelings, and this reaction is stronger for women than for men (Flory et al., 2000).

It is important to be able to focus appropriately. The fact that it is possible to change focus is part of the more general process of *self-regulation* of one's thoughts (Macrae, Bodenhausen, & Milne, 1998). Darwin (1871) recognized the importance of such mental activity when he said that "the highest possible stage in moral culture is when we recognize that we ought to control our thoughts" (p. 123). The key element is the ability to control what you think about; the most beneficial direction for one's focus varies with the situation. For example, a brief period of self-focusing has been found to increase the accuracy with which research participants were able to judge social feedback. And, focusing on self is often a useful way to cope with a stressful situation (see Chapter 13) if it involves taking control of one's affective state and thinking of ways to solve the problem (Taylor et al., 1998). Those who do so are said to take a *reflective orientation* to their moods (McFarland & Buehler, 1998; Trapnell & Campbell, 1999). Self-focusing can also cause difficulties. For example, a *ruminative orientation* involves repeated self-focusing—replaying the same thoughts over and over rather than working on solutions (Conway et al., 1993).

It can be useful to switch to external focusing if you are depressed; external focusing can create positive affect because you "think about something else" (Lyubomirsky & Nolen-Hoeksema, 1995).

In addition to the relationship between self-focusing and positive versus negative affect, Green and Sedikides (1999) propose that *affect orientation* is equally important. Orientation can be *reflective* (the tendency not to act) or *social* (the tendency to act). By asking participants to visualize specific scenarios, the experimenters were able to induce affect; a sadness scenario created feelings such as sorrowful, dejected, and depressed, while a contentment scenario led to feelings such as satisfied, calm, and tranquil. Other scenarios induced affective orientation—the creation of thrill-evoked responses such as overjoyed, exhilarated, and ecstatic—while anger led to such responses as enraged, furious, and mad. When affect is induced, self-focused attention increases. When affective orientation is induced, self-focused attention is reduced. The investigators suggest the following example: "If you win the Publisher's Clearinghouse sweepstakes, you will focus more on the person with the check and your celebrating relatives than on your inner thoughts and feelings. If a loved one dies, you will become more self-focused, withdrawn, and ruminative" (Green & Sedikides, 1999, p. 116).

Because a person's self-concept is made up of many discrete elements, it is not possible to think of all aspects of yourself at once—only one small portion at a time.

The process is analogous to examining the contents of a large, dark room by pointing a flashlight at one object at a time. You can just "let your mind wander" or you can "take charge of the flashlight." Your attention may be directed by cues from the outside or cues that you create yourself (Kunda et al., 1993). As a simple example, let's say that you have a dental appointment tomorrow that involves cleaning and x-rays. I could ask you to tell me about the most unpleasant aspects of the procedure or to tell me about how relieved you will feel when you leave the dentist's office. And, you can decide to dwell on the possible discomfort and pain, or you could think about how useful those procedures can be in preventing serious problems. At the time of this writing, one of my daughters is about to have her wisdom teeth extracted, and the dentist suggested that she bring a favorite CD or cassette tape, prompting her to focus on that rather than on what he is doing inside her mouth. What kind of affect do you think is associated with each of these specific targets of one's focus?

To take a very different example, where is your attention focused when you are stuck in a long line (as in Figure 5.8) waiting to get into a movie? If you think about how you look and if you are concerned about how your are perceived by others in the line, the waiting experience is more negative than if your focus and concerns are elsewhere (Marquis & Filiatrault, 2000).

Some people file positive and negative aspects of their experiences separately in memory—to engage in *compartmentalized self-organization* (Showers, 1992a; Showers & Kling, 1996). When that is done, one's mood can be controlled by deciding whether to focus on the positive or the negative elements. Not only

FIGURE 5.8

Self-Focusing While Waiting in a Long Line.

It seems unlikely that anyone enjoys standing in a line waiting to enter a movie theater or an amusement park ride, or waiting to be served in a post office, fast-food restaurant, or the motor vehicles department. Where you focus your attention while in that line can help determine just how tolerable the experience will be. If you are concerned about yourself and how others perceive you, the experience is a more negative one than if you focus your attention elsewhere, such as on the inefficiency of those in charge or the appearance of the strangers in front of or behind you.

does self-focusing influence mood (Sedikides, 1992), but mood influences the direction of self-focusing (Salovey, 1992). When you are happy, you are more likely to focus on positive aspects of your past and present; when you are sad, the focus is more likely to be on negative aspects. These interconnections are shown in Figure 5.9. Also see Chapter 3 for a discussion of affect and cognition.

People differ in their ability to regulate moods. When a negative mood was induced in a laboratory setting, participants who were characteristically successful at mood regulation were better able to retrieve positive memories, and thus reverse the negative mood, than were participants who were low in the ability to regulate moods (Rusting & DeHart, 2000).

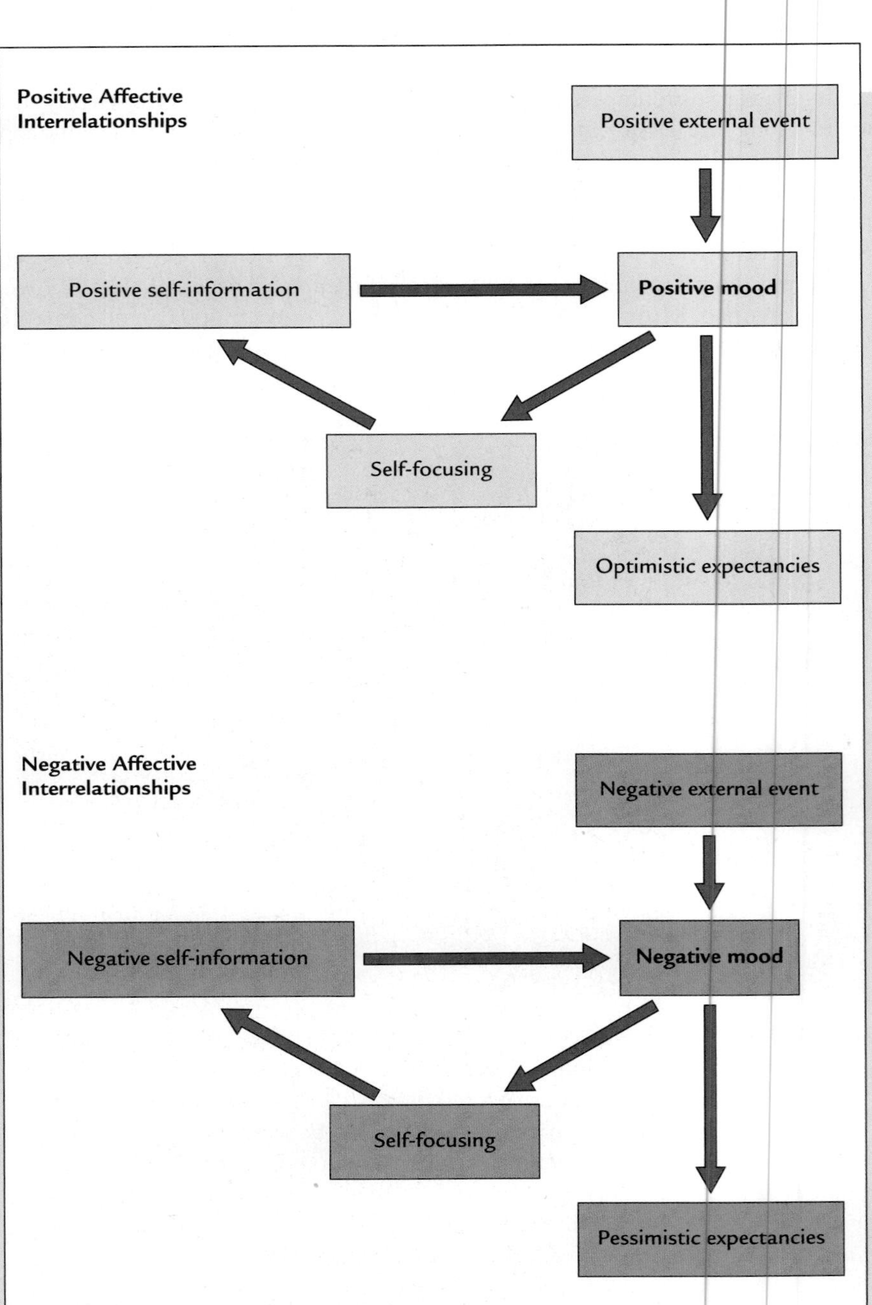

FIGURE 5.9

Interrelationships among External Events, Mood, Expectancies, Self-Focusing, and Self-Information. When positive and negative self-information is stored separately in memory, self-focusing can be directed at either positive or negative information. As a result, the interrelationships among external events, mood, expectancies, self-focusing, and self-information tend to be either all positive or all negative.

Rather than having separate positive and negative mental files, some people store them together in memory (Showers, 1992b). This pattern is called *evaluatively integrated self-organization,* and the result is that self-focusing can never involve purely negative elements because positive elements are also present as part of the same memories. As a result, these individuals experience less severe negative affect and have higher self-esteem. That sounds good, but there are some drawbacks. If you experience severe stress, it is helpful to focus on purely positive self-content. The presence of separate, positive elements of the self makes it easier to protect yourself against depression and anxiety (Showers & Ryff, 1996).

■ MONITORING YOUR BEHAVIOR BY USING INTERNAL OR EXTERNAL CUES. The term **self-monitoring** refers to the tendency to regulate one's behavior on the basis of external cues such as how other people react (high self-monitoring) or on the basis of internal cues such as one's own beliefs and attitudes (low self-monitoring) (Gangestad & Snyder, 1985; Snyder & Ickes, 1985). Low self-monitors tend to behave in a consistent way regardless of the situation, whereas high self-monitors tend to change as the situation changes (Koestner, Bernieri, & Zuckerman, 1992). Scale items such as "I can only argue for ideas that I already believe" are answered as *true* by low self-monitors and *false* by high self-monitors.

self-monitoring: Regulation of one's behavior on the basis of the external situation, such as how other people react (high self-monitoring), or on the basis of internal factors, such as beliefs, attitudes, and values (low self-monitoring).

High self-monitors engage in role playing in order to obtain positive evaluations from other people (Lippa & Donaldson, 1990). This is a useful characteristic for politicians, salespeople, and actors (see Figure 5.10).

Self-monitoring tendencies are revealed in many aspects of social behavior. For example, high self-monitors tend to use the third person (he, she, them, etc.) when

FIGURE 5.10

High Self-Monitoring: Behavior in Response to the Reactions of Others. In interpersonal situations, a person who is a high self-monitor (such as former President Clinton) responds to the reactions of others and then attempts to behave so as to meet their expectations. A low self-monitor, in contrast, responds to his or her own personal standards and then attempts to behave in a way that matches those standards. High self-monitoring is associated with success in politics, acting, and sales.

they verbalize; low self-monitors use the first person (I, me, my, etc.) (Ickes, Reidhead, & Patterson, 1986). More positive self-esteem is characteristic of high self-monitors (Leary et al., 1995), and low self-monitors tend to have fewer and longer lasting romantic relationships than do high do self-monitors (Snyder & Simpson, 1984).

Interestingly, those who are either extremely high or extremely low in self-monitoring are more neurotic and less well adjusted than those who fall in the middle of this dimension (Miller & Thayer, 1989). For high self-monitors, depression and anxiety result from a discrepancy between self-characteristics and what *other people* think those characteristics should be; for low self-monitors, depression and anxiety result from a discrepancy between self-characteristics and what *the individual* thinks they should be (Gonnerman et al., 2000).

There is evidence that self-monitoring is genetic (Gangestad & Simpson, 1993). On some of the questionnaire items used to measure this dispositional variable, identical twins responded in the same way more often than did fraternal twins. Examples are greater similarity in having the ability to imitate others, wanting to impress or entertain people, liking to play charades, and being able to lie. All four of these behaviors are characteristic of high self-monitors, and responses to all four are more similar in identical than in fraternal twins.

■ SELF-EFFICACY: HAVING CONFIDENCE IN ONESELF. **Self-efficacy** is a person's evaluation of his or her ability or competency to perform a task, reach a goal, or overcome an obstacle (Bandura, 1977). This evaluation can vary greatly across situations (Cervone, 1997). For example, I am not upset by the warning "some assembly required." I am very confident that I can assemble a piece of office furniture by following the step-by-step instructions included in the box. I am equally confident that I *cannot* climb to the top of Mt. Everest now or ever.

Performance in both physical (Courneya & McAuley, 1993; Gould & Weiss, 1981; Ng et al., 1999) and academic (Sanna & Pusecker, 1994) tasks, performance on the job (Huang, 1998), and ability to deal with anxiety and depression (Cheung & Sun, 2000) is enhanced by strong feelings of self-efficacy. Unless people believe that they are able to achieve a goal (such as giving up drugs) as the result of what they do, they have little or no incentive to act (Bandura, 1999). People high in such self-confidence also tend to stop working on unsolvable tasks more quickly than those who are low—instead, they prefer to allocate their time and effort to tasks that *can* be solved (Aspinwall & Richter, 1999).

Taking the idea of personal self-efficacy a step further, Bandura (2000) proposes *collective self-efficacy*—the shared belief by members of a group that collective action will produce the desired effects. Those who don't believe in such self-efficacy assume that they can't change things, so they give up and become apathetic about political issues. If the governing system is perceived as trustworthy, collective self-efficacy leads to positive political activism, such as persuading people to vote. If the system is perceived as untrustworthy, the collective behavior leads to confrontational and coercive activism, such as protests and riots.

In the quite different realm of sports, efficacy is also very important. Among basketball players, a shared belief in the collective efficacy of the team (measured at the beginning of the season) is found to be associated with the team's overall success by the end of the season (Watson, Chemers, & Preiser, 2001).

Individuals often lack feelings of self-efficacy in interpersonal situations, based on inadequate social skills (Morris, 1985), inappropriate attributions (Alden, 1986), and an unwillingness to take the initiative in making friends (Fan & Mak, 1998). Among women, feelings of interpersonal self-efficacy are associated with sexual assertiveness (Morokoff et al., 1997). This assertiveness makes it easier to refuse unwanted sexual advances and, if they engage in sex, to insist on protection against sexually transmissible disease and unwanted pregnancy.

self-efficacy: A person's belief in his or her ability or competency to perform a given task, reach a goal, or overcome an obstacle.

Self-efficacy tends to be consistent over time, but it is by no means fixed. Positive feedback about one's skills brings about an increase in self-efficacy (Bandura, 1986). Research on efficacy began with research that dealt with teaching people to conquer snake phobia by means of increasing their sense of efficacy in dealing with snakes (Bandura & Adams, 1977). Those who fear snakes lack confidence in their ability to cope with a snake. Using a form of behavioral therapy, the investigators provided snake-phobic individuals with a series of *desensitizing* experiences. Over a series of sessions, the research participants learned to relax while viewing a photograph of a snake, then a toy snake, then a small snake in a glass cage, and so on. This more and more realistic progression continued until they could eventually feel comfortable with a very large snake crawling on their laps and shoulders, as in Figure 5.11. As the phobia decreased, physiological arousal in response to snakes decreased, and feelings of self-efficacy increased.

More complex behavioral problems—childhood depression and behavioral transgressions—have been investigated in recent research (Bandura et al., 1999, 2001), as summarized in Figure 5.12. In a study of transgressive behavior, the research participants were students at two schools in Italy. Their behavioral transgressions were measured when the children were eleven years of age and then again two years later. The behaviors covered a wide range: physical and verbal aggression, theft, cheating, lying, destructiveness, truancy, and the use of alcohol and drugs.

FIGURE 5.11

Overcoming a Phobia by Developing Self-Efficacy.

A strong fear can be conceptualized as the lack of self-efficacy in perceiving oneself being able to deal with the feared object or activity—"I can't do that!" In an early study of self-efficacy and snake phobia (Bandura & Adams, 1977), feelings of self-efficacy were instilled over a series of sessions. Situations were presented in which the fearful individual could feel relaxed (beginning, for example, with a picture of a snake), then gradually work toward the point where he or she could feel comfortable with a toy snake, a real snake in a glass case, and so on. Over time, feelings of self-efficacy were developed—"I can do that!"

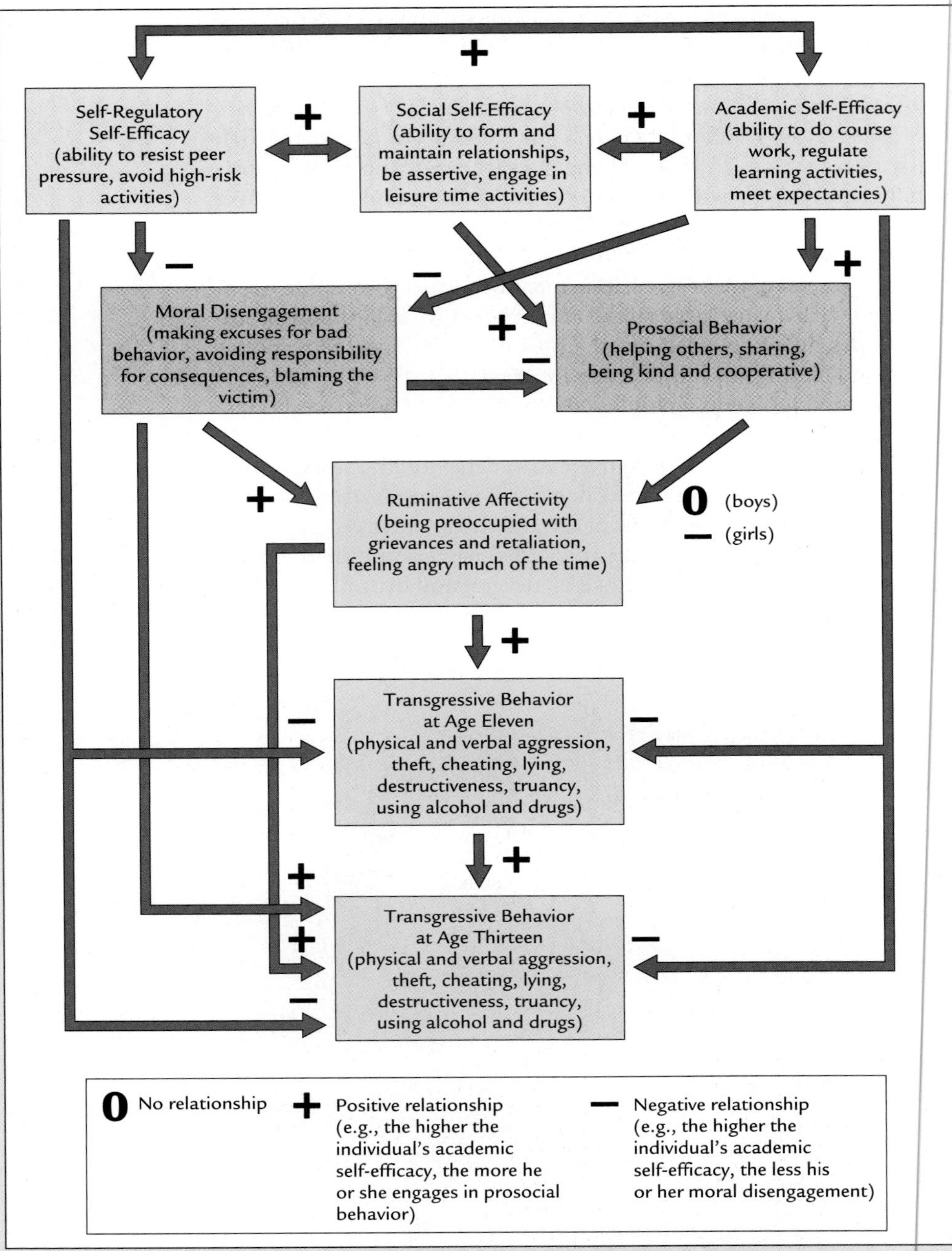

FIGURE 5.12

The Role of Three Types of Self-Efficacy in Influencing Prosocial Behavior, Moral Disengagement, Ruminative Affectivity, and Transgressive Behavior.

A theoretical model of the effect of self-efficacy on transgressive behavior was developed and verified in research with school children. Feelings of self-efficacy with respect to school work, interpersonal interactions, and self-regulation influenced prosocial behavior and whether or not a child could avoid moral responsibility. These two factors influenced whether a child was preoccupied with grievances and feelings of anger. Whether or not a child engaged in transgressions (aggression, cheating, etc.) was influenced by each of these factors.

[SOURCE: BASED ON INFORMATION IN BANDURA ET AL., 2001.]

The investigators proposed that three kinds of self-efficacy were important predictors of the behaviors in question. *Academic self-efficacy* dealt with the students' belief in their ability to do the course work, to regulate their own learning activities, and to live up to the academic expectations of themselves and others. *Social self-efficacy* dealt with their beliefs about their ability to form and maintain relationships, to be assertive, and to engage in leisure time activities. *Self-regulatory self-efficacy* dealt with ability to resist peer pressure and avoid high-risk activities.

It was proposed that these three areas of self-efficacy affect *prosocial behavior* (helping others, sharing, being kind and cooperative) and *moral disengagement* (making excuses for bad behavior, avoiding responsibility for consequences, blaming the victims, etc.). These factors, in turn, influence *ruminative affectivity* (being preoccupied with grievances and retaliation, feeling angry much of the time).

As shown in Figure 5.12, these six factors (three kinds of efficacy, prosocial behavior, moral disengagement, and ruminative affectivity) were found to predict transgressive behavior for both boys and girls. A next applied step could involve attempts to alter these factors in an effort to reduce or eliminate unacceptable behavior.

KEY POINTS

- One's identity, or *self-concept,* consists of self-beliefs and self-perceptions organized as a cognitive schema.
- We can process information about ourselves more efficiently than other types of information—the *self-reference effect.*
- In addition to the personal self, there is a *social-self* that includes interpersonal relationships and a collective identity based on such factors as race, religion, and ethnicity.
- Beyond one's current self-concept, there are many possible different and usually better selves that we can envision in the future—our *possible selves.*
- Self-concepts change as a function of age, but also in response to new information, changes in one's environment or occupational status, and interactions with others.
- *Self-esteem* rests on self-evaluation—the attitudes we hold about ourselves in general and in specific domains. It is based in part on social comparison processes.
- There are many positive (and some negative) factors associated with high self-esteem; negative consequences are consistently found to be associated with variable self-esteem.
- *Self-focusing* refers to the extent to which an individual is directing attention toward self or toward some aspect of the external world.
- How one stores positive and negative information in memory is an important aspect of mood regulation and one's ability to cope with stressful events.
- *Self-monitoring* refers to the tendency to regulate one's behavior on the basis of external factors (high self-monitoring) or on the basis of internal beliefs and values (low self-monitoring).
- *Self-efficacy* refers to an individual's belief that he or she can perform a task, reach a goal, or overcome an obstacle.
- High self-efficacy is crucial to the successful performance of tasks as varied as school work, physical exercise, health, political action, and avoiding behavioral transgressions.

Gender: Being a Male or a Female as a Crucial Aspect of Identity

Perhaps the most crucial element of personal identity is whether we categorize ourselves as either female or male. Most of us may or may not be overly concerned about ethnic identity or social class or whatever, but it would be rare indeed to find an individual who is indifferent about being identified with one sex or the other. Angier (1998b) notes that on the Barney TV show, the cast has included children of all races, children with various disabilities, and thin children and chubby ones—but in all instances, each child was unambiguously and unmistakably either a boy or a girl. In hundreds and hundreds of ways, we are reminded each day of our gender by our first names, the way we dress, and how others respond to us.

Sex and Gender

The terms *sex* and *gender* are often used interchangeably (Gilbert, 1999), but we will adopt the terminology of many in the field (e.g., Beckwith, 1994), who differentiate them in the following way. **Sex** is defined in biological terms based on the anatomical and physiological differences between males and females that are genetically determined. **Gender** refers to everything else associated with an individual's sex, including the roles, behaviors, preferences, and other attributes that define what it means to be a male or a female in a given culture (see Figure 5.13 on page 185).

The origin of gender differences is often a matter of dispute, but we are willing to assume that many gender attributes may be based entirely on what one is taught (such as an association between long hair and femininity). Barbara Mackoff (quoted in Angier, 1998b, p. F5) says, ". . . the biggest difference between girls and boys is in how we treat them." Other attributes may very well be based entirely on biological determinants (such as the presence or absence of facial hair). Young male mammals of many species (including humans across quite varied cultures) engage in play fighting much more often than do young females (Geary, 1999). Eleanor Maccoby (quoted in Carpenter, 2000, p. 35) notes such gender differences across species and concludes, "The parallels are sufficiently strong, I believe, to give us some confidence that there is an evolved, genetic basis for several of the robust gender divergences that have been documented in human children." Finally, some attributes may be influenced by a combination of learning and biology. For example, young primates (including human children) tend to play in same-sex groups, and this self-segregation seems to be based on *biology.* Once in these groups, however, the youngsters *learn* different social skills, styles, and preferences (Martin & Fabes, 2001).

Bem (1995, p. 334) borrows an analogy from anthropologist Kathryn March to make a more general point: "Sex is to gender as light is to color." That is, sex and light are physical phenomena, whereas gender and color are culturally based categories that arbitrarily divide sex and light into specified subgroups. With respect to color, some cultures have only two categories, others three, while in the United States there are Crayola boxes with 256 different hues, each with its own assigned name. With respect to gender, the reverse is true. In the United States and much of the world, two genders are emphasized, whereas other cultures have a Crayola

sex: Maleness or femaleness as determined by genetic factors present at conception that result in anatomical and physiological differences.

gender: The attributes, behaviors, personality characteristics, and expectancies associated with a person's biological sex in a given culture. Gender differences can be based on biology, learning, or a combination of the two.

"How is it gendered?"

FIGURE 5.13

Gender: Over and Above Sex. *Sex* refers to basic biological aspects of maleness and femaleness that is determined at conception, and *gender* refers to all of the attributes, behaviors, personality characteristics, and expectancies associated with biological sex in a given culture. The questioner in this cartoon apparently assumes that gender characteristics are created by environmental factors.

[SOURCE: © THE NEW YORKER COLLECTION 1999 EDWARD KOREN FROM CARTOONBANK.COM. ALL RIGHTS RESERVED.]

box of possibilities ranging from bisexuality to an array of heterosexual and homosexual roles and lifestyles.

Gender Identity and Gender Stereotypes

Each of us has a **gender identity** in that a key part of our self-concept is the label "male" or "female." For the vast majority of people, biological sex and gender identity correspond, though in a small proportion of the population, their gender identity differs from their sex.

gender identity: That part of the self-concept involving a person's identification as a male or a female. Consciousness of gender identity usually develops at about the age of two.

▪ DEVELOPING A GENDER IDENTITY. The first thing most adults ask about a baby (their own or anyone else's) is whether it is a boy or a girl. The birth announcement begins with that information, a male- or female-sounding name is selected, pink or blue clothing is bought, the baby's room is decorated in either a feminine or a masculine style, and "gender appropriate" toys and clothing are provided. As Angier (1998b, p. F5) puts it, "Society still assumes that boys will be boyish and girls not."

Despite this pervasive emphasis on gender definition, infants and even toddlers are usually unaware of either sex or gender until they are about two years of age. (In preschool, one of my daughters saw the genitals of a fellow preschooler and wondered why she and Henry didn't look the same.) For a variety of such reasons, two is the usual age when children learn to call themselves either "girl" or "boy," often without a clear idea as to what those words might mean. Gradually, gender identity is acquired as the child develops a sense of self that includes maleness or femaleness (Grieve, 1980).

Between ages four and seven, children begin to comprehend the importance of **gender consistency.** That is, they accept the principle that gender is a basic attribute of each person—and of pets and cartoon characters as well. Once these cognitions are firmly in place, our subsequent perceptions are strongly affected by what we have been taught about gender.

It is possible to demonstrate just how such beliefs affect us. Imagine that you are a participant in an experiment watching videotapes of nine-month-old infants named Mary, Stephen, Karen, and Matthew. Because the sex of clothed infants (*not* dressed in pink or blue) is not at all obvious, is it possible that your perceptions of these infants would be influenced by the cues to maleness–femaleness provided by their names? For some research participants in an experiment conducted by Vogel and his colleagues (1991), a given baby was identified as Mary, and for other participants the same baby was named Stephen, and so on. The participants (both children and adolescents) agreed that "Mary" and "Karen" were smaller, more beautiful, nicer, and softer than "Stephen" and "Matthew," regardless of which infants were identified by which name. The stereotypes associated with each gender not only have a powerful influence on how individuals are perceived, but they can even lead to false memories (Lenton, Blair, & Hastie, 2001).

■ WHAT IS THE BASIS OF GENDER IDENTITY? Though it has long been widely assumed that most observed differences between males and females are based on biological factors, research of various kinds has shown convincingly that many "typical" masculine and feminine characteristics are in fact acquired (Bem, 1984; Eagly & Wood, 1999). *Gender schema theory* suggests that children have a generalized readiness to organize information about the self on the basis of cultural definitions of appropriate male and female attributes (Bem, 1981, 1983). Such information is applied to self as well as to others. The definitions of appropriate behavior change over time, especially the stereotypes of women in recent history, because there have been greater changes in the roles of women than of men (Diekman & Eagly, 2000). It is often amusing (and, perhaps, not so amusing) to take a look at what previous generations were taught. Consider "The Good Wife's Guide" shown in Figure 5.14.

As children grow older, **sex typing** occurs when they comprehend the "correct" stereotypes associated with maleness and femaleness in their culture. A great deal of what children learn about gender is based on observing their parents and trying to be like them. Generally, children are rewarded for engaging in gender-appropriate behavior and discouraged (often with ridicule) when their behavior is gender-inappropriate.

The influence of gender stereotypes may not be deliberate or obvious, as a recent field study has shown. Video recordings were made of several hundred parents and their offspring (ages one to eight) at the science exhibits in a children's museum (Crowley et al., 2001). Parents were found to be three times more likely to explain scientific information to boys than to girls, even though they were equally likely to talk to their sons and daughters about other topics. This difference was true of both fathers and mothers, and it held true for children regardless of age, as shown in Figure 5.15. Presumably, an interest in science is thought to be more appropriate for boys than for girls. Such findings suggest at least one reason for sex differences in scientific interest in later years.

Sex differences in mathematical reasoning (Benbow et al., 2000) may have an additional situational cause. When high-achieving females engage in problem-solving tasks in a mixed-sex group, they do less well than in an all-female group, though male performance is unaffected (Inzlicht & Ben-Zeev, 2000). These investigators suggested that gender stereotypes about abilities make a mixed-sex situation more threatening for women.

gender consistency: The concept that gender is a basic, enduring attribute of each individual. A grasp of gender consistency usually develops between the ages of four and seven.

sex typing: Comprehension of the stereotypes associated with being a male or a female in one's culture.

FIGURE 5.14
The Stereotype of a Good Wife: 1955. There are many determinants of gender stereotypes, some subtle and some blatant. Looking back almost half a century, it is difficult to believe that some people were writing the kind of material shown here and that some people were probably doing their best to follow this advice. What do you think today's definition of a good wife (and a good husband) would be?

The Good Wife's Guide

- Have dinner ready. Plan ahead, even the night before, to have a delicious meal ready, on time for his return. This is a way of letting him know that you have been thinking about him and are concerned about his needs. Most men are hungry when they come home and the prospect of a good meal (especially his favorite dish) is part of the warm welcome needed.
- Prepare yourself. Take 15 minutes to rest so you'll be refreshed when he arrives. Touch up your makeup, put a ribbon in your hair and be fresh-looking. He has just been with a lot of work-weary people.
- Clear away the clutter. Make one last trip through the main part of the house just before your husband arrives.
- Gather up schoolbooks, toys, paper, etc., and then run a dustcloth over the tables.
- Be happy to see him.
- Listen to him. You may have a dozen important things to tell him, but the moment of his arrival is not the time. Let him talk first—remember, his topics of conversation are more important than yours.
- Make him comfortable. Have him lean back in a comfortable chair or have him lie down in the bedroom. Have a cool or warm drink ready for him.
- Don't ask him questions about his actions or question his judgment or integrity. Remember, he is the master of the house and as such will always exercise his will with fairness and truthfulness. You have no right to question him.
- A good wife always knows her place.

[SOURCE: *HOUSEKEEPING MONTHLY,* MAY 13, 1945.]

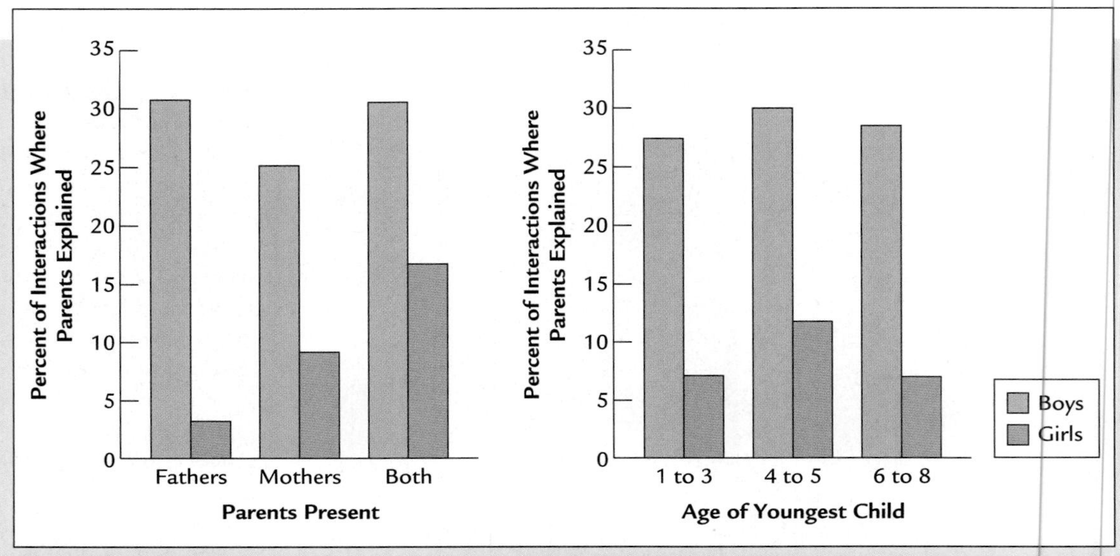

FIGURE 5.15

Explaining Science to Boys and Girls.

Parent–child interactions were videotaped at science exhibits in a museum. It was found that parents (both fathers and mothers) spent much more time explaining the exhibits to their sons than to their daughters, whether the children very young (1 to 3) or older (4 to 8). This kind of gender-specific parental behavior is just one example of the ways that gender stereotypes (e.g., science is for boys, not girls) are passed between generations.

[SOURCE: BASED ON MATERIAL IN CROWLEY ET AL., 2001.]

Do children as well as adults play a role in encouraging and discouraging specific behaviors on the basis of gender? For example, do they notice whether other children are playing "appropriately"? In Israel, fifth- and sixth-grade boys were shown a videotape of a boy their age playing a masculine (soccer), feminine (jump-rope), or neutral (cards) game with either boys or girls (Lobel, 1994). The viewers attributed stereotypic feminine traits to the boy who played a feminine game with girls, and they judged him to be low in popularity. The boy who played a masculine game with other boys was perceived as the most masculine and most popular. (As a footnote, one would guess that with soccer's increased popularity among girls and women, it may now be neutral rather than masculine.)

After a few years spent observing parents and peers and also being exposed to stereotypes in all aspects of the media, a child gradually acquires the gender stereotypes of his or her culture. It is OK for girls to cry and boys to fight. Boys can wrestle, and girls can play cat's cradle. Girls can pretend to be the mother of baby dolls, and boys can wage war with action figures. Clothes and hairstyles and chores around the home tend to be gender-specific. By the time U.S. children reach the sixth grade, they understand the prevailing stereotypes quite well (Carter & McCloskey, 1984). As children reach adolescence, teen magazines supply gender-appropriate scripts (Carpenter, 1988), and we continue to encounter daily examples of the stereotypes throughout life. As a result of all of this experience, most adults are quite accurate in their ability to identify gender stereotypes (Hall & Carter, 1999). The developmental process is summarized in Figure 5.16.

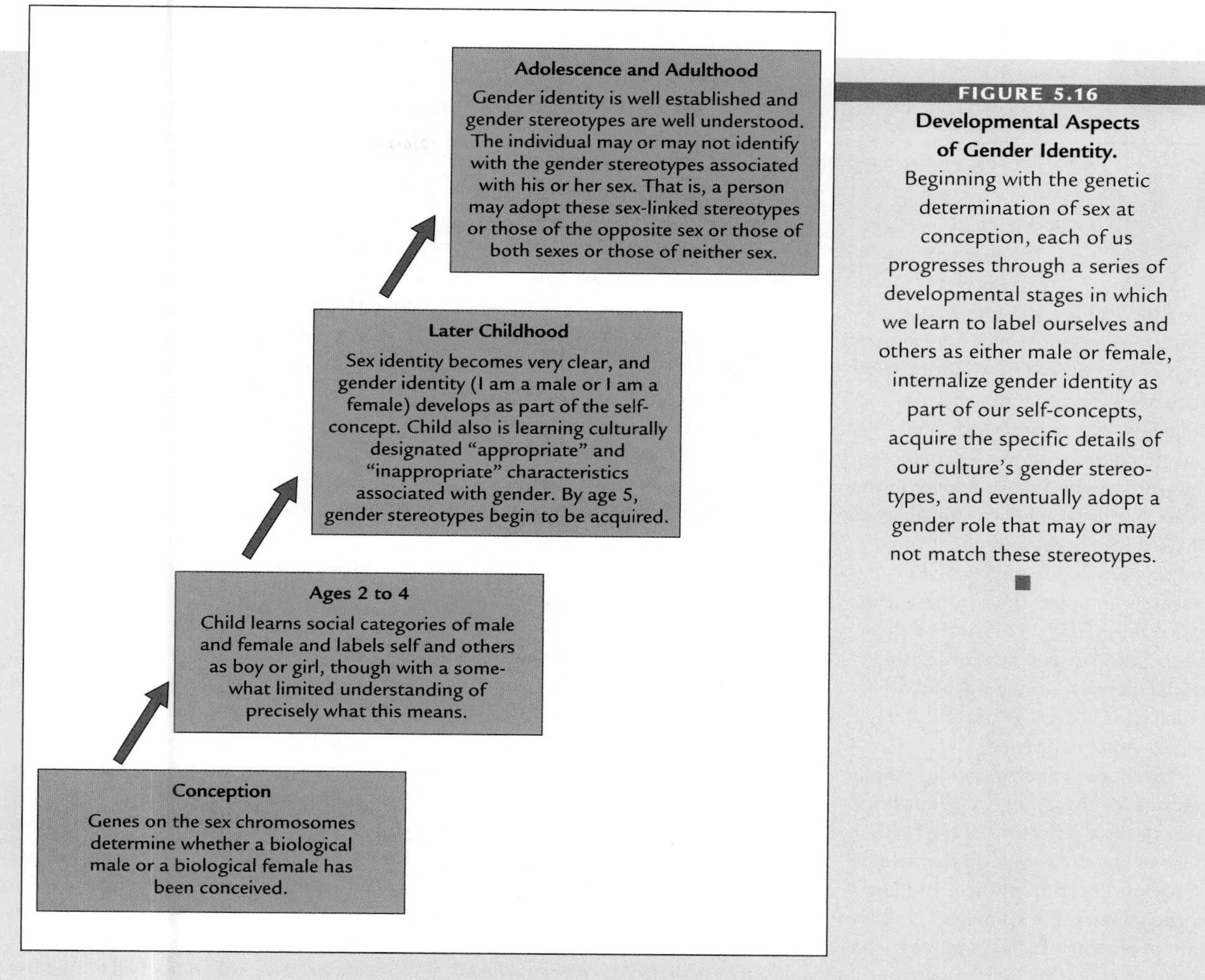

FIGURE 5.16
Developmental Aspects of Gender Identity.
Beginning with the genetic determination of sex at conception, each of us progresses through a series of developmental stages in which we learn to label ourselves and others as either male or female, internalize gender identity as part of our self-concepts, acquire the specific details of our culture's gender stereotypes, and eventually adopt a gender role that may or may not match these stereotypes.

The ideas and issues relating to gender may seem to be an obvious part of social psychology, and, in fact, they now are. But, as you will see in the **Social Psychology: Thirty Years of Progress** on page 190, what you read about today is the culmination of what can only be described as a revolution in the field.

Gender-Role Behavior and Reactions to Gender-Role Behavior

Once we develop a specific set of gender-relevant characteristics, our behavior follows. We hold specific beliefs, make specific assumptions, and act in accordance with specific expectations (Chatterjee & McCarrey, 1991).

■ BEHAVIORS ASSOCIATED WITH GENDER ROLES. To some extent, social norms remain traditional, and gender-typed behavior is expected. That is, men should be powerful, dominant, and self-assertive, while women should be caring, sensitive,

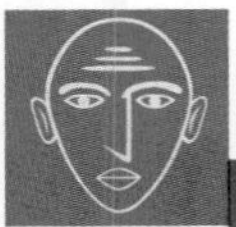

SOCIAL PSYCHOLOGY: THIRTY YEARS OF PROGRESS

SEX, THE GENDER REVOLUTION, AND RELATED ISSUES

We will start with a confession. The first edition of this text was written in the early 1970s and published in 1974. Many of the same topics were covered then as are covered now—attitudes, attraction, aggression, prosocial behavior, and so forth. But there was no coverage of gender. In fact, the word *gender* did not appear in the index. Sex differences (or the absence of sex differences) were mentioned only in connection with specific research findings. The second edition was published in 1977, and by then we included discussions of sexism, sexual identity, sex typing, and a much wider coverage of sex differences. What happened?

There are probably multiple explanations for the change, but our book is basically a reflection of the field of social psychology, and the field is in part a reflection of the prevailing social climate. For whatever combination of reasons, social psychology has changed over time. One aspect of that change is that the study of psychology was originally dominated by men (Milar, 2000; Minton, 2000), but by the mid-1970s that was changing rapidly. In the United States in 1971, 24.7 percent of the Ph.D. degrees in psychology were granted to women; by 1996, the percentage of female Ph.D.s had more than doubled—reaching 62 percent. Similarly, most (72 percent) of those who graduate as psychology majors are now women, and most (67 percent) psychology graduate students are now women (Pion et al., 1996). Such changes, by the way, have not been limited to psychology. In 1900, less than 20 percent of all college graduates were women, but in 2000, the figure was 56 percent (Education, 2001).

One of the many effects of such changes in academia has been a tremendously increased interest in issues that men had scarcely noticed until women brought them up. There are many examples, but we will focus on one.

It was once assumed that masculinity and femininity represented the opposite ends of a single dimension. People simply differed in the extent to which they were masculine or feminine. At about the time that the first edition of this text appeared, Sandra Bem (1974, 1975) offered a new theoretical formulation that dramatically changed how gender is conceptualized and studied. In place of a single dimension, Bem argued that the characteristics associated with masculinity and femininity lie on two separate dimensions. One ranges from low to high in masculinity, and the other ranges from low to high in femininity.

To measure individual differences with respect to masculinity and femininity, the **Bem Sex-Role Inventory (BSRI)** was developed. (Note that in the terminology we mention earlier, this measure would be labeled the "Bem Gender-Role Inventory.") The test was based on earlier investigations in which research participants rated more than four hundred personal characteristics as to whether they were socially desirable for males or females. The final measure contains twenty items perceived as desirable for males but not for females, twenty items desirable for females but not for males (see Table 5.1), and twenty items equally desirable for each sex. Despite cultural changes over the years, there seems to have been very little change in these gender stereotypes (Hosoda & Stone, 2000; Raty & Snellman, 1992).

A person taking the BSRI indicates the accuracy of each item as a description of himself or herself. On the basis of which items are selected as self-descriptive, the individual is classified in terms of sex type (or gender type). This classification indicates **gender-role identification,** or the extent to which an individual does or does not identify with the culture's gender stereotypes. Thus, one can be a sex-typed masculine male or feminine female, a reverse-typed feminine male or masculine female, an **androgynous**

Bem Sex-Role Inventory (BSRI): Bem's measure of the extent to which an individual's self-description involves traditional masculine characteristics, traditional feminine characteristics, both (androgyny), or neither (undifferentiated).

and emotionally expressive. For those who are comfortable with these norms, it is satisfying to conform to them and upsetting when their behavior fails to match the expected pattern (Wood et al., 1997). Gender-stereotyped behavior even extends to bodily posture—men sit with their legs apart and arms away from the trunk, while women sit with their upper legs against each other and arms against the trunk. Women who adopt the male posture are seen as masculine, and men who adopt the female posture are seen as feminine (Vrugt & Luyerink, 2000).

TABLE 5.1

Gender Stereotypes: Self-Descriptions on the Bem Sex-Role Inventory. On the BSRI, each respondent rates himself or herself on each of a series of characteristics as to how descriptive each one is. These items were selected by having research participants judge which ones apply to males and which to females.

CHARACTERISTICS OF THE MALE STEREOTYPE	CHARACTERISTICS OF THE FEMALE STEREOTYPE	CHARACTERISTICS OF THE MALE STEREOTYPE	CHARACTERISTICS OF THE FEMALE STEREOTYPE
Acts as a leader	Affectionate	Has leadership abilities	Loves children
Aggressive	Cheerful	Independent	Loyal
Ambitious	Childlike	Individualistic	Sensitive to the needs of others
Analytical	Compassionate	Makes decisions easily	Shy
Assertive	Does not use harsh language	Masculine	Soft-spoken
Athletic	Eager to soothe hurt feelings	Self-reliant	Sympathetic
Competitive	Feminine	Self-sufficient	Tender
Defends own beliefs	Flatterable	Strong personality	Understanding
Dominant	Gentle	Willing to take a stand	Warm
Forceful	Gullible	Willing to take risks	Yielding

[SOURCE: BASED ON INFORMATION IN BEM, 1974.]

male or female whose self-description fits *both* male and female stereotypes, or an undifferentiated type that endorses few of either male or female stereotypes. Research indicates that about a third of all males taking the test fit the masculine gender type and about a third of the females fit the feminine gender type. Another third of the males and a third of the females fit the androgynous category. The undifferentiated and cross-gender categories made up the rest.

The effect of these gender roles on behavior will be discussed shortly, but the point here is that the stage was set by the mid-1970s for a new era of psychological interest in questions about gender, stereotypes, and self-identity with respect to masculinity and femininity. Throughout this chapter, you will read about research on issues that were not on the agenda of most social psychologists thirty years ago.

With the recognition of androgyny as a possible gender role, much of the research has focused on the hypothesis that it is preferable to be androgynous than to fit into either the usual male or female gender types. Rather than arguing for or against that hypothesis, we find it more useful to conceptualize gender roles as varying along dimensions that include femininity, masculinity, and a combination of the two. The basic research question is to determine the extent to which behavior is associated with these dimensions.

gender-role identification: The degree to which an individual identifies with the gender stereotypes of his or her culture.

androgynous: Characterized by the possession of both traditional masculine characteristics and traditional feminine ones.

There is, however, a large body of research that supports the proposition that "androgyny is good." For example, compared to gender-typed individuals, androgynous men and women are found to be better liked (Major, Carnevale, & Deaux, 1981), more creative and optimistic (Norlander, Erixon, & Archer, 2000), better adjusted (Williams & D'Alessandro, 1994), better able to adapt to the demands of varied situations (Prager & Bailey, 1985), more flexible in coping with stress (McCall & Struthers, 1994), better able to reduce the stress of others (Hirokawa et al., 2001), less likely to develop eating disorders (Thornton, Leo, & Alberg, 1991), more comfortable with their sexuality (Garcia, 1982), and more satisfied with their interpersonal relationships (Rosenzweig & Daley, 1989) and with their lives in general (Dean-Church & Gilroy, 1993).

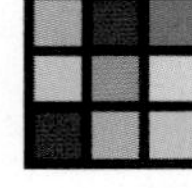

In some cultures, masculinity is as advantageous as androgyny. Abdalla (1995) examined the self-efficacy of Arab students in Qatar and Kuwait with respect to making career decisions. Individuals whose gender roles were either masculine or androgynous were higher in self-efficacy than were those who adhered to feminine or undifferentiated roles.

In other contexts, traditional masculinity seems to create interpersonal problems. For example, among adolescent males, high masculinity is associated with having multiple sex partners, the view that men and women are adversaries, and the belief that impregnating a partner is a positive indication of one's manliness (Pleck, Sonenstein, & Ku, 1993). More surprising, perhaps, is the fact that masculinity (in both males and females) is associated with mortality—the higher the masculinity, the more likely an individual is to die at any given age (Lippa, Martin, & Friedman, 2000). Why? A possible explanation is that masculinity is associated with taking risks and other maladaptive behaviors that reduce life expectancy.

Feminine role identification also has its pitfalls. Those of either gender who are high in femininity tend to have lower self-esteem than either masculine or androgynous individuals (Lau, 1989). High femininity is also associated with depression, especially by the time a woman is middle-aged (Bromberger & Matthews, 1996).

Beyond the kind of masculinity and femininity assessed by the BSRI, there is extreme gender-role identification. The first of these to be studied was **hypermasculinity,** which is characterized by the endorsement of a pattern of attitudes and beliefs associated with an exaggerated version of the traditional male role (Mosher, 1991; Mosher & Tomkins, 1988) (see Figure 5.17). The hypermasculine (or macho) man expresses callous sexual attitudes toward women, believes that violence is manly, and enjoys danger as a source of excitement. Such men engage in sexually coercive behavior (Mosher & Sirkin, 1984), are comfortable with rape fantasies (Mosher & Anderson, 1986), and admit their willingness to commit rape if they could be assured of not getting caught (Smeaton & Byrne, 1987).

The analogous extreme for women is **hyperfemininity** (Murnen & Byrne, 1991). The hyperfeminine woman believes that relationships with men are of central importance in her life, agrees that it is acceptable to use attractiveness and sex to "get a man and keep him," and admits that she "sometimes says no but means yes." Compared with women low on this dimension, hyperfeminine women report having been the target of sexual coercion (Murnen, Perot, & Byrne, 1989) and being attracted to hypermasculine men (Smith, Byrne, & Fielding, 1995).

Both hypermasculinity and hyperfemininity are associated with the endorsement of many legal forms of aggression, for example, spanking one's children, media violence, and the death penalty (Hogben et al., 2001). Even at less extreme levels of masculinity, men who identify strongly with the masculine role behave more violently and aggressively than do men who are only moderately masculine (Finn, 1986).

hypermasculinity: An extreme gender-role identification that consists of an exaggerated version of the traditional male role. Included are callous sexual attitudes toward women, the belief that violence is manly, and the enjoyment of danger as a source of excitement.

hyperfemininity: An extreme gender-role identification that consists of an exaggerated version of the traditional female role. Included are the beliefs that relationships with men are of central importance in one's life, that attractiveness and sexuality should be used to get a man and keep him, and that it is reasonable to sometimes say *no* but mean *yes.*

FIGURE 5.17

Hypermasculinity: The Macho Man. *Hypermasculinity* is a gender type that is a more extreme and exaggerated version of traditional masculinity. Men who score high in hypermasculinity express callous sexual attitudes toward women, believe that violence is manly, and enjoy danger as a source of excitement.

■ GENDER ROLES AT HOME AND ON THE JOB. The happiest marriages consist of two androgynous partners, compared to any other combination (Zammichieli, Gilroy, & Sherman, 1988). Further, when both partners are gender-typed, sexual satisfaction is less than if one or both of them are androgynous (Safir et al., 1982).

Despite remarkable changes in the role of women in Western society in the past few decades, traditional gender roles still exert a strong influence on how men and women interact within the home (Major, 1993). Even when both partners are employed in demanding and high-paying jobs, work around the house is still usually divided along gender lines, as we will discuss in Chapter 8. Altogether, women spend more time doing housework than men, regardless of their gender-role identification (Gunter & Gunter, 1991). When it comes time to clean the bathroom or paint the garage, the culturally prescribed gender roles still exert more influence than a person's self-description on the BSRI (see Figure 5.18 on page 194).

College is also a place where gender affects behavior. Women in traditionally female college majors (e.g., nursing or education) perceive more social discrimination than women in traditionally male majors (e.g., math or physics) (Corning, 2000). Also, women perform less well when they are aware that a given professor is perceived as a sexist who discriminates on the basis of gender (Ruggiero et al., 2000).

The U.S. Bureau of the Census reports that a majority of American women are employed outside of the home. The first major influx of women into the workplace came during World War II. The U.S. government attempted to prepare employers for this strange new phenomenon with a pamphlet, a sample statement from which provides some idea of what gender meant in a man's world at that time (U.S. Secretary of War, 1943):

Remember . . . a woman worker is not a man; in many jobs she is a substitute—like plastic instead of metal—she has special characteristics that lend themselves to new and sometimes much superior uses.

"It's a guy thing."

FIGURE 5.18

Traditional Gender Roles. Despite many changes in attitudes and practices throughout society, many aspects of traditional gender roles are generally accepted as accurate descriptions. That is, there is widespread agreement that some attitudes, behaviors, and other characteristics are "guy things," in contrast to other attributes that are "girl things." The extent to which the differences are based on biological differences (as in this cartoon), learned differences, or a combination of the two is often very difficult to determine.

In the workplace, however, gender and gender roles remain of central importance. For example, occupations are perceived as masculine or feminine, and success is perceived to depend on masculine attributes (vigorous, competitive, mathematical) in masculine jobs and on feminine attributes (beautiful, cooperative, intuitive) in feminine jobs (Cejka & Eagly, 1999). Those occupations requiring masculine attributes for success have higher prestige and higher income. As one example, the U.S. Senate is overwhelmingly male; as of 2001, there are thirteen female and eighty-seven male senators. The majority of these women describe their own characteristics in terms that suggest they are gentle, cooperative, courteous, and civil. As described by other senators and by members of the staff, most of the thirteen are described in much more masculine terms as partisan, brusque, aggressive, tough, tyrannical, mean, cold, and competitive (Cottle, 2001). All that we can conclude, of course, is that these senators don't see themselves as their colleagues and staff do—we don't know which description is more accurate.

In a simulated hiring study, Canadian undergraduates indicated more respect for male than female applicants, and males were also more favored in terms of hiring recommendations (Jackson, Esses, & Burris, 2001). On the job, gender affects expectancies and motivation. Despite equal performance by males and females on intelligence tests and superior performance by women in school, males estimate their own IQs as higher than those of females; both men and women rate their fathers as smarter than their mothers, and their grandfathers as smarter than their grandmothers (Furnham & Rawles, 1995). We will consider the effects of sexism in more detail in Chapter 6.

Men overestimate how well they will do on a new task, while women underestimate their expected performance (Beyer & Bowden, 1997). Similarly, men have higher expectations of occupational success and place more stress on salary than do women (Subich et al., 1986). And, in many situations, men do outperform women, but when women are reminded of the gender stereotypes that may be operating, they react by behaving in a way opposite to the stereotype (Kray, Thompson, & Galinsky, 2001).

For whatever reasons, men have learned to evaluate themselves in a more egotistical way than is true for women, and egotism seems to be rewarded. Consistent with that general idea is Tannen's (1994) stress on gender differences in communication styles. Women are not as likely as men to brag about their accomplishments. One consequence of this difference is that women often fail to receive the appropriate credit, even when their work is exceptionally good (Tannen, 1995). Women are expected to express positive emotions about the successes of others but not about their own achievements (Stoppard & Gruchy, 1993). Though women are traditionally encouraged to be modest about their achievements (Rudman, 1998), they are able to reverse roles when they learn about the effects of sex differences in this respect (Cialdini et al., 1998).

Women in academia still face numerous obstacles. For example, students evaluate instructors differently on the basis of gender; they like a male professor who is enterprising, self-confident, stable, and steady, and a female professor who is jolly and talkative (Burns-Glover & Veith, 1995). Women are also at a disadvantage compared to men with respect to salaries and promotions (Callaci, 1993). One reason is that a woman is more likely to believe that she *deserves* a lower salary (Janoff-Bulman & Wade, 1996). In response to an experimental task, women (compared to men) suggested lower pay for themselves (Desmarais & Curtis, 1997). Women tend to base their estimates of pay on how well they do a job, and men base theirs on their self-esteem, not their performance (Pelham & Hetts, 2001), suggesting that women are not asking to be *underpaid* but that men are demanding to be *overpaid.* Discrimination against women continues when they die: Despite the dramatic increase in the number of women entering science and engineering in the past four decades, only about 5 percent of the obituaries in the scientific journals *Nature* and *Science* over the past ten years were of women scientists, while 95 percent were of males (Falk, 2000).

Sexuality on the job is also a special problem. For example, women in nontraditional female occupations (such as steelworkers) are not as likely to be viewed as the victims of harassment as are women in traditional female occupations (such as secretaries), even when the evidence for harassment and the context are identical (Burgess & Borgida, 1997). In a nationwide survey of U.S. physicians, more than a third of the female doctors reported experiences of sexual harassment while in medical school, during their later training, and after they began practicing medicine (Coleman, 1998).

■ WHY ARE TRADITIONAL GENDER ROLES STILL POWERFUL IN THE TWENTY-FIRST CENTURY? Throughout the world, there is a long history of belief in male–female differences in which males are assumed to be superior to females. In the Judeo-Christian tradition, men were originally designated as the owners of their families (Wolf, 1992). In the Talmud, Jews were taught that categories of property included cattle, women, and slaves. In the New Testament, Ephesians (5:22–24) instructs Christian wives to "be subject to your husbands as you are to the Lord. For the husband is the head of the wife just as Christ is the head of the Church."

Many centuries have passed since those words were first written, but gender differences still have strong cultural support. For example, in 1998 the U.S. Southern Baptist convention (the nation's largest Protestant denomination) agreed on a declaration that a woman should "submit herself graciously" to her husband's leadership and that a man should "provide for, protect, and lead his family" (Niebuhr, 1998).

In a nonreligious context, children's books have traditionally presented males and females of all ages as gender stereotypes (McArthur & Eisen, 1976). Men and boys play active, initiating roles, while women and girls simply follow the male lead or call on males to rescue them from danger. Figure 5.19 suggests that this same tradition continues in our cartoons, and even PBS's *Sesame Street* has tended to portray traditional gender roles (Helman & Bookspan, 1992).

Many of our traditional fairy tales were deliberately designed to teach children moral and behavioral lessons (Lurie, 1993). One example is Little Red Riding Hood, who failed to follow her mother's advice about the best path to take to Grandma's house. The hungry wolf then becomes the instrument of a terrible punishment for her reckless independence. Once that lesson had time to sink in, the woods*man* could rush in with his ax to save Red Riding Hood, and her grandmother, too. Following a similar story line, Snow White, Cinderella, Sleeping Beauty, and all the rest involve a female in serious difficulty. The only hope for a female is to be sufficiently attractive that a handsome prince will kiss her and/or save her from a wicked stepmother so that the couple can live happily ever after.

In more recent times, gender differentiation has continued in the world of computer games and other software. Most of this material is based on male stereotypes, such as action-related sports and games; for females, there are only a few—such as Barbie Fashion Design (Rabasca, 2000). The difference in computer software is possibly why boys outnumber girls in taking computer courses, using computer labs, enrolling in computer camps, and expressing interest in the field of computer science (Cooper, Hall, & Huff, 1990).

Altogether, there has been a long history of the perpetuation of gender stereotypes and male superiority. Perhaps no one should be surprised that the traces of these ideas continue to influence the behavior and the expectations of men and women.

■ INDICATIONS THAT GENDER STEREOTYPES ARE FADING AWAY. There is evidence that we are gradually moving away from gender stereotypes in the United States and elsewhere. Though most individuals are well aware of the traditional assumptions about gender differences, today's college students often ignore these stereotypes and downplay gender differences (Swim, 1994). Assertiveness provides one example of change. American college men were consistently found to be more assertive than college women in studies dating back to 1931, but recent research indicates *no sex differences* in this characteristic (Twenge, 2001).

An important agent of change involves courses in women's studies, and those who take the introductory course in this subject show an increase in feminist consciousness (Henderson-King & Stewart, 1999). There is also some indication that such psychological changes may be attributable to relevant changes in cultural influences.

For example, by the 1970s, quite different children's books began to appear. For example, in *He Bear, She Bear* (1974), the Berenstains instructed their readers that fatherhood is reserved for boy bears and motherhood for girl bears but that activities and occupations are otherwise independent of gender—"There's *nothing* that we cannot try. We can do all these things you see, whether we are he or she."

Children can now read stories in which brave and intelligent heroines fight when necessary, rescue males who are in danger, and otherwise engage in nontraditional feminine behavior (Phelps, 1981). In movies and television programs, women are increasingly found in active, assertive, and sometimes aggressive roles. The women in *Tomb Raider, Charlie's Angels,* and *Hannibal* present images that are quite distant from the images of *Snow White* or June Cleaver on *Leave It to Beaver* (Bellafante, 1997).

FIGURE 5.19

Gender Roles: Even Cartoons Have an Effect. Among the determinants of our attitudes and ideas about appropriate gender behavior are fairy tales, children's books, movies, television, advertising, and—as shown here—cartoons. The images to which we are all exposed are gradually changing, but many gender stereotypes persist.

[SOURCE: © 2001 BY BERKELEY BREATHED. USED BY PERMISSION.]

FIGURE 5.20
Advertising: Nontraditional Gender Roles. Advertising has historically been a major reflector of traditional gender stereotypes. More recently, as this ad of a female volcanologist shows, an increasing proportion of ads has begun to present nontraditional male and female roles. This is one of many small steps that can serve to break down arbitrary gender roles.

Even advertising is beginning to present women and men in nontraditional ways, as illustrated in Figure 5.20. You may wonder whether these new role models for women in children's stories, movies, and advertisements have any effect. They do. When exposed to nontraditional models in the media, females express more confidence in their ability, and both sexes have raised expectancies with respect to female accomplishment (McArthur & Eisen, 1976; Scott & Feldman-Summers, 1979). The impact of such images on behavior in an experimental setting is unmistakable. It is quite reasonable to expect as least as much impact in our everyday world.

When Men and Women Differ: Biology, Acquired Gender Roles, or Both?

Explanations of sex differences in psychological attributes usually emphasize biological factors based on evolution (Archer, 1996), cultural factors (Mischel, 1967), or some combination of the two (Costa, Terracciano, & McCrae, 2001; Wright, 1994). Though this topic can lead to arguments that are political as well as scientific (Eagly, 1995; Hyde & Plant, 1995), college students are found to accept the idea that both social and biological variables are operating, but that learning outweighs genetics (Martin & Parker, 1995).

We will use research on *interpersonal behavior* as an example of the way in which sex differences seem to be shaped by both biology and learning.

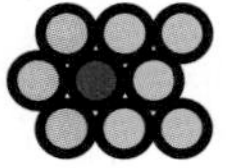

testosterone: The male "sex hormone."

■ SEX DIFFERENCES IN INTERPERSONAL BEHAVIOR. An argument can be made that males and females differ behaviorally because they have different levels of the male hormone **testosterone.** Testosterone is consistently found to be associated with dominant behavior; men have higher levels of testosterone than do women, and men therefore behave in a more dominant way than women. As a plausible evolutionary background, it is proposed that the prehistoric males whose bodies produced the most testosterone were the most combative and dominant, thus being the individuals best able to subdue rival males, obtain mates, and reproduce. Their male descendents have the same biological characteristics. Females also produce testosterone, but high levels provide no special advantages in attracting a mate or reproducing. As a result, today's men are more aggressive and dominant, more strongly motivated to engage in sexual activity, and more willing to take risks than are today's women (Anderson & Aymami, 1993; Baumeister, Catanese, & Vohs, 2001; Berman, Gladue, & Taylor, 1993; Moskowitz, 1993; Wilson et al., 1996). Analogous research on the behavioral effects of the female hormone **estrogen** is lacking.

What are some of the other behavioral correlates of testosterone level? Males with the highest hormone levels tend to choose dominant and controlling occupations; they become trial lawyers, actors, politicians, and criminals (Dabbs, 1992). Even female trial lawyers have higher testosterone levels than other female lawyers. In competitive sports such as basketball, just before the game begins, the team members *and* their male fans show a rise in testosterone level, and these levels go even higher when a team wins (Dabbs, 1993).

Sex differences in other interpersonal behaviors can also be explained in terms of evolutionary differences. For example, women are more likely than men to be aware of their emotions (Barrett et al., 2000), to share rewards (Major & Deaux, 1982), and to be concerned with maintaining relationships rather than controlling them (Timmers, Fischer, & Manstead, 1998). It makes sense that the most successful prehistoric mothers were those who shared with their offspring and pleased their partners. It seems equally possible that such behavior reflects learned gender roles (Major & Adams, 1983). That is, women are subjected to social pressures that induce them to strive for cooperation and generosity rather than competition and selfishness (Nadkarni, Lundgren, & Burlew, 1991). In a similar way, women may have better social skills than men because they *have* to (Margalit & Eysenck, 1990). It is also true that females are twice as likely as males to become depressed, and Aube and her colleagues (2000) propose that the reason for this sex difference is because women feel overly responsible for the welfare of others and find it difficult to be assertive in their relationships. More generally, depression may arise because women are more likely than men to experience repeated negative situations over which they have little control (Nolen-Hoeksema, Larson, & Grayson, 1999).

■ THE DIFFERENT SELF-PERCEPTIONS OF MALES AND FEMALES. Even though young girls in the United States are performing better in school and avoiding unwanted sexual advances more successfully than was true a decade ago, they continue to be more depressed than boys (Mathis, 1998). A major factor in their unhappiness is a pervasive worry about how they look.

Compared to men, women are much more likely to express concern and dissatisfaction about their bodies and their general physical appearance (Hagborg, 1993; Heinberg & Thompson, 1992; Pliner, Chaiken, & Flett, 1990). Even aging is viewed as more negative for women than for men (Deutsch, Zalenski, & Clark, 1986). Columnist Dave Barry (1998) suggests that men think of themselves as average looking, and average is fine; women in contrast, evaluate their appearance as "not good enough." And, these male–female differences have been increasing over the past several decades (Feingold & Mazzella, 1998). Both men and women might gain a better perspective on appearance by considering the *Ideas to Take with You—And Use!* section at the end of this chapter.

For women, especially in Western culture, weight is a special issue. One consequence of female concern about weight is the development of eating disorders, which are more frequent among women than among men (Stice, Shaw, & Nemeroff, 1998; Walsh & Devlin, 1998). We take a closer look at such sex differences in the **Beyond the Headlines** section on page 200.

estrogen: The female "sex hormone."

BEYOND THE HEADLINES: AS SOCIAL PSYCHOLOGISTS SEE IT

LITTLE GIRLS BESET BY BIGGER WORRIES

Kansas City, Kansas, September 16, 2000—Too many little girls are taking on big-girl worries, according to a report from the Girl Scouts of the USA.

An increasing number of girls 8 to 12 worry about their popularity and their appearance. As a result, teen angst has descended upon the elementary school playground.

Girls who may still believe in the tooth fairy fret that they may never get a boyfriend or be accepted by the cool clique at school.

Girls too young to spell "bulimia" are worried about their weight.

Why is appearance a major issue for women? One possibility is that from infancy on, other people place more emphasis on the appearance of females than of males. Women, but not men, are socialized to adopt the perspective of others (they *self-objectify*) with respect to appearance (Fredrickson & Roberts, 1997; Fredrickson et al., 1998). College women report a high frequency of childhood experiences in which they were teased by their peers and siblings about their looks and especially about their weight (Cash, 1995). Even parents discriminate against overweight daughters (but not overweight sons) by being less willing to finance their college education (Crandall, 1995). Presumably, the assumption is that an overweight female won't do well at either finding a husband or getting a job, so college would be a waste of time and money. Even worse than this type of discrimination is the tendency for women to feel guilty and accept the blame for their appearance (Crocker, Cornwell, & Major, 1993).

Some of the differential concern seems to stem from an emphasis on thin women in movies, television, advertising, and modeling (Lavine, Sweeney, & Wagner, 1999). From 1920 to 1999, the Miss America winners have become steadily thinner (Missing America, 2000). There is more direct evidence of the effect of television. In Fiji, before TV was available, only 3 percent of the teenage girls had eating disorders; three years after TV was introduced, the number rose to 15 percent (Numbers, 1999). In Chapter 7, we describe research indicating that when women are exposed to pictures of attractive, ultrathin models, the result is a more negative self-evaluation (Cattarin et al., 2000).

Some new findings suggest that the concern about appearance is specific to male–female interactions. About one out of three college women report being worried about their body image when they are engaged in physical intimacy with a male partner (Wiederman, 2000). Also, while heterosexual females are very concerned about how they look, lesbians are not (Strong et al., 2000).

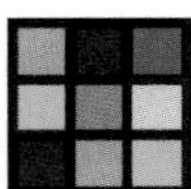

The cultural basis of this dramatic difference between males and females is strongly suggested by the fact that such problems are much more common in Western industrialized nations than in developing countries. Among teenage adolescents and young adults in London schools, whites differed from Asians in the desire to lose weight and in weighing themselves more frequently (Wardle et al., 1993).

Within the United States, Canada, and the United Kingdom, women of Asian and African descent develop eating disorders less frequently than do Caucasian women (O'Neill, 2000). One possible reason is that Asian and African men are less concerned about the weight of their romantic partners than are European and North American men. Caucasian women also denigrate overweight women much more often than do African American women (Hebl & Heatherton, 1998).

Though it sometimes seems that the old adage "you can never be too rich or too thin" is accurate, I (DB) received an e-mail from a nineteen-year-old psychology major at the University of Groningen in The Netherlands. She doesn't agree that the sole problem involves those who are overweight, and she said, in part:

> *I myself am 15 kg [about 33 pounds] UNDERweight . . . when I went to middle school (7th grade) people around me kept telling me how THIN I was, asked whether I had anorexia, compared me to starving people, etc. . . . When people start telling you that you're far from the norm, this can bring on depression or eating disorder or whatever . . . sometimes I still feel ashamed of my thin arms and legs. So my first conclusion is: ultrathin models (whom I now resemble) are NOT the beauty-ideal . . . I'm so tired that this society doesn't pay any attention to the emotions of underweight people . . . Still, when I'm a little bit insecure, my fiance tells me he thinks I'm the most beautiful girl on this planet and this DOES help . . .*
>
> *Muime Paap*

She has a good point, and it is true that being underweight can be as difficult as being overweight, as well as being equally unhealthy. Probably the more general truth is that appearance is a much more serious source of concern for women than for men.

Despite a great deal of research and theorizing, no one can say with certainty the extent to which sex differences are based on biology, learning, or a combination of the two. We realize that such uncertainty is probably frustrating to you. It's frustrating to us, as well. It seems probable, however, that some specific differences are genetically based and some are entirely the result of societal influences, while most such differences represent a blend of biological and external factors.

KEY POINTS

- *Sex* refers to the anatomical and physiological differences between males and females that are genetically determined at conception. *Gender* refers to everything else associated with a person's sex.
- Children begin to understand *gender identity* (the awareness of being a boy or a girl) at about age two. Between ages four and seven, children begin to realize that gender is a basic attribute of each person.
- As childhood progresses, children learn the stereotypes associated with being a male or a female in their culture, and gender-appropriate behavior is strongly encouraged.
- Bem's description of masculinity and femininity as two separate dimensions led to the concept of one's sex role (or gender role) as masculine, feminine, both (*androgynous*), or neither (undifferentiated).
- Much of the research on *gender-role identification* supports the assumption that androgynous individuals have an advantage over those who are sex-typed. Extreme gender-role identification for either males or females seems to be relatively maladaptive.
- Gender roles affect the behavior of men and women at school, in the home, and on the job.
- Traditional gender roles have received powerful support throughout the culture from family, peers, and every aspect of the media. Nevertheless, there is evidence that the content of children's stories, movies, television programs, and advertising is shifting away from traditional portrayals. Perhaps as a result, young people are becoming less bound by traditional stereotypes.
- Males and females often exhibit different behavior or different attitudes, such as a greater concern about appearance by women than by men. In each instance, the explanation may be biological, cultural, or a combination of the two.

CONNECTIONS: INTEGRATING SOCIAL PSYCHOLOGY

IN THIS CHAPTER, YOU READ ABOUT . . .	IN OTHER CHAPTERS, YOU WILL FIND RELATED DISCUSSIONS OF . . .
self-schemas	schemas and information processing (Chapter 3); attitudes as schemas (Chapter 4); and stereotypes as schemas (Chapter 6)
self-esteem	effects of self-esteem on persuasion (Chapter 4); self-esteem after receiving help (Chapter 10)
self-monitoring	effects of self-monitoring on persuasion (Chapter 4)
self-efficacy	effects of self-efficacy on health (Chapter 13)
gender stereotypes	prejudice and stereotypes (Chapter 6)
concern with appearance	the role of attractiveness, weight, and other aspects of appearance in interpersonal attraction (Chapter 7)
male–female interactions	gender differences in romantic and marital relationships (Chapter 8)

THINKING ABOUT CONNECTIONS

1. Try to think of a famous or well-known person who has the same last name or first name as yourself. Now try to think of a famous or well-known person who has the same last name or first name as your psychology instructor. Which task was easier? Were you able to think of more names matching your own or those of your instructor? If there was a difference, why? What cognitive processes described in Chapter 3 were involved in your search for names?

2. Recall situations in which your feelings of self-esteem had an effect on your behavior or situations in which your self-esteem was affected by what occurred in those situations. You might consider incidents in which someone tried to influence your behavior—or vice versa (Chapter 4); in which you met someone for the first time (Chapter 7); in which you were in a relationship that ended (Chapter 8); in which you asked for help (Chapter 10); or a time in which you had an illness (Chapter 13).

3. What do you believe are the most common stereotypes about men and women? Do you personally (or some of your friends) hold these stereotypes? Are these stereotypes at all related to the kind of stereotypes that lead to prejudice and discrimination (Chapter 6)? Do you think that these stereotypes have any effect on interpersonal attraction (Chapter 7) or on romantic relationships (Chapter 8)? Where do you think these stereotypes originated? Can you think of any situations in which your interpersonal behavior was affected by what you believe about typical male or female characteristics?

4. Are you satisfied with your appearance? Why or why not? Do you believe that the way you look has any effect on how much other people like you (Chapter 7) or on your chances of establishing a lasting relationship (Chapter 8)? Do you plan to do something to change your looks? If so, what kind of difference would the change make in your life? What connection is there between your appearance and your self-concept, self-esteem, self-focusing, and feelings of self-efficacy? Try to explain the connections using any of the concepts you read about in this book.

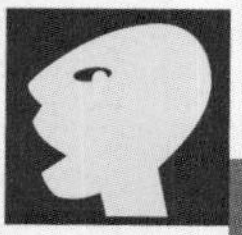

IDEAS TO TAKE WITH YOU—AND USE!

IMPROVING THE NEGATIVE SELF-PERCEPTIONS OF WOMEN

A consistent and pervasive difference between men and women—especially in Western societies—involves the way they perceive and evaluate their appearance. Beginning in adolescence, women are much more concerned about body image than are men. What could be done to decrease such concern?

Be Realistic about the Meaningfulness of Appearance.

"Be realistic" is obviously easier to say than to do. Nevertheless, as you will discover in Chapter 7, the adage that "you can't judge a book by its cover" is true. The most attractive individuals in the world do not differ from the rest of us in intelligence, creativity, character, kindness, or anything else that matters—except in the fact that they are liked on the basis of their looks. Think of the most unkind, dishonest, and totally detestable human being you know. Would you find that person more acceptable if he or she suddenly acquired a stunningly attractive face and body? And, if you meet an attractive person for the first time, try to

Eleanor Roosevelt

remember that appearance gives you no information at all about this individual.

Ask Yourself How Important Your Weight Is to Others.

Women in the United States and other Western nations are often obsessed with their weight. Most men are not nearly as weight-conscious as women with respect to themselves or with respect to the opposite sex. Most people won't even notice if you gain a few pounds or lose a few. And very few people of either sex are really that concerned about how many pounds you weigh.

Rest Assured That Men Are Not That Aware of Every Detail of a Woman's Appearance.

Humorist Dave Barry (1998) said it very well: "Men don't even notice 97 percent of the beauty efforts you make anyway. Take fingernails. The average

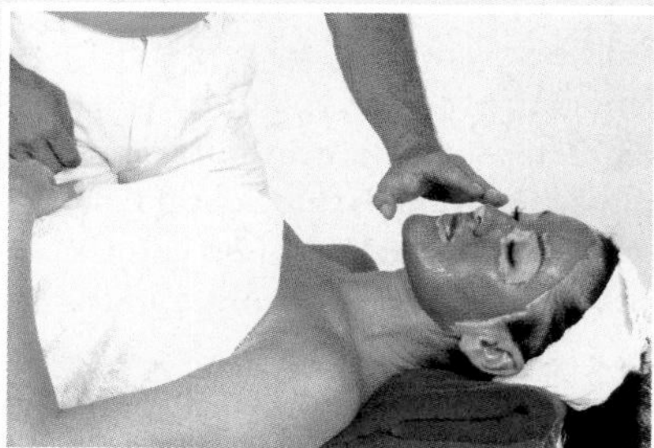

women spends 5,000 hours per year worrying about her fingernails; I have never once, in more than 40 years of listening to men talk about women, heard a man say, 'She has a nice set of fingernails!' Many men would not notice if a woman had upward of four hands." To the extent that some men believe that appearance is the only meaningful characteristic to consider with respect to women, it might be helpful to read Chapter 7, including the opening story.

Select an Appropriate Group for Social Comparison.

When you look through magazines showing page after page of ultrathin models and movie stars, you can easily assume that because you don't measure up to these unrealistic standards, you must be inadequate. You're not. For whatever reason, most men do not feel depressed that they are not as tall as the average NBA star, don't run as

(continued)

IDEAS TO TAKE WITH YOU—AND USE! *(CONTINUED)*

fast as the average NFL halfback, and aren't as cute as actors Brad Pitt or Matt Damon. By definition, most of us lie below the top one tenth of 1 percent of the total population in these characteristics. Rather than comparing yourself to models, movie stars, or sports figures, look around you for more realistic comparisons. Otherwise, you will spend many unhappy hours brooding about not being able to reach an impossible goal. The baby swan was happier when he compared himself to other swans instead of to ducks. In recent months, I had to spend several hours in the waiting rooms of the Albany Family Court and of the U.S. Social Security Office surrounded by random samples of the population. I could be much more positive about my appearance using these citizens as my comparison group rather than superstars. If you are feeling negative about your appearance, I recommend that you seek out such a group for yourself.

SUMMARY AND REVIEW OF KEY POINTS

The Self: Components of One's Unique Identity

- One's identity, or *self-concept,* consists of self-beliefs and self-perceptions organized as a cognitive schema.
- We can process information about ourselves more efficiently than other types of information—the *self-reference effect.*
- In addition to the personal self, there is a *social self* that includes interpersonal relationships and a collective identity based on such factors as race, religion, and ethnicity.
- Beyond one's current self-concept, there are many possible different and usually better selves that we can envision in the future—our *possible selves.*
- Self-concepts change as a function of age, but also in response to new information, changes in one's environment or occupational status, and interactions with others.
- *Self-esteem* consists of self-evaluation—the attitudes we hold about ourselves in general and in specific domains. It is based in part on social comparison processes.
- There are many positive (and some negative) factors associated with high self-esteem; negative consequences are consistently found to be associated with variable self-esteem.
- *Self-focusing* refers to the extent to which an individual is directing attention toward self or toward some aspect of the external world.
- How one stores positive and negative information in memory is an important aspect of mood regulation and one's ability to cope with stressful events.
- *Self-monitoring* refers to the tendency to regulate one's behavior on the basis of external factors (high self-monitoring) or internal beliefs and values (low self-monitoring).
- *Self-efficacy* refers to an individual's belief that he or she can perform a task, reach a goal, or overcome an obstacle.
- High self-efficacy is crucial to the successful performance of tasks as varied as school work, physical exercise, health, political action, and avoiding behavioral transgressions.

Gender: Being a Male or a Female as a Crucial Aspect of Identity

- *Sex* refers to the anatomical and physiological differences between males and females that are genetically determined at conception. *Gender* refers to everything else associated with a person's sex.
- Children begin to understand *gender identity* (the awareness of being a boy or a girl) at about age two. Between ages four and seven, children begin to realize that gender is a basic attribute of each person.
- As childhood progresses, children learn the stereotypes associated with being a male or a female in their culture, and gender-appropriate behavior is strongly encouraged.
- Bem's description of masculinity and femininity as two separate dimensions led to the concept of one's sex role (or gender role) as masculine, feminine, both (*androgynous*), or neither (undifferentiated).
- Much of the research on *gender-role identification* supports the assumption that androgynous individuals have an advantage over those who are sex-typed. Extreme gender-role identification for either males or females seems to be relatively maladaptive.
- Gender roles affect the behavior of men and women at school, in the home, and on the job.

- Traditional gender roles have received powerful support throughout the culture from family, peers, and every aspect of the media. Nevertheless, there is evidence that the content of children's stories, movies, television programs, and advertising is shifting away from traditional portrayals. Perhaps as a result, young people are becoming less bound by traditional stereotypes.

- Males and females often exhibit different behavior or different attitudes, such as a greater concern about appearance by women than by men. In each instance, the explanation may be biological, cultural, or a combination of the two.

KEY TERMS

androgynous (p. 191)
Bem Sex-Role Inventory (BSRI) (p. 190)
downward social comparison (p. 172)
estrogen (p. 199)
gender (p. 184)
gender consistency (p. 186)
gender identity (p. 185)
gender-role identification (p. 191)
hyperfemininity (p. 192)
hypermasculinity (p. 192)
objective self-awareness (p. 163)
paradoxical self-esteem (p. 174)
possible selves (p. 169)
self-concept (p. 162)
self-efficacy (p. 180)
self-esteem (p. 171)
self-focusing (p. 175)
self-monitoring (p. 179)
self-reference effect (p. 164)
sex (p. 184)
sex typing (p. 186)
sexual self-schema (p. 165)
social identity (p. 161)
social self (p. 166)
subjective self-awareness (p. 163)
symbolic self-awareness (p. 164)
testosterone (p. 198)
upward social comparison (p. 173)

FOR MORE INFORMATION

Baumeister, R. F. (Ed.). (1999). *The self in social psychology.* Philadelphia: Psychology Press.

- An up-to-date collection of key articles about the self by a number of leading investigators. Among the many targets covered in this volume are self-knowledge, self-concept, self-esteem, self-regulation, information processing, and self and culture.

Dweck, C. S. (1999). *Self-theories: Their role in motivation, personality, and development.* Philadelphia: Psychology Press.

- A leading researcher in the field, Professor Dweck has written an excellent description of the interaction between ideas and empirical research. She shows clearly the way in which curiosity underlies the development of ideas that can then be tested. The research findings, in turn, lead to still more ideas and experimental tests. As a result of these interacting forces, information accumulates in bits and pieces that lead to a broad, comprehensive understanding of the phenomenon of self.

Eckes, T., & Trautner, H. M. (Eds.). (2000). *The developmental social psychology of gender.* Hillsdale, NJ: Erlbaum.

- Two German psychologists edited this collection of theoretical and research-oriented articles by experts in the field. The contents stress the developmental aspects of gender as influenced by socialization, interpersonal behavior, groups, and culture.

Handler, S. (2000). *The body burden: Living in the shadow of Barbie.* Washington, DC: APA press.

- This book was written by a granddaughter of the woman who created the Barbie doll. It is her personal story of a life-long battle with body image problems. This book is written for all women who have had to deal with food and body issues. The author's goal is to help others as they struggle with the desire for physical perfection.

Worell, J. (Ed.). (2001). *Encyclopedia of women and gender.* Orlando, FL: Academic Press.

- A comprehensive collection of articles in a two-volume set written by leaders in the research field, concentrating on issues involving women and gender. Included among the many topics are discussions of individualism and collectivism, media stereotypes, parenting, prejudice, self-esteem, sex differences, sexuality, social identity, and working environments.

Henri Charles Manguin, *The Gypsies' Caravan.*

6 PREJUDICE: ITS CAUSES, EFFECTS, AND CURES

CHAPTER OUTLINE

I (RAB) am a white male, so in American society, I am not typically seen as a potential victim of prejudice. But in fact, I have been on the receiving end of prejudice more than once in my life. True—such prejudice has been much more subtle than the blatant forms shown toward minority group members in the past; but the effects on me have been real and important, all the same. For instance, my first academic job was at a university in the deep South in 1968. At that time, few persons from the North lived in that part of the South, so my northern accent stuck out like a sore thumb. Even worse, I had grown up in New York, and it soon became clear to me that many people in my new home held a negative stereotype of New Yorkers. They were generally very polite to me—politeness is an important value in Southern culture—but I could pick up their uneasiness over how *I* would act toward them. When I received my course evaluations from my students at the end of my first semester, several wrote comments (anonymously, of course) to the effect that they did not like the idea of having a professor from the North, and that they were sure that underneath my friendly exterior, I was putting them down and felt superior to them. Wow, did that hurt! And in visits to stores, restaurants, and many other places in town, I noticed that people were often a little hesitant about getting into conversations with me. All in all, it was not a pleasant experience—especially because I view myself as a friendly person and one who holds *very* strong views against all kinds of prejudice. Perhaps most interesting of all is how I reacted to this situation. Because there were few other Yankees around at the time, I found myself implicitly assuming that I should just try to be as friendly as possible and ignore the subtle forms of prejudice I confronted every day. I even began to adopt some of the local expressions (e.g., "Hey" instead of "Hi"). In other words, I tried to fit in and downplay my identity as a Northerner and a New Yorker. I think it worked, because I got along just fine and spent several very happy years there.

Why do I (RAB) begin with this incident? Mainly to call your attention to the following point: *At some time or other, virtually everyone comes face to face with prejudice.* It may not be the truly evil form that leads to atrocities such as Nazi death camps, ethnic cleansing in Europe or Africa, or the tragic attacks of hate-filled extremists on the World Trade Center and the Pentagon on September 11, 2001 (see Figure 6.1); and it may focus on age, geographic origin, occupation, or even simply being overweight (e.g., Brown, 1998) rather than on race, gender, or ethnic background. Regardless of its form or focus, however, prejudice is both real and damaging, even when it takes relatively subtle forms (e.g., Shelton, 2000).

Social psychologists have long recognized the importance of prejudice in social behavior and human societies. Thus, they have studied this topic for several decades, and have learned much about its origins, nature, and effects. To provide you with an overview of their major findings, we'll proceed as follows. First, we'll examine the nature of *prejudice* and *discrimination*—two words that are often used as synonyms but that, in fact, refer to very different concepts. Second, we'll con-

FIGURE 6.1
The Evil Face of Prejudice. At one time or other, all of us come face to face with prejudice. We can only hope that our experiences with prejudice will not be as devastating as shown here.

sider the causes of prejudice and discrimination—why they occur and what makes them so intense and persistent. Third, we'll explore various strategies for reducing prejudice and discrimination. As part of this discussion, we'll consider how the targets of prejudice cope with it. I dealt with "anti-Yankee" prejudice in the South by ignoring it and trying to fit in, but as we'll see, the victims of prejudice respond in many other ways as well, and some of these are more adaptive than others. Finally, because it influences the lives of more than half of all human beings, we will focus on *sexism*—prejudice based on gender.

Prejudice and Discrimination: Their Nature and Origins

In everyday speech, the terms *prejudice* and *discrimination* are often used interchangeably. However, social psychologists draw a clear distinction between them.

Prejudice: The Face of Intolerance

We'll begin with a more precise definition: **Prejudice** is *an attitude (usually negative) toward the members of some group, based solely on their membership in that group.* In other words, a person who is prejudiced toward some social group tends to evaluate its members in a specific manner (usually negatively) merely because they belong to that group. Their individual traits or behaviors play little role; they are disliked (or, in a few cases, liked) simply because they belong to a specific group. In contrast, *discrimination* refers to negative actions toward the groups that are the targets of prejudice. We'll have more to say about discrimination later, but here we'll focus on the nature of prejudice.

When prejudice is defined as a special type of attitude, two important implications follow. First, as we saw in Chapters 3 and 4, attitudes often function as **schemas**—cognitive frameworks for organizing, interpreting, and recalling information (e.g., Wyer & Srull, 1994). Thus, individuals who are prejudiced toward particular groups tend to process information about these groups differently from the way they process information about other groups. For example, information relating to the prejudice

prejudice: Negative attitudes toward the members of specific social groups.

schemas: Cognitive frameworks developed through experience that affect the processing of new social information.

is often given more attention, or processed more carefully, than information not relating to it (e.g., Blascovich et al., 1997). Similarly, information that is consistent with individuals' prejudiced views often receives closer attention and so is remembered more accurately than information that is not consistent with these views (e.g., Fiske & Neuberg, 1990; Judd, Ryan, & Parke, 1991). As a result of such effects, prejudice becomes a kind of closed cognitive loop and tends to increase in strength over time.

Second, as an attitude, prejudice also involves negative feelings or emotions on the part of prejudiced persons when they are in the presence of, or merely think about, members of the groups they dislike (Bodenhausen, Kramer, & Susser, 1994b; Vanman et al., 1997). And as we'll soon see, prejudice can also be *implicit*—it can be triggered in a seemingly automatic manner by exposure to members of the groups toward whom it is directed, and can influence overt behavior even when the persons involved are largely unaware of the existence of such views and might deny vigorously that they hold them (e.g., Fazio et al., 1995; Fazio & Hilden, 2001). Like other attitudes, prejudice also includes beliefs and expectations about members of various groups—for instance, beliefs that all members of these groups show certain traits. We'll discuss such beliefs, known as *stereotypes*, later in this chapter (e.g., Jussim, 1991). Finally, prejudice may involve tendencies to act in negative ways toward those who are the object of prejudice; several of these are examined in the next section. When these tendencies are translated into overt behavior, various forms of discrimination result. Before turning to a discussion of the many ways in which prejudice is expressed in overt behavior, however, we should address two related questions: Why, specifically, do people hold prejudiced views? What benefits do they get out of doing so?

Prejudice: Why It Persists

As we noted in Chapters 3 and 4, human beings are "cognitive misers"—they invest the least amount of cognitive effort possible in most situations. Why, then, do so many people form and hold prejudiced views? Research findings point to two conclusions.

First, individuals hold prejudiced views because doing so allows them to bolster their own self-image (e.g., Steele, Spencer, & Lynch, 1993). When prejudiced individuals put down a group toward whom they hold negative views, this allows them to affirm their own self-worth—to feel superior in various ways. In other words, for some persons, prejudice may play an important role in protecting or enhancing their self-concept (see Figure 6.2; Higgins, 1996; Fein & Spencer, 1997).

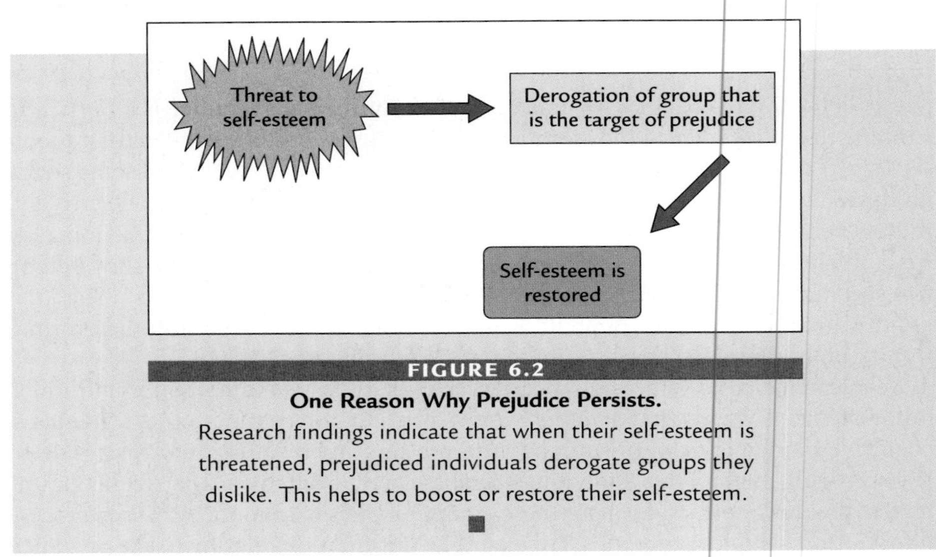

FIGURE 6.2

One Reason Why Prejudice Persists.
Research findings indicate that when their self-esteem is threatened, prejudiced individuals derogate groups they dislike. This helps to boost or restore their self-esteem.

A second basis for holding prejudiced views is that doing so can save us considerable cognitive effort. *Stereotypes,* in particular, seem to serve this function. Once stereotypes are formed, we don't have to bother engaging in careful, systematic processing; after all, because we "know" what members of this group are like, we can rely on quicker, heuristic-driven processing and these preconceived beliefs. The results of several studies offer support for this view (e.g., Bodenhausen, 1993; Macrae, Milne, & Bodenhausen, 1994), so our strong tendency to save mental effort seems to be another reason why prejudices are formed and persist.

KEY POINTS

- *Prejudice* is an attitude (usually negative) toward members of some social group based solely on their membership in that group. It can be triggered in a seemingly automatic manner and can be implicit, as well as explicit, in nature.
- Prejudice, like other attitudes, influences our processing of social information, our beliefs about persons belonging to various groups, and our feelings about them.
- Prejudice persists because disparaging groups we dislike can boost our self-esteem, and because stereotypes save us cognitive effort.

Discrimination: Prejudice in Action

Attitudes, we noted in Chapter 4, are not always reflected in overt actions, and prejudice is definitely no exception to this rule. In many cases, persons holding negative attitudes toward the members of various groups cannot express these views directly. Laws, social pressure, fear of retaliation—all serve to deter people from putting their prejudiced views into open practice. For this reason, blatant forms of **discrimination**—negative actions toward the objects of racial, ethnic, or religious prejudice—have decreased somewhat in recent years in the United States and many other countries (e.g., Swim et al., 1995). Thus, actions such as restricting members of various groups to certain seats on buses or in movie theaters or barring them from public restaurants, schools, or neighborhoods—all common in the past—have now largely vanished in many countries. This is not to suggest that extreme expressions of prejudice have totally vanished, however. On the contrary, dramatic instances of *hate crimes*—crimes based on racial, ethnic, and other types of prejudice—continue to occur with disturbing frequency (see Figure 6.3 on page 212). For instance, in recent years, James Byrd, an African American man, was dragged behind a truck by highly prejudiced white assailants; he died as a result of his injuries. Similarly, Matthew Shepard, a college student, was murdered simply because of his sexual orientation (he was homosexual). The most dramatic recent example of crimes motivated by racial, religious, or ethnic hatred are the tragic attacks by terrorists on the World Trade Center and Pentagon on September 11, 2001. The persons who carried out these crimes were so filled with hatred toward the United States and its citizens that they gladly sacrificed their own lives in order to kill thousands of innocent victims—persons they had never met and who had never done them any direct, personal harm. Actions such as these suggest that extreme expressions of prejudice still occur today; in fact, because of the power of modern weapons and the intricate, interdependent nature of modern societies, such monstrous actions can produce devasting effects in which large numbers of persons are harmed or even killed. But, thank goodness, such events are still relatively rare, and in general, prejudice finds expression in much more

discrimination: Negative behaviors directed toward members of social groups who are the object of prejudice.

FIGURE 6.3
Hate Crimes: Evidence That Blatant Forms of Discrimination Still Exist. Each year, thousands of hate crimes—crimes based largely on racial or ethnic prejudice—are perpetrated in the United States alone. These crimes indicate that extreme forms of prejudice, and the blatant actions they produce, have certainly not vanished.

subtle forms of behavior. What are those *subtle* or *disguised* forms of discrimination like? Research by social psychologists points to several interesting conclusions.

■ MODERN RACISM: MORE SUBTLE, BUT JUST AS DEADLY. At one time, many people felt no qualms about expressing openly racist beliefs (Sears, 1988). Now, of course, very few persons would state such views. Does this mean that racism, a particularly dangerous form of prejudice, has disappeared, or at least decreased? While this is certainly possible (e.g., Martin & Parker, 1995), many social psychologists believe that, in fact, all that has happened is that "old-fashioned" (read "blatant") racism has been replaced by more subtle forms, which they term *modern racism*. (e.g., Swim et al., 1995). What is such racism like? It involves concealing prejudice from others in public settings, but expressing bigoted attitudes when it is safe to do so, for instance, in the company of close friends and family members known to share these views. In addition, it involves attributing various bigoted views to sources other than prejudice, even though they actually do stem from this source. For instance, an individual may state that she or he is against interracial marriage because the children of such marriages may experience many difficulties. In fact, though, such views may stem from prejudice and the belief that members of racial or ethnic groups other than the perceiver's are inferior in various ways.

Because most persons tend to conceal modern racism (and other forms of prejudice), social psychologists have developed unobtrusive means for studying such attitudes. These have revealed much about the nature and causes of prejudice, so let's take a look at their basic nature now.

■ MEASURING IMPLICIT RACIAL ATTITUDES: FROM THE "BOGUS PIPELINE" TO THE "BONA FIDE PIPELINE." The most straightforward approach to measuring prejudice is to simply ask people to express their views toward various racial, ethnic, or gender groups—African Americans, Jews, women. But as we just noted, in the twenty-first century, few persons are willing to openly admit to holding prejudiced views—and certainly not to strangers, such as social psychologists conducting research on their attitudes! How, then, can we measure their actual views? One approach, developed in the past, was known as the "bogus pipeline" (e.g., Sigall & Page, 1971). In this procedure, research participants are told that they will be attached to a special apparatus that, by measuring tiny changes in their muscles (or in brain waves or other reactions), can assess their true opinions no matter what they say (see Figure 6.4). To convince respondents that this is actually so, the researcher asks for their views on several issues—ones on which their real views are known (e.g., because they expressed them several weeks earlier). The researcher then "reads" the machine and reports these views to participants—who are often quite impressed. Once they believe that the machine can, in a sense, "see inside them," there is no reason to conceal their true attitudes. Presumably, then, their responses to questions or to an attitude scale will be quite truthful and provide an accurate picture of their attitudes, including various forms of prejudice.

While the bogus pipeline can be useful for revealing attitudes people normally conceal, it involves deception and can only succeed to the extent that research participants believe false statements about the functions of the apparatus used. Further, the bogus pipeline is only useful for measuring *explicit* attitudes: ones people are aware of and could report if they wished to do so. In recent years, however, social psychologists have recognized the fact that many attitudes people hold are *implicit*—they exist and can influence several forms of behavior, but the persons holding them may not be aware of their existence. In fact, in some cases, these persons would vigorously deny that they have such views, especially when they relate to such "loaded" issues as racial prejudice (e.g., Dovidio & Fazio, 1991; Dovidio et al., 1997; Greenwald & Banaji, 1995). In addition, such attitudes may be elicited

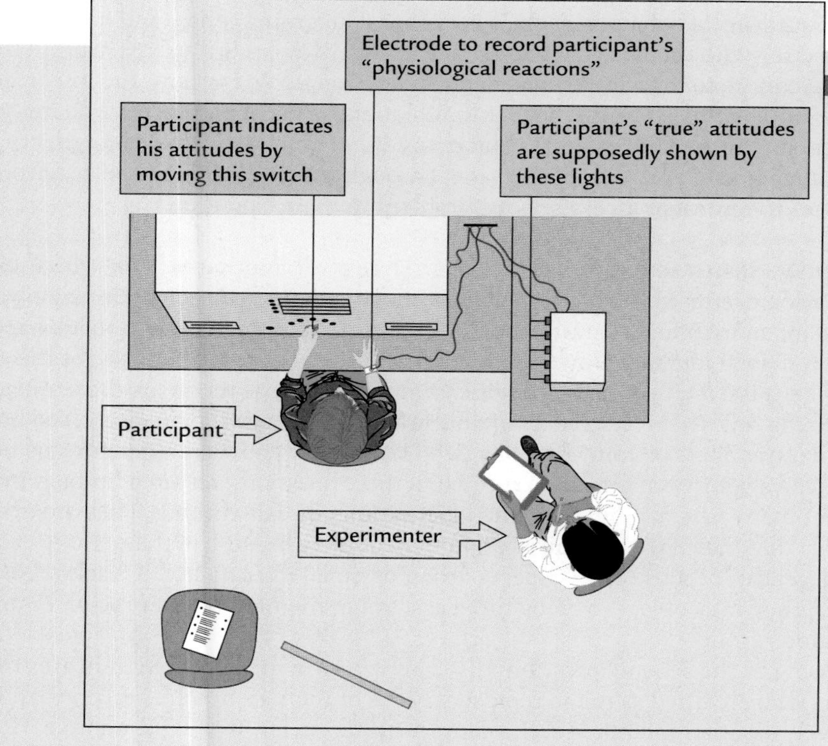

FIGURE 6.4

The "Bogus Pipeline": One Technique for Studying Racial Attitudes and Other Forms of Prejudice. In this procedure, individuals are told that the equipment shown can, by measuring physiological reactions, reveal their true attitudes. If the persons whose attitudes are being measured believe this description, they have no reason to try to conceal their true views; after all, these will be shown by the equipment anyway!

automatically by members of the groups toward whom the prejudice is directed or by stimuli associated with such persons. How can we measure such subtle forms of prejudice? Several different methods have been developed (Kawakami & Dovidio, 2001), but most are based on *priming*—a concept we discussed in Chapter 3. As you may recall, priming refers to the fact that exposure to certain stimuli or events "primes" information held in memory, making it easier to bring to mind or more available to influence our current reactions.

One technique that makes use of priming to study implicit or automatically activated racial attitudes is known as the **bona fide pipeline** (in contrast to the bogus pipeline; Banaji & Hardin, 1996; Towles-Schwen & Fazio, 2001). This procedure involves several stages. In the first, participants see various adjectives and are asked to indicate whether they have a "good" or "bad" meaning by pushing one of two buttons. The adjectives are preceded by a row of asterisks, which signals that the words will appear next. In a second phase, participants in the research see photos of persons belonging to various ethnic or racial groups. Then, in a third phase, they again see the photos and are asked to indicate whether they have seen or not seen each one previously. Half of the photos are ones they have seen and half are not. Finally, in the fourth and crucial phase—the one involving priming—participants are again asked to indicate whether the adjectives are "good" or "bad" in meaning. Before seeing each adjective, however, they are briefly exposed to faces of persons belonging to various racial groups (blacks, whites, Asians, Hispanics). It is reasoned that implicit racial attitudes will be revealed by how quickly participants respond to the words. If, for instance, they hold negative attitudes toward blacks, they will respond faster to words that have a negative meaning. Why? Because the negative attitude triggered by the prime (a picture of a black person's face) is consistent with the word's meaning, which is also negative. In contrast, participants will respond more slowly to words with a positive meaning, because this meaning is inconsistent with the negative attitude elicited by the priming stimulus.

Research findings using this procedure indicate that people do indeed have implicit racial attitudes that are automatically elicited by members of racial or ethnic groups, and that such automatically elicited attitudes, in turn, can influence important forms of behavior, such as decisions concerning others and friendliness in interacting with them (e.g., Fazio & Hilden, 2001; Towles-Schwen & Fazio, 2001). We'll have more to say about such effects in later sections. For now, the important point to note is this: Despite the fact that blatant forms of racism have decreased in public life in the United States and many other countries, this damaging type of prejudice is still very much alive and, through more subtle kinds of reactions, continues to represent a very serious problem in many societies.

■ TOKENISM: SMALL BENEFITS, HIGH COSTS. Here's yet another way in which discrimination occurs in the modern world. Imagine that you are hired for a job you really want and at a higher starting salary than you expected. At first, you are happy about your good fortune. Now assume that one day you learn that you got the job mainly because you belong to a specific group—one whose members the company must hire in order to avoid charges of discrimination. How will you react? And how will other members of your company, who know that you were hired for this reason, perceive you? With respect to the first of these questions, research findings indicate that many persons find this kind of situation quite disturbing. They are upset to realize that they have been hired or promoted solely because of their ethnic background, gender, or some other aspect of their personal identity (e.g., Chacko, 1982). Further, they may object to being hired as a *token* member of their racial, ethnic, or religious group.

Turning to the second question raised above, growing evidence indicates that persons who are hired as token representatives of their groups are perceived quite negatively by other members of the company (Summers, 1991). For example, Heil-

bona fide pipeline: A technique that uses priming to measure implicit racial attitudes.

man, Block, and Lucas (1992) found that job applicants who were identified as "affirmative action hirees" were perceived as less competent by persons who reviewed their files than applicants who were not identified in this manner.

Hiring persons as token members of their groups is just one form of **tokenism;** it occurs in other contexts as well. In its most general form, tokenism involves performing trivial positive actions for the targets of prejudice and then using these as an excuse or justification for later forms of discrimination. "Don't bother me," prejudiced persons who have engaged in tokenism seem to say; "I've done enough for those people already!" (Dutton & Lake, 1973; Rosenfield et al., 1982). Whenever it occurs, tokenism seems to have at least two negative effects. First, it lets prejudiced people off the hook; they can point to tokenistic actions as public proof that they aren't really bigoted. Second, it can be damaging to the self-esteem and confidence of the targets of prejudice, including those few persons who are selected as tokens or who receive minimal aid. Clearly, then, tokenism is one subtle form of discrimination worth preventing.

KEY POINTS

- *Discrimination* involves negative actions toward members of various social groups.
- While blatant discrimination has clearly decreased, more subtle forms such as modern racism and tokenism persist.
- Discrimination can also stem from automatically elicited, implicit attitudes and stereotypes—attitudes of which individuals may not be aware.

The Origins of Prejudice: Contrasting Perspectives

As we have already seen, holding the seemingly irrational negative views that constitute the core of prejudice can produce important benefits for the persons involved. Thus, the existence of prejudice itself is far from mysterious. But precisely how do such negative attitudes emerge? In short, what are the origins of prejudice—the social conditions from which it derives? Research findings provide many insights into this important question.

Direct Intergroup Conflict: Competition as a Source of Prejudice

It is sad but true that the things people want and value most—good jobs, nice homes, high status—are always in short supply. This fact serves as the foundation for what is perhaps the oldest explanation of prejudice—**realistic conflict theory** (e.g., Bobo, 1983). According to this view, prejudice stems from competition among social groups over valued commodities or opportunities. In short, prejudice develops out of the struggle over jobs, adequate housing, good schools, and other desirable outcomes. The theory further suggests that as such competition continues, the members of the groups involved come to view each other in increasingly negative terms (White, 1977). They label each other as "enemies," view their own group as morally superior, and draw the boundaries between themselves and their opponents more and more firmly. The result is that what starts out as simple competition relatively free from hatred gradually develops into full scale, emotion-laden prejudice (see Figure 6.5 on page 216).

tokenism: Instances in which individuals perform trivial positive actions for members of out-groups toward whom they feel strong prejudice. Such tokenistic behaviors are then used as an excuse for refusing more meaningful beneficial actions for these groups.

realistic conflict theory: The view that prejudice sometimes stems from direct competition between various social groups over scarce and valued resources.

FIGURE 6.5

Intergroup Conflict as a Source of Prejudice. When groups compete with each other for valued resources (e.g., jobs, housing, educational opportunities), they may come to view each other in increasingly negative terms. The result may be the development of full-scale ethnic or racial prejudice. And that, unfortunately, often finds expression in overt, harmful actions directed toward the perceived enemy (i.e., the out-group).

Interestingly, competition does not have to be real or direct to start this process. Followers of Osama Bin Laden, for instance, perceive the United States (and all Western nations) as posing a direct threat to their culture and their religion. As a result, they tend to "demonize" the United States and believe that any actions directed toward weakening or destroying it—even killing innocent civilians—are justified. Even the fact that their own religion strongly condemns such actions is not enough to alter their evil intentions.

Evidence from several different studies confirms the occurrence of this process. As competition persists, individuals come to perceive each other in increasingly negative ways. Even worse, such competition often leads to direct, and sometimes violent, conflict. A very dramatic demonstration of such effects is provided by a well-known field study conducted by Sherif and his colleagues (Sherif et al., 1961).

This innovative study involved sending eleven-year-old boys to a special summer camp in a remote area where, free from external influences, the nature of conflict and its role in prejudice could be carefully studied. When the boys arrived at the camp (named "The Robbers' Cave" in honor of a nearby cave that was once, supposedly, used by robbers), they were divided into two separate groups and assigned to cabins located quite far apart. For one week, the campers in each group lived and played together, engaging in such enjoyable activities as hiking, swimming, and other sports. During this initial phase, the boys quickly developed strong attachments to their own groups. They chose names for their teams (*Rattlers* and *Eagles*), stenciled them onto their shirts, and made up flags with their groups' symbols on them.

At this point, the second phase of the study began. The boys in both groups were told that they would now engage in a series of competitions. The winning team would receive a trophy, and its members would earn prizes (pocket knives and medals). Because these were prizes the boys strongly desired, the stage was set for intense competition. Would such conflict generate prejudice? The answer was quick in coming. As the boys competed, the tension between the groups rose. At first it was limited to verbal taunts and name calling, but soon it escalated into more direct acts—for example, the Eagles burned the Rattlers' flag. The next day, the Rattlers struck back by attacking the rival group's cabin, overturning beds, tearing out mosquito netting, and seizing personal property. Such actions continued until the researchers intervened to prevent even more serious incidents. At the same time, the two groups voiced increasingly negative views of each other. They labeled their opponents as "bums" and "cowards," while heaping praise on their own group at every turn. In short, after only two weeks of conflict, the groups showed all the key components of strong prejudice toward each other.

Fortunately, the story had a happy ending. In the study's final phase, Sherif and his colleagues attempted to reduce the negative reactions described above. Merely increasing the amount of contact between the groups failed to accomplish this goal; indeed, it seemed to fan the flames of anger. But when conditions were altered so that the groups found it necessary to work together to reach *superordinate goals*—ones they both desired—dramatic changes occurred. After the boys worked together to restore their water supply (previously sabotaged by the researchers), combined their funds to rent a movie, and jointly repaired a broken-down truck, tensions between the groups largely vanished and many cross-group friendships were established.

There are, of course, major limitations to this research. The study took place over a relatively short period of time; the camp setting was a special one; all participants were boys; and perhaps most important, the boys were quite homogeneous in background—they did not belong to different racial, ethnic, or social groups. Aside from these problems, the study raises important ethical issues: Was it appropriate to place the boys in a situation designed to generate hostility and prejudice, even if doing so could yield important new evidence on the origins of such reactions? Clearly, this is a complex question, deserving of careful attention.

Despite these and other restrictions, however, the findings reported by Sherif and his colleagues are compelling. They offer a chilling picture of how rational competition over scarce resources can quickly escalate into full-scale conflict, which then, in turn, fosters the accompanying negative attitudes toward opponents that form the core of prejudice.

The research reported by Sherif and his colleagues is viewed as a "classic" in the study of prejudice. Yet it was not the first dramatic study of the relationship between conflict and prejudice conducted by social psychologists. That honor goes to a much earlier, and much more disturbing, investigation conducted by Hovland and Sears (1940). The results of this study were very dramatic and were reported in many texts—including this one—for decades. Now, however, more recent findings call these original findings (or at least their generality) into question. Let's take a closer look at both the original research and the modern work in the **Social Psychology: Thirty Years of Progress** feature on page 218.

SOCIAL PSYCHOLOGY: THIRTY YEARS OF PROGRESS

HARD ECONOMIC TIMES AND VIOLENCE AGAINST MINORITY GROUPS: FROM LYNCHINGS IN THE SOUTH TO HATE CRIMES IN NEW YORK

In 1939, several psychologists published an influential book entitled *Frustration and Aggression* (Dollard et al., 1939). In this book, they suggested that aggression often stems from *frustration*—interference with goal-directed behavior. In other words, aggression often occurs in situations in which people are prevented from getting what they want. As we'll see in Chapter 11, this hypothesis is only partially correct. Frustration *can* sometimes lead to aggression, but it is definitely not the only, or most important, cause of such behavior.

The frustration-aggression hypothesis stimulated a great deal of research in psychology, and some of this work was concerned with prejudice. The basic reasoning was as follows: When groups compete for scarce resources, they come to view one another as potential or actual sources of frustration. After all, if "they" get the jobs, the housing, and other benefits, then "we" don't. The result, it was reasoned, is not simply negative attitudes toward opposing groups; in addition, strong tendencies to aggress against opposing groups may also be generated.

Although this possible link among conflict, prejudice, and aggression was studied in several different ways, the most chilling findings were reported by Hovland and Sears (1940). These researchers hypothesized that economic conditions provide a measure of frustration, with "bad times" being high in frustration for many people and "good times" somewhat lower. They reasoned that if this is so, then racially motivated acts of violence such as lynchings should be higher when economic conditions are poor than when they are good. To test this unsettling hypothesis, Hovland and Sears obtained data on the number of lynchings in the United States in each year between 1882 and 1930. Most of these lynchings (a total of 4,761), occurred in fourteen Southern states, and most (but not all) of the victims were African Americans. Next, Hovland and Sears (1940) related the number of lynchings in each year to two economic indexes: the farm value of cotton (the total value of cotton produced that year) and the per-acre value of cotton. Because cotton played a major role in the economies of the states where most lynchings occurred, Hovland and Sears assumed that these measures would provide a good overview of economic conditions in those states.

Results (see Figure 6.6) offered support for the major hypothesis: The number of lynchings rose when economic conditions were poor, but fell when economic conditions improved. So, here, it appeared, was clear evidence for the harmful effects of direct competition between groups. In fact, when depressions or recessions intensify such competition, it appears, overt violence against the weaker minority group may increase.

The findings reported by Hovland and Sears (1940) were dramatic, but the ultimate value of any scientific finding lies in the extent to which it can be replicated by other researchers; only if such replications succeed can we accept initial results with confidence. But in fact, later efforts to replicate these findings reported by Hovland and Sears ran into serious difficulties. One major study by Hepworth and West (1988), using more modern techniques of data analysis, did seem to confirm Hovland and Sears' (1940) original results. However, this was only true when a different index of economic conditions was substituted for the measures relating to cotton used in the initial study. Even worse, this measure (the Ayres index) is one that has subsequently been discarded by economists as having questionable validity.

Even more doubt has been cast on Hovland and Sears' findings by a study conducted by Green, Glaser, and Rich (1998). These researchers obtained records of all *hate crimes* perpetrated in New York City during a nine-year period, and then related the incidence of these crimes to one useful measure of economic conditions—the unemployment rate. (Hate crimes were defined as crimes committed against a person, group, or place because of the race, religion, ethnicity, or sexual orientation of the victim, so they were similar, conceptually, to the lynchings studied by Hovland and Sears.) Green, Glaser, and Rich (1998) conducted these analyses using the most modern statistical techniques available; for instance, they related unemployment rates at a given time to the incidence of hate crimes at twelve later times (e.g., one month later, several months later, etc.) Yet, despite these sophisticated techniques of data analysis, results were generally negative: no strong or stable relationship between unemployment and hate crimes was uncovered (refer to Figure 6.6).

So where does leave us? Why did Hovland and Sears find evidence of a strong relationship between economic hardship and racially motivated violence while modern research, using more sophisticated methods, did not?

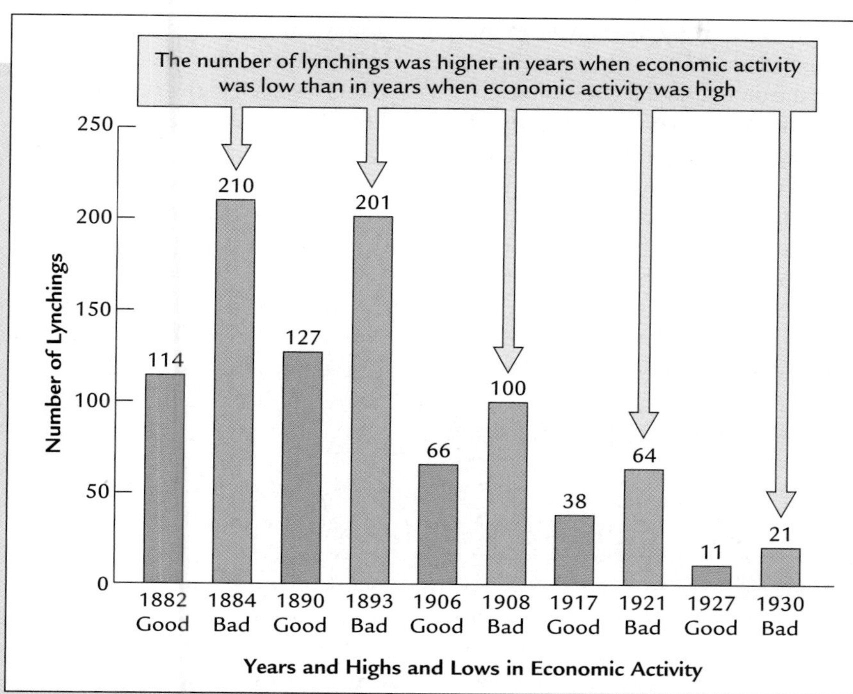

FIGURE 6.6

Racial Violence and Economic Conditions. In a classic study *(upper panel),* Hovland and Sears (1940) found that the number of lynchings in the United States—primarily of African Americans and mainly in Southern states—varied with economic conditions. Lynchings increased when times were bad, but decreased when economic conditions improved. In contrast, more recent research *(lower panel)* has failed to find evidence of a clear link between "hate crimes" and economic conditions. These contrasting results may stem from several different factors.

[SOURCE: BASED ON DATA FROM HOVLAND & SEARS, 1940 AND GREEN, GLASER, & RICH, 1998.]

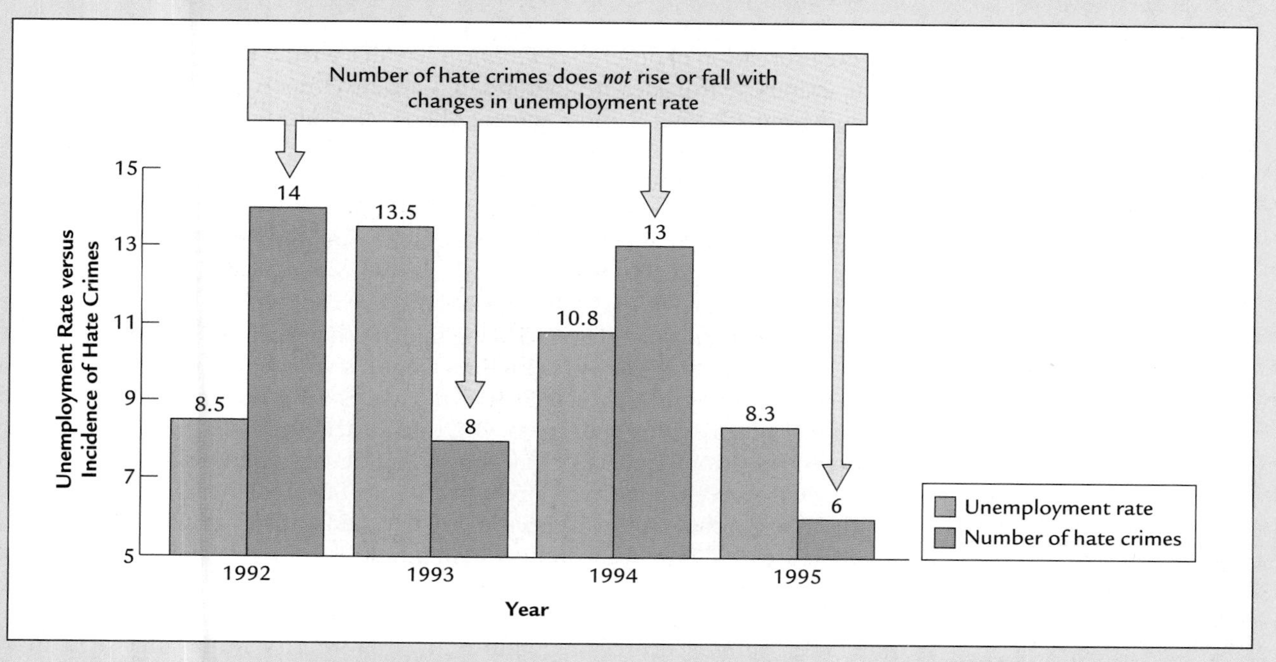

(continued)

SOCIAL PSYCHOLOGY: THIRTY YEARS OF PROGRESS *(CONTINUED)*

One possibility is that there was something unique about the period of time studied by Hovland and Sears; it was, after all, a very unsettled and difficult period for the South, which had still not recovered from the devastation of the Civil War. Perhaps more important, during this period, many political leaders in the South attributed blame for bad times to African Americans; this may have served to focus economic discontent on African Americans and channel it into intergroup violence against them. In contrast, similar action by political leaders was lacking in the later period studied by Green, Glaser, and Rich (1998). Finally, it is possible that the unsophisticated statistical methods used by Hovland and Sears (the best available at the time) and the questionable measures of economic hardship they adopted simply produced spurious findings—ones that were a chance occurrence and could not be replicated. Whatever the reason, comparing the study conducted by Hovland and Sears with more modern research offers a clear illustration of the progress made by social psychology in the intervening years. Our research designs, methods of data analysis, and theoretical frameworks are all much stronger today than they were thirty years ago, when we described the Hovland and Sears research in the first edition of this text. Given these advances, we place greater confidence in the more recent findings and conclude that while there may indeed be a link between economic hardship and violence against minority groups, it is far more complex in nature, and much harder to discern, than the frustration-aggression theory suggests.

Early Experience: The Role of Social Learning

A second explanation for the origins of prejudice is straightforward: it suggests that prejudice is *learned* and that it develops in much the same manner, and through the same basic mechanisms, as other attitudes (refer to our discussion in Chapter 4). According to this **social learning view,** children acquire negative attitudes toward various social groups because they hear such views expressed by parents, friends, teachers, and others, and because they are directly rewarded (with love, praise, and approval) for adopting these views. In addition to direct observation of others, *social norms*—rules within a given group suggesting what actions or attitudes are appropriate—are also important (Pettigrew, 1969). As we will see in Chapter 9, most persons choose to conform to most social norms of groups to which they belong. The development and expression of prejudice toward others often stems from this tendency. "If the members of my group dislike them," many children seem to reason, "then I should, too!" (As we'll soon see, evidence that the members of one's group *like* persons belonging to another group that is the target of strong prejudice can sometimes serve to weaken such negative reactions [e.g. Pettigrew, 1997; Wright et al., 1997]).

Direct experience with persons belonging to other groups also shapes racial attitudes and two other aspects of prejudice—concern with acting in a prejudiced manner, and restraint when interacting with persons outside our own group (mainly to avoid disputes or unpleasantness with them; Fazio & Towles-Schwen, 1999). Evidence for the strong impact of childhood experiences on several aspects of racial prejudice has recently been reported by Towles-Schwen & Fazio (2001).

social learning view (of prejudice): The view that prejudice is acquired through direct and vicarious experience in much the same manner as other attitudes.

These researchers asked Caucasian college students to complete a survey dealing with their childhood encounters with minorities. On this survey, they reported on how frequently they had interacted with various minorities and the extent to which these interactions were negative or positive. In addition, the participants rated their parents' degree of prejudice toward minority groups. In a separate session, an unobtrusive measure of their implicit racial attitudes was obtained, using the *bona fide pipeline* described earlier. In addition, participants also completed a questionnaire that measures motivation to avoid acting in a prejudiced manner and restraint when interacting with minority persons in order to avoid disputes with them.

When all of these variables were examined, intriguing patterns of relationships emerged. Implicit (automatically activated) racial attitudes were related to positive interactions with blacks in high school, but not during earlier periods of life. In contrast, concern with acting in a prejudiced manner was positively related to pleasant interactions with blacks during elementary school; such concern was also related to parental prejudice but in a negative manner: The lower the parental prejudice, the greater the concern participants expressed about acting in a prejudiced manner. Finally, restraint when interacting with minority group members was positively related to parental prejudice but negatively related to positive interactions with blacks during childhood. In other words, the more prejudiced the participants' parents and the less positive the participants' interactions with minority group persons, the greater restraint the participants reported. Because restraint reflects feelings of social awkwardness and anticipation of potential for conflict, these findings make very good sense.

Overall, then, it appears that racial attitudes are indeed shaped by social experience and reflect our parents' attitudes and the frequency and nature of our childhood experiences with minority group members. The less prejudiced our parents are and the more positive our contact with minority group members when we were children, the less prejudiced we are as adults, the greater our concern over acting in a prejudiced manner, and the less restraint we experience when interacting with minority group members (see Figure 6.7).

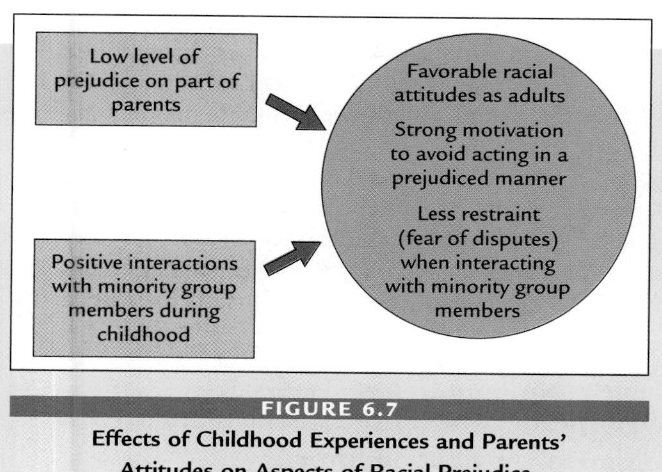

FIGURE 6.7

Effects of Childhood Experiences and Parents' Attitudes on Aspects of Racial Prejudice. Individuals' racial attitudes as adults reflect influences from their parents' attitudes and also from their childhood experiences with minority group members. The less prejudiced peoples' parents and the more positive individuals' interactions with minorities, the more favorable their racial attitudes, the greater their motivation to avoid acting in a prejudiced manner, and the less restraint they experience when interacting with minority persons.

[SOURCE: BASED ON SUGGESTIONS FROM TOWLES-SCHWEN & FAZIO, 2001.]

FIGURE 6.8

The Mass Media: Do They Reflect Reality in Their Presentation of People of Color?

At the present time, the mass media in the United States represent African Americans and other minority groups in a more favorable light than was true in the past. In part, this is due to actual trends in society: persons belonging to minority groups now fill many more high-status positions than before. (*Left photo:* Colin Powell, Secretary of State for the United States; *right photo:* Dr. Shirley Ann Jackson, President of Rensselaer Polytechnic Institute.)

The mass media also play a role in the development of prejudice. Until recently, members of various racial and ethnic minorities were shown infrequently in movies or on television. And when they did appear, they were often cast in low-status or comic roles. Fortunately, this situation has changed greatly in recent years in the United States and elsewhere. Members of various racial and ethnic minorities are now shown in a somewhat more favorable manner than was true in the past—as heroes or heroines and as holding high-status positions, such as physician, scientist, or general. In part, this trend reflects reality: Minority group members do indeed fill more high-status positions than in the past. For instance, Colin Powell was chosen by President Bush to be Secretary of State for the United States, and the president of one of our universities is an African American woman who is a physicist with a Ph.D. degree from the Massachusetts Institute of Technology (see Figure 6.8).

Social Categorization: The Us-versus-Them Effect and the "Ultimate" Attribution Error

social categorization: The tendency to divide the social world into two separate categories: our in-group ("us") and various out-groups ("them").

in-group: The social group to which an individual perceives herself or himself as belonging ("us").

out-group: Any group other than the one to which individuals perceive themselves belonging.

A third perspective on the origins of prejudice begins with a basic fact: People generally divide the social world into two distinct categories—*us* and *them*—referred to as **social categorization.** In short, they view other persons as belonging to either their own group (usually termed the **in-group**) or another group (the **out-group**). Such distinctions are based on many dimensions, including race, religion, sex, age, ethnic background, occupation, and income, to name just a few (see Figure 6.9).

If the process of dividing the social world into "us" and "them" stopped there, it would have little bearing on prejudice. Unfortunately, however, it does not. Sharply contrasting feelings and beliefs are usually attached to members of one's

FIGURE 6.9

Social Categorization: A Fact of Social Life.
As shown here, we have a strong tendency to divide the social world into two opposing camps: "us"—our own in-group—and "them"—everyone else!

in-group and members of various out-groups. Persons in the former (us) category are viewed in favorable terms, while those in the latter (them) category are perceived more negatively. Out-group members are assumed to possess more undesirable traits, are perceived as being more alike (i.e., more homogeneous) than members of the in-group, and are often disliked (Judd, Ryan, & Parke, 1991; Lambert, 1995; Linville & Fischer, 1993). The in-group/out-group distinction also affects *attribution*—the ways in which we explain the actions of persons belonging to these two categories. We tend to attribute desirable behaviors by members of our in-group to stable, internal causes (e.g., their admirable traits), but attribute desirable behaviors by members of out-groups to transitory factors or to external causes (Hewstone, Bond, & Wan, 1983). This tendency to make more favorable and flattering attributions about members of one's own group than about members of other groups is sometimes described as the **ultimate attribution error,** for it carries the self-serving bias we described in Chapter 2 into the area of intergroup relations—with potentially devastating effects.

That strong tendencies to divide the social world into "us" and "them" exist and color our perceptions of these groups have been demonstrated in many studies (e.g., Stephan, 1985; Tajfel, 1982; Harasty, 1997). But how, precisely, does social categorization lead to prejudice? An intriguing answer has been provided by Tajfel and his colleagues (e.g., Tajfel & Turner, 1986; Vanbeselaere, 1991) in **social identity theory.** This theory suggests that individuals seek to enhance their self-esteem by identifying with specific social groups. This tactic can succeed, however, only to the extent that the persons involved perceive these groups as somehow superior to other, competing groups. Because all individuals are subject to the same tendencies, the final result is inevitable: Each group seeks to view itself as different

ultimate attribution error: The tendency to make more favorable and flattering attributions about members of one's own group than about members of other groups.

social identity theory: A theory suggesting that individuals seek to enhance their own self-esteem by identifying with specific social groups.

from—and also better than—its rivals, and prejudice arises out of this clash of social perceptions. Findings indicate that balanced against these tendencies is our desire to be fair-minded, and this may somewhat moderate our propensity to boost our own group and put other groups down (Singh, Choo, and Poh, 1998). However, in general, the strong need to enhance our self-esteem seems to win out, and we see other groups as inferior to our own (e.g., Meindl & Lerner, 1985).

Evidence for this conclusion is provided by a study by Hornsey and Hogg (2000). Drawing on social identity theory, these researchers reasoned that only when individuals feel secure in their own group or cultural identity can they be generous and tolerant toward other groups or cultures. In other words, only when they feel secure with respect to their own group (e.g., secure about its goodness or superiority) will they hold positive attitudes toward other groups or, conversely, show reduced prejudice toward these out-groups. This reasoning leads to an intriguing prediction: Under conditions in which individuals feel that the distinctiveness (superiority) of their own group or culture is somehow threatened, they will react negatively to other groups, and, moreover, these reactions will be intensified by perceived similarity between their own group and the other groups. Why? Because such similarity threatens the distinctiveness of their own group. In contrast, when individuals do not feel that the distinctiveness of their own group is being threatened or challenged, similarity to other groups has opposite effects: the greater the similarity perceived between their own group and these other groups, the more positive their reaction to these groups.

To test these predictions, Hornsey and Hogg (2000) had students at a large university in Australia read short written passages indicating either that math–science students and humanities students are very different in their ideas and attitudes (the *low-similarity* condition) or that they are actually very similar (the *high-similarity* condition). Participants belonged to one group or the other. After reading these passages, half of the participants were induced to think about the fact that they are students at the same university (a procedure designed to threaten the distinctiveness of their own group—either humanities or math–science); this was the *superordinate* condition. The remaining participants were induced to think both about being students at the same university *and* about their identity as either a math–science or a humanities student; this was the *simultaneous* condition.

After these procedures were completed, students rated the extent to which they thought they would enjoy working with a group of humanities or math–science students, and how difficult working with such students would be. Participants rated both their own group and the other group in this manner. It was predicted that in the simultaneous condition, in which the distinctiveness of their own group was not threatened, participants would express less bias toward the other group when it had been described as similar rather than dissimilar to their own. In contrast, in the superordinate condition, in which the distinctiveness of their own group had been threatened, the opposite would be true: participants would actually express more bias toward an out-group described as similar to their own, because this would pose an even bigger threat to their group's distinctiveness or superiority. As you can see from Figure 6.10, both predictions were confirmed.

These findings suggest that efforts to reduce prejudice between groups by breaking down the distinction between "us" and "them" can succeed, but only if doing so does not threaten each group's unique identity or sense of superiority. In other words, our tendency to divide the social world into these two opposing categories seems to serve important esteem-boosting functions for us; if these are overlooked, efforts to reduce prejudice by urging distinct cultural or ethnic groups to view themselves as "one" or as highly similar may well backfire. We'll have more to say about this later, in our discussion of techniques for reducing prejudice.

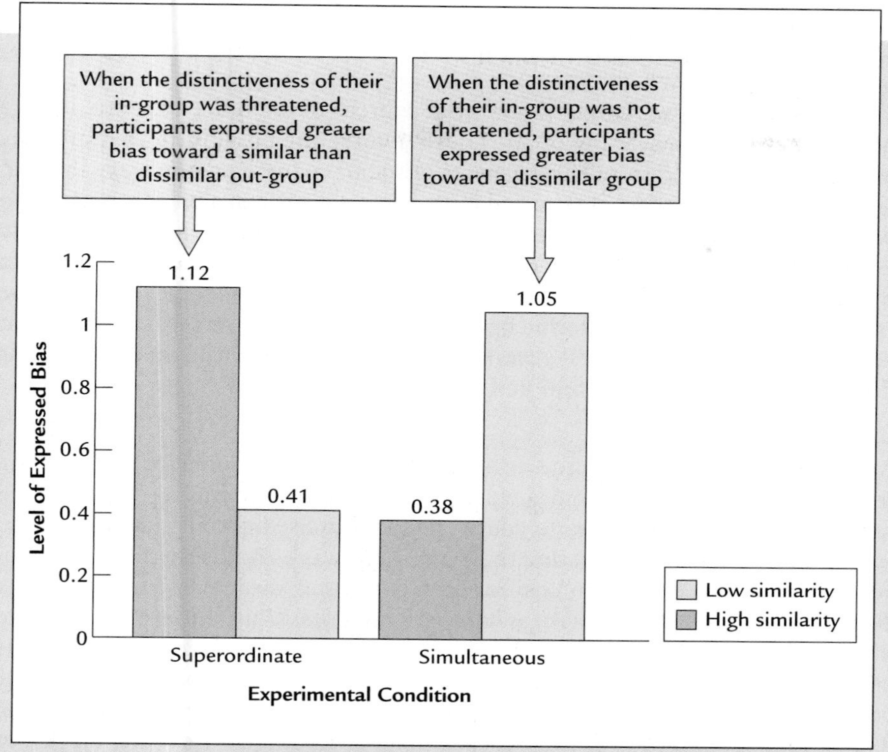

FIGURE 6.10

Social Identity Theory in Action.

When the distinctiveness of their own group was not threatened, individuals reported less bias toward an out-group when it was similar to their own group than when it was dissimilar. However, when the distinctiveness of their own group had been threatened, the participants actually expressed more bias toward an out-group described as similar to their own. These findings are predicted by *social identity theory.*

[SOURCE: HORNSEY & HOGG, 2000.]

KEY POINTS

- Prejudice stems from several different sources. One of these is direct intergroup conflict—situations in which social groups compete for the same scarce resources.
- A second basis for prejudice is early experience and the social learning it involves.
- Findings indicate that parents' degree of prejudice and people's direct experiences with minority groups during childhood both play an important role in shaping racial prejudice.
- Prejudice also derives from our tendencies to divide the world into "us" and "them" and to view our own group much more favorably than various out-groups.

Cognitive Sources of Prejudice: Stereotypes, Explicit and Implicit

Next, we come to potential sources of prejudice that are, in some respects, the most unsettling of all. These involve the possibility that prejudice stems, at least in part, from basic aspects of *social cognition*—the ways in which we think about other persons, store and integrate information about them, and later use this information to draw inferences about them or make social judgments. Because the influence of such factors has been at the very center of recent research on the origins of prejudice, we'll divide our discussion of this topic into two parts. First we'll examine the nature and operation of *stereotypes*—a key cognitive component in prejudice. Then we'll examine other cognitive mechanisms that also play a role in the occurrence of prejudice.

■ STEREOTYPES: WHAT THEY ARE AND HOW THEY OPERATE. Consider the following groups: Korean Americans, homosexuals, Jews, Mexican Americans, African Americans, homeless people. Suppose you were asked to list the traits most characteristic of each. Would you find this to be a difficult task? Probably not. You would probably be able to construct a list for each group and, moreover, you *could probably do so even for groups with whom you have had limited personal contact.* Why? The reason involves the existence and operation of **stereotypes**—cognitive frameworks consisting of knowledge and beliefs about specific social groups and the typical or "modal" traits supposedly possessed by persons belonging to these groups (Judd, Ryan, & Parke, 1991). Stereotypes suggest, in other words, that all persons belonging to social groups possess certain traits, at least to a degree. Once a stereotype is activated, these traits come readily to mind, and it is this fact that explains the ease with which you can probably construct lists like the ones mentioned above. You may not have had much direct experience with Korean Americans, Mexican Americans, Jews, or homeless people, but you *do* have stereotypes for them, so you can readily bring these to mind.

I (RAB) encounter this aspect of stereotypes myself at virtually every party I attend. As soon as I tell a new acquaintance that I'm a psychologist, I can almost see reflections in their eyes of their stereotypes about my field! "Hmm . . . I'd better watch what I say; he's probably analyzing everything. And I'd better not look him in the eye too much . . . he might read my mind or even hypnotize me!" Those are the kind of thoughts many people seem to have.

Like other cognitive frameworks we have considered, stereotypes exert strong effects on how we process social information. Information relevant to an activated stereotype is often processed more quickly, and remembered better, than information unrelated to it (e.g., Dovidio, Evans, & Tyler, 1986; Macrae et al., 1997). Similarly, stereotypes lead persons holding them to pay attention to specific types of information—usually, information consistent with the stereotypes. And when information *inconsistent* with stereotypes does manage to enter consciousness, it may be actively refuted or changed in subtle ways that make it seem *consistent* with the stereotype (Kunda & Oleson, 1995; O'Sullivan & Durso, 1984). For instance, research findings indicate that when we encounter someone who belongs to a group about whom we have a stereotype, and this person does not seem to fit the stereotype (e.g., a highly intelligent and cultivated person who is also a member of a minority group), we do not necessarily alter our stereotype. Rather, we place such persons into a special category or *subtype* consisting of persons who do not confirm the schema or stereotype (e.g., Richards & Hewstone, 2001). Another reaction to information inconsistent with stereotypes involves making *tacit inferences* that change the meaning of this information to *make* it consistent with the stereo-

stereotypes: Beliefs to the effect that all members of specific social groups share certain traits or characteristics. Stereotypes are cognitive frameworks that strongly influence the processing of incoming social information.

type (e.g., Kunda & Sherman-Williams, 1993). In other words, we change the meaning of the information in our minds or draw conclusions about it that make it fit with the stereotype. Here's an example: Suppose you learn that a well-known liberal politician has come out in favor of a large tax cut. This information is inconsistent with your stereotype for liberals, so you quickly draw an inference that permits you to make sense of this unexpected information—for instance, you surmise that the politician did this because most of the cut will go to people with low incomes. This is consistent with your stereotype of liberal politicians, so these tacit inferences help you to retain your stereotype intact, despite the presence of disconfirming information. In view of such effects—which appear to be both strong and general in scope—two social psychologists, Dunning and Sherman (1997), have described stereotypes as *inferential prisons:* once they are formed, they shape our perceptions of other persons so that new information about these persons is interpreted as confirming our stereotypes, even if this is not the case.

■ IMPLICIT STEREOTYPES: WHEN BELIEFS WE DON'T RECOGNIZE INFLUENCE OUR BEHAVIOR. Earlier, we noted that racial attitudes are often implicit: they exist, and can influence many forms of behavior, even when the persons holding them are unaware of their existence or of their impact on behavior. The same seems to be true for stereotypes. As noted by Greenwald and Banaji (1995), we often hold implicit stereotypes that we can't identify easily through introspection, but that still influence our beliefs about the characteristics possessed by members of a particular social category. In other words, racial, ethnic, or gender stereotypes of which we are largely unaware can be activated by various stimuli (e.g., members of the groups to which these stereotypes apply). And once they are activated, these stereotypes influence our thinking, decisions, and even overt behavior concerning persons to whom these stereotypes apply. We have already described one means for measuring implicit attitudes or stereotypes—the bona fide pipeline (e.g., Towles-Schwen & Fazio, 2001). Another was devised by Banaji and Hardin (1996) and also makes use of priming. In this procedure, participants are first shown primes at *subliminal levels*—these stimuli are presented for such a short period of time that participants can't recognize or identify them. For instance, here's how these procedures worked in one recent study (Kawakami & Dovidio, 2001). In this case, the primes were schematic faces of blacks or whites. After the primes were shown for a very short period (fifteen to thirty milliseconds), a specific kind of word category was cued by a letter or symbol—in this study, one letter stood for "houses" and the other for "persons." Finally, words related to racial stereotypes for blacks and whites, or to the neutral category *houses,* were presented and participants were asked to indicate whether these words could ever describe a member of the cued word category (i.e., a person or a house). For instance, one target word related to the racial stereotype for whites was *conventional,* while one target word related to the racial stereotype for blacks was *musical.* An example of the words related to houses was *drafty.*

If implicit racial stereotypes are activated by the priming stimuli (faces of black and white persons), then response times to the target words should vary as a function of these primes. Specifically, participants should respond more quickly to words related to the racial stereotype for whites after seeing a white prime than a black prime, and faster to words related to the racial stereotype for blacks after seeing a black prime than a white prime. As you can see from Figure 6.11 on page 228, this is precisely what was found. Similar results have been reported in many other studies, which, together, indicate that implicit stereotypes can be automatically activated toward blacks (e.g., Devine, 1989; Kawakami, Dion, & Dovidio, 1998), women and men (e.g., Banaji & Hardin, 1996), elderly people (e.g., Hense, Penner, & Nelson,

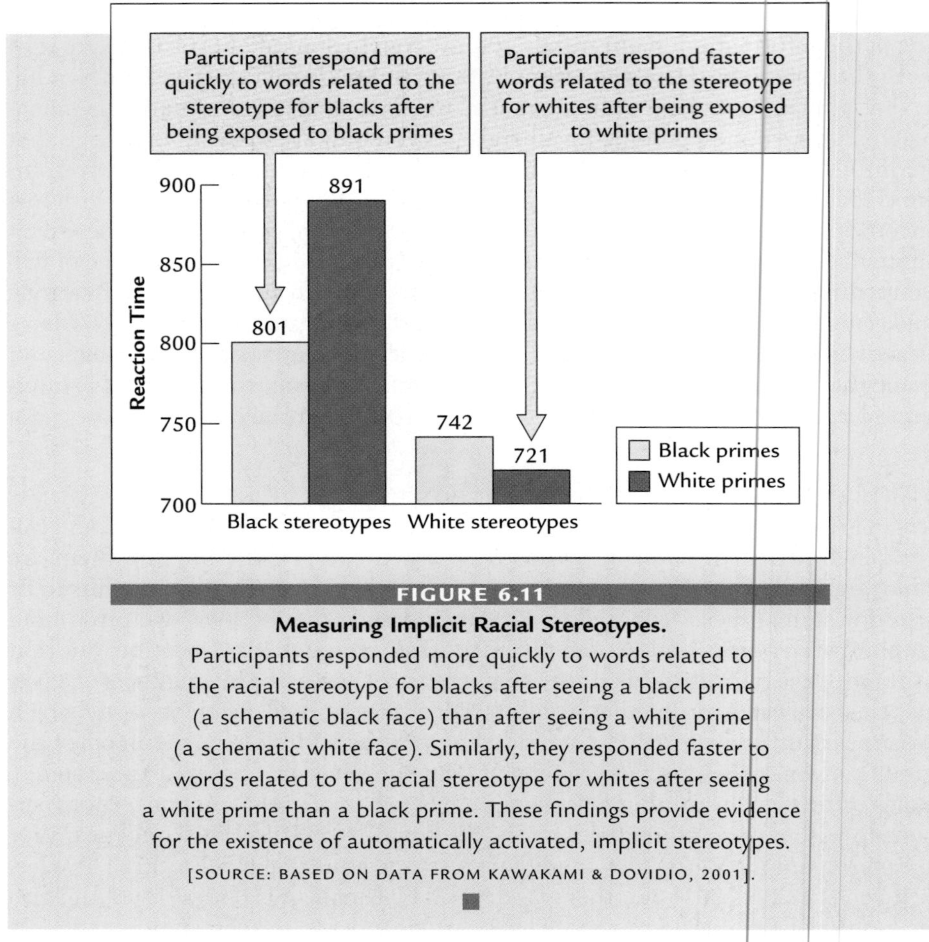

FIGURE 6.11

Measuring Implicit Racial Stereotypes.

Participants responded more quickly to words related to the racial stereotype for blacks after seeing a black prime (a schematic black face) than after seeing a white prime (a schematic white face). Similarly, they responded faster to words related to the racial stereotype for whites after seeing a white prime than a black prime. These findings provide evidence for the existence of automatically activated, implicit stereotypes. [SOURCE: BASED ON DATA FROM KAWAKAMI & DOVIDIO, 2001].

1995), Asians (e.g., Macrae, Bodenhausen, & Milne, 1995), and many other groups (e.g., soccer hooligans, child abusers, skinheads) (e.g., Kawakami et al., 2000)—even professors (Dijksterhuis & van Knippenberg, 1996).

The important thing about such stereotypes is this: We may not be aware of the fact that they are operating, but they can still strongly influence our judgments or decisions about other people, or even how we interact with them. In particular, growing evidence suggests that such implicit stereotypes may be better predictors of subtle or spontaneous expressions of bias than explicit measures obtained through attitude questionnaires or other kinds of self-report (e.g., Dovidio et al., 1997). Clearly, then, implicit stereotypes are something we should definitely not overlook in our efforts to understand the basic nature of prejudice and discrimination.

Other Cognitive Mechanisms in Prejudice: Illusory Correlations and Out-group Homogeneity

Consider the following set of information: (1) There are one thousand members of Group A, but only one hundred members of Group B; (2) one hundred members of Group A were arrested by the police last year, and ten members of Group B were arrested. Suppose you were asked to evaluate the criminal tendencies of these two groups. Would your ratings of them differ? Your first answer is probably "Of course not—why should they?" The rate of criminal behavior is 10 percent in both groups, so why rate them differently? Surprisingly, though, a large body of evidence suggests that you might actually assign a less favorable rating to Group B (Johnson & Mullen, 1994; McConnell, Sherman, & Hamilton, 1994). Social psychologists refer to this tendency to overestimate the rate of negative behaviors in relatively small groups as **illusory correlations.** This term makes a great deal of sense, because such effects involve perceiving links between variables that aren't really there—in this case, links between being a member of Group B and the tendency to engage in criminal behavior.

As you can readily see, illusory correlations, to the extent they occur, have important implications for prejudice. In particular, they help explain why negative behaviors and tendencies are often attributed by majority group members to the members of various minority groups. For example, some social psychologists have suggested that illusory correlation effects help explain why many white persons in the United States overestimate crime rates among African American males (Hamilton & Sherman, 1989). For many complex reasons, young African American men are, in fact, arrested for various crimes at higher rates than are young white men or men of Asian descent (United States Department of Justice, 1994). But white Americans tend to *overestimate* the size of this difference, and this can be interpreted as an instance of illusory correlation.

Why do such effects occur? One explanation is based on the distinctiveness of infrequent events or stimuli. According to this view, infrequent events are distinctive—readily noticed. As such, they are encoded more extensively than are other items when they are encountered, and so become more accessible in memory. When judgments about the groups involved are made at later times, therefore, the distinctive events come readily to mind, and this leads to overinterpretation of their importance. Consider how this explanation applies to the tendency of white Americans to overestimate crime rates among African Americans. African Americans are a minority group (they constitute about 12 percent of the total population); thus, they are high in distinctiveness. Many criminal behaviors, too, are highly distinctive (relatively rare), despite the fact that their incidence has increased greatly in recent decades. When news reports show African Americans being arrested for such crimes, therefore, this information is processed extensively and becomes highly accessible in memory. Thus, it is readily available at later times and may lead to the tendency to overestimate crime rates among minority groups—an instance of illusory correlation. A large number of studies offer support for this *distinctiveness-based interpretation* of illusory correlation (Stroessner, Hamilton, & Mackie, 1992), so with certain modifications, it appears to be quite useful in understanding roots of this kind of cognitive error.

illusory correlations: The perception of a stronger association between two variables than actually exists because each is a distinctive event and the co-occurrence of such events is readily entered into and retrieved from memory.

illusion of out-group homogeneity: The tendency to perceive members of out-groups as more similar to one another (less variable) than the members of one's own in-group.

in-group differentiation: The tendency to perceive members of our own group as showing much larger differences from one another (as being more heterogeneous) than do those of other groups.

■ IN-GROUP DIFFERENTIATION, OUT-GROUP HOMOGENEITY: "THEY'RE ALL THE SAME"—OR ARE THEY? Persons who hold strong prejudice toward some social group often make remarks like these: "You know what they're like; they're all the same." What such comments imply is that the members of an out-group are much more similar to one another (more homogeneous) than are the members of one's own group. This tendency to perceive persons belonging to groups other than one's own as all alike is known as the **illusion of out-group homogeneity** (Linville, Fischer, & Salovey, 1989). The mirror image of this is **in-group differentiation**—the tendency to perceive members of our own group as showing much larger differences from one another (as being more heterogeneous) than do those of other groups.

Existence of the illusion of out-group homogeneity has been demonstrated in many different contexts. For example, individuals tend to perceive persons older or younger than themselves as more similar to one another in terms of personal traits than are persons in their own age group—an intriguing type of generation gap (Linville, Fischer, & Salovey, 1989); they even perceive students from another university as more homogeneous than students at their own university—especially when these persons appear to be biased against *them* (Rothgerber, 1997).

What accounts for the tendency to perceive members of other groups as more homogeneous than members of our own group? One explanation involves the fact that we have a great deal of experience with members of our own group, and so are exposed to a wider range of individual variation within that group. In contrast, we generally have much less experience with members of other groups, and hence less exposure to their individual variations (e.g., Linville, Fischer, & Salovey, 1989). Whatever the precise basis for its existence (see, e.g., Lee and Ottati, 1993), the tendency to perceive other groups as more homogeneous than our own can play an important role in prejudice and in the persistence of negative stereotypes. (Throughout this discussion, we have focused primarily on racial and ethnic prejudice. While these are very important, they are certainly not the only forms of prejudice with harmful effects on their targets. For discussion of another, please see the following **Beyond the Headlines** section.)

BEYOND THE HEADLINES: AS SOCIAL PSYCHOLOGISTS SEE IT

THIN MAY BE "IN," BUT IN THE UNITED STATES, "FAT IS WHERE IT'S AT": COMBATING PREJUDICE AGAINST OBESE PERSONS

Mayor Signs San Francisco Anti-Body Size Discrimination Law

San Francisco, May 26, 2000—Mayor Willie Brown today signed the height/weight ordinance, making it illegal to discriminate against anyone based on their body size. And in related court action, United Airlines lost a weight discrimination case filed in the 9th Circuit Court of Appeals in San Francisco. The courts ruled that United Airlines discriminated against female flight attendants from 1989 to 1994 by demanding they maintain thinner bodies than their male counterparts. Attendants lost pay or were suspended or fired when they didn't manage to maintain the "image" by becoming heavier than the ideal weight range for women with medium body frames. Men, on the other hand, could fall into the large body frame range. United eliminated all weight standards the same year the lawsuit was filed.

As you probably know, there is an epidemic of obesity in the United States; more than 50 percent of the adult population over age forty is significantly overweight. So, in a sense, overweight people are now in the majority, at least in the United States. Yet, like women—a group that constitutes an actual majority of the population—obese persons are often the target of strong prejudice. This is part of a more general phenomenon known as *appearance prejudice*—prejudice against persons who are not considered to be attractive in their societies. In most Western countries (and especially in the United States), thin is indeed "in" right now, with the result that people who are overweight are viewed as unattractive. The result is many kinds of subtle discrimination against them, and some fairly blatant forms as well. Requiring flight attendants to be slim amounts to open discrimination, and it has been declared illegal by the courts. However, there are more subtle effects of prejudice against overweight persons as well. As noted by Berscheid (1996), they are often rejected for jobs for which appearance plays no role and their excess weight would in no way prevent them from performing adequately, simply because they are viewed as being unattractive, therefore conveying the "wrong image" for the company doing the hiring.

It's interesting to note, by the way, that being thin is *not* universally viewed as attractive. For instance, in the Efik community of Nigeria, young girls spend several weeks in "fattening rooms," where they are intensively overfed and told to refrain from exercise so that they can gain weight. "Beauty is in the weight," said a fifty-year-old mother, who was herself sent to a fattening room at age seven. Said a village chief, "People might laugh at parents who didn't have money to allow their child to pass through this rite of passage."

However, in societies in which being overweight is considered unattractive, such persons have recently formed organizations designed to protect their rights—and to combat such prejudice. One such organization, NAAFA (the National Association to Advance Fat Acceptance) urges members to write letters, engage in protests, adopt economic sanctions, and give speeches to promote legislation protecting the rights of obese persons. Another organization, the Fat Activist Task Force, mounts organized campaigns to fight what it terms "size discrimination" (see Figure 6.12).

In sum, prejudice against persons who are overweight appears to be an important and (please excuse the pun!) growing problem in a society in which more and more persons seem to lose the battle of the bulge. Are the steps advocated by the organizations listed above likely to be effective in combating size discrimination? To answer that question, we'll turn next to a discussion of various tactics that do seem to be effective in reducing the impact of prejudice.

FIGURE 6.12

Combating Prejudice Based on Weight: A Sign of the Times.
As the number of persons who are overweight has increased, concern over prejudice toward such people has also increased. This, in turn, has led to the founding of several organizations concerned with protecting the rights of such persons. These organizations urge members to write letters, engage in protests, adopt economic sanctions, and give speeches to promote legislation protecting the rights of obese persons.

KEY POINTS

- Prejudice sometimes stems from basic aspects of social cognition—the ways in which we process social information.
- *Stereotypes* are cognitive frameworks suggesting that all persons belonging to a social group show similar characteristics. Stereotypes strongly influence social thought. For instance, when activated, they lead us to form tacit inferences about others that then make information that is inconsistent with stereotypes seem to be consistent with them.
- Implicit stereotypes can be activated automatically by various stimuli. Even though we are not aware of such activation, it can strongly affect our thinking about, and behavior toward, persons belonging to the groups that are the focus of these stereotypes.
- Findings indicate that stereotypes are closely linked to prejudice; for example, highly prejudiced persons respond more quickly to stereotype-related words than do less prejudiced persons.
- Other cognitive sources of prejudice include *illusory correlations*—the tendency to overestimate the strength of relationships between social categories and negative behaviors—and the *illusion of out-group homogeneity*—the tendency to perceive out-groups as more homogeneous than our own in-group.
- Prejudice takes many forms, and recently it has been directed against persons who are overweight. In response, individuals in this group have taken vigorous steps to protect their rights by lobbying for protective legislation and related actions.

Why Prejudice Is *Not* Inevitable: Techniques for Countering Its Effects

Sad to relate, prejudice appears to be an all too common aspect of life in most, if not all, societies. Does this mean that it is inevitable? Or can prejudice and the repulsive effects it produces be eliminated, or at least reduced? Social psychologists are, by nature, an optimistic group, so they have generally approached this question from the following perspective: "Yes, prejudice *can* be reduced, and it is our job to find out how." Let's now take a look at several promising techniques for reducing prejudice.

Breaking the Cycle of Prejudice: On Learning *Not* to Hate

Few persons would suggest that children are born with prejudices firmly in place. Rather, most would contend that bigots are *made,* not born. Social psychologists share this view: They believe that children acquire prejudice from their parents, other adults, experiences during childhood (e.g., Towles-Schwen & Fazio, 2001), and the mass media. Given this belief, one useful technique for reducing prejudice follows logically: Somehow, we must discourage parents and other adults from training children in bigotry.

Having stated this principle, we must now admit that putting it into practice is far from simple. How can we induce parents who are themselves highly prejudiced to encourage unbiased views among their children? One possibility involves calling parents' attention to their own prejudice. Few persons are willing to describe themselves as bigoted; instead, they view their own negative attitudes toward various groups as entirely justified. A key initial step, therefore, is somehow convincing parents that the problem exists. Once they come face to face with their own prejudices, many do seem willing to modify their words and behavior so as to encourage lower levels of prejudice among their children.

Another argument that can be used to shift parents in the direction of teaching their children tolerance rather than prejudice lies in the fact that prejudice harms not only those who are its victims, but also those who hold such views (Dovidio & Gaertner, 1993; Jussim, 1991). Persons who are prejudiced, it appears, live in a world filled with needless fears, anxieties, and anger. They fear attack from presumably dangerous social groups, they worry about the health risks stemming from contact with such groups, and they experience anger and emotional turmoil over what they view as unjustified incursions by these groups into *their* neighborhoods, schools, or offices. In other words, their enjoyment of everyday activities and life itself is reduced by their own prejudice (Harris et al., 1992). Of course, offsetting such costs is the boost in self-esteem prejudiced persons sometimes feel when they derogate or *scapegoat* out-group members (see our earlier discussion of this topic; Branscombe & Wann, 1994; Fein & Spencer, 1997). Overall, though, it is clear that persons holding intense racial and ethnic prejudices suffer many harmful effects from these intolerant views. Because most parents want to do everything they can to further their children's well-being, calling these costs to their attention may be effective in discouraging them from transmitting prejudiced views to their offspring.

Direct Intergroup Contact: The Potential Benefits of Acquaintance

At the present time, many American cities resemble a social donut: a disintegrating and crime-ridden core inhabited primarily by minority groups, surrounded by a ring of relatively affluent suburbs inhabited mainly by whites and minority group members who have "made it" economically. Needless to say, contact between the people living in these different areas is minimal.

This state of affairs raises an intriguing question: Can prejudice be reduced by somehow increasing the degree of contact between different groups? The idea that it can is known as the **contact hypothesis,** and there are several good reasons for predicting that such a strategy might prove effective (Pettigrew, 1981, 1997). First, increased contact between persons from different groups can lead to a growing recognition of similarities between them. As we will see in Chapter 7, perceived similarity can generate enhanced mutual attraction. Second, although stereotypes are resistant to change, they *can* be altered when sufficient information inconsistent with them is encountered, or when individuals meet a sufficient number of exceptions to their stereotypes (Kunda & Oleson, 1995). Third, increased contact may help counter the illusion of out-group homogeneity described earlier. For these reasons, it seems possible that direct intergroup contact may be one effective means of combating prejudice. Is it? Existing evidence suggests that it is, but only when certain conditions are met: The groups interacting must be roughly equal in social status, the contact between them must involve cooperation and interdependence, the contact must permit them to get to know one another as individuals, norms favoring group equality must exist, and the persons involved must view one another as typical of their respective groups.

When contact between initially hostile groups occurs under these conditions, prejudice between them does seem to decrease (see Figure 6.13 on page 234; Aronson, Bridgeman, & Geffner, 1978; Schwarzwald, Amir, & Crain, 1992). As you can readily see, however, such conditions are rare. Moreover, contact with persons from out-groups, especially when these groups are the target of strong prejudice, can generate negative emotions such as anxiety, discomfort, and fear of appearing to be

contact hypothesis: The view that increased contact between members of various social groups can be effective in reducing prejudice between them. Such efforts seem to succeed only when contact takes place under specific, favorable conditions.

FIGURE 6.13

Intergroup Contact: One Means of Reducing Prejudice. When persons from different racial or ethnic groups have increased contact with each other, prejudice between them may be reduced. For such beneficial effects to occur, however, intergroup contact must occur under certain conditions.

prejudiced (Bodenhausen, 1993; Fazio & Hilden, 2001). Such reactions can work against the potential benefits of contact. In view of such considerations, many social psychologists have voiced pessimism concerning the effectiveness of intergroup contact as a means of reducing prejudice. Recently, however, a modified version of the contact hypothesis, known as the *extended contact hypothesis,* has helped to reverse these gloomy conclusions.

The **extended contact hypothesis** suggests that direct contact between persons from different groups is not essential for reducing prejudice between them. In fact, such beneficial effects can be produced if the persons in question merely *know* that persons in their own group have formed close friendships with persons from the other group (e.g., Pettigrew, 1997; Wright et al., 1997). How can knowledge of such cross-group friendship help to reduce prejudice? In several different ways. For instance, knowledge of such friendship can indicate that contact with out-group members is acceptable—that the norms of the group are not so anti-out-group as individuals might initially have believed. Similarly, knowing that members of one's own group enjoy close friendships with members of an out-group can help to reduce anxiety about interacting with them: If someone we know enjoys such contact, why shouldn't we? Third, the existence of such cross-group friendships suggests that members of an out-group don't necessarily dislike members of our own in-group. Finally, such friendships can generate increased empathy and understanding between groups; in other words, we don't necessarily have to experience close contact with persons from an out-group to feel more positively toward them—learning that members of our own in-group have had such experiences can be sufficient.

extended contact hypothesis: A view suggesting that simply knowing that members of one's own group have formed close friendships with members of an out-group can reduce prejudice against that group.

A growing body of research evidence provides support for the accuracy of this reasoning, and for the extended contact hypothesis. For instance, in one investigation of this hypothesis (Pettigrew, 1997), almost four thousand people living in several European countries completed a questionnaire that measured the extent to which they had friendships with people outside their own cultural group, their level of prejudice toward out-groups generally, their beliefs about immigration, and their feelings toward a very wide range of ethnic and cultural groups (e.g., people from various European countries, North Africans, Turks, black Africans, Asians, West Indians, Jews). Results offered striking support for the benefits of intergroup friendships. The greater the number of cross-group friendships participants reported, the lower their prejudice toward various out-groups and the more favorable their beliefs about immigration into their country. In addition, the greater their experience with intergroup friendships, the more positive their feelings toward many other groups—including ones with which they had experienced little or no contact. This latter finding is very important, for it suggests that reductions in prejudice produced by friendships with persons from one out-group may generalize to other out-groups as well.

Additional support for the value of intergroup friendships has been provided by laboratory as well as survey research (e.g., Wright et al., 1997), so it appears that contact between persons who belong to different groups can be a highly effective means for reducing prejudice between them, especially if these contacts develop into close friendships. Moreover, the beneficial effects of such friendships can readily spread to other persons who have not themselves experienced such contacts: simply knowing about them can be enough. In other words, merely learning that some people in one's own group get along well with persons belonging to other groups can be a highly effective means for countering the detestable effects of prejudice.

KEY POINTS

- Social psychologists believe that prejudice is not inevitable; it can be reduced by several techniques.
- One of these involves changing children's early experiences so that they are not taught bigotry by their parents and other adults.
- Another technique involves direct contact between persons from different groups. When this occurs under certain conditions, prejudice can be reduced.
- Findings indicate that simply knowing that members of one's own group have formed friendships with members of an out-group may be sufficient to reduce prejudice; this is known as the *extended contact hypothesis.*

Recategorization: Redrawing the Boundary between "Us" and "Them"

Think back to your high school days. Imagine that your school's basketball team is playing an important game against a rival school from a nearby town or neighborhood. In this case, you would certainly view your own school as "us" and the other school as "them." But now imagine that the other school's team wins, and goes on to play against a team from another state or province in a national tournament. *Now* how would you view them? The chances are good that, under these conditions, you would view the other school's team as "us"; after all, it represents your state or province. And of course, if a team from a state or province other than your own is playing against teams from other countries, you might now view it as "us" relative to those "foreigners."

Situations like this, in which we shift the boundary between "us" and "them," are quite common in everyday life, and they raise an interesting question: Can such shifts—or **recategorizations,** as they are termed by social psychologists—be used to reduce prejudice? A theory proposed by Gaertner and his colleagues (1989, 1993a) suggests that it can. This theory, known as the **common in-group identity model,** suggests that when individuals belonging to different social groups come to view themselves as members of a *single social entity,* their attitudes toward each other become more positive. These favorable attitudes then promote increased positive contacts between members of the previously separate groups, and this, in turn,

recategorization: Shifts in the boundary between an individual's in-group ("us") and some out-group ("them"). As a result of such recategorization, persons formerly viewed as out-group members may now be viewed as belonging to the in-group.

common in-group identity model: A theory suggesting that to the extent that individuals in different groups view themselves as members of a single social entity, positive contacts between them will increase and intergroup bias will be reduced.

reduces intergroup bias still further. In short, weakening or eliminating initial us–them boundaries starts a process that carries the persons involved toward major reductions in prejudice and hostility.

How can we induce people belonging to different groups to perceive each other as members of a single group? Gaertner and his colleagues (1990) suggest that one crucial factor is the experience of working together cooperatively. When individuals belonging to initially distinct groups work together toward shared goals, they come to perceive themselves as a single social entity. Then, feelings of bias or hostility toward the former out-group—toward "them"—seem to fade away, taking prejudice with them. Such effects have been demonstrated in several studies (e.g., Brewer et al., 1987; Gaertner et al., 1989, 1990, 1993a), both in the laboratory and the field, so it appears that *recategorization* can be another useful technique for reducing many kinds of prejudice.

Cognitive Interventions: Can We Learn to Just Say "No" to Stereotypes?

Throughout this chapter, we have noted that stereotypes play an important role in prejudice. The tendency to think about others in terms of their membership in various groups or categories (known as *category-driven processing*) appears to be a key factor in the occurrence and persistence of several forms of prejudice. If this is so, then interventions designed to reduce the impact of stereotypes may prove highly effective in reducing prejudice and discrimination. How can this goal be attained? Several techniques seem to be effective.

First, the impact of stereotypes can be reduced by motivating others to be nonprejudiced—for example, by making them aware of egalitarian norms and standards requiring that all receive fair treatment (e.g., Macrae, Bodenhausen, & Milne, 1998). Similarly, dependence on stereotypes can be reduced by encouraging individuals to think carefully about others—to pay attention to their unique characteristics rather than their membership in various groups. This can be accomplished by assigning individuals goals that require the acquisition of unique information about a specific group member, in contrast to accepting group-based generalizations about this person (e.g., Fiske & Neuberg, 1990; Monteith, 1993). In sum, when individuals are motivated to be accurate and have sufficient cognitive resources to accomplish this goal, they may show reduced reliance on stereotypes.

Another, and perhaps more surprising, means for reducing the tendency to think stereotypically involves training designed to reduce the automatic activation of stereotypes. When individuals acquire stereotypes, they learn to associate certain characteristics (e.g., negative traits such as "poor," "hostile," or "dangerous") with various racial or ethnic groups; once they do, persons in these groups can serve as primes for the racial or ethnic stereotypes, which are then automatically activated. But what if individuals actively tried to break this stereotype habit by, saying "no" to stereotypic traits supposedly associated with a specific group? Kawakami and her colleagues (2000) reasoned that such procedures might reduce individuals' reliance on stereotypes.

To test this possibility, these researchers conducted several related studies. In one, participants first saw positive or negative words related to stereotypes for blacks and whites—for example, one positive stereotype–related word for blacks was *athletic,* and one negative word was *poor;* for whites, such words included *ambitious* and *uptight,* respectively). These words were followed by photos of white and black persons, and the participants' task was to report on whether each of these persons was black or white. Activation of stereotypes by the initial priming words would be reflected in faster categorization of photos of whites than photos of blacks after presentation of words relating to the white racial stereotype, but faster categorization of photos of blacks than photos of whites after words relating to the black racial stereotype.

Now for the interesting, prejudice-combating part of the study: after the first phase of the research was completed, participants were divided into two groups. One group—those in the *stereotype-maintaining* condition—was instructed to respond "yes" when they were presented with a photograph of a white person and a white stereotype word (a word consistent with the stereotype for whites) or a photograph of a black person and a black stereotype word (a word consistent with the stereotype for blacks). They were told to respond "no" to stereotype-inconsistent word–picture pairings (e.g., a word consistent with the stereotype for whites, but a photo of a black). Those in a second group, the *stereotype-negation* condition, were told to respond "no" when presented with a photo of a white person and a word consistent with this stereotype, or a photo of a black person and a word consistent with the stereotype for blacks. On the other hand, they were told to respond "yes" to stereotype-inconsistent pairings of words and pictures. In other words, they practiced negating their own implicit racial stereotypes. Participants in both groups performed these procedures several hundred times.

Results were clear and offered support for the view that reliance on stereotypes can indeed be reduced through the simple procedures of saying no to them. As shown in Figure 6.14, prior to negation training, participants categorized white faces more quickly than black faces after seeing white stereotype words, but black faces more quickly after seeing black stereotype words. After negation training designed to weaken these implicit stereotypes, however, these differences disappeared.

In sum, it appears that individuals can indeed learn to weaken their own stereotypes simply by saying no to the associations between stereotypic traits and specific social groups. For instance, if individuals learn to reject the implicit cognitive

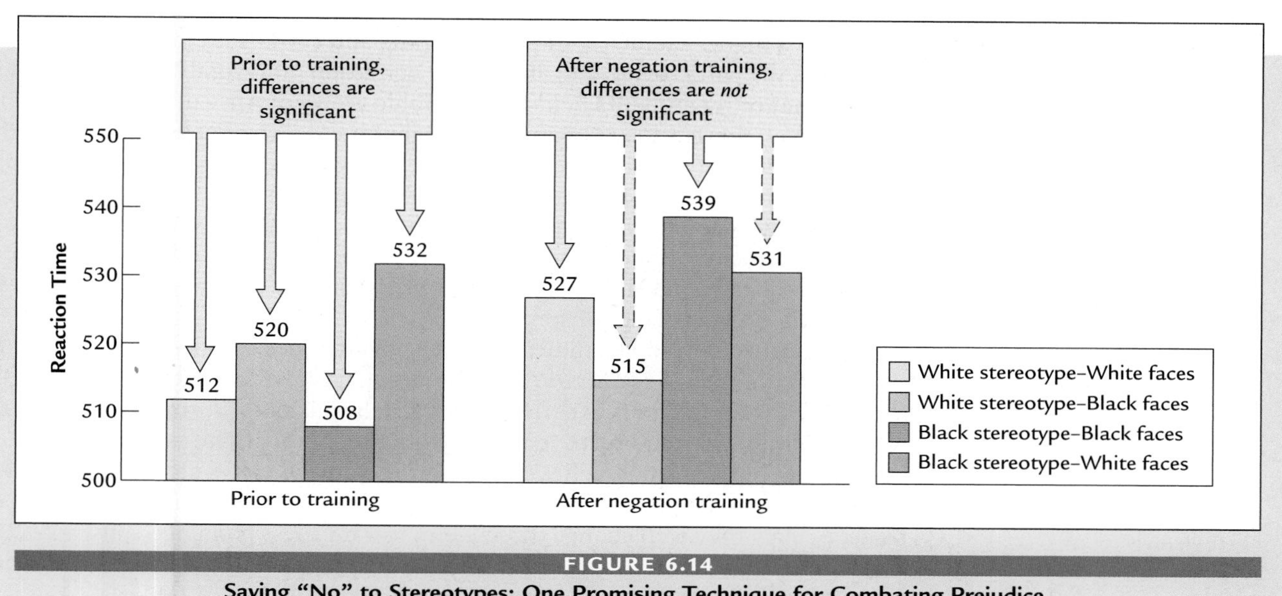

FIGURE 6.14

Saying "No" to Stereotypes: One Promising Technique for Combating Prejudice.
Prior to negation training, during which participants responded "no" to racial stereotypes, participants categorized white faces more quickly than black faces after seeing words related to the stereotype for whites, but categorized black faces more quickly after seeing words related to the stereotype for blacks. After negation training designed to weaken these implicit stereotypes, however, these differences disappeared.
[SOURCE: BASED ON DATA FROM KAWAKAMI ET AL., 2000.]

links between negative traits (e.g., "hostile," "dirty") and racial groups, they can reduce their own tendency to perceive these groups through the filter of racial stereotypes. Clearly, many questions remain concerning this technique—for instance, will it work for all stereotypes or only for some? And how will reduced stereotype activation influence evaluations of category members and actual interactions with them? Only further research can answer such questions, but the possibility that people can readily learn to say no to racial and ethnic stereotypes is encouraging indeed!

Social Influence as a Means of Reducing Prejudice

Earlier, we noted that individuals acquire their racial and ethnic attitudes through the process of social learning. In other words, prejudice and stereotypes arise, at least in part, from social factors and experiences. If this is so, then it seems possible that techniques of social influence might also be used to reduce such reactions. For instance, if individuals learn that their own views are more biased or prejudiced than those of other persons they like, they might well be motivated to change their views so as to be more like those of this reference group. (See Chapter 9 for a full discussion of many techniques of social influence.) Direct evidence that social influence can indeed be used to reduce prejudice has been reported recently by Stangor, Sechrist, and Jost (2001).

These social psychologists asked Caucasian students to estimate the percentage of African Americans possessing each of nineteen stereotypical traits. Nine traits were positive (e.g., outgoing, athletic, musical) and ten were negative (intimidating, hostile, violent). After completing these estimates, they were given information suggesting that other students in their university disagreed with their ratings. In one condition (favorable feedback), they learned that other students held more favorable views of African Americans than they did (i.e., the other students estimated a higher incidence of positive traits and a lower incidence of negative traits than the participants did). In another condition (unfavorable feedback), they learned that other students held less favorable views of African Americans than they did (i.e., these persons estimated a higher incidence of negative traits and a lower incidence of positive traits). After receiving this information, participants again estimated the percentage of African Americans possessing positive and negative traits. Results indicated that participants' racial attitudes were indeed affected by social influence. Endorsement of negative stereotypes increased in the unfavorable feedback condition, while endorsement of such stereotypes decreased in the favorable feedback condition.

Together, these findings indicate that racial attitudes certainly do not exist in a social vacuum; on the contrary, the attitudes that individuals hold are influenced not only by their previous experience, but also by current information indicating where their views stand relative to those of others. The moral is clear: If bigoted persons can be induced to believe that their prejudiced views are out of line with those of most other persons—especially with the views of persons they admire or respect—they may well change those views toward a less prejudiced position. (For an overview of techniques useful in combating prejudice, please see the **Ideas to Take With You—And Use!** feature on page 248.)

Coping with Prejudice: How Targets React to Bigotry

Throughout this section—and this chapter—we have focused on persons who are prejudiced toward others: how they develop these negative views, how they translate them into overt actions, and how prejudice can be reduced. But there is another side of the coin, too: the targets of prejudice. How do such persons react? In other words, what are the effects of prejudice on them, and what techniques do they use for coping with it? These questions were actually among the first ones addressed by social psychologists when they began to study prejudice. For instance, the well-known African American psychologist Kenneth Clark (Clark & Clark, 1947) carried out a series of studies in which white and black children were given the choice between white and black dolls. Clark and Clark found that many black children preferred to play with the white doll and described it as nicer, more attractive, and as looking more like themselves. The researchers interpreted these findings as suggesting that, as a result of prejudice, minority children come to reject their own racial or ethnic identity and suffer such harmful effects as reduced self-esteem.

Fortunately, these chilling results were *not* confirmed in subsequent studies, which indicated that many black children actually prefer to play with black dolls and do not reject their own racial identity. Still, there is little doubt that persons who are the target of prejudice are often well aware of the negative attitudes toward them held by others and that this knowledge, in turn, can exert other harmful effects on them. For instance, Steele and Aronson (1995) suggest that minority persons often experience **stereotype threat**—concern that they will be evaluated in terms of stereotypes relating to their minority status (Steele, 1997), coupled with the fear that they will confirm these negative views. Such concerns, in turn, may disrupt task performance in many contexts. Consistent with this hypothesis, Steele and Aronson (1995) found that black undergraduate students performed more poorly on a cognitive task (answering difficult questions from the Graduate Record Examination) when their race was made salient (called to their attention) and they believed that poor performance would confirm the cultural stereotype that blacks are less intelligent than whites. When race was not made salient, such effects did not occur.

Additional support for the adverse effects of stereotype threat was obtained by Croizet and Claire (1998), who had persons from high or low socioeconomic backgrounds work on a test that was described either as a measure of their intellectual ability or as a measure of the role of attention in memory. The researchers predicted that when the test was described as one of intellectual ability, stereotype threat would be induced among persons from low socioeconomic backgrounds, who would fear that they would be evaluated in terms of the negative stereotype for such persons. Thus, they would actually perform worse on the test than those from high socioeconomic backgrounds. When the test was described as a measure of attention, however, such differences would not occur. Results offered clear support for these predictions. Findings such as these suggest that stereotypes can indeed have harmful effects on the persons to whom they apply—effects that are distinct from those generated by discrimination against such persons.

More recently, social psychologists have begun to adopt a very different perspective on the question of how the targets of prejudice cope with this problem. Instead of viewing such persons as passive victims, this new perspective sees the targets of prejudice as active agents who choose which situations to enter (perhaps ones in which they feel that they have a chance and will *not* be subjected to overt discrimination), think actively about what happens in these situations, and respond in various ways to them (e.g., Crocker, Major, & Steele, 1998; Swim & Stangor, 1998). As noted recently by Shelton (2000), minority group members adopt many strategies to protect their psychological well-being. For instance, they may attribute negative feedback from others to prejudice or choose to compare themselves only with in-group members rather than with the prejudiced majority group. Further, they sometimes choose to view situations or outcomes in which their group is perceived in negative terms as unimportant or irrelevant to them. For instance, some African American teenagers living in economically deprived neighborhoods conclude that success in school is a game they can't win because the dice are loaded

stereotype threat: The concern on the part of persons who are the target of stereotypes that they will be evaluated in terms of this stereotype.

heavily against them, and so perceive such success as unimportant. While this can help protect their self-esteem, it may also limit their economic opportunities, so this is truly unfortunate.

In addition, the victims of prejudice often form racial attitudes and stereotypes of their own. Recent findings indicate that blacks' racial attitudes are based primarily on perceived threat or conflict, coupled with their reactions to white racism (e.g., Duckitt & Mphuthing, 1993; Monteith & Spicer, 2000). In contrast, the racial attitudes of whites seem to stem primarily from their degree of commitment to the principle of egalitarianism (Monteith & Spicer, 2000). Additional findings indicate that, as is true for whites, blacks' racial attitudes vary greatly. Thus, despite having been the target of racism and discrimination for generations, many blacks do not have negative perceptions of whites (e.g., Ryan, 1996). Further, and as might be expected, the more strongly persons belonging to minority groups identify with their group, the more sensitive they are to subtle forms of prejudice and the more strongly they react to it (e.g., Operario & Fiske, 2001).

In sum, a new perspective is emerging in social psychology—one that recognizes the fact that prejudice is a two-way street. It is not only important to understand the mind and behavior of persons who hold racial, ethnic, or gender prejudice; it is equally important to consider how the targets of such attitudes and stereotypes react to these views and to the negative treatment they receive. The hope, of course, is that as we gain more complete knowledge of both aspects of the process, we will be in a better position to counter its occurrence—and its negative effects.

KEY POINTS

- Prejudice can sometimes be reduced through *recategorization*—shifting the boundary between "us" and "them" so as to include former out-groups in the "us" category.
- Cognitive techniques for reducing prejudice are also effective. These are often based on motivating others to be nonprejudiced by, for instance, making them aware of egalitarian norms and standards requiring that all receive fair treatment
- Reductions in prejudice can also be accomplished by training individuals to say no to associations between stereotypes and specific social groups.
- Prejudice can also be reduced through social influence—providing individuals with evidence suggesting that others hold less prejudiced views than they do.
- Recently, a new perspective on prejudice has emerged in social psychology, one that views the targets of prejudice as active agents who choose which situations to enter, think actively about what happens in these situations, and respond in various ways to them.

Prejudice Based on Gender: Its Nature and Effects

More than half of the world's population is female. Yet, despite this fact, many cultures still treat women as a minority group. They have been excluded from economic and political power; they have been the subject of strong negative stereotypes; and they have faced overt discrimination in many areas of life—work settings, higher education, government (Fisher, 1992; Heilman, Block, & Lucas, 1992). This situation is changing in at least some countries and to some degree. Overt discriminatory practices have been banned by laws in many nations, and there has been at least some weakening of negative gender-based stereotypes. For example, I lived in France during the spring of 2001, when mayoral elections occurred all over the country. To counter previous gender bias, a new law required that 50 percent of all the candidates put forward by every major party be women. The result? More women were elected to municipal office than at any previous time. Despite such changes, though, **sexism**—prejudice based on gender—continues to exert harmful effects upon females in many countries (e.g., Glick et al., 2000). Because prejudice based on gender affects more individuals than any other single kind (more than half the human race), it is certainly worthy of our careful attention.

Hostile and Benevolent Sexism: The Two Faces of Prejudice Based on Gender

The term *prejudice* seems to imply hostility or aversion—when we say, in everyday speech, that someone is prejudiced against persons belonging to a specific group, this seems to imply that they hold very negative views of that group. But, in fact, prejudice can have another, sharply contrasting side. Even racists who are strongly prejudiced against African Americans may admit that their athletic and musical talents are very high—perhaps higher than those of whites. The same is true with respect to sexism, which also shows two different faces. One is known as **hostile sexism**—the view that women, if not inferior to men, have many negative traits (e.g., they seek special favors, are overly sensitive, or seek to seize power from men that they don't deserve and should not have). The other is what Glick and his colleagues (2000) describe as **benevolent sexism**—views suggesting that women deserve protection, are superior to men in various ways (e.g., they are more pure, have better taste), and are truly necessary for men's happiness (e.g., no man is truly fulfilled unless he has a woman he adores in his life). According to Glick and his colleagues (2000), both forms of sexism reflect the fact that men have long held a dominant position in most human societies. As a result of this power, they have come to see women as inferior in various ways. At the same time, however, men are dependent on women for the domestic roles they play and for the intimacy and love they provide. These facts, in turn, have contributed to the development of benevolent sexism.

Evidence that both aspects of sexism exist around the world has been provided by Glick and his associates (2000) in a massive study involving more than 15,000 participants in nineteen different countries. The participants (mostly college students) completed questionnaires designed to measure both aspects of sexism. In addition, measures of gender equality in the participants' countries were obtained from the United Nations. Results indicated that both hostile and benevolent sexism seem to exist in every country studied. While men generally express higher hostile sexism than women, this difference disappears or is even reversed, in several nations, for benevolent sexism: women actually subscribe to such views, even more strongly than men in several countries (e.g., Colombia, Turkey, Germany, and Belgium; see Figure 6.15 on page 242).

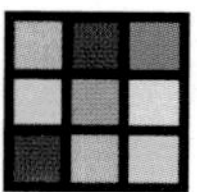

sexism: Prejudice based on gender.

hostile sexism: The view that women, if not inferior to men, have many negative traits (e.g., they seek special favors, are overly sensitive, or seek to seize power from men that they don't deserve to have).

benevolent sexism: Views suggesting that women deserve protection, are superior to men in various ways (e.g., they are more pure, have better taste), and are truly necessary for men's happiness (e.g., no man is truly fulfilled unless he has a woman he adores in his life).

Further, as might be expected, the higher both forms of sexism, the lower the gender equality (in terms of women's presence in high-status jobs, education, and standard of living). This was especially true for men's level of sexism but occurred for women, too. Overall, then, it seems clear that sexism does *not* imply uniformly negative views of women or hostility toward them. It involves what at first might seem to be a kinder, gentler face as well. As noted by Glick and his colleagues (2000), however, benevolent sexism, too, is a form of prejudice: it also serves to keep women in a subordinate role. So benevolent sexism also runs counter to the goal of full equality, which is a central value in the United States and many other countries.

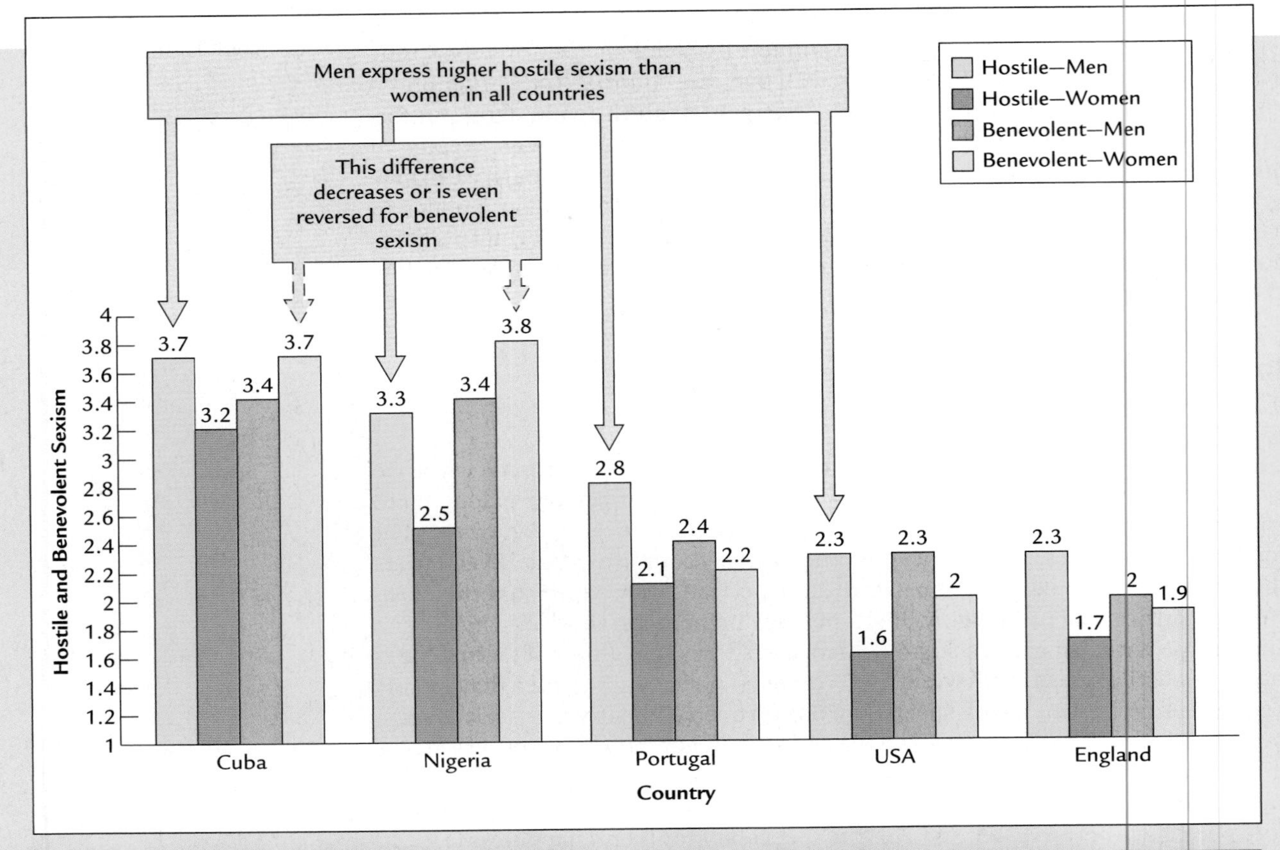

FIGURE 6.15

Hostile and Benevolent Sexism around the Globe.

Two forms of sexism seem to exist—hostile and benevolent. Men generally express *hostile sexism* much more strongly than do women, but this difference decreases or is even reversed with respect to *benevolent sexism*.

[SOURCE: BASED ON DATA FROM GLICK ET AL., 2000.]

The Cognitive Bases of Sexism: Gender Stereotypes and Differential Respect

Now that we have distinguished between the two faces of sexism, let's turn to another important question: Why does it persist? An important part of the answer is that sexism involves **gender stereotypes**—beliefs concerning the supposed characteristics of women and men (see Figure 6.16). These stereotypes exist for both genders and contain both positive and negative traits. For instance, on the positive side of the gender stereotype for women, they are viewed as being kind, nurturant, and considerate. On the negative side of the coin, they are viewed as being indecisive, passive, and overly emotional. Similarly, men, too, are assumed to have both positive and negative traits (e.g., they are viewed as being decisive, assertive, and active, but also as being aggressive, insensitive, and arrogant; Hosada & Stone, in press). Interestingly, the gender stereotype for women actually appears to be somewhat more favorable than the stereotype for men—a finding described by Eagly and Mladinic (1994) as the "women are wonderful" effect. Despite this fact, though, women face a key problem: The traits they supposedly possess, although often positive in nature, tend to be viewed as less appro-

gender stereotypes: Stereotypes concerning the traits supposedly possessed by females and males, and that distinguish the two genders from each other.

SHOE

BY

MACNELLY

PRODUCTIONS

FIGURE 6.16

Gender Stereotypes: An Example.

Gender stereotypes suggest that all men share certain traits and all women share other traits. Obviously, such stereotypes are an exaggeration: some men, at least, can indeed remember anniversaries and pick up their own clothes!

priate for high-level or high-status positions than are the traits supposedly possessed by men. This can serve as an important barrier to advancement by women (e.g., Heilman, 1995).

Are such gender stereotypes accurate? Do men and women really differ in the ways these stereotypes suggest? This question is complex, for such differences between the sexes, even if observed, may be more a reflection of the impact of stereotypes and their self-confirming nature than of basic differences between females and males. Existing evidence, however, points to the following conclusion: *There are indeed some differences between males and females with respect to various aspects of behavior, but in general, the magnitude of such differences is much smaller than prevailing gender stereotypes suggest* (e.g., Betancourt & Miller, 1996; Voyer, Voyer, & Bryden, 1995).

Although gender stereotypes are an important part of the basis for persistent sexism, they are not the only factor in this respect. Jackson, Esses, and Burris (2001) suggest that another variable—differential *respect*—is also important. Specifically, both women and men express higher respect for men. Why? Perhaps because men continue to hold positions of greater power and higher status in society. Higher respect for men may then reflect these differences.

To determine whether differential respect actually does play a role in discrimination toward women, Jackson, Esses, and Burris (2001) conducted a series of studies in which male and female participants evaluated applicants for relatively high status or low status jobs (e.g., regional director of a real estate company versus short-order cook). The applicants were either men or women, and participants rated these persons on the basis of information contained in job applications they had, supposedly, completed. In addition to rating the applicants in terms of whether they should be hired, participants also completed a standard measure of masculine and feminine stereotypes. Finally, they also indicated their level of respect for the applicants.

The researchers predicted that males would receive higher ratings in terms of both hiring recommendations and respect, and, in general, this was the case (although results differed somewhat across the various studies). In addition, and even more important, only ratings of respect for the job applicants significantly predicted hiring recommendations for these persons; gender stereotypes did *not* predict such ratings. In other words, the more respect participants in the study expressed for the applicants, the higher their ratings of these persons in terms of hiring recommendations. In contrast, the extent to which participants rated the applicants as showing the traits contained in gender stereotypes did *not* predict hiring recommendations. Because males received higher ratings of respect, results suggested that this factor does indeed play an important role in at least some forms of discrimination toward women.

In sum, it appears that while gender stereotypes certainly contribute persisting discrimination against women, they are not the entire story. Differential respect for the two genders, too, contributes to this continuing problem.

KEY POINTS

- *Sexism*—prejudice based on gender—affects more than half of the human race.
- Sexism actually occurs in two contrasting forms: *hostile sexism,* which involves negative beliefs about women, and *benevolent sexism,* which involves positive beliefs about them.
- *Gender stereotypes*—cognitive frameworks suggesting that males and females possess sharply different patterns of traits and behavior—play an important role in sexism. While males and females do differ in some respects, gender stereotypes greatly exaggerate these differences.
- Both women and men express greater respect for men, and this factor, too, plays an important role in sexism.

Discrimination against Females: Subtle but Often Deadly

At present, overt discrimination on the basis of gender is illegal in many countries. As a result, businesses, schools, and social organizations no longer reject applicants for jobs or admission simply because they are women (or men). Despite this fact, women continue to occupy a relatively disadvantaged position in many societies in certain respects. They are concentrated in low-paying, low-status jobs (Fisher, 1992), and their average salary remains lower than that for males, even in the same occupations. Why is this the case? One possibility is that sufficient time has not passed for women to have obtained the full benefits of the changes that occurred during the 1970s and 1980s. Another possibility—one supported by a large body of research evidence—is that while overt barriers to female advancement have largely disappeared, other, more subtle forces continue to operate against them in many contexts. We'll now review several of these.

■ THE ROLE OF EXPECTATIONS. One factor impeding the progress of females involves their own expectations. In general, women seem to hold lower expectations about their careers than do men. They expect to receive lower starting and peak salaries (Jackson, Gardner, & Sullivan, 1992; Major & Konar, 1984). And they view lower salaries for females as being somehow fair (Jackson & Grabski, 1988). Why do females hold these lower expectations? Study findings (e.g., Jackson, Gardner, & Sullivan, 1992) indicate that several factors play a role.

First, females expect to take more time out from work (e.g., to spend with their children); this tends to lower their expectations for peak career salaries. Second, women realize that females do generally earn less than males. Thus, their lower expectations may simply reflect their recognition of current reality and its likely impact on their own salaries. Third, as we noted earlier, women tend to perceive relatively low levels of pay as more fair than males do (Jackson, Gardner, & Sullivan, 1992). Finally, and perhaps most important, women tend to compare themselves with other women, and because women earn less than men in many instances, this leads them to conclude that they aren't doing too badly after all (Major, 1993). Whatever the specific basis for women's lower salary expectations, it is a fact of life that, in general, people tend to get what they expect or what they request. Thus, women's lower expectations with respect to such outcomes may be one important factor operating against them in many contexts.

■ THE ROLE OF CONFIDENCE AND SELF-PERCEPTIONS. Confidence, it is often said, is the single best predictor of success. People who expect to succeed often do; those who expect to fail find *that* prediction confirmed. Unfortunately, women tend to express lower self-confidence than men in many achievement-related situations, perhaps because they have been the victims of sexism in such situations. This, in turn, may contribute to the fact that they have not yet attained full equality with men in many work settings.

Another reason why women may be less confident in such contexts is that they have learned, through bitter experience, that tactics which succeed for men often backfire for them. For instance, research findings indicate that self-promoting (impression management) strategies that often succeed very well for men generate negative effects, such as reduced likeability, for women (e.g., Rudman, 1998). In contrast, self-effacement (showing modesty about one's abilities or accomplishments) may reduce ratings of women's competence but increase their attractiveness. Little wonder, then, that women express lower confidence in many situations: they are strongly rewarded for doing so!

■ NEGATIVE REACTIONS TO FEMALE AUTHORITY. At the present time, most people agree that women can definitely be effective leaders. Women have been elected to major offices (prime minister, senator), have been appointed as senior judges (e.g., to the Supreme Court of the United States), hold high ranks in the military, and—in a few cases—head major companies and organizations (see Figure 6.17 on page 246). But how do people react to women in positions of authority? Do they hold them in equally high regard as men? The answer to both questions appears to be no. First, although subordinates often *say* much the same things to female and male leaders, they may actually demonstrate more negative *nonverbal behaviors* toward women leaders (Butler & Geis, 1990).

FIGURE 6.17
Women in Positions of Authority: How Do People React? In recent years, an increasing number of women have attained high-level positions in government and industry. Research findings indicate, however, that many people—women as well as men—continue to prefer and feel more comfortable with men in these positions.

Perhaps even more disturbing than this is the fact that when women serve as leaders, they tend to receive lower evaluations from subordinates than men do (Butler & Geis, 1990; Eagly, Makhijani, & Klonsky, 1992). This is especially true for female leaders who adopt a style of leadership viewed as stereotypically masculine (autocratic, directive), in fields where most leaders are men, and when the persons who evaluate the leaders are men. These findings suggest that women continue to face subtle disadvantages even when they do obtain positions of leadership and authority (Kent & Moss, 1994). (We'll return to the topic of *leadership* in Chapter 13.)

Finally, findings reported by Rudman and Kilianski (2000) indicate that both women and men seem to prefer having men in positions of authority. Indeed, both genders hold implicit attitudes linking men to high-authority roles and women to low-authority roles. The result? Women, as well as men, feel more comfortable when a man is in charge. Clearly, such attitudes operate against women in many contexts.

■ GENDER DIFFERENCES IN CLIMBING THE CORPORATE LADDER: THE "GLASS CEILING"—AND ABOVE. Between the 1970s and the 1990s, the proportion of managers who are women rose from 16 percent to more than 42 percent (U.S. Department of Labor, 1992). Yet, the proportion of *top* managers who are women increased only from 3 percent to 5 percent (Glass Ceiling Commission, 1995). These facts have led many authors to suggest the existence of a **glass ceiling**—a final barrier that prevents women, as a group, from reaching the top positions in many companies. More formally, the U.S. Department of Labor has defined the glass ceiling as "those artificial barriers based on attitudinal or organizational bias that prevent qualified individuals from advancing upward in their organization" (U.S. Department of Labor, 1991).

glass ceiling: Barriers based on attitudinal or organizational bias that prevent qualified women from advancing to top-level positions.

Is this barrier real? And if so, why does it occur? Existing evidence on these issues presents something of a mixed picture. On the one hand, several studies suggest that a glass ceiling exists—that women do experience less favorable outcomes in their careers than men because of their gender (e.g., Heilman, 1995; Morrison, 1992).

On the other hand, however, additional findings point to two more encouraging conclusions. For instance, in one carefully conducted study, Lyness and Thompson (1997) compared the outcomes and experiences of men and women executives in a large company. The two groups were carefully matched in terms of education, work experience, and other factors. Very few differences were found in terms of their salaries, bonuses, and other benefits. The women reported supervising fewer subordinates, more career interruptions, and—importantly—encountering more obstacles (e.g., trying to influence other people without any authority to back up such attempts). But there were few if any gender differences with regard to salary, bonuses, or opportunities to develop their careers.

In a subsequent and closely related study, Lyness and Thompson (2000) expanded the size of their sample and looked more closely at the following question: Do women and men follow different routes to success? More specifically, they focused on the barriers that prevented women from attaining success and the strategies they used to overcome these obstacles. Again, women and men executives in the study were closely matched in terms of their current job, number of years with the company, and performance ratings to assure that differences in these factors would not influence results.

What emerged was evidence that while women and men may ultimately arrive at the same levels in a specific company, they do indeed follow somewhat contrasting routes along the way. With respect to barriers, women reported experiencing greater difficulties with such factors as not fitting into the male-dominated culture, being excluded from informal networks, and securing developmental assignments—ones that would help increase their skills and advance their careers. Turning to the factors and strategies that facilitated their careers, women reported that having a good track record (a good record of achievement) and developing relationships with other persons in the company were more important to their success than did men. For both women and men, access to developmental experiences was a plus for career success.

This study also gathered data on actual career success (salary, bonuses, current job level), and here, relatively few gender differences emerged. However, two factors—having a mentor and receiving large-scale assignments (ones with a lot of responsibility)—were both more strongly related to these tangible measures of career success for men than for women. Overall, then, women did seem to experience more obstacles to success than did men and used different strategies to overcome these. But they managed to surmount these obstacles and attain levels of success comparable to that of men. So, to repeat, is there a glass ceiling? *Yes,* in the sense that women must overcome greater obstacles than men to arrive at similar levels of success. But the fact that they can, ultimately, arrive at these levels (some of the women in the sample had yearly salaries higher than $500,000) points to the following, somewhat optimistic conclusion: The glass ceiling may still exist, but in recent years it has been cracked, if not entirely shattered. Much remains to be done, but it does seem clear that major changes *have* occurred in the world of work and that such changes have increased women's opportunities to at least some extent.

KEY POINTS

- While blatant forms of discrimination based on gender have decreased, females continue to be adversely affected by more subtle forms.
- These include lower expectations by females, low self-confidence and self-perceptions, negative reactions to female leaders, and the *glass ceiling.*
- Recent findings indicate that women may encounter more barriers than men in their careers, but that by adopting effective strategies, they can overcome these barriers and attain high levels of success.

CONNECTIONS: INTEGRATING SOCIAL PSYCHOLOGY

IN THIS CHAPTER, YOU READ ABOUT . . .	IN OTHER CHAPTERS, YOU WILL FIND RELATED DISCUSSIONS OF . . .
stereotypes as mental shortcuts—one means of saving cognitive effort	heuristics and other mental shortcuts (Chapters 3, 4)
the role of economic factors (frustration) in prejudice and racial violence	the role of frustration in aggression and conflict (Chapter 11)
the tendency to divide the social world into "us" and "them" and its effects	other effects of group membership (Chapter 12)
evaluations of women in positions of authority or leadership	other aspects of leadership (Chapter 13)
the effects of perceived similarity on prejudice	the effects of perceived similarity on attraction (Chapter 7)

THINKING ABOUT CONNECTIONS

1. Some observers suggest that as open forms of discrimination have decreased, more subtle forms have increased. In other words, they believe that the attitudes underlying discrimination remain unchanged (see Chapter 4), and that only overt behavior relating to these attitudes has changed. What do you think?
2. Some evidence indicates that prejudice persists because it produces benefits for the people who hold it (e.g., it boosts their self-concept; see Chapter 5). But prejudice also produces harmful effects for the people who hold it (e.g., they experience ungrounded fear of harm from out-group members; see Chapter 11). Which do you think is dominant where prejudice is concerned—its benefits or its costs?
3. In your view, why do we show such a strong tendency to divide the social world into two categories—"us" and "them"? Do you think this tendency could stem, in part, from our biological heritage—for instance, the conditions under which our species evolved (see Chapter 1)? Or is it mainly the result of our tendency to save cognitive effort and other cognitive factors (see Chapter 3)?
4. Sexism appears to have two aspects—hostile and benevolent attitudes toward women. Do you think it is important to eliminate both kinds? Or do you feel that benevolent sexism, which puts women on a pedestal, may actually have some beneficial effects?

IDEAS TO TAKE WITH YOU—AND USE!

TECHNIQUES FOR REDUCING PREJUDICE

Prejudice is an all too common part of social life, but most social psychologists believe that it *can* be reduced—it is not inevitable. Here are some techniques that seem to work.

Teaching Children Tolerance Instead of Bigotry

If children are taught, from an early age, to respect all groups—including ones very different from their own—prejudice can be nipped in the bud, so to speak.

Increased Intergroup Contact—or Merely Knowledge that It Occurs

Findings indicate that if people merely know that friendly contacts occur between members of their own group and members of various

out-groups, their prejudice toward these groups can be sharply reduced.

Recategorization

Once individuals include people they once excluded from their in-group *within* it, prejudice toward them may disappear. This can be accomplished by reminding people that they are part of larger groups—for instance, that they are all Americans, Canadians, and so on.

Undermining Stereotypes

Stereotypes suggest that all persons belonging to specific social groups are alike—that they share the same characteristics. Such beliefs can be weakened by encouraging people to think about others as *individuals,* not simply as members of social groups. Further, if individuals learn to reject implicit links between certain traits and racial or ethnic groups (saying no to stereotypes), the impact of these cognitive frameworks can be reduced.

SUMMARY AND REVIEW OF KEY POINTS

Prejudice and Discrimination: Their Nature and Origins

- *Prejudice* is an attitude (usually negative) toward members of some social group based solely on their membership in that group. It can be triggered in a seemingly automatic manner and can be implicit, as well as explicit, in nature.
- Prejudice, like other attitudes, influences our processing of social information, our beliefs about persons belonging to various groups, and our feelings about them.
- Prejudice persists because disparaging groups we dislike can boost our self-esteem, and because stereotypes save us cognitive effort.
- *Discrimination* involves negative actions toward members of various social groups.
- While blatant discrimination has clearly decreased, more subtle forms, such as modern racism and *tokenism,* persist.
- Discrimination can also stem from automatically elicited implicit attitudes and *stereotypes*—attitudes of which individuals may not be aware.

The Origins of Prejudice: Contrasting Perspectives

- Prejudice stems from several different sources. One of these is direct intergroup conflict—situations in which social groups compete for the same scarce resources.
- A second basis for prejudice is early experience and the social learning it involves.
- Findings indicate that parents' degree of prejudice and people's direct experiences with minority groups during childhood both play an important role in shaping racial prejudice.
- Prejudice also derives from our tendencies to divide the world into "us" and "them" and to view our own group much more favorably than various out-groups.
- Prejudice sometimes stems from basic aspects of social cognition—the ways in which we process social information.
- *Stereotypes* are cognitive frameworks suggesting that all persons belonging to a social group show similar characteristics. Stereotypes strongly influence social thought. For instance, when activated, they lead us to form tacit inferences about others that then make information that is inconsistent with stereotypes seem to be consistent with them.
- Implicit stereotypes can be activated automatically by various stimuli. Even though we are not aware of such activation, it can strongly affect our thinking about, and behavior toward, persons belonging to the groups that are the focus of these stereotypes.
- Findings indicate that stereotypes are closely linked to prejudice; for example, highly prejudiced persons respond more quickly to stereotype-related words than do less prejudiced persons.

- Other cognitive sources of prejudice include *illusory correlations*—the tendency to overestimate the strength of relationships between social categories and negative behaviors—and the *illusion of out-group homogeneity*—the tendency to perceive out-groups as more homogeneous than our own in-group.
- Prejudice takes many forms, and recently it has been directed against persons who are overweight. In response, individuals in this group have taken vigorous steps to protect their rights by lobbying for protective legislation and related actions.

Why Prejudice is *Not* Inevitable: Techniques for Countering Its Effects

- Social psychologists believe that prejudice is not inevitable; it can be reduced by several techniques.
- One of these involves changing children's early experiences so that they are not taught bigotry by their parents and other adults.
- Another technique involves direct contact between persons from different groups. When this occurs under certain conditions, prejudice can be reduced.
- Findings indicate that simply knowing that members of one's in-group have formed friendships with members of an out-group may be sufficient to reduce prejudice; this is known as the *extended contact hypothesis.*
- Prejudice can sometimes be reduced through *recategorization*—shifting the boundary between "us" and "them" so as to include former out-groups in the "us" category.
- Cognitive techniques for reducing prejudice are also effective. These are often based on motivating others to be nonprejudiced by, for instance, making them aware of egalitarian norms and standards requiring that all receive fair treatment.
- Reductions in prejudice can also be accomplished by training individuals to say no to associations between stereotypes and specific social groups.
- Finally, prejudice can be reduced through social influence—providing individuals with evidence suggesting that others hold less prejudiced views than they do.
- Recently, a new perspective on prejudice has emerged in social psychology, one that views the targets of prejudice as active agents who choose which situations to enter, think actively about what happens in these situations, and respond in various ways to them.

Prejudice Based on Gender: Its Nature and Effects

- *Sexism*—prejudice based on gender—affects more than half of the human race.
- Sexism actually occurs in two contrasting forms: *hostile sexism,* which involves negative beliefs about women, and *benevolent sexism,* which involves positive beliefs about them.
- *Gender stereotypes*—cognitive frameworks suggesting that males and females possess sharply different patterns of traits and behavior—play an important role in sexism. While males and females do differ in some respects, gender stereotypes greatly exaggerate these differences.
- Both women and men express greater respect for men, and this factor, too, plays an important role in sexism.
- Although blatant forms of discrimination based on gender have decreased, females continue to be adversely affected by more subtle forms.
- These include lower expectations by females, inaccurately low self-confidence and self-perceptions, negative reactions to female leaders, and the glass ceiling.
- Recent findings indicate that women may encounter more barriers than men in their careers, but that by adopting effective strategies, they can overcome these barriers and attain high levels of success.

KEY TERMS

benevolent sexism (p. 241)
bona fide pipline (p. 214)
common in-group identity model (p. 235)
contact hypothesis (p. 233)
discrimination (p. 211)
extended contact hypothesis (p. 234)
gender stereotypes (p. 242)
glass ceiling (p. 246)
hostile sexism (p. 241)
illusion of out-group homogeneity (p. 229)
illusory correlations (p. 229)
in-group (p. 222)
in-group differentiation (p. 229)
out-group (p. 222)
prejudice (p. 209)
realistic conflict theory (p. 215)
recategorization (p. 235)
schemas (p. 209)
sexism (p. 241)
social categorization (p. 222)
social identity theory (p. 223)
social learning view (of prejudice) (p. 220)
stereotype threat (p. 239)
stereotypes (p. 226)
tokenism (p. 215)
ultimate attribution error (p. 223)

FOR MORE INFORMATION

Eberhardt, J. L., & Fiske, S. T. (Eds.). (1998). *Confronting racism.* Thousand Oaks, CA: Sage.

- This valuable book includes chapters by experts on the issue of racism. The contributors address racism from several perspectives—individual, interpersonal, and intergroup. Implications of the findings of social psychological research for public policy are considered, and the impact of racism on crime, employment, politics, and health are examined.

Stangor, C. (Ed.). (2000). *Stereotypes and prejudice: Essential readings.* Philadelphia: Psychology Press.

- Stereotypes play a key role in all forms of prejudice. This book reviews our current knowledge about this important aspect of social cognition. Topics covered include how stereotypes develop, why they are maintained, when they are used, and how they can be changed. This is an excellent source if you want to know more about the cognitive core of prejudice.

Winstead, B. A., Derlega, V. J., & Rose, S. (1997). *Gender and close relationships.* Thousand Oaks, CA: Sage.

This interesting book examines the nature of gender—including gender stereotypes and gender-role development—and considers the role of gender in close relationships and a wide range of social behavior (e.g., conflict and violence, friendship).

Marc Chagall, *Lovers With Flowers,* 1927. © Copyright Giraudon/Art Resource, NY. © 2002 Artists Rights Society (ARS), New York/ADAGP, Paris.

INTERPERSONAL ATTRACTION: MEETING, LIKING, BECOMING ACQUAINTED

CHAPTER OUTLINE

When I (DB) was younger and (maybe) less wise than now, I was assigned to a biology lab work group; one of the other students in that group was an extremely attractive student named Diana. After a few lab sessions, I was convinced that "Diana must be the one for me." I knew very little about this individual, but that didn't matter at the moment. If she looked that good, she must be a great person. We have all been exposed to the ideas underlying the old sayings "You can't judge a book by its cover" and "Beauty is only skin deep." Nevertheless, simply hearing such folk wisdom doesn't ensure that we have enough sense to pay attention. I didn't.

Diana and I talked from time to time in the coffee shop after class, went to a few movies, had dinner together, and without any actual verbal agreement to that effect, became a couple. Still, we knew very little about one another. She was beautiful and easy to talk to, so what else could matter?

There was another benefit to the relationship beyond the fact that I could look at her and see only perfection. I gained status in the eyes of those who knew me. That is, if someone who was as attractive as Diana liked me, I must somehow be at least a little special myself.

As time passed, however, small problems began to arise. We discovered that we disagreed about many issues, large and small. She enjoyed being surrounded by many acquaintances, and I preferred smaller, closer relationships. That was mildly unpleasant, but not enough to make me realize that we weren't suited for one another. Diana's personality was also different from mine in a great many ways. For example, she was very serious about everything, and I found much to be amused about. Also, she tended to criticize many things I said and did. Whether her comments were valid or not, critical communications are never pleasant. Gradually, our interactions became less and less smooth. She became increasingly angry whenever I didn't totally agree with her views, and we seemed to disagree more and more.

After several weeks of this, I suggested that we might do well to see each other less often. Her response was to call me various unprintable names. Though I couldn't prove that she was the culprit, late one night someone came by where I lived and badly scratched my car doors and hood. It was bad to be called names and to have my car attacked, but it was much better to discover interpersonal problems at that point rather than after having established a long-term, committed relationship. (I had actually thought about marriage.)

Altogether, the greatest benefit of this episode was to teach me that when a person looks great, it is not necessarily a good indication that the person will be great.

Though I didn't know it at the time, my experience with Diana illustrated some of the initial factors in the attraction process: We become acquainted with those with whom we come in contact; our initial response (to appearance, for example) is often a matter of our emotional reactions; similarity is important; and pleasant interactions are crucial. As people become better acquainted, many factors can arise to change the initial liking into disliking.

In this chapter, we will describe how two people first become acquainted, most often as the result of accidental encounters in school, at work, or where they live. The seemingly irrelevant details of *physical proximity* to others can increase or

FIGURE 7.1
They Can't See You on the Internet. Observable characteristics play a major role (sometimes usefully and sometimes not) in our initial attraction toward a stranger. As this canine points out, using the Internet to meet others makes it possible to omit this factor in initial interactions.
[SOURCE: © THE NEW YORKER COLLECTION 1993 PETER STEINER FROM CARTOONBANK.COM. ALL RIGHTS RESERVED.]

decrease the odds that any two individuals will come into contact repeatedly. And such repeated exposure often is the initial basis of attraction. A second very important factor is one's *affective state.* It may sound simplistic (but it is quite accurate) to say that we tend to like people who are associated with positive emotions and to dislike those associated with negative emotions.

Emotional reactions to those we meet are determined in part by how we perceive their *observable characteristics*—such as Diana's physical attractiveness. Figure 7.1 suggests one of the ways we have developed to avoid initial negative reactions to observable characteristics—the Internet. Incidentally, being able to communicate with strangers by means of computers opens up an entirely new interpersonal world (Clay, 2000; Kirn, 2000). With or without the Internet, the attraction process also depends on the needs of the people involved. Depending on the strength of each person's *affiliation motivation,* they may be more or less motivated to establish a relationship.

Given that all four factors (physical proximity, positive emotions, acceptable observable characteristics, and the need to affiliate) are operating, the attraction process can move to the final stage. That is, two people begin to discover the extent to which they are *similar* rather than *dissimilar* with respect to attitudes, beliefs, values, interests, and much else besides. Attraction is enhanced by the extent to which similarities outweigh dissimilarities. A final step occurs when each individual begins to express *mutual liking,* either in words or deeds.

The Beginning of Attraction: Proximity and Emotions

Before going into detail about the variables that determine *attraction,* let's consider just what we mean by this term.

Interpersonal Attraction: An Overview

In Chapter 4, we discussed attitudes and the very human tendency to evaluate just about everything and everyone we encounter, whether it's attitudes

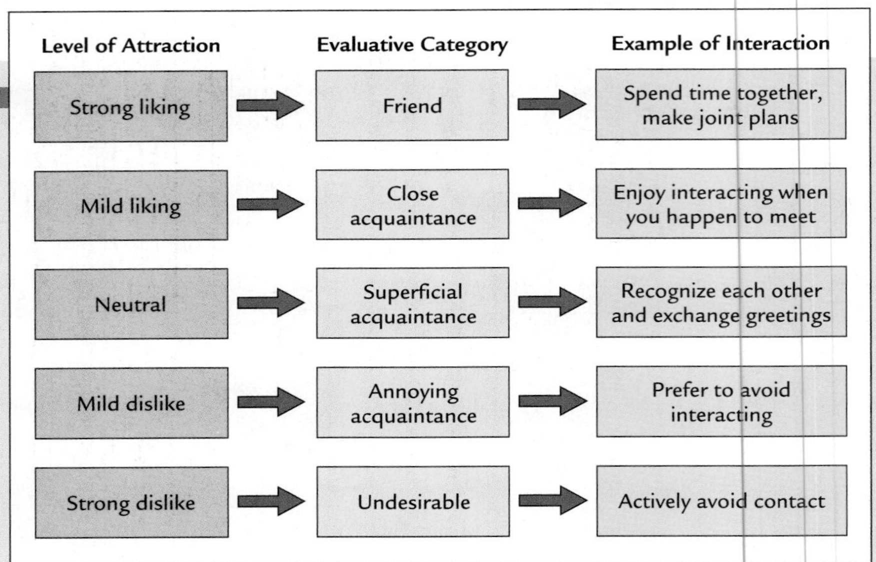

FIGURE 7.2
Interpersonal Attraction: Evaluating Other People. *Interpersonal attraction* refers to one's attitude about another person. Attraction is expressed along a dimension that ranges from strong liking to strong dislike. Attraction research consists of the attempt to identify the factors responsible for these evaluations and to create theoretical formulations that provide an explanation for this aspect of social behavior.

about people, objects, or events. **Interpersonal attraction** refers to an attitude about another person. Such interpersonal evaluations fall along a dimension that ranges from like to dislike (see Figure 7.2). Each of us is liked by some individuals and disliked by others. With respect to most of the people with whom we come in contact, we are not especially liked or disliked—their reaction is a neutral one. In turn, we like some people, dislike others, and are neutral toward most. On what basis do we like, dislike, or remain indifferent to other human beings? The answer to that question has been sought in research by social psychologists and sociologists since the study of human behavior began. In this chapter, we will share with you what has been discovered about attraction over the past decades.

Research on interpersonal attraction is designed to identify in detail the factors responsible for one person's evaluation of another. As you read about each of these factors, it is easy to lose sight of the forest because the discussion necessarily focuses on individual trees. You may find it helpful to keep in mind one very simple but all-important concept. Many social psychologists are convinced that we make positive evaluations whenever we are experiencing positive feelings and negative evaluations whenever we are experiencing negative feelings. Simply put, our interpersonal likes and dislikes are determined by emotions.

If this proposition is true (and we believe it is), any factor that influences a person's emotional state in turn affects attraction. The reasoning that underlies this simple statement should become clear as you progress through the chapter.

You should also note that interpersonal behavior is sometimes more complex than simply the effect of positive and negative emotions on liking and disliking. For example, our evaluations of others can become quite complicated and quite extreme, as you will see when you read about love in Chapter 8 and hate in Chapter 11.

interpersonal attraction: A person's attitude about another person. Attraction involves an evaluation along a dimension that ranges from strong liking to strong disliking.

The Power of Proximity: Unplanned Contacts Can Result in Attraction

Over six billion people live on our planet, and you could possibly like several thousand of them well enough to consider them as your friends. That is

FIGURE 7.3
Proximity: One Way That Strangers Become Acquaintances. At school, at work, or where you live, you encounter strangers. On the basis of *proximity*, you come in contact with some of these individuals over and over again. This repeated exposure leads to recognition, an increasingly positive evaluation, and a greater likelihood that you will become acquainted with those with whom you are brought in contact.

exceedingly unlikely to happen, however. Any one of us will probably become aware of, interact with, and get to know only a tiny percentage of these individuals. In this relatively small subgroup, only a few will become acquaintances, fewer still will become either friends or enemies, and most will remain strangers. What determines awareness, interaction, and level of attraction?

An obvious, but perhaps not entirely obvious, determinant is controlled by our physical surroundings. Many seemingly unimportant details of where we live, work, and go to school represent important and often overlooked influences on our interpersonal behavior. Simply stated, two people tend to become acquainted if external factors (e.g., the location of dormitory rooms, classroom seats, office desks, etc.) bring them into repeated contact, as shown in Figure 7.3. Such contact is the result of physical **proximity**—or closeness.

proximity: In attraction research, the closeness between two individuals' residences, classroom seats, work areas, and so on. The closer the physical distance, the greater the probability that the two people will come into repeated contact and thus experience repeated exposure.

repeated exposure: Frequent contact with a stimulus. According to Zajonc's theory, repeated exposure to any mildly negative, neutral, or positive stimulus results in an increasingly positive evaluation of that stimulus.

■ WHY PROXIMITY MATTERS: REPEATED EXPOSURE. Think back to your first day of college. You probably came in contact with many strangers on the sidewalks, steps, classrooms, cafeteria, library, and in your living quarters. At first, these individuals constituted a confusing blur of people you didn't know. In a relatively short period of time, however, as you walked down your dormitory corridor or sat in your classrooms, some faces began to stand out simply because you passed by or sat beside a few individuals more than once. These casual and unplanned contacts soon led to mutual recognition. You may not have known who these individuals were, but you came to recognize their faces, and they recognized yours. As a result, both of you were more likely to say "Hi" the next time you saw one another and perhaps exchanged a word or two about random topics such as the upcoming exam, the weather, or some event on campus. It feels good to see a familiar face. Why should that be?

It is found that **repeated exposure** to a new stimulus (a stranger's face, an abstract drawing, a product, or whatever) will usually result in an increasingly positive evaluation of that stimulus (Zajonc, 1968). Even infants tend to smile at a photograph of someone they have seen before but not at a photograph of someone they are seeing for the first time (Brooks-Gunn & Lewis, 1981).

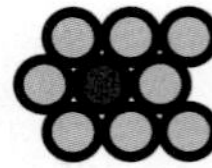

Zajonc's explanation is that we ordinarily respond with at least mild discomfort when we encounter anyone or anything unfamiliar. As we will discuss in more detail later in this chapter, among our early ancestors, it was probably dangerous to trust strangers or to respond positively to almost anything that was new and unknown. With repeated exposure, however, the new and fearful stimulus could gradually become a safe, familiar one. A familiar face not only is evaluated positively, but also elicits positive affect *and* activates facial muscle and brain activity in a way indicative of a positive emotional response (Harmon-Jones & Allen, 2001). The word *familiar* is related to the word *family,* and repeated exposure allows us to include new individuals and new aspects of our world in our expanded family. Even in the absence of language, animals are able to categorize and classify specific individuals in their social encounters as friends and foes (Schusterman, Reichmuth, & Kastak, 2000).

Though the repeated exposure effect has been established in many experiments using many different stimuli, Hansen and Bartsch (2001) suggested the possibility that not all individuals are equally responsive to the exposure effect. Specifically, they proposed that those who most strongly need structure would be most susceptible to the repeated exposure effect. The Personal Need for Structure Scale assesses how much organization a person prefers in his or her world (Neuberg & Newsom, 1993). Those who score high on this scale (compared to those who score low) are more apt to organize their social and nonsocial surroundings in less complex ways, to use stereotypes more readily, and generally to use categories when making judgments. In the experimental portion of the study, research participants were divided into those high versus those low in need for structure. Each individual was shown a series of unfamiliar Turkish words such as *merhaba, pazar,* and *yirmibes.* Some words were shown once, some twice, and so on, up to some being shown nine times. After that, each word was shown a final time and evaluated by the participants. Both high- and low-need-for-structure groups showed the repeated exposure effect—that is, the more times a word had been shown, the more positively it was evaluated. This effect was, however, much stronger for those high in need for structure than for those low in that need. The high-need individuals also responded much more negatively to an unfamiliar word that had not previously been shown at all than did the low-need individuals. The investigators concluded that the statement "Familiarity leads to liking" should be modified to say "Familiarity leads to liking *if* a person has a high need for structure" (Hansen & Bartsch, 2001).

As you might expect from the discussion of subliminal conditioning in Chapter 4, repeated exposure to a stimulus influences a person's evaluation of that stimulus even when he or she is unaware that exposure has taken place. In fact, the effect is stronger under these conditions. Bornstein and D'Agostino (1992) presented stimuli to some research participants at a normal speed and to others at a speed so rapid that they were not aware of having seen them (a speed considered to be *subliminal* or *below threshold*). The repeated exposure effect was found in both conditions, but the effect was greater when the stimuli were presented subliminally rather than at a normal speed.

The subliminal repeated exposure effect influences not only the evaluation of specific stimuli, but also the evaluation of other stimuli (Monahan, Murphy, & Zajonc, 2000). In other words, the positive affect generated by exposure to a specific set of stimuli *generalizes* to other stimuli. In an interesting experiment, undergraduate research participants were subliminally exposed to stimuli that consisted of either Chinese ideographs or drawings of polygons either once or repeatedly. They were then asked to indicate how much they liked each of fifteen stimuli after viewing each one for one second. Some rated the same stimuli to which they had been exposed—the *same* Chinese ideographs if they had been exposed to Chinese ideographs, or the *same* polygons if they had been exposed to polygons. Some rated new but similar stimuli—*different* Chinese ideographs if they had been exposed to Chinese ideographs, or *different* polygons if they had been exposed to polygons. Still other participants rated new but different stimuli—polygons if they had been exposed to Chinese ideographs or Chinese ideographs if they had been exposed to polygons.

As depicted in Figure 7.4, the first group (Chinese ideographs both times or polygons both times) showed the usual repeated exposure effect. The second group (Chinese ideographs the first time and different ideographs the second time, or polygons the first time and different polygons the second time) was also more positive toward novel stimuli to which it had not been exposed *if* it had been repeatedly exposed to similar stimuli. Even the third group (ideographs the first time and polygons the

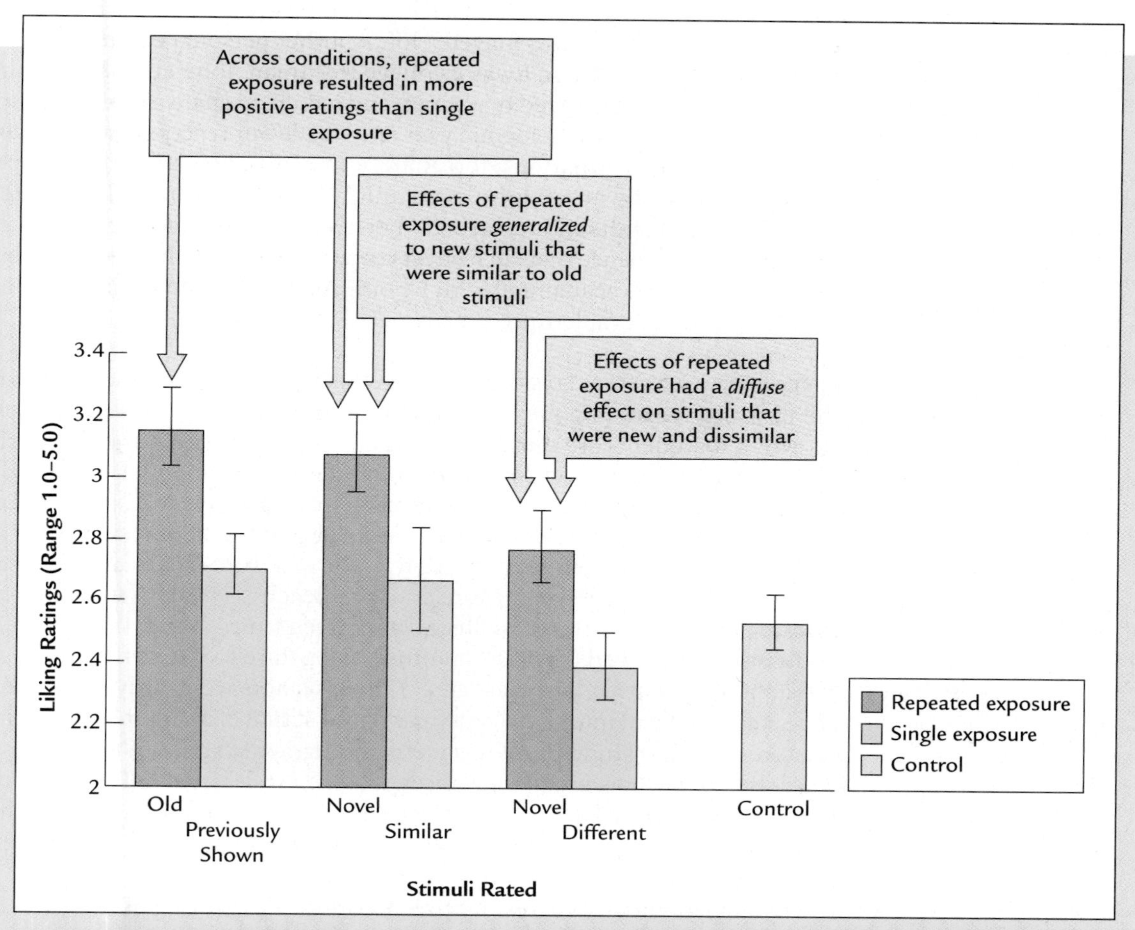

FIGURE 7.4

Repeated Exposure: Specific, General, and Diffuse Effects.

In the first part of an experiment, research participants were subliminally exposed to a given type of stimulus once, twice, or up to nine times. In the second part of the experiment, the participants were asked to rate either the same stimuli they had seen in the first part, stimuli similar to those seen in the first part, or stimuli different from those seen earlier. The control group did not participate in the first part; they simply rated stimuli they were seeing for the first time. (See the text for more specific details.) The usual *repeated exposure effect* was found in the group rating the same stimuli they had seen before, a generalized effect was found in the group rating new stimuli that were similar to those seen before, and a diffuse effect was found in the group rating new, different stimuli.

[SOURCE: BASED ON DATA FROM MONAHAN, MURPHY, & ZAJONC, 2000.]

second, or vice versa) showed the effect, though not quite as strongly. Compared with the control group (not previously exposed to any stimuli), those in the third group were more positive toward the novel stimuli even if they had been repeatedly exposed to quite different stimuli. Presumably, the positive affect aroused by repeated exposure lingers on and has a positive effect on subsequent evaluations of other stimuli.

Note that there are exceptions to the repeated exposure effect. The most important exception is that if one's initial reaction to a person or to anything else is extremely negative, repeated exposure does not increase liking and sometimes even leads to greater dislike (Swap, 1977). One personal example is the song "Copacabana" sung by Barry Manilow; I (DB) disliked it intensely the first time I heard it, and the negative feeling increased each time it was played on the radio. In the late 1970s or early 1980s, it was played a lot. Another personal example is the roommate assigned to me when I was a college freshman. John and I both realized we were incompatible the first day we met, and having to share a room with someone you dislike for an entire academic year only made our reactions more negative. In most interpersonal situations, fortunately, our initial reaction to other people is neutral, only mildly negative, or even mildly positive. As a result, repeated exposure ordinarily results in increasingly positive feelings and friendly relations.

Is there any evidence that such effects occur in everyday life? Do they help determine who becomes acquainted with whom? As you will soon discover, the answer to both questions is a definite yes.

■ PROXIMITY AND REPEATED EXPOSURE IN NATURAL SETTINGS. Numerous studies over the past fifty years in college classrooms in the United States and Europe have shown that students are most likely to become acquainted if they are assigned to sit in adjoining seats (Maisonneuve, Palmade, & Fourment, 1952; Segal, 1974). Sometimes students meet on the basis of an instructor's seating chart and actually become friends (Byrne, 1961a) or even marriage partners (Couple repays . . . , 1997).

To provide experimental evidence that the exposure effect can increase attraction in a classroom setting, Moreland and Beach (1992) instructed one female research assistant to attend a college class fifteen times during the semester, a second assistant to attend the class ten times, and a third to attend five times. A fourth assistant did not attend the class at all. The assistants were fairly similar in appearance, and none had interacted with any of the actual class members. At the end of the semester, the students were shown photographic slides of the four assistants and asked to rate how much they liked each one. As depicted in Figure 7.5, the more times a particular assistant had been in the class, the more she was liked. In this and many other experimental tests of the general proposition, repeated exposure has been found to have a positive effect on attraction.

Beyond the classroom, residential proximity in dwelling places such a dormitories, apartments, and suburban neighborhoods also affects interpersonal relationships, including friendships, romantic partners, and choice of a spouse (Bossard, 1932; Davie & Reeves, 1939). When movies depict a romance with the boy or girl next door, they are accurately reflecting a common occurrence.

In Chapter 1, we cautioned that a correlation between variables does not necessarily indicate a causal relationship. It is possible, for example, that attraction encourages people to select specific housing locations. If so, attraction may cause proximity rather than the opposite. It is even possible that the selection of a dwelling place could be based on some other factor (such as one's ethnic group). If so, this third factor (ethnicity) could lead to attraction *and* to proximity, and thus explain the correlation between those variables. How could you study attraction and proximity in natural settings but still be able to determine whether proximity is the causal factor?

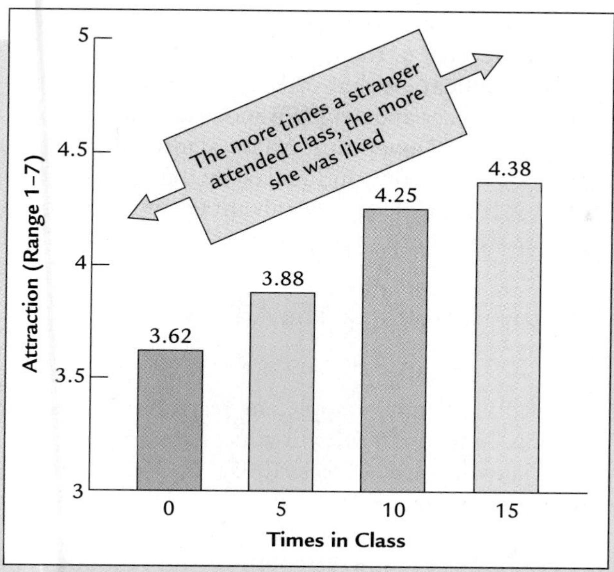

FIGURE 7.5

Frequency of Exposure and Liking in the Classroom. In a test of the repeated exposure effect in a college classroom, four female assistants pretended to be fellow students. One of them did not attend class all semester, another attended the class five times, a third attended ten times, and the fourth came to class fifteen times. At the end of the semester, the students were shown photos of the assistants and were asked to rate how much they liked each of them. The more times the students had been exposed to an assistant, the greater the attraction toward her. [SOURCE: BASED ON DATA FROM MORELAND & BEACH, 1992.]

An example of such research is provided by studies of residential proximity in which the living space had been assigned on a random basis rather than being chosen by the residents (Festinger, Schachter, & Back, 1950). On a university campus, couples were allotted apartments in married student housing on a first-come, first-served basis without their having any choice in the matter. Nevertheless, proximity had a powerful effect on attraction. Couples whose assigned apartments were located within twenty-two feet of one another were very likely to become acquainted. In contrast, if couples were located in apartments more than eighty-eight feet apart, they were quite unlikely to form relationships.

■ APPLYING KNOWLEDGE ABOUT PROXIMITY EFFECTS. If you are not required to live in a specific apartment or sit in a specific seat, it is possible for you to make conscious choices that best fit your needs. You may not have taken advantage of this possibility, but you could. For example, in a classroom, if you want to make new friends, you should select a seat between two likely prospects, not a seat on the end of a row or beside an empty desk. Also, if you find you don't especially like your seat neighbors and if change is permitted, try a new location. At the opposite extreme, if you don't desire new friends or simply want to maintain your privacy (Larson & Bell, 1988), select a classroom seat that is as isolated as possible from other people. Some students seem to do just that, because those who prefer privacy tend to select seats in the back of the room (Pedersen, 1994).

In a more dramatic application that utilizes what is known about proximity, architects have designed offices and neighborhoods in a way that encourages interaction and communication (Giovannini, 2000; Gladwell, 2000). It has long been known that interpersonal behavior is influenced by the details of our physical environment. Altogether, it is possible to take advantage of what we know and create the kind of physical environment that provides the effects we desire.

Positive and Negative Emotions: The Affective Basis for Attraction

Our emotional state (happy, sad, fearful, etc.) at any given moment influences perception, cognition, motivation, decision making, *and* interpersonal attraction (Berry & Hansen, 1996; Forgas, 1995b; Zajonc & McIntosh, 1992) (see Figure 7.6). As you may remember from Chapter 3, psychologists often use the term **affect** when referring to emotions or feelings. The two most important characteristics of affect are *intensity*—the strength of the emotion—and *direction*—whether the emotion is positive or negative.

It is often assumed that all emotions fall along a single dimension—positive at one end and negative at the other. A great deal of research suggests, however, that positive and negative emotions represent two separate and independent dimensions that are reflected in self-ratings (Drake & Myers, 2000; Tellegen, Watson, & Clark, 1999; Yik, Russell, & Barrett, 1999) and in the different brain structures that are activated by positive versus negative emotions (George et al., 1995).

FIGURE 7.6

Affect: A Basis for Our Likes and Dislikes.

Emotions are also known as *affect*, and they have both a direct and an indirect influence on attraction. A direct effect occurs when another person does or says something that makes you feel good or bad. You like those who make you feel good and dislike those who make you feel bad. An indirect effect occurs when your emotional state is aroused by something other than the person you are evaluating. Regardless of the source, your evaluations tend to be influenced by this associated affect.

affect: A person's emotional state—feelings and moods.

If there are two separate emotional dimensions, it is possible for a person to experience a mixture of positive and negative affective states at the same time. Also, one type of emotion can increase or decrease without necessarily having any effect on the other (Barrett & Russell, 1998; Goldstein & Strube, 1994). Such separation of emotions quite possibly has evolutionary significance in that positive affect enables us to seek out and explore novel aspects of the environment; at the same time, negative affect fosters vigilance and the possibility of retreat if that becomes necessary (Cacioppo & Berntson, 1999).

Individual differences also influence affective functioning. For example, some people are found to be more sensitive to positive events in their daily lives, while others are more sensitive to negative events (Gable, Reis, & Elliot, 2000). Also, some individuals—those who are cognitively simple—do tend to report emotions along a single dimension, while cognitively complex individuals give evidence of two independent dimensions (Reich, Zautra, & Potter, 2001).

■ AFFECT AND ATTRACTION. A great many quite varied experiments have consistently found that positive affect leads to positive evaluations of other people—liking—while negative affect leads to negative evaluations—disliking (Dovidio et al., 1995). Affect influences attraction in two different ways. A *direct effect* occurs when another person says or does something that makes you feel good or bad. It is not surprising that you like someone who makes you feel good and dislike one who makes you feel bad (Downey & Damhave, 1991; Shapiro, Baumeister, & Kessler, 1991).

The other way in which affect influences us is less obvious. An *associated effect* occurs when another person is simply present at the moment your emotional state is positive or negative, for reasons that have nothing to do with the person to whom you are responding. Though he or she was not the cause of how you feel, you nevertheless tend to evaluate the other person on the basis of your own affective state. For example, if you meet a stranger on your way to a dental appointment, you are less inclined to like him or her than if you meet on your way to a long-anticipated new movie. We will now take a look at research dealing with both direct and associated effects of emotions.

■ DIRECT EFFECT OF EMOTIONS ON ATTRACTION. We have already described how the positive affect aroused by repeated exposure can determine liking, and we will soon describe how attraction is based on affective reactions to a person's appearance, attitudes, and other attributes.

Even more direct and obvious effects are represented by studies showing that a student in an experiment likes the experimenter better if that person has administered rewards as opposed to punishments (McDonald, 1962). In addition, both males and females tend to dislike strangers who invade their personal space by choosing to sit inappropriately close in a library setting (Fisher & Byrne, 1975), and females dislike males who try to impress them with annoying opening lines such as "Bet I can out-drink you" rather than a neutral opening such as "Hi" (Cunningham, 1989; Kleinke & Dean, 1990).

You can be sure that a stranger will like you better if you do or say something pleasant (e.g., "That's a beautiful dog you've got.") as opposed to something unpleasant (e.g., "Where did you find such an ugly mutt?").

■ INDIRECT EFFECTS OF EMOTIONS ON ATTRACTION. Very often, our positive and negative feelings aren't based on what the individual with whom we are interacting has said or done. Instead, other sources of emotion, such as some recent experience, your physical state, or your current mood, influence not only your feelings, but also your immediate evaluations of others. If another person just happens to be there when your feelings are positive, you tend to like that individual. If the person is present when your feelings are negative, your reaction tends to be one of dislike. The general idea is based on classical conditioning, as outlined in Figure 7.7.

Such indirect influences of affective state on attraction have been demonstrated in many experiments in which emotional states were manipulated in a wide variety of ways. Examples include subliminal presentation of pleasant versus unpleasant pictures (Krosnick et al., 1992), background music (May & Hamilton, 1980), radio news (Kaplan, 1981), and room lighting (Baron, Rea, & Daniels, 1992). In a similar way, existing positive versus negative mood states (not brought on by anything the experimenter did or by anything the other person did) also lead to positive versus negative evaluations of the other person (Berry & Hansen, 1996). In these and numerous other experiments, it has consistently been shown that positive affect results in positive evaluations (liking), while negative affect results in negative evaluations (disliking).

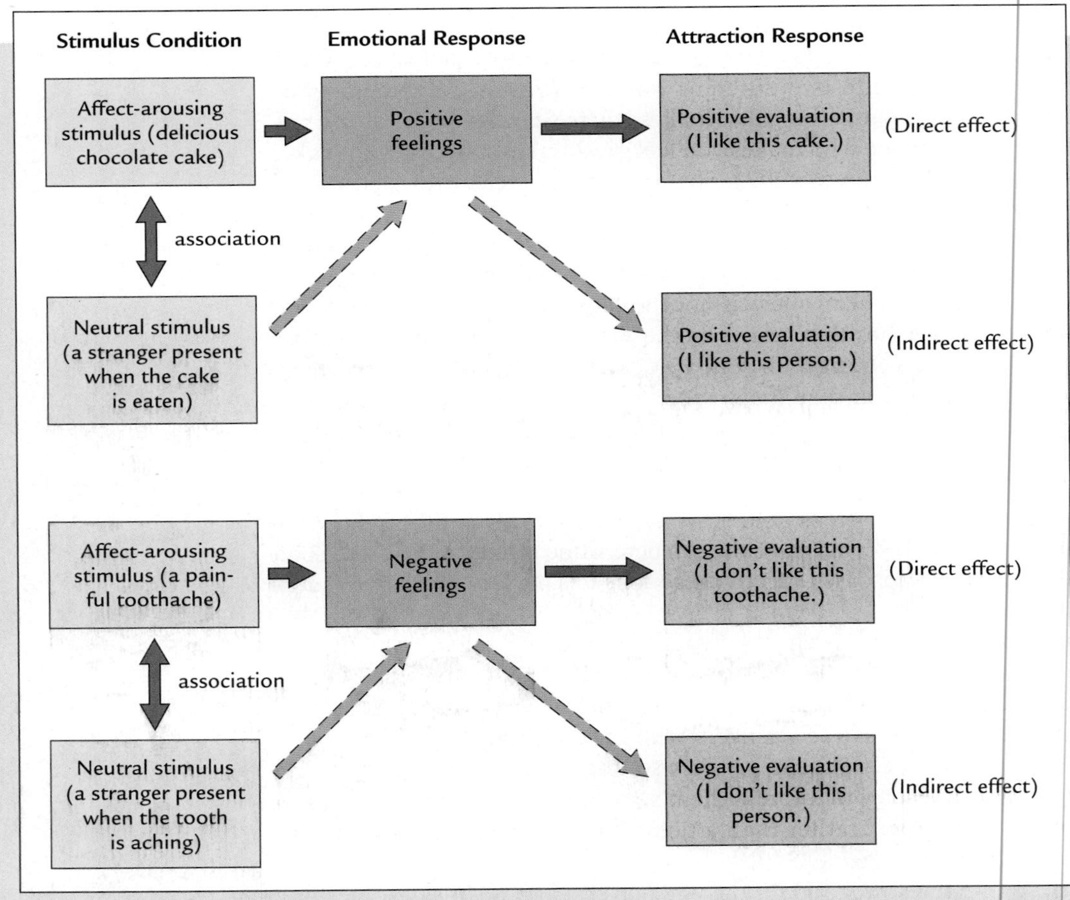

FIGURE 7.7

Direct and Indirect Influences of Affect on Attraction.

When any stimulus (including a person) arouses positive affect, that stimulus is liked. If it arouses negative affect, it is disliked. This is a direct effect. An indirect effect occurs when any neutral stimulus (including a person) is present at the same time that affect is aroused by some unrelated source. The neutral stimulus becomes associated with the affect and is therefore liked or disliked. Such indirect effects represent a type of classical conditioning.

[SOURCE: BASED ON MATERIAL IN BYRNE & CLORE, 1970.]

Taking this model a step further, the affect aroused by one person can become associated with a second person. We have already discussed in Chapter 4 how attitudes in general can be acquired through conditioning, so it should not be surprising that attitudes toward people can be acquired in the same way. If, for example, we have a negative emotional reaction to Person A (for whatever reason), and then observe Person A interacting with Person B, we may well have a negative reaction to Person B. So, if I very much dislike Allen and see him talking to Bill, I will tend to dislike Bill even though I don't know him. This transfer of negative emotions and negative evaluations is often observed with respect to someone who has a **stigma.** Stigma refers any characteristic of a person that at least some people don't like. Stigmas can include race, age, accent, physical disability or disease, unattractiveness, obesity, or sexual orientation (Frable, 1993; Neuberg et al., 1994; Rodin & Price, 1995). When an individual interacts with a stigmatized person, the experience is perceived as threatening, blood pressure increases, and performance is poorer (Blascovich et al., 2001). With continuing contact, however, the threat is diminished. As with any other type of prejudice (see Chapter 6), stigmatization is most often based on irrational assumptions. Nevertheless, the emotions that are aroused may be quite strong and easily transferred to someone else even though the second person does not share the stigma.

We discussed how repeated exposure leads to positive affect and thus to liking, and we described how associated affect also influences liking. Murphy, Monahan, and Zajonc (1995) investigated just what happens when these two independent sources of affect occur simultaneously. They manipulated (1) repeated exposure, which arouses positive affect, and (2) associated affect—happy or angry faces presented so fast that they were subliminal or presented at a normal viewing speed. Both repeated exposure and subliminal association influenced evaluations, combining to yield responses representing their net affective value. Besides showing how different sources of affect combine to influence our evaluations, this experiment suggests the power of subliminal sources of affect.

One question to consider is why the affect aroused by a subliminal presentation of happy and angry faces was more influential than the affect aroused by clearly presented faces. One possible explanation is that people resent having their judgments controlled in obvious ways and are therefore motivated to resist such influences. With subliminal presentations, however, we are unaware of the source of our emotions. As a result, our judgments are easily influenced. Murphy and her colleagues (1995) proposed that in everyday life we are often unaware of the sources of our feelings—we just know that we are sometimes cheerful and sometimes depressed. In that situation, our likes and dislikes can more easily be determined by our moods.

■ ARE WE VULNERABLE TO AFFECT MANIPULATION? It is very clear that our interpersonal evaluations are influenced by direct and indirect affective factors, including indirect subliminal manipulations. Such findings raise the possibility that we could be persuaded to purchase products, vote for political candidates, and support specific issues. Actually, such applications have become a familiar part of our lives. That is, people trying to sell products or services attempt to manipulate our evaluations by offering free samples or by complimenting us. On a more general level, advertisements are designed to arouse positive feelings so that we will be more attracted to whatever or whoever is being "sold."

For example, columnist Molly Ivins suggests that whenever companies known to cut down acres of trees and pollute our streams present an advertisement depicting scenes of a beautiful countryside with green forests and sparkling water, you should immediately be on guard. Such companies are simply trying to manipulate how you evaluate them by arousing your positive affect. In the same way, political strategists have learned to use feel-good campaign techniques—including cheerful music and waving flags—in order to associate positive affect toward a given

stigma: A personal characteristic that at least some other individuals perceive negatively.

candidate so that we will like and vote for him or her. People assume that a candidate's affective expressions (such as smiling) reveal basic personality characteristics of that individual, and thus how much we should like and therefore vote for him or her (Glaser & Salovey, 1998; Hecht & LaFrance, 1998). Even beyond politics, people who express positive emotions are rated more favorably than those who express negative emotions (Harker & Keltner, 2001).

To an equal degree, there is an attempt to associate negative affect with one's opponent. For example, in the New York senatorial race in 2000, candidate Rick Lazio ran multiple ads about his opponent that used the phrase, "Hillary Clinton. You Just Can't Trust Her" (Tomasky, 2000). In that instance, by the way, the tactic failed. Figure 7.8 provides an example of how this process is intended to work.

The media also play a role, in that some events are considered to be more "newsworthy" than others. Political strategist Roger Ailes described campaign coverage in the following way:

> *Let's face it, there are three things that the media are interested in: pictures, mistakes and attacks. It's my orchestra-pit theory of politics. If you have two guys on a stage and one guy says, "I have a solution to the Middle East problems," and the other guy falls into the orchestra pit, who do you think is going to be on the evening news?" (quoted in Wilson, 1993, p. 33).*

Does negative information have an effect? Research suggests that it does. Pentony (1995) presented undergraduates with information about two politicians

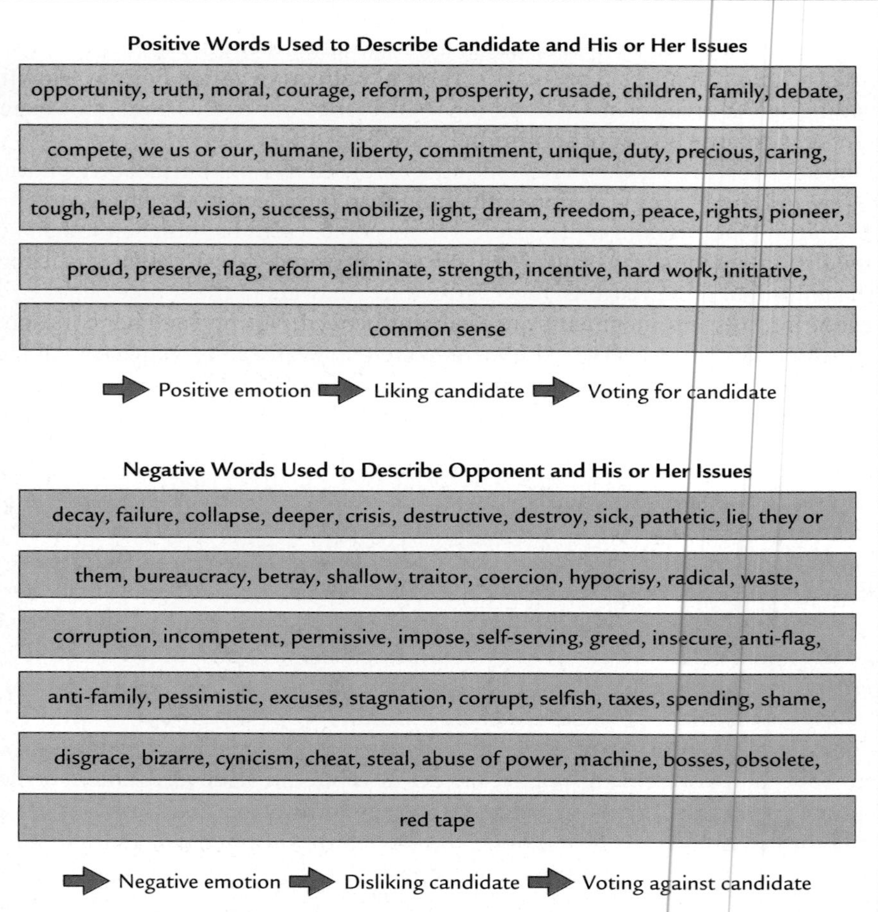

FIGURE 7.8

Positive Words for Your Candidate and Negative Words for the Opponent. The examples above were taken from instructions to political candidates in the United States in 1990 in a mailing entitled "Language: A Key Mechanism of Control." The general idea is to associate "optimistic positive words" with one's candidates and "pessimistic negative words" with one's opponents. Though this particular list was generated by a Republican Action Committee, its general message obviously can be (and has been) used by members of both major political parties.

[SOURCE: BASED ON MATERIAL IN WEISBERG, 1990.]

running for office. Totally positive information was provided about one candidate. Equally positive information was provided about the other candidate, plus one negative allegation (having obtained tax breaks for friends). That single negative element resulted in less positive evaluations of the latter candidate, and it also influenced voting. Even when this candidate was able to refute the negative information, the purely positive candidate won.

Are we helpless in the face of affective influences from candidates and from the media? Ottati and Isbell (1996) provide evidence that the effects of mood on evaluating candidates are greatest when the audience is politically uninformed. In contrast, people who are well informed not only resist affect manipulation, but tend to react in the opposite way. That is, they are even more positive about their candidate when a negative mood is created and even more negative when a positive mood is created.

In a similar way, the mood manipulations work best if the audience is not consciously motivated to evaluate the candidate. When, however, people *are* consciously attempting to make an evaluation, they can adjust their evaluations to compensate for the biasing affective information (Isbell & Wyer, 1999).

Altogether, irrelevant affective factors are most likely to influence potential voters who are uninformed about the candidates and the issues, who are unaware of the source of their current emotional reactions, and who are not actively engaged in evaluating the candidate. You may find it helpful to keep such findings in mind the next time you are exposed to an affect-arousing ad of any kind.

KEY POINTS

- *Interpersonal attraction* refers to the positive and negative attitudes we form about other people.
- The initial contact between two people is very often based on the *proximity* resulting from such physical aspects of the environment as classroom seating assignments, the location of residences, and how workplaces are arranged.
- Proximity, in turn, leads to *repeated exposure* of two individuals to one another. Repeated exposure usually results in positive affect, which results in attraction.
- Positive and negative affective states influence attraction both directly and indirectly. Direct effects occur when another person is responsible for the emotion. Indirect effects occur when the source of the emotion is elsewhere and the other person is simply associated with its presence.
- The application of the power of associated affect to both commercial and political advertising is increasingly common, and we are most influenced by it when we are unaware of the source (as in subliminal presentations) and when we are uninformed about the person or object we are evaluating.

Becoming Acquainted: The Need to Affiliate and the Effect of Observable Characteristics

If two people come into repeated contact and if they experience relatively positive affect, they are at a transition point, and one of two interpersonal patterns is likely to be followed. Quite often, they simply remain *superficial acquaintances* whose only interactions involve the exchange of friendly greetings and a word or two whenever they meet. Sometimes, however, they learn each other's names, exchange bits and pieces of information, and become *close acquaintances.* Which of these two outcomes is more likely depends on the level of *affiliation need* of each of the two acquaintances and the way in which each of them reacts to the *observable characteristics* of the other.

The Need to Affiliate

A good part of our lives is spent interacting with other people, and this tendency to affiliate seems to have a neurobiological basis (Rowe, 1996). The need to affiliate with others and to be accepted by them is hypothesized to be as basic to our psychological makeup as hunger and thirst are to our physical makeup (Baumeister & Leary, 1995). Presumably, it was a distinct advantage to our distant ancestors to interact socially in order to procure food, ward off danger, and reproduce.

Human infants are apparently born with the motivation and the ability to seek understanding of their interpersonal world (Baldwin, 2000), and even newborns are predisposed to look toward faces in preference to other stimuli (Mondloch et al., 1999). Adults also pay special attention to faces, and there is evidence that facial information is processed differently than stimuli of less biological significance (Ro, Russell, & Lavie, 2001). The importance of a facial stimulus is suggested by the fact that there is an automatic response to facial cues such as smiles and frowns (Hassin & Trope, 2000).

It was proposed by Putnam (2000) that one of the current problems with the United States is a decrease in affiliative behavior at the community level. As a consequence, compared with past decades, our lives now consist of fewer interpersonal interactions, less group activity, less interest in taking an active role in seeking improvement in society, and voter apathy. The conclusion is that we are worse off as a result of ignoring our affiliative needs.

People differ, of course, in the strength of their **need for affiliation,** and such differences constitute a relatively stable *trait* (or *disposition*). People learn to seek the amount of social contact that is optimal for them, preferring to be alone part of the time and in social situations part of the time (O'Connor & Rosenblood, 1996). In addition to these individual differences in affiliation motivation, it is also true that specific situations can arouse temporary *states* of affiliation need. We will describe the effects of both types of affiliation need on behavior.

need for affiliation: The basic motive to seek and maintain interpersonal relationships.

■ DISPOSITIONAL DIFFERENCES IN THE NEED TO AFFILIATE. Beginning with the early work of Murray (1938) on the motivational aspects of personality, psychologists have investigated behavioral differences between those high and those low in the need to affiliate. Some of these findings are summarized in Table 7.1.

Attempts to measure the need for affiliation as a trait have involved two approaches, and they seem to tap somewhat different aspects of the need. Self-report measures simply ask direct questions about affiliation-relevant desires and activities, and thus tap an *explicit motive* to affiliate. Projective measures consist of ambiguous pictures in which the respondent is asked to interpret what is going on. This approach is directed at less conscious needs, and thus taps an *implicit motive* to affiliate. College students scoring high on an explicit measure were found to be very sociable, and they interacted with multiple people, whereas those scoring high on an implicit measure were likely to interact in two-person situations involving close relationships (Craig, Koestner, & Zuroff, 1994). It seems that explicit affiliative motives lead to interactions in a social context, and implicit affiliative motives lead to interactions in a close interpersonal context.

In addition to these two somewhat different expressions of the need to affiliate, which Hill (1987) labels the *need for positive stimulation* (explicit motive) and

TABLE 7.1

The Effect of Need for Affiliation on Social Behavior. Over the years, investigators have found differences in interpersonal behavior that are associated with measures of affiliation need. Consistent with Murray's (1938) original definition of this dispositional variable, need for affiliation is related to the tendency to form friendships and to socialize, to interact closely with others, to cooperate and communicate with others in a friendly way, and to fall in love.

INDIVIDUALS WHO ARE COMPARATIVELY HIGH IN THE NEED FOR AFFILIATION
Write more letters and make more local telephone calls (Lansing & Heyns, 1959).
Laugh more and remain physically close to others (McAdams, 1979).
Avoid making negative comments to fellow workers (Exline, 1962).
Desire more dates per week and are more likely to be emotionally involved in a relationship (Morrison, 1954).
Are more likely to express a desire to marry right after college (Bickman, 1975).
Engage in fewer antisocial or negative acts with fellow workers Spend less time alone (Constantian, 1981).
Are more likely to be described by other people as likable, natural, and enthusiastic (McAdams, 1979).

the *need for social support* (implicit motive), are two additional motives. One of these is the *need for attention* that leads some individuals to behave so as to obtain the approval and praise of others. Another motive, *need for social comparison,* results in interactions motivated by the desire to obtain knowledge and reduce uncertainty.

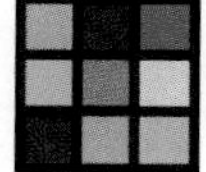

What happens when our affiliative needs are not met? For example, when others ignore us, how do we react? Being ostracized by others is an extremely negative experience, and this can occur throughout the life span (Faulkner & Williams, 1999) and throughout the world (Williams, Cheung, & Choi, 2000). Williams and his colleagues reported a new form of social rejection—ostracism on the Internet—in which an individual enters a chat room and is ignored by the other participants. Studying the reactions of individuals from sixty-two different countries, these investigators found that chat room ostracism led to negative emotions, a feeling of having lost control, and a sense of not belonging.

Such social rejection would be expected to lead to selective memory for socially relevant information. For example, if you had just been ignored or rejected by others, you might pay special attention to social matters such as friendly or unfriendly interpersonal acts. In a test of this proposition, Gardner, Pickett, and Brewer (2000) had undergraduates interact with four other students (actually experimental assistants) by means of computers. The manipulation involved either social acceptance by these strangers or social rejection. In the acceptance condition, a participant's responses were greeted by messages such as "I totally hear you!" and "Cool!" In the rejection condition, the others expressed common interests that could not be shared with the participant (e.g., their fondness for "Hoodoo Meatbucket," an imaginary musical group); thus, the others interacted while the real participant was left out of the electronic conversation. Afterward, each participant read the diary of a same-sex student and then was asked to recall as many events from the diary as possible in ten minutes. Those who had experienced rejection remembered more social events from the diary than did those who had been accepted. Their recall was better for both positive ("My roommate and I went out on the town tonight and had a really great time together") and negative ("My best friend blew me off; we had made weekend plans but I guess they just didn't matter") events in the diary. The investigators concluded that human beings are programmed to monitor and become sensitive to social information when their need to belong is not met. Just as physical hunger increases our sensitivity to food cues, social hunger increases our sensitivity to social cues.

■ SITUATIONAL DETERMINANTS OF THE NEED TO AFFILIATE. Sometimes, external events arouse the affiliation need. Newspaper and television stories quite often describe situations in which strangers come together and interact in a friendly way in response to unusual events. Examples vary from natural disasters (floods, earthquakes, and forest fires) to public events (Mardi Gras, rock concerts, and the Indianapolis 500) (Benjamin, 1998; Byrne, 1991; Humphriss, 1989). Such accounts commonly describe the resulting interactions as friendly, positive, and cheerful, with people doing their best to help one another.

The underlying reason for responding to stress with friendliness and affiliation was first identified by Schachter (1959). His early work revealed that research participants who were expecting to receive electric shock, when given a choice, expressed a preference for being with others who were also expecting to be shocked. In the control group, those not expecting electric shock wanted to be alone or expressed no preference. One conclusion from this line of research was that "misery doesn't just love any kind of company, it loves only miserable company" (Schachter, 1959, p. 24).

Why should real-life events and laboratory manipulations of anxiety arouse the need to affiliate? Why should frightened, anxious people want to be with other frightened, anxious people? As we mentioned earlier, one of the motives for affiliation is the need for social comparison. People tend to seek out others—even strangers—in order to communicate about what is going on, to compare their perceptions, and to make decisions about what to do. People want to compare their emotional reactions with the reactions of others. In short, arousing situations lead us to seek "cognitive clarity" in order to know what is going on (Kulik, Mahler, & Earnest, 1994) and "emotional clarity" in order to understand what we are feeling (Gump & Kulik, 1997).

Not only do we seek out others in such situations, but it is beneficial to do so. The positive effects of affiliation have been shown in studies of hospital patients before and after coronary bypass surgery (Kulik, Mahler, & Moore, 1996). The research participants were males undergoing nonemergency cardiac surgery for the first time. Each patient was assigned to a hospital room with a male roommate who was also hospitalized for surgery—involving either the heart or some other part of the body—and who had either just had the surgery or was still anticipating it. In this real and very stressful situation, those research participants who were given a roommate who had or was expecting cardiac surgery spent more time talking with the other person and seeking cognitive clarity than did patients with a noncardiac roommate. Such conversations often focused on emotions because the patients were also seeking emotional clarity. Being able to obtain both types of clarity from a roommate (a postoperative cardiac patient) resulted in fewer requests for medication and the ability to leave the hospital more quickly following surgery. It seems clear that humans are strongly motivated to affiliate and that affiliation is rewarding.

The Effect of Observable Characteristics: Immediate Determinants of Interpersonal Likes and Dislikes

Whenever we like—or dislike—someone at first sight, this reaction indicates that something about that person elicits positive or negative affect. Presumably such reactions are based on past experiences, stereotypes, and attributions that may or may not be accurate or relevant (Andreoletti, Zebrowitz, & Lachman, 2001). For example, if a stranger reminds you of someone you know and like, you will tend to like him or her (Andersen & Baum, 1994). Or, if the stranger belongs to a subgroup about which you have an existing attitude—for example, he has a Boston accent—you might like him because you like people who sound like the Kennedys or dislike him because you hate people who sound like the Kennedys. As discussed in Chapter 6, such positive and negative stereotypes are poor predictors of behavior.

Nevertheless, reactions to superficial characteristics occur quite often, no matter how unreasonable such reactions may be. One pervasive factor to which most people respond is degree of **physical attractiveness**—those aspects of a person's appearance that people regard as visually appealing or unappealing.

■ PHYSICAL ATTRACTIVENESS: EVALUATING PEOPLE ON THE BASIS OF APPEARANCE. We may say that "beauty is only skin deep," but people are very likely to respond positively to those who are attractive and negatively to those who are unattractive (Collins & Zebrowitz, 1995). There are some individual differences, however. For example, people who are high in the need for cognition (the tendency to engage in and enjoy cognitive activity) are less affected by the attractiveness of a stranger than are those with low cognitive needs (Perlini & Hansen, 2001).

Physical appearance influences many types of interpersonal evaluations, including liking, judgments of guilt or innocence in a courtroom (see Chapter 13), and even the grade that is assigned to an essay (Cash & Trimer, 1984). And people respond more positively to attractive infants than to unattractive ones (Karraker & Stern, 1990). Attractiveness is *especially* crucial, however, with respect to evaluating a potential romantic partner (Sprecher & Duck, 1994). Though both men and women are responsive to the attractiveness of a possible date, lover, or spouse, female attractiveness is more important to men than male attractiveness is to women (Feingold, 1990; Pierce, 1992).

Overall, though, an appealing appearance is perceived as a positive characteristic that influences interpersonal attraction and interpersonal preferences. Numerous stereotypes are consistently associated with appearance, and it would not be surprising if you hold some of them yourself. Before continuing, take a look at Figure 7.9 on page 272. People generally believe that attractive men and women are more poised, interesting, sociable, independent, dominant, exciting, sexy, well adjusted, socially skilled, and successful than unattractive men and women. Handsome men are believed to be more masculine, and beautiful women to be more feminine (Dion & Dion, 1987; Hatfield & Sprecher, 1986a). Altogether, as social psychologists discovered three decades ago, most people assume that "what is beautiful is good" (Dion, Berscheid, & Hatfield, 1972).

Despite the powerful effects of attractiveness, people are not very accurate in estimating how others rate their appearance. Men, especially, overestimate how attractive they are to others (Gabriel, Critelli, & Ee, 1994). The problem is more acute for women than for men, but some members of both sexes respond with **appearance anxiety**—an undue concern with how one looks. Those with the greatest anxiety agree with test items such as "I feel that most of my friends are more physically attractive than myself" and disagree with items such as "I enjoy looking at myself in the mirror" (Dion, Dion, & Keelan, 1990).

physical attractiveness: The combination of characteristics that are evaluated as beautiful or handsome at the most attractive extreme and unattractive at the other extreme.

appearance anxiety: Apprehension or worry about whether one's physical appearance is adequate and about the evaluations of other people.

FIGURE 7.9

What Would You Guess about the Personality Characteristics of These Two Individuals?
Make a list of the characteristics that you think might best describe each of these people. For example, how would you describe each person's sociability, adjustment, intelligence, poise, independence, masculinity/femininity, popularity, vanity, potential for success, integrity, concern for others, adjustment, sexuality, and other qualities? When you are finished, return to the text to find out whether your answers correspond to what most people think and to what psychological research has determined.

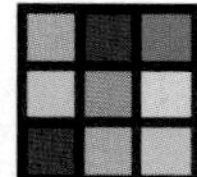

Although cross-cultural research suggests that positive stereotypes about attractiveness are universal, the *specific content* of the stereotypes depends on which characteristics are valued by a particular culture (Dion, Pak, & Dion, 1990). For example, in a collectivist culture such as Korea, attractiveness is assumed to be associated with integrity and concern for others, but these attributes do not appear among the attractiveness stereotypes common among individualistic North Americans (Wheeler & Kim, 1997). There is general agreement across cultures that attractiveness indicates social competence, adjustment, intelligence, and sexual warmth. Nevertheless, a Canadian study reported that women did *not* attribute socially desirable traits to men based on either the man's attractiveness or his age (Perlini, Marcello, & Hansen et al., 2001).

Despite widespread acceptance of the belief that attractiveness is an important cue to personality and character, most of the stereotypes based on appearance are *incorrect* (Feingold, 1992; Kenealy et al., 1991). Serial killers can be very good looking, and a great many people whose looks are considered less than stunning are actually intelligent, interesting, kind, amusing, sensual, and so forth. The stereotypes, in fact, are only valid with respect to a very few characteristics. For example, compared with less beautiful and handsome individuals, those who are most attractive are believed to be more popular (they are) and to have better interpersonal skills and feel better about themselves (they do) (Diener, Wolsic, & Fujita, 1995; Johnstone, Frame, & Bouman, 1992). The more attractive a person is, the more he or she self-discloses to members of the opposite sex, thus facilitating the establishment of a relationship (Stiles et al., 1996). Presumably, the popularity, social skills, high self-esteem, and tendency to self-disclose among those who are attractive occur primarily because such individuals have spent their lives being liked and treated nicely by others who respond positively to their good looks (Zebrowitz, Collins, & Dutta, 1998). In other words, appearance is not directly linked to these attributes; instead, the way other people react to appearance is the causative factor.

It should be added that a few *negative* attributes are also associated with physical attractiveness. For example, beautiful women are sometimes perceived as vain and materialistic (Cash & Duncan, 1984). Also, though handsome male politicians are more likely to be elected than relatively unattractive ones, an attractive woman running for elective office is not helped by her appearance (Sigelman et al., 1986), possibly because someone who is considered "too feminine" is often assumed to be somehow less effective as a legislator or administrator.

■ WHY SHOULD PHYSICAL ATTRACTIVENESS MATTER? If appearance is a poor predictor of other attributes, why in the world should people place great emphasis on it? Is it possible that this is a built-in response based on biological determinants?

Note that attractive people arouse positive affect (Johnston & Oliver-Rodriguez, 1997; Kenrick et al., 1993), and we know that positive affect leads to attraction. But, why should physical attractiveness arouse positive affect? The two basic explanations are (1) we are born with this kind of preference or (2) we learn this preference from various sources in our culture. It has not been possible to obtain convincing proof that would permit us to accept one view and reject the other. What sort of evidence is there?

From the perspective of evolutionary determinants, female beauty is believed to be sexually attractive to men because beauty is associated with youth, health, and fertility. Research supports this relationship, but the association is not a very strong one (Kalick et al., 1998; Shackelford & Larsen, 1999). One side effect of this emphasis on beauty is that women—more than men—seek cosmetic surgery in order to "look as young as they feel" (Grant, 2001).

Note that with respect to one specific aspect of attractiveness, links *are* found between hair length, age, health, and attraction. Men tend to prefer women with long hair (Jacobi & Cash, 1994), and healthy, shiny, strong hair is a sign of youth and health (Etcoff, 1999). In addition, young women tend to have longer hair than older women, and the better the self-reported quality of her hair, the better a woman's health (Hinsz, Matz, & Patience, 2001).

The general evolutionary point is that if men are attracted to and mate with young, healthy, fertile women, this enhances their odds of reproductive success (Johnston & Franklin, 1993). As a result, over hundreds of thousands of years, males with a preference for youthful beauty were more likely to pass on their genes to the next generation than were males for whom youth and beauty were irrelevant. The fact that females are less concerned about male youth and attractiveness is explained by the fact that women have a relatively limited age span in which reproduction is possible, whereas men are usually able to reproduce from puberty well into old age. For prehistoric females, the selection of a fertile male was a matter of less importance because young and old were both fertile. Instead, the choice of a man with the ability to provide resources and to protect her and their offspring

FIGURE 7.10

Mr. Right—Looks or Money?

From the evolutionary perspective, it makes reproductive sense for males to be programmed to emphasize the youth, health, and hence the attractiveness of potential mates. For women, reproductive success is better served by an emphasis on resources.

was crucial (Kenrick et al., 1994). The cartoon in Figure 7.10 suggests how this female preference might be expressed today. Research supports the observation that a male's income is positively associated with his desirability, especially as a marriage partner (Kenrick et al., 2001).

This evolutionary scenario for male and female preferences seems logical enough, but how can one determine the validity of such an explanation? The basic tendency is well established, but the ultimate explanation is more difficult to validate. Studies of undergraduate and graduate students indicate, as predicted by evolutionary theory, that men assess the sexual attractiveness of women on the basis of physical attributes, while women's ratings of male sexual attractiveness is based on social status (Townsend & Wasserman, 1997).

Other studies find that male preference for young, healthy females is universal and not affected by cultural differences (Buss, 1994, 1998), and this is consistent with a biological explanation. These same data also indicate that females prefer males on the basis of their resources (consistent with evolutionary theory), but (consistent with culture-based theories) this preference is greatest in cultures in which women are less well educated and have less control over conception and family size (Kasser & Sharma, 1999).

Still other evidence is consistent with the evolutionary explanation. In the personal ads in which men and women are seeking to find a partner, males and females provide different information. Ads placed by women stress their appearance, while those placed by men focus on material resources (Deaux & Hanna, 1984). A further step is to look at the success of such ads (Baize & Schroeder, 1995). For women, age as stated in the ads is negatively related to the number of replies—the older a woman, the fewer responses she receives. For ads placed by men, the opposite is true—the older the man, the more responses he receives. There may, of course, be limits as to how old a man can be and still attract women. Such limits have not been tested in research, in part because very few 90-year-old men place ads seeking dates. Women are also found to be more likely to respond to a male's ad the higher his income and educational level, but these same factors in a female's ad are unrelated to the number of replies received. So, the most effective male ad is one indicating a mature, rich, educated individual, whereas the most effective female ad is one that simply indicates youthfulness.

A potential problem for the biological theory is the finding that ads placed by gay men indicate a preference for younger male partners in the same way that heterosexual men prefer younger female partners (Kenrick et al., 1995). Such findings could be interpreted to mean that both straight and gay men have been subjected to the same cultural influences stressing the importance of youth and good looks. A biological explanation obviously cannot be based on reproductive success. It may be, however, that the preferences that developed among heterosexual men operate just as strongly among homosexual men despite the fact that such preferences are only relevant for the genetic survival of heterosexuals.

Evidence with respect to the content of personal ads could also be interpreted to mean that preferences across cultures and across sexual orientation simply reflect what most of us have been taught by the media about the importance of females being young and beautiful versus the importance of males being older and richer. Such themes are familiar in ancient fairy tales such as *Beauty and the Beast* and in modern movies. For example, Gallo and Byrne (2001) identified the movies that were most successful at the box office across several decades and found that male actors were ordinarily paired as romantic partners with female actors who were younger (often much younger) than themselves, as shown in Figure 7.11.

FIGURE 7.11

May–December Romance in the Movies: Culture or Biology?

A sampling of the movies that were in the top 40 in box office grosses in various years indicated clearly that when there was an age discrepancy in a romantic couple, the male actor was almost always older than the female actor (Gallo & Byrne, 2001). Shown here is a scene from *Entrapment* (1999), with Sean Connery, who is 196 months older than Catherine Zeta-Jones. Similar findings include *Gone in 60 Seconds* (2000), with Nicholas Cage, who is 137 months older than Angelina Jolie and *When Harry Met Sally* (1989), with Billy Crystal, who is 176 months older than Meg Ryan. Such age differences in films could mean that movies and other cultural influences teach us to accept the older male–younger female stereotype. It could also mean that movies simply reflect what naturally occurs in real life because of evolutionary influences.

Examples of an older woman paired with a younger man were exceedingly rare. Again, such findings could be explained equally well on the basis of biology or culture. A third possibility is that the older men who control the movie industry have a personal bias in encouraging the view that older men are attractive to women.

Some evidence is very difficult to explain in cultural terms. For example, year-old infants prefer attractive adults, and they spend more time playing with attractive dolls than with unattractive ones (Langlois et al., 1991; Langlois & Roggman, 1990). It is not reasonable to argue that the preferences of these infants have been molded by cultural influences. Perhaps the most sensible conclusion at this point is that humans quite possibly are genetically programmed to respond positively to attractiveness and that such preferences are strongly encouraged and supported by cultural factors.

■ WHAT, EXACTLY, CONSTITUTES ATTRACTIVENESS? Judgments of one's own attractiveness may not match very well the judgments of others, but there is surprisingly good agreement when two people are asked to rate a third person (Cunningham et al., 1995). Despite this agreement about who is and is not attractive, it is difficult to specify the exact cues that determine our judgments.

In attempting to identify those cues, investigators have used two approaches. One procedure is to identify a group of individuals who are rated as attractive and then to determine what they have in common. Cunningham (1986) used this method with male undergraduates who rated the photographs of young women. Those rated most attractive were found to fall into one of two groups. Some had "childlike features" with large, widely spaced eyes and a small nose and chin—women such as Meg Ryan, who are characterized as being "cute" (Johnston & Oliver-Rodriguez, 1997; McKelvie, 1993a). The other category of attractive women had mature features with prominent cheekbones, high eyebrows, large pupils, and a big smile—Julia Roberts is an example. These same two general facial types are found among fashion models, and they apply equally to white, African American, and Asian women (Ashmore, Solomon, & Longo, 1996).

A second and quite different approach to identifying what is meant by attractiveness was taken by Langlois and Roggman (1990). They began with facial photographs, then combined several faces into one face by means of computer digitizing. The image in each photo is divided into microscopic squares, and each square is translated into a number that represents a specific shade. Then the numbers are averaged across a group of pictures, and the result is translated back into a composite image.

You might reasonably guess that a face created by averaging would be rated as average in attractiveness. Instead, composite faces are rated as *more* attractive than most of the individual faces used to make the composite (Langlois, Roggman, & Musselman, 1994; Rhodes & Tremewan, 1996). In addition, the more faces that are averaged, the more beautiful the resulting face. Two faces are not enough to make an attractive face, but when you combine as many as thirty-two faces, " . . . you end up with a face that is pretty darned attractive" (Judith Langlois, as quoted in Lemley, 2000, p. 47). (See Figure 7.12).

It is possible to create an even more attractive face by taking initial attractiveness into account. For example, if you start with fifteen extremely attractive faces, their composite is more attractive than a composite of average faces (Perrett, May, & Yoshikawa, 1994). Another way to enhance the attractiveness of an averaged face is to rate each face going into the composite and then assign more weight to those faces rated most attractive. When biopsychologist Victor Johnston did this with a series of twenty generations of composites rated by ten thousand visitors to his web-

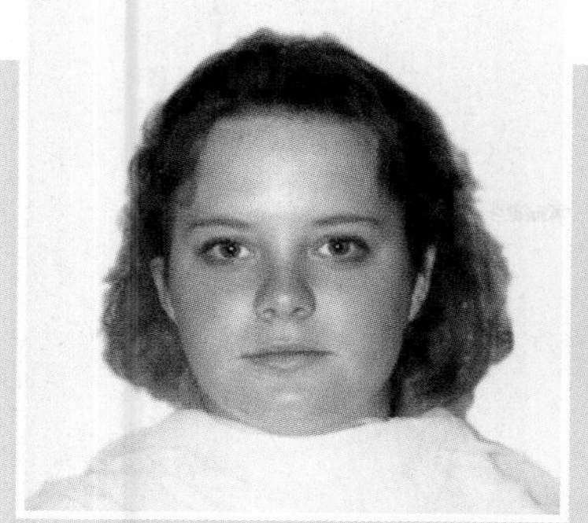

2 Faces

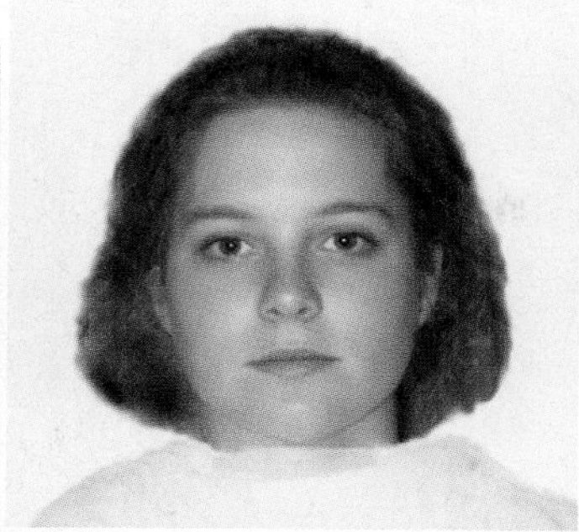

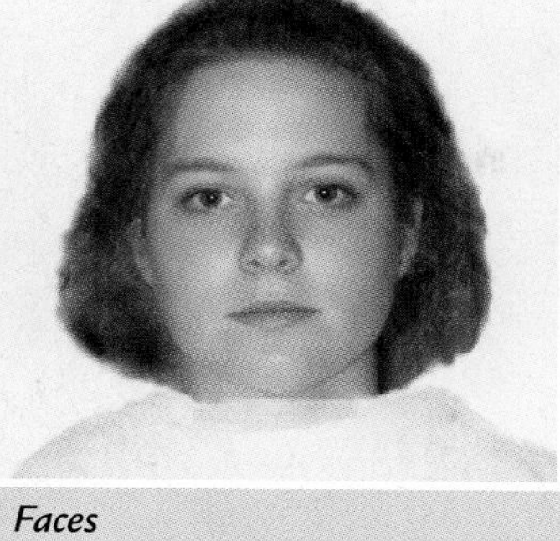

4 Faces

8 Faces

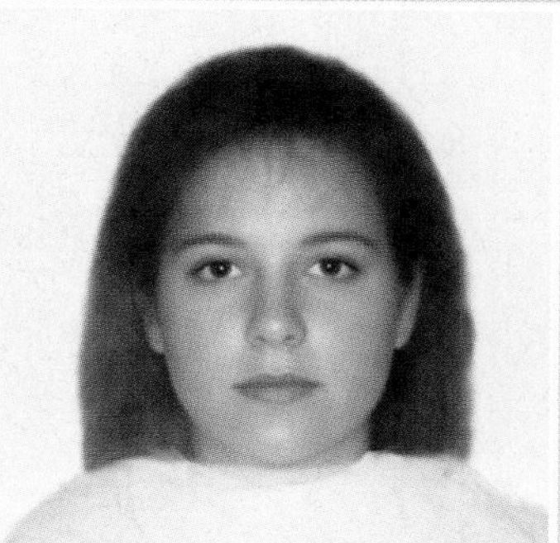

16 Faces

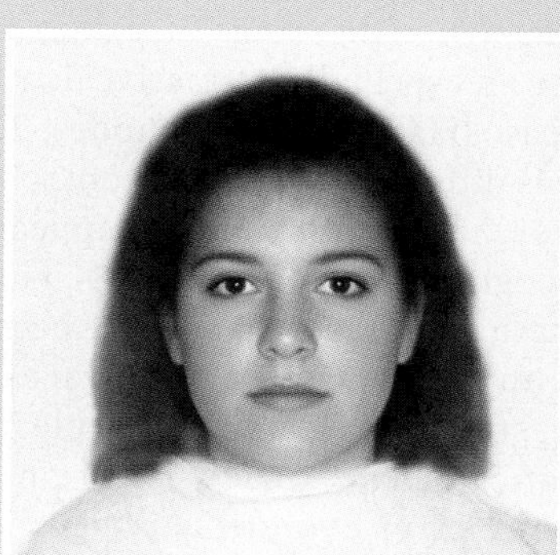

32 Faces

FIGURE 7.12

Composite Faces: The More Faces, the More Attractive. When computer images of faces are combined to form a composite, this average face is perceived as more attractive than individual faces. As the number of faces contributing to the average increases, the attractiveness of the composite increases. [SOURCE: LEMLEY, 2000, P. 47.]

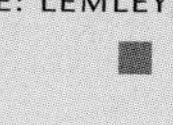

site, the final face was very attractive, and was also perceived to be more feminine than average (Lemley, 2000). A feminine appearance is apparently a plus. For example, a computerized image of either males or females is preferred to the extent that it is feminine rather than masculine (Angier, 1998a). Men with an extremely macho look (big jaw, square face, heavy brow) are perceived as less warm and honest than men with a slender nose, cupid lips, and an "adorable" chin. Think of Russell Crowe and Brad Pitt (see Figure 7.13 on page 278).

Why should composite faces be especially attractive? One possibility is that the average is closer to each person's schema of women and men (see Chapter 3). That is, we form such schemas on the basis of our experiences with many different

FIGURE 7.13
A Relatively Feminine Appearance Is Preferred to a Relatively Maculine One. When faces are created by computer averaging, they are not only perceived as more attractive but also as more feminine. And, both males and females are preferred to the extent that they appear feminine rather than masculine (Angier, 1998a). In the non-computerized examples shown here are two attractive male stars. The relatively feminine features of Brad Pitt tend to be preferred to the relatively masculine features of Russell Crowe.

images, so a composite face is closer to one's schema than is any specific face. If this is accurate, a composite of images of something other than faces should produce similar results. Thus, when drawings fifty dogs and fifty birds are each averaged, the result should be an especially attractive dog and an especially attractive bird, but this is not the case (Halberstadt & Rhodes, 2000). It seems possible that a composite *human* face is different from other composites because human appearance was historically more important than the appearance of dogs and birds as a selection criterion in recognizing potential mates, friends, and enemies.

An alternative explanation suggests that we are born with a preference for symmetry, and a face based on the average of many faces is more symmetrical than individual faces. Further, studies indicate that people find symmetrical faces more attractive than asymmetrical ones (Cowley, 1996) (an example is shown in Figure 7.14). Why do we like symmetry? Evolutionary psychologists once again propose that we respond positively to symmetry because it is an indicator of health and hence reproductive fitness (Mealey, Bridgstock, & Townsend, 1999). Though this idea is plausible, experiments have shown that an average face is preferred even when symmetry is held constant (Rhodes, Sumich, & Byatt, 1999). We can conclude that the attractiveness of a composite face is well established, but explanations of these findings based on simply a preference for familiar schemas or on a preference for symmetry do not seem to be totally convincing. We realize that it would be more satisfactory to provide a final answer to such questions, but science is based on generating ideas and testing them empirically. Sometimes we simply have to wait a bit before a correct solution is offered and tested. In other words, stay tuned.

Situational factors also influence perceptions of attractiveness. For example, a stranger is judged as less attractive by research participants who have just looked at pictures of very attractive people than by participants who have not been shown the attractive pictures (Kenrick et al., 1993). The difference between the attractive people in the photographs and the stranger creates what is known as a "contrast effect." Even a (heterosexual) man's own romantic partner is rated less positively

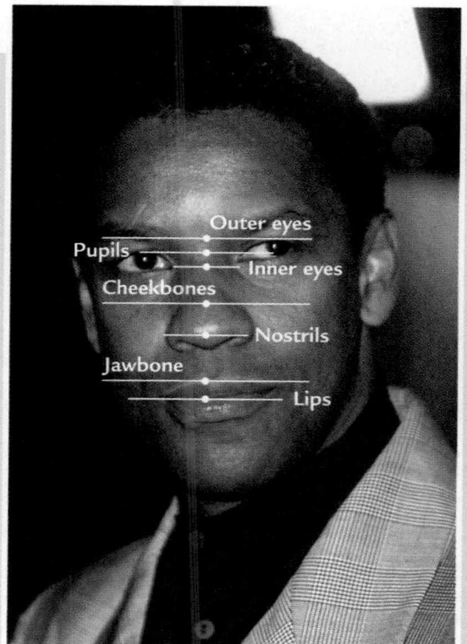

FIGURE 7.14

Attractiveness as a Function of Symmetry. As the symmetry of a face increases, its attractiveness increases. From the evolutionary perspective, symmetry is a cue to health, and a preference for symmetry increases the odds of reproduction. On the left, Denzel Washington's face is an extremely symmetrical one, while on the right, Lyle Lovett's face is not.

if he has just been looking at photographs of very attractive women (Kenrick & Gutierres, 1980). Other aspects of the context also matter. As suggested by Mickey Gilley's song about searching for romance in bars, "the girls all get prettier at closing time." In fact, research indicates that both "girls" and "boys" are perceived as more attractive by members of the opposite sex as the evening progresses (Nida & Koon, 1983; Pennebaker et al., 1979). Ratings of same-sex strangers do not improve as closing time approaches, so alcohol consumption does not explain the effects (Gladue & Delaney, 1990). Rather, as people pair off and the number of available partners decreases, the resulting scarcity results in a more positive evaluation of those who remain unattached.

■ BEYOND FACES: OTHER ASPECTS OF APPEARANCE AND BEHAVIOR. When we meet someone for the first time, we usually react to a variety of factors. Any observable cue, no matter how superficial, may act as the trigger that evokes a stereotype, and the resulting emotional reactions lead to instant likes and dislikes. Examples include clothing (Cheverton & Byrne, 1998; Jarrell, 1998), grooming (Mack & Rainey, 1990), height (Pierce, 1996), disabilities (Fichten & Amsel, 1986), age (McKelvie, 1993b), eyeglasses (Lundberg & Sheehan, 1994), and many other observable details.

Before discussing the research on additional factors, we will suggest the important political role played by observable characteristics in the **Beyond the Headlines** section on page 280.

In addition to attractiveness, stereotypes, emotional reactions, and attraction are also elicited by the details of one's physique. Though it was once thought that body type provided information about personality (Sheldon, Stevens, & Tucker, 1940), decades of research indicated that this assumption was inaccurate. Nevertheless, people still respond to others on the basis of the incorrect idea that a round and fat body indicates a sad and sloppy person, that a hard and muscular body indicates good health and lack of intelligence, and that a thin and angular body indicates intelligence and fearfulness (Gardner & Tockerman, 1994; Ryckman et al., 1989).

BEYOND THE HEADLINES: AS SOCIAL PSYCHOLOGISTS SEE IT

DO LOOKS AND STYLE INFLUENCE VOTERS?

Did Al Gore Need a Fashion Consultant?

Washington, November 8, 1999—In response to disappointing poll results in the U.S. presidential election of 2000, advisors to Vice President Al Gore hired feminist Naomi Wolf as an advisor to his campaign. Many observers described her role as giving advice on how to convince voters that Gore is not a permanent No. 2 but is an "alpha male" who should be in charge. The reference is to studies of primates in which one male stands out as No. 1 in the group—a strong and powerful leader.

Though Wolf denied that she took a salary cut in order to be a "fashion consultant," Mr. Gore did subsequently switch his wardrobe from dark suits to informal clothing and his style from appearing to be a dutiful choir boy to that of a relaxed, regular guy. Clearly, there was an attempt to change his image from that of a somewhat stiff assistant to the President to an informal man's man who could lead the nation.

It has long been known that candidate appeal rests in part on a number of factors related to appearance and to perceptions based on what appearance means. That is, voters respond to stereotypes, and anything that can be done to provide cues to positive stereotypes while avoiding negative stereotypes is likely to be utilized in a campaign.

John Walter and his sister Catherine, the owners of a boutique in New York City, became convinced that the way a man parts his hair is crucial to how he is perceived. They came to the conclusion that a left part indicates an alpha male, while a right part indicates a loser (Schillinger, 2001). For example, in the 1978 movie, Superman parted his hair on the left side, while mild-mannered reporter Clark Kent parted his on the right. Further, only three U.S. chief executives (Buchanan, Harding, and Reagan) maintained a right part throughout their presidencies, and only one of them had lasting popularity. At the time the Walters had their insight about hair parts, Jimmy Carter was president, and he had a right part. As a helpful gesture, the boutique owners contacted him with their advice about what to do to improve his image. Shortly afterward, he changed his part from the right side to the left. It was hypothesized that Carter's favorable post-presidential reputation is based on that change of hair style.

Because Al Gore wears a right part, but wanted to convey an alpha male image in running for the presidency, John and Catherine urged him to change his part. He ignored them and lost the election. For what it is worth, you might notice that President Bush wears a left part. The left-part effect may simply be a matter of familiarity. If most men (including most presidents) part their hair on the left, that appearance is what we see most often and hence prefer.

Is it possible that observable characteristics play a crucial role in national elections? We think so. Just remember that the taller of two male candidates usually wins (Gillis, 1982), the more physically attractive candidate usually wins (Efran & Patterson, 1974), and the candidate with a "soap opera" name like Fairchild is preferred to an opponent with an "ethnic" name like Sangmeister (O'Sullivan et al., 1988). With respect to that last finding, specific ethnic names can be a plus in a given geographic area. For example, French names are helpful in Quebec but not in Ontario, and Hispanic names are helpful in the southwestern United States but not in New England. The general point is that we vote for the person we like best, and liking is in part determined by observable characteristics.

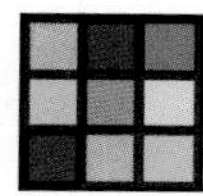

In these and other studies, a consistent finding is that the least-liked physique is one with excess fat (Harris, Harris, & Bochner, 1982; Lundberg & Sheehan, 1994). In Chapter 5, we described the special concern that many women have with respect to weight. Strangely enough, physically attractive women have *greater* weight and diet concerns than do less attractive women (Davis et al., 2001), possibly because of the expectation that being beautiful must be accompanied by being thin. Once again, keep in mind that making assumptions about people on the basis of fatness leads only to inaccuracies (Miller, Rothblum, Brand et al., 1995; Miller, Rothblum, Felicio et al., 1995). Crandall (1994) equates prejudice against obesity with racial prejudice, and he developed a measure of antifat prejudice, as shown in Table 7.2. Though there is a prevailing U.S. prejudice against fatness, in Mexico there is much less concern about weight and a less negative reaction to those who are overweight (Crandall & Martinez, 1996). More generally, it is found that a negative attitude toward fat and the tendency to hold people responsible for their negative attributes together predict antifat prejudice; such tendencies are stronger in individualistic than in collectivistic cultures (Crandall et al., 2001).

Though appearance triggers stereotypes, and thus influences attraction and other interpersonal judgments, behavioral differences are also important. For example, rapid eye blinking is interpreted as a sign of nervousness and carelessness (Omori & Miyata, 2001). A person who has a youthful walking style elicits a more positive response than one who walks in an elderly style, regardless of gender or actual age (Montepare & Zebrowitz-McArthur, 1988). An individual with a firm handshake is perceived as extroverted and emotionally expressive and as neither shy nor neurotic (Chaplin et al., 2000) (see Chapter 1). A positive response is also evoked by expressive, animated behavior (Bernieri et al., 1996), by laughter (Bachorowski & Owren, 2001), and by students who participate in class discussions rather than remaining quiet (Bell, 1995). Actions that suggest arrogance elicit a more negative reaction than does modest behavior (Hareli & Weiner, 2000), but a person who expresses anger is perceived as more competent than one who expresses sadness (Tiedens, 2001).

Also, consistency of behavior is important, possibly because inconsistency suggests hypocrisy. For example, an immoral action by someone who otherwise behaves morally is judged more negatively than the same act by someone who generally behaves in a less moral fashion (Bailey & Vietor, 1996).

In initial encounters, men who behave in a dominant, authoritative, competitive way are preferred to submissive, noncompetitive, less masculine men (Fried-

TABLE 7.2

Antifat Prejudice. A negative reaction to those who are overweight is very much like racial prejudice—negative attitudes and negative attributions based on stereotypes. Sample items from a questionnaire that measures three aspects of antifat attitudes are shown here—dislike of those who are fat, fear of becoming fat, and the belief that people become fat because they lack willpower.

TYPE OF ANTIFAT ATTITUDE	SAMPLE QUESTIONNAIRE ITEM
Dislike	I really don't like fat people much. If I were an employer looking to hire, I might avoid hiring a fat person.
Fear of fat	I feel disgusted with myself when I gain weight. I worry about becoming fat.
Willpower	People who weigh too much could lose some of their weight through a little exercise. Fat people tend to be fat pretty much through their own fault.

[SOURCE: BASED ON INFORMATION IN CRANDALL, 1994.]

TABLE 7.3

What's in a Name? Sometimes the Answer Is Personal Attributions. Initial impressions are sometimes based on a person's first name. Once again, interpersonal attraction is found to be influenced by inaccurate assumptions based on stereotypes.

MALE NAMES	FEMALE NAMES	ATTRIBUTIONS ABOUT THE INDIVIDUAL
Alexander	Elizabeth	*Successful*
Otis	Mildred	*Unsuccessful*
Joshua	Mary	*Moral*
Roscoe	Tracy	*Immoral*
Mark	Jessica	*Popular*
Norbert	Harriet	*Unpopular*
Henry	Ann	*Warm*
Ogden	Freida	*Cold*
Scott	Brittany	*Cheerful*
Willard	Agatha	*Not cheerful*
Taylor	Rosalyn	*Masculine*
Eugene	Isabella	*Feminine*

[SOURCE: BASED ON INFORMATION IN MEHRABIAN & PIERCY, 1993.]

man, Riggio, & Casella, 1988). After additional interactions that provide more information about the individual, however, the preference shifts to men who are prosocial and sensitive (Jensen-Campbell, West, & Graziano, 1995; Morey & Gerber, 1995). It could be said that nice guys finish first.

Interpersonal judgments are also influenced by what a person eats (Stein & Nemeroff, 1995). Regardless of such factors as height and weight, a person who eats "good food" (oranges, salad, whole wheat bread, chicken) is perceived as more likable and even morally superior to one who eats "bad food" (steak, hamburgers, French fries, donuts, and double fudge sundaes).

One final, and perhaps most surprising, influence on interpersonal perceptions is one's first name. Various male and female names are associated with specific positive and negative stereotypes (Mehrabian & Piercy, 1993), as shown in Table 7.3. It also seems likely that the distinctive first name of a well-known individual becomes associated with some of the characteristics of that individual and then transfers to others with that name. What comes to mind when you hear names such as Homer, Monica, Osama, Gwyneth, Timothy, or Hillary?

KEY POINTS

- Individuals high, as opposed to low, in *need for affiliation* are more likely to engage in establishing and maintaining interpersonal relationships, and they are more skilled in dealing with people.
- Under unusual circumstances, such as natural disasters, people are more likely to affiliate with others. It seems that social comparison is the driving force behind this behavior, because people want to interact in order to reduce anxiety by clarifying what is going on and by clarifying their own emotional reactions.

- Interpersonal attraction and interpersonal judgments based on stereotypes are strongly affected by various observable characteristics of those we meet, including *physical attractiveness.* People like and make positive attributions about attractive men and women of all ages, despite the fact that assumptions based on appearance are usually inaccurate. It is still not possible to reach a definitive conclusion about why we react strongly to attractiveness or what constitutes attractiveness.
- In addition to attractiveness, many other observable characteristics influence initial interpersonal evaluations, including physique, weight, behavioral style, food preferences, first names, and other superficial characteristics.

Moving toward Friendship: Similarity and Mutual Liking

We have learned that, in order to form any kind of relationship, two people must come into initial contact, and that this is often facilitated by physical proximity. Once contact occurs, the likelihood that a positive relationship will develop increases if each individual is in a positive emotional state, is motivated by affiliation needs, and reacts positively to the observable characteristics of the other. The next two steps toward interpersonal closeness involve communication. Two crucial aspects of this communication are the degree to which the interacting individuals discover areas of *similarity* and the extent to which they indicate *mutual liking* by what they say and what they do.

Similarity: Birds of a Feather Really Do Flock Together

The role of similarity in fostering interpersonal attraction is now generally accepted (see Figure 7.15). This phenomenon has been observed and discussed for well over two thousand years, beginning with Aristotle's (330 B.C./1932) essay on friendship. Agreement with this early observation can be documented over the centuries from sources as varied as Spinoza (1675/1951) and Samuel Johnson (Boswell, 1791/1963). Empirical support for the "similarity hypothesis" was not available, however, until Sir Francis Galton (1870/1952) obtained correlational data on married couples and found that spouses resembled one another in many respects. In the first

FIGURE 7.15
Attraction to Similar Others and Rejection of Dissimilar Others. As unpleasant as the consequences often are, there seems to be a basic tendency to like those who are similar to self and to dislike those who are dissimilar.
[SOURCE: © THE NEW YORKER COLLECTION 2000 MICHAEL MASLIN FROM CARTOONBANK.COM. ALL RIGHTS RESERVED.]

half of the twentieth century, correlational studies continued to find that pairs of friends and spouses revealed a greater than chance degree of similarity (e.g., Hunt, 1935). Though it was possible that liking led to similarity rather than vice versa, Newcomb (1956) studied university transfer students and found that attitude similarity (measured before the students met) was a predictor of subsequent liking. Though this finding was convincing, scientists prefer experimental data, if experiments are possible (see Chapter 1). As a result, social psychologists (e.g., Schachter, 1951) began manipulating similarity and assessing attraction. We will describe a portion of the resulting research that both supported the earliest philosophical observations and indicated that similarity *caused* attraction and was not simply *correlated* with it.

attitude similarity: The extent to which two individuals share the same attitudes about a range of topics. In practice, the term also includes similarity of beliefs, values, and interests.

proportion of similar attitudes: The number of topics on which two individuals hold the same views divided by the total number of topics on which they compare their views.

■ ATTITUDE SIMILARITY–DISSIMILARITY AS A DETERMINANT OF ATTRACTION. Much of the initial experimental research focused on **attitude similarity,** and this term is generally used to mean similarity of beliefs, values, and interests as well as similarity of attitudes. The typical laboratory study of similarity followed a pattern in which, first, the attitudes of research participants are determined; later, the participants are provided with the attitudes of a stranger and are asked to indicate how much they like that individual (Byrne, 1961b). The results of such experiments indicate clearly that people like those who hold similar attitudes much better than those who hold dissimilar attitudes, and they also evaluate a similar stranger as being more intelligent, better informed, more moral, and better adjusted.

Further research indicated that we respond to the views of others in a surprisingly precise way. Regardless of how many topics are involved, it is as if we classify another person's position on each topic as similar to (positive affect) or different from (negative affect) our own, then add up the number of positive matches, divide by the total number of topics, and then evaluate that person on the basis of the **proportion of similar attitudes** that he or she has expressed (Byrne & Nelson, 1965). The higher the proportion of similar attitudes, the greater the liking, as illustrated in Figure 7.16. We don't actually know how the process works, but the end result is as if people engaged in this kind of simple, affective mathematics.

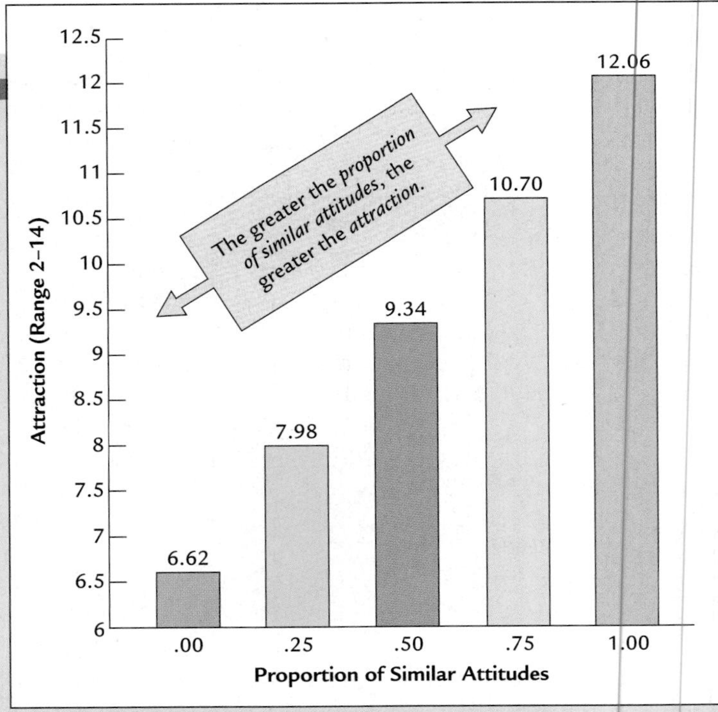

FIGURE 7.16

The Higher the Proportion of Similar Attitudes Expressed by Another Person, the Greater the Attraction toward That Person. The relationship between proportion of similar attitudes and attraction has been found to be a consistent and highly predictable one. The greater the proportion of similar attitudes, the greater the attraction. The linear relationship is found to hold for both genders and despite differences in age, culture, or educational level.

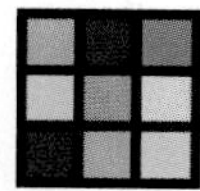

Not only is the relationship between the proportion of similar attitudes and attraction a strong one, it holds true regardless of the number of topics of agreement–disagreement or the importance of those topics. It holds true for both males and females, across age groups, across educational levels, and across cultures (Byrne, 1971). Attempts to find differences among individuals have mostly failed, but individuals in both the United States and Singapore who are high in affiliation need are more positive toward a similar stranger than are those low in affiliation need (Kwan, 1998). And, experiments in France indicate that individuals who seek self-evaluation are not as responsive to similarity–dissimilarity as are those who simply seek validation of their views (Michinov & Michinov, 2000). Also, extroverts reject dissimilar strangers more strongly than do introverts (Singh & Teoh, 1999).

Altogether, the relationship between similarity and attraction was believed to be about as well established as possible (Duck & Barnes, 1992; Cappella & Palmer, 1990, 1992). As we have seen in other areas of research, however, new research and new findings can raise important questions and lead us to modify our conceptualizations. As discussed in the **Social Psychology: Thirty Years of Progress** section on page 286, our understanding of the similarity–attraction link has undergone continued scrutiny and change.

Though much of the research on attraction has concentrated on attitudes, a more general conclusion is that similarity in general is preferable to dissimilarity. People tend to like others who are similar to themselves with respect to many attributes. For example, people prefer others who are similar to themselves in physical attractiveness (Zajonc et al., 1987), and they make more positive assumptions about couples when both individuals are attractive than when one individual is attractive and the other is not (Garcia & Khersonsky, 1997).

Analogously, others are better liked if they are similar to oneself in sociability (Joiner, 1994), marijuana smoking (Eisenman, 1985), religious affiliation (Kandel, 1978), personality traits and affective traits (Watson, Hubbard, & Wiese, 2000), self-concept (LaPrelle et al., 1990), traditional versus nontraditional gender roles (Smith, Byrne, & Fielding, 1995), being a "morning person" versus an "evening person" (Watts, 1982), and laughing at the same jokes (Cann, Calhoun, & Banks, 1995). Why should this be so?

■ WHY DO SIMILARITY AND DISSIMILARITY AFFECT ATTRACTION? A simple answer is that similarity arouses positive affect, while dissimilarity arouses negative affect, and we know that affect influences attraction. But a more basic question is *why* should the similarity or dissimilarity of another person cause us to react emotionally?

The oldest explanation, proposed independently by Newcomb (1961) and by Heider (1958), is **balance theory** (Hummert, Crockett, & Kemper, 1990). This formulation states that people naturally organize their likes and dislikes in a symmetrical way. When two people like each other and find that they are similar in some specific respect, this represents *balance,* and balance is emotionally pleasant. When two people like each other and find that they are dissimilar in some specific respect, the result is *imbalance,* which is emotionally unpleasant. In the latter case, they strive to restore balance by changing one or the other's attitudes and behaviors in order to be more similar, by misperceiving the degree of dissimilarity, or by simply deciding to dislike each other. Dislike creates a state of *nonbalance* that is neither especially pleasant nor unpleasant, because each individual feels indifferent about the similarity or dissimilarity of the other.

balance theory: The formulation that specifies the relationships among (1) an individual's liking for another person, (2) his or her attitude about a given topic, and (3) the other person's perceived attitude about the same topic. Balance results in a positive emotional state, imbalance results in a negative emotional state, and nonbalance leads to indifference.

Although balance theory appears to be correct, it doesn't really explain why similarity should matter in the first place. Why should you care if someone is different from you in musical preferences, religious beliefs, or getting up early in the morning? One answer is provided by Festinger's (1954) social comparison theory. In effect, you compare your attitudes and your behavioral preferences with those of others because that is the primary way in which you can evaluate your accuracy

SIMILARITY, DISSIMILARITY, OR BOTH?

One of the hallmarks of scientific activity is the attempt to discover weaknesses in procedures, findings, and explanations, and thus progress to a better understanding of the phenomenon in question. Many such critical attempts are based on misunderstandings or faulty conclusions; many others are valid and lead to something entirely new or, at least, to modifications.

One such useful criticism of the similarity–attraction research was offered by the late Milt Rosenbaum (1986) when he pointed out a flaw in the experimental manipulations of similarity–dissimilarity. Specifically, research participants have almost always been asked to respond to a stranger who expresses *both* similar and dissimilar attitudes. It was assumed that each type of attitude exerts an influence on attraction. In contrast, Rosenbaum hypothesized that similar attitudes are irrelevant and that people respond only to dissimilarity. He argued, correctly, that the research up to that time had failed to employ a control group whose responses could be compared with those of groups responding to similarity and of groups responding to dissimilarity. To test this proposition, he created a control condition in which no attitudinal information was provided, just a picture of a fellow college student about whom research participants indicated their degree of attraction. Other participants were shown a picture *plus* the similar attitudes of that person, or a picture *plus* the dissimilar attitudes of that person. Rosenbaum found no difference in attraction toward a similar stranger and attraction toward a stranger whose attitudes were unknown. There was, however, a big difference between the control condition and the condition with dissimilar attitudes. On the basis of this and analogous findings, he offered the **repulsion hypothesis,** which states that only dissimilarity, not similarity, plays a role in attraction.

Rosenbaum's findings seemed very clear, so it became necessary to test them further and possibly offer an alternative explanation. One experimental comparison of the similarity–dissimilarity hypothesis and the repulsion hypothesis held the number of dissimilar attitudes constant and varied the number (and hence proportion) of similar attitudes (Smeaton, Byrne, & Murnen, 1989). The results were straightforward; attraction was strongly affected by the proportion of similar attitudes. On that basis, the Rosenbaum hypothesis was rejected because it was clearly incorrect—similarity is *not* irrelevant.

But, why did Rosenbaum obtain the results he did? His "no attitude information" control was the key. Specifically, when we don't know the attitudes of another person, we assume that he or she holds an attitude similar to our own (Hoyle, 1993). The *false consensus effect* refers to the assumption that most other people agree with whatever we believe (Alicke & Largo, 1995; Fabrigar & Krosnick, 1995). In effect, Rosenbaum's "control" group that saw *only* a picture was no different from his "experimental" group that saw a picture *plus* similar attitudes. Both groups were responding to a stranger assumed to be similar to themselves.

If so, it could be said that agreement is expected but disagreement is a surprise (Tan & Singh, 1995). Because of such expectations, information about dissimilarity should have a greater effect on attraction than information about similarity, and that is exactly what Chapman (1995) found among American college students. With students at the National University of Singapore, Singh and Teoh (2000) also found that dissimilar attitudes have a greater impact on attraction than similar attitudes.

One result of all of this is the new realization that all attitudes are not created equal (Singh & Ho, 2000). A dissimilar attitude is more powerful than a similar one. This greater impact of negative versus positive cues is more general than simply the response to attitudes—for example, people are faster and more accurate in detecting threatening than friendly faces (Ohman, Lundqvist, & Esteves, 2001). The false consensus effect also suggests that, everything else being equal, we tend to like those we meet *until* we discover too many areas of dissimilarity. Altogether, Rosenbaum's original proposition about repulsion was not correct as stated, but it contained a partial truth that led to a reformulation as to how we respond to the attitudes of others.

---

repulsion hypothesis: Rosenbaum's provocative but partially inaccurate proposal that attraction is not increased by similar attitudes but only decreased by dissimilar attitudes.

and normality. You turn to others to obtain *consensual validation* (see Chapter 9). It is pleasing to discover that you have sound judgment, are normal, are in contact with reality, and so forth—and not at all pleasing to discover that your judgment is faulty, that you are abnormal, or that you may lack contact with reality. As we discussed in Chapter 5, with respect to seeking information about one's self-concept, we are interested in what other people think and in how they behave not because we are seeking objective information, but because we want to verify what we already believe and what we already do. The anxiety to be correct is based on self-doubt—"It is when we are not sure that we are doubly sure" (Niebuhr, as quoted by Beinart, 1998, p. 25).

A different, but possibly not incompatible, explanation is based on an evolutionary perspective. Proposing that hatred and cruelty have been an integral part of human history, thus demonstrating our genocidal capacity, Gould (1996, p. 64) describes the basic process:

Perhaps we evolved these capacities as active adaptations now gone awry in the modern world. Current genocide may be a sad legacy of behaviors that originated for Darwinian benefit during our ancestral construction as small bands of hunters and gatherers on the savannas of Africa. Darwin's mechanism, after all, encourages only the reproductive success of individuals, not the moral dream of human fellowship across an entire species. Perhaps the traits that lead to modern genocide—xenophobia, tribalism, anathematization of outsiders as subhumans and therefore subject to annihilation—rose to prominence during our early evolution because they enhanced survival in tiny, nontechnological societies based on kinship and living in a world of limited resources under a law of kill-or-be-killed.

. . . Chimpanzees, our closest relatives, will band together and systematically kill members of adjacent groups. Perhaps we are programmed to act in such a manner as well.

Byrne (2001) pursued that theme and made the case that most of human animosity is based on reactions to dissimilarity. As radio personality Howard Stern put it, "If you're not like me, I hate you" (Zoglin, 1993). It seems that the worst acts of barbarism are directed toward those who differ from the perpetrator in terms of race, ethnicity, language, religious beliefs, sexual orientation, political affiliation, and so forth. "Programmed into the human soul is a preference for the near and familiar and a suspicion of the remote and abstract" (McDonald, 2001). Why should that be?

Imagine the time described by Gould when our primitive ancestors only occasionally came in contact with humans from other groups. Horney (1950) has described three possible reactions to the strangers: tendencies to move toward, away from, or against them. Lynn Fairbanks has observed that some monkeys respond to an unfamiliar monkey by rushing up to it, while some avoid it and some engage in aggressive behavior (Carpenter, 2001).

These three patterns of response have different potential consequences. If the prehistoric human strangers were benign, moving toward them in a friendly way would have been beneficial to both groups. If, however, they posed a threat (and that might have been a more likely possibility), then moving toward them with friendliness and trust would be the most dangerous and least adaptive response that could be made. Survival, and hence reproduction, would depend on retreating or attacking, and attacking is probably the best insurance of survival, as depicted in Figure 7.17 on page 288.

Human aggression is notably vicious. Bandura (1999) indicates that it is all too easy to disengage moral control and justify cruel and inhumane acts. For example, it is simple to attribute one's angry, violent impulses to others—if I mean to harm him, it is justified because he means to harm me (Schimel et al., 2000). And once individuals and groups begin harming others, evil behavior increases in intensity (Staub, 1999).

If this account is at all plausible, we are programmed to fear and hate strangers who are observably different from ourselves. Keep in mind that dissimilarity is only one source of provocation; as we will discuss in Chapter 11, there are many other sources of human aggression. There is increasing evidence that we are automatically

FIGURE 7.17

Aggressing against Strangers: A Basic Human Heritage?
There is reason to believe that we and our closest primate relatives tend to fear and hate strangers because those responses enhanced the reproductive success of our ancestors, whereas friendliness and acceptance of strangers did not.

vigilant in reacting to cues that warn us of positive or negative consequences of interaction, and thus to approach or avoid the source of those cues (Bargh, 1997; Bargh & Chartrand, 1999; Chen & Bargh, 1999; Wentura, Rothermund, & Bak, 2000). Though such reactions may have been crucial to survival among our oldest ancestors, today they form the basis for prejudice, hate crimes, and a general dislike of anyone who differs from ourselves.

Mutual Liking: Attraction toward Those Who Are Attracted to Us

Once two people discover that they are sufficiently similar to be able to move toward establishing a friendship, one additional step is crucial. Each individual must somehow communicate liking and a positive evaluation of the other (Condon & Crano, 1988). Most of us are pleased to receive positive feedback and displeased to receive negative evaluations (Gordon, 1996). Even relatively gentle or well-intentioned negative remarks (as suggested in Figure 7.18) are unlikely to be well received.

At the opposite extreme, even a positive evaluation that is inaccurate (Swann et al., 1987) or a clumsy attempt at flattery is *very much* welcomed. To an observer, flattery may seem transparently insincere, but to the person being flattered it is more likely to appear honest and accurate (Gordon, 1996). When an employee is especially nice to a superior in an organization but not nice to subordinates, he or she is seen as especially unlikable—the *slime effect* (Vonk, 1998). This pattern of "licking

"Theresa, what I am about to say should not be construed as criticism."

FIGURE 7.18

Positive Evaluations from Others Are Much Better Than Even Well-Intended Negative Evaluations.

We like to be liked and evaluated positively, and we hate to be disliked and evaluated negatively. When two people interact, even a mild, potentially helpful, and well-meant criticism can have a negative effect on emotions and hence on attraction.

upward but kicking downward" is greatly disliked by the ones being kicked and even by those not personally involved, but the positive behavior toward a superior is nevertheless an effective interpersonal strategy. In a study of almost 150 managers in public and private organizations, bragging was not useful, but those who used ingratiation techniques on the job reported the greatest salary increases and the most promotions over a five-year period (Orpen, 1996). Such behavior is not new. When Alexis de Tocqueville journeyed from France in 1831 to study the United States, he observed that Americans had a special talent for ingratiating themselves with anybody and everybody who could do something for them (Lapham, 1996).

Under normal circumstances, however, most people don't like to criticize others. Many times, people make positive interpersonal statements in order to be polite and to avoid hurt feelings rather than to get something in return. DePaulo and Bell (1996) asked research participants to discuss student paintings, some of which the participants liked and some of which they disliked. When the artist was present, however, the participants did not give totally honest feedback. Instead, they tried to make as many positive statements as possible, including some outright lies.

Though liking and positive evaluations are often expressed in words, at times the first sign of attraction may be nonverbal cues (discussed in Chapter 2). For example, when a woman maintains eye contact while conversing with a man and leans toward him, the man tends to interpret these acts (sometimes incorrectly) to mean that she likes him. Such positive signs, in turn, often lead him to like her (Gold, Ryckman, & Mosley, 1984).

■ ATTRACTION: THE BIGGER PICTURE. Throughout this chapter, we have stressed the idea that attraction is based on affective responses. This general concept is known as the **affect-centered model of attraction.** The emphasis on affect does not mean, however, that cognitive processes are irrelevant. As shown in Figure 7.19, Person B's affective state (whether directly aroused by Person A or simply associated with him or her) is believed to play a major role in determining the evaluation that B makes of A, and B's subsequent behavior toward A. We automatically form and store such evaluations in memory (Betsch et al., 2001). It is also necessary, however, for B to engage in cognitively processing all available information about A. Because this information (including stereotypes, beliefs, and factual knowledge) can be affectively arousing, it contributes to B's evaluation of A.

affect-centered model of attraction: A conceptual framework in which attraction is assumed to be based on positive and negative emotions. These emotions can be aroused directly by another person, simply associated with that person, and/or mediated by cognitive processes.

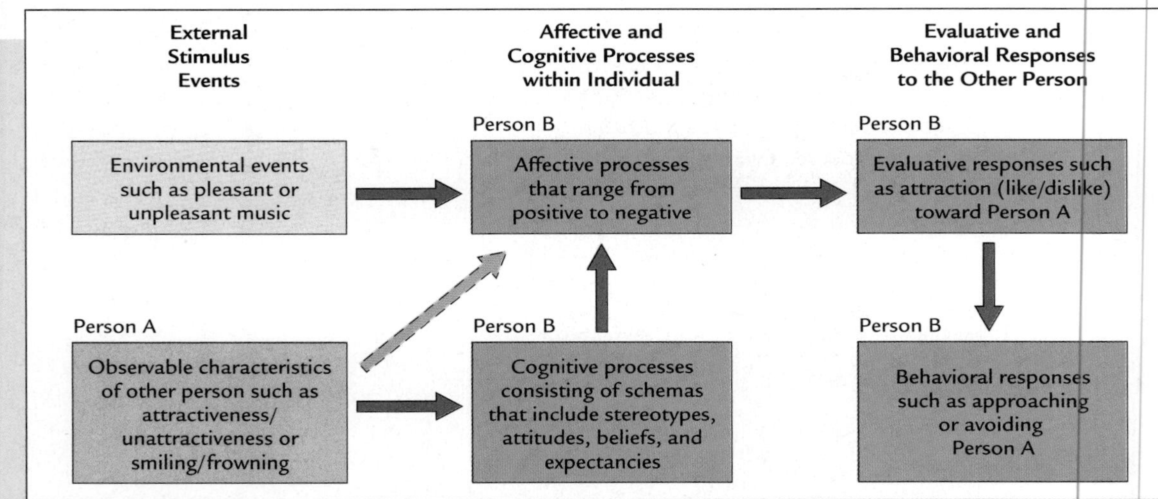

FIGURE 7.19

The Affect-Centered Model of Attraction.

Essentially, attraction to a given person is based on affective responses that are aroused by various events (e.g., pleasant versus unpleasant music), by relatively stable characteristics of the person (e.g., physical appearance), and by changeable characteristics of the person (e.g., smiling versus frowning). Some of the person's characteristics have a relatively direct effect on one's emotional responses (e.g., flattering comments or hostile insults); other characteristics must be processed cognitively in ways that activate schemas involving stereotypes, attitudes, beliefs, and expectancies (e.g., attractiveness, race, similarities and differences, etc.). The net affective state leads to an evaluative response along a dimension ranging from liking to dislike and to approach or avoidant behavior consistent with the evaluation.

[SOURCE: BASED ON MATERIAL IN BYRNE, 1992.]

At the same time that B is reacting to and processing information about A, A is, of course, doing the same thing with respect to B. One possible end result is a positive relationship between A and B.

Most of the information in this chapter has very practical value in the real world. Assuming that you would prefer to be liked than disliked, take a look at the **Ideas to Take with You—And Use!** section on page 292 for some helpful suggestions.

KEY POINTS

- One of many factors determining attraction toward another person is similarity of attitudes, beliefs, values, and interests.
- Though dissimilarity has a greater impact on attraction than similarity, we respond to both. Thus, the higher the *proportion of similar attitudes,* the greater the attraction.
- The positive affective response to similarity and the negative affective response to dissimilarity have been hypothesized to rest on social comparison processes that lead to consensual validation or invalidation. A different explanation rests on the adaptive utility of our ancestors for reacting to dissimilar, and potentially dangerous, strangers with either fear or anger.
- We also like other people who indicate in word or deed that they like and positively evaluate us. We dislike those who dislike and negatively evaluate us.
- An overall summary of the major determinants of attraction is provided by the *affect-centered model of attraction,* which specifies that attraction is determined by direct and associated sources of affect, often mediated by cognitive processes.

CONNECTIONS: INTEGRATING SOCIAL PSYCHOLOGY

IN THIS CHAPTER, YOU READ ABOUT . . .	IN OTHER CHAPTERS, YOU WILL FIND RELATED DISCUSSIONS OF . . .
attitudes about people	attitudes (Chapter 4)
conditioning of attraction	conditioning of attitudes (Chapter 4)
correlational versus experimental findings in similarity–attraction research	types of research (Chapter 1)
similarity and attraction	similarity and friendship, love, and marriage (Chapter 8)
effects of physical attractiveness	attractiveness and love (Chapter 8); effects of attractiveness in the courtroom (Chapter 13)
appearance and stereotypes	prejudice and stereotypes (Chapter 6)
preferring positive information about self	seeking positive information about self (Chapter 5)

(continued)

THINKING ABOUT CONNECTIONS

1. Pick one person you know (or once knew) very well. Can you remember exactly how you met? When did you decide that you liked this individual, and why? If the relationship no longer exists, what happened to end it? Are there any connections between your personal experience with this person and the discussion in this chapter about the factors influencing attraction?
2. Consider some issues about which you have strong attitudes and beliefs. Do you ever discuss these issues with your acquaintances, friends, or family? How do you react when others agree with you? What happens when they disagree with you? Have disagreements ever caused you to stop interacting with someone you once liked? Think about your reactions and about why agreement and disagreement might matter to you.
3. Give some thought to the physical appearance of someone you don't know very well but see in class, in your dormitory, or at work. On the basis of the person's attractiveness, physique, accent, clothing, or whatever else you observe about him or her, what can you conclude about this person? Have you ever talked to him or her? Why or why not? Do you see any connections between prejudice and your evaluation of this individual?
4. Do you ever compliment other people, tell them you like them, or comment favorably on something they have done? If so, how did they respond? Describe what you believe is going on in this kind of interaction. Consider the opposite situation, in which you have criticized another person, indicated dislike, or given a negative evaluation. What happens in this kind of interaction?

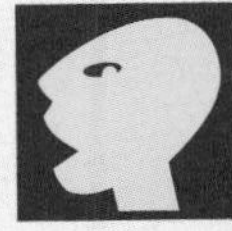

IDEAS TO TAKE WITH YOU—AND USE!

MAKING IT EASY FOR PEOPLE TO LIKE YOU

Most of us would much rather be liked than disliked, but many of us seem to have difficulty in getting to know others and establishing positive interpersonal relationships. The suggestions here are solidly based on social psychological research, and you may find them helpful. If, of course, you want to be disliked and left alone, just do the opposite.

Take Control of Proximity Factors.

Whenever possible, play an active role in arranging what are usually the *accidental* contacts that determine who gets to know one another. In a classroom, for example, sit beside others and avoid seats on the end of rows or in the corners. After a while, if you haven't become acquainted with those sitting near you, move to a new location and start over.

Create Positive Affect.

In situations in which you hope to make friends, do your part in creating a pleasant mood. Depending on the situation, this could involve making sure the temperature is comfortable, playing popular music, finding agreeable topics of conversation, providing something good to eat and drink, and so forth.

Reach Out to Others in Emotion-Arousing Situations.

From time to time, we find ourselves in unexpected situations,

including floods and blizzards, power outages, accidents, and so forth. At such times, most people want to interact with others (including total strangers) because they want to know what is going on and what is the most appropriate emotional response. It helps if you initiate conversations, provide information, and disclose your own reactions. Instant interpersonal closeness is uniquely possible when we encounter an unusual situation, even a very stressful one.

Make the Most of Your Own Appearance and Look beyond the Appearance of Others.

Because observable characteristics play an important role in how others react to you, do anything reasonable you can in order to improve your physical appearance and outward style. On the other hand, try very hard not to accept inaccurate stereotypes of other people based on superficial characteristics; this will clearly increase your pool of potential friends.

Emphasize Similarities and Overlook Differences.

Remember that people respond positively to agreement and similarity. You don't need to deceive anyone about your own views, but there is no need to concentrate on talking about areas of dissimilarity when you can find areas of similarity instead. Try hard to approach any disagreements in an open-minded and nondogmatic way, and don't attack the beliefs of others or become threatened and defensive whenever you encounter disagreement.

Remember to Express Positive—Not Negative—Sentiments.

It is as easy to be nice as to be obnoxious, and "nice" includes saying sincerely positive things to others. Compliments, praise, congratulations, and positive evaluations are almost always guaranteed to cause pleasure. Insults, criticisms, derogatory remarks, cruel teasing, and negative evaluations are almost always guaranteed to cause a negative reaction.

SUMMARY AND REVIEW OF KEY POINTS

The Beginning of Attraction: Proximity and Emotions

- *Interpersonal attraction* refers to the positive and negative attitudes we form about other people.
- The initial contact between two people is very often based on the *proximity* that is determined by such physical aspects of the environment as classroom seating assignments, the location of residences, and how workplaces are arranged.
- Proximity, in turn, leads to *repeated exposure* of two individuals to one

another. Repeated exposure usually results in positive *affect,* which results in attraction.

- Positive and negative affective states influence attraction both directly and indirectly. Direct effects occur when another person is responsible for the emotion. Indirect effects occur when the source of the emotion is elsewhere and the other person is simply associated with its presence.

Becoming Acquainted: The Need to Affiliate and the Effect of Observable Characteristics

- Individuals high, as opposed to low, in *need for affiliation* are more likely to engage in establishing and maintaining interpersonal relationships, and they are more skilled in dealing with people.

- Under unusual circumstances, such as natural disasters, people are more likely to affiliate with others. It seems that social comparison is the driving force behind this behavior because people want to interact, in order to reduce anxiety by clarifying what is going on and by clarifying their own emotional reactions.

- Interpersonal attraction and interpersonal judgments based on stereotypes are strongly affected by various observable characteristics of those we meet, including *physical attractiveness.* People like and make positive attributions about attractive men and women of all ages, despite the fact that assumptions based on appearance are usually inaccurate. It is still not possible to reach a definitive conclusion about why we react strongly to attractiveness or what constitutes attractiveness.

- In addition to attractiveness, many other observable characteristics influence initial interpersonal evaluations, including physique, weight, behavioral style, food preferences, first names, and other superficial characteristics.

Moving toward Friendship: Similarity and Mutual Liking

- One of many factors determining attraction toward another person is similarity of attitudes, beliefs, values, and interests.

- Though dissimilarity has a greater impact on attraction than does similarity, we respond to both. Thus, the higher the *proportion of similar attitudes,* the greater the attraction.

- The positive affective response to similarity and the negative affective response to dissimilarity have been hypothesized to rest on social comparison processes that lead to consensual validation or invalidation. A different explanation rests on the adaptive utility of our ancestors for reacting to dissimilar, and potentially dangerous, strangers with either fear or anger.

- We also like other people who indicate in word or deed that they like and positively evaluate us. We dislike those who dislike and negatively evaluate us.

- An overall summary of the major determinants of attraction is provided by the *affect-centered model of attraction,* which specifies that attraction is determined by direct and associated sources of affect, often mediated by cognitive processes.

KEY TERMS

affect (p. 262)

affect-centered model of attraction (p. 290)

appearance anxiety (p. 271)

attitude similarity (p. 284)

balance theory (p. 285)

interpersonal attraction (p. 256)

need for affiliation (p. 268)

physical attractiveness (p. 271)

proportion of similar attitudes (p. 284)

proximity (p. 257)

repeated exposure (p. 257)

repulsion hypothesis (p. 286)

stigma (p. 265)

FOR MORE INFORMATION

Hatfield, E., & Sprecher, S. (1986). *Mirror, mirror . . . : The importance of looks in everyday life.* Albany: SUNY Press.

- A well-written and extremely interesting summary of research dealing with the effects of physical attractiveness on interpersonal relationships. The scientific literature is well covered, and the findings are illustrated throughout with anecdotes, photographs, and drawings that consistently enliven the presentation.

Heatherton, T. F., Kleck, R. E., Hebl, M. R., & Hull, J. G. (2000). *The social psychology of stigma.* New York: Guilford.

- Leading researchers in the field summarize our current knowledge about why people stigmatize others, how it feels to be stigmatized, and the effects of such behavior on social interactions.

David Hockney, *My Parents,* 1977. Oil on canvas, 72 x 72". © David Hockney. © Tate Gallery, London/Art Resource, NY.

CLOSE RELATIONSHIPS: FAMILY, FRIENDS, LOVERS, AND SPOUSES

CHAPTER OUTLINE

Because my (DB's) early life was spent moving between two states, four towns, and more neighborhoods than I care to remember, I have had many acquaintances and many friendships. Let me briefly identify three of these relationships to provide a subjective view of how they differed, probably as a function of age.

In elementary school (or, in my case, schools), a "friend" tends to mean someone with whom you interact pleasantly and with whom you have something in common. I began the fourth grade, for example, as a newcomer from another state, and Frank was friendly to me. We enjoyed playing marbles at recess, and that's about all I remember of the many hours we spent together.

In high school, I knew and liked many people. One of my friends, Bill, was very bright and witty and a member of the football team. We, along with several others in our group, spent our time saying things we thought were funny, playing touch football during the lunch hour, going to movies, drinking beer, talking about sex, and—once—ditching school in order to go swimming in the Kern River. Our families met and interacted socially, and Bill was great at finding the "dirty parts" of novels (though in the late 1940s, the content was not very explicit and would today be rated PG-13 at most). Though Bill and I were friends, it wasn't until near the end of our senior year, as we were making college plans, that I discovered that he intended to become a Jesuit priest. His vocational goal came as quite a surprise and indicated to me that we really didn't know each other as well as had I thought. This friendship involved more than playing marbles and was undoubtedly closer than the one with Frank in the fourth grade, but it was still relatively superficial. We enjoyed each other's company, spent time together, and yet maintained our distance. He did enter the priesthood after graduation, and I visited him once during his first year of training. Several years later, after he was ordained, my wife and I had lunch with Bill and his parents. In retrospect, I can see that he and I were simply friendly acquaintances.

In college, I became friends with an entirely new set of individuals. This group did many of the same things as my group had done in high school a couple of years earlier—spent time together, drank beer, said funny things, talked about sex, and so forth. One difference was the fact that we also talked more seriously and honestly about many things—from the existence of God to racial prejudice to our plans for the future. In other words, we were close enough and trusting enough to self-disclose. We eventually knew each other in sufficient detail that there was little chance that any one of us was harboring a dramatic secret. I remained in close contact with two of these individuals after college and after our respective marriages. We socialized as couples, said funny things, drank cocktails, talked about sex, played charades, went to plays and movies, and shared meals at restaurants and at our homes. Though about five decades have passed since those days and though we live on opposite coasts, I still maintain contact with Bob and Nairn through e-mail and Christmas notes, and from time to time we meet in person when vacations or professional trips provide the opportunity. I feel as close and comfortable with them now as I did many years ago.

One key difference in my friendships from elementary school to high school to college and afterward is, I believe, the greater openness, honesty, and trust that came with growing older. It seems that close relationships fall along a continuum from relatively superficial to relatively open and honest to completely open and honest. The last category, by the way, is associated with love and marriage, and those topics are also part of this chapter.

The study of *interpersonal attraction* (see Chapter 7) was a major focus of social psychological research for most of the twentieth century, but the investigation of *close interpersonal relationships* has tended to lag far behind. In part, this is because interrelationships are more complex and more difficult to study than the attraction felt by one person toward another.

In relatively recent years, however, social psychologists have made up for lost time by turning their attention to relationships in general (Berscheid & Reis, 1998), relationships within families (Boon & Brussoni, 1998), love and intimacy (Hatfield & Rapson, 1993b), and marriage (Sternberg & Hojjat, 1997).

Given the importance of family, friendship, love, and marriage to most people, knowledge about the factors underlying success and failure in relationships is almost certainly of interest to each of us. The science of relationships is actively pursued in many parts of the world, and it cuts across traditional fields of research, including social, developmental, and clinical psychology (Berscheid, 1999; Harvey & Pauwels, 1999).

In this chapter, we will first describe what is known about two important kinds of *interdependent relationships*—those within the family and those involving friendships. We will also discuss the difficulty some people have in establishing lasting relationships and the resultant discomfort of *loneliness.* We next examine *intimate relationships* and the factors involved in romance, love, and sexual intimacy. The final topic, *marital relationships,* focuses on the factors responsible for successful versus unsuccessful marriages and the often painful aspects of ending a relationship.

Interdependent Relationships with Family and Friends versus Loneliness

The common element of all close relationships is **interdependence,** an interpersonal association in which two people consistently influence each other's lives, focus their thoughts and emotions on one another, and regularly engage in joint activities whenever possible. Close relationships with friends, family members, and one's spouse also include an element of commitment (Fehr, 1999). Interdependence occurs across age groups and across quite different kinds of interactions. The importance of forming bonds with other people is underscored by Ryff and Singer (2000, p. 30), who state, "Quality ties to others are universally endorsed as central to optimal living."

interdependence: The characteristic common to all close relationships—an interpersonal association in which two people influence each other's lives and engage in many joint activities.

The affection of mothers for their offspring appears to be based, at least in part, on hormones (Maestripieri, 2001). Do other interpersonal bonds also rest on biological factors? There is good reason to believe that our need for companionship has evolutionary roots. DNA evidence indicates that, among other species, chimpanzees and bonobos are our closest evolutionary relatives, and they are more closely related to us than to gorillas or orangutans (Smuts, 2000/2001). Field studies of these primates indicate that they interact much as we do. That is, they hug,

FIGURE 8.1

The Evolutionary Roots of Our Need for Friendship. A good argument can be made for the biological basis of the human need for close relationships, including friends. DNA evidence indicates our common ancestry with the great apes, and field studies of apes show many behavioral similarities. For example, both young humans *(left)* and young orangutans *(right)* provide examples of the joys and comforts of friendship that we share.

kiss, and form long-term bonds between individuals such as mother and offspring, friendship pairs (see Figure 8.1), and mates.

Observing the forest apes in their natural environments suggests many behavioral similarities to human interactions. As one example, Smuts (2000) states,

> *In chimps and bonobos, in particular, emotional expression is uninhibited, at least from the point of view of staid human observers. When two groups meet after a separation of days or even hours, it is as if they have not seen one another in ages. Animals rush into each other's arms, jump up and down, and shriek with delight. (p. 80)*

Evolutionary theory argues that the tendency to form emotional bonds contributed to reproductive success in terms of increasing the odds that an individual was able to conceive and care for offspring. It was also beneficial to cooperate with peers in the search for food and to defend one another against rivals and predators. Altogether, studies of DNA, field studies of apes, and evolutionary theory suggest strongly that natural selection has shaped the emotional and social tendencies of humans and of our closest animal relatives. We will now take a closer look at human family relationships.

Family: The First Relationships

Most parent–child interactions have later implications because the family is the setting in which each of us learns how to deal with other people. Dissanayake (2000) suggests that we come into the world ready to interact with other human beings. During the first year of life, when the range of possible behaviors is obviously limited, human infants are extremely sensitive to certain sounds, facial expressions, and bodily movements, as shown in Figure 8.2. And most caregivers

A

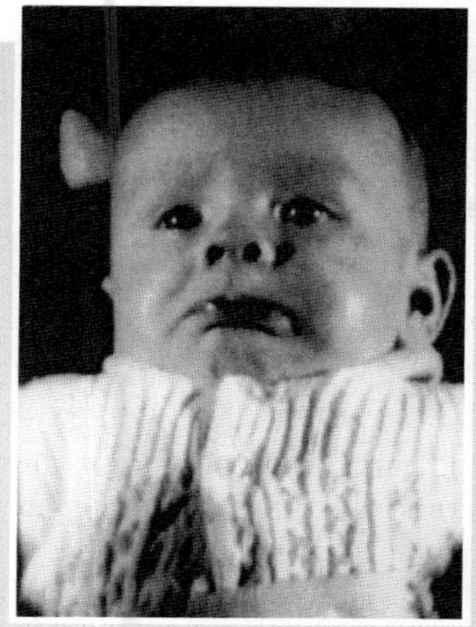

B

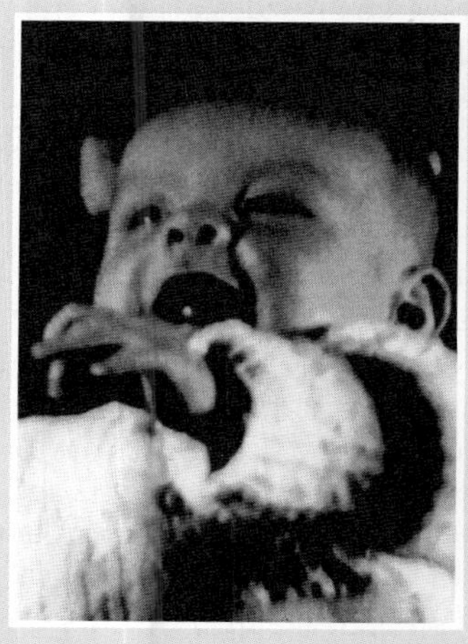

FIGURE 8.2

Communication between Infant and Mother. Beginning early in their first year of life, human infants are extremely sensitive to the specific sounds, facial expressions, and bodily movements of their caregivers (typically their mothers). And their caregivers are equally sensitive to the infant's sounds, expressions, and movements. The result is interactive communication between mother and infant.

In the first set of these video stills *(A),* the baby hears a frightening noise, pouts, and then the mother shows concern, immediately sensing the baby's fear, and says, "Aargh! I don't want to see a pouty face." In the second set of stills *(B),* the baby is laughing in response to the mother's animation which occurred when the baby smiled and cooed at her.

Altogether infants are very sensitive to maternal signals, and they are also active communicators who express themselves. Mothers, in turn, are very sensitive to what babies do. Such interactions constitute a very early aspect of interpersonal behavior.

are equally sensitive to what the infant does. In the resulting interaction, infant and caregiver communicate and reinforce one another (Murray & Trevarthen, 1986; Trevarthen, 1993). The caregiver shows interest in the infant's communication in various ways such as engaging in baby talk and displaying exaggerated facial expressions. In turn, the infant shows interest in the adult with appropriate sounds and expressions. The resulting interaction can be a positive interpersonal experience for both participants, and both learn something from such a relationship.

THE INTERACTIONS OF PARENTS AND THEIR OFFSPRING. Because of the lasting effects of early experience on later interpersonal behavior, the study of family relationships extends beyond the usual boundaries of social psychology. By the time you finish reading this chapter, however, you may be convinced that some aspects of developmental psychology are quite relevant to social psychology. As a very brief overview, the general idea is that the quality of the interaction between a mother (or other caregiver) and her infant determines how that tiny individual responds to other people throughout his or her life. Research provides evidence that men and women show consistent patterns in their relationships with their mothers, fathers, same-sex friends, and romantic partners (Foltz et al., 1999). We will get into this topic more directly when we discuss *attachment style* in an upcoming section.

Mothers, fathers (Maio, Fincham, & Lycett, 2000; Rohner, 1998), grandparents (Boon & Brussoni, 1996), and others in the family interact in a multitude of ways with infants, toddlers, young children, and adolescents. To some degree, the nature of the interactions depends on the personality characteristics of those interacting with the youngster (Clark, Kochanska, & Ready, 2000). For example, the effect of an outgoing, affectionate mother can be quite different from that of a withdrawn, aloof one. All interactions with parents and other family members have some effect on what the child learns about relationships with other people (O'Leary, 1995). For example, when parents play games with their children (from patty cake to Monopoly), they are providing information about how people deal with one another in a social situation, follow certain procedures, and engage in cooperative behavior—all of which is relevant to children's ability to deal with other adults and also with their peers (Lindsey, Mize, & Pettit, 1997).

As the infant becomes a child and then an adolescent, parenting can constitute more of a challenge. To some degree, the belief that parent–offspring relations become less pleasant as puberty arrives seems to be an accurate one. Despite this general truth, however, most adolescents express very positive feelings about their parents, even though they are less close to and less dependent on them than they were in childhood (Galambos, 1992). Adolescents are found to love their parents to the extent that they *like* them and to the extent that the adolescent is a *decent* person who behaves in a moral and ethical way (Jeffries, 1993). Most teenagers feel such love toward their mother and father and feel loved in return. This kind of happy and satisfying relationship within a family is associated with the ability to experience empathy, high self-esteem, and interpersonal trust.

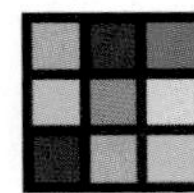

Interactions within a family are influenced not only by genetics and personality characteristics, but also by culture. For example, Mexican Americans, compared to Anglo-Americans, place a greater stress on collectivism and the importance of family support and family membership (Freeberg & Stein, 1996). In Mexican American families, the offspring are more likely than those in Anglo-American families to help their parents, less likely to want to interact with others outside of the home, and more likely to feel an obligation toward their parents rather than expecting parents always to be the ones who provide help.

RELATIONSHIPS BETWEEN AND AMONG SIBLINGS. Most children (about 80 percent) grow up in a household with at least one sibling, and sibling interactions provide another way in which we learn patterns of interpersonal behavior (Dunn, 1992).

Sibling relationships differ from those between parents and their children, and often combine feelings of affection, hostility, and rivalry (Boer et al., 1997). A familiar refrain for siblings is some version of "Mom always liked you best," but parents are reluctant to admit to any such favoritism. In fact, however, when mothers in their sixties and seventies are asked about differential liking, they report being closer to at least one of their grown offspring than to the others (Suitor & Pillemer, 2000).

In the United States, with a divorce rate of about 50 percent, remarriages add to the complexity of these interactions, because stepchildren and stepparents may be involved as well as siblings, which often include half-siblings and stepsiblings (Coleman et al., 2001). We don't yet have extensive data on the effect of these various combinations within a family.

An affectionate relationship between siblings is most likely if each sibling has a warm relationship with each parent, and if the parents perceive their marriage in positive terms (McGuire, McHale, & Updegraff, 1996; Stocker & McHale, 1992). Sibling relationships are important because the positive or negative affect associated with siblings is likely to be aroused over and over in interactions with peers, romantic partners, and spouses (Klagsbrun, 1992). For example, schoolyard bullies tend to have had negative relationships with their siblings (Bowers, Smith, & Binney, 1994). Other research indicates that most behavior problems occur among boys who have had a high level of conflict with their siblings plus a rejecting, punitive mother (Garcia & Shaw, 2000).

Siblings are most likely to feel close if they are able to share attitudes and memories, stand up for one another, experience companionship, and help one another cope with difficulties (Floyd, 1996). Even when siblings are very close in childhood, they tend to grow apart in adolescence and young adulthood (Rosenthal, 1992). By the time they reach middle age, however, the vast majority of them once again establish positive relationships (see Figure 8.3). Sometimes, one sibling takes the role of parent, but in other instances middle-aged siblings function as close buddies or casual acquaintances, or they simply remain in contact because they feel it is a family responsibility (Stewart, Verbrugge, & Beilfuss, 1998). As they grow older, most elderly siblings rely heavily on one another; as a result, when one dies,

G. W. H. Bush *G. W. Bush* *Jebb Bush*

FIGURE 8.3

Siblings: Close in Childhood, Distant in Adolescence, Close Again as They Grow Older. It is a common pattern for siblings to feel close when they are children and then to drift apart in adolescence and young adulthood. By the time they reach middle age, the vast majority once again establish close, positive relationships.

the impact can be devastating (Van Volkom, 2000). At the other extreme, about 20 percent of adult siblings never establish any degree of closeness—about half of these are simply indifferent to their siblings, and half actively dislike their brothers and sisters (Folwell et al., 1997).

Relationships beyond the Family: Establishing a Close Friendship

Beginning in childhood, most of us establish casual friendships with peers who share common interests. These early relationships, as discussed in Chapter 7, tend to consist of mutual liking based on positive affect (Lydon, Jamieson, & Holmes, 1997). Generally, having friends is positive because they boost one's self-esteem and help in coping with stress, but friends can have a negative effect if they are antisocial, withdrawn, nonsupportive, argumentative, or unstable (Hartup & Stevens, 1999).

▪ CLOSE FRIENDS VERSUS OTHER FRIENDLY RELATIONSHIPS. As we mature, **close friendships** have several distinctive characteristics. For example, people tend to engage in self-enhancing behavior such as bragging with nonfriends, but they are more likely to exhibit modesty about their accomplishments when interacting with friends (Tice et al., 1995). And friends tend to avoid lying to one another—unless the purpose of the lie is to make the other person feel better (DePaulo & Kashy, 1998).

Once established, a close relationship, compared to a casual relationship, results in the two individuals spending more time together, interacting in more varied situations, self-disclosing, providing mutual emotional support, and differentiating between the close friend and other friends (Kenney & Kashy, 1994; Laurenceau, Barrett, & Pietromonaco, 1998; Parks & Floyd, 1996) (see Figure 8.4). A casual friend is someone who is fun to be with, while a close friend is valued for his or her generosity, sensitivity, and honesty—someone with whom you can relax and be yourself (Urbanski, 1992).

▪ GENDER AND FRIENDSHIPS. Women report having more close friends than men do (Fredrickson, 1995), and there are benefits to having close friends. For example, job satisfaction (see Chapter 13) is greater among those who have such friends than among those without that kind of relationship (Winstead et al., 1995).

The downside is the pain associated with losing or being separated from a highly valued friend. For example, when a close friendship is interrupted by college graduation, the two individuals must adapt to the separation because it constitutes an emotional threat (Fredrickson, 1995). As a result, graduating seniors, especially women, report more intense emotional involvement when interacting with close friends than is true for students not facing graduation.

Do the conversations of two male friends differ from those of two female friends? Martin (1997) identified several gender-specific aspects that characterize what friends talk about. Two males tend to talk about women and sex, being trapped in a relationship, sports, and alcohol. Two females tend to talk about relationships with men, clothes, problems with roommates, and giving or receiving presents.

Can a male and a female have a friendship that is not sexual? Relatively little research has been done on such relationships, but it was recently reported that men and women differ in their expectations about opposite-sex friendships (Bleske-Rechek & Buss, 2001). For example, men tend to initiate such friendships when the woman is attractive, and they tend to expect a sexual relationship to develop.

close friendship: A relationship in which two people spend a great deal of time together, interact in a variety of situations, exclude others from the relationship, and provide mutual emotional support.

FIGURE 8.4
A Close Friendship.
When two individuals establish a close relationship, they spend time together, interact in a variety of situations, disclose confidential information, provide mutual emotional support, and exclude outsiders from the relationship.

If physical intimacy is absent, men perceive this as a reason for ending the relationship. Women, in contrast, tend to initiate such a friendship to gain physical protection, and, in the absence of such protection, they feel justified in dissolving the relationship.

Adult Relationships and Attachment Style

We indicated earlier that the study of relationships is a more recent concern of social psychology than the study of initial attraction. Over the past three decades, the focus of relationship research has increasingly focused on the concept of **attachment style,** as will be described in the **Social Psychology: Thirty Years of Progress** section on page 306.

THREE ATTACHMENT STYLES OR FOUR? Though many investigators have accepted the three attachment styles as defined by Bowlby, Bartholomew and her associates (Bartholomew, 1990; Bartholomew & Horowitz, 1991) suggested a different approach. Given Bowlby's emphasis on two basic attitudes (about self and others), it was assumed that many aspects of interpersonal behavior are influenced by the extent to which a person's self-evaluation is positive or negative *and* by the extent to which other people are perceived as positive (trustworthy) or negative (untrustworthy).

attachment style: The degree of security experienced in interpersonal relationships. Differential styles are initially developed in infancy, but attachment differences appear to affect interpersonal behavior throughout life.

THE IMPORTANCE OF ADULT ATTACHMENT STYLE IN INTERPERSONAL BEHAVIOR

One of the interesting fringe benefits of writing a textbook is the necessity of becoming aware of research trends and developments. One such new trend in social psychology was the sudden interest in *adult attachment style* that burst upon the scene near the end of the twentieth century. In the first six editions of this book (1974 to 1991), the concept of attachment was not mentioned at all. In the 1994 edition, the topic appeared on two pages, with references to the work of Bringle and Bagby (1992), Hazan and Shaver (1990), and Shaver and Brennan (1992). By 1997, the total had increased to fourteen pages of coverage, followed by over twenty pages in the 2000 edition. What was this "new" phenomenon all about?

The concept of attachment originated in the study of the interaction between an infant and his or her caregiver (most often, the mother). Bowlby (1969, 1973) proposed that in the course of this interaction, the child develops cognitions centering on two crucial attitudes (Bowlby's term for these attitudes is *working models*). One basic attitude, evaluation of oneself, is termed *self-esteem.* In effect, the behavior and emotional reactions of the caregiver provide information to the infant that he or she is a valued, important, loved individual or, at the other extreme, relatively valueless, unimportant, and unloved. The many consequences of high versus low self-esteem are described in Chapter 5, and Bowlby proposed that individual differences in this characteristic are formed in infancy.

The second basic attitude that babies acquire is an aspect of the social self consisting of one's beliefs and expectancies about other people —**interpersonal trust.** The general idea is that the infant experiences the caregiver as trustworthy, dependable, and reliable or as relatively untrustworthy, undependable, and unreliable. As the infant grows and interacts with other people within and outside of the family, the basic attitude about self remains constant, and the basic attitude about the caregiver generalizes to other individuals.

If Bowlby is correct, long before we have acquired language skills, we are able to form basic schemas about ourselves and about other people, schemas that guide our interpersonal behavior throughout our lives. As a result, our interactions with family members, strangers, peers, friends, romantic partners, and spouses are to some degree influenced by what we learned in early infancy (Hazan & Shaver, 1990).

Based on his conceptualizations about mother–child interactions and the resulting schemas that are learned, Bowlby (1982) proposed that infants develop one of three types of attachment style: *secure, insecure–avoidant,* or *insecure–ambivalent.* These same styles can be observed beyond infancy in the interactions between mother and child (Ainsworth et al., 1978). In the Ainsworth paradigm, the mother and child are observed in a controlled setting, and the mother is instructed to leave the room briefly on two occasions and then return to her child. The three attachment styles can be observed in the child's response to this situation. Secure children are mildly upset by the mother's absence but are quickly soothed by her return. Avoidant children tend to reject the mother and to show emotional control and restraint when they are once again with her. Ambivalent children reveal a state of conflict—they cry when separated from the mother, but her return only leads to more crying and to anger.

Following infancy and early childhood, these same attachment patterns can still be observed in the way preschool children interact with their peers (Kerns, 1994; Kerns & Barth, 1995), in the way that preadolescents form friendships at summer camp (Shulman, Elicker, & Sroufe, 1994), in the way that adolescents establish and maintain friendships (Cooper, Shaver, & Collins, 1998), and in the way that some individuals have turbulent and unstable relationships (Simpson, Ickes, & Grich, 1999). Observations of adults at an airport when one member of a couple is departing and the other is staying behind indicate parallels with the children in the Ainsworth studies. When a partner leaves, the remaining individual may be mildly upset, rejecting, and restrained, or express both sadness and anger (Fraley & Shaver, 1998) (see Figure 8.5).

Attitudes about self and others are important because people are not at all accurate in determining whether they are liked or disliked by strangers

FIGURE 8.5
Attachment Style Predicts Response to Separation. Studies of small children experiencing brief separation from their mothers and of adult couples facing separation at an airport show similarities with respect to how individuals with secure and insecure attachment styles react to this kind of stress.

(Marcus & Askari, 1999). Those with a positive attitude about self and about other people expect to be liked, and they usually are. Among both children and adults, a secure attachment style is also associated with adaptive behavior, such as curiosity about and exploration of one's environment (Green & Campbell, 2000). During pregnancy, securely attached women report stronger bonding with the fetus than do insecure women (Mikulincer & Florian, 1999).

As a general summary, secure individuals of whatever age interact well with others, avoidant individuals have the most interpersonal difficulties, and ambivalent individuals fall someplace in between. As you might guess from these differences among attachment styles, most people prefer a secure romantic partner rather than one who is avoidant or ambivalent, regardless of their own attachment style (Chappell & Davis, 1998; Latty-Mann & Davis, 1996).

Cross-cultural research (such as that in the Netherlands) provides evidence of the universality of the attachment phenomenon (Gerlsma, Buunk, & Mutsaers, 1994). For example, among twelve-year-olds in Maastricht, an insecure attachment style was found to be associated with anxiety and depression (Muris, Mayer, & Meesters, 2000). It has been suggested, however, that security as defined in attachment research is biased toward individualistic concepts of the value of autonomy and having a secure base, whereas a collectivist approach to attachment is needed to understand interpersonal behavior in non-Western cultures (Rothbaum et al., 2000).

In any event, once social psychologists recognized the applicability of these concepts to the study of interpersonal relationships, love, and marriage, the research floodgates opened for attachment research. You will read about much of this research in the remaining sections of this chapter.

Think about the positive–negative dimensions that underlie attachment and how they might affect interpersonal behavior. A person with a positive self-image expects to be liked and accepted and thus should find it easy to make friends. A negative self-image leads to the expectation that others will respond negatively. Thus, the individual with a negative self-image fears new relationships and has difficulty in making friends.

interpersonal trust: A dimension underlying styles of attachment that involves the belief that other people are trustworthy, dependable, and reliable versus the belief that others are untrustworthy, undependable, and unreliable.

secure attachment style: In Bartholomew's model, a style characterized by high self-esteem and high interpersonal trust; usually described as the most successful and most desirable attachment style.

With respect to the other basic attitude, a positive image of other people leads to positive expectations about a stranger's intentions and motives—trust. A negative image of others leads to negative expectations about what a stranger intends and wants—mistrust. These negative expectations arouse fears of being exploited (McGowan, Daniels, & Byrne, 2001). Bartholomew's conceptualization goes a further step and suggests that the two dimensions should be considered simultaneously. As shown in Figure 8.6, the resulting combination of positive–negative attitudes about self and positive–negative attitudes about others yields *four attachment styles* rather than the original three. What characteristics are associated with these four adult attachment styles?

A person with a **secure attachment style** has high self-esteem and is positive about other people, so he or she seeks interpersonal closeness and feels comfortable in relationships. For example, secure adults express trust in their partners (Mikulincer, 1998b) and are able to work together to solve problems (Lopez et al., 1997). Those

Working Model of Others

Positive = Interpersonal Trust

Negative = Interpersonal Mistrust

Working Model of Self: Negative = Low Self-Esteem; Positive = High Self-Esteem

	Negative = Low Self-Esteem	Positive = High Self-Esteem
Positive = Interpersonal Trust	**Preoccupied Attachment Style** I am more affectionate than my partner. I fall in love easily. Sometimes I tell people too much about myself. My most important goal is to be truly appreciated by another person.	**Secure Attachment Style** I find it easy to meet new people. I enjoy looking at myself in the mirror. I'm very happy with my life right now. It's easy to make me smile and laugh.
Negative = Interpersonal Mistrust	**Fearful-avoidant Attachment Style** Whenever I hear the doorbell ring, I'm usually a little worried about who it might be. I feel that most people don't like me. I don't have much to be proud of. It's really much safer just to think about a relationship instead of actually initiating one.	**Dismissing Attachment Style** I had rather depend on myself than on other people. I don't like to reveal things about myself to others. My friends seldom live up to my expectations. I can get along quite well without a close emotional relationship in my life.

FIGURE 8.6

Four Attachment Styles Based on Attitudes about Self and Others.
Griffin and Bartholomew (1994a, 1994b) extended Bowlby's work on *attachment styles* in infancy by identifying four adult styles. The two underlying dimensions are based on positive versus negative attitudes about self (self-esteem) and about other people (*interpersonal trust*). Representing a combination of these two dimensions are four attachment styles: *secure, dismissing, fearful–avoidant,* and *preoccupied.* The sample statements associated with each style are taken from the *Albany Measure of Attachment Style (AMAS)* [SOURCE: MCGOWAN, DANIELS, & BYRNE, 2000].

with a secure style report having had a warm relationship with their parents (Bringle & Bagby, 1992) and perceive their past and present family life in positive terms (Diehl et al., 1998; Levy, Blatt, & Shaver, 1998; Scher & Mayseless, 1994). Compared to those with other attachment styles, secure individuals are less prone to becoming angry, attribute less hostile intent to others, and expect conflicts to have positive and constructive outcomes (Mikulincer, 1998a). Secure individuals are best able to form lasting, committed, satisfying relationships (Shaver & Brennan, 1992).

An important reason that relationship satisfaction is associated with secure attachment was identified by Osland (2001). She was able to pinpoint *empathy* (see Chapter 10) as the underlying mechanism. Secure individuals experience greater empathy and are thus able to perceive the relationship from the perspective of their partner as well as from their own (see Figure 8.7). Those whose attachment styles are dismissing, fearful–avoidant, or preoccupied tend to lack this empathic ability, and their relationships suffer as a result.

Altogether, a secure style is associated with getting along with other people, feeling close to one's parents, and evaluating relationships in a positive way (McGowan, Daniels, & Byrne, 2000). Shaver and his associates (1996) suggest that secure attachment is similar to *androgyny* (see Chapter 5), constituting a combination of masculine and feminine characteristics.

A person with a **fearful–avoidant attachment style** is low in self-esteem and negative about other people. By minimizing interpersonal closeness and avoiding close relationships, they hope to protect themselves from the pain of being rejected. Fearful–avoidant individuals describe their parents in negative terms (Levy et al., 1998), are hostile and become angry without realizing it (Mikulincer, 1998a), and experience less intimacy and enjoyment in interacting with current or potential romantic partners (Tidwell, Reis, & Shaver, 1996). This attachment style is associated with negative interpersonal relationships, feelings of jealousy, and the use of alcohol to reduce their anxiety about social situations (McGowan, Daniels, & Byrne, 2000).

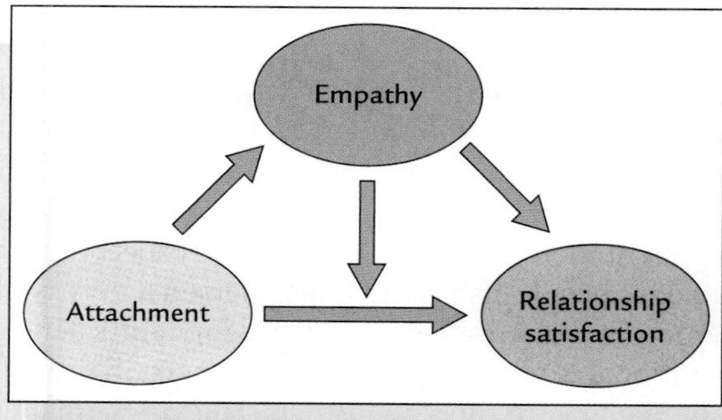

FIGURE 8.7

Attachment Style, Empathy, and Relationship Satisfaction.

Those with a *secure attachment style* have been found to express greater relationship satisfaction than those with the other three, less secure styles. Osland (2001) confirmed this association and was able to show that one of the underlying reasons is that secure individuals (compared to those who are dismissing, fearful-avoidant, or preoccupied) experience greater feelings of empathy and are thus able to perceive the relationship from the perspective of the partner as well as from their own perspective.

fearful–avoidant attachment style: In Bartholomew's model, a style characterized by low self-esteem and low interpersonal trust. This is the most insecure and least adaptive style of attachment.

The remaining two attachment patterns involve inconsistency between self-image and the image of others. A **preoccupied attachment style** is defined by a negative view of self combined with positive expectations that other people will be loving and accepting. As result, preoccupied individuals seek closeness in relationships (sometimes excessive closeness), but they also experience anxiety and shame because they feel they are not "worthy" of the other person's love (Lopez et al., 1997). Distress about the possibility of being rejected is extreme. The need for love and approval plus self-criticism leads to depression whenever a relationship goes badly (Whiffen et al., 2000).

A very positive self-image (sometimes unrealistically positive) is characteristic of the **dismissing attachment style,** and the self-descriptions of these individuals differ greatly from the way others describe them (Onishi, Gjerde, & Block, 2001). The dismissing individual views himself or herself as worthwhile, independent, and very much entitled to a close relationship; other people are more likely to view them less positively and to describe them as unfriendly and limited in social ability. A major problem is that they expect the worst of others, so they are likely to fear genuine closeness. Both dismissing and fearful–avoidant individuals avoid face-to-face interactions in favor of impersonal contacts such as notes or e-mail, and when they drink, they drink alone rather than in a social context (McGowan, Daniels, & Byrne, 2000).

■ EFFECTS OF ATTACHMENT STYLE ON OTHER BEHAVIOR. A general point is that attachment style is most likely to influence social interactions to the extent that the interactions are relevant to interpersonal concerns (Pietromonaco & Barrett, 1997). For example, interacting with a grocery clerk at the checkout counter should have little or nothing to do with attachment, but interacting with a date is likely to be closely related to attachment style. Canadian undergraduates reported having attachment-relevant relationships with an average of about five people, including family members, romantic partners, and friends (Trinke & Bartholomew, 1997). Attachment is associated not only with response to other individuals, but also with response to groups (Smith, Murphy, & Coats, 1999).

It is assumed that people who differ in attachment style are predisposed to think, feel, and behave in specific ways in their relationships. In part, then, one's attachment style has an effect on behavior because of differences in social perception (see Chapters 2 and 3) (Mikulincer & Horesh, 1999) and in the ability to regulate affect (Mikulincer & Sheffi, 2000). For example, in responding to events in a relationship, preoccupied individuals interpret what is going on in more negative ways than do secure individuals, report more emotional distress, and expect more conflict (Collins, 1996). Fearful–avoidant people also explain interpersonal events in a negative way but without the emotional distress. Fearful–avoidant adults defend themselves by failing to recall emotional experiences (Fraley, Garner, & Shaver, 2000). As an additional example, compared with those who are insecure, secure individuals process information about social situations in ways that involve curiosity and the tendency to rely on new information in making social judgments (Mikulincer, 1997).

Consider another situation in which attachment is relevant. What do you do when you are experiencing stress? A common coping response is to think about something else (see Chapter 13). For example, if you have a significant other, it could be comforting and anxiety-reducing to think about him or her. McGowan (1999) tested this possibility in an experiment that induced stress—informing participants that they would be giving a lecture in front of a class. At this point, they were asked to write a description of a significant other or a description of an acquaintance. Their general mood and level of anxiety were measured both before they learned about giving a lecture and after they wrote the description of another person. Thinking about a significant other was obviously helpful to those with positive self-views (secure and dismissive)—their anxiety level was lowered. In contrast, those with negative self-views (preoccupied and fearful–avoidant) were not able to use significant others as a secure base. Instead, for them, it was more com-

preoccupied attachment style: In Bartholomew's model, a style characterized by low self-esteem and high interpersonal trust; usually described as a conflicted and somewhat insecure style in which the individual strongly desires a close relationship but feels that he or she is unworthy of the partner and thus vulnerable to being rejected.

dismissing attachment style: In Bartholomew's model, a style characterized by high self-esteem and low interpersonal trust. It is usually described as a conflicted and somewhat insecure style in which the individual feels that he or she "deserves" a close relationship but mistrusts potential partners. The result is the tendency to reject the other person at some point in the relationship in order to avoid being the one who is rejected.

forting to think about an acquaintance. McGowan concluded that when preoccupied and fearful–avoidant individuals are asked to think about a significant other, doing so reminds them of concerns about rejection and therefore increases rather than decreases anxiety.

In research on the effect of similarity–dissimilarity on attraction (see Chapter 7), securely attached individuals responded in the expected way, indicating more attraction toward a similar than toward a dissimilar stranger. Unexpectedly, however, fearful–avoidant individuals were *not* responsive to similarity–dissimilarity (Dye, 2001). One possible explanation is that secure individuals are sensitive to cues that indicate a good versus a bad relationship, while fearful–avoidant individuals are not—they expect the relationship to be bad, no matter what. In analogous research on the need for affiliation, those relatively high in this need are most responsive to similarity–dissimilarity, while those low in need for affiliation are relatively indifferent to such information (Byrne, 1971).

Somewhat surprising is the fact that, with academic ability held constant, secure college students have a higher grade point average than do students with other attachment styles (Cutrona et al., 1994). A possible explanation is that having a secure relationship with one's parents makes it easier to establish a similar relationship with professors (Lopez, 1997).

We will return to the topic of attachment from time to time in this chapter (and in other chapters as well) because self-esteem and interpersonal trust are relevant to many aspects of social behavior. You should note, however, that the attachment styles observed in infancy and childhood may not be perfect predictors of adult attachment styles. It seems plausible that the basic attitudes and expectancies developed in infancy simply continue through adolescence and adulthood. Though there is considerable consistency across the life span (Klohnen & Bera, 1998), our images of ourselves and others (and therefore our attachment styles) can be changed by good and bad relationship experiences (Brennan & Bosson, 1998; Shaver & Hazan, 1994). For example, dating couples were studied on two occasions over a five-month period. Among those who experienced a breakup during that time period, secure attachment *decreased;* secure attachment increased when the couple remained in a relationship (Ruvolo, Fabin, & Ruvolo, 2001).

There is evidence that people differ in the extent to which their attachment style remains constant or changes over time (Davila, Burge, & Hammen, 1997). There is also evidence that the security of one's attachment varies in response to mother, father, romantic partner, and best friend (La Guardia et al., 2000). It seems clear that attachment style is an important determinant of interpersonal behavior, but it is by no means certain that each person's interpersonal future is etched in stone during the first months of life.

Loneliness: Life without Close Relationships

Though there may well be a biological need to establish relationships and though the rewards of relationships are well established, many individuals find it difficult to achieve that goal. The result is **loneliness**—an emotional and cognitive reaction to having fewer and less satisfying relationships than one desires (Archibald, Bartholomew, & Marx, 1995; Peplau & Perlman, 1982). An individual who doesn't want friends is not lonely, but someone who wants friends and doesn't have them is (Burger, 1995).

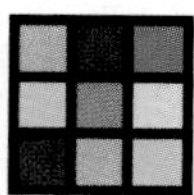

loneliness: The unhappy emotional and cognitive state that results from desiring close relationships but being unable to attain them.

Loneliness appears to be a common phenomenon throughout the world, as indicated by studies of British Asian (Shams, 2001), Spanish (Rokach et al., 2001), Portuguese (Neto & Barrios, 2000), Chinese Canadian (Goodwin, Cook, & Yung, 2001), Turkish, and Argentinean participants (Rokach & Bacanli, 2001), as well as by the many studies of Canadians and Americans (Rokach & Neto, 2000). An investigation of Dutch students found that lack of reciprocity in a relationship resulted in loneliness, especially among those who perceived themselves as giving more than they were receiving (Buunk & Prins, 1998). A move to a new location can lead to loneliness, but North American college students studying in Israel were found to be only temporarily lonely because they were able to establish new relationships in a few weeks (Wiseman, 1997).

■ THE CONSEQUENCES OF LONELINESS. As you might expect, people who feel lonely tend to spend their leisure time in solitary activity, to have very few dates, and to have only casual friends or acquaintances (R. A. Bell, 1991; Berg & McQuinn, 1989). Lonely individuals feel left out and believe they have very little in common with those they meet (Bell, 1993; Russell, Peplau, & Cutrona, 1980).

Loneliness is accompanied by negative affect, including feelings of depression, anxiety, unhappiness, and dissatisfaction associated with pessimism, self-blame, and shyness (Anderson et al., 1994; Jackson, Soderlind, & Weiss, 2000; Jones, Carpenter, & Quintana, 1985). Lonely individuals are perceived as maladjusted by those who know them (Lau & Gruen, 1992; Rotenberg & Kmill, 1992).

■ HOW DOES LONELINESS DEVELOP? The answer to this question seems to be a combination of genetics, individual experiences, and cultural influences.

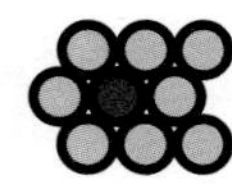

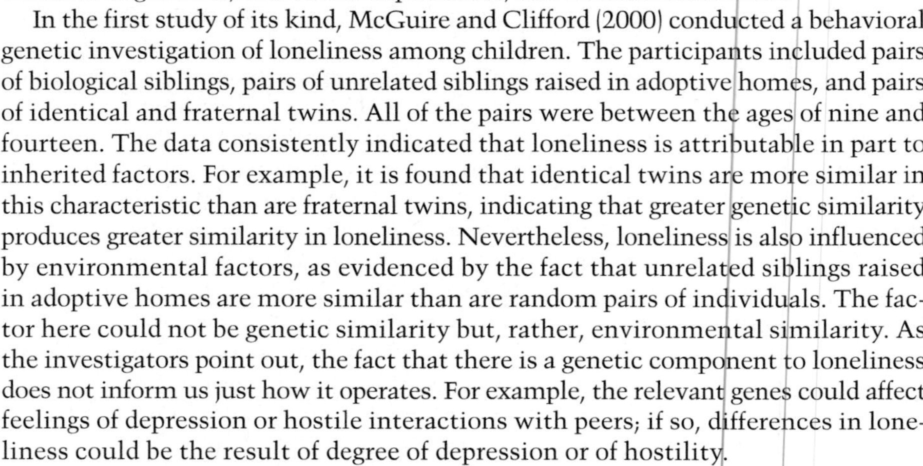

In the first study of its kind, McGuire and Clifford (2000) conducted a behavioral genetic investigation of loneliness among children. The participants included pairs of biological siblings, pairs of unrelated siblings raised in adoptive homes, and pairs of identical and fraternal twins. All of the pairs were between the ages of nine and fourteen. The data consistently indicated that loneliness is attributable in part to inherited factors. For example, it is found that identical twins are more similar in this characteristic than are fraternal twins, indicating that greater genetic similarity produces greater similarity in loneliness. Nevertheless, loneliness is also influenced by environmental factors, as evidenced by the fact that unrelated siblings raised in adoptive homes are more similar than are random pairs of individuals. The factor here could not be genetic similarity but, rather, environmental similarity. As the investigators point out, the fact that there is a genetic component to loneliness does not inform us just how it operates. For example, the relevant genes could affect feelings of depression or hostile interactions with peers; if so, differences in loneliness could be the result of degree of depression or of hostility.

Duggan and Brennan (1994) trace the failure to establish friendships to attachment style. For example, we have described how both dismissing and fearful–avoidant individuals resist forming relationships because of the potential for rejection—a fear of intimacy (Sherman & Thelen, 1996). Individuals with these same two attachment styles tend to mistrust others, and loneliness is associated with a lack of interpersonal trust (Rotenberg, 1994).

Relationships within the family can also be crucial. Loneliness in late adolescence is found to be greater among those who do not have a close relationship with a sibling, especially if there is conflict between siblings (Ponzetti & James, 1997). It also appears that a failure to develop appropriate social skills in childhood results in unsuccessful interactions with peers, and thus to loneliness (see Figure 8.8) (Braza et al., 1993). For example, a child who is either too hostile and aggressive or too shy and withdrawn is very likely to be rejected as a playmate (Johnson, Poteat, & Ironsmith, 1991; Ray et al., 1997). Some engage in teasing peers about their appearance or their intelligence or other attributes and fail to realize the hurt and anger they cause (Kowalski, 2000). Unless there is some form of intervention to alter self-defeating behaviors such as aggressiveness, shyness, or teasing, interpersonal difficulties typically continue throughout childhood and adolescence and into adulthood—they don't simply go away with the passage of time (Asendorpf, 1992). Among senior citizens aged sixty-five and older, feelings of loneliness are strongest among those who have no offspring and no friends (Hall-Elston & Mullins, 1999).

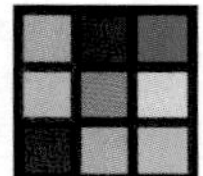

Culture also has an influence on loneliness and its possible origins. North Americans place the primary blame on unfulfilled intimate relationships, but South

FIGURE 8.8

Loneliness: Wanting Friends but Not Having Them. From childhood through adulthood, many people are lonely. They desire close interpersonal relationships but are unsuccessful in attaining that goal. Loneliness seems to be based on a combination of factors: heredity, experiences within one's family, and cultural determinants.

Asians are more likely to attribute loneliness to personal inadequacies, such as shortcomings in character (Rokach, 1998).

LONELINESS IN ADULTHOOD. Without the appropriate intervention, the lonely child becomes a lonely adult. What are the implications of that?

The inadequate social skills of children become the inadequate social skills of adolescents and adults. The socially unskilled individual tends to be shy, to have low self-esteem, and to feel self-conscious when interacting with a stranger (Bruch, Hamer, & Heimberg, 1995). Specific behavioral differences are found to be associated with good or bad social skills. A person with good skills is friendly, able to avoid angry responses, and comfortable in making conversation (Reisman, 1984). An unskilled person is generally uninterested in and insensitive to the other person and makes many references to himself or herself (Kowalski, 1993). A lonely individual does not want to hear the intimate disclosures of others (Rotenberg, 1997) and tends to disclose either very little or too much (R. A. Bell, 1991). At the extreme, an unskilled person may be disagreeable and engage in bullying behavior that generates feelings of hurt and unhappiness in others (Keltner et al., 1998). Just as is true for children, these various awkward, insensitive, and unpleasant acts in adulthood drive away potential friends (Meleshko & Alden, 1993). This unpopularity adds to the lonely individual's negativity and pessimism (Carver, Kus, & Scheier, 1994).

A key characteristic of lonely, friendless adults is *personal negativity*—the general tendency to be unhappy and dissatisfied with oneself. This is associated with a spiraling of negative events: Personal negativity leads to the belief that other people perceive the individual negatively, as is true of his or her self-perception, and social interactions become increasingly maladaptive. In time, other people *do* respond negatively, and the result is even more personal negativity (Furr & Funder, 1998).

Those who cannot deal successfully with social interactions are usually very much aware of how badly they function in interpersonal situations (Duck, Pond, & Leatham, 1994). One solution is to avoid other people as much as possible to minimize embarrassment and humiliation (Herbert, 1995). When a teenager is sufficiently lonely and fearful, he or she can feel a sense of complete *hopelessness,* and the resulting despair may culminate in suicide (Page, 1991). Can anything be done to prevent this from occurring?

The two primary interventions—sometimes used simultaneously—are *cognitive therapy* and *social skills training.* Research indicates that socially successful and unsuccessful college students think differently about social situations (Langston & Cantor, 1989; Salmela-Aro & Nurmi, 1996). Those who are socially unskilled appraise social interactions negatively and react with anxiety. To avoid rejection, they interact with others in a restrained way, taking few initiatives and revealing very little about themselves. This strategy creates a negative impression, and so it is self-defeating. The goal of cognitive therapy is to disrupt this pattern and encourage new cognitions more like those of socially successful individuals. When it is possible to alter cognitions, perceptions, and expectations, more adaptive social behavior is likely to follow.

Social skills training is helpful in providing some specific guidelines for such new behavior (Hope, Holt, & Heimberg, 1995). In this teaching process, examples of appropriate social behavior are provided on videotape, followed by role playing in which the client tries to model his or her behavior to match what is shown on the videotape. With sufficient practice in a nonthreatening therapeutic setting, the new skills can then be tried out in actual situations. The outcome can consist of a remarkable change in social behavior, and social success results in decreased loneliness and a more positive self-concept. Among the key social skills are impression management and accurate social perception (see Chapter 2), resulting in a higher level of "emotional intelligence" (Baron & Markman, 1998). Just as people can be taught the multiplication tables and how to drive a car, they can be taught social skills and how to interact with other people.

KEY POINTS

- Close relationships are characterized by *interdependence,* in which two people influence each other's lives, share their thoughts and emotions, and engage in joint activities.
- Evolutionary theory proposes that emotional bonding with friends and with mates increased the odds of reproductive success. As a result, humans and other primates are "hard-wired" to seek emotional closeness.
- The first relationships are within the family, and children learn what to expect from others and how to interact with them as they interact with parents, siblings, grandparents, and other family members.
- Friendships outside of the family begin in childhood and are initially based simply on interpersonal attraction. Many individuals are able to form a *close friendship* that involves spending time together, interacting in many different situations, providing mutual social support, and engaging in self-disclosure.
- At all ages, *attachment style* exerts a major influence on the ease with which people make friends, on the way they interact with others, and on their success in maintaining relationships.
- Adult attachment style is characterized as the combination of a person's level of self-esteem and degree of *interpersonal trust*. These positive–negative dimensions yield four resulting attachment styles: *secure, dismissing, fearful–avoidant,* and *preoccupied.* Those who are secure are best able to form long-lasting, committed, satisfying relationships.
- *Loneliness* occurs when a person has fewer and less satisfying relationships than he or she desires. The result is depression and anxiety. The causes of loneliness can be a combination of genetic predisposition, specific learning experiences early in life, and cultural influences. Interventions can help, especially a combination of cognitive therapy and social skills training.

Romantic Relationships, Love, and Physical Intimacy

Because of the upsurge of research on close relationships, social psychologists have learned a great deal in recent years about the factors that lead to romance, love, and physical intimacy. In a developing relationship, one or any combination of these three aspects may be involved, and they may take place simultaneously or in any sequence. We will first discuss romantic relationships. Because most of the existing research has dealt with heterosexual couples, that will be our major focus, but we will take note whenever corresponding data are available with respect to gays and Lesbians. For example, both homosexual and heterosexual men have the same expectations with respect to a romantic relationship, and these expectancies include having similar attitudes and values, providing mutual support, being honest and loyal, spending time together, sharing resources, and having something special together—"something magic" (Baccman, Folkesson, & Norlander, 1999).

Romance: Beyond Friendship

Among the defining characteristics of a romantic relationship are sexual attraction and some degree of physical intimacy, as suggested in Figure 8.9. Depending on the individuals and on what is culturally acceptable, intimacy may involve simply holding hands, embracing, or kissing, but it can also involve more explicitly sexual interactions, ranging from caresses to sexual intercourse. One or both partners are also likely to have thoughts of love and the possibility of eventual marriage.

FIGURE 8.9

Romantic Relationships Include Physical Intimacy. Romantic relationships almost always include some degree of physical intimacy. In close friendships, verbal intimacy is important, but physical intimacy tends to be limited, especially for male-male friendships. The degree of physical intimacy that is acceptable varies considerably across cultures.

■ CLOSE FRIENDSHIP AND ROMANCE: SIMILARITIES AND DIFFERENCES. In many respects, romantic attraction is much like any other type of interpersonal attraction. Just as we described with respect to acquaintances in Chapter 7 and to friends in this chapter, romance is likely to begin as a function of proximity, affect arousal, the motivation to have a relationship, our beliefs about the observable characteristics of the other person, similarity, and mutual liking. As an example, we will describe the workplace as one familiar setting for romance.

On the job, people who were once strangers work in close proximity, react to one another on the basis of how they look, talk to one another and discover ways in which they are similar and dissimilar, and—sometimes—experience sexual attraction (Seal, 1997). The effects of these familiar factors have been described by Pierce, Byrne, and Aguinis (1996), and they function as shown in Figure 8.10. There are, however, some special issues that are unique to the workplace setting, such as the effect of romance on productivity and job satisfaction (see Chapter 13) (Pierce, 1998) and possible accusations of sexual harassment (Pierce & Aguinis, 1997), especially

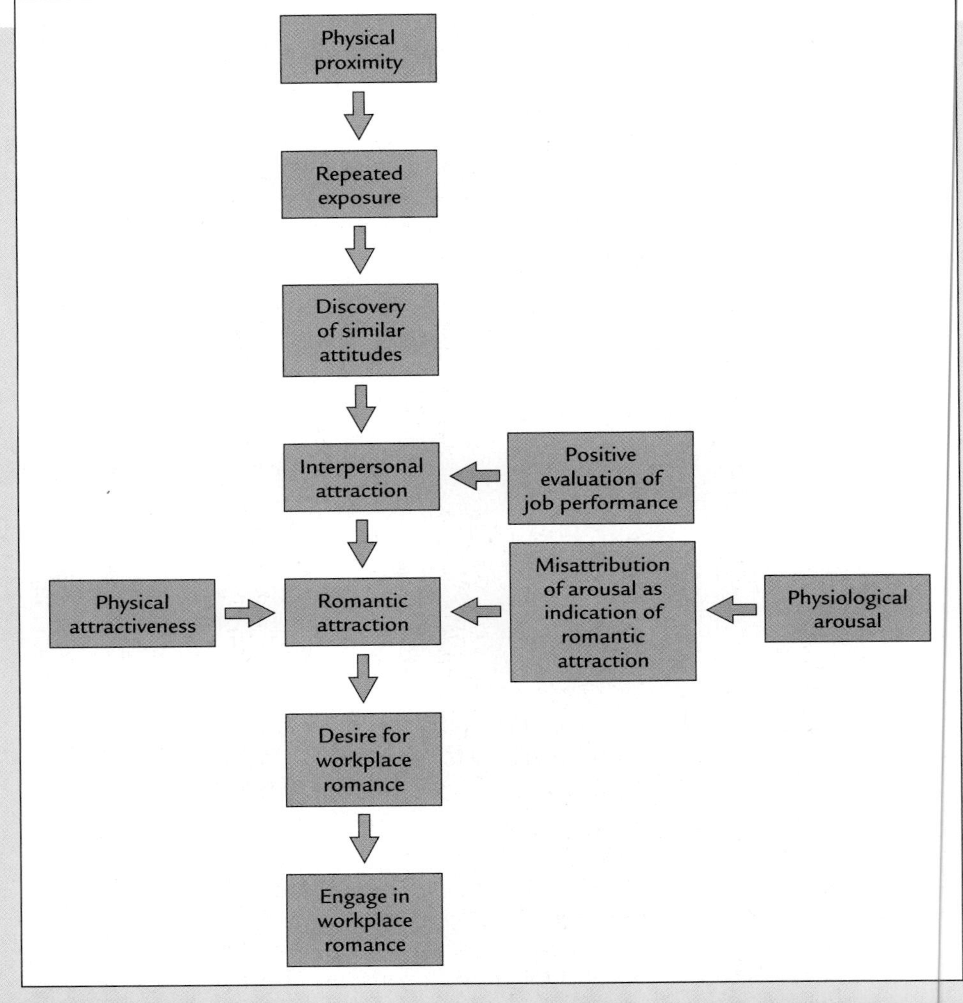

FIGURE 8.10

Factors That Facilitate Workplace Romance.

Romance in the workplace is a common occurrence, and the factors that facilitate it are many of the same factors that lead to interpersonal attraction, romance, and love in any setting.

[SOURCE: ADAPTED FROM INFORMATION IN PIERCE, BYRNE, & AGUINIS, 1996.]

if the relationship dissolves (Pierce & Aguinis, 2001a, 2001b; Pierce, Aguinis, & Adams, 2000; Pierce, Broberg, & Aguinis, 2001).

In addition to physical intimacy, some aspects of a romantic relationship are different from those of a friendly relationship. For example, Swann, De La Ronde, and Hixon (1994) report that among friends, college roommates, and even married couples, most people prefer a partner who provides accurate feedback relevant to his or her self-concept, someone who can be a source of verification and accuracy (De La Ronde & Swann, 1998). We like having a friend who knows us well enough to recognize our best and worst characteristics. A romantic relationship, in contrast, is different. At least at the beginning, two people are not looking for accuracy as much as they are looking for acceptance—wanting to like and to be liked unconditionally, as demonstrated by compliments and praise. People go out together to have a good time, and they are on their best behavior. Judgments of one another are often unrealistic, because each individual wants to believe that he or she has found the perfect partner and wants uncomplicated, totally positive feedback from that partner (Simpson, Ickes, & Blackstone, 1995). As gratifying as it may be to have a totally adoring companion, partners who are able to provide feedback that is both self-enhancing and self-verifying are the most attractive of all (Katz & Beach, 2000).

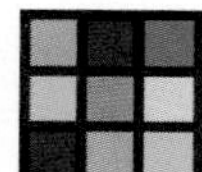

From the perspective of an outside observer, a romantic couple can seem unrealistic, but one way to understand romance is to recognize that it is built in part on fantasy and positive illusions. In fact, such illusions seem to help create a better relationship (Martz et al., 1998; Murray & Holmes, 1997; Murray, Holmes, & Griffin, 1996). Perceptions of one's partner tend to be biased, and the other person is perceived to be more like one's ideal self than is actually the case (Klohnen & Mendelsohn, 1998). The partner's virtues are emphasized, and any perceived faults are minimized (Murray & Holmes, 1999). One consequence of these tendencies is that, as documented in the United States, Canada, and the Netherlands, as well as among Asian Canadians, couples judge their own relationships to be better than the relationships other people have (Buunk & van der Eijnden, 1997; Endo, Heine, & Lehman, 2000; Van Lange & Rusbult, 1995), especially when they are induced to think about the possible failure of their relationships (Rusbult et al., 2000).

These shared illusions about romance are often based on the *belief in romantic destiny*—the conviction that two people are meant for each other. In fact, if two people care for each other and believe that they are meant to be together, that affection and those beliefs can help maintain the relationship (Knee, 1998).

This emphasis on the positive makes it difficult for partners to imagine the relationship ever ending; as a result, their ability to predict how long the relationship will last is less accurate than predictions made by their roommates or their parents (MacDonald & Ross, 1999).

Relationships can be conceptualized in terms of overlapping schemas, as presented in Figure 8.11 on page 318 (Fletcher et al., 1999). In a relationship, there is a cognitive schema involving the self (as we described in Chapter 5), a second schema that involves the partner, and a third schema that deals with the relationship between the two. Some cognitions represent qualities of the ideal partner: partner warmth and trustworthiness, vitality and attractiveness, and status and resources (Fletcher & Simpson, 2000). The closer the partner is to the ideal, the better the relationship is perceived to be and the more likely it is to last (Fletcher, Simpson, & Thomas, 2000). Also, people are happier in the relationship the more closely they match their partner's ideals (Campbell et al., 2001).

Let's go back now to the initial step in a relationship—meeting the other person for the first time. In ordinary life, proximity is extremely important, but those seeking a romantic relationship often take additional, more deliberate steps to meet another person than is true in the case of friendship. That is, people go on blind dates, get "fixed up" by someone who knows them both, place ads in the personal columns, seek out dating services in the hope of meeting the right romantic partner, and call

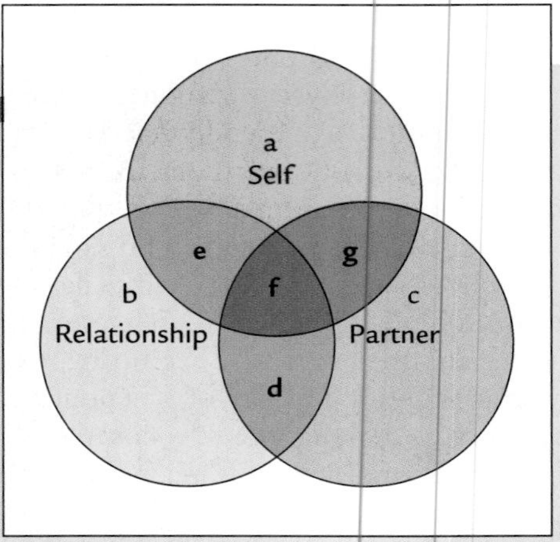

FIGURE 8.11

Cognitive Schemas in a Romantic Relationship. In addition to the schema that constitutes one's self-concept, an intimate relationship also includes a schema for one's partner and for the relationship itself. In the drawing, a, b, and c represent content that involves each of these three schemas. Overlapping content between pairs of schemas are labeled d, e, and g; and f indicates content that includes all three schemas. Examples from the perspective of a female: *a,* I am intelligent; *b,* relationships fail without good communication; *c,* men are aggressive; *d,* relationships work well when one partner is dominant; *e,* I want an exciting relationship; *f,* I want an honest relationship with a partner I can trust; *g,* I am suited to someone who is sporting and athletic.

[SOURCE: ADAPTED FROM FLETCHER ET AL., 1999.]

the Psychic Hotline to get Miss Cleo's advice. Comparable actions are almost never involved in the search for a friend.

Old television programs such as *The Dating Game* exploited the process of competition for an attractive date and overemphasized the importance of first impressions based on clever responses. More recent television programs, such as *Blind Date* (on UPN) and *Dating Story* (on TLC), provide graphic documentary evidence as to how difficult initial meetings can be and how often the individuals discover over the course of several hours that "this is not the one for me." To compound the difficulty of such dating situations, women tend to assume that men are sexually motivated. Men therefore present themselves in a deceptive way (Keenan et al., 1997). All such problems lead to the obvious question, "Isn't there a better way?"

The many obstacles involved in finding an appropriate romantic partner have led to new and possibly more efficient approaches to romance, including the phenomenon of "fast dating," as discussed in the following **Beyond the Headlines** section.

BEYOND THE HEADLINES: AS SOCIAL PSYCHOLOGISTS SEE IT

ARE SEVEN-MINUTE DATES THE SOLUTION?

Hello, Goodbye, Hey Maybe I Love You?

U.S. News and World Report, June 4, 2001—Romance is always a thriving market—if not the most efficient one. But wait, there's hope. At a suburban Virginia coffeehouse one night last week, attractive young singles paid $25 to interact with a week's worth of dates in a single evening.

The basic plan is to set up seven face-to-face conversations lasting seven minutes each. So avid were some of those taking part in the Virginia date-a-thon that they drove for 90 minutes to participate, despite tornado warnings in the area.

The formula is simple. At the Virginia meeting [see Figure 8.12], the organizer's role was to match men and women, ensure that they rotated among tables, and ring a bell to end each short-lived "date." Perhaps because of the enforced time limits, bland conversations about the weather soon gave way to comparisons of evil bosses, questions about the other person's most romantic evening, debates over the correct use of herbal medicine, and other matters of importance to each individual.

Fast dating has some appealing aspects. If the seven-minute interaction goes badly, the couple doesn't have to suffer through the awkward hours of a disastrous first date. If you don't like the other person, you part when the bell rings without having to pretend that you enjoyed it and without regrets. You need never see each other again, and no harm is done.

Several firms are now running this kind of service in over 30 cities, including Paris and Kiev. Most report that they have a high rate of success and that over 50 percent of the participants meet someone with whom there is mutual interest in another date.

(Based on an article by Kurlantzick, 2001.)

FIGURE 8.12

Fast Dating: Seeking a Romantic Partner.
The phenomenon of fast dating represents a way to meet a series of strangers in a safe setting, converse for several minutes, and then decide which (if any) of them you might like to see again. The idea is to provide a quick evaluation process that eliminates some of the problems associated with a first date.

Beyond the phenomenon of fast dating, there are other relatively recent innovations that provide alternative ways to initiate a relationship. On the Internet, there are websites, chat rooms, and personal listings designed to bring people together on line. The movie, *You've Got Mail,* illustrated how two people could meet and decide they liked one another by means of Internet communication. In the film, the same two people clearly weren't destined for romance on the basis of their real-life contact. There are obviously very serious dangers in interacting with strangers who might turn out to be serial killers, rapists, or pedophiles, but such problems can be avoided with a few simple precautions, such as withholding one's name, address, and telephone number until much more is known about the other person.

McKenna and Bargh (2000) suggest that computer technology provides us with something new and different with respect to social identity, social interaction, and relationship formation. They point out some major advantages of the Internet compared to real life: greater anonymity, the reduced importance of physical appearance and physical distance in relationship development, and one's greater control over the time and the place of interactions. We would add another advantage—freedom from the necessity in real life of having to make the first move and risking the possibility of a painful rejection (Snell, 1998).

McKenna and Bargh (2000) point out that, like all past technological advances, the Internet can be used for good or evil—it's up to the users. One thing is obvious: Up to now, our technological advances have brought about great changes in many aspects of our lives,

(continued)

from transportation to communication to the quality of life, but the way we go about initiating relationships has not changed appreciably since the first humans appeared on the planet. Maybe that is changing.

Will these new approaches to romance be successful? We don't know, but there are about eighty-five million singles in the United States alone, and the traditional ways to find a romantic partner are inefficient and time consuming. It may come as an unexpected bonus, but technology and innovative business ventures could prove to be a blessing for romance.

As you may guess from our earlier discussion, those individuals who are most successful in establishing close friendships are also likely to be the most successful in forming and maintaining romantic relationships (Connolly & Johnson, 1996). Relationships do fail, of course, and couples break up (Arriaga, 2001). The end of a relationship causes the least emotional upset among those with a secure attachment style, and the most upset for those whose style is preoccupied (Choo, Levine, & Hatfield, 1996).

Difficulties are caused by such things as betrayal of trust (using personal information against a partner), rebuff (canceling plans in order to do something else), unwarranted criticism (negative comments about small mistakes or about appearance), and lack of consideration (forgetting the partner's birthday) (Fehr et al., 1999). When teenage romantic partners break up, a common consequence is depression, especially among young women (Joyner & Udry, 2000). We will return to the topic of relationship failure later in the chapter, in the segment dealing with marriage.

What Is This Thing Called Love?

Love is one of the most common themes in our songs, movies, and everyday lives. Most people in our culture accept love as a common human experience, and a 1993 poll found that almost three out of four Americans said they were currently "in love." In part, love is an emotional reaction as familiar and as basic as anger, sadness, happiness, and fear (Shaver, Morgan, & Wu, 1996). Maybe love is even good for you, because Aron, Paris, and Aron (1995) found that falling in love leads to an increase in self-efficacy and self-esteem (see Chapter 5). So, what is meant by *love?* When children aged four to eight were asked that question, they gave a variety of answers (Hughes, 2000), some of which appear in Table 8.1. Strangely enough, social psychologists didn't get involved in trying to answer that same question until the latter part of the twentieth century.

The specific details of what love means vary from culture to culture (Beall & Sternberg, 1995), but there is reason to believe that the general phenomenon is a universal one (Hatfield & Rapson, 1993). At the very least, research has shown that love is something more than a simple friendship and more than being romantically or sexually interested in someone. As suggested in the cartoon in Figure 8.13, love contains cognitive components (such as making a commitment) in addition to emotional ones. We will now describe some of what is known about both the cognitive and the emotional aspects of love.

love: A combination of emotions, cognitions, and behaviors that can be involved in intimate relationships.

passionate love: An intense and often unrealistic emotional response to another person. The person experiencing this emotion usually interprets it as "true love," whereas outside observers are more likely to label it as "infatuation."

■ PASSIONATE LOVE. Aron and his colleagues (1989) pointed out that many people fall in love, but no one ever seems to have "fallen in friendship." Unlike attraction, friendship, or even romance, **passionate love** involves an intense and often unre-

TABLE 8.1

The Meaning of Love—In the Words of Children. When a group of children, aged four to eight, were asked the meaning of love, the following were some of their responses. They managed to give some specific examples of the basic components of love that have been identified by social psychologists.

"Love is that first feeling you feel before all the bad stuff gets in the way."
"Love is when a girl puts on perfume and a boy puts on shaving cologne and they go out and smell each other."
"Love is when you go out to eat and give somebody most of your French fries without making them give you any of theirs."
"Love is what makes you smile when you're tired."
"Love is when mommy sees daddy smelly and sweaty and still says he looks like Robert Redford."
"Love is when your puppy licks your face even after you left him alone all day."

[SOURCE: HUGHES, 2000.]

alistic emotional reaction to another person. It often occurs suddenly, as Elaine Hatfield once said, "like slipping on a banana peel." And the experience is described as "falling head over heels in love."

Passionate love usually begins as an instant, overwhelming, surging, all-consuming positive reaction to another person—a reaction that feels as if it's beyond your control, like an unpredictable accident. A person in love is preoccupied with the loved one and can think of little else. The emotion is so intense that merely thinking about a past love can create a positive mood (Clark & Collins, 1993). I (DB) remember first responding in this way to a girl with beautiful red hair who was a fellow fourth-grader (we eventually became good friends in high school) and have

FIGURE 8.13

Love: Making a Commitment. One of the cognitive elements that differentiates love from friendship, a casual romance, or sexual intimacy is that of commitment. As the woman in the cartoon indicates, her partner has to decide whether he is serious about their relationship.

experienced that same reaction several additional times after the fourth grade—including once quite recently.

Meyers and Berscheid (1997) note that sexual attraction is a necessary but not sufficient condition for being in love with another person, and surveys show that college students agree (Regan, 1998). That is, you can be sexually attracted without being in love, but you aren't likely to be in love in the absence of sexual attraction (Regan, 2000). In fact, love makes sex more acceptable, and people are more comfortable about sex if it is romanticized (Goldenberg et al., 1999). For example, it is much more acceptable for two people to "make love" than simply to copulate like animals in heat.

Altogether, passionate love seems to be a mixture of sexual attraction, physiological arousal, a desire to be physically close, and an intense need to be loved as much as you are loved—all of this accompanied by a recurring fear that something may happen to end the relationship. Hatfield and Sprecher (1986b) developed the *Passionate Love Scale* to measure this emotion with items such as "I would feel deep despair if _____ left me" and "For me, _____ is the perfect romantic partner."

You might think it would only happen in the movies, but most people report having had the experience of falling in love with a stranger—love at first sight (Averill & Boothroyd, 1977). Even in a laboratory setting, something like this can occur. When two opposite-sex strangers are asked to gaze into each other's eyes for two minutes or to self-disclose, the result is a mutual feeling of affection (Aron et al., 1997; Kellerman, Lewis, & Laird, 1989). Acts such as gazing and holding hands are most likely to have positive effects on those who strongly believe in romantic phenomena such as love at first sight and the notion that "love conquers all" (Williams & Kleinke, 1993).

It is even possible to love someone who does not love you. This one-way flow of affection is known as **unrequited love,** and it is most common among those with an anxious–ambivalent attachment style (Aron, Aron, & Allen, 1998). In one large survey, about 60 percent of the respondents said that they had had such an experience within the past two years (Bringle & Winnick, 1992). Men, especially in late adolescence and early adulthood, report more instances of unrequited love than women do, and men say they have experienced unrequited love more often than mutual love (Hill, Blakemore, & Drumm, 1997). The individual who loves in vain feels rejected, while the one who fails to respond feels guilty (Baumeister, Wotman, & Stillwell, 1993).

For passionate love to occur, Hatfield and Walster (1981) suggest that three common factors must be in place. First, individuals need to be exposed throughout their lives to romantic images in fairy tales, love songs, and stories about love. In part, such images motivate us to experience similar emotions in our own lives, and they provide a script as to how we should react (Sternberg, 1996). Second, an appropriate love object must be present. "Appropriate" is likely to mean a physically attractive person of the opposite sex—a youthful female or a male with adequate resources—for example, one who is intelligent, educated, and employed (Buss, 1988; Greer & Buss, 1994). Third, based on Schachter's (1964) two-factor theory of emotion, the individual must be in a state of arousal that he or she labels as "love" (Foster et al., 1998). It doesn't matter if the arousal involves fear (Dutton & Aron, 1974), frustration and anger (Driscoll, Davis, & Lipetz, 1972), or sexual excitement (Istvan, Griffitt, & Weidner, 1983) as long as the aroused state is interpreted as an indication of love. In the words of an old Broadway song, "You're not sick, you're just in love."

■ WHY LOVE? It has not been easy to explain why human beings experience love. Love could be only a collective fantasy that many of us share. It could be based on psychoanalytical concepts, as we transfer unconscious lust for a parent into more appropriate channels. It appears, however, that the most accepted explanation today is based on evolutionary factors (Buss & Schmitt, 1993; Fisher, 1992).

Several million years ago, our early hominid ancestors first began to walk in an upright position and forage for whatever food could be carried back to a safe shel-

unrequited love: Love felt by one person for another who does not feel love in return.

ter (Lemonick & Dorfman, 2001). The survival of these ancient humans, and later of *Homo sapiens,* depended on their reproductive success (Buss, 1994). Among many factors, this meant that potential mates had to be sexually attracted and, ideally, willing to invest time and effort in feeding and protecting their offspring. These two important characteristics (lust and commitment) were most likely to occur if biologically based sexual desire were combined with a biologically based tendency to bond with one's mate and with one's children (Rensberger, 1993). With the emotional attachment of bonding, early human male–female pairs were more than simply sex partners. It was an advantage to like and trust one another and to divide up tasks such as hunting, gathering food, and caring for children. According to this scenario, feeling an emotion such as love would enhance reproductive success. As a consequence, today's humans are genetically primed to seek sex, fall in love, and care for offspring. Monogamy may depend in part on brain chemistry (Insel & Carter, 1995), and most young adults expect their relationship to be a monogamous one (Wiederman & Allgeier, 1996).

Keep in mind that even if this evolutionary explanation is totally accurate, cultural influences still have the ability to guide lust and commitment into quite specific and varied forms based on our experiences with fictional presentations, religious teachings, and even the laws enacted by societies (Allgeier & Wiederman, 1994).

■ LOVE MAY BE A MANY-SPLENDORED THING. Though passionate love is a common experience, it is too intense and too overwhelming to be maintained as a permanent state. Love that is based totally on emotion is fragile and is based more on fantasy than on rational details (Wilson & Kraft, 1993).

Other kinds of love *can,* however, be long lasting. Hatfield (1988, p. 205) describes **companionate love** as the "affection we feel for those with whom our lives are deeply entwined." Unlike passionate love, companionate love is based on a very close friendship in which two people are sexually attracted, have a great deal in common, care about each other's well-being, and express mutual liking and respect (Caspi & Herbener, 1990). This is a kind of love that can sustain a relationship over time—even though it does not lend itself quite as easily to songs and movies as does passionate love.

companionate love: Love that is based on friendship, mutual attraction, common interests, mutual respect, and concern for each other's welfare.

Hendrick and Hendrick (1986) extended the conception of love by adding four additional "love styles" to passionate and companionate love, and they constructed a measure of these six styles (see Table 8.2). Research indicates that men tend to endorse both passionate love and game-playing love more than do women, while

TABLE 8.2

Styles of Love. In addition to passionate and companionate (or friendship) love, four additional love styles have been proposed. The six styles are shown here along with their Greek names and sample items from a test designed to measure individual differences in love styles. These different styles represent quite different attitudes about interpersonal relationships.

SIX LOVE STYLES	SAMPLE TEST ITEMS THAT INDICATE ONE'S STYLE
Eros: Passionate love	My lover and I were attracted to each other immediately after we first met.
Storge: Friendship or companionate love	Love is really a deep friendship, not a mysterious, mystical emotion.
Ludus: Game-playing love	I have sometimes had to keep two of my lovers from finding out about each other.
Mania: Possessive love	I cannot relax if I suspect that my lover is with someone else.
Pragma: Logical love	It is best to love someone with a similar background.
Agape: Selfless love	I would rather suffer myself than let my lover suffer.

[SOURCE: BASED ON MATERIAL FROM HENDRICK & HENDRICK, 1986.]

women favor companionate love, logical love, and possessive love more than do men (Hendrick et al., 1984). Women who endorse possessive love report high levels of verbal and physical aggression in their dating relationships (Bookwala, Frieze, & Grote, 1994). Game-playing love is most characteristic of those who are concerned with themselves and their own independence (Dion & Dion, 1991). A game-playing style leads to multiple sexual partners, unhappy relationships, loneliness, and coercive sexual behavior (Hensley, 1996; Kalichman et al., 1993; Rotenberg & Korol, 1995). Very religious individuals are likely to be highest in friendship, logical, and selfless love (Hendrick & Hendrick, 1987). And, in general, people express a preference for those whose love style is similar to their own (Morrow, Clark, & Brock, 1995), though there is agreement that companionate love and selfless love are the most desirable and game-playing love the least desirable (Hahn & Blass, 1997).

Cultural differences in love styles are also found. For example, Chinese residents in Hong Kong stress the importance of *yuan,* the belief that love is predestined and a matter of fate. In other words, love is a matter of external forces beyond one's control; two people fall in love because it is "written in the stars." Belief in yuan is rare among Westerners, and it is associated with logical and selfless love (Goodwin & Findlay, 1997).

triangular model of love: Sternberg's conceptualization of love relationships as encompassing three basic components: intimacy, passion, and decision/commitment.

Still another major conceptualization of love is Sternberg's (1986, 1988a, 1988b) **triangular model of love,** which is depicted in Figure 8.14. This formulation sug-

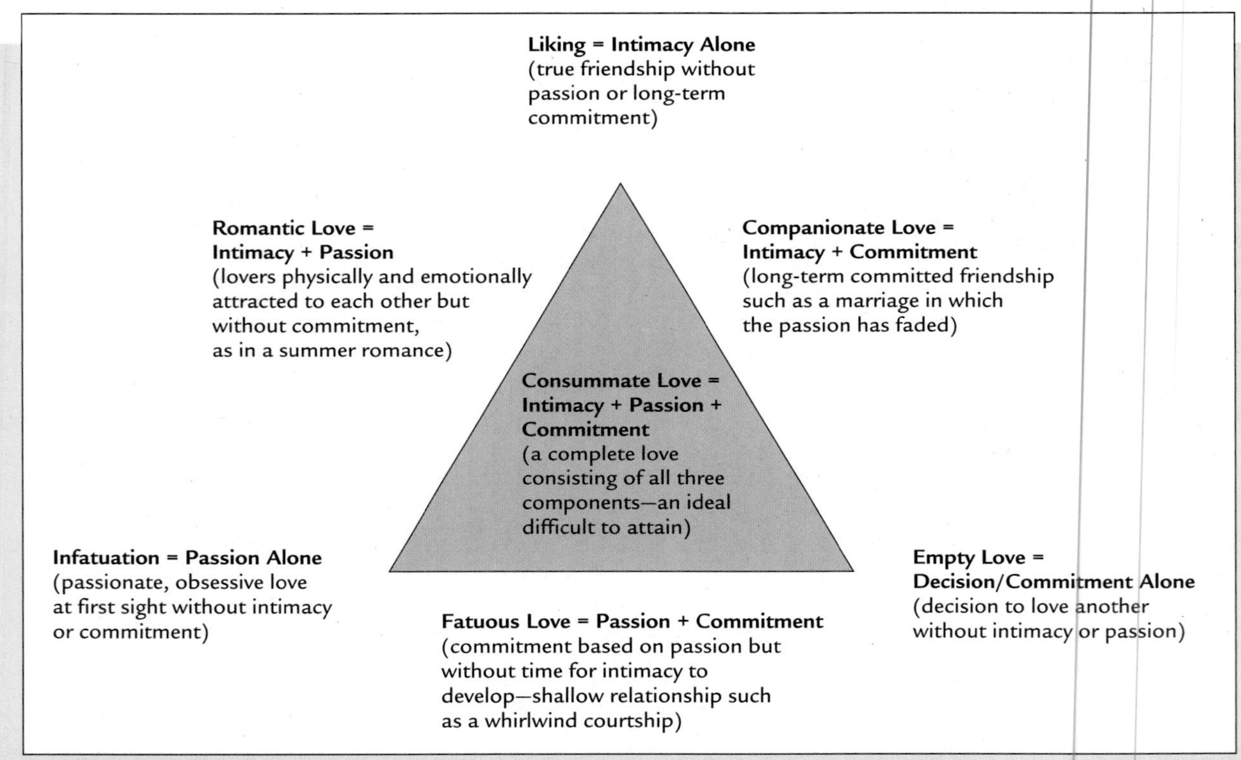

FIGURE 8.14

Sternberg's Triangular Model of Love.
Sternberg proposes a triangular model of love with three basic components: *intimacy, passion*, and *decision/commitment*. Love can be based primarily on any one of these three components, on a combination of any two of them, or on all three. As shown in the figure, these various possibilities yield seven types of relationship, with the ideal (*consummate love*) consisting of all three basic components included equally.

gests that each love relationship contains three basic components that are present in varying degrees for different couples (Aron & Westbay, 1996). One component is **intimacy**—the closeness two people feel and the strength of the bond that holds them together. Intimacy is essentially companionate love. Partners high in intimacy are concerned with each other's welfare and happiness, and they value, like, count on, and understand one another. The second component, **passion,** is based on romance, physical attraction, and sexuality—in other words, passionate love. Men are more likely to stress this component than are women (Fehr & Broughton, 2001). The third component suggests a new element: **Decision/commitment** represents cognitive factors such as the decision that you love and want to be with the other person plus a commitment to maintain the relationship. Actual lovers subjectively experience these three components as overlapping and related aspects of love, but any given relationship may be characterized primarily by one component or by two components—as suggested in Figure 8.14. When all three corners of the triangle are equally strong and balanced, the result is **consummate love**; this is defined as the ideal form of love, but one that is difficult to attain.

Though the effects of physical attractiveness on attraction are well documented (see Chapter 7), its importance in love and romance has been somewhat neglected. In Spain, almost two thousand individuals ranging in age from eighteen to sixty-four were asked questions about physical attractiveness, falling in love, and each of the components of Sternberg's model (Sangrador & Yela, 2000). The findings suggest that appearance is an important aspect not only of passion, but also of intimacy and decision/commitment. And attractiveness was important both at the early stages of a relationship and at the later stages, including degree of satisfaction with the relationship. In the words of these Spanish psychologists, "What is beautiful is loved." Such findings are a bit unsettling, but the investigators suggest that we should at least acknowledge the continuing influence of physical attractiveness on relationships or make an attempt to reduce that influence—or both.

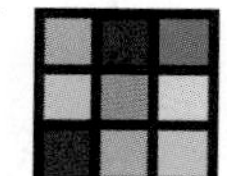

Now that we have discussed the many varieties of love, you may find it useful to consider some of the love-related issues that are raised in the **Ideas to Take with You—And Use!** section on page 342.

Sexuality in Romantic Relationships

Religious and legal sanctions against premarital sex have a long history in many cultures, but dramatic changes in attitudes about sex and in sexual behavior took place during the twentieth century. Attitudes about sexuality became increasingly permissive, and sexual interactions became a common and widely accepted component of romantic relationships in much of the world.

■ CHANGES IN SEXUAL ATTITUDES AND BEHAVIOR. Surveys taken before and after World War II provide evidence of a major shift toward sexual permissiveness, especially in the United States, Canada, Europe, and Australia. In the late 1940s, even the statistical tables summarizing the survey findings of Alfred Kinsey and his colleagues were denounced as an unacceptable attack on the moral values that held society together (Jones, 1997). Twenty years later, changes in views about sexuality had been sufficiently dramatic and pervasive that they were characterized as a "sexual revolution" of the 1960s (see Figure 8.15). As just one example of the changes, in the first half of that century, oral sex was considered both a psychological perversion and (in many states of the U.S.) a criminal act. By the 1970s, most American men and women reported that they frequently engaged in oral sex and enjoyed it (Michael et al., 1994). More recently, perhaps influenced by the words of President Clinton, not all college undergraduates even define such activity as "having sex" (Bogart et al., 2000).

intimacy: In Sternberg's triangular model of love, the closeness felt by two partners—the extent to which they are bonded.

passion: In Sternberg's triangular model of love, the sexual motives and sexual excitement associated with a couple's relationship.

decision/commitment: In Sternberg's triangular model of love, the cognitive elements involved in the decision that you love the other person and the commitment to maintain the relationship.

consummate love: In Sternberg's triangular model of love, a complete and ideal love that combines intimacy, passion, and decision/commitment.

FIGURE 8.15
Sexual Revolution: The Times Were a-Changin'. In the 1960s and 1970s in the United States, protests against the war in Vietnam, experiments with illegal drugs, a new kind of music, and the cause of sexual freedom combined into a collective criticism of the status quo. Among the lasting legacies of that period was sexual liberation. At the very least, sexual attitudes shifted toward greater permissiveness and tolerance. ■

Though the 1950s are often portrayed as the last decade of sexual innocence in the United States, that was actually the time when premarital sex became an increasingly common experience for couples in a relationship (Coontz, 1992). By the 1980s, only 17 percent of American college students reported *not* having had intercourse (Christopher & Cate, 1985). The average age of first intercourse has dropped since 1970 and is now seventeen for girls and sixteen for boys (Stodghill, 1998). As of the 1990s, only 5 percent of the women and 2 percent of the men in the United States reported having intercourse for the first time on their wedding night (Laumann et al., 1994; Michael et al., 1994).

One of the possible explanations for changes in sexual attitudes and behavior lies in the messages provided by the media. On the TV shows most popular with adolescents, talking about sex and engaging in sex is extremely common, and intercourse is depicted or strongly implied in one of every eight television programs (Kunkel, Cope, & Biely, 1999). Soap operas often have sexual story lines featuring sexual intercourse among unmarried partners, and such content has increased over time (Greenberg & Woods, 1999). And research indicates that the sexual content of such shows is found to affect adolescents' sexual attitudes, expectations, and behavior (Ward & Rivadeneyra, 1999).

There is not, of course, perfect uniformity in sexuality. People differ a great deal in their sexual knowledge, attitudes, and practices. Attitudes about sexual issues range from extremely positive and permissive—*erotophilic*—to extremely negative and restrictive—*erotophobic* (Byrne, 1997; Fisher & Barak, 1991), and males tend to be more erotophilic than females. Behavioral differences are equally varied. For example, Simpson and Gangestad (1991, 1992) describe a dispositional continuum of *sociosexuality.* At one end of the continuum are people (predominantly male) who express an *unrestricted sociosexual orientation* in which the members of the opposite sex are sought simply as sexual partners without any need for closeness, commitment, or emotional bonding. At the other end of this dimension are individuals (predominantly female) who express a *restricted sociosexual orientation* in which a sexual relationship is acceptable only when accompanied by affection and tenderness. For both males and females, a secure attachment style is associated with restricted sociosexuality (Brennan & Shaver, 1995).

Though gender differences in the incidence of sexual behavior have essentially disappeared (Breakwell & Fife-Schaw, 1992; Weinberg, Lottes, & Shaver, 1995), they nevertheless differ, as we have noted, in erotophilic attitudes and in sociosexual restrictiveness. Men still play a traditional role as the ones who initiate sexual activity (O'Sullivan & Byers, 1992). College men and women also differ with respect to how long one must know another person before it is acceptable to engage in intercourse. As depicted in Figure 8.16, men are more willing than women to have sex with someone they've known for a day or less, but women prefer to know someone for a longer time period before becoming intimate (Buss & Schmitt, 1993). Casual sex is still part of college life, and the term *hookup* is applied to a brief sexual encounter between two people who are strangers or brief acquaintances. In one study, approximately one of three students reported having experienced a hookup, most often when intoxicated with a partner who adopts a game-playing love style (Paul, McManus, & Hayes, 2000).

■ IS THE SEXUAL REVOLUTION OVER? Though the "flower children" of the late 1960s and early 1970s had high hopes that the world would become a better place when people chose to "make love, not war," warning signs of a backlash began to appear

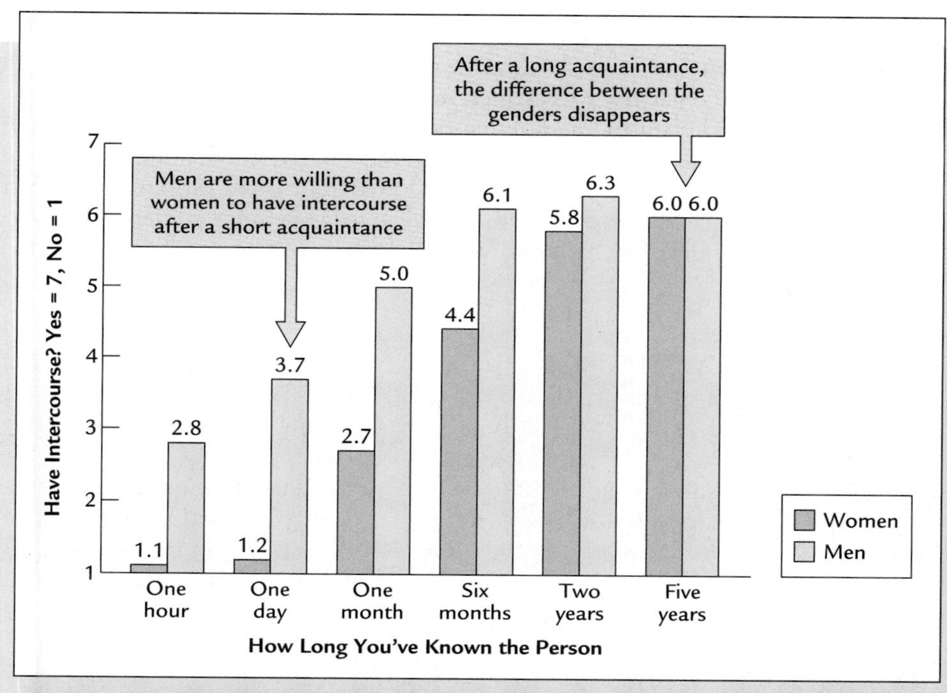

FIGURE 8.16

After What Time Period Is Sex Appropriate: Gender Differences.

College students were asked, "If the conditions were right, would you consider having sexual intercourse with someone you viewed as desirable if you had known that person for one hour?" "One day?" (And so on, up to five years.) The respondents answered on a seven-point scale ranging from "definitely not" to "definitely yes." While both men and women were more likely to say yes as the time period increased, men more than women say yes to sex at every acquaintance level up through two years. At the five-year point, gender differences disappear.

[SOURCE: BASED ON DATA FROM BUSS & SCHMITT, 1993.]

by the end of that time period. It seemed that permissive sexuality was not the all-purpose solution to political problems or even problems associated with love and relationships.

For one thing, many people came to the realization that engaging in sex was not necessarily a personal decision. Sex wasn't always an enjoyable expression of freedom so much as a matter of conforming to social pressure (see Chapter 9). Anyone who abstained was likely to be characterized as uptight, repressed, and out of it (DeLamater, 1981). Many women reported that they felt vulnerable, guilty, and exploited (Townsend, 1995; Weis, 1983).

In addition to these subjective concerns, the 1980s and 1990s brought heightened awareness of two very serious potential consequences of indiscriminate sex. Casual sex was not just fun and games but an activity that could result in *unwanted pregnancies* and/or *sexually transmitted diseases* or *STDs* (see Figure 8.17).

Unintended, unwanted, and unwise pregnancies sounded the first alarm. A surprisingly large proportion of sexually active teenagers and young adults failed to use effective contraceptives or used them inconsistently, in part because obtaining, using, and even talking about contraceptives was seen as both nonspontaneous and embarrassing (Buysse & Ickes, 1999; Byrne & Fisher, 1983). In addition, men said that proposing condom use diminished the chance of the woman agreeing to have sexual intercourse (Bryan, Aiken, & West, 1999). Alcohol and other drugs played a role, because they reduce the fear of taking risks (Murphy, Monahan, & Miller, 1998). Even the physical attractiveness of the partner had an influence. Both men and women said they were less likely to discuss the risk of unprotected sex if the partner was attractive, and men even perceived an attractive partner as less risky than an unattractive one (Agocha & Cooper, 1999). The combination of casual sex and casual contraception in the 1970s resulted in more than one million teenage pregnancies each year in the United States, and similar data were reported in many other countries as well. This *teenage pregnancy epidemic* became an acute source of stress for the individuals directly involved and for society at large.

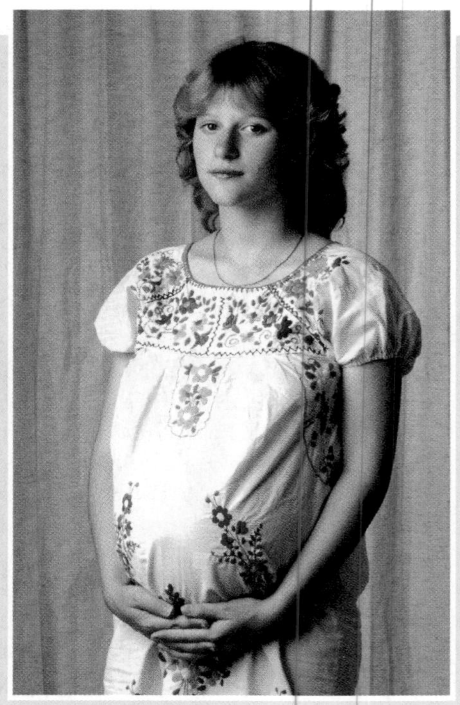

FIGURE 8.17

The Dark Consequences of the Sexual Revolution. Increased sexual permissiveness and greater sexual freedom were found to have negative consequences. The Age of Aquarius began to seem less bright and hopeful in light of the reality of unwanted pregnancies and HIV infections that are likely to develop into AIDS.

Sexually transmitted disease constituted the second negative consequence of the new sexual freedom. The familiar, treatable infections such as syphilis, gonorrhea, genital herpes, and chlamydia were serious enough. These STDs were soon followed, however, by a viral disease for which no cure is yet available—HIV (human immunodeficiency virus) infection, which can develop into AIDS (acquired immuno deficiency syndrome). AIDS is a painful, wasting disease that is fatal. Medical evidence indicates that the disease first spread from apes to humans as early as the seventeenth century, but only in the 1980s did it suddenly burst on the world scene as an epidemic (Boyce, 2001). At first, the disease seemed limited to the "four H's"—homosexuals, Haitians, hemophiliacs, and heroin users—but it soon was learned that the risk was a general one (Boyce, 2001).

Women who are sexually intimate with only one male partner are not safe from acquiring these diseases. For example, in the United States, about three and a half million women are at risk of contracting STDs because they mistakenly believe they are in a monogamous relationship, when, in fact, their partners are being unfaithful (Lowy, 1999).

The realization of the problems of unwanted pregnancy and incurable diseases did not have an immediate effect on sexual practices. One explanation for this is that young people often view such threats as not personally relevant. There is a general tendency to believe in one's invulnerability to diseases and accidents (Buzwell & Rosenthal, 1995; Rosenthal & Shepherd, 1993). I (DB) will illustrate with a nonsexual example. With each of my four offspring, I remember numerous instances in which the interchange went something like this: "Don't climb on those rocks, you might fall." "I didn't fall." "But you might." "No, I won't." It is very comforting, though incorrect, to believe that it hasn't happened to me, and it won't happen to me because it can't happen to me. Unfortunately, it can and it might. As we discussed in Chapter 4, it is very difficult to bring about attitudinal and behavioral change, even with adults.

In time, however, the reality of words like *epidemic* became difficult to ignore. The impetus for change was aided by public service campaigns (Middlestadt et al., 1995) and a focus on the impact of unwanted pregnancy or a fatal disease on specific individuals—both real and fictional. In the United States, we seem to have experienced the peak in both respects and to be moving slowly toward improvement.

For example, teen births in the United States have dropped to a record low (Schmid, 2001), and a report from the Centers for Disease Control and Prevention indicates a 20 percent drop in teen pregnancy from its all-time high in 1991 (Bjerklie, 2001). According to the U.S. Department of Health and Human Services, the most dramatic decline in pregnancies has been among African American teens aged fifteen to seventeen, with a 30 percent decrease over the past decade (Song, 2000). The explanation for the decline appears to be not less sexual activity, but more consistent and more effective contraception (Dickinson, 1999).

With respect to HIV infections and AIDS, the news contains a few bright spots, but the prospect for improvement is much less hopeful. To date, the "deadliest microbe in the world" has killed more than fifteen million people, and forty million more have the viral infection that will slowly destroy their immune systems (Ho, 1999). New drugs have helped prolong life, and, presumably because of changes in sexual practices, the incidence of HIV infections has actually *decreased* in Australia, New Zealand, and Western Europe. There is, however, explosive growth of the infection in Sub-Saharan Africa, Eastern Europe, China, the Caribbean, and the islands of the Pacific (Altman, 1998b; Fang, 2001; The spread of . . . , 1999). The rate of growth in the United States is less than 1 percent, but the figure is at least ten times higher than this among the poor, minority groups, gay men, and teenage women in the fifteen to nineteen age group (A really scary . . . , 2001; Brown, 2001; Ho, 1999; Numbers, 2000; Okie, 2001).

KEY POINTS

- One defining characteristic of romantic relationships is some degree of physical intimacy, ranging from holding hands to sexual interactions.
- As is true for attraction and friendship, romantic attraction is influenced by factors such as physical proximity, appearance, and similarity. In addition, romance includes sexual attraction, the desire for total acceptance by the other person, and a degree of fantasy based on positive illusions.
- *Love* involves multiple possibilities. For example, *passionate love* is a sudden, overwhelming emotional response. *Companionate love,* in contrast, is more like a close friendship that includes caring, mutual liking, and respect.
- Besides passionate and companionate love, Hendrick and Hendrick add four other "love styles," and Sternberg conceptualizes love in terms of a triangle, with the three corners representing companionate love, passionate love, and *decision/commitment.*
- Widespread changes in sexual attitudes and sexual practices were labeled the "sexual revolution" of the 1960s and 1970s. The lasting result has been greater permissiveness with respect to all aspects of sexuality. One consequence is that premarital sex has become the norm.
- The most dramatic consequences of this newfound sexual freedom were unwanted pregnancies and incurable STDs such as HIV and AIDS. Recent attitudinal and behavioral changes appear to be having a positive effect on teenage pregnancies, but the AIDS epidemic continues to expand rapidly in many parts of the world as well as in specific segments of the U.S. population.

Marriage: The Ultimate Close Relationship

As you might expect, all of the factors that have been discussed with respect to attraction, friendship, romance, love, and sex are also relevant to the selection of a marital partner (for example, similarity, personality dispositions, and illusions). New issues have also become relevant, including such challenges as dealing with economic issues, parenthood, and careers plus the very difficult task of maintaining a long-term relationship.

Marital Success and Marital Satisfaction: Similarity, Assumed Similarity, Personality, and Sex

Given the fact that most people do get married and that half or more of these marriages fail, it would be beneficial to all of us to know as much as possible about the factors that differentiate successful and unsuccessful couples (see Figure 8.18). Some of the negative factors develop over time in response to the stresses of a long-term relationship, and we will discuss them shortly. Other predictive factors, however, are present at the beginning and could served as warning signs.

SIMILARITY AND ASSUMED SIMILARITY. Not surprisingly, a century of research has indicated consistently that spouses are similar in their attitudes, values, interests, and other attributes (Pearson & Lee, 1903; Terman & Buttenwieser, 1935a, 1935b; Smith et al., 1993). Further, a longitudinal study of couples from the time they became engaged through twenty years of marriage indicated very little change in the degree of similarity over time (Caspi, Herbener, & Ozer, 1992). In other words,

FIGURE 8.18
Predicting Whether They Will or Won't Live Happily Ever After.
More than half of all marriages fail, and often the problems develop slowly over time as the result of events that change the relationship. To some extent, however, factors present at the very beginning of the marriage predict success versus failure.

similar people marry, and the similarity neither increases nor decreases as the years pass. Because greater similarity is associated with a positive relationship (Acitelli, Kenny, & Weiner, 2001; Nemechek & Olson, 1999), a couple contemplating marriage might do well to think beyond physical attractiveness and sex in order to look closely at their similarities and dissimilarities.

Not only do similar people marry, but a positive relationship is also characterized by **assumed similarity.** Spouses tend to assume greater similarity than is actually the case (Byrne & Blaylock, 1963; Schul & Vinokur, 2000), and marital satisfaction is positively related to both similarity and assumed similarity.

Are similarity and assumed similarity equally strong in other kinds of relationships? Watson, Hubbard, and Wiese (2000) answered this question by comparing married couples, dating couples, and friendship pairs with respect to the Big Five Personality Dispositions and for measures of positive and negative affect. The pairs of individuals in each type of relationship were more similar than chance, but the spouses were more similar than were the dating couples or friends. Assumed similarity, however, was highest in the dating couples, perhaps reflecting the romantic illusions we discussed earlier. Friends and spouses were slightly more realistic. If married couples indicate more actual similarity and less assumed similarity than is true for dating couples, this suggests that many couples are making relatively wise and realistic decisions before deciding on marriage. It is also true that two people who are committed to a relationship tend to shift their attitudes toward greater similarity (Davis & Rusbult, 2001).

A few decades ago, some women began retaining their own surnames or adopting a hyphenated last name (Helms, 2001). Because this break with tradition coincided with the rising divorce rate, some suggested there might be a causal connection. In fact, marital success is unaffected by whether the woman's surname is her own, her husband's, or a hyphenated combination (Kline, Stafford, & Miklosovic, 1996).

■ PERSONALITY FACTORS. Similarity is not everything. It is also found that specific personality dispositions are related to marital success. In other words, some people are more likely to have positive relationships than others.

In some instances, a given person's particular needs can best be met *not* by a similar spouse, but by one who is able to satisfy those needs. As an extreme example,

assumed similarity: The extent to which two people believe they are similar in certain respects, as opposed to the extent to which they are actually similar.

consider **narcissism,** a personality disposition that goes beyond high self-esteem. The extreme narcissist feels superior to most people, seeks admiration, is sensitive to criticism, lacks empathy for others, and is exploitative (American Psychiatric Association, 1994). This kind of person would not seem to be a very good marital bet because what she or he seeks in an ideal partner is someone who is highly positive and admiring rather than someone similar to themselves or even someone who offers emotional intimacy (Campbell, 1999). In effect, the narcissist wants praise, *not* another narcissist and *not* a sense of closeness.

Other personality characteristics that appear to be crucial are those associated with interpersonal behavior and attachment styles. For example, individuals with negative self models (preoccupied and fearful–avoidant styles), compared to those with positive self models (secure and dismissing), find themselves in less satisfying relationships because they underestimate how much they are loved by their partners (Murray et al., 2001). Thus, insecurity leads to misperception, and, based on the misperception, there is a less positive evaluation of the partner and of the relationship, as well as less optimism about the future. Over time, the vulnerability of those with low self-esteem gets worse rather than better (Murray, Holmes, & Griffin, 2000).

Other personality characteristics, such as anxiety, negative affect, and neuroticism (measured when the spouses were newlyweds), have been found to be associated with interpersonal negativity in a marriage and a partner's subsequent dissatisfaction at various points in the marriage (Huston et al., 2001) (see Figure 8.19). Data indicate that the negative characteristics present when the marriage began predicted marital happiness over the subsequent thirteen years of marriage (Caughlin, Huston, & Houts, 2000).

Such longitudinal research suggests that negative affectivity results in disillusionment over time as love fades, overt affection declines, and ambivalence increases. Consistent with these findings, people are happiest with a relationship in which the partner tends *not* to express negative emotions such as fear, anxiety, and anger (Robins, Caspi, & Moffitt, 2000). When a partner behaves badly (for example, being inconsiderate or yelling at the other person), the most common reaction is to criticize the lack of consideration or to yell back. For the sake of the relationship, however, it is best to resist the impulse to respond destructively. That kind of accommodation requires a great deal of self-control, more than some of us can muster (Finkel & Campbell, 2001). As we stressed in Chapter 7, positive interpersonal evaluations of another person are based on positive emotions associated with that person. It appears that a negative spouse can easily create a negative relationship.

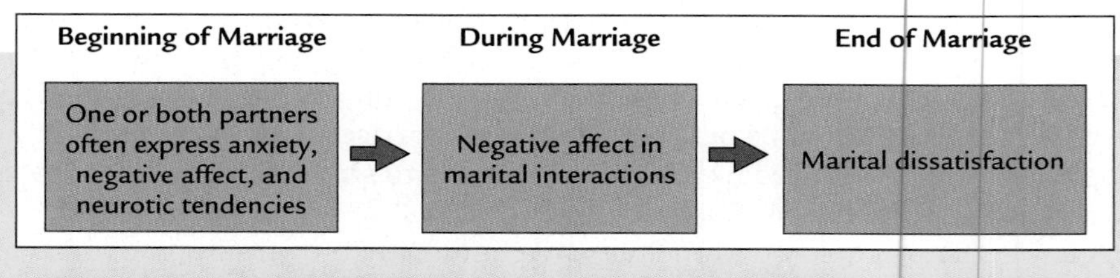

FIGURE 8.19

Negative Affectivity and Marital Dissatisfaction.
Some factors present at the time of a wedding predict later negative interactions and marital dissatisfaction. For example, when one or both spouses are disposed to behave in ways that indicate anxiety, negative affect, and neurotic behavior, the result is repeated negative marital interactions. Over time, the continued negative affect leads to dissatisfaction with the marriage.

[SOURCE: BASED ON INFORMATION IN CAUGHLIN, HUSTON, & HOUTS, 2000; HUSTON ET AL., 2001.]

narcissism: A personality disposition in which the individual goes beyond high self-esteem, and also feels superior to most people, seeks admiration, is sensitive to criticism, lacks empathy for others, and is exploitative.

■ MARITAL SEX. Surveys of married couples reveal that sexual interactions become less frequent over time, and that the most rapid decline occurs during the first four years of marriage (Udry, 1980). Still, 41 percent of all married couples have sex twice a week or more often, whereas only 23 percent of single individuals have sex that frequently.

The most sexually active couples are those who are living together but not married (*cohabiting*)—56 percent have sex at least twice a week (Laumann et al., 1994; Michael et al., 1994). According to the latest U.S. census, the number of cohabiting couples has nearly doubled—from 3.1 million couples during the 1990s to 5.5 million by 2000 (Schmitt, E., 2001). Because this pattern is increasingly common, it is reasonable to ask whether the experience of living together has any effect on later marriages. Despite the hopes of some that living together as a couple will lead to more realistic expectations concerning marriage, and the fears of others that such behavior will destroy the family, research indicates little or no effect of premarital sexual experiences on subsequent relationships. That is, premarital intercourse, including cohabitation, has no effect on the likelihood of marriage, no effect on marital satisfaction, and no effect on marital success or failure (Cunningham & Antill, 1994; Markman, 1981).

Marital Love, Careers, Parenthood, and the Changing Composition of Families

The reality of marriage entails much more than falling in love, having a wedding ceremony, and then experiencing unending bliss. After the honeymoon, two people must interact on a daily basis and find ways to deal with a multitude of challenges, such as deciding how to share household chores, dealing with the ups and downs of daily life, and meeting the demands of an outside job (or jobs). In addition, economic concerns (Conger, Rueter, & Elder, 1999), the stresses of parenthood (Kurdek, 1999), and nontraditional family composition can add unexpected complications. What do we know about the effects of such factors on marital satisfaction? A longitudinal study of over five hundred couples suggests that the quality of their relationship began declining shortly after they said, "I do" (Kurdek, 1999). Based on such data, you might ask, "Is marriage worth it?"

■ IS BEING MARRIED BETTER THAN BEING SINGLE? More people are remaining single than ever before, but singles still represent only about 10 percent of the population, according to U.S. Census data (Edwards, 2000; Households, 2001). The overwhelming majority of adults want to get married, and do get married—women at age twenty-five, men at age twenty-seven (Frazier et al., 1996; People, 2001).

Compared to single individuals, those who are married consistently report being happier and healthier (Steinhauer, 1995). In Norway, married people, compared to those who are single, report a greater sense of well-being and have a lower suicide rate—at least until they reach their late thirties; after that, the advantages of being married begin to disappear (Mastekaasa, 1995).

■ LOVE AND MARRIAGE. Usually, passionate love decreases over the years of a marriage (Tucker & Aron, 1993). Those women who continue to feel such love toward their husbands, however, express more satisfaction with their marriages than women who do not. Male satisfaction in a marriage, however, is unrelated to passionate love (Aron & Henkemeyer, 1995). For both men and women, satisfaction is related to behavior that suggests companionate love—sharing activities, exchanging ideas, laughing together, and working together on projects. Altogether, companionate love seems to be the key ingredient in a happy marriage, but women are even happier if they also continue to feel the spark of passionate love.

■ WORK INSIDE AND OUTSIDE THE HOME. As discussed in Chapter 5, husbands do 71 percent of the household repairs, but women do 75 percent of the cooking and 70 percent of the household cleaning, even when they have an active career (Yu, 1996).

Perceived unfairness in the division of chores is associated with marital conflict and dissatisfaction (Grote & Clark, 2001). In fact, compared with heterosexual and gay couples, only Lesbian partners seem to be able to share household labor in a fair and equitable manner (Kurdek, 1993).

Any married individual who is employed faces a potential conflict between the motivation to do a good job at work and the motivation to engage in family activities (Senecal, Vallerand, & Guay, 2001). These two motivations can easily lead to conflict, alienation, and eventually to emotional exhaustion. The conflicts between work and family affect both men and women and can lead to dissatisfaction with one's job and also with one's life (Perrewe & Hochwarter, 2001). If both spouses work outside of the home, the potential for conflict becomes even more intense. A major task for two employed spouses is to discover how best to adjust to the demands of a two-career family (Gilbert, 1993), and there seem to be no easy answers.

It is sometimes assumed that a couple's sexual relationship suffers if an outside job is too demanding, especially if the wife is employed outside of the home. In fact, however, surveys of over 1,700 married participants indicated that employment—either part time or full time—had no effect on the sexual functioning of the participants (Hyde, DeLamater, & Durik, 2001).

■ PARENTHOOD. Some form of caregiving and attachment to one's offspring is characteristic of all mammals, and even of mammal-like reptiles, beginning about 240 million years ago. Bell (2001) suggests that evolution has produced a neurobiological basis for the emotional attraction of parents to their children that goes beyond logic or other cognitive considerations.

Despite these biological pressures that encourage having offspring, becoming a parent can interfere with marital sexuality and also create a variety of other problems in the relationship (Alexander & Higgins, 1993; Hackel & Ruble, 1992). Parenthood is often found to be associated with a decline in marital satisfaction, but this negative effect is less if the couple has a strong, companionate relationship (Shapiro & Gottman, 2000). Not surprisingly, men and women with secure adult attachment styles are found to be best able to cope with the stresses created by the transition to parenthood (Alexander et al., 2001), and secure women express the most positive feelings about motherhood (Berant, Mikulincer, & Florian, 2001).

Despite the problems that children bring to the marriage, parents consistently report that they are very glad they have children (Feldman & Nash, 1984). It is possible, of course, that dissonance reduction is operating—if you have offspring, you may tend to convince yourself that parenthood is worthwhile. As the number of children increases, women report less satisfaction with the marriage, and men report more (Grote, Frieze, & Stone, 1996). One reason for the gender difference is that women spend more time taking care of the child or children (Bjorklund & Shackelford, 1999). With the increasing numbers of two-career families, parents (especially mothers) spend an average of twenty-two fewer hours with their children each week than they did in 1969 (137 hours then versus 160 now), and much of that change is due to women working outside of the home (Levy, 1999b).

The problem of unequal male–female participation in child rearing decreases when couples actively strive to share parenting on an equal basis (Deutsch, 2001). Sharing becomes more difficult as the number of children increases, so another solution to the problem is to have fewer children. For a variety of reasons, the trend toward smaller families has been the norm for some time. According to U.S. Census data, one out of three American couples who are starting their families now plan to have only one child (Levy, 1999a). Extrapolating, the future norm is expected to be one-child families.

Despite the problems, most people say that they want to have children, and outsiders assume that men and women who remain childless are relatively less warm, kind, and caring than those who become parents (LaMastro, 2001). It seems that parenthood is a desired goal, and the absence of children is attributed to personal failings.

■ CHANGES IN FAMILY COMPOSITION. When we speak of marriage, parenthood, and families, many of us have an idealized image of a traditional household, such as that represented by the TV shows *Leave It to Beaver* and *Ozzie and Harriet.* Today, however, families take many forms.

Is "married with children" the norm in the United States? The answer is *no,* and it hasn't been the norm for several decades. In the early 1970s, only 45 percent of American families consisted of a married couple and their offspring, and that figure had dropped to 23.5 percent by the end of the century (Irvine, 1999; Schmitt, E., 2001). Comparing U.S. Census Bureau figures for 1990 and 2000, the greatest increase has been in the number of households consisting of a single mother. Single-mother families grew five times faster in the 1990s than did the number of married-couple families (Schmitt, 2001).

In addition to single-parent households, there has also been an increase in the number of remarriages in which the wife, the husband, or both have offspring from a previous marriage; the number of cohabiting couples who become parents; and the number of gay and Lesbian couples with children (either adopted or the offspring of one of the partners) (McLaughlin, 2001a; Stacy & Biblarz, 2001). We don't yet know the possible ramifications of these quite different family arrangements either for the adults or for their children.

Relationship Problems, Reactions to the Problems and the Effects of Relationship Failure

People usually enter marriage with high hopes, and they tend to be quite optimistic about their chances of marital success. Though more than half of the marriages in the United States end in divorce, unmarried respondents and those married more than ten years estimate for themselves only about a 10 or 11 percent likelihood of a future divorce. In fact, for people getting married now, the divorce rate is expected to be about 64 percent (Fowers et al., 2001). This is not a unique American problem; for example, the divorce rate in Japan jumped 55 percent between 1990 and 2000 (Bright, 2000).

The optimism that most married couples feel is easy to explain—our earlier discussion of love and romance described the way that fantasies and positive illusions strongly influence our ideas. A more puzzling issue is why most couples fail to succeed at marriage, no matter how optimistic they may be.

■ PROBLEMS BETWEEN SPOUSES. What happens to transform a loving romantic relationship into one characterized by unhappiness, dissatisfaction, and—often—hate? One problem is the need to understand the reality of a relationship. That is, no spouse (including oneself) is perfect. No matter how ideal the other person may have seemed, one eventually realizes that he or she has negative as well as positive qualities. For example, the discovery that the *actual* similarity between spouses is less than the *assumed* similarity can be a disappointment (Sillars et al., 1994). And negative personal characteristics become less tolerable over time. Even characteristics that once seemed to be cute and "different" can come to seem annoying and unlikable (Felmlee, 1995; Pines, 1997). Felmlee's (1998) research suggests that if you are initially drawn to someone because that person is very different from yourself or even unique, chances are good that disenchantment will eventually set in.

Some marital problems are universal, because being in any kind of close relationship involves a degree of compromise. By yourself, you can do as you wish. When two people live together, however, they must jointly decide what to eat for dinner, who prepares it, and when to serve it. Similar decisions must be made about whether to watch TV and which program to watch, whether to wash the dishes or let them wait until the next day, where to set the thermostat, whether to have sex right now or at some other time—along with hundreds of other major and minor decisions. The necessity of considering the needs of both partners means that there is an inevitable conflict between the desire for independence and the need for closeness (Baxter, 1990). As a consequence, 98.8 percent of those who are married report they have disagreements, and most indicate that conflicts arise once a month or more often (McGonagle, Kessler, & Schilling, 1992).

communal behavior: Benevolent acts in a relationship that "cost" the one who performs those acts and benefit the partner and the relationship itself.

It is possible to conceptualize many of the interactions in a marriage in terms of costs and benefits. Presumably, the greater the number of benefits relative to the number of costs, the higher the quality of the relationship. Clark and Grote (1998) identified several types of costs and benefits, some of which are intentionally positive or negative and some of which are unintentional. Still other costs involve voluntary decisions to engage in difficult or undesired behavior in order to meet the needs of one's partner. The latter acts constitute **communal behavior**—a "cost" for one individual that actually benefits the partner as well as the relationship. Examples of the various types of costs and benefits are shown in Figure 8.20.

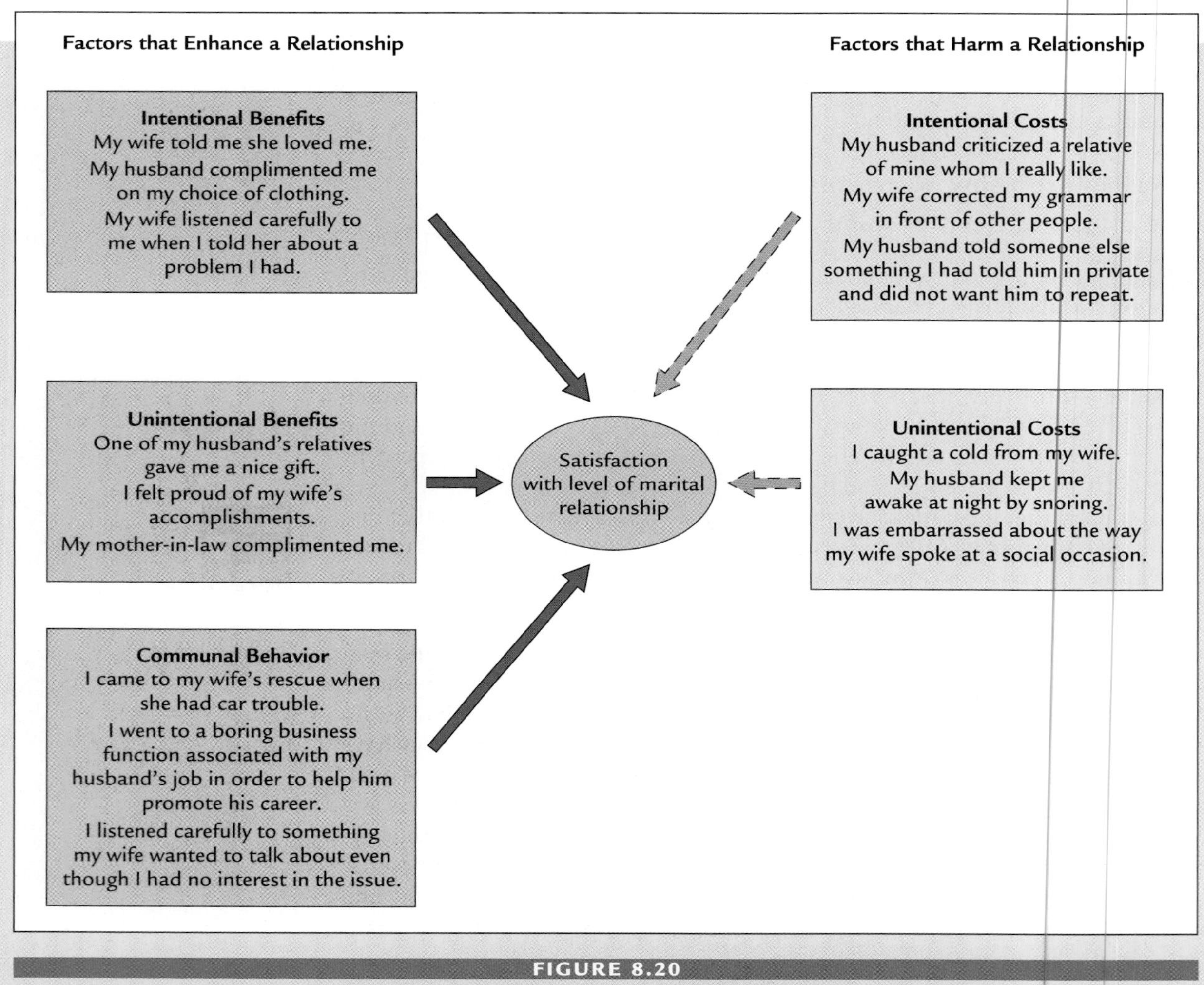

FIGURE 8.20

Costs and Benefits of a Marital Relationship.

Relationship success and failure can be conceptualized as the result of the costs and benefits involved. Shown here are some representative intentional and unintentional costs and benefits. In addition, there is *communal behavior*, which represents a "cost" to the one engaging in the behavior but a benefit to the partner and to the relationship itself. Marital satisfaction depends on the relative number of costs and benefits that spouses experience in the marriage.

[SOURCE: BASED ON INFORMATION IN CLARK & GROTE, 1998.]

In addition to dissimilarities and disagreements, costs and benefits, additional challenges are inevitable. We have already discussed conflicts between the workplace and home and the stresses of parenthood. In addition, people may become ill, have accidents, lose their jobs, develop chronic physical or emotional disorders, experience jealousy (Buss et al., 1992; Buunk, 1995; Dijkstra & Buunk, 1998; Dreznick, 2001; Knobloch, Solomon, & Cruz, 2001; Nannini & Meyers, 2000), or have extramarital affairs (Christian-Herman, O'Leary, & Avery-Leaf, 2001; Dreznick, 2001; Schmitt & Buss, 2001), and on and on.

When a spouse needs to be cared for, attachment styles become especially important. Insecure individuals have difficulty in seeking help for themselves and in providing effective support for a partner in need (Collins & Feeney, 2000; Feeney & Hohaus, 2001). The key to marital success and failure is not the ability to avoid all such difficulties, but the ability to deal with the problems and with each other in a satisfactory way, as we will discuss next.

■ REACTING TO MARITAL PROBLEMS. When there are arguments or disagreements, it is not helpful to focus on winning versus losing or on being right versus being wrong, as suggested in Figure 8.21. Marital disagreement is not a sport in which you need to score points, and trying to win is not helpful. Men are more likely than women simply to avoid talking about a conflict, but this is not a satisfactory solution either (Bodenmann et al., 1998; Oggins, Veroff, & Leber, 1993). Probably the most common and most maladaptive response to conflict is for disagreeing partners to lash out with hostile words or engage in hostile acts, which only provoke still more negative and destructive responses.

What are the alternatives to an insistence on being right and winning the argument, pretending the conflict doesn't exist, or attacking one another in insulting and destructive ways? People need to pause and consider the long-term consequences of these actions for the relationship, because this consideration is likely to encourage a constructive response (Yovetich & Rusbult, 1994). It is helpful if each individual can resist trying to tear down the other person's positive self-evaluation (Mendolia, Beach, & Tesser, 1996). It is important to be able to disagree and to deal with problems in an agreeable way (Graziano, Jensen-Campbell, & Hair, 1996), to show empathy (Arriaga & Rusbult, 1998), and to avoid hostility and defensiveness

"Well, if it doesn't matter who's right and who's wrong, why don't I be right and you be wrong?"

FIGURE 8.21

"I'm Right, and You're Wrong": Not a Helpful Approach. When conflicts and disagreements arise in a relationship, they all too often develop into a contest with right versus wrong or winner versus loser as the focus of the interaction. There are much more constructive ways to deal with problems.

(Newton et al., 1995; Thompson, Whiffen, & Blain, 1995). As you might have guessed, the more secure one's attachment style, the more likely the possibility of a committed and satisfying marriage (Radecki-Bush, Farrell, & Bush, 1993). For whatever reason, gay and Lesbian couples express less hostility when they argue and are better able to calm down afterward (McLaughlin, 2001b).

A more comprehensive way of characterizing these various ways of interacting with a partner can be summarized simply. Whatever is said or done that creates negative affect is bad for a relationship, and whatever is said or done that creates positive affect is good for a relationship (Levenson, Carstensen, & Gottman, 1994). For example, a study of cohabiting couples revealed that satisfaction was greatest if the two individuals frequently experienced *intimacy.* That is, they engaged in pleasant interactions, disclosed their emotions and other private information about themselves, expressed positive feelings, and felt understood by their partner (Lippert & Prager, 2001).

Also, a long-term relationship can become boring (negative affect) because people perceive themselves as being in a rut, doing the same things over and over (Byrne & Murnen, 1988). When, however, couples participate together in novel and arousing activities (positive affect), the perceived quality of the relationship improves (Aron et al., 2000).

Videotapes of interactions between satisfied and dissatisfied partners reveal much more negative verbal and nonverbal behavior in the latter pairs than in the former (Halford & Sanders, 1990). As the amount of negative affect increases and the amount of positive affect decreases, the relationship becomes less and less satisfactory for both heterosexual and homosexual couples (Kurdek, 1996, 1997). Perhaps because they have discovered the secret of successful relationships, older couples who have remained married express more positive affect than do young or middle-aged couples (Levenson, Carstensen, & Gottman, 1994).

Jeff Herring, marriage and family therapist, has provided ten tips to strengthen a marriage (Herring, 2001), and his suggestions (see Table 8.3) reinforce much of what has been discussed here.

TABLE 8.3

Ten Tips to Strengthen a Marriage. Marriage and family therapist Jeff Herring provides these suggestions as a way to maintain a happy marital relationship. You may notice that these tips from clinical practice are quite consistent with the research findings discussed in this chapter.

1. You can be right or you can be happy—not both. Choose wisely.
2. Learn the gentle art of cooperation.
3. Talk about the important stuff.
4. Forgive as much or more than you would like to be forgiven.
5. Celebrate what you want to see more of. Appreciation can go a long way.
6. Listen to the heart more than you listen to the words. This can lead to conflict resolution and to taking care of each other.
7. Don't be like Darren in *Bewitched* who wanted Samantha to stop using her magic witch powers. Encourage your partner in her or his gifts.
8. Check out your communication. It's easy to talk, but it's more difficult to communicate.
9. Take responsibility for your contributions to the problems.
10. Don't assume that just because you are married, you know how to be married.

[SOURCE: BASED ON INFORMATION FROM HERRING, MAY 20, 2001, KNIGHT RIDDER.]

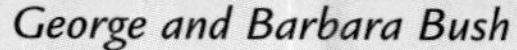

George and Barbara Bush

Jimmy and Rosalynn Carter

FIGURE 8.22
Marriages Can Be Successful. Though there is often an emphasis on marital failure and the fact that more than half of all marriages end in divorce, it is equally true that marriages can succeed and that almost half of all marriages last a lifetime. Among the key ingredients are an emphasis on friendship, commitment, similarity, and the expression and creation of positive affect.

Though most of the research on marriage (and most of the discussion in this chapter) focuses on problems, it should be remembered that almost half of all marriages succeed, as illustrated in Figure 8.22. A successful marriage seems to emphasize friendship, commitment, trust, social support, similarity, and a consistent determination to create positive affect (Adams & Jones, 1997; Cobb, Davila, & Bradbury, 2001; Lauer & Lauer, 1985; Wieselquist et al., 1999).

Though successful marriages can be achieved, unsuccessful ones are all too familiar, and we will now take a look at the unpleasant consequences of relationship dissolution.

■ RELATIONSHIP FAILURE: THE EFFECTS OF DISSOLUTION. It is possible for two friends simply to drift apart, but the partners in a relationship as intimate as marriage are much more likely to feel intense distress and anger when the relationship fails (Fischman, 1986). In part, lovers and spouses find the end of the relationship more difficult than the end of a friendship because they have invested considerable time in one another, engaged in many mutually rewarding activities, and expressed a lasting commitment to the relationship (Simpson, 1987). There is the feeling that all such experiences were a waste of time, and, of course, that the other person is entirely to blame.

In some respects, a divorced spouse is analogous to a deceased spouse. In the case of death, the surviving partner can be angry at the spouse because he or she died (resulting in chronic grief) or can be proud of the deceased and of self (resulting in improved functioning over time) (Bonanno, Mihalecz, & LeJeune, 1999). In the case of divorce, anger is much more likely than pride, and this emotion is detrimental to improved functioning.

Rusbult and Zembrodt (1983) point out that people respond either actively or passively to an unhappy partnership. An active response consists of either ending the relationship (*exit*—"Here's my lawyer's business card; I've filed for divorce") or working to improve it (*voice*—"I believe we should give marital counseling a try"). A passive response involves one simply waiting for improvement to occur (*loyalty*—"I'll stand by my partner until things get better") or waiting for what is perceived as the inevitable breakup (*neglect*—"I won't do anything until the situation

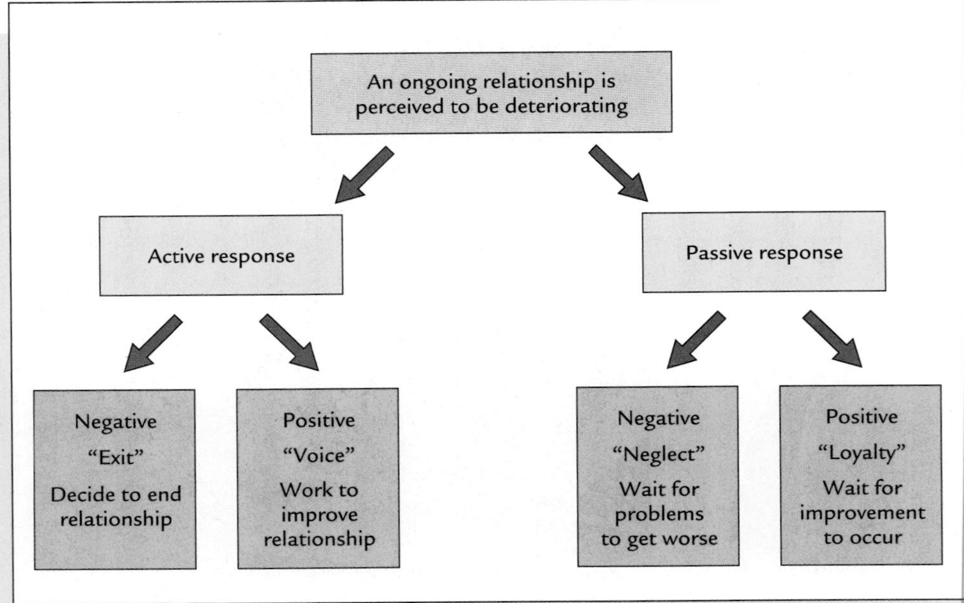

FIGURE 8.23

Responding to a Troubled Relationship.

When a relationship is beginning to fail, the partners can respond in either an active or a passive way. Within each of these two alternatives, the response can be either positive or negative. Rusbult and Zembrodt label the active-negative decision (to end the relationship) as "exit," and the active-positive decision (to attempt to improve the relationship) as "voice." A passive-negative response (simply waiting for the problems to get worse) is labeled "neglect"; a passive-positive response (simply waiting for improvement) is known as "loyalty."

[SOURCE: BASED ON INFORMATION FROM RUSBULT & ZEMBRODT, 1983.]

becomes totally impossible"). These alternatives are summarized in Figure 8.23. If the goal is to save the relationship, then *exit* and *neglect* are clearly the least constructive choices. Compared to secure individuals, those with insecure attachment styles are more likely to react with exit or neglect and less likely to react with voice. Men and women with high self-esteem tend to respond to a bad relationship by exiting, while those with low self-esteem choose neglect (Rusbult, Morrow, & Johnson, 1990).

Although it is very difficult to reverse a deteriorating relationship, it is possible to save a marriage if the conditions are right. The couple can reconcile if (1) the partnership satisfies the needs of each individual, (2) each remains committed to staying together, and (3) alternative lovers are not readily available (Arriaga & Agnew, 2001; Rusbult, Martz, & Agnew, 1998). And relationships are sometimes maintained because one partner is overly dependent on the other. For example, a dependent spouse is often reluctant to give up the relationship even when she is the victim of physical abuse (Drigotas & Rusbult, 1992; Holtzworth-Munroe, 2000; Rusbult & Martz, 1995).

The totally innocent victims of relationship failure and divorce are, of course, the couple's children. About one out of three American children has had this experience (Bumpass, 1984). The negative consequences of divorce for children include long-term effects on their health and well-being (Friedman et al., 1995a; Vobejda, 1997), behavior problems at school (O'Brien & Bahadur, 1998), a higher risk of mortality throughout their lives, and a greater likelihood of getting a divorce themselves

(Tucker et al., 1997). Such findings have been instrumental in motivating a growing movement to make it more difficult for couples to divorce, especially when children are involved (Kirn, 1997).

Despite the shattered hopes of living happily ever after and despite the emotional pain of a marital breakup, it is interesting to note that most divorced individuals marry again, especially men. In fact, nearly half of all marriages in the United States are remarriages for one or both partners (Koch, 1996). The desire for future love and happiness in a relationship seems to have a greater influence on behavior than the negative interactions with a former spouse. Or, as Samuel Johnson put it over a century ago, "Remarriage, sir, represents the triumph of hope over experience."

KEY POINTS

- In the United States, about 50 percent of marriages end in divorce, but people do not believe that their own marriages will fail.
- Most married couples have some degree of conflict and disagreement. When difficulties are resolved constructively, the marriage is likely to endure. When the problems are made worse by destructive interactions, the marriage is likely to fail.
- Constructive responses include taking the other person's viewpoint, protecting his or her self-esteem, compromising, increasing the benefits and decreasing the costs of the marriage, being agreeable, and, above all, maximizing positive affect and minimizing negative affect.
- If dissatisfaction becomes too great, individuals tend to respond either actively or passively in an attempt to restore the relationship or to end it.
- Divorce is a painful process with negative emotional and economic effects, but the most vulnerable and most innocent victims are the children. Despite this experience, though, most people who divorce (especially men) decide to marry again.

CONNECTIONS: INTEGRATING SOCIAL PSYCHOLOGY

IN THIS CHAPTER, YOU READ ABOUT . . .	IN OTHER CHAPTERS, YOU WILL FIND RELATED DISCUSSIONS OF . . .
the association between self-esteem and attachment style and the effect of love on self-esteem	self-esteem (Chapter 5)
similarity as a factor in friendships, romantic relationships, and marriage	similarity and attraction (Chapter 7)
social skills and cognitive processes	cognitive processes (Chapter 7)
love as emotional misattribution	misattribution and emotions (Chapter 3)
affect and relationships	affect and attraction (Chapter 7)
responses to conflicts between spouses	response to conflicts in organizations (Chapter 13)

(continued)

THINKING ABOUT CONNECTIONS

1. Do you believe that your relationship with your parents has anything to do with how you react to other people? Did your mother and father make you feel good about yourself? Do you still feel the same way about yourself? In your childhood, were the adults in your life dependable? Did they keep their promises? Did you think of them as kind? How do you feel about most of the people you meet? Do you believe they are more or less trustworthy?
2. Think of someone who is (or was) your closest friend. What was it about that person that first attracted you? Did proximity, similarity, positive affect, or appearance play a role in your getting to know one another? What do (or did) you do when together? Are there any parallels between your childhood friendships and your current friendships?
3. Think about yourself in a close romantic relationship—either in the past, in the present, or in a possible future romance. What is it about the other person that you find attractive? Do you think romance is something that grows gradually, or is it love at first sight? Is there any match between your own experience and such research questions as the role of misattributed emotions, evolutionary reproductive strategies, or expectancies based on stories about love to which you have been exposed since childhood?
4. When you find yourself disagreeing with a romantic partner, a friend, or anyone else, what do you do? Is the interaction constructive, or do you just get mad and exchange insults? Have you ever broken up with someone to whom you once felt very close? Why did it happen? Who initiated the breakup, and how was it done? Could either of you have handled the situation more constructively?

IDEAS TO TAKE WITH YOU—AND USE!

ALL YOU NEED IS LOVE?

There are few (if any) words that appear more often in songs, stories, movies, fairy tales, and our everyday lives than "love." Nevertheless, a question people frequently ask themselves (and advice columnists as well) is "How do I know if I'm really in love?" A common answer is "If you have to ask, you're not." That's cute, but don't count on being accurate just because you are so sure of yourself that you don't have to ask. You might find it more helpful to consider what has been learned about this topic in empirical research.

Emotional Arousal Is Not Necessarily Love.

When you are near someone who appeals to you, it is easy to confuse a variety of arousal states with "love." Social psychologist Elaine Hatfield once suggested that we often fall in lust and interpret it as love. More generally, research on emotional misattribution indicates that the physiological arousal associated with excitement, fear, happiness, anxiety, and even anger can be mislabeled. Think of common experiences on a date (from kissing to watching a frightening movie to riding on a motorcycle) that can potentially be arousing. You may label your feelings as sexual arousal, fear, or excitement, but it is also very easy to identify them as love. If you find yourself surging with emotion and thinking that you must be madly in love, take a deep breath and consider alternative explanations for what you may be feeling.

What Do You Know about This Person?

It is difficult to get to know someone in depth. It's not acceptable to administer a detailed questionnaire to a potential date, lover, or spouse. A simple, but reasonable, alternative is for two people to learn as much as they can about one another by talking, writing, chatting on line (as Meg Ryan and Tom Hanks did in the movie *You've Got Mail*), or whatever else they find

comfortable. And if any specific topic is extremely important to you—religion, politics, sex, vegetarianism, or whatever—it is better to discover incompatibilities early in the relationship rather than later. It may seem awkward to ask about such things, but it's better to feel awkward now than to be unpleasantly surprised later.

What Does Love Mean to You?

Look back in the chapter at the definitions of the six love styles, the three corners of the love triangle, and the Chinese concept of love as a matter of fate and predestination. To you, is love simply close friendship, a fun game, a logical arrangement, what you say to justify sex, or something else? Does your partner define love in the same way you do? If the two of you match in this respect, you are likely to encounter fewer romantic problems than if you conceive of love in two quite different ways.

Is Consummate Love a Realistic Possibility?

In Sternberg's triangular model of love, the ideal or "consummate" match is between two individuals for whom intimacy, passion, and commitment are all present in equal strength. Is that possible? Well, few relationships are perfect, but consummate love is surely an ideal worth striving for. At the very least, two people who are at all serious about each other should know where each of them fits on the triangle.

SUMMARY AND REVIEW OF KEY POINTS

Interdependent Relationships with Family and Friends versus Loneliness

- Close relationships are characterized by *interdependence,* in which two people influence each other's lives, share their thoughts and emotions, and engage in joint activities.
- Evolutionary theory proposes that emotional bonding with friends and with mates increases the likelihood of reproductive success. As a result, humans and other primates are "hard-wired" to seek emotional closeness.
- The first relationships are within the family, and children learn what to expect from others and how to interact with them as they interact with parents, siblings, grandparents, and other family members.
- Friendships outside of the family begin in childhood and are based initially simply on interpersonal attraction. Many individuals are able to form a *close friendship* that involves spending time together, interacting in many different situations, providing mutual social support, and engaging in self-disclosure.
- At all ages, *attachment style* exerts a major influence on the ease with which people make friends, on the way they interact with others, and on their success in maintaining relationships.
- Adult attachment style is characterized as the combination of a person's level of self-esteem and degree of interpersonal trust. These positive–negative dimensions yield four resulting attachment styles: *secure, dismissing, fearful–avoidant,* and *preoccupied.* Those who are secure are best able to form long-lasting, committed, satisfying relationships.

- *Loneliness* occurs when a person has fewer and less satisfying relationships than he or she desires. The result is depression and anxiety. The causes of loneliness can be a combination of genetic predisposition, specific learning experiences early in life, and cultural influences. Interventions can help, especially a combination of cognitive therapy and social skills training.

Romantic Relationships, Love, and Physical Intimacy

- One defining characteristic of romantic relationships is some degree of physical intimacy, ranging from holding hands to sexual interactions.
- As is true for attraction and friendship, romantic attraction is influenced by factors such as physical proximity, appearance, and similarity. In addition, romance includes sexual attraction, the desire for total acceptance by the other person, and a degree of fantasy based on positive illusions.
- *Love* involves multiple possibilities. For example, *passionate love* is a sudden, overwhelming emotional response. *Companionate love,* in contrast, is more like a close friendship that includes caring, mutual liking, and respect.
- Besides passionate and companionate love, Hendrick and Hendrick add four other "love styles," and Sternberg conceptualizes love in terms of a triangle, with the three corners representing companionate love, passionate love, and *decision/commitment.*
- Widespread changes in sexual attitudes and sexual practices were labeled the "sexual revolution" of the 1960s and 1970s. The result is greater permissiveness with respect to all aspects of sexuality. One consequence of this shift is that premarital sex has become the norm.
- The most dramatic consequences of the newfound sexual freedom of the 1960s and 1970s were unwanted pregnancies and incurable STDs, such as HIV. Recent attitudinal and behavioral changes appear to be having a positive effect on the incidence of teenage pregnancies, but the HIV/AIDS epidemic continues to expand rapidly in many parts of the world as well as in specific segments of the U.S. population.

Marriage: The Ultimate Close Relationship

- In the United States, about 50 percent of marriages end in divorce, but people do not believe that their own marriages will fail.
- Most married couples have some degree of conflict and disagreement. When difficulties are resolved constructively, the marriage is likely to endure. When the problems are made worse by destructive interactions, the marriage is likely to fail.
- Constructive responses include taking the other person's viewpoint, protecting his or her self-esteem, compromising, increasing the benefits and decreasing the costs of the marriage, being agreeable, and, above all, maximizing positive affect and minimizing negative affect.
- If dissatisfaction becomes too great, individuals tend to respond either actively or passively in an attempt to either restore the relationship or to end it.
- Divorce is a painful process with negative emotional and economic effects, but the most vulnerable and most innocent victims are the children. Despite this experience, most people who divorce (especially men) decide to marry again.

KEY TERMS

assumed similarity (p. 331)
attachment style (p. 305)
close friendship (p. 304)
communal behavior (p. 336)
companionate love (p. 323)
consummate love (p. 325)
decision/commitment (p. 325)
dismissing attachment style (p. 310)
fearful-avoidant attachment style (p. 309)
interdependence (p. 299)
interpersonal trust (p. 308)
intimacy (p. 325)
loneliness (p. 311)
love (p. 320)
narcissism (p. 332)
passion (p. 325)
passionate love (p. 320)
preoccupied attachment style (p. 310)
secure attachment style (p. 308)
triangular model of love (p. 324)
unrequited love (p. 322)

FOR MORE INFORMATION

Booth, A., Crouter, A. C, & Clements, M. (2001). *Couples in conflict.* Hillsdale, NJ: Erlbaum.

- Based on presentations at a national symposium on couples in conflict, this collection of chapters focuses on many family issues. The content addresses four major issues: the societal and evolutionary underpinnings of couple conflict, the interpersonal roots of couple conflict and its consequences, the effects on children, and policies and programs dealing with couple conflict.

Harvey, J. H., & Wenzel, A. (Eds.). (2001). *Close romantic relationships: Maintenance and enhancement.* Hillsdale, NJ: Erlbaum.

- This book comprises a collection of chapters by some of the leading investigators and theorists in the field of relationships and deals with theoretical approaches and applied issues.

Regan, P. C., & Berscheid, E. (1999). *Lust: What we know about human sexual desire.* Thousand Oaks, CA: Sage.

- Part of the Sage series on close relationships, this interesting book deals with sexual desire in the context of attraction, social interactions between men and women, romance, and love.

Simpson, J. A., & Rholes, W. S. (Eds.). (1998). *Attachment theory and close relationships.* New York: Guilford.

- An up-to-date collection of chapters by psychologists directly involved in research on attachment theory, this book provides an invaluable summary of progress in this active field of research.

Renato Guttuso, *The Discussion,* 1959–60. © 2002 Artists Rights Society (ARS), New York/SIAE, Rome. © Tate Gallery/London/Art Resource, NY.

9 SOCIAL INFLUENCE: CHANGING OTHERS' BEHAVIOR

CHAPTER OUTLINE

Where course grades are concerned, I (RAB) have a simple policy: Once they are assigned, I never change them—and I mean *never*—unless, of course, there has been some error in addition. I announce this policy to my classes at the start of the semester and repeat it before and after every exam. I urge my students to come to see me during the semester if they want to discuss their grades, but remind them over and over again that once the semester is done, I will stick firmly to my "no change" policy. Despite these efforts, though, there are always several students in my class who make appointments to see me after final grades have been posted. And when they come to my office, they use every tactic of **social influence**—techniques designed to change my attitudes, beliefs, perceptions, or behavior (Cialdini, 1994)—under the sun. They offer excuses for poor exam scores, tell me how disappointed their parents will be, describe the health or personal problems that interfered with their performance, plead, and even, in some cases, threaten ("If you won't help me, I'll go to the Dean"). None of these tactics works because I decided long ago that it was simply not fair to change grades; after all, if I did so, I would be assigning grades on the basis of students' ability to exert social influence—not on their performance in the course. But believe me, I am frequently tempted because some of the students put on a great performance!

Clearly, this is far from the only time I am exposed to efforts by other persons to exert social influence—to change my attitudes or behavior. Every time I see a TV commercial, drive by an advertising sign, or look through a magazine, I am exposed to efforts to change my attitudes and behavior. So I am definitely on the receiving end of such attempts all through the day (see Figure 9.1).

Where social influence is concerned, however, we don't merely receive it—we "dish it out" as well. How many times each day do *you* try to influence others—friends, roommates, family members, romantic partners? If you are like most people, you practice many forms of social influence each day.

Because social psychologists have long recognized the importance of social influence in our daily lives, this topic has long been a central focus of our field. We have already considered some of this work in Chapter 4, where we examined the process of *persuasion.* Here, we'll expand on that earlier discussion by examining many other aspects of social influence. First, we'll focus on the topic of **conformity**—behaving in ways that are viewed as acceptable or appropriate in our group or society. As we'll soon see, such pressure to conform can be very hard to resist. Next, we'll turn to **compliance**—efforts to get others to say yes to various requests. Finally, we'll examine two extreme forms of social influence: **obedience**—a form of social influence in which one person simply orders one or more others to do what they want—and **intense indoctrination**—efforts by extremist groups to recruit new members and induce them to accept the group's beliefs in an unquestioning manner (Baron, R. S., 2000).

FIGURE 9.1

Social Influence in Action.

Many techniques for exerting *social influence*—for changing others' attitudes or behavior—exist. Some are obvious, but others are more subtle, such as the one shown here.

[SOURCE: REPRINTED WITH SPECIAL PERMISSION OF KING FEATURES SYNDICATE.]

Conformity: Group Influence in Action

Have you ever found yourself in a situation in which you felt that you stuck out like the proverbial sore thumb? If so, you have already had direct experience with pressures toward *conformity.* In such situations, you probably experienced a strong desire to "get back into line"—to fit in with the other people around you. Such pressures toward conformity stem from the fact that in many contexts there are explicit or unspoken rules indicating how we *should* or *ought to* behave. These rules are known as **social norms,** and they often exert powerful effects on our behavior. (Actually, there are several kinds of social norms, and here we are discussing primarily one important type known as *injunctive norms*—the kind that tells us what we *should* do in a given situation. We'll consider other types of social norms below; Kallgren, Reno, & Cialdini, 2000).

social influence: Efforts by one or more individuals to change the attitudes, beliefs, perceptions, or behaviors of one or more others.

conformity: A type of social influence in which individuals change their attitudes or behavior in order to adhere to existing social norms.

compliance: A form of social influence involving direct requests from one person to another.

obedience: A form of social influence in which one person simply orders one or more others to perform some action(s).

intense indoctrination: A process through which individuals become members of extreme groups and come to accept the beliefs and rules of the groups in a totally unquestioning way.

social norms: Rules indicating how individuals are expected to behave in specific situations.

In some instances, social norms are both detailed and stated explicitly. For instance, governments generally function through written constitutions and laws; athletic contests are usually regulated by written rules; and signs in many public places (e.g., along highways, in parks, at airports) describe expected behavior in considerable detail, as in SPEED LIMIT: 55, NO SWIMMING, NO PARKING, and KEEP OFF THE GRASS (see Figure 9.2 on page 350).

In contrast, other norms are unspoken or implicit. Most of us obey such unwritten rules as "Don't stand too close to strangers" and "Don't arrive at parties exactly on time." Similarly, we are often influenced by current and rapidly changing standards of dress, speech, and grooming. Regardless of whether social norms are explicit or implicit, though, one fact is clear: *Most people obey them most of the time.* For instance, few persons visit restaurants without leaving a tip for the server, and virtually everyone, regardless of personal political beliefs, stands when the national anthem of their country is played at sports events or other public gatherings. Most people even follow the norm indicating that they should clean up after their dogs (Webley & Siviter, 2000; see Figure 9.2 on page 350).

At first glance, this strong tendency toward conformity—toward going along with society's or the group's expectations about how we should behave in various

FIGURE 9.2
Social Norms: Regulators of Everyday Life. Social norms tell us what we should do (or not do) in a given situation. They are often stated explicitly (e.g., in signs such as the one shown here), and most people do in fact obey most of the time.

situations—may strike you as objectionable. After all, it does place restrictions on personal freedom. Actually, though, there is a strong basis for so much conformity: without it, we would quickly find ourselves facing social chaos. Imagine what would happen outside movie theaters, at stadiums, or at supermarket checkout counters if people did *not* obey the norm "Form a line and wait your turn." And consider the danger to both drivers and pedestrians if there were *not* clear and widely followed traffic regulations. In many situations, then, conformity serves a very useful function.

Given that strong pressures toward conformity exist in many social settings, it is surprising to learn that conformity, as a social process, received relatively little attention in social psychology until the 1950s. At that time, Solomon Asch (1951), whose research on impression formation we considered in Chapter 2, carried out a series of experiments on conformity that yielded dramatic results. Because Asch's research had a strong influence on later studies of this aspect of social influence, it's worth a close look here.

Asch's Research on Conformity: Social Pressure—the Irresistible Force?

Suppose that just before an important math exam, you discover that your answer to a homework problem—a problem of the type that will be on the test—is different from that obtained by one of your friends. How would you react? Probably with mild concern. Now imagine that you learn that a second person's answer, too, is different from yours. To make matters worse, it agrees with the answer reported by the first person. How would you feel *now*? The chances are good that your anxiety will be considerable. Next, you discover that a third person agrees with the other two. At this point, you know that you are in big trouble. Which answer should you accept? Yours or the one obtained by your three friends? The exam is about to start, so you have to decide quickly.

Life is filled with such dilemmas—instances in which we discover that our own judgments, actions, or conclusions are different from those reached by other persons. What do we do in such situations? Important insights into our behavior were provided by studies conducted by Solomon Asch (1951, 1955), research that is viewed as a true "classic" in social psychology.

In his research, Asch asked participants to respond to a series of simple perceptual problems, such as the one in Figure 9.3. On each problem, participants indi-

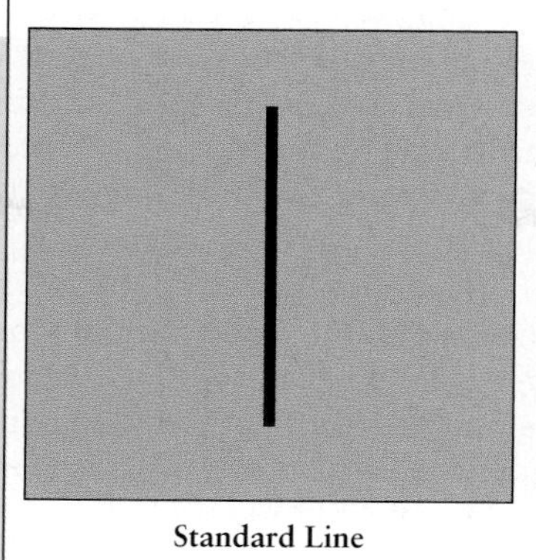

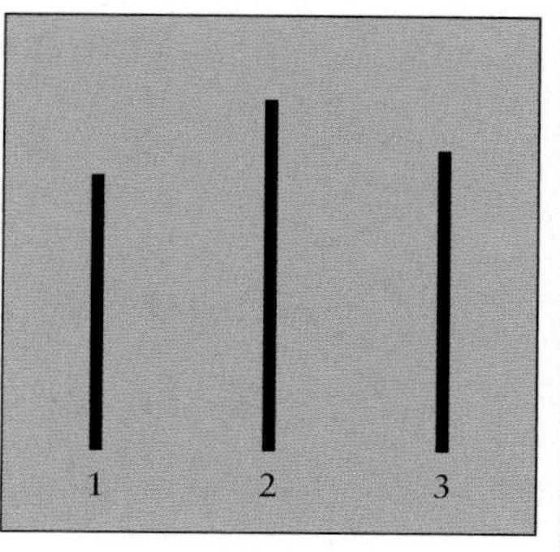

FIGURE 9.3

Solomon Asch and the Line-Judgment Task He Used to Study Conformity. Participants in Asch's research were asked to report their judgments on problems such as this one. Their task was to indicate which of the comparison lines (1, 2, or 3) best matched the standard line in length. To study conformity, he had participants make these judgments out loud, only after hearing the answers of several other people—all of whom were Asch's assistants. On certain critical trials, the assistants all gave wrong answers. This exposed participants to strong pressures toward conformity.

Solomon Asch is one of the founders of modern social psychology. His research on several important topics—impression formation, conformity—started new lines of work and played an important role in shaping the nature of the field. I (RAB) met him in the late 1970s, and we soon struck up a friendship. I found Professor Asch to be as kind and considerate as he was intelligent and insightful.

cated which of three comparison lines matched a standard line in length. Several other persons (usually six to eight) were also present during the session, but, unknown to the real participant, all were assistants of the experimenter. On certain occasions, known as *critical trials* (twelve out of the eighteen problems), the accomplices offered answers that were clearly wrong: they unanimously chose the wrong line as a match for the standard line. Moreover, they stated their answers *before* the real participants responded. Thus, on these critical trials, the persons in Asch's study faced precisely the type of dilemma described above. Should they go along with the other individuals present or stick to their own judgments? Results were clear: A large majority of the persons in Asch's research chose conformity. Across several different studies, fully 76 percent of those tested went along with the group's false answers at least once; overall, they voiced agreement with these errors 37 percent of the time. In contrast, only 5 percent of the participants in a control group, who responded to the same problems alone, made such errors.

Of course, there were large individual differences in this respect. Almost 25 percent of the participants *never* yielded to the group pressure. At the other extreme, some persons went along with the majority nearly all the time. When Asch questioned them, some of these persons stated, "I am wrong, they are right"; they had little confidence in their own judgments. Others, however, said they felt that the other persons present were suffering from some sort of optical illusion or were merely sheep following the responses of the first person. Yet, when it was their turn, these people, too, went along with the group.

In further studies, Asch (1951, 1956) investigated the effects of shattering the group's unanimity by having one of the accomplice's break with the others. In one study, this person gave the correct answer, becoming an "ally" of the real participant; in another study, he chose an answer in between the one given by the group and the correct one; and in a third, he chose the answer that was even more incorrect than that chosen by the majority. In the latter two conditions, in other words, he broke from the group but still disagreed with the real participants. Results indicated that conformity was reduced under all three conditions. However, somewhat surprisingly, this reduction was greatest when the dissenting assistant expressed views even more extreme (and wrong) than the majority. Together, these findings suggest that it is the unanimity of the group that is crucial; once it is broken, no matter how, resisting group pressure becomes much easier.

There's one more aspect of Asch's research that it is important to mention. In later studies, he repeated his basic procedure, but with one important change: Instead of stating their answers out loud, participants wrote them down on a piece of paper. As you might guess, conformity dropped sharply because there was no way for the real participants to know what the other persons were doing. This finding points to the importance of distinguishing between *public conformity*—doing or saying what others around us say or do—and *private acceptance*—actually coming to feel or think as others do. Often, it appears, we follow social norms overtly but don't actually change our private views (Maas & Clark, 1984). This distinction between public conformity and private acceptance is an important one, and we'll refer to it at several points in this book.

Asch's research was the catalyst for much activity in social psychology, as many other researchers rushed to investigate the nature of conformity, to identify factors that influence it, and to establish its limits (e.g., Crutchfield, 1955; Deutsch & Gerard, 1955). Indeed, such research is continuing today and is still adding to our understanding of this crucial form of social influence (e.g., Baron, Vandello, & Brunsman, 1996; Bond & Smith, 1996; Buehler & Griffin, 1994).

KEY POINTS

- *Social influence*—efforts by one or more persons to change the attitudes or behavior of one or more others—is a common part of life.
- Most people behave in accordance with *social norms* most of the time; in other words, they show strong tendencies toward *conformity*.
- Conformity was first systematically studied by Solomon Asch, whose classic research indicated that many persons will yield to social pressure from a unanimous group.

Factors Affecting Conformity: Variables That Determine the Extent to Which We "Go Along"

Asch's research demonstrated the existence of powerful pressures toward conformity, but even a moment's reflection suggests that conformity does not occur to the same degree in all settings. For instance, bell-bottom jeans and short hair (especially for men) are "in" right now, with the result that many teenagers and some young adults experience strong pressures to adopt these fashions. Yet, despite this fact, many do not. They don't wear bell-bottoms and don't cut their hair short. Why? In other words, what factors determine the extent to which individuals yield to conformity pressure or resist it? Systematic research suggests that many factors play a role; here, we'll examine the ones that appear to be most important.

COHESIVENESS AND CONFORMITY: ACCEPTING INFLUENCE FROM THOSE WE LIKE. As we just stated, short hair is in right now, especially for men (but also, to some extent, for women). But suppose that suddenly, some of the most popular people in your school or neighborhood let their hair grow until it is shoulder length. Would their adoption of this new style lead to its rapid spread? Perhaps; after all, these people are popular, and it is often the popular people who set the trends. But now suppose that, instead, the only persons who adopt this style are true losers—people who are viewed as weird and unpopular. Would *their* adoption of the new fashion lead to its rapid spread? Probably not; after all, who wants to be like them?

This example illustrates one factor that plays an important role where conformity is concerned: **cohesiveness,** which can be defined as the degree of attraction felt by individuals toward some group. When cohesiveness is high—when we like and admire some group of persons—pressures toward conformity are magnified. After all, we know that one way of gaining the acceptance of such persons is to be like them in various ways. On the other hand, when cohesiveness is low, pressures toward conformity, too, are low; why should we change our behavior to be like other people we don't especially like or admire (see Figure 9.4)? Research findings

cohesiveness: With respect to conformity, the degree of attraction felt by an individual toward an influencing group.

FIGURE 9.4

Cohesiveness and Conformity. Would you be more likely to change your behavior (e.g., your hairstyle, mode of dress) to be like the persons in the photo on the *top* or the photo on the *bottom?* This depends on which group you find more attractive.

indicate that cohesiveness exerts strong effects on conformity (Crandall, 1988; Latané & L'Herrou, 1996), so it is definitely one important determinant of the extent to which we yield to this type of social pressure.

■ CONFORMITY AND GROUP SIZE: WHY MORE IS BETTER WITH RESPECT TO SOCIAL PRESSURE. A second factor that exerts important effects on the tendency to conform is the size of the influencing group. Asch (1956) and other early researchers (e.g., Gerard, Wilhelmy, & Conolley, 1968) found that conformity increases with group size, but only up to about three members; beyond that point, it appears to level off or even decrease. However, more recent research has failed to confirm these early findings (e.g., Bond & Smith, 1996). Instead, these later studies found that conformity tended to increase with group size up to eight group members and beyond. So it appears that the larger the group, the greater our tendency to go along with it, even if this means behaving differently than we'd really prefer.

■ DESCRIPTIVE AND INJUNCTIVE SOCIAL NORMS: WHEN NORMS DO—OR DO NOT—AFFECT BEHAVIOR. Social norms, we have already seen, can be formal or informal in nature—as different as rules printed on large signs and informal guidelines such as "Don't leave your shopping cart in the middle of a parking spot outside the supermarket." This is not the only way in which norms differ, however. Another important distinction is that between **descriptive norms** and **injunctive norms** (e.g., Cialdini, Kallgren, & Reno, 1991; Reno, Cialdini, & Kallgren, 1993). Descriptive norms are ones that simply describe what most people do in a given situation. They influence behavior by informing us about what is generally seen as effective or adaptive in that situation. In contrast, injunctive norms specify what *ought* to be done—what is approved or disapproved behavior in a given situation. Both norms can exert strong effects upon behavior (e.g., Brown, 1998). However, Cialdini and his colleagues believe that in certain situations—especially ones in which antisocial behavior (behavior not approved of by a given group or society) is likely to occur—injunctive norms may exert somewhat stronger effects. This is true for two reasons. First, such norms tend to shift attention away from *how* people are acting in a particular situation (e.g., littering) to how they *should be* behaving (e.g., putting trash into containers). Second, such norms may activate the social motive to do what's right in a given situation regardless of what others have done.

When, precisely, do injunctive norms influence behavior? It is clear that they don't always produce such effects. For instance, although there is an injunctive norm stating "Clean up after your dog," and despite the fact that my village has a law requiring this, I frequently observe my neighbors looking the other way while their dog "does its thing" on my property. Why do people sometimes disobey or ignore even strong injunctive norms? One answer is provided by **normative focus theory** (e.g., Cialdini et al., 1990). This theory suggests that norms will influence behavior only to the extent that they are focal for the persons involved at the time the behavior occurs. In other words, people will obey injunctive norms only when they think about them and see them as related to their own actions. Cialdini and his colleagues have conducted several studies that provide support for this view (e.g., Cialdini, Reno, and Kallgren, 1990), but perhaps the clearest evidence is that reported by Kallgren, Reno, and Cialdini (2000).

In one study, which took place not in the laboratory but in an enclosed stairwell, these researchers first exposed participants to brief written passages relating to the injunctive norm against littering in public places. These passages varied in how closely linked they were to this norm: some participants read passages that were closely related to littering (e.g., the passages discussed graffiti and water pollution), others read passages moderately related to littering (they discussed the issue of containers and turning down stereo sets at night), and still other participants read passages that were only distantly related to littering (voting, returning library books on time). A final group read passages that did not focus on any injunctive norms.

descriptive norms: Norms that simply indicate what most people do in a given situation.

injunctive norms: Norms specifying what ought to be done—what is approved or disapproved behavior in a given situation.

normative focus theory: A theory suggesting that norms will influence behavior only to the extent that they are focal for the persons involved at the time the behavior occurs.

All of the written passages used had previously been rated by a large group of raters for closeness to the norm against littering.

After reading these written passages, participants were told that to test a new physiological measure, some would exercise while others would not. Those in the exercise group walked up and down the stairs for three minutes, while the others simply sat and rested. The purpose of these procedures was to increase arousal among some participants, because past findings suggest that arousal intensifies dominant (strong) responses. Thus, presumably, effects of the closeness of the written passages to the injunctive norm against littering would be stronger for the aroused participants than for the nonaroused participants. Heart rate was measured for both groups before and after exercising or sitting quietly, and as part of these procedures, the experimenter placed a sticky ointment on participants' hands. At the end of the study, participants were given a paper towel to remove this ointment. They were then observed as they left the study to determine whether they threw the towel on the ground—that is, engaged in littering. The major prediction was that the more closely related the passages were to the anti-littering norm, the less likely participants would be to litter and that this effect would be stronger for those in the high-arousal group. As shown in Figure 9.5, this is precisely what happened.

In additional studies, Kallgren, Reno, and Cialdini (2000) found further support for the view that norms affect behavior only when they are salient to us—when we focus on them. For instance, seeing themselves on a TV screen (a procedure that made personal views more salient) reduced littering among persons who agreed with the norm against such behavior; it had less effect on people who did not strongly

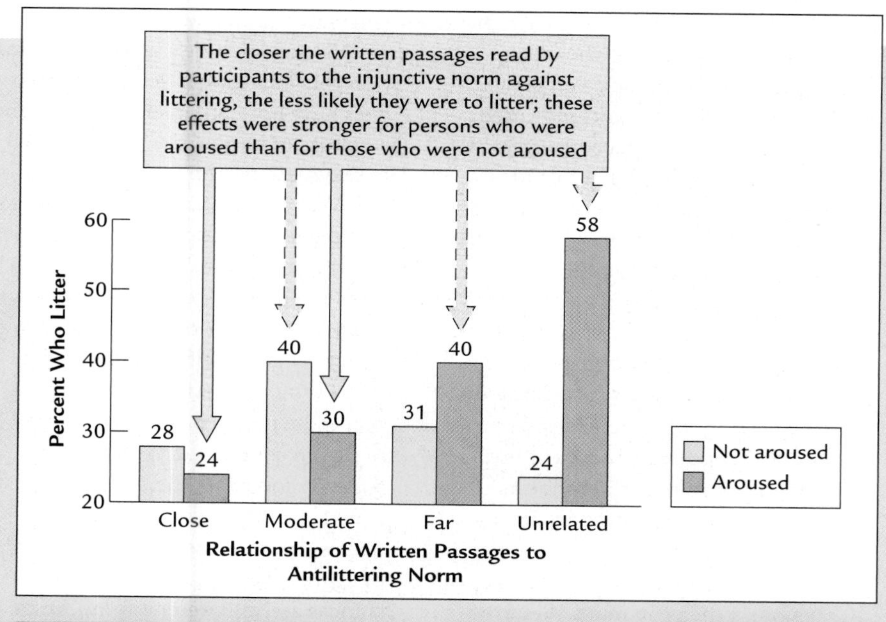

FIGURE 9.5

When Injunctive Norms Do, and Do Not, Affect Behavior.

Research participants who read passages closely related to the injunctive norm against littering were less likely to engage in littering than were those who read passages less closely related to this norm. Moreover, this effect was much stronger among persons who had exercised, and so were experiencing high arousal. These findings provide support for *normative focus theory*—the view that norms affect overt behavior only to the extent that they are focal (i.e., salient) to the persons involved.

[SOURCE: BASED ON DATA FROM KALLGREN, RENO, & CIALDINI, 2000.]

SOCIAL PSYCHOLOGY: THIRTY YEARS OF PROGRESS

THE PERSISTENCE OF SOCIAL NORMS: FROM THE AUTOKINETIC PHENOMENON TO THE "CULTURE OF HONOR"

That norms often exert important effects on behavior is clear; indeed, most people conform to them most of the time. But this in no way implies that norms themselves are set in stone; on the contrary, what is considered appropriate behavior in a given society often changes over time. For instance, when I was a boy, it was considered very rude for children to address adult neighbors by their first names—they were always "Mrs. Kelly" or "Mr. Colasano." Now, though, this seems to have changed, and many of my neighbors' children think it is perfectly OK to call me "Bob" or "Robert." These informal observations point to an important question long studied by social psychologists: Just how stable *are* social norms? The first research evidence on this topic was gathered by Muzafer Sherif, one of the founders of our field, who performed this early research in the 1930s and 1940s (e.g., Sherif, 1937).

In his research, Sherif used a technique known as the *autokinetic phenomenon.* This refers to the fact that when individuals are placed in a completely dark room and exposed to a single, stationary point of light, they often perceive it as moving about, even though it remains still. Putting this illusion to good use, Sherif placed groups of persons in this situation together. He found that, over time, they seemed to establish agreed-upon norms about how much the light was moving. Although the members of the group would differ slightly from each other about how much the light moved, each group seemed settled on a fairly narrow range. For instance, the judgments of the members of one group might cluster around an average movement of five feet, while those in another group might cluster around an average of two feet. Here's the interesting part: When individuals then responded to the light alone, they continued to stick to the norm of their group. More recent studies using somewhat different procedures investigated whether norms established during brief group meetings would remain stable across "generations"—when new people enter the group (e.g., Weick & Gifillan, 1971). Results indicated that they would: as each new person entered the group, she or he quickly adopted the existing norm, responding much as other members did. This was true even when old members left as new ones entered. So it appears that even norms created in relatively meaningless situations tend to persist.

More recent research has examined this question in a different and more dramatic context. In some cultures—ones anthropologists describe as **cultures of honor**—there are strong norms condoning violence as a means of answering an affront to one's honor. This was a theme in many Westerns I saw at the movies when I was a boy, in which characters felt compelled to have a shoot-out with another person because their honor had somehow been sullied (see Figure 9.6).

Why did such norms develop? Cohen and Nisbett (1994, 1997) suggest that they may be traced to the fact that, in some geographic areas, wealth was once concentrated mainly in assets that could readily be stolen. For this reason, it became important for individuals to demonstrate that they would not tolerate such thefts, or any other affront to their honor. The result? Norms condoning violence in response to insults to one's honor emerged and were widely accepted.

Once again, here's where the situation gets interesting: Social psychologists have noted that such norms—and a culture of honor—are alive and well in two sections of the United States: the West and the South. In these areas, wealth was in cattle, which, of course, could be readily stolen, so norms developed condoning violence in response to such threats or other slurs on one's honor. This in itself is not surprising. What is more unexpected, though, is that these norms persist even today. Research conducted by Cohen and Nisbett, and other social psychologists (1994, 1996), suggest that traces of norms condoning or even approving of aggression under certain circumstances are still present in the South

---

agree with this norm. Overall, then, it seems clear that norms influence our actions primarily when they seem relevant to us at the time when we can choose either to obey or to ignore them. (Once established, norms tend to persist unless something happens to change them. To see how research on this topic—the persistence of norms—has changed and advanced in social psychology, see the **Social Psychology: Thirty Years of Progress** section above.)

cultures of honor: Cultures in which strong social norms condone violence as a means of answering an affront to one's honor.

FIGURE 9.6

The Culture of Honor: How Hollywood Once Saw It.
In many old Westerns, an affront to the honor of one character led to duels such as this one. Research suggests that norms condoning or requiring such behavior are still active in certain regions of the United States.

and West of the United States. As evidence for this conclusion, Cohen and Nisbett (1997) point to such facts as these: The West and South, in comparison to other sections of the United States, have looser gun controls, more laws allowing people to use violence in defense of self, and a higher rate of murders stemming from brawls and arguments.

How powerful are these norms? Stronger than you might guess (e.g., Cohen, 1998; Cohen & Nisbett, 1997). In the study by Cohen and Nisbett (1997), a fictitious job applicant wrote letters to almost one thousand organizations throughout the United States, requesting an application form and other information. In half of the letters, the individual indicated that he had killed a man in a fight brought on by strong insults to his honor (the victim of his assault claimed to be having an affair with the man's fiancée and insulted both the job applicant's fiancée and his mother). In the other letters, the individual indicated that he had performed a different crime—car theft.

Cohen and Nisbett (1997) reasoned that if the culture of honor was still operating in the West and South, the job applicant who mentioned a crime of honor would receive greater compliance with his requests for information and friendlier letters from these sections of the country than from other sections. In fact, this is what happened; there were no differences in compliance or tone of response between the North and the South and West in responses to the letter that mentioned car theft. However, significant differences *did* emerge in responses to the letter that mentioned the crime of honor: for both measures, responses from companies in the South and West were more favorable.

This research is very different from Sherif's early research using the autokinetic phenomenon, but it agrees with his finding that norms, once created, tend to persist. In addition, these more recent studies also clearly illustrate how the methods used by social psychologists to study this topic have become increasingly sophisticated, and realistic, over the past few decades. By almost any standard, we believe, this represents real scientific progress.

The Bases of Conformity: Why We Often Choose to "Go Along"

As we have just seen, several factors determine whether and to what extent conformity occurs. Yet this does not alter the essential point: Conformity is a basic fact of social life. Most people conform to the norms of their groups or societies much, if not most, of the time. Why is this so? Why do people often choose to go along with these social results or expectations instead of resisting them? The answer seems to involve two powerful motives possessed by all human beings—the desire to be liked or accepted by others and the desire to be right, to have accurate understanding of the social world (Deutsch & Gerard, 1955; Insko, 1985)—plus cognitive processes that lead us to view conformity as fully justified after it has occurred (e.g., Buehler & Griffin, 1994).

■ NORMATIVE SOCIAL INFLUENCE: THE DESIRE TO BE LIKED AND THE FEAR OF REJECTION. How can we get others to like us? This is one of the eternal puzzles of social life. As we saw in Chapters 2 and 7, many tactics can prove effective in this regard. One of the most successful of these is to appear to be as similar to others as possible. From our earliest days, we learn that agreeing with the persons around us, and behaving as they do, causes them to like us. Parents, teachers, friends, and others often heap praise and approval on us for showing such similarity (see our discussion of attitude formation in Chapter 4). One important reason we conform, therefore, is this: We have learned that doing so can help us win the approval and acceptance we crave. This source of conformity is known as **normative social influence,** because it involves altering our behavior to meet others' expectations.

If our tendency to conform to social norms stems, at least in part, from our desire to be liked and accepted by others, then it stands to reason that anything that increases our fear of rejection by these persons will increase our conformity. And one thing that can trigger fears of rejection is witnessing another person being held up to ridicule (see Figure 9.7). When we witness such scenes, we wish to avoid rejection ourselves, and one way of doing this is to stick more closely to what is viewed as "acceptable" or "appropriate" in our group—in other words, to conform even more with existing social norms. Two researchers, Janes and Olson (2000) have tested these suggestions, and have coined the phrase *jeer pressure* (suggestive of *peer pressure*) to describe such effects. Their research offered support for the prediction that when people fear rejection from others (potential jeer pressure), they do indeed show a greater tendency to conform. These findings provide additional support for

normative social influence: Social influence based on individuals' desire to be liked or accepted by other persons.

FIGURE 9.7

Jeer Pressure: When the Fear of Rejection Leads to Increased Conformity. When we see another person being ridiculed, we may fear similar rejection ourselves. One result may be an increased tendency to stick more closely to behavior that is considered to be acceptable or appropriate—that is, to conform to social norms.

the view that one reason we conform is to be liked by others—or, at least, to avoid rejection by them.

■ THE DESIRE TO BE RIGHT: INFORMATIONAL SOCIAL INFLUENCE. If you want to know your weight, you can step onto a scale. If you want to know the dimensions of a room, you can measure them directly. But how can you establish the accuracy of your own political or social views or decide which hairstyle suits you best? There are no simple physical tests or measuring devices for answering these questions. Yet we want to be correct about such matters, too. The solution to this dilemma is obvious: To answer such questions, we refer to other people. We use *their* opinions and actions as guides for our own. Such reliance on others, in turn, is often a powerful source of the tendency to conform. Other people's actions and opinions define social reality for us, and we use these as a guide for our own actions and opinions. This basis for conformity is known as **informational social influence**, because it is based on our tendency to depend on others as a source of information about many aspects of the social world.

Research evidence suggests that because our motivation to be correct or accurate is very strong, informational social influence is a very powerful source of conformity. However, as you might expect, this is more likely to be true in situations in which we are highly uncertain about what is "correct" or "accurate" than in situations in which we have more confidence in our own ability to make such decisions. That this is so is clearly illustrated by the results of a study conducted by Baron, Vandello, and Brunsman (1996). (Robert S. Baron is *not* the Robert Baron who is a coauthor of this text.) In this investigation, the researchers used an ingenious modification of the Asch line-judging task. They showed participants a drawing of a person and then asked them to identify this person from among several other drawings in a kind of simulated eyewitness lineup. In one condition, the drawing was shown for only 0.5 second; this made the identification task quite difficult to perform. In another condition, it was shown for 5.0 seconds, and the task was much easier. Another aspect of the study involved the importance of making an accurate decision. Half the participants were told that the study was only preliminary in nature, so results were not very important. The others were told that the results were very important to the researchers.

To measure conformity, participants were exposed to the judgments of two assistants, who identified the *wrong* person before making their own choice in the simulated lineup. The overall prediction was that when the study was described as being very important, participants would be more likely to conform when the task was difficult (when they saw the drawings for only 0.5 second) than when the task was easy (when they saw the photos for 5.0 seconds). This would be so because, under these conditions, participants would be uncertain of their own decisions and would rely on the judgments of the assistants. When the study was described as being relatively unimportant, however, task difficulty wouldn't matter: conformity would be the same in both conditions. As you can see from Figure 9.8 on page 360, results offered clear support for these predictions. These findings suggest that our desire to be correct or accurate can be a strong source of conformity, but primarily when we are uncertain about what is correct or accurate in a given situation.

■ JUSTIFYING CONFORMITY: THE COGNITIVE CONSEQUENCES OF GOING ALONG WITH THE GROUP. Asch (1951, 1955) reported that some people who conform do so without any reservations: they conclude that they are wrong and the others are right. For these people, conforming poses only a very temporary dilemma at most. But for many persons, the decision to yield to group pressure and do as others do is more

informational social influence: Social influence based on individuals' desire to be correct—to possess accurate perceptions of the social world.

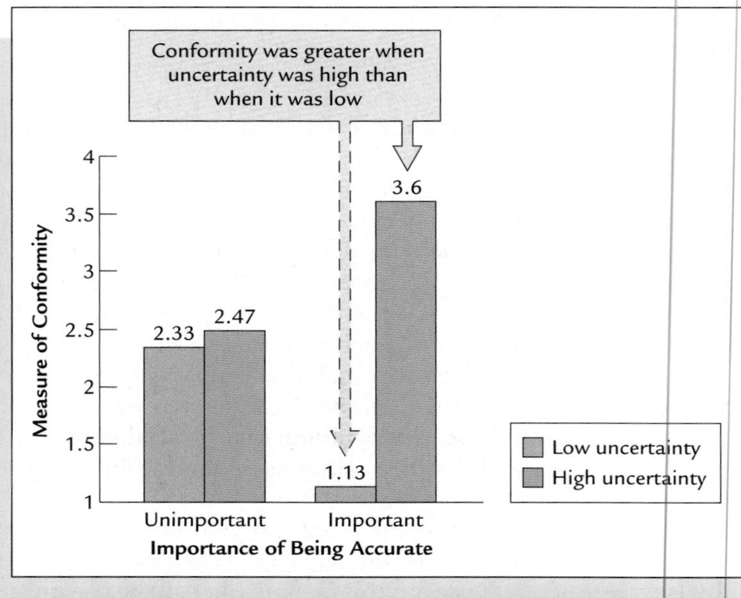

FIGURE 9.8

Evidence for the Operation of Informational Social Influence. When the motivation to be accurate was high (the task was described as important) research participants showed a greater tendency to conform to the judgments of others when they were uncertain about the correct answer (the task was difficult) than when they had greater confidence in their own judgments (the task was easy). When motivation to be accurate was low (the task was described as unimportant), no such differences occurred. These findings suggest that our susceptibility to informational social influence varies with several factors. [SOURCE: BASED ON DATA FROM BARON, VANDELLO, & BRUNSMAN, 1996.]

complex. Such persons feel that their own judgment is correct, but at the same time, they don't want to be different; so they behave in ways that are inconsistent with their private beliefs. What are the effects of conformity on such persons? Research findings (e.g., Griffin & Buehler, 1993; Buehler & Griffin, 1994) suggest that one effect may involve a tendency to alter their perceptions of the situation so that conformity appears, in fact, to be justified. As John Kenneth Galbraith stated, "Faced with the choice between changing one's mind and proving that there is no need to do so, almost everyone gets busy on the proof!" (cited in Buehler & Griffin, 1994, p. 993).

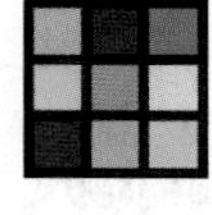

Several studies suggest that the decision to conform may be followed by changes in perceptions of the facts—changes that tend to justify conformity (e.g., Buehler & Griffin, 1994). Given these results, an interesting question arises: Would this same pattern occur in all cultures? In cultures that value individuals' individual choice backed by rational analysis of available information (e.g., the United States and many Western countries), such effects would be expected to occur: People feel a strong need to explain why they conformed. In cultures that place greater value on group judgments and on avoiding disagreements with others, however, the pressures toward such cognitive justification may be weaker (Bond & Smith, 1996). As noted by Buehler and Griffin (1994), this is an intriguing issue well deserving of further study.

KEY POINTS

- Many factors determine whether, and to what extent, conformity occurs. These include *cohesiveness*—the degree of attraction felt by an individual toward some group, group size, and type of social norm operating in that situation—*descriptive* or *injunctive*.
- We are most likely to behave in ways consistent with norms when they are relevant to us.
- Norms tend to persist over time. This is one reason why a *culture of honor* still exists in the South and West of the United States.
- Two important motives underlie our tendency to conform: the desire to be liked by others and the desire to be right or accurate. These two motives are reflected in two distinct types of social influence, *normative* and *informational social influence*.
- The desire to be liked by others, or fear of rejection by them, results in *jeer pressure*—the desire to avoid rejection by sticking even closer to existing social norms.
- Once we show conformity in a given situation, we tend to view it as justified, even if it has required us to behave in ways contrary to our true beliefs.

Resisting Pressures to Conform: Why, Sometimes, We Choose *Not* to Go Along

Having read our discussion of normative and informational social influence, you may now have the distinct impression that pressures toward conformity are so strong that they are all but impossible to resist. If so, take heart. In many cases, individuals—or groups of individuals—*do* resist (see Figure 9.9). This

"You are so stubborn."

FIGURE 9.9
Resisting Pressures to Conform. Like the character in this cartoon, most of us sometimes resist even strong pressures to conform.
[SOURCE:]

was certainly true in Asch's research; as you may recall, most of the participants yielded to social pressure, but *only part of the time.* On many occasions, they stuck to their guns, even in the face of a unanimous majority that disagreed with them. If you want other illustrations, just look around you: you will find that while most persons adhere to social norms most of the time, many do not. For example, the former Dean of my College almost never wore a tie, even in situations in which all other men were wearing them. Clearly, he chose not to conform to this particular social norm. Most of us make similar choices: we conform to most social norms, but not completely, and certainly not to all of them. What accounts for this ability to resist even powerful pressures toward conformity? Many factors appear to be important (e.g., Burger, 1992), but two seem to be most important: the need to maintain our individuality, and the need to maintain control over our own lives.

The need to maintain our individuality, in particular, appears to be a powerful one. Yes, we want to be like others—but not, it seems, to the extent that we lose our personal identity. In other words, along with the needs to be right and to be liked, most of us possess a desire for **individuation**—for being distinguishable from others in some respects (e.g., Maslach, Santee, & Wade, 1987). In general, we want to be like others—especially others we like or respect—but we don't want to be *exactly* like these persons, because that would involve giving up our individuality (e.g., Snyder & Fromkin, 1979).

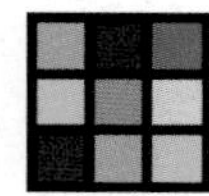

If this is so, then an interesting prediction relating to cultural diversity follows: The tendency to conform will be lower in cultures that emphasize individuality (individualistic cultures) than in ones that emphasize being part of the group (collectivist cultures). A large study by Bond and Smith (1996) examined this hypothesis by comparing conformity in seventeen different countries. They examined the results of 133 past studies that used the Asch line-judging task to measure conformity. Among these studies, they identified ones conducted in countries with collectivistic cultures (e.g., countries in Africa and Asia) and ones with individualistic cultures (ones in North America and Western Europe). Then they compared the amount of conformity shown in these two groups of countries. Results indicated that more conformity did indeed occur in the countries with collectivistic cultures, where the motive to maintain one's individuality was expected to be lower, and this was true regardless of the size of the influencing group. Similar results have been obtained in other studies (e.g., Hamilton & Sanders, 1995), so it does appear that the need for individuation varies greatly across different cultures, and that these differences, in turn, influence the tendency to conform.

Another reason why individuals often choose to resist group pressure involves their desire to maintain control over the events in their lives (e.g., Daubman, 1993). Most persons want to believe that they can determine what happens to them, and yielding to social pressure sometimes runs counter to this desire. After all, going along with a group implies behaving in ways one might not ordinarily choose, and this, in turn, can be viewed as a restriction of personal freedom and control. The results of many studies suggest that the stronger individuals' need for personal control, the less likely they are to yield to social pressure; so this factor, too, appears to be an important one where resisting conformity is concerned.

In sum, two motives—the desire to retain our individuality and the desire to retain control over our own lives—serve to counter our desires to be liked and to be accurate, and so reduce conformity. Whether we conform in a given situation, then, depends on the relative strength of these various motives and the complex interplay between them. Once again, therefore, we come face to face with the fact that trying to understand the roots of social behavior is often as complex as it is fascinating.

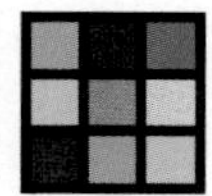

individuation: The need to be distinguishable from others in some respects.

■ PEOPLE WHO CANNOT CONFORM. So far in this discussion, we have been focusing on people who can conform but choose not to do so. There are also many persons who cannot conform for physical, legal, or psychological reasons. For instance, consider persons who are physically challenged. While they can certainly lead rich, full

FIGURE 9.10

Persons Who Cannot Conform.

Some persons who would like to conform to existing social norms cannot do so because of physical, psychological, or legal barriers. For instance, in most countries, homosexual couples cannot marry, even if they are in a long-term stable relationship and wish to do so. Only in one country—the Netherlands—are such marriages legal.

lives and participate in many activities that other persons enjoy, they cannot adhere to some social norms because of their physical limitations. For instance, some cannot stand when the national anthem is played, and others cannot adhere to accepted styles of dress for similar reasons.

Homosexuals, too, face difficulties in adhering to social norms. Many persons in this group participate in stable, long-term relationships with a partner and would like to conform to the social norm stating that those who love each other may get married. Until, recently, however, this was not possible in most countries. Even now, marriage between homosexuals is fully legal in only one—the Netherlands (see Figure 9.10). While this is a complex issue relating to moral, religious, and ethical concerns, and is outside the realm of science, it is important to note that many people find it difficult or impossible to adhere to existing social norms even when they wish to, and that, as a result, they face difficulties and conflicts unfamiliar to others.

Minority Influence: Does the Majority Always Rule?

As we just stated, individuals can, and often do, resist group pressure. Lone dissenters or small minorities can dig in their heels and refuse to go along. Yet there is more to the story than this; in addition, there are instances in which such persons—*minorities* within their groups—can turn the tables on the majority and exert rather than merely receive social influence. History provides many examples of such events. Giants of science, such as Galileo, Pasteur, and Freud, faced virtually unanimous majorities who initially rejected their views. Yet, over time, these famous persons overcame such resistance and won widespread acceptance for their theories. More recent examples of minorities influencing majorities are provided by the successes of environmentalists. Initially, such persons were viewed as wild-eyed radicals with strange ideas. Gradually, however, they succeeded in changing the attitudes of the majority so that today, many of their views are widely accepted.

But when, precisely, do minorities succeed in influencing majorities? Research findings suggest that they are most likely to do so under certain conditions (Moscovici, 1985). First, the members of such groups must be *consistent* in their opposition to majority opinions. If they waver or seem to be divided, their impact is reduced. Second, members of the minority must avoid appearing to be rigid and dogmatic (Mugny, 1975). A minority that merely repeats the same position over and over again is less persuasive than one that demonstrates a degree of flexibility. Third, the general social context in which a minority operates is important. If a minority argues for a position that is consistent with current social trends (e.g., conservative views at a time of growing conservatism), its chances of influencing the majority are greater than if it argues for a position out of step with wider trends.

Of course, even when these conditions are met, minorities face a tough uphill fight. The power of majorities is great, especially in ambiguous or complex social situations, in which majorities are viewed as more reliable sources of information about what is true than are minorities. In this sense, however, the threat posed by majorities to minorities may actually be of help to these minorities. Recent findings indicate that because they feel greater concern over being right (i.e., holding correct views), minorities tend to overestimate the number of persons who share their views. In other words, they perceive more support for their positions than actually exists (Kenworthy & Miller, 2001). This can be encouraging, and serve to strengthen the resolve of minorities to persevere in the face of daunting odds.

If minorities persist, they may ultimately triumph and find that *their* views are now in the majority; that is precisely what happened with respect to the environmental movement, as noted above. But what happens to minorities when they become the majority? And what happens to majorities when they fall from their favored position? Prislin, Limbert, and Bauer (2000) have investigated these questions, and have obtained some surprising results. On the basis of earlier research, they predicted that the loss experienced by majorities who become minorities would be greater than the gain experienced by minorities who become majorities (an *asymmetry model*). To test this hypothesis, they had four-person groups discuss their views about preservation of the environment. Unknown to participants, three of the persons in each group were assistants of the researchers, and two of them either agreed with the participant on most issues (thus placing this person in the majority) or disagreed with the participant (thus placing this person in the minority). As the discussion progressed, either all three assistants maintained their position (the no-change condition) or one of them changed (to *agreeing* with the participant if the assistant initially agreed or to *disagreeing* if this person initially agreed; this was the partial change condition). Finally, in a third condition (the complete-change condition), two of the assistants changed their views.

After the group discussion was completed, participants rated their similarity toward the group and how much they liked it. The asymmetry model predicts greater change for the participants who moved from being a majority to being a minority than for participants who experienced the opposite pattern (those who moved from being a minority to being a majority). As Figure 9.11 illustrates, results confirmed this prediction. In short, losing one's majority position had stronger effects on participants' reactions toward the group (making these less favorable) than did gaining a majority position after being a minority (in which case, views became more favorable, but to a lesser extent). These findings have important implications, suggesting that minorities whose views gain ascendance may be on somewhat shaky ground, at least for a while. The defeated majority experiences strong negative reactions, while the newly powerful minority (now in the majority) shows weaker positive reactions. As a result, the newly triumphant minority may be in a vulnerable position, at least initially. If they do not take actions to cement their victory, it may, in fact, be short-lived.

Before concluding this discussion, we should note one more point: Additional evidence suggests that one positive effect produced by minorities is that they induce the majority to exert increased cognitive effort in order to understand *why* the

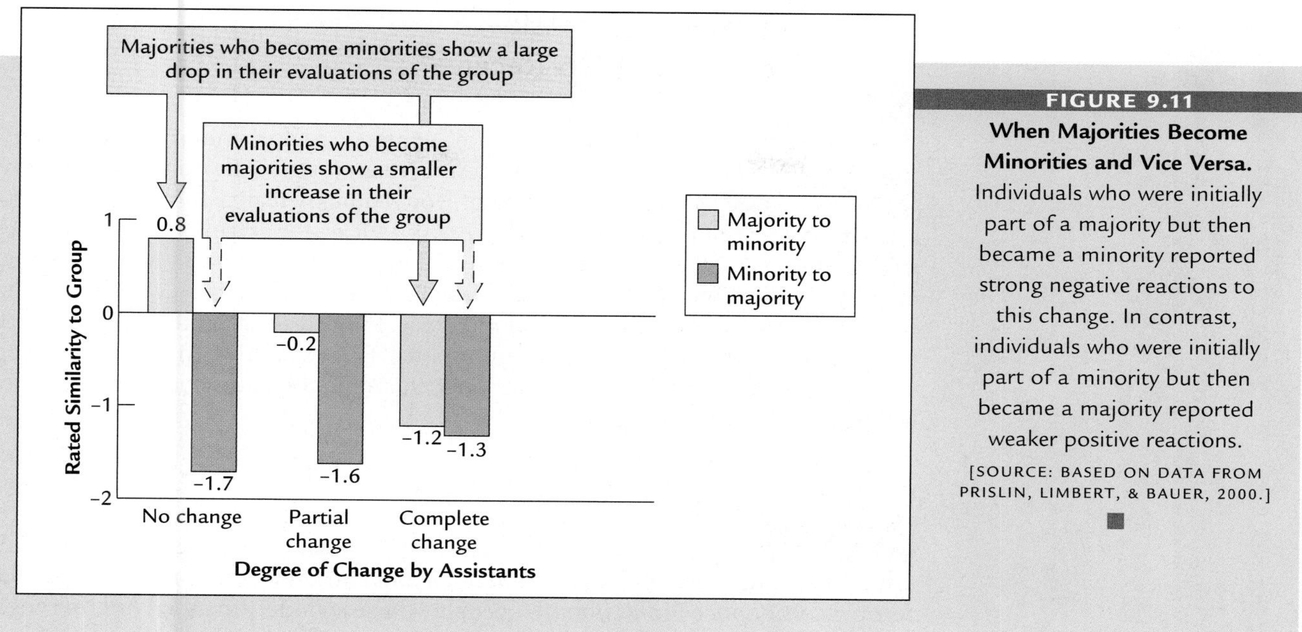

FIGURE 9.11

When Majorities Become Minorities and Vice Versa. Individuals who were initially part of a majority but then became a minority reported strong negative reactions to this change. In contrast, individuals who were initially part of a minority but then became a majority reported weaker positive reactions.

[SOURCE: BASED ON DATA FROM PRISLIN, LIMBERT, & BAUER, 2000.]

minority holds its unusual and unpopular views (Nemeth, 1995; Vonk & van Knippenberg, 1995). In other words, deeply committed and vocal minorities can encourage members of the majority to engage in *systematic processing* with respect to information they provide (e.g., Smith, Tindale, & Dugoni, 1996; Wood et al., 1996). Similarly, minority members may engage in more careful (systematic) thought themselves concerning their unpopular views. This, in turn, may lead them to generate stronger arguments with which to influence the majority (Zdaniuk & Levine, 1996). So even if minorities fail to sway majorities initially, they may initiate processes, such as more careful consideration of opposing ideas, that ultimately lead to large-scale social change (e.g., Alvaro & Crano, 1996).

KEY POINTS

- While pressures toward conformity are strong, many persons resist them, at least part of the time. This resistance seems to stem from two strong motives: the desire to retain one's individuality, and the desire to exert control over one's own life.
- Under some conditions, minorities can induce even large majorities to change their attitudes or behavior.
- Because their views are threatened, minorities often overestimate the number of persons who share their beliefs.
- Majorities who become minorities experience strong negative reactions; in contrast, the positive reactions of minorities who become majorities are somewhat weaker.
- One positive effect of minorities is that they induce majorities to think more systematically about the issues minorities raise. This may facilitate large-scale social change.

Compliance: To Ask—Sometimes—Is to Receive

Suppose that you wanted someone to do something for you; how would you go about getting them to agree? If you think about this question for a moment, you'll quickly realize that you have quite a few tricks up your sleeve for gaining *compliance*—for getting others to say yes to your requests. What are these techniques like? Which ones work best? These are among the questions studied by social psychologists in their efforts to understand this, the most frequent form of social influence. In the discussion that follows, we'll examine many tactics for gaining compliance. Before turning to these, however, we'll introduce a basic framework for understanding the nature of all of these procedures and why they often work.

Compliance: The Underlying Principles

Some years ago, one well-known social psychologist (Robert Cialdini) decided that the best way to find out about compliance was to study what he termed *compliance professionals*—people whose success (financial or otherwise) depends on their ability to get others to say yes. Who are such persons? They include salespeople, advertisers, political lobbyists, fund-raisers, politicians, con artists, professional negotiators, and many others. Cialdini's technique for learning from these people was simple: he temporarily concealed his true identity and took jobs in various settings in which gaining compliance is a way of life. In other words, he worked in advertising, direct (door-to-door) sales, fund-raising, and other compliance-focused fields. On the basis of these first-hand experiences, he concluded that although techniques for gaining compliance take many different forms, they all rest to some degree on six basic principles (Cialdini, 1994):

- *Friendship/liking:* In general, we are more willing to comply with requests from friends or from people we like than with requests from strangers or people we don't like.
- *Commitment/consistency:* Once we have committed ourselves to a position or action, we are more willing to comply with requests for behaviors that are consistent with this position or action than with requests that are inconsistent with it.
- *Scarcity:* In general, we value, and try to secure, outcomes or objects that are scarce or decreasing in their availability. As a result, we are more likely to comply with requests that focus on scarcity than with ones that make no reference to this issue.
- *Reciprocity:* We are generally more willing to comply with a request from someone who has previously provided a favor or concession to us than to oblige someone who has not. In other words, we feel compelled to pay people back in some way for what they have done for us.
- *Social validation:* We are generally more willing to comply with a request for some action if this action is consistent with what we believe persons similar to ourselves are doing (or thinking). We want to be correct, and one way to do so is to act and think like others.
- *Authority:* In general, we are more willing to comply with requests from someone who holds legitimate authority—or who simply appears to do so.

According to Cialdini (1994), these basic principles underlie many techniques used by professionals—and ourselves—for gaining compliance from others. We'll now examine techniques based on these principles, plus a few others as well.

Tactics Based on Friendship or Liking: Ingratiation

We've already considered several techniques for increasing compliance through liking in our discussion of *impression management* (Chapter 2). As you may recall, impression management involves various procedures for making a good impression on others. While this can be an end in itself, impression management techniques are often used for purposes of **ingratiation**—for getting others to like us so that they will be more willing to agree to our requests (Jones, 1964; Liden & Mitchell, 1988).

Which ingratiation techniques work best? A review of existing studies on this topic (Gordon, 1996) suggests that *flattery*—praising others in some manner—is one of the best. As the cartoon in Figure 9.12 suggests, flattery doesn't have to focus on the recipient to succeed; it can also heap praise on someone close to this individual (e.g., his or her children). Other techniques that seem to work are improving one's own appearance, emitting many positive nonverbal cues, and doing small favors for the target persons (Gordon, 1996; Wayne & Liden, 1995). We described many of these tactics in detail in Chapter 2, so we won't repeat that information here. Suffice it to say that many of the tactics used for purposes of impression management are also successful from the point of view of increasing compliance.

ingratiation: A technique for gaining compliance in which requesters first induce target persons to like them, then attempt to change their behavior in some desired manner.

FIGURE 9.12

Flattery: A Powerful Tool for Gaining Compliance. Flattery is one highly effective technique for gaining compliance. As shown here, it doesn't have to focus on the recipient to be effective; compliments for persons close to the recipient (e.g., his or her children) can also succeed. [SOURCE: UNIVERSAL PRESS SYNDICATE, MAY 6, 2000.]

Tactics Based on Commitment or Consistency: The Foot-in-the-Door and the Lowball

Every time I (RAB) visit the food court of our local shopping mall, I am approached by one or more persons who offer me free samples of various foods. The reason behind these actions is obvious: The persons offering the free samples hope that once I have accepted these gifts, I'll like the taste of the food and will then be more willing to buy my lunch at their business. This is the basic idea behind an approach for gaining compliance known as the **foot-in-the-door technique.** In operation, this tactic involves inducing target persons to agree to a small initial request ("Accept this free sample") and then making a larger request—the one desired all along. The results of many studies indicate that this tactic works; it succeeds in inducing increased compliance (e.g., Beaman et al., 1983; Freedman & Fraser, 1966). Why is this the case? Because the foot-in-the-door technique rests on the principle of *consistency*: once we have said yes to the small request, we are more likely to say yes to subsequent and larger ones, too, because refusing these would be inconsistent with our previous behavior. For example, imagine that you wanted to borrow lecture notes for several weeks' classes from one of your friends. You might begin by asking for the notes from one lecture. After copying these, you might come back with a larger request: the notes for all the other classes. If your friend complied, it might well be because refusing would be inconsistent with his or her initial yes (e.g., DeJong & Musilli, 1982).

The foot-in-the-door technique is not the only tactic based on the consistency/commitment principle, however. Another is the **lowball technique.** In this procedure, which is often used by automobile salespersons, a very good deal is offered to a customer. After the customer accepts, however, something happens that makes it necessary for the salesperson to change the deal and make it less advantageous for the customer—for example, the sales manager rejects the deal. The totally rational reaction for customers, of course, would be to walk away. Yet often they agree to the changes and accept the less desirable arrangement (Cialdini et al., 1978; see Figure 9.13). In instances such as this, an initial commitment seems to make it more difficult for individuals to say no, even though the conditions that led them to say yes in the first place are now changed.

Tactics Based on Reciprocity: The Door-in-the-Face and the "That's-Not-All" Techniques

Reciprocity is a basic rule of social life: we usually do unto others as they have done unto us. If they have done a favor for us, therefore, we feel that we should be willing to do one for them in return. While this convention is viewed by most persons as being fair and just, the principle of reciprocity also serves as the basis for several techniques for gaining compliance. One of these is, on the face of it, the opposite of the foot-in-the-door technique. Instead of beginning with a small request and then escalating to a larger one, persons seeking compliance sometimes start with a very large request and then, after this is rejected, shift to a smaller request—the one they wanted all along. This tactic is known as the **door-in-the-face technique** (because the first refusal seems to slam the door in the face of the requester), and several studies indicate that it can be quite effective. For example, in one well-known experiment, Cialdini and his colleagues (1975) stopped college students on the street and presented a huge request: Would the students serve as unpaid counselors for juvenile delinquents two hours a week for the net *two years!* As you can guess, no one agreed. When the experimenters then scaled down their request to a much smaller one—would the same students take a group of delinquents on a two-hour trip to the zoo—fully 50 percent agreed. In contrast, fewer than 17 percent of those in a control group agreed to this smaller request when it was presented cold rather than after the larger request.

foot-in-the-door technique: A procedure for gaining compliance in which requesters begin with a small request and then, when this is granted, escalate to a larger one (the one they actually desired all along).

lowball technique: A technique for gaining compliance in which an offer or deal is changed (made less attractive) after the target person has accepted it.

door-in-the-face technique: A procedure for gaining compliance in which requesters begin with a large request and then, when this is refused, retreat to a smaller one (the one they actually desired all along).

FIGURE 9.13

The Lowball Technique: A Procedure for Gaining Compliance Based on the Principle of Commitment.

Many automobile salespersons use the *lowball technique.* In this procedure for gaining compliance, customers are offered a very attractive deal which they accept. The deal is then rejected by the sales manager, who raises the price or makes some other change unfavorable to the customer. Rationally, people should walk away from such deals, but because of prior commitment, they often accept them.

The same tactic is often used by negotiators, who may begin with a position that is extremely advantageous to themselves but then retreat to a position much closer to the one they really hope to obtain. Similarly, sellers often begin with a price they know buyers will reject, then lower the price to a more reasonable one—but one that is still quite favorable to themselves, and close to what they wanted all along.

A related procedure for gaining compliance is known as the **"that's-not all" technique.** Here, an initial request is followed, *before the target person can say yes or no,* by something that sweetens the deal—a small extra incentive from the persons using this tactic (e.g., a reduction in price, "throwing in" something additional for the same price). For example, television commercials for various products frequently offer something extra to induce viewers to pick up the phone and place an order. Several studies confirm informal observations suggesting that the "that's-not-all technique" really works (Burger, 1986). Why is this so? One possibility is that this tactic succeeds because it is based on the principle of reciprocity: Persons on the receiving end of this technique view the "extra" thrown in by the other side as an added concession, and so feel obligated to make a concession themselves. The result: They are more likely to say yes.

Another possibility is that creating the appearance of a bargain by reducing the price of an item or offering to add something extra causes individuals to think about the situation in an automatic or, as social psychologists sometimes put it, *mindless* way (e.g., Langer, 1984). "This is a bargain," people might reason, and in accordance with this heuristic thinking, become more likely to say yes than would be true if they were thinking more systematically. Evidence for this suggestion was reported by Pollock and his colleagues (1998). They found that a small price reduction produced the "that's-not-all" effect for a low-cost item (a $1.25 box of chocolates reduced to $1.00), but did not produce this effect for a more expensive item (a $6.25 box

"that's-not-all" technique: A technique for gaining compliance in which requesters offer target persons additional benefits before they have decided whether to comply with or reject specific requests.

reduced to $5.00). Apparently, individuals thought more carefully about spending $5.00, and this countered their tendency to respond automatically—and favorably—to a small price reduction. Whatever its precise basis, the "that's-not-all" technique can often be an effective means for increasing the likelihood that others will say yes to various requests.

Tactics Based on Scarcity: Playing Hard to Get and the Fast-Approaching-Deadline Technique

It's a general rule of life that things that are scarce, rare, or difficult to obtain are viewed as being more valuable than those that are plentiful or easy to obtain. Thus, we are often willing to expend more effort or go to greater expense to obtain items or outcomes that are scarce than to obtain ones that are in large supply. This principle serves as the foundation for several techniques for gaining compliance. One of the most common of these is **playing hard to get.**

Many people know that this can be an effective tactic in the area of romance: by suggesting that it is difficult to win their affection or that there are many rivals for their love, individuals can greatly increase their desirability (e.g., Walster et al., 1973). This tactic is not restricted to interpersonal attraction, however; research findings indicate that it is also sometimes used by job candidates to increase their attractiveness to potential employers, and hence to increase the likelihood that these employers will offer them a job. Persons using this tactic let the potential employer know that they have other offers and so are a very desirable employee. And in fact, research findings indicate that this technique often works (Williams et al., 1993).

A related procedure also based on the same what's-scarce-is-valuable principle is one frequently used by department stores. Ads using this **deadline technique** state that a special sale will end on a certain date, implying that after that the prices will go up. In many cases, the time limit is false: the prices won't go up after the indicated date and may, in fact, continue to drop if the merchandise remains unsold. Yet many persons reading such ads, or seeing signs like the one in Figure 9.14, believe them and hurry down to the store to avoid missing out on a great opportunity. So when you encounter an offer suggesting that the clock is ticking and may soon run out, be cautious: this may simply be a technique for boosting sales.

Before concluding, we should note that the principle of *social validation,* another one of Cialdini's (1994) basic principles, is closely related to conformity, and especially to informational social influence. Social validation suggests that we often comply with requests for actions that we view as being consistent with what persons similar to ourselves are doing (or thinking). So the next time someone suggests to you that you should do something they want you to do because "it's what people like us are doing," you should be on guard: the chances are good that this is a tactic for gaining compliance rather than a simple description of what is appropriate behavior.

KEY POINTS

- Individuals use many different tactics for gaining *compliance*—getting others to say yes to various requests. Many of these rest on basic principles well known to social psychologists.
- Two widely used tactics, the *foot-in-the-door* and the *lowball procedure* rest on the principle of commitment/consistency. In contrast, the *door-in-the-face* and the *"that's-not-all"* techniques rest on the principle of reciprocity.
- *Playing hard to get* and the *deadline technique* are based on the principle of scarcity—the idea that what is scarce or hard to obtain is valuable.
- Social validation, another basic principle underlying compliance, is closely related to informational social influence and conformity.

playing hard to get: A technique that can be used for increasing compliance by suggesting that a person or object is scarce and hard to obtain.

deadline technique: A technique for increasing compliance in which target persons are told that they have only limited time to take advantage of some offer or to obtain some item.

FIGURE 9.14
The Deadline Technique in Action.
Advertisers often use the *deadline technique* to convince customers to buy now—before it's too late!

Other Tactics for Gaining Compliance: The Pique Technique and Putting Others in a Good Mood

A few days ago, I (RAB) was invited to dinner at a good French restaurant. The meal was excellent, but on the way out, we were met by a very persistent panhandler who kept asking us, "How was that chicken dinner?" followed by "And how about some money for a homeless person?" We ignored her, and kept on walking. Later, though, I wondered why. We are not a hard-hearted group—far from it. The answer, I think, is that we were acting on "automatic"—following a well-learned tendency to ignore panhandlers because there are many in my city, and stopping to help all of them is really impossible.

If our tendency to ignore requests from strangers is indeed often the result of such thinking on automatic (or *mindlessness,* as it is sometimes termed), then anything that gets us out of this state and causes us to really think about a request from a stranger might increase our tendency to comply. This is the basis for another technique for gaining compliance, known as the **pique technique.** It involves *piquing* (stimulating) the target person's interest. Evidence that the pique technique really works is provided by several studies. For example, Santos, Leve, and Pratkanis (1994) conducted research in which female assistants played the role of panhandlers and asked passersby for money. In two conditions not expected to pique interest, they asked, "Can you spare any change?" or "Can you spare a quarter?" In two other conditions, expected to pique the interest of passersby and prevent them from

pique technique: A technique for gaining compliance in which target persons' interest is piqued (stimulated) by unusual requests. As a result, they do not refuse requests automatically, as is often the case.

rejecting the requests automatically, the assistants made unusual requests: "Can you spare 17 cents?" or "Can you spare 37 cents?" Results indicated that the pique technique was very effective: while about 75 percent of passersby exposed to the pique technique conditions gave money to the assistants, only about half (on average) gave money in the other two conditions.

These findings suggest that charitable organizations might increase the amount of money they collect by doing something that makes their requests unusual or attention-getting. In fact, this is actually done on my own campus where faculty are "arrested" once a year by students taking part in a charity drive. The faculty members can only be released from jail if they—or others—pay their "bail." This procedure is highly successful, and I have always believed that it works because the props it uses (students dressed as sheriffs, large cages to hold faculty members) all pique the interest of passersby. Of course, I can't tell for sure in the absence of systematic research, but it does seem to be one reasonable interpretation of why these procedures work so well.

Another tactic for gaining compliance is one with which we're sure you are already familiar: putting others in a good mood before making your request. Flattery and other tactics of ingratiation are often used for this purpose, and as we noted earlier, they can be quite successful if not overdone (Gordon, 1996). But many other techniques can—and apparently do—accomplish the same end (e.g., Rind, 1996).

For example, consider an intriguing study by Rind and Bordia (1996). These researchers asked waitpersons of both genders either to draw a smiling face on the back of the checks they gave to customers or to leave this artwork off the checks. On the basis of previous studies (e.g., Rind & Bordia, 1996), the researchers predicted that the smiling face would be interpreted as a sign of friendliness on the part of female waitpersons, and this, in turn, would put customers in a slightly better mood. As a result, they would leave larger tips than would customers who did not see the smiling face. However, such effects would not occur for male waitpersons, because drawing the smiling face would be seen as less gender appropriate for them. Results confirmed these predictions: The tips received by female waitpersons rose almost 19 percent when they drew the smiling face; similar effects were *not* observed for male waitpersons. These results, and those of many other studies conducted both in the lab and field (e.g., Baron, 1997a; Rind, 1996), suggest that almost *anything* that puts people in a better mood (i.e., that induces positive affect) can increase their tendency to say yes to various requests.

For an overview of various tactics for gaining compliance, see the **Ideas to Take with You—and Use!** feature on page 383. And for an unsettling illustration of how techniques for gaining compliance are used by unscrupulous persons in real-life situations, see the following **Beyond the Headlines** section.

KEY POINTS

- In the *pique technique,* compliance with requests is increased by piquing (stimulating) target persons' interest, so that they do not refuse requests automatically.
- Another tactic for gaining compliance involves putting others in a good mood before making a request. Evidence indicates that this tactic is especially likely to succeed if something about the request induces target persons to think systematically about it.
- While everyone engages in efforts to exert social influence on others, research findings indicate that the specific tactics individuals choose are related to their own traits and characteristics.

BEYOND THE HEADLINES: AS SOCIAL PSYCHOLOGISTS SEE IT

HIGH-PRESSURE TACTICS FOR GAINING COMPLIANCE: DO YOU REALLY NEED A $1500 VACUUM CLEANER? DOES ANYONE?

How Kirby Persuades Uncertain Consumers: The Door-to-Door Hard Sell Brings Profits

Wall Street Journal, October 4, 1999—In the world of home appliances, Kirby Co. likes to consider its product the Porsche of vacuum cleaners. . . . With a price tag of around $1500, it costs more than four times what other top-of-the-line vacuum cleaners do. And after 64 years, it is still being marketed exclusively door-to-door—often to people who can ill afford a $1500 gadget but succumb to the sales pitch nonetheless. . . . For example, in May 1996, Stephen and Wilma Tucker were sitting down to dinner when three Kirby salesmen showed up at their Springfield, Vermont home and spent five hours selling their product despite protests from the 60-year-old Mr. Tucker that he was disabled, unemployed, and incapable of buying so expensive a machine. One salesman even helped himself to some fried chicken, the Tuckers say. Finally, "More or less just to get them out of there, we agreed to it," Mr. Tucker says. In another case, 78-year-old Henrietta Taylor and her husband Dennis, 79, answered a knock on the door of their mobile home in Fort Meade, Florida, to find two Kirby salesmen standing on the stoop. The Taylors didn't need a vacuum, but the salesmen persisted with an hour-and-a-half demonstration that included dumping dirt on the carpet to show off the Kirby's cleaning power. "They were the pushiest people I ever saw," Mrs. Taylor says. The Taylors agreed to buy the machine for $1,749. That far exceeded the value of their own carpet. It also exceeded their monthly income of $1,100 in Social Security. To finance the purchase, the salesmen arranged for a loan—with a 21.19% annual interest rate—that brought the total in payments to $2553.06. The company says it has a "Golden-Ager Policy" requiring distributors to agree to cancel sales to customers over the age of 65, up to a year after the transaction, with no questions asked. But this policy didn't help Thorhild Christopher, who died in December 1996 at age 76. She lived alone in a mobile home, scraping by on about $1,000 a month in Social Security payments and her husband's pension. When she died, she owned two Kirby vacuum cleaners, the last one sold to her in September 1995. . . .

What's going on here? Why would elderly persons living on small pensions and in mobile homes agree to buy a vacuum cleaner worth more than all the rugs they own (see Figure 9.15 on page 374)? What mysterious tactics do Kirby salespersons use to induce such customers to go into debt (at high interest) for a product they don't need? On closer inspection, the mystery vanishes. In fact, the tactics used by these salespersons for gaining sales—and compliance—are very familiar to social psychologists. For example, the Kirby salespersons often use the foot-in-the-door approach. At first, they offer to shampoo the potential customer's rugs free of charge. Only after they have finished do they begin their sales pitch for the vacuum.

In addition, of course, the "free shampoos" create a sense of obligation in the customers. The salespersons have done something for them, so now the potential customers feel that they should reciprocate by doing something for the salespersons. They don't plan to spend this much on a vacuum cleaner, so at this point, the salespersons often switch to other tactics. They alternate praising the potential customers ("Surely someone as intelligent as you can see what a wonderful machine this is!") with statements about a "special price" that is only available today (the approaching-deadline technique). And then they simply refuse to leave, thus putting customers in a confused and fatigued state in which their resistance is greatly weakened. The door-in-the-face tactic, too, is often employed. The $1500 price is "reduced" to payments of only "$30 or $40" per month. This sounds like a major concession to exhausted, elderly customers, who reciprocate by saying yes.

In short, there is no mystery here: Kirby salespersons succeed because they combine a large array of techniques for gaining compliance and

(continued)

FIGURE 9.15

Social Influence in Action.
What makes one vacuum cleaner worth several times the price of another? One answer involves high-pressure tactics of social influence used by salespersons to promote these products. Door-to-door salespersons, in particular, often use such techniques to convince consumers to pay $1,000 or more for a vacuum cleaner, when others of equal quality can be purchased in stores for much lower prices.

high motivation to make a sale with a lack of concern for the well-being of their customers. I (RAB) personally knew an elderly couple who had purchased one of these vacuums, as well as several costly options (e.g., an air filter for cleaning the air as you vacuum), and they praised it strongly any time it was mentioned. In truth, what choice did they have? They had already spent much more than they could afford on this appliance, so the only route left to them was to perceive it as "worth very penny." (Recall our discussion of cognitive dissonance in Chapter 4.) How sad that tactics of social influence are often used for such selfish ends!

Extreme Forms of Social Influence: Obedience to Authority and Intense Indoctrination

In this final section, we will focus on social influence carried to the extreme. Specifically, we'll examine two topics, *obedience* and *intense indoctrination.* In both, social influence is used to produce dramatic changes in behavior—changes far greater than that produced by other types of influence.

Destructive Obedience: Would You Harm an Innocent Stranger If Ordered to Do So?

Have you ever seen a military officer shout commands at troops, who then carry out these orders instantly? Have you ever watched a sports coach deliver a lecture to a player who towers over him but who listens meekly and quickly obeys the coach's commands? If so, you are aware of another form of social influence: *obedience*—instances in which someone in a position of authority simply tells or orders one or more other persons to do something—and they do it! Obedience is less frequent than conformity or compliance, because even persons who possess authority and could use it often prefer to exert influence through the *velvet glove*—through requests rather than direct orders (e.g., Yukl & Falbe, 1991). Still, obedience is far from rare; it occurs in many settings, ranging from schools (wouldn't you obey an order from your principal when you were in high school?) to military bases. Obedience to the commands of persons who possess authority is far from surprising; such persons usually have effective means for enforcing their orders. More surprising is the fact that, often, persons lacking in such power can also induce high levels of submission from others. The clearest and most dramatic evidence for such effects was reported by Stanley Milgram in a series of famous—and controversial—studies (Milgram, 1963, 1965a, 1974).

■ STUDYING DESTRUCTIVE OBEDIENCE IN THE LABORATORY. In his research, Milgram wished to find out whether individuals would obey commands from a relatively powerless stranger requiring them to inflict what seemed to be considerable pain on another person—a totally innocent victim. Milgram's interest in this topic derived from tragic events in which seemingly normal, law-abiding persons actually obeyed such directives. For example, during World War II, troops in the German army frequently obeyed commands to torture and murder millions of unarmed civilians. In fact, the Nazis established horrible but highly efficient death camps designed to eradicate Jews, Gypsies, and other groups they felt were inferior or a threat to their own racial purity. These events are described in vivid detail in the National Holocaust Museum in Washington, D.C., and we strongly recommend that you visit this museum if you ever get the chance to do so (see Figure 9.16).

FIGURE 9.16
Destructive Obedience: Its Ultimate Costs. The Holocaust Museum in Washington, D.C. presents dramatic evidence for the tragic results that may occur when destructive obedience is carried to extreme levels. ■

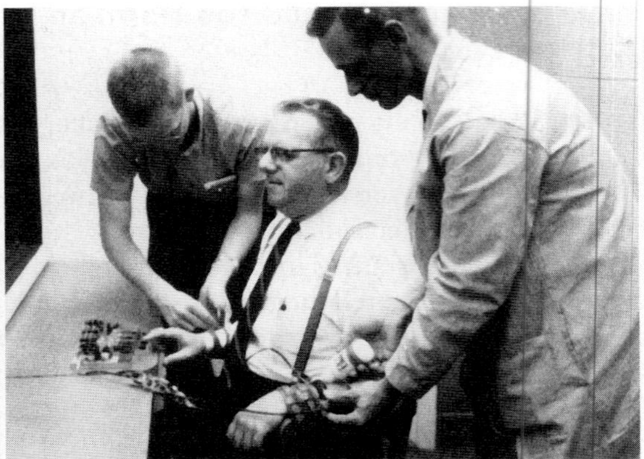

FIGURE 9.17

Studying Obedience in the Laboratory.

The photo on the left shows the apparatus Stanley Milgram used in his famous experiments on destructive obedience. The photo on the right shows the experimenter *(right front)* and a participant *(rear)* attaching electrodes to the learner's (accomplice's) wrist.

[SOURCE: FROM THE FILM *OBEDIENCE*, DISTRIBUTED BY THE NEW YORK UNIVERSITY FILM LIBRARY, COPYRIGHT 1965 BY STANLEY MILGRAM. REPRINTED BY PERMISSION OF THE COPYRIGHT HOLDER.]

In an effort to gain insights into the nature of such events, Milgram designed an ingenious, if unsettling, laboratory simulation. The experimenter informed participants in the study (all males) that they were taking part in an investigation of the effects of punishment on learning. One person in each pair of participants would serve as a "learner" and would try to perform a simple task involving memory (supplying the second word in previously memorized pairs of words after hearing only the first word). The other participant, the "teacher," would read these words to the learner and would punish errors by the learner (failures to provide the second word in each pair) through electric shock. These shocks would be delivered by means of the equipment shown in Figure 9.17. As you can see from the photo, this device contained thirty numbered switches ranging from 15 volts (the first) through 450 volts (the thirtieth). The two persons present—a real participant and a research assistant—then drew slips of paper from a hat to determine who would play each role; as you can guess, the drawing was rigged so that the real participant always became the teacher. The teacher was then told to deliver a shock to the learner each time he made an error on the task. Moreover—and this is crucial—teachers were told that they had to *increase the strength of the shock each time the learner made an error.* This meant that if the learner made many errors, he would soon be receiving strong jolts of electricity. It's important to note that this information was false: in reality, the assistant (the learner) *never received any shocks during the experiment.* The only real shock ever used was a mild pulse from button number 3 to convince participants that the equipment was real.

During the session, the learner (following prearranged instructions) made many errors. Thus, participants soon found themselves facing a dilemma: Should they continue punishing this person with what seemed to be increasingly painful shocks? Or should they refuse to go on? If they hesitated, the experimenter pressured them to continue with a graded series of "prods": "Please continue"; "The experiment requires that you continue"; "It is absolutely essential that you continue"; "You have no other choice—you *must* go on."

Because participants were all volunteers and were paid *in advance,* you might predict that most would quickly refuse the experimenter's orders. In reality, though, *fully 65 percent showed total obedience*—they proceeded through the entire series to the final 450-volt level. Many participants, of course, protested and asked that the session be ended. When ordered to proceed, however, a majority yielded to the experimenter's influence and continued to obey. Indeed, they continued doing so even when the victim pounded on the wall as if in protest over the painful shocks (at the 300-volt level), and even when he *no longer responded,* as if he had passed out. The experimenter told participants to treat failures to answer as errors; so from this point on, many participants believed that they were delivering dangerous shocks to someone who might already be unconscious!

In further experiments, Milgram (1965b, 1974) found that similar results could be obtained even under conditions that might be expected to reduce such obedience. When the study was moved from its original location on the campus of Yale University to a run-down office building in a nearby city, participants' level of obedience remained virtually unchanged. Similarly, a large proportion continued to obey, even when the accomplice complained about the painfulness of the shocks and begged to be released. Most surprising of all, many (about 30 percent) obeyed even when they were required to grasp the victim's hand and force it down upon a metal shock plate! That these chilling results are not restricted to a single culture is indicated by the fact that similar findings were soon reported in several different countries (e.g., Jordan, Germany, Australia) and with children as well as adults (e.g., Kilham & Mann, 1974; Shanab & Yahya, 1977). Thus, Milgram's findings seemed to be alarmingly general in scope.

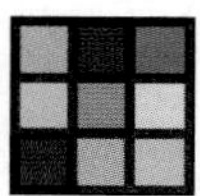

I (RAB) went to high school with Milgram's niece, and I can remember the disbelief with which students in my class reacted when she told us about her uncle's findings, several years before they were published. Psychologists, too, found Milgram's findings highly disturbing. On the one hand, psychologists were shaken by the results: Milgram's studies seemed to suggest that ordinary people are willing, although with some reluctance, to harm an innocent stranger if ordered to do so by someone in authority. This led to an important question: What factors lie behind this tendency to obey, even when obedience results in potential harm to others? Before turning to this question, though, we should comment on another reaction many psychologists had to Milgram's research: Was it ethical to conduct such studies? Some participants experienced extreme stress when faced with the dilemma of either harming an innocent stranger or disobeying a white-coated authority figure. And when they did, Milgram virtually ordered them to continue. (Seeing whether they would do so was one of the key goals of the study.) To deal with these issues, Milgram conducted a complete and thorough debriefing after each session (see Chapter 1); he tried to assure that no participant left the laboratory feeling distressed or disturbed. Still, it is possible that later, when they thought about their own behavior in this situation, some persons *did* become upset; after all, they had assumed they were harming an innocent person who never did anything to them, and for no strong reason.

The ethical issues raised by Milgram's research were so disturbing that they contributed to the adoption, by the field of psychology, of strict ethical guidelines designed to protect the rights and welfare of research participants. In view of these guidelines, it is probably safe to say that Milgram could not conduct his studies in the United States or many other countries today—these studies would not be approved by the Internal Review Boards that carefully evaluate all research involving human beings for potential risks to the participants. Please keep this fact in mind as you read further.

■ DESTRUCTIVE OBEDIENCE: ITS SOCIAL PSYCHOLOGICAL BASIS. As we noted earlier, one reason why Milgram's results are so disturbing is that they seem to parallel many real-life events involving atrocities against innocent victims. So we repeat the question raised above: Why does such *destructive obedience* occur? Why were participants in these experiments—and why are many persons in tragic situations outside the laboratory—so willing to yield to this powerful form of social influence? Social psychologists have identified several factors that seem to play a role, and several of these are related to other aspects of social influence we have already considered.

First, in many situations, the persons in authority relieve those who obey of the responsibility for their own actions. "I was only carrying out orders" is the defense many offer after obeying harsh or cruel commands. In life situations, this transfer of responsibility may be implicit; the person in charge (e.g., the military or police officer) is assumed to have the responsibility for what happens. In Milgram's experiments, this transfer of responsibility was explicit. Participants were told at the start that the experimenter (the authority figure), not they, would be responsible for the learner's well-being. In view of this fact, it is not surprising that many obeyed; after all, they were completely off the hook.

Second, persons in authority often possess visible badges or signs of their status. They wear special uniforms or insignia, have special titles, and so on. These serve to remind many persons of the social norm "Obey the persons in charge." This is a powerful norm, and when confronted with it, most people find it difficult to disobey. After all, we do not want to do the wrong thing, and obeying the commands of those who are in charge usually helps us avoid such errors. In a sense, then, informational social influence—a key factor in conformity to social norms—may have contributed to Milgram's results (e.g., Bushman, 1988; Darley, 1995).

A third reason for obedience in many situations in which the targets of such influence might otherwise resist involves the gradual escalation of the authority figure's orders. Initial commands may call for relatively mild actions, such as merely arresting people. Only later do orders come to require behavior that is dangerous or objectionable. For example, police or military personnel may at first be ordered only to question or threaten potential victims. Gradually, demands are increased to the point where these personnel are commanded to beat, torture, or even murder unarmed civilians. In a sense, persons in authority use the foot-in-the-door technique, asking for small actions first but ever-larger ones later. In a similar manner, participants in Milgram's research were first required to deliver only mild and harmless shocks to the victim. Only as the sessions continued did the intensity of these "punishments" rise to potentially harmful levels.

Finally, events in many situations involving destructive obedience move very quickly: demonstrations quite suddenly turn into riots, arrests into mass beatings or mass murder. The fast pace of such events gives participants little time for reflection or systematic processing: people are ordered to obey and—almost automatically—they do so. Such conditions prevailed in Milgram's research; within a few minutes of entering the laboratory, participants found themselves faced with commands to deliver strong electric shocks to the learner. This fast pace, too, may tend to increase obedience.

In sum, the high levels of obedience generated in Milgram's studies are not as mysterious as they may seem. A social psychological analysis of the conditions existing both there and in many real-life situations identifies several factors that, together, may make it very difficult for individuals to resist the commands they receive. The consequences, of course, can be truly tragic for innocent and often defenseless victims.

■ DESTRUCTIVE OBEDIENCE: RESISTING ITS EFFECTS. Now that we have considered some of the factors responsible for the strong tendency to obey sources of authority, we will turn to a related question: How can this type of social influence be resisted? Several strategies may be helpful in this respect.

First, individuals exposed to commands from authority figures can be reminded that they—not the authorities—are responsible for any harm produced. Under these conditions, sharp reductions in the tendency to obey have been observed (e.g., Hamilton, 1978; Kilham & Mann, 1974).

Second, individuals can be provided with a clear indication that beyond some point, total submission to destructive commands is inappropriate. One procedure that is highly effective in this regard involves exposing individuals to the actions of *disobedient models*—persons who refuse to obey an authority figure's commands. Research findings indicate that such models can greatly reduce unquestioning obedience (e.g., Rochat & Modigliani, 1995.) When we see one or more persons refuse to obey the commands of an authority figure, we may be strongly encouraged to do the same—with the ultimate result that the power of those in authority is severely weakened.

Third, individuals may find it easier to resist influence from authority figures if they question the expertise and motives of these figures. Are those in authority really in a better position to judge what is appropriate and what is not? What motives lie behind their commands—socially beneficial goals or selfish gains? Dictators always claim that their brutal orders reflect their undying love for their fellow citizens and are in the people's best interest, but to the extent that large numbers of persons question these motives, the power of such dictators can be eroded and perhaps, ultimately, be swept away.

Finally, simply knowing about the power of authority figures to command blind obedience may helpful in itself. Some research findings (e.g., Sherman, 1980) suggest that when individuals learn about the results of social psychological research, they often recognize these as important (Richard, Bond, & Stokes-Zoota, 2001) and sometimes change their behavior in light of this new knowledge. With respect to destructive obedience, there is some hope that knowing about this process can enhance individuals' resolve to resist. To the extent this is so, then even exposure to findings as disturbing as those reported by Milgram can have positive social value.

To conclude: The power of authority figures to command obedience is certainly great, but it is *not* irresistible. Under appropriate conditions, it can be countered or reduced. As in many other areas of life, there *is* a choice. Deciding to resist the commands of persons in authority can, of course, be highly dangerous. For example, dictators usually control most of the weapons, the army, and the police. Yet, as events in Eastern Europe and Russia in the 1980s and 1990s and in Serbia during the past few years indicate, even powerful regimes can crumble when confronted by committed groups of citizens who choose to resist their authority. Ultimately, victory may go to those on the side of freedom and decency rather than to those who wish to exert ruthless and total control over their fellow citizens.

KEY POINTS

- *Obedience* is a form of social influence in which one person orders one or more to do something, and they do it. It is, in a sense, the most direct form of social influence.
- Research by Stanley Milgram indicates that many persons readily obey orders from a relatively powerless source of authority, even if these orders require them to harm an innocent stranger.
- Such destructive obedience, which plays a role in many real-life atrocities, stems from several factors. These include the shifting of responsibility to the authority figure, outward signs of authority on the part of these persons (which remind many persons of the norm "Obey those in authority"), a gradual escalation of the scope of the commands given (related to the foot-in-the-door technique), and the rapid pace with which such situations proceed.
- Several strategies can help to reduce the occurrence of destructive obedience. These include reminding individuals that they share in the responsibility for any harm produced, reminding them that beyond some point obedience is inappropriate, calling the motives of authority figures into question, and informing the general public of the findings of social psychological research on this topic.

Intense Indoctrination: Social Influence Carried to the Extreme

In 1978, 914 members of the People's Temple committed suicide when ordered to do so by their leader. In 1992, members of the Branch Davidian cult engaged in what amounted to suicidal resistance to the demands of government agents—resistance that resulted in the deaths of many members of the group. These tragic events have focused much public attention on extreme religious groups, and have revealed some truly shocking things about conditions in them. In many of these groups, new members must give all of their possessions to the group on joining, and they must agree to live by rules and regulations that most of us would find completely incomprehensible. For example, among the Branch Davidians, all members, except the leader, were forbidden to engage in sexual relations; he reserved this right strictly for himself.

The extreme and often bizarre conditions of life in these groups raise an intriguing question: How do they manage to exert such total control over the lives of their members? In other words, how do these groups succeed in exercising profound levels of social influence over the persons who join them? At first glance, it might seem as though they achieve this goal by means of mysterious forces and processes outside the realm of science. A recent analysis of conditions in these groups by one social psychologist, though, suggests that, actually, the powerful influence of extreme groups over their members can be fully understood in terms of the principles and processes considered in this chapter (Baron, R. S., 2000). Let's see how this can be so.

In his analysis of *intense indoctrination*—a process through which individuals become members of extreme groups and come to accept the beliefs and rules of the group in a totally unquestioning and highly committed way—Baron (2000) suggests that such indoctrination involves four distinct stages, and that at each stage, factors well known to social psychologists play an important role. We'll first describe these stages and then indicate what aspects of social influence shape them.

■ STAGES OF INTENSE INDOCTRINATION. In the first, or *softening-up*, stage, new recruits are isolated from friends and family, and efforts are made to keep them confused, tired, disoriented, and emotionally aroused. The main goal here is to cut new recruits off from their former lives and to put them in a state in which they are receptive to the group's message (see Figure 9.18).

This stage is followed by a second one, known as *compliance*. During this stage, recruits are asked to pay lip service to the demands and beliefs of the group and actively "try out" the role of member. A third stage, *internalization*, quickly follows. Now, recruits begin to accept the views of the group as correct and to actually believe these views. In other words, public compliance is replaced by inner acceptance.

Finally, in the *consolidation* stage recruits solidify their membership by engaging in costly acts that make it difficult, if not impossible, to go back: they donate all their personal possessions to the group, cut off all ties with former friends and family, begin to actively recruit new members, and so on. The result is that the new members now accept the beliefs and philosophy of the group in an unquestioning manner, and come to hold negative views about "outsiders."

■ SOCIAL PSYCHOLOGICAL PROCESSES: WHY INTENSE INDOCTRINATION SUCCEEDS. Now for *the* central question: Why do individuals continue through these phases? Why do they gradually surrender almost total control over their own lives to the groups they join? According to R. S. Baron (2000), a key part of the answer involves the fact that, in these groups, vigorous efforts are made to place members in a state that maximizes the impact of tactics of social influence upon them at each of the stages described above. This key state is *reduced attentional capacity.* In other words, extreme groups use various tactics to ensure that new recruits are rendered incapable of

FIGURE 9.18
Intense Indoctrination: How Extreme Groups Gain New Members.
Extreme groups like the one shown here expose new recruits to conditions designed to reduce their attentional capacity. This, in turn, increases the susceptibility of new recruits to various tactics of social influence, and it makes it more and more difficult for them to withdraw before becoming fully committed members.

thinking carefully or systematically. This, in turn, increases their susceptibility to the group's efforts to reshape their attitudes and behavior. How do extreme groups do this? As noted above, by keeping new recruits exhausted (e.g., through lack of sleep or poor nutrition), emotionally aroused, and isolated from their former lives.

The resulting state of reduced attentional capacity, in turn, plays a key role in each of the stages described above. For example, consider internalization, the stage at which members begin to accept the group's extreme views. Here, reduced attentional capacity lowers the recruits' ability to think carefully and systematically about the information they are receiving. It also increases their tendency to conform, because conformity is often enhanced when people are confused, uncertain about how to act, and are experiencing reduced confidence (e.g., Baron, Vandello, & Brunsman, 1996). At the same time, reduced attentional capacity increases the tendency of new recruits to think stereotypically—for instance, to develop negative views about nonmembers (e.g., Paulhus, Martin, & Murphy, 1992).

Other social psychological factors are at work during the consolidation stage. Here, individuals who have made public statements supporting the group's views or who have engaged in actions such as donating all their possessions to the group may experience strong dissonance (see Chapter 4), accompanied by powerful motives to justify these past actions. Previous research indicates that reduced attentional capacity (or emotional arousal) can intensify such effects (e.g., Stalder & Baron, 1998). The result? Their commitment to the group's extreme views is increased.

In sum, by placing new recruits in a state that lessens their attentional capacity (i.e., their capacity to think carefully and systematically), extreme groups increase the susceptibility of these persons to various influence tactics. These tactics (e.g., intense peer pressure, inducing recruits to make public statements supporting the group's views) are then applied to potential members forcefully and consistently over prolonged periods of time, until recruits reach a point where they accept the group's views in a totally unquestioning manner. In short, while the level of influence exerted by extreme groups over their members is indeed unsettling, it is by no means mysterious. Rather, it can be fully understood in terms of principles and processes of social influence—factors and events very familiar to social psychologists.

KEY POINTS

- Extreme groups subject new recruits to a process of *intense indoctrination* directed toward the goal of inducing recruits to accept the beliefs and rules of the group in a totally unquestioning and highly committed way.
- New members pass through four stages in this process: softening up, compliance, internalization, and consolidation.
- At each of these stages, reduced attentional capacity increases recruits' susceptibility to various tactics of social influence. Thus, their powerful commitment to the group can be understood in terms of processes and principles well known to social psychologists.

CONNECTIONS: INTEGRATING SOCIAL PSYCHOLOGY

IN THIS CHAPTER, YOU READ ABOUT . . .	IN OTHER CHAPTERS, YOU WILL FIND RELATED DISCUSSIONS OF . . .
the role of social norms in conformity	the role of social norms in attraction (Chapter 7), helping (Chapter 10), aggression (Chapter 11), and group decision making (Chapter 12)
the basic principles underlying many different techniques for gaining compliance	the role of these principles in other aspects of social behavior: . . . the role of reciprocity in attraction (Chapter 7), aggression (Chapter 11), and cooperation (Chapter 12) . . . the role of the desire to be consistent in attitude change (Chapter 4), the self-concept (Chapter 5), and helping (Chapter 10) . . . the role of liking or friendship in social perception (Chapter 2), social relationships (Chapter 8), leadership (Chapter 12), and the legal process (Chapter 13)
the role of mood in compliance	the effects of mood on social cognition (Chapter 3), attitudes (Chapter 4), and helping (Chapter 10)

THINKING ABOUT CONNECTIONS

1. The level of violence seems to have increased in many countries. Do you think this reflects changing norms concerning aggression—that norms now define aggression as more appropriate or acceptable than was true in the past? If so, why have such changes occurred?
2. As we'll describe in Chapter 13, charismatic leaders are often viewed as masters of social influence: they seem to possess an amazing ability to bend others to their will. Do you think they use the principles and tactics for gaining compliance described in this chapter? And which of these do you feel might be most important to such leaders in their efforts to influence their followers?
3. It has sometimes been argued that social influence is the most basic and important aspect of social behavior. Do you agree? Can you think of any forms of social behavior (e.g., aggression, Chapter 11; helping, Chapter 10) in which influence does *not* play a role? What about attraction and love (Chapters 7 and 8); are these aspects of social behavior affected by social influence?

IDEAS TO TAKE WITH YOU—AND USE!

TACTICS FOR GAINING COMPLIANCE

How can we get other persons to say yes to our requests? This is an eternal puzzle of social life. Research by social psychologists indicates that all of the techniques described here can be useful—and that they are widely used. So, whether or not you use these approaches yourself, you are likely to be on the receiving end of many of them during your lifetime. Here are tactics that are especially common.

Ingratiation: Getting others to like us so that they will be more willing to agree to our requests. We can ingratiate ourselves through flattery, by making ourselves attractive, and by showing liking for and interest in the target person.

The Foot-in-the-Door Technique: Starting with a small request and, after it is accepted, escalating to a larger one.

The Door-in-the-Face Technique: Starting with a large request and then, when this is refused, backing down to a smaller one.

Playing Hard to Get: Making it appear as though we are much in demand, thereby making it more likely that others will value us and agree to our requests—implicit or explicit.

The Pique Technique: Using unusual or attention-getting requests, which are often more successful in gaining compliance, so that the recipients cannot say no in an automatic manner.

Putting Others in a Good Mood: Putting other people in a good mood, so they are more likely to say yes to our various requests.

SUMMARY AND REVIEW OF KEY POINTS

Conformity: Group Influence in Action

- *Social influence*—efforts by one or more persons to change the attitudes or behavior of one or more others—is a common part of life.
- Most people behave in accordance with *social norms* most of the time; in other words, they show strong tendencies toward *conformity*.
- Conformity was first systematically studied by Solomon Asch, whose classic research indicated that many persons will yield to social pressure from a unanimous group.
- Many factors determine whether, and to what extent, conformity occurs. These include *cohesiveness*—the degree of attraction felt by an individual toward some

group—group size, and type of social norm operating in that situation—*descriptive* or *injunctive*.

- We are most likely to behave in ways consistent with norms when they are relevant to us.
- Norms tend to persist over time. This is one reason why *cultures of honor* still exist in the South and West of the United States.
- Two important motives underlie our tendency to conform: the desire to be liked by others and the desire to be right or accurate. These two motives are reflected in two distinct types of social influence, *normative* and *informational* social influence.
- The desire to be liked by others, or fear of rejection by them, results in jeer pressure—the desire to avoid rejection by sticking even closer to existing social norms.
- Once we show conformity in a given situation, we tend to view it as justified, even if it has required us to behave in ways contrary to our true beliefs.
- Although pressures toward conformity are strong, many persons resist them, at least part of the time. This resistance seems to stem from two strong motives: the desire to retain one's individuality, and the desire to exert control over one's own life.
- Under some conditions, minorities can induce even large majorities to change their attitudes or behavior.
- Because their views are threatened, minorities often overestimate the number of persons who share their beliefs.
- Majorities who become minorities experience strong negative reactions; in contrast, the positive reactions of minorities who become majorities are somewhat weaker.
- One positive effect of minorities is that they induce majorities to think more systematically about the issues they raise. This may facilitate large-scale social change.

Compliance: To Ask—Sometimes—Is to Receive

- Individuals use many different tactics for gaining *compliance*—getting others to say yes to various requests. Many of these rest on basic principles well known to social psychologists.
- Two widely used tactics, the *foot-in-the-door* technique and the *lowball procedure,* rest on the principle of commitment/consistency. In contrast, the *door-in-the-face* technique and the *"that's-not-all" technique* rest on the principle of reciprocity.
- *Playing hard to get* and the *deadline technique* are based on the principle of scarcity—the idea that what is scarce or hard to obtain is valuable.
- Social validation, another basic principle underlying compliance, is closely related to informational social influence and conformity.
- In the *pique technique,* compliance with requests is increased by piquing (stimulating) target persons' interest, so that they do not refuse requests automatically.
- Another tactic for gaining compliance involves putting others in a good mood before making a request. Research evidence indicates that this tactic is especially likely to succeed if something about the request induces target persons to think systematically about it.
- Although everyone engages in efforts to exert social influence on others, research findings indicate that the specific tactics individuals choose are related to their own traits and characteristics.

Extreme Forms of Social Influence: Obedience to Authority and Intense Indoctrination

- *Obedience* is a form of social influence in which one person orders one or more persons to do something, and they do it. It is, in a sense, the most direct form of social influence.
- Research by Stanley Milgram indicates that many persons readily obey orders from a relatively powerless source of authority, even if these orders require them to harm an innocent stranger.
- Such destructive obedience, which plays a role in many real-life atrocities, stems from several factors. These include the shifting of responsibility to the authority figure, outward signs of authority on the part of these persons (which remind many persons of the norm "Obey those in authority"), a gradual escalation of the scope of the commands given (related to the foot-in-the-door technique), and the rapid pace with which such situations proceed.
- Several strategies can help to reduce the occurrence of destructive obedience. These include reminding individuals that they share in the responsibility for any harm produced, reminding them that beyond some point obedience is inappropriate, calling the motives of authority figures into question, and informing the general public of the findings of social psychological research on this topic.
- Extreme groups subject new recruits to a process of *intense indoctrination* directed toward the goal of inducing them to accept the beliefs and rules of the group in a totally unquestioning and highly committed way.
- New members pass through four stages in this process: softening up, compliance, internalization, and consolidation.
- At each of these stages, reduced attentional capacity increases recruits' susceptibility to various tactics of social influence. Thus, their powerful commitment to the group can be understood in terms of processes and principles well known to social psychologists.

KEY TERMS

cohesiveness (p. 353)
compliance (p. 349)
conformity (p. 349)
cultures of honor (p. 356)
deadline technique (p. 370)
descriptive norms (p. 354)
door-in-the-face technique (p. 368)
foot-in-the-door technique (p. 368)
individuation (p. 362)
informational social influence (p. 359)
ingratiation (p. 367)
injunctive norms (p. 354)
intense indoctrination (p. 349)
lowball technique (p. 368)
normative focus theory (p. 354)
normative social influence (p. 358)
obedience (p. 349)
pique technique (p. 371)
playing hard to get (p. 370)
social influence (p. 349)
social norms (p. 349)
"that's-not-all" technique (p. 369)

FOR MORE INFORMATION

Cialdini, R. B. (1994). *Influence: Science and practice* (3rd ed.). New York: HarperCollins.

- This book is an insightful and very readable account of the major techniques people use to influence others. The book draws both on the findings of systematic research and on informal observations made by the author in a wide range of practical settings (e.g., sales, public relations, fund-raising).

McIlveen, R., & Gross, R. (1999). *Social influence.* Mahwah, NJ: Erlbaum.

- This book summarizes what we know about many aspects of social influence. It is brief and easy to read, and a good source to consult if you'd like to know more about the topics covered in this chapter.

Milgram, S. (1974). *Obedience to authority.* New York: Harper & Row.

- More than twenty-five years after it was written, this book remains the definitive work on obedience as a social psychological process. The untimely death of its author only adds to its value as a lasting contribution to our field.

Beauford Delaney, *Can Fire in the Park,* 1946. Oil on canvas, 24 x 30". © Copyright Smithsonian American Art Museum, Washington, DC/Art Resource, NY.

10

PROSOCIAL BEHAVIOR: HELPING OTHERS

CHAPTER OUTLINE

Several years ago, I (DB) was flying from my home in West Lafayette, Indiana, to San Marcus, Texas, in order to give a talk. Across the aisle from me, a young mother was traveling with her two children, an infant and a little boy who was about three. I'm not one to strike up a conversation with a stranger, even an attractive one, or to try to amuse someone else's child.

As I changed planes in the Dallas–Fort Worth airport by taking a tram from one terminal to another, I noticed that this family was doing the same thing and that the little boy (I heard his mother call him Teddy) seemed to be frightened. People were hurrying in various directions, it was noisy, and the mother had all that she could do to handle the baby and the carry-on bags.

Clearly, she needed help, and Teddy could use—literally—a helping hand. We were the only ones boarding that particular tram. Because I knew how difficult it is to travel with children, and because I felt sorry for Teddy, and because there was no one else around to offer assistance, I did. She seemed relieved when I took Teddy's hand to lead him to a seat next to me.

When the tram started moving, accelerating rapidly, Teddy became increasingly frightened—he didn't know where he was or what was happening. I had recently taken my own son and daughter to Disney World, so it popped into my head to tell him that this was just like one of the rides there. I told him that we were on the Donald Duck train under Magic Mountain (or something like that). As soon as Teddy heard my well-intentioned lie, his fear quickly dissipated, and he began to enjoy himself. After we reached the next terminal, Teddy squeezed my hand, his mother thanked me, and we went our separate ways.

My brief interaction with this mother and her children is a minor example of *prosocial behavior.* These people were strangers to me (beyond "Teddy," I didn't even know their names), and I could have easily have let them take care of themselves. Social psychological research on such behavior has attempted to determine why people sometimes provide help to strangers and sometimes stand back and do nothing. As we describe some of this research in the following pages, remember my small act of helpfulness and ask yourself, "Why did he offer help to these people he didn't know when he could more easily have simply minded his own business?" Also keep in mind that prosocial actions always seem to involve a mixture of making at least some mild personal sacrifice in order to provide assistance and, at the same time, obtaining some degree of personal satisfaction from having done so. This mixture of sacrifice and satisfaction holds true whether the act is something relatively simple and safe, such as helping a mother and her small son in an airport, or something complicated and dangerous, such as saving a stranger who is drowning.

With respect to such behavior, the goal of social psychologists is to understand and predict **prosocial behavior**—any act that benefits others. Generally, the term is applied to acts that do not provide any direct benefit to the person who performs the act, and may even involve some degree of risk. Even simple acts can sometimes involve some type of risk, as the cautious Boy Scout in Figure 10.1 is aware. The term **altruism** is sometimes used interchangeably with *prosocial behavior,* but true altruism is an *unselfish* concern for the welfare of others. As we will discuss later, it may be that *no* behavior is purely altruistic.

In this chapter, we will first describe the basic factors that influence the likelihood that a given individual will or will not *respond to an emergency* with a prosocial act. Next, we will examine some of the dispositional and emotional characteristics of *those who help others and those who are helped,* both in emergencies and in long-lasting situations. The third major topic is a presentation of the

"Before we set out, there's this little matter of a waiver."

FIGURE 10.1

Prosocial Behavior Sometimes Involves Risk.

Prosocial acts do not provide direct benefits to the person who performs them, and they may involve a degree of risk. This Boy Scout doesn't want his helpfulness to lead to future legal problems.

prosocial behavior: A helpful action that benefits other people without necessarily providing any direct benefits to the person performing the act, and may even involve a risk for the person who helps.

altruism: Behavior that reflects an unselfish concern for the welfare of others.

diffusion of responsibility: The proposal that the amount of responsibility assumed by bystanders to an emergency is shared among them. If there is only one bystander, he or she has total responsibility. If there are two bystanders, each has 50 percent of the responsibility. If there are one hundred bystanders, each has only 1 percent of the responsibility. The more bystanders, the less any one of them feels responsible to act.

major theoretical *explanations of prosocial motivation,* ranging from theories based on self-centered versus unselfish motivation to the proposition that the helping process is based—at least in part—on genetic determinants.

Responding to an Emergency: Why Are Bystanders Sometimes Helpful, Sometimes Indifferent?

You can easily find stories in the newspaper describing incidents in which bystanders witnessed an emergency and refused to help. As one example, a middle-aged woman developed car trouble in rush-hour traffic one morning, and then had to push her automobile to the side of the road. Despite the fact that many people drove past,

SOCIAL PSYCHOLOGY: THIRTY YEARS OF PROGRESS

THE STUDY OF PROSOCIAL BEHAVIOR BEGAN WITH A MURDER

Just ten years before the first edition of this book was published, in the early morning hours of March 13, 1964, a woman was murdered in New York City. Catherine (Kitty) Genovese was returning home from her job as manager of a bar. As she crossed the street from her car to the apartment building where she lived, a man armed with a knife approached her. She ran away from him, but he chased Ms. Genovese, caught up with her, and then stabbed her. She screamed for help, and lights went on in many of the apartments overlooking the street as people looked out to see what was going on. The attacker started to leave, but when he saw that no one was coming to help his victim, he returned to kill her. She screamed again, but he stabbed her repeatedly until she lay dead. It was later determined that this horrifying forty-five-minute attack was seen and heard by thirty-eight witnesses, but no one took any direct action or bothered to call the police (Rosenthal, 1964).

The failure of the bystanders to provide help led many in the media to attempt to answer the question "Why didn't they help?" Maybe people in the 1960s had become apathetic, cold, and indifferent to the problems of others. Perhaps life in a big city had resulted in a callous outlook. Perhaps aggression on TV and in the movies had simply desensitized viewers to real violence. Less than a year before this murder, President Kennedy was assassinated in Dallas, and the drama was recorded on film; on the following Sunday morning, the shooting of the suspected assassin took place in front of still and video cameras. Perhaps the accumulated effect of such events had made it impossible to empathize with the plight of a stranger screaming for help.

It is somehow comforting to think that people used to be better in the good old days, and that something has gone wrong with society to make today's citizens apathetic. Even at the anecdotal level, however, it is as easy to find everyday examples of prosocial behavior as to find examples of apathy. If people have become so bad, why would an individual who finds a bag full of money seek out the owner and return his $70,000 (Hurewitz, 1998)? Why would a man risk death by diving 150 feet off of a bridge in order to save a woman who was trying to commit suicide (Fitzgerald, 1996)?

Such striking behavioral contrasts led two social psychologists, John Darley and Bibb Latané, to begin speculating in order to suggest testable explanations. Both Darley and Latané were professors at universities in New York at the time of the Genovese murder, and they discussed what had happened over lunch. As they talked, a novel idea was generated, and that idea became the first step in thirty years of research and theorizing about the determinants of prosocial behavior. An initial basic assumption was: the failure of the bystanders to respond was not that they didn't care about the crime victim, but that something about the situation must have made them hesitate. As Darley and Latané talked, they began to outline proposed experiments on their tablecloth (Krupat, 1975).

The first hypothesis to be tested was that bystanders fail to respond to an emergency if there is **diffusion of responsibility.** In other words, the more bystanders there are, the less responsibility any one of them accepts in dealing with the emergency. If this idea is correct, it follows that in a situno one stopped to ask what was wrong or to inquire whether they could help by calling someone (Cotterell, 1997). A worse example is that of a woman who was injured in an accident on a busy interstate highway; dozens of drivers passed as she lay beside her car, but no one stopped or even reported the problem (Drivers indifferent, 1998).

bystander effect: The fact that the likelihood of a prosocial response to an emergency is affected by the number of bystanders who are present. As the number of bystanders increases, the probability that any one bystander will help decreases and the amount of time that passes before help occurs increases.

Why Didn't Someone Help?

In each instance, the obvious question is "Why didn't someone help?" The answer is *not* obvious, but just such an incident led two social psychologists to attempt to find the answer, as will be described in the **Social Psychology: Thirty Years of Progress** section on pages 390–392.

ation with only one bystander, help is very likely to be given. In the incident involving the mother and her frightened son in the Texas airport, I was the only bystander; any responsibility for helping was mine alone, and I did help. With multiple bystanders, as in the attack on Kitty Genovese, any one of thirty-eight people looking out of their windows *could* have acted, but each had only one thirty-eighth of the total responsibility, and that was apparently not enough to motivate any one of them do something. The general prediction at this point was a simple but very important one: As the number of bystanders to an emergency *increases,* the likelihood of a prosocial response *decreases.* An experiment was designed to test the prediction of what became known as the **bystander effect.**

Note that the basic task of behavioral science is to generate just such imaginative predictions, devise ways to test their accuracy with empirical data, and then, based on what is found, expand the ideas and test them.

The groundbreaking experiment devised by Darley & Latané (1968) involved the creation of what appeared to be an emergency in their research laboratory. They arranged for different numbers of bystanders to be present and then assessed whether or not the number of bystanders had the expected effect on prosocial responsiveness.

Male students took part in what was supposedly a study of campus life. Each one sat alone and talked to other students (by means of an intercom) about the problems encountered in adjusting to college. After this bogus study was underway, the participants were suddenly confronted by an emergency—what seemed to be a severe medical problem experienced by a fellow student. This student said that he sometimes had seizures when confronted by stress, and soon after that he began choking, had difficulty speaking, and said he was going to die and needed help, after which he made no further sound.

This stranger in need was actually only a tape recording that was played for each participant—one aspect of the deception necessary to create the needed conditions. The second deception involved varying the number of bystanders. Participants were assigned to one of three groups. In one group, each participant was led to believe that he was one of two students, so he was the only one aware of the emergency. In the second group, each participant believed that he was in a three-person experiment, so he was one of two bystanders; in the third group, each was supposedly one of five bystanders. Not only was the "victim" a tape recording, so were the fellow bystanders.

The experimental design was meant to create a situation analogous to that experienced by the neighbors of Kitty Genovese: A stranger is having a serious problem, and the bystander is faced with a decision. Because the experimenters had supposedly left for another location, the only way to help was for the student to leave the experimental cubicle and search the nearby rooms in an effort to locate the person having a seizure. Helpfulness was measured in terms of (1) the percentage of the participants in each experimental group who attempted to help and (2) among those who helped, the time they waited before acting. Would you have helped? Would you have hesitated, not knowing how best to respond? Would you have done nothing at all and simply waited for the experimenters to return?

(continued)

Would you have been most likely to help if you were alone and least likely if you were one of five bystanders? In other words, would your behavior have been influenced by diffusion of responsibility, as predicted?

As you might have guessed, and is shown in Figure 10.2, the prediction was correct: the bystander effect was shown to occur, and the findings were consistent with the concept of diffusion of responsibility. The more bystanders, the lower the percentage of students who responded and the longer they waited before responding.

A question that always arises after a successful experiment is "What do we do next?" There is no guide as to what should be done next, but what ordinarily happens is that research and theory tend to take off in several directions at once. One could generate many possible new questions. Does the bystander effect occur in other types of emergencies? What additional factors may operate in determining helpfulness? What if the other bystanders are friends rather than strangers? Are some people more likely *to help* than others? Are some people more likely *to be helped* than others? What motivates anyone to help in the first place? The list of questions could go on and on, as you will see, because the remainder of this chapter describes the next thirty years of progress in the study of prosocial behavior. That is, we don't have only one example of how this research progressed, but a chapter full of such examples.

As is usually the case, it is difficult or impossible to predict the effect of an idea or of a research finding on subsequent developments in a field. One of the original investigators (Darley, 1991) wrote that neither he nor his colleague could have foreseen the flood of research that their experiment initiated. Their creative insight about diffusion of responsibility was only the beginning.

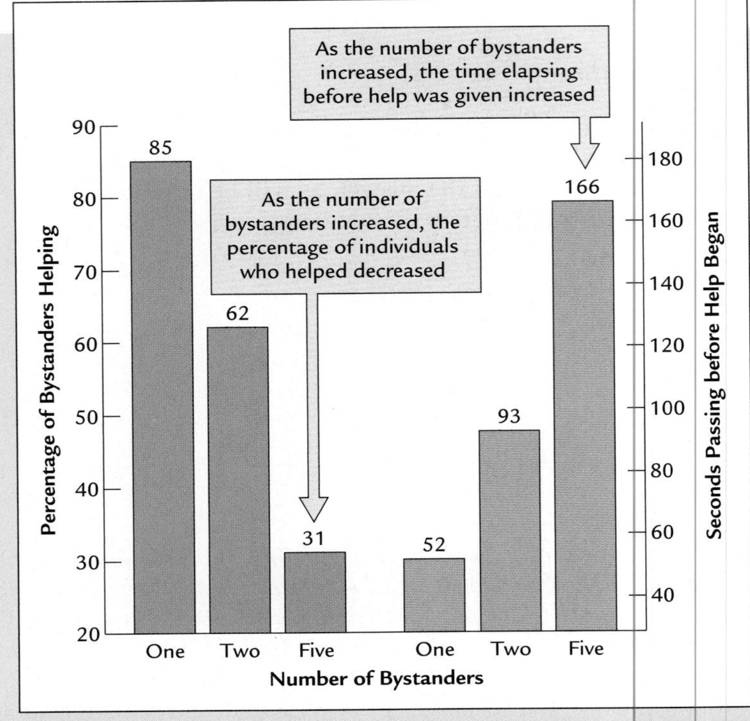

FIGURE 10.2

The More Numerous the Bystanders, the Less Help Offered. In the initial research designed to test the proposed *bystander effect,* students heard what seemed to be a fellow student experiencing a seizure and calling out for help. Each research participant believed himself to be either the only bystander aware of the emergency, one of two bystanders, or one of five. As the number of bystanders increased, the percentage of individuals who tried to help the victim decreased. In addition, among those who did attempt to provide help, the more bystanders, the greater the delay prior to initiating helpful behavior. It was proposed that this effect is the result of *diffusion of responsibility* among those who could potentially provide assistance.

The Decision to Help in an Emergency: Five Essential Steps

As research on prosocial behavior expanded beyond the original question and the original experiment, theoretical formulations expanded to take into account additional factors that influence why help does and does not occur. Any one of us can sit in a comfortable chair and figure out instantly what bystanders should do. For example, the drivers should have helped the woman with car trouble and the woman who lay injured on the highway. The apartment dwellers should have called the police when they heard Kitty Genovese scream or perhaps intervened directly by shouting at the attacker or even by coming to the woman's rescue as a group. The students in the laboratory experiment should have rushed out immediately to help in what was apparently a medical emergency.

When you are actually face to face with such emergencies, however, the situation is not that simple. Beyond diffusion of responsibility, there are numerous factors that influence how people respond. As their research progressed, Latané and Darley (1970) conceptualized an individual's response in emergency situations as a series of five essential steps—five choice points that can either lead toward a prosocial act or toward doing nothing. These steps and the necessary decisions are summarized in Figure 10.3 on page 394. At each step, the easiest choice is the path of least resistance—doing nothing. By failing to help a victim in distress, you avoid a lot of potential problems for yourself. The five-step model provides a framework that helps us understand why people often choose not to help.

■ STEP 1: NOTICING THE EMERGENCY. By definition, emergencies don't happen on schedule, so there is no way to anticipate when or where an unexpected problem will arise. As a result, we usually are doing something else and thinking about quite different matters when suddenly we encounter a stranded motorist, an accident on the highway, screams in the night, or a fellow research participant having a seizure. In many instances, people simply *do not notice;* as a result, for them, the problem does not exist. In our everyday lives, we ignore or screen out many sights and sounds because they are personally irrelevant. If we did not, we would be overwhelmed by an overload of information. I (DB) was with my two younger daughters at a restaurant recently. At the next table were two couples talking loudly about people they knew, an amazing cleaning product available at a local hardware store, and similar topics of no interest to the three of us. We did our best to tune them out. We actively tried to have our own conversation and ignore what was being said by our "neighbors." Most often, it is beneficial *not* to pay attention to much of what goes on around us, and this makes it easy to overlook significant events on those rare occasions when they do occur. If, for example, the other diners in the restaurant had been plotting a terrorist crime, we would not have noticed because we were doing our best *not* to hear what they were saying.

An interesting verification of the importance of this first step was provided by a field study. Darley and Batson (1973) proposed that when a person is preoccupied by personal concerns, prosocial behavior is unlikely to occur. Their research was conducted with seminary students, individuals who should be especially likely to help someone in need. To make helpfulness as salient as possible, the experimenters asked some of the participants to walk to a nearby building on campus to talk to a group about a topic either related to helpfulness or unrelated. In order to vary the degree of preoccupation, the investigators created three different conditions. Some of the seminarians were told that they had plenty of extra time to reach the other

FIGURE 10.3

Five Essential Steps to a Prosocial Response in an Emergency. Latané and Darley (1971) conceptualized prosocial behavior as the end point of a series of five steps—five choice points in confronting an emergency that lead toward either making or not making a prosocial response. At each step, the choices consist of either (1) no—leading away from behaving in a helpful, prosocial way; or (2) yes—leading toward such a response.

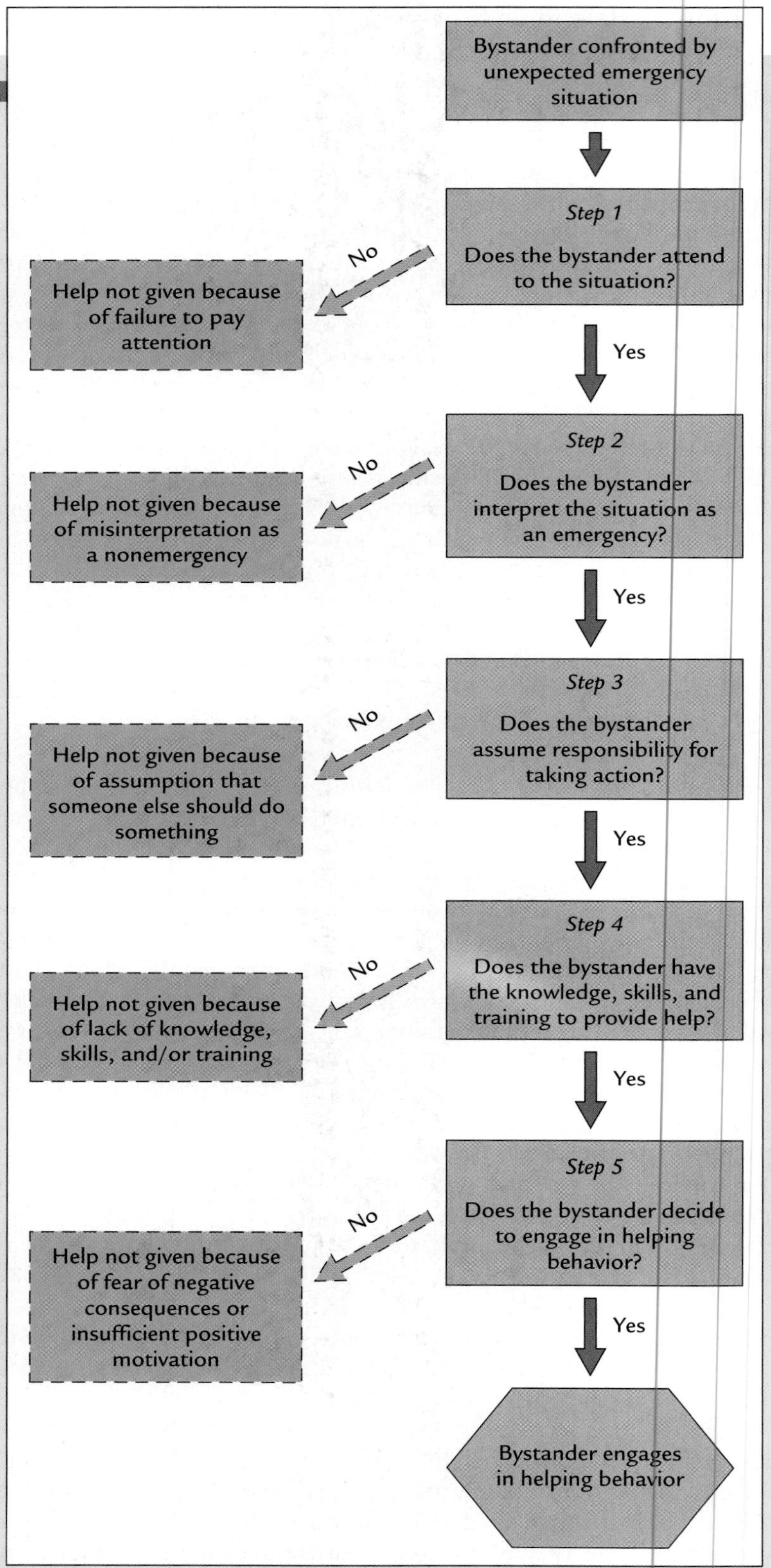

building, some were told they were right on schedule with just enough time to get there, and the third group was told that they were late for the speaking engagement and needed to hurry. Presumably, in walking across the campus, the first group would be the least preoccupied, and the third group would be the most preoccupied. Would the degree of preoccupation influence whether or not they engaged in prosocial behavior?

Along the route to the building where each participant was supposed to give a talk, an emergency was staged. A stranger (actually a research assistant) was slumped in a doorway, coughing and groaning. Would the participants notice this apparently sick or injured individual? Would they stop to help him? Though the topic of their upcoming talk had no effect on their responses, degree of preoccupation had a major effect. As you can see in Figure 10.4, 63 percent of the participants who had time to spare provided help. Among those who were on schedule, 45 percent helped. In the most preoccupied group (those who had to hurry), only 10 percent provided aid. Many of the preoccupied seminarians paid little or no attention to the person who was coughing and groaning; they simply stepped over him and kept on going.

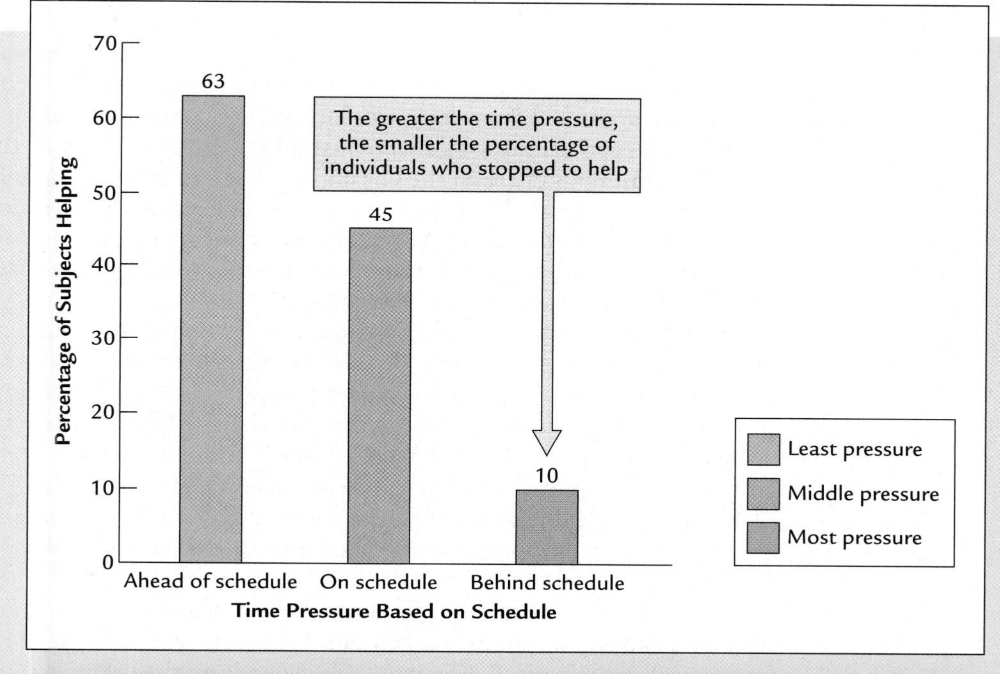

FIGURE 10.4

Too Preoccupied to Notice an Emergency.

When bystanders are preoccupied with other concerns, they are relatively less likely to attend to events in their surroundings and so are less likely to help a person in need. When research participants were told that they were ahead of schedule in reaching an appointment, most stopped and helped a stranger who was slumped over, coughing and groaning, in a doorway. When others were told that they were behind schedule in reaching the appointment, only one out of ten stopped and provided help.

[SOURCE: BASED ON DATA FROM DARLEY & BATSON, 1973.]

It could be concluded that a person who is too busy to pay attention to his or her surroundings fails to notice even an obvious emergency. No help is given because there is no awareness that the emergency exists.

■ STEP 2: INTERPRETING AN EMERGENCY AS AN EMERGENCY. Even when we do pay attention to what is going on around us, we have only limited and incomplete information about what strangers might be doing. Most of the time, it doesn't matter, and it's none of our business. I (DB) was once in a hotel in Chicago, looking out of the window. I was surprised to see a man running down the sidewalk, holding a briefcase. It passed through my mind that he probably was running to work, but it was also possible that he could have just robbed a bank. Rather than call the police about a possible thief, it was easier (and probably more accurate) to assume that he was on legitimate business. Most of the time, it is better to assume a routine, everyday explanation than a highly unusual and unlikely one (Macrae & Milne, 1992). When there really is an emergency, however, the inclination to perceive such events as a nonemergency inhibits any tendency to make a prosocial response.

Whenever potential helpers are not completely sure as to what is going on, they tend to hold back and wait for further information. It's quite possible that in the early morning hours when Kitty Genovese was murdered, her neighbors could not clearly see what was happening, even though they heard the screams and knew that a man and a woman were having an unpleasant confrontation. It could have just been a loud argument between a woman and her boyfriend. Perhaps a man and a woman had been drinking and were just joking around. Either of those two possibilities is more likely than the possibility that a man was stabbing a woman to death just outside their apartment. With ambiguous information as to whether one is witnessing a serious problem or something inconsequential, most people are inclined to accept a comforting and nonstressful interpretation that indicates no need to do anything (Wilson & Petruska, 1984).

All of this suggests that multiple witnesses may inhibit helping not only because of the diffusion of responsibility, but also because it would be embarrassing to misinterpret the situation and act inappropriately. Making such a serious mistake in front of several strangers might lead them to label your behavior as stupid or as a silly overreaction. As discussed in Chapter 7, when we want evidence about the correctness of our opinions, we utilize social comparison (see also Chapters 4 and 9). If other people do not appear to be alarmed about what is going on and if they are not taking steps to intervene, it is safer to follow their lead. Who wants to look foolish or to lose one's cool?

The tendency for those in a group of strangers to hesitate and do nothing is based on what is known as **pluralistic ignorance.** That is, because none of the bystanders knows for sure what is happening, each depends on the others to provide cues; as a result, no one responds. Latané and Darley (1968) provided a dramatic demonstration of just how far people will go to avoid making an "inappropriate" response to what may or may not be an emergency. The investigators placed research participants in a room alone or with two other participants as they filled out questionnaires. After several minutes had passed, the experimenters pumped smoke into the research room through a vent. When individuals were alone, most (75 percent) stopped what they were doing when the smoke appeared and went out to report the problem. When three people were in the room, however, only 38 percent reacted to the smoke. Even after the smoke became so thick that it was difficult to see, 62 percent did nothing. Being with other people who fail to respond seems to be a powerful inhibitor. It is as if risking death would be preferable to making a fool of yourself.

pluralistic ignorance: The tendency of bystanders in an emergency to rely on what other bystanders do and say, even though none of them is sure about what is happening or what to do about it. Very often, all of the bystanders hold back and behave as if there is no problem, and use this "information" to justify their failure to act.

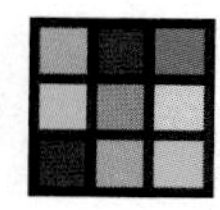

The fear of misinterpreting a situation and making a blunder is reduced under certain conditions, however. For example, social inhibitions are much weaker if the other bystanders are friends rather than strangers, because friends are much more likely to communicate with one another about what is going on and what to do about it. As a result, with friends, the bystander effect is much less strong. (Rutkowski, Gruder, & Romer, 1983).

People in small towns are much more likely to help a stranger than are people in large cities (Levine et al., 1994), both in the United States and in Australia (Amato, 1983). Why? In part, people in small towns tend to know many of their fellow citizens and can communicate with them, thus moving forward at Step 2. In contrast, people in large cities tend to move faster, avoiding eye contact with those around them and paying attention primarily to themselves, thus being inhibited at Step 1 *and* at Step 2 (McCauley, Coleman, & Defusco, 1977; Walmsley & Lewis, 1989).

The fear of doing the wrong thing can also be reduced by consumption of alcohol, because the effect of alcohol reduces anxiety about the opinions of others, thus increasing the tendency to provide help (Steele, Critchlow, & Liu, 1985). Think of the experiment with the smoke coming under the door. It seems very likely that three friends drinking beer would not remain quietly seated while the room filled with smoke.

■ STEP 3: ASSUMING THAT IT IS YOUR RESPONSIBILITY TO HELP. Once an individual pays attention to some external event and interprets it as an emergency, a prosocial act will follow only if the person takes responsibility for providing help. In many instances, the responsibility is clear. Firefighters are the ones to do something about a burning house; police officers are the ones to do something about a crime; medical personnel deal with injuries and illnesses. When responsibility is not as clear as in those examples, people tend to assume that anyone in a leadership role must be responsible (Baumeister et al., 1988). For example, professors are responsible for dealing with classroom emergencies and bus drivers for emergencies involving their vehicles. When there is one adult and several children, the adult is expected to take charge.

One of the reasons that a lone bystander is more likely to act than a bystander in a group is that there is no one else present who *could* take responsibility. With a group that has no obvious leader, there is diffusion of responsibility, as was hypothesized in the original experiment discussed earlier.

■ STEP 4: KNOWING WHAT TO DO. Even if a bystander reaches Step 3 and assumes responsibility, nothing useful can be done unless that person knows *how* to be helpful. Some emergencies are sufficiently simple that almost everyone has the necessary skills. If you see someone slip on an icy sidewalk, you are very probably able to help that person get back on his or her feet. If you see a scruffy, suspicious stranger trying to break into a parked car, you know how to find a phone and dial 911.

Some emergencies require special knowledge and skills that are not possessed by most bystanders. For example, you can help someone who is drowning only if you know how to swim *and* how to guide a floundering swimmer to safety. When there is an accident and possible injury, a registered nurse is more likely to assume responsibility and more likely to help than someone not employed in a medical profession (Cramer et al., 1988).

■ STEP 5: MAKING THE DECISION TO HELP. Even if a bystander's response at each of the first four steps is yes, help will not occur unless he or she makes the final decision to act. Helping at this final point can be inhibited by fears (often realistic ones) about potential negative consequences. In effect, people seem to engage in "cognitive algebra" as they weigh the positive versus the negative aspects of helping (Fritzsche, Finkelstein, & Penner, 2000). And the potential costs are many. For example, if you stop to help a person who slipped on the ice, you might fall yourself. A sick person who has collapsed in a doorway may throw up on your shoes when you try to provide help. Worst of all, the person who seems to be in need may be a criminal who is only pretending to have a problem. Ted Bundy, the serial killer, was a good-looking, well-educated man who repeatedly played on the sympathies of unsuspecting women. Sometimes he would limp, ask a young woman to help him into his car, and then abduct her as his next victim (Byrne, R. L., 2001).

A special type of unpleasant consequence may arise when you observe an individual being threatened by someone in his or her own family. The well-meaning outsider who attempts to help often arouses only anger. Possibly this explains why bystanders rarely offer help when they believe that a woman is being attacked by her husband or boyfriend (Shotland & Strau, 1976) or that a child is being physically abused by a parent (Christy & Voigt, 1994). Even police are wary when they have been called to deal with an angry domestic scene. Intervention in family violence can be more dangerous than interference in a hostile interaction between two strangers.

For some very good reasons, then, bystanders may decide to hold back and avoid the risks that can be associated with performing prosocial acts.

While the five steps are still fresh in your mind, you might want to take a look at the **Ideas to Take with You—And Use!** section on page 429.

Situational Factors That Enhance or Inhibit Helping: Attraction, Attributions, and Prosocial Models

Beyond the five decision-making steps that influence prosocial behavior, additional factors also have an effect on whether or not a bystander is likely to provide help. The most important of these are the extent to which a bystander evaluates the victim positively (*attraction*), the *attributions* made by the bystander as to the victim's responsibility for his or her plight, and the bystander's exposure to *prosocial models* either in the present situation or in the past.

■ HELPING THOSE YOU LIKE. In most of the examples of actual emergencies reported in the newspapers and of bogus emergencies devised by social psychologists, the person in need is usually a total stranger. What if, instead of a stranger, the woman being stabbed or the student having a seizure were a close friend of yours? Would that make you more inclined to go to their aid? The answer is obviously yes. An extreme example of the risks one will take for a loved one is provided by the case of a husband found guilty of manslaughter because he assisted in the suicide of his wife. After thirty-three years of marriage, she developed a form of Lou Gehrig's disease and repeatedly begged him to set her free from the total paralysis and the mental deterioration she would otherwise experience before she died. The husband finally did as she wished, despite having to having to face up to fifteen years in prison as a consequence (Thompson, 1998).

Consider a less obvious situation. The victim is a stranger but because of similarity, physical attractiveness, and other factors discussed in Chapter 7, you feel that this is someone you would like. Would such characteristics have any effect on your prosocial tendencies? Again, the answer is yes. Whatever factors increase a bystander's attraction toward a victim increases the probability of a prosocial response if the individual needs help (Clark et al., 1987). Appearance provides one example: a physically attractive victim receives more help than an unattractive one

(Benson, Karabenick, & Lerner, 1976). Also, you will not be surprised to learn that bystanders are more likely to help a victim who is similar to themselves than one who is dissimilar (Dovidio & Morris, 1975; Hayden, Jackson, & Guydish, 1984).

We also mentioned in Chapter 7 that homosexuality is stigmatized by many people in our society. On this basis, Shaw, Borough, and Fink (1994) predicted that a homosexual stranger in need would receive less help than a comparable heterosexual stranger. Using the "wrong number technique," a male research assistant, named "Mike," dialed random telephone numbers from a pay phone and pretended to have a flat tire. He supposedly had used his last quarter to make this emergency call, but because he had dialed a "wrong number," he could not tell his friend that he would arrive late. Mike asked the person whose number he had called "by mistake" to please make the call for him. The stranger was requested to call either Mike's girlfriend ("Lisa") or his boyfriend ("Rick") to say that Mike would be late for the celebration of their first anniversary together. The phone number provided by Mike was actually that of another research assistant, so the experimenters were able to determine which calls were actually made. As shown in Figure 10.5, 70 percent of the women and 90 percent of the men responded helpfully by calling Mike's girlfriend. When the requested call was to Mike's boyfriend, however, only 35 percent of the women and 30 percent of the men made the call. Clearly, random citizens were much more willing to assist a heterosexual stranger than a homosexual one. Presumably, most of the people who were asked to help were heterosexuals, and they were not inclined to help someone whose sexual orientation differed from their own.

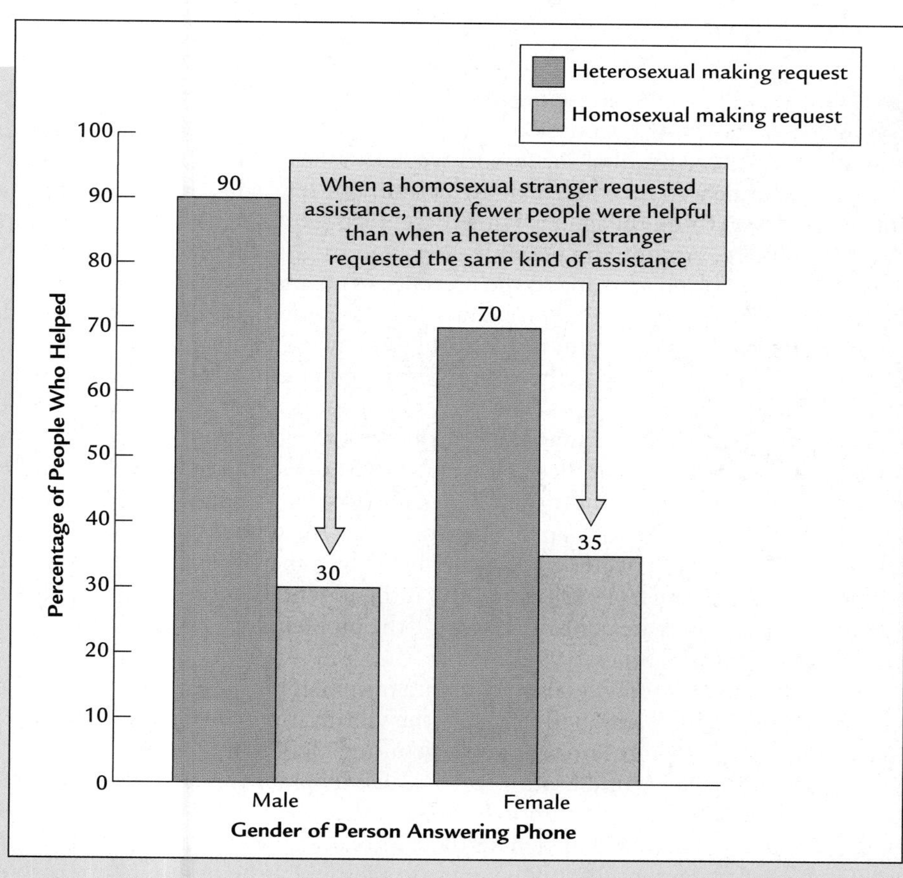

FIGURE 10.5

Heterosexuals Helping a Heterosexual versus Helping a Homosexual. When a male research assistant asked strangers to help him by making a telephone call to his girlfriend, or to his boyfriend, to say that he would be late for their anniversary celebration, the odds of his receiving assistance depended on his perceived sexual orientation. He received twice as much help from women and three times as much help from men when he asked them to call his girlfriend as when he asked them to call his boyfriend. Apparently, a negative attitude about a sexual orientation different from one's own can inhibit prosocial behavior.

[SOURCE: BASED ON DATA FROM SHAW, BOROUGH, & FINK, 1994.]

FIGURE 10.6

Would You Help This Stranger? Why Is He Lying There?

Depending on why you think the man is lying there, you might be more or less inclined to provide help. If you think he is responsible for his condition, you are probably less likely to help. If you think he is an innocent victim, you are probably more likely to help.

ATTRIBUTIONS CONCERNING VICTIM RESPONSIBILITY. If you were taking a walk and came across a man lying unconscious by the curb, your tendency to help or not help would be influenced by all of the factors we discussed earlier—from the presence of other bystanders to interpersonal attraction. But let's add a further consideration. Why do you think the man is lying there? (See Figure 10.6.) What attributions might you make? Among the possible cues, you might react to the fact that his clothing is stained and torn and to the presence of an empty wine bottle in a paper sack. You might decide that he probably drank too much and passed out. Would you be more likely to help him if his clothes are neat and clean and you notice a bruise on his forehead? Under these circumstances, you might decide that he had an accident or had been mugged. The odds are, of course, that you would probably be less motivated to help the man with the dirty clothes and the wine bottle. Why? Despite the fact that both of these strangers might need assistance, you would be less motivated to help if you made the attribution that the man was personally responsible for his situation than if he seemed to be the innocent victim of an accident or a mugging. Help is not given as freely if a bystander assumes that "the victim is to blame" (Weiner, 1980), especially if the potential helper tends to assume that most misfortunes are controllable. If so, the problems are perceived as the victim's fault (Higgins & Shaw, 1999).

Even very religious individuals may refrain from helping if they attribute responsibility to the victim (Campbell, 1975). If the victim is perceived as one who violated your religious values (for example, drinking alcohol), you are less likely to help. In Canada, Jackson and Esses (1997) studied religious fundamentalists whose values were violated by the "immoral" sexual behavior of homosexuals and single mothers. When gay men and unwed mothers were described as having employment problems, the fundamentalists believed that such individuals should not receive help, but, rather, that they should change their lifestyles. In response to victims who did not behave in a way that violated their religious values (strangers simply described as Native Canadians or students), those with employment problems were perceived as free of blame and deserving of aid.

The general tendency is to attribute more personal responsibility for misfortunes to those who are different from ourselves than to those who are similar. Consider the crime of rape. Most sexual assaults are committed by men, and most of the victims are women. Because of this gender difference in perpetrators and victims, women perceive themselves as similar to the person who is attacked, while men perceive themselves as similar to the person who commits the crime (Bell, Kuriloff, & Lottes, 1994). Further, the more similar a woman feels to the female victim, the *less* she blames the victim for the attack. In contrast, the more similar a man feels to the accused rapist, the *more* he blames the victim for what happened. Because of these different attributions, women are motivated to help those assumed to be innocent rape victims, and men are more willing to help those perceived to be falsely accused of the crime.

Despite the power of similarity demonstrated in such investigations, there are times that it is threatening to encounter a victim who is too much like yourself. How could that be? When something bad happens to someone who is like you with respect to gender, age, race, and so forth, this raises the unpleasant possibility that you, too, could be a victim. This is why it is strangely comforting to discover that the victims of a plane crash or an earthquake or some other misfortune differ from you in race, ethnicity, age, nationality, economic status, or any other characteristics. It's a relief to find that this terrible thing happened to "them" and not to "us." Even if the victims *are* similar to you, your discomfort can be reduced if you misperceive them as being dissimilar to you in some way (Drout & Gaertner, 1994) or attribute their misfortune to something they did that you surely wouldn't be foolish enough to do. Blaming the victim is one way to restore your own sense of perceived control over events (Murrell & Jones, 1993) and thus relieve your feelings of anxiety (Thornton, 1992).

■ PROSOCIAL MODELS: THE POWER OF POSITIVE EXAMPLES. If you are out shopping and notice someone collecting money for the homeless or for needy children, do you react by making a contribution? That is, assuming that you responded to the earlier decision steps with a yes, do you then decide to help? An important factor at this final step is whether you observe someone else make a donation. If others give money, you are more likely to do so (Macauley, 1970). Even the presence of coins and bills that were apparently contributed earlier in the day encourages you to make a charitable response. The various compliance techniques described in Chapter 9 are directly relevant to this type of helping behavior. Collecting money for charity involves some of the same psychological processes as are involved in panhandling or selling a product.

In an emergency situation, we indicated that the presence of fellow bystanders who fail to respond inhibits helpfulness. It is equally true, however, that the presence of a helpful bystander provides a strong *social model,* and the result is an increase in helping behavior among the remaining bystanders. An example of such modeling is provided by a field experiment in which a young woman (a research assistant) with a flat tire on her car had parked just off of a road. Motorists were much more inclined to stop and help this woman if they had previously driven past a staged scene in which another woman with car trouble could be observed receiving assistance (Bryan & Test, 1967).

In addition to prosocial models in the real world, helpful models in the media also contribute to the creation of a social norm that encourages prosocial behavior. For example, the prosocial responsiveness of six-year-olds is in part a function of what they have seen on TV (Sprafkin, Liebert, & Poulous, 1975). In a demonstration of the power of television, some youngsters were shown an episode of *Lassie* in which there was a rescue scene—a model for providing help. A second

FIGURE 10.7

TV Models for Children: Which Do You Prefer? Research consistently indicates that children tend to respond in a prosocial fashion after exposure to prosocial models in the media. If you were a victim in an emergency situation, would you prefer to have bystanders and potential helpers who modeled their attitudes and behavior on those of Big Bird or on those of Bart Simpson?

group watched a *Lassie* episode that did not center on a prosocial theme. A third group watched a humorous episode of *The Brady Bunch*—also without prosocial content. After watching one of these shows, the children played a game in which the winner could receive a prize. During the game, it was arranged that the children would pass a group of whining, hungry puppies. Each child was faced with a choice between pausing to help the little dogs (and thus lose the chance to win a prize) and ignoring the puppies and going on with the game. Their decision depended on which TV show they had watched. The children who had viewed the *Lassie* rescue episode stopped and spent much more time trying to comfort the animals than did the children who watched either of the other two television programs. As expected, those who watched prosocial behavior on TV then engaged in prosocial behavior in real life.

Additional experiments have confirmed the influence of positive TV models on children (see Figure 10.7). For example, preschool children who watch prosocial programs—such as *Mister Rogers' Neighborhood, Sesame Street,* or *Barney and Friends*—are much more apt to respond in a prosocial way than are children who do not watch such shows (Forge & Phemister, 1987).

It should be noted that negative effects also occur. For example, playing violent video games such as "Mortal Kombat" and "Street Fighter" leads to a *decrease* in prosocial behavior (Anderson & Bushman, 2001).

Thus, a prosocial model encourages prosocial behavior, and video violence inhibits it. What about models that are *not* violent but appear unconcerned about the plight of others? Such non-prosocial models seem to be increasingly popular—for example, in shows such as *The Simpsons* and *South Park.* However entertaining they may be, they provide behavioral models very different from Big Bird and Barney. It seems possible that the level of prosocial behavior among children could be negatively affected, but the relevant research has not yet been done.

Self-Interest, Moral Integrity, and Moral Hypocrisy

Most of us would not deliberately choose to be heartless and uncaring, but we can be nudged in that direction by convincing ourselves that there is no reason to help (Bersoff, 1999). All too often, people choose to ignore a victim for a variety of reasons, including some that we have discussed, such as "It's not my responsibility" and "It's her own fault." We know, then, that multiple factors can lead us to set aside or disengage moral standards (Bandura, 1999). We usually believe that we, personally, are more likely to engage in selfless and kind behavior than are other people, but this mistaken belief is based on the fact that we tend to overestimate our own moral actions. The result is a self-assessment that "I am holier than thou" (Epley & Dunning, 2000).

More generally, it can be concluded that otherwise moral people sometimes fail to act morally. Much of our discussion so far has explained the absence of a prosocial response on the basis of various details of the situation and a person's cognitive assessment of what is occurring. How else might we explain the absence of a prosocial response?

■ MOTIVATION AND MORALITY. Batson and Thompson (2001) suggest that motivational issues must also be considered. They indicate that three major motives are relevant when a person is faced with a moral dilemma: *self-interest* (sometimes called **egoism**), *moral integrity,* and *moral hypocrisy.* People can be roughly categorized with respect to which motive is primary for them. What is meant by these motives, and how do they affect behavior?

Most of us are motivated, at least in part, by **self-interest,** and much of our behavior is based on seeking whatever provides us with the most satisfaction. People for whom this is the primary motive are not bothered by questions of right and wrong or fair and unfair—they simply do what is best for them.

Other individuals truly want to be moral and thus give evidence of a quite different motive—**moral integrity.** For those who are motivated by moral integrity, considerations of goodness and fairness frequently require some sacrifice of self-interest in order to do "the right thing." For a moral person, the conflict between self-interest and moral integrity can be resolved by making the moral choice, a choice that is also influenced by the presence of internal and external support. For example, the odds of making a moral decision are increased if the individual reflects on his or her values or is reminded of them by others. Sometimes the motive to behave with moral integrity is overpowered in a specific situation if self-interest is sufficiently strong.

A third category of individuals consists of those who want to *appear* moral while avoiding the costs of actually *being* moral; they are motivated by **moral hypocrisy.** That is, they are driven by self-interest but are also concerned with outward appearances. This combination means that it is important to them to *seem* to care about doing the right thing, while they in fact continue to follow their own interests.

How could one investigate the behavioral effects of self-interest, moral integrity, and moral hypocrisy? Batson and his colleagues (Batson et al., 1997) did so by creating a situation in which research participants faced a moral dilemma. Each was given the power to assign himself or herself to one of two experimental tasks. The more desirable task included the chance to win raffle tickets. The less desirable task was described as dull and boring (and involved no raffle tickets). Most participants (over 90 percent) agreed that assigning the dull task to oneself was the moral thing to do in the sense that it is more polite and that you should "do unto others as you would have them do unto you." However, most (70 to 80 percent) actually did the opposite. In this simple situation, most people made a choice based on self-interest, but note that 20 to 30 percent did what they thought was right.

■ MAKING MORALITY SALIENT. Using the same experimental situation just described, Batson and his colleagues (Batson, Thompson et al., 1999) added a new element. To make the moral standard of fairness salient, some participants were told, "Most participants feel that giving both people an equal chance—for example, by flipping a coin—is the fairest way to assign themselves and the participant to the tasks."

egoism: An exclusive concern with one's own personal needs and welfare rather than with the needs and welfare of others. See *self-interest.*

self-interest: The motivation to engage in whatever behavior provides the greatest satisfaction. See *egoism.*

moral integrity: The motivation to be moral and actually to engage in moral behavior.

moral hypocrisy: The motivation to appear moral while doing one's best to avoid the costs involved in actually being moral.

The experimenters then provided a coin for the participants to use if they wished to use that method.

Again, there is very good agreement about the most moral thing to do—almost all agreed that a fair procedure, such as tossing the coin or assigning the other person to the more desirable task, would be the proper decision. Nevertheless, only about half of the participants tossed the coin. Again, most (80 to 90 percent) of those who did not flip a coin assigned themselves to the positive task (the chance to win a raffle). More surprisingly, of those who did toss the coin, the same percentage still assigned themselves to the positive task! Because the assignments should have been fifty-fifty based on the coin toss, many participants obviously cheated if the random assignment did not come out the way they wanted it to. Some individuals tossed the coin in order to be fair, reflecting moral integrity. Others simply used the coin in order to *appear* fair, but then ignored the outcome when it conflicted with what they wanted. In other words, those individuals displayed moral hypocrisy.

To make the moral decision even more salient, still other participants had the option of flipping a coin or having the experimenter do it. Most (80 percent) of those who chose to have a coin flipped wanted the experimenter to do the flipping (Batson, Tsang, & Thompson, 2000). In this way, there could be no temptation to cheat, and that made it easier to behave with moral integrity.

One further step was to make the cost of morality more difficult by providing a choice between a positive task and a negative one that involved receiving electric shock. Under these conditions, almost all of the participants assigned themselves to the positive task without even pretending to be fair.

In summary, as shown in Figure 10.8, it seems that some people simply choose to act in their own self-interest even though they realize this is the less fair and less moral choice (for example, assigning themselves to the preferred task). Others are motivated to act in a moral way and do so. A moral decision is even more likely when they can avoid the temptation to do the wrong thing (for example, allowing the experimenter to toss the coin). These individuals sometimes fail to make the

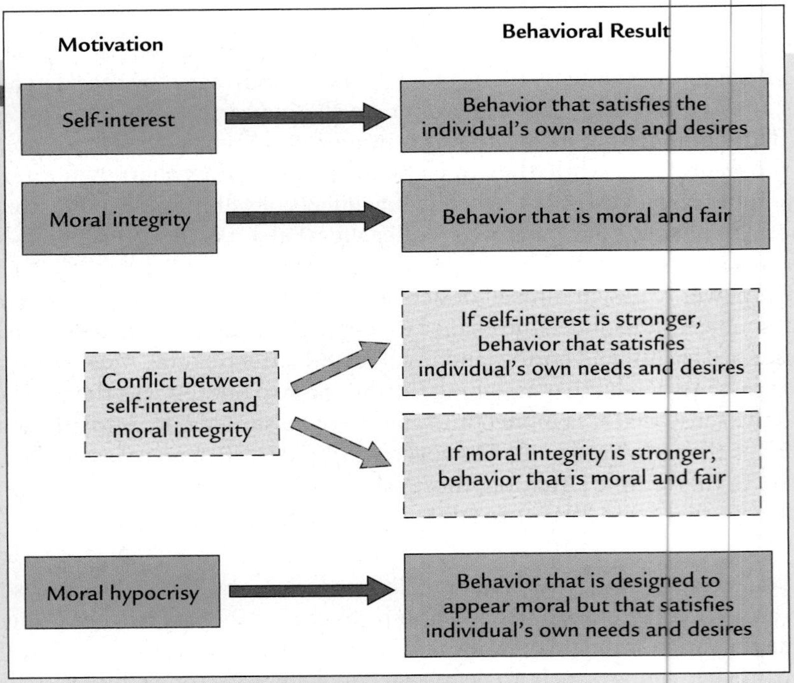

FIGURE 10.8

Motivation and Moral Behavior. People differ in their motivations when faced with a moral decision. Some are motivated primarily by *self-interest* and do what is best for them. Some are motivated primarily by *moral integrity* and do what is moral and fair. Moral integrity often conflicts with self-interest, and the outcome of the conflict depends on a variety of factors. Some are motivated primarily by *moral hypocrisy* and behave so as to appear moral but actually meet their own personal needs. [SOURCE: BASED ON INFORMATION IN BATSON & THOMPSON, 2001.]

moral choice; however, when self-interest is quite strong (for example, avoiding electric shock), it is likely to prevail. Still other individuals might *seem* to be doing the moral thing, but their actual behavior is based on self-interest. These moral hypocrites toss a coin but then cheat if they don't like the outcome.

KEY POINTS

- In part because of *diffusion of responsibility,* the more bystanders present as witnesses to an emergency, the less likely each of them is to provide help and the greater the delay before help occurs.
- When faced with an emergency, a bystander must go through five crucial steps involving decisions that either inhibit or enhance the likelihood of a prosocial response. He or she must notice the emergency, correctly interpret what is occurring, assume responsibility for helping, have the necessary skills and knowledge to help, and then actually decide to provide assistance.
- Prosocial acts occur most often when the bystander feels attraction toward the person in need and attributes the problem to circumstances beyond the victim's control.
- Exposure to prosocial models in real life and in the media has a positive effect on prosocial acts.
- People can be differentiated in terms of their primary motivation in situations involving a moral choice: *self-interest, moral integrity,* and *moral hypocrisy.*

The Helpers and Those Who Receive Help

Up to this point in the description of prosocial behavior, we have primarily stressed the importance of the situation (for example, the number of bystanders), of cognition (for example, attributions about victim responsibility), and of motivation (for example, moral integrity). We now turn to other determinants of prosocial behavior. Some people under some circumstances are much more likely to help than are others, and we will first examine the way in which affect and personality influence helping behavior. First, we will describe how variations in *emotional state* (mood and the affective changes that accompany good and bad events) have somewhat complex effects on prosocial responding. Then, we will indicate how the tendency to act in a prosocial manner is influenced by *dispositional differences* (traits or personality characteristics). Next, we will examine prosocial responses to ongoing problems that are not acute emergencies—people in need of long-term help that requires *volunteerism* and continued commitment to providing help. Finally, we turn to the other major participant in prosocial interactions as we look at the *effects of helping on those who receive help.*

Helping as a Function of the Bystander's Emotional State

Offhand, it might seem that being in a good mood would increase the probability of helping others, while a bad mood would interfere with helping. There is a good deal of evidence that supports such assumptions (Forgas, 1998a). Nevertheless, research indicates that the effects of emotional state on prosocial behavior are somewhat more complicated than you might guess.

For a potential helper, the effect of emotional state is complicated by several additional factors that must be taken into account (Salovey, Mayer, & Rosenhan, 1991). We will discuss some of these complications, indicating the circumstances under which positive and negative emotions have expected but sometimes unexpected effects on one's willingness to help others.

■ POSITIVE EMOTIONS AND PROSOCIAL BEHAVIOR. Most children seem to believe that it's better to request something from a parent when he or she is in a good mood rather than in a bad one. Most often, this is true, and the effect extends to prosocial acts as well. When research participants are in a positive mood as a result of listening to a comedy recording (Wilson, 1981), finding money in the coin return slot of a public phone (Isen & Levin, 1972), or spending time outdoors on a pleasant sunny day (Cunningham, 1979), they are more likely to engage in prosocial acts to help a stranger.

Emotions also can be affected by what we smell, and for that reason we spend money on perfume, aftershave lotion, and air fresheners. If pleasant fragrances make us feel better, it follows that our behavior should also be affected by odors (Baron, 1990b). In a study of prosocial effects, Baron and Thomley (1994) exposed participants to one of two pleasant odors (a lemon or a floral fragrance); as a result, there was increased willingness to volunteer their time in response to a request for help. Another source of pleasant smells is less obvious—but have you ever been in a shopping mall and sniffed the air while passing a bakery or a coffee shop? Baron (1997a) found that such pleasant odors not only induce positive affect, but also increase helpful behavior such as picking up a stranger's dropped pen or making change for a dollar. Altogether, these various laboratory and field studies consistently indicate the beneficial effect of positive emotions on prosocial behavior.

Other factors can alter the relationship, however. What if a bystander is in a very positive mood when he or she encounters an ambiguous emergency situation? When the problem is not clear and one is feeling happy, most people tend to assume that no real emergency exists. It is as if a person decides, "Why spoil my mood by deciding that someone needs help?" By not interpreting what you see as an emergency, you can pass on by and remain in a good mood. Even if the emergency is unmistakable, a good mood can inhibit a prosocial act that requires you to do something difficult and unpleasant (Rosenhan, Salovey, & Hargis, 1981). For example, do you really want to assist someone who has vomited all over his clothing? The fact that you feel good actually provides a sense of power, including the power to refuse to be helpful.

The general conclusion is that if the need for help is very clear and helping doesn't involve negative consequences for the helper, positive emotions increase the probability of a prosocial response. If, however, prosocial acts might spoil a person's good mood, the good mood actually results in *less* helpfulness (Isen, 1984).

■ NEGATIVE EMOTIONS AND PROSOCIAL BEHAVIOR. Again, a common belief is that someone in a negative mood is less likely to be helpful. When you are in a bad mood and you are focusing attention on yourself and your own problems, you are less likely to help someone in need (Amato, 1986; Rogers et al., 1982; Thompson, Cowan, & Rosenhan, 1980).

As with positive emotions, however, negative emotions can have the opposite effect under specific conditions. For example, if the act of helping involves an interaction that would make you feel better, negative emotions increase the probability of prosocial acts (Cialdini, Kenrick, & Bauman, 1982). The positive effect of negative emotions is most likely to be observed if the negative feelings are *not too*

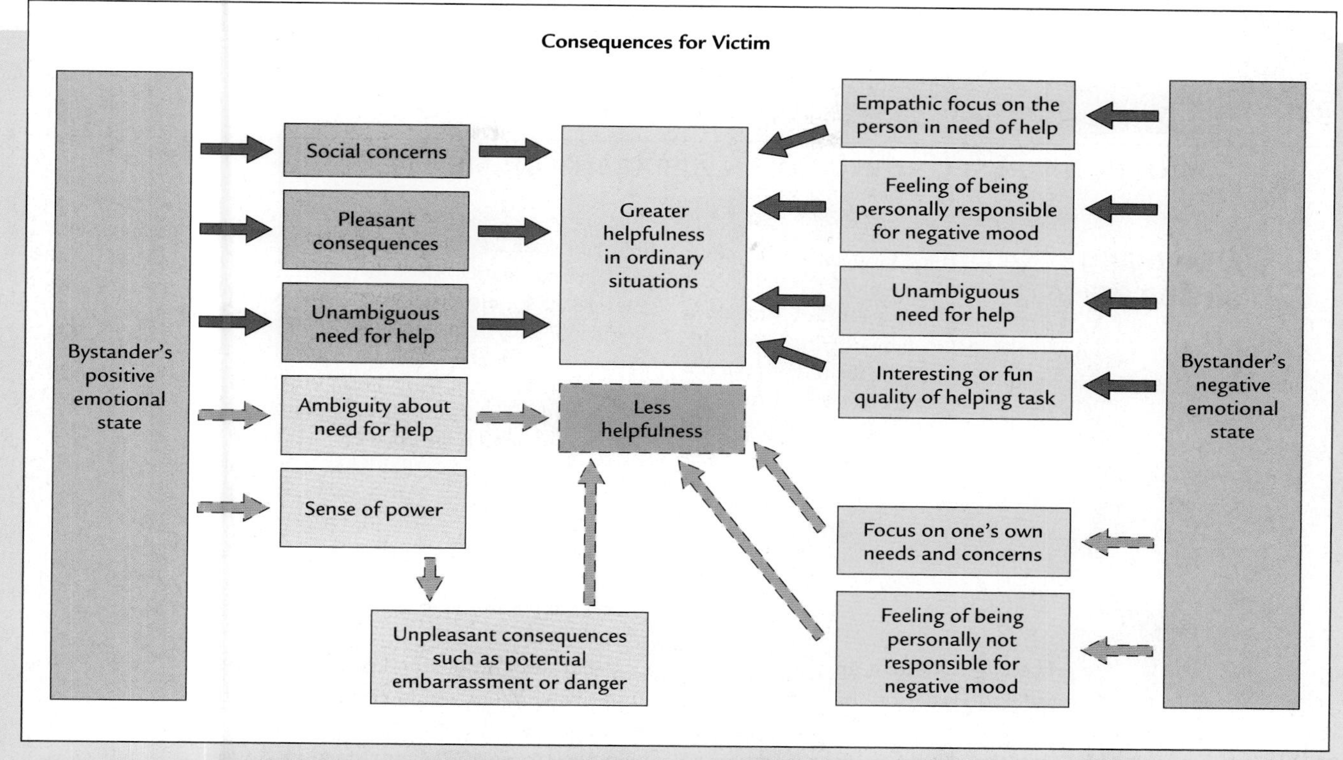

FIGURE 10.9

Positive and Negative Emotions Sometimes Enhance and Sometimes Inhibit Prosocial Behavior. Depending on several specific factors, a positive emotional state can either increase or decrease the likelihood of a prosocial response—and the same is true of a negative emotional state. This diagram summarizes the factors that influence the effect of emotions on helping behavior.

intense, if the emergency is *not ambiguous,* and if the act of helping is *interesting and satisfying* rather than *difficult and unpleasant* (Berkowitz, 1987; Cunningham et al., 1990). See Figure 10.9 for a summary of these positive and negative effects of positive and negative emotions.

Dispositional Differences in Prosocial Responding

In addition to all of the factors discussed so far as influences on prosocial behavior, it seems clear that some individuals are more likely to help than are others. Whether dispositions differ on the basis of genetics, learning experiences, or a combination of the two, the result is differences in prosocial behavior.

There also seems to be consistency over time. Children who are prosocial in early childhood (engaging in cooperating, helping, sharing, and consoling behavior) become adolescents who are liked by their peers and do well academically (Caprara et al., 2000).

Before getting into a description of the characteristics of those who are most likely to engage in prosocial acts, consider the story of the cab driver in the **Beyond the Headlines** section on page 408.

BEYOND THE HEADLINES: AS SOCIAL PSYCHOLOGISTS SEE IT

PROSOCIAL RESPONDING TO AN APPARENT CRIME

A Mugging on Camera

The New Yorker, December 1, 1997—I am a director, and was involved one day in shooting a scene for a television sketch which depicted a purse snatcher's attack on a young tourist couple.

There was to be a struggle at the Columbus Circle fountain, after which the thief would run about fifty feet down Broadway. To get a wide establishing shot, the camera was looking down from the seventh floor of a nearby building, and after rehearsals the crew and the security detail were moved well away from the action so they would not be visible on screen.

Take One: while the thief was grappling with the couple the driver of a passing yellow cab stopped, sprang out of the car, and collared the actor who played the thief just as he completed his run. It ruined the take, of course, but none of us cared (Barnhizer, 1997).

The preceding vignette is an example of bystander intervention that was based on an incorrect interpretation of the "emergency," but the cab driver was clearly motivated to provide help in an emergency, help that involved possible risk to himself. His intentions were sufficiently prosocial that the people involved in the TV production applauded what he did and didn't complain about having to redo the scene.

What does it take for a person to respond in this way? What would compel this man to abandon his taxi and risk danger in order to help two strangers? Many other cab drivers would probably have driven away, happy to be able to remove themselves from the situation. The characteristic most basic to this and other types of prosocial behavior, *empathy*, is described in the following section.

empathy: A complex affective and cognitive response to another person's emotional distress. Empathy includes being able to feel the other person's emotional state, feeling sympathetic and attempting to solve the problem, and taking the perspective of the other person. One can be empathetic toward fictional characters as well as toward real-life victims.

■ EMPATHY: A BASIC REQUIREMENT. Much of the interest in individual differences in helpfulness has concentrated on altruistic motives based on **empathy** (Clary & Orenstein, 1991; Grusec, 1991). Empathy involves both *affective* and *cognitive* components (Duan, 2000). Affectively, an empathetic person *feels* what another person is feeling (Darley, 1993). Cognitively, an empathetic person *understands* what another person is feeling and why (Azar, 1997). Thus, empathy means not only former President Clinton's familiar statement, "I feel your pain," but also, "I understand your pain."

The affective component is essential to empathy, and children as young as twelve months seem clearly to feel distress in response to the distress of others (Brothers, 1990). This same characteristic is also observed in other primates (Ungerer et al., 1990) and perhaps among dogs and dolphins as well (Azar, 1997), as suggested by Figure 10.10. Humans even show empathy by blushing when another person engages in an embarrassing act, such as singing offkey on video (Shearn et al., 1999). Evolutionary psychologists interpret such findings as indications of the biological underpinnings of prosocial behavior. Helping others and being helped by others clearly enhance the chances of the person in need being able to survive and reproduce. The affective component of empathy also includes *feeling sympathetic*—not only feeling another's pain but also expressing concern and attempting to do some-

FIGURE 10.10
Empathy Is Rooted in Biology. The affective aspects of empathy—responding with distress to the distress of others and indicating concern—can be observed in human infants, other primates, and perhaps in a few other mammals, such as dogs and dolphins.

thing to relieve the pain. For example, individuals high in empathy are more highly motivated to help a friend than are those low in empathy (Schlenker & Britt, 2001).

The cognitive component of empathy seems to be a uniquely human quality that develops only as we progress beyond infancy. Relevant cognition includes the ability to consider the viewpoint of another person, sometimes referred to as *perspective taking*—being able to "put yourself in someone else's shoes" or, in a Native American expression, "walking a mile in my moccasins."

Social psychologists have identified three different types of perspective taking (Batson, Early, & Salvarani, 1997; Stotland, 1969): (1) You can imagine how the other person perceives an event and how he or she must feel as a result—taking the "imagine other" perspective. (2) You can imagine how *you* would feel if you were in that situation—taking the "imagine self" perspective. Each of these two types of perspective taking results in an emotional response to the person in need, but the emotions are specific to each type. Those who take the "imagine other" perspective experience relatively pure empathy that motivates altruistic behavior. Those who take the "imagine self" perspective also experience empathy; in addition, the feelings of distress arouse egoistic or self-interest motives that can interfere with altruism. (3) The third type of perspective taking involves *fantasy*—feeling empathy for a fictional character. As a result, there is an emotional reaction to the joys, sorrows, and fears of a person—or an animal—in a book, movie, or TV program. For example, it is not unusual for children to cry when Bambi discovers that his mother has been killed or express fear when Snow White runs

FIGURE 10.11

Feeling Empathy for a Fictional Character. The cognitive aspects of empathy include perspective taking, and one aspect of perspective taking is the ability to feel empathy for a fictional character. An empathetic member of the audience experiences sadness, fear, or joy when these emotions are experienced by a character in the story.

through the forest after the huntsman tells her than her stepmother wants her killed. See Figure 10.11.

HOW DOES EMPATHY DEVELOP, AND WHY DO PEOPLE DIFFER IN EMPATHY? Despite the biological roots of empathy, humans differ greatly in how they respond to the emotional distress of others. The range extends from highly empathetic individuals who consistently feel distress whenever someone else is upset to sociopathic individuals who are emotionally indifferent to anyone else's emotional state. Why do people differ so widely in this respect?

Genetic differences in empathy were investigated by Davis, Luce, and Kraus (1994). They examined more than 800 sets of identical and nonidentical twins and found that inherited factors underlie the two affective aspects of empathy (personal distress and sympathetic concern) but not cognitive empathy. Genetic factors account for about a third of the variations among people in affective empathy. Presumably, external factors account for differences in cognitive empathy and for two thirds of the variation in affective empathy. Psychologist Janet Strayer (quoted in Azar, 1997a) suggests that we are all born with the biological and cognitive capacity for empathy, but that our specific experiences determine whether this innate potential is blocked or becomes a vital part of our selves.

What kinds of specific experiences might enhance or inhibit the development of empathy? One answer is the role of schools in developing character education programs (Lord, 2001). In the United States, forty of the fifty states have instituted such programs to teach children to be honest, behave, respect others, and be responsible. Under President Bush, millions of federal dollars are being devoted to this attempt to build character. Whether these programs, with their slogans, banners, and focus on character, will have lasting behavioral effects has yet to be established, but research is in progress.

Earlier, we described research indicating the effect of prosocial models seen on television, and that is another factor that can enhance the development of empathy. More influential than models provided by media, however, are the models provided by parents. Psychiatrist Robert Coles (1997) emphasizes the importance of mothers and fathers in shaping such behavior in his book, *The Moral Intelligence of Children.* Coles suggests that the key is to teach children to be "good" or "kind" and to think about other people rather than just about themselves. Good children who are not self-centered are more likely to respond to the needs of others. This kind of moral intelligence is not based on memorizing rules and regulations or on learning abstract definitions. Instead, children learn by observing what their parents do and say in their everyday lives. Such experiences are important at any age, but Coles believes that the elementary school years are the crucial time during which a child develops or fails to develop a conscience. Without appropriate models and appropriate experiences, children can easily grow into selfish and rude adolescents and then into equally unpleasant adults. You may even have known one or two people like that. Coles quotes novelist Henry James, whose nephew asked what he ought to do in his life. James replied, "Three things in human life are important. The first is to be kind. The second is to be kind. And the third is to be kind." Coles suggests that those who learn to be kind have a strong commitment to helping others rather than hurting them.

Research has provided other examples of specific experiences that enhance the development of empathy. These include a mother's warmth and clear and forceful messages from parents emphasizing how others are affected by hurtful behavior. Also, it is beneficial to learn to distinguish feeling justified guilt about any harm that we cause from unjustified guilt about bad events for which we are not to blame. A child's sense of empathy is enhanced when parents are able to discuss emotions; but a major *inhibitor* of empathic development is the use of anger by parents as the primary way to control their children (Azar, 1997a). Psychologist Gustavo Carlo (quoted in Carpenter, 2001, p. 76) says,

> *There are wide individual differences in dispositional sympathy, and we now know that kids who are sympathetic tend to come from family environments that are warm and supportive. Kids who are highly sympathetic also tend to be kids who are pretty sophisticated in their moral reasoning and tend to be good at regulating their emotions.*

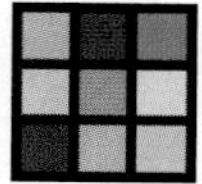

Either because of genetic differences or because of different socialization experiences, women express higher levels of empathy than do men (Trobst, Collins, & Embree, 1994). Consistent with such findings are studies of non-Jewish Germans who helped rescue Jews from the Nazis in World War II. By a ratio of two to one, women outnumbered men in this brave (and very dangerous) prosocial activity (Anderson, 1993).

Empathy is greatest toward anyone (or anything) similar to oneself. To take an obvious example, humans are much more likely to respond empathetically to difficulties encountered by cuddly fellow mammals such as puppies, kittens, and baby seals than to similar difficulties encountered by noncuddly reptiles, fish, and insects. Within our own species, we are also most empathetic to other humans who are most like ourselves.

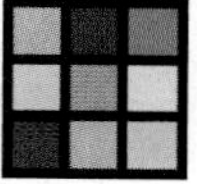

A special instance of such empathy is the response of people to catastrophes (for example, an earthquake, a bombing, a long-lasting drought) experienced by total strangers. Most people respond with sympathy and sometimes with material assistance, but the greatest concern occurs when the victims resemble oneself. When freak tornadoes in 1998 damaged many homes in upstate New York, there was an outpouring of help in the form of money, supplies, and volunteers from nearby communities. In contrast, equally bad or worse disasters in Africa, Asia, and South America generate only mild interest. In addition to the similarity of the victims, people express greater empathy if they themselves have faced a similar disaster (Batson, Sager et al., 1997). For example, those who have experienced a hurricane are especially responsive to hurricane victims (Sattler, Adams, & Watts, 1995), and those who have experienced floods in the Netherlands are more responsive to flood victims in Bangladesh than are those who have not (den Ouden & Russell, 1997). Finally, political ideology also plays a role. In response to a catastrophe such as a flood, conservatives, compared to liberals, were more likely to hold flood victims responsible for needing such assistance (victims choose to live in such a location) and thus for solving their own problems (Skitka, 1999).

■ A VERY SPECIAL CATASTROPHE. The factors we have just described (similarity to self, experience with a similar disaster, political ideology) are apparently irrelevant when the catastrophe is a compelling one. This was shown in the response to the truly catastrophic horror of September 11, 2001. Terrorist attacks on the World Trade Center in New York City, on the Pentagon in Washington, D.C., and on the planes that were hijacked—including the one that crashed in a field in Pennsylvania after the passengers prevented the terrorists from reaching their goal—resulted in over three thousand deaths. The immediate response of those near the scenes of the attack and of those who watched the story unfold on television was overwhelming. In New York, for example, police, firefighters, doctors, and members of the clergy were the first to arrive at the scene, directing people out of harm's way, rescuing survivors, and providing medical treatment and spiritual comfort. These people risked their lives to help, and many lost their lives doing so (Piekarski, 2001). Many ordinary citizens also rushed to the scene to help. As the extent of the horror became known, people shed tears, stood in long lines to donate blood, and quickly began contributing money and supplies.

In the same city where people were accused of being indifferent when Kitty Genovese was killed, New Yorkers volunteered their time and skills in an effort to help, including the removal of the rubble of the two giant skyscrapers that lay in ruin (see Figure 10.12). The emotional response among those involved was much like we described as a response to disasters in Chapter 7. Affiliation needs were aroused, and many of the helpers expressed a feeling of closeness and a sense of bonding with others who were helping.

The outpouring of sympathy and the desire to provide aid was not limited to the residents of New York and Washington, D.C., or even to residents of the United States. There was a worldwide response. An American tourist described his experience on the day of the tragedy:

> *After one evening out in Queenstown, New Zealand, I returned to the hotel to find teary-eyed employees waiting for me to break the news. . . . The next morning, the outpouring of sympathy was unbelievable. People were crying in the street as though it had happened to their country. . . .*
>
> *The local community had American banners with cards of sympathy around town. . . .*
>
> *These folks are our friends and allies, indeed, and if needed they will be there for us. I just wanted everyone to know. (Lynch, 2001, p. B4)*

Clearly, this horrific event had a powerful emotional effect on a great many people and motivated countless instances of prosocial behavior.

■ BEYOND EMPATHY: ADDITIONAL PERSONALITY FACTORS ASSOCIATED WITH PROSOCIAL BEHAVIOR. Empathy and altruistic motivation are associated with other positive characteristics, such as a sense of well-being, achievement motivation, sociability, and a positive emotional state, but *negatively* related to aggressiveness (Krueger, Hicks, & McGue, 2001; Menesini, 1997; Miller & Jansen-op-de-Haar, 1997).

Among other dispositional factors that are characteristic of those who are most likely to help others is *need for approval.* Individuals high in this need respond best

FIGURE 10.12

Sympathy and Widespread Prosocial Responsiveness.

When terrorists flew two jet airliners into the twin towers of the World Trade Center in New York City on September 11, 2001, more people were killed than in any previous terrorist attack. Within hours, there began an unprecedented wave of helpful behavior in which people volunteered their skills, time, blood, finances, and prayers in an effort to provide aid to the wounded, to those who died, and to the surviving family members of the victims.

to rewards such as praise and similar signs of appreciation. When they are rewarded in this way for prosocial acts, helpfulness increases on subsequent occasions (Deutsch & Lamberti, 1986). People high in *interpersonal trust* engage in more prosocial acts than do people who tend to distrust others (Cadenhead & Richman, 1996). *Machiavellianism* refers to people who are characterized by distrust, cynicism, egocentricity, and the tendency to manipulate others; those scoring highest on this dimension are *least* likely to show prosocial tendencies (McHoskey, 1999). Studies with children suggest that prosocial tendencies can become part of the self-schema (see Chapter 5), and are then applied to specific situations in which help is needed (Froming, Nasby, & McManus, 1998).

The fact that multiple aspects of the personality are involved in prosocial acts has led some investigators to suggest that a combination of relevant factors constitutes what has been designated as an *altruistic personality.* In order to specify the components of an altruistic personality, Bierhoff, Klein, and Kramp (1991) selected several personality variables that had previously been found to predict prosocial behavior and then tested their predictive power by comparing people who helped in real-life emergencies with people who failed to help. These participants were matched with respect to gender, age, and social class and differed only in their prosocial responsiveness. All had been at the scene of an accident, but some had administered first aid before an ambulance arrived on the scene (the altruistic group) and some did nothing (the nonaltruistic group). All of these bystanders were given a series of personality tests and were found to differ on five characteristics. These dispositional factors that make up the **altruistic personality** are as follows:

1. *Empathy.* As you might expect, those who helped were found to be higher in empathy than those who did not. The most altruistic participants described themselves as responsible, socialized, conforming, tolerant, self-controlled, and motivated to make a good impression.
2. *Belief in a just world.* Helpful people perceive the world as a fair and predictable place in which good behavior is rewarded and bad behavior is punished. This belief leads to the conclusion that helping those in need is the right thing to do *and* to the expectation that the person who helps will actually benefit from doing a good deed.
3. *Social responsibility.* Those who are most helpful express the belief that each person is responsible for doing his or her best to help those in need.
4. *Internal locus of control.* This is an individual's belief that he or she can choose to behave in ways that maximize good outcomes and minimize bad ones. Those who help are high on this dimension. Those who don't help, in contrast, tend to have an *external locus of control* and believe that what they do is irrelevant, because what happens is controlled by luck, fate, powerful people, and other uncontrollable factors.
5. *Low egocentrism.* Those who help do *not* tend to be egocentric, self-absorbed, and competitive.

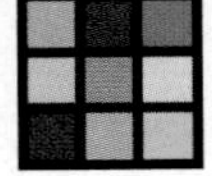

These same five personality characteristics were found among people throughout Europe who were active in the 1940s in rescuing Jews from Nazi persecution (Oliner & Oliner, 1988).

Volunteering: Motivation for Long-Term Help

Helping in response to personal emergencies or to international disasters tends to be a one-time event that occurs within a brief time period. Quite different prosocial behavior is required when the person in need has a chronic, continuing problem that requires help (Williamson & Schulz, 1995). Anyone who volunteers to provide assistance must commit his or her time, special skills, and/or money over an extended period of time. In the United States alone, almost one hundred million adults volunteer 20.5 billion hours each year, averaging 4.2 hours of prosocial activity each week (Moore, 1993). In the United States, in the year 2000, donations to charities increased 6.6 percent over 1999 for a total of $203.5 billion (Sweet charity, 2001). It is reasonable to assume that, around the world, people are spending an enormous amount of time and money engaged in just such voluntary acts of helpfulness.

The five steps required to respond to an emergency that were described earlier also apply to volunteering one's time. In order to help those who are homeless, for example, you must become aware of the problem (usually through the news media), interpret the situation accurately (the need for food, shelter, and medical assistance), assume responsibility to provide help, decide on a course of action that is possible for you (volunteering your time or donating money), and then actually respond. We will now consider some of the motives that determine that crucial last step.

altruistic personality: A combination of dispositional variables associated with prosocial behavior. Among the many components are empathy, belief in a just world, acceptance of social responsibility, and having an internal locus of control.

■ MOTIVES FOR VOLUNTEERING. Patients with AIDS provide an example of a continuing problem that requires the time-consuming commitment of volunteers. In 1981, the Centers for Disease Control issued the first reports on that then unknown disease (see Chapter 8). Despite the efforts of medical research, there is still no effective way to immunize against HIV infections or to cure AIDS. On every continent, a growing number of individuals require assistance as they await death. Volunteers can provide emotional support, and they can help with household chores and transportation. In addition, they can staff hot lines and become political activists in the cause of awareness, preventive behavior, and research funding.

There are a great many reasons *not* to help, of course. As we discussed earlier, there is little sympathy or assistance when the victim is perceived to be responsible for his her difficulty—"They have only themselves to blame." Such reasoning is very often applied to the sexual practices and the intravenous drug use that put people at risk for HIV infections. As Pullium (1993) found, there is much less empathy for and willingness to help an AIDS patient who is homosexual or who shares needles than for someone who contracted the disease from a blood transfusion. The individuals in the first two categories are seen as bringing it on themselves, while those in the latter category are viewed as "innocent victims." Such reactions are associated with political beliefs as suggested earlier, in that conservatives are less generous than liberals toward those perceived as being responsible for their plight (Farwell & Weiner, 2000). Even if potential volunteers don't react by pointing the finger of blame, they nevertheless may feel that the costs of working with such patients are too high. Altogether, most AIDS patients are perceived as undeserving, the possibility of contracting the disease through contact with them is frightening, and there is a reluctance to acquire a stigma by association (see Chapter 7) and interaction with AIDS patients.

Given these powerful negative considerations, a person must be strongly motivated to volunteer to help with this particular problem. For homosexuals, a major motive is to gain knowledge and understanding, but for heterosexuals, the motive involves the expression of humanitarian values (Simon, Sturmer, & Steffens, 2000).

More generally, Clary and Snyder (1999) have identified six basic functions that are served by volunteer work, and these are summarized in Table 10.1. The decision

TABLE 10.1

Why Volunteer? Six different functions can be served by engaging in volunteer activity. Appeals for volunteers are most effective if they recognize that different individuals have different reasons for engaging in such activity. The sample items are taken from the *Volunteer Functions Inventory.*

FUNCTION SERVED	DEFINITION	SAMPLE ITEM
Values	To express or act on important values such as humanitarianism	"I feel it is important to help others."
Understanding	To learn more about the world or exercise skills that are often not used	"Volunteering lets me learn through direct, hands-on experience."
Enhancement	To grow and develop psychologically through volunteer activities	"Volunteering makes me feel better about myself."
Career	To gain career-related experience	"Volunteering can help me to get my foot in the door at a place where I would like to work."
Social	To strengthen social relationships	"People I know share an interest in community service."
Protective	To reduce negative feelings, such as guilt, or to address personal problems	"Volunteering is a good escape from my own problems."

[SOURCE: BASED ON INFORMATION IN CLARY & SNYDER, 1999.]

to volunteer can be based on personal values, the need to understand the phenomenon, the desire to enhance one's own development, the chance to gain career-related experience, the need to improve one's own personal relationships, and/or the desire to reduce negative feelings such as guilt and to solve personal problems. In other words, volunteers may work side by side doing exactly the same job, but for quite different reasons.

A practical implication of identifying these motivational differences is that efforts to recruit volunteers can be most successful when there is an emphasis on multiple reasons to become involved rather than just a single reason. The greatest success occurs when it is possible to match the recruitment message to the recipient's motivation (Clary et al., 1998).

Note that recruitment is not the only issue in volunteer work. Retaining volunteers over time is a more difficult problem (Grube & Piliavin, 2000; Omoto & Snyder, 1995). About half of those who volunteer quit within a year. Why? Once again, motivational differences are crucial. People who continue working as volunteers for a least two and half years tend to be motivated by the need to gain self-understanding, enhance self-esteem, and help their own personal development. These seemingly "selfish" needs are better predictors of continuing volunteer work than the seemingly "selfless" needs centering on humanitarianism and the desire to help others.

Does it help to mandate volunteerism? There are some college programs in which it is mandatory to spend time in volunteer work in order to graduate, but for some students the sense of being forced to engage in such work actually decreases their interest in future volunteer activity (Stukas, Snyder, & Clary, 1999).

■ VOLUNTEERING: IS ALTRUISM INVOLVED? As you might expect from the previous discussion of other types of prosocial behavior, volunteerism is also influenced by dispositional factors. For example, volunteers tend to be high in empathy (Penner & Finkelstein, 1998), specifically perspective taking, empathic concern, and personal distress (Unger & Thumuluri, 1997). Those who volunteer also express internal rather than external locus of control (Guagnano, 1995).

A different approach to understanding individual differences in willingness to volunteer is offered by McAdams and his colleagues (1997). They define **generativity** as an adult's interest in and commitment to the well-being of future generations. People high in generativity show this interest and commitment by becoming parents, by teaching what they know to young people, and by engaging in acts that will have positive effects beyond their own lifetimes.

Generative adults believe that people need to care for one another. They possess enduring moral values that give purpose and meaning to their lives, perceive bad events as opportunities to create good outcomes, and make an effort to contribute to the progressive development of a better society. Figure 10.13 lists the many personality dispositions—including generativity—that characterize altruistic individuals.

Who Receives Help, and How Do People Respond to Being Helped?

Most of the research on prosocial behavior has focused on those who provide or fail to provide help. We will now turn briefly to what is known about those who are in need of assistance. Specifically, we will discuss the effect of *gender* on the likelihood of receiving help, the importance of *asking for help*, and *how people react to receiving help.*

generativity: An adult's concern for and commitment to the well-being of future generations.

■ GENDER: ARE FEMALES MORE LIKELY TO BE HELPED THAN MALES? Though it sounds like a sexist stereotype, research has consistently shown that men are very likely to provide help to women in distress (Latané & Dabbs, 1975; Piliavin & Unger,

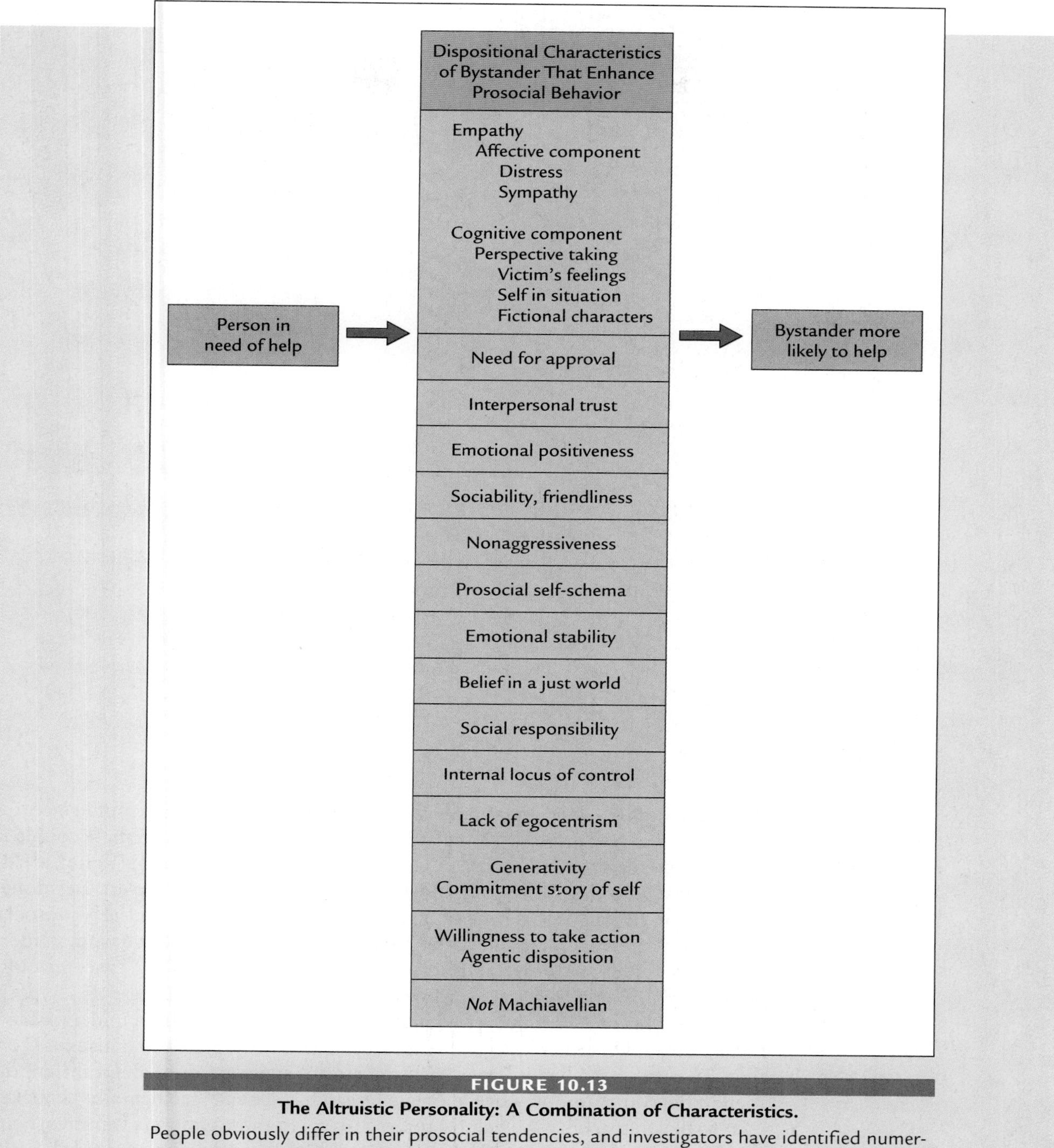

FIGURE 10.13

The Altruistic Personality: A Combination of Characteristics.
People obviously differ in their prosocial tendencies, and investigators have identified numerous personality differences between those who help and those who don't. Shown here are most of the relevant traits (or dispositions) that enhance or inhibit prosocial responsiveness. ■

1985), even though females of all ages are higher in empathy than males (Shigetomi, Hartmann, & Gelfand, 1981). So, why do men help women?

One possible answer lies in Step 4 of the decision-making mode. Many emergency situations require certain skills and knowledge that are more common among men than women (for example, changing a flat tire). Other situations require strength or special training associated with men (for example, fighting off an

FIGURE 10.14

Why Do Men Help a Woman in Distress?

In many situations, women are more likely to receive help than either men or male–female couples, and men are more likely to provide help than are women. Because attractive women receive more help than unattractive ones, and because men exposed to erotic stimuli are more helpful to women than are men exposed to neutral stimuli, it seems reasonable to suggest that the motivation for male helpfulness in these instances is based in part on sexual attraction rather than pure altruism.

attacker). Perhaps this explains why a female motorist with car trouble (see Figure 10.14) receives more assistance than either a male or a male–female couple in the same predicament (Pomazal & Clore, 1973; Snyder, Grether, & Keller, 1974). Also, those who stop to help are most often young males who are driving alone.

The motivation for this kind of male helpfulness may not be entirely prosocial or altruistic, however. For one thing, men stop to help an attractive woman more frequently than to help an unattractive one (West & Brown, 1975). It seems quite possible that the motivation is primarily romantic or sexual. To test this hypothesis, Przybyla (1985) conducted a laboratory experiment in which undergraduate men were shown either an erotic videotape or a control tape with nonsexual content. The men who had just watched the erotic tape were more helpful than the men in the control group when a female research assistant "accidentally" knocked over a stack of papers. The helpful males also spent more time (six minutes) helping this female stranger than other males spent (thirty seconds) helping a male assistant who had knocked over a stack of papers. Note that viewing or not viewing an erotic tape had no effect on the helping behavior of female participants, and the gender of the person needing help also had no effect on females.

■ ASKING FOR HELP. We have pointed out that uncertainty about what is happening in an emergency and about what to do can inhibit a bystander's prosocial response. Ambiguity leads potential helpers to hold back and wait for clarification. The most direct and most effective way for a victim to reduce ambiguity is to *ask for help* in very clear terms. If possible, the person in need would do well to make a specific request. Though saying "Help!" is better than nothing, it is better still to say, "Please call the police" or "Would you help me get back up on my feet?"

It may seem obvious (and easy) to ask for help, but those in need often fail to do so for a variety of reasons. For example, shy men and women are reluctant to seek help from a member of the other gender (DePaulo et al., 1989). Students whose attachment style is secure are more likely to seek the support of a counselor than are those with ambivalent or avoidant styles (LaRose, Boivin, & Doyle, 2001). Women ask for help more often than men, young adults ask more often than elderly adults, and help is more likely to be requested by someone high in socioeconomic status than by someone whose status is low (Nadler, 1991). The decision to seek help is also influenced by stereotypes (see Chapter 6) associated with potential helpers. For example, white college students often hold positive stereotypes about the quantitative skills of Asians, and they request help on a math test more frequently from an Asian American student than from a fellow white student (Bogart, 1998).

As with potential helpers, the person in need of help does not want to overreact with inappropriate emotionality (Yates, 1992). Victims also fear that others will perceive them as incompetent if they ask for help (DePaulo & Fisher, 1980). Being dependent on others can be stigmatizing, especially in Western cultures (Nadler, 1993). When a great deal of help seems to be required, the person receiving it may be viewed inappropriately as stupid or unskilled (Gilbert & Silvera, 1996). Thus, it can be uncomfortable to receive help, as will be discussed in more detail in the following section.

■ HOW DOES IT FEEL TO RECEIVE HELP? You are in need of help, and someone comes along to provide assistance. Offhand, it seems that you should react positively and with gratitude, but often your reaction is not like that at all. As suggested above, a person who receives help may experience negative emotions such as discomfort and feel resentful toward the person who provided assistance. Elderly adults who are physically impaired need help, but many nevertheless feel depressed as a consequence (Newsom, 1999).

Receiving help can lower self-esteem (see Chapter 5), especially if the helper is a friend or someone who is similar to you in age, education, or other characteristics (DePaulo et al., 1981; Nadler, Fisher, & Itzhak, 1983). When self-esteem is threatened, the resulting negative affect creates feelings of dislike toward the good Samaritan (see Chapter 7). An equally negative response is common when a member of a stigmatized group (for example, a black student) receives unsolicited help from a member of a nonstigmatized group (for example, a white student). In this instance, the help may be perceived as a patronizing insult (Schneider et al., 1996).

Help from a sibling can also be unpleasant, especially from a younger brother (Searcy & Eisenberg, 1992). Help from a nonsibling or from a dissimilar (nonstigmatized) stranger is relatively nonthreatening, however, and the resulting affect is much more positive (Cook & Pelfrey, 1985). In the airport incident described at the beginning of this chapter, the young mother with her two children might have felt less grateful if the assistance had come from another young mother with children rather than from me. That is, if someone very much like herself (a woman traveling alone with children) were able to offer assistance, it might appear that the helper is more competent than the one receiving help. Help from a man traveling by himself would not constitute a threat to her competence.

Whenever a person responds negatively to receiving help, there is also a positive aspect that is not obvious. When being helped is sufficiently unpleasant that the person wants to avoid appearing incompetent again, he or she is motivated to engage in self-help in the future (Fisher, Nadler, & Whitcher-Alagna, 1982; Lehman et al., 1995). Among other benefits, this motivation can reduce feelings of dependence

(Daubman, 1995). I (DB) have learned many things about the use of my computer because I don't want to depend on my two youngest daughters to help me copy a file on a disk, move a paragraph from one location to another, or add an attachment to an e-mail. In contrast, when I receive help from a relative stranger who is a computer expert, I'm not at all motivated to help myself by learning all there is to know. The various effects of receiving help from different sources are shown in Figure 10.15.

What are some of the implications of such emotional and motivational effects to being helped? Help for major problems (e.g., financial difficulties) that is provided by friends, family, and neighbors can lead to feelings of inadequacy and resentment, but this can motivate the individual to work hard to avoid such problems in the future. If, in contrast, the help comes from strangers, such as employees in a government agency, the person in need retains a positive self-image and appreciates the help, but there is little motivation to avoid future crises. The choice may be between recipients who are unhappy and motivated to change and those who are happy and unmotivated. Which do you think is preferable?

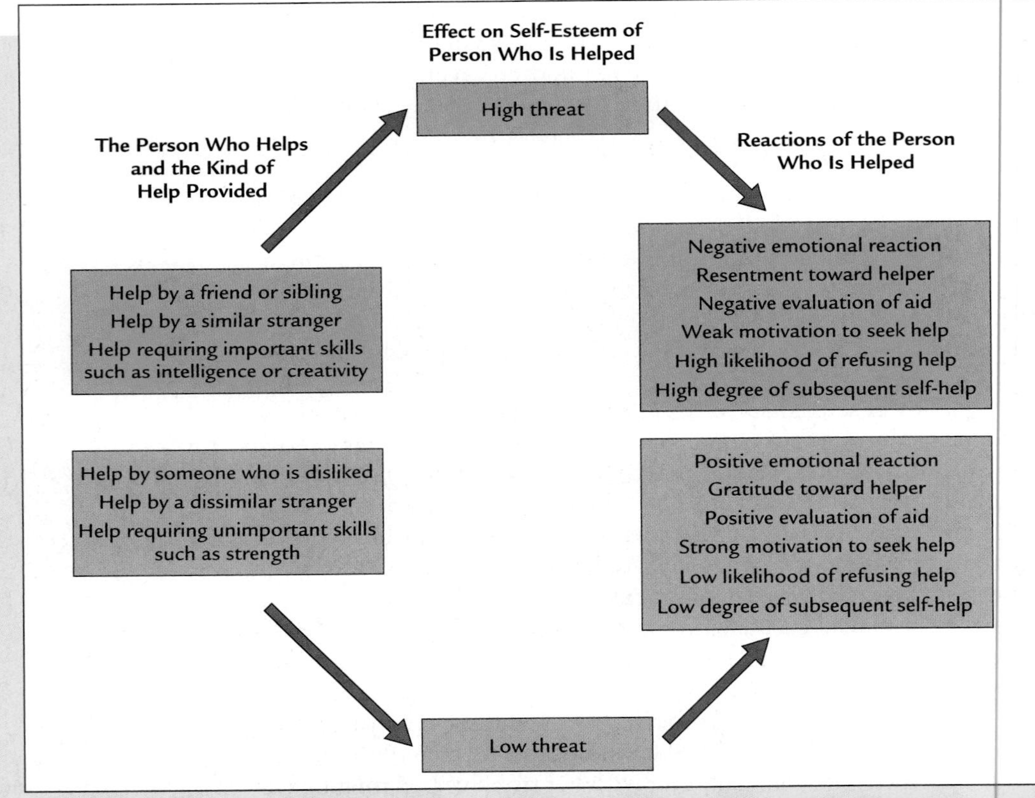

FIGURE 10.15

Reactions to Receiving Help: It Depends.

A person who receives help sometimes responds negatively and sometimes positively. It is threatening to be helped by a friend or by a stranger similar to oneself. The effect on the person receiving assistance is lowered self-esteem and negative affect—but a stronger motivation to attempt self-help in the future. Receiving help from a dissimilar stranger is not threatening, does not lower self-esteem, and arouses positive affect—but leads to less self-help in the future.

[SOURCE: BASED ON INFORMATION IN FISHER, NADLER, & WHITCHER-ALAGNA, 1982.]

KEY POINTS

- Positive and negative emotional states can either enhance or inhibit prosocial behavior, depending on specific factors in the situation and on the nature of the required assistance.
- Individual differences in altruistic behavior are based in large part on *empathy,* a complex response that includes both affective and cognitive components. The extent to which a person is able to respond with empathy depends on both genetics and learning experiences.
- The *altruistic personality* consists of empathy plus additional relevant dispositional variables.
- People volunteer to provide help on a long-term basis as a function of various selfish and selfless motives and specific dispositional variables.
- Help is given most often by men to women, at least in part because of differential skills associated with gender and also by the fact that males are motivated by romance or sex in addition to altruism.
- Asking for help reduces ambiguity and increases the probability of receiving help.
- When the helper and the recipient are similar, the person who is helped tends to react negatively and to feel incompetent, to experience decreased self-esteem, and to resent the helper. These negative responses also tend to motivate self-help in the future.

Explaining Prosocial Behavior: Why Do People Help?

Based on the discussion so far, it is obvious that many factors influence whether or not an individual will engage in prosocial behavior. The situation is very important, and there are important dispositional variables that affect the probability of helping or not helping. Also, various characteristics of the person in need influence how potential helpers respond. We now turn to a different kind of question about prosocial responses: not who will help under what circumstances, but rather *why* anyone would ever engage in such behavior. In other words, what motivates a prosocial act? Many theories have been formulated, but most rest on the familiar assumption that people attempt to maximize rewards and minimize punishments.

Existing theories tend to stress either relatively selfish or relatively unselfish motives for behaving in a prosocial manner (Campbell & Sprecht, 1985). As you might guess, people tend to attribute their own helpful behavior to unselfish motives, usually suggesting basic moral values—"It was the right thing to do" or "That was the way my parents raised me" or "The Lord put me there for a reason."

When, however, the help is provided by someone else, an observer is equally likely to attribute either unselfish motives—"She was heroic"—or selfish ones—"She was just hoping for a reward." (Doherty, Weigold, & Schlenker, 1990). Even those who spend their lives trying to deal with massive problems such as global warming or a cure for cancer are often viewed as acting in terms of their own self-interest (Baron, J., 1997). The ultimate example of such attributions is to say that the person who does good deeds is doing so only because of the prospect of being rewarded by spending all eternity in heaven (see Figure 10.16).

FIGURE 10.16

Altruism in Return for a Place in Heaven.

It is sometimes suggested that all prosocial behavior can be explained by self-interest of one kind or another. Even if there is no direct reward in this life, it is possible that people behave in an altruistic fashion because, like the gentleman in this cartoon, they expect a reward after dying.

[SOURCE: © THE NEW YORKER COLLECTION 2000 FRANK COTHAM FROM CARTOONBANK.COM. ALL RIGHTS RESERVED.]

"I contributed a lot to charity back when I thought I was going to die."

It is possible, then, to explain all prosocial behavior as selfish and self-centered. We, however, prefer to take the position that prosocial actions are probably based in part on selfish motives and in part on unselfish ones.

We now turn to the four major theories that attempt to explain prosocial motivation. These formulations are summarized in Figure 10.17, and you might find it helpful to take a good look at that information before you read the following discussion.

Empathy–Altruism: It Feels Good to Help Those in Need

Perhaps the least selfish explanation of prosocial behavior is that empathetic people help others because "it feels good to do good." On this underlying assumption, Batson and his colleagues (1981) proposed the **empathy–altruism hypothesis.** They suggest that at least some prosocial acts are motivated solely by the unselfish desire to help someone in need (Batson & Oleson, 1991). This motivation to help can be sufficiently strong that the individual who provides help is willing to engage in unpleasant, dangerous, and even life-threatening activity (Batson, Batson et al., 1995). The feelings of compassion can be sufficiently strong that they outweigh all other considerations (Batson, Klein et al., 1995). The powerful feeling of empathy provides validating evidence to the individual that he or she must *truly value* the other person's welfare (Batson, Turk et al., 1995).

To test this altruistic view of helping behavior, Batson and his colleagues devised an experimental procedure in which they aroused a bystander's empathy by describing him or her as being either similar to or dissimilar from the victim (see Chapter 7). The bystander was then presented with an opportunity to be helpful (Batson et al., 1983; Toi & Batson, 1982). Each undergraduate research participant was given the role of an "observer" who watched a "fellow student" on a TV monitor as she performed a task while (supposedly) receiving random electric shocks. This fellow student was in fact a research assistant recorded on videotape. After the task was underway, the assistant said that she was in pain and confided that as a child she

empathy–altruism hypothesis: The proposal that prosocial behavior is motivated solely by the desire to help someone in need.

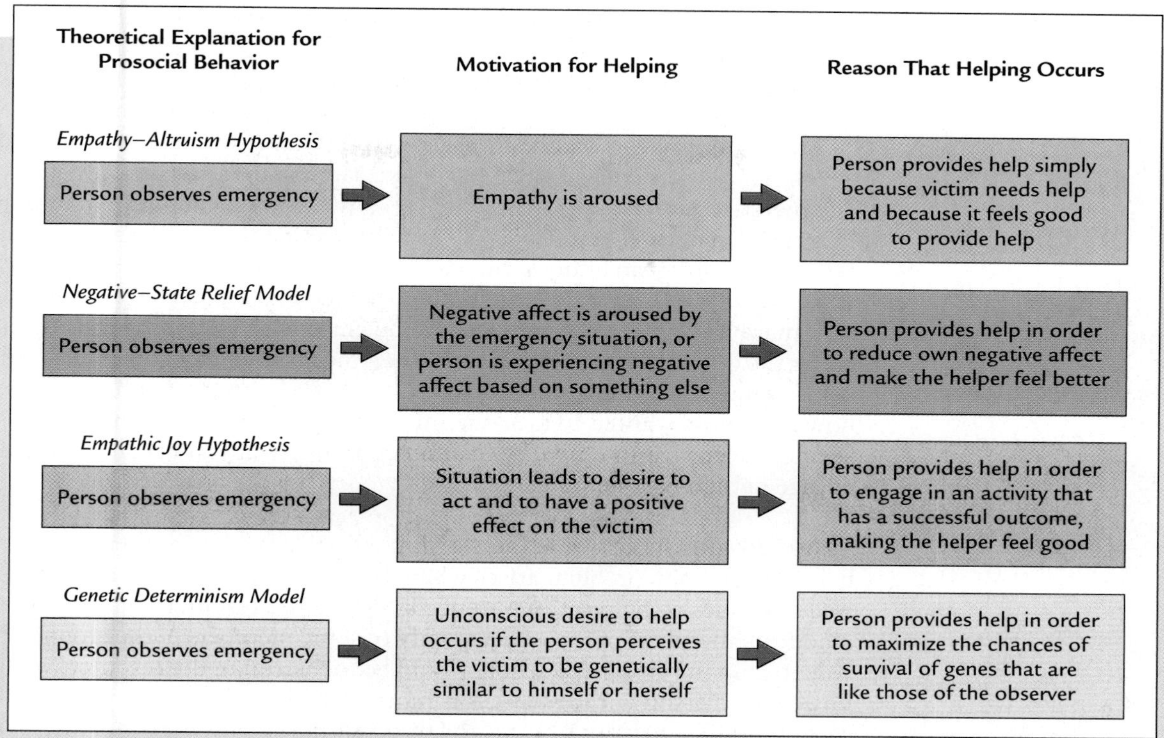

FIGURE 10.17

What Motivates Prosocial Behavior?

Four major explanations of the motivation underlying prosocial behavior are outlined here: *empathy–altruism hypothesis, negative–state relief model, empathic joy hypothesis,* and *genetic determinism model.* The first three formulations stress the importance of increasing positive affect or decreasing negative affect. The fourth formulation rests on the assumption that prosocial behavior is genetically determined and that such behavior evolved because it enhanced reproductive success.

had had a traumatic experience with electricity. She agreed to continue if necessary, but the experimenter asked whether the observer would be willing to trade places with her or whether they should simply discontinue the experiment. When empathy was low (dissimilar victim and participant), the participants preferred to end the experiment rather than engage in a painful prosocial act. When empathy was high (similar victim and participant), the participants agreed to take the victim's place and receive the shocks. It appears that this altruistic act was motivated solely by empathic concern for the victim. Further, other research indicates that when empathy-based helping is unsuccessful, the helper experiences negative emotion (Batson & Weeks, 1996). In other words, high empathy not only leads to prosocial action because such behavior feels good, but an unsuccessful attempt to provide help feels bad.

Arguing against this unselfish view of prosocial behavior, Cialdini and his colleagues (1997) agreed that empathy leads to altruistic behavior but argued that this only occurs when the participant perceives an overlap between self and other. If another person overlaps oneself—in effect, is part of one's own self-concept—then a helpful participant is simply helping himself or herself. These investigators presented evidence that without this feeling of oneness, empathic concern does *not* increase helping. Batson and his colleagues (1997) responded with additional evidence indicating that the perception of overlapping is *not* necessary—empathy leads to helping even in the absence of oneness.

■ EMPATHY AVOIDANCE. Do you suppose that most people *like* to have their empathy aroused? Given a choice, would people want to receive information that increased their empathy level? Apparently, such information is aversive—most individuals seek to avoid it, thus avoiding the need to engage in something difficult.

This tendency was shown in research conducted by Shaw, Batson, and Todd (1994). They asked college students to take part in a new program designed to help a homeless man. The cost of helping was either low (spending an hour preparing letters that requested donations) or high (interacting with the homeless man himself for more than an hour on three separate occasions). After learning about the task (low cost or high cost), the students could choose between receiving factual information about the man or receiving an emotional, empathy-arousing message about the difficulties he was having. When the cost of helping was low, most students wanted to hear the emotional message. When the cost of helping was high, however, most wanted to hear the informational message. In other words, they seemed to engage in *empathy avoidance* in order not to become motivated to engage in high-cost helping.

■ EMPATHY AND SELECTIVE ALTRUISM. Empathy plays still another role in helping behavior. A major problem arises when decisions must be made about using limited resources to help a group in need. Should the resources be divided equally among all members of the group or only to some members of the group? The best way to help the group as a whole would be to distribute the resources equally. If, however, a person with resources is motivated either by egoism ("First you take care of number one") or by empathy directed at a single group member (*selective altruism* for an individual who arouses your emotions), the group as a whole will be neglected (Batson, Ahmed et al., 1999). Either of these alternatives poses a threat to the common good.

Though the negative effect of egoism is not surprising, the effect of selective altruism is much less obvious. A specific example of the latter is provided by appeals to support a specific child in need (see Figure 10.18). It is undoubtedly much more difficult to generate helpfulness for thousands of underfed children than for a specific child who has a name and whose face can be seen in a photograph. Keep-

FIGURE 10.18
Selective Altruism: Helping One and Ignoring the Common Good?
For any group of individuals in need, an equal distribution of needed resources would be best for the common good. Very often, however, people are more willing to help on the basis of *selective altruism;* that is, they will assist one member of the group who engages them emotionally. You might try to answer this question: Is it fair to help one and ignore the rest?

ing the resources for yourself (egoism) is obviously frowned upon, but deciding to help one member of the group (selective altruism) is generally commended. In either instance the question remains—Is it fair to help one and ignore the rest? How would you answer that question?

Negative-State Relief: Helping Can Reduce Your Negative Affect

Another theory suggests that people sometimes help because they are in a bad mood and want to make themselves feel better. This explanation of prosocial behavior is known as the **negative–state relief model** (Cialdini, Baumann, & Kenrick, 1981). In other words, prosocial behavior can act as a self-help undertaking to reduce one's negative affect.

Research indicates that it doesn't matter whether the bystander's negative emotions were aroused before the emergency arose or were aroused by the emergency itself. That is, you might be upset about receiving a bad grade or about seeing an injured stranger. In either instance, you may engage in a prosocial act primarily in order to improve your own mood (Dietrich & Berkowitz, 1997; Fultz, Schaller, & Cialdini, 1988). In such situations, sadness leads to prosocial behavior, and empathy is not a necessary component (Cialdini et al., 1987).

Empathic Joy: Helping Can Make You Feel Better—If You Know That You Accomplished Something

It is generally true that it feels good to have a positive impact on other people. It can literally be better to give than to receive. Helping can thus be explained on the basis of the **empathic joy hypothesis** (Smith, Keating, & Stotland, 1989). From this perspective, a helper responds to the needs of a victim because he or she wants to feel good about accomplishing something.

One implication of this formulation is that it is crucial for the person who helps to know that his or her actions have a positive impact on the victim. It is argued that if helping were based entirely on empathy, feedback about its effect would be irrelevant. Is that accurate? To find out, Smith, Keating, and Stotland (1989) asked research participants to watch a videotape in which a female student said she might drop out of college because she felt isolated and distressed. After they watched the videotape, the participants were given the opportunity to offer advice. Some were told that they would receive feedback about the effectiveness of their advice, and others were told that they would not be told what the woman decided to do. The woman was described as either similar to a participant (high empathy) or dissimilar (low empathy). Under these conditions, empathy alone was not enough to bring about a prosocial response. Rather, empathy *and* feedback about one's impact were required.

In each of the three theoretical models that have just been described—1) empathy–altruism hypothesis, 2) negative state relief model, and 3) empathic joy hypothesis—affective state is a crucial element. That is, prosocial behavior occurs because such actions increase positive affect or decrease negative affect. All three formulations rest on the assumption that people engage in helpful behavior either because it feels good or because it makes one feel less bad. The emotion that is elicited by performing a prosocial act is sometimes labeled *helper's high*—a feeling of calmness, self-worth, and warmth (Luks, 1988). Depending on the specific circumstances, each of the three models can make accurate predictions about how people will respond.

There is, however, a fourth explanation of prosocial behavior that approaches the question in an entirely different way—perhaps the tendency to help others is based on genetics rather than emotion.

negative–state relief model: The proposal that prosocial behavior is motivated by the bystander's desire to reduce his or her own uncomfortable negative emotions.

empathic joy hypothesis: The proposal that prosocial behavior is motivated by the positive emotion a helper anticipates experiencing as a the result of having a beneficial impact on the life of someone in need.

Genetic Determinism: Helping Others Maximizes Gene Survival

The **genetic determinism model** is based on a general theory of human behavior (Pinker, 1998). Evolutionary psychologists stress that we are not conscious of responding to genetic influences—we simply do so because we are built that way (Rushton, 1989b). In effect, humans are programmed to help just as they are programmed with respect to prejudice (Chapter 6), attraction (Chapter 7), mate selection (Chapter 8), aggression (Chapter 11), and other behaviors.

Archer (1991) describes how sociobiological theories are based on the concept of natural selection. As is well established for physical characteristics, many behavioral characteristics are also assumed to be genetically based. In each instance, the characteristics are "selected" through evolution purely on the basis of their relevance to reproductive success. The individual's only "goal" is the unconscious need to ensure that his or her genes are passed on to the next generation. Any physical or behavioral characteristic that furthers that goal is more likely to be represented in future generations than are other characteristics that either interfere with genetic transmission or are irrelevant to it.

Note that the enthusiasm sometimes generated by an evolutionary explanation may lead to selective perception. For example, biologists have observed that meerkats seem to be altruistic in that one stands guard while the others eat. The guard meerkat's job is to watch for hawks in order to be able to give a warning and thus protect his fellow meerkats (Clutton-Brock et al., 1999; Yoon, 1999) (see Figure 10.19). However, it has more recently been discovered that the seemingly unselfish "guards" first eat their fill and then stand up to watch. And this task is not simply to help their fellow meerkats—those that stand guard are the first to spot a predator and are thus able to dive for safety when danger threatens (Clutton-Brock et al., 1999). In other words, this "altruistic" sentinel is actually acting in his own self-interest.

As we have indicated throughout this chapter, both empathy and prosocial acts depend in part on the similarity between victim and bystander. Studies of various species indicate that the greater the genetic similarity between two individual organisms, the more likely it is that one will help the other when help is needed (Ridley & Dawkins, 1981). Evolutionary theorists assume that prosocial behavior results from the "selfish gene." That is, the more similar Individual A is to Individual B, the more genes they probably have in common. If so, when A helps B, some portion of A's genes will be more likely to be represented in future generations even if A dies in the process of helping (Rushton, Russell, & Wells, 1984). More generally, the genetic "fitness" of each individual organism requires that it live long enough to reproduce *or* to enhance the reproductive odds of another individual whose genetic makeup is similar to his or her own (Browne, 1992).

A slightly different approach that leads to the same conclusion was offered by Burnstein, Crandall, and Kitayama (1994). They argued that it was not in the best interest of prehistoric humans to help one another—natural selection would favor not helping. Anyone who helped another person in an emergency such as drowning or being attacked by predatory animals would risk being killed and thus not be able to pass along her or his own genes. One exception to this outcome is the case in which the person in need of help was a close relative. In this instance, natural selection would favor those who helped *relatives* who were young enough *to reproduce.* Helpfulness to a close relative is perceived as rational, ethical, and a matter of obligation—but, this is true only if helping would affect survival or reproductive success (Kruger, 2001) and only if the individual feels emotionally close to the relative (Korchmaros & Kenny, 2001). Burnstein and his colleagues conducted a series of studies based on hypothetical decisions about who should be helped. As predicted on the basis of genetic similarity, research participants were more likely to help a close relative than either a distant relative or a nonrelative. And as pre-

genetic determinism model: The proposal that behavior is driven by genetic attributes that evolved because they enhanced the probability of transmitting one's genes to subsequent generations.

FIGURE 10.19
The Meerkat Sentry: Altruism or Self-Interest?
Sometimes, we project altruism onto other species when other motives can explain the behavior. For example, while the rest of his group is busy searching for food, one meerkat stands alone scanning the sky for hawks, ready to sound the warning if one appears. This behavior has long been assumed to be an instance of self-sacrifice and altruism in this species. More recent observations suggest, however, that a meerkat only goes on guard duty after he is well fed, and the reason for doing so is to be the first to see a predator and thus be able to dive down a hole for safety.

dicted on the basis of reproductive ability, more help was offered to young relatives than to old ones—for example, more help was given to a female relative young enough to bear children than to a female relative past menopause.

In a review of the altruism literature, Buck and Ginsberg (1991) concluded that there is no evidence of a gene that determines prosocial behavior. Among humans, however, and among other animals as well (de Waal, 1996), there *are* genetically based abilities to communicate emotions and to form social bonds. It may be these inherited capacities that increase the odds that one person will help another when problems arise. In effect, humans are inherently sociable and capable of empathy. When people interact with each other in social relationships, "they are always prosocial, usually helpful, and often altruistic" (Fiske, 1991, p. 209).

You would probably find it more satisfying if we used this final paragraph to announce which of these competing explanations of prosocial behavior is the correct one. Instead, it seems quite possible that we respond to the needs of others on the basis of a variety of motives. Further, different individuals in different situations may well be helpful for quite different reasons. *Regardless of the underlying reason for any specific prosocial response, it can be agreed that one very positive aspect of human behavior is that we frequently are willing to help those in need.*

KEY POINTS

- The *empathy–altruism* hypothesis proposes that, because of empathy, we help those in need simply because it feels good to do so.
- The *negative–state relief model* proposes that people help other people in order to relieve and make less negative their own emotional discomfort.
- The *empathic joy hypothesis* bases helping on the positive feelings of accomplishment that arise when the helper knows that he or she was able to have a beneficial impact on the person in need.
- The *genetic determinism model* traces prosocial behavior to the general effects of natural selection. To the extent that prosocial acts increase the odds of that person's genes being transmitted to future generations. As a result, they become part of our biological heritage.

CONNECTIONS: INTEGRATING SOCIAL PSYCHOLOGY

IN THIS CHAPTER, YOU READ ABOUT . . .	IN OTHER CHAPTERS, YOU WILL FIND RELATED DISCUSSIONS OF . . .
bystanders' response to the nonverbal cues of other bystanders	interpretation of nonverbal cues (Chapter 2)
social comparison processes among the witnesses to an emergency	the importance of social comparison in the study of attitudes (Chapter 4), affiliation (Chapter 7), and social influence (Chapter 9)
attributions as to the cause of a victim's problem	attribution theory (Chapter 2)
self-concept as a determinant of helping behavior and the effect of receiving help on self-esteem	research and theory on self-concept and self esteem (Chapter 5)
similarity of victim and bystander as a determinant of helping	similarity and attraction (Chapters 7 and 8)
genetics and helping	genetics as a factor in prejudice (Chapter 6), attraction (Chapter 7), mate selection (Chapter 8), and aggression (Chapter 11)
affective state and helping	affect as a factor in attitudes (Chapter 4), prejudice (Chapter 6), attraction (Chapter 7), relationships (Chapter 8), and aggression (Chapter 11)

THINKING ABOUT CONNECTIONS

1. As you are walking out of the building after your social psychology class, you see an elderly man lying face down on the sidewalk. Three students are standing nearby, not speaking but looking at the man. How would you interpret this situation? What might you observe in the facial expressions and bodily gestures of the three bystanders (Chapter 2)? As you take a closer look at the man lying on the sidewalk, you may make some guesses as to why he is there. Many different attributions are possible (Chapter 2). Suggest some of the possibilities that might occur to you.

2. Your car won't start, and you are in a hurry. You know that you have plenty of gas, and the battery is almost new. You open the hood but don't see anything obviously wrong. A fellow student comes along and offers to help. She looks under the hood, taps something or other, and says, "Try it now." You turn the key, and the car starts easily. How do you feel at that moment? Do you like the student

who helped you (Chapter 7)? Does being helped raise or lower your self-esteem (Chapter 5)? Do you think you might be motivated to learn more about automobiles so this won't happen again (Chapter 10)?

3. On the evening news, you learn about a devastating earthquake in southern California that has destroyed a great many homes, leaving a large number of people without shelter or food. The announcer gives a telephone number and an address for those who want to contribute money or food. Also, volunteers are needed to help with the cleanup. Do you ignore this message, or do you decide to contribute money, food, or your time? What factors with respect to the disaster itself, where it occurred, and your experiences with such a situation might influence your decision? List the kinds of social psychological processes that could be operating.

4. You are in a building that is on fire. You can get out, but there is time to help only one other person escape from the fast-moving blaze. You know that you could select your teenage cousin or his mother (your middle-aged aunt). Which one would you choose to save? On what basis would you make this decision? Think about what you have read in this chapter about genetic influences as well as in other chapters about attraction (Chapter 7) and relationships (Chapter 8).

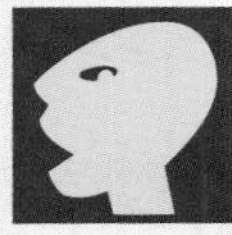

IDEAS TO TAKE WITH YOU—AND USE!

BEING A RESPONSIVE BYSTANDER

Throughout this chapter, you have read examples of real and staged emergencies. In your own life you probably will come across numerous unexpected situations in which your help is badly needed. How you respond is your own business, of course, but at least consider the following suggestions that might be useful if you want to make an informed decision.

Pay Attention to What Is Going on around You.

In our everyday lives we often think more about ourselves (our plans, worries, expectations, etc.) than about our surroundings. It is useful, however, to be aware of what is happening around us. Remember the seminary students who were behind schedule and in such a hurry that they ignored a man who appeared to have collapsed in a doorway? It is sometimes worthwhile to pay attention to and think about other people and their welfare.

If You Notice Something Unusual, Consider Multiple Alternatives.

A child crying in a grocery store may just want another piece of candy, or she might be the victim of abuse. The man who is running down the street may be exercising, or he might be escaping with something he has stolen. The smoke you smell might be burnt toast, or it might indicate a fire in your apartment. It might be cool to do nothing, and it might be foolish to jump to false conclusions. The best move is to consider various possibilities and seek additional information. Is someone hurting the child? Is the man carrying a large plastic bag with money sticking out of the top? Is there smoke coming out of your bedroom? Many (maybe most) such events turn out to be of no importance, but you need to be alert to the possibility that there are times when you are a bystander who could help.

Remember That You Are as Responsible as Anyone Else to Help a Stranger in Need.

When help is needed, everyone who is aware of the problem is equally responsible. Once I (DB) was with my two youngest daughters at a multiplex movie theater in a mall. When it was time for the film to begin, nothing happened. A roomful of people of various ages sat in their seats and stared at the blank screen. This seemed ridiculous to me, so I left my daughters, went to the refreshment counter, and asked the person stirring the popcorn to inform whoever was in

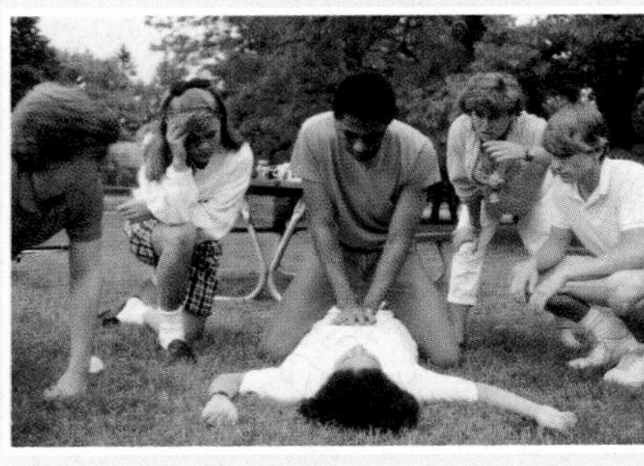

(continued)

IDEAS TO TAKE WITH YOU—AND USE! *(CONTINUED)*

charge that there was no movie on screen 12. She told the manager, he found someone to push the right button, and the movie began. Unlike my airport experience described at the beginning of this chapter, I was not the only bystander, but anyone there could have done what I did. If you always allow your fellow unresponsive bystanders to guide your behavior, you are acting as foolishly as they are. If I had not taken charge in the movie, I wonder how long the others might have continued sitting quietly in their seats.

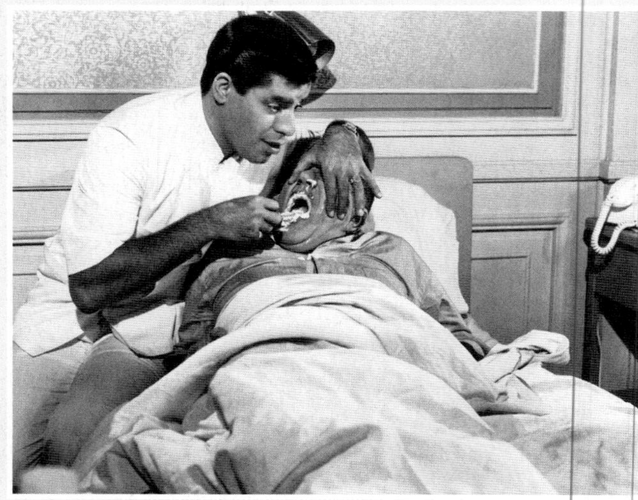

Be Willing to Take a Chance and Do Something.

Sometimes, when others fail to act, and you believe something is wrong, they can be correct and you can do something foolish. Being foolish is not the end of the world, and you will probably never see the other bystanders again. Better to make a foolish decision and offer help to someone who doesn't need it than to make a less obvious but equally foolish decision to stand back when help is badly needed. Do what you think is the right thing to do.

SUMMARY AND REVIEW OF KEY POINTS

Responding to an Emergency: Why Are Bystanders Sometimes Helpful, Sometimes Indifferent?

- In part because of *diffusion of responsibility,* the more bystanders present as witnesses to an emergency, the less likely is help to be given and the greater the delay before help occurs.
- When faced with an emergency, a bystander must go through five crucial steps involving decisions that either inhibit or enhance the likelihood of a prosocial response. He or she must notice the emergency, correctly interpret what is occurring, assume responsibility for helping, have the necessary skills and knowledge to help, and then actually decide to provide assistance.
- Prosocial acts occur most often when the bystander feels attraction toward the person in need and attributes the problem to circumstances beyond the victim's control.
- Exposure to prosocial models in real life and in the media has a positive effect on prosocial acts.
- People can be differentiated in terms of their primary motivation in situations involving a moral choice—*self-interest, moral integrity,* and *moral hypocrisy.*

The Helpers and Those Who Receive Help

- Positive and negative emotional states can either enhance or inhibit prosocial behavior, depending on specific factors in the situation and in the nature of the required assistance.
- Individual differences in altruistic behavior are based in large part on *empathy,* a complex response that includes both affective and cognitive components. The extent to which a person is able to respond with empathy depends on both genetics and learning experiences.
- The *altruistic personality* consists of empathy plus additional relevant dispositional variables.
- People volunteer to provide help on a long-term basis as a function of various selfish and selfless motives and specific dispositional variables.
- Help is given most often by men to women, at least in part because of differential skills associated with gender and also because of the fact that males are motivated by romance or sex in addition to altruism.
- Asking for help reduces ambiguity and increases the probability of receiving help.
- When the helper and the recipient are similar, the person who is

helped tends to react negatively and to feel incompetent, to experience decreased self-esteem, and to resent the helper. These negative responses also tend to motivate self-help in the future.

Explaining Prosocial Behavior: Why Do People Help?

- The *empathy–altruism hypothesis* proposes that, because of empathy, we help those in need simply because it feels good to do so.
- The *negative–state relief model* proposes that people help other people in order to relieve and make less negative their own emotional discomfort.
- The *empathic joy hypothesis* bases helping on the positive feelings of accomplishment that arise when the helper knows that he or she was able to have a beneficial impact on the person in need.
- The *genetic determinism model* traces prosocial behavior to the general effects of natural selection. To the extent that prosocial acts increase the odds of one's genes being transmitted to future generations, they become part of our biological heritage.

KEY TERMS

altruism (p. 389)

altruistic personality (p. 414)

bystander effect (p. 391)

diffusion of responsibility (p. 390)

egoism (p. 403)

empathic joy hypothesis (p. 425)

empathy (p. 408)

empathy–altruism hypothesis (p. 422)

generativity (p. 416)

genetic determinism model (p. 426)

moral hypocrisy (p. 403)

moral integrity (p. 403)

negative–state relief model (p. 425)

pluralistic ignorance (p. 396)

prosocial behavior (p. 389)

self-interest (p. 403)

FOR MORE INFORMATION

Coles, R. (1997). *The moral intelligence of children.* New York: Random House.

- A thought provoking discussion by psychiatrist Robert Coles, who is a Harvard professor and winner of the Pulitzer Prize for a previous book. Coles describes the many ways that parents and other adults shape the behavior of their children. He indicates how they direct or fail to direct children toward developing a conscience, concern for others, kindness, and a willingness to help.

Gladwell, M. (2000). *The tipping point: How little things can make a difference.* New York: Little, Brown.

- For a wide variety of human behaviors, it can be shown that people will act or fail to act as a function of what other people are doing *if* a sufficient number of others behave in a particular way. That sufficient number is the "straw that broke the camel's back" or the "tipping point." For a great many people, there is a tendency not to act until a certain number of others have done so first. Thus, people can provide extraordinary help to others in an emergency, or they can hold back and fail to respond. The same phenomenon can be observed in such diverse behaviors as deciding to give up cigarettes, joining a political protest, recycling, littering, rioting, mowing your lawn, and much else besides. Gladwell proposes that any widespread behavioral change occurs when a small number of people take the initiative to act, when what they do is memorable, and when small changes in the situation facilitate the behavior. This book has an optimistic message that societal changes can and do occur with a little nudging by the right people in the right place.

Shroeder, D. A., Penner, L. A., Dovidio, J. F., & Piliavin, J. A. (1995). *The social psychology of helping and altruism: Problems and puzzles.* New York: McGraw-Hill.

- This is the first text devoted entirely to the topic of prosocial behavior. The authors cover much of the material discussed in Chapter 10, plus such topics as the developmental aspects of helping, cooperation, and collective helping. They also present an integrative conceptual framework based on affect and cognition, and make suggestions for future research.

Wright, R. (1994). *The moral animal: The new science of evolutionary psychology.* New York: Pantheon.

- A readable and creative explanation of how evolutionary factors affect human genetics and how genes, in turn, affect behavior. Wright's discussion includes prosocial behavior and feelings of compassion, along with many other aspects of social behavior.

Jackson Pollock, *Untitled (Naked Man with Knife)*, 1938–41. © 2002 The Pollock-Krasner Foundation/ Artists Rights Society (ARS), New York. © Tate Gallery, London/Art Resource, NY.

AGGRESSION: ITS NATURE, CAUSES, AND CONTROL

CHAPTER OUTLINE

Most people who know me (RAB) would, I think, describe me as a fairly happy type—cheerful, optimistic, and upbeat. Yet I have had a career-long interest in human **aggression**—the intentional infliction of some form of harm on others (e.g., Baron & Richardson, 1994; Berkowitz, in press). I did not work with a famous researcher in this area when I was a graduate student, and it was not the topic of my Ph.D. dissertation, so I have often wondered: "Where—and when—did I first develop this interest?" I'm not sure, but I think I can trace it back to the summer when I was thirteen. At that time, I hung out with a group of friends who were about the same age as myself. One of them—a fellow named Joel—was, for reasons I will probably never understand, the scapegoat of our group. No matter what he said or did, he was always on the receiving end: the butt of our jokes, our sarcastic remarks, or worse. If there was a trick to be played, Joel was always the one on whom it was tried. And when we chose up sides to play baseball, basketball, or football, he was always the last selected; further, the team that got him generally complained loud and long about being stuck with such a loser. I never gave any of this much thought because (lucky me) I was a very fast runner and got along well with everyone, so I was rarely in Joel's lonely place (although from time to time, all of us were the temporary scapegoat). But one day, I was riding home on my bicycle and took a shortcut through the park. There, behind a tree, I spotted Joel, sobbing as if his heart would break and, even more disturbing to me, hitting his head against the trunk. I pulled to a stop, got off my bicycle, and asked, "What the heck are you doing?" He turned and in a flash, I could see the pain, frustration, and misery on his face. I kept pressing him to explain what was bothering him, so finally he did: he was sick and tired of being rejected and humiliated. And who could blame him? As I listened to his words, uttered between choking sobs, I began to realize how much misery we had inflicted on him. Worst of all, when I thought about it, I couldn't understand *why* we had done this to him. Actually, Joel was a pretty nice guy, and he really wasn't that much worse at sports or that much funnier-looking than the rest of us. I began to feel pretty guilty; after all, he had never done anything to *me,* so how could I justify treating him with so much cruelty? I decided right then and there that I would no longer join the others in taunting him—and in fact, after that day, I didn't. From that time on, I became much more aware of human cruelty and its consequences. So, in one sense, I can trace my interest in the origins of human aggression—and how we can reduce it—to that long-vanished summer day.

Sad to say, human aggression is not restricted to the kinds of things my friends and I did to Joel; on the contrary, if you ever read the newspapers or watch the evening news, you already know very well that aggression is far from rare, and that it often takes much more deadly forms than our childish taunts (see Figure 11.1). It will come as no surprise, then, to learn that this unsettling form of social behavior has long been the subject of systematic research by social psychologists who have tried to understand its nature, origins, and functions (e.g., Baron & Richardson, 1994; Berkowitz, in press; Geen & Donnerstein, 1998). In this chapter, we will provide you with an overview of the key findings of this work. Specifically, we will focus on the following topics.

FIGURE 11.1
The Deadly Face of Human Aggression.
Often, human *aggression* takes devastating forms and results in injury or death to large numbers of persons.

First, we'll describe several *theoretical perspectives* on aggression, contrasting views about its nature and origin. Next, we'll examine several important determinants of human aggression. These include *social factors* involving the words or deeds of other persons; *personal factors,* or traits that predispose specific persons toward aggressive outbursts; and *situational factors,* aspects of the external world such as high temperatures and alcohol. Third, we'll consider two forms of aggression that are especially disturbing because they occur within the context of long-term, ongoing relationships rather than between total strangers: *bullying* (which can occur among adults as well as among children or teenagers such as my friends) and *workplace aggression.* Finally, to conclude on an optimistic note, we'll examine various techniques for the *prevention and control* of aggression.

Theoretical Perspectives on Aggression: In Search of the Roots of Violence

Why do human beings aggress against others? What makes them turn, with fierce brutality, on their fellow human beings? Thoughtful persons have pondered these questions for centuries and have proposed many contrasting explanations for the paradox of human violence. We'll examine several that have been especially influential, concluding with the modern answer provided by social psychologists.

The Role of Biological Factors: From Instincts to the Evolutionary Psychological Perspective

The oldest and probably best known explanation for human aggression is the view that human beings are somehow "programmed" for violence by their basic nature. Such theories suggest that human violence stems from built-in (i.e., inherited) tendencies to aggress against others. The most famous supporter of this theory was Sigmund Freud, who held that aggression stems mainly from a powerful *death wish* (thanatos) possessed by all persons. According to Freud, this instinct is initially aimed at self-destruction but is soon redirected outward, toward others.

aggression: Behavior directed toward the goal of harming another living being who is motivated to avoid such treatment.

A related view was proposed by Konrad Lorenz, a Nobel Prize–winning scientist. Lorenz (1966, 1974) suggested that aggression springs mainly from an inherited *fighting instinct* that human beings share with many other species. Presumably, this instinct developed during the course of evolution because it helped ensure that only the strongest and most vigorous individuals would pass their genes on to the next generation. If you have ever seen nature programs showing scenes in which males fight for dominance—and the right to mate with females—you can see why this view has been so popular: it does seem to fit with careful observations of the natural world around us.

Until a few years ago, few social psychologists accepted such views. Among the many reasons for their objections to the idea that human aggression is genetically programmed were these: (1) Human beings aggress against others in many different ways—everything from ignoring target persons or spreading false rumors about them to the kind of brutal acts that are often reported on the evening news. How could such a huge range of behaviors be determined by genetic factors? (2) The frequency of aggressive actions varies tremendously across human societies—being as much as fifty times more common in some societies than in others (e.g., Fry, 1998). Again, social psychologists asked, "How can aggressive behavior be determined by genetic factors if such huge differences exist?" On the basis of these and other considerations, social psychologists generally concluded that genetic and biological factors play little if any role in human aggression, even though they may influence aggression by other species.

With the advent of the evolutionary perspective in psychology, however, this situation has changed considerably. While most social psychologists continue to reject the view that human aggression stems largely from innate factors, many now accept the possibility that genetic factors play *some* role in human aggression. For instance, consider the following reasoning, based on an evolutionary perspective (please see our discussion of this theory in Chapter 1). In the past (and even at present to some extent), males seeking desirable mates found it necessary to compete with other males. One way of eliminating such competition, of course, is through successful aggression, which drives such rivals away or may even eliminate them entirely by proving fatal. Because males who were adept at such behavior may have been more successful in securing mates and in transmitting their genes to offspring, this may have led to the development of a genetically influenced tendency for males to aggress against other males. In contrast, males would not be expected to acquire a similar tendency to aggress against females, because females may view males who engage in such behavior as too dangerous to themselves and potential future children, and so may reject these males as potential mates. As a result, males may have weaker tendencies to aggress against females than against other males. In contrast, females might aggress equally against males and females, or even more frequently against males than other females. In fact, the results of several recent studies confirm such predictions (e.g., Hilton, Harris, & Rice, 2000). Male teenagers are more likely to engage in aggression against other males than against females, while, for females, corresponding differences do not occur. Findings such as these suggest that biological or genetic factors may indeed play some role in human aggression, although in a much more complex manner than Freud, Lorenz, and other early theorists suggested. We will return to this possibility at later points in this chapter, but we wanted to note early on that where the role of biological factors in human aggression is concerned, the pendulum of scientific opinion has shifted considerably in recent years.

Drive Theories: The Motive to Harm Others

When social psychologists rejected the instinct views of aggression proposed by Freud and Lorenz, they countered with an alternative of their own: the view that aggression stems mainly from an externally elicited *drive* to harm oth-

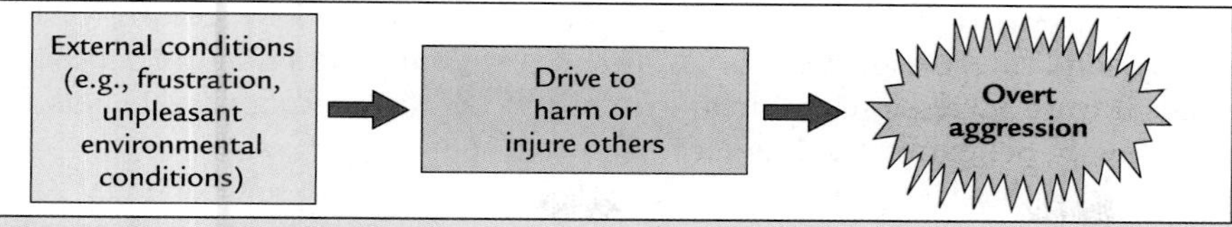

FIGURE 11.2

Drive Theories of Aggression: Motivation to Harm Others.

Drive theories of aggression suggest that aggressive behavior is pushed from within by drives to harm or injure others. These drives, in turn, stem from external events such as frustration. Such theories are no longer accepted as valid by most social psychologists, but one such view—the famous *frustration–aggression hypothesis*—continues to influence modern research.

ers. This approach is reflected in several different **drive theories** of aggression (e.g., Berkowitz, 1989; Feshbach, 1984). These theories propose that external conditions—especially *frustration*—arouse a strong motive to harm others. This aggressive drive, in turn, leads to overt acts of aggression (see Figure 11.2)

By far the most famous of these theories is the well-known *frustration–aggression hypothesis* (Dollard et al., 1939). According to this view, frustration leads to the arousal of a drive whose primary goal is that of harming some person or object—primarily the perceived cause of frustration (Berkowitz, 1989). As we'll see in a later discussion, the central role assigned to frustration by the frustration–aggression hypothesis has turned out to be largely false: frustration is only of many different causes of aggression, and a fairly weak one at that. Moreover, aggression stems from many causes others than frustration. However, while social psychologists have largely rejected this theory as false, it still enjoys widespread acceptance outside our field. Further, as we'll see in a later section, some aspects of the frustration–aggression theory have received support in recent research (e.g., the suggestion that if aggression toward a source of anger may be displaced to other, innocent targets; Marcus-Newhall et al., 2000). In this way, drive theories have had a lasting impact on the study of human aggression.

Modern Theories of Aggression: Taking Account of Learning, Cognitions, Mood, and Arousal

Unlike earlier views, modern theories of aggression (e.g., Anderson, 1997; Berkowitz, 1993; Zillmann, 1994) do not focus on a single factor as the primary cause of aggression. Rather, they draw on advances in many fields of psychology in order to gain added insight into the factors that play a role in the occurrence of such behavior. While no single theory includes all the factors that social psychologists now view as important, one approach—the **general affective aggression model**—proposed by Anderson (Anderson et al., 1996; Anderson, 1997) provides a good illustration of the breadth and sophistication of these new perspectives.

According to this theory (known as the *GAAM* for short), aggression is triggered by a wide range of *input variables*—aspects of the current situation or tendencies individuals bring with them to a given situation. Variables falling into the first category include frustration, some kind of attack from another person (e.g., an insult), exposure to other persons behaving aggressively (*aggressive models*), the presence of cues associated with aggression (e.g., guns or other weapons), and virtually anything that causes individuals to experience discomfort—everything from uncomfortably

drive theories (of aggression): Theories suggesting that aggression stems from external conditions that arouse the motive to harm or injure others. The most famous of these is the frustration–aggression hypothesis.

general affective aggression model: A modern theory of aggression suggesting that aggression is triggered by a wide range of input variables; these influence arousal, affective stages, and cognitions.

high temperatures to a dentist's drill or even an extremely dull lecture. Variables in the second category (*individual differences*) include traits that predispose individuals toward aggression (e.g., high irritability), certain attitudes and beliefs about violence (e.g., believing that it is acceptable and appropriate), values about violence (e.g., the view that it is a "good" thing—perhaps that it shows an individual's worth or masculinity), and specific skills related to aggression (e.g., knowing how to fight, knowing how to use various weapons).

According to the GAAM, these situational and individual difference variables can then lead to overt aggression through their impact on three basic processes: *arousal*—they may increase physiological arousal or excitement; *affective states*—they can arouse hostile feelings and outward signs of these (e.g., angry facial expressions); and *cognitions*—they can induce individuals to think hostile thoughts or bring hostile memories to mind. Depending on individuals' interpretations (*appraisals*) of the current situation and restraining factors (e.g., the presence of police or the threatening nature of the intended target person), aggression either occurs or does not occur (see Figure 11.3 for an overview of this theory.)

Modern theories like the GAAM are, admittedly, much more complex than the early ones offered by Freud and Lorenz, or even the famous frustration–aggression hypothesis (Dollard et al., 1939). But they are also supported by a growing body of evidence (e.g., Lieberman & Greenberg, 1999) and are much more likely to provide an accurate and complete picture of the origins of human aggression—and that, of course, is what science is all about.

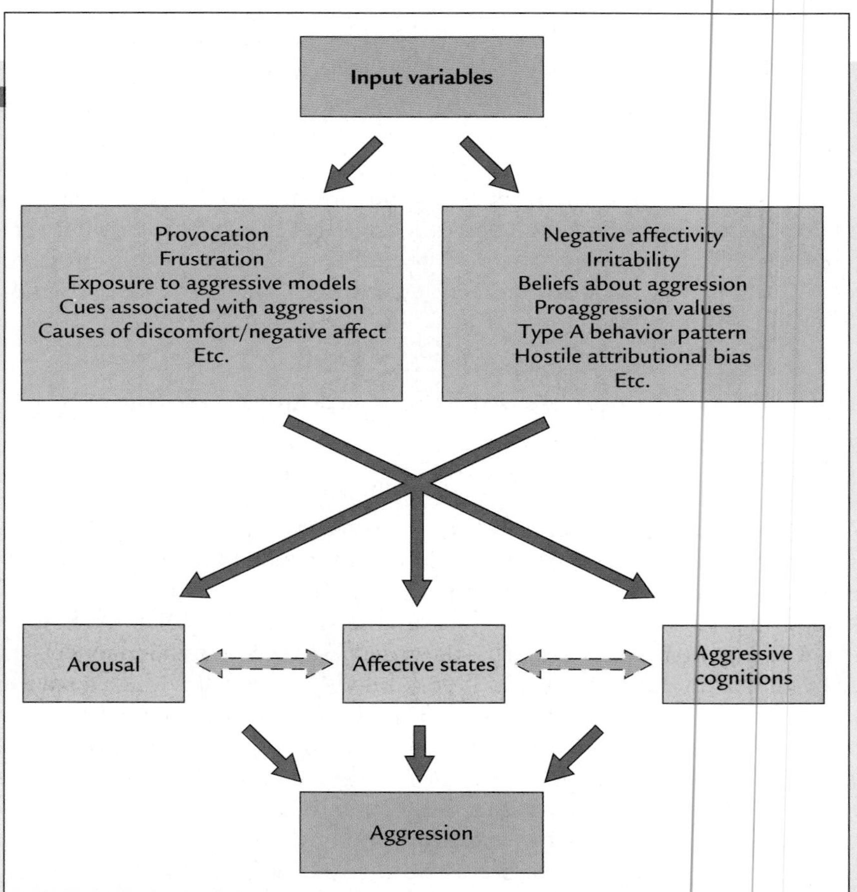

FIGURE 11.3
The GAAM: One Modern Theory of Human Aggression.
As shown here, the *general affective aggression model* suggests that human aggression stems from many different factors. A wide range of input variables influences cognitions, affect, and arousal, and these internal states plus other factors determine whether, and in what form, aggression occurs.
[SOURCE: BASED ON SUGGESTIONS BY ANDERSON, 1997.]

KEY POINTS

- *Aggression* is the intentional infliction of harm on others. While most social psychologists reject the view that human aggression is strongly determined by genetic factors, many now accept an evolutionary perspective that recognizes the potential role of such factors.
- *Drive theories* suggest that aggression stems from externally elicited drives to harm or injure others. The frustration–aggression hypothesis is the most famous example of such theories.
- Modern theories of aggression, such as the *general affective aggression model,* recognize the importance in aggression of learning, various eliciting input variables, cognitions, individual differences, and affective states.

Determinants of Human Aggression: Social, Personal, Situational

Think back to the last time you lost your temper. What made you blow your cool? Something another person said or did (Harris, 1993)? Something about yourself—are you easily annoyed, do you perceive that others often treat you unfairly? Or was it something about the situation—had you been drinking, was the weather hot and steamy? In fact, research findings indicate that all of these factors can play a role in human aggression. As we noted earlier, such behavior appears to stem from a wide range of *social, personal,* and *situational* variables. In this section, we'll examine the effects of variables in each of these major categories. Before turning to this task, however, we will first turn to a critical preliminary question: *How can human aggression—especially physical aggression—be studied in a systematic manner without the risk of harm to the participants in such research?* One important answer was provided by Arnold Buss (1961), in research that, in a sense, made much of the work described in this chapter possible. Buss's ingenious research, plus other techniques for measuring human aggression, are described below.

Techniques for Studying Human Aggression: Harm without Risk?

Creative minds, it seems, often move along parallel courses. Do you remember our description of Stanley Milgram's research on obedience in Chapter 9? If so, you may recall that procedures he devised involved ordering research participants to deliver stronger and stronger electric shocks to an innocent victim. The key question: Would participants obey? As you probably recall, they did—to an alarming extent. At the same time that Milgram was developing these procedures, Arnold Buss (see Figure 11.4) was working on a different but related question—the one we posed above. *How could researchers wishing to study human aggression do so in a way that would eliminate the risk of actual harm to participants?*

The solution Buss formulated seems, on the surface, to be quite similar to the technique developed by Milgram. However, I (RAB) knew both Stanley Milgram and Arnold Buss (I say "knew" because Milgram passed away several years ago), and they both confirmed what I suspected all along: they developed their similar research techniques simultaneously, but in a totally independent manner.

How do the procedures developed by Buss differ from those devised by Milgram? Let's take a closer look to see. In the approach designed by Buss, research participants

FIGURE 11.4
Arnold Buss: Inventor of the "Aggression Machine."
Arnold Buss devised a technique for studying physical aggression under safe laboratory conditions. He developed this technique at almost precisely the same time that Stanley Milgram was devising his own procedures for studying obedience to authority. I (RAB) first met Arnie when I was a visiting professor at the University of Texas, and have remained friends with him ever since. His book, *The Psychology of Aggression,* published in 1961, is a true classic in the field, and it stimulated many social psychologists—including myself—to conduct systematic research on human aggression. Arnie's son, David Buss, is a well-known social psychologist who has also made many important contributions to the rapidly growing field of evolutionary psychology.

are told that they are taking part, along with another person, in a study of the effects of punishment on learning. One of the two persons present serves as a *teacher* and the other as a *learner.* The teacher (always the real participant) presents various materials to the learner, who is actually an accomplice. This person attempts to learn these materials, and each time he or she makes a correct response, the teacher rewards the learner with a signal indicating "correct." Each time the learner makes an error, however, the teacher delivers an electric shock to this person, using an apparatus like that shown in Figure 11.5.

So far, this sounds very much like the procedures we described in Chapter 9. But here is where they differ: *The teachers in Buss's study were given free choice as to how strong the shocks should be.* In fact, they were told that they could choose any button on the apparatus and hold it down for as long as they wished. The higher the number on the button, the stronger, supposedly, was the shock to the learner; and as in Milgram's procedures, teachers (real participants) were given several sample shocks to convince them that the equipment actually worked.

During each session, the learner (accomplice) made many errors, thus providing participants with lots of opportunities to deliver painful shocks. Buss reasoned that because participants were free to choose any shock they wished, these procedures would, in fact, measure participants' desire to hurt the accomplice; after all, if they wished, they could stick to the mildest shock (from button 1), which was described as being so mild that the learner would probably not even feel it.

Social psychologists interested in studying human aggression quickly seized on Buss's apparatus, sometimes known as the **aggression machine,** as a valuable new

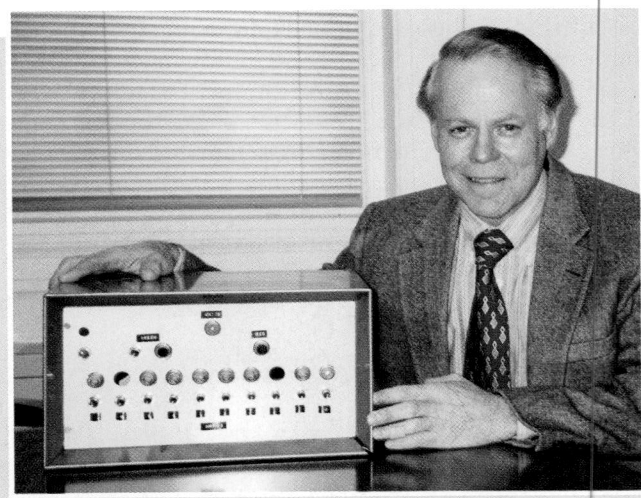

FIGURE 11.5

An Aggression Machine Similar to the One Developed by Arnold Buss. The apparatus shown here was widely used, in the past, to study physical aggression under safe laboratory conditions. Participants are told that they can deliver shocks of varying strength to another person by pushing buttons on this machine; the higher the number of the button, the stronger the shock. In recent years, the *aggression machine* has been employed in a decreasing number of studies, mainly because many researchers are concerned about the ethical issues raised by its use.

aggression machine: Apparatus used to measure physical aggression under safe laboratory conditions.

research tool. Before its appearance, studies of aggression were largely limited to asking individuals how they would respond in various imaginary situations or to measuring their *verbal* reactions to provocations or frustrations from others (usually, from accomplices). Here, it seemed, was a means of studying not what people guessed they would do in such situations but what they actually *would* do. Thus, the Buss technique and related procedures, such as one devised by Stuart Taylor (1967), were soon used in a large number of studies designed to examine many aspects of aggression (see, e.g., Baron & Richardson, 1994). But questions concerning the external validity of Buss's procedures were quickly raised. Did pushing buttons on an aggression machine really provide a valid measure of individuals' willingness to harm another person? Or were social psychologists simply fooling themselves by putting faith in such procedures?

This question has never been totally resolved, and because of this continuing controversy, several additional techniques for measuring aggression under safe laboratory conditions have been devised. For instance, in one, known as the *Point Subtraction and Aggression Paradigm* (the PSAP for short), participants play a game with another person in which each can decide to push buttons that (1) give the opponent money, (2) subtract money from the opponent's total, or (3) protect against the possibility that the opponent will remove the player's money. In reality, the opponent is fictitious, so the experimenter can make it seem as though this person is behaving provocatively (removing money from the participant's total on many occasions) or in a more friendly manner (e.g., adding money to the participant's total). These procedures eliminate the need for any mention of electric shock or other unpleasant physical outcomes, but seem to capture the essence of aggression: intentional infliction of harm on opponents (e.g., Cherek et al., 1997).

Several lines of evidence suggest that Buss's procedures, the PSAP, and related techniques do indeed provide valid and useful measures of human aggression. First, many studies found that people with a history of real aggressive behavior—for instance, violent criminals—chose stronger shocks or subtracted money from their opponent in the PSAP more often than did persons without such a history of aggression (e.g., Cherek et al., 1996; Gully & Dengerink, 1983; Wolfe & Baron, 1971). For instance, in one recent study, Cherek and his colleagues (2000) had female parolees who had been convicted of either aggressive crimes (e.g., assaults or aggravated robbery) or nonaggressive crimes (drug offenses, forgery, theft) participate in the PSAP procedure. Results were clear: Following provocations by the fictitious opponent, parolees who had been convicted of violent crimes were much more likely to behave aggressively, removing money from their opponents' total.

Additional evidence for the validity of laboratory measures of aggression is provided by the findings, in many studies, that variables found to influence aggression in real-life settings also influence aggression in laboratory studies using the procedures devised by Buss and others (e.g., Taylor, 1967). For instance, as reported by Anderson and Bushman (1997), aggression in laboratory studies is strongly increased by such factors as direct provocation, exposure to media violence, high temperatures, and the consumption of alcohol—variables that have also been found to influence aggression outside the laboratory.

On the basis of such evidence, many researchers have concluded that the procedures developed by Buss and many other social psychologists do indeed provide at least a rough index of the central concept we wish to measure in research on aggression: people's willingness to inflict harm—physical or otherwise—on another human being. However, even the strongest supporters of these methods admit that they are far from perfect, so the most reasonable conclusion may be something like this: By all means, use these techniques if they seem appropriate, but always do so with great caution, never take their external validity for granted, and combine them with observations of aggression in real-life settings whenever possible.

Social Determinants of Aggression: Frustration, Provocation, Displaced Aggression, Media Violence, and Heightened Arousal

Now, let's return to the major task we started above: describing some of the key social, personal, and situational causes of aggression.

■ FRUSTRATION: WHY NOT GETTING WHAT YOU WANT (OR WHAT YOU EXPECT) CAN SOMETIMES LEAD TO AGGRESSION. Suppose that you asked twenty people you know to name the single most important cause of aggression. What would they say? The chances are good that most would reply *frustration.* And if you asked them to define frustration, many would say, "The way I feel when something—or someone—prevents me from getting what I want or expect to get in some situation." This widespread belief in the importance of frustration as a cause of aggression stems, at least in part, from the famous **frustration–aggression hypothesis** mentioned in our discussion of drive theories of aggression (Dollard et al., 1939). In it is original form, this hypothesis made two sweeping assertions: (1) Frustration *always* leads to some form of aggression, and (2) aggression *always* stems from frustration. In short, the theory held that frustrated persons always engage in some type of aggression and that all acts of aggression, in turn, result from frustration. Bold statements like these are appealing, but this doesn't imply that they are necessarily accurate. In fact, existing evidence suggests that both portions of the frustration–aggression hypothesis assign far too much importance to frustration as a determinant of human aggression. Research findings indicate that, when frustrated, individuals do *not* always respond with aggression. On the contrary, they show many different reactions, ranging from sadness, despair, and depression on the one hand, to a direct attempt to overcome the source of their frustration on the other. Aggression is definitely *not* an automatic response to frustration.

frustration–aggression hypothesis: The suggestion that frustration is a very powerful determinant of aggression.

Second, it is equally clear that not all aggression stems from frustration. People aggress for many different reasons and in response to many different factors. For example, professional boxers hit their opponents because they wish to win valued prizes—not because of frustration (see Figure 11.6). Similarly, during wars, air force

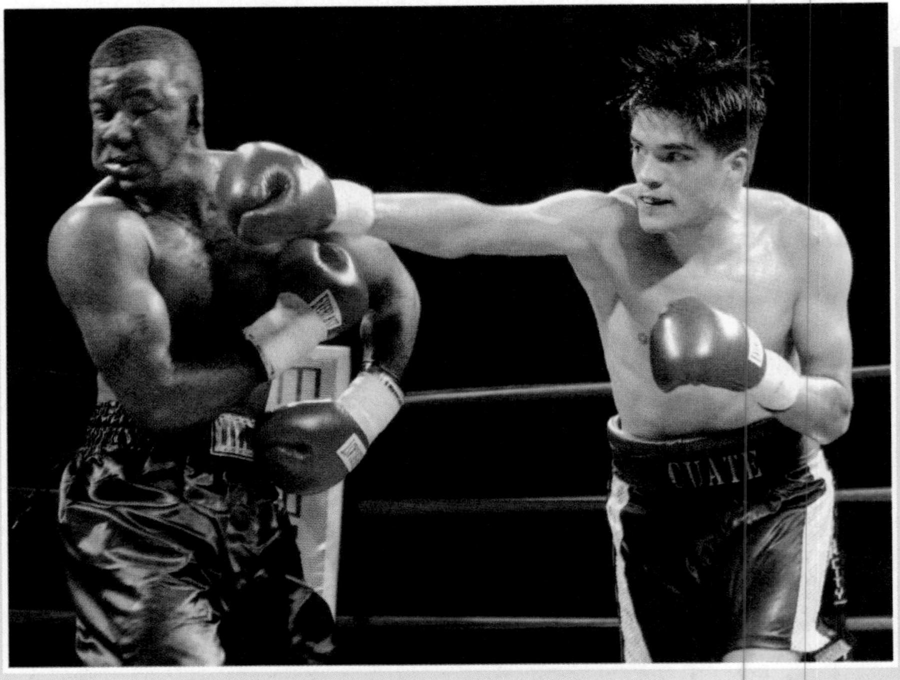

FIGURE 11.6
An Illustration of the Fact That Aggression Does Not Always Stem from Frustration. Professional boxers and wrestlers attempt to inflict harm on their opponents, primarily in order to gain various prizes or win large amounts of money—not because they are frustrated by these persons. ■

pilots report that flying their planes is a source of pleasure, and they bomb enemy targets while feeling elated or excited—not frustrated. In these and many other cases, aggression stems from factors other than frustration. We'll consider many of these other causes of aggression below.

In view of these facts, few social psychologists now accept the idea that frustration is the only, or even the most important, cause of aggression. Instead, most believe that it is simply one of many factors that can potentially lead to aggression. Along these lines, Berkowitz (1989, 1993) has proposed a revised version of the frustration–aggression hypothesis that seems consistent with a large amount of evidence about the effects of frustration. According to this view, frustration is an unpleasant experience, and it may lead to aggression largely because of this fact. In other words, frustration sometimes produces aggression because of a basic link between negative affect (unpleasant feelings) and aggressive behavior—a relationship that has been confirmed in many studies (e.g., da Gloria et al., 1994).

We should add that frustration *can* serve as a powerful determinant of aggression under certain conditions—especially when it is viewed as illegitimate or unjustified (e.g., Folger & Baron, 1996). For instance, if an individual believes that she deserves a large raise and then receives a much smaller one with no explanation for why this is so, she may conclude that she has been treated very unfairly—that her legitimate needs have been thwarted. The result: She may have hostile thoughts, experience intense anger, and seek revenge against the perceived source of such frustration—her boss or company. As we'll see in a later section, such reactions may play a key role in *workplace aggression* and in the aggressive reactions of some employees who lose their jobs through downsizing (e.g., Catalano, Novaco, & McConnell, 1997; Greenberg & Alge, 1997).

■ DIRECT PROVOCATION: WHEN AGGRESSION BREEDS AGGRESSION. Look at the cartoon in Figure 11.7 on page 444. Can you understand why the two pirates are reluctant to tell the captain that they don't like the ship's flag? I'm sure you can, because it is clear that, often, aggression is the result of physical or verbal **provocation** from others. When we are on the receiving end of some form of aggression from others—criticism we consider unfair, sarcastic remarks, or physical assaults—we rarely turn the other cheek. Instead, we tend to reciprocate, returning as much aggression as we have received—or perhaps even slightly more, especially if we are certain that the other person *meant* to harm us (Chermack, Berman, & Taylor, 1997; Ohbuchi & Kambara, 1985).

■ DISPLACED AGGRESSION: THE EFFECTS OF TRIVIAL TRIGGERING PROVOCATIONS. Have you ever had the following kind of experience? You are strongly provoked by someone toward whom you are very reluctant to retaliate—for instance a professor, a boss, or a state trooper—and you don't aggress: you somehow manage to hold your temper in check. Then, at a later time, someone else says or does something irritating that, under normal conditions, you would ignore or shrug off. Instead, you lash out at this person, just as if he or she had strongly provoked you. Experiences like this refer to what the authors of the famous frustration–aggression hypothesis termed **displaced aggression**—aggression against someone other than the source of strong, initial provocation (Dollard et al., 1939). The existence of such displaced aggression suggests that the impact of a provocation of a given magnitude is not always the same; rather, this depends on what else has happened to us recently. If we are having a pleasant day, a mild provocation may evoke weak aggression or even no aggression at all. But if we are having a bad day, in which one or more other persons have previously annoyed us, we may explode and aggress strongly—much more strongly than the mild provocation seems to deserve. Social psychologists refer to such reactions as instances of *triggered displaced aggression:* a mild triggering event by one person results in that individual becoming the target of strong displaced aggression—intense aggression that comes as a real surprise to the person in question (Marcus-Newhall et al., 2000).

provocation: Actions by others that tend to trigger aggression in the recipient, often because they are perceived as stemming from malicious intent.

displaced aggression: Aggression against someone other than the source of strong provocation; displaced aggression occurs because the persons who perform it are unwilling or unable to aggress against the initial source of provocation.

"*You* tell him that you find the flag offensive."

FIGURE 11.7
Direct Provocation: A Powerful Elicitor of Aggression.
The characters in this cartoon are well aware of the fact that verbal *provocations* (in this case, in the form of criticism) often evoke an angry, aggressive response from others.
[SOURCE: © THE NEW YORKER COLLECTION 2000 FRANK COTHAM FROM CARTOONBANK.COM. ALL RIGHTS RESERVED.]

Research by Pederson, Gonzales, and Miller (2000) provides clear insight into the operation of this process. In their research, participants worked on a series of anagrams (word puzzles) under one of two conditions. In the first (no provocation), the anagrams were fairly easy, participants worked in the presence of a soothing sound (falling rain), and they were treated in a neutral manner by the experimenter. In the second (provocation), the anagrams were difficult, participants worked in the presence of loud, distracting music, and they were treated in a rude manner by the experimenter. Following these events, they received an evaluation of their work from another participant (actually an assistant of the researchers). This evaluation was either slightly negative, thus serving as a triggering event for displaced aggression, or neutral in nature. Finally, participants evaluated the assistant on several dimensions; these ratings provided a means for them to aggress or not aggress against this person.

As shown in Figure 11.8, results were clear: In the no provocation condition, the triggering event (mild negative ratings from the assistant) produced little or no aggression toward this person. In the provocation condition, in contrast, participants reacted strongly to the mild triggering event: they showed evidence of displaced aggression against this person. Another interesting effect was the occurrence of a *contrast effect:* participants rated the accomplice who evaluated them in a neutral manner more favorably when they had previously been provoked by the experimenter than when they had not been provoked. In other words, the accomplice seemed nicer in comparison with the rude researcher.

Why does triggered displaced aggression occur? One possibility is that the earlier provocations cause individuals to *ruminate*—to think about the wrongs they

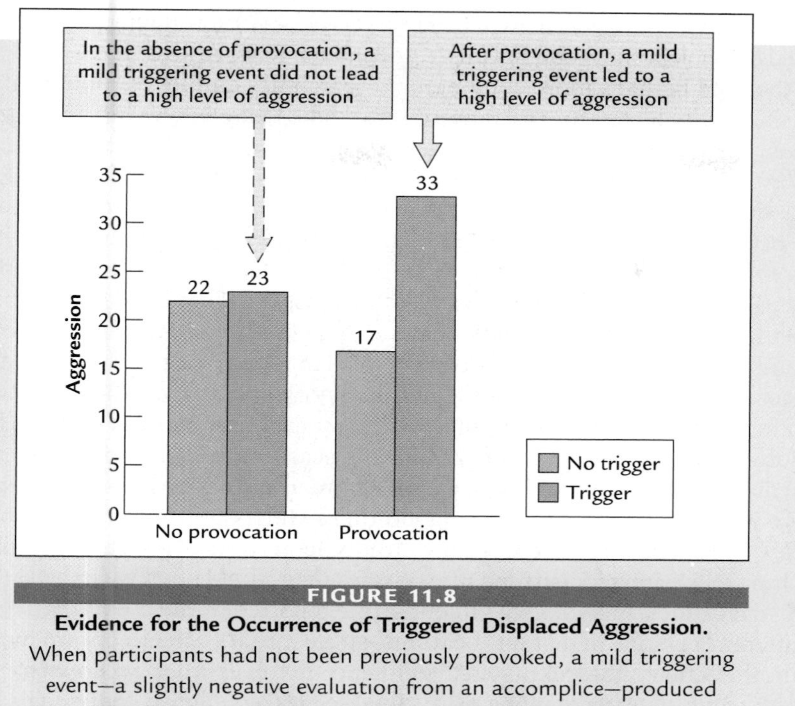

FIGURE 11.8

Evidence for the Occurrence of Triggered Displaced Aggression. When participants had not been previously provoked, a mild triggering event—a slightly negative evaluation from an accomplice—produced little effect on their behavior toward this person. When they had previously been strongly provoked but given no opportunity to retaliate for this treatment, however, a mild triggering event led to much stronger aggression against the accomplice, who, of course, was not the person who had previously annoyed them. [SOURCE: BASED ON DATA FROM PEDERSON ET AL., 2000.]

have suffered at the hands of other persons. This, in turn, raises their sensitivity to even minor provocations and causes them to lash out at persons who annoy them even in trivial ways. Whatever the precise mechanisms involved, however, triggered displaced aggression can have serious consequences, causing individuals who are angered in one context and by other persons to aggress strongly, perhaps dangerously, against persons who have done little or nothing to deserve such treatment.

■ EXPOSURE TO MEDIA VIOLENCE: THE EFFECTS OF WITNESSING AGGRESSION. List several films you have seen in recent months. Now, answer the following question: How much aggression or violence did each of these contain? How often did characters in these movies hit, shoot at, or otherwise attempt to harm others? Unless you have chosen very carefully, you probably recognize that many of the films you have seen contain a great deal of violence—much more than you are ever likely to see in real life (Reiss & Roth, 1993; Waters et al., 1993).

This fact raises an important question that social psychologists have studied for decades: Does exposure to **media violence** increase aggression among children or adults? Literally hundreds of studies have been performed to test this possibility, and the results seem clear: *Exposure to media violence may indeed be one factor contributing to high levels of violence in countries where such materials are viewed by large numbers of persons* (e.g., Anderson, 1997; Berkowitz, 1993; Paik & Comstock, 1994; Wood, Wong, & Cachere, 1991). Many kinds of evidence lend support to this conclusion. For example, in *short-term laboratory experiments,* children or adults have viewed either violent films and television programs or nonviolent ones; then, their tendency to aggress against others has been measured. In general, the results

media violence: Depictions of violent actions in the mass media.

of such experiments have revealed higher levels of aggression among participants who viewed the violent films or programs (e.g., Bandura, Ross, & Ross, 1963; Geen, 1991b).

Other and perhaps more convincing research has employed *longitudinal* procedures, in which the same participants are studied for many years (e.g., Huesmann & Eron, 1984, 1986). Results of such research, too, are clear: The more violent films or television programs participants watched as children, the higher their levels of aggression as teenagers or adults—for instance, the higher the likelihood that they have been arrested for violent crimes. Such findings have been replicated in many different countries—Australia, Finland, Israel, Poland, and South Africa (Botha, 1990). Thus, these findings appear to hold across different cultures.

While these longitudinal studies have been carefully conducted, it's important to remember that they are still only correlational in nature. As we noted in Chapter 1, the fact that two variables are correlated does *not* imply that one necessarily causes the other. However, when the results of these studies are combined with the findings of short-term laboratory experiments, a strong case for the suggestion that exposure to media violence is one potential cause of human aggression does seem to emerge.

But why, you may be wondering, do these effects occur? A number of possibilities exist. First, individuals may simply learn new ways of aggressing from watching television program and films—ways they would not have imagined before. "Copycat crimes," in which a violent crime reported in the media is then copied by different persons in distant locations, suggest that such effects are real.

Another effect of watching media violence involves what is known as *densensitization effects.* After viewing many vivid scenes of violence, individuals become hardened to the pain and suffering of other persons: they experience less emotional reaction to such cues than was originally true (e.g., Baron, 1974a), and this may lessen their own restraints against engaging in aggression.

Research indicates that a third effect may occur as well: watching scenes of violence may serve to "prime" hostile thoughts, so that these come to mind more readily—they become more accessible to conscious thought. This, in turn, can increase the likelihood that a person will engage in overt aggression (Anderson, 1997). Because repeated exposure to media violence may strengthen such priming effects over time, the impact of watching violence may be cumulative—and even more important than was previously assumed.

Because exposure to media violence may have harmful effects on society, why, you may be wondering, is there so much of it on television and in films? One answer is that the advertisers who pay for these programs believe that "violence sells"—it is one way to increase audience size. While this may be true, findings reported by Bushman (1998) suggest that media violence may actually backfire from the point of view of increasing the sales of products advertised on such shows. He found that audiences who watch violent programs are significantly *less* likely to remember the content of commercials shown during these programs than are audiences who watch nonviolent programs. Apparently, violent images on the television screen trigger memories of other violent scenes, and such thoughts distract viewers from paying attention to commercials. These findings suggest that sponsoring violent television programs is not just questionable from a moral point of view; it may also make little economic sense for sponsors!

■ HEIGHTENED AROUSAL: EMOTION, COGNITION, AND AGGRESSION. Suppose that you are driving to the airport to meet a friend. On the way there, another driver cuts you off and you almost have an accident. Your heart pounds wildly and your blood pressure shoots through the roof; but, fortunately, no accident occurs. Now you arrive at the airport. You park and rush inside. When you get to the security check, an elderly man in front of you sets off the buzzer. He becomes confused and can't seem to understand that the security guard wants him to empty his pockets. You are irritated by this delay. In fact, you begin to lose your temper and mutter, "What's wrong with him? Can't he get it?"

Now for the key question: Do you think that your recent near miss in traffic may have played any role in your sudden surge of anger? Could the emotional arousal from that incident have somehow transferred to the scene inside the airport? Growing evidence suggests that it could (Zillmann, 1988, 1994). Under some conditions, heightened arousal—whatever its source—can enhance aggression in response to provocation, frustration, or other factors. In fact, in various experiments, arousal stemming from such varied sources as participation in competitive games (Christy, Gelfand, & Hartmann, 1971), vigorous exercise (Zillmann, 1979), and even some types of music (Rogers & Ketcher, 1979) has been found to increase subsequent aggression. Why is this the case? A compelling explanation is offered by **excitation transfer theory** (Zillmann, 1983, 1988).

This theory suggests that because physiological arousal tends to dissipate slowly over time, a portion of such arousal may persist as a person moves from one situation to another. In the example above, some portion of the arousal you experienced because of the near miss in traffic may still be present as you approach the security gate in the airport. Now, when you encounter minor annoyance, that arousal intensifies your emotional reactions to the annoyance. The result: You become enraged rather than just mildly irritated. Excitation transfer theory further suggests that such effects are most likely to occur when the persons involved are relatively unaware of the presence of residual arousal—a common occurrence, as small elevations in arousal are difficult to notice (Zillmann, 1994). Excitation transfer theory also suggests that such effects are likely to occur when the persons involved recognize their residual arousal but attribute it to events occurring in the present situation (Taylor et al., 1991). In the airport incident, for instance, your anger would be intensified if you recognized your feelings of arousal but attributed them to the elderly man's actions (see Figure 11.9.)

excitation transfer theory: A theory suggesting that arousal produced in one situation can persist and intensify emotional reactions occurring in later situations.

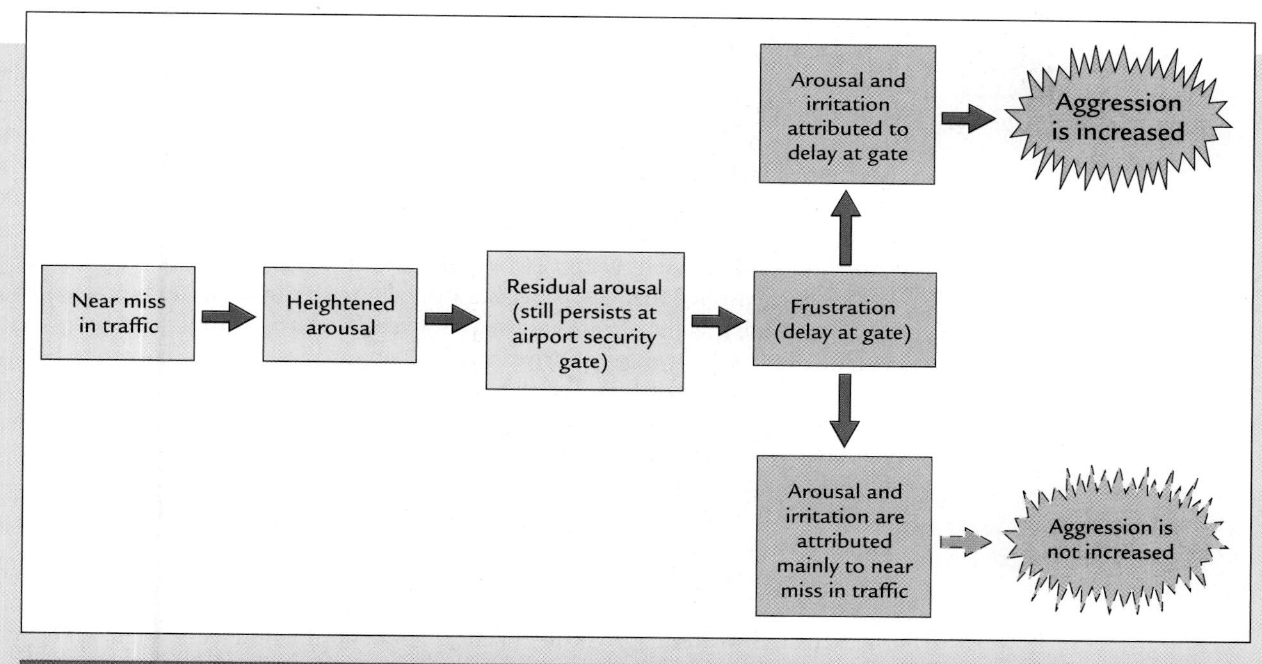

FIGURE 11.9

Excitation Transfer Theory.

Excitation transfer theory suggests that arousal occurring in one situation can persist and intensify emotional reactions in later, unrelated situations. Thus, the arousal produced by a near miss in traffic can intensify feelings of annoyance stemming from delays at an airport security gate.

[SOURCE: BASED ON SUGGESTIONS BY ZILLMANN, 1988, 1994.]

■ SEXUAL AROUSAL AND AGGRESSION: EMOTIONAL AND COGNITIVE LINKS. Are sexual arousal and aggression somehow linked? Freud felt that they were, and suggested that the desire to hurt or be hurt by one's lover is often a normal part of sexual relations. Whether this is true or not, there is indeed some evidence for important links between sexual arousal—or even, as we will soon see, merely being exposed to sex-related words—and subsequent aggression. Let's take a closer look at this intriguing research.

First, there is some evidence for the view that sexual arousal can actually reduce overt aggression. In several early studies (e.g., Baron, 1974b, 1979; Ramirez, Bryant, & Zillmann, 1983), the following procedures were followed: Participants were first annoyed by a stranger. Then they examined stimuli that were either mildly sexually arousing (e.g., pictures of attractive nudes) or neutral (e.g., pictures of scenery, abstract art). Finally, they had an opportunity to retaliate against their provoker. Results indicated that people exposed to mildly arousing sexual materials showed lower levels of aggression than those exposed to the neutral stimuli.

The word *mild* should be emphasized, however. In subsequent studies in which participants were exposed to more arousing sexual materials, higher levels of arousal were found to *increase* rather than reduce aggression (e.g., Jaffe et al., 1974; Zillmann, 1984). Together, these findings suggest that the relationship between sexual arousal and aggression is *curvilinear* in nature. Mild sexual arousal reduces aggression to a level below that shown in the absence of such arousal, while higher levels of arousal actually increase it above this level. Why? Perhaps because mild erotic materials generate mainly positive feelings that inhibit aggression, while more explicit sexual stimuli generate mainly negative feelings that can, through excitation transfer, increase aggression (Zillmann, 1984). The findings of several studies are consistent with this reasoning (e.g., Ramirez, Bryant, & Zillmann, 1983), so it appears to provide a useful explanation for the curvilinear relationship between sexual arousal and aggression.

In addition to these affective or emotional links between sexual arousal and aggression, however, more recent research suggests that there may be cognitive links, too. Do you remember the principle of *priming,* which we discussed in Chapter 3? This suggests that specific stimuli may activate schemas or other knowledge structures in our minds, and so influence our thinking and judgments. For instance, after being exposed to stimuli that prime the trait "dishonest" (e.g., words such as "thief," "crime," and "prison"), we may interpret an ambiguous description of another person as suggesting that he or she is dishonest because we have been primed to think in such terms. Two social psychologists, Mussweiler and Forster (2000), have reasoned that such effects may occur with respect to the sex–aggression link. Specifically, when we are exposed to sexually related stimuli (e.g., words such as "skin" or "bed"), we may primed to think about aggression—or even to behave aggressively. More importantly, these researchers also suggest that while sex and aggression may be linked in the minds of both men and women, the influence of such links may differ for the two genders. Specifically, because men are more often the aggressor in sexual situations, priming with sexual stimuli may prime not just aggressive thoughts, but also aggressive actions. In contrast, this would not be expected to occur for women.

To test this reasoning, Mussweiler and Forster (2000) conducted a study in which both women and men were exposed either to neutral words (e.g., "clock," "roof") or sex-related words (e.g., "skin," "bed"). Then, both women and men were given a chance to throw darts either at a photo of a human face or at physical objects (e.g., a vase). The authors predicted that when exposed to sex-related words, men would throw more darts at the human face, while this would not be true for women. This is precisely what happened. The results of a follow-up study that used somewhat different procedures indicated that these effects occurred only if the target was a female; males primed with sex-related words aggressed more than males primed with neutral words, but only against a woman. Women showed no differences of this kind.

These results suggest that the link between sex and aggression may be more complex than was initially believed. Not only does sexual arousal influence aggression through the generation of positive and negative affect (i.e., moods or feelings); in addition, exposure to sex-related stimuli may activate schemas or other mental frameworks that can, in turn, influence overt behavior toward specific targets. If these findings remind you of the general affective model of aggression (GAMA) we described early in this chapter, you are right on track: as this model suggests, in order to fully understand human aggression, we must take careful account of a wide range of factors—social, affective, cognitive, and personal. We have already discussed variables relating to the first three categories, so we turn next to *personal* causes of aggression—traits and characteristics of individuals that can influence when, where, and toward whom they choose to aggress.

KEY POINTS

- In order to study aggression, social psychologists often use procedures in which individuals are led to believe that they can harm others in various ways—delivery of painful electric shocks or reducing their winnings in a competitive game.
- Contrary to the famous *frustration–aggression hypothesis,* all aggression does not stem from frustration, and frustration does not always lead to aggression. Frustration is a strong elicitor of aggression only under certain limited conditions.
- In contrast, *provocation* from others is a powerful elicitor of aggression. We rarely turn the other cheek; rather, we match—or slightly exceed—the level of aggression we receive from others.
- One exception to such matching occurs in triggered displaced aggression. In such situations, persons who were strongly provoked previously but did not aggress respond very strongly to mild provocations, thus displacing aggression to largely innocent targets.
- Exposure to *media violence* has been found to increase aggression among viewers. This is due to several factors, such as the priming of aggressive thoughts and a weakening of restraints against aggression.
- Heightened arousal can increase aggression if it persists beyond the situation in which it was induced and is falsely interpreted as anger.
- Mild levels of sexual arousal reduce aggression, while higher levels increase such behavior. Even exposure to sex-related words can increase aggression through the priming of schemas and other knowledge structures related to aggression.

Personal Causes of Aggression

Are some persons "primed" for aggression by their personal characteristics? Informal observation suggests that this is so (see Figure 11.10 on page 450). While some individuals rarely lose their tempers or engage in aggressive actions, others seem to be forever losing it, with potentially serious consequences. In this section, we will consider several traits or characteristics that seem to play an important role in aggression.

THE TYPE A BEHAVIOR PATTERN: WHY THE *A* IN TYPE A COULD STAND FOR *AGGRESSION*. Do you know anyone you could describe as (1) extremely competitive, (2) always in a hurry, and (3) especially irritable and aggressive? If so, this person shows the characteristics of what psychologists term the **Type A behavior pattern** (Glass, 1977; Strube, 1989). At the opposite end of the continuum are persons who

Type A behavior pattern: A pattern consisting primarily of high levels of competitiveness, time urgency, and hostility.

FIGURE 11.10

Personality and Aggression. Are some persons primed for aggression by their own personalities? Research findings agree with this cartoon in suggesting that this is so.

[SOURCE: © THE NEW YORKER COLLECTION 1999 GAHAN WILSON FROM CARTOONBANK.COM. ALL RIGHTS RESERVED.]

"What are you doing outside of coach?"

do not show these characteristics—individuals who are *not* highly competitive, who are *not* always fighting the clock, and who do *not* readily lose their temper; such persons are described as showing the **Type B behavior pattern.**

Given the characteristics mentioned above, it seems only reasonable to expect that Type A's would tend to be more aggressive than Type B's in many situations. In fact, the results of several experiments indicate that this is actually the case (Baron, Russell, & Arms, 1985; Carver & Glass, 1978; Berman, Gladue, & Taylor, 1993).

Additional findings indicate that Type A's are truly hostile people: they don't merely aggress against others because this is a useful means for reaching other goals, such as winning athletic contests or furthering their own careers. Rather, they are more likely than Type B's to engage in what is known as **hostile aggression**—aggression in which the prime objective is inflicting some kind of harm on the victim (Strube et al., 1984). In view of this fact, it is not surprising to learn that Type A's are more likely than Type B's to engage in such actions as child abuse or spouse abuse (Strube et al., 1984). In contrast, Type A's are *not* more likely than Type B's to engage in **instrumental aggression**—aggression performed primarily to attain other goals aside from harming the victim, goals such as control of valued resources or praise from others for behaving in a "tough" manner.

Type B behavior pattern: A pattern consisting of the absence of characteristics associated with the Type A behavior pattern.

hostile aggression: Aggression in which the prime objective is inflicting some kind of harm on the victim.

instrumental aggression: Aggression in which the primary goal is not harm to the victim but attainment of some other goal, such as access to valued resources.

PERCEIVING EVIL INTENT IN OTHERS: HOSTILE ATTRIBUTIONAL BIAS. Suppose that while you are in a supermarket, another shopper hits you with her cart and then shouts angrily at you to get out of her way. In this case, it would be fairly clear that her actions were done on purpose: they stemmed from *hostile intentions.* But what if after hitting you she had said, "Oh, I'm sorry. Please excuse me." If she appeared to be genuinely sorry, the chances are good that you would not become angry and would not seek to retaliate against her. This is because our *attributions* concerning the causes of others' behavior play an important role in aggression, just as they do in many other forms of social behavior (see our discussion of this topic in Chapter 2). But what if she muttered, "Oh, I'm sorry," but at the same time had a malicious look on her face? In both cases, your actions would depend strongly on your attributions concerning her behavior. If you attributed her hitting you with her cart to hostile intentions, you would still become angry; if you decided to believe her, you might simply walk away instead.

The fact that attributions play an important role in our reactions to others' behavior—and especially to apparent provocations—is the starting point for another important personal characteristic that influences aggression—the **hostile attributional bias** (e.g., Dodge et al., 1986). This term refers to the tendency to perceive hostile intentions or motives in others' actions when these actions are ambiguous. In other words, persons high in hostile attributional bias rarely give others the benefit of the doubt: they simply *assume* that any provocative actions by others are intentional, and they react accordingly. The results of many studies offer support for the potential impact of this factor (e.g., Dodge & Coie, 1987), so it seems to be another important personal (individual difference) factor in the occurrence of aggression.

■ NARCISSISM, EGO-THREAT, AND AGGRESSION: ON THE DANGERS OF WANTING TO BE SUPERIOR. Do you know the story of Narcissus? He was a character in Greek mythology who fell in love with his own reflection in the water and drowned trying to reach it. His name has now become a synonym for excessive self-love—for holding an over-inflated view of one's own virtues or accomplishments. Research findings indicate that this trait may be linked to aggression in important ways. Specifically, studies by Bushman and Baumeister (1998) suggest that persons high in *narcissism* (ones who agree with items such as "If I ruled the world it would be a much better place" and "I am more capable than other people") react with exceptionally high levels of aggression to slights from others—feedback that threatens their inflated self-image. Why? Perhaps because such persons have nagging doubts about the accuracy of their inflated egos and so react with intense anger toward anyone who threatens to undermine them.

These findings have important implications because, at the present time, many schools in the United States focus on building high self-esteem within their students. Up to a point, this may indeed be beneficial. But if such esteem-building tactics are carried too far and produce children whose opinions of themselves are unrealistically high (i.e., narcissistic), the result may actually be an increased potential for violence. Clearly, this is a possibility worthy of further, careful study.

■ GENDER DIFFERENCES IN AGGRESSION: DO THEY EXIST? Are males more aggressive than females? Folklore suggests that they are, and research findings suggest that, in this case, informal observation is correct: when asked whether they have ever engaged in any of a wide range of aggressive actions, males report a higher incidence of many aggressive behaviors than do females (Harris, 1994, 1996). On close examination, however, the picture regarding gender differences in aggression becomes more complex. On the one hand, males are generally more likely than females both to perform aggressive actions and to serve as the target for such behavior (Bogard, 1990; Harris, 1992, 1994; Walker, Richardson, & Green, 2000). Further, this difference seems to persist throughout the life span, occurring even among people in their seventies and eighties (Walker, Richardson, & Green, 2000). On the other hand, however, the size of these differences appears to vary greatly across situations.

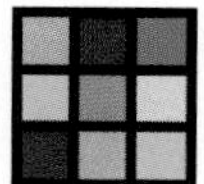

First, gender differences in aggression are much larger in the absence of provocation than in its presence. In other words, males are significantly more likely than females to aggress against others when these persons have *not* provoked them in any manner (Betancourt & Miller, 1996). In situations in which provocation *is* present, and especially when it is intense, females may be just as aggressive as males.

Second, the size—and even direction—of gender differences in aggression seems to vary greatly with the *type* of aggression in question. Research findings indicate

hostile attributional bias: The tendency to perceive hostile intentions or motives in others' actions when these actions are ambiguous.

that males are more likely than females to engage in various forms of *direct* aggression—actions that are aimed directly at the target and that clearly stem from the aggressor (e.g., physical assaults, pushing, shoving, throwing something at another person, shouting, making insulting remarks; Björkqvist, Österman, & Hjelt-Bäck, 1994). However, females are more likely than males to engage in various forms of *indirect* aggression—actions that allow the aggressor to conceal his or her identity from the victim and that, in some cases, make it difficult for the victim to know that they have been the target of intentional harm-doing. Such actions include spreading vicious rumors about the target person, gossiping behind this person's back, telling others not to associate with the intended victim, making up stories to get the victim in trouble, and so on. Research findings indicate that gender differences with respect to indirect aggression are present among children as young as eight years old and increase through age fifteen (Björkqvist, Lagerspetz, & Kaukiainen, 1992; Österman et al., 1998), and they seem to persist into adulthood as well (Björkqvist, Österman, & Hjelt-Bäck, 1994; Green, Richardson, & Lago, 1996). Further, these differences have been observed in several different countries—Finland, Sweden, Poland, Italy, and Australia (Österman et al., 1998; Owens, Shute, & Slee, 2000), so they appear to be quite general in scope.

Before concluding this discussion, we should make one final point: Men and women also differ considerably with respect to one other kind of aggression—*sexual coercion.* Such behavior involves words and deeds designed to overcome a partner's objections to engaging in sexual behavior, and they can range from verbal tactics such as false statements of love to threats of harm and actual physical force (see Figure 11.11). As we noted earlier, males are far more likely to engage in such behavior than are females (e.g., Mussweiler & Forster, 2000). Further, findings reported by Hogben and his colleagues (Hogben et al., 2001) indicate that this difference may stem, at least in part, from greater acceptance by males than females of the idea that aggression is a legitimate and acceptable form of behavior. Specifically, Hogben and associates (2001) found that the more strongly males endorsed such beliefs, the greater their tendency to engage in sexual coercion; in contrast, this was not the case for females.

FIGURE 11.11
Sexual Coercion: One Form of Aggression Related to Gender.
Large gender differences exist with respect to one form of aggression: sexual coercion. Males are much more likely to engage in such behavior than are females.

In sum, gender differences with respect to aggression do exist and can be substantial in some contexts. But overall, the nature of such differences is far more complex than common sense suggests.

KEY POINTS

- Persons showing the *Type A behavior pattern* are more irritable and aggressive than persons with the *Type B behavior pattern.*
- Individuals high in *hostile attributional bias* attribute others' actions to hostile intent. As a result, they are more aggressive than persons low in this characteristic.
- Persons high in narcissism hold an over-inflated view of their own worth. They react with exceptionally high levels of aggression to feedback from others that threatens their inflated egos.
- Males are more aggressive overall than are females, but this difference decreases in the context of strong provocation. Males are more likely to use direct forms of aggression, but females are more likely to use indirect forms of aggression. Males are much more likely than females to engage in sexual coercion.

Situational Determinants of Aggression: The Effects of High Temperatures and Alcohol Consumption

While aggression is often strongly influenced by social factors and personal characteristics, it is also affected by factors relating to the situation or context in which it occurs—including the extent to which aggression is viewed as acceptable within a given culture (e.g., Cohen et al., 1996). Here, we'll examine two of the many *situational factors* that can influence aggression: high temperatures and alcohol. Research on the first of these topics has continued for many years and provides a clear illustration of how social psychologists make progress in understanding complex topics, so we'll examine it in the **Social Psychology: Thirty Years of Progress** section on page 454.

ALCOHOL AND AGGRESSION: A POTENTIALLY DANGEROUS MIX. It is widely believed that some persons, at least, become more aggressive when they consume alcohol. This idea is supported by the fact that bars and nightclubs are frequently the scenes of violence. However, while alcohol is certainly consumed in these settings, other factors might be responsible for the fights—or worse—that often erupt: competition for desirable partners, crowding (which leads people to jostle one another), and even cigarette smoke, which irritates some people (Zillmann, Baron, & Tamborini, 1981). What does systematic research reveal about a possible link between alcohol and aggression? Interestingly, it tends to confirm the existence of an alcohol–aggression link. In several experiments, participants who consumed substantial doses of alcohol—enough to make them legally drunk—have been found to behave more aggressively, and to respond to provocations more strongly, than those who did not consume alcohol (e.g., Bushman & Cooper, 1990; Gustafson, 1990). (Needless to state, participants in such research are always warned in advance that they may be receiving alcoholic beverages, and only those who consent to such procedures actually take part.) An interesting study by Pihl, Lau, and Assad (1997) illustrates such effects very clearly.

These researchers had young male volunteers consume drinks containing either substantial doses of alcohol (1 ml per kilogram of body weight) or no alcohol. Then the volunteers competed with a fictitious opponent in a competitive reaction-time task in which they could set the level of shock to be received by their opponent on each trial if this person lost in the game (i.e., responded more slowly than they did on that trial).

SOCIAL PSYCHOLOGY: THIRTY YEARS OF PROGRESS

STUDYING HEAT AND AGGRESSION: FROM THE LABORATORY TO POLICE RECORDS OF ASSAULT

In the heat of anger. Boiling mad. Hot-tempered. Phrases like these suggest that there may well be a link between temperature and human aggression. In fact, many people report that they often feel especially irritable and short-tempered on hot and steamy days. Is there really a link between climate and human aggression? Social psychologists have been studying this question for three decades, and during this period, the methods they have used and the results they have obtained have become increasingly sophisticated. (The most current answer to the question, by the way, is *yes,* heat does increase aggression—*but only up to a point.* Beyond some level, aggression may actually decline as temperatures rise, because people become so uncomfortable and fatigued that they are actually less likely to engage in overt aggression.) But let's see how social psychologists have attempted to study this complex question.

Actually, I (RAB) conducted some of the original studies on this topic in the early 1970s (Baron, 1972a; Baron & Lawton, 1972). At that time, two factors led me to conduct studies on the "heat and aggression" question. First, I was a professor at the University of South Carolina. Being from the North, I had never experienced such unrelenting heat before, and I began to wonder whether it was affecting my behavior, making me irritable and short-tempered. Second, a series of frightening riots had occurred recently in cities throughout the United States. Most of these, I noticed, took place during the summer months. Did high temperatures play a role in such events, I wondered?

These speculations led me to conduct an initial laboratory study in which participants took part in a modified version of the teacher–learner procedures devised by Buss. Participants in this study (Baron, 1972a) were first provoked (by insults from an accomplice) or not provoked, and then provided with an opportunity to aggress against this person by means of the aggression machine. In addition, we varied the temperatures in the experimental rooms. In one condition, the air conditioning was on, so the rooms were comfortably cool (about 70 to 72 degrees Fahrenheit). In the other condition, we shut off the air conditioning and opened the windows; this raised the temperatures to the mid- to upper 90s—the typical outdoor temperatures from June through September in Columbia, South Carolina. Results were both clear and surprising: High temperature *reduced* aggression for both provoked and unprovoked persons.

This unexpected pattern of results led me to consider the possibility that perhaps heat increases aggression, but only up to a point. Beyond some level, people become so uncomfortable that they lack the energy for engaging in aggression or any other kind of vigorous activity. To test this hypothesis—known as the *negative-affect escape model*—Paul Bell and I conducted a series of studies in which we varied temperature over a wider range (Baron & Bell, 1975; Bell & Baron, 1976). The results: Aggression did increase as temperatures rose into the mid-80s Fahrenheit, but then dropped off at higher levels. So it appeared that heat does increase aggression, but only up to a point.

At this point, a number of other social psychologists became interested in this topic, and they quickly pointed to a serious question about my research: It was conducted in the laboratory under restricted and artificial conditions. Would a link between heat and aggression be found in the real world as well? To find out, other researchers adopted very different procedures in their studies (e.g., Anderson, 1989a; Anderson & Anderson, 1996; Bell, 1992). Specifically, they examined long-term records of temperatures and police records of various aggressive crimes to determine whether the frequency of such crimes increased with rising temperatures. For instance, consider a carefully conducted study by Anderson, Bushman, and Groom (1997).

These researchers collected average annual temperatures for fifty cities in the United States over a forty-five-year period (1950–1995). In addition, they obtained information on the rate of both violent crimes (aggravated assault, homicide) and property crimes (burglary, car theft), as well as another crime that has often been viewed as primarily aggressive in nature: rape. They then performed analyses to determine whether temperature were related to these crimes. Results indicated that hotter years did indeed produce higher rates of violent crimes, but that they did *not* produce increases in property crimes or rape. This was true even when the effect of many other variables that might also influence aggressive crimes (e.g., poverty, age distribution of the population) was eliminated. These findings, and those of related studies (e.g., Anderson, Anderson, & Deuser, 1996), suggest that heat is indeed linked to aggression. As noted by Anderson, Bushman, and Groom (1997), their results have very serious implications, because if global warming actually occurs in the years ahead, this may lead to increased violence—something our species can clearly do without.

Although sophisticated field studies such as those conducted by Anderson and his colleagues pointed to a significant link between high temperatures and aggression, they did not resolve one key question: Does this heat–aggression relationship have any limits? In other words, does aggression increase with heat indefinitely, or only up to some point, beyond which aggression actually declines as temperatures continue to rise? As you may recall, that is the pattern uncovered in initial laboratory studies on this topic.

Recent studies by Rotton and Cohn (Cohn & Rotton, 1997; Rotton & Cohn, 2000) have helped to resolve this issue. These researchers reasoned that if the negative affect escape model is accurate, the relationship between heat and aggression should be stronger in the evening hours, when temperatures are below their peak, than at midday. In other words, a finer grained analysis would reveal a curvilinear relationship between heat and aggression during the day, but a linear one at night. This would also be true because people are more likely to leave their homes on hot nights, and so are more likely to come into contact with dangerous persons who may assault them. To test these hypotheses, Rotton and Cohn examined records of physical assaults during a two-year period in two different cities in the United States—Dallas and Minneapolis. Temperature ranges contrast sharply in these cities, with Dallas having many more very hot days than Minneapolis, so having data from the two cities adds to the generality of the findings. Records of both assaults and temperatures were obtained for each three-hour period of the day. Results in both cities were similar: The relationship between heat and aggression was indeed linear at night but curvilinear during the day. In fact, as you can see in Figure 11.12, when assaults were related to temperature for each three-hour segment of the day, the relationship between heat and aggression was strongly curvilinear. In contrast, when data were combined for all hours of the day, this relationship appeared to be linear in nature.

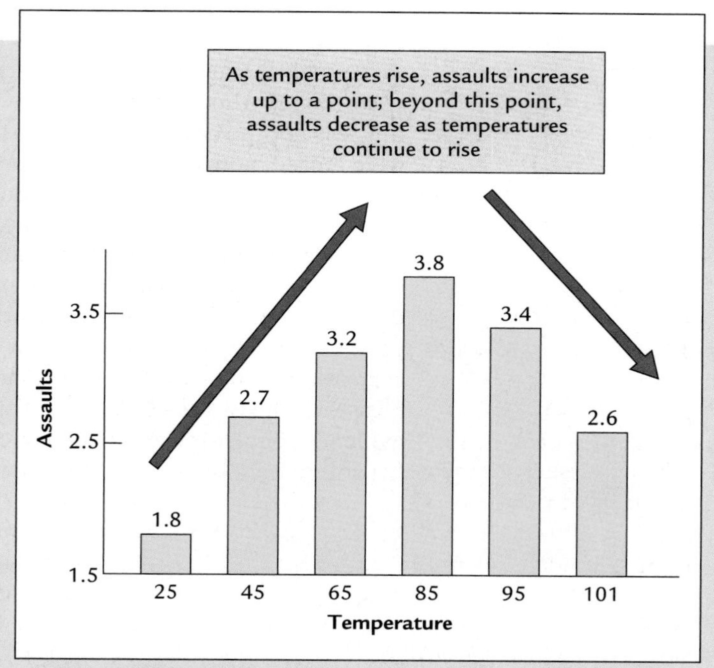

FIGURE 11.12

Heat and Aggression: Evidence That the Relationship between Them Is Curvilinear.

In two large U.S. cities, the incidence of violent assaults rose with increasing temperatures, but only up to a point; beyond this level, as temperatures continued to rise, the incidence of assaults actually dropped. These findings suggest that the relationship between heat and aggression may be curvilinear in nature.

[SOURCE: BASED ON DATA FROM ROTTON & COHN, 2000.]

(continued)

SOCIAL PSYCHOLOGY: THIRTY YEARS OF PROGRESS *(CONTINUED)*

In sum, research on the effects of heat on aggression (sometimes referred to as the "long, hot summer effect") has progressed from straightforward, but limited, laboratory research to sophisticated field studies focused on long-term records of both climate and acts of violence. The methods used in these more recent studies are far more sophisticated and complex than those I (RAB) used in my early laboratory studies, but I would be the first to state that they have brought us much closer to a full understanding of how one important aspect of the physical world influences our behavior. To my way of thinking, that is indeed real scientific progress.

Their opponent, in turn, could set the shocks participants would receive if *they* lost. During the reaction-time task, participants were exposed either to strong provocation—their opponent set increasing shocks for them to receive—or low provocation—the opponent set very low shocks.

Prior to the start of the study, participants had completed a questionnaire and an interview designed to determine whether they were low or high in the tendency to behave aggressively. It was predicted that in the presence of high provocation, those high in aggressive tendencies (high aggressors) would be more aggressive regardless of whether they consumed alcohol. As shown in Figure 11.13, however, this was *not* the case. While persons with a strong tendency to behave aggressively were indeed more aggressive than low aggressors when both groups were sober, this difference disappeared after the consumption of alcohol. High aggressors became slightly *less* aggressive when intoxicated, while low aggressors became significantly *more* aggressive. These findings, and those of many other studies (e.g., Gantner & Taylor, 1992), suggest that alcohol may indeed be one situational factor contributing to the occurrence of aggression, and that such effects may be especially strong for persons who do not normally engage in aggression (persons low in the tendency to aggress). (For an overview of the many factors that play a role in human aggression, please see the **Ideas to Take with You—And Use!** feature on page 468. And for more evidence concerning the impact of environmental factors on aggression, please see the following **Beyond the Headlines** section on page 457.)

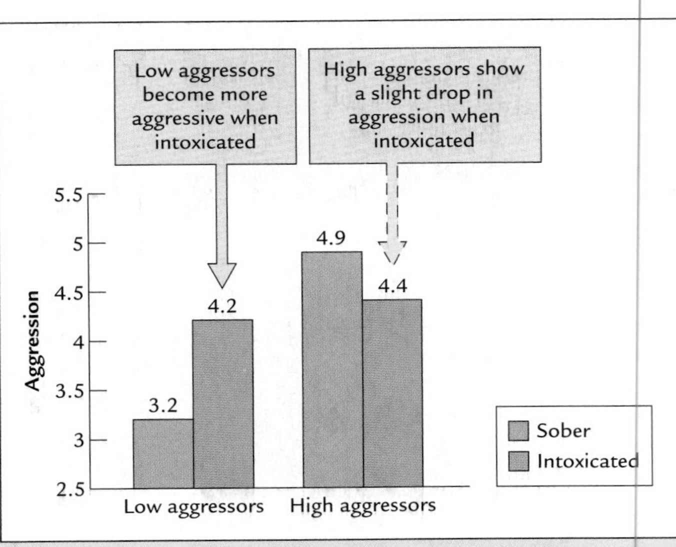

FIGURE 11.13

The Effects of Alcohol on Aggression: Empirical Evidence. Individuals with relatively weak tendencies to aggress (low aggressors) became more aggressive when intoxicated. In contrast, individuals with strong aggressive tendencies became slightly less aggressive when intoxicated. [SOURCE: BASED ON DATA FROM PIHL, LAU, & ASSAD, 1997.]

BEYOND THE HEADLINES: AS SOCIAL PSYCHOLOGISTS SEE IT

AGGRESSION IN THE AIR—AND NO WONDER!

Tension on a Crowded Plane Nears the Breaking Point

United Press, April 28, 1999—The 757's toilets overflowed. A hysterical passenger vowed to blow an emergency door and jump into the freezing darkness. A grown man wept and begged to be freed. Babies screamed. Adults screamed, too. These were the conditions on Northwest Airlines Flight 1829 from Tampa to Detroit which arrived about 22 hours late and was trapped on the tarmac at its destination for nearly seven hours before being permitted to taxi to a gate and release its long-suffering passengers. . . . Five hours into its wait on the ground in Detroit, Capt. Stabler phoned the Northwest duty manager and stated: "People are starting to lose their composure here . . . I'm afraid somebody will make a panic evacuation." "There are thousands of people in here," the flight manager replied. "There are fistfights. The airport police are arresting people." On the plane, conditions worsened. In Row 9, passenger D, Christina Ward, screamed: "I've had enough of this! I have to get off this plane! I'm going to open this door!" Crying hysterically, she prepared to pull the emergency-exit lever next to her seat and leap into the night. "No! No!" other passengers pleaded. Still others made plans to follow her out the door. Finally, after seven hours, the jet was towed to the gate. The passengers, numb and exhausted, moved slowly through the door. Tragedy had been averted . . . but by a seemingly razor-thin margin. . . .

These days, everyone experiences delays while traveling by air. But what the passengers on the ill-fated flight endured was something else again—a true nightmare of modern transportation (or of a modern transportation system in danger of imminent collapse!). And given the findings of social psychological research on human aggression, the passengers' behavior is far from surprising. They were, after all, exposed to highly unpleasant physical conditions, to intense frustration, and to the mounting belief that they were suffering needlessly, primarily because no one cared to help them. So it is not surprising that many became angry and emotional and threatened to open the emergency doors—or worse! What is *more* surprising is that they did not actually do these things and that fistfights and open assaults against the crew or other passengers did not occur. Witnesses on board the plane, however, are unanimous in their observation that it was a very near thing; the risk that some people, at least, would resort to acts of violence was not only real—it became increasingly palpable as the hours passed and passenger discomfort and annoyance continued to rise.

There is a real lesson here for the airline industry, whose record of delays, lost luggage, and other annoyances to passengers—continues to deteriorate: People can be pushed only so far. And when the breaking point is reached, they may engage in actions that are extremely dangerous under any conditions, but which are especially frightening in the cramped quarters of modern jets.

KEY POINTS

- *High temperatures* tend to increase aggression, but only up to a point. Beyond some level, aggression declines as temperatures rise.
- Consuming alcohol can increase aggression—especially, it appears, in individuals who normally show low levels of aggression.

Aggression in Long-Term Relationships: Bullying and Workplace Violence

Reports of instances in which people are attacked by total strangers are disturbing. Even more unsettling, however, are situations in which people are harmed by others they know or with whom they have long-term relationships—family members, schoolmates, coworkers. While such aggression takes many different forms, we'll focus here on two important topics: *bullying* (e.g., Ireland & Ireland, 2000; Smith & Brain, 2000) and *workplace violence* (Baron & Neuman, 1999; Baron, Neuman, & Geddes, 1999).

Bullying: Singling out Others for Repeated Abuse

Do you remember Joel—the teenager in my neighborhood who was constantly taunted and humiliated by my other friends—and, often, by me? Clearly, he was the target of **bullying** in our group; he was the target of repeated aggression in a context in which he had less power or prestige than the persons who aggressed against him—other members of the group (Olweus, 1993). Although he wasn't smaller or weaker than the rest of us (victims of bullies often are), he was somehow less able to stand up for himself and bring our bullying to an end, and so became the target of unrelenting attacks. While bullying has been studied primarily as something that occurs between children and teenagers, it is also common in other contexts, too, such as workplaces and prisons. Indeed, recent findings indicate that fully 50 percent of persons in prison are exposed to one or more episodes of bullying each week (Ireland & Ireland, 2000). Because most research has focused on bullying among children, though, we will focus on this work here. Two basic questions have been considered in research on bullying among children: (1) What are the characteristics of bullies and victims—in other words, why do some persons become bullies and others victims, while still others are not involved in bullying; and (2) what steps can be taken to reduce or prevent bullying?

bullying: A pattern of behavior in which one individual is chosen as the target of repeated aggression by one or more others; the target person (the victim) generally has less power than those who engage in aggression (the bullies).

THE CHARACTERISTICS OF BULLIES AND VICTIMS. Perhaps we should start with two basic facts. First, research on bullying indicates that relatively few children are purely victims or purely bullies; rather, a larger number play both roles: they bully some people and are bullied, in turn, by others (e.g., see Figure 11.14; Vermande et

FIGURE 11.14
Bullying: All Too Common in Many Schools. *Bullying*—repeated assaults by one or more persons against a target person who is weaker or lower in power—is very common among children. Research findings indicate that it can have devastating effects on the victims, and on the bullies, too.

al., 2000). Second, bullying seems to be common all around the globe. Indeed, at the time I (RAB) wrote these words, I was living in France, where I was a visiting professor at the Université des Sciences Sociales in Toulouse. Almost every night, the evening news reported growing concern with bullying and other forms of violence in the public schools in France. Not surprisingly, then, research on this topic has been truly international in scope, and has examined the occurrence of bullying in many different cultures.

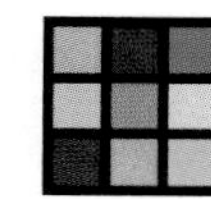

But now, returning to the central question, what, specifically, has research on bullying discovered about the characteristics of bullies and their victims? First, that they differ in their perceptions of the social world. For instance, bullies tend to perceive others as acting the way they do because they are that kind of person or because they intended to act in the way they did (Smorti & Ciucci, 2000). In contrast, victims tend to perceive others as acting as they do at least in part because they are responding to external events of conditions, including how others have treated *them.* What this implies is that bullies may be more likely than victims to fall prey to the hostile attributional bias described earlier in this chapter. So, in a sense, they strike at others repeatedly because they perceive them to be potentially dangerous and wish to subdue such opponents in advance.

Additional findings indicate that while bullies and victims are not easy to differentiate in terms of specific characteristics, children who play both roles (*bully/victims,* as they are often termed) do differ from children who are not involved in bullying. Such bully/victims are lower in self-esteem, lower in the belief that they can control their own outcomes, and higher in Machiavellianism—a tendency to adopt a ruthless, manipulative approach to dealing with other persons (e.g., Mynard & Joseph, 1997; Andreou, 2000). As one researcher (Andreou, 2000, p. 54) puts it, "These children believe that they live in a world in which they can be either bullies or victims, and they choose to be both to be consistent with their low self-esteem and their Machiavellian strategy for dealing with other people."

Finally, we should note that bullies and bully/victims seem to be less effective in coping with stress than are other children, especially those not involved in bullying. Bullies and bully/victims are more likely to respond to stress with aggression (lashing out at someone physically or verbally) or by engaging in self-destructive behaviors (doing something dangerous, smoking, taking drugs). In contrast, children not involved in bullying are more likely to react to stress in more adaptive ways, for instance, by distracting themselves (taking their minds off the stress by engaging in hobbies or exercise). Overall, then, it seems fair to say that children who become bullies or bully/victims have a more negative view of the world than other children and show personal characteristics that may interfere with their personal happiness and adjustment.

■ REDUCING THE OCCURRENCE OF BULLYING: SOME POSITIVE STEPS. As I (RAB) discovered many years ago while listening to my friend Joel, bullying can have devastating effects on its victims. In fact, there have been several cases in which children that are bullied repeatedly and brutally by their classmates have actually committed suicide (O'Moore, 2000). These distressing facts lead to the following question: What can be done to reduce or even eliminate bullying? Many research projects—some involving the entire school systems of several countries—have been conducted to find out, and the results have been at least moderately encouraging.

First, it appears that students themselves can be every effective in reducing bullying. When children are trained to intervene rather than to simply stand by when bullying occurs, the incidence of such behavior can be substantially reduced (e.g., Cowei, 2000). However, it appears that girls are more willing to intervene than are boys, who tend to perceive bullying as part of being masculine: "real" boys can both take it and dish it out. Special efforts may be necessary, therefore, to induce boys as well as girls to intervene when bullying occurs.

Teachers, too, can play a very helpful role in reducing bullying. One recent project conducted in Ireland (O'Moore, 2000) indicates that teachers often do not fully grasp the importance of low self-esteem in bullying, so programs designed to call this point to the attention of teachers can be very useful. Once they understand that bullies as well as victims suffer from low self-esteem, teachers can take steps to enhance childrens' feelings of self-worth, and this, in turn, can be a very useful initial step toward reducing bullying.

Additional projects carried out in the Netherlands (e.g., Limper, 2000) and in Norway (e.g., Roland, 2000) have enlisted the aid of parents, through parents associations and the help of outside experts such as psychologists and professors, to reduce bullying. In these programs, efforts are made to change the entire school environment so that it is clear to students, teachers, and parents alike that bullying is *not* a normal part of growing up and is *not* to be tolerated. For example, in the Netherlands, the following points have been stressed:

1. Bullying must been seen to be a problem by all involved parties—teachers, parents, and students.
2. If bullying occurs, teachers must draw attention to it and take an unequivocal stand against it.
3. Students must be provided with direct means for dealing with bullying—they must be told precisely what to do and whom to see when bullying occurs.
4. If a teacher or school refuses to address the problem, then an outside expert must be called in to help.

The effects of programs emphasizing such steps are encouraging and suggest that when concerted action is taken, bullying can indeed be reduced.

Workplace Violence: Aggression on the Job

> City of Industry, California—A postal worker walked up to his boss, pulled a gun from a paper bag and shot him dead, the latest incident in an alarming increase in workplace violence. (*Los Angeles Times,* July 18, 1995.)
>
> Portland, Oregon—A man accused of shooting two people and taking four others hostage in an office tower appeared in court Friday. . . . Police initially said Rancor intended to shoot female office workers for having him fired from his job . . . but investigators said Friday that Rancor had problems with authority in general. (Associated Press, 1996.)

Reports of incidents such as these have appeared with alarming frequency in recent years, and appear to reflect a rising tide of violence in workplaces. In fact, more than eight hundred people are murdered at work each year in the United States alone (National Institute for Occupational Safety and Health, 1993). While these statistics seem to suggest that workplaces are becoming truly dangerous locations where disgruntled employees frequently attack or even shoot one another, two facts should be carefully noted: (1) A large majority of violence occurring in work settings is performed by outsiders—people who do not work there but who enter a workplace to commit robbery or other crimes (see Figure 11.15). And (2) surveys indicate that threats of physical harm or actual harm in work settings are actually quite rare—in fact, the chances of being killed at work (by outsiders or coworkers combined) are something like 1 in 450,000 (although this is considerably higher in some high-risk occupations, such as taxi driving or police work; Leonard & Sloboda, 1996).

workplace aggression: any form of behavior through which individuals seek to harm others in their workplace.

In sum, growing evidence suggests that while workplace *violence* is certainly an important topic worthy of careful study, it is relatively rare, and is, in fact, only the dramatic tip of the much larger problem of **workplace aggression**—any form of behavior through which individuals seek to harm others in their workplace

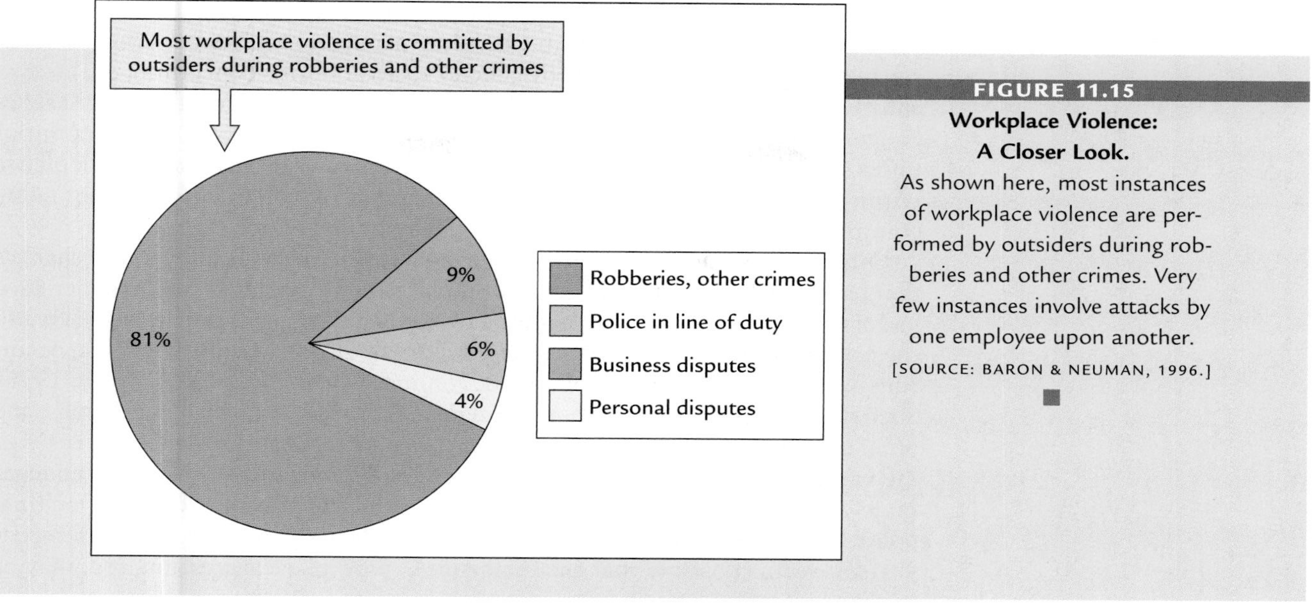

FIGURE 11.15
Workplace Violence: A Closer Look.
As shown here, most instances of workplace violence are performed by outsiders during robberies and other crimes. Very few instances involve attacks by one employee upon another.
[SOURCE: BARON & NEUMAN, 1996.]

(Baron & Neuman, 1996; Neuman & Baron, 1998). What is such aggression like? Growing evidence suggests that it is largely *covert* rather than *overt* in nature. That is, like *indirect aggression,* which we discussed earlier, covert aggression is relatively subtle in nature and allows aggressors to harm other persons while simultaneously preventing such persons from identifying them as the source of the harm. This type of aggression is strongly preferred in workplaces for the following reason: Aggressors in such settings expect to interact with their intended victims frequently in the future. Using covert forms of aggression reduces the likelihood that the victims will retaliate against them.

What specific forms of aggression do individuals actually use in workplaces? Evidence on this issue is provided by research conducted by Baron, Neuman, and Geddes (1999). These researchers asked almost five hundred employed persons to rate the frequency with which they had personally experienced a wide range of aggressive behaviors at work. Careful analysis of their responses indicated that most aggression occurring in workplaces falls into three major categories:

1. *Expressions of hostility:* Behaviors that are primarily verbal or symbolic in nature (e.g., belittling others' opinions, talking behind their backs).
2. *Obstructionism:* Behaviors designed to obstruct or impede the target's performance (e.g., failure to return phone calls or respond to memos, failure to transmit needed information, interfering with activities important to the target).
3. *Overt aggression:* Behaviors that have typically been included under the heading "workplace violence" (e.g., physical assault, theft or destruction of property, threats of physical violence).

Additional findings indicated that expressions of hostility and instances of obstructionism are much more frequent than instances of overt aggression. Thus, covert forms of aggression do seem to be the preferred ones in most work settings.

What are the causes of workplace aggression? Again, as is true of aggression in any context, many factors seem to play a role. However, one that has emerged again and again in research on this topic is *perceived unfairness* (e.g., Skarlicki & Folger, 1997; Neuman & Baron, 1997). When individuals feel that they have been treated unfairly by others in their organization—or by their organization itself—they experience intense feelings of anger and resentment and often seek to even the score by harming the people they hold responsible in some manner. In addition, research in work settings seems to be influenced by general societal norms concerning the acceptability of such behavior. For instance, in one recent study, Folger and his colleagues (Folger et al., in press) found that the greater the incidence of violence in communities surrounding U.S. post offices, the higher the rates of aggression and violence within these branch offices. It was as if acceptance of violence in the surrounding communities paved the way for similar behavior inside this organization.

Other factors that seem to play a role in workplace aggression relate to changes that have occurred recently in many workplaces: downsizing, layoffs, and increased use of part-time employees, to name a few. Several studies indicate that the greater the extent to which such changes have occurred, the greater the aggression occurring in such workplaces (e.g., Baron & Neuman, 1996; Neuman & Baron, 1998). Such findings are only correlational in nature, but because downsizing, layoffs, and other changes have been found to produce negative feelings among employees (e.g., increased anxiety and feelings of resentment), it seems possible that these changes may well contribute, through such reactions, to increased aggression. One final point: Because such changes have occurred with increasing frequency in recent years, it seems possible that the incidence of workplace aggression, too, may be increasing for this reason.

In sum, media attention to dramatic instances of workplace violence may be somewhat misleading; while such actions do indeed occur, they are far less frequent than more subtle but still harmful instances of workplace aggression. And such behavior, in turn, appears to be influenced by many of the same factors that influence aggression in other contexts. Our conclusion: Workplace aggression is not a new or unique form of behavior; rather, it is simply aggression occurring in one kind of setting. Thus, efforts to understand it—and to reduce it—should be linked as closely as possible to the large body of research on human aggression summarized in this chapter and in other sources.

KEY POINTS

- *Bullying* involves repeated aggression against individuals who, for various reasons, are unable to defend themselves against such treatment. Bullying occurs in many contexts, including schools, workplaces, and prisons. Few children are solely bullies or victims; more play both roles. Bullies and bully/victims appear to have lower self-esteem than children who are not involved in bullying.
- *Workplace aggression* takes many different forms, but is usually covert in nature. It stems from a wide range of factors, including perceptions of having been treated unfairly and the many disturbing changes that have occurred in workplaces in recent years.

The Prevention and Control of Aggression: Some Useful Techniques

If there is one idea in this chapter we hope you'll remember in the years ahead, it is this: Aggression is *not* an inevitable or unchangeable form of behavior. On the contrary, because aggression stems from a complex interplay of external events, cognitions, and personal characteristics, it *can* be prevented or reduced. In fact, we have already mentioned this fact repeatedly in our discussion of bullying. In this final section, we'll consider several procedures that, when used appropriately, can be effective in reducing the frequency or intensity of human aggression.

Punishment: An Effective Deterrent to Violence?

In New York state, where we both live, a key issue in one recent election for governor was *capital punishment*—the death penalty. One of the candidates was strongly against capital punishment, while the other favored it. Although the two candidates had many reasons for these opposing views, the one that was emphasized throughout the election campaign was the potential value of capital punishment as a *deterrent* to crimes of violence. One of the candidates felt that capital punishment would *not* deter criminals from engaging in aggressive acts, while the other felt that it would. As we'll explain below, this is a complex issue, and evidence relating to it is mixed. Thus, we can't resolve it here. What we *can* do, however, is point out a few pertinent facts about the use of **punishment**—delivery of aversive consequences in order to decrease some behavior—as a technique for reducing aggression.

First, we should note that, taken as a whole, existing evidence suggests that punishment *can* succeed in deterring individuals from engaging in many forms of behavior. However, such effects are neither automatic nor certain. Unless punishment is administered in accordance with basic principles, it can be totally *ineffective* in this respect. What conditions must be met for punishment to succeed? Four are most important: (1) It must be *prompt*—it must follow aggressive actions as quickly as possible. (2) It must be *certain*—the probability that it will follow aggression must be very high. (3) It must be *strong*—strong enough to be highly unpleasant to potential recipients. And (4) it must be perceived by recipients as *justified* or deserved.

punishment: Procedures in which aversive consequences are delivered to individuals when they engage in specific actions.

Unfortunately, as you can readily see, these conditions are often *not* present in the criminal justice systems of many nations. In many societies, the delivery of punishment for aggressive actions is delayed for months or even years; in the United States, for example, convicted murderers often spend more than a decade on death row, awaiting execution (see Figure 11.16). Similarly, many criminals avoid arrest

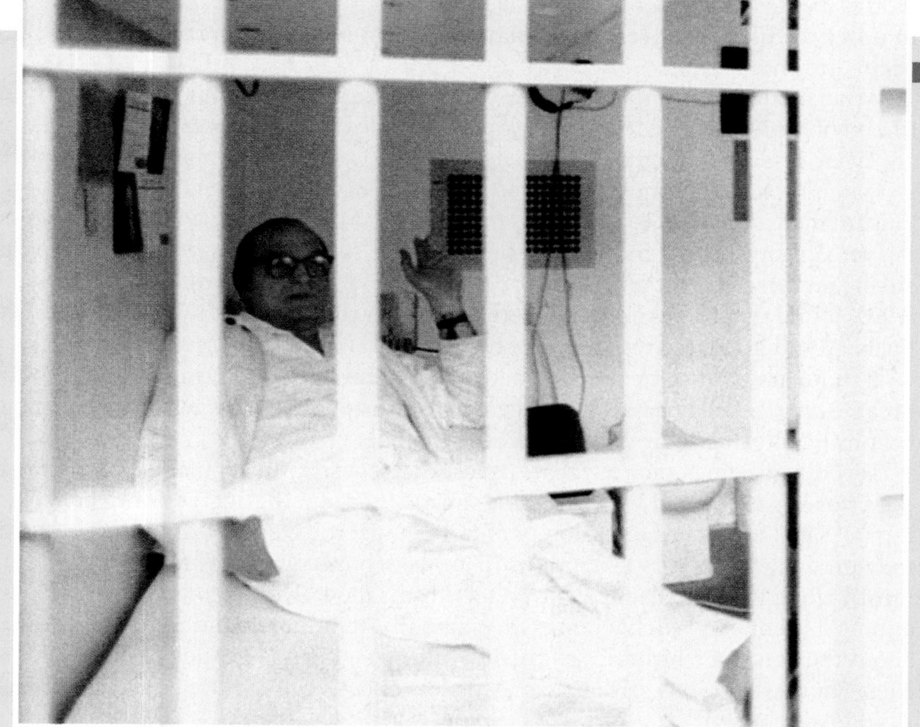

FIGURE 11.16
Why Punishment Often Fails to Deter Violent Crime. In the United States and many other countries, punishment for crimes is far from swift. In fact, convicted murderers often spend years on death row while legal battles are fought concerning their execution. Such delays make it unlikely that the threat of even this extreme form of punishment can be effective in deterring future crimes.

and conviction, so the certainty of punishment is low. The magnitude of punishment itself varies from one city, state, or even courtroom to another. In view of these conditions, it is hardly surprising that the threat of punishment—even the most severe punishment (execution)—does not seem to be effective in deterring violent crime. The conditions necessary for it to be effective are simply not present. This raises an intriguing question: Could punishment prove effective as a deterrent to violence if it were used more effectively? We can't say for sure, but existing evidence suggests that it could, potentially, exert such effects *if* it were used in accordance with the principles described above. But again, instituting such conditions would raise complex issues relating to ethical and religious beliefs, so scientific data are clearly only one consideration, and for that reason, we cannot offer a clear position here. Rather, this is a matter each person must decide for her- or himself.

Catharsis: Does Getting It Out of Your System Really Help?

When I (RAB) was a little boy, my grandmother used to greet my temper tantrums by saying, "That's right, get it out . . . don't keep it bottled up inside—that will hurt you." In other words, she was a true believer in the **catharsis hypothesis**—the view that if individuals give vent to their anger and hostility in relatively nonharmful ways, their tendencies to engage in more dangerous types of aggression will be reduced (Dollard et al., 1939).

Is this actually true? Contrary to common belief, existing evidence offers a mixed picture (Feshbach, 1984; Geen, 1991b). On the one hand, participation in various activities that are not harmful to others (e.g., vigorous sports activities, shouting obscenities into an empty room) can reduce emotional arousal stemming from frustration or provocation (Zillmann, 1979). Unfortunately, though, such effects appear to be temporary. Arousal stemming from provocation may reappear as soon as individuals bring the incidents that made them angry to mind (Caprara et al., 1994). In other words, cognitive factors may often ensure that cathartic effects, if they occur, are short-lived.

What about the idea that performing "safe" aggressive actions reduces the likelihood of more harmful forms of aggression? The results of research on this issue are even less encouraging. Overt aggression, it appears, it is not reduced by (1) watching scenes of media violence (Geen, 1998), (2) attacking inanimate objects (Bushman, Baumeister, & Stack, 1999; Mallick & McCandless, 1966), or (3) aggressing verbally against others. Indeed, some findings suggest that aggression may actually be *increased* by these activities. For instance, Bushman, Baumeister, and Stack (1999) found that aggression was increased rather than reduced by hitting a punching bag. And in related research, Bushman (2001) found that research participants who thought about someone who had angered them while hitting a punching bag became *angrier* and behaved more aggressively than participants who thought about becoming physically fit while punching the bag.

Together, findings such as these suggest that, contrary to popular belief, catharsis does *not* appear to be a very effective means for reducing aggression. Participating in "safe" forms of aggression or merely in vigorous, energy-draining activities may produce temporary reductions in arousal; but feelings of anger may quickly return when individuals meet, or merely think about, the persons who previously annoyed them. And such feelings may actually be intensified if individuals think about the persons who annoyed them while engaging in so-called cathartic activities. For these reasons, catharsis may be less effective in reducing aggression than is widely believed.

catharsis hypothesis: The view that providing angry persons with an opportunity to express their aggressive impulses in relatively safe ways will reduce their tendencies to engage in more harmful forms of aggression.

Cognitive Interventions: Apologies and Overcoming Cognitive Deficits

Do you find it easy or hard to apologize to others? If your answer is "hard," I suggest that you work on this particular social skill, because research findings agree with what common sense suggests: *apologies*—admissions of wrongdoing that include requests for forgiveness—often go a long way toward defusing aggression (e.g., Ohbuchi, Kameda, & Agarie, 1989). Similarly, good excuses—ones that make reference to factors beyond the excuse-giver's control—can also be quite effective in reducing anger and overt aggression by persons who have been provoked in some manner (e.g., Baron, 1989b; Weiner et al., 1987). So if you feel that you are making another person angry, apologize without delay. The trouble you will save makes it quite worthwhile to say "I'm sorry."

Here's one old saying that I like a lot: "When emotions run high, reason flies right out the window." Applied to the question of controlling or reducing aggression, this saying calls attention to the fact that when we are very angry, our ability to thinking clearly—for instance, to evaluate the consequences of our own actions—may be sharply reduced. When this occurs, restraints that normally serve to hold aggression in check (e.g., fear of retaliation) may also diminish. In addition, as noted by Lieberman and Greenberg (1999), when we are emotionally aroused, we may adopt modes of thought in which we process information in a quick and impetuous manner. This, in turn, may increase the chances that we will "lash out against" someone else—including other persons who are *not* the cause of our annoyance or irritation (the kind of *displaced aggression* discussed earlier in this chapter).

Given these basic facts, any procedures that help us avoid or overcome such *cognitive deficits* can be helpful from the point of view of reducing aggression (Zillmann, 1993). One such technique involves *preattribution*—attributing annoying actions by others to *unintentional* causes before the provocation actually occurs. For example, before meeting with someone you know who can be irritating, you could remind yourself that she or he doesn't mean to make you angry—it is just the result of an unfortunate personal style. Another technique involves preventing yourself (or others) from dwelling on previous real or imagined wrongs. You can accomplish this by distracting yourself in some way—for instance, by reading, by watching an absorbing movie or television program, or by working on a complex puzzle). Such activities allow for a cooling-off period during which anger can dissipate, and also help to reestablish cognitive controls over behavior—controls that help to hold aggression in check.

Other Techniques for Reducing Aggression: Exposure to Nonaggressive Models, Training in Social Skills, and Incompatible Responses

Many other techniques for reducing overt aggression have been developed and tested. Here, briefly, are three more that appear to be quite effective.

■ EXPOSURE TO NONAGGRESSIVE MODELS: THE CONTAGION OF RESTRAINT. If exposure to aggressive actions by others in the media or in person can increase aggression, it seems possible that exposure to *non*aggressive actions might produce opposite effects. In fact, the results of several studies indicate that this is so (e.g., Baron, 1972b; Donnerstein & Donnerstein, 1976). When individuals who have been provoked are exposed to others who either demonstrate or urge restraint, the tendency of potential aggressors to lash out is reduced. These findings suggest that it may be useful to place restrained, nonaggressive models in tense and potentially dangerous situations. Their presence may well tip the balance against overt violence.

■ TRAINING IN SOCIAL SKILLS: LEARNING TO GET ALONG WITH OTHERS. One reason many persons become involved in aggressive encounters is that they are sorely lacking in basic social skills. They don't know how to respond to provocations from others in a way that will soothe these persons rather than annoy them (see Figure 11.17). They don't know how to make requests or how to say no to requests from others without making these people angry. Persons lacking in basic social skills seem to account for a high proportion of violence in many societies (Toch, 1985), so equipping such persons with improved social skills may go a long way toward reducing aggression.

Fortunately, procedures for teaching individuals such skills exist and are not very complex. For example, both adults and children can rapidly acquire improved social skills from watching other persons (social models) demonstrate both effective and ineffective behaviors (Schneider, 1991). Such gains can be obtained through just a few hours of treatment (Bienert & Schneider, 1993), so they are practical and cost-effective as well as successful.

■ INCOMPATIBLE RESPONSES: IT'S HARD TO STAY ANGRY IF YOU SMILE. Suppose you were in a situation in which you felt yourself growing angry and then someone told a joke that made you laugh. Would you remain angry? Probably not. The chances are good

FIGURE 11.17

Training in Social Skills: A Useful Technique for Reducing Aggression.

Many persons have aggressive encounters with others because they are lacking in social skills—for instance, they don't know how to soothe others when they become angry, and they don't know how to refuse requests in a way that does not anger the requester.

that once you laughed, you would feel less angry. Why? Because laughter and the positive affect it generates are incompatible with feeling angry and actually aggressing. This is the basis for another approach for reducing aggression, known as the **incompatible response technique** (e.g., Baron, 1993b). This technique suggests that if individuals are exposed to events or stimuli that cause them to experience affective states incompatible with anger or aggression, these reactions are reduced.

What stimuli or experiences produce such incompatible affective states? Research findings indicate that humor, mild sexual arousal, and feelings of empathy toward the victim are all effective in this respect (e.g., Baron, 1983b, 1993b; Richardson et al., 1994). Of course, this technique can be overdone: trying to make someone laugh when they are already extremely angry can backfire and make them even angrier. But if used early in the process—before individuals have become enraged—efforts to replace negative internal states such as annoyance with positive ones can be quite effective.

incompatible response technique: A technique for reducing aggression in which individuals are exposed to events or stimuli that cause them to experience affective states incompatible with anger or aggression.

KEY POINTS

- *Punishment* can be effective in reducing aggression, but only when it is delivered under certain conditions.
- The *catharsis hypothesis* appears to be mainly false. Engaging in vigorous activities may produce reductions in arousal, but these are only temporary. Similarly, aggression is not reduced by engaging in apparently "safe" forms of aggression.
- Aggression can be reduced by apologies—admissions of wrongdoing that include a request for forgiveness—and by engaging in activities that distract attention away from causes of anger.
- Aggression can also be reduced by exposure to nonaggressive models, training in social skills, and the induction of affective states incompatible with aggression.

CONNECTIONS: INTEGRATING SOCIAL PSYCHOLOGY

IN THIS CHAPTER, YOU READ ABOUT . . .	IN OTHER CHAPTERS, YOU WILL FIND RELATED DISCUSSIONS OF . . .
the role of cognitive and affective variables in aggression	the role of these factors in attitude change (Chapter 4), prejudice (Chapter 6), and helping (Chapter 10)
social factors that play a role in aggression	the effects of these factors on social models (Chapter 10), attributions (Chapter 2), and arousal (Chapter 7)
personal characteristics that influence aggression	the role of these factors in social perception (Chapter 2), helping behavior (Chapter 10), and leadership (Chapter 13)

THINKING ABOUT CONNECTIONS

1. Attorneys sometimes defend individuals who commit violent acts—including murder—by suggesting that these persons were "overwhelmed" by emotions beyond their control. In view of our discussions in other chapters (e.g., Chapters 3 and 10) of the effects of emotions on social thought and social behavior, what are your reactions to such defenses?

(continued)

2. Many social psychologists now accept the view that genetic factors play some role in human aggression. Do you think that such factors also influence bullying, predisposing some children to show such behavior?

3. Violence and other forms of aggression appear to be increasing in many workplaces. Do you think it would be possible to screen potential employees, so as to reject those who have a high propensity for engaging in such behavior? If so, what aspects of their self-concept (Chapter 5), attitudes (Chapter 4), or past behavior (e.g., the kind of relationships they have had with others; see Chapter 8) might be useful predictors of the likelihood that they would engage in workplace aggression if hired?

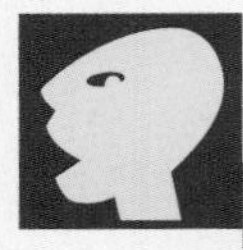

IDEAS TO TAKE WITH YOU—AND USE!

CAUSES OF AGGRESSION

Research findings indicate that aggression stems from a wide range of variables—social factors, personal characteristics, and situational factors. Here is an overview of the most important factors identified by systematic research.

Social Determinants of Aggression

Frustration →
Direct provocation →
Exposure to media violence →
Heightened arousal →

Aggression

Personal Determinants of Aggression

Type A behavior pattern →
Hostile attributional bias →
Gender →

Aggression

Situational Determinants of Aggression

High temperatures →

Alcohol →

Cultural beliefs, values →

Aggression

SUMMARY AND REVIEW OF KEY POINTS

Theoretical Perspectives on Aggression: In Search of the Roots of Violence

- *Aggression* is the intentional infliction of harm on others. While most social psychologists reject the view that human aggression is strongly determined by genetic factors, many now accept an evolutionary perspective that recognizes the potential role of such factors.

- *Drive theories* suggest that aggression stems from externally elicited drives to harm or injure others. The frustration–aggression hypothesis is the most famous example of such theories.

- Modern theories of aggression, such as the *general affective aggression model,* recognize the importance in aggression of learning, various eliciting input variables, cognitions, individual differences, and affective states.

Determinants of Human Aggression: Social, Personal, Situational

- In order to study aggression, social psychologists often use procedures in which individuals are led to believe that they can harm others in various ways—delivery of painful electric shocks or reducing their winnings in a competitive game.

- Contrary to the famous *frustration–aggression hypothesis,* all aggression does not stem from frustration, and frustration does not always lead to aggression. Frustration is a strong elicitor of aggression only under certain limited conditions.

- In contrast, *provocation* from others is a powerful elicitor of aggression. We rarely turn the other cheek; rather, we match—or slightly exceed—the level of aggression we receive from others.

- One exception to such matching occurs in triggered *displaced aggression.* In such situations, persons who were strongly provoked previously but did not aggress respond very strongly to mild provocations, thus displacing aggression to largely innocent targets.

- Exposure to *media violence* has been found to increase aggression among viewers. This is due to several factors, such as the priming of aggressive thoughts and a weakening of restraints against aggression.

- *Heightened arousal* can increase aggression if it persists beyond the situation in which it was induced and is falsely interpreted as anger.

- Mild levels of *sexual arousal* reduce aggression, while higher levels increase such behavior. Even exposure to sex-related words can increase aggression through the priming of schemas and other knowledge structures related to aggression.

- Persons showing the *Type A behavior pattern* are more irritable and aggressive than persons with the *Type B behavior pattern.*

- Individuals high in *hostile attributional bias* attribute others' actions to hostile intent. As a result, they are more aggressive than persons low in this characteristic.

- Persons high in narcissism hold an over-inflated view of their own worth. They react with exceptionally high levels of aggression to feedback from others that threatens their inflated egos.

- Males are more aggressive overall than are females, but this difference decreases in the context of strong provocation. Males are more likely to use direct forms of aggression, but females are more likely to use indirect forms of aggression. Males are much more likely than females to engage in sexual coercion.
- High temperatures tend to increase aggression, but only up to a point. Beyond some level, aggression declines as temperatures rise.
- Consuming alcohol can increase aggression, especially, it appears, by individuals who normally show low levels of aggression.

Aggression in Long-Term Relationships: Bullying and Workplace Violence

- *Bullying* involves repeated aggression against individuals who, for various reasons, are unable to defend themselves against such treatment. Bullying occurs in many contexts, including schools, workplaces, and prisons. Few children are solely bullies or victims; more play both roles. Bullies and bully/victims appear to have lower self-esteem than children who are not involved in bullying.
- *Workplace aggression* takes many different forms, but is usually covert in nature. It stems from a wide range of factors, including perceptions of having been treated unfairly and the many disturbing changes that have occurred in workplaces in recent years.

The Prevention and Control of Aggression: Some Useful Techniques

- *Punishment* can be effective in reducing aggression, but only when it is delivered under certain conditions.
- The *catharsis hypothesis* appears to be mainly false. Engaging in vigorous activities may produce reductions in arousal, but these are only temporary. Similarly, aggression is not reduced by engaging in apparently "safe" forms of aggression.
- Aggression can be reduced by apologies—admissions of wrongdoing that include requests for forgiveness—and by engaging in activities that distract attention away from causes of anger.
- Aggression can also be reduced by exposure to nonaggressive models, training in social skills, and the induction of affective states incompatible with aggression.

KEY TERMS

aggression (p. 435)
aggression machine (p. 440)
bullying (p. 458)
catharsis hypothesis (p. 464)
displaced aggression (p. 443)
drive theories (p. 437)
excitation transfer theory (p. 447)
frustration-aggression hypothesis (p. 442)
general affective aggression model (p. 437)
hostile aggression (p. 450)
hostile attributional bias (p. 451)
incompatible response technique (p. 467)
instrumental aggression (p. 450)
media violence (p. 445)
provocation (p. 443)
punishment (p. 463)
Type A behavior pattern (p. 449)
Type B behavior pattern (p. 450)
workplace aggression (p. 460)

FOR MORE INFORMATION

Baron, R. A., & Richardson, D. R. (1994). *Human aggression* (2nd ed.). New York: Plenum.

- This book provides a broad overview of current knowledge about human aggression. Separate chapters focus on the biological, social, environmental, and personal determinants of aggression. Additional chapters examine the development of aggression, the prevention and control of such behavior, and its occurrence in many natural contexts.

Moeller, T. G. (2001). *Youth aggression and violence: A psychological approach.* Mahwah, NJ: Erlbaum.

- This book examines the causes of aggression by young persons in schools and other settings. It considers genetic and biological underpinnings of such aggression, family and social factors, and examines the findings of current research employing a wide range of methods. This is a very timely book on an important topic closely related to issues examined in this chapter.

Raoul Dufy, *Les Cavaliers sous Bois.*

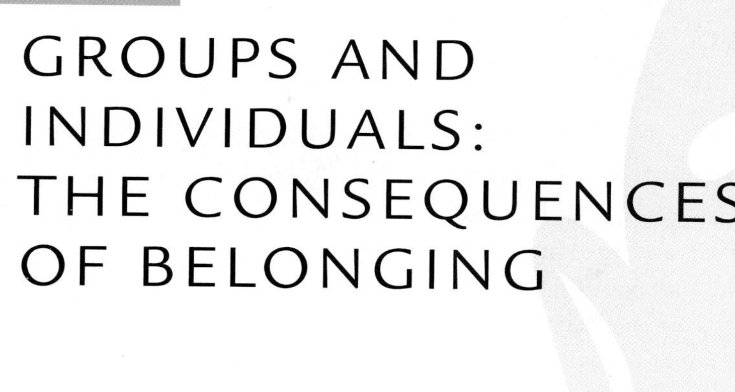

12 GROUPS AND INDIVIDUALS: THE CONSEQUENCES OF BELONGING

CHAPTER OUTLINE

For many years, I (RAB) worked at a large state university. Because all faculty members were state employees, our salaries could not be kept secret. In fact, salary information was readily available in a government office. But as far as I know, no one ever chose this route to get this information—or if they did, they didn't talk about it. One year, though, someone visited the state capital and recorded the salaries of all faculty. Then, this person printed copies and distributed them to every department on campus. Soon, shouts of anger and dismay could be heard from every direction! Many people were shocked to learn that they earned less than some of their colleagues, and they made these feelings known to everyone who would listen. One of my friends, in particular, was extremely upset when he learned that his salary was lower than that of several other persons, including me. He burst into my office, shouting, "It's so unfair! I always suspected that I was being exploited, but now I know it for certain. I can see why *you* get more than I do, but how about ______" (and he named one of our colleagues). "I'm worth twice what he is!" I did my best to calm him down, pointing out that his salary was only a few hundred dollars less than this other person's and reminding him that he doubled his yearly salary by consulting. After a while, he calmed down and left, but from that day on, troubles plagued our department. Faculty who felt they were not being treated fairly remained disgruntled, and their annoyance showed up in many ways. They stopped being team players, so cooperation took a nose dive. And organizational politics of the nastiest kind increased. Ultimately, several of the people who were most upset about their salaries took other jobs; so, over a period of several years, we lost some of our best people. In short, the day our salaries were made public marked the start of problems that persisted for years.

At the time this unhappy chain of events took place, I was too close to them to fully grasp what was happening. But now, looking back, I see that these events clearly illustrate several important facts about *groups*—collections of persons perceived to form coherent units to some degree (e.g., Lickel et al., 2000). First, and most obviously, this incident calls attention to the importance of feelings of fairness within groups. When people conclude that they are not being treated fairly, their willingness to cooperate with others may be greatly reduced; instead, conflict may be triggered. The result of these processes, in turn, may be reduced performance by the group; this was certainly true for our department, which became less effective in several ways. For instance, people seemed to work less hard on projects that required joint efforts to succeed (e.g., plans for new, team-taught courses). And it became harder for us to recruit new faculty members, because instead of praising our department, several persons began making negative remarks about it to job applicants when they visited campus. Decision making, too, became much harder: we could no longer reach consensus on important issues, and our meetings often turned into angry shouting matches rather than logical discussions. In short, the internal workings of our department changed in important ways, and these changes, in turn, exerted negative effects, one way or another, on all of us. So, yes, that anonymous person stirred up a lot of trouble when she or he decided to make everyone's salary public!

During the course of our daily lives, we all belong to many groups, and these groups, in turn, often exert powerful effects upon us. For this reason, the topic of *group influence*—how being part of a social group can influence the ways in which think and behave—has long been of major interest to social psychologists (e.g., Sedikides, Schopler, & Insko, 1998). To provide you with an overview of what research on this topic has revealed, we'll focus on several related issues. First, we'll take a closer look at the basic nature of groups—what they are and how they affect their members. Next, we'll examine the impact of groups on *task performance*—how our performance on various tasks can be affected by working with others or, in some cases, merely by their presence on the scene. Third, we'll turn to the question of what might be termed *coordination* within groups—the extent to which individuals pool their efforts and work together toward certain goals (i.e., cooperate with one another) or, instead, choose to work against each other in what is known as *conflict.* Fourth, we'll examine the question of perceived *fairness* in groups—the central process at work in the salary incident described earlier. Finally, we'll consider *decision making* in groups; as we'll soon see, this differs from decision making by individuals in several important ways. (We'll consider another important aspect of group functioning—*leadership*—in Chapter 13.)

Groups: What They Are and How They Function

Look at the photos in Figure 12.1. Which shows a group? Probably you would identify the one on the left as a group but the one on the right as showing a mere collection of persons. Why? Because, implicitly, you already accept a definition of the term **group** close to the one adopted by social psychologists: A collection of persons who are

group: A collection of persons who are perceived to be bonded together in a coherent unit to some degree.

FIGURE 12.1

Entiativity: What Makes a Group a Group?

The photo on the left shows a group high in entiativity: the members in this group interact with one another and have shared goals and outcomes. The photo on the right shows a group very low in entiativity: it is a mere collection of people who happen to be in the same location at the same time.

perceived to be bonded together in a coherent unit to some degree (e.g., Dasgupta, Banaji, & Abelson, 1999; Lickel et al., 2000). Social psychologists refer to this property of groups as *entiativity*—the extent to which a group is perceived as being a coherent entity (Campbell, 1958). Entiativity varies greatly, ranging from mere collections of people who happen to be in the same place at the same time but have little or no connection with one another, to highly intimate groups such as our family or persons with whom we have romantic relationships. So clearly, some groups are much closer to our conception of what a group is like than others. But what determines whether, and to what extent, we perceive several persons as forming a coherent group? This question has received growing attention from researchers in recent years, and a clear answer has begun to emerge. For instance, consider research on this issue by Lickel and his colleagues (Lickel et al., 2000).

These researchers presented the names of forty different kinds of groups (e.g., sports teams, the audience at a movie) to research participants and asked them to rate each on several dimensions, including these: the extent to which it is a coherent unit (entiativity), how important it is to group members, how much group members interact with one another, the extent to which they share common goals and common outcomes, how similar they are to one another, and how long these groups are likely to last. In addition, participants were asked to place the groups into *categories*—clusters of groups that seem to go together.

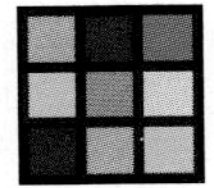

As shown in Table 12.1, participants perceived the groups as differing greatly in terms of entiativity: some (e.g., families, rock bands, close friends) were rated as being very high on this dimension, while others (e.g., plumbers, people at a bus stop) were perceived as very low in this respect. Perhaps more important, other findings indicated that several factors influenced these ratings: the degree to which group

TABLE 12.1

Entiativity of Various Groups. Participants in a recent study rated some groups as much higher on entiativity—being a coherent entity. Ratings could range from 1 to 9.

GROUPS	ENTIATIVITY RATINGS
Members of a professional sports team	8.27
Members of a family	8.16
Members of a rock band	8.16
Friends who do things together	7.75
Members of an orchestra	7.21
Members of a labor union	6.89
Women	5.16
People who live in the same neighborhood	4.78
Teachers	4.70
People attending an athletic contest	3.69
People in line at a bank	2.40

[SOURCE: BASED ON DATA FROM LICKEL ET AL., 2000.]

members interacted with one another (this was the strongest predictor of ratings of entiativity), the group's importance to members, the extent to which members shared outcomes and common goals, and their similarity to each other. The higher groups were on these dimensions, the more they were seen as forming coherent entities. Other findings indicated that four distinct types of groups emerged from participants' efforts to divide them into categories: *intimacy groups* (family, two people in a romantic relationship), *task-oriented groups* (e.g., committees, work groups), *social categories* (e.g., women, Americans), and *weak social relationships or associations* (e.g., people who live in the same neighborhood, people who enjoy classical music). To test the generality of these findings, Lickel and his colleagues (2000) then repeated this study in another country—Poland. Results were virtually identical, so it appears that at least in two different cultures, the factors that lead individuals to perceive groups as forming coherent units (i.e., as being high in entiativity) are very much the same.

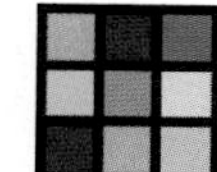

Additional research indicates that judgments concerning a group's entiativity exert important effects on how we think about such groups—for instance, our overall impression of the group (e.g., Susskind et al., 1999) and the attributions we make about it (e.g., Yzerbyt et al., 1998). Indeed, judgments concerning a group's entiativity, once made, seem to influence our processing of information about the group at an implicit (nonconscious) level of thought. For instance, when we perceive a group as being high in entiativity, we tend to compare the members with each other to a greater extent than is true for groups low in entiativity (Pickett, 2001). And such comparisons seem to occur implicitly, without conscious thought or intention. Clearly, then, entiativity is a key dimension from the point of view of understanding precisely what constitutes a group and how being part of a group can influence our behavior.

How Groups Function: Roles, Status, Norms, and Cohesiveness

That groups often exert powerful effects upon their members is obvious and will be a basic theme of this chapter. Before turning to specific aspects of group influence, however, we should address a basic issue: How, precisely, do groups affect their members? A complete answer to this question involves many processes we have already examined in this book (e.g., conformity, persuasion, and attraction). In addition, four aspects of groups themselves play a key role in this regard: *roles, status, norms,* and *cohesiveness.*

■ ROLES: DIFFERENTIATION OF FUNCTIONS WITHIN GROUPS. Think of a group to which you belong or have belonged—anything from the Scouts to a professional association. Now consider this question: Did everyone in the group act in the same way or perform the same functions? Your answer is probably *no.* Different persons performed different tasks and were expected to accomplish different things for the group. In short, they played different **roles.** Sometimes roles are assigned; for instance, a group may select different individuals to serve as its leader, treasurer, or secretary. In other cases, individuals gradually acquire certain roles without being formally assigned to them. Regardless of how roles are acquired, people often *internalize* them; they link their roles to key aspects of their self-concept (see Chapters 2 and 5). When this happens, a role may exert profound effects on a person's behavior, even when she or he is not in the group. For instance, a professor, used to lecturing to students, may lecture his or her family when at home—something I've been accused of doing myself!

roles: Sets of behaviors that individuals occupying specific positions within a group are expected to perform.

Roles help to clarify the responsibilities and obligations of group members, so in this respect, they are very useful. They do have a downside, though. Group members sometimes experience *role conflict*—stress stemming from the fact that two roles they play are somehow at odds with each other. For instance, the parents of young children often experience conflict between their role as *parent* and their role as *student* or *employee,* and this can be highly stressful for them (Williams et al., 1992).

■ STATUS: HIERARCHIES IN GROUPS. When the president of my university enters the room, everyone stands; and no one sits down until she has taken a seat. Why? One answer involves an important aspect of groups or, rather, positions within them: **status**—position or rank within a group. Different roles or positions in a group are often associated with different levels of status, and our president is clearly very high on this dimension. People are often extremely sensitive to status because it is linked to a wide range of desirable outcomes—everything from salary and "perks" to first choice among potential romantic partners (Buss, 1998). For this reason, groups often use status as a means of influencing the behavior of their members: only "good" members—ones who follow the group's rules—receive high status.

Evolutionary psychologists attach considerable importance to status, noting that in many different species, including our own, high status confers important advantages on those who possess it. Specifically, high-status persons have greater access than lower status persons to key resources relating to survival and reproduction, such as food and access to mates. For instance, throughout human history, and in many different societies, high-status males have had access to a larger number of potential mates. As a result, some theorists contend, evolution has favored stronger motivation for status among men than among women. And in fact, men tend to score higher on measures of status motivation than do women (e.g., Pratto, 1996). Whether this is due to evolutionary pressures or other factors, of course, is unclear, but there seems little doubt that high status brings important rewards for persons of both genders, so it is not surprising that people seek to gain it. In short, status is one of the rewards that groups offer members, and as such may be one factor in group influence.

How, precisely, do people acquire high status? As noted by Buss (1998), sheer size may play some role—taller men have an edge. For instance, presidents and heads of large corporations tend to be taller than average (e.g., Gillis, 1982). Whether this advantage of being tall will fade as women move increasingly into such high-status positions remains to be seen, but at least for men, "bigger" does seem to be "better" where status is concerned.

Factors relating to individuals' behavior, too, play a role in acquiring status. Recent research by Tiedens (2001), for instance, suggests that people can sometimes boost their status through intimidation—by appearing angry and threatening. In one intriguing study, Tiedens (2001) showed participants videotapes of President Clinton's grand jury testimony about the Monica Lewinsky scandal. (As you recall, Clinton had an affair with Ms. Lewinsky, who was a young White House intern at the time.) In one segment, Clinton appeared to be sad and expressed regret over his affair with Ms. Lewinsky. In the other, he wagged his finger and appeared to be angry about the investigation into his private life. After watching one of these tapes, participants rated their approval of President Clinton. As shown in Figure 12.2, they expressed higher approval when he was angry than when he was sad.

status: Position or rank within a group.

Several other studies offered additional support for the suggestion that displays of anger can boost one's status. For instance, in another study, participants (employees of a software company) rated each other in terms of how frequently they each

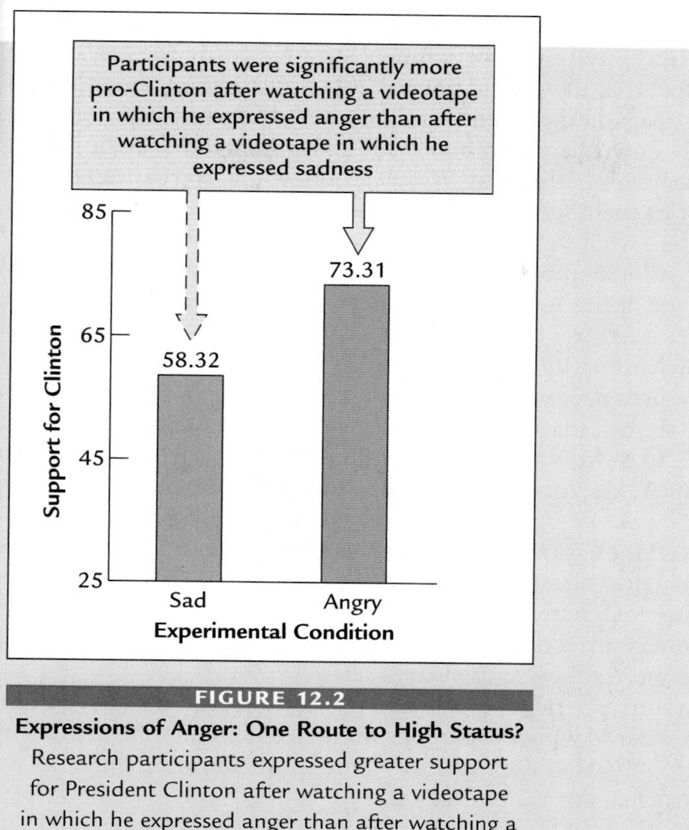

FIGURE 12.2

Expressions of Anger: One Route to High Status? Research participants expressed greater support for President Clinton after watching a videotape in which he expressed anger than after watching a videotape in which he expressed sadness. These findings, and other, related results, suggest that expressing anger may be one technique for acquiring status. [SOURCE: BASED ON DATA FROM TIEDENS, 2001.]

expressed several emotions, including anger and sadness. These ratings were then related to several measures of status in the company—the number of previous promotions they had received, current salary, and predictions of future promotions by the manager. Results indicated that the frequency of sadness was not related to any of these measures, but frequency of expressing anger was strongly related to all three. In other words, the more often employees expressed anger, the higher their current and future predicted status.

Of course, there may be important limits to these findings: Too much anger may reduce rather than increase status, and calm anger may be more effective than overt rage. But overall, Tiedens' (2001) findings suggest that expressing anger may be one means of acquiring status in at least some groups.

■ NORMS: THE RULES OF THE GAME. A third factor responsible for the powerful impact of groups on their members is **norms**—rules established by groups that tell their members how they are supposed to behave. We discussed norms in detail in Chapter 9, so here we simply want to note, again, that they often exert powerful effects on behavior. Moreover, as noted above, adherence to such norms is often a necessary condition for gaining status and other rewards controlled by groups.

norms: Rules within a group indicating how its members should or should not behave.

■ COHESIVENESS: THE FORCE THAT BINDS. Consider two groups. In the first, members like one another very much, strongly desire the goals their group is seeking, and feel that they could not possibly find another group that would better satisfy their needs. In the second, the opposite is true: members don't like one another very much, don't share common goals, and are actively seeking other groups that might offer them a better deal. Which group would exert stronger effects on the behavior of its members? The answer is obvious: the first. The reason for this difference involves what social psychologists describe as **cohesiveness**—all the forces (factors) that cause members to remain in the group, such as liking for the other members and the desire to maintain or increase one's status by belonging to the "right" groups (Festinger et al., 1950). At first glance, it might seem that cohesiveness would involve primarily liking between group members. However, evidence suggests that it involves *depersonalized attraction*—liking for other group members stemming from the fact that they belong to the group and embody or represent its key features, quite apart from their traits as individuals (Hogg & Haines, 1996).

Several factors influence cohesiveness, including (1) status within the group (Cota et al., 1995)—cohesiveness is often higher for high- than for low-status members; (2) the effort required to gain entry into the group—the greater these costs, the higher the cohesiveness (see our discussion of dissonance theory in Chapter 4); (3) the existence of external threats or severe competition—such threats increase members' attraction and commitment to the group; and (4) size—small groups tend to be more cohesive than large ones.

In sum, several aspects of groups—roles, status, norms, and cohesiveness—shape the extent to which the groups influence their members' behavior. We'll have reason to refer to these factors at later points in this chapter, as we discuss specific forms of such group influence.

KEY POINTS

- A *group* is a collection of persons perceived to form a coherent unit to some degree. The extent to which the group is perceived to form a coherent entity is known as entiativity.
- Groups influence their members in many ways, but such effects are often produced through *roles, status, norms,* and *cohesiveness.*
- Men are higher in status motivation than are women; evolutionary psychologists attribute this to the fact that high-status men obtain access to a greater number of mates than do lower status men.
- Recent findings indicate that one technique for gaining status is by expressing anger.

■ How Groups Affect Individual Performance: From Social Facilitation to Social Loafing

Sometimes, when we perform a task, we work totally alone; for instance, you might study alone in your room, and as I write these words, I am alone in my office. In many other cases, even if we are working on a task by ourselves, other people *are* present—for instance, you might study in a crowded library or in your room while your roommate

cohesiveness: All forces (factors) that cause group members to remain in the group.

sleeps or also studies. In other situations, we work on tasks together with other persons as part of a task-performing group. What are the effects of the presence of others on our performance in these various settings? Let's see what research findings have revealed.

Social Facilitation: Performance in the Presence of Others

Imagine that you are a young athlete—an ice-skater, for example—and that you are preparing for your first important competition. You practice your routines alone for several hours each day, month after month. Finally, the big day arrives and you skate out onto the ice in a huge arena filled with the biggest crowd you've ever seen (see Figure 12.3). How will you do? Better or worse than

FIGURE 12.3
Presence of an Audience: Does It Improve or Impair Performance?
Athletes such as the one shown here usually practice alone, but then often perform in front of a large audience. Will this improve or impair their performance? Social psychologists have made interesting discoveries about this issue.

when you practiced alone? This was one of the first topics ever studied in social psychology, and early results (e.g., Allport, 1920) suggested that performance was better when people worked in the presence of others than when they worked alone. For instance, in one study, Allport (1920) asked participants to write down as many associations as they could think of to words printed at the top of an otherwise blank sheet of paper (e.g., "building," "laboratory"). They were allowed to work for three one-minute periods, and they performed this task both alone and in the presence of two other persons. Results were clear: Ninety-three percent of the participants produced more associations when working in the presence of others than when working alone. On the basis of such findings, Allport and other researchers referred to the effects on performance of the presence of other persons as **social facilitation,** because it appeared that when others were present, performance was enhanced. But other research soon called the accuracy of this phrase into question. It was soon clear that sometimes the presence of others facilitated task performance, but sometimes it actually reduced performance (Pessin, 1933). Taking note of this result, researchers today sometimes refer to it as *social facilitation–inhibition,* a phrase that more accurately reflects the complex effects of the presence of other persons. But *why* does the presence of others sometimes enhance and sometimes reduce performance? One elegant answer to this mystery was offered by Robert Zajonc.

■ ZAJONC'S DRIVE THEORY OF SOCIAL FACILITATION: OTHER PERSONS AS A SOURCE OF AROUSAL. Imagine that you are performing some task alone. Then, several other people arrive on the scene and begin to watch you intently. Will your pulse beat quicker because of this audience? Informal experience suggests that it may—that the presence of other persons in the form of an interested audience can increase our activation or arousal. Zajonc suggested that this might provide the solution to the puzzle of social facilitation. Here's how.

When arousal increases, our tendency to perform *dominant responses*—the ones that are most likely to occur in a given situation—also rises. Such dominant responses, in turn, can be correct or incorrect. If this is so, then it follows logically that if the presence of an audience increases arousal, this factor will *improve* performance when dominant responses are correct ones, but may *impair* performance when such responses are incorrect (see Figure 12.4).

Another implication of Zajonc's reasoning—which is known as the **drive theory of social facilitation** because it focuses on arousal or drive—is this: The presence of others will improve individuals' performance when they are highly skilled at the task in question (in this case, their dominant responses would tend to be correct), but will interfere with performance when they are not highly skilled—for instance, when they are learning to perform it. (Under these conditions, their dominant responses would *not* be correct.)

Many studies soon provided support for Zajonc's theory. Individuals were more likely to perform dominant responses in the presence of others than when alone, and their performance on various tasks was either enhanced or impaired, depending on whether these responses were correct or incorrect in each situation (e.g., Geen, 1989; Zajonc & Sales, 1966).

But the story does not end there. Additional research raised an important question: Does social facilitation stem from the *mere physical presence of others?* Or do other factors such as concern about others' evaluations of us also play a role? This question was raised very early in research on social facilitation, and, in essence, it asks, "*How* do audiences or coactors (other persons performing the same task), influence performance?" Is it through increased drive, as

social facilitation: Effects upon performance resulting from the presence of others.

drive theory of social facilitation: A theory suggesting that the mere presence of others is arousing and increases the tendency to perform dominant responses.

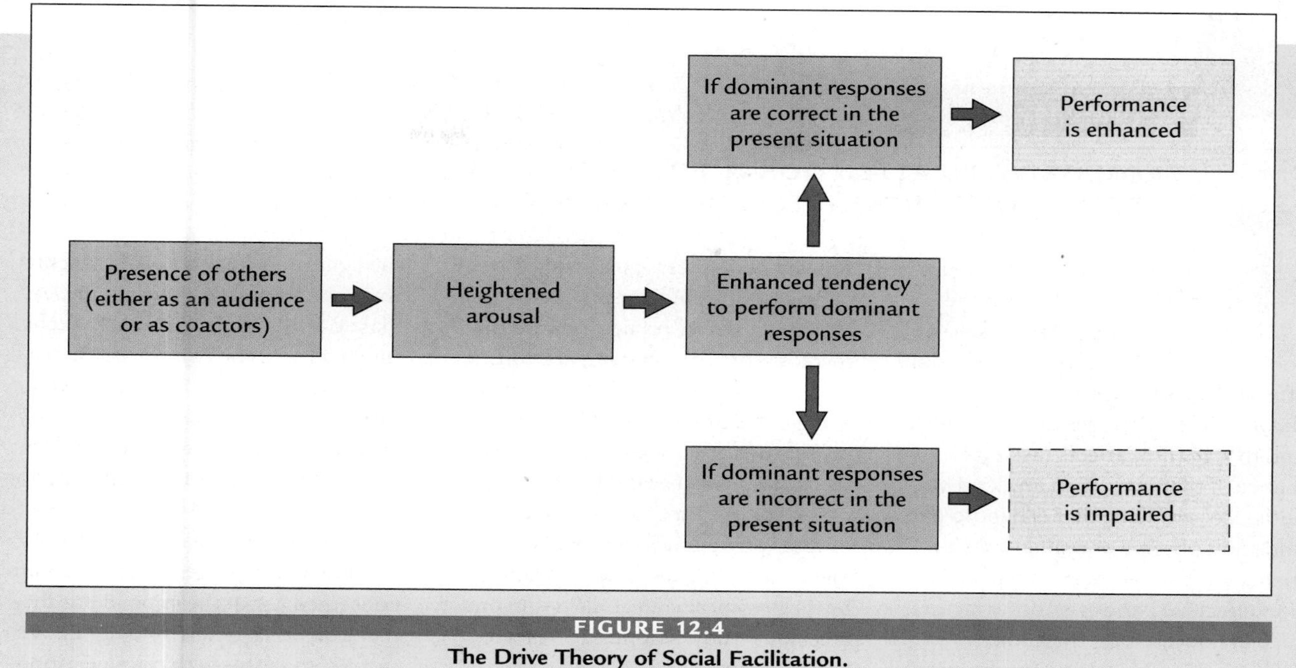

FIGURE 12.4

The Drive Theory of Social Facilitation.
According to the *drive theory of social facilitation* (Zajonc, 1965), the presence of others increases arousal and this, in turn, increases the tendency to perform dominant responses. If these responses are correct, performance is enhanced; if they are incorrect, performance is impaired.

Zajonc suggested, or do other mechanisms also play a role? To see how social psychologists have attempted to answer this question, please read the **Social Psychology: Thirty Years of Progress** section on page 484.

KEY POINTS

- The mere presence of other persons either as an audience or as coactors can influence our performance on many tasks. Such effects are known as *social facilitation* (or as social facilitation–inhibition effects).
- The *drive theory of social facilitation* suggests that the presence of others is arousing and can either increase or reduce performance, depending on whether dominant responses in a given situation are correct or incorrect.
- The *distraction–conflict theory* suggests that the presence of others induces conflicting tendencies to focus on the task being performed and on an audience or coactors. This can result both in increased arousal and narrowed attentional focus.
- Recent findings offer support for the view that several kinds of audiences produce narrowed attentional focus among persons performing a task. This cognitive view of social facilitation helps explain why social facilitation occurs among animals as well as people.

FROM DRIVE TO ATTENTIONAL FOCUS: HOW DOES THE PRESENCE OF OTHERS INFLUENCE TASK PERFORMANCE?

The drive theory of social facilitation suggests that it is the mere presence of other persons that is crucial in social facilitation effects. The presence of others, this theory states, increases drive (arousal) and this, in turn, affects task performance. If that is so, then any kind of audience—even one that is blindfolded and can't observe or evaluate performance—should produce social facilitation effects. If, however, other factors, such as concern over the audience's evaluations (**evaluation apprehension**) play a role, then *type* of audience should matter. In fact, several studies found this to be the case: for instance, social facilitation effects did *not* occur if the audience was blindfolded or showed no interest in watching the person performing a task (Cottrell et al., 1968). Such findings indicate that there is more to social facilitation than just increased drive; concern over being evaluated also plays a role.

Reasonable as these conclusions seem, however, they didn't apply in all cases. For instance, other studies conducted with animals found that performance of simple tasks was facilitated by the presence of an audience. In one ingenious study, Zajonc, Heingartner, and Herman (1969) placed cockroaches in simple mazes where the animals had to run straight ahead to escape from a bright light, or in more complex ones in which they had to choose the correct path to escape from the light. Audiences of other roaches were placed next to the maze in clear plastic boxes so that the cockroaches running through the maze could see them (see Figure 12.5). Results were fully consistent with Zajonc's drive theory: The presence of an audience of four other roaches facilitated performance on the simple maze but reduced it on the complex maze. Because it seems weird to suggest that insects are concerned about the impressions they make on others, these findings do not seem compatible with the suggestion that social facilitation stems solely from evaluation apprehension. So what's the final answer? Modern research suggests that it may involve cognitive mechanisms relating to attentional focus.

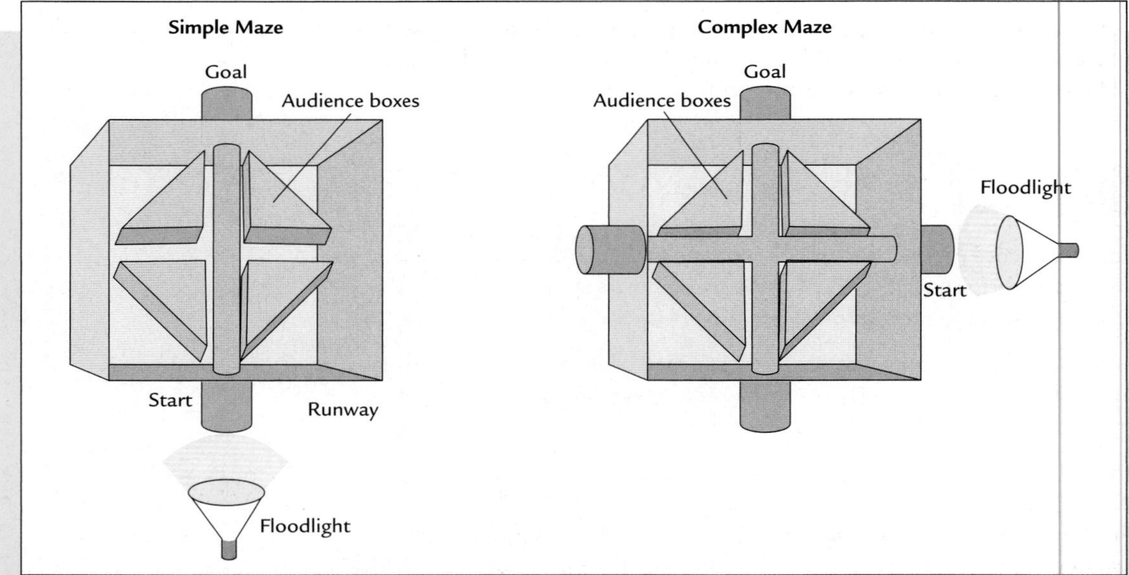

FIGURE 12.5

Social Facilitation among Insects? In an ingenious (and amusing!) study (Zajonc et al., 1969), cockroaches ran through a simple *(left-hand drawing)* or complex *(right-hand drawing)* maze to escape from a bright light. They performed both tasks either in the presence of an audience of four other roaches or alone. Results indicated that an audience facilitated performance on the simple maze but interfered with performance on the more complex maze. These findings are consistent with Zajonc's (1965) *drive theory of social facilitation.*

According to one researcher—Robert S. Baron (not the author of this text)—the presence of other persons, either as an audience or as coactors, can be distracting; and because this presence is distracting, it can threaten the organism performing a task with cognitive overload (e.g., Baron, 1986). Specifically, task performers must divide their attention between the task and the audience, and this generates both increased arousal *and* the possibility of cognitive overload. Cognitive overloads, in turn, can lead to a tendency to restrict one's attention so as to focus only on essential cues or stimuli while "screening out" nonessential ones.

Several findings offer support for this view, known as **distraction–conflict theory** (Baron, 1986). For example, audiences produce social facilitation effects only when directing attention to them conflicts in some way with task demands (Groff, Baron, & Moore, 1983). Similarly, individuals experience greater distraction when they perform various tasks in front of an audience than when they perform them alone (Baron, Moore, & Sanders, 1978).

But a key question remains: Which is more important—increased drive or this tendency toward a narrowed attentional focus? According to Baron (1986), the two theories (drive theory and distraction-conflict theory) make contrasting predictions with respect to one type of task: a poorly learned task that involves only a few key stimuli. Drive theory predicts that the presence of others will facilitate dominant responses, which, on a poorly learned task, are errors. Thus, performance will be reduced by the presence of an audience. In contrast, the attentional focus perspective predicts that the presence of others will cause individuals to focus more closely on the important task-relevant cues, with the result that performance will be improved.

These predictions were tested by Huguet and his colleagues (1999) in a series of ingenious studies. These researchers employed the Stroop task—a task that involves only a small number of stimuli but is poorly learned. On the Stroop task, the names of colors (red, green) are printed either in the color named by the word (e.g., the word *red* is printed in red) or in another, different color (e.g., the word *red* is printed in green). Typically, individuals perform more slowly (i.e., read more slowly) when the word and ink color do not match—this is known as *Stroop interference.*

In several studies, Huguet and his colleagues (1999) had participants perform the Stroop task either alone or in the presence of several kinds of audience: an audience that was busy reading a book (*inattentive–busy* audience), an audience hidden from the participants' view (*invisible* audience), and an audience that watched the participants as they performed (*attentive* audience). In addition, after completing the task, participants were asked to recognize the words they had previously seen among other words they had not seen. As you can see in Figure 12.6, results offered strong support for the attentional focus

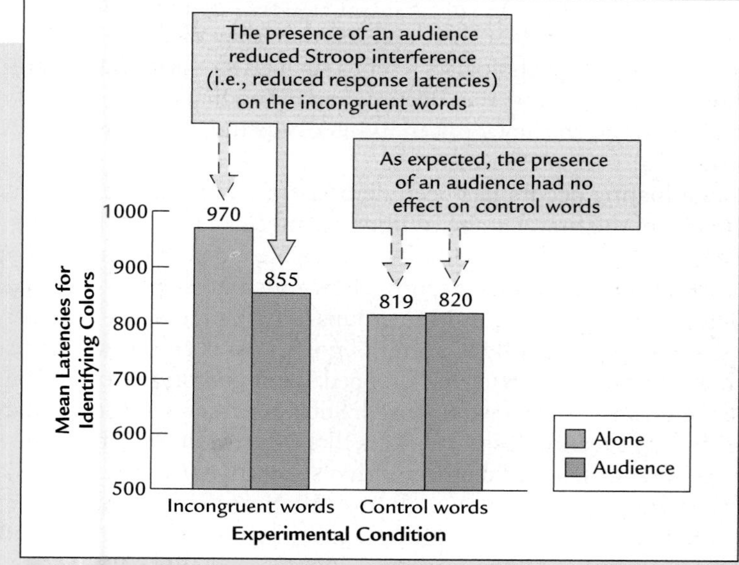

FIGURE 12.6

Social Facilitation: The Role of Attentional Focus. The presence of an audience reduced interference on the Stroop task—a sign that the presence of others caused persons performing this task to narrow their attentional focus. Interestingly, an attentive audience or one that was not visible to task-performers produced stronger effects than an inattentive audience.

[SOURCE: BASED ON DATA FROM HUGUET ET AL., 1999.]

(continued)

theory: Stroop interference was greatest in the alone condition but was reduced in the audience conditions—and especially in the attentive and invisible audience conditions. This would be expected if the presence of an audience caused participants to focus their attention on the ink colors (the essential cues) while ignoring the words. In addition, participants did better on the recognition memory task in the alone condition than in the others; this was predicted, because if an audience is distracting, this would interfere with memory.

In sum, it appears that cognitive processes—not just increased arousal—play an important role in social facilitation. The presence of others may well produce increased arousal, but it may do so because of the cognitive demands of paying attention both to an audience and to the task being performed, as distraction–conflict theory suggests; and it may influence task performance by inducing a narrowed attention focus. One advantage of this cognitive perspective is that it helps explain why animals as well as people are affected by the presence of an audience. After all, animals, too (even cockroaches), can experience conflicting tendencies to work on a task *and* pay attention to an audience. A theory that can explain similar patterns of behavior among organisms ranging from cockroaches to human beings is powerful, indeed. So, clearly, social psychologists have made considerable progress in their efforts to answer the question, "Why does social facilitation occur?"

Social Loafing: Letting Others Do the Work When Part of a Group

Suppose that you and several other people are helping a friend move. In order to lift the heaviest pieces of furniture, you all pitch in. Will all of the people helping exert equal effort? Probably not. Some will take as much of the load as they can, while others will simply hang on, perhaps grunting loudly in order to pretend that they are helping more than they are.

This pattern is quite common in situations in which groups perform what are known as **additive tasks**—ones in which the contributions of each member are combined into a single group output. On such tasks, some persons work hard while others goof off, doing less than their share and less than they might do if working alone (see Figure 12.7). Social psychologists refer to such effects as **social loafing**—reductions in motivation and effort that occur when individuals work collectively in a group compared to when they work individually as independent coactors (Karau & Williams, 1993).

That social loafing occurs has been demonstrated in many experiments. For example, in one of the first, Latané, Williams, and Harkins (1979) asked groups of male students to clap or cheer as loudly as possible at specific times, supposedly so that the experimenter could determine how much noise people make in social settings. They performed these tasks in groups of two, four, or six persons. Results indicated that although the total amount of noise rose as group size increased, the amount produced *by each participant* dropped. In other words, each person put out less and less effort as group size increased. Such effects are not restricted to simple and seemingly meaningless situations like this; on the contrary, they appear to be quite general in scope and occur with respect to many different tasks—cognitive ones as well as ones involving physical effort (Weldon & Mustari, 1988; Williams & Karau, 1991). Moreover, they appear among both genders, and among children as well as adults. The only exception to the generality of such effects seems

evaluation apprehension: Concern over being evaluated by others. Such concern can increase arousal and so contribute to social facilitation.

distraction–conflict theory: A theory suggesting that social facilitation stems from the conflict produced when individuals attempt, simultaneously, to pay attention to other persons and to the task being performed.

additive tasks: Tasks for which the group product is the sum or combination of the efforts of individual members.

social loafing: Reductions in motivation and effort when individuals work collectively in a group compared to when they work individually or as independent coactors.

FIGURE 12.7
Social Loafing: A Danger When People Work Together.
When several persons work on a task, some may engage in *social loafing*—they pretend to work hard but, in fact, put out less effort than they would if they were working alone.

to be a cultural one: social loafing effects don't seem to occur in *collectivistic* cultures, such as those in many Asian countries—cultures in which the collective good is more highly valued than individual accomplishment or achievement (Earley, 1993). In fact, in such cultures, people seem to work *harder* when in groups than they do when alone. So, as we've noted repeatedly, cultural factors sometimes play a very important role in social behavior.

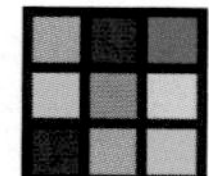

Aside from this important exception, however, social loafing appears to be a pervasive fact of social life. If this is indeed true, then two important questions arise: *Why* do such effects occur? And what steps can be taken to reduce their occurrence?

■ THE COLLECTIVE EFFORT MODEL: AN EXPECTANCY THEORY OF SOCIAL LOAFING. While many different explanations for the occurrence of social loafing have been proposed (e.g., Latané, 1981), perhaps the most comprehensive explanation of social loafing offered to date, however, is the **collective effort model** (CEM for short), proposed by Karau and Williams (1993). These researchers suggest that social loafing can be understood by extending a basic theory of individual motivation—*expectancy–valence theory*—to situations involving group performance. Expectancy–valence theory suggests that individuals will work hard on a given task only to the extent that the following conditions exist: (1) They believe that working hard will lead to better performance (*expectancy*); (2) they believe that better performance will be recognized and rewarded (*instrumentality*); and (3) the rewards obtained are ones they value and desire (*valence*).

According to Karau and Williams (1993), these links often appear weaker when individuals work together in groups than when they work alone. Consider *expectancy*—the belief that increased effort will lead to better performance. This may be high when individuals work alone but lower when they work together in groups, because people realize that other factors aside from their own effort will determine the group's performance—for instance, the amount of effort exerted by other members. Similarly, *instrumentality*—the belief that good performance will be recognized and rewarded—may also be weaker when people work together in groups. They realize that valued outcomes are divided among all group members and that,

collective effort model: An explanation of social loafing suggesting that perceived links between individuals' effort and their outcomes are weaker when they work together with others in a group. This, in turn, produces tendencies toward social loafing.

as a result, they may not get their fair share given their level of effort. CEM theory suggests that because there is more uncertainty between how hard people work and the rewards they receive, they engage in social loafing. After all, why work hard when this may fail to produce the outcomes you desire?

Research findings have confirmed many predictions derived from the CEM (e.g., Karau & Williams, 1993), so this model appears to offer a useful framework for understanding the nature of social loafing and why it occurs. For example, the CEM predicts that social loafing will be weakest when (1) individuals work in small rather than large groups; (2) when they work on tasks that are intrinsically interesting or important to them; (3) when they work with respected others (friends, teammates, etc.); (4) when they perceive that their contributions to the group product are unique or important; (5) when they expect their coworkers to perform poorly; and (6) when they come from cultures that emphasize individual effort and outcomes rather than group outcomes (Western cultures versus Asian ones, for instance). The results of the meta-analysis offered support for all of these predictions. In others words, social loafing was weakest and strongest under conditions predicted by CEM theory.

While the CEM provides a useful framework for understanding the nature and causes of social loafing, it also suggests that this effect is a potentially serious problem for task-performing groups. According to the CEM, social loafing is most likely to occur under conditions in which individuals' contributions can't be evaluated, when people work on tasks they find boring or uninspiring, and when they work with others they don't greatly respect or don't know very well. Unfortunately, these conditions exist in many settings in which groups of persons work together. If social loafing is a common occurrence, then an important question arises: What steps can be taken to reduce it? Let's see what research findings suggest.

■ REDUCING SOCIAL LOAFING: SOME USEFUL TECHNIQUES. The most obvious way to reduce social loafing involves making the output or effort of each participant readily identifiable (e.g., Williams, Harkins, & Latané, 1981). Under these conditions, people can't sit back and let others do their work, so social loafing is in fact reduced. Second, groups can reduce social loafing by increasing group members' commitment to successful task performance (Brickner, Harkins, & Ostrom, 1986). Pressures toward working hard will then serve to offset temptations to engage in social loafing. Third, social loafing can be reduced by increasing the apparent importance or value of a task (Karau & Williams, 1993). Fourth, social loafing declines when individuals view their contributions to the task as unique rather than merely redundant with those of others (Weldon & Mustari, 1988).

Together, these steps can sharply reduce social loafing—and the temptation to "goof off" at the expense of others. (Please see the **Ideas to Take with You—And Use!** feature on page 513 for some practical suggestions on how you can both benefit from social facilitation and protect yourself against social loafing by others.)

KEY POINTS

- When individuals work together on a task, *social loafing*—reduced output by each group member—sometimes occurs.
- According to the *collective effort model,* such effects occur because when working together with others as compared to working alone, individuals experience weaker links between their effort and their outcomes.
- Social loafing can be reduced in several ways: by making outputs individually identifiable, by increasing commitment to the task and sense of task importance, and by assuring that each member's contributions to the task are unique.

Coordination in Groups: Cooperation or Conflict?

In Chapter 10, we noted that individuals often engage in *prosocial behavior*—actions that benefit others but have no obvious or immediate benefits for the persons who perform them. While such behavior is far from rare, another pattern—one in which helping is mutual and both sides benefit—is even more common. This pattern is known as **cooperation** and involves situations in which groups work together to attain shared goals. Cooperation can be highly beneficial; indeed, through this process, groups of persons can attain goals they could never hope to reach by themselves. Surprisingly, though, cooperation *does* not always develop. Frequently, persons belonging to a group try to coordinate their efforts but somehow fail in the attempt.

Even worse, they may perceive their personal interests as incompatible, with the result that instead of working together and coordinating their efforts, they work *against* each other, often, in this way, producing negative results for both sides. This is known as **conflict**—a process in which individuals or groups perceive that others have taken or will soon take actions incompatible with their own interests (see Figure 12.8). Conflict is indeed a process, for as you probably know from your own experience, it has a nasty way of escalating, starting, perhaps, with simple mistrust and quickly moving through a spiral of anger, resentment, and actions designed to harm the other side. When carried to extremes, the ultimate effects can be very harmful to both sides. Let's see what social psychologists have learned about both patterns of behavior.

cooperation: Behavior in which groups work together to attain shared goals.

conflict: A process in which individuals or groups perceive that others have taken or will soon take actions incompatible with their own interests.

Cooperation: Working with Others to Achieve Shared Goals

Cooperation is often highly beneficial to the persons involved. A key question, then, is this: Why don't group members always coordinate their activities in this manner? One answer is straightforward: They don't cooperate because

FIGURE 12.8

Conflict: Actions Incompatible with Others' Interests.
Conflict is often defined as a process in which individuals or groups perceive that others have taken or will soon take actions incompatible with their own interests. That is certainly the case in this cartoon!
[SOURCE: DILBERT REPRINTED BY PERMISSION OF UNITED FEATURE SYNDICATE, INC.]

some goals that people seek simply can't be shared. Several people seeking the same job, promotion, or romantic partner can't combine forces to attain these goals: the rewards can go to only one in each case. In such cases, cooperation is not possible, and *conflict* may quickly develop as each person (or group) attempts to maximize his or her own outcomes (Tjosvold, 1993).

In many other situations, however, cooperation *could* develop but does not. This is precisely the kind of situation that has been of most interest to social psychologists, who have tried to identify the factors that tip the balance either toward or away from cooperation. We'll now consider some of the most important of these factors.

■ SOCIAL DILEMMAS: SITUATIONS IN WHICH COOPERATION COULD OCCUR BUT OFTEN DOESN'T. Many situations in which cooperation could develop but does not can be described as ones involving **social dilemmas;** these are situations in which each person can increase his or her individual gains by acting in a purely selfish manner, but if all (or most) persons do the same thing, the outcomes experienced by all are reduced (Komorita & Parks, 1994). As a result, the persons in such situations must deal with *mixed motives:* there are reasons to cooperate (avoid negative outcomes for all), but also reasons to *defect*—to do what is best for oneself. After all, if only one or a few persons engage in such behavior, they will benefit while the others will not. A classic illustration of this kind of situation, and one in which it is reduced to its simplest form, is known as the *prisoner's dilemma* (see Figure 12.9). Here,

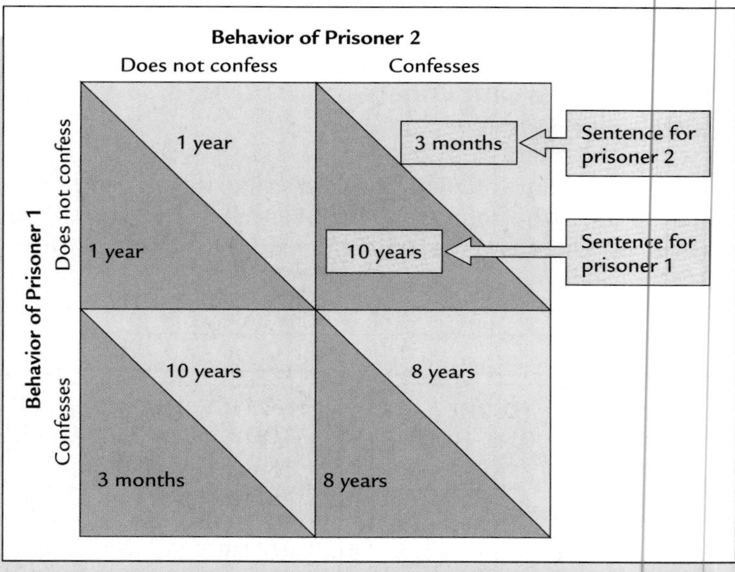

FIGURE 12.9

The Prisoner's Dilemma: To Cooperate or Compete—That Is the Question!

In the prisoner's dilemma, a simple form of social dilemma, two persons can choose either to cooperate or to compete with one another. If both choose to cooperate, each receives very favorable outcomes. If both choose to compete, each receives negative outcomes. If one chooses to compete while the other chooses to cooperate, the first person receives a much better outcome than the second person. Research findings indicate that many factors influence the choices people make in this kind of mixed-motive situation.

social dilemmas: Situations in which each person can increase his or her individual gains by acting in one way, but if all (or most) persons do the same thing, the outcomes experienced by all are reduced.

there are two persons, and each can choose either to cooperate or to compete. If both cooperate, then they both experience large gains. If both compete, each person experiences much smaller gains, or actual losses. The most interesting pattern occurs if one chooses to compete while the other chooses to cooperate. In this case, the first person experiences much larger gains than the second, trusting one. This situation is called the "prisoner's dilemma" because it reflects a dilemma faced by two suspects who have been caught by police. Assume that the police do not have enough evidence to convict either person. If both stick to their stories (i.e., they both cooperate), they will be set free or receive a very short sentence for a minor crime. If both confess, they will both be convicted and receive stiff sentences. If one confesses (i.e., turns states' evidence) but the other does not, the police will have enough evidence to convict both, but the person who confesses will receive a lighter sentence because of the help she or he has given. As you can see, this situations captures the essence of many social dilemmas: each suspect experiences pressures both to cooperate and to compete. Social psychologists have used this type of situation, or ones very much like it (simulated, of course!), to examine the factors that tip the balance toward trust and cooperation or mistrust and competition (e.g., Insko et al., 2001). The findings of such research indicate that many factors play a role in whether cooperation or competition develops. (For another real-life example of a social dilemma, see the **Beyond the Headlines** section on page 492.)

■ FACTORS INFLUENCING COOPERATION: RECIPROCITY, PERSONAL ORIENTATIONS, AND COMMUNICATION. While many different factors determine whether individuals will choose to cooperate with others in situations involving the mixed motives generated by social dilemmas, three appear to be most important: tendencies toward *reciprocity, personal orientations* concerning cooperation, and *communication.*

Reciprocity is probably the most obvious of these factors. Throughout life, we tend to follow this principle, treating others very much as they have treated us (e.g., Pruitt & Carnevale, 1993). In choosing between cooperation and competition, too, we seem to adopt this general rule. When others cooperate with us and put their selfish interests aside, we usually respond in kind. In contrast, if they defect and pursue their own interests, we generally do the same (Kerr & Kaufman-Gilliland, 1994).

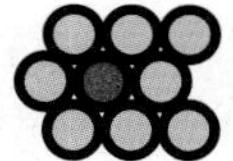

Evolutionary psychologists have noted that this tendency to adopt reciprocity where cooperation is concerned is not restricted to human beings; it has been observed among other species, too (e.g., bats and chimpanzees; Buss, 1999). This, in turn, raises an intriguing question: Because "cheaters" (those who do not return cooperation after receiving it) often gain an advantage, how could a strong tendency toward reciprocity have evolved? One possible answer is provided by the theory of *reciprocal altruism* (e.g., Cosmides & Tooby, 1992). This theory suggests that by sharing resources such as food, organisms increase their chances of survival, and thus the likelihood that they will pass their genes on to the next generation. Further, they tend to share in such a way that the benefits are relatively great for the recipients of such cooperation while the costs are relatively minimal to the provider. For instance, if one hunter has more meat than he and his family can eat, while another is starving, the costs to the first for sharing are minimal, while the gains to the second are great. When the situation is reversed, cooperation will again benefit both parties and increase their chances of survival. In contrast, organisms that act in a purely selfish manner do not gain such benefits.

A second factor that exerts strong effects on cooperation is *personal orientation* toward such behavior. Think about the many people you have known during your life. Can you remember ones who strongly preferred cooperation—people who could be counted on to try work together with other group members in almost every situation? In contrast, can you remember others who usually preferred to pursue their own selfish interests and could *not* be relied on to cooperate?

reciprocity: A basic rule of social life suggesting that individuals tend to treat others as these persons have treated them.

BEYOND THE HEADLINES: AS SOCIAL PSYCHOLOGISTS SEE IT

"WE'RE ALL IN THIS TOGETHER, SO WHY DOESN'T EVERYONE DO THEIR SHARE?": A SOCIAL DILEMMA IN THE OFFICE

The Scariest Thing in Many Offices Is the Scuzzy Fridge

Wall Street Journal, June 22, 1998—A monster is lurking in companies across the nation. It's the office refrigerator, bulging at the seams with leftover plastic–foam boxes, forgotten Tupperware containers, and open cans of Coke. . . . Marc Grendon in San Francisco didn't think condiments could go bad until he tried to use some mustard and ketchup from the office fridge shared by 60 people. The ketchup was putrid and the mustard looked fossilized. "I thought these things could last forever," Mr. Grendon says. "After this kind of experience, you don't put anything directly on your food until you test it first." But crusty condiments are nothing compared to what Kay Norberg has seen at S&S Public Relations in Northbrook, Illinois. Sure, there was moldy fruit salad but what really got to her was the frozen lizard. It turns out that the reptile had died in her sleep and her owner, Allison Clark, wanted to have her autopsied. But Mrs. Norberg, who calls herself the "office mom" because she is always picking up after her co-workers, had no idea whom the cryogenic creature belonged to. The problem of course, is that while everyone contributes to the mess in an office fridge, few take ownership for what's inside. . . .

Steven J. Brams, a professor of politics at New York University, attributes the multiplying mold in many office refrigerators to a "free rider" effect. As he puts it, it's "the idea that you don't have to pay for a public good or something that everybody can share. In other words," Dr. Brams explains, "you'd be a sucker to clean up after others."

Karen Johnson concedes she falls into that category. "Chief of the Kitchen Police," in her Washington, D.C. office, Ms. Johnson refuses to use the fridge in her office because it gets so gross. But somehow, she always winds up cleaning it on what she calls a "day of purging." "I've tried going as long as three months, thinking somebody who puts food in there will get so disgusted they will do it. But it never happens," says Ms. Johnson. "They outwait me every time. They know sooner or later I'll clean it. . . ."

Can you figure out what's going on here? Wouldn't it be to everyone's advantage to help keep the refrigerator clean? Why not cooperate on this simple chore? The answer, we think, lies in the fact that this situation is simply a social dilemma. Every person who uses the refrigerator gets the benefits of this appliance, but all hope that someone else will keep it clean. In other words, each person wishes to reap the benefits without incurring any of the costs. True: If people cooperated in keeping the refrigerator clean (e.g., by taking turns), everyone would benefit—it would remain clean and safe to use. But by failing to do their share, they can maximize their own gains, at least in the short run.

What do you think of Dr. Bram's comments about "free riders"? This term is often used to refer to the people who don't do their share in situations involving social loafing. Do you think this is a factor, too? Perhaps, but because keeping the refrigerator clean is not an assigned task or one toward which everyone is working, we think that it is more appropriate to view this situation as a social dilemma. We realize that this is not the most earth-shaking example of a social dilemma—the consequences of failing to cooperate are not very great. But it is precisely the kind of social dilemma we all encounter in our daily lives—a situation in which we can choose to cooperate with others or pursue our own selfish ends. Can people be encouraged to behave in a more cooperative manner in such contexts? Absolutely. Please read on to find out what social psychologists have learned about this issue—which certainly far transcends office refrigerators in its importance!

You probably have little difficulty in bringing examples of both types to mind, for large individual differences in the tendencies to cooperate exist. Such differences, in turn, seem to reflect contrasting perspectives toward working with others—perspectives that individuals carry with them from situation to situation, even over relatively long periods of time (e.g., Knight & Dubro, 1984). Specifically, research findings indicate that individuals can possess any one of three distinct orientations toward situations involving social dilemmas: (1) a *cooperative* orientation, in which they prefer to maximize the joint outcomes received by all the persons involved; (2) an *individualistic* orientation, in which they focus primarily on maximizing their own outcomes; or (3) a *competitive* orientation, in which they focus primarily on defeating others—on obtaining better outcomes than other persons do (DeDreu & McCusker, 1997; Van Lange & Kuhlman, 1994). These orientations exert strong effects on how people behave in many situations, so they are an important factor in whether cooperation does or does not develop.

A third factor that influences the choice between cooperation and competition is *communication.* Common sense suggests that if individuals can discuss the situation with others, they may soon conclude that the best option is for everyone to cooperate; after all, this will result in gains for all. Surprisingly, though, early research on this possibility produced mixed results. In many situations, the opportunity for group members to communicate with each other about what they should do in the situation did *not* increase cooperation. On the contrary, group members seemed to use this opportunity primarily to *threaten* one another, with the result that cooperation did not occur (e.g., Deutsch & Krauss, 1960; Stech & McClintock, 1981). Is this always the case? Fortunately, research findings point to more optimistic conclusions: apparently, communication between group members *can* lead to increased cooperation, provided certain conditions are met (e.g., Kerr & Kaufman-Gilliland, 1994; Sally, 1998). Specifically, beneficial effects can and do occur if group members make personal commitments to cooperate with one another and if these commitments are backed up by strong, personal norms to honor them (see Chapter 9 for a discussion of the nature and impact of social norms; e.g., Kerr et al., 1997).

In sum, several factors determine what individuals do in situations in which they can choose between cooperation and defection. The choice, in short, is neither simple nor automatic; rather, it emerges from a complex interaction between social and personal factors.

■ THE DISCONTINUITY EFFECT: WHY GROUPS ARE MORE COMPETITIVE THAN INDIVIDUALS. So far, we have focused on cooperation between individuals. But this is not the only situation that exists where cooperation is concerned. Groups, too, can choose to cooperate or compete with each other. Businesses, for instance, usually compete for customers and markets, but sometimes, they form a *consortium*—an association whose members cooperate with one another. For example, hospitals in the United States have recently begun to cooperate in this manner, so that one specializes in heart surgery, another in reconstructive surgery for persons after serious accidents, and so on. The reason for such cooperation is clear: The facilities for each of these specialties are so expensive, it makes more sense for the hospitals to divide them rather than try to compete by offering every service.

Research findings indicate, however, that such *intergroup cooperation* may be difficult to achieve. Specifically, many studies have found evidence for a *discontinuity effect*—a greater tendency for groups than individuals to compete in mixed-motive situations of the type discussed above (e.g., the prisoner's dilemma; e.g., Insko et al., 2001; Schopler et al., 2001). Why is this so? Insko and colleagues (2001) point to three factors that may play a role. First, people tend to distrust other groups more than other persons; in fact, they expect individuals to cooperate with them, but they are much less optimistic about receiving such treatment from groups. Second, when groups act in a selfish, competitive manner, their members can convince each other that this is appropriate; individuals, in contrast, must handle such selfishness without social support. Third, individuals know that they are readily identifiable to their opponents; members of groups, in contrast, can enjoy a degree of anonymity. Evidence for the influence of all of these factors exists, so it appears that the tendency for groups to be more competitive than individuals stems from several factors (e.g., Schopler & Insko, 1999). For instance, consider one study conducted by Insko and his colleagues (Insko et al., 2001).

In this experiment, participants played a prisoner's dilemma game either as individuals or as three-person groups. Half were led to believe that they would make the choice to cooperate or compete with their opponent only once, while others were lead to believe that they would make this choice a number of times. Insko and his colleagues (2001) predicted that when groups anticipated continuing interactions, they would become less competitive because a longer term orientation would work against the three factors mentioned above—distrust, social support for acting in a purely selfish manner, and reduced identifiability. In contrast, because individuals already show a much higher level of cooperation, this factor would not influence their choices concerning cooperation or competition to as large a degree. As you can see from Figure 12.10, this is precisely what happened: groups showed a much lower tendency to make a competitive choice when they anticipated multiple contacts with their opponent, while individuals showed a much smaller reduction.

In sum, cooperation can occur between groups as well as within them, and research findings confirm what is apparent in the social world around us: Intergroup cooperation may be even harder to attain, for several reasons, than intragroup cooperation.

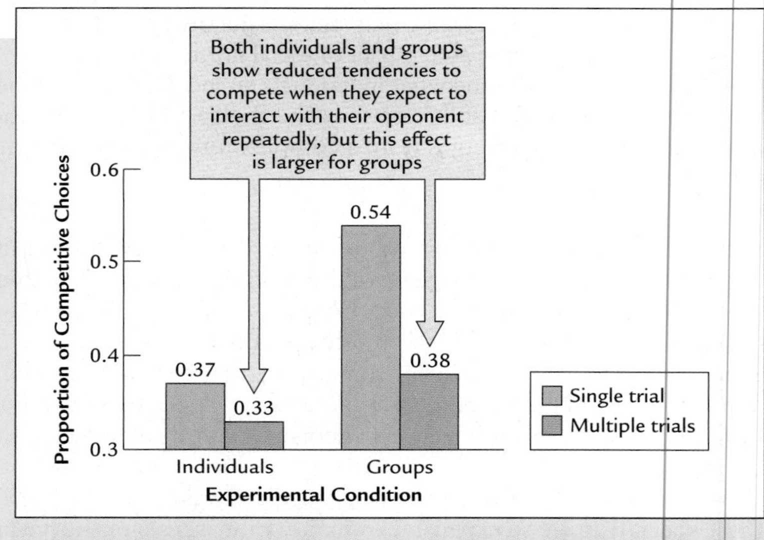

FIGURE 12.10

Reducing the Discontinuity Effect: The Potential Benefits of a Long-Term Orientation.

When participants expected to interact with their opponents repeatedly, both individuals and groups showed reduced tendencies to compete. However, these reductions were much larger for groups. These findings are consistent with theoretical explanations for the discontinuity effect—why groups are more competitive than individuals.

[SOURCE: BASED ON DATA FROM INSKO ET AL., 2001.]

KEY POINTS

- *Cooperation*—working together with others to obtain shared goals—is a common aspect of social life.
- However, cooperation does not develop in many situations in which it is possible. One reason is that because such situations often involve *social dilemmas,* in which individuals can increase their own gains by defection.
- Several factors influence whether cooperation occurs in such situations. These include strong tendencies toward *reciprocity,* personal orientation toward cooperation, and communication.
- Evolutionary psychologists suggest that our tendency to reciprocate may result from the fact that organisms that cooperate are more likely to survive and reproduce than organisms that do not.
- The discontinuity effect refers to the fact that groups are more likely to compete with one another than are individuals. In short, intergroup cooperation may be more difficult to attain than intragroup cooperation.

Conflict: Its Nature, Causes, and Effects

If prosocial behavior (see Chapter 10) and cooperation constitute one end of a dimension describing how individuals and groups work together, then *conflict* lies at or near the other end. As we noted earlier, conflict is a process in which one individual or group perceives that others have taken or will soon take actions incompatible with its own interests. The key elements in conflict, then, seem to include (1) opposing interests between individuals or groups, (2) recognition of such opposition, (3) the belief by each side that the other will act to interfere with these interests, and (4) actions that in fact produce such interference (see Figure 12.11).

Unfortunately, conflict is an all too common part of social life and can be extremely costly to both sides. What factors cause such seemingly irrational

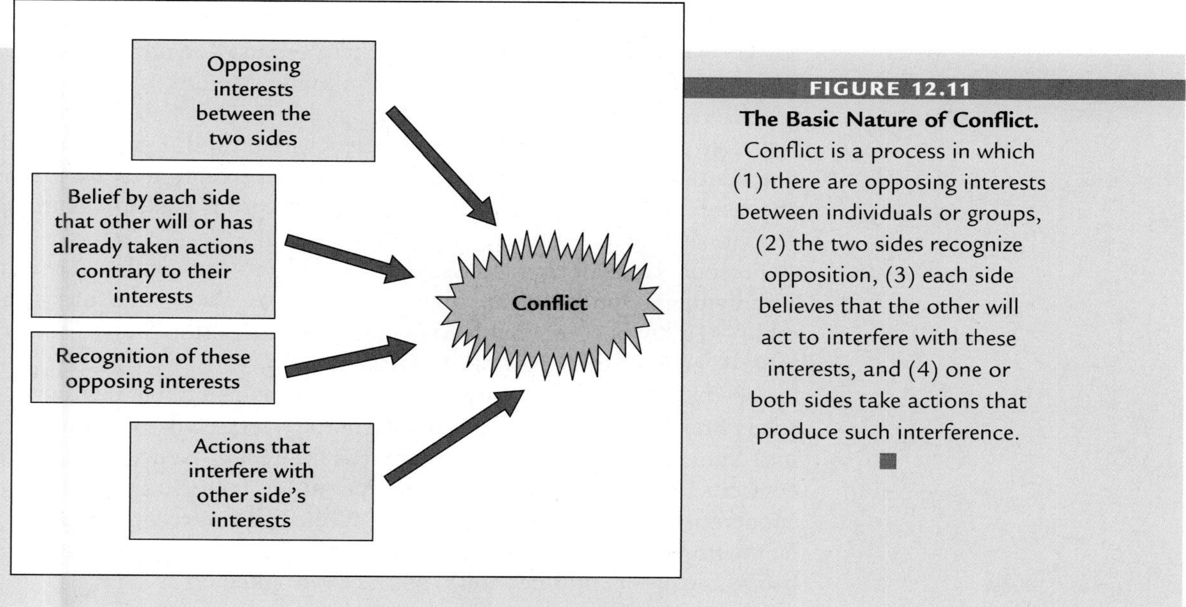

FIGURE 12.11
The Basic Nature of Conflict. Conflict is a process in which (1) there are opposing interests between individuals or groups, (2) the two sides recognize opposition, (3) each side believes that the other will act to interfere with these interests, and (4) one or both sides take actions that produce such interference.

behavior? Perhaps even more important, what can be done to reduce it? These are the key questions that social psychologists have addressed in their research.

■ MAJOR CAUSES OF CONFLICT. Our definition of conflict emphasizes the existence of incompatible interests, and recognition of this fact by the parties involved. Indeed, this is *the* defining feature of conflicts. Interestingly, though, conflicts sometimes fail to develop even though both sides have incompatible interests; and in other cases, conflicts occur when the two sides don't really have opposing interests—they may simply *believe* that these exist (e.g., DeDreu & Van Lange, 1995; Tjosvold & DeDreu, 1997). In short, conflict involves much more than opposing interests. In fact, a growing body of evidence suggests that *social* factors may play as strong a role as incompatible interests in initiating conflicts.

One social factor that plays a role in this respect consists of what have been termed *faulty attributions*—errors concerning the causes behind others' behavior (e.g., Baron, 1989b). When individuals find that their interests have been thwarted, they generally try to determine *why* this occurred. Was it bad luck? A lack of planning on their part? A lack of needed resources? Or was it due to intentional interference by another person or group? If they conclude that the latter is true, then the seeds for an intense conflict may be planted—*even if other persons actually had nothing to do with the situation.* In other words, erroneous attributions concerning the causes of negative outcomes can and often do play an important role in conflicts, and sometimes cause them to occur when they could readily have been avoided. (See Chapter 11 for a related discussion of the effects of the hostile attributional bias.)

Another social factor that seems to play an important role in conflict is what might be termed *faulty communication*—the fact that individuals sometimes communicate with others in a way that angers or annoys them, even though it is not their intention to do so. Have you ever been on the receiving end of harsh criticism—criticism you felt was unfair, insensitive, and not in the least helpful? The results of several studies indicate that feedback of this type, known as *destructive criticism,* can leave the recipient hungry for revenge—and so set the stage for conflicts that, again, do not necessarily stem from incompatible interests (e.g., Baron, 1990a; Cropanzano, 1993).

A third social cause of conflict involves the tendency to perceive our own views as objective and as reflecting reality, but those of others as biased by their ideology (e.g., Keltner & Robinson, 1997; Robinson et al., 1995). As a result of this tendency, we tend to magnify differences between our views and those of others, and so also exaggerate conflicts of interest between us. Research findings indicate that this tendency is stronger for groups or individuals who currently hold a dominant or powerful position (Keltner & Robinson, 1997). This, in turn, often leads to what is known as the *status quo bias*—a tendency for powerful groups defending the current status quo to be less accurate at intergroup perception than the groups that are challenging them. For instance, they perceive their position as much more reasonable or objective than it is.

Personal traits or characteristics, too, play a role in conflict. For example, *Type A* individuals—ones who are highly competitive, always in a hurry, and quite irritable—tend to become involved in conflicts more often than calmer and less irritable Type B persons (Baron, 1989a).

So where does all this leave us? With the conclusion that conflict does *not* stem solely from opposing interests. On the contrary, it often derives from social factors—long-standing grudges or resentment, the desire for revenge, inaccurate social perceptions, poor communication, and similar factors. In short, conflict, like cooperation, has many different roots. While the most central of these may indeed be incompatible interests, this is far from the entire story, and the social and cognitive causes of conflict should not be overlooked.

Resolving Conflicts: Some Useful Techniques

Because conflicts are often very costly, the persons involved in such situations usually want to resolve them as quickly as possible. What steps are most useful for reaching this goal? While many steps may succeed, two seem especially useful—*bargaining* and *superordinate goals.*

■ BARGAINING: THE UNIVERSAL PROCESS. By far the most common strategy for resolving conflicts is **bargaining** or negotiation (e.g., Pruitt & Carnevale, 1993). In this process, opposing sides exchange offers, counteroffers, and concessions, either directly or through representatives. If the process is successful, a solution acceptable to both sides is attained and the conflict is resolved. If, instead, bargaining is unsuccessful, costly deadlock may result and the conflict will intensify. What factors determine which of these outcomes occurs? As you can probably guess, many factors play a role.

First, and perhaps most obvious, the outcome of bargaining is determined, in part, by the specific tactics adopted by the bargainers. Many of these are designed to accomplish a key goal: to reduce the opponent's *aspirations* so that this person or group becomes convinced that it cannot get what it wants and should, instead, settle for something quite favorable to the other side. Tactics for accomplishing this goal include (1) beginning with an extreme initial offer—one that is very favorable to the side proposing it; (2) the "big lie" technique—convincing the other side that one's break-even point is much higher than it is so that they offer more than would otherwise be the case (for example, a used car salesperson may claim that she will lose money on the deal if she lowers the price when, in fact, this is false); and (3) convincing the other side that you have an "out"—if they won't make a deal with you, you can go elsewhere and get even better terms (Thompson, L., 1998).

Do these tactics seem ethical to you? This is a complex question on which individuals may well differ, but social psychologists who have conducted research on this question (Robinson et al., 1998) have found that there is general agreement that four types of tactics are questionable from an ethical standpoint: (1) *attacking an opponent's network*—manipulating or interfering with an opponent's network of support and information; (2) *false promises*—offering false commitments or lying about future intentions; (3) *misrepresentation*—providing misleading or false information to an opponent; and (4) *inappropriate information gathering*—collecting information in an unethical manner (e.g., through theft, spying, etc.). These tactics are measured by a questionnaire known as the Self-reported Inappropriate Negotiation Strategies Scale (or SINS for short).

Perhaps more interesting than the fact that such tactics exist is the finding that, depending on their role as a negotiator, individuals find them more or less acceptable. At first glance, you might expect that aggressive negotiators intent on winning might view such tactics as more appropriate than will negotiators who adopt a more defensive posture. In fact, though, exactly the opposite seems to be true. Negotiators who must defend themselves against opponents they view as unprincipled and aggressive actually rate various tactics such as those listed above as *more* acceptable (e.g., Ford & Blegen, 1992). Why? Apparently because they feel that they have to do whatever they can to defend against the harsh assaults they fully expect to follow.

Clear evidence for the effects of negotiators' roles on their perceptions of the appropriateness of questionable negotiating tactics has been provided by Garcia, Darley, and Robinson (2001). These researchers asked both public defenders (attorneys assigned by courts to defend people charged with crimes) and district attorneys (attorneys who prosecute persons charged with crimes) to rate the appropriateness of various tactics measured by SINS (see Figure 12.12 on page 498). Included were the following tactics: (1) In return for concessions now, offer to make

bargaining (negotiation): A process in which opposing sides exchange offers, counteroffers, and concessions, either directly or through representatives.

FIGURE 12.12
Negotiating Tactics in the Courtroom: Which Are Acceptable?
Negotiators often use tactics that are questionable from the standpoint of being ethical. Surprisingly, negotiators who play a defensive role, such as public defenders in the court system, view such tactics as more appropriate than do negotiators who play an offensive, aggressive role, such as district attorneys.

future concessions that you know you will not really offer; (2) make an opening demand that is far greater than what you really hope to get; (3) deny the validity of information that your opponent has that weakens your negotiating position, even though that information is true and valid; (4) threaten to postpone or speed up a trial, whichever is worse for your opponent; and (5) intentionally misrepresent information to your opponent in order to strengthen your negotiating arguments or positions. Participants (actual public defenders and district attorneys) rated the appropriateness of each of these tactics both in the abstract and in response to their use by an opponent (i.e., how appropriate is it for you to use these tactics if they have been used by your opponent?) Garcia, Darley, and Robinson (2001) predicted that public defenders would rate the tactics as more appropriate than would district attorneys, and that both groups would rate these tactics as more appropriate in response to their use by an opponent. Results confirmed both hypotheses.

A second and very important determinant of the outcome of bargaining involves the over all orientation of the bargainers to the process (Pruitt & Carnevale, 1993). People taking part in negotiations can approach such discussions from either of two distinct perspectives. In one, they can view the negotiations as "win–lose" situations in which gains by one side are necessarily linked with losses for the other. Or they can approach negotiations as potential "win–win" situations, in which the interests of the two sides are not necessarily incompatible and in which the potential gains of both sides can be maximized.

Not all situations offer the potential for win–win agreements, but many provide such possibilities. If participants are willing to explore all options carefully, they can sometimes attain what are known as *integrative agreements*—ones that offer greater joint benefits than simple compromise—splitting all differences down the middle. An example: Suppose that two cooks are preparing recipes that call for an entire orange, and they have only one orange between them. What should they do? One possibility is to divide the orange in half. That leaves both with less than they need. Suppose, however, that one cook needs all the juice while the other needs all the peel. Here, a much better solution is possible: they can share the orange, each using the part she or he needs. Many techniques for attaining such integrative solutions exist; a few of these are summarized in Table 12.2.

TABLE 12.2

Tactics for Reaching Integrative Agreements. Many different strategies can be useful in attaining integrative agreements—ones that offer better outcomes than simple compromise. A few of those are summarized here.

TACTIC	DESCRIPTION
Broadening the pie	Available resources are increased so that both sides can obtain their major goals.
Nonspecific compensation	One side gets what it wants; the other is compensated on an unrelated issue.
Logrolling	Each party makes concessions on low-priority issues in exchange for concessions on issues it values more highly.
Bridging	Neither party gets its initial demands, but a new option that satisfies the major interests of both sides is developed.
Cost cutting	One party gets what it desires, and the costs to the other party are reduced in some manner.

■ SUPERORDINATE GOALS: "WE'RE ALL IN THIS TOGETHER." As we saw in Chapter 6, individuals often divide the world into two opposing camps—"us" and "them." They perceive members of their own group (us) as quite different from, and usually better than, people belonging to other groups (them). These tendencies to magnify differences between one's own group and others and to disparage outsiders are very powerful and often play a role in the occurrence and persistence of conflicts. Fortunately, they can be countered through the induction of **superordinate goals**—goals that both sides seek and that tie their interests together rather than drive them apart (e.g., Sherif et al., 1961; Tjosvold, 1993). When opposing sides can be made to see that they share overarching goals, conflict is often sharply reduced and may, in fact, be replaced by overt cooperation.

Conflict across Ethnic and Cultural Boundaries

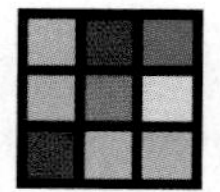

When individuals engage in conflict, they often focus primarily on the outcomes they attain: Have they won or lost? As noted by Tyler and Lind (1992) and other social psychologists (e.g., Ohbuchi, Chiba, & Fukushima, 1994), this is far from the entire story. In addition, persons involved in conflicts are also often interested in the *quality* of their relationship with their opponent. Have they been treated with respect and dignity? Does the other side behave in a way suggesting that it can be trusted? According to a perspective known as the *relational model,* individuals often consider such questions carefully (e.g., Huo et al., 1996).

At this point, another interesting issue arises. In recent decades, the world's economy has become increasingly globalized. In addition, immigration has risen to unprecedented heights. This means that large numbers of people from different cultural and ethnic backgrounds now come into contact with each other and, inevitably, experience conflict. Are relational concerns stronger or weaker in this cross-cultural context? The relational model suggests that they may be *weaker* for two important reasons. First, how we are treated by members of our own group may tell us more about how they view us—our relations with them—than how we are treated by people outside our own group. Second, we are less confident of

superordinate goals: Goals that both sides to a conflict seek and that tie their interests together rather than drive them apart.

our ability to "read" people from other cultures accurately, so we may be less likely to rely on their treatment of us as a source of useful information. Thus, we may focus more on the outcomes we experience when interacting with people from other groups.

Support for this reasoning has been provided by several studies. For instance, Tyler and colleagues (1998) asked employees of a large university to describe recent conflicts with their supervisors and to rate both the *outcomes* they received (e.g., "How favorable was the outcome to you?") and their *treatment* by these people (e.g., "How politely were you treated?" "How much concern was shown for your rights?"). In addition, participants also rated their willingness to accept their supervisors' decision in this dispute. Because participants and their supervisors varied in ethnic background, it was possible to compare their concern with how they were treated with their concern over outcomes in cases in which these individuals were of the same ethnic background and in cases in which they were different. Results indicated that when conflicts occurred within groups, relational factors were more important in determining acceptance of the supervisors' decisions; when conflicts occurred between groups, outcomes were more important.

These findings, which have been replicated in several other contexts (e.g., disputes between Japanese and Western teachers of English in Japan), have important implications. In many conflicts, one or even both sides of a dispute may find the outcomes they receive disappointing. Yet individuals can still accept such results if they feel that they were treated with dignity and respect (e.g., Tyler & Smith, 1997). Unfortunately, such "relational adjustments" seem less likely to occur in conflicts between persons from different cultures, because in such situations, each side focuses primarily on the outcomes it receives (see Figure 12.13). In short, relational factors may combine with stereotyping, the "us–them" division, and several other factors to make cross-cultural conflicts especially difficult to resolve, because in such conflicts, people focus on outcomes and not on developing effective relationships with their opponents. In a world where such conflicts seem likely to be increasingly common, this suggests the need for vigorous steps to develop new strategies for resolving them effectively.

FIGURE 12.13

Culture and Conflict: Focus on Relations or Outcomes?

Research findings indicate that individuals tend to focus more on relational factors in conflicts within their own cultural or ethnic group, but more on outcomes in conflicts that occur across cultural or ethnic boundaries. These findings have important implications for efforts to resolve social conflicts.

KEY POINTS

- *Conflict* is a process that begins when individuals or groups perceive that others' interests are incompatible with their own.
- Conflict can also stem from social factors such as faulty attributions, poor communication, the tendency to perceive our own views as objective, and personal traits.
- Conflict can be reduced in many ways, but *bargaining* and the induction of *superordinate goals* seem to be most effective.
- When individuals experience conflicts with members of their own cultural or ethnic groups, they often focus on relational concerns. In conflicts with persons from other groups, however, they tend to focus on outcome concerns.

Perceived Fairness in Groups: Its Nature and Effects

Have you ever been in a situation in which you felt that you were getting less than you deserved from some group to which you belonged—less status, less approval, less pay? If so, you probably remember that your reactions to such *perceived unfairness* were probably very strong, and not at all pleasant. Perhaps you experienced anger, resentment, and powerful feelings of injustice (e.g., Cropanzano, 1993; Scher, 1997). If you did, you probably did not sit around waiting for the situation to improve; on the contrary, you may have taken some concrete action to rectify it and get whatever it was you felt you deserved (see Figure 12.14). Whatever you did—demand more, reduce your con-

FIGURE 12.14

The Effects of Perceived Injustice.

When people feel that they are getting less than they deserve from some group (e.g., an organization that employs them), they often take steps to reduce such perceived unfairness. The character in this cartoon is demonstrating one way of handling this kind of situation.

[SOURCE: LUANN REPRINTED BY PERMISSION OF UNITED FEATURE SYNDICATE, INC.]

tributions to the group, or even leave it—may well have affected the functioning of the group. (Remember what happened in my academic department when faculty learned each others' salaries?) Social psychologists have recognized such effects for many years and have conducted many studies to understand (1) the factors that lead individuals to decide they have been treated fairly or unfairly, and (2) what they do about it—their efforts to deal with perceived unfairness (e.g., Adams, 1965). We'll now consider both questions.

Judgments of Fairness: Outcomes, Procedures, and Courtesy

The summer before I (RAB) entered college, I worked in the finance office of a large labor union. I was a summer fill-in, so the work was totally *boring.* My hours were long, and I had to punch a time clock when I arrived and when I left. I had only forty-five minutes for lunch and one fifteen-minute break in the morning. I needed the money for college, so I would have gladly put up with all of this except for one thing: another student also working there was treated much better. Tom, who was a year older than I was, arrived late every morning and often left early. He disappeared for long periods of time during the day, and often took two-hour lunches. Worst of all, he was given the most interesting jobs to do. The final blow came when, by mistake, I received his paycheck. It was 50 percent higher than mine! My head nearly exploded over the unfairness of it all. "Who the heck is this guy to get such special treatment?" I wondered. I soon found out: he was the nephew of the president of the union. End of the mystery—but not of my feelings of being treated unfairly.

This situation provides a clear illustration of one set of conditions that leads individuals to conclude that they are being treated unfairly—an imbalance between the *contributions* they make to a group and the *outcomes* (rewards) they receive, *relative to those of other persons* (Adams, 1965). In general, we expect this ratio of contributions and rewards to be about the same for everyone in the group: the more each person contributes, the larger the rewards he or she receives. In other words, we seek **distributive justice** (or *equity*)—conditions under which available rewards are divided fairly among group members, according to what each has contributed to the group (e.g., Brockner & Wiesenfeld, 1996; Greenberg, 1993a). It was the absence of this kind of fairness that upset me in the summer job described above: my contributions were actually *larger* than those of the other student, yet his rewards were greater the mine (see Figure 12.15).

Two more points are worth carefully noting. First, judgments about distributive justice are very much in the eye of the beholder; *we* do the comparing and *we* decide whether our share of available rewards is fair relative to that of other group members (Greenberg, 1990). Second, we are much more sensitive about receiving less than we feel we deserve than to receiving *more* than we feel we deserve. In other words, the *self-serving bias* that we described in Chapter 2 operates strongly in this context (Greenberg, 1996; Diekmann et al., 1997).

distributive justice (equity): Refers to individuals' judgments about whether they are receiving a fair share of available rewards—a share proportionate to their contributions to the group (or to any social relationship).

procedural justice: The fairness of the procedures used to distribute available rewards among group members.

interactional (interpersonal) justice: The extent to which persons who distribute rewards explain or justify their decisions and show considerateness and courtesy to those who receive the rewards.

■ PROCEDURAL AND INTERPERSONAL JUSTICE: WHY PROCEDURES AND COURTESY MATTER, TOO. Although distributive justice plays a key role in shaping perceptions of fairness, it is not the entire story. In addition to concern over how much we receive relative to others, we are also interested in other issues, too: (1) the *procedures* followed in dividing available rewards—**procedural justice,** and (2) the extent to which persons who distribute rewards explain or justify their decisions and show considerateness and courtesy to us—**interactional (or interpersonal) justice** (e.g., Folger & Baron, 1996). In other words, in reaching conclusions about whether we have been treated fairly, we do not focus solely on our actual outcomes: we also care

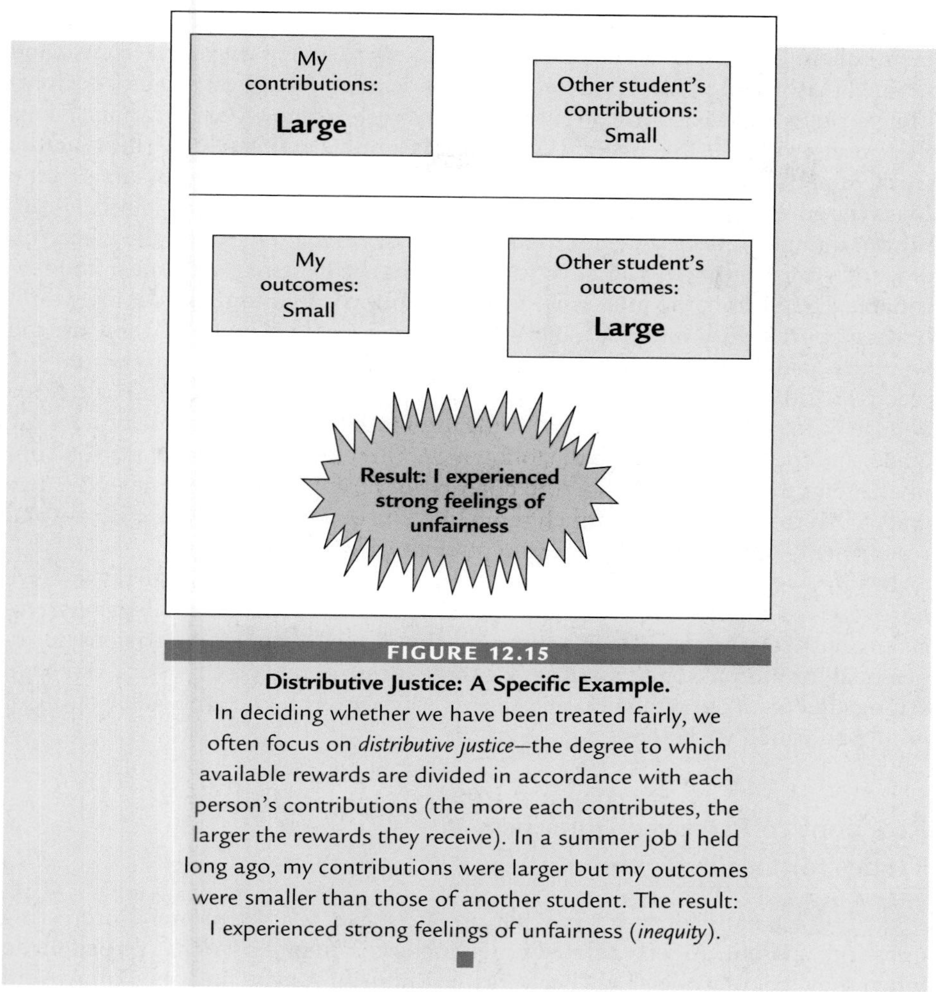

FIGURE 12.15

Distributive Justice: A Specific Example. In deciding whether we have been treated fairly, we often focus on *distributive justice*—the degree to which available rewards are divided in accordance with each person's contributions (the more each contributes, the larger the rewards they receive). In a summer job I held long ago, my contributions were larger but my outcomes were smaller than those of another student. The result: I experienced strong feelings of unfairness (*inequity*).

about how the decisions to distribute rewards in a specific way were reached (the procedures followed) and about how we were treated throughout the process (interactional fairness).

What factors influence judgments concerning the fairness of procedures? Ones such as these: (1) The consistency of procedures—the extent to which they are applied in the same manner to all persons; (2) accuracy—the extent to which procedures are based on accurate information about the relative contributions of all group members; (3) opportunity for corrections—the extent to which any errors in distributions that are made can be adjusted; (4) bias suppression—the extent to which decision makers avoid being influenced by their own self-interest; and (5) ethicality—the extent to which decisions are made in a manner compatible with ethical and moral values held by the people affected.

Evidence that such factors really do influence our judgments concerning procedural justice has been obtained in many studies (e.g., Brockner et al., 1994; Leventhal, Karuza, & Fry, 1980). For instance, in one recent investigation, Magner and colleagues (2000) asked property owners in a medium-sized city to rate the extent to which their taxes were determined through fair procedures. Results indicated that ethicality, accuracy, and bias suppression were important factors in taxpayers' decisions about procedural justice: the more these factors were present, the more the people perceived the process of setting each person's taxes to be fair.

Turning to *interactional justice,* two factors seem to play a key role in our judgments about how we have been treated: the extent to which we are given clear and rational reasons for *why* rewards were divided as they were (Bies, Shapiro, & Cummings, 1988), and the courtesy and sensitivity with which we are informed about these divisions (e.g., Greenberg, 1993b). Here's an illustration of how these factors work: Suppose you receive a term paper back from one of your professors. On the top is the grade "C–." You expected at least a B, so you are quite disappointed. Reading on, though, you see a detailed explanation of why you received the grade you did, and after reading it, you have to admit that the explanation is clear and reasonable. In addition, the professor inserts the following comment: "I know you'll be disappointed with this grade, but I feel you are capable of much better work and would be glad to work with you to help you improve your grade." How would you react? Probably by concluding that the grade is low but the professor has treated you fairly. In contrast, imagine how you'd react if there were no explanation for the grade, and the professor wrote the following comment: "Very poor work; you simply haven't met my standards. And don't bother to try to see me. I never change grades." In this case, you are much more likely to experience feelings of anger and resentment, and to view your treatment by the professor as unfair.

In sum, we judge fairness in several different ways—in terms of the rewards we have received (distributive justice), the procedures used to reach these divisions (procedural justice), and the style in which we are informed about these divisions (interpersonal, or interactional, justice). All three forms of perceived justice can have strong effects on our behavior, and in this way, can influence the functioning of groups to which we belong.

Reactions to Perceived Unfairness: Tactics for Dealing with Injustice

Now let's turn to what, in one sense, is an even more interesting question, and one directly related to what goes on in groups: What do people do when they feel that they have been treated unfairly? As you probably know from your own experience, many different things. First, if unfairness centers around rewards (distributive justice), people may focus on changing the balance between their contributions and their outcomes. For example, they may reduce contributions or demand larger rewards. If these are not delivered, they may take more drastic actions, such as leaving the group altogether. All of these reactions are readily visible in workplaces—one setting in which judgments concerning fairness play a key role. Employees who feel that they are being underpaid may come in late, leave early, do less on the job, and request more benefits—higher pay, more vacation, and so on. If these tactics fail, they may protest, join a union and go out on strike, or, ultimately, quit and look for another job. Such reactions are also visible in intimate relationships: when members of a couple feel that they are being treated unfairly by their spouse or significant other (e.g., they have to do more than their share of the housework), they often react with anger and resentment, and they may take steps to change the situation (e.g., Sprecher, 1992). This can range from direct requests to their partner to deciding to leave the relationship for another. Interestingly, recent findings indicate that perceived unfairness not only may lead to marital distress, it may be a result of it. In a carefully conducted longitudinal study, Grote and Clark (2001) asked married couples to rate their marital satisfaction, their marital conflict, and the perceived fairness of division of household tasks at three different times: while the wife was pregnant, six months after their child was born, and twelve to fifteen months after their child was born. Results indicated that the more conflict couples reported before the child was born, the greater their perceptions of unfairness at the later times (after the child was born). These findings

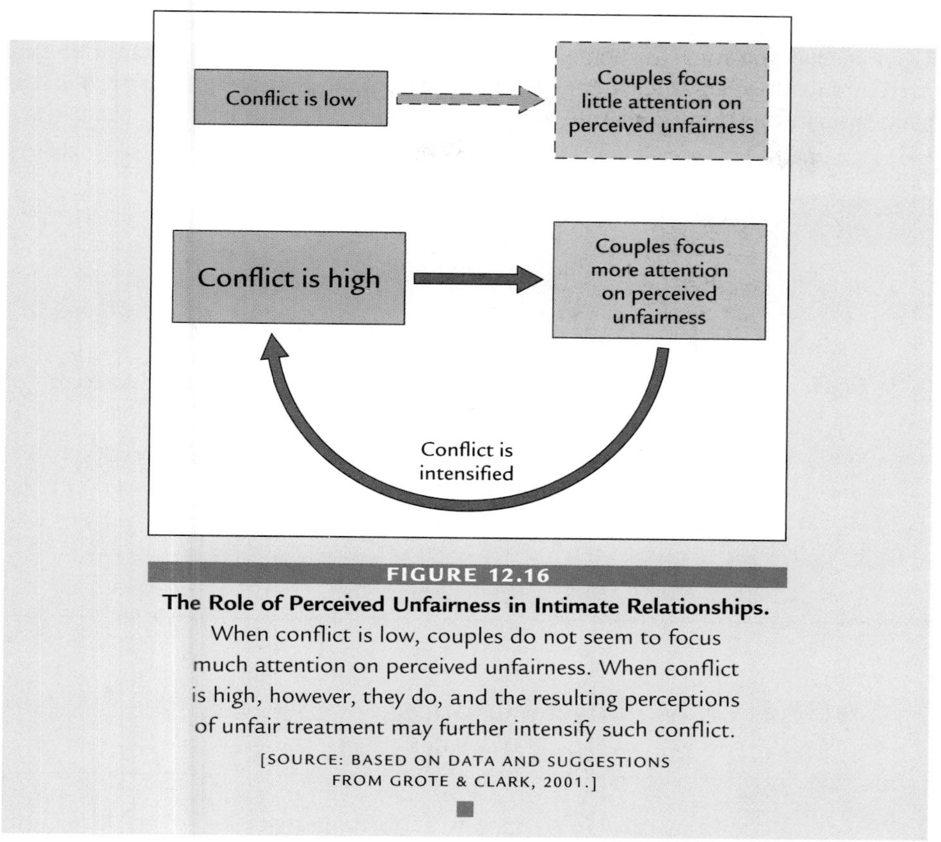

FIGURE 12.16

The Role of Perceived Unfairness in Intimate Relationships. When conflict is low, couples do not seem to focus much attention on perceived unfairness. When conflict is high, however, they do, and the resulting perceptions of unfair treatment may further intensify such conflict.

[SOURCE: BASED ON DATA AND SUGGESTIONS FROM GROTE & CLARK, 2001.]

occurred for both genders but were, not surprisingly, somewhat stronger for women, who, in fact, do more than half of the household chores in most couples. These results suggest that when couples are getting along well and conflict is low, they do *not* pay much attention to unfairness, even if it exists. But when conflict is high, their attention is focused on unfairness, and this, in turn, may serve to intensify conflict still further (see Figure 12.16). In sum, perceived unfairness can be the result of marital conflict as well as a cause of such difficulties for couples.

When unfairness centers around procedures (procedural justice) or a lack of courtesy on the part of the persons who determine reward divisions (interactional justice) rather than on rewards themselves (distributive justice), individuals may adopt somewhat different tactics. Procedures are often harder to change than specific outcomes because they go on behind closed doors and may depart from announced policies in many ways. Similarly, changing the negative attitudes or personality traits that lie behind insensitive treatment by bosses, professors, or other reward allocators is a difficult, if not impossible, task. The result? Individuals who feel that they have been treated unfairly in these ways often turn to more covert (hidden) techniques for evening the score. For instance, a growing body of evidence suggests that such feelings of unfairness lie behind many instances of employee theft and sabotage (e.g., Greenberg & Scott, 1996). And, as we noted in Chapter 11, feelings of unfairness also play a major role in many forms of workplace aggression—especially in subtle, hidden actions individuals perform to "get even" with others who, they believe, have treated them unfairly.

Finally, individuals who feel that they have been treated unfairly and conclude that there is little they can do about this may cope with this situation simply by changing their perceptions. They can conclude, for instance, that other persons who receive larger rewards than they do *deserve* this special treatment because they possess something "special": extra talent, greater experience, a bigger reputation, or some other special qualities. In such cases, individuals who feel that they cannot eliminate unfairness can at least cope with it and reduce the discomfort it produces, even though they may continue to be treated unfairly by others.

KEY POINTS

- Individuals wish to be treated fairly by the groups to which they belong. Fairness can be judged in terms of outcomes (*distributive justice*), in terms of procedures (*procedural justice*), or in terms of courteous treatment (*interactional justice*).
- When individuals feel that they have been treated unfairly, they often take steps to restore fairness.
- These steps range from overt actions such as reducing their contributions to covert actions such as employee theft or sabotage, or changes in perception, suggesting that others deserve better treatment.
- In intimate relationships, conflict can lead to increased feelings of unfair treatment, and this, in turn, can further intensify conflict.

Decision Making by Groups: How It Occurs and the Pitfalls It Faces

Groups are called upon to perform many tasks—everything from conducting surgical operations to entertaining large crowds. One of the most important activities they perform, however, is **decision making**—combining and integrating available information in order to choose one out of several possible courses of action. Governments, large corporations, military units, sports teams—these and many other groups entrust key decisions to groups. Why? While many factors play a role, the most important seems to be this: Most people believe that groups usually reach better decisions than do individuals. After all, groups can pool the expertise of their members and avoid extreme decisions.

Are such beliefs accurate? Do groups really make better or more accurate decisions than individuals? In their efforts to answer this question, social psychologists have focused on three major questions: (1) How do groups actually make their decisions and reach consensus? (2) Do decisions reached by groups differ from those reached by individuals? (3) What accounts for the fact that groups sometimes make truly disastrous decisions—ones so bad it is hard to believe they were actually reached?

The Decision-Making Process: How Groups Attain Consensus

When groups first begin to discuss any issue, their members rarely voice unanimous agreement. Rather, they come to the decision-making task with different information and so support a wide range of views (e.g., Larson, Foster-Fishman, & Franz, 1998; Gigone & Hastie, 1997). After some period of discussion, however, groups usually reach a decision. This does not always happen—juries become "hung," and other decision-making groups, too, sometimes deadlock. But in general, some decision is reached. How is this accomplished, and can the final outcome be predicted from the views initially held by a group's members? Here is what research findings suggest.

decision making: Processes involved in combining and integrating available information in order to choose one of several possible courses of action.

SOCIAL DECISION SCHEMES: BLUEPRINTS FOR DECISIONS. Let's begin with the question of whether a group's decisions can be predicted from the views held by its members at the start. Here, the answer itself is quite straightforward, even though the processes involved are more complex: Yes. The final decisions reached by groups can often be predicted quite accurately by relatively simple rules known as **social decision schemes.** These rules relate the initial distribution of members' views or preferences to the group's final decisions. For example, one scheme—the *majority-wins rule*—suggests that, in many cases, the group will opt for whatever position is initially supported by most of its members (e.g., Nemeth et al., 2001). According to this rule, discussion serves mainly to confirm or strengthen the most popular initial view; it is generally accepted no matter how passionately the minority argues for a different position. A second decision scheme is the *truth-wins rule.* This indicates that the correct solution or decision will ultimately be accepted as its correctness is recognized by more and more members. A third decision rule is known as the *first-shift rule.* Groups tend to adopt a decision consistent with the direction of the first shift in opinion shown by any member.

Surprising as it may seem, the results of many studies indicate that these simple rules are quite successful in predicting even complex group decisions. Indeed, they have been found to be accurate up to 80 percent of the time (e.g., Stasser, Taylor, & Hanna, 1989). Thus, they seem to provide important insights into how groups move toward agreement.

NORMATIVE AND INFORMATIONAL INFLUENCE IN GROUPS: HOW GROUP MEMBERS INFLUENCE EACH OTHERS' VIEWS. Many studies indicate that, in general, decision-making groups move toward consensus; indeed, as we'll see below, this strong tendency to seek uniformity or agreement is one of the potential dangers of decision making by groups. But how, precisely, do members influence each other so that the group moves toward such consensus? The answer seems to be through the two kinds of influence we described in Chapter 9: *normative social influence* and *informational social influence.* Normative social influence is based on our desire to be liked or accepted, and groups certainly use this tactic to influence disagreeing members to go along. Similarly, groups also employ informational social influence, which is based on our desire to be right—to hold the correct views. Many studies in which decision-making groups have been carefully observed indicate that both forms of social influence are used by members to bring "mavericks" (disagreeing members) into line (e.g., Kaplan, 1989; Kelley et al., 1997; Larrey & Paulus, 1999). Moreover, this appears to be true in a wide range of decision-making groups, ranging from juries to cabinet-level groups in governments. In short, there is no real mystery as to why groups move toward the position adopted by the majority of their members initially; they attain consensus through reciprocal social influence among their members.

The Nature of Group Decisions: Moderation or Polarization?

Truly important decisions are rarely left to individuals. Instead, they are usually assigned to groups—and highly qualified groups at that. Even total dictators usually consult with groups of highly skilled advisers before taking major actions. As we noted earlier, the major reason behind this strategy is the belief that groups are far less likely than individuals to make serious errors—to rush blindly over the edge. Is this really true? Research on this issue has yielded surprising findings. Contrary to popular belief, a large body of evidence indicates that groups are actually *more* likely to adopt extreme positions than are individuals making decisions alone. In fact, across many different kinds of decisions and many different contexts, groups show a pronounced tendency to shift toward views more extreme than

social decision schemes: Rules relating the initial distribution of members' views to final group decisions.

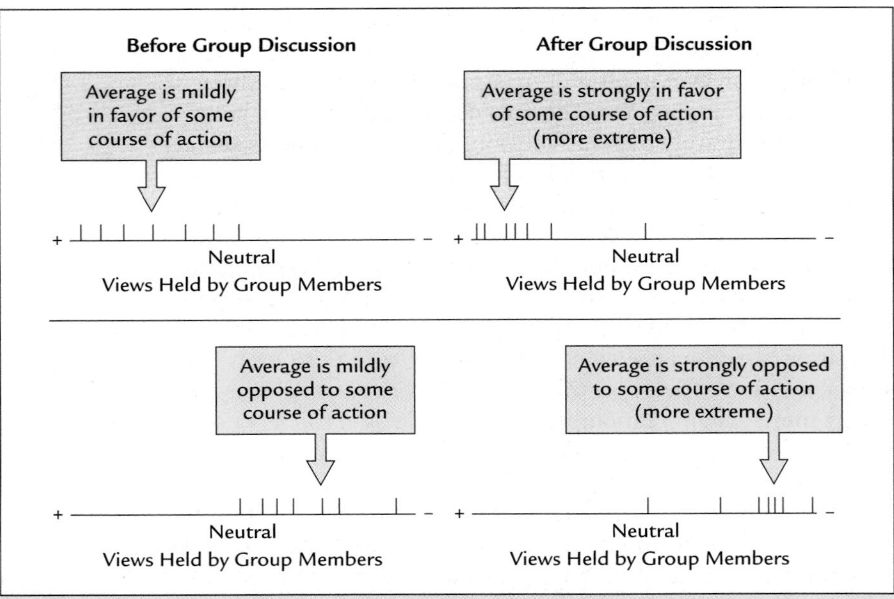

FIGURE 12.17

Group Polarization: Its Basic Nature.

As shown here, *group polarization* involves the tendency for decision-making groups to shift toward views that are more extreme than the ones with which they initially began, but in the same general direction. Thus, if groups start out slightly in favor of one view or position, they often end up holding this view more strongly or extremely after deliberations. The shift toward extremity can be quite dangerous in many settings.

the ones with which they initially began (Burnstein, 1983; Lamm & Myers, 1978). This is known as **group polarization,** and its major effects can be summarized as follows: Whatever the initial leaning or preference of a group prior to its discussions, it is strengthened during the group's deliberations. The result: Not only does the *group* shift toward more extreme views, but individual members, too, often show such a shift (see Figure 12.17). (Note: The term *group polarization* does not refer to a tendency of groups to split apart into two opposing camps or poles; on the contrary, it refers to a strengthening of the group's initial preferences.)

Why does this effect occur? Two major factors seem to be involved. First, it appears that *social comparison*—a process we examined earlier—plays an important role. Everyone wants to be "above average," and where opinions are concerned, this implies holding views that are "better" than those of other group members. What does "better" mean? This depends on the specific group: Among a group of liberals, "better" would mean "more liberal." Among a group of conservatives, it would mean "more conservative." Among a group of racists, it would mean "even more bigoted." In any case, during group discussions, at least some members discover—to their shock!—that their views are *not* "better" than those of most other members. The result: After comparing themselves with these persons, they shift to even more extreme views, and the group polarization effect is off and running (Goethals & Zanna, 1979).

A second factor involves the fact that, during group discussion, most arguments presented are ones favoring the group's initial leaning or preference. As a result of hearing such arguments, persuasion occurs (presumably through the *central route* described in Chapter 4), and members shift, increasingly, toward the majority view. These shifts increase the proportion of arguments favoring this view, and, ultimately, members convince themselves that this is the "right" view and shift toward it with increasing strength. Group polarization results from this process (Vinokur & Burnstein, 1974).

group polarization: The tendency of group members, as a result of group discussion, to shift toward more extreme positions than those they initially held.

Regardless of the precise basis for group polarization, it definitely has important implications. The occurrence of polarization may lead many decision-making groups to adopt positions that are increasingly extreme, and therefore increasingly dangerous. In this context, it is chilling to speculate about the potential role of such shifts in disastrous decisions by political, military, or business groups that should, by all accounts, have known better—for example, the decision by the hard-liners in the now-vanished Soviet Union to stage a coup to restore firm communist rule, or the decision by Apple computer *not* to license its software to other manufacturers—a decision that ultimately cost it most of its sales. Did group polarization influence these and other disastrous decisions? It is impossible to say for sure, but research findings suggest that this is a real possibility.

Potential Dangers of Group Decision Making: Groupthink, Biased Processing, and the Tendency of Group Members to Tell Each Other What They Already Know

The drift of many decision-making groups toward polarization is a serious problem—one that can interfere with their ability to make accurate decisions. Unfortunately, this is not the only process that can exert such negative effects. Several others, too, emerge during group discussions and can lead groups to make costly, even disastrous, decisions (Hinsz, 1995). Among the most important of these are (1) *groupthink,* (2) biased processing of information by group members, and (3) groups' seeming inability to share and use information held by some but not all of their members.

■ GROUPTHINK: WHEN TOO MUCH COHESIVENESS IS A DANGEROUS THING. Earlier, we suggested that tendencies toward group polarization may be one reason why decision-making groups sometimes go off the deep end, with catastrophic results. However, another even more disturbing factor may also contribute to such outcomes. This is a process known as **groupthink**—a strong tendency for decision-making groups to close ranks, cognitively, around a decision, assuming that the group *can't* be wrong, that all members must support the decision strongly, and that any information contrary to it should be rejected (Janis, 1972, 1982). Once this collective state of mind develops, it appears, groups become unwilling—and perhaps *unable*—to change their decisions, even if external events suggest that these decisions are very poor ones. For example, consider the repeated decisions by three United States presidents (Kennedy, Johnson, and Nixon) to escalate the war in Vietnam. Each escalation brought increased American casualties and no visible progress toward the goal of assuring the survival of South Vietnam as an independent country; yet the cabinets of each president continued to recommend escalation. According to Janis (1982), the social psychologist who originated the concept of *groupthink,* this process—and the increasing unwillingness to consider alternative courses of action that it encourages among group members—may well have contributed to this tragic chain of events. And other psychologists noted the possible effects of groupthink in a wide range of other contexts (e.g., Hilton, 1998).

Why does groupthink occur? Research findings (e.g., Tetlock et al., 1992; Kameda & Sugimori, 1993) suggest that two factors may be crucial. The first is a very high level of *cohesiveness* among group members: they are similar in background, interests, and values, and so tend to like each other very much. The second is *emergent group norms*—norms suggesting that the group is both infallible and morally superior, and that because of these factors, there should be no further discussion of the issues at hand: the decision has been made, and the only task now is to support it as strongly as possible. Once groupthink takes hold in a decision-making group, Janis (1982) argues, pressure toward maintaining high levels of group consensus overrides the motivation to evaluate all potential courses of action as accurately as possible. The result: Such groups shift from focusing on making the best decisions possible

groupthink: The tendency of the members of highly cohesive groups to assume that their decisions can't be wrong, that all members must support the group's decisions strongly, and that information contrary to it should be ignored.

to focusing on maintaining a high level of consensus, and this, in turn, can yield truly disastrous effects.

■ BIASED PROCESSING OF INFORMATION IN GROUPS. While groupthink is a dramatic process, other more subtle but equally costly sources of bias exist in decision-making groups. One of the most important of these is the tendency for such groups to process available information in a biased manner. Groups, like individuals, are not always motivated to maximize accuracy; on the contrary, they are often motivated to find support for the views they initially favor. In other words, they act more like "intuitive lawyers," searching for evidence that supports their case (initial preferences) than as "intuitive scientists," seeking truth and accuracy (e.g., Baumeister & Newman, 1994). Such tendencies do not always stem from the selfish pursuit of self-interest; rather, they may derive from adherence to values or principles that are generally accepted in society and viewed in a positive light. A clear illustration of this kind of potential clash between positive values and accuracy in decision making occurs in juries—especially those concerned with settling civil suits in which one side seeks damages from the other.

In such cases, judges often instruct juries to follow one of three legal rules: *comparative negligence*—reduce the award sought by the plaintiff in proportion to the extent the plaintiff was negligent (responsible for the harm she or he suffered); *contributory negligence*—award the plaintiff *no damages* if she or he was negligent to any extent; *strict liability*—award *full damages* to the plaintiff if the defendant was negligent to any extent. As you can see, only the first of these rules is consistent with distributive justice; the other rules, although often used in legal proceedings, violate this common-sense rule. Taking account of this fact, Sommer, Horowitz, and Bourgeois (2001) predicted that juries would engage in biased processing of information in order to adhere to distributive justice, even if instructed by a judge to follow the other two rules. To test this prediction, they conducted a study in which participants listened to an audiotape of a civil trial in which a plaintiff was suing an automobile manufacturer for one million dollars in damages; the case involved a faulty fuel filter that caused a gas tank to explode, resulting in the death of the plaintiff's wife. In three different conditions, jurors were told to follow each of the rules above in making their decisions. Sommer, Horowitz, & Bourgeois (2001) reasoned that jurors would engage in biased processing of information concerning the trial in order to adhere to distributive justice. Thus, for example, they would discuss more pro-plaintiff evidence under the contributory negligence rule (which strongly favors the defendant) than under the strict liability rule (which strongly favors the plaintiff). As you can see from Figure 12.18, this is precisely what happened. Other measures indicated that jurors did actually engage in biased processing of available evidence in order to obtain the decisions they wanted—ones consistent with the principle of distributive justice.

These findings and those of related research (e.g., Frey, Schulz-Hardt, & Stahlberg, 1996) indicate that juries and other decision-making groups do indeed engage in biased processing: in other words, they process available information in ways that allow them to reach the decisions they want!

■ WHY GROUPS OFTEN FAIL TO SHARE INFORMATION UNIQUE TO EACH MEMBER. A third potential source of bias for decision-making groups involves the fact that contrary to what common sense suggests, such groups do not always pool their resources—share information and ideas that are unique to each member. In fact, research on this issue (Gigone & Hastie, 1993, 1997; Stasser, 1992) indicates that such pooling of resources or information may be the exception rather than the rule. When groups discuss a given issue and try to reach a decision about it, they tend to discuss information shared by most if not all members, rather than information that is known to only one or a few. The result: The decisions they make tend to reflect the shared information (e.g., Gigone & Hastie, 1993). This is not a problem

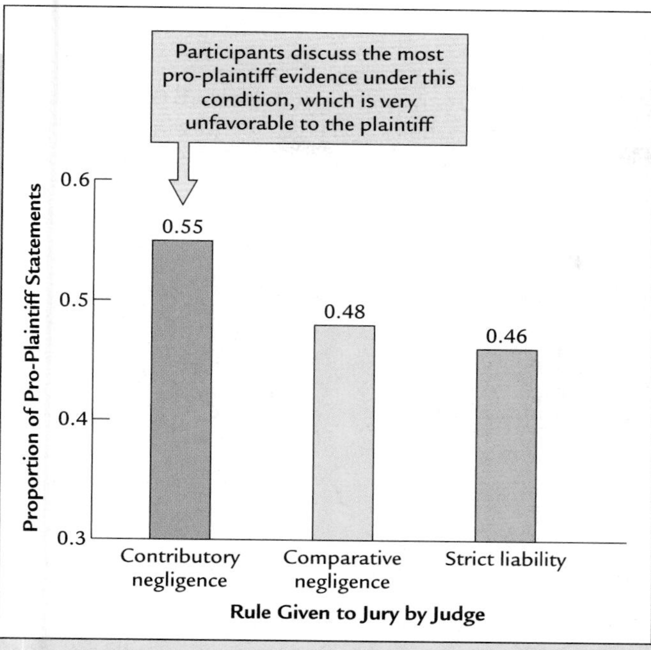

FIGURE 12.18

Biased Processing and Group Decisions. Mock jurors told to follow legal rules in deciding a damage case engaged in biased processing in order to ignore these rules and adhere to the principle of distributive justice (fairness). Specifically, they discussed more pro-plaintiff evidence under the contributory negligence rule (which strongly favors the defendant) than under the strict liability rule (which strongly favors the plaintiff).

[SOURCE: BASED ON DATA FROM SOMMER, HOROWITZ, & BOURGEOIS, 2001.]

if such information points to the best decision. But consider what happens when information pointing to the best decision is *not* shared by most members. In such cases, the tendency of group members to discuss mainly the information they all already possess may prevent them from reaching the best decision.

Disturbingly, research findings suggest that this tendency is strong indeed. For instance, even with respect to medical diagnoses, which can involve life-and-death decisions, teams of interns and medical students discussed more shared than unshared information during group discussions. However, the more they pooled *unshared* information (information known, initially, to only some members), the more accurate were the groups' diagnoses (e.g., Larson et al., 1998; Winquist & Larson, 1998).

■ IMPROVING GROUP DECISIONS. Groupthink, biased processing, discussing information already known to all the members—these are discouraging barriers to effective decision making by groups. Can these potential pitfalls be overcome? Many studies have addressed this issue, and together, they do point to some promising techniques. Several of these involve encouraging dissent, because doing so may slow the rapid movement of groups toward consensus. One such approach is the **devil's advocate technique** (e.g., Hirt & Markman, 1995), in which one group member is assigned the task of disagreeing with and criticizing whatever plan or decision is under consideration. This tactic often works because it induces members to think carefully about the decision toward which they are moving.

Another approach involves calling in outside experts who offer their recommendations and opinions on the group's plans (e.g., Janis, 1982). Recent studies suggest that most effective of all may be **authentic dissent,** in which one or more group members actively disagree with the group's initial preference without being assigned this role. For instance, a study by Nemeth and her colleagues (2001) found that authentic dissent was more likely to encourage original thinking by group members, greater consideration of alternative views, and more attitude change away from the group's initial position than was the devil's advocate approach. In any case, it is clear that decision making by groups *can* be improved; however, active steps must be taken to achieve this goal. Left to their own devices, and without outside intervention, groups often do slip easily into the mental traps outlined here—often with disastrous results.

devil's advocate technique: A technique for improving the quality of group decisions in which one group member is assigned the task of disagreeing with and criticizing whatever plan or decision is under consideration.

authentic dissent: A technique for improving the quality of group decisions in which one or more group members actively disagree with the group's initial preference without being assigned this role.

KEY POINTS 

- It is widely believed that groups make better decisions than do individuals. However, research findings indicate that groups are often subject to *group polarization* effects, which lead them to make more extreme decisions than do individuals.
- In addition, groups often suffer from *groupthink*—a tendency to assume that they can't be wrong and that information contrary to the group's view should be rejected.
- Groups often engage in biased processing of information in order to reach the decisions they initially prefer, or to adhere to general values such as the principle of *distributive justice*.

CONNECTIONS: INTEGRATING SOCIAL PSYCHOLOGY

IN THIS CHAPTER, YOU READ ABOUT . . .	IN OTHER CHAPTERS, YOU WILL FIND RELATED DISCUSSIONS OF . . .
the role of *norms* in the functioning of groups	the nature of norms and their role in social influence (Chapter 9) and aggression (Chapter 11)
the nature of cooperation and conflict and factors that affect their occurrence	other forms of behavior that either assist or harm others: discrimination (Chapter 6) helping behavior (Chapter 10) aggression (Chapter 11)
individuals' concern with others' evaluations of their performance	the effects of others' evaluations on our self-concept (Chapter 5) and on our liking for others (Chapter 7)
perceived fairness	the effects of perceived fairness on many other forms of social behavior, such as helping (Chapter 10) and aggression (Chapter 11), and its role in close relationships (Chapter 8)
the role of persuasion and other forms of social influence in group decision making	the nature of persuasion (Chapter 4); various forms of social influence (Chapter 9)

THINKING ABOUT CONNECTIONS

1. Do you see any connection between social loafing and perceived fairness? (Hint: Have you ever been in a group in which you suspected that other people were engaging in social loafing? If so, what did you do about it? And if you did take action, why?)
2. Many situations in our lives involve social dilemmas—if we cooperate with others, everyone gains, but it is tempting to pursue our own self-interests because, in the short-run, doing so is easier and offers immediate gains. Can you think of such a situation in your own life? What did you do when you found yourself in it—the "right" thing or the "easy" thing? Do you think that after reading this chapter, you might behave differently in such situations than you have in the past?
3. Decision making by groups is a complex process. Drawing on previous discussions of gender throughout this book (Chapters 6, 7, 10, and 11), do you think that decision making would be different in groups consisting of females than in groups consisting of males? If so, in what ways?

IDEAS TO TAKE WITH YOU—AND USE!

MAXIMIZING YOUR OWN PERFORMANCE AND COMBATING SOCIAL LOAFING BY OTHERS

Social facilitation effects seem to occur because the presence of others is arousing. Arousal increases our tendency to perform dominant responses. If these are correct, performance is improved; if they are incorrect, performance is impaired. This leads to several practical suggestions:

Study Alone but Take Tests in the Presence of Others.

If you study alone, you'll avoid the distraction caused by other persons and so will learn new materials more efficiently. If you have studied hard, your dominant responses will probably be correct ones; so when you take a test, the increased arousal generated by other persons will improve your performance.

Work on Simple Tasks (e.g., Ones Requiring Pure Physical Effort) in Front of an Audience.

The presence of an audience will increase your arousal, and so your ability to put out physical effort on such tasks.

Social loafing occurs when persons working together put out less effort than they would if they were working alone. This can be costly to you if *you* work hard but others goof off. Here's how you can avoid such outcomes:

Make Sure That the Contribution of Each Member of the Group Can Be Assessed Individually—Don't Let Social Loafers Hide!

Try to Work Only with People Who Are Committed to the Group's Goals.

Make Sure That Each Person's Contribution Is Unique—Not Redundant to That of Others.

In this way, each person can be personally responsible for what she or he produces.

SUMMARY AND REVIEW OF KEY POINTS

Groups: What They Are and How They Function

- A *group* is a collection of persons perceived to form a coherent unit to some degree. The extent to which the group is perceived to form a coherent entity is known as entiativity.
- Groups influence their members in many ways, but such effects are often produced through *roles, status, norms,* and *cohesiveness.*
- Men are higher in status motivation than are women; evolutionary psychologists attribute this to the fact that high-status men obtain access to a greater number of mates than do lower status men.
- Research findings indicate that one technique for gaining status is by expressing anger.

How Groups Affect Individual Performance: From Social Facilitation to Social Loafing

- The mere presence of other persons either as an audience or as coactors can influence our performance on many tasks. Such effects are known as *social facilitation* (or as social facilitation–inhibition effects).
- The *drive theory of social facilitation* suggests that the presence of others is arousing and can either increase or reduce performance, depending on whether dominant responses in a given situation are correct or incorrect.
- The *distraction–conflict* theory suggests that the presence of others is arousing because it induces conflicting tendencies to focus on the task being performed and on an audience or coactors. This can result both in increased arousal and in narrowed attentional focus.
- Research findings offer support for the view that several kinds of audiences produce narrowed attentional focus among persons performing a task. This cognitive view of social facilitation helps explain why social facilitation occurs among animals as well as people.
- When individuals work together on a task, *social loafing*—reduced output by each group member—sometimes occurs.
- According to the *collective effort model,* such effects occur because when working together with others as compared to working alone, individuals experience weaker links between their effort and their outcomes.
- Social loafing can be reduced in several ways: by making outputs individually identifiable, by increasing commitment to the task and sense of task importance, and by assuring that each member's contributions to the task are unique.

Coordination in Groups: Cooperation or Conflict?

- *Cooperation*—working together with others to obtain shared goals—is a common aspect of social life.
- However, cooperation does not develop in many situations in which it is possible, partly because such situations involve *social dilemmas,* in which individuals can increase their own gains by defection.
- Several factors influence whether cooperation occurs in such situations. These include strong tendencies toward *reciprocity,* personal orientation toward cooperation, and communication.
- Evolutionary psychologists suggest that our tendency to reciprocate may result from the fact that organisms that cooperate are more likely to survive and reproduce than are organisms that do not.
- The discontinuity effect refers to the fact that groups are more likely to compete with one another than are individuals. In short, intergroup cooperation may be more difficult to attain than intragroup cooperation.
- *Conflict* is a process that begins when individuals or groups perceive that others' interests are incompatible with their own.
- Conflict can also stem from social factors such as faulty attributions, poor communication, the tendency to perceive our own views as objective, and personal traits.
- Conflict can be reduced in many ways, but *bargaining* and the induction of *superordinate goals* seem to be most effective.
- When individuals experience conflicts with members of their own cultural or ethnic groups, they often focus on relational concerns. In conflicts with persons from other groups, however, they tend to focus on outcome concerns.

Perceived Fairness in Groups: Its Nature and Effects

- Individuals wish to be treated fairly by the groups to which they belong. Fairness can be judged in terms of outcomes (*distributive justice*), in terms of procedures (*procedural justice*), or in terms of courteous treatment (*interactional,* or *interpersonal, justice*).
- When individuals feel that they have been treated unfairly, they often take steps to restore fairness.
- These steps range from overt actions such as reducing their contributions to covert actions such as employee theft or sabotage, or changes in perception, suggesting that others deserve better treatment.

- In intimate relationships, conflict can lead to increased feelings of unfair treatment, and this, in turn, can further intensify conflict.

Decision Making by Groups: How It Occurs and the Pitfalls It Faces

- It is widely believed that groups make better decisions than do individuals. However, research findings indicate that groups are often subject to *group polarization* effects, which lead them to make more extreme decisions than would individuals.
- In addition, groups often suffer from *groupthink*—a tendency to assume that they can't be wrong and that information contrary to the group's view should be rejected.
- Groups often engage in biased processing of information in order to reach the decisions they initially prefer, or to adhere to general values such as the principle of distributive justice.

KEY TERMS

additive tasks (p. 486)
authentic dissent (p. 511)
bargaining (negotiation) (p. 497)
cohesiveness (p. 480)
collective effort model (p. 487)
conflict (p. 489)
cooperation (p. 489)
decision making (p. 506)
devil's advocate technique (p. 511)
distraction-conflict theory (p. 486)
distributive justice (equity) (p. 502)
drive theory of social facilitation (p. 482)
evaluation apprehension (p. 486)
group (p. 475)
group polarization (p. 508)
groupthink (p. 509)
interactional (interpersonal) justice (p. 502)
norms (p. 479)
procedural justice (p. 502)
reciprocity (p. 491)
roles (p. 477)
social decision schemes (p. 507)
social dilemmas (p. 490)
social facilitation (p. 482)
social loafing (p. 486)
status (p. 478)
superordinate goals (p. 499)

FOR MORE INFORMATION

Foddy, M., Smithson, M., Schneider, S., & Hogg, M. A. (Eds.). (2000). *Resolving social dilemmas: Dynamic, structural, and intergroup aspects* (pp. 281–293). Philadelphia: Psychology Press.

- In this book, experts on social dilemmas—and on cooperation and competition—discuss the nature of such situations and techniques for resolving them in a way that maximizes the outcomes of all persons concerned. This is an excellent source to consult if you'd like to know more about how people behave in situations involving conflicting pressures to cooperate and compete.

Thompson, L. (1998). *The mind and heart of the negotiator.* Upper Saddle River, NJ: Prentice Hall.

- In this well-written and relatively brief book, a noted researcher describes the nature of negotiation from the perspective of modern social psychology. The roles of various cognitive processes and biases, perceived fairness, past experience, and group processes are all described. This is an excellent source to consult if you'd like to know more about bargaining.

Tyler, T. R., & Blader, S. (2000). *Cooperation in groups: Procedural justice, social identity, and behavioral engagement.* Philadelphia: Psychology Press.

- Why do people choose to cooperate—or to compete—with others? The authors of this thought-provoking book examine people's views about the extent to which procedures in a group are fair and how this perception affects their motivation to cooperate or be helpful. This is an intriguing book if you want to know more about perceived justice (fairness) and its role in important group processes.

Witte, E., & Davis, J. H. (Eds.). (1996). *Understanding group behavior: Consensual action by small groups.* Hillsdale, NJ: Erlbaum.

- In this book, noted experts summarize existing knowledge about many aspects of group behavior. The sections on decision making are especially interesting, and expand greatly upon the information on this topic presented in this chapter.

Jacob Lawrence, *The 1920's . . . The Migrants Cast Their Ballots,* 1974. Silkscreen print, 32" × 25". Collection of the Newark Museum, 75.227. Artwork © Copyright Gwendolyn Knight Lawrence, courtesy of the Jacob and Gwendolyn Lawrence Foundation. © Copyright The Newark Museum, Newark, New Jersey, USA/Art Resource, NY.

SOCIAL PSYCHOLOGY IN ACTION: APPLICATIONS TO LAW, MEDICINE, AND ORGANIZATIONS

CHAPTER OUTLINE

Each of the two authors of this book spent several years serving as Chair of their respective departments (DB for five years and RAB for six). We had many similar experiences, and the following example highlights one of a Chair's less satisfying duties, illustrating how difficult it can be to remove an unsatisfactory member of the faculty.

During the time that I (RAB) served as Department Chair, by far the worst experience I had involved the firing of a junior faculty member. She had come to us from a top-rated university, and we expected great things of her. But soon after she arrived on campus and started teaching, I began receiving complaints from her students. Several students came to my office to tell me that she was treating them in an arrogant, offhand manner—and they didn't like it! When I asked for more specific information, they told me that she belittled members of her classes when they offered their opinions and frequently reminded them that *she* was the professor while they were "only" the students. After the third complaint, I spoke to her about the situation, suggesting—very mildly—that she avoid criticizing students or saying anything that might make them feel put down. She agreed, but the complaints continued. Again I spoke with her and urged her to adjust her teaching style and again she agreed, but the situation didn't change. After visits from two more students—one was enraged and the other burst into tears in my office—I went to see the Dean. He scheduled a meeting with the young faculty member and also urged her to make some changes. In addition, we both attended another meeting with her in which we offered to help in any way we could—for instance, by providing a "teaching mentor" or by allowing her to choose different courses to teach. The Dean even mentioned in passing that if she was upset about anything in her personal life, the university would pay for counseling. She declined the help, saying that she didn't need it, and again promised to change her teaching style.

When the semester ended, I was not surprised to find that she received the lowest student ratings in the department; in fact, they were the lowest ratings I had ever seen. The situation did not improve in the spring when she switched from teaching undergraduate to graduate courses. The complaints began again almost at once. But one thing did change: while the undergraduate students in her classes had made only verbal complaints, several Ph.D. students chose to write formal letters. These letters were quite detailed and charged that her language was both offensive and abusive. One female student, for example, stated that the professor had said to her, in class, "Why do you wear that short skirt—because you can't attract a man any other way than by showing your thighs?" I didn't see any choice but to take these letters to the Dean. He, in turn, took them to the Vice President and, soon, a decision came down from above: We would *not* renew her contract. When I told her, she threatened to sue me, the Department, and the University. In fact, she did hire an attorney. After reading the files that described the many student complaints and all of our efforts to help her deal with the problem, the attorney advised her simply to leave: there was not the slightest indication of any form of discrimination against her—sexual or otherwise. The day she gave me the key to her office and left the building was a melancholy one for me. On the one hand, I was relieved because she had, indeed, had a very negative impact on students and on the Department. On the other hand, I couldn't help thinking, "What a waste of talent."

Why do we start with this incident? Because it relates closely to the major theme of this chapter—the application of social psychology's findings to important practical issues. As we noted in Chapter 1, other people play a crucial role in our lives, and we interact with and think about them in virtually every situation we encounter. As a result, the findings of social psychology are very useful for understanding important questions relating to the *legal system, medical system,* and *organizations* (the workplace), because all of these settings involve social interactions between two or more persons (see Figure 13.1).

In the remainder of this chapter, we will examine the many ways in which social psychology has contributed to our understanding of events and processes in (1) the *legal system* (for example, how a jury's decisions are affected by what is said and done by attorneys, judges, and defendants), (2) the *medical system* (for example, how stress affects health and strategies for coping with stress, and (3) *organizations* (for example, why people like or dislike their jobs, prosocial behavior at work, and leadership).

Applying Social Psychology to the Interpersonal Aspects of the Legal System

If the real world lived up to our ideals, the judicial process would provide an elaborate and totally fair set of procedures that ensured objective, unbiased, and consistent decisions about violations of criminal and civil laws. At the opposite extreme, our worst nightmares of injustice would be realized if all judges were corrupt, the police always coerced confessions by mistreating defendants, all lawyers were dishonest, and all jurors were ignorant, disinterested, and biased. In fact, the legal system is neither as perfect as it could ideally be nor as imperfect as inadequate and unethical participants could ideally make it. Instead, research indicates that the people involved in the legal process usually try to do what they believe to be the right thing.

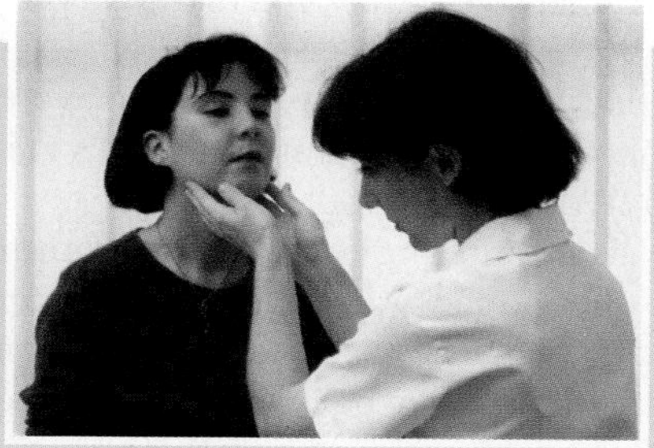

FIGURE 13.1

Applying Social Psychology.
The findings and knowledge of social psychology have proved to be quite useful in the search for answers to important questions relating to the *legal system, medical system,* and *organizations* (work settings), because each of these realms involves the social interactions of two or more persons.

Nevertheless, there are problems. As we have shown over and over again in the previous chapters, the perceptions, cognitions, emotions, and judgments of human beings are influenced by many factors other than objectivity. The psychological study of legal issues—**forensic psychology**—deals with the effects of psychological factors on legal processes (Davis, 1989). Among the many consequences of human fallibility influencing legal matters are biased judgments, reliance on stereotypes, faulty memories, and incorrect or unfair decisions. Because of these connections between psychology and the law, psychologists are often asked to serve as expert witnesses (Sleek, 1998) and as consultants in the courtroom. The role of these experts and consultants raises questions about how best to train them for these functions and whether they should be licensed (Moran, 2001).

Before the Trial Begins: Effects of Police Procedures and Media Coverage

Long before a criminal case reaches a courtroom, two major factors influence both the testimony that will eventually be presented and the pretrial attitudes of the jurors: (1) how the police deal with witnesses and suspects, and (2) how information about the case is presented in the media.

Why do most people obey the law? Why do they usually accept judicial decisions? Social psychological research indicates that people obey the law and accept judicial decisions as long as they believe that the procedures and the laws are fair and just (Tyler et al., 1997). When, however, people have reason to believe that the system is unfair—that, for example, the police are racist (Wilson, 2000)—lawful behavior and trust in the system declines. In a similar way, when there is a discrepancy between the average person's sense of justice and the law, people tend to ignore the law and to exert pressure to change it (Darley, 2001). For example, laws prohibiting the manufacture and sale of alcohol in the United States in the 1920s were widely unpopular; prohibition laws were broken by many otherwise upright citizens, and the constitutional ban on alcohol was eventually repealed.

■ EFFECTS OF POLICE PROCEDURES. Do police procedures affect perceptions of fairness? In both the United Kingdom and the United States, most people agree that the correct role for police in investigating a crime is to search for the truth as inquisitors, not to attempt to prove that someone is guilty as adversaries. An extreme example of the adversarial approach occurred in the investigation of the JonBenet Ramsey murder by Boulder, Colorado, police detectives. Assuming that one or both of the little girl's parents were guilty, the detectives planted a hidden microphone and camera at the child's grave, hoping to overhear a graveside confession (Woodbury, 2000).

The attempt to prove guilt more commonly involves the way a witness or suspect is questioned. As suggested in Figure 13.2, the image of manipulation by a "good cop" versus a "bad cop" is a common one. In Great Britain, a law was passed requiring that police be trained not to seek confessions but simply to gather the facts. Does such training help?

To answer that question, a Scotland Yard study was designed to determine exactly how British detectives go about the interrogation process (Williamson, 1993). Observations were made of actual interactions between detectives and suspects, and the officers were found to differ in their goals and in their style. Despite the new training that stressed fact-finding to obtain evidence, many of the detec-

forensic psychology: Psychological research and theory that deals with the effects of cognitive, affective, and behavioral factors on legal processes.

"Before we begin, may I ask which of you is the good cop, and which is the bad?"

FIGURE 13.2

Styles of Police Interrogation.

Two common styles used to interrogate suspects are a friendly, conversational approach versus an angry, confrontational approach. These styles have come to be known as "good cop" and "bad cop."

tives remained oriented toward obtaining a confession. Beyond differing in their goals, detectives also differed in their style—they were either friendly and cooperative or angry and confrontational. When the detectives were classified with respect to their goals and their styles, as shown in Figure 13.3 on page 522, they were split about fifty-fifty with respect to seeking evidence versus seeking a confession, but 70 percent were found to employ a cooperative approach rather than a confrontational one. Some observers believe, however, that most law officers actually do seek confessions but have learned to limit such questioning to times when their behavior is not being observed or recorded (Moston & Stephenson, 1993).

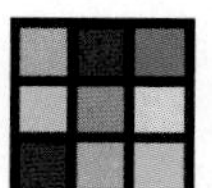

Beyond goals and styles, most interrogations take place in an atmosphere that is intimidating to the person being questioned. A person finds himself or herself in a police station being questioned by an official who is clearly in charge of the interaction. The situation is one in which social influence processes (see Chapter 9) are designed to obtain compliance and even obedience (Gudjonsson & Clark, 1986; Schooler & Loftus, 1986). How do these procedures influence what is said?

When we try to remember *any* event or past experience, the result is a blend of fact and fiction (Roediger & McDermott, 2000). Our cognitive system is *not* a recorder; rather, its function is to attempt to make sense out of the world. Whether we are telling a friend about something we did last week or an investigator about

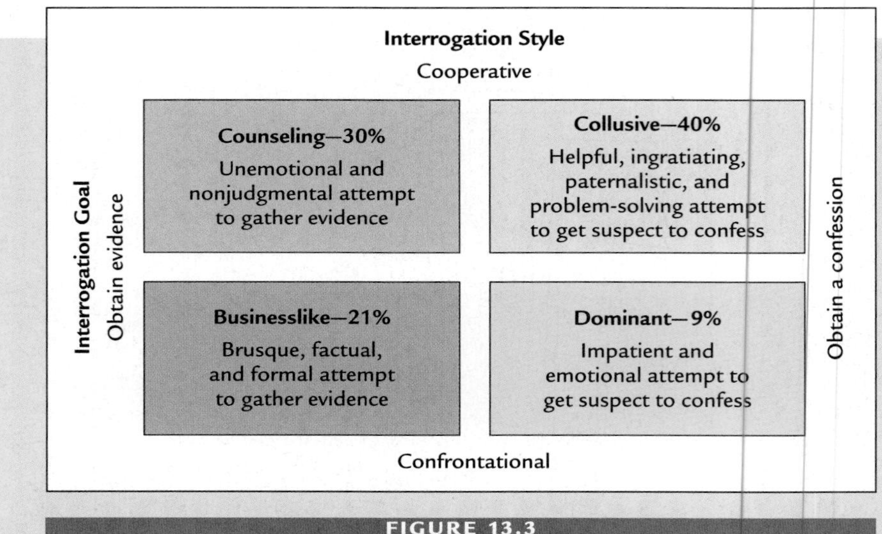

FIGURE 13.3

Evidence versus a Confession, Cooperation versus Confrontation. Police interrogations can be classified according to the goal of the interrogator (to obtain factual evidence or to obtain a confession) and the style of the interrogator (friendly and cooperative or angry and confrontational). In a British study, about half of the detectives were oriented toward obtaining facts and half toward obtaining a confession. With respect to style, however, over two thirds engaged in cooperative behavior and less than a third in confrontational behavior.

[SOURCE: BASED ON DATA FROM WILLIAMSON, 1993.]

what we saw at the crime scene, memory errors occur because we make inferences about what we see and hear. This natural tendency to create a meaningful story can be guided in a specific direction by a skilled questioner and thus exploited.

This natural tendency to tell a coherent story is combined with social influence processes, and three specific factors encourage compliant and obedient responding. Suspect and witnesses usually have (1) some *uncertainty* about the "right" answers, (2) some degree of *trust* in the officer asking the questions, and (3) the *expectation* that he or she is supposed to know what the answers should be. All of this makes it more difficult to say, "I don't know" or "I don't remember," so most people tend to provide some kind of answer. Even if the answer is qualified by "maybe" or "I believe" or whatever, the person who gave the answer becomes convinced that it must have been correct, especially if the interrogator reinforces the behavior with a nod, with a smile, or by saying, "Good." This subtle approach can be very effective when dealing with someone suspected of committing a crime, especially if the interrogator induces a false sense of security by suggesting that the evidence is weak, that the charge is not a serious one, or even that the victim was to blame (Kassin & McNall, 1991).

In such an interaction, the person being questioned can come to believe and even "remember" the details of an event that never happened, confessing to a crime of which he or she is actually innocent. Kassin and Kiechel (1996) were able to obtain such false confessions from college students in a laboratory setting. Each male research participant interacted with a female student who was actually an experimental assistant. The two individuals were assigned a task in which the assistant read letters of the alphabet, which the participant then typed on a keyboard. They were warned *never* to press the ALT key because this would cause the program to crash and the data to be lost. No one actually did hit that key, but during the experiment, the computer suddenly ceased functioning. The experimenter rushed in, pretending to be upset, and accused the participant of having ruined everything by pressing the forbidden key. Each participant was asked, "Did you press the ALT key?" The innocent student could (1) *comply* by signing a false confession, (2) *internalize* the false confession by telling another student privately that he really did press the key, or (3) *confabulate* by later "recalling" false details of his supposed "crime." Two conditions were varied to determine their effects on false confessions. One, the accomplice either read the letters at a fast or a slow pace. Presumably, the participant would be less able to remember exactly what he did in the fast condition. Two, the accomplice either said that she had not seen what happened or that she had seen the student hit the key—thus providing false evidence against him.

Altogether, even though all were innocent of wrongdoing, 69 percent of the students signed the false confession, 28 percent internalized their guilt, and 9 percent confabulated and "remembered" false details about what happened. As shown in Figure 13.4, false confessions were more likely when the pace was fast and also

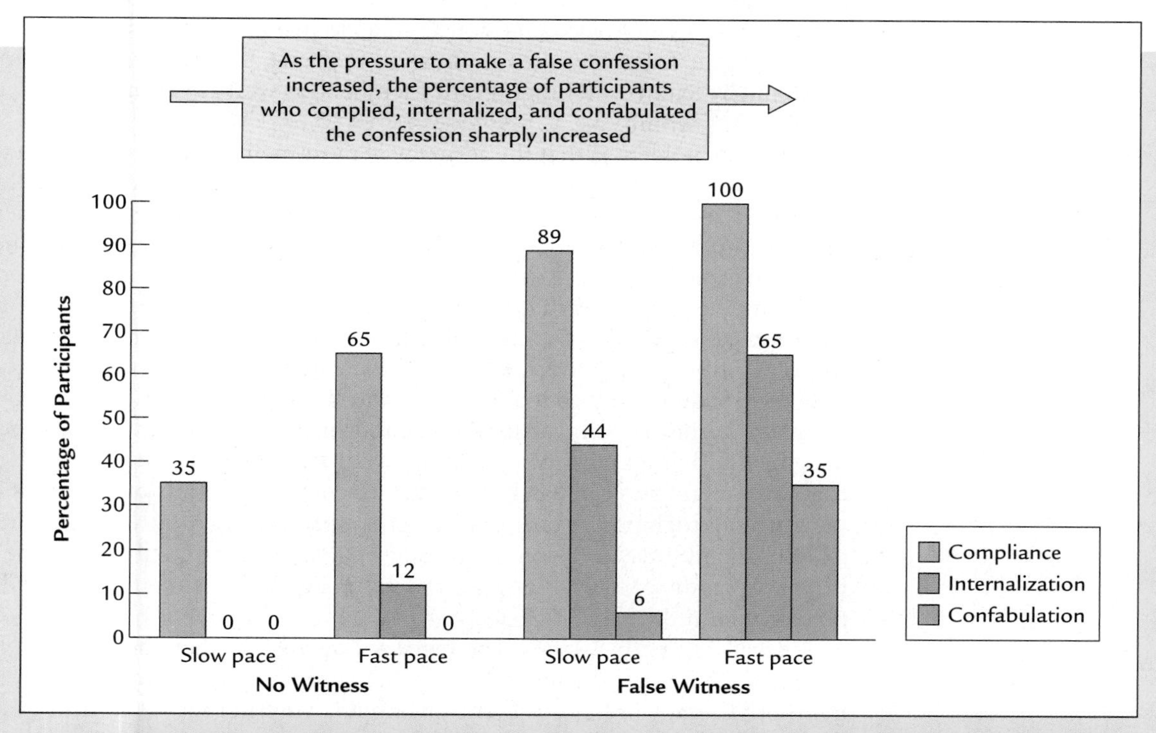

FIGURE 13.4

Innocent People Make False Confessions of Guilt.

It is possible to persuade an innocent individual not only to comply with a request to confess guilt for something he or she didn't do, but also to internalize the guilt (believing that he or she actually did it) and to *confabulate* ("remembering" details of the "crime"). In a lab study, false confessions increased when a witness gave false evidence and when a fast pace made it more difficult to pay attention to details. In the condition in which there was a false witness and a fast pace, all of the participants confessed to the crime, two thirds internalized the guilt and believed they had done it, and about a third confabulated false details.

[SOURCE: BASED ON DATA FROM KASSIN & KIECHEL, 1996.]

when the accomplice said that she saw the key being pushed. In the condition that created the greatest vulnerability—a fast pace and a false witness, every participant *confessed,* most *internalized* their guilt, and more than a third *confabulated* by remembering details of their "crime" that hadn't really been committed.

If such confessions can be obtained in a laboratory experiment at a university, it seems very likely that they can take place in actual interrogations as well. Kassin (1997) concludes that the criminal justice system does not provide adequate protection for the innocent person who becomes a suspect. He further argues that a confession obtained by means that involve manipulations such as providing the suspect with fake evidence should not be considered credible in a court of law.

■ INTERROGATION (AND THERAPY) AS AN IMPETUS TO RECOVERED MEMORIES. Beyond the issue of false confessions is the related but more general question of "recovered memories." When, for example, an adult (often during questioning about a crime or during psychotherapy) remembers a traumatic criminal act in his or her past, how accurate is that memory? There are many highly publicized accounts of the sudden recovery of memories of being sexually abused in childhood, but Humphreys (1998) suggests that many of these recollections are false. He notes that in addition to credible accounts of incest and other crimes, other so-called memories center on sexual abuse by aliens from another planet, by strangers in a previous lifetime, and by Satan-worshipping cult members, as well as prenatal experiences in the mother's womb.

A general problem is that the accuracy of most memories decreases with the passage of time. One study documented major changes in the memories of college students with respect to the details of how they had heard the news about the verdict in the O. J. Simpson murder trial (Schmolck, Buffalo, & Squire, 2000). Their recollections three days after the event were compared with what they remembered fifteen months and thirty-two months later. After fifteen months, half of the recollections were highly accurate, though 11 percent contained major errors or distortions. After thirty-two months, only 29 percent were highly accurate, and more than 40 percent contained major distortions. It seems likely that if memories associated with a news event can deteriorate this badly over time, memories about sexual abuse and other personal experiences can be at least as faulty. It is also found that false memories can easily be constructed out of various experiences such as viewing photographs, hearing what other people say, and even daydreaming (Henkel, Franklin, & Johnson, 2000). Such experiences are combined in one's mind into a coherent story, and the result is a firm belief that something actually happened when it did not.

A debate currently is focused on **repressed memory**—when the memory of a traumatic incident is completely forgotten. When such memories are recovered in the course of therapy or hypnosis, the question is whether they constitute valid evidence that could be relevant to a criminal prosecution (Brown, 1997) or false memories that pose a threat to innocent individuals accused of committing criminal acts (Loftus, 1998).

As we described with respect to false confessions, false recovered memories can also be created in the laboratory (Loftus, Coan, & Pickrell, 1996; Loftus & Pickrell, 1995). If you were told about something that supposedly happened to you when you were a child, would you then "remember" it? Quite possibly you would. When adults (aged eighteen to fifty-three) were told three true stories of events in their childhood (provided by relatives) along with one false story about an event that did not occur, 25 percent of the participants said they "remembered" the imaginary incident. It is possible to convince an even higher percentage of people to accept

repressed memory: A form of psychogenic amnesia; forgetting the details of a traumatic event as a way of defending oneself from having to deal with the anxiety and fear associated with the event.

false memories when the recovery is encouraged by an experimenter's questions or by hypnotic suggestion. For example, under such circumstances, 60 percent of the participants say they remember events occurring on the day they were born (DuBreuil, Garry, & Loftus, 1998; Loftus, 1997). As Loftus concludes, "Planting memories is not a particularly difficult thing to do" (1997, p. 64).

Recent research has shown, however, that those who report having recovered memories differ in some respects from those who do not. For example, in a laboratory setting, women with recovered memories are also especially likely to "recognize" words as having been shown to them by the experimenter when that was not true (Clancy et al., 2000). Further, some people are more easily led to false memories than are others, and some are better at leading another person to have such memories than are others (Porter, Birt et al., 2000). As one example, the creation of a false memory is facilitated when the participant is low in extroversion and the interviewer is high in extroversion.

The overall problem is highlighted by studies of recovered memories of events for which independent evidence is available (Arrigo & Pezdek, 1997). Events such as automobile accidents, natural disasters, combat, attempted suicide, and the death of a parent can be forgotten as a psychological mechanism to reduce fear and anxiety, and this is known as *psychogenic amnesia.* When such memories are gradually recovered, some are found to be totally accurate while some are found to be totally false. It seems very likely that the same level of accuracy and inaccuracy holds for recovered memories of childhood events (Poole & Lindsay, 1998; Newcombe et al., 2000). What is needed, but not yet available, is a way to distinguish between accurate and inaccurate memories.

■ EFFECTS OF THE MEDIA. A Gallup poll (in the 1990s) reported that Americans consider crime to be their most important concern. Crime is obviously something that none of us wants to experience, but the general belief is that it is widespread and threatening, more so than is actually the case (Ostrow, 1995). Surveys show that U.S. citizens believe that criminal activity has reached epidemic proportions and is getting progressively worse (Hull, 1995; Jackson, 1996). In fact, FBI statistics indicate that the number of crimes has been dropping steadily since 1992 (Crime and punishment . . . , 2001; Ho, 2000; Sniffen, 1999). For example, the Bureau of Justice Statistics reported a 15 percent drop in violent crime in 2000 and a 2.7 percent drop in car theft (Crime, 2001). Why the discrepancy between beliefs and facts?

A plausible explanation is the availability heuristic, discussed in Chapter 3. The news presented on radio and television and in newspapers is heavily weighted toward what is of dramatic interest—murder, assault, rape, robbery, arson, and so forth, primarily because the public finds such stories more interesting than stories about good people doing good deeds (Pooley, 1997). The result is that we overestimate the frequency of illegal activity and underestimate the frequency of prosocial behavior. A second explanation is that negative information has a greater impact than positive information (Skowronski & Carston, 1989), as discussed in Chapters 3 and 7.

Despite the good news about the crime rate, it should be noted that the rate of murders by teenagers is rapidly increasing (Lacayo, 1997). The U.S. Bureau of Justice Statistics indicates that youngsters aged twelve to fifteen have a 1 in 8 chance of being a crime victim. Those most worried about crime, however, are aged sixty-five and older, and their chance of being a crime victim is only 1 in 179 (Teens top . . . , 1995).

Media reports of crime clearly influence our general perceptions, but a more serious problem is the way in which the media cover specific crimes and specific

FIGURE 13.5
Guilty or Innocent?
When a crime suspect is arrested, the general public (including some individuals who will eventually become jurors) is exposed to media coverage of the crime and of the suspect. Such coverage leads the public to assume guilt. This assumption on the part of jurors results in an increased likelihood of a decision that a defendant is guilty. Thus, pretrial publicity strengthens the case of the prosecution and weakens the case for the defense.

individuals who are suspected of committing those crimes. Whenever a suspect is arrested in such cases, we quickly learn a great deal about that person and are shown photographs and videotapes of the accused wearing handcuffs and being surrounded by law officers, as in Figure 13.5. If the suspect has been arrested, it is assumed there must be some compelling evidence indicating guilt. Because the public is not provided with any opposing evidence indicating the suspect's possible innocence, there is a strong tendency to form a negative impression based on the primacy effect (see Chapter 2).

Additional factors add to the media's influence. People tend to believe assertions made in the media—"They wouldn't say it on television unless it were true" (Gilbert, Tafarodi, & Malone, 1993). In addition, those crimes that make the news are often terrible ones, and the public is eager to identify and punish the individual responsible for the evil deed. Altogether, people tend to leap to assumptions of guilt long before the evidence with respect to guilt or innocence is presented in court.

The assumptions of the public may be wrong, but what harm does that do? The most serious problem is that the members of the jury will be drawn from that same public whose opinions have been influenced by the media. As a result, pretrial publicity tends to help the prosecution and harm the defense, as Moran and Cutler (1991) have documented. Because the individuals who serve as jurors have already formed opinions before the trial even begins, there is a potential effect on the final decision made by the jury. In fact, the greater the amount of publicity about a crime, the greater the tendency of jurors to convict whoever is accused of committing it (Linz & Penrod, 1992). Government officials take advantage of these effects by providing as much crime information as possible to the media so that potential jurors will form a negative impression of the accused and thus support the government's case (G. Moran, personal communication, February 23, 1993).

One solution to such bias and to its manipulation would be to change the law. For example, the United States allows publicity about a case before and during trials, whereas Canada restricts such coverage in order to avoid "polluting" the jury (Farnsworth, 1995). Another solution to the media problem is suggested by the findings of Fein, McClosky, and Tomlinson (1997). The biasing effect of pretrial publicity is greatly weakened if the jurors are provided with a good reason to be suspicious about *why* incriminating evidence was made available to the media. This shifts attention away from the content of the leaked evidence to the underlying *motivation* of those who did the leaking.

You may someday find yourself serving on a jury. If so and if you would like to avoid the kind of juror errors just described and others to be described in the following pages, please see the **Ideas to Take with You—And Use!** section on page 564.

Eyewitness Testimony: Problems and Solutions

Anyone who witnesses a crime or something relevant to a crime may be asked to testify and thus provide crucial information in an investigation or in a trial. Each year, witnesses in U.S. courtrooms provide crucial positive or negative evidence involving 75,000 suspects (Goldstein, Chance, & Schneller, 1989). Eyewitness testimony has a major impact on the decisions of juries (Wolf & Bugaj, 1990). Obviously, the accuracy of those witnesses is crucial. What have psychologists learned about this topic?

■ WHEN WITNESSES ARE WRONG. There are many dramatic instances in which witnesses, including the victims of crimes, have identified the wrong suspect, who has then been convicted and imprisoned (Loftus, 1992a).

Even the most honest, intelligent, and well-meaning witnesses to an event can make mistakes, and we have known about this since the beginning of the twentieth century, when empirical research on witness accuracy was first conducted in Germany (e.g., Munsterberg, 1907). One of the early studies took place in a law school class in Berlin in 1901 (Gawande, 2001). During the lecture, a student interrupted the professor by shouting an objection to what was being said. Another student angrily responded to the first, and they exchanged insults. With clenched fists, they threatened each other, and one drew a gun. The professor ran toward the students and placed himself between them; there was a struggle, and then a shot was heard. The excited members of the class were then surprised to see the two students return to their seats. The professor then returned to his lectern and told the audience that the incident had been planned. At that point, all of the students were asked to describe exactly what had occurred. Some were asked to write an account immediately, some delayed the writing for a day or a week, and some were subjected to cross-examination about the events they had witnessed. What was found?

> *The results were dismal. The most accurate witness got twenty-six per cent of the significant details wrong; others up to eighty per cent. Words were put in people's mouths. Actions were described that had never taken place. Events that* had *taken place disappeared from memory. (Gawande, 2001, p. 50)*

After over a century of research on this topic, we now know that those early findings in Germany are as relevant today as they were a hundred years ago. Sadly enough, it has been found that inaccurate eyewitnesses constitute the single most important factor in the wrongful conviction of innocent defendants (Wells, 1993; Wells, Luus, & Windschitl, 1994). A more positive fact is that we now know a great deal about why such mistakes are made, and it is now possible to avoid at least some of them.

Loftus (1992b) has pointed out that a major obstacle to accuracy is the passage of time between the time an event is witnessed and the time testimony is given. During that interval, the witness is almost always exposed to *misleading postevent information* from police questioning, news stories, and the statements that other people make. All such information becomes incorporated into what the witness remembers (see Chapter 3). The information blends into a "story" that consists of details the person *seems* to remember.

Besides the passage of time, what other factors influence accuracy? A study by Kassin and his colleagues (2001) asked sixty-four psychologists who were experts on this topic. Eighty percent of them agreed on the effects of each of the phenomena that are indicated in Table 13.1. You can see that accuracy is impaired, for example, when the witness experiences a high level of stress during the event, when a weapon was present, when only one person is asked to be identified (a show-up) rather than selected out of a group of people (a lineup), and when members of a lineup are fairly similar to one another in appearance.

The list in Table 13.1 suggests that many of the problems are based on familiar psychological principles that we have discussed in the previous chapters. For example, witnesses are better at identifying an individual of their own race rather than someone of another race who "all look alike." The problem is not an inability to distinguish individuals of another race but rather the tendency to respond to race first and then rush to utilize a racial schema containing racial stereotypes (Levin, 2000). Because people often process the information in this manner, they

TABLE 13.1

Factors That Influence Eyewitness Accuracy. A group of sixty-four psychologists with courtroom experience were asked their opinions about factors affecting eyewitness testimony. There was 80 percent agreement among these experts with respect to fifteen factors that influence accuracy, including the ones shown here.

FACTOR	EFFECT ON ACCURACY OF EYEWITNESS
Mug shot–induced bias	Exposure to mug shots of a suspect increases the likelihood that the witness will later choose that suspect in a lineup.
Postevent information	Eyewitness testimony about an event often reflects not only what the witness actually saw, but information he or she obtained later on.
Alcoholic intoxication	Alcoholic intoxication impairs an eyewitness's later ability to recall persons and events.
Cross-race bias	Eyewitnesses are more accurate when identifying members of their own race than members of other races.
Weapon focus	The presence of a weapon impairs an eyewitness's ability to accurately identify the perpetrator's face.
Child suggestibility	Young children are more vulnerable than adults to interviewer suggestion, peer pressures, and other social influences.

[SOURCE: BASED ON INFORMATION IN KASSIN ET AL., 2001.]

FIGURE 13.6

Recognizing Suspects Recorded on Videotape.
When suspects are videotaped by a surveillance camera, the relatively poor quality of the resulting picture makes identification difficult. Based on video stills such as that on the left, both undergraduates and experienced police officers were inaccurate in identifying the individual (as shown in the well-lighted photograph on the right) *unless* they already knew the person.

don't get around to examining the specific individual and how he or she looks (Carpenter, 2000b).

In any event, it should be useful to develop guidelines as to when testimony is most and least likely to be reliable, and about the wisdom of avoiding certain procedures.

A somewhat different problem involves recognizing people who have been videotaped while committing a crime (Burton et al., 1999). It is increasingly common to have evidence available from surveillance cameras installed in banks, department stores, and other public places. Consider the photographs in Figure 13.6. Most of us could identify the individual on the basis of the photograph on the right. But how well could you do with the still from a video shown on the left? Unless the man in the video still is someone they already know, research participants do very poorly in attempts to identify him, and experienced police officers do just as poorly. Altogether, poor-quality video images result in poor-quality identifications, unless the suspect is a friend of yours.

■ INCREASING EYEWITNESS ACCURACY. Despite the very real possibility of errors, you should not conclude that eyewitnesses are *always* wrong; often, they are extremely accurate (Youille & Cutshall, 1986). In addition, many attempts have been made to increase accuracy (Foxhall, 2000). The result is a nationwide change in the way that eyewitness testimony is gathered by police (Wells et al., 2000). Responding to many cases in which DNA analysis indicated wrongful convictions and to decades of relevant psychological research, U.S. Attorney General Janet Reno ordered the National Institute of Justice to develop nationwide guidelines designed to improve the accuracy of evidence provided by eyewitnesses (Technical Working Group for Eyewitness Evidence, 1999).

A major target for improvement has been the police lineup in which witnesses examine several individuals (the suspect plus several nonsuspects) and try to identify the one who is guilty. Wells and Luus (1990) suggest that a lineup is analogous to a social psychological experiment. The officer conducting the lineup is the *experimenter,* the eyewitnesses are the *research participants,* the suspect is the primary *stimulus,* a witness's positive identification constitutes the *behavioral data,* and the presence of nonsuspects plus the arrangement of the lineup constitute the *research design.* And, most often the police investigators have a *hypothesis* about the guilt of the suspect. Finally, for both experimental findings and legal testimony, the data should be stated in terms of *probability,* because neither procedure can provide absolute certainty.

blank-lineup control: A procedure in which a witness views a police lineup that does not include a suspect. If a witness does not identify a suspect, this increases confidence in his or her testimony. If the witness *does* identify an innocent person, he or she is told of the mistake and cautioned to be more careful. In either instance, witness accuracy is increased.

In Chapter 1 you read about factors that can interfere with obtaining accurate experimental results—for example, demand characteristics, experimenter bias, and the absence of a control group. The same factors can interfere with witness accuracy in responding to police lineups. Accuracy is improved, for example, when police use a **blank-lineup control** procedure. A witness is first shown a lineup containing only innocent individuals and not the suspect (Wells, 1984). If the witness fails to identify any of them, there is increased confidence in his or her accuracy. If an innocent person *is* identified, the witness is informed of his or her mistake and cautioned about the danger of making a false identification. Such an experience improves the accuracy of witnesses when actual lineups are then presented. The parallels between lineups and experiments, as well as suggestions for improving accuracy, are summarized in Table 13.2.

TABLE 13.2

Lineups and Experiments: How to Obtain Reliable and Objective Information. There are many parallels between police lineups and social psychological experiments, according to Wells and Luus (1990). Based on this analogy, it follows that police officers can improve the accuracy of lineups by following well-established experimental procedures that provide safeguards against contaminated data. In lineups as well as in experiments, it is crucial to avoid biasing the data, to eliminate demand characteristics, and so forth.

RECOMMENDED PROCEDURES FOR POLICE LINEUPS AND PHOTO LINEUPS	ANALOGOUS PROCEDURES IN PSYCHOLOGICAL EXPERIMENTS
Witnesses should be separated and not permitted to interact.	Participants cannot communicate with one another before responding; otherwise, their data are not independent.
A witness should not be told or led to believe that the actual perpetrator is in the lineup.	Experimental instructions should be worded so as not to create demands that the participants respond in a given way.
The officer conducting the lineup should not know the identity of the suspected perpetrator.	The experimental assistants who interact with the participants should be kept "blind" as to both the hypothesis and the experimental condition to which the participant is assigned.
If there is more than one witness, the position of the suspect in the lineup should be different for each witness.	The order in which stimuli are presented should be randomized or counterbalanced across participants.
Not until the lineup procedure is totally concluded should cues of any kind be given to a witness with respect to whether or not the person he or she identified is actually the suspect in the case.	Not until the experiment is concluded and all dependent measures collected should a participant be debriefed and told the experimenter's hypothesis.

Other procedures for improving accuracy include the presentation of pictures of the crime scene and the victim to the witness before an identification is made (Cutler, Penrod, & Martens, 1987), showing the lineup one person at a time rather than as a group (Leary, 1988), and encouraging witnesses to give their first impressions (Dunning & Stern, 1994). Further, those conducting the lineup should refrain from giving feedback such as "Good. You identified the actual suspect." Such reinforcement increases the witness's confidence in his or her judgment, even if that judgment is actually incorrect (Wells & Bradfield, 1999).

The Central Participants in a Trial: Effects of Attorneys, Judges, Jurors, and Defendants

Research has repeatedly shown that the outcome of a trial is not simply a matter of evidence and logic. Those elements matter, but their effects are combined with the seemingly irrelevant aspects of what is said and done and thought by attorneys, judges, jurors, and the defendants.

■ ATTORNEYS: ADVERSARIES FOR THE PROSECUTION AND FOR THE DEFENSE. In our legal system, the two sides do not cooperate in order to reach a common goal such as "the truth." Instead, they compete in a struggle to win rather than lose the case (Garcia, Darley, & Robinson, 2001). The prosecutor does everything possible to make the defendant look bad, and the defender attempts to make him or her look good. The opposing attorneys also strive to make themselves liked and trusted by the members of the jury, as shown in Figure 13.7.

A crucial phase of courtroom procedure that occurs just before a trial is jury selection through the **voir dire** procedure, in which attorneys for each side can "see

voir dire: A French term ("to see and to speak") used in law to mean the examination of prospective jurors in order to determine their competence to serve. The judge and the opposing attorneys may dismiss prospective jurors for specific reasons or, within limits, for no stated reason.

FIGURE 13.7

Opposing Attorneys: Presenting Evidence and Playing a Role.
In addition to dealing with legal issues, each attorney in a criminal case has two messages to convey. First, he or she must be perceived by the jury as knowledgeable, honest, and likable. Second, he or she must weave a convincing and believable story that makes the defendant appear either guilty or not guilty. In many respects, then, the ideal trial lawyer is both a legal expert and a skilled actor. ■

and speak with" potential jurors to determine who is acceptable and who is not. The stated goal is to choose the most competent and impartial citizens to serve, but in fact the opposing legal representatives do their best to select jurors they believe will be helpful to their side of the case and/or harmful to the other side.

Abramson (1994) suggests that jury trials have become a game in which each side does its best to load the jury with those most likely to be biased one way or the other. Sometimes this attempt to stack the deck goes to extremes, but not quite as bad as the example in Figure 13.8. Perhaps the best news in the interest of fairness is that both experienced lawyers and untrained college students are more often wrong than right in predicting how prospective jurors will actually respond to the opposing arguments.

During the trial itself, attorneys are *not* permitted to ask **leading questions**—questions designed to elicit specific answers—when examining their own witnesses. For example, a leading question would be "How much blood did you see on Mrs. Johnson's car seat?" An acceptable version would be, "Would you describe what you observed when you looked into Mrs. Johnson's car?" In cross-examination, however, leading questions *are* permitted, and, not surprisingly, they are found to influence how a witness responds (Smith & Ellsworth, 1987).

When they make closing arguments, attorneys for each side get one last chance to influence how jurors will vote, and much of what they say is designed to do just that. In capital trials (those involving the charge of first-degree murder), the jury not only decides guilt or innocence in Phase I of the trial, but also recommends in Phase I to the judge whether a guilty defendant should be sentenced to life in prison or to be put to death. In some states, the jury actually makes the decision rather than recommending it to the judge. Whether recommending or deciding, the only criterion that jurors should use is whether there are "aggravating and mitigating circumstances." Prosecutors seeking the death penalty often stray from that guideline, however, and make statements designed to convince jurors to decide in favor

leading questions: Questions designed to elicit specific answers rather than simply to elicit information.

"I'm afraid we'll have to excuse you, madam. Your pronounced aversion to armed robbery makes it unlikely that you could serve impartially."

FIGURE 13.8

Voir Dire: Selecting Jurors Who Are Biased in the Desired Direction.
The jury selection process is intended to detect and eliminate prospective jurors who are unable to make objective, impartial judgments based on the evidence presented in the trial. To a significant degree, the process permits the opposing sides to select jurors who are biased in their favor, though not as obviously as the defense attorney in this cartoon.

of the death penalty (Platania & Moran, 1999). Platania and Moran determined the effect of such statements by presenting over three hundred jury-eligible individuals with a videotaped enactment of the summaries, closing arguments, and judge's instructions in the penalty phase of a capital case. Participants in the control condition viewed a tape in which the prosecutor's arguments were legally acceptable; those in the experimental group viewed a tape in which the prosecutor engaged in verbal misconduct by making twelve inappropriate statements, as shown in Table 13.3. In the control condition, the percentages of jurors recommending that

TABLE 13.3

Improper Statements Made by Prosecutor in Closing Arguments of a Capital Case. Though the closing arguments in the penalty phase of a capital case are supposed to be limited to issues involving aggravating and mitigating circumstances, the prosecutor sometimes makes improper statements that convince jurors to recommend the death penalty. The following statements were taken from the statements of the prosecutor in an actual case in which the defendant (Brooks) had been convicted of armed robbery, rape, kidnapping, and first-degree murder. When used in an experimental setting, these statements (compared to a closing argument in which there were no improper statements) resulted in significantly more recommendations for the death penalty by the jurors.

1. "He was just walking along with a pistol in his pocket, and decided: 'Well, I'll just make a hustle,' to use their language, his language."
2. The prosecutor's statement of his own personal opinion regarding capital punishment: "If you have to take sides, I take the side of capital punishment."
3. Comparing Brooks to a "cancer on the body of society."
4. Discussing the "dangerous criminal element," then seeking death for Brooks by stating, "He's a member of the dangerous criminal element."
5. Reference to taking the death penalty seriously, "In the seven and half years I've been District Attorney, I believe we've only asked for the death penalty less than a dozen times."
6. "The last person in Georgia was electrocuted in 1964," asserting that crime has increased since that time.
7. Discussion of the victim by emphasizing her youth, attractiveness, and kind disposition.
8. Diluting the jury's sense of responsibility by arguing that *it* would not be "responsible" for Brooks' death. "Brooks himself pulled the switch" on the day he murdered the victim.
9. Reminding the jury of the tragedy to the victim's family: "Next week when it's Thanksgiving and they are sitting around the table, Carol Jeannine won't be there and never will be there again."
10. Reference to the cost to taxpayers if the defendant spends the rest of his life in prison.
11. Focusing on the future dangerousness of the defendant by asking, "Whose daughter will it be next time?"
12. Arguing that the defendant believed in the death penalty: "He executed her in a whole lot more horrible way than the electric chair."

[SOURCE: BASED ON INFORMATION IN PLATANIA AND MORAN, 1999.]

the sentence be life in prison and recommending a death sentence were about equal. The effect of the prosecutor's words were dramatically evident in the experimental condition, in which 66 percent favored execution, compared to 46 percent in the control condition. Clearly, the words (appropriate or not) of the prosecutor have a significant effect on what the jurors decide.

■ THE JUDGE: ENFORCING RULES AND MINIMIZING BIAS. Ideally, judges are entirely objective and fair, but they are also human beings who can make mistakes and hold biases. Juries are instructed to base their verdicts entirely on factual evidence, but sometimes the evidence is challenged and then ruled inadmissible by the judge—"The jury will disregard the witness's last statement." Unless jurors believe that the *reason* for dismissing the evidence is a good one, many jurors simply ignore what the judge ruled (Kassin & Sommers, 1997). For example, in a mock trial, wiretap evidence was introduced in which the defendant told a friend, "I killed Marylou and some bastard she was with. God, I don't . . . yeah, I ditched the blade." After the defense objected, the judge ruled the evidence either admissible, inadmissible because the police made the recording without first obtaining a warrant, or inadmissible because the recording was barely audible and difficult to understand. The jurors were much more inclined to accept the judge's ruling when the reason was a bad tape, but many simply ignored the judge when the reason was a procedural error by the police.

Generally, jurors only comply selectively with instructions about inadmissibility, and some jurors do this more than others. For example, disregarding unreliable evidence but not illegally obtained evidence is most common among jurors high in the *need for cognition*—those who tend to engage in and enjoy difficult cognitive activity such as learning something new or solving puzzles (Sommers & Kassin, 2001). Such individuals seem to be more concerned with accuracy than with legal niceties.

In theory, neither the judge nor the jury is supposed to make a final decision about guilt or innocence until the end of the trial (Hastie, 1993), but most humans find it difficult or impossible to suspend judgment over the course of a trial. Even judges may form a private opinion and frequently speculate to their colleagues about what the verdict is likely to be. To test the possible effects of these unstated opinions on jurors, Hart (1995) showed research participants videotapes of one trial followed by tapes of a judge (actually one from a different trial) reading standard jury instructions. Then, the mock jurors decided on a verdict. The judge on each tape had told the experimenter whether he or she expected a guilty verdict. Even though these private beliefs involved a different trial and a different defendant from the one viewed by the research participants, these unspoken opinions about guilt or innocence somehow were communicated to the jury and influenced their decision. As shown in Figure 13.9, when a judge believed that a defendant was guilty, most of the mock jurors actually gave that verdict. When a judge believed that a defendant was not guilty, the jury split fifty-fifty on the verdict. Presumably, the judges' beliefs were communicated by their nonverbal behavior, such as facial expressions and gestures (as described in Chapter 2), and such cues in turn influenced how the jurors voted.

■ THE EFFECTS OF DEFENDANT AND JUROR CHARACTERISTICS. If you think of the defendant as a stranger encountered for the first time by a juror who then automatically evaluates that stranger, you might well guess that many of the factors studied by social psychologists would influence these evaluations (Niedermeier, Kerr, & Messe, 1999). Especially important determinants are nonverbal commu-

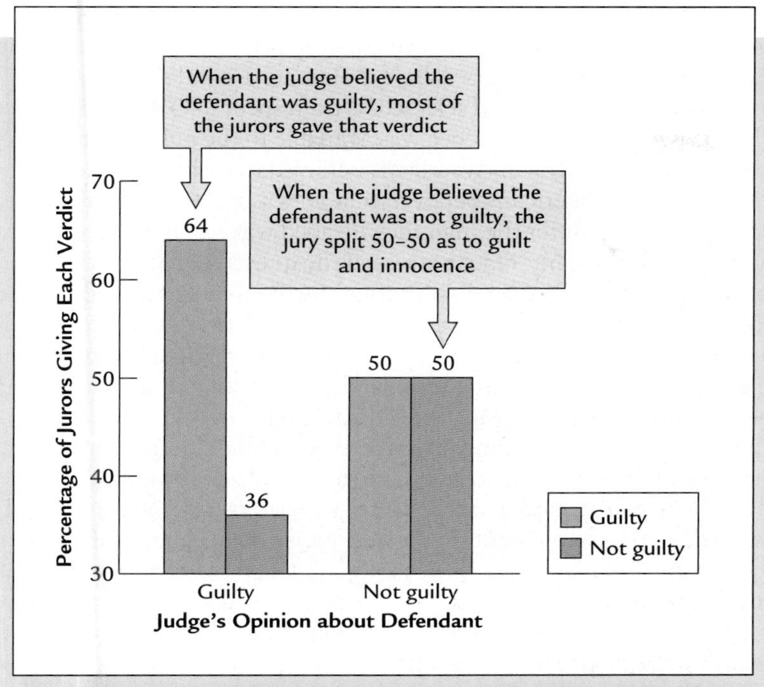

FIGURE 13.9

A Judge's Influence: Unintentional and Nonverbal. Mock jurors drawn from a jury pool were shown videotapes of an actual court trial and of a judge (actually one from a different trial) giving standard instructions to the jury. The experimenter had determined whether the videotaped judge in each case privately believed in the guilt or in the innocence of the defendant. When the judge believed the person was guilty, the research participants overwhelmingly returned a guilty verdict. When the judge believed the person was not guilty, the "jurors" split fifty-fifty. It seems that, through inadvertent nonverbal cues, the judge communicated his or her opinion, and this opinion affected the jurors' decisions.

[SOURCE: BASED ON DATA FROM HART, 1995.]

nication, attribution, impression formation, and impression management (Chapter 2), prejudice (Chapter 6), and interpersonal attraction (Chapter 7). Matters such as first impressions, stereotypes, and attraction should, of course, be irrelevant in the courtroom, but they are found to influence the outcomes of both real and simulated trials (Dane, 1992).

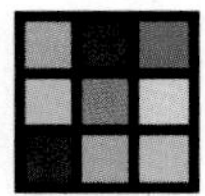

The question of race was brought up earlier with respect to eyewitnesses making less accurate identifications of members of another race than of their own. Do such cross-racial problems play any role in the courtroom? It may come as no surprise—the answer is *yes* (Sommers & Ellsworth, 2000). When, for example, the defendant is African American, the racial composition of the jury is extremely important. When O. J. Simpson was charged with the murder of his former wife and her male acquaintance, he faced a criminal trial in which a predominantly black jury drawn from downtown Los Angeles found him innocent. At a later date, in a civil trial involving responsibility for "wrongful death," a predominantly white jury drawn from Santa Monica found him guilty. Same defendant, same evidence, different juries, different verdicts. Why? Goleman (1994a) suggests that most trials are over once the jury has been selected. With respect to O. J. Simpson, before either trial began and before any evidence was available to the public, surveys consistently indicated that most African Americans believed that the defendant was innocent, while most white Americans believed that he was guilty. Whites stressed the need for severe punishment for the man they decided was responsible for murdering two innocent individuals, but blacks stressed the questionable evidence and, at most, the need for the defendant's rehabilitation. Such racial differences were consistent before the first trial, midway in the first trial, and after the second trial (Graham, Weiner, & Zucker, 1997; Lafferty, 1997; Toobin, 1995). In addition, racial attitudes were actually found to become more stable and consistent following the verdict in the criminal case (Nier, Mottola, & Gaertner, 2000).

Though the race of a defendant is a crucial (and obviously unfair) factor in the courtroom, jurors are also affected by the same (and equally unfair) factors that influence interpersonal attraction (see Chapter 7). For example, those accused of a crime are *less* likely to be found guilty if they are physically attractive, female, and of high socioeconomic status (Mazzella & Feingold, 1994). Attractiveness is surprisingly influential. In both real and mock trials, attractive defendants have the advantage over unattractive ones with respect to being acquitted, receiving a light sentence, and gaining the sympathy of the jurors (Downs & Lyons, 1991; Quigley, Johnson, & Byrne, 1995; Wuensch, Castellow, & Moore, 1991). It is even found that a smiling defendant is more likely to be recommended for leniency than a nonsmiling one (LaFrance & Hecht, 1995).

Beyond race, it also matters who a juror is and what he or she believes. For example, in cases involving rape, female jurors are less likely than males to conclude that the victim had engaged in consensual sex (Harris & Weiss, 1995). In cases of rape and child abuse, women are more likely than men to vote for conviction (Schutte & Hosch, 1997).

Jurors also differ in the way they process information, and these differences can lead to incompetent decisions. For example, about a third of those chosen as jurors have already made up their minds about the trial by the time the opening arguments are made. As the trial progresses, 75 to 85 percent begin to favor one side over the other, and this bias affects how subsequent evidence is processed (Carlson & Russo, 2001). Once a juror's bias is established, a guilty or a not-guilty schema is formed, and all of the evidence and testimony that follows is either (1) interpreted so as to fit the schema or (2) ignored if it absolutely doesn't fit (Kuhn, Weinstock, & Flaton, 1994).

Jurors whose minds are made up are very certain about their beliefs, give extreme verdicts, and are responsible for hung juries, because they resist changing their minds. In contrast, the most competent jurors process trial information by constructing at least two alternate schemas so that each bit of evidence can fit into one schema or the other.

Various decisions made by jurors are associated with specific personality dispositions and specific attitudes and beliefs. Some of these dispositional effects are summarized in Table 13.4.

Altogether, research on the legal system provides evidence that judicial fairness and objectivity often fail because of quite common human characteristics. The increased use of technology such as videotaped testimony, computer animation, and simulations in the courtroom (Carpenter, 2001) quite possibly will only add to problems with objectivity. The total elimination of biases in the courtroom is a laudable goal, but it may not be a reachable one.

TABLE 13.4

Juror Characteristics as Predictors of Juror Decisions. Various attitudes, beliefs, and personality dispositions of jurors have been found to be related to the decisions that those jurors make. A few of the findings are summarized here.

JUROR CHARACTERISTIC	JUROR DECISION
Leniency Bias (assumption that the defendant is also a victim)	less likely to vote guilty (MacCoun & Kerr, 1988)
Authoritarianism (tendency to hold authoritarian beliefs and attitudes)	more likely to vote guilty (Narby, Cutler, & Moran, 1993) and to react to all offenses as serious and deserving punishment (Feather, 1996)
Attributional Complexity (preference for complex over simple explanations)	less likely to vote guilty and to consider external causes for defendant's behavior (Pope & Meyer, 1999)
Epistemic Understanding (ability to differentiate whether a claim makes sense and whether it is true)	tendency to understand that a fact and an opinion differ and that a claim represents a theory that must be substantiated by evidence (Kuhn, 2001)
Opposed to Death Penalty	more likely to vote not guilty (Bersoff, 1987) and less likely to accept insanity defense (Poulson, Braithwaite et al., 1997; Poulson, Wuensch et al., 1997)
Negative Attitude about Psychiatry	less likely to accept testimony about defendant's mental state (Cutler, Moran, & Narby, 1992)
Entity Theorists (those who believe that traits are fixed and unchangeable)	more likely to rely on cues they believe to indicate character, such as the defendant's clothing (Gervey et al., 1999)

KEY POINTS

- People obey the law and accept legal decisions so long as they perceive the procedures to be fair and just.
- Most people would prefer police to search for the truth rather than attempt to prove guilt, but both interrogation approaches are common.
- There are several factors that contribute to false confessions and to a belief in one's guilt by an individual who is actually innocent.
- A serious and controversial legal problem is the recovery of *repressed memories* of past criminal events that often turn out to be false memories.
- People are interested in details about crime, and extensive media coverage leads to overestimations of the frequency of murder, assault, and other crimes.
- Media concentration on a person accused of a crime leads to widespread assumptions of guilt among the general public, including those who will become jurors. Because such assumptions help the prosecution, government officials tend to provide the media with as much information as possible.
- Eyewitnesses to a crime often make mistakes, but a variety of procedures have been developed to help ensure greater accuracy.
- Attorneys act as adversaries who attempt to select juries biased toward their side and to convince the jurors that their version of the truth is the correct one.
- The words and even the unspoken beliefs of judges can influence the verdict.

(continued)

KEY POINTS (CONTINUED)

- Defendants are judged in part on irrelevant characteristics such as appearance, gender, socioeconomic status, and behavior in the courtroom.
- A juror's response to the evidence and to the defendant depends on his or her affective evaluations, cognitive processing, and various personality characteristics.

Applying Social Psychology to Health-Related Behavior

Until the second half of the nineteenth century, illness was assumed to be caused by such things as inherited weaknesses, immorality, bad air, or witchcraft. Though the idea of "invisible" bacteria and viruses was originally rejected both by physicians and by the general public, people now understand the role of microbes (Tomes, 1998). Despite the central importance of these tiny organisms, it is now increasingly clear that psychological factors affect all aspects of our physical well-being (Rodin & Salovey, 1989; Rabasca, 2000). As a result, investigators interested in **health psychology** focus on the psychological processes that influence the development, prevention, and treatment of physical illness (Glass, 1989). You may be puzzled as to how psychological and physiological processes can be interconnected, but we hope that the next few pages will convince you that they are.

Responding to Health-Related Information

The initial step in dealing with health issues is to obtain the relevant factual information and then to act on it. Obviously, what we learn, remember, and accept depends on both cognitive and affective factors, and our subsequent behavior depends on motivational factors. Even with respect to obtaining factual information, our health behavior is determined by psychological variables.

COMPREHENDING AND EVALUATING HEALTH INFORMATION. If headlines were our main source of knowledge, we would live in constant fear of AIDS, Lyme disease, mad cow disease, flesh-eating bacteria, and viruses from African monkeys that turn one's insides into a spaghetti-like mass. We also regularly receive very positive news indicating that medical science is on the brink of preventing or curing cancer, diabetes, and other dread diseases (e.g., Lemonick & Park, 2001).

Some stories manage to do both—providing frightening information about a new epidemic and comforting information about how to deal with it (Fischman, 2001). Just as we overestimate the amount of crime, we overestimate the threat of rare diseases and also the promise of instant cures on the basis of the availability heuristic (see Chapter 3).

While the truth is not nearly as bad as the epidemic headlines nor quite as good as the miracle cure headlines, people are living longer than ever; in the United States, the number of people eighty-five and older increased 38 percent in the past decade (Armas, 2001). Also, the U.S. death rates from heart disease, cancer, stroke, lung disease, and pneumonia–influenza have all been dropping (Latest figures, 1994). Such data include the first-ever decline in the incidence of cancer and even a decrease in the rate of accidental deaths (Easterbrook, 1999).

health psychology: The study of the effects of psychological factors in the development, prevention, and treatment of physical illness.

In additional to medical advances, much of the improvement seems to be the result of people being better informed, obtaining earlier diagnoses, and changing their habits.

■ REJECTING HEALTH INFORMATION VERSUS ACCEPTING IT. In response to a barrage of information about health from television, newspaper and magazine articles, sources on the Internet, and medical personnel, people tend to accept only portions of it. Even if acceptance is total, that doesn't necessarily mean that an individual follows through with the appropriate behavior. That is, some people quit smoking cigarettes and others do not; some begin a regular exercise program and others remain on the couch clutching a TV remote; some get a physical examination once a year and others avoid seeing a doctor until they are seriously ill. Why do people react in such divergent ways with respect to matters of health?

One factor is the affective content of health warnings. Often the message is very frightening because the goal is to motivate the recipient into action. An example is a billboard campaign in which a coffin was depicted along with a message in black print, "CIGARETTES ARE KILLING YOU." Unfortunately, people often reject that kind of disturbing and anxiety-arousing message by deciding that it is untrue (Liberman & Chaiken, 1992). It is obviously more comforting to believe that cigarettes are not killing you than to believe the reverse. Not only does that conclusion make you feel better, but you also are able to avoid the physical discomfort that accompanies giving up nicotine.

In a similar way, contemplating something as frightening as breast cancer can activate defense mechanisms that interfere with a woman's ability to pay attention to a message about early detection, remember it, and take the appropriate action (Miller, 1997). One problem is that messages about health risks threaten the self, and so there is a tendency to respond defensively in order to maintain a positive self-image (see Chapter 5). This defensiveness can be reduced by *self-affirmation,* such as a positive experience with an unrelated task. After a success experience, for example, people are more likely to respond to a health-related message, accept it, and then change their behavior (Sherman, Nelson, & Steele, 2000).

A common way to deal with anxiety about health issues is to drink alcohol, and one consequence can be what is called *alcohol myopia* (Steele & Josephs, 1990). For example, drinking can lead to unsafe sex (MacDonald, Zanna, & Fong, 1996), unsafe driving, and unsafe dining.

While a negative message may evoke fear and avoidance, health messages can be *positively framed,* suggesting that altered behavior will result in a gain. Positive framing is most effective in motivating *preventive* behavior, whereas a *negatively framed* message, suggesting a loss from failing to act, is best for motivating *detection* behavior (Rothman et al., 1999). This difference was demonstrated in research focusing on dental messages. A positive dental pamphlet—"People who use a mouth rinse daily are taking advantage of a safe and effective way to reduce plaque accumulation"—heightened interest in using a plaque-fighting mouth rinse. In contrast, a negative dental pamphlet—"Failing to use a disclosing rinse before brushing limits your ability to detect areas of plaque accumulation"—heightened interest in using a plaque-detecting rinse.

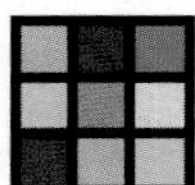

Beliefs and expectations also contribute to whether or not a person engages in the necessary health-related behavior. For example, almost everyone is exposed to information indicating the importance of breast self-examination for early detection of disease. Many women do and many do not comply with such messages. Studies in the United States and in Australia indicate that the two strongest predictors of such behavior are (1) perceived confidence that one has the ability to carry out a self-exam and (2) perceived susceptibility to breast cancer (Ashton, Karnilowicz, & Fooks, 2001). On the basis of such findings, it is possible to increase self-confidence by having a nurse teach the procedure in a one-to-one interaction with a patient. An increase in perceived susceptibility is possible when patients are given information about the factors that increase the likelihood of developing breast cancer (Murray & McMillan, 1993).

People who ignore various health messages often have a sense of *unrealistic optimism* or an *optimistic bias.* There's no reason to alter your behavior if you are convinced that bad things are not going to happen to you. With unrealistic optimism, you feel free to drive while intoxicated, eat as much saturated fat as you like, and go bungee jumping (Helweg-Larsen & Shepperd, 2001; Middleton, Harris, & Surman, 1996).

Risky behavior can also occur in a limited specific situation. Would you drink from a stranger's water bottle? The answer seems to depend on whether you are challenged to do so and whether you are concerned about how you are viewed by others. Martin and Leary (1999) designed an unusual experiment in which a research participant was asked to drink three mildly unpleasant liquids, after which another participant (actually a research assistant) offered a partially empty bottle of water from his backpack to wash out the bad taste. (Though it was made to appear that the assistant had been drinking from the bottle, actually only clean, nonused bottles were used.) The assistant either offered the bottle in a nonchallenging way—"That stuff must have tasted pretty nasty. Do you want a drink of my water?" In the challenging condition, he said the same thing and added ". . . if you're not worried about drinking out of the same bottle as me." A questionnaire measured *social-image concern*—the degree to which each participant was concerned about how other people assess them. As shown in Figure 13.10, those in the high image concern group drank more than those in the low image concern group, and those who were challenged drank more than those who were not challenged. You can see that

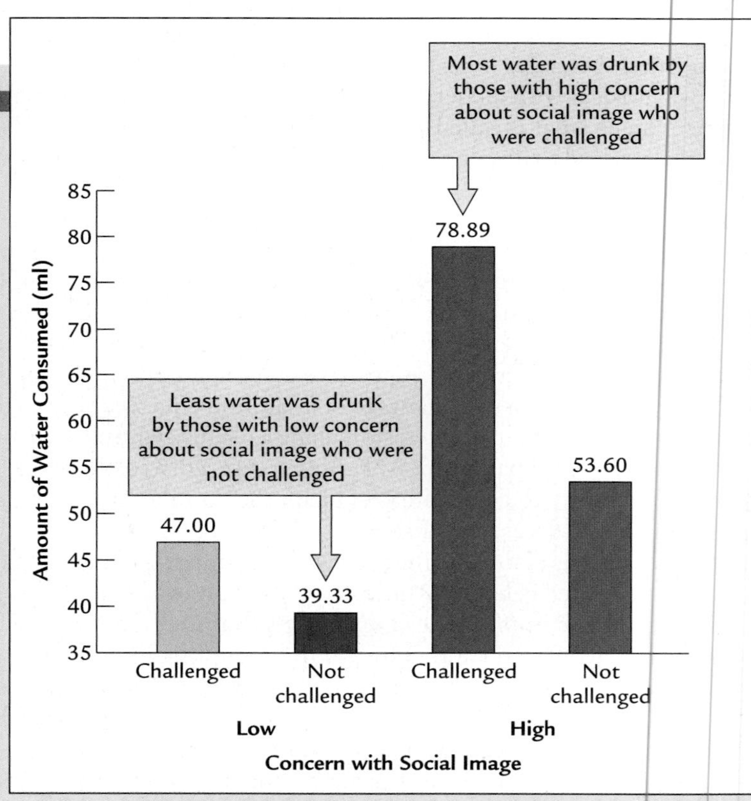

FIGURE 13.10

Taking a Health Risk: Challenge and Concern about Social Image. The amount of water consumed when drinking from a stranger's water bottle was affected by whether or not this behavior had been challenged and whether the research participant was high or low in concern about social image. Those who were challenged drank more, and those high in social image concern also drank more.

[SOURCE: BASED ON DATA IN MARTIN & LEARY, 1999.]

risky health behavior was a function of situational factors (challenge or no challenge) and dispositional factors—concern with self-image. Now that you have this information, how would you answer the question "Would you drink from a stranger's water bottle?"

The Emotional and Physiological Effects of Stress

During World War II, psychologists became increasingly interested in stress and its impact on cognition, overt behavior, and health (Lazarus, 1993; Somerfield & McCrae, 2000). **Stress** is defined as any physical or psychological event that is perceived as a potential threat to physical or emotional well-being. Among college students, the resulting distress often includes anxiety and depression, which may, in turn, lead to alcohol abuse and eating problems (Oliver et al., 1999). **Coping** refers to the way in which people deal with threats and with their emotional consequences (Taylor, Buunk, & Aspinwall, 1990; Tennen et al., 2000). Of special interest is the effect of stress on health.

■ PHYSICAL ILLNESS AS A CONSEQUENCE OF STRESS. There seems to be no doubt that as stress increases, illness is more likely to occur. Research has documented multiple sources of stress in our daily lives.

For example, college students experience stress caused by such factors as low grades, the ups and downs of romantic and sexual relationships, and living in a new environment (Gall, Evans, & Bellrose, 2000). At work, stress is frequently the result of negative interpersonal relationships, work overload, and the loss of one's job (Schwarzer, Jerusalem, & Hahn, 1994). Everyday hassles include marital stress, crowded living conditions, commuting, and excessive noise (Chapman, Hobfoll, & Ritter, 1997; Evans, Bullinger, & Hygge, 1998; Evans, Lepore, & Schroeder, 1996; Foxhall, 2001). Being the victim of a natural disaster such as a tornado or a man-made disaster such as a terrorist attack is obviously stressful, and a major component is the perception of oneself as vulnerable and threatened by the inability to control what happens (Weinstein et al., 2000). And the effects continue long after the disaster has ended. For the same reasons, women who have been sexually assaulted continue to experience stress after the assault, and they are likely to have long-term physical health problems ranging from pelvic pain to gastrointestinal disorders (Golding, 1999).

The fact that African Americans have a higher incidence of high blood pressure than do European Americans has been known for many years (Obrist, 1981), but why would this be? The explanation could rest on genetic differences (Rotini et al., 1994) or on differences in the level of stress they experience. One possible source of additional stress among African Americans is known as *stereotype threat*—being in an interpersonal situation in which other people are likely to perceive them in terms of stereotypical assumptions (Clark et al., 1999; Steele, 1997).

This kind of stress has been created experimentally. For example, stereotype stress is experienced by African American research participants when they are led to believe that they will be compared unfavorably to whites on an intelligence test. In the laboratory, they are told by a European American experimenter that they will be given a new intelligence test developed at Princeton, Stanford, and the University of Michigan, and they will be part of a nationally representative sample (Blascovich et al., 2001). In a low-stress condition, other participants are told by an African American experimenter that the test was developed at Tulane, Howard, and the University of Michigan to provide a culturally unbiased measure on which black and white students perform equally well. Compared to European American participants in either condition or to African Americans in the low-stress condition, African Americans in the high-stress condition were found to have higher blood pressure readings while taking the test, and they also performed less well on the

stress: Any physical or psychological event perceived as potentially constituting physical harm or emotional distress.

coping: Responding to stress in a way that reduces the threat and its effects; includes what a person does, feels, or thinks in order to master, tolerate, or decrease the negative effects of a stressful situation.

test. The assumption is that African Americans experience similar stress in their everyday lives, and one result is high blood pressure. In addition, blacks and other racial and ethnic groups experience not only stereotype stress, but also stress resulting from acts of discrimination by the members of other groups and conformity pressures exerted by their own group members (Contrada et al., 2000).

Thus, various kinds of stress result in illness. In addition, the fear of illness, illness itself, and medical procedures for diagnosis and treatment all constitute additional sources of stress (Azar, 1999b; Meyerowitz et al., 2000). Even the race and gender of the health care provider can be a problem; in evaluating dentists, people view males as more competent than females, and the first choice is a white male (Newton et al., 2001). It appears that prejudices and stereotypes influence the choice of a practitioner or the reaction to that individual when it is not possible to choose.

The best way to reduce the stress caused by illness or diagnostic and treatment procedures is to know as much as possible about your condition. Read about it, look it up on the Internet, ask your physician questions, and talk to others who have gone through the same process (Rall, Peskoff, & Byrne, 1994; Sanchez, 2001). Knowledge provides a sense of control, and even knowing that a procedure will be painful is less stressful than ignorance and fear of the unknown (Suls & Wan, 1989). In effect, predictability is what we want and need, rather than unpredictability (Carpenter, 2000a; Pham, Taylor, & Seeman, 2001). When we can't predict, we feel helpless and lacking in control. Lack of control results in negative affect and increased dissatisfaction (Lachman & Weaver, 1998). Even an unrealistic belief about one's ability to control illness is helpful in adapting to disease (Griffin & Rabkin, 1998).

Whatever the source of stress, as the number and severity of negative events increase, their cumulative effect increases the risk of physical illness (Cohen, Tyrrell, & Smith, 1993; King et al., 1998). Monkeys as well as humans become more susceptible to disease under conditions of stress (Shively, 1998), and experiments with rats indicate that stress promotes the development of cancerous tumors (Azar, 1999a). Pleasant feelings, by the way, have the opposite effect on physical functioning, in that a positive emotional state is associated with good health (Salovey et al., 2000).

How, exactly, could stress cause physical illness? Baum (1994) proposes that direct and indirect effects of stress each lead to an increase in illness, as shown in Figure 13.11. The indirect effects occur when the negative emotional effects of stress interfere with health-related behavior, such as eating a balanced diet or scheduling a physical examination.

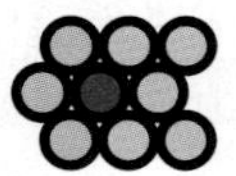

The direct physical effects are somewhat more surprising in that stress delays the healing process in wounds, has a negative effect on the endocrine system, and interferes with the functioning of the immune system (Kiecolt-Glaser et al., 1998). **Psychoneuroimmunology** is the research field that explores the relationships among stress, emotional and behavioral reactions, and the body's immune system (Ader, 2001). One example of such research focused on the well established fact that college students show an increase in upper respiratory infections as exam time approaches (Dorian et al., 1982). To study the mechanism underlying this relationship, Jemmott and Magloire (1988) obtained samples of students' saliva over several weeks to assess the presence of *secretory immunoglobulin A*—the body's primary defense against infections. They found that the level of this substance dropped during final exams and then returned to normal levels when the exams were over. In a work setting, parallel findings indicate that the immune system suffers when projects turn out badly, especially for workers who blame themselves for what went wrong (Schaubroeck, Jones, & Xie, 2001). The psychological–physiological connection works in both directions. Not only is there an effect of psychological variables on the immune system, but the activation of the immune system alters neural activity and thus affects behavior, mood, and cognitive functioning (Maier & Watkins, 2000).

psychoneuroimmunology: The research field that explores the relationships among stress, emotional and behavioral reactions, and the immune system.

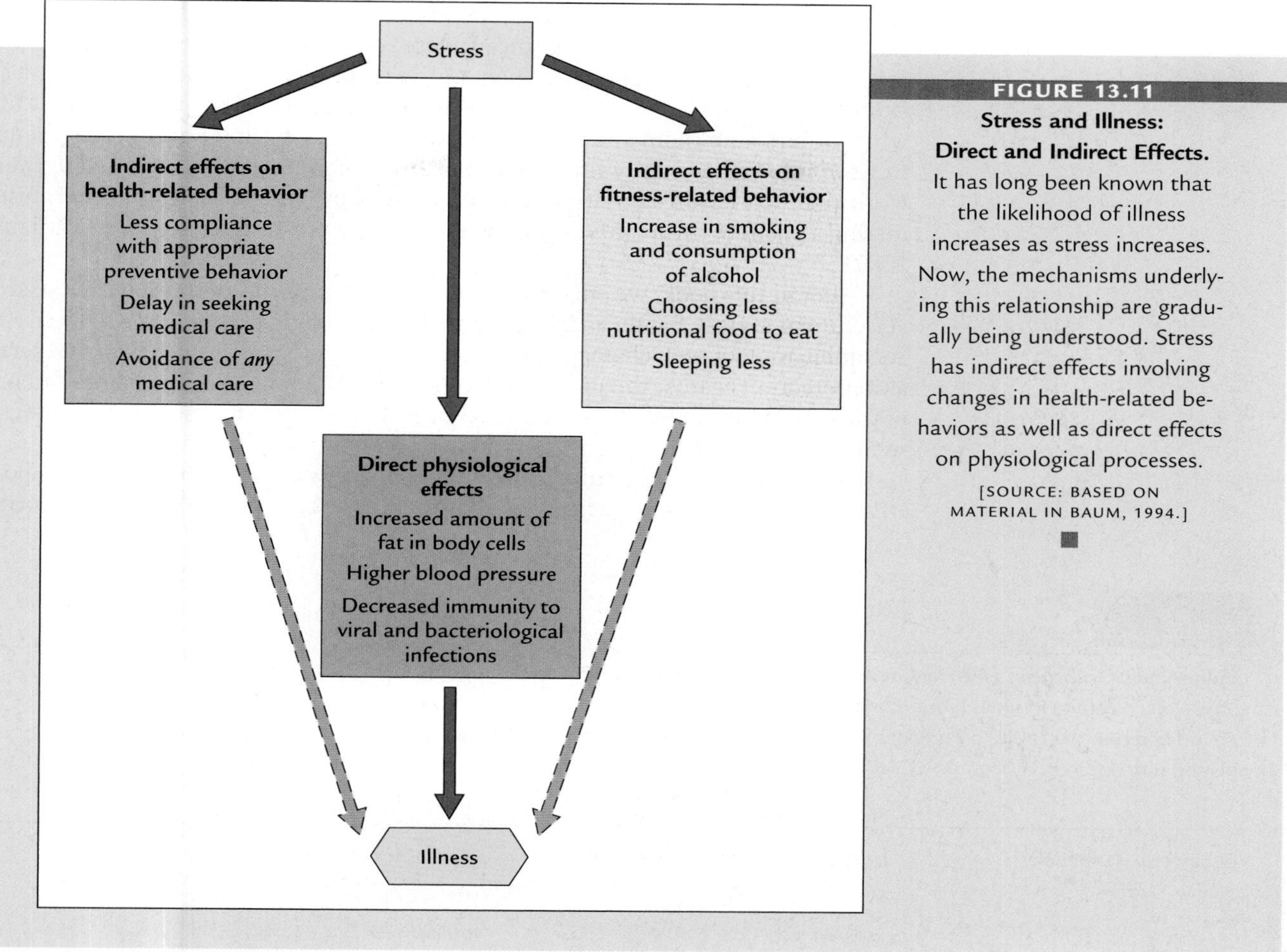

FIGURE 13.11

Stress and Illness: Direct and Indirect Effects. It has long been known that the likelihood of illness increases as stress increases. Now, the mechanisms underlying this relationship are gradually being understood. Stress has indirect effects involving changes in health-related behaviors as well as direct effects on physiological processes.

[SOURCE: BASED ON MATERIAL IN BAUM, 1994.]

As stress increases, anxiety and anger also increase (Martin et al., 1999), and these negative emotions bring about increased risk of illness, the malfunctioning of the immune system, pain, and even a greater possibility of dying (Suinn, 2001). A related phenomenon is the effect of a pessimistic outlook on risk-taking behavior; one result is the association between pessimism and untimely death, especially among males (Peterson et al., 1998). In general, people with an optimistic outlook live 19 percent longer than those who are pessimistic (Horowitz, 2000). A study of Catholic nuns found that positive emotions expressed in autobiographies written when they were in their twenties were associated with longevity and living to ages seventy-five to ninety-five; those who expressed negative emotions in their twenties had a much shorter life span (Danner, Snowden, & Friesen, 2001).

■ INDIVIDUAL DIFFERENCES IN THE EFFECTS OF STRESS. Given the same amount and intensity of stress, some people react more negatively than others and are thus more likely to become ill. Each of us falls somewhere along a dispositional continuum that ranges from those most susceptible to the negative effects of stress—**disease-prone personality**—to those most resistant to stress—**self-healing personality** (Friedman, Hawley, & Tucker, 1994). A person at the disease-prone end of the spectrum responds to stress with intensely negative emotions and a pattern of unhealthy behavior, resulting in illness and a shorter life span. For a self-healing person, in contrast, stress is unpleasant, but it is perceived as something to be managed. Healthy behavior is maintained, and illness is either avoided

disease-prone personality: A personality characterized by negative emotional reactions to stress, ineffective coping strategies, and unhealthy behavior patterns. Among the correlates are a higher incidence of illness and a shorter life span.

self-healing personality: A personality characterized by effective coping with stress. Self-healing individuals are energetic, responsive to others, and positive about life.

or of brief duration. There is a general tendency for such individuals to be enthusiastic about life, emotionally balanced, alert, responsive to others, energetic, curious, secure, and constructive. Such individuals have also been described as expressing *subjective well-being* and as being *optimistic*. They express gratitude when others help them and forgiveness when others do them harm. They benefit from interpreting daily life in positive terms, being strongly involved in their work and their leisure activities, feeling a sense of purpose in their lives, and anticipating a positive future (Myers & Diener, 1995; Segerstrom et al., 1998; Vaillant, 2002).

Earlier in this book, we encountered similar descriptions of those with a secure attachment style (Chapter 8) and those with an altruistic personality (Chapter 10). A combination of such characteristics seems to promote positive behavior and serve as a protection against the negative effects of stress. Table 13.5 summarizes many of the personality differences between those who are most disease-prone and those who are self-healing.

Note that a long, happy life is most likely to occur among people with this positive outlook, along with a lifestyle that includes exercise, an interest in contin-

TABLE 13.5

Vulnerability to Stress: Self-Healing Personality versus Disease-Prone Personality.
Stress often results in illness, but some individuals are far more vulnerable than others. As indicated in the table, differences in vulnerability are associated with a variety of personality differences.

	SELF-HEALING PERSONALITY	DISEASE-PRONE PERSONALITY
Behavioral Tendencies	avoids interpersonal conflicts	gets into interpersonal conflicts
	nonperfectionist	perfectionist
	extroverted	introverted
	completes school assignments on time	procrastinates
Expectancies and Beliefs	positive bias in interpreting stressful events	negative bias in interpreting stressful events
	internal locus of control	external locus of control
	believes in a just world	does not believe in a just world
	high self-efficacy	low self-efficacy
	optimistic	pessimistic
	approaches goals, focusing on positive outcomes	avoids goals, focusing on negative outcomes
Personal Characteristics	not neurotic	neurotic
	well adjusted	maladjusted
	high self-esteem	low self-esteem
	independent	dependent
	accessible attitudes—knows his or her likes and dislikes	inaccessible attitudes—unsure of his or her likes and dislikes

[SOURCE: AMIRKHAN, RISINGER, & SWICKERT, 1995; BANDURA, 1993; BIRKIMER, LUCAS, & BIRKIMER, 1991; BERNARD & BELINSKY, 1993; BOLGER & ZUCKERMAN, 1995; BOOTH-KEWLEY & VICKERS, 1994; BORNSTEIN, 1995; CAMPBELL, CHEW, & SCRATCHLEY, 1991; DYKEMA, BERGBOWER, & PETERSON, 1995; ELLIOT & SHELDON, 1998; FAZIO & POWELL, 1997; GUNTHERT, COHEN, & ARMELI, 1999; HEMENOVER, 2001; JOINER & SCHMIDT, 1995; TICE & BAUMEISTER, 1997; TOMAKA & BLASCOVICH, 1994.]

ued learning, and the avoidance of cigarette smoking, alcohol abuse, and obesity (Vaillant, 2002).

A somewhat different personality pattern (*Type A*)—associated with coronary disease—was described in Chapter 11. Type A individuals, compared with the more placid Type B individuals, are more hostile, have higher blood pressure (Contrada, 1989), and are twice as likely to develop heart disease (Weidner, Istvan, & McKnight, 1989).

Coping with Stress

Each of us inevitably encounters stressful situations throughout life. Beyond those fortunate enough to have self-healing personalities, what kind of strategies can be developed to help deal with stress? We will briefly describe some of the most effective.

■ INCREASING PHYSICAL FITNESS. It should not come as a surprise to learn that eating nutritious foods, getting enough sleep, and engaging in regular exercise results in increased **fitness**—that is, being in good physical condition as indicated by endurance and strength. Even fifteen to twenty minutes of aerobic exercise (jogging, biking, swimming, dancing, etc.) each day or every other day increases fitness. Just one hour a week spent walking cuts the rate of heart disease in half (Lee et al., 2001). The result of being fit is a sense of well-being and self-efficacy (see Chapter 5), along with the perception of being able to handle stress (Brown, 1991; Jessor, Turbin, & Costa, 1998; Rudolph & Kim, 1996; Winett, 1998).

Overeating, eating less nutritious food, and becoming overweight constitute a special set of problems that undermine fitness. Because, in the past, food supplies were scarce and unpredictable, humans and other animals evolved to eat as much as possible whenever food was available (Pinel, Assanand, & Lehman, 2000). The excess was stored in the body as a buffer against starvation whenever food became difficult to obtain. Though overeating was adaptive for our ancestors, most of us who live in the industrialized world are surrounded by a wide variety of readily available, good-tasting food containing many more calories and much more fat and sugar than we need. For most people, overeating in the twenty-first century is not at all adaptive, but the fight to maintain an optimal weight is a difficult one because we are genetically programmed to eat too much. To establish different eating habits, the best approach is to begin in infancy with breast-feeding rather than formula from a bottle (O'Neil, 1999) and to continue throughout childhood with a balanced diet at home and in school (Berger, 1999). In adulthood, those who avoid becoming overweight are more healthy and have a longer life span (Calle et al., 1999).

Almost everyone should be able to become fit, but most of us do not. To change from being a "couch potato" to someone with a better diet, an adequate amount of sleep, and regular exercise requires strong motivation, continuing commitment, and the ability to regulate one's own behavior (Mullan & Markland, 1997; Schwarzer, 2001).

■ COPING STRATEGIES: POSITIVE EMOTIONS AND REGULATORY CONTROL. Compas and his colleagues (1991) proposed that *coping* with stress is a process consisting of two levels. As outlined in Figure 13.12 on page 546, the first level involves *emotion-focused coping*—attempts to reduce the negative emotional response elicited by the threat and to increase positive affect (Folkman & Moskowitz, 2000a, 2000b; Stanton et al., 2000). Even if the threat is still there, we prefer to feel less anxious and less angry, and we seek ways to increase our positive feelings. At the second level is *problem-focused coping*, which involves an attempt to deal with the threat itself and to gain control of the situation.

fitness: Being in good physical condition as indicated by endurance and strength.

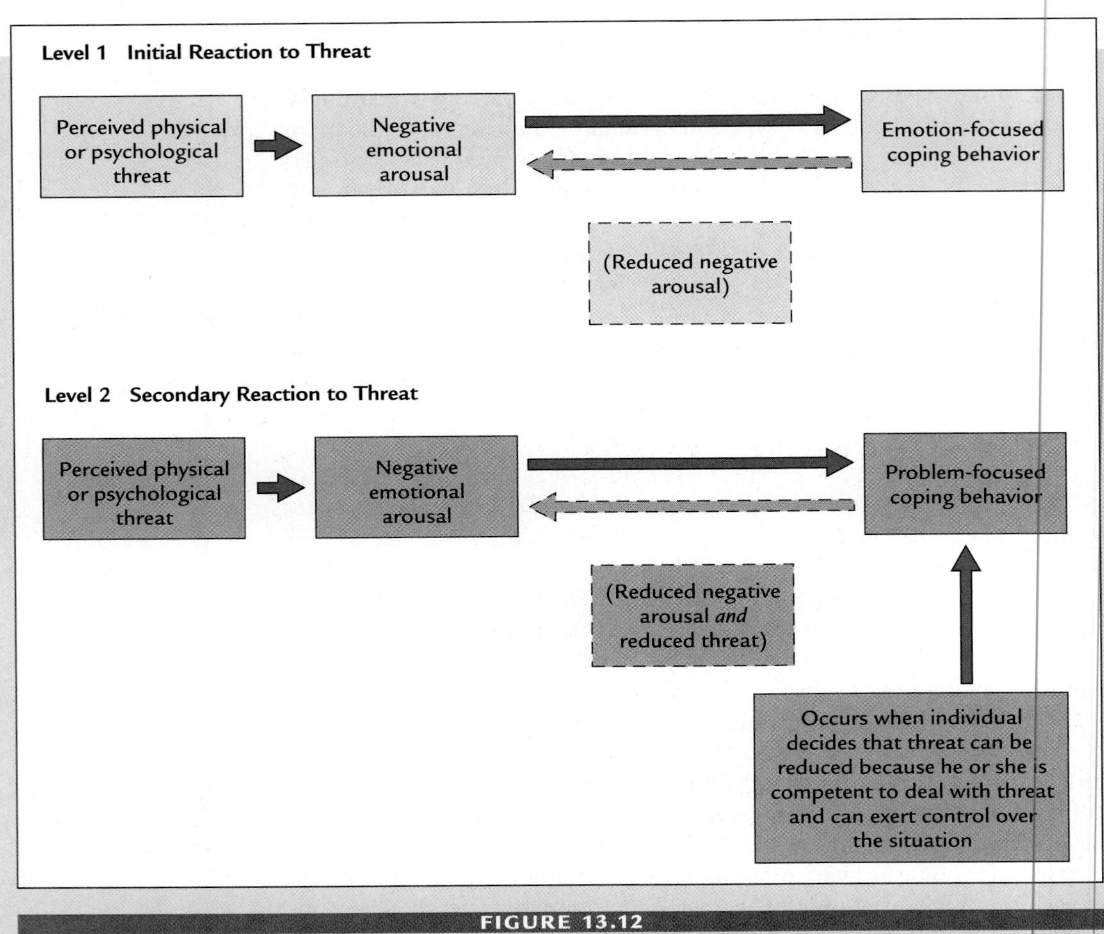

FIGURE 13.12

Coping: Emotion-Focused and Problem-Focused.

We respond to whatever is stressful and threatening in two ways. The initial reaction is emotion-focused (level 1), meaning that we seek ways to cope with our feelings of distress. If it is possible to remove or modify the threat, however, a problem-focused (level 2) type of coping can be employed.

[SOURCE: BASED ON INFORMATION IN COMPAS ET AL., 1991.]

At Level 1, how can you decrease negative emotions and increase positive ones? Some attempts to change one's affective state are temporarily effective, but essentially maladaptive—for example, drinking alcohol or taking drugs (Armeli et al., 2000; Cooper et al., 1995). You may feel better after several drinks, but then wake up with the original threat still hanging over you plus the unpleasantness of a hangover. Equally ineffective is to deny that anything is wrong and thus ignore the problem (Smith, 1996). And some people make matters worse by engaging in *counterfactual thinking* (see Chapter 3)—dwelling on things they might have done to prevent the stressful situation from occurring in the first place (Davis et al., 1995).

A better path is to find ways to experience positive, happy feelings and to think optimistically despite negative events (Chang, 1998; Mayer & Salovey, 1995). When President Lincoln was asked how he could possibly make jokes during the worst days of the Civil War, he replied, "I laugh because I must not cry." And he was correct. Laughter provides a buffer against stressful events (Francis, Monahan, & Berger, 1999; Kuiper & Martin, 1998). In a similar way, it is helpful to seek out positive experiences such as spending time with family or friends (Stone, Neal et al., 1994), engaging in enjoyable work (Csikszentmihalyi & LeFevre, 1989), experiencing love (Levin, J., 2000), or seeking comfort in religion and spirituality (George et al., 2000; Seybold & Hill, 2001). Anything that improves one's mood helps to counteract the negative effects of stress.

Before discussing problem-focused coping, we'll examine a special way to reduce stress and increase positive emotions in the **Beyond the Headlines** section below.

At Level 2 of the coping process, what can you do about the stress itself? Successful coping involves *regulatory control*—the processes that enable an individual to guide his or her goal-directed activities over time and across situations. Some people have learned to control what they think, how they feel, what they do, and where they direct their attention (Karoly, 1993). Regulatory control includes holding

BEYOND THE HEADLINES: AS SOCIAL PSYCHOLOGISTS SEE IT

PETS CAN HELP REDUCE STRESS

Pets Are Good Medicine: Healthy Pets Make for Healthier People

New York, PR Newswire, May 9, 2000—Their names may be "Fluffy," "Fido," or "Frenchy," but to millions of Americans our companion animals—the dogs, cats, birds, fish, reptiles, and small animals that we hold so dear—are much more than pets, they're part of the family.

The American Pet Products Manufacturers Association today issued a report indicating a strong correlation between pet ownership and improved physical and mental health. A survey of 500 pet owners across the U.S. indicated that personal well-being may be directly related to a strong human–animal bond. Pets help people relax, and the survey indicates why this may be.

Most of the survey respondents said that pets make their life healthier—emotionally or physically—by counteracting the effect of too much technology and by having a calming effect when there is stress and worry. In addition, people are more courteous and less likely to lose their temper when interacting with their pets than with other members of their family.

In the 1960s, I (DB) remember seeing the title of a paper at a psychological convention, "The Dog as Co-Therapist." I laughed about it at the time with my colleagues, but the effects of pets on emotions now seem quite clear and no longer amusing. "Pet therapy" is widely used in nursing homes, prisons, hospitals, and schools to reduce loneliness, depression, and stress. Pets are found to lower blood pressure and to decrease anxiety (Pets reduce . . . , 1996; Study: Pets . . . , 1999). Elderly people with pets make fewer visits to the doctor's office, and the survival rate of cardiac patients is higher for pet owners than for those without an animal companion (Pets and stress . . . , 1996).

For almost everyone, but especially for elderly people, a pet provides comfort, companionship, something to think about besides oneself, and a being to care for. The majority of pet owners over the age of sixty-five report that if they and a pet were both sick, they would take care of the pet first. It has been suggested that a pet is preferable to a spouse because a pet never argues with you, never disagrees, never criticizes you, and never files for divorce.

If, at any time in your life, you ever talked to your dog or hugged your purring cat, you know how important such interactions can be. I will never again snicker at the idea of a dog as co-therapist.

positive beliefs (Reed & Aspinwall, 1998), engaging in constructive behavior (Fabes & Eisenberg, 1997), giving up short-term pleasures to gain long-term satisfactions (Mayer & Salovey, 1995), and having positive expectations about the future—a feeling of hope (Chang & DeSimone, 2001; Snyder, 2000).

■ THE IMPORTANCE OF SOCIAL SUPPORT. **Social support**—the physical and psychological comfort provided by other people (Sarason, Sarason, & Pierce, 1994)—also is beneficial in times of stress, and it is effective regardless of the kind of coping strategies that are used (Frazier et al., 2000). In part, contact with others like yourself is a source of comfort when you experience stress (Morgan, Carder, & Neal, 1997), and monkeys respond in the same way (Cohen et al., 1992). The presence of social support helps to ward off illness and enables one to recover from illness more quickly (Roy, Steptoe, & Kirschbaum, 1998), but the most effective support is "invisible"—possibly because awareness of receiving help is sometimes negative, as we discussed in Chapter 10 (Bolger, Zuckerman, & Kessler, 2000). Though a person facing stress may need support, awkward attempts to provide comfort can actually make things worse. Unhelpful support efforts include trying to minimize the problem, suggesting that the difficulty is the stressed person's fault, and simply bumbling efforts to help (Ingram et al., 2001).

Individuals with a secure attachment style (see Chapter 8) are best able to seek out social support, and they tend to receive more social support than individuals with the other styles of attachment (Davis, Morris, & Kraus, 1998; Mikulincer & Florian, 1995). Women are more likely than men to give and to receive social support (Barbee et al., 1993; Porter, Marco et al., 2000). People who focus excessively on their feelings about a stressor also receive more social support and benefit from it (Nolen-Hoeksema & Davis, 1999).

Disease support groups are also helpful, even if the communication is online, but some diseases are more likely to motivate seeking this kind of support than others. Support seeking is most apt to occur when the disease is stigmatizing (for example, AIDS, alcoholism, breast and prostate cancer) and least likely for a non-embarrassing disease such as a coronary problem (Davison, Pennebaker, & Dickerson, 2000).

Social support networks are larger among Mexican Americans than among Anglo-Americans (Gamble & Dalla, 1997). Also, the social support provided by religion possibly explains why those who attend weekly services live longer than those who do not (Crumm, 1998). Among African Americans, an individual involved in religious activity lives about fourteen years longer than one who is not actively religious.

Why does social support have the effect that it does? We have already suggested that simply being with other people (or even pets) reduces anxiety (emotion-focused). In addition, friends and family may help in solving problems (problem-focused). People sometimes seek compassion and sometimes seek advice (Horowitz et al., 2001). Both kinds of support have a positive effect on the cardiovascular, endocrine, and immune systems (Uchino, Uno, & Holt-Lunstad, 1999). There is an additional source of help—simply the act of talking to someone. When we experience stress, telling others about our difficulties not only reduces negative feelings, but also reduces the incidence of health problems (Clark, 1993). And talking seems to help, whether it is to a relative, friend, therapist, or minister.

More surprisingly, simply writing about your feelings makes you feel better (Lepore, 1997), improves your memory functioning (Klein & Boals, 2001), and has a positive physiological effect (Hughes, Uhlmann, & Pennebaker, 1994; Pennebaker, 1997; Pennebaker & Graybeal, 2001). The writing cannot, however, involve just a list of thoughts and feelings—it must consist of a narrative or story that ties together experiences and responses (Smyth, True, & Souto, 2001).

social support: The physical and psychological comfort provided by one's friends and family members.

Further, writing about nontraumatic topics such as the perceived benefits of the trauma or even verbalizing one's life goals can be beneficial (King, 2001; King & Miner, 2000). It also helps to write about secrets (Kelly et al., 2001) or to reveal personal secrets to someone who is discreet and nonjudgmental (Kelly, 1999). Sometimes, this involves a confession, with or without a religious connotation.

Just *thinking* about traumatic events has a positive effect on illness (Greenberg, Wortman, & Stone, 1996; Rivkin & Taylor, 1999). Suppressing negative thoughts has the opposite effect and interferes with the immune system (Petrie, Booth, & Pennebaker, 1998). Finally, having forgiving thoughts is beneficial to health, while have chronic, unforgiving thoughts results in negative health consequences (VanOyen, Witvliet, Ludwig, & Laan, 2001). Presumably, the negative emotions associated with lack of forgiveness are harmful, and it is better for one's health to forgive and reinterpret the past in a more positive way (Vaillant, 2002). Those who cling to negative thoughts over the years are less happy. For example, continually blaming your parents for your rotten childhood seems to impede maturity (Walker, 2001).

KEY POINTS

- We receive health-related information on a daily basis, and all of us need to remain informed and willing to change our minds in response to new findings.
- *Stress* refers to any event that is perceived as a potential source of physical or emotional harm. Stress can lead to physical illness indirectly through its effect on health-related behavior and directly by interfering with the immune system.
- A variety of dispositional factors are associated with differential vulnerability to illness that is initiated by stress. The negative effects of stress have the greatest effect on those with *disease-prone personality* characteristics but are resisted by those with *self-healing personality* characteristics.
- Effective strategies for *coping* with stress include increasing one's physical *fitness;* engaging in regulatory control of feelings, thoughts, and activities; seeking sources of positive affect (including the presence of pets); and establishing a network of *social support.*

Applying Social Psychology to the World of Work: Job Satisfaction, Helping, and Leadership

What single activity fills more of most persons' time than any other? We can answer with a single word: work. It's not surprising, then, that the principles and findings of social psychology have often been applied to the task of understanding what happens in work settings—mainly with an eye toward making this key part of life both more satisfying and more productive. In many cases, social psychologists themselves have used the knowledge of their field to address important questions and to solve practical problems relating to work. In other cases, however, the findings and principles of our field have been put to use by *industrial/organizational psychologists*—psychologists who specialize in studying all aspects of behavior in work settings (Murnighan, 1993). Similarly, many findings of social psychology have been adapted and put to practical use by persons in management—especially in a field known as *organizational behavior,* which, as its name suggests, studies human behavior in organizations (e.g., Greenberg & Baron, 2002).

In this section, we will consider some of the contributions made by social psychologists to understanding four important topics: *job satisfaction*—employees' attitudes toward their jobs; *organizational citizenship behavior*—prosocial behavior (e.g., helping) at work; the role of *personality* in work-related behavior; and *leadership*—the process through which one member of a group (its leader) influences other members to work toward attaining shared group goals (e.g., Vecchio, 1997; Yukl, 1998).

Job Satisfaction: Attitudes about Work

As we saw in Chapter 4, we are rarely neutral in responding to the social world. On the contrary, we hold strong *attitudes* about many aspects of it. Jobs are no exception to this rule. If asked, most persons can readily report their attitudes toward their jobs, and also toward the organizations that employ them. Attitudes concerning one's own job or work are generally referred to by the term **job satisfaction** (e.g., Wanous, Reichers, & Hudy, 1997), while attitudes toward one's company are known as *organizational commitment* (e.g., Brown, 1996; Keller, 1997). Because job satisfaction is linked more directly to basic research on attitudes in social psychology, we'll focus on this topic.

job satisfaction: Attitudes concerning one's job or work.

■ FACTORS AFFECTING JOB SATISFACTION. While most people tend to report being at least moderately satisfied with their jobs, others do not. This raises an important question: What factors contribute to these differences in job satisfaction? Research on this issue indicates that two major groups of factors are important: *organizational factors* related to a company's practices or the working conditions it provides (see Figure 13.13), and *personal factors* related to the traits of individual employees.

The organizational factors that influence job satisfaction contain few surprises: people report higher satisfaction when they feel that the reward systems in their companies are fair (when raises, promotions, and other rewards are distributed fairly) (see Chapter 12), when they like and respect their bosses and believe these persons have their best interests at heart, when they can participate in the decisions

FIGURE 13.13

Organizational Factors in Job Satisfaction.

How an organization treats its employees is an important factor in their job satisfaction. Clearly, the organization shown here is not interested in generating high levels of job satisfaction among its workers!

[SOURCE: DILBERT REPRINTED BY PERMISSION OF UNITED FEATURE SYNDICATE, INC.]

that affect them, when the work they perform is interesting rather than boring and repetitious, and when they are neither *overloaded* with too much to do in a given amount of time nor *underloaded* with too little to do (e.g., Callan, 1993; Melamed et al., 1995; Miceli & Lane, 1991). Physical working conditions, too, play a role: when employees are comfortable, they report higher job satisfaction than when they are uncomfortable (e.g., too hot, too noisy, too crowded; Baron, 1994).

Turning to personal factors, both seniority and status are important. The longer people have been in a given job and the higher their status, the greater their satisfaction (Zeitz, 1990). Similarly, the greater the extent to which jobs are closely matched to individuals' personal interests, the greater their satisfaction (Fricko & Beehr, 1992). In addition, certain personal traits are closely related to job satisfaction. For instance, research findings indicate that differences in what have been termed *core self-evaluations*—individuals' basic assessment about themselves and their self-worth—may play a key role (see Chapter 5) (e.g., Judge, Locke, & Durham, 1997). Such core self-evaluations involve four basic factors: self-esteem, generalized feelings of self-efficacy, locus of control (people's beliefs about their ability to influence their own outcomes), and emotional stability. As you would probably guess, persons with positive core self-evaluations tend to express higher job satisfaction than do those with negative core self-evaluations in many different settings (Judge et al., 1998). Additional evidence indicates that this may be so because persons high in core self-evaluations (i.e., persons who hold a favorable view of themselves and their own abilities) tend to hold more complex, challenging jobs. Such jobs, in turn, offer more autonomy and variety in the tasks they involve (more favorable *job characteristics*), and this, in turn, leads to high job satisfaction, as can be seen in Figure 13.14. Research by Judge, Bono, and Locke (2000) provides clear support for this reasoning, so it does appear that core self-evaluations are an important factor in job satisfaction.

So far, our discussion of job satisfaction has contained few surprises. But now, get ready for the unexpected: Research findings also indicate that job satisfaction may actually have an important *genetic* component, and that, as a result, some individuals have a tendency to express either relatively high or relatively low levels of job satisfaction *no matter where they work.* The first research pointing to such conclusions was conducted by Arvey and his colleagues (1989) more than twelve years ago. These researchers measured current job satisfaction in thirty-four pairs of identical (monozygotic) twins who had been separated at an early age and then reared apart. Because such twins have identical genetic inheritance but have had different life experiences (being reared in different homes), the extent to which they report

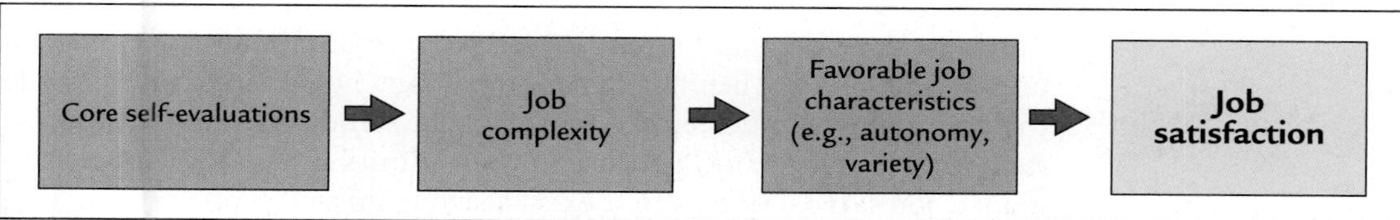

FIGURE 13.14

Core Self-Evaluations: An Important Determinant of Job Satisfaction.
Persons who are high in their core self-evaluations—their basic assessment of themselves and their own self-worth—report higher job satisfaction than do persons low in core self-evaluations. Recent findings (e.g., Judge, Bono, & Locke, 2000) suggest that this is because persons high in core self-evaluations select more complex jobs. Such jobs offer more favorable characteristics (e.g., they are more challenging, provide more autonomy). These favorable characteristics, in turn, lead to high levels of job satisfaction.

similar levels of job satisfaction provides information on the potential role of genetic factors in such attitudes. Results obtained by Arvey and his associates (1989) indicated that the level of job satisfaction reported by these pairs of twins correlated significantly, and that these correlations were higher than was true for unrelated persons who, of course, do not share the same genes. Additional findings indicated that as much as 30 percent of the variation in job satisfaction may stem from genetic factors!

Although these same results remain somewhat controversial (e.g., Cropanzano & James, 1990), they have been replicated in other studies (e.g., Keller et al., 1992). Thus, it appears that job satisfaction my stem, at least in part, from genetic factors. How can such effects occur? One possibility involves genetically influenced differences in *affective temperament* (e.g., Weiss & Cropanzano, 1996). In other words, genetic factors influence temperament—general tendencies to be upbeat, positive, and happy at one extreme versus depressed, negative, and unhappy at the other. Differences in temperament do indeed seem to stem, at least in part, from genetic factors, and are visible even in very young infants (e.g., Lemery et al., 1999). Such differences may influence how individuals experience emotionally significant events at work (e.g., praise or criticism from one's boss; an argument with a coworker), and such contrasting experiences, in turn, may affect job satisfaction. At present, this explanation is only speculative in nature. But the finding that work-related attitudes such as job satisfaction are highly stable over time is consistent with it (e.g., Steel & Rentsch, 1997). Because of such stability, persons who express high levels of satisfaction in one job at a given time are likely to express high levels of satisfaction in a different job at a later time, and the same is true for persons who express low levels of satisfaction—they tend to be dissatisfied no matter where they work. This doesn't in any way imply that job satisfaction can't be changed—it can. But together, these findings indicate that, as we saw in Chapter 4, changing strongly held attitudes is always a challenging task for those who want to produce such shifts.

■ THE EFFECTS OF JOB SATISFACTION ON TASK PERFORMANCE: WEAKER THAN YOU MIGHT GUESS. Are happy workers—people who like their jobs—productive workers? Common sense seems to suggest that they are, but remember, as we noted in Chapter 4, attitudes are not always strong predictors of overt behavior. In view of this, you should not be surprised to learn that while job satisfaction is related to performance in many jobs, this relationship is relatively weak—correlations in the range of .15 to .20 (e.g., Judge, 1993; Tett & Meyer, 1993).

Why isn't this relationship stronger? Because several factors may tend to weaken or moderate the impact of job satisfaction on performance. One of the most important of these is this: Many jobs leave little room for variations in performance. Think about production-line employees, for example. If they don't perform at a minimum level, they get behind "the line" and can't hold the job. But they can't *exceed* this minimum by much either: they'd just be standing around waiting for the next item on which to work. Because of these limits in the range of possible performance, job satisfaction cannot exert a strong influence on performance.

Another reason why job satisfaction is not strongly related to task performance involves the possibility that positive attitudes toward one's job—or toward coworkers or the entire organization—may be reflected primarily in forms of behavior other than performance (e.g., Keller, 1997). In other words, individuals who hold positive attitudes toward their jobs may express these attitudes through actions that *are* consistent with such views but are not directly or immediately linked to task performance—for instance, through praising their company to people outside it, conserving its resources, or helping other coworkers. Such actions can have quite beneficial effects on an organization, so let's take a closer look at them now.

Organizational Citizenship Behavior: Prosocial Behavior at Work

In Chapter 10, we examined many aspects of *prosocial behavior*—helpful actions that benefit others but have no obvious benefits for the persons who perform them. As we saw in that chapter, prosocial behavior stems from many different factors and can yield a wide range of effects. That prosocial actions occur in work settings, too, is obvious: employees often help each other with difficult tasks and sometimes even volunteer to do more than is required for their jobs. Research on prosocial behavior in work settings, therefore, has focused on two important questions: What forms of prosocial behavior do employees show? And what factors encourage or discourage such behavior? Let's see what research on these questions has revealed.

■ PROSOCIAL BEHAVIOR AT WORK: THE FORMS IT TAKES. While a number of different terms have been used to describe prosocial behavior in work settings (e.g., Van Dyne & LePine, 1998), most researchers refer to such behavior as **organizational citizenship behavior** (*OCB* for short)—prosocial behavior occurring within an organization that may or may not be rewarded by the organization (e.g., Organ, 1997). The fact that such behavior is not automatically or necessarily rewarded (e.g., through a bonus or a raise in pay) is important, because it suggests that sometimes, at least, OCB is performed without any hope of external reward. How do individuals working in an organization seek to help one another? Research findings suggest that they do so in many different ways, and that these actions can be directed at helping either other persons (individual OCB) or their organization (organizational OCB). Examples of individual OCB include *helping others who have a heavy work load, volunteering to do things that are not required,* and *always being on time and refraining from taking unnecessary breaks.* Examples of organizational OCB include "saying positive things about the organization to persons outside it," "attending functions that are not required," and "reading—and paying attention to—memos concerning new company policies or procedures" (Bettencourt, Gwinner, & Meuter, 2001; Skarlicki & Latham, 1997; see Figure 13.15).

organizational citizenship behavior (OCB): Prosocial behavior occurring within an organization that may or may not be rewarded by the organization.

FIGURE 13.15
Organizational Citizenship Behavior: Prosocial Behavior at Work. Prosocial behavior at work takes many different forms and can be directed toward other employees or toward the organization itself.

■ OCB: FACTORS CONTRIBUTING TO ITS OCCURRENCE. What factors lead individuals to engage in various forms of OCB? Recent findings indicate that a number of different factors play a role. Not surprisingly, one factor is job satisfaction—the higher employees' satisfaction with their jobs, the more likely they are to engage in OCB, especially actions that show *loyalty* to the organization, such as telling outsiders that it is a good place to work and actively promoting the company's products and services (Bettencourt, Gwinner, & Meuter, 2001). *Perceived justice*, too, plays a role. When individuals feel that they are being treated fairly by their organization, they are more likely to engage in citizenship behavior than when they feel they are being treated unfairly (see our discussion of perceived justice in Chapter 12; Skarlicki & Latham, 1997). A recent study by Aryee and Chay (2001) indicates that perceived justice exerts its effects most strongly when individuals feel that their organization actively supports them (i.e., cares about their welfare) and when it helps them to reach their goals. These researchers studied union members and found that perceptions by the members that they were being treated fairly by the union strongly predicted behaviors designed to help it (organizational OCB) and other members (individual OCB). But this was especially true when participants in the study also perceived that the union actively supported them (e.g., cared about their well-being) and was instrumental in helping them reach important goals (e.g., improving working conditions, improving job security).

Another factor that influences OCB involves employees' perceptions of the breadth of their jobs—which behaviors are required and which are voluntary. The more broadly employees define their jobs, the more likely they are to engage in instances of OCB (Morrison, 1994; Van Dyne & LePine, 1998). For instance, if a professor believes that helping other professors is part of her job—that this is simply the right thing to do—she may be much more willing to engage in such behavior than if she believes that helping other professors is definitely *not* part of her job and *not* her responsibility.

Interestingly, research findings indicate that employees do not always engage in OCB without any hope of reward for doing so. On the contrary, growing evidence suggests that managers often take subordinates' willingness to engage in OCB into account when making decisions about their raises and promotions (e.g., Podsakoff, MacKenzie, & Hui, 1993). In other words, managers take note of employees' willingness to be a good team player and tend to reward such behavior. An intriguing study by Hui, Lam, and Law (2000) indicates that employees are well aware of this fact and often engage in OCB as a means of gaining desirable outcomes, such as a promotion.

In their study, Hui, Lam, and Law (2000) asked tellers at a large international bank to rate the extent to which they believed that their chances of promotion would be higher if they engaged in OCB (e.g., volunteered for things that are not required, helped others who had heavy work loads). At the same time, the tellers' supervisors also rated the extent to which the subordinates engaged in OCB. These initial ratings were made three months prior to a decision concerning the tellers' promotions. Three months after this decision, managers again rated the tellers' tendencies to engage in OCB. Hui, Lam, and Law (2000) predicted that the greater the tellers' tendencies to engage in OCB, the more likely they would be to receive a promotion, and that the more strongly the tellers believed that OCB was instrumental to promotion, the more they would engage in such behavior. Both predictions were supported by the findings. In addition, and most interesting of all, Hui, Lam, and Law (2000) also predicted that employees who perceived OCB as instrumental to their promotion would be more likely to show an actual *drop* in such behavior after receiving a promotion; in contrast, they predicted that such a drop would not occur among tellers who did not perceive OCB as instrumental for promotion or who were not promoted. As you can see in Figure 13.16, this is precisely what happened: among tellers who were promoted, those who believed that engaging in OCB was

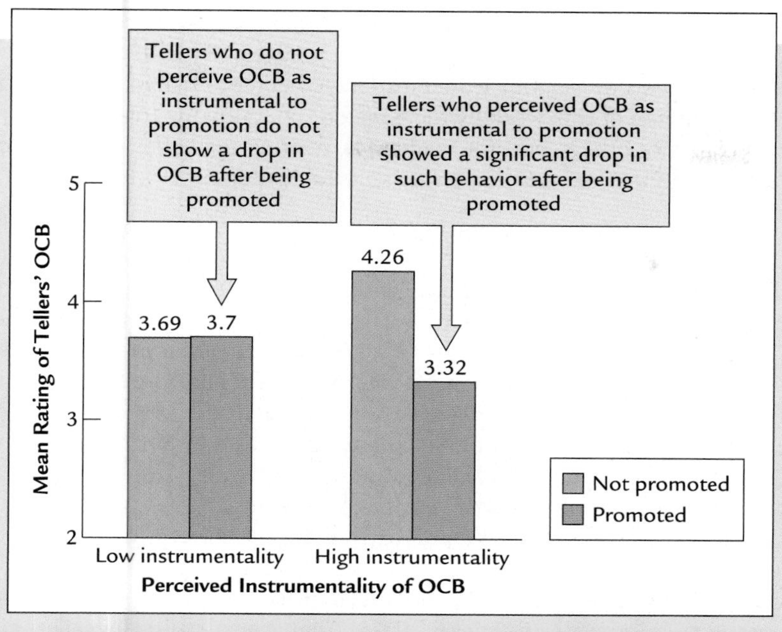

FIGURE 13.16

Evidence That Employees Sometimes Engage in OCB in Order to Gain Promotion.

Tellers in a large bank who believed that engaging in OCB would increase their chances of promotion actually showed a drop in such behavior after gaining the promotion they sought. In contrast, tellers who did not perceive OCB as instrumental in gaining promotion or who were not promoted did not show a similar decline in their willingness to help others.

[SOURCE: BASED ON DATA FROM HUI, LAM, & LAW, 2000.]

important to gaining this reward showed a substantial drop in OCB after receiving the promotion. Other tellers did not show a similar pattern. These findings indicate that OCB at work is often *not* pure altruism. On the contrary, many employees recognize that engaging in OCB will boost their image and further their careers.

In sum, as is true of prosocial behavior in other settings, individuals' tendencies to engage in such actions at work are influenced by several different factors. To the extent that these are present, OCB will be a frequent occurrence in an organization; to the extent these factors are lacking, such behavior will occur at a lower rate.

Leadership: Patterns of Influence within Groups

Try this simple demonstration with your friends. Ask them to rate themselves on a scale ranging from 1 (very low) to 7 (very high) on *leadership potential.* Unless your friends are a very unusual group, here's what you'll find: Most will rate themselves as *average* or *above* on this dimension. This suggests that they view leadership very favorably. But what *is* leadership? To a degree, it's like attractiveness: easy to recognize but hard to define. However, psychologists generally use this term to mean *the process through which one member of a group (the leader) influences other group members toward attainment of shared group goals* (Vecchio, 1997; Yukl, 1998). In other words, being a leader involves *influence*—a leader is the group member who exerts the most influence within the group.

Research on leadership has long been part of social psychology, but it is also an applied topic studied by other fields as well (e.g., Bass, B. I., 1998); literally thousands of research studies about leadership have been published. Here, we'll consider a small portion of this work by focusing on the following topics: (1) why some individuals, but not others, become leaders; (2) contrasting *styles* of leadership; and (3) the nature of *transformational* (*charismatic*) leadership.

■ WHO BECOMES A LEADER? DO TRAITS REALLY MATTER? Are some people born to lead? Common sense suggests that this is so. Famous leaders such as Alexander the Great, Queen Elizabeth I, and Abraham Lincoln seem to differ from ordinary people in several respects. Such observations led early researchers to formulate the **great person theory** of leadership—the view that great leaders possess certain traits that set them apart from most human beings, traits that are possessed by all such leaders, no matter when or where they lived (see Figure 13.17).

great person theory: A view of leadership suggesting that great leaders possess certain traits that set them apart from most human beings, traits that are possessed by all such leaders no matter when or where they lived.

These are intriguing ideas, but research designed to test them was not encouraging. Try as they might, researchers could not come up with a short list of key traits shared by all great leaders (Yukl, 1998). In recent years, however, this situation has changed greatly. More sophisticated research methods, coupled with a better understanding of the basic dimensions of human personality, have led many researchers to conclude that leaders do indeed differ from other persons in several important ways (Kirkpatrick & Locke, 1991). What special traits do leaders possess? Research findings point to the conclusion that leaders rate higher than most people

FIGURE 13.17

The Great Person Theory of Leadership. According to the great person theory, all great leaders share certain traits that set them apart from other persons, and they possess these traits no matter where or when they lived. Research findings offer little support for this view but *do* suggest that leaders differ from other persons with respect to some traits.

Queen Elizabeth I

Abraham Lincoln

Alexander the Great

on the following traits: *drive*—the desire for achievement, coupled with high energy and resolution; *self-confidence; creativity;* and *leadership motivation*—the desire to be in charge and exercise authority over others. Perhaps the most important single characteristic of leaders, however, is a high level of *flexibility*—the ability to recognize what actions or approaches are required in a given situation and then to act accordingly (Zaccaro, Foti, & Kenny, 1991).

In addition, research findings suggest that several basic dimensions of personality, too, may be related to becoming a leader and being effective in this role (e.g., Watson & Clark, 1997). Specifically, recent findings (e.g., Judge & Bono, 2000) suggest that several of what psychologists often term the **Big Five dimensions of personality** may play an important role in leadership (e.g., Barrick & Mount, 1991). Briefly, these five dimensions seem to represent very basic aspects of personality—dimensions along which individuals vary, and ones that are often readily apparent in others' behavior. The five dimensions are as follows (for each, we'll describe the *high* end of the dimension): *extraversion*—the tendency to be outgoing, assertive, and active; *agreeableness*—the tendency to be kind, gentle, trusting, and trustworthy; *conscientiousness*—being organized, dependable, and achievement-oriented; *openness to experience*—the tendency to be creative, imaginative, perceptive, and thoughtful; and *emotional adjustment or stability*—the tendency to be calm, not depressed, and not moody. (This fifth dimension is often described, at the low end, as *neuroticism,* and this involves the opposite: tendencies to be anxious, fearful, depressed, and moody.)

What do these dimensions have to do with leadership? According to the findings of recent studies, quite a lot. For instance, in one large-scale investigation, Judge and Bono (2000) had hundreds of persons who were participating in community leadership programs throughout the U.S. Midwest complete questionnaires designed to measure their standing on each of the Big Five dimensions and the extent to which they showed a certain kind of leadership behavior (specifically, *transformational* leadership—an important style of leadership that we'll consider in detail below). Results indicated that agreeableness was strongly related to such leadership. In addition, both extraversion and openness to experience were also related to showing this kind of leadership. These and related findings indicate that some aspects of leadership, at least, are linked to basic dimensions of personality.

So, are some persons more suited for leadership than others? Research suggests that, to some extent, the answer is yes—persons who possess certain traits are more likely to become leaders and to succeed in this role than are persons who do not possess these traits or who possess them to a lesser degree. It is also clear, however, that leaders do *not* operate in a social vacuum. On the contrary, different groups, facing different tasks and problems, seem to require different types of leaders, or at least leaders who demonstrate contrasting styles (House & Podsakoff, 1994; Locke, 1991). So traits, while they do indeed matter where leadership is concerned, are only part of the total picture. With this thought in mind, let's take a closer look at precisely *how* leaders lead—the contrasting styles they can adopt.

■ HOW LEADERS LEAD: CONTRASTING STYLES AND APPROACHES. All leaders are definitely not alike. They may share certain traits to a degree, but they differ greatly in terms of personal *style* or approach to leadership (e.g., George, 1995; Peterson, 1997). While there are probably as many different styles of leadership as there are leaders, research on leader behavior or style suggests that, in fact, most leaders can be placed along a small number of dimensions relating to their overall approach to leadership. Two such dimensions emerged in very early research on leadership (e.g., Weissenberg & Kavanagh, 1972) and have been repeatedly confirmed. The first is known as **initiating structure** (or *production orientation*). Leaders high on this dimension are primarily concerned with getting the job done. They engage in actions such as organizing work, urging subordinates to follow the rules, setting goals, and making leader and subordinate roles explicit. In contrast, leaders low on this dimension engage in such actions to a lesser degree.

Big Five dimensions of personality: Basic dimensions of personality; where individuals stand along these dimensions (for example, extroversion, agreeableness, neuroticism) is often apparent in their behavior.

initiating structure: (production-orientation). A key dimension of leader behavior. Leaders high on this dimension are primarily concerned with getting the job done (that is, with production).

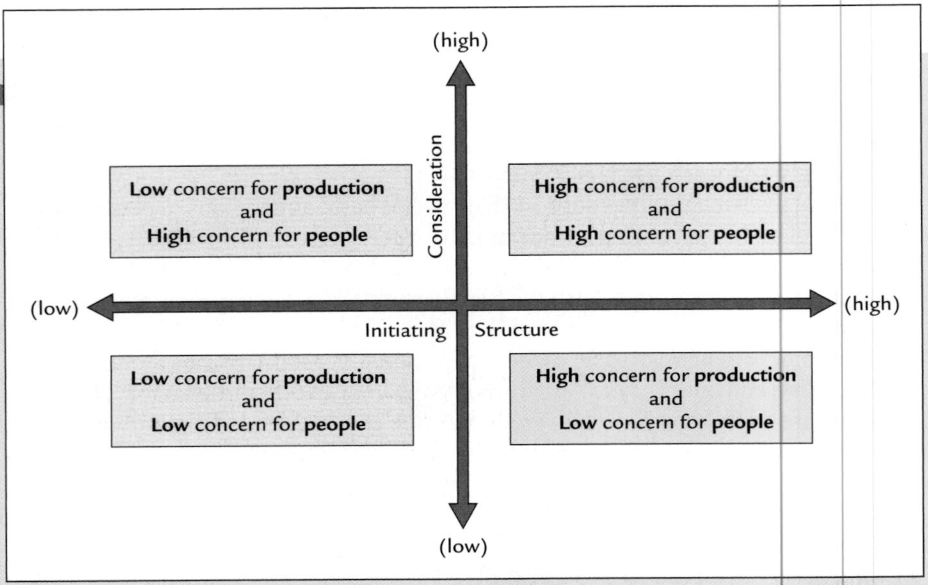

FIGURE 13.18

Leader Behavior: Two Basic Dimensions. The behavior of leaders has been found to vary along the two dimensions shown here: *consideration,* which involves concern for people and good relations with them, and *initiating structure,* which involves concern for production and task completion. Any given leader can be high or low on each of these dimensions.

The second dimension is known as **consideration** (or *person orientation*). Leaders high on this dimension focus on establishing good relations with their subordinates and on being liked by them. They engage in such actions as doing favors for subordinates, explaining things to them, and watching out for their welfare. Leaders low on this dimension, in contrast, do not really care how well they get along with their subordinates. (See Figure 13.18 for an overview of these two basic dimensions of leader behavior.)

Is either of these two styles superior? Not really. Both offer a mixed pattern of advantages and disadvantages. High consideration (high concern for people) can result in improved group morale, but because such leaders do not like to tell subordinates what to do or give them negative feedback, efficiency sometimes suffers. In contrast, when leaders are high on initiating structure, efficiency may be high but subordinates may conclude that the leader does not really care about them. As a result, their commitment to the organization may suffer. Overall, though, it appears that leaders who are high on both dimensions may have an edge in many situations. In other words, leaders who are concerned with establishing good relations with their subordinates *and* with maintaining efficiency and productivity may often prove superior to leaders showing other patterns of behavior.

Two additional dimensions of leader behavior that have been uncovered by careful research involve the extent to which leaders make all the decisions themselves or allow participation by group members (an *autocratic–participative* dimension), and the extent to which leaders try to run the show by closely directing the activities of all group members (a *directive–permissive* dimension) (Muczyk & Reimann, 1987; Peterson, 1997). If you think back over your own experiences, you can probably recall leaders who were high or low on both of these dimensions. For instance, in a summer job I (RAB) once held, the manager of the department was squarely on the directive end of the directive–permissive dimension: he was constantly looking over our shoulders and telling us how to do virtually everything. Many employees dislike this micro-management because it suggests that their boss has no confidence in them; in fact, that's just how I felt. Again, being high or low on each of these dimensions is not necessarily good or bad from the point of view of leader effectiveness—it depends on the situation. For instance, under emergency conditions, when decisions have to be made quickly, an autocratic style may be helpful; under more relaxed conditions, though, most persons prefer participative leaders

consideration: (person-orientation). A key dimension of leader behavior. Leaders high on this dimension focus on establishing good relations with their subordinates and on being liked by them.

who let them have input into the decision-making process. The same is true for the directive–permissive dimension; when subordinates are new at their jobs, they need direction from the leader; once they have mastered their jobs, though, it is usually better for the leader to take a step back and leave them alone.

■ **TRANSFORMATIONAL (CHARISMATIC) LEADERS: LEADERS WHO CHANGE THE WORLD—OR AT LEAST THEIR ORGANIZATIONS.** Have you ever seen films of John F. Kennedy? Franklin Roosevelt? Martin Luther King, Jr.? If so, you may have noticed that there seems to be something special about these leaders. As you listened to their speeches, you may have found yourself being moved by their words and stirred by the vigor of their presentations. You are definitely not alone in such reactions: these leaders exerted powerful effects on many millions of persons and by doing so, changed their societies. Leaders who accomplish such feats are termed **transformational** (or *charismatic*) **leaders** (House & Howell, 1992; Kohl, Steers, & Terborg, 1995). What characteristics make certain leaders charismatic? While there is not complete agreement on this point, most researchers who have studied charismatic leaders generally agree that they show these characteristics (e.g., Bass, 1985; Judge & Bono, 2000): (1) *idealized influence*—they serve as a charismatic role model to followers (i.e., they show charisma); (2) *intellectual stimulation*—they stimulate creativity among followers by questioning assumptions and the status quo; (3) *inspirational motivation*—they articulate a clear, inspiring vision to followers; and (4) *individual consideration*—they pay attention to and support the individual needs of followers.

Transformational leaders often exert profound effects on their followers—and on organizations or even society in general. And it seems clear that they do so through their ability to induce extraordinary levels of motivation and commitment among followers. How do they do this? Research findings emphasize the importance of the following factors. First, as noted above, this type of leader often states a compelling *vision* of the future or of what an organization or group can—and should—accomplish (Howell & Frost, 1989). To the extent that followers accept this vision, their level of commitment to the leader and the leader's goals can become intense.

Second, charismatic leaders go beyond stating a vision: they also offer a route for reaching it. They tell their followers, in straightforward terms, how to get from here to there. This, too, seems crucial, for a vision that seems out of reach is unlikely to motivate people to work to attain it.

Third, charismatic leaders engage in *framing* (Conger, 1991). They define the goals for their group in a way that gives extra meaning and purpose to the goals and actions needed to attain them. A clear illustration of such framing is provided by the story of two stonecutters working on a cathedral in the Middle Ages. When asked what they were doing, one replied, "Cutting this stone, of course." The other answered, "Building the world's most beautiful temple to the glory of God." Which person would be likely to work harder, and perhaps accomplish extraordinary things? The answer is obvious, and it is also clear that any leader who can induce such thinking in her or his followers can also have profound effects upon them.

Other behaviors shown by charismatic leaders include high levels of self-confidence, an excellent communication style, and an exciting personal style (House, Spangler, & Woycke, 1991). Finally, transformational leaders are often masters of *impression management,* a process we described in Chapter 2. When this skill is added to the traits and behaviors mentioned above, and combined with a charismatic leader's use of vision and framing, the ability of such leaders to influence large numbers of followers loses some of its mystery. Transformational leaders produce the profound effects they do because they possess characteristics that, together, arm them with an impressive personal style—one that many people find hard to resist.

So, in a sense, research on leadership has come full cycle, from initial efforts to understand the style and behavior of run-of-the-mill leaders to the style and behavior of extraordinary ones. For an overview of how research on leadership has progressed, please see the **Social Psychology: Thirty Years of Progress** section on page 560.

transformational (charismatic) leaders: Leaders who exert profound effects on their followers and by doing so, change their organizations or societies.

UNDERSTANDING THE DIMENSIONS—AND LIMITS—OF LEADERSHIP STYLE: FROM AUTOCRATIC AND DEMOCRATIC LEADERS TO CHARISMA

That leaders differ in style—in their approach to leadership—is obvious. What is less obvious, though, is how leaders' style influences the groups they direct. Social psychologists have long recognized the importance of this question, and for this reason, it has been a central one in the study of leadership for several decades. In fact, one of the earliest investigations of leadership—a famous one by Lewin, Lippitt, and White (1939)—focused on this issue.

Lewin and his colleagues were interested in comparing the effects of three styles of leadership: *autocratic, laissez-faire,* and *democratic.* To study this issue, they arranged for ten- and eleven-year-old boys to meet in five-member groups after school, to engage in hobbies such woodworking and painting. Each group was led by an adult who assumed one of the three styles of leadership listed above.

The *autocratic* leader gave many orders and made all of the decisions himself. He determined what activities the group would perform, and in what order, and simply assigned each boy a work partner without considering their personal preferences. In contrast, the *democratic* leader allowed the boys to participate in reaching decisions and often sought their input. He rarely gave orders or commands, allowed them to choose their own work partners, and permitted them to approach their work in whatever way they wished. Finally, the *laissez-faire* leader adopted a hands-off approach (the French words *laissez-faire* mean "let people do what they choose"). He avoided participating in group activities and did not intervene in any way. Rather, his role was primarily that of an interested observer, there to provide technical information about the hobby activities if requested to do so by the boys.

Trained observers watched the groups as they worked and rated their behavior in several respects—for example, the amount of time spent working while the leader was present, the amount of time spent working when he left the room, aggressive activities such as hostility among group members, demands for attention, destructiveness, and *scapegoating*—a tendency to single out one group member as the target of continuous verbal abuse. These ratings revealed a number of differences in the boys' behavior across the three conditions. For example, boys in the autocratic and democratic groups spent about an equal amount of time working when the leader was present; those in the laissez-faire groups worked less. When the leader left the room, however, work dropped off sharply in the groups headed by an autocratic leader; in contrast, it remained unchanged in the democratic groups; work actually increased slightly in the laissez-faire groups. In addition, boys in the autocratic condition seemed more at a loss when the leader left the room: they appeared to be heavily dependent on the leader for direction and did not know how to proceed without his commands and guidance. With respect to the measures of aggressiveness, it appeared that there were more signs of such behavior in the autocratic groups than in the democratic or laissez-faire ones. For example, boys in the autocratic groups expressed more discontent and made more aggressive demands for attention. Those in the democratic groups tended to be friendlier. Not surprisingly, the boys tended to prefer the democratic leaders to the other two.

These findings suggest that leaders' style or behavior can indeed exert strong effects on the groups they lead. Specifically, Lewin and his colleagues suggested that, overall, a democratic style of leadership may be best. It encourages a high level of productivity that persists even when the leader is absent. Further, it fosters positive and cooperative relations among group members. In contrast, an autocratic style of leadership produces high productivity only when the leader is present and seems to increase both dependence on the leader and higher levels of aggression.

Research on leaders' style has continued without interruption since this initial, ingenious study. At first, the focus was on the dimensions we described earlier—for instance, the extent to which leaders show consideration or initiate structure. More recently, though, the focus has shifted to examining the impact of transformational leaders and a contrasting type known as **transactional leaders.** While transformational (charismatic) leaders focus on stating an inspiring vision, transactional leaders act more like traditional managers. They direct their groups by rewarding them for desired behavior, by taking action to correct mistakes or departures from existing rules, and generally by strengthening existing structures and strategies within an organization.

Clearly, transactional and transformational leaders differ sharply in style, and this, in turn, leads to an intriguing question: Which is better from the point of view of maximizing organizational performance? To find out, Waldman and his colleagues (2001) asked several hundred high-level executives in more than one hundred different companies to rate the CEO (leader) of their company in terms of both styles of leadership. These ratings were then related to the companies' financial performance (how successful they were in making a profit). An additional aspect of the study involved the extent to which the companies faced an uncertain and unpredictable environment. Waldman and his associates (2001) predicted that charismatic leaders would be especially beneficial in uncertain, rapidly changing environments because such leaders would be more effective than transactional leaders in gaining high commitment and effort from employees.

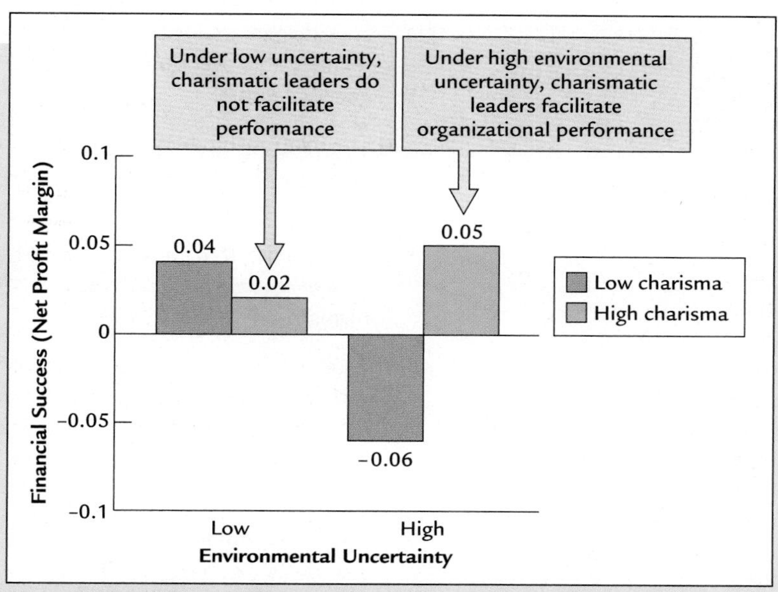

FIGURE 13.19

Charismatic Leaders: When Do They Facilitate Organizational Performance?

When organizations faced rapidly changing, unpredictable environments, they performed significantly better if their leaders were high in charisma rather than low in charisma. When organizations faced stable, predictable environments, in contrast, the leaders' charisma had little effect on organizational performance.

[SOURCE: BASED ON DATA FROM WALDMAN ET AL., 2001.]

As you can see in Figure 13.19, results confirmed this prediction. Whether leaders were low or high in charisma did not matter in stable, unchanging environments. But in rapidly changing, chaotic environments, companies whose leaders were high in charisma outperformed those whose leaders were low in charisma. Interestingly, the extent to which leaders were low or high in transactional leadership style did not influence the companies' financial performance.

In sum, several decades of research employing a wide range of participants and many different measures of group performance indicate that leader style does indeed matter. While there does not appear to be one single style of leadership that is always best, it is clear that some styles are preferred by most group members and that, depending on the circumstances faced by a group, some leaders are more likely than others to facilitate performance. The final message in all this? Choosing the right leader is a crucial task for all groups.

KEY POINTS

- People spend more time at work than in any other single activity. Because they often work with others, the findings and principles of social psychology help to explain behavior in work settings.
- Job satisfaction is an individual's attitude toward her or his job. Job satisfaction is influenced by organizational factors, such as working conditions and the fairness of reward systems, and personal factors, such as seniority, status, and specific personality traits. Recent findings suggest that job satisfaction is often highly stable over time for many persons and that it may be influenced by genetic factors.
- The relationship between job satisfaction and task performance is relatively weak, partly because many factors other than these work-related attitudes influence performance.
- Individuals often engage in prosocial behavior at work. This is known as *organizational citizenship behavior (OCB),* and it can take many different forms.
- OCB is influenced by several factors, including job satisfaction, the extent to which employees feel they are being treated fairly by their organization, and the extent to which they define their job responsibilities broadly.
- OCB can also be performed because employees perceive it as instrumental to obtaining promotions.
- Leadership refers to the process through which one member of a group (its leader) influences the other group members toward the attainment of shared group goals.
- While the great person theory of leadership has been shown to be false, recent findings suggest that leaders do indeed differ from other persons with respect to several traits. For instance, two of the *Big Five dimensions of personality*—extroversion and openness to experience—seem to be related to becoming a leader and succeeding in this role.
- In addition, leaders vary with respect to their behavior or style. Classic research in social psychology suggested that leaders vary in terms of two basic dimensions: *consideration* and *initiating structure.* In addition, leaders vary along two other key dimensions: autocratic–participative and directive–permissive.
- Transformational (charismatic) leaders exert profound effects on their followers and often change their societies. Research on the nature of such leadership suggests that it stems from certain behaviors by leaders, such as stating a clear vision, framing the group's goals in ways that magnify their importance, and possessing a strong personal style. Together, such actions produce a special relationship between charismatic leaders and their followers that maximizes the leader's influence.
- Recent research on transformational leadership suggests that it enhances organizations' performance, but only when organizations face rapidly changing, unpredictable environments.

transactional leaders: Leaders who direct their groups by rewarding them for desired behavior and by taking action to correct mistakes or departures from existing rules. Such leaders generally strengthen existing structures and strategies within an organization.

CONNECTIONS: INTEGRATING SOCIAL PSYCHOLOGY

IN THIS CHAPTER, YOU READ ABOUT . . .	IN OTHER CHAPTERS, YOU WILL FIND RELATED DISCUSSIONS OF . . .
forming attitudes about a suspect based on pre-trial publicity	first impressions (Chapter 2) and attitude formation (Chapter 4)
accuracy of eyewitness testimony	information processing and information retrieval (Chapter 3)
the similarity of police lineups and social psychological experiments	designing experiments to maximize the odds of obtaining objective and reliable results (Chapter 1)
nonverbal communication from judge to jurors	basic channels of nonverbal communication (Chapter 2)
attraction toward and evaluation of defendants	factors influencing interpersonal attraction (Chapter 7)
stereotypes and prejudice in evaluating defendants	stereotypes and prejudice based on race and gender (Chapter 6)
processing health-related information	use of the availability heuristic and the resulting distortions (Chapter 3) and the use of persuasive appeals (Chapter 4)
self-efficacy in responding to stress	the general effects of self-efficacy (Chapter 5)
self-healing personality	secure attachment style (Chapter 8) and the altruistic personality (Chapter 10)
hostile Type A behavior as a health risk	Type A behavior and aggression (Chapter 11)
seeking social support as a coping strategy	the importance of affiliation (Chapter 7) and relationships versus loneliness (Chapter 8)
attachment style as a determinant of social support behavior	attachment style in interpersonal relationships (Chapter 8)
job satisfaction	the basic nature of attitudes (Chapter 4)
organizational citizenship behavior	prosocial behavior (Chapter 10)
leadership	other aspects of influence (Chapter 9) and other group processes (Chapter 12)

THINKING ABOUT CONNECTIONS

1. A theft has taken place where you work, and all of the employees are being questioned by the police about what they know. You are asked to remember where you were at noon on Friday of the previous week, the actions of your fellow employees that day, and precisely what you may have seen. Think about what it is you actually remember (Chapter 3) and what you only seem to remember (Chapter 13). Is it possible that the person interrogating you has already made up his mind and simply wants you to provide confirmation? Do the questions suggest that certain answers are expected? Are you comfortable in honestly saying such things as "I don't know" and "I can't remember," or do you feel that you *should* come up with tentative guesses?

2. In the past year you have probably experienced at least one or two (and maybe many more) stressful situations. How did you respond? Were you physically fit at the time, or had you skipped exercise, stayed up late and missed sleep, and dined primarily on junk food? Did you feel depressed? Did you think of options that might help remove the source of stress or at

(continued)

least help you deal with it? Did you seek the support of other people? How closely do you feel that you resemble the self-healing personality versus the disease-prone personality? Finally, did you get sick and, if so, does it appear that your illness occurred because of the stress and the way you tried to cope with it?

3. Prosocial behavior at work is often difficult to measure—it occurs in subtle ways between employees who assist each other without making a big deal about it, or it occurs away from the organization, when employees say positive things about it or promote its image in other ways. Given the measurement problem, how can we be certain that encouraging such behavior is a good thing for organizations? In other words, how can we determine whether prosocial behavior (organizational citizenship behavior) yields beneficial effects for organizations and their employees?

4. At the present time, many people feel that there are no longer any great leaders in the world. Do you agree? If you do, why do you think this is so? And if there are no great leaders now, could we take any steps to produce such individuals by training them in the required leadership qualities?

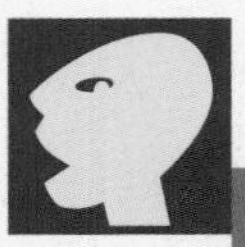

IDEAS TO TAKE WITH YOU—AND USE!

DON'T RUSH TO JUDGMENT

Whether as a potential juror or as an official member of a jury, you will be exposed to a great deal of information, many arguments, and diverse facts about any given crime and about the suspected criminal. Even if you are simply a member of the general public with no formal role to play, it is still useful for you to keep in mind some of the issues involved in reaching valid conclusions about legal matters. If you are actually a member of the jury, your ability to remain open-minded can literally be a matter of life and death.

Remember: The Arrest of a Suspect Is Not Automatically an Indication of Guilt.

When you hear the details of a brutal crime and then learn on TV or in the newspapers that a suspect has been arrested, don't assume that the crime is necessarily solved or that the arrested individual is known to be guilty. Before guilt or innocence is determined, there must be an indictment, a trial, the presentation of evidence for and against the defendant, a consideration of precise legal issues, and an attempt by a jury to reach consensus. The most reasonable position to take is that *either* the prosecution or the defense might be correct, so you would be wise to construct two alternative schemas for yourself—one in which you store all of the information indicating guilt and one in which you store all of the information indicating innocence. Wait until the facts are in before deciding which schema is more convincing.

Separate Interpersonal Attraction toward the Defendant from Judgments Based on the Evidence.

It is probably not possible to enter any situation with a totally objective, open mind. Remember, research findings suggest that we automatically respond to stimuli with relatively positive or relatively negative attitudes. The best we can do is to separate how much

we *like* the defendant from what we *know* about his or her probable guilt based on testimony and physical evidence. No matter how you feel about the defendant's appearance, ethnic background, political views, sexual orientation, or whatever else, the question is not your attraction toward the individual but whether the bulk of the evidence indicates guilt beyond a reasonable doubt. In everyday life, we often blur the distinction between attraction toward someone and factual knowledge about that person. For a juror, it is crucial that such distinctions be made.

Don't Let Your Opinion Be Swayed by Emotional Appeals.

We all know that the prosecutor and the defense attorney have very specific and quite different scenarios to "sell." Each side wants to convince the onlookers (including the jurors) that there is only one version of the truth. Each side will try to appeal to your feelings, your prejudices, your similarity to the defendant or your differences, or whatever else might be effective in convincing you to vote "the right way." Again, your task is not to deny the disgust you may feel about a brutal crime or the sympathy you may feel toward a possibly innocent citizen dragged into court and unfairly accused of committing a criminal act. Both feelings are reasonable. The question, however, is once again a matter of what is indicated by the legally relevant evidence. The courtroom is clearly a place where it is important to separate emotional processes from cognitive ones.

Don't Let the Judge Persuade You to Agree with His or Her Opinion.

It is your job to provide a verdict, and it is the judge's job to maintain orderly proceedings and enforce the rules with respect to the kinds of questions asked and the kinds of evidence that are acceptable. Like you, the judge may be tempted to jump to conclusions or to be swayed by emotions. At times, he or she may be unable to conceal a positive or negative opinion. Your task, however, is to avoid responding to irrelevant factors, including the judge's personal belief about guilt or innocence.

SUMMARY AND REVIEW OF KEY POINTS

Applying Social Psychology to the Interpersonal Aspects of the Legal System

- People obey the law and accept legal decisions so long as they perceive the procedures to be fair and just.
- Most people would prefer police to search for the truth rather than attempt to prove guilt, but both interrogation approaches are common.
- There are several factors that contribute to false confessions and to a belief in one's guilt by an individual who is actually innocent.
- A serious and controversial legal problem is the recovery of *repressed memories* of past criminal events that often turn out to be false memories.
- People are interested in details about crime, and extensive media coverage leads to over-estimations of the frequency of murder, assault, and other crimes.
- Media concentration on a person accused of a crime leads to widespread assumptions of guilt among the general public, including those who will become jurors. Because such assumptions help the prosecution, government officials tend to provide the media with as much information as possible.
- Eyewitnesses to a crime often make mistakes, but a variety of procedures have been developed to help ensure greater accuracy.
- Attorneys act as adversaries who attempt to select juries biased toward their side and to convince the jurors that their version of the truth is the correct one.
- The words and even the unspoken beliefs of judges can influence the verdict.
- Defendants are judged in part on irrelevant characteristics such as appearance, gender, socioeconomic status, and behavior in the courtroom.
- A juror's response to the evidence and to the defendant depends on his or her affective evaluations, cognitive processing, and personality characteristics.

Applying Social Psychology to Health-Related Behavior

- We receive health-related information on a daily basis, and all of us need to remain informed and willing to change our minds in response to new findings.
- *Stress* refers to any event that is perceived as a potential source of physical or emotional harm. Stress can lead to physical illness indirectly through its effect on health-related behavior and directly by interfering with the immune system.
- A variety of dispositional factors are associated with differential vulnerability to illness that is initiated by stress. The negative effects of stress have the greatest effect on those with *disease-prone personality* characteristics but are resisted by those with *self-healing personality* characteristics.
- Effective strategies for *coping* with stress include increasing one's physical *fitness;* engaging in regulatory control of feelings, thoughts, and activities; seeking sources of positive affect (including the presence of pets); and establishing a network of *social support.*

Applying Social Psychology to the World of Work: Job Satisfaction, Helping, and Leadership

- People spend more time at work than in any other single activity. Because they often work with others, the findings and principles of social psychology help to explain behavior in work settings.
- *Job satisfaction* is an individual's attitude toward her or his job. Job satisfaction is influenced by organizational factors, such as working conditions and the fairness of reward systems, and personal factors, such as seniority, status, and specific personality traits. Recent findings suggest that job satisfaction is often highly stable over time for many persons and that it may be influenced by genetic factors.
- The relationship between job satisfaction and task performance is relatively weak, partly because many factors other than these work-related attitudes influence performance.
- Individuals often engage in prosocial behavior at work. This is known as *organizational citizenship behavior* (OCB), and it can take many different forms.
- OCB is influenced by several factors, including job satisfaction, the extent to which employees feel they are being treated fairly by their organization, and the extent to which they define their job responsibilities broadly.
- OCB can also be performed because employees perceive it as instrumental to obtaining promotions.
- Leadership refers to the process through which one member of a group (its leader) influences the other group members toward the attainment of shared group goals.
- While the great person theory of leadership has been shown to be false, recent findings suggest that leaders do indeed differ from other persons with respect to several traits. For instance, two of the *Big Five dimensions of personality*—extroversion and openness to experience—seem to be related to becoming a leader and succeeding in this role.
- In addition, leaders vary with respect to their behavior or style. Classic research in social psychology suggested that leaders vary in terms of two basic dimensions: *consideration* and *initiating structure.* In addition, leaders vary along two other key dimensions: autocratic–participative and directive–permissive.
- *Transformational (charismatic) leaders* exert profound effects on their followers and often change their societies. Research on the nature of such leadership suggests that it stems from certain behaviors by leaders, such as stating a clear vision, framing the group's goals in ways that magnify their importance, and possessing a strong personal style. Together, such actions produce a special relationship between charismatic leaders and their followers that maximizes the leader's influence.
- Recent research on transformational leadership suggests that it enhances organizations' performance, but only when organizations face rapidly changing, unpredictable environments.

KEY TERMS

Big Five dimensions of personality (p. 557)
blank-lineup control (p. 530)
consideration (p. 558)
coping (p. 541)
disease-prone personality (p. 543)
fitness (p. 545)
forensic psychology (p. 520)
great person theory (p. 556)
health psychology (p. 538)
initiating structure (p. 557)
job satisfaction (p. 550)
leading questions (p. 532)
organizational citizenship behavior (OCB) (p. 553)
psychoneuroimmunology (p. 542)
repressed memory (p. 524)
self-healing personality (p. 543)
social support (p. 548)
stress (p. 541)
transactional leaders (p. 562)
transformational (charismatic) leaders (p. 559)
voir dire (p. 531)

FOR MORE INFORMATION

Amsterdam, A. G., & Bruner, J. (2000). *Minding the law.* Cambridge, MA: Harvard University Press.

- In this collaborative effort by a lawyer and a psychologist, the way that cognitive processes influence judicial decision making is described in detail. They use actual court cases as examples of how psychological phenomena can shape the judicial process.

Bass, B. M. (1998). *Transformational leadership: Industrial, military, and educational impact.* Mahwah, NJ: Erlbaum.

- In this book, an expert who has studied leadership for several decades reviews existing evidence concerning the nature and effects of transformational leadership. Transformational leadership is compared with other types and styles of leadership, and ways in which the principles of transformational leadership can be applied in many different settings are described. A stimulating, thought-provoking book.

Greenberg, J., & Baron, R. A. (2002). *Behavior in organizations* (8th ed). Upper Saddle River, NJ: Prentice-Hall.

- This book provides a broad overview of our knowledge about behavior in work settings. Many of the topics covered represent applications of social psychology to issues relating to organizations.

Le Fanu, J. (2000). *The rise and fall of modern medicine.* New York: Carroll and Graf.

- This is an interesting book that deals with medical knowledge past and present, demonstrating the way in which medical beliefs and medical decisions have been shaped by cultural beliefs as much as by science. Much of this material (especially the portion dealing with current medical practices) may be controversial, but it is consistently intriguing.

Pope, K. S., & Brown, L. S. (1996). *Recovered memories of abuse: Assessment, therapy, forensics.* Washington, DC: American Psychological Association.

- This is a guide that presents an overview of the problem of recovered memories, dealing with both legal and psychological issues. The authors cover such topics as the study of memory, the effects of trauma, the way in which people are questioned about their memories, and the issues that face therapists and expert witnesses.

Radley, A. (1994). *Making sense of illness: The social psychology of health and disease.* Thousand Oaks, CA: Sage.

- This book cuts across the field of health psychology, sociology, and medicine to describe the importance of psychological factors in responding to stress, coping with acute and chronic health problems, and behaving in ways that promote good health and prevent disease.

Glossary

actor–observer effect: The tendency to attribute our own behavior mainly to situational causes but the behavior of others mainly to internal (dispositional) causes.

additive tasks: Tasks for which the group product is the sum or combination of the efforts of individual members.

affect: A person's emotional state—feelings and moods.

affect-centered model of attraction: A conceptual framework in which attraction is assumed to be based on positive and negative emotions. These emotions can be aroused directly by another person, simply associated with that person, and/or mediated by cognitive processes.

aggression: Behavior directed toward the goal of harming another living being who is motivated to avoid such treatment.

aggression machine: Apparatus used to measure physical aggression under safe laboratory conditions.

altruism: Behavior that reflects an unselfish concern for the welfare of others.

altruistic personality: A combination of dispositional variables associated with prosocial behavior. Among the many components are empathy, belief in a just world, acceptance of social responsibility, and having an internal locus of control.

androgynous: Characterized by the possession of both traditional masculine characteristics and traditional feminine ones.

appearance anxiety: Apprehension or worry about whether one's physical appearance is adequate and about the evaluations of other people.

assumed similarity: The extent to which two people believe they are similar in certain respects, as opposed to the extent to which they are actually similar.

attachment style: The degree of security experienced in interpersonal relationships. Differential styles are initially developed in infancy, but attachment differences appear to affect interpersonal behavior throughout life.

attitude ambivalence: Refers to the fact that we often have positive and negative evaluations of the same attitude object; thus, our attitude toward it is ambivalent.

attitude polarization: The tendency to evaluate mixed evidence or information in such a way that it strengthens our initial views and makes them more extreme.

attitude similarity: The extent to which two individuals share the same attitudes about a range of topics. In practice, the term also includes similarity of beliefs, values, and interests.

attitude-to-behavior process model: A model of how attitudes guide behavior that emphasizes the influence of both attitudes and stored knowledge of what is appropriate in a given situation on an individual's definition of the present situation. This definition, in turn, influences overt behavior.

attitudes: Evaluations of various aspects of the social world.

attribution: The process through which we seek to identify the causes of others' behavior and so gain knowledge of their stable traits and dispositions.

augmenting: The tendency to attach greater importance to potential causes of behavior if the behavior occurs despite the presence of other, inhibitory causes.

authentic dissent: A technique for improving the quality of group decisions in which one or more group members actively disagree with the group's initial preference without being assigned this role.

automatic processing: This occurs when, after extensive experience with a task or type of information, we reach the stage where we can perform the task or process the information in a seemingly effortless, automatic, and nonconscious manner.

availability heuristic: A strategy for making judgments on the basis of how easily specific kinds of information can be brought to mind.

balance theory: The formulation that specifies the relationships among (1) an individual's liking for another person, (2) his or her attitude about a given topic, and (3) the other person's perceived attitude about the same topic. Balance results in a positive emotional state, imbalance results in a negative emotional state, and nonbalance leads to indifference.

bargaining (negotiation): A process in which opposing sides exchange offers, counteroffers, and concessions, either directly or through representatives.

Bem Sex-Role Inventory (BSRI): Bem's measure of the extent to which an individual's self-description involves traditional masculine characteristics, traditional feminine characteristics, both (androgyny), or neither (undifferentiated).

benevolent sexism: Views suggesting that women deserve protection, are superior to men in various ways (e.g., they are more pure, have better taste), and are truly necessary for men's happiness (e.g., no man is truly fulfilled unless he has a woman he adores in his life).

biased assimilation: The tendency to evaluate information that disconfirms our existing views as less convincing or reliable than information that confirms these views.

Big Five dimensions of personality: Basic dimensions of personality; where individuals stand along these dimensions (for example, extroversion, agreeableness, neuroticism) is often apparent in their behavior.

blank-lineup control: A procedure in which a witness views a police lineup that does not include a suspect. If a witness does not identify a suspect, this increases confidence in his or her testimony. If the witness *does* identify an innocent person, he or she is is told of the mistake and cautioned to be more careful. In either instance, witness accuracy is increased.

body language: Cues provided by the position, posture, and movement of others' bodies or body parts.

bona fide pipeline: A technique that uses priming to measure implicit racial attitudes.

bullying: A pattern of behavior in which one individual is chosen as the target of repeated aggression by one or more others; the target person (the victim) generally has less power than those who engage in aggression (the bullies).

bystander effect: The fact that the likelihood of a prosocial response to an emergency is affected by the number of bystanders who are present. As the number of bystanders increases, the probability that any one bystander will help decreases and the amount of time that passes before help occurs increases.

catharsis hypothesis: The view that providing angry persons with an opportunity to express their aggressive impulses in relatively safe ways will reduce their tendencies to engage in more harmful forms of aggression.

central route (to persuasion): Attitude change resulting from systematic processing of information presented in persuasive messages.

classical conditioning: A basic form of learning in which one stimulus, initially neutral, acquires the capacity to evoke reactions through repeated pairing with another stimulus. In a sense, one stimulus becomes a signal for the presentation or occurrence of the other.

close friendship: A relationship in which two people spend a great deal of time together, interact in a variety of situations, exclude others from the relationship, and provide mutual emotional support.

cognitive dissonance: An unpleasant internal state that results when individuals notice inconsistency between two or more of their attitudes or between their attitudes and their behavior.

cohesiveness: (1) All forces (factors) that cause group members to remain in the group. (2) With respect to conformity, the degree of attraction felt by an individual toward an influencing group.

collective effort model: An explanation of social loafing suggesting that perceived links between individuals' effort and their outcomes are weaker when they work together with others in a group. This, in turn, produces tendencies toward social loafing.

common in-group identity model: A theory suggesting that to the extent that individuals in different groups view themselves as members of a single social entity, positive contacts between them will increase and intergroup bias will be reduced.

communal behavior: Benevolent acts in a relationship that "cost" the one who performs those acts and benefit the partner and the relationship itself.

companionate love: Love that is based on friendship, mutual attraction, common interests, mutual respect, and concern for each other's welfare.

compliance: A form of social influence involving direct requests from one person to another.

conflict: A process in which individuals or groups perceive that others have taken or will soon take actions incompatible with their own interests.

conformity: A type of social influence in which individuals change their attitudes or behavior in order to adhere to existing social norms.

consensus: The extent to which other persons react to some stimulus or even in the same manner as the person we are considering.

consideration: (person-orientation). A key dimension of leader behavior. Leaders high on this dimension focus on establishing good relations with their subordinates and on being liked by them.

consistency: The extent to which an individual responds to a given stimulus or situation in the same way on different occasions (i.e., across time).

consummate love: In Sternberg's triangular model of love, a complete and ideal love that combines intimacy, passion, and decision/commitment.

contact hypothesis: The view that increased contact between members of various social groups can be effective in reducing prejudice between them. Such efforts seem to succeed only when contact takes place under specific, favorable conditions.

cooperation: Behavior in which groups work together to attain shared goals.

coping: Responding to stress in a way that reduces the threat and its effects; includes what a person does, feels, or thinks in order to master, tolerate, or decrease the negative effects of a stressful situation.

correlational method: A method of research in which a scientist systematically observes two or more variables to determine whether changes in one are accompanied by changes in the other.

correspondence bias (fundamental attribution error): The tendency to explain others' actions as stemming from dispositions, even in the presence of clear situational causes.

correspondent inference (theory of): A theory describing how we use others' behavior as a basis for inferring their stable dispositions.

counterfactual thinking: The tendency to imagine other outcomes in a situation than the ones that actually occurred—to think about "what might have been."

cultures of honor: Cultures in which strong social norms condone violence as a means of answering an affront to one's honor.

deadline technique: A technique for increasing compliance in which target persons are told that they have only limited time to take advantage of some offer or to obtain some item.

debriefing: Procedures at the conclusion of a research session in which participants are given full information about the nature of the research and the hypothesis or hypotheses under investigation.

deception: A technique whereby researchers withhold information about the purposes or procedures of a study from persons participating in it.

decision/commitment: In Sternberg's triangular model of love, the cognitive elements involved in the decision that you love the other person and the commitment to maintain the relationship.

decision making: Processes involved in combining and integrating available information in order to choose one of several possible courses of action.

dependent variable: The variable that is measured in an experiment.

descriptive norms: Norms that simply indicate what most people do in a given situation.

devil's advocate technique: A technique for improving the quality of group decisions in which one group member is assigned the task of disagreeing with and criticizing whatever plan or decision is under consideration.

diffusion of responsibility: The proposal that the amount of responsibility assumed by bystanders to an emergency is shared among them. If there is only one bystander, he or she has total responsibility. If there are two bystanders, each has 50 percent of the responsibility. If there are one hundred bystanders, each has only 1 percent of the responsibility. The more bystanders, the less any one of them feels responsible to act.

discounting: The tendency to attach less importance to one potential cause of some behavior when other potential causes are also present.

discrimination: Negative behaviors directed toward members of social groups who are the object of prejudice.

disease-prone personality: A personality characterized by negative emotional reactions to stress, ineffective coping strategies, and unhealthy behavior patterns. Among the correlates are a higher incidence of illness and a shorter life span.

dismissing attachment style: In Bartholomew's model, a style characterized by high self-esteem and low interpersonal trust. It is usually described as a conflicted and somewhat insecure style in which the individual feels that he or she "deserves" a close relationship but mistrusts potential partners. The result is the tendency to reject the other person at some point in the relationship in order to avoid being the one who is rejected.

displaced aggression: Aggression against someone other than the source of strong provocation; displaced aggression occurs because the persons who perform it are unwilling or unable to aggress against the initial source of provocation.

distinctiveness: The extent to which an individual responds in the same manner to different stimuli or events.

distraction–conflict theory: A theory suggesting that social facilitation stems from the conflict produced when individuals attempt, simultaneously, to pay attention to other persons and to the task being performed.

distributive justice (equity): Refers to individuals' judgments about whether they are receiving a fair share of available rewards—a share proportionate to their contributions to the group (or to any social relationship).

door-in-the-face technique: A procedure for gaining compliance in which requesters begin with a large request and then, when this is refused, retreat to a smaller one (the one they actually desired all along).

downward social comparison: Comparing yourself to someone who is worse off than you with respect to a particular attribute.

drive theories (of aggression): Theories suggesting that aggression stems from external conditions that arouse the motive to harm or injure others. The most famous of these is the frustration–aggression hypothesis.

drive theory of social facilitation: A theory suggesting that the mere presence of others is arousing and increases the tendency to perform dominant responses.

egoism: An exclusive concern with one's own personal needs and welfare rather than with the needs and welfare of others. See *self-interest.*

elaboration likelihood model (of persuasion): A theory suggesting that persuasion can occur in either of two distinct ways, which differ in the amount of cognitive effort or elaboration they require.

empathic joy hypothesis: The proposal that prosocial behavior is motivated by the positive emotion a helper anticipates experiencing as a the result of having a beneficial impact on the life of someone in need.

empathy: A complex affective and cognitive response to another person's emotional distress. Empathy includes being able to feel the other person's emotional state, feeling sympathetic and attempting to solve the problem, and taking the perspective of the other person. One can be empathetic toward fictional characters as well as toward real-life victims.

empathy–altruism hypothesis: The proposal that prosocial behavior is motivated solely by the desire to help someone in need.

estrogen: The female "sex hormone."

evaluation apprehension: Concern over being evaluated by others. Such concern can increase arousal and so contribute to social facilitation.

evolutionary psychology: A new branch of psychology that seeks to investigate the potential role of genetic factors in various aspects of human behavior.

excitation transfer theory: A theory suggesting that arousal produced in one situation can persist and intensify emotional reactions occurring in later situations.

experimentation (experimental method): A method of research in which one or more factors (the independent variables) are systematically changed to determine whether such variations affect one or more other factors (dependent variables).

experimenter effects: Unintended effects on participants' behavior produced by researchers.

extended contact hypothesis: A view suggesting that simply knowing that members of one's own group have formed close friendships with members of an out-group can reduce prejudice against that group.

external validity: The extent to which findings of an experiment can be generalized to real-life social situations and perhaps to persons different from those who participated in the research.

fearful–avoidant attachment style: In Bartholomew's model, a style characterized by low self-esteem and low interpersonal trust. This is the most insecure and least adaptive style of attachment.

fitness: Being in good physical condition as indicated by endurance and strength.

foot-in-the-door technique: A procedure for gaining compliance in which requesters begin with a small request and then, when this is granted, escalate to a larger one (the one they actually desired all along).

forensic psychology: Psychological research and theory that deals with the effects of cognitive, affective, and behavioral factors on legal processes.

forewarning: Advance knowledge that one is about to become the target of an attempt at persuasion. Forewarning often increases resistance to the persuasion that follows.

frustration–aggression hypothesis: The suggestion that frustration is a very powerful determinant of aggression.

fundamental attribution error (correspondence bias): The tendency to overestimate the impact of dispositional cues on others' behavior.

gender: The attributes, behaviors, personality characteristics, and expectancies associated with a person's biological sex in a given culture. Gender differences can be based on biology, learning, or a combination of the two.

gender consistency: The concept that gender is a basic, enduring attribute of each individual. A grasp of gender consistency usually develops between the ages of four and seven.

gender identity: That part of the self-concept involving a person's identification as a male or a female. Consciousness of gender identity usually develops at about the age of two.

gender-role identification: The degree to which an individual identifies with the gender stereotypes of his or her culture.

gender stereotypes: Stereotypes concerning the traits supposedly possessed by females and males, and that distinguish the two genders from each other.

general affective aggression model: A modern theory of aggression suggesting that aggression is triggered by a wide range of input variables; these influence arousal, affective stages, and cognitions.

generativity: An adult's concern for and commitment to the well-being of future generations.

genetic determinism model: The proposal that behavior is driven by genetic attributes that evolved because they enhanced the probability of transmitting one's genes to subsequent generations.

glass ceiling: Barriers based on attitudinal or organizational bias that prevent qualified women from advancing to top-level positions.

great person theory: A view of leadership suggesting that great leaders possess certain traits that set them apart from most human beings, traits that are possessed by all such leaders no matter when or where they lived.

group: A collection of persons who are perceived to be bonded together in a coherent unit to some degree.

group polarization: The tendency of group members, as a result of group discussion, to shift toward more extreme positions than those they initially held.

groupthink: The tendency of the members of highly cohesive groups to assume that their decisions can't be wrong, that all members must support the group's decisions strongly, and that information contrary to it should be ignored.

health psychology: The study of the effects of psychological factors in the development, prevention, and treatment of physical illness.

heuristic processing: Processing of information in a persuasive message that involves the use of simple rules of thumb or mental shortcuts.

heuristics: Simple rules for making complex decisions or drawing inferences in a rapid and seemingly effortless manner.

hostile aggression: Aggression in which the prime objective is inflicting some kind of harm on the victim.

hostile attributional bias: The tendency to perceive hostile intentions or motives in others' actions when these actions are ambiguous.

hostile sexism: The view that women, if not inferior to men, have many negative traits (e.g., they seek special favors, are overly sensitive, or seek to seize power from men that they don't deserve to have).

hyperfemininity: An extreme gender-role identification that consists of an exaggerated version of the traditional female role. Included are the beliefs that relationships with men are of central importance in one's life, that attractiveness and sexuality should be used to get a man and keep him, and that it is reasonable to sometimes say *no* but mean *yes.*

hypermasculinity: An extreme gender-role identification that consists of an exaggerated version of the traditional male role. Included are callous sexual attitudes toward women, the belief that violence is manly, and the enjoyment of danger as a source of excitement.

hypocrisy: Publicly advocating some attitudes or behavior but then acting in a way that is inconsistent with these attitudes or behavior.

hypothesis: An as yet unverified prediction based on a theory.

illusion of out-group homogeneity: The tendency to perceive members of out-groups as more similar to one another (less variable) than the members of one's own in-group.

illusory correlations: The perception of a stronger association between two variables than actually exists because each is a distinctive event and the co-occurrence of such events is readily entered into and retrieved from memory.

impression formation: The process through which we form impressions of others.

impression management (self-presentation): Efforts by individuals to produce favorable first impressions on others.

incompatible response technique: A technique for reducing aggression in which individuals are exposed to events or stimuli that cause them to experience affective states incompatible with anger or aggression.

independent variable: The variable that is systematically changed (i.e., varied) in an experiment.

individuation: The need to be distinguishable from others in some respects.

induced or forced compliance: Situations in which individuals are somehow induced to say or do things inconsistent with their true attitudes.

inferential statistics: A special form of mathematics that allows us to evaluate the likelihood that a given pattern of research results occurred by chance alone.

information overload: Instances in which our ability to process information is exceeded.

informational social influence: Social influence based on individuals' desire to be correct—to possess accurate perceptions of the social world.

informed consent: A procedure in which research participants are provided with as much information as possible about a research project before deciding whether to participate in it.

ingratiation: A technique for gaining compliance in which requesters first induce target persons to like them, then attempt to change their behavior in some desired manner.

in-group: The social group to which an individual perceives herself or himself as belonging ("us").

in-group differentiation: The tendency to perceive members of our own group as showing much larger differences from one another (as being more heterogeneous) than do those of other groups.

initiating structure: (production-orientation). A key dimension of leader behavior. Leaders high on this dimension are primarily concerned with getting the job done (that is, with production).

injunctive norms: Norms specifying what ought to be done—what is approved or disapproved behavior in a given situation.

instrumental aggression: Aggression in which the primary goal is not harm to the victim but attainment of some other goal, such as access to valued resources.

instrumental conditioning: A basic form of learning in which responses that lead to positive outcomes or that permit avoidance of negative outcomes are strengthened.

intense indoctrination: A process through which individuals become members of extreme groups and come to accept the beliefs and rules of the groups in a totally unquestioning way.

interactional (interpersonal) justice: The extent to which persons who distribute rewards explain or justify their decisions and show considerateness and courtesy to those who receive the rewards.

interdependence: The characteristic common to all close relationships—an interpersonal association in which two people influence each other's lives and engage in many joint activities.

interpersonal attraction: A person's attitude about another person. Attraction involves an evaluation along a dimension that ranges from strong liking to strong disliking.

interpersonal trust: A dimension underlying styles of attachment that involves the belief that other people are trustworthy, dependable, and reliable versus the belief that others are untrustworthy, undependable, and unreliable.

intimacy: In Sternberg's triangular model of love, the closeness felt by two partners—the extent to which they are bonded.

job satisfaction: Attitudes concerning one's job or work.

leading questions: Questions designed to elicit specific answers rather than simply to elicit information.

less-leads-to-more effect: The fact that offering individuals small rewards for engaging in counterattitudinal behavior often produces more dissonance, and so more attitude change, than offering them larger rewards.

loneliness: The unhappy emotional and cognitive state that results from desiring close relationships but being unable to attain them.

love: A combination of emotions, cognitions, and behaviors that can be involved in intimate relationships.

lowball technique: A technique for gaining compliance in which an offer or deal is changed (made less attractive) after the target person has accepted it.

magical thinking: Thinking involving assumptions that don't hold up to rational scrutiny—for example, the belief that things that resemble one another share fundamental properties.

media violence: Depictions of violent actions in the mass media.

mental contamination: A process in which our judgments, emotions, or behaviors are influenced by mental processing that is unconscious and uncontrollable.

meta-analysis: A statistical technique for combining data from independent studies in order to determine whether specific variables (or interactions between variables) have significant effects across these studies.

microexpressions: Fleeting facial expressions lasting only a few tenths of a second.

mood congruence effects: Our tendency to store or remember positive information when in a positive mood and negative information when in a negative mood.

mood-dependent memory: The fact that what we remember while in a given mood may be determined, in part, by what we learned when previously in that mood.

moral hypocrisy: The motivation to appear moral while doing one's best to avoid the costs involved in actually being moral.

moral integrity: The motivation to be moral and actually to engage in moral behavior.

multicultural perspective: A focus on understanding the cultural and ethnic factors that influence social behavior.

narcissism: A personality disposition in which the individual goes beyond high self-esteem, and also feels superior to most people, seeks admiration, is sensitive to criticism, lacks empathy for others, and is exploitative.

need for affiliation: The basic motive to seek and maintain interpersonal relationships.

negative–state relief model: The proposal that prosocial behavior is motivated by the bystander's desire to reduce his or her own uncomfortable negative emotions.

negativity bias: Refers to the fact that we show greater sensitivity to negative information than to positive information.

noncommon effects: Effects produced by a particular cause that could not be produced by any other apparent cause.

nonverbal communication: Communication between individuals that does not involve the content of spoken language. It relies instead on an unspoken language of facial expressions, eye contact, and body language.

normative focus theory: A theory suggesting that norms will influence behavior only to the extent that they are focal for the persons involved at the time the behavior occurs.

normative social influence: Social influence based on individuals' desire to be liked or accepted by other persons.

norms: Rules within a group indicating how its members should or should not behave.

obedience: A form of social influence in which one person simply orders one or more others to perform some action(s).

objective self-awareness: An organism's capacity to be the object of its own attention, to be aware of its own state of mind, and to know that it knows and remember that it remembers.

observational learning: A basic form of learning in which individuals acquire new forms of behavior or thought through observing others.

optimistic bias: Our predisposition to expect things to turn out well overall.

organizational citizenship behavior (OCB): Prosocial behavior occurring within an organization that may or may not be rewarded by the organization.

out-group: Any group other than the one to which individuals perceive themselves belonging.

paradoxical self-esteem: Unrealistically high or unrealistically low self-esteem.

passion: In Sternberg's triangular model of love, the sexual motives and sexual excitement associated with a couple's relationship.

passionate love: An intense and often unrealistic emotional response to another person. The person experiencing this emotion usually interprets it as "true love," whereas outside observers are more likely to label it as "infatuation."

peripheral route (to persuasion): Attitude change that occurs in response to persuasion cues—information concerning the expertise or status of would-be persuaders.

perseverance effect: The tendency for beliefs and schemas to remain unchanged even in the face of contradictory information.

persuasion: Efforts to change others' attitudes through the use of various kinds of messages.

physical attractiveness: The combination of characteristics that are evaluated as beautiful or handsome at the most attractive extreme and unattractive at the other extreme.

pique technique: A technique for gaining compliance in which target persons' interest is piqued (stimulated) by unusual requests. As a result, they do not refuse requests automatically, as is often the case.

planning fallacy: The tendency to make optimistic predictions concerning how long a given task will take for completion.

playing hard to get: A technique that can be used for increasing compliance by suggesting that a person or object is scarce and hard to obtain.

pluralistic ignorance: The tendency of bystanders in an emergency to rely on what other bystanders do and say, even though none of them is sure about what is happening or what to do about it. Very often, all of the bystanders hold back and behave as if there is no problem, and use this "information" to justify their failure to act.

possible selves: Mental representations of what we might become, or should become, in the future.

prejudice: Negative attitudes toward the members of specific social groups.

preoccupied attachment style: In Bartholomew's model, a style characterized by low self-esteem and high interpersonal trust; usually described as a conflicted and somewhat insecure style in which the individual strongly desires a close relationship but feels that he or she is unworthy of the partner and thus vulnerable to being rejected.

priming: Increased availability of information in memory or consciousness, resulting from exposure to specific stimuli or events.

procedural justice: The fairness of the procedures used to distribute available rewards among group members.

proportion of similar attitudes: The number of topics on which two individuals hold the same views divided by the total number of topics on which they compare their views.

prosocial behavior: A helpful action that benefits other people without necessarily providing any direct benefits to the person performing the act, and may even involve a risk for the person who helps.

provocation: Actions by others that tend to trigger aggression in the recipient, often because they are perceived as stemming from malicious intent.

proximity: In attraction research, the closeness between two individuals' residences, classroom seats, work areas, and so on. The closer the physical distance, the greater the probability that the two people will come into repeated contact and thus experience repeated exposure.

psychoneuroimmunology: The research field that explores the relationships among stress, emotional and behavioral reactions, and the immune system.

punishment: Procedures in which aversive consequences are delivered to individuals when they engage in specific actions.

random assignment of participants to experimental conditions: A basic requirement for conducting valid experiments. According to this principle, research participants must have an equal chance of being exposed to each level of the independent variable.

reactance: Negative reaction to threats to one's personal freedom. Reactance often increases resistance to persuasion.

realistic conflict theory: The view that prejudice sometimes stems from direct competition between various social groups over scarce and valued resources.

recategorization: Shifts in the boundary between an individual's in-group ("us") and some out-group ("them"). As a result of such recategorization, persons formerly viewed as out-group members may now be viewed as belonging to the in-group.

reciprocity: A basic rule of social life suggesting that individuals tend to treat others as these persons have treated them.

regulatory focus theory: A theory suggesting that in regulating their own behavior in order to attain desired goals, individuals adopt one of two different perspectives: a promotion focus, in which they emphasize the presence and absence of positive outcomes; or a prevention focus, in which they emphasize negative outcomes.

repeated exposure: Frequent contact with a stimulus. According to Zajonc's theory, repeated exposure to any mildly negative, neutral, or positive stimulus results in an increasingly positive evaluation of that stimulus.

representativeness heuristic: A strategy for making judgments based on the extent to which current stimuli or events resemble other stimuli or categories.

repressed memory: A form of psychogenic amnesia; forgetting the details of a traumatic event as a way of defending oneself from having to deal with the anxiety and fear associated with the event.

repulsion hypothesis: Rosenbaum's provocative but partially inaccurate proposal that attraction is not increased by similar attitudes but only decreased by dissimilar attitudes.

roles: Sets of behaviors that individuals occupying specific positions within a group are expected to perform.

schemas: (1) Cognitive frameworks developed through experience that affect the processing of new social information. (2) Mental frameworks centering around a specific theme that help us to organize social information.

secure attachment style: In Bartholomew's model, a style characterized by high self-esteem and high interpersonal trust; usually described as the most successful and most desirable attachment style.

selective avoidance: A tendency to direct attention away from information that challenges existing attitudes. Such avoidance increases resistance to persuasion.

self-concept: One's self-identity, a basic schema consisting of an organized collection of beliefs and attitudes about oneself.

self-efficacy: A person's belief in his or her ability or competency to perform a given task, reach a goal, or overcome an obstacle.

self-esteem: The self-evaluation made by each individual; one's attitude toward oneself along a positive–negative dimension.

self-focusing: The act of directing one's attention toward oneself as opposed to toward one's surroundings.

self-fulfilling prophecies: Predictions that, in a sense, make themselves come true.

self-healing personality: A personality characterized by effective coping with stress. Self-healing individuals are energetic, responsive to others, and positive about life.

self-interest: The motivation to engage in whatever behavior provides the greatest satisfaction. See *egoism.*

self-monitoring: Regulation of one's behavior on the basis of the external situation, such as how other people react (high self-monitoring), or on the basis of internal factors, such as beliefs, attitudes, and values (low self-monitoring).

self-reference effect: The effect on attention and memory that occurs because the cognitive processing of information relevant to the self is more efficient than the processing of other types of information.

self-serving bias: The tendency to attribute positive outcomes to internal causes (e.g., one's own traits or characteristics) but negative outcomes or events to external causes (e.g., chance, task difficulty).

sex: Maleness or femaleness as determined by genetic factors present at conception that result in anatomical and physiological differences.

sexism: Prejudice based on gender.

sex typing: Comprehension of the stereotypes associated with being a male or a female in one's culture.

sexual self-schema: Cognitive representations of the sexual aspects of oneself.

slime effect: A tendency to form very negative impressions of others who "lick upward but kick downward"; that is, persons in a work setting who play up to their superiors but treat subordinates with disdain and contempt.

social categorization: The tendency to divide the social world into two separate categories: our in-group ("us") and various out-groups ("them").

social cognition: The manner in which we interpret, analyze, remember, and use information about the social world.

social comparison: The process through which we compare ourselves to others in order to determine whether our view of social reality is or is not correct.

social decision schemes: Rules relating the initial distribution of members' views to final group decisions.

social dilemmas: Situations in which each person can increase his or her individual gains by acting in one way, but if all (or most) persons do the same thing, the outcomes experienced by all are reduced.

social facilitation: Effects upon performance resulting from the presence of others.

social identity: A person's definition of who he or she is, including personal attributes and attributes shared with others, such as gender and race.

social identity theory: A theory suggesting that individuals seek to enhance their own self-esteem by identifying with specific social groups.

social influence: Efforts by one or more individuals to change the attitudes, beliefs, perceptions, or behaviors of one or more others.

social learning: The process through which we acquire new information, forms of behavior, or attitudes from other persons.

social learning view (of prejudice): The view that prejudice is acquired through direct and vicarious experience in much the same manner as other attitudes.

social loafing: Reductions in motivation and effort when individuals work collectively in a group compared to when they work individually or as independent coactors.

social norms: Rules indicating how individuals are expected to behave in specific situations.

social perception: The process through which we seek to know and understand other persons.

social psychology: The scientific field that seeks to understand the nature and causes of individual behavior and thought in social situations.

social self: A collective identity that includes interpersonal relationships plus those aspects of identity that are derived from membership in larger, less personal groups based on race, ethnicity, and culture.

social support: The physical and psychological comfort provided by one's friends and family members.

staring: A form of eye contact in which one person continues to gaze steadily at another regardless of what the recipient does.

status: Position or rank within a group.

stereotypes: Beliefs to the effect that all members of specific social groups share certain traits or characteristics. Stereotypes are cognitive frameworks that strongly influence the processing of incoming social information.

stereotype threat: The concern on the part of persons who are the target of stereotypes that they will be evaluated in terms of this stereotype.

stigma: A personal characteristic that at least some other individuals perceive negatively.

stress: Any physical or psychological event perceived as potentially constituting physical harm or emotional distress.

subjective self-awareness: The ability of an organism to differentiate itself, however crudely, from its physical and social environment.

subliminal conditioning (of attitudes): Classical conditioning that occurs through exposure to stimuli that are below individuals' thresholds of conscious awareness.

superordinate goals: Goals that both sides to a conflict seek and that tie their interests together rather than drive them apart.

survey method: A method of research in which a large number of persons answer questions about their attitudes or behavior.

symbolic self-awareness: An organism's ability to form an abstract concept of self through language. This ability enables the organism to communicate, form relationships, set goals, evaluate outcomes, develop self-related attitudes, and defend itself against threatening communications.

systematic observation: A method of research in which behavior is systematically observed and recorded.

systematic processing: Processing of information in a persuasive message that involves careful consideration of message content and ideas.

testosterone: The male "sex hormone."

"that's-not-all" technique: A technique for gaining compliance in which requesters offer target persons additional benefits before they have decided whether to comply with or reject specific requests.

theories: Frameworks constructed by scientists in any field to explain why certain events or processes occur as they do.

theory of planned behavior: An extension of the *theory of reasoned action,* suggesting that in addition to attitudes toward a given behavior and subjective norms about it, individuals also consider perceived behavioral control—their ability to perform the behavior.

theory of reasoned action: A theory suggesting that the decision to engage in a particular behavior is the result of a rational process in which behavioral options are considered, consequences or outcomes of each are evaluated, and a decision is reached to act or not to act. That decision is then reflected in behavioral intentions, which strongly influence overt behavior.

thought suppression: Efforts to prevent certain thoughts from entering consciousness.

tokenism: Instances in which individuals perform trivial positive actions for members of out-groups toward whom they feel strong prejudice. Such tokenistic behaviors are then used as an excuse for refusing more meaningful beneficial actions for these groups.

transactional leaders: Leaders who direct their groups by rewarding them for desired behavior and by taking action to correct mistakes or departures from existing rules. Such leaders generally strengthen existing structures and strategies within an organization.

transformational (charismatic) leaders: Leaders who exert profound effects on their followers and by doing so, change their organizations or societies.

triangular model of love: Sternberg's conceptualization of love relationships as encompassing three basic components: intimacy, passion, and decision/commitment.

trivialization: A technique for reducing dissonance in which the importance of attitudes and behaviors that are inconsistent with each other is cognitively reduced.

Type A behavior pattern: A pattern consisting primarily of high levels of competitiveness, time urgency, and hostility.

Type B behavior pattern: A pattern consisting of the absence of characteristics associated with the Type A behavior pattern.

ultimate attribution error: The tendency to make more favorable and flattering attributions about members of one's own group than about members of other groups.

unrequited love: Love felt by one person for another who does not feel love in return.

upward social comparison: Comparing yourself to someone who is better off than you with respect to a particular attribute.

voir dire: A French term ("to see and to speak") used in law to mean the examination of prospective jurors in order to determine their competence to serve. The judge and the opposing attorneys may dismiss prospective jurors for specific reasons or, within limits, for no stated reason.

workplace aggression: any form of behavior through which individuals seek to harm others in their workplace.

References

A really scary adolescent worry: HIV. (2001, August 6). *U.S. News & World Report*, 6.

Abdalla, I. A. (1995). Sex, sex-role self-concepts and career decision-making self-efficacy among Arab students. *Social Behavior and Personality, 23,* 389–402.

Abramson, J. (1994). *We, the jury.* New York: Basic Books.

Abu-Hilal, M. M., & Bahri, T. M. (2000). Self-concept: The generalizability of research on the SDQ, Marsh/Shavelson model, and I/E frame of reference model to United Arab Emirates students. *Social Behavior and Personality, 28,* 309–322.

Acitelli, L. K., Kenny, D. A., & Weiner, D. (2001). The importance of similarity and understanding of partners' marital ideals to relationship satisfaction. *Personal Relationships, 8,* 167–185.

Adams, J. M., & Jones, W. H. (1997). The conceptualization of marital commitment: An integrative analysis. *Journal of Personality and Social Psychology, 72,* 1177–1196.

Adams, J. S. (1965). Inequity in social exchange. In L. Berkowitz (Ed.), *Advances in experimental social psychology* (Vol. 2, pp. 267–299). New York: Academic Press.

Ader, R. (2001). Psychoneuroimmunology. *Current Directions in Psychological Science, 10,* 94–98.

Agocha, V. B., & Cooper, M. L. (1999). Risk perceptions and safer-sex intentions: Does a partner's physical attractiveness undermine the use of risk-relevant information? *Personality and Social Psychology Bulletin, 25,* 746–759.

Ainsworth, M. D. S., Blehar, M. C., Waters, E., & Wall, S. (1978). *Patterns of attachment.* Hillsdale, NJ: Erlbaum.

Ajzen, I. (1987). Attitudes, traits, and actions: Dispositional prediction of behavior in personality and social psychology. In L. Berkowitz (Ed.), *Advances in experimental social psychology* (Vol. 20). San Diego, CA: Academic Press.

Ajzen, I. (1991). The theory of planned behavior: Special issue: Theories of cognitive self-regulation. *Organizational Behavior and Human Decision Processes, 50,* 179–211.

Ajzen, I., & Fishbein, M. (1980). *Understanding attitudes and predicting social behavior.* Englewood Cliffs, NJ: Prentice-Hall.

Alagna, F. J., Whitcher, S. J., & Fisher, J. D. (1979). Evaluative reactions to interpersonal touch in a counseling interview. *Journal of Counseling Psychology, 26,* 465–472.

Albarracin, D., & Wyer, R. S., Jr. (2000). The cognitive impact of past behavior: Influences on beliefs, attitudes, and future behavioral decisions. *Journal of Personality and Social Psychology, 79,* 5–22.

Alden, L. (1986). Self-efficacy and causal attributions for social feedback. *Journal of Research in Personality, 20,* 460–473.

Alexander, M. J., & Higgins, E. T. (1993). Emotional trade-offs of becoming a parent: How social roles influence self-discrepancy effects. *Journal of Personality and Social Psychology, 65,* 1259–1269.

Alexander, R., Feeney, J., Hohaus, L., & Noller, P. (2001). Attachment style and coping resources as predictors of coping strategies in the transition to parenthood. *Personal Relationships, 8,* 137–152.

Alicke, M. D., & Largo, E. (1995). The role of the self in the false consensus effect. *Journal of Experimental Social Psychology, 31,* 28–47.

Allgeier, E. R., & Wiederman, M. W. (1994). How useful is evolutionary psychology for understanding contemporary human sexual behavior? *Annual Review of Sex Research, 5,* 218–256.

Allport, F. H. (1920). The influence of the group upon association and thought. *Journal of Experimental Psychology, 3,* 159–182.

Allport, F. H. (1924). *Social psychology.* Boston: Houghton Mifflin.

Allyn, J., & Festinger, L. (1961). The effectiveness of unanticipated persuasive communications. *Journal of Abnormal and Social Psychology, 62,* 35–40.

Al-Simadi, F., & Atoum, A. (2000). Family environment and self-concept of Palestinian youth living in Jordanian refugee camps. *Social Behavior and Personality, 28,* 377–386.

Altman, L. K. (1998a, June 24). Report: AIDS an epic scourge. *New York Times.*

Altman, L. K. (1998b, November 24). Dismaying experts, H.I.V. infections soar. *New York Times,* F7.

Alvaro, E. M., & Crano, W. D. (1996). Cognitive responses to minority- or majority-based communications: Factors that underlie minority influence. *British Journal of Social Psychology, 34,* 105–121.

Amato, P. R. (1983). Helping behavior in urban and rural environments: Field studies based on a taxonomic organization of helping episodes. *Journal of Personality and Social Psychology, 45,* 571–586.

Amato, P. R. (1986). Emotional arousal and helping behavior in a real-life emergency. *Journal of Applied Social Psychology, 16,* 633–641.

Ambady, N., & Rosenthal, R. (1992). Thin slices of expressive behavior as predictors of interpersonal consequences: A meta-analysis. *Psychological Bulletin, 111,* 256–274.

American Psychiatric Association. (1994). *Diagnostic and statistical manual of mental disorders* (4th ed.). Washington, DC: American Psychiatric Association.

Amirkhan, J. H., Risinger, R. T., & Swickert, R. J. (1995). Extraversion: A "hidden" personality factor in coping? *Journal of Personality, 63,* 189–212.

Andersen, B. L., & Cyranowski, J. M. (1994). Women's sexual self-schema. *Journal of Personality and Social Psychology, 67,* 1079–1100.

Andersen, B. L., Cyranowski, J. M., & Espindle, D. (1999). Men's sexual self-schema. *Journal of Personality and Social Psychology, 76,* 645–661.

Andersen, S. M., & Baum, A. (1994). Transference in interpersonal relations: Inferences and affect based on significant-other representations. *Journal of Personality, 62,* 459–497.

Anderson, C. A. (1989a). Temperature and aggression: Effects on quarterly, yearly, and city rates of violent and nonviolent crime. *Journal of Personality and Social Psychology, 52,* 1161–1173.

Anderson, C. A. (1989b). Temperature and aggression: The ubiquitous effects of heat on the occurrence of human violence. *Psychological Bulletin, 106,* 74–96.

Anderson, C. A. (1997). Effects of violent movies and trait hostility on hostile feelings and aggressive thoughts. *Aggressive Behavior, 23,* 161–178.

Anderson, C. A., & Anderson, K. B. (1996). Violent crime rate studies in philosophical context: A destructive testing approach to heat and Southern culture of violence effects. *Journal of Personality and Social Psychology, 70,* 740–756.

Anderson, C. A., & Bushman, B. J. (1997). External validity of "trivial" experiments: The case of laboratory aggression. *Review of General Psychology, 1,* 19–41.

Anderson, C. A., & Bushman, B. J. (2001). Effects of violent video games on aggressive behavior, aggressive cognition, aggressive affect, physiological arousal, and prosocial behavior: A meta-analytic review of the scientific literature. *Psychological Science, 12,* 353–359.

Anderson, C. A., Anderson, K. B., & Deuser, W. E. (1996). Examining an affective aggression framework: Weapon and temperature effects on aggressive thoughts, affect, and attitudes. *Personality and Social Psychology Bulletin, 22,* 366–376.

Anderson, C. A., Bushman, B. J., & Groom, R. W. (1997). Hot years and serious and deadly assault: Empirical tests of the heat hypothesis. *Journal of Personality and Social Psychology, 73,* 1213–1223.

Anderson, C. A., Miller, R. S., Riger, A. L., Dill, J. C., & Sedikides, C. (1994). Behavioral and characterological attributional styles as predictors of depression and loneliness: Review, refinement, and test. *Journal of Personality and Social Psychology, 66,* 549–558.

Anderson, N. H. (1965). Averaging versus adding as a stimulus combination rule in impression formation. *Journal of Experimental Social Psychology, 70,* 394–400.

Anderson, N. H. (1968). Application of a linear-serial model to a personality impression task. Using serial presentation. *Journal of Personality and Social Psychology, 10,* 354–362.

Anderson, N. H. (1973). Cognitive algebra: Integration theory applied to social attribution. In L. Berkowitz (Ed.), *Advances in experimental social psychology.* New York: Academic Press.

Anderson, P. B., & Aymami, R. (1993). Reports of female initiation of sexual contact: Male and female differences. *Archives of Sexual Behavior, 22,* 335–343.

Anderson, V. L. (1993). Gender differences in altruism among holocaust rescuers. *Journal of Social Behavior and Personality, 8,* 43–58.

Andreoletti, C., Zebrowitz, L. A., & Lachman, M. E. (2001). *Personality and Social Psychology Bulletin, 27,* 969–981.

Andreou, E. (2000). Bully/victim problems and their association with psychological constructs in 8- to 12-year-old Greek schoolchildren. *Aggressive Behavior, 26,* 49–58.

Angier, N. (1998a, September 1). Nothing becomes a man more than a woman's face. *New York Times,* p. F3.

Angier, N. (1998b, November 24). Condemning our kids to life on Mars or Venus. *New York Times,* F5.

Archer, J. (1991). Human sociobiology: Basic concepts and limitations. *Journal of Social Issues, 47*(3), 11–26.

Archer, J. (1996). Sex differences in social behavior: Are the social role and evolutionary explanations compatible? *American Psychologist, 51,* 909–917.

Archibald, F. S., Bartholomew, K., & Marx, R. (1995). Loneliness in early adolescence: A test of the cognitive discrepancy model of loneliness. *Personality and Social Psychology Bulletin, 21,* 296–301.

Aristotle. (1932). *The rhetoric* (L. Cooper, Trans.). New York: Appleton-Century-Crofts. (Original work published c. 330 B.C.)

Armas, G. C. (2001, May 15). 85-plus population soaring. Associated Press.

Armeli, S., Carney, M. A., Tennen, H., Affleck, G., & O'Neil, T. P. (2000). Stress and alcohol use: A daily process examination of the stressor–vulnerability model. *Journal of Personality and Social Psychology, 78,* 979–994.

Armitage, C. J., & Conner, M. (2000). Attitudinal ambivalence: A test of three key hypotheses. *Personality and Social Psychology Bulletin, 26,* 1421–1432.

Aron, A., & Henkemeyer, L. (1995). Marital satisfaction and passionate love. *Journal of Social and Personal Relationships, 12,* 139–146.

Aron, A., & Westbay, L. (1996). Dimensions of the prototype of love. *Journal of Personality and Social Psychology, 70,* 535–551.

Aron, A., Aron, E. N., & Allen, J. (1998). Motivations for unreciprocated love. *Personality and Social Psychology Bulletin, 24,* 787–796.

Aron, A., Paris, M., & Aron, E. N. (1995). Falling in love: Prospective studies of self-concept change. *Journal of Personality and Social Psychology, 69,* 1102–1112.

Aron, A., Dutton, D. G., Aron, E. N., & Iverson, A. (1989). Experiences of falling in love. *Journal of Social and Personal Relationships, 6,* 243–257.

Aron, A., Melinat, E., Aron, E. N., Vallone, R. D., & Bator, R. J. (1997). The experimental generation of interpersonal closeness: A procedure and some preliminary findings. *Personality and Social Psychology Bulletin, 23,* 363–377.

Aron, A., Norman, C. C., Aron, E. N., McKenna, C., & Heyman, R. E. (2000). Couples' shared participation in novel and arousing activities and experienced relationship quality. *Journal of Personality and Social Psychology, 78,* 273–284.

Aronoff, J., Woike, B. A., & Hyman, L. M. (1992). Which are the stimuli in facial displays of anger and happiness? Configurational bases of emotion recognition. *Journal of Personality and Social Psychology, 62,* 1050–1066.

Aronson, E. (1968). Dissonance theory: Progress and problems. In R. Abelson, E. Aronson, W. McGuire, T. Newcomb, M. Rosenberg, & P. Tannenbaum (Eds.), *The cognitive consistency theories: A source book* (pp. 5–27). Chicago: Rand McNally.

Aronson, E., Bridgeman, D. L., & Geffner, R. (1978). Interdependent interactions and prosocial behavior. *Journal of Research and Development in Education, 12,* 16–27.

Aronson, E., Fried, C., & Stone, J. (1991). Overcoming denial: Increasing the intention to use condoms through the induction of hypocrisy. *American Journal of Public Health, 18,* 1636–1640.

Arriaga, X. B. (2001). The ups and downs of dating: Fluctuations in satisfaction in newly formed romantic relationships. *Journal of Personality and Social Psychology, 80,* 754–765.

Arriaga, X. B., & Agnew, C. R. (2001). Being committed: Affective, cognitive, and conative components of relationship commitment. *Personality and Social Psychology Bulletin, 27,* 1190–1203.

Arriaga, X. B., & Rusbult, C. E. (1998). Standing in my partner's shoes: Partner perspective taking and reactions to accommodative dilemmas. *Personality and Social Psychology Bulletin, 24,* 927–948.

Arrigo, J. M., & Pezdek, K. (1997). Lessons from the study of psychogenic amnesia. *Current Directions in Psychological Science, 6,* 148–152.

Arvey, R. D., Bouchard, T. J. Jr., Segal, N. L., & Abraham, L. M. (1989). Job satisfaction: Genetic and environmental components. *Journal of Applied Psychology, 74,* 187–192.

Aryee, S., & Chay, Y. W. (2001). Workplace justice, citizenship behavior, and turnover intentions in a union context: Examining the mediating role of perceived union support and union instrumentality. *Journal of Applied Psychology, 86,* 154–160.

Asch, S. (1946). Forming impressions of personality. *Journal of Abnormal and Social Psychology, 41,* 258–290.

Asch, S. E. (1951). Effects of group pressure upon the modification and distortion of judgment. In H. Guetzkow (Ed.), *Groups, leadership, and men.* Pittsburgh: Carnegie.

Asch, S. E. (1955). Opinions and social pressure. *Scientific American, 193*(5), 31–35.

Asch, S. E. (1956). Studies of independence and conformity: A minority of one against unanimous majority. *Psychological Monographs, 70* (Whole No. 416).

Asendorpf, J. B. (1992). A Brunswickean approach to trait continuity: Application to shyness. *Journal of Personality, 60,* 55–77.

Ashmore, R. D., Solomon, M. R., & Longo, L. C. (1996). Thinking about fashion models' looks: A multidimensional approach to the structure of perceived physical attractiveness. *Personality and Social Psychology Bulletin, 22,* 1083–1104.

Ashton, L., Karnilowicz, W., & Fooks, D. (2001). The incidence and belief structures associated with breast self-examination. *Social Behavior and Personality, 29,* 223–230.

Aspinwall, L. G., & Richter, L. (1999). Optimism and self-mastery predict more rapid disengagement from unsolvable tasks in the presence of alternatives. *Motivation and Emotion, 23,* 221–245.

Attitudinal ambivalence toward parents and attachment style. *Personality and Social Psychology Bulletin, 26,* 1451–1464.

Aube, J., Fichman, L., Saltaris, C., & Koestner, R. (2000). Gender differences in adolescent depressive symptomatology: Towards an integrated social-developmental model. *Journal of Social and Clinical Psychology, 19,* 297–313.

Averill, J. R., & Boothroyd, P. (1977). On falling in love: Conformance with romantic ideal. *Motivation and Emotion, 1,* 235–247.

Azar, B. (1997, November). Defining the trait that makes us human. *APA Monitor,* 1, 15.

Azar, B. (1999a, June). Probing links between stress, cancer. *APA Monitor,* 15.

Azar, B. (1999b, June). Anxiety over cancer keeps people from genetic tests. *APA Monitor,* 16.

Baccman, C., Folkesson, P., & Norlander, T. (1999). Expectations of romantic relationships: A comparison between homosexual and heterosexual men with regard to Baxter's criteria. *Social Behavior and Personality, 27,* 363–374.

Bachorowski, J., & Owren, M. J. (2001). Not all laughs are alike: Voiced but not unvoiced laughter readily elicits positive affect. *Psychological Science, 12,* 252–257.

Bailey, R. C., & Vietor, N. A. (1996). A religious female who engages in casual sex: Evidence of a boomerang effect. *Social Behavior and Personality, 24,* 215–220.

Baize, H. R., Jr., & Schroeder, J. E. (1995). Personality and mate selection in personal ads: Evolutionary preferences in a public mate selection process. *Journal of Social Behavior and Personality, 10,* 517–536.

Baldwin, D. A. (2000). Interpersonal understanding fuels knowledge acquisition. *Current Directions in Psychological Science, 9,* 40–45.

Banaji, M., & Hardin, C. (1996). Automatic stereotyping. *Psychological Science, 7,* 136–141.

Bandura, A. (1977). Self-efficacy: Toward a unifying theory of behavior change. *Psychological Review, 84,* 191–215.

Bandura, A. (1986). The explanatory and predictive scope of self-efficacy theory. *Journal of Social and Clinical Psychology, 4,* 359–373.

Bandura, A. (1993). Self-efficacy mechanisms in psychobiological functioning. *Stanford University Psychologist, 1,* 5–6.

Bandura, A. (1997). *Self-efficacy: The exercise of control.* New York: Freeman.

Bandura, A. (1999). A sociocognitive analysis of substance abuse: An agentic perspective. *Psychological Science, 10,* 214–216.

Bandura, A. (1999). Moral disengagement in the perpetration of inhumanities. *Personality and Social Psychology Review, 3,* 193–209.

Bandura, A. (2000). Exercise of human agency through collective efficacy. *Current Directions in Psychological Science, 9,* 75–78.

Bandura, A., & Adams, N. E. (1977). Analysis of self-efficacy theory of behavioral change. *Cognitive Therapy and Research, 1,* 287–310.

Bandura, A., Ross, D., & Ross, S. (1963). Imitation of film-mediated aggressive models. *Journal of Abnormal and Social Psychology, 66,* 3–11.

Bandura, A., Pastorelli, C., Barbaranelli, C., & Caprara, G. V. (1999). Self-efficacy pathways to childhood depression. *Journal of Personality and Social Psychology, 76,* 258–269.

Bandura, A., Caprara, G. V., Barbaranelli, C., Pastorelli, C., & Regalia, C. (2001). Sociocognitive self-regulatory mechanisms governing transgressive behavior. *Journal of Personality and Social Psychology, 80,* 125–135.

Barbee, A. P., Cunningham, M. R., Winstead, B. A., Derlega, V. J., Gulley, M. R., Yankeelov, P. A., & Druen, P. B. (1993). Effects of gender role expectations on the social support process. *Journal of Social Issues, 49,* 175–190.

Bargh, J. A. (1997). The automaticity of everyday life. In R. S. Wyer (Ed.), *Advances in social cognition* (Vol. 10, pp. 1–61). Mahwah, NJ: Erlbaum.

Bargh, J. A., & Chartrand, T. L. (1999). The unbearable automaticity of being. *American Psychologist, 54,* 462–479.

Bargh, J. A., & Pietromonaco, P. (1982). Automatic information processing and social perception: The influence of trait information presented outside of conscious awareness on impression formation. *Journal of Personality and Social Psychology,* 43, 437–449.

Bargh, J. A., Chen, M., & Burrows, L. (1996). Automaticity of social behavior: Direct effects of trait construct and stereotype activation on action. *Journal of Personality and Social Psychology, 71,* 230–234.

Barnhizer, D. (1997, December 1). Mugging for the camera. *The New Yorker,* 16.

Baron, J. (1997). The illusion of morality as self-interest: A reason to cooperate in social dilemmas. *Psychological Science, 8,* 330–335.

Baron, R. A. (1972a). Aggression as a function of ambient temperature and prior anger arousal. *Journal of Personality and Social Psychology, 21,* 183–189.

Baron, R. A. (1972b). Reducing the influence of an aggressive model: The restraining effects of peer censure. *Journal of Experimental Social Psychology, 8,* 266–275.

Baron, R. A. (1974a). Aggression as a function of victim's pain cues, level of prior anger arousal, and exposure to an aggressive model. *Journal of Personality and Social Psychology, 29,* 117–124.

Baron, R. A. (1974b). The aggression-inhibiting influence of heightened sexual arousal. *Journal of Personality and Social Psychology, 30,* 318–322.

Baron, R. A. (1976). The reduction of human aggression: A field study of the influence of incompatible responses. *Journal of Applied Social Psychology, 6,* 260–674.

Baron, R. A. (1977). *Human aggression.* New York: Plenum.

Baron, R. A. (1979). Aggression, empathy, and race: Effects of victim's pain cues, victim's race, and level of instigation on physical aggression. *Journal of Applied Social Psychology, 9,* 103–114.

Baron, R. A. (1983a). The "sweet smell of success"? The impact of pleasant artificial scents (perfume or cologne) on evaluations of job applicants. *Journal of Applied Psychology, 68,* 709–713.

Baron, R. A. (1983b). The control of human aggression: An optimistic perspective. *Journal of Social and Clinical Psychology, 1,* 97–119.

Baron, R. A. (1989a). Applicant strategies during job interviews. In G. R. Ferris & R. W. Eder (Eds.), *The employment interview: Theory, research, and practice* (pp. 204–216). Newbury Park, CA: Sage.

Baron, R. A. (1989b). Personality and organizational conflict: The Type A behavior pattern and self-monitoring. *Organizational Behavior and Human Decision Processes, 44,* 281–297.

Baron, R. A. (1990a). Attributions and organizational conflict. In S. Graha & V. Folkes (Eds.), *Attribution theory: Applications to achievement, mental health, and interpersonal conflict* (pp. 185–204). Hillsdale, NJ: Erlbaum.

Baron, R. A. (1990c). Environmentally induced positive affect: Its impact on self-efficacy, task performance, negotiation, and conflict. *Journal of Applied Social Psychology, 20,* 368–384.

Baron, R. A. (1993a). Effects of interviewers' moods and applicant qualifications on ratings of job applicants. *Journal of Applied Social Psychology, 23,* 254–271.

Baron, R. A. (1993b). Reducing aggression and conflict: The incompatible response approach, or why people who feel good usually won't be bad. In G. C. Brannigan & M. R. Merrens (Eds.), *The undaunted psychologist* (pp. 203–218). Philadelphia: Temple University Press.

Baron, R. A. (1994). The physical environment of work settings: Effects of task performance, interpersonal relations, and job satisfaction. In M. Staw & L. L. Cummings (Eds.), *Research in organizational behavior* (Vol. 16, pp. 1–46). Greenwich, CT: JAI Press.

Baron, R. A. (1997). The sweet smell of helping: Effects of pleasant ambient fragrance on prosocial behavior in shopping malls. *Personality and Social Psychology Bulletin, 23,* 498–503.

Baron, R. A., (2000). Counterfactual thinking and venture formation: The potential effects of thinking about "What might have been." *Journal of Business Venturing, 15,* 79–92.

Baron, R. A., & Bell, P. A. (1975). Aggression and heat: Mediating effects of prior provocation and exposure to an aggressive model. *Journal of Personality and Social Psychology, 31,* 825–832.

Baron, R. A., & Lawton, S. F. (1972). Environmental influences on aggression: The facilitation of modeling effects by high ambient temperatures. *Psychonomic Science, 26,* 80–82.

Baron, R. A., & Markman, G. D. (in press). Beyond social capital: The role of entrepreneurs' social competence in their financial success. *Journal of Business Venturing.*

Baron, R. A., & Markman, G. D. (1998). *Social skills and entrepreneural success: A framework and initial data.* Manuscript submitted for publication.

Baron, R. A., & Neuman, J. H. (1996). Workplace violence and workplace aggression: Evidence on their relative frequency and potential causes. *Aggressive Behavior, 22,* 161–173.

Baron, R. A., & Neuman, J. H. (1998). Workplace aggression—the iceberg beneath the tip of workplace violence: Evidence on its forms, frequency, and potential causes. *Public Administration Quarterly, 21,* 446–464.

Baron, R. A., & Richardson, D. R. (1994). *Human Aggression* (2nd ed.). New York: Plenum.

Baron, R. A., & Thomley, J. (1994). A whiff of reality: Positive affect as a potential mediator of the effects of pleasant fragrances on task performance and helping. *Environment and Behavior, 26,* 766–784.

Baron, R. A., Markman, G. D., & Hirsa, A. (2001). Perceptions of women and men as entrepreneurs. Evidence for differential effects of attributional augmenting. *Journal of Applied Psychology, 86,* 923–929.

Baron, R. A., Neuman, J. H., & Geddes, D. (1999). Social and personal determinants of workplace aggression: Evidence for the impact of perceived injustice and the Type A behavior pattern. *Aggressive Behavior,* 25.

Baron, R. A., Rea, M. S., & Daniels, S. G. (1992). Lighting as a source of environmentally-generated positive affect in work settings: Impact on cognitive tasks and interpersonal behaviors. *Motivation and Emotion, 14,* 1–34.

Baron, R. A., Russell, G. W., & Arms, R. L. (1985). Negative ions and behavior: Impact on mood, memory, and aggression among Type A and Type B persons. *Journal of Personality and Social Psychology, 48,* 746–754.

Baron, R. S. (1986). Distraction/conflict theory: Progress and problems. In L. Berkwoitz (Ed.), *Advances in* experimental social psychology (Vol. 19, pp. 1–40). Orlando: Academic Press.

Baron, R. S. (2000). Arousal, capacity, and intense indoctrination. *Personality and Social Psychology Review, 4,* 238–254.

Baron, R. S., Moore, D., & Sanders, G. S. (1978). Distraction as a source of drive in social facilitation research. *Journal of Personality and Social Psychology, 36,* 816–824.

Baron, R. S., Vandello, U. A., & Brunsman, B. (1996). The forgotten variable in conformity research: Impact of task importance on social influence. *Journal of Personality and Social Psychology, 71,* 915–927.

Barrett, L. F., & Russell, J. A. (1998). Independence and bipolarity in the structure of current affect. *Journal of Personality and Social Psychology, 74,* 967–984.

Barrett, L. F., Lane, R. D., Sechrest, L., & Schwartz, G. E. (2000). Sex differences in emotional awareness. *Personality and Social Psychology Bulletin, 26,* 1027–1035.

Barrick, M. R., & Mount, M. K. (1991). The Big Five personality dimensions and job performance: A meta-analytic analysis. *Personnel Psychology, 44,* 1–26.

Barry, D. (1998, February 1). A question that drives guys totally crazy. *Miami Herald.*

Bartholomew, K. (1990). Avoidance of intimacy: An attachment perspective. *Journal of Social and Personal Relationships, 7,* 147–178.

Bartholomew, K., & Horowitz, L. M. (1991). Attachment styles among young adults: A test of a four category model. *Journal of Personality and Social Psychology, 61,* 226–244.

Bass, B. I. (1998). *Leadership* (2nd ed.). New York: Free Press.

Bass, B. M. (1985). *Leadership and performance beyond expectations.* New York: Free Press.

Bass, B. M. (1998). *Transformational leadership: Industry, military, and educational impact.* Mahwah, NJ: Erlbaum.

Batson, C. D., & Oleson, K. C. (1991). Current status of the empathy–altruism hypothesis. In M. S. Clark (Ed.), *Prosocial behavior* (pp. 62–85). Newbury Park, CA: Sage.

Batson, C. D., & Thompson, E. R. (2001). Why don't moral people act morally? Motivational considerations. *Current Directions in Psychological Science, 10,* 54–57.

Batson, C. D., & Weeks, J. L. (1996). Mood effects of unsuccessful helping: Another test of the empathy–altruism hypothesis. *Personality and Social Psychology Bulletin, 22,* 148–157.

Batson, C. D., Early, S., & Salvarani, G. (1997). Perspective taking: Imagining how another feels versus imagining how you would feel. *Personality and Social Psychology Bulletin, 23,* 751–758.

Batson, C. D., Tsang, J., & Thompson, E. R. (2000). *Weakness of will: Counting the cost of being moral.* Unpublished manuscript, University of Kansas, Lawrence.

Batson, C. D., Klein, T. R., Highberger, L., & Shaw, L. L. (1995). Immorality from empathy-induced altruism: When compassion and justice conflict. *Journal of Personality and Social Psychology, 68,* 1042–1054.

Batson, C. D., Turk, C. L., Shaw, L. L., & Klein, T. R. (1995). Information function of empathic emotion: Learning that we value the other's welfare. *Journal of Personality and Social Psychology, 68,* 300–313.

Batson, C. D., Duncan, B. D., Ackerman, P., Buckley, T., & Birch, K. (1981). Is empathic emotion a source of altruistic motivation? *Journal of Personality and Social Psychology, 40,* 290–302.

Batson, C. D., Kobrynowicz, D., Donnerstein, J. L., Kampf, H. C., & Wilson, A. D. (1997). In a very different voice: Unmasking moral hypocrisy. *Journal of Personality and Social Psychology, 72,* 1335–1348.

Batson, C. D., O'Quin, K., Fultz, J., Vanderplas, M., & Isen, A. M. (1983). Influence of self-reported distress and empathy on egoistic versus altruistic motivation to help. *Journal of Personality and Social Psychology, 45,* 706–718.

Batson, C. D., Thompson, E. R., Seuferling, G., Whitney, H., & Strongman, J. A. (1999). Moral hypocrisy: Appearing moral to oneself without being so. *Journal of Personality and Social Psychology, 77,* 525–537.

Batson, C. D., Batson, J. G., Todd, R. M., Brummett, B. H., Shaw, L. L., & Aldeguer, C. M. R. (1995). Empathy and the collective good: Caring for one of the others in a social dilemma. *Journal of Personality and Social Psychology, 68,* 619–631.

Batson, C. D., Sager, K., Garst, E., Kang, M., Rubchinsky, K., & Dawson, K. (1997b). Is empathy-induced helping due to self–other merger? *Journal of Personality and Social Psychology, 73,* 495–509.

Batson, C. D., Ahmed, N., Yin, J., Bedell, S. J., Johnson, J. W., Templin, C. M., & Whiteside, A. (1999). Two threats to the common good: Self-interested egoism and empathy-induced altruism. *Personality and Social Psychology Bulletin, 25,* 3–16.

Baum, A. (1994). Behavioral, biological, and environmental interactions in disease processes. In S. Blumenthal, K. Matthews, & S. Weiss (Eds.), *New research frontiers in behavioral medicine: Proceedings of the national conference* (p. 62). Washington, DC: NIH Publications.

Baumeister, R., Smart, L., & Boden, J. (1996). Relation of threatened egotism to violence and aggression: The dark side of high self-esteem. *Psychological Review, 103,* 5–33.

Baumeister, R. F., & Leary, M. R. (1995). The need to belong: Desire for interpersonal attachments as a fundamental human motivation. *Psychological Bulletin, 117,* 497–529.

Baumeister, R. F., & Newman, L. S. (1994). Self-regulation of cognitive inference and decision processes. *Personality and Social Psychology Bulletin, 20,* 3–19.

Baumeister, R. F., Bushman, B. J., & Campbell, W. K. (2000). Self-esteem, narcissism, and aggression: Does violence result from low self-esteem or from threatened egotism? *Current Directions in Psychological Science, 9,* 26–29.

Baumeister, R. F., Catanese, K. R., & Vohs, K. D. (2001). Is there a gender difference in strength of sex drive? Theoretical views, conceptual distinctions, and a review of relevant evidence. *Personality and Social Psychology Review, 5,* 242–273.

Baumeister, R. F., Wotman, S. R., & Stillwell, A. M. (1993). Unrequited love: On heartbreak, anger, guilt, scriptlessness, and humiliation. *Journal of Personality and Social Psychology, 64,* 377–394.

Baumeister, R. F., Chesner, S. P., Sanders, P. S., & Tice, D. M. (1988). Who's in charge here? Group leaders do lend help in emergencies. *Personality and Social Psychology Bulletin, 14,* 17–22.

Baxter, L. A. (1990). Dialectical contradictions in relationship development. *Journal of Social and Personal Relationships, 7,* 69–88.

Beall, A. E., & Sternberg, R. J. (1995). The social construction of love. *Journal of Social and Personal Relationships, 12,* 417–438.

Beaman, A. I., Cole, M., Preston, M., Klentz, B., & Steblay, N. M. (1983). Fifteen years of the foot-in-the-door-research: A meta-analysis. *Personality and Social Psychology Bulletin, 9,* 181–186.

Beckwith, J. B. (1994). Terminology and social relevance in psychological research on gender. *Social Behavior and Personality, 22,* 329–336.

Beinart, P. (1998, October 19). Battle for the 'burbs. *The New Republic,* 25–29.

Bell, B. (1993). Emotional loneliness and the perceived similarity of one's ideas and interests. *Journal of Social Behavior and Personality, 8,* 273–280.

Bell, B. E. (1995). Judgments of the attributes of a student who is talkative versus a student who is quiet in class. *Journal of Social Behavior and Personality, 10,* 827–832.

Bell, D. C. (2001). Evolution of parental caregiving. *Personality and Social Psychology Review, 5,* 216–229.

Bell, P. A. (1992). In defense of the negative affect escape model of heat and aggression. *Psychological Bulletin, 111,* 342–346.

Bell, P. A., & Baron, R. A. (1976). Aggression and heat: The mediating role of negative affect. *Journal of Applied Social Psychology, 6,* 18–30.

Bell, R. A. (1991). Gender, friendship network density, and loneliness. *Journal of Social Behavior and Personality, 6,* 45–56.

Bell, S. T., Kuriloff, P. J., & Lottes, I. (1994). Understanding attributions of blame in stranger rape and date rape situations: An examination of gender, race, identification, and students' social perceptions of rape victims. *Journal of Applied Social Psychology, 24,* 1719–1734.

Bellafante, G. (1997, May 5). Bewitching teen heroines. *Time,* 82–84.

Bem, S. L. (1974). The measurement of psychological androgyny. *Journal of Consulting and Clinical Psychology, 42,* 155–162.

Bem, S. L. (1975). Sex role adaptability: One consequence of psychological androgyny. *Journal of Personality and Social Psychology, 31,* 634–643.

Bem, S. L. (1981). Gender schema theory: A cognitive account of sex typing. *Psychological Review, 88,* 354–364.

Bem, S. L. (1983). Gender schema theory and its implications for child development: Raising gender-schematic children in a gender-schematic society. *Signs: Journal of Women in Culture and Society, 8,* 598–616.

Bem, S. L. (1984). Androgyny and gender-schema theory: A conceptual and empirical integration. *Nebraska Symposium on Motivation: Psychology and Gender, 32,* 179–226.

Bem, S. L. (1995). Dismantling gender polarization and compulsory heterosexuality: Should we turn the volume down or up? *Journal of Sex Research, 32,* 329–334.

Benbow, C. P., Lubinski, D., Shea, D. L., & Eftekhari-Sanjani, H. (2000). Sex differences in mathematical reasoning ability at age 13: Their status 20 years later. *Psychological Science, 11,* 474–480.

Benjamin, E. (1998, January 14). Storm brings out good, bad and greedy. Albany *Times Union,* pp. A1, A6.

Benson, P. L., Karabenick, S. A., & Lerner, R. M. (1976). Pretty pleases: The effects of physical attractiveness, race, and sex on receiving help. *Journal of Experimental Social Psychology, 12,* 409–415.

Berant, E., Mikulincer, M., & Florian, V. (2001). The association of mothers' attachment style and their psychological reactions to the diagnosis of infant's congenital heart disease. *Journal of Social and Clinical Psychology, 20,* 208–232.

Berg, J. H., & McQuinn, R. D. (1989). Loneliness and aspects of social support networks. *Journal of Social and Personal Relationships, 6,* 359–372.

Berger, A. (1999, July 20). An early start for healthier habits. *New York Times,* F7.

Berkowitz, L. (1987). Mood, self-awareness, and willingness to help. *Journal of Personality and Social Psychology, 52,* 721–724.

Berkowitz, L. (1989). Frustration-aggression hypothesis: Examination and reformulation. *Psychological Bulletin, 106,* 59–73.

Berkowitz, L. (1993). *Aggression: Its causes, consequences, and control.* New York: McGraw Hill.

Berkowitz, L. (2001). *Aggression.* New York: Academic Press.

Berkowitz, L. (in press). Affect, aggression, and antisocial behavior. In R. J. Davidson, K. Scherer, & H. H. Goldsmith (Eds.), *Handbook of affective sciences.* New York: Oxford.

Berman, M., Gladue, B., & Taylor, S. (1993). The effects of hormones, Type A behavior pattern and provocation on aggression in men. *Motivation and Emotion, 17,* 125–138, 182–199.

Bernard, L. C., & Belinsky, D. (1993). Hardiness, stress, and maladjustment: Effects on self-reported retrospective health problems and prospective health center visits. *Journal of Social Behavior and Personality, 8,* 97–110.

Bernieri, F. J., Gillis, J. S., Davis, J. M., & Grahe, J. E. (1996). Dyad rapport and the accuracy of its judgment across situations: A lens model analysis. *Journal of Personality and Social Psychology, 71,* 110–129.

Berry, D. S. (1991). Accuracy in social perception: Contributions of facial and vocal information. *Journal of Personality and Social Psychology, 68,* 291–307.

Berry, D. S., & Hansen, J. S. (1996). Positive affect, negative affect, and social interaction. *Journal of Personality and Social Psychology, 71,* 796–809.

Berscheid, E. (1996). Appearance prejudice: Impression management or discrimination? In P. C. Smith & J. M. Hanebury (Eds.), *Issues in the workplace: Human resource dilemmas.* New York: Dame Publications, Inc.

Berscheid, E. (1999). The greening of relationship science. *American Psychologist, 54,* 260–266.

Berscheid, E., & Reis, H. T. (1998). Attraction and close relationships. In D. T. Gilbert, S. T. Fiske, & G. Lindzey (Eds.), *The handbook of social psychology* (Vol. 2, 4th ed., pp. 193–281). New York: McGraw-Hill.

Bersoff, D. (1987). Social science data and the Supreme Court: Lockhart as a case in point. *American Psychologist, 42,* 52–58.

Bersoff, D. M. (1999). Why good people sometimes do bad things: Motivated reasoning and unethical behavior. *Personality and Social Bulletin, 25,* 28–39.

Betancourt, B. A., & Miller, N. (1996). Gender differences in aggression as a function of provocation: A meta-analyis. *Psychological Bulletin, 119,* 422–447.

Betsch, T., Plessner, H., Schwieren, C., & Gutig, R. (2001). I like it but I don't know why: A value-account approach to implicit attitude formation. *Personality and Social Psychology Bulletin, 27,* 242–253.

Bettencourt, L. A., Gwinner, K. P., & Meuter, M. L. (2001). Comparison of attitude, personality, and knowledge predictors of service-oriented organizational citizenship behaviors. *Journal of Applied Psychology, 86,* 29–41.

Beyer, S., & Bowden, E. M. (1997). Gender differences in self-perceptions: Convergent evidence from three measures of accuracy and bias. *Personality and Social Psychology Bulletin, 23,* 157–172.

Bickman, L. D. (1975). *Personality constructs of senior women planning to marry or to live independently after college.* Unpublished doctoral dissertation, University of Pennsylvania.

Bienert, H., & Schneider, B. H. (1993). Diagnosis-specific social skills training with peer-nominated aggressive–disruptive and sensitive–isolated preadolescents. *Journal of Applied Developmental Psychology, 26* 182–199.

Bierhoff, H. W., Klein, R., & Kramp, P. (1991). Evidence for the altruistic personality from data on accident research. *Journal of Personality, 59,* 263–280.

Bies, R. J., Shapiro, D. L., & Cummings, L. L. (1988). Causal accounts and managing organizational conflict: Is it enough to say it's not my fault? *Communication Research, 15,* 381–399.

Birkimer, J. C., Lucas, M., & Birkimer, S. J. (1991). Health locus of control and status of cardiac rehabilitation graduates. *Journal of Social Behavior and Personality, 6,* 629–640.

Bjerklie, D. (2001, June 25). Teen sense. *Time,* 74.

Bjorklund, D. F., & Shackelford, T. K. (1999). Differences in parental investment contribute to important differences between men and women. *Current Directions in Psychological Science, 8,* 86–89.

Björkqvist, K., Lagerspetz, K. M., & Kaukiainen, A. (1992). Do girls manipulate and boys fight? Developmental trends in regard to direct and indirect aggression. *Aggressive Behavior, 18,* 117–127.

Björkqvist, K., Österman, K., & Hjelt-Bäck, M. (1994). Aggression among university employees. *Aggressive Behavior, 20,* 173–184.

Blaney, P. H. (1986). Affect and memory: A review. *Psychological Bulletin, 99,* 229–246.

Blascovich, J., Spencer, S. J., Quinn, D., & Steele, C. (2001). African Americans and high blood pressure: The role of stereotype threat. *Psychological Science, 12,* 225–229.

Blascovich, J., Wyer, N. A., Swart, L. A., & Kibler, J. L. (1997). Racism and racial categorization. *Journal of Personality and Social Psychology, 72,* 1364–1372.

Blascovich, J., Mendes, W. B., Hunter, S. B., Lickel, B., & Kowaii-Bell, N. (2001). Perceiver threat in social interactions with stigmatized others. *Journal of Personality and Social Psychology, 80,* 253–267.

Blazer, D. G., Kessler, R. C., McGonagle, K. A., & Swartz, M. S. (1994). The prevalence and distribution of major depression in a national community sample: The National Comorbidity Survey. *American Journal of Psychiatry, 151,* 979–986.

Bleske-Rechek, A. L., & Buss, D. M. (2001). Opposite-sex friendship: Sex differences and similarities in initiation, selection, and dissolution. *Personality and Social Psychology Bulletin, 27,* 1310–1323.

Bober, S., & Grolnick, W. (1995). Motivational factors related to differences in self-schemas. *Motivation and Emotion, 19,* 307–327.

Bobo, L. (1983). Whites' opposition to busing: Symbolic racism or realistic group conflict? *Journal of Personality and Social Psychology, 45,* 1196–1210.

Bodenhausen, G. F. (1993). Emotion, arousal, and stereotypic judgment: A heuristic model of affect and stereotyping. In D. Mackie & D. Hamilton (Eds.), *Affect, cognition, and stereotyping: Intergroup processes in intergroup perception* (pp. 13–37). San Diego, CA: Academic Press.

Bodenhausen, G. V., Kramer, G. P., & Susser, K. (1994b). Happiness and stereotypic thinking in social judgment. *Journal of Personality and Social Psychology, 66,* 621–632.

Bodenmann, G., Kaiser, A., Hahlweg, K., & Fehn-Wolfsdorf, G. (1998). Communication patterns during marital conflict: A cross-cultural replication. *Personal Relationships, 5,* 343–356.

Boer, F., Westenberg, M., McHale, S. M., Updegraff, K. A., & Stocker, C. M. (1997). The factorial structure of the Sibling Relationship Inventory (SRI) in American and Dutch samples. *Journal of Social and Personal Relationships, 14,* 851–859.

Bogard, M. (1990). Why we need gender to understand human violence. *Journal of Interpersonal Violence, 5,* 132–135.

Bogart, L. M. (1998). The relationship of stereotypes about helpers to help-seeking judgments, preferences, and behaviors. *Personality and Social Psychology Bulletin, 24,* 1264–1275.

Bogart, L. M., Cecil, H., Wagstaff, D. A., Pinkerton, S. D., & Abramson, P. R. (2000). Is it "sex"?: College students' interpretations of sexual behavior terminology. *Journal of Sex Research, 37,* 108–116.

Bolger, N., & Zuckerman, A. (1995). A framework for studying personality in the stress process. *Journal of Personality and Social Psychology, 69,* 890–902.

Bolger, N., Zuckerman, A., & Kessler, R. C. (2000). Invisible support and adjustment to stress. *Journal of Personality and Social Psychology, 79,* 953–961.

Bonanno, G. A., Mihalecz, M. C., & LeJeune, J. T. (1999). The core emotion themes of conjugal love. *Motivation and Emotion, 23,* 175–199.

Bond, C. F., Jr., & Atoum, A. O. (2000). International deception. *Personality and Social Psychology Bulletin, 26,* 385–395.

Bond, R., & Smith, P. B. (1996). Culture and conformity: A meta-analysis of studies using Asch's (1952b, 1956) line judgment task. *Psychological Bulletin, 119,* 111–137.

Bookwala, J., Frieze, I. H., & Grote, N. K. (1994). Love, aggression and satisfaction in dating relationships. *Journal of Social and Personal Relationships, 11,* 625–632.

Boon, S. D., & Brussoni, M. J. (1996). Young adults' relationships with their "closest" grandparents: Examining emotional closeness. *Journal of Social Behavior and Personality, 11,* 439–458.

Boon, S. D., & Brussoni, M. J. (1998). Popular images of grandparents: Examining young adults' views of their closest grandparents. *Personal Relationships, 5,* 105–119.

Booth-Kewley, S., & Vickers, R. R. Jr. (1994). Associations between major domains of personality and health behavior. *Journal of Personality, 62,* 281–298.

Bornstein, R. F. (1995). Interpersonal dependency and physical illness: The mediating roles of stress and social support. *Journal of Social and Clinical Psychology, 14,* 225–243.

Bornstein, R. F., & D'Agostino, P. R. (1992). Stimulus recognition and the mere exposure effect. *Journal of Personality and Social Psychology, 63,* 545–552.

Bossard, J. H. S. (1932). Residential propinquity as a factor in marriage selection. *American Journal of Sociology, 38,* 219–224.

Bosson, J. K., & Swann, W. B., Jr. (1999). Self-liking, self-competence, and the quest for self-verification. *Personality and Social Psychology Bulletin, 25,* 1230–1241.

Boswell, J. (1963). *The life of Samuel Johnson L.L.D.* (Vol. 2). New York: Heritage. (Original work published 1791.)

Botha, M. (1990). Television exposure and aggression among adolescents: A follow-up study over 5 years. *Aggressive Behavior, 16,* 361–380.

Bouchard, T. J., Jr., Arvey, R. D., Keller, L. M., & Segal, N. L. (1992). Genetic influences on job satisfaction: A reply to Cropanzano and Hames. *Journal of Applied Psychology, 77,* 89–93.

Bower, G. H. (1991). Mood congruity of social judgments. In J. P. Forgas (Ed.), *Emotion and social judgments* (pp. 31–55). Oxford: Pergamon Press.

Bowers, L., Smith, P. K., & Binney, V. (1994). Perceived family relationships of bullies, victims and bully/victims in middle childhood. *Journal of Social and Personal Relationships, 11,* 215–232.

Bowlby, J. (1969). *Attachment and loss: Vol. 1. Attachment.* New York: Basic Books.

Bowlby, J. (1973). *Attachment and loss: Vol. 2. Separation.* New York: Basic Books.

Bowlby, J. (1982). *Attachment and loss: Vol. 1. Attachment* (2nd ed.). New York: Basic Books.

Boyce, N. (2001, June 4). Cruel lessons from an epidemic. *U.S. News and World Report,* 48–49.

Branscombe, N. R., & Wann, D. L. (1994). Collective self-esteem consequences of outgroup derogation when a valued social identity is on trial. *European Journal of Social Psychology, 24,* 641–657.

Braza, P., Braza, F., Carreras, M. R., & Munoz, J. M. (1993). Measuring the social ability of preschool children. *Social Behavior and Personality, 21,* 145–158.

Breakwell, G. M., & Fife-Schaw, C. (1992). Sexual activities and preferences in a United Kingdom sample of 16- to 20-year-olds. *Archives of Sexual Behavior, 21,* 271–293.

Brehm, J. W. (1966). *A theory of psychological reactance.* New York: Academic Press.

Brennan, K. A., & Bosson, J. K. (1998). Attachment-style differences in attitudes toward and reactions to feedback from romantic partners: An exploration of the relational bases of self-esteem. *Personality and Social Psychology Bulletin, 24,* 699–714.

Brennan, K. A., & Shaver, P. R. (1995). Dimensions of adult attachment, affect regulation, and romantic relationship functioning. *Personality and Social Psychology Bulletin, 21,* 267–283.

Brewer, M. B., & Gardner, W. (1996). Who is this "we"? Levels of collective identity and self representations. *Journal of Personality and Social Psychology, 71,* 83–93.

Brewer, M. B., Ho, H., Lee, J., & Miller, M. (1987). Social identity and social distance among Hong Kong schoolchildren. *Personality and Social Psychology Bulletin, 13,* 156–165.

Brickner, M., Harkins, S., & Ostrom, T. (1986). Personal involvement: Thought provoking implications for social loafing. *Journal of Personality and Social Psychology, 51,* 763–769.

Bright, S. (2000, August/September). Rubber baby boom. *Civilization,* 28.

Bringle, R. G., & Bagby, G. J. (1992). Self-esteem and perceived quality of romantic and family relationships in young adults. *Journal of Research in Personality, 26,* 340–356.

Bringle, R. G., & Winnick, T. A. (1992, October). *The nature of unrequited love.* Paper presented at the first Asian Conference in Psychology, Singapore.

Brockner, J. M., & Wiesenfeld, B. M. (1996). An integrative framework for explaining reactions to decisions: Interactive effects of outcomes and procedures. *Psychological Bulletin, 120,* 189–208.

Brockner, J., Konovsky, M., Cooper-Schneider, R., Folger, R., Martin, C., & Bies, R. J. (1994). Interactive effects of procedural justice and outcome negativity on victims and survivors of job loss. *Academy of Management Journal, 37,* 397–409.

Brody, L. R., & Hall, J. A. (1993). Gender and emotion. In M. Lewis & J. Haviland (Eds.), *Handbook of emotions* (pp. 447–460). New York: Guilford.

Brooks-Gunn, J., & Lewis, M. (1981). Infant social perception: Responses to pictures of parents and strangers. *Developmental Psychology, 17,* 647–649.

Bromberger, J. T., & Matthews, K. A. (1996). A "feminine" model of vulnerability to depressive symptoms: A longitudinal investigation of middle-aged women. *Journal of Personality and Social Psychology, 70,* 591–598.

Brothers, L. (1990). The neural basis of primate social communication. *Motivation and Emotion, 14,* 81–91.

Brown, D. (2001, June 1). HIV rate surges again for gay men. *Washington Post.*

Brown, J. D. (1991). Staying fit and staying well: Physical fitness as a moderator of life stress. *Journal of Personality and Social Psychology, 60,* 555–561.

Brown, J. D., & Dutton, K. A. (1995). The thrill of victory, the complexity of defeat: Self-esteem and people's emotional reactions to success and failure. *Journal of Personality and Social Psychology, 68,* 712–722.

Brown, J. D., & Rogers, R. J. (1991). Self-serving attributions: The role of physiological arousal. *Personality and Social Psychology Bulletin, 17,* 501–506.

Brown, L. M. (1998). Ethnic stigma as a contextual experience: Possible selves perspective. *Personality and Social Psychology Bulletin, 24,* 165–172.

Brown, L. S. (1997). The private practice of subversion: Psychology as *tikkun olam. American Psychologist, 52,* 449–462.

Brown, R. P., Charnsangavej, T., Keough, K. A., Newman, M. L., & Rentfrow, P. J. (2000). Putting the "affirm" into affirmative action: Preferential selection and academic performance. *Journal of Personality and Social Psychology, 79,* 736–747.

Brown, S. L. (1998). Associations between peer drink driving, peer attitudes toward drink, driving, and personal drink driving. *Journal of Applied Social Psychology, 28,* 423–436.

Brown, S. P. (1996). A meta-analysis and review of organizational research on job involvement. *Psychological Bulletin, 120,* 235–255.

Browne, M. W. (1992, April 14). Biologists tally generosity's rewards. *New York Times,* pp. C1, C8.

Bruch, M. A., Hamer, R. J., & Heimberg, R. G. (1995). Shyness and public self-consciousness: Additive or interactive relation with social interaction? *Journal of Personality, 63,* 47–63.

Bruder, G. E., Stewart, M. M., Mercier, M. A., Agosti, V., Leite, P., Donovan, S., & Quitkin, F. M. (1997). Outcome of cognitive–behavioral therapy for depression: Relation to hemispheric dominance for verbal processing. *Journal of Abnormal Psychology, 106,* 138–144.

Bryan, A. D., Aiken, L. S., & West, S. G. (1999). The impact of males proposing condom use on perceptions of an initial sexual encounter. *Personality and Social Psychology Bulletin, 25,* 275–286.

Bryan, J. H., & Test, M. A. (1967). Models and helping: Naturalistic studies in aiding behavior. *Journal of Personality and Social Psychology, 6,* 400–407.

Buck, R., & Ginsburg, B. (1991). Spontaneous communication and altruism: The communicative gene hypothesis. In M. S. Clark (Ed.), *Prosocial behavior* (pp. 149–175). Newbury Park, CA: Sage.

Budesheim, T. L., & Bonnelle, K. (1998). The use of abstract trait knowledge and behavioral exemplars in causal explanations of behavior. *Personality and Social Psychology Bulletin, 24,* 575–587.

Buehler, R., & Griffin, D. (1994). Change-of-meaning effects in conformity and dissent: Observing construal processes over time. *Journal of Personality and Social Psychology, 67,* 984–996.

Buehler, R., Griffin, D., & MacDonald, H. (1997). The role of motivated reasoning in optimistic time predictions. *Personality and Social Psychology Bulletin, 23,* 238–247.

Buehler, R., Griffin, D., & Ross, M. (1994). Exploring the "planning fallacy": Why people underestimate their task completion times. *Journal of Personality and Social Psychology,* 67, 366–381.

Bumpass, L. (1984). Children and marital disruption: A replication and update. *Demography, 21,* 71–82.

Burger, J. M. (1986). Increasing compliance by improving the deal: The that's-not-all technique. *Journal of Personality and Social Psychology, 51,* 277–283.

Burger, J. M. (1992). *Desire for control: Personality, social, and clinical perspectives.* New York: Plenum.

Burger, J. M. (1995). Individual differences in preference for solitude. *Journal of Research in Personality, 29,* 85–108.

Burgess, D., & Borgida, E. (1997). Sexual harassment: An experimental test of sex-role spillover theory. *Personality and Social Psychology Bulletin, 23,* 63–75.

Burns-Glover, A. L., & Veith, D. J. (1995). Revisiting gender and teaching evaluations: Sex still makes a difference. *Journal of Social Behavior and Personality, 10,* 69–80.

Burnstein, E. (1983). Persuasion as argument processing. In M. Brandstatter, J. H. Davis, & G. Stocker-Kriechgauer (Eds.), *Group decision processes.* London: Academic Press.

Burnstein, E., Crandall, C., & Kitayama, S. (1994). Some neo-Darwinian rules for altruism: Weighing cues for inclusive fitness as a function of the biological importance of the decision. *Journal of Personality and Social Psychology, 67,* 773–789.

Burton, A. M., Wilson, S., Cowan, M., & Bruce, V. (1999). Face recognition in poor-quality video: Evidence from security surveillance. *Psychological Science, 10,* 243–248.

Bushman, B. J. (1988). The effects of apparel on compliance: A field experiment with a female authority figure. *Personality and Social Psychology Bulletin, 14,* 459–467.

Bushman, B. J. (1998). Effects of television violence on memory for commercial messages. *Journal of Experimental Psychology: Applied, 4,* 1–17.

Bushman, B. J. (2001). Does venting anger feed or extinguish the flame? Catharsis, rumination, distraction, anger, and aggressive responding. Manuscript under review.

Bushman, B. J., & Baumeister, R. F. (1998). Threatened egotism, narcissism, self-esteem, and direct and displaced aggression: Does self-love or self-hate lead to violence? *Journal of Personality and Social Psychology, 75,* 219–229.

Bushman, B. J., & Cooper, H. M. (1990). Effects of alcohol on human aggression: An integrative research review. *Psychological Bulletin, 107,* 341–354.

Bushman, B. J., Baumeister, R. F., & Stack, A. D. (1999). Catharsis messages and anger-reducing activities. *Journal of Personality and Social Psychology, 76,* 367–376.

Buss, A. M. (1961). *The psychology of aggression.* New York: Wiley.

Buss, D. M. (1988). Love acts: The evolutionary biology of love. In R. J. Sternberg & M. L. Barnes (Eds.), *The psychology of love* (pp. 100–118). New Haven, CT: Yale University Press.

Buss, D. M. (1994). The strategies of human mating. *American Scientist, 82,* 238–249.

Buss, D. M. (1995). Evolutionary psychology: A new paradigm for psychological science. *Psychological Inquiry, 6,* 1–30.

Buss, D. M. (1998). *Evolutionary psychology.* Boston: Allyn and Bacon.

Buss, D. M. (1999). *Evolutionary psychology: The new science of the mind.* Boston: Allyn and Bacon.

Buss, D. M., & Schmitt, D. P. (1993). Sexual strategies theory: An evolutionary perspective on human mating. *Psychological Review, 100,* 204–232.

Buss, D. M., & Shackelford, T. K. (1997). From vigilance to violence: Mate retention tactics in married couples.

Journal of Personality and Social Psychology, 72, 346–361.

Buss, D. M., Larsen, R. J., Westen, D., & Semmelroth, J. (1992). Sex differences in jealousy: Evolution, physiology, and psychology. *Psychological Science, 3,* 251–255.

Butler, A. C., Hokanson, J. E., & Flynn, H. A. (1994). A comparison of self-esteem lability and low trait self-esteem as vulnerability factors for depression. *Journal of Personality and Social Psychology, 66,* 166–177.

Butler, D., & Geis, F. L. (1990). Nonverbal affect responses to male and female leaders: Implications for leadership evaluations. *Journal of Personality and Social Psychology, 58,* 48–59.

Buunk, B. P. (1995). Sex, self-esteem, dependency and extradyadic sexual experience as related to jealousy responses. *Journal of Social and Personal Relationships, 12,* 147–153.

Buunk, B. P., & Prins, K. S. (1998). Loneliness, exchange orientation, and reciprocity in friendships. *Personal Relationships, 5,* 1–14.

Buunk, B. P., & van der Eijnden, R. J. J. M. (1997). Perceived prevalence, perceived superiority, and relationship satisfaction: Most relationships are good, but ours is the best. *Personality and Social Psychology Bulletin, 23,* 219–228.

Buysse, A., & Ickes, W. (1999). Communication patterns in laboratory discussions of safer sex between dating versus non-dating partners. *Journal of Sex Research, 36,* 121–134.

Buzwell, S., & Rosenthal, D. (1995). Exploring the sexual world of the unemployed adolescent. *Journal of Community and Applied Social Psychology, 5,* 161–166.

Byrne, B. M., & Shavelson, R. J. (1996). On the structure of social self-concept for pre-, early, and late adolescents: A test of the Shavelson, Hubner, and Stanton (1976) model. *Journal of Personality and Social Psychology, 70,* 599–613.

Byrne, D. (1961a). The influence of propinquity and opportunities for interaction on classroom relationships. *Human Relations, 14,* 63–69.

Byrne, D. (1961b). Interpersonal attraction and attitude similarity. *Journal of Abnormal and Social Psychology, 62,* 713–715.

Byrne, D. (1971). *The attraction paradigm.* New York: Academic Press.

Byrne, D. (1991). Perspectives on research classics: This ugly duckling has yet to become a swan. *Contemporary Social Psychology, 15,* 84–85.

Byrne, D. (1992). The transition from controlled laboratory experimentation to less controlled settings: Surprise! Additional variables are operative. *Communication Monographs, 59,* 190–198.

Byrne, D. (1997). Why would anyone conduct research on sexual behavior? In G. G. Brannigan, E. R. Allgeier, & A. R. Allgeier (Eds.), *The sex scientists* (pp. 15–30). New York: Addison Wesley Longman.

Byrne, D. (2001). Interpersonal dissimilarity as an initiator of fear and anger: Reactions that once enhanced reproductive success now facilitate interpersonal hate and violence. In M. E. Sutherland, B. Matthies, & C. A. Bailey (Eds.), *Psychology and Caribbean development.* Kingston, Jamaica: University of the West Indies Press.

Byrne, D., & Blaylock, B. (1963). Similarity and assumed similarity of attitudes among husbands and wives. *Journal of Abnormal and Social Psychology, 67,* 636–640.

Byrne, D., & Clore, G. L. (1970). A reinforcement–affect model of evaluative responses. *Personality: An International Journal, 1,* 103–128.

Byrne, D., & Fisher, W. A. (Eds.). (1983). *Adolescents, sex, and contraception.* Hillsdale, NJ: Lawrence Erlbaum Associates.

Byrne, D., & Murnen, S. K. (1988). Maintaining loving relationships. In R. J. Sternberg & M. L. Barnes (Eds.), *The psychology of love* (pp. 293–310). New Haven, CT: Yale University Press.

Byrne, D., & Nelson, D. (1965). Attraction as a linear function of proportion of positive reinforcements. *Journal of Personality and Social Psychology, 1,* 659–663.

Byrne, R. L. (2001, June 1). Good safety advice. Internet.

Cacioppo, J. T., & Berntson, G. G. (1999). The affect system: Architecture and operating characteristics. *Current Directions in Psychological Science, 8,* 133–136.

Cacioppo, J. T., Gardner, W. L., & Berntson, G. G. (1999). The affect system has parallel and integrative processing components: Form follows function. *Journal of Personality and Social Psychology, 76,* 839–855.

Cadenhead, A. C., & Richman, C. L. (1996). The effects of interpersonal trust and group status on prosocial and aggressive behaviors. *Social Behavior and Personality, 24,* 169–184.

Callaci, D. (1993, March 3). The glass is half full. *New York Teacher,* 9–11.

Callan, V. J. (1993). Subordinate manager communication in different sex-dyads: Consequences for job satisfaction. *Journal of Occupational and Organizational Psychology, 66,* 13–27.

Calle, E. E., Thun, M. J., Petrelli, J. M., Rodriguez, M. P. H., & Heath, C. W. (1999). Body-mass index and mortality in a prospective cohort of U.S. adults. *New England Journal of Medicine, 341,* 1097–1105.

Campbell, D. T. (1958). Common fate, similarity, and other indices of the status of aggregates of persons as social entities. *Behavioral Science, 4,* 14–25.

Campbell, D. T. (1975). On the conflicts between biological and social evolution and between psychological and moral tradition. *American Psychologist, 30,* 1103–1126.

Campbell, D. T., & Specht, J. C. (1985). Altruism: Biology, culture, and religion. *Journal of Social and Clinical Psychology, 3,* 33–42.

Campbell, J. D., Chew, B., & Scratchley, L. S. (1991). Cognitive and emotional reactions to daily events: The effects of self-esteem and self-complexity. *Journal of Personality, 59,* 473–505.

Campbell, L., Simpson, J. A., Kashy, D. A., & Fletcher, G. J. O. (2001). Ideal standards, the self, and flexibility of ideals in close relationships. *Personality and Social Psychology Bulletin, 27,* 447–462.

Campbell, W. K. (1999). Narcissism and romantic attraction. *Journal of Personality and Social Psychology, 77,* 1254–1270.

Cann, A., Calhoun, L. G., & Banks, J. S. (1995). On the role of humor appreciation in interpersonal attraction: It's no joking matter. *Humor: International Journal of Humor Research.*

Cappella, J. N., & Palmer, M. T. (1990). Attitude similarity, relational history, and attraction: The mediating effects of kinesic and vocal behaviors. *Communication Monographs, 57,* 161–183.

Cappella, J. N., & Palmer, M. T. (1992). *Communication Monographs, 59,* 180–189.

Caprara, G. V., Barbaranelli, C., Pastorelli, C., & Perugini, M. (1994). Individual differences in the study of human aggression. *Aggressive Behavior, 20,* 291–303.

Caprara, G. V., Barbaranelli, C., Pastorelli, C., Bandura, A., & Zimbardo, P. G. (2000). Prosocial foundations of children's academic achievement. *Psychological Science, 11,* 302–306.

Carey, M. P., Morrison-Beedy, D., & Johnson, B. T. (1997). The HIV-Knowledge Questionnaire: Development and evaluation of a reliable, valid, and practical self-administered questionnaire. *AIDS and Behavior, 1,* 61–74.

Carlson, K. A., & Russo, J. E. (2001). Biased interpretation of evidence by mock jurors: A meta-analysis. *Journal of Experimental Psychology: Applied, 7,* 91–103.

Carpenter, L. M. (1988). From girls into women: Scripts for sexuality and romance in *Seventeen* magazine, 1974–1994. *Journal of Sex Research, 35,* 158–168.

Carpenter, S. (2000, October). Biology and social environments jointly influence gender development. *Monitor on Psychology,* 35.

Carpenter, S. (2000a, December). Preferring the predictable. *Monitor on Psychology,* 42–43.

Carpenter, S. (2000b, December). Why do 'they all look alike'? *Monitor on Psychology,* 44–46.

Carpenter, S. (2001, March). Fools rush in. *Monitor on Psychology,* 66–67.

Carpenter, S. (2001, July/August). They're positively inspiring. *Monitor on Psychology,* 74–76.

Carpenter, S. (2001, October). Technology gets its day in court. *Monitor on Psychology,* 30–32.

Carroll, J. M., & Russell, H. A. (1996). Do facial expressions signal specific emotions? Judging emotion from the face in context. *Journal of Personality and Social Psychology, 70,* 205–218.

Carter, D. B., & McCloskey, L. A. (1984). Peers and the maintenance of sex-typed behavior: The development of children's conceptions of cross-gender behavior in their peers. *Social Cognition, 2,* 294–314.

Carver, C. S., & Glass, D. C. (1978). Coronary-prone behavior pattern and interpersonal aggression. *Journal of Personality and Social Psychology, 376,* 361–366.

Carver, C. S., Kus, L. A., & Scheier, M. F. (1994). Effects of good versus bad mood and optimistic versus pessimistic outlook on social acceptance versus rejection. *Journal of Social and Clinical Psychology, 13,* 138–151.

Carver, C. S., Reynolds, S. L., & Scheier, M. F. (1994). The possible selves of optimists and pessimists. *Journal of Research in Personality, 28,* 133–141.

Cash, T. F. (1995). Developmental teasing about physical appearance: Retrospective descriptions and relationships with body image. *Social Behavior and Personality, 23,* 123–130.

Cash, T. F., & Duncan, N. C. (1984). Physical attractiveness stereotyping among black American college students. *Journal of Social Psychology, 122,* 71–77.

Cash, T. F., & Trimer, C. A. (1984). Sexism and beautyism in women's evaluation of peer performance. *Sex Roles, 10,* 87–98.

Caspi, A., & Herbener, E. S. (1990). Continuity and change: Assortative marriage and the consistency of personality in adulthood. *Journal of Personality and Social Psychology, 58,* 250–258.

Caspi, A., Herbener, E. S., & Ozer, D. J. (1992). Shared experiences and the similarity of personalities: A longitudinal study of married couples. *Journal of Personality and Social Psychology, 62,* 281–291.

Catalano, R., Novaco, R., & McConnell, W. (1997). A model of the net effect of job loss on violence. *Journal of Personality and Social Psychology, 72,* 1440–1447.

Cattarin, J. A., Thompson, J. K., Thomas, C., & Williams, R. (2000). Body image, mood, and televised images of attractiveness: The role of social comparison. *Journal of Social and Clinical Psychology, 19,* 220–239.

Caughlin, J. P., Huston, T. L., & Houts, R. M. (2000). How does personality matter in marriage? An examination of trait anxiety, interpersonal negativity, and marital satisfaction. *Journal of Personality and Social Psychology, 78,* 326–336.

Cejka, M. A., & Eagly, A. H. (1999). Gender-stereotypic images of occupations correspond to the sex segregation of employment. *Personality and Social Psychology Bulletin, 25,* 413–423.

Cervone, D. (1997). Social–cognitive mechanisms and personality coherence: Self-knowledge, situational beliefs, and cross-situational coherence in perceived self-efficacy. *Psychological Science, 8,* 43–50.

Chacko, T. I. (1982). Women and equal employment opportunity: Some unintended effects. *Journal of Applied Psychology, 67,* 119–123.

Chaiken, S., Giner-Sorolla, R., & Chen, S. (1996). Beyond accuracy: Defense and impression motives in heuristic and systematic processing. In P. M. Gollwitzer & J. A. Bargh (Eds.), *The psychology action: Linking motivation and cognition to behavior* (pp. 553–578). New York: Guilford.

Chaiken, S., Liberman, A., & Eagly, A. H. (1989). Heuristic and systematic processing within and beyond persuasion context. In J. S. Uleman & J. A. Bargh (Eds.), *Unintended thought* (pp. 212–252). New York: Guilford.

Chang, E. C. (1998). Dispositional optimism and secondary appraisal of a stressor: Controlling for confounding influences and relations to coping and psychological and physical adjustment. *Journal of Personality and Social Psychology, 74,* 1109–1120.

Chang, E. C., & DeSimone, S. L. (2001). The influence of hope on appraisals, coping, and dysphoria: A test of hope theory. *Journal of Social and Clinical Psychology, 20,* 117–129.

Chaplin, W. F., Phillips, J. B., Brown, J. D., Clanton, N. R., & Stein, J. L. (2000). Handshaking, gender, personality, and first impressions. *Journal of Personality and Social Psychology, 79,* 110–117.

Chapman, B. L. (1995). *The Byrne-Nelson formula revisited: The additional impact of number of dissimilar attitudes on attraction.* Unpublished masters thesis, University at Albany, State University of New York.

Chapman, H. A., Hobfoll, S. E., & Ritter, C. (1997). Partners' stress under-estimations lead to women's distress: A study of pregnant inner-city women. *Journal of Personality and Social Psychology, 73,* 418–425.

Chappell, K. D., & Davis, K. E. (1998). Attachment, partner choice, and perception of romantic partners: An experimental test of the attachment-security hypothesis. *Personal Relationships, 5,* 327–342.

Chatterjee, J., & McCarrey, M. (1991). Sex-role attitudes, values, and instrumental-expressive traits of women trainees in traditional vs. non-traditional programmes. *Applied Psychology: An International Review, 40,* 282–297.

Chen, M., & Bargh, J. A. (1999). Consequences of automatic evaluation: Immediate behavioral predispositions to approach or avoid the stimulus. *Personality and Social Psychology Bulletin, 25,* 215–224.

Cheney, D. L., & Seyfarth, R. M. (1992). Précis of how monkeys see the world. *Behavioral and Brain Sciences, 15,* 135–182.

Cherek, D. R., Moeller, F. G., Schnapp, W., & Dougherty, D. M. (1997). Studies of violent and nonviolent male parolees. I: Laboratory and psychometric measurements of aggression. *Biological Psychiatry, 41,* 514–522.

Cherek, D. R., Schnapp, W., Gerard Moeller, F., & Dougherty, D. M. (1996). Laboratory measures of aggressive responding in male parolees with violent and nonviolent histories. *Aggressive Behavior 22,* 37–36.

Cherek, D. R., Lane, S. C., Dougherty, D. M., Moeller, F. G., & White, S. (2000). Laboratory and questionnaire measures of aggression among female parolees with violent or nonviolent histories. *Aggressive Behavior, 26,* 291–307.

Chermack, S. T., Berman, M., & Taylor, S. P. (1997). Effects of provocation on emotions and aggression in males. *Aggressive Behavior, 23,* 1–10.

Cheung, S.-K., & Sun, S. Y. K. (2000). Effects of self-efficacy and social support on the mental health conditions of mutual-aid and organization members. *Social Behavior and Personality, 28,* 413–422.

Cheverton, H. M., & Byrne, D. (1998, February). *Development and validation of the Primary Choice Clothing Questionnaire.* Presented at the meeting of the Eastern Psychological Association, Boston.

Choi, I., & Nisbett, R. E. (1998). Situational salience and cultural differences in the correspondence bias and actor-observer bias. *Personality and Social Psychology Bulletin, 24,* 949–960.

Choo, P., Levine, T., & Hatfield, E. (1996). Gender, love schemas, and reactions to romantic break-ups. *Journal of Social Behavior and Personality, 11,* 143–160.

Christian-Herman, J. L., O'Leary, K. D., & Avery-Leaf, S. (2001). The impact of severe negative events in marriage on depression. *Journal of Social and Clinical Psychology, 20,* 24–40.

Christopher, F. S., & Cate, R. M. (1985). Premarital sexual pathways and relationship development. *Journal of Social and Personal Relationships, 2,* 271–288.

Christy, C. A., & Voigt, H. (1994). Bystander responses to public episodes of child abuse. *Journal of Applied Social Psychology, 24,* 824–847.

Christy, P. R., Gelfand, D. M., & Hartmann, D. P. (1971). Effects of competition-induced frustration on two classes of modeled behavior. *Developmental Psychology, 5,* 104–111.

Cialdini, R. B., Reno, R. R., & Kallgren, C. A. (1990). A focus theory of normative conduct: Recycling the concept of norms to reduce littering in public places. *Jour-*

nal of Personality and Social Psychology, 58, 1015–1026.

Cialdini, R. B. (1994). Interpersonal influence. In S. Shavitt & T. C. Brock (Eds.), *Persuasion* (pp. 195–218). Boston: Allyn & Bacon.

Cialdini, R. B., & Petty, R. (1979). Anticipatory opinion effects. In B. Petty, T. Ostrom, & T. Brock (Eds.), *Cognitive responses in persuasion.* Hillsdale, NJ: Erlbaum.

Cialdini, R. B., Baumann, D. J., & Kenrick, D. T. (1981). Insights from sadness: A three-step model of the development of altruism as hedonism. *Developmental Review, 1,* 207–223.

Cialdini, R. B., Kallgren, C. A., & Reno, R. R. (1991). A focus theory of normative conduct. *Advances in Experimental Social Psychology, 24,* 201–234.

Cialdini, R. B., Kenrick, D. T., & Baumann, D. J. (1982). Effects of mood on prosocial behavior in children and adults. In N. Eisenberg-Berg (Ed.), *Development of prosocial behavior.* New York: Academic Press.

Cialdini, R. B., Cacioppo, J. T., Bassett, R., & Miller J. A. (1978). A low-ball procedure for producing compliance: Commitment then cost. *Journal of Personality and Social Psychology, 36,* 463–476.

Cialdini, R. B., Brown, S. L., Lewis, B. P., Luce, C., & Neuberg, S. L. (1997). Reinterpreting the empathy–altruism relationship: When one into one equals oneness. *Journal of Personality and Social Psychology, 73,* 481–494.

Cialdini, R. B., Wosinska, W., Dabul, A. J., Whetstone-Dion, R., & Heszen, I. (1998). When social role salience leads to social role rejection: Modest self-presentation among women and men in two cultures. *Personality and Social Psychology Bulletin, 24,* 473–481.

Cialdini, R. B., Schaller, M., Houlainham, D., Arps, K., Fultz, J., & Beaman, A. L. (1987). Empathy-based helping: Is it selflessly or selfishly motivated? *Journal of Personality and Social Psychology, 52,* 749–758.

Cialdini, R. B., Vincent, J. E., Lewis, S. K., Catalan, J., Wheeler, D., & Darby, B. L. (1975). Reciprocal concessions procedure for inducing compliance: The door-in-the-face technique. *Journal of Personality and Social Psychology, 31,* 206–215.

Clancy, S. A., Schacter, D. L., McNally, R. J., & Pilman, R. K. (2000). False recognition in women reporting recovered memories of sexual abuse. *Psychological Science, 11,* 26–31.

Clark, K., & Clark, M. (1947). Racial identification and racial preference in Negro children. In T. M. Newcomb & E. L. Hartley (Eds.), *Reading in social psychology* (pp. 169–178). New York: Holt.

Clark, L. A., Kochanska, G., & Ready, R. (2000). Mothers' personality and its interaction with child temperament as predictors of parenting behavior. *Journal of Personality and Social Psychology, 79,* 274–285.

Clark, L. F. (1993). Stress and the cognitive–conversational benefits of social interaction. *Journal of Social and Clinical Psychology, 12,* 25–55.

Clark, L. F., & Collins, J. E. II. (1993). Remembering old flames: How the past affects assessments of the present. *Personality and Social Psychology Bulletin, 19,* 399–408.

Clark, M. S., & Grote, N. K. (1998). Why aren't indices of relationship costs always negatively related to indices of relationship quality? *Personality and Social Psychology Review, 2,* 2–17.

Clark, M. S., Ouellette, R., Powel, M. C., & Milberg, S. (1987). Recipient's mood, relationship type, and helping. *Journal of Personality and Social Psychology, 53,* 94–103.

Clark, R., Anderson, N. B., Clark, V. R., & Williams, D. R. (1999). Racism as a stressor for African-Americans: A biopsychosocial model. *American Psychologist, 54,* 805–816.

Clary, E. G., & Orenstein, L. (1991). The amount and effectiveness of help: The relationship of motives and abilities in helping behavior. *Personality and Social Psychology Bulletin, 17,* 58–64.

Clary, E. G., & Snyder, M. (1999). The motivations to volunteer: Theoretical and practical considerations. *Current Directions in Psychological Science, 8,* 156–159.

Clary, E. G., Snyder, M., Ridge, R. D., Copeland, J., Stukas, A. A., Haugen, J., & Miene, P. (1998). Understanding and assessing the motivations of volunteers: A functional approach. *Journal of Personality and Social Psychology, 74,* 1516–1530.

Clay, R. A. (2000, April). Linking up online. *Monitor on Psychology,* 20–23.

Cliff, J. E. (1998). Does one size fit all? Exploring the relationship between attitudes toward growth, gender, and business size. *Journal of Business Venturing, 13,* 523–542.

Clore, G. L., Schwarz, N., & Conway, M. (1993). Affective causes and consequences of social information processing. In R. S. Wyer & T. K. Srull (Eds.), *Handbook of social cognition* (2nd ed.). Hilldsale, NJ: Erlbaum.

Clutton-Brock, T. H., O'Riain, M. J., Brotherton, D. N. M., Gaynor, D., Kansky, R., Griffin, A. S., & Manser, M. Selfish sentinels in cooperative mammals. *Science, 284,* 1640–1644.

Cobb, R. J., Davila, J., & Bradbury, T. N. (2001). Attachment security and marital satisfaction: The role of positive perceptions and social support. *Personality and Social Psychology Bulletin, 27,* 1131–1143.

Cohen, D. (1998). Culture, social organization, and patterns of violence. *Journal of Personality and Social Psychology, 75,* 408–419.

Cohen, D., & Nisbett, R. E. (1994). Self-protection and the culture of honor: Explaining southern violence.

Personality and Social Psychology Bulletin, 20, 551–567.

Cohen, D., & Nisbett, R. E. (1997). Field experiments examining the culture of honor: The role of institutions in perpetuating norms about violence. *Personality and Social Psychology Bulletin, 23,* 1188–1199.

Cohen, D., Nisbett, R. E., Bowdle, B. F., & Schwarz, N. (1996). Insult, aggression, and the Southern culture of honor: An "experimental ethnography." *Journal of Personality and Social Psychology, 70,* 945–960.

Cohen, G. L., Aronson, J., & Steele, C. M. (2000). When beliefs yield to evidence: Reducing biased evaluation by affirming the self. *Personality and Social Psychology Bulletin, 26,* 1151–1164.

Cohen, S., Tyrrell, D. A. J., & Smith, A. P. (1993). Negative life events, perceived stress, negative affect, and susceptibility to the common cold. *Journal of Personality and Social Psychology, 64,* 131–140.

Cohen, S., Nisbett, R. E., Bowdle, B. F., & Schwarz, N. (1996). Insult, aggression, and the Southern culture of honor: An "experimental ethnography." *Journal of Personality and Social Psychology, 70,* 945–960.

Cohen, S., Kaplan, J. R., Cunnick, J. E., Manuck, S. B., & Rabin, B. S. (1992). Chronic social stress, affiliation, and cellular immune response in non-human primates. *Psychological Science, 3,* 301–304.

Cohn, E. G., & Rotton, J. (1997). Assault as a function of time and temperature: A moderator-variable time-series analysis. *Journal of Personality and Social Psychology, 72,* 1322–1334.

Coleman, B. C. (1998, February 23). Female doctors face high harassment rate. Associated Press.

Coleman, M., Fine, M. A., Ganong, L. H., Downs, K. J. M., & Pauk, N. (2001). When you're not the Brady Bunch: Identifying perceived conflicts and resolution strategies in stepfamilies. *Personal Relationships, 8,* 55–73.

Coles, R. (1997). *The moral intelligence of children.* New York: Random House.

Collins, M. A., & Zebrowitz, L. A. (1995). The contributions of appearance to occupational outcomes in civilian and military settings. *Journal of Applied Social Psychology, 25,* 129–163.

Collins, N. L. (1996). Working models of attachment: Implications for explanation, emotion, and behavior. *Journal of Personality and Social Psychology, 71,* 810–832.

Collins, N. L., & Feeney, B. C. (2000). A safe haven: An attachment theory perspective on support seeking and caregiving in intimate relationships. *Journal of Personality and Social Psychology, 78,* 1053–1073.

Colvin, C. R., Block, J., & Funder, D. C. (1995). Overly positive self-evaluations and personality: Negative implications for mental health. *Journal of Personality and Social Psychology, 68,* 1152–1162.

Compas, B. E., Banez, G. A., Malcarne, V., & Worsham, N. (1991). Perceived control and coping with stress: A developmental perspective. *Journal of Social Issues, 47*(4), 23–34.

Condon, J. W., & Crano, W. D. (1988). Inferred evaluation and the relation between attitude similarity and interpersonal attraction. *Journal of Personality and Social Psychology, 54,* 789–797.

Conger, J. A. (1991). Inspiring others: The language of leadership. *Academy of Management Executive, 5*(1), 31–45.

Conger, R. D., Rueter, M. A., & Elder, G. H., Jr. (1999). Couple resilience to economic pressure. *Journal of Personality and Social Psychology, 76,* 54–71.

Conner, M. T., & McMillan, B. (1999). Interaction effects in the theory of planned behaviour: Studying cannabis use. *British Journal of Social Psychology, 38,* 195–222.

Connolly, J. A., & Johnson, A. M. (1996). Adolescents' romantic relationships and the structure and quality of their close interpersonal ties. *Personal Relationships, 3,* 185–195.

Constantian, C. (1981). *Solitude, attitudes, beliefs, and behavior in regard to spending time alone.* Unpublished doctoral dissertation, Harvard University.

Contrada, R. J. (1989). Type A behavior, personality hardiness, and cardiovascular responses to stress. *Journal of Personality and Social Psychology, 57,* 895–903.

Contrada, R. J., Ashmore, R. D., Gary, M. L., Coups, E., Egeth, J. D., Sewell, A., Ewell, K., Goyal, T. M., & Chasse, V. (2000). Ethnicity-related sources of stress and their effects on well-being. *Current Directions in Psychological Science, 9,* 136–139.

Conway, M., Giannopoulos, C., Csank, P., & Mendelson, M. (1993). Dysphoria and specificity in self-focused attention. *Personality and Social Psychology Bulletin, 19,* 265–268.

Cook, S. W., & Pelfrey, M. (1985). Reactions to being helped in cooperating interracial groups: A context effect. *Journal of Personality and Social Psychology, 49,* 1231–1245.

Coontz, S. (1992). *The way we never were: American families and the nostalgia trap.* New York: Basic Books.

Cooper, A., Gimeno-Gascon, F. J., & Woo, C. (1994). Initial human and financial capital as predictors of new venture performance. *Journal of Business Venturing, 9,* 371–395.

Cooper, J., & Scher, S. J. (1994). Actions and attitudes: The role of responsibility and aversive consequences in persuasion. In T. Brock & S. Shavitt (Eds.), *Persuasion* (pp. 95–111). San Francisco: Freeman.

Cooper, J., Fazio, R. H., & Rhodewalt, F. (1978). Dissonance and humor: Evidence for the undifferentiated nature of dissonance arousal. *Journal of Personality and Social Psychology, 36,* 280–285.

Cooper, J., Hall, J., & Huff, C. (1990). Situational stress as a consequence of sex-stereotyped software. *Personality and Social Psychology Bulletin, 16,* 419–429.

Cooper, M. L., Shaver, P. R., & Collins, N. L. (1998). Attachment styles, emotion regulation, and adjustment in adolescence. *Journal of Personality and Social Psychology, 74,* 1380–1397.

Cooper, M. L., Frone, M. R., Russell, M., & Mudar, P. (1995). Drinking to regulate positive and negative emotions: A motivational model of alcohol use. *Journal of Personality and Social Psychology, 69,* 990–1005.

Corning, A. F. (2000). Assessing perceived social inequity: A relative deprivation framework. *Journal of Personality and Social Psychology, 78,* 463–477.

Cosmides, L., & Tooby, J. (1992). Cognitive adaptations for social exchange. In J. Barkow, L. Cosmides, & J. Tooby (Eds.), *The adapted mind* (pp. 163–228). New York: Oxford University Press.

Costa, P. T., Jr., Terracciano, A., & McCrae, R. R. (2001). Gender differences in personality traits across cultures: Robust and surprising findings. *Journal of Personality and Social Psychology, 81,* 322–331.

Cota, A. A., Evans, C. R., Dion, K. L., Kilik, L., & Longman, R. S. (1995). The structure of group cohesion. *Personality and Social Psychology Bulletin, 21,* 572–580.

Cotterell, J. (1997, September 1). Where are all the good Samaritans? Albany *Times Union,* A10.

Cottle, M. (2001, January 1 & 8). Sugar and spice: Our shy, retiring female senators. *The New Republic,* 14, 16.

Cottrell, N. B., Wack, K. L., Sekerak, G. J., & Rittle, R. (1968). Social facilitation of dominant responses by the presence of an audience and the mere presence of others. *Journal of Personality and Social Psychology, 9,* 245–250.

Couple repays university for bringing them together. (1997, October 29). *University Update.*

Courneya, K. S., & McAuley, E. (1993). Efficacy, attributional, and affective responses of older adults following an acute bout of exercise. *Journal of Social Behavior and Personality, 8,* 729–742.

Cowei, H. (2000). Bystanding or standing by: Gender issues in coping with bullying in English schools. *Aggressive Behavior, 26,* 85–98.

Cowley, G. (1996, June 3). The biology of beauty. *Newsweek,* 61–66.

Craig, J.-A., Koestner, R., & Zuroff, D. C. (1994). Implicit and self-attributed intimacy motivation. *Journal of Social and Personal Relationships, 11,* 491–507.

Craik, F. I. M., Moroz, T. M., Moscovitch, M., Stuss, D. T., Winocur, G., Tulving, E., & Kapur, S. (1999). In search of the self: A positron emission tomography study. *Psychological Science, 10,* 26–34.

Cramer, R. E., McMaster, M. R., Bartell, P. A., & Dragma, M. (1988). Subject competence and minimization of the bystander effect. *Journal of Applied Social Psychology, 18,* 1133–1148.

Crandall, C. S. (1988). Social contagion of binge eating. *Journal of Personality and Social Psychology, 55,* 588–598.

Crandall, C. S. (1994). Prejudice against fat people: Ideology and self-interest. *Journal of Personality and Social Psychology, 66,* 882–894.

Crandall, C. S. (1995). Do parents discriminate against their heavyweight daughters? *Personality and Social Psychology Bulletin, 21,* 724–735.

Crandall, C. S., & Martinez, R. (1996). Culture, ideology, and anti-fat attitudes. *Personality and Social Psychology Bulletin, 22,* 1165–1176.

Crandall, C. S., D'Anello, S., Sakalli, N., Lazarus, E., Wieczorkowska, G., & Feather, N. T. (2001). An attribution–value model of prejudice: Anti-fat attitudes in six nations. *Personality and Social Psychology Bulletin, 27,* 30–37.

Crano, W. D. (1995). Attitude strength and vested interest. In R. E. Petty & J. A. Krosnick (Eds.), *Attitude strength: Antecedents and consequences* (Vol. 4, pp. 131–157). Hillsdale, NJ: Erlbaum.

Crano, W. D. (1997). Vested interest, symbolic politics, and attitude–behavior consistency. *Journal of Personality and Social Psychology, 72,* 485–491.

Crano, W. D., & Prislin, R. (1995). Components of vested interest and attitude–behavior consistency. *Basic and Applied Social Psychology, 17,* 1–21.

Crelia, R., & Tesser, A. (1996). Attitude heritability and attitude reinforcement: A replication. *Personality and Individual Differences, 21,* 803–808.

Crime and punishment: Time to try another tack? (2001, June 11). *U.S. News & World Report,* 12.

Crime. (2001, June 25). *Time,* 22.

Crites, S. L., Jr., Cacioppo, J. T., Gardner, W. L., & Bernston, G. G. (1995). Bioelectrical echoes from evaluative categorization: II. A late positive brain potential that varies as a function of attitude registration rather than attitude report. *Journal of Personality and Social Psychology, 68,* 997–1013.

Crocker, J. (1993). Memory for information about others: Effects of self-esteem and performance feedback. *Journal of Research in Personality, 27,* 35–48.

Crocker, J., & Major, B. (1993). *When bad things happen to bad people: The perceived justifiability of negative outcomes based on stigma.* Manuscript submitted for publication.

Crocker, J., Cornwell, B., & Major, B. (1993). The stigma of overweight: Affective consequences of attributional ambiguity. *Journal of Personality and Social Psychology, 64,* 60–70.

Crocker, J., Major, B., & Steele, C. (1998). Social stigma. In D. Gilbert, S. T. Fiske, & G. Lindzey (Eds.), *Handbook of social psychology* (4th ed., pp. 504–553). Boston: McGraw-Hill.

Croizet, J. C., & Claire, T. (1998). Extending the concept of stereotype threat to social class: The intellectual underperformance of students from low socioeconomic backgrounds. *Personality and Social Psychology Bulletin, 24,* 588–594.

Cropanzano, R. (Ed.). (1993). *Justice in the workplace* (pp. 79–103). Hillsdale, NJ: Erlbaum.

Cropanzano, R., & James, K. (1990). Some methodological considerations for the behavioral–genetic analysis of work attitudes. *Journal of Applied Psychology, 71,* 433–439.

Crowley, K., Callanan, M. A., Tenenbaum, H. R., & Allen, E. (2001). Parents explain more often to boys than to girls during shared scientific thinking. *Psychological Science, 12,* 258–261.

Crumm, D. (1998, December 11). Keeping the faith may keep mind, body going. Knight Ridder.

Crutchfield, R. A. (1955). Conformity and character. *American Psychologist, 10,* 191–198.

Csikszentmihalyi, M., & LeFevre, J. (1989). Optimal experience in work and leisure. *Journal of Personality and Social Psychology, 56,* 815–822.

Cunningham, J. D., & Antill, J. K. (1994). Cohabitation and marriage: Retrospective and predictive comparisons. *Journal of Social and Personal Relationships, 11,* 77–93.

Cunningham, M. R. (1979). Weather, mood, and helping behavior: Quasi-experiments with the sunshine Samaritan. *Journal of Personality and Social Psychology, 37,* 1947–1956.

Cunningham, M. R. (1986). Measuring the physical in physical attractiveness: Quasi-experiments on the sociobiology of female facial beauty. *Journal of Personality and Social Psychology, 50,* 925–935.

Cunningham, M. R. (1989). Reactions to heterosexual opening gambits: Female selectivity and male responsiveness. *Personality and Social Psychology Bulletin, 15,* 27–41.

Cunningham, M. R., Roberts, A. R., Wu, C.-H., Barbee, A. P., & Druen, P. B. (1995). "Their ideas of beauty are, on the whole, the same as ours": Consistency and variability in the cross-cultural perception of female physical attractiveness. *Journal of Personality and Social Psychology, 68,* 261–279.

Cunningham, M. R., Shaffer, D. R., Barbee, A. P., Wolff, P. L., & Kelley, D. J. (1990). Separate processes in the relation of elation and depression to helping: Social versus personal concerns. *Journal of Experimental Social Psychology, 26,* 13–33.

Cutler, B. L., Moran, G., & Narby, D. J. (1992). Jury selection in insanity defense cases. *Journal of Research in Personality, 26,* 165–182.

Cutler, B. L., Penrod, S. D., & Martens, T. K. (1987). Improving the reliability of eyewitness identification: Putting content into context. *Journal of Applied Psychology, 72,* 629–637.

Cutrona, C. E., Cole, V., Colangelo, N., Assouline, S. G., & Russell, D. W. (1994). Perceived parental social support and academic achievement: An attachment theory perspective. *Journal of Personality and Social Psychology, 66,* 369–378.

Cyranowski, J. M., & Andersen, B. L. (2000). Evidence of self-schematic cognitive processing in women with differing sexual self-views. *Journal of Social and Clinical Psychology, 19,* 519–543.

da Gloria, J., Pahlavan, F., Duda, D., & Bonnet, P. (1994). Evidence for a motor mechniasm of pain-induced aggression instigation in humans. *Aggressive Behavior, 20,* 1–7.

Dabbs, J. M., Jr. (1992). Testosterone measurements in social and clinical psychology. *Journal of Social and Clinical Psychology, 11,* 302–321.

Dabbs, J. M., Jr. (1993). Salivary testosterone measurements in behavioral studies. In D. Malamud & L. A. Tabak (Eds.), *Saliva as a diagnostic fluid* (pp. 177–183). New York: New York Academy of Sciences.

Damasio, A. R. (1994). *Descartes' error: Emotion, reason and the human brain.* New York: Putnam.

Dana, E. R., Lalwani, N., & Duval, S. (1997). Objective self-awareness and focus of attention following awareness of self-standard discrepancies: Changing self or changing standards of correctness. *Journal of Social and Clinical Psychology, 16,* 359–380.

Dane, F. C. (1992). Applying social psychology in the courtroom: Understanding stereotypes in jury decision making. *Contemporary Social Psychology, 16,* 33–36.

Danner, D. D., Snowden, D. A., & Friesen, W. V. (2001). Positive emotions in early life and longevity: Findings from the nun study. *Journal of Personality and Social Psychology, 80,* 804–813.

Darley, J. M. (1991). Altruism and prosocial behavior research: Reflections and prospects. In M. S. Clark (Ed.), *Prosocial behavior* (pp. 312–327). Newbury Park, CA: Sage.

Darley, J. M. (1993). Research on morality: Possible approaches, actual approaches. *Psychological Science, 4,* 353–357.

Darley, J. M. (1995). Constructive and destructive obedience: A taxonomy of principal-agent relationships. *Journal of Social Issues, 125,* 125–154.

Darley, J. M. (2001). Citizens' sense of justice and the legal system. *Current Directions in Psychological Science, 10,* 10–12.

Darley, J. M., & Batson, C. D. (1973). From Jerusalem to Jericho: A study of situational dispositional variables in helping behavior. *Journal of Personality and Social Psychology, 27,* 100–108.

Darley, J. M., & Latané, B. (1968). Bystander intervention in emergencies: Diffusion of responsibility. *Journal of Personality and Social Psychology, 8,* 377–383.

Darwin, C. (1871). *The descent of man.* London: J. Murray.

Dasgupta, N., Banji, M. R., & Abelson, R. P. (1999). Group entiativity and group perception: Association between physical features and psychological judgment. *Journal of Personality and Social Psychology, 75,* 991–1005.

Daubman, K. A. (1993). *The self-threat of receiving help: A comparison of the threat-to-self-esteem model and the theat-to-interpersonal-power model.* Unpublished manuscript, Gettysburg College, Gettysburg, PA.

Daubman, K. A. (1995). Help which implies dependence: Effects on self-evaluations, motivation, and performance. *Journal of Social Behavior and Personality, 10,* 677–692.

Davie, M. R., & Reeves, R. J. (1939). Propinquity of residence before marriage. *American Journal of Sociology, 44,* 510–517.

Davila, J., Burge, D., & Hammen, C. (1997). Why does attachment style change? *Journal of Personality and Social Psychology, 73,* 826–838.

Davis, C., Shuster, B., Dionne, M., & Claridge, G. (2001). Do you see what I see?: Facial attractiveness and weight preoccupation in college women. *Journal of Social and Clinical Psychology, 20,* 147–160.

Davis, C. G., Lehman, D. R., Wortman, C. B., Silver, R. C., & Thompson, S. C. (1995). The undoing of traumatic life events. *Personality and Social Psychology Bulletin, 21,* 109–124.

Davis, J. H. (1989). Psychology and the law: The last 15 years. *Journal of Applied Social Psychology, 19,* 119–230.

Davis, J. L., & Rusbult, C. E. (2001). Attitude alignment in close relationships. *Journal of Personality and Social Psychology, 81,* 65–84.

Davis, M. H., Luce, C., & Kraus, S. J. (1994). The heritability of characteristics associated with dispositional empathy. *Journal of Personality, 62,* 369–391.

Davis, M. H., Morris, M. M., & Kraus, L. A. (1998). Relationship-specific and global perceptions of social support: Associations with well-being and attachment. *Journal of Personality and Social Psychology, 74,* 468–481.

Davis, P. J. (1999). Gender differences in autobiographical memory for childhood emotional experiences. *Journal of Personality and Social Psychology, 76,* 498–510.

Davison, K. P., Pennebaker, J. W., & Dickerson, S. S. (2000). The social psychology of illness support groups. *American Psychologist, 55,* 205–217.

De La Ronde, C., & Swann, W. B., Jr. (1998). Partner verification: Restoring shattered images of our intimates. *Journal of Personality and Social Psychology, 75,* 374–382.

de Waal, F. (1996). *Good natured: The origins of right and wrong in humans and other animals.* Cambridge, MA: Harvard University Press.

Dean-Church, L., & Gilroy, F. D. (1993). Relation of sex-role orientation to life satisfaction in a healthy elderly sample. *Journal of Social Behavior and Personality, 8,* 133–140.

Deaux, K. (1993). Reconstructing social identity. *Personality and Social Psychology Bulletin, 19,* 4–12.

Deaux, K., & Hanna, R. (1984). Courtship in the personals column: The influence of gender and sexual orientation. *Sex Roles, 11,* 363–375.

Deaux, K., Reid, A., Mizrahi, K., & Ethier, K. A. (1995). Parameters of social identity. *Journal of Personality and Social Psychology,* 68, 280–291.

DeBono, K. G., & Snyder, M. (1995). Acting on one's attitudes: The role of a history of choosing situations. *Personality and Social Psychology Bulletin, 21,* 629–636.

DeBruin, E. N., & Van Lange, P. A. M. (2000). What people look for in others: Influences of the perceiver and the perceived on information selection. *Personality and Social Psychology Bulletin, 26,* 206–219.

DeDreu, C. K. W., & McCusker, C. (1997). Gain–loss frames and cooperation in two-person social dilemmas: A transformational analysis. *Journal of Personality and Social Psychology, 72,* 1093–1106.

DeDreu, C. K. W., & Van Lange, P. A. M. (1995). Impact of social value orientation on negotiator cognition and behavior. *Personality and Social Psychology Bulletin, 21,* 1178–1188.

DeJong, W., & Musilli, L. (1982). External pressure to comply: Handicapped versus nonhandicapped requesters and the foot-in-the-door phenomenon. *Personality and Social Psychology Bulletin, 8,* 522–527.

DeLamater, J. (1981). The social control of sexuality. *Annual Review of Sociology, 7,* 263–290.

den Ouden, M. D., & Russell, G. W. (1997). Sympathy and altruism in response to disasters: A Dutch and Canadian comparison. *Social Behavior and Personality, 25,* 241–248.

DePaulo, B. M. (1992). Nonverbal behavior and self-presentation. *Psychological Bulletin, 111,* 203–243.

DePaulo, B. M. (1994). Spotting lies: Can humans learn to do better? *Current Directions in Psychological Science, 3,* 873–886.

DePaulo, B. M., & Bell, K. L. (1996). Truth and investment: Lies are told to those who care. *Journal of Personality and Social Psychology, 71,* 703–716.

DePaulo, B. M., & Fisher, J. D. (1980). The costs of asking for help. *Basic and Applied Social Psychology, 1,* 23–35.

DePaulo, B. M., & Kashy, D. A. (1998). Everyday lies in close and casual relationships. *Journal of Personality and Social Psychology, 74,* 63–79.

DePaulo, B. M., Stone, J. L., & Lassiter, G. D. (1985). Deceiving and detecting deceit. In B. R. Schlenker (Ed.), *The self and social life* (pp. 3230–3370). New York: McGraw-Hill.

DePaulo, B. M., Brown, P. L., Ishii, S., & Fisher, J. D. (1981). Help that works: The effects of aid on subsequent task performance. *Journal of Personality and Social Psychology, 41,* 478–487.

DePaulo, B. M., Dull, W. R., Greenberg, J. M., & Swaim, G. W. (1989). Are shy people reluctant to ask for help? *Journal of Personality and Social Psychology, 56,* 834–844.

DePaulo, B. M., Kashy, D. A., Kirkendol., S. E., Wyer, M. M., & Epstein, J. A. (1996). Lying in everyday life. *Journal of Personality and Social Psychology, 70,* 979–995.

Desmarais, S., & Curtis, J. (1997). Gender and perceived pay entitlement: Testing for effects of experience with income. *Journal of Personality and Social Psychology, 72,* 141–150.

Deutsch, F. M. (2001). Equally shared parenting. *Current Directions in Psychological Science, 10,* 25–28.

Deutsch, F. M., & Lamberti, D. M. (1986). Does social approval increase helping? *Personality and Social Psychology Bulletin, 12,* 149–157.

Deutsch, F. M., Zalenski, C. M., & Clark, M. E. (1986). Is there a double standard of aging? *Journal of Applied Social Psychology, 16,* 771–785.

Deutsch, M., & Gerard, H. B. (1955). A study of normative and informational social influences upon individual judgment. *Journal of Abnormal and Social Psychology, 51,* 629–636.

Deutsch, M., & Krauss, R. M. (1960). The effect of threat upon interpersonal bargaining. *Journal of Abnormal and Social Psychology, 61,* 181–189.

Devine, P. G. (1989). Automatic and controlled processes in prejudice: The role of stereotypes and personal beliefs. In A. R. Pratkanis, S. J. Brcekler, & A. G. Greenwalr (Eds.), *Attitude structure and function* (pp. 181–212). Hillsdale, NJ: Erlbaum.

Dickinson, A. (1999, November 8). Teenage sex. *Time,* 160.

Diehl, M., Elnick, A. B., Bourbeau, L. S., & Labouvie-Vief, G. (1998). Adult attachment styles: Their relations to family context and personality. *Journal of Personality and Social Psychology, 74,* 1656–1669.

Diekman, A. B., & Eagly, A. H. (2000). Stereotypes as dynamic constructs: Women and men of the past, present, and future. *Personality and Social Psychology Bulletin, 26,* 1171–1188.

Diekmann, K. A., Samuels, S. M., Ross, L., & Bazerman, M. H. (1997). Self-interest and fairness in problems of response allocation: Allocators versus recipients. *Journal of Personality and Social Psychology, 72,* 1061–1074.

Diener, E., Wolsic, B., & Fujita, F. (1995). Physical attractiveness and subjective well-being. *Journal of Personality and Social Psychology, 69,* 120–129.

Dietrich, D. M., & Berkowitz, L. (1997). Alleviation of dissonance by engaging in prosocial behavior or receiving ego-enhancing feedback. *Journal of Social Behavior and Personality, 12,* 557–566.

Dijksterhuis, A., & van Knippenberg, A. (1996). The knife that cuts both ways: Facilitated and inhibited access to traits as a result of stereotype-activation. *Journal of Experimental Social Psychology, 32,* 271–288.

Dijkstra, P., & Buunk, B. P. (1998). Jealousy as a function of rival characteristics: An evolutionary perspective. *Personality and Social Psychology Bulletin, 24,* 1158–1166.

Dion, K. K., & Dion, K. L. (1991). Psychological individualism and romantic love. *Journal of Social Behavior and Personality, 6,* 17–33.

Dion, K. K., Berscheid, E., & Hatfield (Walster), E. (1972). What is beautiful is good. *Journal of Personality and Social Psychology, 24,* 285–290.

Dion, K. K., Pak, A. W.-P., & Dion, K. I. (1990). Stereotyping physical attractiveness: A sociocultural perspective. *Journal of Cross-Cultural Psychology, 21,* 158–179.

Dion, K. L., & Dion, K. K. (1987). Belief in a just world and physical attractiveness stereotyping. *Journal of Personality and Social Psychology, 52,* 775–780.

Dion, K. L., Dion, K. K., & Keelan, J. P. (1990). Appearance anxiety as a dimension of social-evaluative anxiety: Exploring the ugly duckling syndrome. *Contemporary Social Psychology, 14,* 220–224.

Dodge, K. A., & Coie, J. D. (1987). Social-information-processing factors in reactive and proactive aggression in children's peer groups. *Journal of Personality and Social Psychology, 53,* 1146–1158.

Dodge, K. A., Pettit, G. S., McClaskey, C. L., & Brown, M. M. (1986). Social competence in children. *Monographs of the Society for Research in Child Development, 51*(2), 1–85.

Dodgson, P. G., & Wood, J. V. (1998). Self-esteem and the cognitive accessibility of strengths and weaknesses after failure. *Journal of Personality and Social Psychology, 75,* 178–197.

Doherty, K., Weigold, M. F., & Schlenker, B. R. (1990). Self-serving interpretations of motives. *Personality and Social Psychology Bulletin, 16,* 485–495.

Dollard, J., Doob, L., Miller, N., Mowerer, O. H., & Sears, R. R. (1939). *Frustration and aggression.* New Haven, CT: Yale University Press.

Donnerstein, E., & Donnerstein, M. (1976). Research in the control of interracial aggression. In R. G. Geen & E. C. O'Neal (Eds.), *Perspectives on aggression.* New York: Academic Press.

Dorian, B. J., Keystone, E., Garfinkel, P. E., & Brown, J. M. (1982). Aberrations in lymphocyte subpopulations and function during psychological stress. *Clinical and Experimental Immunology, 50,* 132–138.

Dovidio, J., & Fazio, R. (1991). New technologies for the direct and indirect assessment of attitudes. In N. J. Tanur (Ed.), *Questions about survey questions: Meaning, memory, attitudes, and social interaction* (pp. 204–237). New York: Russell Sage.

Dovidio, J., Kawakami, K., Johnson, C., Johnson, B., & Howard, A. (1997). On the nature of prejudice: Automatic and controlled processes. *Journal of Experimental Social Psychology, 33,* 510–540.

Dovidio, J. F., & Gaertner, S. L. (1993). Stereotype and evaluative intergroup bias. In D. M. Mackie & D. L. Hamilton (Eds.), *Affect, cognition, and stereotyping: Interactive processes in group perception.* Orlando, FL: Academic Press.

Dovidio, J. F., & Morris, W. N. (1975). Effects of stress and commonality of fate on helping behavior. *Journal of Personality and Social Psychology, 31,* 145–149.

Dovidio, J. F., Evans, N., & Tyler, R. B. (1986). Racial stereotypes: The contents of their cognitive representations. *Journal of Experimental Social Psychology, 22,* 22–37.

Dovidio, J. F., Brigham, J., Johnson, B. & Gaertner, S. (1996). Stereotyping, prejudice, and discrimination: Another look. In N. Macrae, C. Stangor, & M. Hwestone (Eds.), *Stereotypes and stereotyping* (pp. 1276–1319). New York: Guilford.

Dovidio, J. F., Gaertner, S. L., Isen, A. M., & Lowrance, R. (1995). Group representations and intergroup bias: Positive affect, similarity, and group size. *Personality and Social Psychology Bulletin, 21,* 856–865.

Downey, J. L., & Damhave, K. W. (1991). The effects of place, type of comment, and effort expended on the perception of flirtation. *Journal of Social Behavior and Personality, 6,* 35–43.

Downs, A. C., & Lyons, P. M. (1991). Natural observations of the links between attractiveness and initial legal judgments. *Personality and Social Psychology Bulletin, 17,* 541–547.

Drake, R. A., & Myers, L. R. (2001, in press). Visual perception and emotion: Relative rightward attention predicts positive arousal. *Cognitive Brain Research.*

Dreznick, M. T. (2001). *The reasons that women and men engage in extrarelational sex: A meta-analysis.* Unpublished manuscript, University at Albany, State University of New York.

Drigotas, S. M., & Rusbult, C. E. (1992). Should I stay or should I go? A dependence model of breakups. *Journal of Personality and Social Psychology, 62,* 62–87.

Drigotas, S. M., Rusbult, C. E., Wieselquist, J., & Whitton, S. W. (1999). Close partner as sculptor of the idea self: Behavioral affirmation and the Michelangelo phenomenon. *Journal of Personality and Social Psychology, 77,* 293–323.

Driscoll, R., Davis, K. E., & Lipetz, M. E. (1972). Parental interference and romantic love: The Romeo and Juliet effect. *Journal of Personality and Social Psychology, 24,* 1–10.

Drivers indifferent to victim on road. (1998, April 22). *Washington Post.*

Drout, C. E., & Gaertner, S. L. (1994). Gender differences in reactions to female victims. *Social Behavior and Personality, 22,* 267–278.

Duan, C. (2000). Being empathic: The role of motivation to empathize and the nature of target emotions. *Motivation and Emotion, 24,* 29–49.

Dubois, D. L., & Tevendale, H. D. (1999). Self-esteem in childhood and adolescence: Vaccine or epiphenomenon? *Applied and Preventive Psychology, 8,* 103–117.

DuBreuil, S. C., Garry, M., & Loftus, E. F. (1998). Tales from the crib. In S. J. Lynn & K. M. McConkey (Eds.), *Truth in memory.* New York: Guilford.

Duck, J. M., Terry, D. J., & Hogg, M. A. (1998). Perceptions of a media campaign: The role of social identity and the changing intergroup context. *Personality and Social Psychology Bulletin, 24,* 3–16.

Duck, S., & Barnes, M. K. (1992). Disagreeing about agreement: Reconciling differences about similarity. *Communication Monographs, 59,* 199–208.

Duck, S., Pond, K., & Leatham, G. (1994). Loneliness and the evaluation of relational events. *Journal of Social and Personal Relationships, 11,* 253–276.

Duckitt, J., & Mphuthing, T. (1993). Group identification and intergroup attitudes: A longitudinal analysis in South Africa. *Journal of Personality and Social Psychology, 74,* 80–85.

Duggan, E. S., & Brennan, K. A. (1994). Social avoidance and its relation to Bartholomew's adult attachment typology. *Journal of Social and Personal Relationships, 11,* 147–153.

Dunn, J. (1992). Siblings and development. *Current Directions in Psychological Science, 1,* 6–11.

Dunning, D., & Sherman, D. A. (1997). Stereotypes and tacit inference. *Journal of Personality and Social Psychology, 73,* 459–471.

Dunning, D., & Stern, L. B. (1994). Distinguishing accurate from inaccurate eyewitness identification via inquiries about decision processes. *Journal of Personality and Social Psychology, 67,* 818–835.

Dutton, D. G., & Aron, A. P. (1974). Some evidence for heightened sexual attraction under conditions of high anxiety. *Journal of Personality and Social Psychology, 30,* 510–517.

Dutton, D. G., & Lake, R. A. (1973). Threat of own prejudice and reverse discrimination in interracial situations. *Journal of Personality and Social Psychology, 28,* 94–100.

Dye, M. R. (2001). *Adult attachment style, similarity of general attitudes, and similarity of attachment-relevant attitudes as determinants of attraction.* Unpublished masters thesis, University at Albany, State University of New York.

Dykema, J., Bergbower, K., & Peterson, C. (1995). Pessimistic explanatory style, stress, and illness. *Journal of Social and Clinical Psychology, 14,* 357–371.

Eagly, A. H. (1995). The science and politics of comparing women and men. *American Psychologist, 50,* 145–158.

Eagly, A. H., & Chaiken, S. (1998). Attitude structure and function. In G. Lindsey, S. T., Fiske, & D. T. Gilbert (Eds.), *Handbook of social psychology* (4th ed.). New York: Oxford University Press and McGraw-Hill.

Eagly, A. H., & Mladinic, A. (1994). Are people prejudiced against women? Some answers from research on attitudes, gender stereotypes, and judgments of competence. In W. Sroebe & M. Hewstone (Eds.), *European review of social psychology* (Vol. 5, pp. 1–35). New York: Wiley.

Eagly, A. H., & Wood, W. (1999). The origins of sex differences in human behavior: Evolved dispositions versus social roles. *American Psychologist, 54,* 408–423.

Eagly, A. H., Makhijani, M. G., & Klonsky, B. G. (1992). Gender and the evaluation of leaders: A meta-analysis. *Psychological Bulletin, 111,* 3–22.

Eagly, A. H., Wood, W., & Chaiken, S. (1996). Principles of persuasion. In E. T. Higgins & A. W. Kruglanski (Eds.), *Social psychology: Handbook of basic principles* (pp. 702–742). New York: Guilford.

Eagly, A. H., Chen, S., Chaiken, S., & Shaw-Barnes, K. (1999). The impact of attitudes on memory: An affair to remember. *Psychological Bulletin, 124,* 64–89.

Eagly, A. H., Kulesa, P., Brannon, L. A., Shaw, K., & Hutson-Comeaux, S. (2000). Why counterattitudinal messages are as memorable as proattitudinal messages: The importance of active defense against attack. *Personality and Social Psychology Bulletin, 26,* 1392–1408.

Earley, P. C. (1993). East meets West meets Mideast: Further explorations of collectivistic and individualistic work groups. *Academy of Management Journal, 36,* 319–348.

Easterbrook, G. (1999, January 4 and 11). America the O.K. *The New Republic,* pp. 19–25.

Education. (2001, August 6). *U.S. News & World Report,* 17.

Edwards, K., & Bryan, T. S. (1997). Judgmental biases produced by instructions to disregard: The (paradoxical) case of emotional information. *Personality and Social Psychology Bulletin, 23,* 849–864.

Edwards, K., Heindel, W., & Louis-Dreyfus, E. (1996). *Directed forgetting of emotional and non-emotional words: Implications for implicit and explicit memory processes.* Manuscript submitted for publication.

Edwards, T. M. (2000, August 28). Flying solo. *Time,* 46–52.

Effects of a dissolved workplace romance and rater characteristics of responses to a sexual harassment accusation. *Academy of Management Journal, 43,* 869–880.

Efran, M. G., & Patterson, E. W. J. (1974). Voters vote beautiful: The effect of physical appearance on a national election. *Canadian Journal of Behavioral Science, 6,* 352–356.

Eich, E. (1995). Searching for mood dependent memory. *Psychological Science, 6,* 67–75.

Eisenman, R. (1985). Marijuana use and attraction: Support for Byrne's similarity-attraction concept. *Perceptual and Motor Skills, 61,* 582.

Eisenstadt, D., & Leippe, M. R. (1994). The self-comparison process and self-discrepant feedback: Consequences of learning you are what you thought you were not. *Journal of Personality and Social Psychology, 67,* 611–626.

Ekman, P. A. (1985). *Telling lies.* New York: Norton.

Ekman, P. (1992). Are there basic emotions? *Psychology Review, 99,* 550–553.

Ekman, P., & Friesen, W. V. (1975). *Unmasking the face.* Englewood Cliffs, NJ: Prentice-Hall.

Ekman, P., & Heider, K. (1988). The universality of a contempt expression: A replication. *Motivation and Emotion, 12,* 303–308.

Elkin, R., & Leippe, M. (1986). Physiological arousal, dissonance, and attitude change: Evidence for a dissonance–arousal link and "don't remind me" effect. *Journal of Personality and Social Psychology, 51,* 55–65.

Elliot, A. J., & Devine, P. G. (1994). On the motivational nature of cognitive dissonance: Dissonance as psychological discomfort. *Journal of Personality and Social Psychology, 67,* 382–394.

Elliot, A. J., & Sheldon, K. M. (1998). Avoidance personal goals and the personality-illness relationship. *Journal of Personality and Social Psychology, 75,* 1282–1299.

Ellsworth, P. C., & Carlsmith, J. M. (1973). Eye contact and gaze aversion in aggressive encounter. *Journal of Personality and Social Psychology, 33,* 117–122.

Endo, Y., Heine, S. J., & Lehman, D. R. (2000). Culture and positive illusions in close relationships: How my relationships are better than yours. *Personality and Social Psychology Bulletin, 26,* 1571–1586.

Epley, N., & Dunning, D. (2000). Feeling "holier than thou": Are self-serving assessments produced by errors in self- or social prediction? *Journal of Personality and Social Psychology, 79,* 861–875.

Epley, N., & Huff, C. (1998). Suspicion, affective response, and educational benefit as a result of deception in psychology research. *Personality and Social Psychology Bulletin, 24,* 759–768.

Estrada, C. A., Isen, A. M., & Young, M. J. (1995). Positive affect improves creative problem solving and influences reported source of practice satisfaction in physicians. *Motivation and Emotion, 18,* 285–300.

Etcoff, N. (1999). *Survival of the prettiest: The science of beauty.* New York: Doubleday.

Ethier, K. A., & Deaux, K. (1994). Negotiating social identity when contexts change: Maintaining identification and responding to threat. *Journal of Personality and Social Psychology, 67,* 243–251.

Evans, G. W., Bullinger, M., & Hygge, S. (1998). Chronic noise exposure and physiological response: A prospective study of children living under environmental stress. *Psychological Science, 9,* 75–77.

Evans, G. W., Lepore, S. J., & Schroeder, A. (1996). The role of interior design elements in human responses to crowding. *Journal of Personality and Social Psychology, 70,* 41–46.

Exline, R. (1962). Need affiliation and initial communication behavior in problem-solving groups characterized by low interpersonal visibility. *Psychological Reports, 10,* 79–89.

Fabes, R. A., & Eisenberg, N. (1997). Regulatory control and adults' stress-related responses to daily life events. *Journal of Personality and Social Psychology, 73,* 1107–1117.

Fabrigar, L. R., & Krosnick, J. A. (1995). Attitude importance and the false consensus effect. *Personality and Social Psychology Bulletin, 21,* 468–479.

Falk, D. (2000). Careers in science offer women an unusual bonus: Immortality. *Nature, 407,* 833–834.

Fan, C., & Mak, A. S. (1998). Measuring social self-efficacy in a culturally diverse student population. *Social Behavior and Personality, 26,* 131–144.

Fang, B. (2001, September 3). On the trail of a killer. *U.S. News & World Report,* 22–26.

Farnsworth, C. H. (1995, June 4). Canada puts different spin on sensational murder trial. *Albany Times Union,* pp. E-8.

Farwell, L., & Weiner, B. (2000). Bleeding hearts and the heartless: Popular perceptions of liberal and conservative ideologies. *Personality and Social Psychology Bulletin, 26,* 845–852.

Faulkner, S. J., & Williams, K. D. (1999, April). *After the whistle is blown: The aversive impact of ostracism.* Paper presented at the meeting of the Midwestern Psychological Association, Chicago.

Fazio, R. H. (1989). On the power and functionality of attitudes: The role of attitude accessibility. In A. R. Pratkanis, S. J. Breckler, & A. G. Greenwald (Eds.), *Attitude structure and function* (pp. 153–179). Hillsdale, NJ: Erlbaum.

Fazio, R. H., & Hilden, L. E. (2001). Emotional reactions to a seemingly prejudiced response: The role of automatically activated racial attitudes and motivation to control prejudiced reactions. *Personality and Social Psychology Bulletin, 27,* 538–549.

Fazio, R. H., & Powell, M. C. (1997). On the value of knowing one's likes and dislikes: Attitude accessibility, stress, and health in college. *Psychological Science, 8,* 430–436.

Fazio, R. H., & Roskos-Ewoldsen, D. R. (1994). Acting as we feel: When and how attitudes guide behavior. In S. Shavitt & T. C. Brock (Eds.), *Persuasion* (pp. 71–93). Boston: Allyn and Bacon.

Fazio, R. H., & Towles-Schwen, T. (1999). The MODE model of attitude–behavior processes. In S. Chaiken & Y. Trope (Eds.), *Dual process theories in social psychology* (pp. 97–116). New York: Guilford.

Fazio, R., Jackson, J., Dunton, B., & Williams, C. (1995). Variability in automatic activation as an unobtrusive measure of racial attitudes: A bona fide pipeline. *Journal of Personality and Social Psychology, 69,* 1013–1028.

Feather, N. T. (1996). Reactions to penalties for an offense in relation to authoritarianism, values, perceived responsibility, perceived seriousness, and deservingness. *Journal of Personality and Social Psychology, 71,* 571–587.

Feeney, J. A., & Hohaus, L. (2001). Attachment and spousal caregiving. *Personal Relationships, 8,* 21–39.

Fehr, B. (1999). Laypeople's conceptions of commitment. *Journal of Personality and Social Psychology, 76,* 90–103.

Fehr, B., & Broughton, R. (2001). Gender and personality differences in conceptions of love: An interpersonal theory analysis. *Personal Relationships, 8,* 115–136.

Fehr, B., Baldwin, M., Collins, L., Patterson, S., & Benditt, R. (1999). Anger in close relationships: An interpersonal script analysis. *Personality and Social Psychology Bulletin, 25,* 299–312.

Fein, S., & Spencer, S. J. (1997). Prejudice as self-image maintenance: Affirming the self through derogating others. *Journal of Personality and Social Psychology, 73,* 31–44.

Fein, S., McCloskey, A. L., & Tomlinson, T. M. (1997). Can the jury disregard that information? The use of suspicion to reduce the prejudicial effects of pretrial publicity and inadmissible testimony. *Personality and Social Psychology Bulletin, 23,* 1215–1226.

Feingold, A. (1990). Gender differences in effects of physical attractiveness on romantic attraction: A comparison across five research paradigms. *Journal of Personality and Social Psychology, 59,* 981–993.

Feingold, A. (1992). Good-looking people are not what we think. *Psychological Bulletin, 111,* 304–341.

Feingold, A. (1994). Gender differences in personality: A meta-analysis. *Psychological Bulletin, 116,* 412–456.

Feingold, A., & Mazzella, R. (1998). Gender differences in body image are increasing. *Psychological Science, 9,* 190–195.

Feldman, S. S., & Nash, S. C. (1984). The transition from expectancy to parenthood: Impact of the firstborn child on men and women. *Sex Roles, 11,* 61–78.

Felmlee, D. H. (1995). Fatal attractions: Affection and disaffection in intimate relationships. *Journal of Social and Personal Relationships, 12,* 295–311.

Felmlee, D. H. (1998). "Be careful what you wish for . . . ": A quantitative and qualitative investigation of "fatal attractions." *Personal Relationships, 5,* 235–253.

Fenigstein, A., & Abrams, D. (1993). Self-attention and the egocentric assumption of shared perspectives. *Journal of Experimental Social Psychology, 29,* 287–303.

Feshbach, S. (1984). The catharsis hypothesis, aggressive drive, and the reduction of aggression. *Aggressive Behavior, 10,* 91–101.

Festinger, L. (1950). Informal social communication. *Psychological Review, 57,* 271–282.

Festinger, L. (1954). A theory of social comparison processes. *Human Relations, 7,* 117–140.

Festinger, L. (1957). *A theory of cognitive dissonance.* Evanston, IL: Row, Peterson.

Festinger, L., & Carlsmith, J. M. (1959). Cognitive consequences of forced compliance. *Journal of Abnormal and Social Psychology, 58,* 203–210.

Festinger, L., Schachter, S., & Back, K. (1950). *Social pressures in informal groups: A study of a housing community.* New York: Harper.

Fichten, C. S., & Amsel, R. (1986). Trait attributions about college students with a physical disability: Circumplex analyses and methodological issues. *Journal of Applied Social Psychology, 16,* 410–427.

Finkel, E. J., & Campbell, W. K. (2001). Self-control and accommodation in close relationships: An interdependence analysis. *Journal of Personality and Social Psychology, 81,* 263–277.

Finn, J. (1986). The relationship between sex role attitudes and attitudes supporting marital violence. *Sex Roles, 14,* 235–244.

Fischman, J. (1986, January). Women and divorce: Ten years after. *Psychology Today,* 15.

Fischman, J. (2001, June 25). Facing down a killer disease. *U.S. News & World Report,* 58–61, 64–65, 67.

Fisher, A. B. (1992, September 21). When will women get to the top? *Fortune,* pp. 44–56.

Fisher, H. (1992). *Anatomy of love.* New York: Norton.

Fisher, J. D., & Byrne, D. (1975). Too close for comfort: Sex differences in response to invasions of personal space. *Journal of Personality and Social Psychology, 32,* 15–21.

Fisher, J. D., Nadler, A., & Whitcher-Alagna, S. (1982). Recipient reactions to aid. *Psychological Bulletin, 91,* 27–54.

Fisher, W. A., & Barak, A. (1991). Pornography, erotica, and behavior: Most questions than answers. *International Journal of Love and Psychiatry, 14,* 65–83.

Fiske, A. P. (1991). The cultural relativity of selfish individualism: Anthropological evidence that humans are inherently sociable. In M. S. Clark (Ed.), *Prosocial behavior* (pp. 176–214), Newbury Park, CA: Sage.

Fiske, S., & Neuberg, S. (1990). A continuum of impression formation from category-based to individuating processes. In M. Zanna (Ed.), *Advances in experimental social psychology* (Vol. 23, pp. 1–73). San Diego: Academic Press.

Fiske, S. T. (1993). Social cognition and social perception. In L. W. Porter & M. R. Rosenzweig (Eds.), *Annual Review of Psychology, 44,* 155–194.

Fiske, S. T., & Taylor, S. E. (1991). *Social cognition.* New York: McGraw-Hill.

Fiske, S. T., Lin, M. H., & Neuberg, S. L. (1999). The continuum model: Ten years later. In S. Chaiken & Y. Trope (Eds.), *Dual process theories in social psychology* (pp. 231–254). New York: Guilford.

Fitzgerald, J. (1996, September 11). A hero leaps from bridge into breach. *Albany Times Union,* p. B2.

Fletcher, G. J. O., & Simpson, J. A. (2000). Ideal standards in close relationships: Their structure and functions. *Current Directions in Psychological Science, 9,* 102–105.

Fletcher, G. J. O., Simpson, J. A., & Thomas, G. (2000). Ideals, perceptions, and evaluations in early relationship development. *Journal of Personality and Social Psychology, 79,* 933–940.

Fletcher, G. J. O., Simpson, J. A., Thomas, G., & Giles, L. (1999). Ideals in intimate relationships. *Journal of Personality and Social Psychology, 76,* 72–89.

Flory, J. D., Raikkonen, K., Matthews, K. A., & Owens, J. F. (2000). Self-focused attention and mood during everyday social interactions. *Personality and Social Psychology Bulletin, 26,* 875–883.

Floyd, K. (1996). Brotherly love I: The experience of closeness in the fraternal dyad. *Personal Relationships, 3,* 369–385.

Folger, R., & Baron, R. A. (1996). Violence and hostility at work: A model of reactions to perceived injustice. In G. R. VandenBos and E. Q. Bulato (Eds.), *Violence on the job: Identifying risks and developing solutions* (pp. 51–85). Washington, DC: American Psychological Association.

Folger, R., Robinson, S. L., Dietz, J., McLean Parks, J., & Baron, R. A. (in press). Aggression in organizations: The impact of societal violence and organizational unjustice on workplace assaults and threats. *Academy of Management Journal.*

Folkman, S., & Moskowitz, J. T. (2000a). Positive affect and the other side of coping. *American Psychologist, 55,* 647–654.

Folkman, S., & Moskowitz, J. T. (2000b). Stress, positive emotions, and coping. *Current Directions in Psychological Science, 9,* 115–118.

Foltz, C., Barber, J. P., Weinryb, R. M., Morse, J. Q., & Chittams, J. (1999). Consistency of themes across interpersonal relationships. *Journal of Social and Clinical Psychology, 18,* 204–222.

Folwell, A. L., Chung, L. C., Nussbaum, J. F., Bethes, L. S., & Grant, J. A. (1997). Differential accounts of closeness in older adult sibling relationships. *Journal of Social and Personal Relationships, 14,* 843–849.

Ford, R., & Blegen, M. (1992). Offensive and defensive use of punitive tactics in explicit bargaining. *Social Psychology Quarterly, 55,* 351–362.

Forgas, J. P. (1995a). Mood and judgment: The affect infusion model (AIM). *Psychological Bulletin, 117,* 39–66.

Forgas, J. P. (1995b). Strange couples: Mood effects on judgments and memory about prototypical and atypical targets. *Personality and Social Psychology Bulletin, 21,* 747–765.

Forgas, J. P. (1998a). Asking nicely? The effects of mood on responding to more or less polite requests. *Personality and Social Psychology Bulletin, 24,* 173–185.

Forgas, J. P., & Fiedler, K. (1996). Us and them: Mood effects on intergroup discrimination. *Journal of Personality and Social Psychology, 70,* 28–40.

Forge, K. L., & Phemister, S. (1987). The effect of prosocial cartoons on preschool children. *Child Study Journal, 17,* 83–88.

Forrest, J. A., & Feldman, R. S. (2000). Detecting deception and judge's involvement; lower task involvement leads to better lit detection. *Personality and Social Psychology Bulletin, 26,* 118–125.

Foster, C. A., Witcher, B. S., Campbell, W. K., & Green, J. D. (1998). Arousal and attraction: Evidence for automatic and controlled processes. *Journal of Personality and Social Psychology, 74,* 86–101.

Fowers, B., Lyons, E., Montel, K., & Shaked, N. (2001). Positive illusions about marriage among married and single individuals. *Journal of Family Psychology,* 95–109.

Foxhall, K. (2000, January). Suddenly, a big impact on criminal justice. *Monitor on Psychology,* 36–37.

Foxhall, K. (2001, March). Study finds marital stress can triple women's risk of recurrent coronary event. *Monitor on Psychology,* 14.

Frable, D. E. S. (1993). Dimensions of marginality: Distinctions among those who are different. *Personality and Social Psychology Bulletin, 19,* 370–380.

Fraley, R. C., & Shaver, P. R. (1998). Airport separations: A naturalistic study of adult attachment dynamics in separating couples. *Journal of Personality and Social Psychology, 75,* 1198–1212.

Fraley, R. C., Garner, J. P., & Shaver, P. R. (2000). Adult attachment and the defensive regulation of attention and memory: Examining the role of preemptive and postemptive defensive processes. *Journal of Personality and Social Psychology, 79,* 816–826.

Francis, L., Monahan, K., & Berger, C. (1999). A laughing matter? The uses of humor in medical interaction. *Motivation and Emotion, 23,* 155–174.

Frazier, P. A., Tix, A. P., Klein, C. D., & Arikian, N. J. (2000). Testing theoretical models of the relations between social support, coping, and adjustments to stressful life events. *Journal of Social and Clinical Psychology, 19,* 314–335.

Frazier, P. A., Byer, A. L., Fischer, A. R., Wright, D. M., & DeBord, K. A. (1996). Adult attachment style and partner choice: Correlational and experimental findings. *Personal Relationships, 3,* 117–136.

Fredrickson, B. L. (1995). Socioemotional behavior at the end of college life. *Journal of Social and Personal Relationships, 12,* 261–276.

Fredrickson, B. L., & Roberts, T. A. (1997). Objectification theory: Toward understanding women's lived experiences and mental health risks. *Psychology of Women Quarterly, 21,* 173–206.

Fredrickson, B. L., Roberts, T. A., Noll, S. M., Quinn, D. M., & Twenge, J. M. (1998). That swimsuit becomes you: Sex differences in self-objectification, restrained eating, and math performance. *Journal of Personality and Social Psychology, 75,* 269–284.

Frey, D., Schulz-Hardt, S., & Stahlberg, D. (1996). Information seeking among individuals and groups and possible consequences for decision making in business and politics. In E. Witte & J. H. Davis (Eds.), *Understanding group behavior: Small group processes and interpersonal relation* (Vol. 2, pp. 211–225). Mahwah, NJ: Lawrence Erlbaum.

Freeberg, A. L., & Stein, C. H. (1996). Felt obligation towards parents in Mexican–American and Anglo–American young adults. *Journal of Social and Personal Relationships, 13,* 457–471.

Freedman, J. L., & Fraser, S. C. (1966). Compliance without pressure: The foot-in-the-door technique. *Journal of Personality and Social Psychology, 4,* 195–202.

Fricko, M. A. M., & Beehr, T. A. (1992). A longitudinal investigation of interest congruence and gender concentration as predictors of job satisfaction. *Personnel Psychology, 45,* 99–117.

Fried, C. B., & Aronson, E. (1995). Hypocrisy, misattribution, and dissonance reduction. *Personality and Social Psychology Bulletin, 21,* 925–933.

Friedman, H. S., Hawley, P. H., & Tucker, J. S. (1994). Personality, health, and longevity. *Current Directions in Psychological Science, 3,* 37–41.

Friedman, H. S., Riggio, R. E., & Casella, D. F. (1988). Nonverbal skill, personal charisma, and initial attraction. *Personality and Social Psychology Bulletin, 14,* 203–211.

Friedman, H. S., Tucker, J. S., Schwartz, J. E., Martin, L. R., Tomlinson-Keasey, C., Wingard, D. L., & Criqui, M. H. (1995a). Childhood conscientiousness and longevity: Health behaviors and cause of death. *Journal of Personality and Social Psychology, 68,* 696–703.

Fritzsche, B. A., Finkelstein, M. A., & Penner, L. A. (2000). To help or not to help: Capturing individuals' decision policies. *Social Behavior and Personality, 28,* 561–578.

Froming, W. J., Nasby, W., & McManus, J. (1998). Prosocial self-schemas, self-awareness, and children's prosocial behavior. *Journal of Personality and Social Psychology, 75,* 766–777.

Fry, D. P. (1998). Anthropological perspectives on aggression: Sex differences and cultural variation. *Aggressive Behavior, 24,* 81–95.

Fultz, J., Shaller, M., & Cialdini, R. B. (1988). Empathy, sadness, and distress: Three related but distant vicarious affective responses to another's suffering. *Personality and Social Psychology Bulletin, 14,* 312–325.

Furnham, A., & Rawles, R. (1995). Sex differences in the estimation of intelligence. *Journal of Social Behavior and Personality, 10,* 741–748.

Furr, R. M., & Funder, D. C. (1998). A multimodal analysis of personal negativity. *Journal of Personality and Social Psychology, 74,* 1580–1591.

Gable, S. L., Reis, H. T., & Elliot, A. J. (2000). Behavioral activation and inhibition in everyday life. *Journal of Personality and Social Psychology, 78,* 1135–1149.

Gabriel, M. T., Critelli, J. W., & Ee, J. S. (1994). Narcissistic illusions in self-evaluations of intelligence and attractiveness. *Journal of Personality, 62,* 143–155.

Gaertner, L., Sedikides, C., & Graetz, K. (1999). In search of self-definition: Motivational primacy of the individual self, motivational primacy of the collective self, or contextual primacy? *Journal of Personality and Social Psychology, 76,* 5–18.

Gaertner, S. L., Mann, J., Murrell, A., & Dovidio, J. F. (1989). Reducing intergroup bias: The benefits of recategorization. *Journal of Personality and Social Psychology, 57,* 239–249.

Gaertner, S. L., Dovidio, J. F., Anastasio, P. A., Bachman, B. A., & Rust, M. C. (1993b). The common ingroup identity model: Recategorization and the reduction of intergroup bias. In W. Stroebe & H. Hewstone (Eds.), *European Review of Social Psychology, 4,* 1–26.

Gaertner, S. L., Mann, J. A., Dovidio, J. F., Murrell, A. J., & Pomare, M. (1990). How does cooperation reduce intergroup bias? *Journal of Personality and Social Psychology, 59,* 692–704.

Gaertner, S. L., Rust, M. C., Dovidio, J. F., Bachman, B. A., & Anastasio, P. A. (1993b). The contact hypothesis: The role of a common ingroup identity on reducing intergroup bias. *Small Groups Research, 25*(2), 224–249.

Galambos, N. L. (1992). Parent–adolescent relations. *Current Directions in Psychological Science, 1,* 146–149.

Gall, T. L., Evans, D. R., & Bellerose, S. (2000). Transition to first-year university: Patterns of change in adjustment across life domains and time. *Journal of Social and Clinical Psychology, 19,* 544–567.

Gallo, J., & Byrne, D. (2001). *May–December romances in the movies: A cultural influence or a reflection of biological determinants?* Unpublished manuscript, University at Albany, SUNY.

Gallup, G. G. (1994). Monkeys, mirrors, and minds. *Behavioral and Brain Sciences, 17,* 572–573.

Galton, F. (1952). *Hereditary genius: An inquiry into its laws and consequences.* New York: Horizon. (Original work published 1870.)

Gamble, W. C., & Dalla, R. L. (1997). Young children's perceptions of their social worlds in single- and two-parent, Euro– and Mexican–American families. *Journal of Social and Personal Relationships, 14,* 357–372.

Gangestad, S., & Snyder, M. (1985). On the nature of self-monitoring: An examination of latent causal structure. In P. Shaver (Ed.), *Review of Personality and Social Psychology* (Vol. 6, pp. 65–85). Beverly Hills, CA: Sage.

Gangestad, S. W., & Simpson, J. A. (1993). Development of a scale measuring genetic variation related to expressive control. *Journal of Personality, 61,* 133–158.

Gantner, A. B., & Taylor, S. P. (1992). Human physical aggression as a function of alcohol and threat of harm. *Aggressive Behavior, 18,* 29–36.

Garcia, L. T. (1982). Sex role orientation and stereotypes about male–female sexuality. *Sex Roles, 8,* 863–876.

Garcia, M., & Shaw, D. (2000). Destructive sibling conflict and the development of conduct problems in young boys. *Developmental Psychology, 36,* 44–53.

Garcia, S. D., & Khersonsky, D. (1997). "They are a lovely couple": Further examination of perception of couple attractiveness. *Journal of Social Behavior and Personality, 12,* 367–380.

Garcia, S. M., Darley, J. M., & Robinson, R. J. (2001). Morally questionable tactics: Negotiations between district attorneys and public defenders. *Personality and Social Psychology Bulletin, 27,* 731–743.

Gardner, R. M., & Tockerman, Y. R. (1994). A computer–TV methodology for investigating the influence of somatotype on perceived personality traits. *Journal of Social Behavior and Personality, 9,* 555–563.

Gardner, W. L., Pickett, C. L., & Brewer, M. B. (2000). Social exclusion and selective memory: How the need to belong influences memory for social events. *Personality and Social Psychology Bulletin, 26,* 486–496.

Gawande, A. (2001, January 8). Under suspicion: The fugitive science of criminal justice. *The New Yorker,* 50–53.

Geary, D. C. (1999). Evolution and developmental sex differences. *Current Directions in Psychological Science, 8,* 115–120.

Geen, R., & Donnerstein, E. (Eds.). (1998). *Human aggression: Theories, research and implications for policy.* Pacific Grove, CA: Brooks/Cole.

Geen, R. G. (1989). Alternative conceptions of social facilitation. In P. B. Paulus (Ed)., *Psychology of group influence* (2nd ed., pp. 10037). New York: Academic Press.

Geen, R. G. (1991a). *Human aggression.* Pacific Grove, CA: Brooks/Cole.

Geen, R. G. (1991b). Behavioral and physiological reactions to observed violence: Effects of prior exposure to aggressive stimuli. *Journal of Personality and Social Psychology, 40,* 868–875.

Geen, R. G. (1998). Some effects of observing violence upon the behavior of the observer. In B. A. Maher (Ed.), *Progress in experimental personality research* (Vol. 8). New York: Academic Press.

George, J. M. (1990). Personality, affect, and behavior in groups. *Journal of Applied Psychology, 75,* 107–116.

George, J. M. (1995). Leader positive mood and group performance: The case of customer service. *Journal of Applied Social Psychology, 25,* 778–794.

George, L. K., Larson, D. B., Koenig, H. G., & McCullough, M. E. (2000). Spirituality and health: What we know, what we need to know. *Journal of Social and Clinical Psychology, 19,* 102–116.

George, M. S., Ketter, T. A., Parekh-Priti, I., Horwitz, B., et al. (1995). Brain activity during transient sadness and happiness in healthy women. *American Journal of Psychiatry, 152,* 341–351.

Gerard, H. B., Wilhelmy, R. A., & Conolley, E. S. (1968). Conformity and group size. *Journal of Personality and Social Psychology, 8,* 79–82.

Gerlsma, C., Buunk, B. P., & Mutsaers, W. C. M. (1996). Correlates of self-reported adult attachment styles in a Dutch sample of married men and women. *Journal of Social and Personal Relationships, 13,* 313–320.

Gervey, B. M., Chiu, C.-y., Hong, Y.-y., & Dweck, C. S. (1999). Differential use of person information in decisions about guilt versus innocence: The role of implicit theories. *Personality and Social Psychology Bulletin, 25,* 17–27.

Gibbons, F. X., Eggleston, T. J., & Benthin, A. C. (1997). Cognitive reactions to smoking relapse: The reciprocal relation between dissonance and self-esteem. *Journal of Personality and Social Psychology, 72,* 184–195.

Gifford, R. (1994). A lens-mapping framework for understanding the encoding and decoding of interpersonal dispositions in nonverbal behavior. *Journal of Personality and Social Psychology, 66,* 398–412.

Gigone, D., & Hastie, R. (1993). The common knowledge effect: Information sharing and group judgment. *Journal of Personality and Social Psychology, 65,* 959–974.

Gigone, D., & Hastie, R. (1997). The impact of information on small group choice. *Journal of Personality and Social Psychology, 72,* 132–140.

Gilbert, D. T., & Malone, P. S. (1995). The correspondence bias. *Psychological Bulletin, 117,* 21–38.

Gilbert, D. T., & Silvera, D. H. (1996). Overhelping. *Journal of Personality and Social Psychology, 70,* 678–690.

Gilbert, D. T., Tafarodi, R. W., & Malone, P. S. (1993). You can't not believe everything you read. *Journal of Personality and Social Psychology, 65,* 221–233.

Gilbert, L. A. (1993). *Two careers/one family.* Newbury Park, CA: Sage.

Gilbert, L. A. (1999). Reproducing gender in counseling and psychotherapy: Understanding the problem and changing the practice. *Applied and Preventive Psychology, 8,* 119–127.

Gillis, J. S. (1982). *Too small, too tall.* Champaign, IL: Institute for Personality and Ability Testing.

Gilovich, T., & Medvec, V. H. (1994). The temporal pattern to the experience of regret. *Journal of Personality and Social Psychology, 67,* 357–365.

Giner-Sorolla, R., & Chaiken, S. (1994). The causes of hostile media effects. *Journal of Experimental Social Psychology, 30,* 165–180.

Giner-Sorolla, R., & Chaiken, S. (1997). Selective use of heuristic and systematic processing under defense motivation. *Personality and Social Psychology Bulletin, 23,* 84–97.

Giovannini, J. (2000, November 27). Lost in space. *New York.* 146, 148.

Gladue, B. A., & Delaney, H. J. (1990). Gender differences in perception of attractiveness of men and women in bars. *Personality and Social Psychology Bulletin, 16,* 378–391.

Gladwell, M. (2000, December 11). Designs for working. *The New Yorker,* 60, 62, 64–65, 68–70.

Glaser, J., & Salovey, P. (1998). Affect in electoral politics. *Personality and Social Psychology Review, 2,* 156–172.

Glass Ceiling Commission. (1995). *Good for business: Making full use of the nation's human capital.* Washington, DC: Glass Ceiling Commission.

Glass, D. C. (1977). *Behavior patterns, stress, and coronary disease.* Hillsdale, NJ: Erlbaum.

Glass, D. C. (1989). Psychology and health: Obstacles and opportunities. *Journal of Applied Social Psychology, 19,* 1145–1163.

Gleason, J. H., Alexander, A. M., & Somers, C. L. (2000). Later adolescents' reactions to three types of childhood teasing: Relations with self-esteem and body image. *Social Behavior and Personality, 28,* 471–480.

Gleicher, F., Boninger, D., Strathman, A., Armor, D., Hetts, J., & Ahn, M. (1995). With an eye toward the future: Impact of counterfactual thinking on affect, attitudes, and behavior. In N. J. Roses & J. M. Olson (Eds.), *What might have been: the social psychology of counterfactual thinking.* (pp. 283–304). Mahwah, NJ: Erlbaum.

Glick, P., Fiske, S. T., et al. (2000). Beyond prejudice as simple antipathy: Hostile and benevolent sexism across cultures. *Journal of Personality and Social Psychology, 79,* 763–775.

Goethals, G. R., & Zanna, M. P. (1979). The role of social comparison in choice shifts. *Journal of Personality and Social Psychology, 37,* 1469–1476.

Gold, J. A., Ryckman, R. M., & Mosley, N. R. (1984). Romantic mood induction and attraction to a dissimilar other: Is love blind? *Personality and Social Psychology Bulletin, 10,* 358–368.

Goldenberg, J. L., McCoy, S. K., Greenberg, J., Pyszczynski, T., & Solomon, S. (2000). The body as a source of self-esteem: The effect of mortality salience on identification with one's body, interest in sex, and appearance monitoring. *Journal of Personality and Social Psychology, 79,* 118–130.

Goldenberg, J. L., Pyszczynski, T., Greenberg, J., McCoy, S. K., & Solomon, S. (1999). Death, sex, love, and neuroticism: Why is sex such a problem? *Journal of Personality and Social Psychology, 77,* 1173–1187.

Golding, J. M. (1999). Sexual-assault history and long-term physical health problems: Evidence from clinical and population epidemiology. *Current Directions in Psychological Science, 8,* 191–194.

Goldstein, A. G., Chance, J. E., & Schneller, G. R. (1989). Frequency of eyewitness identification in criminal cases: A survey of prosecutors. *Bulletin of the Psychonomic Society, 27,* 71–74.

Goldstein, M. D., & Strube, M. J. (1994). Independence revisited: The relation between positive and negative affect in a naturalistic setting. *Personality and Social Psychology Bulletin, 20,* 57–64.

Goleman, D. (1994, November 29). Study finds jurors often hear evidence with a closed mind. *New York Times,* C1, C2.

Gonnerman, M. E., Jr., Parker, C. P., Lavine, H., & Huff, J. (2000). The relationship between self-discrepancies and affective states: The moderating roles of self-monitoring and standpoints on the self. *Personality and Social Psychology Bulletin, 26,* 810–819.

Goodwin, R., & Findlay, C. (1997). "We were just fated together" . . . Chinese love and the concept of *yuan* in England and Hong Kong. *Personal Relationships, 4,* 85–92.

Goodwin, R., Cook, O., & Yung, Y. (2001). Loneliness and life satisfaction among three cultural groups. *Personal Relationships, 8,* 225–230.

Gordon, R. A. (1996). Impact of ingratiation in judgments and evaluations: A meta-analytic investigation. *Journal of Personality and Social Psychology, 71,* 54–70.

Gould, D., & Weiss, M. (1981). Effect of model similarity and model self-talk on self-efficacy in muscular endurance. *Journal of Sport Psychology, 3,* 17–29

Gould, S. J. (1996, September). The Diet of Worms and the defenestration of Prague. *Natural History,* 18–24, 64, 66–67.

Graham, S., & Folkes, V. (Eds.). (1990). *Attribution theory: Applications to achievement, mental health, and interpersonal conflict.* Hillsdale, NJ: Erlbaum.

Graham, S., Weiner, B., & Zucker, G. S. (1997). An attributional analysis of punishment goals and public reactions to O. J. Simpson. *Personality and Social Psychology Bulletin, 23,* 331–346.

Grant, P. (2001, March/April). Face time. *Modern Maturity,* 56–63.

Graziano, W. G., Jensen-Campbell, L. A., & Hair, E. C. (1996). Perceiving interpersonal conflict and reacting to it: The case for agreeableness. *Journal of Personality and Social Psychology, 70,* 820–835.

Green, D. P., Glaser, J., & Rich, A. (1998). From lynching to gay bashing: The elusive connection between economic conditions and hate crime. *Journal of Personality and Social Psychology, 75,* 82–92.

Green, J. D., & Campbell, W. K. (2000). Attachment and exploration in adults: Chronic and contextual accessibility. *Personality and Social Psychology Bulletin, 26,* 452–461.

Green, J. D., & Sedikides, C. (1999). Affect and self-focused attention revisited: The role of affect orientation. *Personality and Social Psychology Bulletin, 25,* 104–119.

Green, L. R., Richardson, D. R., & Lago, T. (1996). How do friendship, indirect, and direct aggression relate? *Aggressive Behavior, 22,* 81–86.

Greenbaum, P., & Rosenfield, H. W. (1978). Patterns of avoidance in responses to interpersonal staring and proximity: Effects of bystanders on drivers at a traffic intersection. *Journal of Personality and Social Psychology, 36,* 575–587.

Greenberg, B. S., & Woods, M. G. (1999). The soaps: Their sex, gratifications, and outcomes. *Journal of Sex Research, 36,* 250–257.

Greenberg, J. (1990). Employee theft as a reaction to underpayment inequity: The hidden cost of pay cuts. *Journal of Applied Psychology, 75,* 561–568.

Greenberg, J. (1996). *The quest for justice: Essays and experiments.* Thousand Oaks, CA: Sage Publications.

Greenberg, J. (1993a). The social side of fairness: Interpersonal and informational classes of organizational justice. In R. Cropanzano (Ed.), *Justice in the workplace* (pp. 79–103). Hillsdale, NJ: Erlbaum.

Greenberg, J. (1993b). Stealing in the name of justice: Informational and interpersonal moderators of theft reactions to underpayment inequity. *Organizational Behavior and Human Decision Processes, 54,* 81–103.

Greenberg, J., & Alge, B. J. (1997). Aggressive reactions to workplace injustice. In R. W. Griffin, A. O'Leary-Kelly, & J. Collins (Eds.), *Dysfunctional behavior in organizations: Vol. 1. Violent behaviors in organizations.* Greenwich, CT: JAI Press.

Greenberg, J., & Baron, R. A. (2002). *Behavior in organizations* (8th ed.). Upper Saddle River, NJ: Prentice-Hall.

Greenberg, J., & Scott, K. S. (1996). Why do workers bite the hands that feed them? Employee theft as social exchange process. In B. M. Staw & L. L. Cummings (Eds.), *Research in organizational behavior* (Vol. 18, pp. 111–156). Greenwich, CT: JAI Press.

Greenberg, J., Pyszczynski, T., & Solomon, S. (1982). The self-serving attributional bias: Beyond self-presentation. *Journal of Experimental Social Psychology, 18,* 56–67.

Greenberg, J., Solomon, S., Pyszczynski, T., Rosenblatt, A., Burling, J., Lyon, D., Simon, L., & Pinel, E. (1992). Why do people need self-esteem? Converging evidence that self-esteem serves an anxiety-buffering function. *Journal of Personality and Social Psychology, 63,* 913–922.

Greenberg, M. A., Wortman, C. B., & Stone, A. A. (1996). Emotional expression and physical health: Revising traumatic memories or fostering self-regulation? *Journal of Personality and Social Psychology, 71,* 588–602.

Greenwald, A. G., & Banaji, M. R. (1995). Implicit social cognition: Attitudes, self-esteem, and stereotypes. *Psychological Review, 102,* 4–27.

Greenwald, A. G., & Farnham, S. D. (2000). Using the implicit association test to measure self-esteem and self-concept. *Journal of Personality and Social Psychology, 79,* 1022–1038.

Greenwald, A. G., McGhee, D. E., & Schwartz, J. L. K. (1998). Measuring individual differences in implicit cognition: The implicit association test. *Journal of Personality and Social Psychology, 74,* 1464–1480.

Greer, A. E., & Buss, D. M. (1994). Tactics for promoting sexual encounters. *Journal of Sex Research, 31,* 185–201.

Grieve, N. (1980). Beyond sexual stereotypes. Androgyny: A model or an ideal? In N. Grieve & P. Grimshaw (Eds.), *Australian women: Feminist perspectives* (pp. 247–257). Melbourne, Australia: Oxford University Press.

Griffin, D. W., & Bartholomew, K. (1994a). The metaphysics of measurement: The case of adult attachment. In K. Bartholomew & D. Perlman (Eds.), *Advances in personal relationships: Vol. 5. Attachment processes in adulthood* (pp. 17–52). London: Jessica Kingsley.

Griffin, D. W., & Bartholomew, K. (1994b). Models of the self and other: Fundamental dimensions underlying measures of adult attachment. *Journal of Personality and Social Psychology, 67,* 430–445.

Griffin, D. W., & Buehler, R. (1993). Role of construal process in conformity and dissent. *Journal of Personality and Social Psychology, 65,* 657–669.

Griffin, K. W., & Rabkin, J. G. (1998). Perceived control over illness, realistic acceptance, and psychological adjustment in people with AIDS. *Journal of Social and Clinical Psychology, 17,* 407–424.

Groff, D. B., Baron, R. S., & Moore, D. L. (1983). Distraction, attentional conflict, and drivelike behavior. *Journal of Experimental Social Psychology, 19,* 359–380.

Grote, N. K., & Clark, M. S. (2001). Perceiving unfairness in the family: Cause of consequence of marital distress? *Journal of Personality and Social Psychology, 80,* 281–289.

Grote, N. K., Frieze, I. H., & Stone, C. A. (1996). Children, traditionalism in the division of family work, and marital satisfaction: "What's love got to do with it?" *Personal Relationships, 3,* 211–228.

Grube, J. A., & Piliavin, J. A. (2000). Role identity, organizational experiences, and volunteer performance.

Personality and Social Psychology Bulletin, 26, 1108–1119.

Grusec, J. E. (1991). The socialization of altruism. In M. S. Clark (Ed.), *Prosocial behavior* (pp. 9–33). Newbury Park, CA: Sage.

Guagnano, G. A. (1995). Locus of control, altruism and agentic disposition. *Population and Environment, 17,* 63–77.

Gudjonsson, G. H., & Clark, N. K. (1986). Suggestibility in police interrogation: A social psychological model. *Social Behavior, 1,* 83–104.

Gully, K. J., & Dengerink, H. A. (1983). The dyadic interaction of persons with violent and nonviolent histories. *Aggressive Behavior, 9,* 13–20.

Gump, B. B., & Kulik, J. A. (1997). Stress, affiliation, and emotional contagion. *Journal of Personality and Social Psychology, 72,* 305–319.

Gunter, B. G., & Gunter, N. C. (1991). Inequities in household labor: Sex role orientation and the need for cleanliness and responsibility as predictors. *Journal of Social Behavior and Personality, 6,* 559–572.

Gunthert, K. C., Cohen, L. H., & Armeli, S. (1999). The role of neuroticism in daily stress and coping. *Journal of Personality and Social Psychology, 77,* 1087–1100.

Gustafson, R. (1990). Wine and male physical aggression. *Journal of Drug Issues, 20,* 75–86.

Hackel, L. S., & Ruble, D. N. (1992). Changes in the marital relationship after the first baby is born: Predicting the impact of expectancy disconfirmation. *Journal of Personality and Social Psychology, 62,* 944–957.

Hagborg, W. J. (1993). Gender differences on Harter's Self-Perception Profile for Adolescents. *Journal of Social Behavior and Personality, 8,* 141–148.

Hahn, J., & Blass, T. (1997). Dating partner preferences: A function of similarity of love styles. *Journal of Social Behavior and Personality, 12,* 595–610.

Halberstadt, J., & Rhodes, G. (2000). The attractiveness of nonface averages: Implications for an evolutionary explanation of the attractiveness of average faces. *Psychological Science, 11,* 285–289.

Halford, W. K., & Sanders, M. R. (1990). The relationship of cognition and behavior during marital interaction. *Journal of Social and Clinical Psychology, 9,* 489–510.

Hall, J. A., & Carter, J. D. (1999). Gender-stereotype accuracy as an individual difference. *Journal of Personality and Social Psychology, 77,* 350–359.

Hall-Elston, C., & Mullins, L. C. (1999). Social relationships, emotional closeness, and loneliness among older meal program participants. *Social Behavior and Personality, 27,* 503–518.

Hamilton, D. L., & Sherman, S. J. (1989). Illusory correlations: Implications for stereotype theory and research. In D. Bar-Tal, C. F. Graumann, A. W. Kruglanski, & W. Stroebe (Eds.), *Stereotyping and prejudice: Changing conceptions* (pp. 59–82). New York: Springer-Verlag.

Hamilton, G. V. (1978). Obedience and responsibility: A jury simulation. *Journal of Personality and Social Psychology, 36,* 126–146.

Hamilton, V. L., & Sanders, J. (1995). Crimes of obedience and conformity in the workplace: Surveys of Americans, Russians, and Japanese. *Journal of Social Issues, 51,* 67–88.

Hansen, T., & Bartsch, R. A. (2001). The positive correlation between personal need for structure and the mere exposure effect. *Social Behavior and Personality, 29,* 271–276.

Harasty, A. S. (1997). The interpersonal nature of social stereotypes: Differential discussion patterns about in-groups and out-groups. *Personality and Social Psychology Bulletin, 23,* 270–284.

Hareli, S., & Weiner, B. (2000). Accounts for success as determinants of perceived arrogance and modesty. *Motivation and Emotion, 24,* 215–236.

Harker, L., & Keltner, D. (2001). Expressions of positive emotion in women's college yearbook pictures and their relationship to personality and life outcomes across adulthood. *Journal of Personality and Social Psychology, 80,* 112–124.

Harmon-Jones, E. (2000). Cognitive dissonance and experienced negative affect: Evidence that dissonance increases experienced negative affect even in the absence of aversive consequences. *Personality and Social Psychology Bulletin, 26,* 1490–1501.

Harmon-Jones, E., & Allen, J. J. B. (2001). The role of affect in the mere exposure effect: Evidence from psychophysiological and individual differences approaches. *Personality and Social Psychology Bulletin, 27,* 889–898.

Harris, L. R., & Weiss, D. J. (1995). Judgments of consent in simulated rape cases. *Journal of Social Behavior and Personality, 10,* 79–90.

Harris, M. B. (1992). Sex, race, and experiences of aggression. *Aggressive Behavior, 18,* 201–217.

Harris, M. B. (1993). How provoking! What makes men and women angry? *Journal of Applied Social Psychology, 23,* 199–211.

Harris, M. B. (1994). Gender of subject and target as mediators of aggression. *Journal of Applied Social Psychology, 24,* 453–471.

Harris, M. B. (1996). Aggressive experiences and aggressiveness: Relationship to gender, ethnicity, and age. *Journal of Applied Social Psychology, 26,* 843–870.

Harris, M. B., Harris, R. J., & Bochner, S. (1982). Fat, four-eyed, and female: Stereotypes of obesity, glasses, and gender. *Journal of Applied Social Psychology, 12,* 503–516.

Harris, M. J., Milch, R., Corbitt, E. M., Hoover, D. W., Brady, M. (1992). Self-fulfilling effects of stigmatizing information on children's social interaction. *Journal of Personality and Social Psychology, 63,* 41–50.

Hart, A. J. (1995). Naturally occurring expectation effects. *Journal of Personality and Social Psychology, 68,* 109–115.

Hartup, W. W., & Stevens, N. (1999). Friendships and adaptation across the life span. *Current Directions in Psychological Science, 8,* 76–79.

Harvey, J. H., & Pauwels, B. G. (1999). Recent developments in close-relationships theory. *Current Directions in Psychological Science, 8,* 93–95.

Hassin, R., & Trope, Y. (2000). Facing faces: Studies on the cognitive aspects of physiognomy. *Journal of Personality and Social Psychology, 78,* 837–852.

Hastie, R. (Ed.). (1993). *Inside the juror: The psychology of juror decision making.* Cambridge, England: Cambridge University Press.

Hatfield, E. (1988). Passionate and companionate love. In R. J. Sternberg & M. I. Barnes (Eds.), *The psychology of love* (pp. 191–217). New Haven, CT: Yale University Press.

Hatfield, E., & Rapson, R. L. (1999). Historical and cross-cultural perspectives on passionate love and sexual desire. *Annual Review of Sex Research, 4,* 67–97.

Hatfield, E., & Sprecher, S. (1986a). *Mirror, mirror . . . :* The importance of looks in everyday life. Albany, NY: S.U.N.Y. Press.

Hatfield, E., & Sprecher, S. (1986b). Measuring passionate love in intimate relations. *Journal of Adolescence, 9,* 383–410.

Hatfield, E., & Walster, G. W. (1981). *A new look at love.* Reading, MA: Addison-Wesley.

Hayden, S. R., Jackson, T. T., & Guydish, J. N. (1984). Helping behavior of females: Effects of stress and commonality of fate. *Journal of Psychology, 117,* 233–237.

Hazan, C., & Shaver, P. R. (1990). Love and work: An attachment-theoretical perspective. *Journal of Personality and Social Psychology, 59,* 270–280.

Hebl, M. R., & Heatherton, T. E. (1998). The stigma of obesity in women: The difference is black and white. *Personality and Social Psychology Bulletin, 24,* 417–426.

Hecht, M. A., & LaFrance, M. (1998). License or obligation to smile: The effect of power and sex on amount and type of smiling. *Personality and Social Psychology Bulletin, 24,* 1332–1342.

Heider, F. (1958). *The psychology of interpersonal relations.* New York: Wiley.

Heilman, M. E. (1995). Sex stereotypes and their effects in the workplace: What we know and what we don't know. *Journal of Social Behavior and Personality, 10,* 3–26.

Heilman, M. E., Block, C. J., & Lucas, J. A. (1992). Presumed incompetent? Stigmatization and affirmative action efforts. *Journal of Applied Psychology, 77,* 536–544.

Heinberg, L. J., & Thompson, J. K. (1992). Social comparison: Gender, target importance ratings, and relation to body image disturbance. *Journal of Social Behavior and Personality, 7,* 335–344.

Heine, S. J., & Lehman, D. R. (1997a). Culture, dissonance, and self-affirmation. *Personality and Social Psychology Bulletin, 23,* 389–400.

Heine, S. J., & Lehman, D. R. (1997b). The cultural construction of self-enhancement: An examination of group-serving bias. *Journal of Personality and Social Psychology, 72,* 1268–1283.

Heine, S. J., & Lehman, D. R. (1999). Culture, self-discrepancies, and self-satisfaction. *Personality and Social Psychology Bulletin, 25,* 915–925.

Helman, D., & Bookspan, P. (1992, February 8). In Big Bird's world, females are secondary. *Albany Times Union,* E–2.

Helms, A. D. (2001, July 22). With this ring, I thee hyphenate? Knight Ridder.

Helweg-Larsen, M., & Shepperd, J. A. (2001). Do moderators of the optimistic bias affect personal or target risk estimates? A review of the literature. *Personality and Social Psychology Review, 5,* 74–95.

Hemenover, S. H. (2001). Self-reported processing bias and naturally occurring mood: Mediators between personality and stress appraisals. *Personality and Social Psychology Bulletin, 27,* 387–394.

Henderson-King, D., & Stewart, A. J. (1999). Educational experiences and shifts in group consciousness: Studying women. *Personality and Social Psychology Bulletin, 25,* 390–399.

Hendrick, C., & Hendrick, S. S. (1986). A theory and method of love. *Journal of Personality and Social Psychology, 50,* 392–402.

Hendrick, C., Hendrick, S. S., Foote, F. H., & Slapion-Foote, M. J. (1984). Do men and women love differently? *Journal of Social and Personal Relationships, 1,* 177–195.

Hendrick, S. S., & Hendrick, C. (1987). Love and sex attitudes and religious beliefs. *Journal of Social and Clinical Psychology, 5,* 391–398.

Henkel, L. A., Franklin, N., & Johnson, M. K. (2000). Cross-model source monitoring confusions between perceived and imagined events. *Journal of Experimental Psychology: Learning, Memory, and Cognition, 26,* 321–335.

Hense, R., Penner, L., & Nelson, D. (1995). Implicit memory for age stereotypes. *Special Cognition, 13,* 399–415.

Hensley, W. E. (1996). The effect of a ludus love style on sexual experience. *Social Behavior and Personality, 24,* 205–212.

Hepworth, J. T., & West, S. G. (1988). Lynchings and the economy: A time-series reanalysis of Hovland and Sears (1940). *Journal of Personality and Social Psychology, 55,* 239–247.

Herbert, J. D. (1995). An overview of the current status of social phobia. *Applied and Preventive Psychology, 4,* 39–51.

Herring, J. (2001, May 20). 10 tricks to a happy marriage. Knight Ridder.

Hershberger, S. L., Lichtenstein, P., & Knox, S. S. (1994). Genetic and environmental influences on perceptions of organizational climate. *Journal of Applied Psychology, 79,* 24–33.

Hewstone, M., Bond, M. H., & Wan, K. C. (1983). Social factors and social attributions: The explanation of intergroup differences in Hong Kong. *Social Cognition, 2,* 142–157.

Higgins, E. T. (1996). Emotional experiences: The pains and pleasures of distinct regulatory systems. In D. Kavanaugh, B. Zimmerberg, & S. Fein (Eds.), *Emotion: Interdisciplinary perspectives* (pp. 203–241). Mahwah, NJ: Erlbaum.

Higgins, E. T. (1998). Promotion and prevention: Regulatory focus as a motivational principle. In. M. P. Zanna (Ed.), *Advances in experimental social psychology* (Vol. 30, pp. 1–46). New York: Academic Press.

Higgins, E. T., & Bargh, J. A. (1987). Social cognition and social perception. *Annual Review of Psychology, 38,* 369–425.

Higgins, E. T., & King, G. (1981). Accessibility of social constructs: Information processing consequences of individual and contextual variability. In N. Cantor & J. Kihlstrom (Eds.), *Personality, cognition, and social interaction* (pp. 69–121). Hillsdale, NJ: Erlbaum.

Higgins, E. T., Rohles, W. S., & Jones, C. R. (1977). Category accessibility and impression formation. *Journal of Experimental Social Psychology, 13,* 141–154.

Higgins, N. C., & Shaw, J. K. (1999). Attributional style moderates the impact of causal controlability information on helping behavior. *Social Behavior and Personality, 27,* 221–236.

Hill, C. A. (1987). Affiliation motivation: People who need people but in different ways. *Journal of Personality and Social Psychology, 52,* 1008–1018.

Hill, C. A., Blakemore, J. E. O., & Drumm, P. (1997). Mutual and unrequited love in adolescence and young adulthood. *Personal Relationships, 4,* 15–23.

Hilton, D. J. (1998). *Psychology and the city: Applications to trading, dealing, and investment analysis.* London: Center for the Study of Financial Innovation.

Hilton, N. Z., Harris, G. T., & Rice, M. E. (2000). The functions of aggression by male teenagers. *Journal of Personality and Social Psychology, 79,* 988–994.

Hinde, R. A., Finkenauer, C., Auhagen, A. E. (2001). Relationships and the self-concept. *Personal Relationships, 8,* 187–204.

Hinkley, K., & Andersen, S. M. (1996). The working self-concept in transference: Significant-other activation and self change. *Journal of Personality and Social Psychology, 71,* 1279–1295.

Hinsz, V. B. (1995). Goal setting by groups performing an additive task: A comparison with individual goal setting. *Journal of Applied Social Psychology, 25,* 965–990.

Hinsz, V. B., Matz, D. C., & Patience, R. A. (2001). Does women's hair signal reproductive potential? *Journal of Experimental Social Psychology, 37,* 166–172.

Hirokawa, K., Yamada, F., Dohi, I., & Miyata, Y. (2001). Effect of gender-types on interpersonal stress measured by blink rate and questionnaires: Focusing on stereotypically sex-typed and androgynous types. *Social Behavior and Personality, 29,* 375–384.

Hirt, E. R., & Markman, K. D. (1995). Multiple explanation: A consider-an-alternative strategy for debiasing judgments. *Personality and Social Psychology Bulletin, 69,* 1069–1086.

Ho, D. (1999, November 8). . . . And will we ever cure AIDS? *Time,* 84.

Ho, D. (2000, December 19). Crime decline slows, FBI says. Associated Press.

Hogben, M., Byrne, D., Hamburger, M. E., & Osland, J. (2001). Legitimized aggression and sexual coercion: Individual differences in cultural spillover. *Aggressive Behavior, 29,* 26–43.

Hogg, M. A., & Haines, S. C. (1996). Intergroup relations and group solidarity: Effects of group identification and social beliefs on depersonalized attraction. *Journal of Personality and Social Psychology, 70,* 25–309.

Holtzworth-Munroe, A. (2000). A typology of men who are violent toward their female partners: Making sense of the heterogeneity in husband violence. *Current Directions in Psychological Science, 9,* 140–143.

Hope, D. A., Holt, C. S., & Heimberg, R. G. (1995). Social phobia. In T. R. Giles (Ed.), *Handbook of effective psychotherapy* (pp. 227–251). New York: Plenum.

Horney, K. (1950). *Neurosis and human growth: The struggle toward self-realization.* New York: Norton.

Hornsey, M. J., & Hogg, M. A. (2000). Intergroup similarity and subgroup relations: Some implications for assimilation. *Personality and Social Psychology Bulletin, 26,* 948–958.

Horowitz, J. M. (2000, February 21). Pangloss power. *Time,* 138.

Horowitz, L. M., Krasnoperova, E. N., Tatar, D. G., Hansen, M. B., Person, E. A., Galvin, K. L., & Nelson, K. L. (2001). The way to console may depend on the goal: Experimental studies of social support. *Journal of Experimental Social Psychology, 37,* 49–61.

Hosoda, M., & Stone, D. L. (in press). Current gender stereotypes and their evaluative content. *Perceptual and Motor Skills.*

House, R. J., & Howell, J. M. (1992). Personality and charismatic leadership. *Leadership Quarterly, 3,* 81–108.

House, R. J., & Podsakoff, P. M. (1994). Leadership effectiveness: Past perspectives and future directions for research. In J. Greenberg (Ed.), *Organizational behavior: The state of the science* (pp. 45–82). Hillsdale, NJ: Erlbaum.

House, R. J., Spangler, W. D., & Woycke, J. (1991). Personality and charisma in the U.S. presidency: A psychological theory of leader effectiveness. *Administrative Science Quarterly, 36,* 364–396.

Households. (2001, August 6). *U.S. News & World Report,* 15.

Hovland, C. I., & Sears, R. R. (1940). Minor studies in aggression: VI. Correlation of lynchings with economic indices. *Journal of Psychology, 9,* 301–310.

Hovland, C. I., & Weiss, W. (1951). The influence of source credibility on communication effectiveness. *Public Opinion Quarterly, 15,* 635–650.

Hovland, C. I., Janis, I. L., & Kelley, H. H. (1953). *Communication and persuasion: Psychological studies of opinion change.* New Haven, CT: Yale University Press.

Howell, J. M., & Frost, P. J. (1989). A laboratory study of charismatic leadership. *Organizational Behavior and Human Decision Processes, 43,* 243–269.

Hoyle, R. H. (1993). Interpersonal attraction in the absence of explicit attitudinal information. *Social Cognition, 11,* 309–320.

Huang, I.-C. (1998). Self-esteem, reaction to uncertainty, and physician practice variation: A study of resident physicians. *Social Behavior and Personality, 26,* 181–194.

Huesmann, L. R., & Eron, L. D. (1984). Cognitive processes and the persistence of aggressive behavior. *Aggressive Behavior, 10,* 243–251.

Huesmann, L. R., & Eron, L. D. (1986). *Television and the aggressive child: A cross-national comparison.* Hillsdale, NJ: Erlbaum.

Hughes, C. F., Uhlmann, C., & Pennebaker, J. W. (1994). The body's response to processing emotional trauma: Linking verbal text with autonomic activity. *Journal of Personality, 62,* 565–585.

Hughes, J. (2000, December 12). What does love mean? From the Internet. jeh66@aol.com.

Huguet, P., Galvaing, M. P., Monteil, J. M., & Dumas, F. (1999). Social presence effects in the Stroop task: Further evidence for an attentional view of social facilitation. *Journal of Personality and Social Psychology, 77,* 1011–1025.

Hui, C., Lam, S. S. K., & Law, K. K. S. (2000). Instrumental values of organizational citizenship behavior for promotion: A field quasi-experiment. *Journal of Applied Psychology, 85,* 822–828.

Hull, J. D. (1995, January 30). The state of the union. *Time,* 52–57, 60.

Hummert, M. L., Crockett, W. H., & Kemper, S. (1990). Processing mechanisms underlying use of the balance scheme. *Journal of Personality and Social Psychology, 58,* 5–21.

Humphreys, L. G. (1998). A little noticed consequence of the repressed memory epidemic. *American Psychologist, 53,* 485–486.

Humphriss, N. (1989, November 20). Letters. *Time,* 12.

Hunt, A. McC. (1935). A study of the relative value of certain ideals. *Journal of Abnormal and Social Psychology, 30,* 222–228.

Huo, Y. J., Smith, H. J., Tyler, T. R., & Lind, E. A. (1996). Superordinate identification subgroup identification and justice concerns: Is separation the problem, is assimilation the answer? *Psychological Science, 7,* 40–45.

Hur, Y.-M., McGue, M., & Iacono, W. G. (1998). The structure of self-concept in female preadolescent twins: A behavioral genetic approach. *Journal of Personality and Social Psychology, 74,* 1069–1077.

Hurewitz, M. (1998, March 26). Young man finds honesty has its rewards. Albany *Times Union,* pp. B1, B7.

Huston, T. L., Caughlin, J. P., Houts, R. M., Smith, S. E., & George, L. J. (2001). The connubial crucible: Newlywed years as predictors of marital delight, distress, and divorce. *Journal of Personality and Social Psychology, 80,* 237–252.

Hyde, J. S., & Plant, E. A. (1995). Magnitude of psychological gender differences: Another side to the story. *American Psychologist, 50,* 159–161.

Hyde, J. S., DeLamater, J. D., & Durik, A. M. (2001). Sexuality and the dual-earner couple, Part II: Beyond the baby years. *Journal of Sex Research, 38,* 10–23.

Ickes, W., Reidhead, S., & Patterson, M. (1986). Machiavellianism and self-monitoring: As different as "me" and "you." *Social Cognition, 4,* 58–74.

Ingram, K. M., Betz, N. E., Mindes, E. J., Schmitt, M. M., & Smith, N. G. (2001). Unsupportive responses from others concerning a stressful life event: Development of the Unsupportive Social Interactions Inventory. *Journal of Social and Clinical Psychology, 20,* 171–207.

Insel, T. R., & Carter, C. S. (1995, August). The monogamous brain. *Natural History,* 12–14.

Insko, C. A. (1985). Balance theory, the Jordan paradigm, and the West tetrahedron. In L. Berkowitz (Ed.), *Advances in experimental social psychology.* New York: Academic Press.

Insko, C. A., Schopler, H. J., Gaertner, G., Wildschutt, T., Kozar, R., Pinter, B., Finkel, E. J., Brazil, D. M., Cecil, C. L., & Montoya, M. R. (2001). Interindividual-intergroup discontinuity reduction through the anticipation of future interaction. *Journal of Personality and Social Psychology, 80,* 95–111.

Interpersonal trust and fear of exploitation: An exploration of the other-model underlying adult attachment style. Manuscript submitted for publication.

Inzlicht, M., & Ben-Zeev, T. (2000). A threatening intellectual environment: Why females are susceptible to experiencing problem-solving deficits in the presence of males. *Psychological Science, 11,* 365–371.

Ireland, C. A., & Ireland, J. L. (2000). Descriptive analysis of the nature and extent of bullying behavior in a maximum security prison. *Aggressive Behavior, 26,* 213–222.

Irvine, M. (1999, November 24). American families in flux. Associated Press.

Isbell, L. M., & Wyer, R. S., Jr. (1999). Correcting for mood-induced bias in the evaluation of political candidates: The roles of intrinsic and extrinsic motivation. *Personality and Social Psychology Bulletin, 25,* 237–249.

Isen, A. M. (1970). Success, failure, attention, and reaction to others: The warm glow of success. *Journal of Personality and Social Psychology, 15,* 294–301.

Isen, A. M. (1984). Toward understanding the role of affect in cognition. In S. R. Wyer & T. K. Srull (Eds.), *Handbook of social cognition* (Vol. 3, pp. 179–236). Hillsdale, NJ: Erlbaum.

Isen, A. M., & Baron, R. A. (1991). Affect and organizational behavior. In B. M. Staw & L. L. Cummings (Eds.), *Research in organizational behavior* (Vol. 15, pp. 1–53).

Isen, A. M., & Levin, P. A. (1972). Effect of feeling good on helping: Cookies and kindness. *Journal of Personality and Social Psychology, 21,* 384–388.

Istvan, J., Griffitt, W., & Weidner, G. (1983). Sexual arousal and the polarization of perceived sexual attractiveness. *Basic and Applied Social Psychology, 4,* 307–318.

Ito, T. A., Larsen, J. T., Smith, N. K., & Cacioppo, J. T. (1998). Negative information weighs more heavily on the brain: The negativity bias in evaluative categorizations. *Journal of Personality and Social Psychology, 75,* 887–900.

Izard, C. (1991). *The psychology of emotions.* New York: Plenum.

Jackson, J. W., & Smith, E. R. (1999). Conceptualizing social identity: A new framework and evidence for the impact of different dimensions. *Personality and Social Psychology Bulletin, 25,* 120–135.

Jackson, L. A., & Grabski, S. V. (1988). Perceptions of fair play and the gender wage gap. *Journal of Applied Social Psychology, 18,* 606–625.

Jackson, L. A., Gardner, P., & Sullivan, L. (1992). Explaining gender differences in self-pay expectations: Social comparison standards and perceptions of fair pay. *Journal of Applied Psychology, 77,* 651–663.

Jackson, L. M., & Esses, V. M. (1997). Of scripture and ascription: The relation between religious fundamentalism and intergroup helping. *Personality and Social Psychology Bulletin, 23,* 893–906.

Jackson, L. M., Esses, V. M., & Burris, C. T. (2001). Contemporary sexism and discrimination: The importance of respect for men and women. *Personality and Social Psychology Bulletin, 27,* 48–61.

Jackson, R. L. (1996, September 18). Violent crime down sharply, survey says. *Los Angeles Times.*

Jackson, T., Soderlind, A., & Weiss, K. E. (2000). Personality traits and quality of relationships as predictors of future loneliness among American college students. *Social Behavior and Personality, 28,* 463–470.

Jacobi, L., & Cash, T. F. (1994). In pursuit of the perfect appearance: Discrepancies among self-ideal percepts of multiple physical attributes. *Journal of Applied Social Psychology, 24,* 379–396.

Jaffe, Y., Malamuth, N., Feingold, J., & Feshbach, S. (1974). Sexual arousal and behavioral aggression. *Journal of Personality and Social Psychology, 30,* 759–764.

James, W. (1890). *The principles of psychology.* New York: Holt.

Janes, L., & Olson, J. M. (2000). Jeer pressure: The behavioral effects of observing ridicule of others. *Personality and Social Psychology Bulletin, 26,* 474–485.

Janis, I. L. (1972). *Victims of groupthink.* Boston: Houghton Mifflin.

Janis, I. L. (1982). *Victims of groupthink* (2nd ed.). Boston: Houghton Mifflin.

Janoff-Bulman, R., & Wade, M. B. (1996). The dilemma of self-advocacy for women: Another case of blaming the victim? *Journal of Social and Clinical Psychology, 15,* 143–152.

Jarrell, A. (1998, October 4). Date that calls for judicious attire. *New York Times,* 9-1–9-2.

Jeffries, V. (1993). Virtue and attraction: Validation of a measure of love. *Journal of Social and Personal Relationships, 10,* 99–117.

Jemmott, J. B. III, & Magloire, K. (1988). Academic stress, social support, and secretory immunoglobulin. *Journal of Personality and Social Psychology, 55,* 803–810.

Jensen-Campbell, L. A., West, S. G., & Graziano, W. G. (1995). Dominance, prosocial orientation, and female preferences: Do nice guys really finish last? *Journal of Personality and Social Psychology, 68,* 427–440.

Jessor, R., Turbin, M. S., & Costa, F. M. (1998). Protective factors in adolescent health behavior. *Journal of Personality and Social Psychology, 75,* 788–800.

Jex, S. M., Cvetanovski, J., & Allen, S. J. (1994). Self-esteem as a moderator of the impact of unemployment. *Journal of Social Behavior and Personality, 9,* 69–80.

Johnson, B. T. (1994). Effects of outcome-relevant involvement and prior information on persuasion. *Journal of Experimental Social Psychology, 30,* 556–579.

Johnson, C., & Mullen, B. (1994). Evidence for the accessibility of paired distinctiveness in the distinctiveness-based illusory correlation in stereotyping. *Personality and Social Psychology Bulletin, 20,* 65–70.

Johnson, J. C., Poteat, G. M., & Ironsmith, M. (1991). Structural vs. marginal effects: A note on the importance of structure in determining sociometric status. *Journal of Social Behavior and Personality, 6,* 489–508.

Johnson, M. K., & Sherman, S. J. (1990). Constructing and reconstructing the past and the future in the present. In E. T. Higgins & R. M. Sorrentino (Eds.), *Handbook of motivation and social cognition: Foundations of social behavior* (pp. 482–526). New York: Guilford.

Johnston, V. S., & Franklin, M. (1993). Is beauty in the eye of the beholder? *Ethology and Sociobiology, 14,* 183–199.

Johnston, V. S., & Oliver-Rodriguez, J. C. (1997). Facial beauty and the late positive component of event-related potentials. *Journal of Sex Research, 34,* 188–198.

Johnstone, B., Frame, C. L., & Bouman, D. (1992). Physical attractiveness and athletic and academic ability in controversial–aggressive and rejected–aggressive children. *Journal of Social and Clinical Psychology, 11,* 71–79.

Joiner, T. E., Jr. (1994). The interplay of similarity and self-verification in relationship formation. *Social Behavior and Personality, 22,* 195–200.

Joiner, T. E., Jr., & Schmidt, N. B. (1995). Dimensions of perfectionism, life stress, and depressed and anxious symptoms: Prospective support for diathesis–stress but not specific vulnerability among male undergraduates. *Journal of Social and Clinical Psychology, 14,* 165–183.

Joiner, T. E., Jr., Katz, J., & Lew, A. (1999). Harbingers of depressotypic reassurance seeking: Negative life events, increased anxiety, and decreased self-esteem. *Personality and Social Psychology Bulletin, 25,* 630–637.

Jonas, E., Schulz-Hardt, S., Frey, D., & Thelen, N. (2001). Confirmation bias in sequential information search after preliminary decisions: An expansion of dissonance theoretical research on selective exposure to information. *Journal of Personality and Social Psychology, 80,* 557–571.

Jones, E. E. (1964). *Ingratiation: A social psychology analysis.* New York: Appleton-Century-Crofts.

Jones, E. E. (1979). The rocky road from acts to dispositions. *American Psychologist, 34,* 107–117.

Jones, E. E., & Davis, K. E. (1965). From acts to disposition: The attribution process in person perception. In L. Berkowitz (Ed.), *Advances in experimental social psychology* (Vol. 2, pp. 219–266). New York: Academic Press.

Jones, E. E., & McGillis, D. (1976). Corresponding inferences and attribution cube: A comparative reappraisal. In J. H. Har, W. J. Ickes, & R. F. Kidd (Eds.), *New directions in attribution research* (Vol. 1). Morristown, NJ: Erlbaum.

Jones, E. E., & Nisbett, R. E. (1971). *The actor and the observer: Divergent perceptions of the causes of behavior.* Morristown, NJ: General Learning Press.

Jones, J. H. (1997, August 25 and September 1). Dr. Yes. *New Yorker,* 98–110, 112–113.

Jones, W. H., Carpenter, B. N., & Quintana, D. (1985). Personality and interpersonal predictors of loneliness in two cultures. *Journal of Personality and Social Psychology, 48,* 1503–1511.

Joyner, K., & Udry, R. J. (2000). You don't bring me anything but down: Adolescent romance and depression. *Journal of Health and Social Behavior, 41,* 369–391.

Judd, C. M., Ryan, C. S., & Parke, B. (1991). Accuracy in the judgment of in-group and out-group variability. *Journal of Personality and Social Psychology, 61,* 366–379.

Judge, T. A. (1993). Does affective disposition moderate the relationships between job satisfaction and voluntary turnover? *Journal of Applied Psychology, 78,* 395–401.

Judge, T. A., & Bono, J. E. (2000). Five-factor model of personality and transformational leadership. *Journal of Applied Psychology, 85,* 751–765.

Judge, T. A., Bono, J. E., & Locke, E. Q. (2000). Personality and job satisfaction: The mediating role of job characteristics. *Journal of Applied Psychology, 85,* 237–249.

Judge, T. A., Locke, E. Q., & Durham, C. C. (1997). The dispositional causes of job satisfaction: A core evaluation approach. *Research in Organizational Behavior, 19,* 151–188.

Judge, T. A., Locke, E. A., Durham, C. C., & Kluger, A. N. (1998). Dispositional effects on job and life satisfaction: The role of core evaluations. *Journal of Applied Psychology, 83,* 17–34.

Jussim, L. (1991). Interpersonal expectations and social reality: A reflection–construction model and reinterpretation of evidence. *Psychological Review, 98,* 54–73.

Kaiser, C. R., & Miller, C. T. (2001). Stop complaining! The social costs of making attributions to discrimination. *Personality and Social Psychology Bulletin, 27,* 254–263.

Kalichman, S. C., Sarwer, D. B., Johnson, J. R., Ali, S. A., Early, J., & Tuten, J. T. (1993). Sexually coercive behavior and love styles: A replication and extension. *Journal of Psychology & Human Sexuality, 6,* 93–106.

Kalick, S. M., Zebrowitz, L. A., Langlois, J. H., & Johnson, R. M. (1998). Does human facial attractiveness honestly advertise health? Longitudinal data on an evolutionary question. *Psychological Science, 9,* 8–13.

Kallgren, C. A., Reno, R. R., & Cialdini, R. B. (2000). A focus theory of normative conduct: When norms do and do not affect behavior. *Personality and Social Psychology Bulletin, 26,* 1002–1012.

Kameda, T., & Sugimori, S. (1993). Psychological entrapment in group decision making: An assigned decision rule and a groupthink phenomenon. *Journal of Personality and Social Psychology, 65,* 282–292.

Kanagawa, C., Cross, S. E., & Markus, H. R. (2001). "Who am I?" The cultural psychology of the conceptual self. *Personality and Social Psychology Bulletin, 27,* 90–103.

Kandel, D. B. (1978). Similarity in real-life adolescent friendship pairs. *Journal of Personality and Social Psychology, 36,* 306–312.

Kaplan, M. F. (1981). State dispositions in social judgment. *Bulletin of the Psychonomic Society,* 18, 27–29.

Kaplan, M. F. (1989). Task, situational and perceived determinants of influence processes in group decision making. In E. Lawler & B. Markovsky (Eds.), *Advances in group processes* (Vol. 6, pp. 87–1050). Greenwich, CT: JAI.

Karau, S. J., & Williams, K. D. (1993). Social loafing: A meta-analytic review and theoretical integration. *Journal of Personality and Social Psychology, 65,* 681–706.

Karoly, P. (1993). Mechanisms of self-regulation: A systems view. *Annual Review of Psychology, 44,* 23–52.

Karraker, K. H., & Stern, M. (1990). Infant physical attractiveness and facial expression: Effects on adult perceptions. *Basic and Applied Social Psychology,* 11, 371–385.

Kasser, T., & Sharma, Y. S. (1999). Reproductive freedom, educational equality, and female's preference for resource-acquisition characteristics in mates. *Psychological Science, 10,* 374–377.

Kassin, S. M. (1997). The psychology of confession evidence. *American Psychologist, 52,* 221–233.

Kassin, S. M., & Kiechel, K. L. (1996). The social psychology of false confessions: Compliance, internalization, and confabulation. *Psychological Science, 7,* 125–128.

Kassin, S. M., & McNall, K. (1991). Police interrogations and confessions: Communicating promises and threats by pragmatic implication. *Law and Human Behavior, 15,* 233–251.

Kassin, S. M., & Sommers, S. R. (1997). Inadmissible testimony, instructions to disregard, and the jury: Substantive versus procedural considerations. *Personality and Social Psychology Bulletin, 23,* 1046–1054.

Kassin, S. M., Tubb, V. A., Hosch, H. M., & Memon, A. (2001). On the "general acceptance" of eyewitness testimony research. *American Psychologist, 56,* 405–416.

Katz, D. (1960). The functional approach to the study of attitudes. *Journal of Abnormal and Social Psychology, 70,* 1037–1051.

Katz, J., & Beach, S. R. H. (2000). Looking for love? Self-verification and self-enhancement effects on initial romantic attraction. *Personality and Social Psychology Bulletin, 26,* 1526–1539.

Kawakami K., & Dividio, J. F. (2001). The reliability of implicit stereotyping. *Personality and Social Psychology Bulletin, 27,* 212–225.

Kawakami, K., Dion, K. L., & Dovidio, J. F. (1998). Racial prejudice and stereotype activation. *Personality and Social Psychology Bulletin, 24,* 407–416.

Kawakami K., Dovidio, J. F., Moll, J., Hermsen, S., & Russn, A. (2000). Just say no (to stereotyping): Effects of training in the negation of stereotypic associations on stereotype activation. *Journal and Personality and Social Psychology, 78,* 871–888.

Keenan, J. P., Gallup, G. G., Jr., Goulet, N., & Kulkarni, M. (1997). Attributions of deception in human mating strategies. *Journal of Social Behavior and Personality, 12,* 45–52.

Keller, L. M., Bouchard, T. J., Jr., Arvey, R. D., Segal, N. L., & Dawis, R. V. (1992). Work values: Genetic and environmental influences. *Journal of Applied Psychology, 77,* 79–88.

Keller, R. T. (1997). Job involvement and organizational commitment as longitudinal predictors of job performance: A study of scientists and engineers. *Journal of Applied Psychology, 82,* 539–545.

Kellerman, J., Lewis, J., & Laird, J. D. (1989). Looking and loving: The effects of mutual gaze on feelings of romantic love. *Journal of Research in Personality, 23,* 145–161.

Kelley, H. H. (1972). Attribution in social interaction. In E. E. Jones et al. (Eds.), *Attribution: Perceiving the causes of behavior.* Morristown, NJ: General Learning Press.

Kelley, H. H., & Michela, J. L. (1980). Attribution theory and research. *Annual Review of Psychology, 31,* 57–501.

Kelly, A. E. (1999). Revealing personal secrets. *Current Directions in Psychological Science, 8,* 105–109.

Kelly, A. E., & Kahn, J. H. (1994). Effects of suppression of personal intrusive thoughts. *Journal of Personality and Social Psychology, 66,* 998–1026.

Kelly, A. E., & Nauta, M. M. (1997). Reactance and thought suppression. *Personality and Social Psychology Bulletin, 23,* 1123–1132.

Kelly, A. E., Klusas, J. A., von Weiss, R. T., & Kenny, C. (2001). What is it about revealing secrets that is beneficial? *Personality and Social Psychology Bulletin, 27,* 651–665.

Kelly, J. R., Jackson, J. W., & Hutson-Comeaux, S. L. (1997). The effects of time pressure and task differences on influence modes and accuracy in decision-making groups. *Personality and Social Psychology Bulletin, 23,* 10–22.

Kelman, H. C. (1967). Human use of human subjects: The problem of deception in social psychological experiments. *Psychological Bulletin, 67,* 1–11.

Keltner, D., & Robinson, R. J. (1997). Defending the status quo: Power and bias in social conflict. *Personality and Social Psychology Bulletin, 23,* 1066–1077.

Keltner, D., Young, R. C., Heerey, E. A., Oemig, C., & Monarch, N. D. (1998). Teasing in hierarchical and intimate relations. *Journal of Personality and Social Psychology, 75,* 1231–1247.

Kendzierski, D., & Whitaker, D. J. (1997). The role of self-schema in linking intentions with behavior. *Personality and Social Psychology Bulletin, 23,* 139–147.

Kenealy, P., Gleeson, K., Frude, N., & Shaw, W. (1991). The importance of the individual in the 'causal' relationship between attractiveness and self-esteem. *Journal of Community and Applied Social Psychology,* 1, 45–56.

Kenney, D. A., & Kashy, D. A. (1994). Enhanced co-orientation in the perception of friends: A social relations analysis. *Journal of Personality and Social Psychology, 67,* 1024–1033.

Kenney, D. A., Albright, L., Malloy, T. E., & Kashy, D. A. (1994). Consensus in interpersonal perception: Acquaintance and the big five. *Journal of Personality and Social Psychology, 116,* 245–258.

Kenrick, D. T., & Gutierres, S. E. (1980). Contrast effects and judgments of physical attractiveness: When beauty becomes a social problem. *Journal of Personality and Social Psychology, 38,* 131–140.

Kenrick, D. T., Groth, G. E., Trost, M. R., & Sadalla, E. K. (1993). Integrating evolutionary and social exchange perspectives on relationships: Effects of gender, self-appraisal, and involvement level on mate selection criteria. *Journal of Personality and Social Psychology, 64,* 951–969.

Kenrick, D. T., Montello, D. R., Gutierres, S. E., & Trost, M. R. (1993). Effects of physical attractiveness on affect and perceptual judgments: When social comparison overrides social reinforcement. *Personality and Social Psychology Bulletin, 19,* 195–199.

Kenrick, D. T., Neuberg, S. L., Zierk, K. L., & Krones, J. M. (1994). Evolution and social cognition: Contrast effects as a function of sex, dominance, and physical attractiveness. *Personality and Social Psychology Bulletin, 20,* 210–217.

Kenrick, D. T., Sundie, J. M., Nicastle, L. D., & Stone, G. O. (2001). Can one ever be too wealthy or too chaste? Searching for nonlinearities in mate judgement. *Journal of Personality and Social Psychology, 80,* 462–471.

Kenrick, D. T., Keefe, R. C., Bryan, A., Barr, A., & Brown, S. (1995). Age preferences and mate choice among homosexuals and heterosexuals: A case for modular psychological mechanisms. *Journal of Personality and Social Psychology, 69,* 1166–1172.

Kent, R. L., & Moss, S. E. (1994). Effects of sex and gender role on leader emergence. *Academy of Management Journal, 37,* 1335–1346.

Kenworthy, J. B., & Miller, N. (2001). Perceptual asymmetry in consensus estimates of majority and minority members. *Journal of Personality and Social Psychology, 80,* 597–612.

Kernis, M. H., Paradise, A. W., Whitaker, D. J., Wheatman, S. R., & Goldman, B. N. (2000). Master of one's psychological domain? Not likely if one's self-esteem is unstable. *Personality and Social Psychology Bulletin, 26,* 1297–1305.

Kernis, M. H., Whisenhunt, C. R., Waschull, S. B., Greenier, K. D., Berry, A. J., Herlocker, C. E., & Anderson, C. A. (1998). Multiple facets of self-esteem and their relations to depressive symptoms. *Personality and Social Psychology Bulletin, 24,* 657–668.

Kerns, K. A. (1994). A longitudinal examination of links between mother–child attachment and children's friendships in early childhood. *Journal of Social and Personal Relationships, 11,* 379–381.

Kerns, K. A., & Barth, J. M. (1995). Attachment and play: Convergence across components of parent–child relationships and their relations to peer competence. *Journal of Social and Personal Relationships, 12,* 243–260.

Kerr, N. L., & Kaufman-Gilliland, C. M. (1994). Communication, commitment, and cooperation in social dilemmas. *Journal of Personality and Social Psychology, 66,* 513–529.

Kerr, N. L., Garst, J., Lewandowski, D. A., & Harris, S. E. (1997). That still, small voice: Commitment to cooperate as an internalized versus a social norm. *Personality and Social Psychology Bulletin, 23,* 1300–1311.

Kiecolt-Glaser, J. K., Page, G. G., Marucha, P. T., MacCallum, R. C., & Glaser, R. (1998). Psychological influences on surgical recovery: Perspectives from psychoneuroimmunology. *American Psychologist, 53,* 1209–1218.

Kilduff, M., & Day, D. V. (1994). Do chameleons get ahead? The effects of self-monitoring on managerial careers. *Academy of Management Journal, 37,* 1047–1060.

Kilham, W., & Mann, L. (1974). Level of destructive obedience as a function of transmitter and executant roles in the Milgram obedience paradigm. *Journal of Personality and Social Psychology, 29,* 696–702.

Killeya, L. A., & Johnson, B. T. (1998). Experimental induction of biased systematic processing: The directed through technique. *Personality and Social Psychology Bulletin, 24,* 17–33.

King, L. A. (2001). The health benefits of writing about life goals. *Personality and Social Psychology Bulletin, 27,* 798–807.

King, L. A., & Miner, K. N. (2000). Writing about the perceived benefits of traumatic events: Implications for physical health. *Personality and Social Psychology Bulletin, 26,* 220–230.

King, L. A., King, D. W., Fairbank, J. A., Keane, T. M., & Adams, G. A. (1998). Resilience-recovery factors in post-traumatic stress disorder among female and male Vietnam veterans: Hardiness, postwar social support, and additional stressful life events. *Journal of Personality and Social Psychology, 74,* 420–434.

Kirkpatrick, S. A., & Locke, E. A. (1991). Leadership: Do traits matter? *Academy of Management Executive, 5*(2), 48–60.

Kirn, W. (1997, August 18). The ties that bind. *Time,* 48–50.

Kirn, W. (2000, February 14). The love machines. *Time,* 73–74.

Kitayama, S., Markus, H. R., Matsumoto, H., & Norasakkunkit, V. (1997). Individual and collective processes in the construction of the self: Self-enhancement in the United States and self-criticism in Japan. *Journal of Personality and Social Psychology, 72,* 1245–1267.

Klagsbrun, F. (1992). *Mixed feelings: Love, hate, rivalry, and reconciliation among brothers and sisters.* New York: Bantam.

Klein, K., & Boals, A. (2001). Expressive writing can increase working memory capacity. *Journal of Experimental Psychology: General, 130,* 520–533.

Klein, S. B., & Loftus, J. (1988). The nature of self-referent encoding: The contributions of elaborative and organizational processes. *Journal of Personality and Social Psychology, 55,* 5–11.

Klein, S. B., & Loftus, J. (1993). Behavioral experience and trait judgments about the self. *Personality and Social Psychology Bulletin, 16,* 740–745.

Klein, S. B., Loftus, J., & Burton, H. A. (1989). Two self-reference effects: The importance of distinguishing between self-descriptiveness judgments and autobiographical retrieval in self-referent encoding. *Journal of Personality and Social Psychology, 56,* 853–865.

Klein, S. B., Loftus, J., & Plog, A. E. (1992). Trait judgments about the self: Evidence from the encoding specificity paradigm. *Personality and Social Psychology Bulletin, 18,* 730–735.

Klein, S. B., Loftus, J., Trafton, J. G., & Fuhrman, R. W. (1992). Use of exemplars and abstractions in trait judgments: A model of trait knowledge about the self and others. *Journal of Personality and Social Psychology, 63,* 739–753.

Kleinke, C. L. (1986). Gaze and eye contact: A research review. *Psychological Bulletin, 100,* 78–100.

Kleinke, C. L., & Dean, G. O. (1990). Evaluation of men and women receiving positive and negative responses with various acquaintance strategies. *Journal of Social Behavior and Personality, 5,* 369–377.

Kline, S. L., Stafford, L., & Miklosovic, J. D. (1996). Women's surnames: Decisions, interpretations and associations with relational qualities. *Journal of Social and Personal Relationships, 13,* 593–617.

Kling, K. C., Ryff, C. D., & Essex, M. J. (1997). Adaptive changes in the self-concept during a life transition. *Personality and Social Psychology Bulletin, 23,* 981–990.

Klohnen, E. C., & Bera, S. (1998). Behavioral and experiential patterns of avoidantly and securely attached women across adulthood: A 31-year longitudinal perspective. *Journal of Personality and Social Psychology, 74,* 211–223.

Klohnen, E. C., & Mendelsohn, G. A. (1998). Partner selection for personality characteristics: A couple-centered approach. *Personality and Social Psychology Bulletin, 24,* 268–278.

Knee, C. R. (1998). Implicit theories of relationships: Assessment and prediction of romantic relationship initiation, coping, and longevity. *Journal of Personality and Social Psychology, 74,* 360–370.

Knight, G. P., & Dubro, A. (1984). Cooperative, competitive, and individualistic social values: An individualized regression and clustering approach. *Journal of Personality and Social Psychology, 46,* 98–105.

Knobloch, L. K., Solomon, D. H., & Cruz, M. G. (2001). The role of relationship development and attachment in the experience of romantic jealousy. *Personal Relationships, 8,* 205–224.

Koch, W. (1996, March 10). Marriage, divorce rates indicate Americans are hopelessly in love. *Albany Times Union*, p. A11.

Koehler, J. J. (1993). The base rate fallacy myth. *Psychology, 4.*

Koestner, R., Bernieri, F., & Zuckerman, M. (1992). Self-regulation and consistency between attitudes, traits, and behaviors. *Personality and Social Psychology Bulletin, 18,* 52–59.

Kohl, W. L., Steers, R., & Terborg, Jr. (1995). The effects of transformational leadership on teacher attitudes and student performance in Singapore. *Journal of Organizational Behavior, 73,* 695–702.

Komorita, M., & Parks, G. (1994). Interpersonal relations: Mixed-motive interaction. *Annual Review of Psychology, 46,* 183–207.

Koole, S. L., Dijksterhuis, A., & van Knippenberg, A. (2001). What's in a name: Implicit self-esteem and the automatic self. *Journal of Personality and Social Psychology, 80,* 669–685.

Korchmaros, J. D., & Kenny, D. A. (2001). Emotional closeness as a mediator of the effect of genetic relatedness on altruism. *Psychological Science, 12,* 262–265.

Kowalski, R. M. (1993). Interpreting behaviors in mixed-gender encounters: Effects of social anxiety and gender. *Journal of Social and Clinical Psychology, 12,* 239–247.

Kowalski, R. M. (2000). "I was only kidding!": Victims' and perpetrators' perceptions of teasing. *Personality and Social Psychology Bulletin, 26,* 231–241.

Kraus, S. J. (1995). Attitudes and the prediction of behavior: A meta-analysis of the empirical literature. *Personality and Social Psychology Bulletin, 21,* 58–75.

Kray, L. J., Thompson, L., & Galinsky, A. (2001). Battle of the sexes: Gender stereotype confirmation and reactance in negotiations. *Journal of Personality and Social Psychology, 80,* 942–958.

Krosnick, J. A. (1988). The role of attitude importance in social evaluation: A study of political preferences, presidential candidate evaluations, and voting behavior. *Journal of Personality and Social Psychology, 55,* 196–210.

Krosnick, J. A. (1989). Attitude importance and attitude accessibility. *Personality and Social Psychology Bulletin, 15,* 297–308.

Krosnick, J. A., Betz, A. L., Jussim, L. J., & Lynn, A. R. (1992). Subliminal conditioning of attitudes. *Personality and Social Psychology Bulletin, 18,* 152–162.

Krosnick, J. A., Boninger, D. S., Chuang, Y. C., Berent, M. K., & Carnot, C. G. (1993). Attitude strength: One construct or many related constructs? *Journal of Personality and Social Psychology, 65,* 1132–1151.

Krueger, R. F., Hicks, B. M., & McGue, M. (2001). Altruism and antisocial behavior: Independent tendencies, unique personality characteristics, distinct etiologies. *Psychological Science, 12,* 397–402.

Kruger, D. J. (2001). Psychological aspects of adaptations for kin directed altruistic helping behaviors. *Social Behavior and Personality, 29,* 323–330.

Kruger, J., & Dunning, D. (1999). Unskilled and unaware of it: How difficulties in recognizing one's own incompetence lead to inflated self-assessments. *Journal of Personality and Social Psychology, 77,* 1121–1134.

Krupat, E. (1975). *Psychology is social.* Glenview, IL: Scott Foresman.

Kuhn, D. (2001). How do people know? *Psychological Science, 12,* 1–8.

Kuhn, D., Weinstock, M., & Flaton, R. (1994). How well do jurors reason? Competence dimensions of individual variation in a juror reasoning task. *Psychological Science, 5,* 289–296.

Kuiper, N. A., & Martin, R. A. (1998). Laughter and stress in daily life: Relation to positive and negative affect. *Motivation and Emotion, 22,* 133–153.

Kulik, J. A., Mahler, H. I. M., & Earnest, A. (1994). Social comparison and affiliation under threat: Going beyond the affiliate-choice paradigm. *Journal of Personality and Social Psychology, 66,* 301–309.

Kulik, J. A., Mahler, H. I. M., & Moore, P. J. (1996). Social comparison and affiliation under threat: Effects on recovery from major surgery. *Journal of Personality and Social Psychology, 71,* 967–979.

Kunda, Z. (1999). *Social cognition: Making sense of people.* Cambridge, MA: MIT Press.

Kunda, Z., & Oleson, K. C. (1995). Maintaining stereotypes in the face of disconfirmation: Constructing grounds for subtyping deviants. *Journal of Personality and Social Psychology, 68,* 565–579.

Kunda, Z., & Sherman-Williams, B. (1993). Stereotypes and the construal of individuating information. *Personality and Social Psychology Bulletin, 19,* 90–99.

Kunda, Z., Fong, G. T., Sanitioso, R., & Reber, E. (1993). Directional questions direct self-conceptions. *Journal of Experimental Social Psychology, 29,* 63–86.

Kunkel, D., Cope, K. M., & Biely, E. (1999). Sexual messages on television: Comparing findings from three studies. *Journal of Sex Research, 36,* 230–236.

Kurdek, L. (1999). The nature and predictors of the trajectory of change in marital quality for husbands and wives over the first 10 years of marriage: Predicting the seven-year itch. *Journal of Developmental Psychology, 35,* 1283–1296.

Kurdek, L. A. (1993). The allocation of household labor in gay, lesbian, and heterosexual married couples. *Journal of Social Issues, 49(3),* 127–139.

Kurdek, L. A. (1996). The deterioration of relationship quality for gay and lesbian cohabiting couples: A five-year prospective longitudinal study. *Personal Relationships, 3,* 417–442.

Kurdek, L. A. (1997). Adjustment to relationship dissolution in gay, lesbian, and heterosexual partners. *Personal Relationships, 4,* 145–161.

Kurlantzick, J. (2001, June 4). Hello, goodbye, hey maybe I love you? *U.S. News & World Report,* 43.

Kwan, L. K. (1998). *Attitudes and attraction: A new view on how to diagnose the moderating effects of personality.* Unpublished master's thesis, National University of Singapore.

Kwan, V. S. Y., Bond, M. H., & Singelis, T. M. (1997). Pancultural explanations for life satisfaction: Adding relationship harmony to self-esteem. *Journal of Personality and Social Psychology, 73,* 1038–1051.

Kwon, Y.-H. (1994). Feeling toward one's clothing and self-perception of emotion, sociability, and work competency. *Journal of Social Behavior and Personality, 9,* 129–139.

La Guardia, J. G., Ryan, R. M., Couchman, C. E., & Deci, E. L. (2000). Within-person variation in security of attachment: A self-determination theory perspective on attachment, need fulfillment, and well-being. *Journal of Personality and Social Psychology, 79,* 367–384.

Lacayo, R. (1997, July 21). Teen crime. *Time,* 26–29.

Lachman, M. E., & Weaver, S. L. (1998). The sense of control as a moderator of social class differences in health and well-being. *Journal of Personality and Social Psychology, 74,* 763–773.

Lafferty, E. (1997, February 17). The inside story of how O. J. lost. *Time,* 29–36.

LaFrance, M., & Hecht, M. A. (1995). Why smiles generate leniency. *Personality and Social Psychology Bulletin, 21,* 207–214.

LaMastro, V. (2001). Childless by choice? Attributions and attitudes concerning family size. *Social Behavior and Personality, 29,* 231–244.

Lambert, A. J. (1995). Stereotypes and social judgment: The consequences of group variability. *Journal of Personality and Social Psychology, 68,* 388–403.

Lamm, H. & Myers, D. G. (1978). Group-induced polarization of attitudes and behavior. In L. Berkowitz (Ed.), *Advances in experimental social psychology.* New York: Academic Press.

Langer, E. (1984). *The psychology of control.* Beverly Hills, CA: Sage.

Langlois, J. H., & Roggman, L. A. (1990). Attractive faces are only average. *Psychological Science, 1,* 115–121.

Langlois, J. H., Roggman, L. A., & Musselman, L. (1994). What is average and what is not average about attractive faces? *Psychological Science, 5,* 214–220.

Langlois, J. H., Ritter, J. M., Roggman, L. A., & Vaughn, L. S. (1991). Facial diversity and infant preferences for attractive faces. *Developmental Psychology, 27,* 79–84.

Langston, C. A., & Cantor, N. (1989). Social anxiety and social constraint: When making friends is hard. *Journal of Personality and Social Psychology, 56,* 649–661.

Lansing, J. B., & Heyns, R. W. (1959). Need affiliation and frequency of four types of communication. *Journal of Abnormal and Social Psychology, 58,* 365–372.

Lapham, L. H. (1996, September). Back to school. *Harper's Magazine,* 10–11.

LaPiere, R. T. (1934). Attitude and actions. *Social Forces, 13,* 230–237.

LaPrelle, J., Hoyle, R. H., Insko, C. A., & Bernthal, P. (1990). Interpersonal attraction and descriptions of the traits of others: Ideal similarity, self similarity, and liking. *Journal of Research in Personality, 24,* 216–240.

LaRose, S., Boivin, M., & Doyle, A. B. (2001). Parental representation and attachment style as predictors of support-seeking behaviors and perceptions of support in an academic counseling relationship. *Personal Relationships, 8,* 93–113.

Larrey, T. S., & Paulus, P. B. (1999). Group preference and convergent tendencies in groups: A content analysis of group brainstorming performance. *Creativity Research Journal, 12,* 175–184.

Larson, J. H., & Bell, N. J. (1988). Need for privacy and its effects upon interpersonal attraction and interaction. *Journal of Social and Clinical Psychology, 6,* 1–10.

Larson, J. R., Jr., Foster-Fishman, P. G., & Franz, T. M. (1998). Leadership style and the discussion of shared and unshared information in decision-making groups. *Personality and Social Psychology Bulletin, 24,* 482–495.

Larson, J. R. Jr., Christensen, C., Franz, T. M., & Abbott, A. S. (1998). Diagnosing groups: The pooling, management, and impact of shared and unshared case information in team-based medical decision making. *Jounral of Personality and Social Psychology, 75,* 93–108.

Latané, B. (1981). The psychology of social impacts. *American Psychologist, 36,* 343–356.

Latané, B., & Dabbs, J. M., Jr. (1975). Sex, group size, and helping in three cities. *Sociometry, 38,* 180–194.

Latané, B., & Darley, J. M. (1968). Group inhibition of bystander intervention in emergencies. *Journal of Personality and Social Psychology, 10,* 215–221.

Latané, B., & Darley, J. M. (1970). *The unresponsive bystander: Why doesn't he help?* New York: Appleton-Century-Crofts.

Latané, B., & L'Herrou, T. (1996). Spatial clustering in the conformity game: Dynamic social impact in electronic groups. *Journal of Personality and Social Psychology, 70,* 1218–1230.

Latané, B., Williams, K., & Harkins, S. (1979). Many hands make light the work: The causes and consequences of social loafing. *Journal of Personality and Social Psychology, 37,* 822–832.

Latest figures: U.S. death rate is lower. (1994, December 16). Associated Press.

Latty-Mann, H., & Davis, K. E. (1996). Attachment theory and partner choice: Preference and actuality. *Journal of Social and Personal Relationships, 13,* 5–23.

Lau, S. (1989). Sex role orientation and domains of self esteem. *Sex Roles, 21,* 415–422.

Lau, S., & Gruen, G. E. (1992). The social stigma of loneliness: Effect of target person's and perceiver's sex. *Personality and Social Psychology Bulletin, 18,* 182–189.

Lau, S., & Kwok, L.-K. (2000). Relationship of family environment to adolescents' depression and self-concept. *Social Behavior and Personality, 28,* 41–50.

Lau, S., & Pun, K.-L. (1999). Parental evaluations and their agreement: Relationship with children's self-concepts. *Social Behavior and Personality, 27,* 639–650.

Lauer, J., & Lauer, R. (1985, June). Marriages made to last. *Psychology Today,* 22–26.

Laumann, E. O., Gagnon, J. H., Michael, R. T., & Michaels, S. (1994). *The social organization of sexuality: Sexual practices in the United States.* Chicago: University of Chicago Press.

Laurenceau, J.-P., Barrett, L. F., & Pietromonaco, P. R. (1998). Intimacy as an interpersonal process: The importance of self-disclosure, partner disclosure, and perceived partner responsiveness in interpersonal exchanges. *Journal of Personality and Social Psychology, 74,* 1238–1251.

Lavine, H., Sweeney, D., & Wagner, S. H. (1999). Depicting women as sex objects in television advertising: Effects on body dissatisfaction. *Personality and Social Psychology Bulletin, 25,* 1049–1058.

Lavine, H., Thomsen, C. J., & Gonzales, M. H. (1997). The development of interattitudinal consistency: The shared-consequences model. *Journal of Personality and Social Psychology, 72,* 735–749.

Lazarus, R. S. (1993). From psychological stress to the emotions: A history of changing outlooks. *Annual Review of Psychology, 44,* 1–21.

Lea, M., Spears, R., & de Groot, D. (2001). Knowing me, knowing you: Anonymity effects on social identity processes within groups. *Personality and Social Psychology Bulletin, 27,* 526–537.

Leary, M. R. (1999). Making sense of self-esteem. *Current Directions in Psychological Science, 8,* 32–35.

Leary, M. R., Schreindorfer, L. S., & Haupt, A. L. (1995). The role of low self-esteem in emotional and behavioral problems: Why is low self-esteem dysfunctional? *Journal of Social and Clinical Psychology, 14,* 297–314.

Leary, M. R., Tambor, E. S., Terdal, S. K., & Downs, D. L. (1995). Self-esteem as an interpersonal monitor: The sociometer hypothesis. *Journal of Personality and Social Psychology, 68,* 518–530.

Leary, M. R., Spinger, C., Negel, L., Ansell, E., & Evans, K. (1998). The causes, phenomenology, and consequences of hurt feelings. *Journal of Personality and Social Psychology, 74,* 1225–1237.

Leary, W. E. (1988, November 19). Novel methods unlock witnesses' memories. *New York Times,* pp. C1, C15.

Lee, I.-M., Rexrode, K. M., Cook, N. R., Manson, J. A. E., Buring, J. E. (2001). Physical activity and coronary heart disease in women: Is "no pain, no gain" passé? *Journal of the American Medical Association, 285,* 1447–1454.

Lee, Y. T., & Ottati, V. (1993). Determinants of ingroup and out-group perceptions of heterogeneity: An investigation of Sino-American differences. *Journal of Cross-Cultural Psychology, 25,* 146–158.

Lee, Y. T., & Seligman, M. E. P. (1997). Are Americans more optimistic than the Chinese? *Personality and Social Psychology Bulletin, 23,* 32–40.

Lehman, T. C., Daubman, K. A., Guarna, J., Jordan, J., & Cirafesi, C. (1995, April). *Gender differences in the motivational consequences of receiving help.* Paper presented at the meeting of the Eastern Psychological Association, Boston.

Lemery, K. S., Goldsmith, H. H., Klinnert, M. D., & Mrazek, D. A. (1999). Developmental models of infant and childhood temperament. *Developmental Psychology, 35,* 189–204.

Lemley, B. (2000, February). Isn't she lovely? *Discover,* 42–49.

Lemonick, M. D., & Dorfman, A. (2001, July 23). One giant step for mankind. *Time,* 54–61.

Lemonick, M. D., & Park, A. (2001, May 28). New hope for cancer. *Time,* 62–69.

Lenton, A. P., Blair, I. V., & Hastie, R. (2001). Illusions of gender: Stereotypes evoke false memories. *Journal of Experimental Social Psychology, 37,* 3–14.

Leonard, J. R., & Sloboda, B. A. (1996, April). Workplace violence: A review of current literature. Paper presented at the Annual Meeting of the Society for Industrial and Organizational Psychology. San Diego, CA.

Lepore, S. J. (1997). Expressive writing moderates the relation between intrusive thoughts and depressive symptoms. *Journal of Personality and Social Psychology, 73,* 1030–1037.

Levenson, R. W., Carstensen, L. L., & Gottman, J. M. (1994). The influence of age and gender on affect, physiology, and their interrelations: A study of long-term marriages. *Journal of Personality and Social Psychology, 67,* 56–68.

Leventhal, G. S., Karuza, J., & Fry, W. R. (1980). Beyond fairness: A theory of allocation preferences. In G. Mikula (Ed.), *Justice and social interaction* (pp. 167–218). New York: Springer-Verlag.

Leventhal, H., Singer, R., & Jones, S. (1965). The effects of fear and specificity of recommendation upon attitudes and behavior. *Journal of Personality and Social Psychology, 2,* 20–29.

Levin, D. (2000). Race as a visual feature: Using visual search and perceptual discrimination tasks to understand face categories and the cross-race recognition deficit. *Journal of Experimental Psychology: General, 129,* 559–574.

Levin, J. (2000). A prolegomenon to an epidemiology of love: Theory, measurement, and health outcomes. *Journal of Social and Clinical Psychology, 19,* 117–136.

Levine, R. V., Martinez, T. S., Brase, G., & Sorenson, K. (1994). Helping in 36 U.S. cities. *Journal of Personality and Social Psychology, 67,* 69–82.

Levy, D. S. (1999a, June 7). And baby makes three. *Time,* 86.

Levy, D. S. (1999b, June 21). Hello, I must be going. *Time,* 86.

Levy, K. N., Blatt, S. J., & Shaver, P. R. (1998). Attachment styles and parental representations. *Journal of Personality and Social Psychology, 74,* 407–419.

Lewin, K., Lippitt, R., & White, R. K. (1939). Patterns of aggressive behavior in experimentally created "social climates." *Journal of Social Psychology, 10,* 271–299.

Lewis, M. (1992). Will the real self or selves please stand up? *Psychological Inquiry, 3,* 123–124.

Liberman, A., & Chaiken, S. (1992). Defensive processing of personally relevant health messages. *Personality and Social Psychology Bulletin, 18,* 669–679.

Liberman, N., Molden, D. C., Idson, L. C., & Higgins, E. T. (2001). Promotion and prevention focus on alternative hypotheses: Implications for attributional functions. *Journal of Personality and Social Psychology, 80,* 5–18.

Lickel, B., Hamilton, D. L., Wieczorkowski, G., Lewis, A., Sherman, S. J., & Uhles, A. N. (2000). Varieties of groups and the perception of group entiativity. *Journal of Personality and Social Psychology, 78,* 223–246.

Liden, R. C., & Mitchell, T. R. (1988). Ingratiatory behaviors in organizational settings. *Academy of Management Review, 13,* 572–587.

Lieberman, J. D., & Greenberg, J. (1999). Cognitive-experiential self-theory and displaced aggression. *Journal of Personality and Social Psychology,* in press.

Limper, R. (2000). Cooperation between parents, teachers, and school boards to prevent bullying in education: An overview of work done in the Netherlands. *Aggressive Behavior, 26,* 113–124.

Linden, E. (1992). Chimpanzees with a difference: Bonobos. *National Geographic, 18*(3), 46–53.

Lindsey, E. W., Mize, J., & Pettit, G. S. (1997). Mutuality in parent–child play: Consequences for children's peer competence. *Journal of Social and Personal Relationships, 14,* 523–538.

Linville, P. W., & Fischer, G. W. (1993). Exemplar and abstraction models of perceived group variability and stereotypicality. *Social Cognition, 11,* 92–125.

Linville, P. W., Fischer, G. W., & Salovey, P. (1989). Perceived distributions of the characteristics of in-group and out-group members: Empirical evidence and a computer simulation. *Journal of Personality and Social Psychology, 57,* 165–188.

Linz, D., & Penrod, S. (1992). Exploring the first and sixth amendments: Pretrial publicity and jury decision making. In D. K. Kagehiro & W. S. Laufer (Eds.), *Handbook of psychology and law.* New York: Springer-Verlag.

Lipkus, I. M., Green, J. D., Feaganes, J. R., & Sedikides, C. (2001). The relationships between attitudinal ambivalence and desire to quite smoking among college smokers. *Journal of Applied Social Psychology, 31,* 113–133.

Lippa, R., & Donaldson, S. I. (1990). Self-monitoring and idiographic measures of behavioral variability across interpersonal relationships. *Journal of Personality, 58,* 465–479.

Lippa, R. A., Martin, L. R., & Friedman, H. S. (2000). Gender-related individual differences and mortality in the Terman longitudinal study: Is masculinity hazardous to your health? *Personality and Social Psychology Bulletin, 26,* 1560–1570.

Lippert, T., & Prager, K. J. (2001). Daily experiences of intimacy: A study of couples. *Personal Relationships, 8,* 283–298.

Lobel, T. E. (1994). Sex typing and the social perception of gender stereotypic and nonstereotypic behavior: The uniqueness of feminine males. *Journal of Personality and Social Psychology, 66,* 379–385.

Locke, E. A. (1991). *The essence of leadership.* New York: Lexington Books.

Lockwood, P., & Kunda, Z. (1999). Increasing the salience of one's best selves can undermine inspiration by outstanding role models. *Journal of Personality and Social Psychology, 76,* 214–228.

Loftus, E. F. (1992a). *Witness for the defense.* New York: St. Martin's Press.

Loftus, E. F. (1992b). When a lie becomes memory's truth: Memory distortion after exposure to misinformation. *Current Directions in Psychological Science, 1,* 121–123.

Loftus, E. F. (1997). Memory for a past that never was. *Current Directions in Psychological Science, 6,* 60–65.

Loftus, E. F. (1996). The private practice of misleading direction. *American Psychologist, 53,* 484–485.

Loftus, E. F., & Pickrell, J. E. (1995). The formation of false memories. *Psychiatric Annals, 25,* 720–725.

Loftus, E. F., Coan, J. A., & Pickrell, J. E. (1996). Manufacturing false memories using bits of reality. In L. Reder (Ed.), *Implicit memory and metacognition* (pp. 195–220). Mahwah, NJ: Erlbaum.

Lopez, F. G. (1997). Student–professor relationship styles, childhood attachment bonds and current academic orientations. *Journal of Social and Personal Relationships, 14,* 271–282.

Lopez, F. G., Gover, M. R., Leskela, J., Sauer, E. M., Schirmer, L., & Wyssmann, J. (1997). Attachment styles, shame, guilt, and collaborative problem-solving orientations. *Personal Relationships, 4,* 187–199.

Lord, C. G., Ross, L., & Lepper, M. R. (1979). Biased assimilation and attitude polarization: The effects of prior theories on subsequently considered evidence. *Journal of Personality and Social Psychology, 37,* 2098–2109.

Lord, M. (2001, June 4). Morality goes to school. *U.S. News & World Report,* 50–51.

Lorenz, K. (1966). *On aggression.* New York: Harcourt, Brace, & World.

Lorenz, K. (1974). *Civilized man's eight deadly sins.* New York: Harcourt, Brace, Jovanovich.

Losch, M., & Cacioppo, J. (1990). Cognitive dissonance may enhance sympathetic tonis, but attitudes are changed to reduce negative affect rather than arousal. *Journal of Experimental Social Psychology, 26,* 289–304.

Lowy, J. (1999, October 7). Monogamous women risk diseases. Scripps Howard.

Luks, A. (1988, October). Helper's high. *Psychology Today,* 39–40.

Lundberg, J. K., & Sheehan, E. P. (1994). The effects of glasses and weight on perceptions of attractiveness and intelligence. *Journal of Social Behavior and Personality, 9,* 753–760.

Lurie, A. (Ed.). (1993). *The Oxford book of modern fairy tales.* Oxford, England: Oxford University Press.

Lydon, J. E., Jamieson, D. W., & Holmes, J. G. (1997). The meaning of social interactions in the transition from acquaintanceship to friendship. *Journal of Personality and Social Psychology, 73,* 536–548.

Lynch, D. (2001, September 23). New Zealand residents show support for U.S. *Albany Times Union,* B4.

Lyness, K. S., & Thompson, D. E. (1997). Above the glass ceiling? A comparison of matched samples of female and male executives. *Journal of Applied Psychology, 82,* 359–375.

Lyness, K. S., & Thompson, D. E. (2000). Climbing the corporate ladder: Do female and male executives follow the same route? *Journal of Applied Psychology, 85,* 86–101.

Lyubomirsky, S., & Nolen-Hoeksema, S. (1995). Effects of self-focused rumination on negative thinking and interpersonal problem solving. *Journal of Personality and Social Psychology, 69,* 176–190.

Maas, A., & Clark, R. D. III (1984). Hidden impact of minorities: Fifteen years of minority influence research. *Psychological Bulletin, 95,* 233–243.

Macaulay, J. (1970). A shill for charity. In J. Macaulay & L. Berkowitz (Eds.), *Altruism and helping behavior* (pp. 43–59). New York: Academic Press.

MacCoun, R. J., & Kerr, N. L. (1988). Asymmetric influence in mock jury deliberation: Jurors' bias for leniency. *Journal of Personality and Social Psychology, 54,* 21–33.

MacDonald, T. K., & Ross, M. (1999). Assessing the accuracy of predictions about dating relationships: How and why do lovers' predictions differ from those made by observers? *Personality and Social Psychology Bulletin, 25,* 1417–1429.

MacDonald, T. K., Zanna, M. P., & Fong, G. T. (1996). Why common sense goes out the window: Effects of alcohol on intentions to use condoms. *Personality and Social Psychology Bulletin, 8,* 763–775.

Mack, D., & Rainey, D. (1990). Female applicants' grooming and personnel selection. *Journal of Social Behavior and Personality, 5,* 399–407.

Macrae, C., Bodenhausen, G., & Milne, A. (1995). The dissection of selection in person perception: Inhibitory processes in social stereotyping. *Journal of Personality and Social Psychology, 69,* 397–407.

Macrae, C. N., & Milne, A. B. (1992). A curry for your thoughts: Empathic effects on counterfactual thinking. *Personality and Social Psychology Bulletin, 18,* 625–630.

Macrae, C. N., Bodenhausen, G. V., & Milne, A. B. (1998). Saying no to unwanted thoughts: Self-focus and the regulation of mental life. *Journal of Personality and Social Psychology, 74,* 578–589.

Macrae, C. N., Milne, A. B., & Bodenhausen, G. V. (1994). Stereotypes as energy-saving devices: A peek inside the cognitive toolbox. *Journal of Personality and Social Psychology, 66,* 37–47.

Macrae, C. N., Bodenhausen, G. V., Milne, A. B., & Ford, R. (1997). On the regulation of recollection: The intentional forgetting of sterotypical memories. *Journal of Personality and Social Psychology, 72,* 709–719.

Maestripieri, D. (2001). Biological bases of maternal attachment. *Current Directions in Psychological Science, 10,* 79–82.

Magner, N. R., Johnson, G. G., Sobery, J. S., & Welker, R. B. (2000). Enhancing procedural justice in local government budget and tax decision making. *Journal of Applied Social Psychology, 30,* 798–815.

Maheswaran, D., & Chaiken, S. (1991). Promoting systematic processing in low-motivation settings: Effect of incongruent information on processing and judgment. *Journal of Personality and Social Psychology, 61,* 13–25.

Maier, S. F., & Watkins, L. R. (2000). The immune system as a sensory system: Implications for psychology. *Current Directions in Psychological Science, 9,* 98–102.

Maio, G. R., Esses, V. M., & Bell, D. W. (1994). The formation of attitudes toward new immigrant groups. *Journal of Applied Social Psychology, 24,* 1762–1776.

Maio, G. R., Fincham, F. D., & Lycett, E. J. (2000). Attitudinal ambivalence toward parents and attachment style. *Personality and Social Psychology Bulletin, 26,* 1451–1464.

Maisonneuve, J., Palmade, G., & Fourment, C. (1952). Selective choices and propinquity. *Sociometry, 15,* 135–140.

Major, B. (1993). Gender, entitlement, and the distribution of family labor. *Journal of Social Issues, 49*(3), 141–159.

Major, B., & Adams, J. B. (1983). Roles of gender, interpersonal orientation, and self-presentation in distributive justice behavior. *Journal of Personality and Social Psychology, 45,* 598–608.

Major, B., & Deaux, K. (1982). Individual differences in justice behavior. In J. Greenberg & R. L. Cohen (Eds.), *Equity and justice in social behavior.* New York: Academic Press.

Major, B., & Konar, E. (1984). An investigation of sex differences in pay expectations and their possible causes. *Academy of Management Journal, 27,* 777–792.

Major, B., Carnevale, P. J. D., & Deaux, K. (1981). A different perspective on androgyny: Evaluations of masculine and feminine personality characteristics. *Journal of Personality and Social Psychology, 41,* 988–1001.

Major, B., Sciacchitano, A. M., & Crocker, J. (1993). In-group versus out-group comparisons and self-esteem. *Personality and Social Psychology Bulletin, 19,* 711–721.

Malle, B. F. (1999). How people explain behavior: A new theoretical framework. *Personality and Social Psychology Review, 3,* 21–43.

Malle, B. F., & Horowitz, L. M. (1995). The puzzle of negative self-views: An exploration using the schema concept. *Journal of Personality and Social Psychology, 68,* 470–484.

Malle, B. F., Knobe, J., O'Laughlin, M. J., Pearce, G. E., & Nelson, S. E. (2000). Conceptual structure and social functions of behavior explanations: Beyond person–situation attribution. *Journal of Personality and Social Psychology, 79,* 309–326.

Mallick, S. K., & McCandless, B. R. (1966). A study of catharsis of aggression. *Journal of Personality and Social Psychology, 4,* 591–596.

Marcus, D. K., & Askari, N. H. (1999). Dysphoria and interpersonal rejection: A social relations analysis. *Journal of Social and Clinical Psychology, 18,* 370–384.

Marcus-Newhall, A., Pederson, W. C., Carlson, M., & Miller, N. (2000). Displaced aggression is alive and well: A meta-analytic review. *Journal of Personality and Social Psychology, 78,* 670–689.

Margalit, M., & Eysenck, S. (1990). Prediction of coherence in adolescence: Gender differences in social skills, personality, and family climate. *Journal of Research in Personality, 24,* 510–521.

Markman, H. J. (1981). Prediction of marital distress: A 5-year follow-up. *Journal of Consulting and Clinical Psychology, 49,* 760–762.

Markus, H., & Nurius, P. (1986). Possible selves. *American Psychologist, 41,* 954–969.

Marquis, M., & Filiatrault, P. (2000). Cognitive and affective reactions when facing an additional delay while waiting in line: A matter of self-consciousness disposition. *Social Behavior and Personality, 28,* 355–376.

Marsh, H. W. (1995). A Jamesian model of self-investment and self-esteem: Comment on Pelham (1995). *Journal of Personality and Social Psychology, 69,* 1151–1160.

Martin, C. L., & Fabes, R. A. (2001). The stability and consequences of young children's same-sex peer interactions. *Developmental Psychology, 37,* 431–446.

Martin, C. L., & Parker, S. (1995). Folk theories about sex and race differences. *Personality and Social Psychology Bulletin, 21,* 45–57.

Martin, K. A., & Leary, M. R. (1999). Would you drink after a stranger? The influence of self-presentational motives on willingness to take a health risk. *Personality and Social Psychology Bulletin, 25,* 1092–1100.

Martin, R. (1997). "Girls don't talk about garages!": Perceptions of conversation in same- and cross-sex friendships. *Personal Relationships, 4,* 115–130.

Martin, R., Wan, C. K., David, J. P., Wegner, E. L., Olson, B. D., & Watson, D. (1999). Style of anger expression: Relation to expressivity, personality, and health. *Personality and Social Psychology Bulletin, 25,* 1196–1207.

Martz, J. M., Verette, J., Arriaga, X. B., Slovik, L. F., Cox, C. L., & Rusbult, C. E. (1998). Positive illusion in close relationships. *Personal Relationships, 5,* 159–181.

Maslach, C., Santee, R. T., & Wade, C. (1987). Individuation, gender role, and dissent: Personality mediators of situational forces. *Journal of Personality and Social Psychology, 53,* 1088–1094.

Mastekaasa, A. (1995). Age variation in the suicide rates and self-reported subjective well-being of married and never married persons. *Journal of Community and Applied Social Psychology, 5,* 21–39.

Mathis, D. (1998, June 17). Report on girls' lives offers mixed assessment. Gannett News Service.

May, J. L., & Hamilton, P. A. (1980). Effects of musically evoked affect on women's interpersonal attraction and perceptual judgments of physical attractiveness of men. *Motivation and Emotion, 4,* 217–228.

Mayer, J. D., & Hanson, E. (1995). Mood-congruent judgment over time. *Personality and Social Psychology Bulletin, 21,* 237–244.

Mayer, J. D., & Salovey, P. (1995). Emotional intelligence and the construction and regulation of feelings. *Applied & Preventive Psychology, 4,* 197–208.

Mazzella, R., & Feingold, A. (1994). The effects of physical attractiveness, race, socioeconomic status, and gender of defendants and victims on judgments of mock jurors: A meta-analysis. *Journal of Applied Social Psychology, 24,* 1315–1344.

McAdams, D. P. (1979). *Validation of a thematic coding system for the intimacy motive.* Unpublished doctoral dissertation, Harvard University.

McAdams, D. P., Diamond, A., Aubin, E. de S., & Mansfield, E. (1997). Stories of commitment: The psychosocial construction of generative lives. *Journal of Personality and Social Psychology, 72,* 678–694.

McArthur, L. Z., & Eisen, S. V. (1976). Achievements of male and female storybook characters as determinants of achievement behavior by boys and girls. *Journal of Personality and Social Psychology, 33,* 467–473.

McCall, M. (1997). Physical attractiveness and access to alcohol: What is beautiful does not get carded. *Journal of Applied Social Psychology, 23,* 453–562.

McCall, M. E., & Struthers, N. J. (1994). Sex, sex-role orientation and self-esteem as predictors of coping style. *Journal of Social Behavior and Personality, 9,* 801–810.

McCauley, C., Coleman, G., & DeFusco, P. (1977). Commuters' eye contact with strangers in city and suburban train stations: Evidence of short-term adaptation to interpersonal overload in the city. *Environmental Psychology and Nonverbal Behavior, 2,* 215–225.

McClure, J. (1998). Discounting causes of behavior: Are two reasons better than one? *Journal of Personality and Social Psychology, 74,* 7–20.

McConnell, A. R., Sherman, S. J., & Hamilton, D. L. (1994). Illusory correlation in the perception of groups: An extension of the distinctiveness-based account. *Journal of Personality and Social Psychology, 67,* 414–429.

McDonald, F. (2001). *States' rights and the union: Imperium in imperio, 1776–1876.* Lawrence: University of Kansas Press.

McDonald, H. E., & Hirt, E. R. (1997). When expectancy meets desire: Motivational effects in reconstructive memory. *Journal of Personality and Social Psychology, 72,* 5–23.

McDonald, R. D. (1962). *The effect of reward–punishment and affiliation need on interpersonal attraction.* Unpublished doctoral dissertation, University of Texas.

McFarland, C., & Buehler, R. (1995). Collective self-esteem as a moderator of the frog-pond effect in reactions to performance feedback. *Journal of Personality and Social Psychology, 68,* 1055–1070.

McFarland, C., & Buehler, R. (1998). The impact of negative affect on autobiographical memory: The role of self-focused attention to moods. *Journal of Personality and Social Psychology, 75,* 1424–1440.

McGonagle, K. A., Kessler, R. C., & Schilling, E. A. (1992). The frequency and determinants of marital disagreements in a community sample. *Journal of Social and Personal Relationships, 9,* 507–524.

McGowan, S. (2001, in press). Mental representations in stressful situations: The calming effect of significant others. *Journal of Experimental Social Psychology.*

McGowan, S., Daniels, L. K., & Byrne, D. (2000). The Albany Measure of Attachment Style: A multi-item measure of Bartholomew's four-category model. Manuscript submitted for publication.

McGowan, S., Daniels, L. K., & Byrne, D. (2001). *Interpersonal trust and fear of exploitation: An exploration of the other-model underlying adult attachment style.* Manuscript submitted for publication.

McGuire, S., & Clifford, J. (2000). Genetic and environmental contributions to loneliness in children. *Psychological Science, 11,* 487–491.

McGuire, S., McHale, S. M., & Updegraff, K. A. (1996). Children's perceptions of the sibling relationship in middle childhood: Connections within and between family relationships. *Personal Relationships, 3,* 229–239.

McGuire, W. J. (1961). Resistance to persuasion confirmed by active and passive prior refutation of the same and alternate counterarguments. *Journal of Abnormal and Social Psychology, 63,* 326–332.

McGuire, W. J., & McGuire, C. V. (1996). Enhancing self-esteem by directed-thinking tasks: Cognitive and affective positivity asymmetries. *Journal of Personality and Social Psychology, 70,* 1117–1125.

McGuire, W. J., & Papageorgis, D. (1961). The relative efficacy of various types of prior belief-defense in producing immunity against persuasion. *Journal of Abnormal and Social Psychology, 62,* 327–337.

McHoskey, J. W. (1999). Machiavellianism, intrinsic versus extrinsic goals, and social interest: A self-determination theory analysis. *Motivation and Emotion, 23,* 267–283.

McKelvie, S. J. (1993a). Perceived cuteness, activity level, and gender in schematic babyfaces. *Journal of Social Behavior and Personality, 8,* 297–310.

McKelvie, S. J. (1993b). Stereotyping in perception of attractiveness, age, and gender in schematic faces. *Social Behavior and Personality, 21,* 121–128.

McKenna, K. Y. A., & Bargh, J. A. (2000). Plan 9 from cyberspace: The implications of the internet for personality and social psychology. *Personality and Social Psychology Review, 4,* 57–75.

McLaughlin, L. (2001a, April 30). Happy together. *Time,* 82.

McLaughlin, L. (2001b, May 21). Gay and lesbian couples. *Time,* G10.

McNulty, S. E., & Swann, W. B., Jr. (1994). Identity negotiation in roommate relationships: The self as architect and consequence of social reality. *Journal of Personality and Social Psychology, 67,* 1012–1023.

McWhirter, B. T. (1997). A pilot study of loneliness in ethnic minority college students. *Social Behavior and Personality, 25,* 295–304.

Mealey, L., Bridgstock, R., & Townsend, G. C. (1999). Symmetry and perceived facial attractiveness: A monozygotic co-twin comparison. *Journal of Personality and Social Psychology, 76,* 151–158.

Medvec, V. H., & Savitsky, K. (1997). When doing better means feeling worse: The effects of categorical cutoff points on counterfactual thinking and satisfaction. *Journal of Personality and Social Psychology, 72,* 1284–1296.

Medvec, V. H., Madey, S. F., & Gilovich, T. (1995). When less is more: Counterfactual thinking and satisfaction among Olympic athletes. *Journal of Personality and Social Psychology, 69,* 603–610.

Mehrabian, A., & Piercy, M. (1993). Affective and personality characteristics inferred from length of first names. *Personality and Social Psychology Bulletin, 19,* 755–758.

Meindl, J. R., & Lerner, M. J. (1985). Exacerbation of extreme responses to an outgroup. *Journal of Personality and Social Psychology, 47,* 71–84.

Melamed, S., Ben-Avi, I., Luz, J., & Green, M. S. (1995). Objective and subjective work monotony: Effects on job satisfaction, psychological distress, and absenteeism in blue-collar workers. *Journal of Applied Psychology, 80,* 29–42.

Meleshko, K. G. A., & Alden, L. E. (1993). Anxiety and self-disclosure: Toward a motivational model. *Journal of Personality and Social Psychology, 64,* 1000–1009.

Mendolia, M., Beach, S. R. H., & Tesser, A. (1996). The relationship between marital interaction behaviors and affective reactions to one's own and one's spouse's self-evaluation needs. *Personal Relationships, 3,* 279–292.

Mendoza-Denton, R., Ayduk, O., Mischel, W., Shoda, Y., & Testa, A. (2001). Person X situation interactionism in self-encoding (*I am . . . When . . .*): Implications for affect regulation and social information processing. *Journal of Personality and Social Psychology, 80,* 533–544.

Menesini, E. (1997). Behavioural correlates of friendship status among Italian schoolchildren. *Journal of Social and Personal Relationships, 14,* 109–121.

Meyerowitz, B. E., Formenti, S. C., Ell, K. O., & Leedham, B. (2000). Depression among Latina cervical cancer patients. *Journal of Social and Clinical Psychology, 19,* 352–371.

Meyers, S. A., & Berscheid, E. (1997). The language of love: The difference a preposition makes. *Personality and Social Psychology Bulletin, 23,* 347–362.

Miceli, M. P., & Lane, M. C. (1991). Antecedents of pay satisfaction: A review and extension. In K. Rowland & O. R. Ferris (Eds.), *Research in personnel and human resources management* (Vol. 9, pp. 235–309). Greenwich, CT: JAI Press.

Michael, R. T., Gagnon, J. H., Laumann, E. O., & Kolata, G. (1994). *Sex in America: A definitive survey.* Boston: Little, Brown.

Michinov, E., & Michinov, N. (in press). The similarity hypothesis: A test of the moderating role of social comparison orientation. *European Journal of Social Psychology.*

Michinov, N. (2001). When downward comparison produces negative affect: The sense of control as a moderator. *Social Behavior and Personality, 29,* 427–444.

Middlestadt, S. E., Fishbein, M., Albarracin, D., Francis, C., Eustace, M. A., Helquist, M., & Schneider, A. (1995). Evaluating the impact of a national AIDS prevention radio campaign in St. Vincent and the Grenadines. *Journal of Applied Social Psychology, 25,* 21–34.

Middleton, W., Harris, P., & Surman, M. (1996). Give 'em enough rope: Perception of health and safety risks in bungee jumpers. *Journal of Social and Clinical Psychology, 15,* 68–79.

Mikulincer, M. (1997). Adult attachment style and information processing: Individual differences in curiosity and cognitive closure. *Journal of Personality and Social Psychology, 72,* 1217–1230.

Mikulincer, M. (1998a). Adult attachment style and individual differences in functional versus dysfunctional experiences of anger. *Journal of Personality and Social Psychology, 74,* 513–524.

Mikulincer, M. (1998b). Attachment working models and the sense of trust: An exploration of interaction goals and affect regulation. *Journal of Personality and Social Psychology, 74,* 1209–1224.

Mikulincer, M., & Florian, V. (1995). Appraisal of and coping with a real-life stressful situation: The contribution of attachment styles. *Personality and Social Psychology Bulletin, 21,* 406–414.

Mikulincer, M., & Florian, V. (1999). Maternal-fetal bonding, coping strategies, and mental health during pregnancy: The contribution of attachment style. *Journal of Social and Clinical Psychology, 18,* 255–276.

Mikulincer, M., & Horesh, N. (1999). Adult attachment style and the perception of others: The role of projective mechanisms. *Journal of Personality and Social Psychology, 76,* 1022–1034.

Mikulincer, M., & Sheffi, E. (2000). Adult attachment style and cognitive reactions to positive affect: A test of mental categorization and creative problem solving. *Motivation and Emotion, 24,* 149–174.

Milar, K. S. (2000). The first generation of women psychologists and the psychology of women. *American Psychologist, 55,* 616–619.

Miles, S. M., & Carey, G. (1997). Genetic and environmental architecture of human aggression. *Journal of Personality and Social Psychology, 72,* 207–217.

Milgram, S. (1963). Behavior study of obedience. *Journal of Abnormal and Social Psychology, 67,* 371–378.

Milgram, S. (1965a). Liberating effects of group pressure. *Journal of Personality and Social Psychology, 1,* 127–134.

Milgram, S. (1965b). Some conditions of obedience and disobedience to authority. *Human Relations, 18,* 57–76.

Milgram, S. (1974). *Obedience to authority.* New York: Harper.

Millar, M. G. (1997). The effects of emotion on breast self-examination: Another look at the health belief model. *Social Behavior and Personality, 25,* 223–232.

Miller, A. G., McHoskey, J. W., Bane, C. M., & Dowd, T. G. (1993). The attitude polarization phenomenon: Role of response measure, attitude extremity, and behavioral consequences of reported attitude change. *Journal of Personality and Social Psychology, 64,* 516–574.

Miller, C. T., Rothblum, E. D., Brand, P. A., & Felicio, D. M. (1995). Do obese women have poorer social relationships than nonobese women? Reports by self, friends, and coworkers. *Journal of Personality, 63,* 65–85.

Miller, C. T., Rothblum, E. D., Felicio, D., & Brand, P. (1995). Compensating for stigma: Obese and nonobese women's reactions to being visible. *Personality and Social Psychology Bulletin, 21,* 1093–1106.

Miller, D. T. (1999). The norm of self-interest. *American Psychologist, 54,* 1053–1060.

Miller, D. T., & Ross, M. (1975). Self-serving biases in attribution of causality: Fact or fiction? *Psychological Bulletin, 82,* 313–325.

Miller, M. L., & Thayer, J. F. (1989). On the existence of discrete classes in personality: Is self-monitoring the correct joint to carve? *Journal of Personality and Social Psychology, 57,* 143–155.

Miller, N., Maruayama, G., Beaber, R. J., & Valone, K. (1976). Speed of speech and persuasion. *Journal of Personality and Social Psychology, 34,* 615–624.

Miller, P. A., & Jansen-op-de-Haar, M. A. (1997). Emotional, cognitive, behavioral, and temperament characteristics of high empathy children. *Motivation and Emotion, 21,* 109–125.

Minton, H. L. (2000). Psychology and gender at the turn of the century. *American Psychologist, 55,* 613–615.

Mischel, W. (1967). A social learning view of sex differences in behavior. In E. E. Maccoby (Ed.), *The development of sex differences* (pp. 56–81). London: Tavistock.

Missing America. (2000, April 4). *Time,* 22.

Monahan, J. L., Murphy, S. T., & Zajonc, R. B. (2000). Subliminal mere exposure: Specific, general, and diffuse effects. *Psychological Science, 11,* 462–466.

Mondloch, C. J., Lewis, T. L., Budreau, D. R., Maurer, D., Dannemiller, J. L., Stephens, B. R., & Kleiner-Gathercoal, K. A. (1999). Face perception during early infancy. *Psychological Science, 10,* 419–422.

Monteith, M. (1993). Self-regulation of prejudiced responses: Implications for progress in prejudice-reduction efforts. *Journal of Personality and Social Psychology, 65,* 469–485.

Monteith, M. J., & Spicer, C. V. (2000). Contents and correlates of Whites' and Blacks' racial attitudes. *Journal of Experimental Social Psychology, 36,* 125–154.

Montepare, J. M., & Zebrowitz-McArthur, L. (1988). Impressions of people created by age-related qualities of their gates. *Journal of Personality and Social Psychology, 55,* 547–556.

Moore, T. (1993, August 16). Millions of volunteers counter image of a selfish society. *Albany Times Union,* p. A-2.

Moran, G. (1993, February 23). Personal communication.

Moran, G. (in press). Trial consultation: Why licensure is not necessary. *Journal of Forensic Psychology Practice.*

Moran, G., & Cutler, B. L. (1991). The prejudicial impact of pretrial publicity. *Journal of Applied Social Psychology, 21,* 345–367.

Moreland, R. L., & Beach, S. R. (1992). Exposure effects in the classroom: The development of affinity among students. *Journal of Experimental Social Psychology, 28,* 255–276.

Morey, N., & Gerber, G. L. (1995). Two types of competitiveness: Their impact on the perceived interpersonal attractiveness of women and men. *Journal of Applied Social Psychology, 25,* 210–222.

Morgan, D., Carder, P., & Neal, M. (1997). Are some relationships more useful than others? The value of similar others in the networks of recent widows. *Journal of Social and Personal Relationships, 14,* 745–759.

Morgan, H. J., & Janoff-Bulman, R. (1994). Positive and negative self-complexity: Patterns of adjustment following traumatic versus non-traumatic life experiences. *Journal of Social and Clinical Psychology, 13,* 63–85.

Morojele, N., & Stephenson, G. M. (1994). Addictive behaviors: Prediction of abstinence intentions and expectations in the theory of planned behavior. In D. R. Rutter & L. Quine (Eds.), *Social psychology and health: European perspectives* (pp. 47–70). Aldershot, UK: Avesbury.

Morokoff, P. J., Quina, K., Harlow, L. L., Whitmire, L., Grimley, D. M., Gibson, P. R., & Burkholder, G. J. (1997). Sexual Assertiveness Scale (SAS) for women: Development and validation. *Journal of Personality and Social Psychology, 73,* 790–804.

Morris, K. J. (1985). *Discriminating depression and social anxiety: Self-efficacy analysis.* Unpublished master's thesis, Texas Tech University, Lubbock.

Morris, M. W., & Larrick, R. P. (1995). When one cause casts doubt on another: A normative analysis of discounting in causal attribution. *Psychological Review, 102,* 331–335.

Morris, M. W., & Pang, K. (1994). Culture and cause: American and Chinese attributions for social and physical events. *Journal of Personality and Social Psychology, 67,* 949–971.

Morrison, A. M. (1992). *The new leaders: Guidelines on leadership diversity.* San Francisco: Jossey-Bass.

Morrison, E. W. (1994). Role definitions and organizational citizenship behavior: The importance of employees' perspective. *Academy of Management Journal, 37,* 1543–1567.

Morrison, E. W., & Bies, R. J. (1991). Impression management in the feedback-seeking process: A literature review and research agenda. *Academy of Management Review, 16,* 322–341.

Morrison, H. W. (1954). *The validity and behavioral manifestations of female need for affiliation.* Unpublished master's thesis, Wesleyan University.

Morrow, G. D., Clark, E. M., & Brock, K. F. (1995). Individual and partner love styles: Implications for the quality of romantic involvements. *Journal of Social and Personal Relationships, 12,* 363–387.

Moscovici, S. (1985). Social influence and conformity. In G. Lindzey & E. Aronson (Eds.), *Handbook of social psychology* (3rd ed.). New York: Random House.

Mosher, D. L. (1991). Macho men, machismo, and sexuality. *Annual Review of Sex Research, 2,* 199–247.

Mosher, D. L., & Anderson, R. D. (1986). Macho personality, sexual aggression, and reactions to guided imagery of realistic rape. *Journal of Research in Personality, 20,* 77–94.

Mosher, D. L., & Sirkin, M. (1984). Measuring a macho personality constellation. *Journal of Research in Personality, 18,* 150–163.

Mosher, D. L., & Tomkins, S. S. (1988). Scripting the macho man: Hypermasculine socialization and enculturation. *Journal of Sex Research, 15,* 60–84.

Moskowitz, D. S. (1990). Convergence of self-reports and independent observers: Dominance and friendliness. *Journal of Personality and Social Psychology, 58,* 1096–1106.

Moskowitz, D. S. (1993). Dominance and friendliness: On the interaction of gender and situation. *Journal of Personality, 61,* 387–409.

Moston, S., & Stephenson, G. M. (1993). The changing face of police interrogation. *Journal of Community and Applied Social Psychology, 3,* 101–115.

Muczyk, J. P., & Reimann, B. C. (1987). The case for directive leadership. *Academy of Management Review, 12,* 637–647.

Mueller, U., & Mazur, A. (1996). Facial dominance of West Point cadets as predictors of later military rank. *Social Forces, 74,* 823–850.

Mugny, G. (1975). Negotiations, image of the other and the process of minority influence. *European Journal of Social Psychology, 5,* 209–229.

Mullan, E., & Markland, D. (1997). Variations in self-determination across the stages of change for exercise in adults. *Motivation and Emotion, 21,* 349–362.

Munro, G. D., & Ditto, P. H. (1997). Biased assimilation, attitude polarization, and affect in reactions to stereotype-relevant scientific information. *Personality and Social Psychology Bulletin, 23,* 636–653.

Munsterberg, H. (1907). *On the witness stand: Essays in psychology and crime.* New York: McClure.

Muris, P., Mayer, B., & Meesters, C. (2000). Self-reported attachment style, anxiety, and depression in children. *Social Behavior and Personality, 28,* 157–162.

Murnen, S. K., & Byrne, D. (1991). Hyperfemininity: Measurement and initial validation of the construct. *Journal of Sex Research, 28,* 479–489.

Murnen, S., K., Perot, A., & Byrne, D. (1989). Coping with unwanted sexual activity: Normative responses, situational determinants, and individual differences. *Journal of Sex Research, 26,* 85–106.

Murnighan, K. (Ed.). (1993). *Handbook of social psychology in organizations.* Englewood Cliffs, N.J.

Murphy, S. T., Monahan, J. L., & Miller, L. C. (1998). Inference under the influence: The impact of alcohol and inhibition conflict on women's sexual decision making. *Personality and Social Psychology Bulletin, 24,* 517–528.

Murphy, S. T., Monahan, J. L., & Zajonc, R. B. (1995). Additivity of nonconscious affect: Combined effects of priming and exposure. *Journal of Personality and Social Psychology, 69,* 589–602.

Murray, H. A. (1938). *Explorations in personality.* New York: Oxford University Press.

Murray, L., & Trevarthen, C. (1985). Emotional regulation of interactions between two-month-olds and their mothers. In T. M. Field & N. A. Fox (Eds.), *Social perception in infants* (pp. 177–197). Norwood, NJ: Ablex.

Murray, L., & Trevarthen, C. (1986). The infant's role in mother-infant communications. *Journal of Child Language, 13,* 15–29.

Murray, M., & McMillan, C. (1993). Health beliefs, locus of control, emotional control and women's cancer screening behaviour. *British Journal of Clinical Psychology, 32,* 87–100.

Murray, S. L., & Holmes, J. G. (1997). A leap of faith? Positive illusions in romantic relationships. *Personality and Social Psychology Bulletin, 23,* 586–604.

Murray, S. L., & Holmes, J. G. (1999). The (mental) ties that bind: Cognitive structures that predict relationship resilience. *Journal of Personality and Social Psychology, 77,* 1228–1244.

Murray, S. L., Holmes, J. G., & Griffin, D. W. (1996). The benefits of positive illusions: Idealization and the construction of satisfaction in close relationships. *Journal of Personality and Social Psychology, 70,* 79–98.

Murray, S. L., Holmes, J. G., & Griffin, D. W. (2000). Self-esteem and the quest for felt security: How perceived regard regulates attachment processes. *Journal of Personality and Social Psychology, 78,* 478–498.

Murray, S. L., Holmes, J. G., Griffin, D. W., Bellavia, G., & Rose, P. (2001). The mismeasure of love: How self-doubt contaminates relationship beliefs. *Personality and Social Psychology Bulletin, 27,* 423–436.

Murrell, A. J., & Jones, J. M. (1993). Perceived control and victim derogation: Is the world still just? *Journal of Social Behavior and Personality, 8,* 545–554.

Mussweiler, T., & Forster, J. (2000). The sex–aggression link: A perception–behavior dissociation. *Journal of Personality and Social Psychology, 79,* 507–520.

Mussweiler, T., Gabriel, S., & Bodenhausen, G. V. (2000). Shifting social identities as a strategy for deflecting threatening social comparisons. *Journal of Personality and Social Psychology, 79,* 398–409.

Myers, D. G., & Diener, E. (1995). Who is happy? *Psychological Science, 6,* 10–19.

Mynard, H., & Joseph, S. (1997). Bully victim problems and their association with Eysenck's personality dimensions in 8 to 13 year olds. *British Journal of Educational Psychology, 67,* 51–54.

Nadkarni, D. V., Lundgren, D., & Burlew, A. K. (1991). Gender differences in self-depriving behavior as a reaction to extreme inequity. *Journal of Social Behavior and Personality, 6,* 105–117.

Nadler, A. (1991). Help-seeking behavior: Psychological costs and instrumental benefits. In M. S. Clark (Ed.), *Prosocial behavior* (pp. 290–311). Newbury Park, CA: Sage.

Nadler, A. (1993, March). Personal communication.

Nadler, A., Fisher, J. D., & Itzhak, S. B. (1983). With a little help from my friend: Effect of a single or multiple acts of aid as a function of donor and task characteristics. *Journal of Personality and Social Psychology, 44,* 310–321.

Nannini, D. K., & Meyers, L. S. (2000). Jealousy in sexual and emotional infidelity: An alternative to the evolutionary explanation. *Journal of Sex Research, 37,* 117–122.

Narby, D. J., Cutler, B. L., & Moran, G. (1993). A meta-analysis of the association between authoritarianism and jurors' perceptions of defendant culpability. *Journal of Applied Psychology, 78,* 34–42.

National Institute for Occupational Safety and Health, Center for Disease Control and Prevention. "Homicide in the workplace." Document #705003, December 5, 1993.

Nemechek, S., & Olson, K. R. (1999). Five-factor personality similarity and marital adjustment. *Social Behavior and Personality, 27,* 309–318.

Nemeth, C. J. (1995). Dissent as driving cognition, attitudes, and judgments. *Social Cognition, 13,* 273–291.

Nemeth, C. J., Connell, J. B., Rogers, J. D., & Brown, K. S. (2001). Improving decision making by means of dissent. *Journal of Applied Social Psychology, 31,* 45–58.

Neto, F., & Barrios, J. (2000). Predictors of loneliness among adolescents from Portuguese immigrant families in Switzerland. *Social Behavior and Personality, 28,* 193–206.

Neuberg, S. L., & Newsom, J. T. (1993). Personal need for structure: Individual differences in the desire for simple structure. *Journal of Personality and Social Psychology, 65,* 113–131.

Neuberg, S. L., Smith, D. M., Hoffman, J. C., & Russell, F. J. (1994). When we observe stigmatized and "normal" individuals interacting: Stigma by association. *Personality and Social Psychology Bulletin, 20,* 196–209.

Neuman, J. H., & Baron, R. A. (1997). Aggression in the workplace. In Giacalone, R. A., & Greenberg, J. (Eds.), *Anti-social behavior in organizations.* Thousand Oaks, CA: Sage.

Neuman, J. H., & Baron, R. A. (1998). Workplace violence and workplace aggression: Evidence concerning specific forms, potential causes, and preferred targets. *Journal of Management, 24,* 391–420.

Neumann, R., & Strack, F. (2000). "Mood contagion": The automatic transfer of mood between persons. *Journal of Personality and Social Psychology, 79,* 211–223.

New survey reveals pets are good medicine: Report further indicates healthy pets make for healthier people. (2000, May 9). *PR Newswire.*

Newcomb, T. M. (1956). The prediction of interpersonal attraction. *Psychological Review, 60,* 393–404.

Newcomb, T. M. (1961). *The acquaintance process.* New York: Holt, Rinehart and Winston.

Newcombe, N. S., Drummey, A. B., Fox, N. A., Lie, E., & Ottinger-Alberts, W. (2000). Remembering early childhood: How much, how, and why (or why not). *Current Directions in Psychological Science, 9,* 55–58.

Newsom, J. T. (1999). Another side to caregiving: Negative reactions to being helped. *Current Directions in Psychological Science, 8,* 183–187.

Newton, J. T., Davenport-Jones, L., Idle, M., Patel, M., Setchell, A., & Turpin, C. (2001). Patients' perceptions of general dental practitioners: The influence of ethnicity and sex of dentist. *Social Behavior and Personality, 29,* 601–606.

Newton, T. L., Kiecolt-Glaser, J. K., Glaser, R., & Malarkey, W. B. (1995). Conflict and withdrawal during marital interaction: The roles of hostility and defensiveness. *Personality and Social Psychology Bulletin, 21,* 512–524.

Nezlek, J. B., & Plesko, R. M. (2001). Day-to-day relationships among self-concept clarity, self-esteem, daily events, and mood. *Personality and Social Psychology Bulletin, 27,* 201–211.

Nezlek, J. B., Kowalski, R. M., Leary, M. R., Blevins, T., & Holgate, S. (1997). Personality moderators to reactions to interpersonal rejection: Depression and trait self-esteem. *Personality and Social Psychology Bulletin, 23,* 1235–1244.

Ng, J. Y. Y., Tam, S. F., Yew, W. W., & Lam, W. K. (1999). Effects of video modeling on self-efficacy and exercise performance of COPD patients. *Social Behavior and Personality, 27,* 475–486.

Nida, S. A., & Koon, J. (1983). They get better looking at closing time around here, too. *Psychological Reports, 52,* 657–658.

Niebuhr, G. (1998, June 10). Baptists amend beliefs on family. *New York Times.*

Niedenthal, P. M., Setterlund, M. B., & Wherry, M. B. (1992). Possible self-complexity and affective reactions to goal-relevant evaluation. *Journal of Personality and Social Psychology, 63,* 5–16.

Niedermeier, K. E., Kerr, N. L., & Messe, L. A. (1999). Jurors' use of naked statistical evidence: Exploring biases and implications of the Wells Effect. *Journal of Personality and Social Psychology, 76,* 533–542.

Nienhuis, A. E., Manstead, A. S. R., & Spears, R. (2001). Multiple motives and persuasive communication: Creative elaboration as a result of impression motivation and accuracy motivation. *Personality and Social Psychology Bulletin, 27,* 118–132.

Nier, J. A., Mottola, G. R., & Gaertner, S. L. (2000). The O. J. Simpson criminal verdict as a racially symbolic event: A longitudinal analysis of racial attitude change. *Personality and Social Psychology Bulletin, 26,* 507–516.

Nisbett, R. E. (1990). Evolutionary psychology, biology, and cultural evolution. *Motivation and Emotion, 14,* 255–264.

Nolen-Hoeksema, S., & Davis, C. G. (1999). "Thanks for sharing that": Ruminators and their social support networks. *Journal of Personality and Social Psychology, 77,* 801–814.

Nolen-Hoeksema, S., Larson, J., & Grayson, C. (1999). Explaining the gender differences in depressive symptoms. *Journal of Personality and Social Psychology, 77,* 1061–1072.

Norlander, T., Erixon, A., & Archer, T. (2000). Psychological androgyny and creativity: Dynamics of gender-role and personality trait. *Social Behavior and Personality, 28,* 423–436.

Numbers. (1999, May 31). *Time,* 29.

Numbers. (2000, July 17). *Time,* 21.

Nunn, J. S., & Thomas, S. L. (1999). The angry male and the passive female: The role of gender and self-esteem in anger expression. *Social Behavior and Personality, 27,* 145–154.

O'Brien, M., & Bahadur, M. A. (1998). Marital aggression, mother's problem-solving behavior with children, and children's emotional and behavioral problems. *Journal of Social and Clinical Psychology, 17,* 249–272.

O'Connor, S. C., & Rosenblood, L. K. (1996). Affiliation motivation in everyday experience: A theoretical comparison. *Journal of Personality and Social Psychology, 70,* 513–522.

O'Leary, S. G. (1995). Parental discipline mistakes. *Current Directions in Psychological Science, 4,* 11–13.

O'Moore, M. N. (2000). Critical issues for teacher training to counter bullying and victimization in Ireland. *Aggressive Behavior, 26,* 99–112.

O'Neil, J. (1999, July 20). In infancy, reducing the odds of obesity. *New York Times,* F7.

O'Neill, S. K. (2000). *Ethnicity and eating disorders in women and adolescent girls: A meta-analysis.* Unpublished manuscript, University at Albany, State University of New York.

O'Sullivan, C. S., & Durso, F. T. (1984). Effects of schema-incongruent information on memory for stereotypical attributes. *Journal of Personality and Social Psychology, 47,* 55–70.

O'Sullivan, C. S., Chen, A., Mohapatra, S., Sigelman, L., & Lewis, E. (1988). Voting in ignorance: The politics of smooth-sounding names. *Journal of Applied Social Psychology, 18,* 1094–1106.

O'Sullivan, L. F., & Byers, E. S. (1992). College students' incorporation of initiator and restrictor roles in sexual dating interactions. *Journal of Sex Research, 29,* 435–446.

Obrist, P. A. (1981). *Cardiovascular psychophysiology: A perspective.* New York: Plenum.

Oettingen, G. (1995). Explanatory style in the context of culture. In G. M. Buchanan & M. E. P. Seligman (Eds.)., *Explanatory style.* Hillsdale, NJ: Erlbaum.

Oettingen, G., & Seligman, M. E. P. (1990). Pessimism and behavioral signs of depression in East versus West Berlin. *European Journal of Social Psychology, 201,* 207–220.

Oggins, J., Veroff, J., & Leber, D. (1993). Perceptions of marital interaction among black and white newlyweds. *Journal of Personality and Social Psychology, 65,* 494–511.

Ohbuchi, K., & Kambara, T. (1985). Attacker's intent and awareness of outcome, impression management, and retaliation. *Journal of Experimental Social Psychology, 21,* 321–330.

Ohbuchi, K., Chiba, S., & Fukushima, O. (1994). *Mitigation of interpersonal conflict: Politeness and time pressure.* Unpublished manuscript, Tohoku University.

Ohbuchi, K., Kameda, M., & Agarie, N. (1989). Apology as aggression control: Its role in mediating appraisal of and response to harm. *Journal of Personality and Social Psychology, 56,* 219–227.

Ohman, A., Lundqvist, D., & Esteves, F. (2001). The face in the crowd revisited: Threat advantage with schematic stimuli. *Journal of Personality and Social Psychology, 80,* 381–396.

Okie, S. (2001, August 14). Decline of AIDS begins to level off. *Washington Post.*

Oliner, S. P., & Oliner, P. M. (1988). *The altruistic personality: Rescuers of Jews in Nazi Europe.* New York: Free Press.

Oliver, J. M., Reed, C. K. S., Katz, B. M., & Haugh, J. A. (1999). Students' self-reports of help-seeking: The impact of psychological problems, stress, and demographic variables on utilization of formal and informal support. *Social Behavior and Personality, 27,* 109–128.

Oliver, M. B., & Hyde, J. S. (1993). Gender differences in sexuality: A meta-analysis. *Psychological Bulletin, 114,* 29–51.

Olmstead, R. E., Guy, S. M., O'Malley, P. M., & Bentler, P. M. (1991). Longitudinal assessment of the relationship between self-esteem, fatalism, loneliness, and substance use. *Journal of Social Behavior and Personality, 6,* 749–770.

Olweus, D. (1993). *Bullying at school: What we know and what we can do.* Oxford: Blackwell.

Omori, Y., & Miyata, Y. (2001). Estimates of impressions based on frequency of blinking. *Social Behavior and Personality, 29,* 159–168.

Omoto, A. M., & Snyder, M. (1995). Sustained helping without obligation: Motivation, longevity of service, and perceived attitude change among AIDS volunteers. *Journal of Personality and Social Psychology, 68,* 671–686.

Onishi, M., Gjerde, P. F., & Block, J. (2001). Personality implications of romantic attachment patterns in young adults: A multi-method, multi-informant study. *Personality and Social Psychology Bulletin, 27,* 1097–1110.

Orbell, S., Blair, C., Sherlock, K., & Conner, M. (2001). The theory of planned behavior and ecstasy use: Roles for habit and perceived control over taking versus obtaining substances. *Journal of Applied Social Psychology, 31,* 31–47.

Organ, D. W. (1997). Organizational citizenship behavior: It's construct clean-up time. *Human Performance, 10,* 85–98.

Orpen, C. (1996). The effects of ingratiation and self promotion tactics on employee career success. *Social Behavior and Personality, 24,* 213–214.

Osborne, J. W. (1995). Academics, self-esteem, and race: A look at the underlying assumptions of the disidentification hypothesis. *Personality and Social Psychology Bulletin, 21,* 449–455.

Osland, J. A. (2001). *Theoretical models of the relationships among attachment, empathy, and relationship satisfaction.* Unpublished doctoral dissertation, University at Albany, State University of New York.

Osperio, D., & Fiske, S. T. (2001). Ethnic identity moderates perceptions of prejudice: Judgments of personal versus group discrimination and subtle versus blatant bias. *Personality and Social Psychology Bulletin, 27,* 550–561.

Österman, K., Björkqvist, K., Lagerspetz, K. M. J., Kaukiainen, A., Landua, S. F., Fraczek, A., & Caprara, G. V. (1998). Cross-cultural evidence of female indirect aggression. *Aggressive Behavior, 24,* 1–8.

Ostrow, R. J. (1995, November 19). As crime fears rise, actual crime falls. *Los Angeles Times.*

Ottati, V. C., & Isbell, L. M. (1996). Effects of mood during exposure to target information on subsequently reported judgments: An on-line model of misattribution and correction. *Journal of Personality and Social Psychology, 71,* 39–53.

Owen, P. R., & Laurel-Seller, E. (2000). Weight and shape ideals: Thin is dangerously in. *Journal of Applied Social Psychology, 30,* 979–990.

Owens, L., Shute, R., & Slee, P. (2000). "Guess what I just heard!": Indirect aggression among teenage girls in Australia. *Aggressive Behavior, 26,* 57–66.

Oyserman, D., Gant, L., & Ager, J. (1995). A socially contextualized model of African American identity: Possible selves and school persistence. *Journal of Personality and Social Psychology, 69,* 1216–1232.

Page, R. M. (1991). Loneliness as a risk factor in adolescent hopelessness. *Journal of Research in Personality, 25,* 189–195.

Paik, H., & Comstock, G. (1994). The effects of television violence on antisocial behavior: A meta-analysis. *Communication Research, 21,* 516–546.

Park, J., & Banaji, M. R. (2000). Mood and heuristics: The influence of happy and sad states on sensitivity and bias in stereotyping. *Journal of Personality and Social Psychology, 78,* 1005–1023.

Parks, M. R., & Floyd, K. (1996). Meanings for closeness and intimacy in friendship. *Journal of Social and Personal Relationships, 13,* 85–107.

Paul, E. L., McManus, B., & Hayes, A. (2000). "Hookups": Characteristics and correlates of college students' spontaneous and anonymous sexual experiences. *Journal of Sex Research, 37,* 76–88.

Paulhus, D. L., Bruce, M. N., & Trapnell, P. D. (1995). Effects of self-presentation strategies on personality profiles and their structure. *Personality and Social Psychology Bulletin, 21,* 100–108.

Paulhus, D. L., Martin, C. L., & Murphy, G. K. (1992). Some effects of arousal on sex stereotyping. *Personality and Social Psychology Bulletin, 18,* 325–330.

Pearson, K., & Lee, A. (1903). On the laws of inheritance in man: I. Inheritance of physical characters. *Biometrika, 2,* 357–462.

Pedersen, D. M. (1994). Privacy preferences and classroom seat selection. *Social Behavior and Personality, 22,* 393–398.

Pederson, W. C., Gonzales, C., & Miller, N. (2000). The moderating effect of trivial triggering provocation on displaced aggression. *Journal of Personality and Social Psychology, 78,* 913–947.

Pelham, B. W. (1995a). Self-investment and self-esteem: Evidence for a Jamesian model of self-worth. *Journal of Personality and Social Psychology, 69,* 1141–1150.

Pelham, B. W. (1995b). Further evidence for a Jamesian model of self-worth: Reply to Marsh (1995). *Journal of Personality and Social Psychology, 69,* 1161–1165.

Pelham, B. W., & Hetts, J. J. (2001). Underworked and overpaid: Elevated entitlement in men's self-pay. *Journal of Experimental Social Psychology, 37,* 93–103.

Pelham, B. W., & Wachsmuth, J. O. (1995). The waxing and waning of the social self: Assimilation and contrast in social comparison. *Journal of Personality and Social Psychology, 69,* 825–838.

Pennebaker, J. W. (1997). Writing about emotional experiences as a therapeutic process. *Psychological Science, 8,* 162–166.

Pennebaker, J. W., & Graybeal, A. (2001). Patterns of natural language use: Disclosure, personality, and social integration. *Current Directions in Psychological Science, 10,* 90–93.

Pennebaker, J. W., Dyer, M. A., Caulkins, R. S., Litowicz, D. L., Ackerman, P. L., & Anderson, D. B. (1979). Don't the girls all get prettier at closing time: A country and western application to psychology. *Personality and Social Psychology Bulletin, 5,* 122–125.

Penner, L. A., & Finkelstein, M. A. (1998). Dispositional and structural determinants of volunteerism. *Journal of Personality and Social Psychology, 74,* 525–537.

Pentony, J. F. (1995). The effect of negative campaigning on voting, semantic differential, and thought listing. *Journal of Social Behavior and Personality, 10,* 631–644.

People. (2001, August 6). *U.S. News & World Report,* 14.

Peplau, L. A., & Perlman, D. (1982). Perspective on loneliness. In L. A. Peplau & D. Perlman (Eds.), *Loneliness: A sourcebook of current theory, research, and therapy.* New York: Wiley.

Perlini, A. H., & Hansen, S. D. (2001). Moderating effects of need for cognition on attractiveness stereotyping. *Social Behavior and Personality, 29,* 313–322.

Perlini, A. H., Marcello, A., Hansen, S. D., & Pudney, W. (2001). The effects of male age and physical appearance on evaluations of attractiveness, social desirability and resourcefulness. *Social Behavior and Personality, 29,* 277–288.

Perrett, D. I., May, K. A., & Yoshikawa, S. (1994). Facial shape and judgements of female attractiveness. *Nature, 368,* 239–242.

Perrewe, P. L., & Hochwarter, W. A. (2001). Can we really have it all? The attainment of work and family values. *Current Directions in Psychological Science, 10,* 29–32.

Personality implications of romantic attachment patterns in young adults: A multi-method, multi-informant study. *Personality and Social Psychology Bulletin, 27,* 1097–1110.

Pessin, J. (1933). The comparative effects of social and mechanical stimulation on memorizing. *American Journal of Psychology, 45,* 263–270.

Peterson, C., Seligman, M. E. P., Yurko, K. H., Martin, L. R., & Friedman, H. S. (1998). Catastrophizing and untimely death. *Psychological Science, 9,* 127–130.

Peterson, R. S. (1997). A directive leadership style in group decision making can be both a virtue and vice: Evidence from elite and experimental groups. *Journal of Personality and Social Psychology, 72,* 1107–1121.

Petkova, K. G., Ajzen, I., & Driver, B. L. (1995). Salience of anti-abortion beliefs and commitment to an attitudinal position: On the strength, structure, and predictive validity of anti-abortion attitudes. *Journal of Applied Social Psychology, 25,* 463–483.

Petrie, K. J., Booth, R. J., & Pennebaker, J. W. (1998). The immunological effects of thought suppression. *Jour-*

nal of Personality and Social Psychology, 75, 1264–1272.

Pets and stress management. (1996, May 24). *Go Ask Alice.* Columbia University's Health Question and Answer Internet Service.

Pets reduce blood pressure: Sydney conference. (1996, November 5). *Media Release, Australian Veterinary Association.*

Pettigrew, T. F. (1969). Racially separate or together? *Journal of Social Issues, 24,* 43–69.

Pettigrew, T. F. (1981). Extending the stereotype concept. In D. L. Hamilton (Ed.), *Cognitive processes in stereotyping and intergroup behavior* (pp. 303–331). Hillsdale, NJ: Erlbaum.

Pettigrew, T. F. (1997). Generalized intergroup contact effects on prejudice. *Personality and Social Psychology Bulletin, 23,* 173–185.

Petty, R. E., & Cacioppo, J. T. (1986). The elaboration likelihood model of persuasion. In L. Berkowitz (Ed.), *Advances in experimental social psychology,* (Vol. 19, pp. 123–205). New York: Academic Press.

Petty, R. E., & Cacioppo, J.T. (1990). Involvement and persuasion: Tradition versus integration. *Psychological Bulletin, 107,* 367–374.

Petty, R. E., Cacioppo, J. T., Strathman, A. J., & Priester, J. R. (1994). To think or not to think: Exploring two routes to persuasion. In S. Shavitt & T. C. Brock (Eds.), *Persuasion* (pp. 113–147). Boston: Allyn and Bacon.

Petty, R. J., & Krosnick, J. A. (Eds.). (1995). *Attitude strength: Antecedents and consequences* (Vol. 4). Hillsdale, NJ: Erlbaum.

Pham, L. B., Taylor, S. E., & Seeman, T. E. (2001). Effects of environmental predictability and personal mastery on self-regulatory and physiological processes. *Personality and Social Psychology Bulletin, 27,* 611–620.

Phelps, E. J. (1981). *The maid of the North.* New York: Holt, Rinehart, & Winston.

Pickett, C. L. (2001). The effects of entiativity beliefs on implicit comparisons between group members. *Personality and Social Psychology Bulletin, 27,* 515–525.

Piekarski, M. (2001, September 23). Heroism should never be defined too narrowly. Albany *Times Union,* B1–B2.

Pierce, C. A. (1992). *The effects of physical attractiveness and height on dating choice: A meta-analysis.* Unpublished masters thesis, University at Albany, State University of New York, Albany, NY.

Pierce, C. A. (1996). Body height and romantic attraction: A meta-analytic test of the male-taller norm. *Social Behavior and Personality, 24,* 143–150.

Pierce, C. A. (1998). Factors associated with participating in a romantic relationship in a work environment. *Journal of Applied Social Psychology, 28,* 1712–1730.

Pierce, C. A., & Aguinis, H. (1997). Bridging the gap between romantic relationships and sexual harassment in organizations. *Journal of Organizational Behavior, 18,* 197–200.

Pierce, C. A., & Aguinis, H. (2001a). A framework for investigating the link between workplace romance and sexual harassment. *Group & Organization Management, 26,* 206–229.

Pierce, C. A., & Aguinis, H. (2001b). Romantic relationships in organizations: A test of a model of formation and impact factors. Manuscript submitted for publication.

Pierce, C. A., Aguinis, H., & Adams, S. K. R. (2000). Effects of a dissolved workplace romance and rater characteristics of responses to a sexual harassment accusation. *Academy of Management Journal, 43,* 869–880.

Pierce, C. A., Broberg, B. J., & Aguinis, H. (2001). Effects of characteristics of a dissolved workplace romance on the legitimization of sexually harassing behavior. Manuscript submitted for publication.

Pierce, C. A., Byrne, D., & Aguinis, H. (1996). Attraction in organizations: A model of workplace romance. *Journal of Organizational Behavior, 17,* 5–32.

Pietromonaco, P. R., & Barrett, L. F. (1997). Working models of attachment and daily social interactions. *Journal of Personality and Social Psychology, 73,* 1409–1423.

Pihl, R. O., Lau, M. L., & Assad, J. M. (1997). Aggressive disposition, alcohol, and aggression. *Aggressive Behavior, 23,* 11–18.

Piliavin, J. A., & Unger, R. K. (1985). *The helpful but helpless female: Myth or reality?* In V. E. O'Leary, R. K. Unger, & B. S. Wallston (Eds.), *Women, gender, and social psychology* (pp. 149–189). Hillsdale, NJ: Erlbaum.

Pinel, J. P. J., Assanand, S., & Lehman, D. R. (2000). Hunger, eating, and ill health. *American Psychologist, 55,* 1105–1116.

Pines, A. (1997). Fatal attractions or wise unconscious choices: The relationship between causes for entering and breaking intimate relationships. *Personal Relationship Issues, 4,* 1–6.

Pinker, S. (1998). *How the mind works.* New York: Norton.

Pion, G. M., Mednick, M., Astin, H. S., Hall, C. C. I., Kenkel, M. B., Keita, G. P., Kohout, J. L., & Kelleher, J. C. (1996). The shifting gender composition of psychology: Trends and implications for the discipline. *American Psychologist, 51,* 509–528.

Pittman, T. S. (1993). Control motivation and attitude change. In G. Weary, F. Gleicher, & K. L. Marsh (Eds.), *Control motivation and social cognition* (pp. 157–175). New York: Springer-Verlag.

Platania, J., & Moran, G. (1999). Due process and the death penalty: The role of prosecutorial misconduct in closing arguments in capital trials. *Law and Human Behavior, 23,* 471–486.

Pleck, J. H., Sonenstein, F. L., & Ku, L. C. (1993). Masculinity ideology: Its impact on adolescent males' heterosexual relationships. *Journal of Social Issues, 49*(3), 11–29.

Pliner, P., Chaiken, S., & Flett, G. L. (1990). Gender differences in concern with body weight and physical appearance over the life span. *Personality and Social Psychology Bulletin, 16,* 263–273.

Podaskoff, P. M., Mackenzie, S. B., & Hui, C. (1993). Organizational citizenship behaviors and managerial evaluations of employee performance: A review and suggestions for future research. In G. R. Ferris (Ed.), *Research in personnel and human resources management* (Vol. 11, pp. 1–40). Greenwich, CT: JAI Press.

Polivy, J., & Herman, C. P. (2000). The false-hope syndrome: Unfulfilled expectations of self-change. *Current Directions in Psychological Science, 9,* 128–131.

Pollock, C. L., Smith, S. D., Knowles, E. S., & Bruce, H. J. (1998). Mindfulness limits compliance with the that's-not-all technique. *Personality and Social Psychology Bulletin, 24,* 1153–1157.

Pomazal, R. J., & Clore, G. L. (1973). Helping on the highway: The effects of dependency and sex. *Journal of Applied Social Psychology, 3,* 150–164.

Pomerantz, E. M., Chaioken, S., & Tordesilla, S. (1995). Attitude strength and resistance processes. *Journal of Personality and Social Psychology, 69,* 408–419.

Pontari, B. A., & Schlenker, B. R. (2000). The influence of cognitive load on self-presentation: Can cognitive busyness help as well as harm social performance? *Journal of Personality and Social Psychology, 78,* 1092–1108.

Ponzetti, J. J., Jr., & James, C. M. (1997). Loneliness and sibling relationships. *Journal of Social Behavior and Personality, 12,* 103–112.

Poole, D. A., & Lindsay, D. S. (1998). Assessing the accuracy of young children's reports: Lessons from the investigation of child sexual abuse. *Applied & Preventive Psychology, 7,* 1–26.

Pooley, E. (1997, May 19). Too good to be true? *Time,* 28–33.

Pope, J., & Meyer, R. (1999). An attributional analysis of jurors' judgments in a criminal case: A preliminary investigation. *Social Behavior and Personality, 27,* 563–574.

Porter, L. S., Marco, C. A., Schwartz, J. E., Neale, J. M., Shiffman, S., & Stone, A. A. (2000). Gender differences in coping: A comparison of trait and momentary assessments. *Journal of Social and Clinical Psychology, 19,* 480–498.

Porter, S., Birt, A. R., Yuille, J. C., & Lehman, D. R. (2000). Negotiating false memories: Interviewer and rememberer characteristics relate to memory distortion. *Psychological Science, 11,* 507–510.

Poulson, R. L., Braithwaite, R. L., Brondino, M. J., & Wuehsch, K. L. (1997). Mock jurors' insanity defense verdict selections: The role of evidence, attitudes, and verdict options. *Journal of Social Behavior and Personality, 12,* 743–758.

Poulson, R. L., Wuensch, K. L., Brown, M. B., & Braithwaite, R. L. (1997). Mock jurors' evaluations of insanity defense verdict selection: The role of death penalty attitudes. *Journal of Social Behavior and Personality, 12,* 1065–1078.

Prager, K. J., & Bailey, J. M. (1985). Androgyny, ego development, and psychosocial crisis. *Sex Roles, 13,* 525–536.

Pratto, F. (1996). Sexual politics: The gender gap in the bedroom, the cupboard, and the cabinet. In D. M. Buss & N. M. Malamuth (Eds.), *Sex, power, conflict: Evolutionary and feminist perspectives* (pp. 179–230). New York: Oxford University Press.

Pratto, F., & Bargh, J. A. (1991). Stereotyping based on apparently individuating information: Trait and global components of sex stereotypes under attentional overload. *Journal of Experimental Social Psychology, 27,* 26–47.

Priester, J. R., & Petty, R. E. (2001). Extending the bases of subjective attitudinal ambivalence: Interpersonal and intrapersonal antecedents of evaluative tension. *Journal of Personality and Social Psychology, 80,* 19–34.

Prislin, R., Limbert, W. M., & Bauer, E. (2000). From majority to minority and vice versa: The asymmetrical effects of losing and gaining majority position within a group. *Journal of Personality and Social Psychology, 79,* 385–397.

Pruitt, D. G., & Carnevale, P. J. (1993). *Negotiation in social conflict.* Pacific Grove, CA: Brooks/Cole.

Przybyla, D. P. J. (1985). *The facilitating effect of exposure to erotica on male prosocial behavior.* Unpublished doctoral dissertation, University at Albany, State University of New York.

Pullium, R. M. (1993). Reactions to AIDS patients as a function of attributions about controllability and promiscuity. *Social Behavior and Personality, 21,* 297–302.

Putnam, R. D. (2000). *Bowling alone: The collapse and revival of American community.* New York: Simon & Schuster.

Quigley, B. M., Johnson, A. B., & Byrne, D. (1995, June). *Mock jury sentencing decisions: A meta-analysis of the attractiveness–leniency effect.* Paper presented at the meeting of the American Psychological Society, New York.

Rabasca, L. (2000, February). Proving psychologists' value. *Monitor on Psychology,* 42–44.

Rabasca, L. (2000, October). The internet and computer games reinforce the gender gap. *Monitor on Psychology,* 32–33.

Radecki-Bush, C., Farrell, A. D., & Bush, J. P. (1993). Predicting jealous responses: The influence of adult attachment and depression on threat appraisal. *Journal of Social and Personal Relationships, 10,* 569–588.

Rall, M. L., Peskoff, F. S., & Byrne, J. J. (1994). The effects of information-giving behavior and gender on the perceptions of physicians: An experimental analysis. *Social Behavior and Personality, 22,* 1–16.

Ramirez, J., Bryant, J., & Zillmann, D. (1983). Effects of erotica on retaliatory behavior as a function of level of prior provocation. *Journal of Personality and Social Psychology, 43,* 971–978.

Raty, H., & Snellman, L. (1992). Does gender make any difference? Common-sense conceptions of intelligence. *Social Behavior and Personality, 20,* 23–34.

Ray, G. E., Cohen, R., Secrist, M. E., & Duncan, M. K. (1997). Relating aggressive victimization behaviors to children's sociometric status and friendships. *Journal of Social and Personal Relationships, 14,* 95–108.

Read, S. J., & Miller, L. C. (1998). *Connectionist and PDP models of social reasoning and social behavior.* Mahwah, NJ: Erlbaum.

Reed, M. B., & Aspinwall, L. G. (1998). Self-affirmation reduces biases processing of health-risk information. *Motivation and Emotion, 22,* 99–132.

Regan, P. C. (1998). Of lust and love: Beliefs about the role of sexual desire in romantic relationships. *Personal Relationships, 5,* 139–157.

Regan, P. C. (2000). The role of sexual desire and sexual activity in dating relationships. *Social Behavior and Personality, 28,* 51–60.

Regan, P. C., Snyder, M., & Kassin, S. M. (1995). Unrealistic optimism: Self-enhancement or person positivity? *Personality and Social Psychology Bulletin, 21,* 1073–1082.

Reich, J. W., Zautra, A. J., & Potter, P. T. (2001). Cognitive structure and the independence of positive and negative affect. *Journal of Social and Clinical Psychology, 20,* 99–115.

Reis, T. J., Gerrard, M., & Gibbons, F. X. (1993). Social comparison and the pill: Reactions to upward and downward comparison of contraceptive behavior. *Personality and Social Psychology Bulletin, 19,* 13–20.

Reisman, J. M. (1984). Friendliness and its correlates. *Journal of Social and Clinical Psychology, 2,* 143–155.

Reiss, A. J., & Roth, J. A. (Eds.). (1993). *Understanding and preventing violence.* Washington, DC: National Academy Press.

Reno, R. R., Cialdini, R. B., & Kallgren, C. A. (1993). The transsituational influence of social norms. *Journal of Personality and Social Psychology, 64,* 104–112.

Rensberger, B. (1993, November 9). Certain chemistry between vole pairs. *Albany Times Union,* pp. C-1, C-3.

Rentsch, J. R., & Heffner, T. S. (1994). Assessing self-concept: Analysis of Gordon's coding scheme using "Who am I?" responses. *Journal of Social Behavior and Personality, 9,* 283–300.

Rhodes, G., & Tremewan, T. (1996). Averageness, exaggeration, and facial attractiveness. *Psychological Science, 7,* 105–110.

Rhodes, G., Sumich, A., & Byatt, G. (1999). Are average facial configurations attractive only because of their symmetry? *Psychological Science, 10,* 52–58.

Rhodewalt, F., & Davison, J., Jr. (1983). Reactance and the coronary-prone behavior pattern: The role of self-attribution in response to reduced behavioral freedom. *Journal of Personality and Social Psychology, 44,* 220–228.

Richard, F. D., Bond, C. F., Jr., & Stokes-Zoota, J. J. (2001). "That's completely obvious . . . and important." Lay judgments of social psychological findings. *Personality and Social Psychology Bulletin, 27,* 497–505.

Richards, Z., & Hewstone, M. (2001). Subtyping and subgrouping: Processes for the prevention and promotion of stereotype change. *Personality and Social Psychology Review, 5,* 52–73.

Richardson, D. R., Hammock, G. S., Smith, S. M., Gardner, W., & Signo, M. (1994). Empathy as a cognitive inhibitor of interpersonal aggression. *Aggressive Behavior, 20,* 275–289.

Ridley, M., & Dawkins, R. (1981). The natural selection of altruism. In J. P. Rushton & R. M. Sorrentino (Eds.), *Altruism and helping behavior.* Hillsdale, NJ: Erlbaum.

Riess, M., & Schlenker, B. R. (1977). Attitude change and responsibility avoidance as modes of dilemma resolution in forced-compliance situations. *Journal of Personality and Social Psychology, 35,* 21–30.

Rind, B. (1996). Effect of beliefs about weather conditions on tipping. *Journal of Applied Social Psychology, 26,* 137–147.

Rind, B., & Bordia, P. (1996). Effect on restaurant tipping of male and female servers drawing a happy, smiling face on the backs of customers' checks. *Journal of Applied Social Psychology, 26,* 218–225.

Rivkin, I. D., & Taylor, S. E. (1999). The effects of mental stimulation on coping with controllable stressful events. *Personality and Social Psychology Bulletin, 25,* 1451–1462.

Ro, T., Russell, C., & Lavie, N. (2001). Changing faces: A detection advantage in the flicker paradigm. *Psychological Science, 12,* 94–99.

Robberson, N. R., & Rogers, R. W. (1988). Beyond fear appeals: Negative and positive persuasive appeals to health and self-esteem. *Journal of Applied Social Psychology, 18,* 277–287.

Robbins, T. L., & DeNisi, A. S. (1994). A closer look at interpersonal affect as a distinct influence on cognitive processing in performance evaluations. *Journal of Applied Psychology, 79,* 341–353.

Robins, R. W., & Beer, J. S. (2001). Positive illusions about the self: Short-term benefits and long-term costs. *Journal of Personality and Social Psychology, 80,* 340–352.

Robins, R. W., Caspi, A., & Moffitt, T. E. (2000). Two personalities, one relationship: Both partners' personality traits shape the quality of their relationship. *Journal of Personality and Social Psychology, 79,* 251–259.

Robins, R. W., Hendin, H. M., & Trzesniewski, K. H. (2001). *Personality and Social Psychology Bulletin, 27,* 151–161.

Robins, R. W., Spranca, M. D., & Mendelsohn, G. A. (1996). The actor–observer effect revisited: Effects of individual differences and repeated social interactions on actor and observer attribution. *Journal of Personality and Social Psychology, 71,* 375–389.

Robinson, L. A., Berman, J. S., & Neimeyer, R. A. (1990). Psychotherapy for the treatment of depression: A comprehensive review of controlled outcome research. *Psychological Bulletin, 108,* 30–49.

Robinson, R., Keltner, D., Ward, A., & Ross, L. (1995). Actual versus assumed differences in construal: "Naïve realism" in intergroup perception and conflict. *Journal of Personality and Social Psychology, 68,* 404–417.

Robinson, R. J., Lewicki, R. J., & Donahue, E. M. (1998). *Extending and testing a five factor model of ethical and unethical bargaining tactics: Introducing the SINS Scale.* Unpublished manuscript, Harvard University, Business School.

Rochat, F., & Modigliani, A. (1995). The ordinary quality of resistance: From Milgram's laboratory to the village of Le Chambon. *Journal of Social Issues, 5,* 195–210.

Rodin, J., & Salovey, P. (1989). Health psychology. *Annual Review of Psychology, 40,* 533–579.

Rodin, M., & Price, J. (1995). Overcoming stigma: Credit for self-improvement or discredit for needing to improve? *Personality and Social Psychology Bulletin, 21,* 172–181.

Roediger, H. L., III, & McDermott, K. B. (2000). Tricks of memory. *Current Directions in Psychological Science, 9,* 123–127.

Roese, N. J. (1997). Counterfactual thinking. *Psychological Bulletin, 121,* 133–148.

Rogers, C. R. (1951). *Client-centered therapy.* Boston: Houghton Mifflin.

Rogers, M., Miller, N., Mayer, F. S., & Duvall, S. (1982). Personal responsibility and salience of the request for help: Determinants of the relations between negative affect and helping behavior. *Journal of Personality and Social Psychology, 43,* 956–970.

Rogers, R. W. (1980). *Subjects' reactions to experimental deception.* Unpublished manuscript, University of Alabama, Tuscaloosa.

Rogers, R. W., & Ketcher, C. M. (1979). Effects of anonymity and arousal on aggression. *Journal of Psychology, 102,* 13–19.

Rohner, R. P. (1998). Father love and child development: History and current evidence. *Current Directions in Psychological Science, 7,* 157–161.

Rokach, A. (1998). The relation of cultural background to the causes of loneliness. *Journal of Social and Clinical Psychology, 17,* 75–88.

Rokach, A., & Bacanli, H. (2001). Perceived causes of loneliness: A cross-cultural comparison. *Social Behavior and Personality, 29,* 169–182.

Rokach, A., & Neto, F. (2000). Coping with loneliness in adolescence: A cross-cultural study. *Social Behavior and Personality, 28,* 329–342.

Rokach, A., Moya, M. C., Orzeck, T., & Exposito, F. (2001). Loneliness in North America and Spain. *Social Behavior and Personality, 29,* 477–490.

Roland, E. (2000). Bullying in school: Three national innovations in Norwegian schools in 15 years. *Aggressive Behavior, 26,* 135–143.

Rosenbaum, M. E. (1986). The repulsion hypothesis: On the nondevelopment of relationships. *Journal of Personality and Social Psychology, 51,* 1156–1166.

Rosenberg, E. L., & Ekman, P. (1995). Conceptual and methodological issues in the judgment of facial expressions of emotion. *Motivation and Emotion, 19,* 111–138.

Rosenfield, D., Greenberg, J., Folger, R., & Borys, R. (1982). Effect of an encounter with a black panhandler on subsequent helping for blacks: Tokenism or conforming to a negative stereotype? *Personality and Social Psychology Bulletin, 8,* 664–671.

Rosenhan, D. L., Salovey, P., & Hargis, K. (1981). The joys of helping: Focus of attention mediates the impact of positive affect on altruism. *Journal of Personality and Social Psychology, 40,* 899–905.

Rosenthal, A. M. (1964). *Thirty-eight witnesses.* New York: McGraw-Hill.

Rosenthal, R. (1994). Interpersonal expectancy effects: A thirty year perspective. *Current Direction in Psychological Science, 3,* 176–179.

Rosenthal, D. A., & Shepherd, H. (1993). A six-month follow-up of adolescents' sexual risk-taking, HIV/AIDS knowledge, and attitudes to condoms. *Journal of Community and Applied Social Psychology, 3,* 53–65.

Rosenthal, E. (1992, August 18). Troubled marriage? Sibling relations may be at fault. *New York Times,* pp. C1, C9.

Rosenthal, R., & Jacobson, L. (1968). *Pygmalion in the classroom: Teacher expectation and student intellectual development.* New York: Holt, Rinehart, & Winston.

Rosenzweig, J. M., & Daley, D. M. (1989). Dyadic adjustment/sexual satisfaction in women and men as a function of psychological sex role self-perception. *Journal of Sex and Marital Therapy, 15,* 42–56.

Ross, L. (1977). The intuitive scientist and his shortcoming. In L. Berkowitz (Ed.), *Advances in experimental social psychology* (Vol. 10, pp. 174–221). New York: Academic Press.

Rotenberg, K. J. (1994). Loneliness and interpersonal trust. *Journal of Social and Clinical Psychology, 13,* 152–173.

Rotenberg, K. J. (1997). Loneliness and the perception of the exchange of disclosures. *Journal of Social and Clinical Psychology, 16,* 259–276.

Rotenberg, K. J., & Kmill, J. (1992). Perception of lonely and non-lonely persons as a function of individual differences in loneliness. *Journal of Social and Personal Relationships, 9,* 325–330.

Rotenberg, K. J., & Korol, S. (1995). The role of loneliness and gender in individuals' love styles. *Journal of Social Behavior and Personality, 10,* 537–546.

Rothbaum, F., Weisz, J., Pott, M., Miyake, K., & Morelli, G. (2000). Attachment and culture: Security in the United States and Japan. *American Psychologist, 55,* 1093–1104.

Rothgerber, H. (1997). External intergroup threat as an antecedent to perceptions of in-group and out-group homogeneity. *Journal of Personality and Social Psychology, 73,* 1206–1212.

Rothman, A. J., & Hardin, C. D. (1997). Differential use of the availability heuristic in social judgment. *Personality and Social Psychology Bulletin, 23,* 123–138.

Rothman, A. J., Martino, S. C., Bedell, B. T., Detweiler, J. B., & Salovey, P. (1999). The systematic influence of gain- and loss-framed messages on interest in and use of different types of health behavior. *Personality and Social Psychology Bulletin, 25,* 1355–1369.

Rotini, C., Cooper, R., Cao, G., Sundarum, C., & McGee, D. (1994). Familial aggregation of cardiovascular diseases in African-American pedigrees. *Genetic Epidemiology, 11,* 397–407.

Rotton, J., & Cohn, E. G. (2000). Violence is a curvilinear function of temperature in Dallas: A replication. *Journal of Personality and Social Psychology, 78,* 1074–1081.

Rotton, J., & Kelley, I. W. (1985). Much ado about the full moon: A meta-analysis of lunar-lunacy research. *Psychological Bulletin, 97,* 286–306.

Rowatt, W. C., Cunningham, M. R., & Druen, P. B. (1998). Deception to get a date. *Personality and Social Psychology Bulletin, 24,* 1228–1242.

Rowe, P. M. (1996, September). On the neurobiological basis of affiliation. *APS Observer,* 17–18.

Roy, M. P., Steptoe, A., & Kirschbaum, C. (1998). Life events and social support as moderators of individual differences in cardiovascular and cortisol reactivity. *Journal of Personality and Social Psychology, 75,* 1273–1281.

Rozin, P., & Nemeroff, C. (1990). The laws of sympathetic magic: A psychological analysis of similarity and contagion. In W. Stigler, R. A. Shweder, & G. Herdt (Eds.), *Cultural psychology: Essays in comparative human development* (pp. 205–232). Cambridge, England: Cambridge University Press.

Rozin, P., Lowery, L., & Ebert, R. (1994). Varieties of disgust faces and the structure of disgust. *Journal of Personality and Social Psychology, 66,* 870–881.

Rozin, P., Markwith, M., & Nemeroff, C. (1992). Magical contagion beliefs and fear of AIDS. *Journal of Applied Social Psychology, 22,* 1081–1092.

Rubin, J. Z. (1985). Deceiving ourselves about deception: Comment on Smith and Richardson's "Amelioration of deception and harm in psychological research." *Journal of Personality and Social Psychology, 48,* 252–253.

Rubin, M., & Hewstone, M. (1998). Social identity theory's self-esteem hypothesis: A review and some suggestions for clarification. *Personality and Social Psychology Review, 2,* 40–62.

Rudich, E. A., & Vallacher, R. R. (1999). To belong or to self-enhance? Motivational bases for choosing interaction partners. *Personality and Social Psychology Bulletin, 25,* 1387–1404.

Rudman, L. A. (1998). Self-promotion as a risk factor for women: The costs and benefits of counterstereotypical impression management. *Journal of Personality and Social Psychology, 74,* 629–645.

Rudman, L. A., & Kilianski, S. E. (2000). Implicit and explicit attitudes toward female authority. *Personality and Social Psychology Bulletin, 26,* 1315–1329.

Rudolph, D. L., & Kim, J. G. (1996). Mood responses to recreational sport and exercise in a Korean sample. *Journal of Social Behavior and Personality, 11,* 841–849.

Ruggiero, K. M., Steele, J., Hwang, A., & Marx, D. M. (2000). "Why did I get a 'D'?" The effects of social comparisons on women's attributions to discrimination. *Personality and Social Psychology Bulletin, 26,* 1271–1283.

Rusbult, C. E., & Martz, J. M. (1995). Remaining in an abusive relationship: An investment model analysis of nonvoluntary dependence. *Personality and Social Psychology Bulletin, 21,* 558–571.

Rusbult, C. E., & Zembrodt, I. M. (1983). Responses to dissatisfaction in romantic involvements: A multidimensional scaling analysis. *Journal of Experimental Social Psychology, 19,* 274–293.

Rusbult, C. E., Martz, J. M., & Agnew, C. R. (1998). The Investment Model Scale: Measuring commitment level, satisfaction level, quality of alternatives, and investment size. *Personal Relationships, 5,* 467–484.

Rusbult, C. E., Morrow, G. D., & Johnson, D. J. (1990). Self-esteem and problem-solving behavior in close relationships. *British Journal of Social Psychology,*

Rusbult, C. E., Van Lange, P. A. M., Wildschut, T., Yovetich, N. A., & Verette, J. (2000). Perceived superiority in close relationships: Why it exists and persists. *Journal of Personality and Social Psychology, 79,* 521–545.

Ruscher, J. B., & Hammer, E. D. (1994). Revising disrupted impressions through conversation. *Journal of Personality and Social Psychology, 66,* 530–541.

Rushton, J. P. (1989a). Genetic similarity in male friendships. *Ethology and Sociobiology, 10,* 361–373.

Rushton, J. P. (1989b). Genetic similarity, human altruism, and group selection. *Behavioral and Brain Sciences, 12,* 503–559.

Rushton, J. P., Russell, R. J. H., & Wells, P. A. (1984). Genetic similarity theory: Beyond kin selection. *Behavior Genetics, 14,* 179–193.

Russell, D., Peplau, L. A., & Cutrona, C. E. (1980). The revised UCLA Loneliness Scale: Concurrent and discriminant validity evidence. *Journal of Personality and Social Psychology, 39,* 472–480.

Russell, J. A. (1994). Is there universal recognition of emotion from facial expressions? A review of cross-cultural studies. *Psychological Bulletin, 115,* 102–141.

Rusting, C. L., & DeHart, T. (2000). Retrieving positive memories to regulate negative mood: Consequences for mood-congruent memory. *Journal of Personality and Social Psychology, 78,* 737–752.

Rutkowski, G. K., Gruder, C. L., & Romer, D. (1983). Group cohesiveness, social norms, and bystander intervention. *Journal of Personality and Social Psychology, 44,* 542–552.

Ruvolo, A. P., Fabin, L. A., & Ruvolo, C. M. (2001). Relationship experiences and change in attachment characteristics of young adults: The role of relationship breakups and conflict avoidance. *Personal Relationships, 8,* 265–281.

Ryan, C. S. (1996). Accuracy of Black and White college students' in-group and out-group stereotypes. *Personality and Social Psychology Bulletin, 22,* 1114–1127.

Ryckman, R. M., Robbins, M. A., Kaczor, L. M., & Gold, J. A. (1989). Male and female raters' stereotyping of male and female physiques. *Personality and Social Psychology Bulletin, 15,* 244–251.

Ryff, C. D., & Singer, B. (2000). Interpersonal flourishing: A positive health agenda for the new millennium. *Personality and Social Psychology Review, 4,* 30–44.

Sadker, M., & Sadker, D. (1994). *Failing at fairness: How America's schools cheat girls.* New York: Charles Scribners Sons.

Safir, M. P., Peres, Y., Lichtenstein, M., Hoch, Z., & Shepher, J. (1982). Psychological androgyny and sexual adequacy. *Journal of Sex and Marital Therapy, 8,* 228–240.

Saki, R. [H. H. Munro]. (1924). Clovis on the alleged romance of business. In *The Square Egg.* New York: Viking.

Sally, D. (1998). Conversation and cooperation in social dilemmas: A meta-analysis of experiments from 1958–1992. *Rationality and Society.*

Salmela-Aro, K., & Nurmi, J.-E. (1996). Uncertainty and confidence in interpersonal projects: Consequences for social relationships and well-being. *Journal of Social and Personal Relationships, 13,* 109–122.

Salmivalli, C., Kaukiainen, A., Kaistaniemi, L., & Lagerspetz, K. M. J. (1999). Self-evaluated self-esteem, peer-evaluated self-esteem, and defensive egotism as predictors of adolescents' participation in bullying situations. *Personality and Social Psychology Bulletin, 25,* 1268–1278.

Salovey, P. (1992). Mood-induced self-focused attention. *Journal of Personality and Social Psychology, 62,* 699–707.

Salovey, P., Mayer, J. D., & Rosenhan, D. L. (1991). Mood and helping: Mood as a motivator of helping and helping as a regulator of mood. In M. S. Clark (Ed.), *Prosocial behavior* (pp. 215–237). Newbury Park, CA: Sage.

Salovey, P., Rothman, A. J., Detweiler, J. B., & Steward, W. T. (2000). Emotional stress and physical health. *American Psychologist, 55,* 110–121.

Sanchez, M. M. (2001). Effects of assertive communication between doctors and patients in public health outpatient surgeries in the city of Seville (Spain). *Social Behavior and Personality, 29,* 63–70.

Sangrador, J. L., & Yela, C. (2000). 'What is beautiful is loved': Physical attractiveness in love relationships in a representative sample. *Social Behavior and Personality, 28,* 207–218.

Sanna, L. J. (1997). Self-efficacy and counterfactual thinking: Up a creek with and without a paddle. *Personality and Social Psychology Bulletin, 23,* 654–666.

Sanna, L. J., & Pusecker, P. A. (1994). Self-efficacy, valence of self-evaluation, and performance. *Personality and Social Psychology Bulletin, 20,* 82–92.

Santos, M. D., Leve, C., & Pratkanis, A. R. (1994). Hey buddy, can you spare seventeen cents? Mindful persuasion and pique technique. *Journal of Applied Social Psychology, 24,* 755–764.

Sarason, I. G., Sarason, B. R., & Pierce, G. R. (1994). Social support: Global and relationship-based levels of analysis. *Journal of Social and Personal Relationships, 11,* 295–312.

Sattler, D. N., Adams, M. G., & Watts, B. (1995). Effects of personal experience on judgments about natural disasters. *Journal of Social Behavior and Personality, 10,* 891–898.

Schachter, D. L., & Kihlstrom, J. F. (1989). Functional amnesia. In F. Boller & J. Grafman (Eds.), *Handbook of neuropsychology* (Vol. 3, pp. 209–230). New York: Elsevier.

Schachter, S. (1951). Deviation, rejection, and communication. *Journal of Abnormal and Social Psychology, 46,* 190–207.

Schachter, S. (1959). *The psychology of affiliation.* Stanford, CA: Stanford University Press.

Schachter, S. (1964). The interaction of cognitive and physiological determinants of emotional state. In L. Berkowitz (Ed.), *Advances in experimental social psychology* (Vol. 1, pp. 48–81). New York: Academic Press.

Schaubroeck, J., Jones, J. R., & Xie, J. L. (2001). Individual differences in utilizing control to cope with job demands: Effects on susceptibility to infectious disease. *Journal of Applied Psychology, 86,* 265–278.

Scher, A., & Mayseless, O. (1994). Mothers' attachment with spouse and parenting in the first year. *Journal of Social and Interpersonal Relationships, 11,* 601–609.

Scher, S. J. (1997). Measuring the consequences of injustice. *Personality and Social Psychology Bulletin, 23,* 482–497.

Schillinger, L. (2001, January 29). Optical delusions: Al Gore's hair problem. *The New Yorker,* 34–35.

Schimel, J., Arndt, J., Pyszczynski, T., & Greenberg, J. (2001). Being accepted for who we are: Evidence that social validation of the intrinsic self reduces general defensiveness. *Journal of Personality and Social Psychology, 80,* 35–52.

Schimel, J., Pyszczynski, T., Greenberg, J., O'Mahen, H., & Arndt, J. (2000). Running from the shadow: Psychological distancing from others to deny characteristics people fear in themselves. *Journal of Personality and Social Psychology, 78,* 446–462.

Schlenker, B. R., & Britt, T. W. (2001). Strategically controlling information to help friends: Effects of empathy and friendship strength on beneficial impression management. *Journal of Experimental Social Psychology, 37,* 357–372.

Schlenker, B. R., & Pontari, B. A. (in press). The strategic control of information: Impression management and self-presentation in daily life. In A. Tesser, R. Felson, & J. Suls (Eds.), *Perspectives on self and identity.* Washington, DC: American Psychological Association.

Schlenker, B. R., Pontari, B. A., & Christopher, A. N. (2001). Excuses and character: Personal and social implications of excuses. *Personality and Social Psychology Review, 5,* 15–32.

Schmid, R. E. (2001, April 18). Teen pregnancy drops to record low. Associated Press.

Schmitt, D. P., & Buss, D. M. (2001). Human mate poaching: Tactics and temptations for infiltrating existing mateships. *Journal of Personality and Social Psychology, 80,* 894–917.

Schmitt, E. (2001, May 15). In census, families changing. *New York Times.*

Schmolck, H., Buffalo, E. A., & Squire, L. R. (2000). Memory distortions develop over time: Recollections of the O. J. Simpson trial verdict after 15 and 32 months. *Psychological Science, 11,* 39–45.

Schneider, B. H. (1991). A comparison of skill-building and desensitization strategies for intervention with aggressive children. *Aggressive Behavior, 17,* 301–311.

Schneider, M. E., Major, B., Luhtanen, R., & Crocker, J. (1996). Social stigma and the potential costs of assumptive help. *Personality and Social Psychology Bulletin, 22,* 201–209.

Schooler, J. W., & Engstler-Schooler, T. Y. (1990). Verbal overshadowing of visual memories: Some things are better left unsaid. *Cognitive Psychology, 22,* 36–71.

Schooler, J. W., & Loftus, E. F. (1986). Individual differences and experimentation: Complementary approaches to interrogative suggestibility. *Social Behavior, 1,* 105–112.

Schopler, J., & Insko, C. A. (1999). The reduction of the interindividual–intergroup discontinuity effect: The role of future consequences. In M. Foddy, M. Smithson, S. Schneider, & M. Hogg (Eds.), *Resolving social dilemmas: Dynamic, structural, and intergroup aspects* (pp. 281–293). Philadelphia: Psychology Press.

Schopler, J., Insko, C. A., Wieslquist, J., Pemberton, M., Witcher, B., Koazr, R., Roddenberry, C., & Wildschut, T. (2001). When groups are more competitive than individuals: The domain of the discontinuity effect. *Journal of Personality and Social Psychology, 80,* 632–644.

Schul, Y., & Vinokur, A. D. (2000). Projection in person perception among spouses as a function of the similarity in their shared experiences. *Personality and Social Psychology Bulletin, 26,* 987–1001.

Schusterman, R. J., Reichmuth, C. J., & Kastak, D. (2000). How animals classify friends and foes. *Current Directions in Psychological Science, 9,* 1–6.

Schutte, J. W., & Hosch, H. M. (1997). Gender differences in sexual assault verdicts: A meta-analysis. *Journal of Social Behavior and Personality, 12,* 759–772.

Schwarz, N., Bless, H., Strack, F., Klumpp, G., Rittenauer-Schatka, G., & Simons, A. (1991b). Ease of retrieval as information: Another look at the availability heuristic. *Journal of Personality and Social Psychology, 61,* 195–202.

Schwarzer, R. (1994). Optimism, vulnerability, and self-beliefs as health-related cognitions: A sytematic overview. *Psychology and Health, 9,* 161–180.

Schwarzer, R. (2001). Social–cognitive factors in changing health-related behaviors. *Current Directions in Psychological Science, 10,* 47–51.

Schwarzer, R., Jerusalem, M., & Hahn, A. (1994). Unemployment, social support and health complaints: A longitudinal study of stress in East German refugees. *Journal of Community and Applied Social Psychology, 4,* 31–45.

Schwarzwald, J., Amir, Y., & Crain, R. L. (1992). Long-term effects of school desegregation experiences on interpersonal relations in the Israeli defense forces. *Personality and Social Psychology Bulletin, 18,* 357–368.

Scott, K. P., & Feldman-Summers, S. (1979). Children's reactions to textbook stories in which females are portrayed in traditionally male roles. *Journal of Educational Psychology, 71,* 396–402.

Seal, D. W. (1997). Inter-partner concordance of self-reported sexual behavior among college dating couples. *Journal of Sex Research, 34,* 39–55.

Searcy, E., & Eisenberg, N. (1992). Defensiveness in response to aid from a sibling. *Journal of Personality and Social Psychology, 62,* 422–433.

Sears, D. O. (1988). Symbolic racism. In P. A. Katz & D. A. Taylor (Eds.), *Eliminating racism: Profiles in controversy* (pp. 53–84). New York: Plenum.

Sedikides, C. (1992). Attentional effects on mood are moderated by chronic self-conception valence. *Personality and Social Psychology Bulletin, 18,* 580–584.

Sedikides, C. (1993). Assessment, enhancement, and verification determinants of the self-evaluation process. *Journal of Personality and Social Psychology, 65,* 317–338.

Sedikides, C. (1995). Central and peripheral self-conceptions are differentially influenced by mood: Test of the differential sensitivity hypothesis. *Journal of Personality and Social Psychology, 69,* 759–777.

Sedikides, C., & Green, J. D. (2000). On the self-protective nature of inconsistency-negativity management: Using the person memory paradigm to examine self-referent memory. *Journal of Personality and Social Psychology, 79,* 906–922.

Sedikides, C., & Skowronski, J. J. (1997). The symbolic self in evolutionary context. *Personality and Social Psychology Review, 1,* 80–102.

Sedikides, C., Schopler, J., & Insko, C. A. (Eds.). (1998). *Intergroup cognition and intergroup behavior.* Mahwah, NJ: Erlbaum.

Segal, M. M. (1974). Alphabet and attraction: An unobtrusive measure of the effect of propinquity in a field setting. *Journal of Personality and Social Psychology, 30,* 654–657.

Segerstrom, S. C., Taylor, S. E., Kemeny, M. E., & Fahey, J. L. (1998). Optimism is associated with mood, coping, and immune change in response to stress. *Journal of Personality and Social Psychology, 74,* 1646–1655.

Senecal, C., Vallerand, R. J., & Guay, F. (2001). Antecedents and outcomes of work-family conflict: Toward a motivational model. *Personality and Social Psychology Bulletin, 27,* 176–186.

Seta, C. E., Hayes, N. S., & Seta, J. J. (1994). Mood, memory, and vigilance: The influence of distraction on recall and impression formation. *Personality and Social Psychology Bulletin, 20,* 170–177.

Seybold, K. S., & Hill, P. C. (2001). The role of religion and spirituality in mental and physical health. *Current Directions in Psychological Science, 10,* 21–24.

Shackelford, T. K., & Larsen, R. J. (1999). Facial attractiveness and physical health. *Evolution and Human Behavior, 20,* 71–76.

Shams, M. (2001). Social support, loneliness and friendship preference among British Asian and non-Asian adolescents. *Social Behavior and Personality, 29,* 399–404.

Shanab, M. E., & Yahya, K. A. (1977). A behavioral study of obedience in children. *Journal of Personality and Social Psychology, 35,* 530–536.

Shapiro, A., & Gottman, J. (2000). The baby and the marriage: Identifying factors that buffer against decline in marital satisfaction after the first baby arrives. *Journal of Family Psychology, 14,* 59–70.

Shapiro, J. P., Baumeister, R. F., & Kessler, J. W. (1991). A three-component model of children's teasing: Aggression, humor, and ambiguity. *Journal of Social and Clinical Psychology, 10,* 459–472.

Sharp, M. J., & Getz, J. G. (1996). Substance use as impression management. *Personality and Social Psychology Bulletin, 22,* 60–67.

Sharp, D., Adair, J. G., & Roese, N. J. (1992). Twenty years of deception research: A decline in subjects' trust? *Personality and Social Psychology Bulletin, 18,* 585–590.

Shaver, J. (1993, August 9). America's legal immigrants: Who they are and where they go. *Newsweek,* pp. 20–21.

Shaver, P. R., & Brennan, K. A. (1992). Attachment styles and the "big five" personality traits: Their connections with each other and with romantic relationship outcomes. *Personality and Social Psychology Bulletin, 18,* 536–545.

Shaver, P. R., & Hazan, C. (1994). Attachment. In A. L. Weber & J. H. Harvey (Eds.), *Perspectives on close relationships* (pp. 110–130). Boston: Allyn & Bacon.

Shaver, P. R., Morgan, H. J., & Wu, S. (1996). Is love a "basic" emotion? *Personal Relationships, 3,* 81–96.

Shavitt, S. (1989). Operationalizing functional theories of attitudes. In A. R. Pratkanis, S. J. Breckler, & A. G. Greenwald (Eds.), *Attitude structure and function* (pp. 311–377). Hillsdale, NJ: Erlbaum.

Shavitt, S. (1990). The role of attitude objects in attitude functions. *Journal of Experimental Social Psychology, 26,* 124–148.

Shaw, J. I., Borough, H. W., & Fink, M. I. (1994). Perceived sexual orientation and helping behavior by males and females: The wrong number technique. *Journal of Psychology and Human Sexuality, 6,* 73–81.

Shaw, L. L., Batson, C. D., & Todd, R. M. (1994). Empathy avoidance: Forestalling feeling for another in order to escape the motivational consequences. *Journal of Personality and Social Psychology, 67,* 879–887.

Shearn, D., Spellman, L., Straley, B., Meirick, J., & Stryker, K. (1999). Empathic blushing in friends and strangers. *Motivation and Emotion, 23,* 307–316.

Shechtman, Z. (1993). School adjustment and small-group therapy: An Israeli study. *Journal of Counseling and Development, 72,* 77–81.

Sheeran, P., & Abraham, C. (1994). Unemployment and self-conception: A symbolic interactionist analysis. *Journal of Community & Applied Social Psychology, 4,* 115–129.

Sheldon, W. H., Stevens, S. S., & Tucker, W. B. (1940). *The varieties of human physique.* New York: Harper.

Shelton, J. N. (2000). A reconceptualization of how we study issues of racial prejudice. *Personality and Social Psychology Review, 4,* 374–390.

Shepperd, J. A., Ouellette, J. A., & Fernandez, J. K. (1996). Abandoning unrealistic optimistic performance estimates and the temporal proximity of self-relevant feedback. *Journal of Personality and Social Psychology, 70,* 844–855.

Shepperd, J. A., Findley-Klein, C., Kwavnick, K., Walker, D., & Perez, S. (2000). Bracing for loss. *Journal of Personality and Social Psychology, 78,* 620–634.

Sherif, M. (1937). An experimental approach to the study of attitudes. *Sociometry, 1,* 90–98.

Sherif, M., Harvey, D. J., White, B. J., Hood, W. R, & Sherif, C. W. (1961). *The Robbers' cave experiment.* Norman, OK: Institute of Group Relations.

Sherman, D. A. K., Nelson, L. D., & Steele, C. M. (2000). Do messages about health risks threaten the self? Increasing the acceptance of threatening health messages via self-affirmation. *Personality and Social Psychology Bulletin, 26,* 1046–1058.

Sherman, J. W., & Klein, S. B. (1994). Development and representation of personality impressions. *Journal of Personality and Social Psychology, 67,* 972–983.

Sherman, M. D., & Thelen, M. H. (1996). Fear of intimacy scale: Validation and extension with adolescents. *Journal of Social and Personal Relationships, 13,* 507–521.

Sherman, S. R. (1994). Changes in age identity: Self-perceptions in middle and late life. *Journal of Aging Studies, 8,* 397–412.

Sherman, S. S. (1980). On the self-erasing nature of errors of prediction. *Journal of Personality and Social Psychology, 16,* 388–403.

Shigetomi, C. C., Hartmann, D. P., & Gelfand, D. M. (1981). Sex differences in children's altruistic behavior and reputations for helpfulness. *Developmental Psychology, 17,* 434–437.

Shively, C. A. (1998, March/April). Social stress and disease susceptibility in female monkeys. *Psychological Science Agenda,* 6–7.

Shotland, R. I., & Strau, M. K. (1976). Bystander response to an assault: When a man attacks a woman. *Journal of Personality and Social Psychology, 34,* 990–999.

Showers, C. (1992a). Compartmentalization of positive and negative self-knowledge: Keeping bad apples out of the bunch. *Journal of Personality and Social Psychology, 62,* 1036–1049.

Showers, C. (1992b). Evaluative integrative thinking about characteristics of the self. *Personality and Social Psychology Bulletin, 18,* 719–729.

Showers, C. J., & Kling, K. C. (1996). Organization of self-knowledge: Implications for recovery from sad mood. *Journal of Personality and Social Psychology, 70,* 578–590.

Showers, C. J., & Ryff, C. D. (1996). Self-differentiation and well-being in a life transition. *Personality and Social Psychology Bulletin, 22,* 448–460.

Shulman, S., Elicker, J., & Sroufe, L. A. (1994). Stages of friendship growth in preadolescence as related to attachment history. *Journal of Social and Personal Relationships, 11,* 341–361.

Sigall, H. (1997). Ethical considerations in social psychological research: Is the bogus pipeline a special case? *Journal of Applied Social Psychology, 27,* 574–581.

Sigall, H., & Page, R. (1971). Current stereotypes: A little fading, a little faking. *Journal of Personality and Social Psychology, 18,* 247–255.

Sigelman, C. K., Thomas, D. B., Sigelman, L., & Robich, F. D. (1986). Gender, physical attractiveness, and electability: An experimental investigation of voter biases. *Journal of Applied Social Psychology, 16,* 229–248.

Sillars, A. L., Folwell, A. L., Hill, K. C., Maki, B. K., Hurst, A. P., & Casano, R. A. (1994). *Journal of Social and Personal Relationships, 11,* 611–617.

Silverstein, R. (1994). Chronic identity diffusion in traumatized combat veterans. *Social Behavior and Personality, 22,* 69–80.

Simon, B., & Klandermans, B. (2001). Politicized collective identity: A social psychological analysis. *American Psychologist, 56,* 319–331.

Simon, B., Sturmer, S., & Steffens, K. (2000). Helping individuals or group members? The role of individual and collective identification in AIDS volunteerism. *Personality and Social Psychology Bulletin, 26,* 497–506.

Simon, L., Greenberg, J., & Brehm, J. (1995). Trivialization: The forgotten mode of dissonance reduction. *Journal of Personality and Social Psychology, 68,* 247–260.

Simpson, J. A. (1987). The dissolution of romantic relationships: Factors involved in relationship stability and emotional stress. *Journal of Personality and Social Psychology, 53,* 683–692.

Simpson, J. A., & Gangestad, S. W. (1991). Individual differences in sociosexuality: Evidence for convergent and discriminant validity. *Journal of Personality and Social Psychology, 60,* 870–883.

Simpson, J. A., & Gangestad, S. W. (1992). Sociosexuality and romantic partner choice. *Journal of Personality, 60,* 31–51.

Simpson, J. A., Ickes, W., & Blackstone, T. (1995). When the head protects the heart: Empathic accuracy in dating relationships. *Journal of Personality and Social Psychology, 69,* 629–641.

Simpson, J. A., Ickes, W., & Grich, J. (1999). When accuracy hurts: Reactions of anxious-ambivalent dating partners to a relationship-threatening situation. *Journal of Personality and Social Psychology, 76,* 754–769.

Singh, R., & Ho, S. Y. (2000). Attitudes and attraction: A new test of the attraction, repulsion and similarity–dissimilarity asymmetry hypotheses. *British Journal of Social Psychology, 39,* 197–211.

Singh, R., & Teoh, J. B. P. (1999). Attitudes and attraction: A test of two hypotheses for the similarity–dissimilarity asymmetry. *British Journal of Social Psychology, 38,* 427–443.

Singh, R., & Teoh, J. B. P. (2000). Impression formation from intellectual and social traits: Evidence for behavioural adaptation and cognitive processing. *British Journal of Social Psychology, 39,* 537–554.

Singh, R., Choo, W. M., & Poh, L. L. (1998). In-group bias and fair-mindedness as strategies of self-presentation in intergroup perception. *Personality and Social Psychology Bulletin, 24,* 147–162.

Sivacek, J., & Crano, W. D. (1982). Vested interest as a moderator of attitude-behavior consistency. *Journal of Personality and Social Psychology, 43,* 210–221.

Skarlicki, D. P., & Folger, R. (1997). Retaliation in the workplace: The roles of distributive, procedural, and interactional justice. *Journal of Applied Psychology, 821,* 434–443.

Skarlicki, D. P., & Latham, G. P. (1997). Leadership training in organizational justice to increase citizenship behavior within a labor union: A replication. *Personnel Psychology, 50,* 617–633.

Skitka, L. J. (1999). Ideological and attributional boundaries on public compassion: Reactions to individuals and communities affected by a natural disaster. *Personality and Social Psychology Bulletin, 25,* 793–808.

Skowronski, J. J., & Carston, D. E. (1989). Negativity and extremity biases in impression formation: A review of explanations. *Psychological Bulletin, 105,* 131–142.

Sleek, S. (1998, February). Is psychologists' testimony going unheard? *APA Monitor, 1,* 34.

Smeaton, G., & Byrne, D. (1987). The effects of R-rated violence and erotica, individual differences, and victim characteristics on acquaintance rape proclivity. *Journal of Research in Personality, 21,* 171–184.

Smeaton, G., Byrne, D., & Murnen, S. K. (1989). The repulsion hypothesis revisited: Similarity irrelevance or dissimilarity bias? *Journal of Personality and Social Psychology, 56,* 54–59.

Smith, B. W. (1996). Coping as a predictor of outcomes following the 1993 Midwest flood. *Journal of Social Behavior and Personality, 11,* 225–239.

Smith, C. M., Tindale, R. S., & Dugoni, B. L. (1996). Minority and majority influence in freely interacting groups: Qualitative versus quantitative differences. *British Journal of Social Psychology, 35,* 137–149.

Smith, D. E., Gier, J. A., & Willis, F. N. (1982). Interpersonal touch and compliance with a marketing request. *Basic and Applied Social Psychology, 3,* 35–38.

Smith, E. R., & Henry, S. (1996). An in-group becomes part of the self: Response time evidence. *Personality and Social Psychology Bulletin, 22,* 635–642.

Smith, E. R., & Zarate, M. A. (1992). Exemplar-based model of social judgment. *Psychological Review, 99,* 3–21.

Smith, E. R., Byrne, D., & Fielding, P. J. (1995). Interpersonal attraction as a function of extreme gender role adherence. *Personal Relationships, 2,* 161–172.

Smith, E. R., Murphy, J., & Coats, S. (1999). Attachment to groups: Theory and measurement. *Journal of Personality and Social Psychology, 77,* 94–110.

Smith, E. R., Byrne, D., Becker, M. A., & Przybyla, D. P. J. (1993). Sexual attitudes of males and females as predictors of interpersonal attraction and marital compatibility. *Journal of Applied Social Psychology, 23,* 1011–1034.

Smith, K. D., Keating, J. P., & Stotland, E. (1989). Altruism reconsidered: The effect of denying feedback on a victim's status to empathetic witnesses. *Journal of Personality and Social Psychology, 57,* 641–650.

Smith, P. B., & Bond, M. H. (1993). *Social psychology across cultures.* Boston: Allyn & Bacon.

Smith, P. K., & Brain, P. (2000). Bullying in schools; lessons from two decades of research. *Aggressive Behavior, 26,* 1–9.

Smith, S. S., & Richardson, D. (1985). On deceiving ourselves about deception: Reply to Rubin. *Journal of Personality and Social Psychology, 48,* 254–255.

Smith, V. I., & Ellsworth, P. C. (1987). The social psychology of eyewitness accuracy: Misleading questions and communicator expertise. *Journal of Applied Psychology, 72,* 294–300.

Smorti, A., & Ciucci, E. (2000). Narrative strategies in bullies and victims in Italian schoolchildren. *Aggressive Behavior, 26,* 33–48.

Smuts, B. (2001, December/January). Common ground. *Natural History,* 78–83.

Smyth, J., True, N., & Souto, J. (2001). Effects of writing about traumatic experiences: The necessity for narrative structuring. *Journal of Social and Clinical Psychology, 20,* 161–172.

Snell, W. E., Jr. (1998). The Relationship Awareness Scale: Measuring relational-consciousness, relational-monitoring, and relational-anxiety. *Contemporary Social Psychology, 18,* 23–49.

Sniffen, M. J. (1999, November 22). Serious crime declines sharply. Associated Press.

Snyder, C. R. (2000). The past and possible futures of hope. *Journal of Social and Clinical Psychology, 19,* 11–28.

Snyder, C. R., & Fromkin, H. L. (1979). *Uniqueness: The human pursuit of difference.* New York: Plenum.

Snyder, M., & Ickes, W. (1985). Personality and social behavior. In G. Lindzey & E. Aronson (Eds.), *Handbook of social psychology* (3rd ed.) (Vol. 2, pp. 883–947). New York: Random House.

Snyder, M., & Simpson, J. A. (1984). Self-monitoring and dating relationships. *Journal of Personality and Social Psychology, 47,* 1281–1291.

Snyder, M., Grether, J., & Keller, K. (1974). Staring and compliance: A field experiment on hitchhiking. *Journal of Applied Social Psychology, 4,* 165–170.

Somerfield, M. R., & McCrae, R. R. (2000). Stress and coping research: Methodological challenges, theoretical advances, and clinical applications. *American Psychologist, 55,* 620–625.

Sommer, K. L., Horowitz, I. A., & Bourgeois, M. J. (2001). When juries fail to comply with the law: Biased evidence processing in individual and group decision making. *Personality and Social Psychology Bulletin, 27,* 309–320.

Sommers, S. R., & Ellsworth, P. C. (2000). Race in the courtroom: Perceptions of guilt and dispositional attributions. *Personality and Social Psychology Bulletin, 26,* 1367–1379.

Sommers, S. R., & Kassin, S. M. (2001). On the many impacts of inadmissible testimony: Selective compliance, need for cognition, and the overcorrection bias. *Personality and Social Psychology Bulletin, 27,* 1368–1377.

Song, S. (2000, August 21). Teen moms. *Time,* 84.

Spinoza, B. (1951). *The ethics.* New York: Dover. (Original work published 1675.)

Sprafkin, J. N., Liebert, R. M., & Poulous, R. W. (1975). Effects of a prosocial televised example on children's helping. *Journal of Personality and Social Psychology, 48,* 35–46.

Sprecher, S. (1992). How men and women expect to feel and behave in response to inequity in close relationships. *Social Psychology Quarterly, 55,* 57–69.

Sprecher, S., & Duck, S. (1994). Sweet talk: The importance of perceived communication for romantic and friendship attraction experienced during a get-acquainted date. *Personality and Social Psychology Bulletin, 20,* 391–400.

Stacey, J., & Biblarz, T. (2001). Does the sexual orientation of parents matter? *American Sociological Review, 66,* 159–183.

Stalder, D. R., & Baron, R. S. (1998). Attributional complexity as a moderator of dissonance-produced attitude change. *Journal of Personality and Social Psychology, 75,* 449–455.

Stangor, C., & McMillan, D. (1992). Memory for expectancy-congruent and expectancy-incongruent information: A review of the social and social developmental literatures. *Psychological Bulletin, 111,* 42–61.

Stangor, C., Sechrist, G. B., & Jost, T. J. (2001). Changing racial beliefs by providing consensus information. *Personality and Social Psychology Bulletin, 27,* 486–496.

Stanton, A. L., Kirk, S. B., Cameron, C. L., & Danoff-Burg, S. (2000). Coping through emotional approach: Scale construction and validation. *Journal of Personality and Social Psychology, 78,* 1150–1169.

Stasser, G. (1992). Pooling of unshared information during group discussion. In S. Worchel, W. Wood, & J. H. Simpson (Eds.), *Group process and productivity* (pp. 48–67). Newbury Park, CA: Sage.

Stasser, G., Taylor, L. A., & Hanna, C. (1989). Information sampling in structured and unstructured discussions of three- and six-person groups. *Journal of Personality and Social Psychology, 57,* 67–78.

Staub, E. (1999). The roots of evil: Social conditions, culture, personality, and basic human needs. *Personality and Social Psychology Review, 3,* 179–192.

Stech, F., & McClintock, C. G. (1981). Effects of communication timing on duopoly bargaining outcomes. *Journal of Personality and Social Psychology, 40,* 664–674.

Steel, R. P., & Rentsch, J. R. (1997). The dispositional model of job attitudes revisited: Findings of a 10-year study. *Journal of Applied Psychology, 82,* 873–879.

Steele, C. M. (1988). The psychology of self-affirmation: Sustaining the integrity of the self. In L. Berkowitz (Ed.), *Advances in experimental social psychology* (pp. 261–302). Hillsdale, NJ: Erlbaum.

Steele, C. M. (1992, April). Race and the schooling of Black Americans. *The Atlantic Monthly, 269*(4), 68–78.

Steele, C. M. (1997). A threat in the air: How stereotypes shape the intellectual identities and performance of women and African-Americans. *American Psychologist, 52,* 613–629.

Steele, C. M., & Aronson, J. (1995). Stereotype threat and the intellectual test performance of African Americans. *Journal of Personality and Social Psychology, 69,* 797–811.

Steele, C. M., & Josephs, R. A. (1990). Alcohol myopia: Its prized and dangerous effects. *American Psychologist, 45,* 921–933.

Steele, C. M., & Lui, T. J. (1983). Dissonance processes as self-affirmation. *Journal of Personality and Social Psychology, 45,* 5–19.

Steele, C. M., Critchlow, B., & Liu, T. J. (1985). Alcohol and social behavior: The helpful drunkard. *Journal of Personality and Social Psychology, 48,* 35–46.

Steele, C. M., Southwick, L., & Critchlow, B. (1981). Dissonance and alcohol: Drinking your troubles away. *Journal of Personality and Social Psychology, 41,* 831–846.

Steele, C. M., Spencer, S. J., & Lynch, M. (1993). Self-image resilience and dissonance: The role of affirmational resources. *Journal of Personality and Social Psychology, 64,* 885–896.

Stein, R. I., & Nemeroff, C. J. (1995). Moral overtones of food: Judgments of others based on what they eat. *Personality and Social Psychology Bulletin, 21,* 480–490.

Steinhauer, J. (1995, April 10). Big benefits in marriage, studies say. *New York Times,* p. A10.

Stephan, W. G. (1985). Intergroup relations. In G. Lindzey & E. Aronson (Eds.), *Handbook of social psychology* (Vol. 3, pp. 599–658). New York: Addison-Wesley.

Sternberg, R. J. (1986). A triangular theory of love. *Psychological Review, 93,* 119–135.

Sternberg, R. J. (1988a). *The triangle of love.* New York: Basic Books.

Sternberg, R. J. (1988b). Triangulating love. In R. J. Sternberg & M. J. Barnes (Eds.), *The psychology of love* (pp. 119–138). New Haven, CT: Yale University Press.

Sternberg, R. J. (1996). Love stories. *Personal Relationships, 3,* 59–79.

Sternberg, R. J., & Hojjat, M. (Eds.). (1997). *Satisfaction in close relationships.* New York: Guilford.

Stevens, C. K., & Kristof, A. L. (1995). Making the right impression: A field study of applicant impression management during job interviews. *Journal of Applied Psychology, 80,* 587–606.

Stevens, L. E., & Fiske, S. T. (2000). Motivated impressions of a powerholder: Accuracy under task dependency and misperception under evaluation dependency. *Personality and Social Psychology Bulletin, 26,* 907–922.

Stewart, R. B., Verbrugge, K. M., & Beilfuss, M. C. (1998). Sibling relationships in early adulthood: A typology. *Personal Relationships, 5,* 59–74.

Stice, E., Shaw, H., & Nemeroff, C. (1998). Dual pathway model of bulimia nervosa: Longitudinal support for dietary restraint and affect-regulation mechanisms. *Journal of Social and Clinical Psychology, 17,* 129–149.

Stiff, J. B., Miller, G. R., Sleight, C., Mongeau, P. J., Gardelick, R., & Rogan, R. (1989). Explanation for visual cue primacy in judgments of honesty and deceit. *Journal of Personality and Social Psychology, 56,* 555–564.

Stiff, J. B., Miller, G. R., Sleight, C., Mongeau, P. I., Gardelick, R., Strack, F., & Neumann, R. (2000). Furrowing the brow may undermine perceived fame: The role of facial feedback in judgments of celebrity. *Personality and Social Psychology Bulletin, 26,* 762–768.

Stiles, W. B., Walz, N. C., Schroeder, M. A. B., Williams, L. L., & Ickes, W. (1996). Attractiveness and disclosure in initial encounters of mixed-sex dyads. *Journal of Social and Personal Relationships, 13,* 303–312.

Stocker, C. M., & McHale, S. M. (1992). The nature and family correlates of preadolescents' perceptions of their sibling relationships. *Journal of Social and Personal Relationships, 9,* 179–195.

Stodghill, R., III. (1998, June 15). Where'd you learn that? *Time,* 52–59.

Stone, A. A., Neale, J. M., Cox, D. S., Napoli, A., Valdimarsdottir, H., & Kennedy-Moore, E. (1994). Daily events are associated with a secretory immune response to an oral antigen in men. *Health Psychology, 13,* 440–446.

Stone, J., Wiegand, A. W., Cooper, J., & Aronson, E. (1997). When exemplification fails: Hypocrisy and the motives for self-integrity. *Journal of Personality and Social Psychology, 72,* 54–65.

Stone, J., Aronson, E., Crain, A. L., Winslow, M. P., & Fried, C. B. (1994). Inducing hypocrisy as a means of encouraging young adults to use condoms. *Personality and Social Psychology Bulletin, 20,* 116–128.

Stoppard, J. M., & Gruchy, C. D. G. (1993). Gender, context, and expression of positive emotion. *Personality and Social Psychology Bulletin, 19,* 143–150.

Story, A. L. (1998). Self-esteem and memory for favorable and unfavorable personality feedback. *Personality and Social Psychology Bulletin, 24,* 51–64.

Stotland, E. (1969). Exploratory investigations of empathy. *Advances in Experimental Social Psychology, 4,* 271–313.

Stradling, S. G., Crowe, G., & Tuohy, A. P. (1993). Changes in self-concept during occupational socialization of new recruits to the police. *Journal of Community & Applied Social Psychology, 3,* 131–147.

Strauman, T. J. (1996). Stability within the self: A longitudinal study of the structural implications of self-discrepancy theory. *Journal of Personality and Social Psychology, 71,* 1142–1153.

Strauman, T. J., Lemieux, A. M., & Coe, C. L. (1993). Self-discrepancy and natural killer cell activity: Immunological consequences of negative self-evaluation. *Journal of Personality and Social Psychology, 64,* 1042–1052.

Stroessner, S. J., Hamilton, D. L., & Mackie, D. M. (1992). Affect and stereotyping: the effect of induced mood on distinctiveness-based illusory correlations. *Journal of Personality and Social Psychology, 62,* 564–576.

Strong, S. M., Williamson, D. A., Netemeyer, R. G., & Geer, J. H. (2000). Eating disorder symptoms and concerns about body differ as a function of gender and sexual orientation. *Journal of Social and Clinical Psychology, 19,* 240–255.

Strube, M., Turner, C. W., Cerro, D., Stevens, J., & Hinchey, F. (1984). Interpersonal aggression and the Type A coronary-prone behavior pattern: A theoretical distinction and practical implications. *Journal of Personality and Social Psychology, 47,* 839–847.

Strube, M. J. (1989). Evidence for the Type in Type A behavior: A taxonometric analysis. *Journal of Personality and Social Pychology, 56,* 972–987.

Study: Pets curb dangerous rises in blood pressure. (1999, November 8). CNN.com.

Stukas, A. A., Snyder, M., & Clary, E. G. (1999). The effects of "mandatory volunteerism" on intentions to volunteer. *Psychological Science, 10,* 59–64.

Subich, L. M., Cooper, E. A., Barrett, G. V., & Arthur, W. (1986). Occupational perceptions of males and females as a function of sex ratios, salary, and availability. *Journal of Vocational Behavior, 28,* 123–134.

Suinn, R. M. (2001). The terrible twos—Anger and anxiety: Hazardous to your health. *American Psychologist, 56,* 27–36.

Suitor, J. J., & Pillemer, K. (2000). Did Mom really love you best? Developmental histories, status transitions, and parental favoritism in later life families. *Motivation and Emotion, 24,* 105–120.

Suls, J., & Rosnow, J. (1988). Concerns about artifacts in behavioral research. In M. Morawski (Ed.), *The rise of experimentation in American psychology* (pp. 163–187). New Haven, CT: Yale University Press.

Suls, J., & Wan, C. K. (1989). The effects of sensory and procedural information on coping with stressful medical procedures and pain: A meta-analysis. *Journal of Consulting and Clinical Psychology, 57,* 372–379.

Summers, R. J. (1991). The influence of affirmative action on perceptions of a beneficiary's qualifications. *Journal of Applied Social Psychology, 21,* 1265–1276.

Susskind, J., Maurer, K. L., Thakkar, V., Hamilton, D. L., & Sherman, J. (1999). Perceiving individuals and groups: Expectancies, inferences, and causal attribution. *Journal of Personality and Social Psychology, 76,* 181–191.

Sussman, N. M. (2000). The dynamic nature of cultural identity throughout cultural transitions: Why home is not so sweet. *Personality and Social Psychology Review, 4,* 355–373.

Swann, W. B., Jr. (1997). The trouble with change: Self-verification and allegiance to the self. *Psychological Science, 8,* 177–180.

Swann, W. B., Jr., & Gill, M. J. (1997). Confidence and accuracy in person perception: Do we know what we think we know about our relationship partners? *Journal of Personality and Social Psychology, 73,* 747–757.

Swann, W. B., Jr., De La Ronde, C., & Hixon, J. G. (1994). Authenticity and positivity strivings in marriage and courtship. *Journal of Personality and Social Psychology, 66,* 857–869.

Swann, W. B., Jr., Griffin, J. J. Jr., Predmore, S. C., & Gaines, B. (1987). Cognitive–affective crossfire: When self-consistency meets self-enhancement. *Journal of Personality and Social Psychology, 52,* 881–889.

Swap, W. C. (1977). Interpersonal attraction and repeated exposure to rewarders and punishers. *Personality and Social Psychology Bulletin, 3,* 248–251.

Sweet charity. (2001, June 4). *U.S. News & World Report,* 10.

Swim, J. K. (1994). Perceived versus meta-analytic effect sizes: An assessment of the accuracy of gender stereotypes. *Journal of Personality and Social Psychology, 66,* 21–36.

Swim, J. K., & Stangor, C. (1998). *Prejudice: The target's perspective.* New York: Academic Press.

Swim, J. K., Aikin, K. J., Hall, W. S., & Hunter, B. A. (1995). Sexism and racism: Old-fashioned and modern prejudices. *Journal of Personality and Social Psychology, 68,* 199–214.

Tafarodi, R. W. (1998). Paradoxical self-esteem and selectivity in the processing of social information. *Journal of Personality and Social Psychology, 74,* 1181–1196.

Tafarodi, R. W., & Vu, C. (1997). Two-dimensional self-esteem and reactions to success and failure. *Personality and Social Psychology Bulletin, 23,* 626–635.

Tajfel, H. (1982). *Social identity and intergroup relations.* Cambridge, England: Cambridge University Press.

Tajfel, H., & Turner, J. C. (1986). The social identity theory of intergroup behavior. In S. Worchel & W. Austin (Eds.), *Psychology of intergroup relations.* Chicago: Nelson-Hall.

Takata, T., & Hashimoto, H. (1973). Effects of insufficient justification upon the arousal of cognitive dissonance: Timing of justification and evaluation of task. *Japanese Journal of Experimental Social Psychology, 13,* 77–85.

Tan, D. T. Y., & Singh, R. (1995). Attitudes and attraction: A developmental study of the similarity–attraction and dissimilarity–repulsion hypotheses. *Personality and Social Psychology Bulletin, 21* 975–986.

Tannen, D. (1994). *Talking from 9 to 5.* New York: William Morrow.

Tannen, D. (1995, January 9–15). And rarely the twain shall meet. *Washington Post National Weekly Edition* 25.

Tassinary, L. G., & Hansen, K. A. (1998). A critical test of the waist-to-hip ratio hypothesis of female physical attractiveness. *Psychological Science, 9,* 150–155.

Taylor, K. M., & Shepperd, J. A. (1998). Bracing for the worst: Severity, testing, and feedback timing as moderators of the optimistic bias. *Personality and Social Psychology Bulletin, 24,* 915–926.

Taylor, S. E., & Brown, J. D. (1988). Illusion and well-being: A social psychological perspective on mental health. *Psychological Bulletin, 103,* 193–210.

Taylor, S. E., Buunk, B. P., & Aspinwall, L. G. (1990). Social comparison, stress, and coping. *Personality and Social Psychology Bulletin, 16,* 74–89.

Taylor, S. E., Helgeson, V. S., Reed, G. M., & Skokan, L. A. (1991). Self-generated feelings of control and adjustment to physical illness. *Journal of Social Issues, 47,* 91–109.

Taylor, S. E., Neter, E., & Wayment, H. A. (1995). Self-evaluation processes. *Personality and Social Psychology Bulletin, 21,* 1278–1287.

Taylor, S. E., Pham, L. B., Rivkin, I. D., & Armor, D. A. (1998). Harnessing the imagination: Mental stimulation, self-regulation, and coping. *American Psychologist, 53,* 429–439.

Taylor, S. P. (1967). Aggressive behavior and physiological arousal as a function of provocation and the tendency to inhibit aggression. *Journal of Personality, 35,* 297–310.

Technical Working Group for Eyewitness Evidence. (1999). *Eyewitness evidence: A guide for law enforcement* [Booklet]. Washington, DC: United States Department of Justice, Office of Justice Programs.

Teens top elderly as victims of crime. (1995, June 1). Albany *Times Union,* p. A13.

Tellegen, A., Watson, D., & Clark, L. A. (1999). On the dimensional and hierarchical structure of affect. *Psychological Science, 10,* 297–309.

Tennen, H., Affleck, G., Armeli, S., & Carney, M. A. (2000). A daily process approach to coping: Linking theory, research, and practice. *American Psychologist, 55,* 626–636.

Terman, L. M., & Buttenwieser, P. (1935a). Personality factors in marital compatibility: I. *Journal of Social Psychology, 6,* 143–171.

Terman, L. M., & Buttenwieser, P. (1935b). Personality factors in marital compatibility: II. *Journal of Social Psychology, 6,* 267–289.

Terry, R. L., & Krantz, J. H. (1993). Dimensions of trait attributions associated with eyeglasses, men's facial hair, and women's hair length. *Journal of Applied Social Psychology, 23,* 1757–1769.

Tesser, A. (1993). On the importance of heritability in psychological research: The case of attitudes. *Psychological Review, 100,* 129–142.

Tesser, A. (2001). On the plasticity of self-defense. *Current Directions in Psychological Science, 10,* 66–69.

Tesser, A., & Martin, L. (1996). The psychology of evaluation. In E. T. Higgins & A. W. Kruglanski (Eds.), *Social psychology: Handbook of basic principles* (pp. 400–423). New York: Guilford Press.

Tesser, A., Martin, L. L., & Cornell, D. P. (1996). On the substitutability of the self-protecting mechanisms. In P. Gollwitzer & J. Bargh (Eds.), *The psychology of action* (pp. 48–68). New York: Guilford.

Tetlock, P. E., Peterson, R. S., McGuire, C., Change, S., & Feld, P. (1992). Assessing political group dynamics: A test of the groupthink model. *Journal of Personality and Social Psychology, 63,* 403–425.

Tett, R. P., & Meyer, J. P. (1993). Job satisfaction, organizational commitment, turnover intention, and turnover: Path analyses based on meta-analytic findings. *Personnel Psychology, 46,* 259–293.

The spread of HIV. (1999, November 8). *Time,* 84.

Thompson, C. (1998, February 21). Associated Press.

Thompson, D. (1992). The danger in doomsaying. *Time, 139*(10), 61.

Thompson, J. M., Whiffen, V. E., & Blain, M. D. (1995). Depressive symptoms, sex and perceptions of intimate relationships. *Journal of Social and Personal Relationships, 12,* 49–66.

Thompson, L. (1998). *The mind and heart of the negotiator.* Upper Saddle River, NJ: Prentice-Hall.

Thompson, M. M., Zanna, M. P., & Griffin, D. W. (1995). Let's not be indifferent about attitudinal ambivalence. In R. E. Petty & J. A. Krosnick (Eds.), *Attitude strength: Antecedents and consequences* (pp. 361–386). Mahwah, NJ: Erlbaum.

Thompson, W. C., Cowan, C. L., & Rosenhan, D. L. (1980). Focus of attention mediates the impact of negative affect on altruism. *Journal of Personality and Social Psychology, 38,* 291–300.

Thoreau, H. D. (1906). Journal entry for 20 Feb. 1859.1.

Thornton, B. (1992). Repression and its mediating influence on the defensive attribution of responsibility. *Journal of Research in Personality, 26,* 44–57.

Thornton, B., Leo, R., & Alberg, K. (1991). Gender role typing, the superwoman ideal, and the potential for eating disorders. *Sex Roles, 25,* 469–484.

Tice, D. M., & Baumeister, R. F. (1997). Longitudinal study of procrastination, performance, stress, and health: The costs and benefits of dawdling. *Psychological Science, 8,* 454–458.

Tice, D. M., Bratslavsky, E., & Baumeister, R. F. (2000). Emotional distress regulation takes precedence over impulse control: If you feel bad, do it! *Journal of Personality and Social Psychology, 80,* 53–67.

Tice, D. M., Butler, J. L., Muraven, M. B., & Stillwell, A. M. (1995). When modesty prevails: Differential favorability of self-presentation to friends and strangers. *Journal of Personality and Social Psychology, 69,* 1120–1138.

Tidwell, M.-C. O., Reis, H. T., & Shaver, P. R. (1996). Attachment, attractiveness, and social interaction: A diary study. *Journal of Personality and Social Psychology, 71,* 729–745.

Tiedens, L. Z. (2001). Anger and advancement versus sadness and subjugation: The effect of negative emotion expressions on social status control. *Journal of Personality and Social Psychology, 80,* 86–94.

Timmers, M., Fischer, A. H., & Manstead, A. S. R. (1998). Gender differences in motives for regulating emotions. *Personality and Social Psychology Bulletin, 24,* 974–985.

Tjosvold, D. (1993). *Learning to manage conflict: Getting people to work together productively.* New York: Lexington.

Tjosvold, D., & DeDreu, C. (1997). Managing conflict in Dutch organizations: A test of the relevance of Deutsch's cooperation theory. *Journal of Applied Social Psychology, 27,* 2213–2227.

Toch, H. (1985). *Violent men* (rev. ed.). Cambridge, MA: Schenkman.

Toi, M., & Batson, C. D. (1982). More evidence that empathy is a source of altruistic motivation. *Journal of Personality and Social Psychology, 43,* 281–292.

Tomaka, J., & Blascovich, J. (1994). Effects of justice beliefs on cognitive appraisal of and subjective, physiological, and behavioral responses to potential stress. *Journal of Personality and Social Psychology, 67,* 732–740.

Tomasky, M. (2000, September 11). The N-word. *New York,* 40–41.

Tomes, N. (1998). *The gospel of germs: Men, women, and the microbe in American life.* Cambridge, MA: Harvard University Press.

Toobin, J. (1995, July 17). Putting it in black and white. *New Yorker,* 31–34.

Towles-Schwen, T., & Fazio, R. H. (2001). On the origins of racial attitudes: Correlates of childhood experiences. *Personality and Social Psychology Bulletin, 27,* 162–175.

Townsend, J. M. (1995). Sex without emotional involvement: An evolutionary interpretation of sex differences. *Archives of Sexual Behavior, 24,* 173–206.

Townsend, J. M., & Wasserman, T. (1997). The perception of sexual attractiveness: Sex differences in variability. *Archives of Sexual Behavior, 26,* 243–268.

Trapnell, P. D., & Campbell, J. D. (1999). Private self-consciousness and the five-factor model of personality: Distinguishing rumination from reflection. *Journal of Personality and Social Psychology, 76,* 284–304.

Trevarthen, C. (1993). The function of emotions in early infant communication and development. In J. Nadel & L. Camaioni (Eds.), *New perspectives in early communication development* (pp. 48–81). London: Routledge.

Triandis, H. C. (1990). Cross-cultural studies of individualism and collectivism. In J. J. Berman (Ed.), *Nebraska symposium on motivation, 1989* (pp. 41–133). Lincoln: University of Nebraska Press.

Trinke, S. J., & Bartholomew, K. (1997). Hierarchies of attachment relationships in young adulthood. *Journal of Social and Personal Relationships, 14,* 603–625.

Trobst, K. K., Collins, R. L., & Embree, J. M. (1994). The role of emotion in social support provision: Gender, empathy, and expressions of distress. *Journal of Social and Personal Relationships, 11,* 45–62.

Trope, Y., & Liberman, A. (1996). Social hypothesis testing: Cognitive and motivational mechanisms. In E. T. Higgins & A. W. Kruglanski (Eds.), *Social psychology: Handbook of basic principles* (pp. 239–270). New York: Guilford.

Tschanz, B. T., & Rhodewalt, F. (2001). Autobiography, reputation, and the self: On the role of evaluative valence and self-consistency of the self-relevant information. *Journal of Experimental Social Psychology, 37,* 32–48.

Tucker, J. S., Friedman, H. S., Schwartz, J. E., Criqui, M. H., Tomlinson-Keasey, C., Wingard, D. L., & Martin, L. R. (1997). Parental divorce: Effects on individual behavior and longevity. *Journal of Personality and Social Psychology, 73,* 381–391.

Tucker, P., & Aron, A. (1993). Passionate love and marital satisfaction at key transition points in the family life cycle. *Journal of Social and Clinical Psychology, 12,* 135–147.

Tversky, A., & Kahneman, D. (1973). Availability: A heuristic for judging frequency and probability. *Cognitive Psychology, 5,* 207–232.

Tversky, A., & Kahneman, D. (1982). Judgment under uncertainty: Heuristics and biases. In D. Kahneman, P. Slovic, & A. Tversky (Eds.), *Judgment under uncertainty* (pp. 3–20). New York: Cambridge University Press.

Twenge, J. M. (2001). Changes in women's assertiveness in response to status and roles: A cross-temporal meta-analysis, 1931–1993. *Journal of Personality and Social Psychology, 81,* 133–145.

Twenge, J. M., & Manis, M. M. (1998). First-name desirability and adjustment: Self-satisfaction, others' ratings, and family background. *Journal of Applied Social Psychology, 24,* 41–51.

Tykocinski, O. E. (2001). I never had a chance: Using hindsight tactics to mitigate disappointments. *Personality and Social Psychology Bulletin, 27,* 376–382.

Tykocinski, O. E., & Pittman, T. S. (1998). The consequences of doing nothing: Inaction inertia as avoidance of anticipated counterfactual regret. *Journal of Personality and Social Psychology, 73,* 607–616.

Tykocinski, O. E., Pittman, T. S., & Tuttle, E. E. (1995). Inaction inertia: Foregoing future benefits as a result of an initial failure to act. *Journal of Personality and Social Psychology, 68,* 793–803.

Tyler, T. R., & Lind, E. A. (1992). A relational model of authority in groups. In M. Zanna (Ed.), *Advances in experimental social psychology* (Vol. 27, pp. 115–191). New York: Academic Press.

Tyler, T. R., & Smith, H. J. (1997). Social justice and social movements. In D. Gilbert, S. T. Firks, & G. Lindzey (Eds.), *Handbook of social psychology* (Vol. 2, 2nd ed., pp. 595–629. New York: McGraw-Hill.

Tyler, T. R., Boeckmann, R. J., Smith, H. J., & Huo, Y. J. (1997). *Social justice in a diverse society.* Boulder, CO: Westview.

Tyler, T. R., Lind, E. A., Ohbuchi, K. I., Sugawara, I., & Huo, Y. J. (1998). Conflict with outsiders: Disputing within and across cultural boundaries. *Personality and Social Psychology Bulletin, 24,* 137–146.

U.S. Department of Justice. (1994). *Criminal victimization in the United States, 1992.* Washington, DC: Office of Justice Programs, Bureau of Justice Statistics.

U.S. Department of Labor. (1991). *A report on the glass ceiling initiative.* Washington, DC: U.S. Department of Labor.

U.S. Department of Labor. (1992). *Employment and earnings* (Vol. 39, No. 5: Table A-22). Washington, DC: U.S. Department of Labor.

Uchino, B. N., Uno, D., & Holt-Lunstad, J. (1999). Social support, physiological processes, and health. *Current Directions in Psychological Science, 8,* 145–148.

Udry, J. R. (1980). Changes in the frequency of marital intercourse from panel data. *Archives of Sexual Behavior, 9,* 319–325.

Ullman, C. (1987). From sincerity to authenticity: Adolescents' view of the "true self." *Journal of Personality, 55,* 583–595.

Unger, L. S., & Thumuluri, L. K. (1997). Trait empathy and continuous helping: The case of volunteerism. *Journal of Social Behavior and Personality, 12,* 785–800.

Ungerer, J. A., Dolby, R., Waters, B., Barnett, B., Kelk, N., & Lewin, V. (1990). The early development of empathy: Self-regulation and individual differences in the first year. *Motivation and Emotion, 14,* 93–106.

Urbanski, L. (1992, May 21). Study uncovers traits people seek in friends. *The Evangelist,* 4.

Vaillant, G. E. (2002). *Aging well.* New York: Little, Brown.

Vallone, R., Ross, L., & Lepper, M. (1985). Social status, cognitive alternatives, and intergroup relations. In H. Tajfel (Ed.), *Differentiation between social groups* (pp. 201–226). London: Academic Press.

Van Dyne, L., & LePine, J. A. (1998). Helping and voice extra-role behaviors: Evidence of construct and predictive validity. *Academy of Management Journal, 41,* 108–119.

Van Hook, E., & Higgins, E. T. (1988). Self-related problems beyond the self-concept: Motivational consequences of discrepant self-guides. *Journal of Personality and Social Psychology, 55,* 625–633.

Van Lange, P. A. M., & Kuhlman, M. D. (1994). Social value orientation and impressions of partner's honesty and intelligence: A test of the might versus morality effect. *Journal of Personality and Social Psychology, 67,* 126–141.

Van Lange, P. A. M., & Rusbult, C. E. (1995). My relationship is better than—and not as bad as—yours is: The perception of superiority in close relationships. *Personality and Social Psychology Bulletin, 21,* 32–44.

Van Overwalle, F. (1997). Dispositional attributions require the joint application of the methods of difference and agreement. *Personality and Social Psychology Bulletin, 23,* 974–980.

Van Overwalle, F. (1998). Causal explanation as constraint satisfaction: A critique and a feedforward connectionist alternative. *Journal of Personality and Social Psychology, 74,* 312–328.

VanOyen Witvliet, C., Ludwig, T. E., & Laan, K. L. V. (2001). Granting forgiveness or harboring grudges:

Implications for emotion, physiology, and health. *Psychological Science, 12,* 117–123.

Van Volkom, M. (2000). *Sibling relationships in middle and older adulthood.* Unpublished manuscript, University at Albany, State University of New York.

Vanbeselaere, N. (1991). The different effects of simple and crossed categorizations: A result of the category differentiation process of differential category salience? In W. Stroebe & M. Hewstone (Eds.), *European review of social psychology* (Vol. 2, pp. 247–278). Chichester, UK: Wiley.

Vanderbilt, A. (1957). *Amy Vanderbilt's complete book of etiquette.* Garden City, NY: Doubleday.

Vanman, E. J., Paul, B. Y., Ito, T. A., & Miller, N. (1997). The modern face of prejudice and structure features that moderate the effect of cooperation on affect. *Journal of Personality and Social Psychology, 73,* 941–959.

Vecchio, R. (1997). *Leadership.* Notre Dame, IN: University of Notre Dame Press.

Vermande, M. M., van den Oord, E. J. C. G., Goudena, P. P., & Rispens, J. (2000). Structural characteristics of aggressor–victim relationships in Dutch school classes of 4- to 5-year-olds. *Aggressive Behavior, 26,* 11–32.

Vinokur, A., & Burnstein, E. (1974). Effects of partially shared persuasive arguments on group-induced shifts: A group problem-solving approach. *Journal of Personality and Social Psychology, 29,* 305–315.

Vobejda, B. (1997, June 3). Pain of divorce follows children. *Washington Post.*

Vogel, D. A., Lake, M. A., Evans, S., & Karraker, K. H. (1991). Children's and adults' sex-stereotyped perceptions of infants. *Sex Roles, 24,* 605–616.

Vonk, R. (1998). The slime effect: Suspicion and dislike of likeable behavior toward superiors. *Journal of Personality and Social Psychology, 74,* 849–864.

Vonk, R., & van Knippenberg, A. (1995). Processing attitude statements from in-group and out-group members: Effects of within-group and within-person inconsistencies on reading times. *Journal of Personality and Social Psychology, 68,* 215–227.

Voyer, D., Voyer, S., & Bryden, M. P. (1995). Magnitude of sex differences in spatial abilities: A meta-analysis and consideration of critical variables. *Psychological Bulletin, 117,* 250–270.

Vrugt, A., & Luyerink, M. (2000). The contribution of bodily posture to gender stereotypical impressions. *Social Behavior and Personality, 28,* 91–104.

Waldman, D. A., Ramiriz, G. G., House, R. J., & Puranam, P. (2001). Does leadership matter? CEO leadership attributes and profitability under conditions of perceived environmental uncertainty. *Academy of Management Journal, 44,* 134–143.

Walker, L. A. (2001, September 16). We can control how we age. *Parade,* 4–5.

Walker, S., Richardson, D. S., & Green, L. R. (2000). Aggression among older adults: The relationship of interaction networks and gender role to direct and indirect responses. *Aggressive Behavior, 26,* 145–154.

Waller, N. G., Kojetin, B. A., Bouchard, T. J. Jr., Lykken, D. T., & Tellegen, A. (1990). Genetic and environmental influences on religious interests, attitudes, and values: A study of twins reared apart and together. *Psychological Science, 1,* 138–142.

Walmsley, D. J., & Lewis, G. J. (1989). The pace of pedestrian flows in cities. *Environment and Behavior, 21,* 123–150.

Walsh, T., & Devlin, M. J. (1998). Eating disorders: Progress and problems. *Science, 280,* 1387–1390.

Walster, E., & Festinger, L. (1962). The effectiveness of "overheard" persuasive communication. *Journal of Abnormal and Social Psychology, 65,* 395–402.

Walster, E., Walster, G. W., Piliavin, J., & Schmidt, L. (1973). "Playing hard-to-get": Understanding an elusive phenomenon. *Journal of Personality and Social Psychology, 26,* 113–121.

Wanous, J. P., Reiches, A. E., & Hudy, M. J. (1997). Overall job satisfaction: How good are single-item measures? *Journal of Applied Psychology, 82,* 247–252.

Ward, L. M., & Rivadeneyra, R. (1999). Contributions of entertainment television to adolescents' sexual attitudes and expectations: The role of viewing amount versus viewer involvement. *Journal of Sex Research, 36,* 237–249.

Wardle, J., Bindra, R., Fairclough, B., & Westcombe, A. (1993). Culture and body image: Body perception and weight concern in young Asian and Caucasian British women. *Journal of Community & Applied Social Psychology, 3,* 173–181.

Waters, H. F., Block, D., Friday, C., & Gordon, J. (1993, July 12). Networks under the gun. *Newsweek,* 64–66.

Watson, C. B., Chemers, M. M., & Preiser, N. (2001). Collective efficacy: A multilevel analysis. *Personality and Social Psychology Bulletin, 27,* 1057–1068.

Watson, D., & Clark, L. A. (1997). Extraversion and its positive emotional core. In R. Hogan, J. A. Johnson, & S. R. Briggs (Eds.), *Handbook of personality psychology* (pp. 767–793). San Diego, CA: Academic Press.

Watson, D., Hubbard, B., & Wiese, D. (2000). Self–other agreement in personality and affectivity: The role of acquaintanceship, trait visibility, and assumed similarity. *Journal of Personality and Social Psychology, 78,* 546–558.

Watts, B. L. (1982). Individual differences in circadian activity rhythms and their effects on roommate relationships. *Journal of Personality, 50,* 374–384.

Wayment, H. A., & Taylor, S. E. (1995). Self-evaluation processes: Motives, information use, and self-esteem. *Journal of Personality, 63,* 729–757.

Wayne, S. J., & Ferris, G. R. (1990). Influence tactics, and exchange quality in supervisor–subordinate interactions: A laboratory experiment and field study. *Journal of Applied Psychology, 75,* 487–499.

Wayne, S. J., & Kacmar, K. M. (1991). The effects of impression management on the performance appraisal process. *Organizational Behavior and Human Decision Processes, 48,* 70–88.

Wayne, S. J., & Liden, R. C. (1995). Effects of impression management on performance ratings: A longitudinal study. *Academy of Management Journal, 38,* 232–260.

Wayne, S. J., Liden, R. C., Graf, I. K., & Ferris, G. R. (1997). The role of upward influence tactics in human resource decisions. *Personnel Psychology, 50,* 979–1006.

Webley, P., & Siviter, C. (2000). Why do some owners allow their dogs to foul the pavement? The social psychology of a minor rule infraction. *Journal of Applied Social Psychology, 30,* 1371–1380.

Wegner, D. M. (1992a). The premature demise of the solo experiment. *Personality and Social Psychology Bulletin, 18,* 504–508.

Wegner, D. M. (1992b). You can't always think what you want: Problems in the suppression of unwanted thoughts. In M. Zanna (Ed.), *Advances in experimental social psychology* (Vol. 25, pp. 193–225). San Diego, CA: Academic Press.

Wegner, D. M. (1994). Ironic processes of mental control. *Psychological Review, 101,* 34–54.

Wegner, D. M., & Bargh, J. A. (1998). Control and automaticity in social life. In D. T. Gilbert, S. T. Fiske, & G. Lindsey (Eds.), *Handbook of social psychology* (4th ed.). New York: McGraw-Hill.

Wegner, D. M., & Gold, D. B. (1995). Fanning old flames: Emotional and cognitive effects of suppressing thoughts of a past relationship. *Journal of Personality and Social Psychology, 68,* 782–792.

Wegner, D. M., & Zanakos, S. (1994). Chronic thought suppression. *Journal of Personality, 62,* 615–640.

Weick, K. E., & Gifillan, D. P. (1971). Fate of arbitrary traditions in a laboratory microculture. *Journal of Personality and Social Psychology, 17,* 179–191.

Weidner, G., Istvan, J., & McKnight, J. D. (1989). Clusters of behavioral coronary risk factors in employed women and men. *Journal of Applied Social Psychology, 19,* 468–480.

Weinberg, M. S., Lottes, I. L., & Shaver, F. M. (1995). Swedish or American heterosexual college youth: Who is more permissive? *Archives of Sexual Behavior, 24,* 409–437.

Weiner, B. (1980). A cognitive (attribution) emotion–action model of motivated behavior: An analysis of judgments of help-giving. *Journal of Personality and Social Psychology, 39,* 186–200.

Weiner, B. (1985). An attributional theory of achievement motivation and emotion. *Psychological Review, 92,* 548–573.

Weiner, B. (1993). On sin versus sickness: A theory of perceived responsibility and social motivation. *American Psychologist, 48,* 957–965.

Weiner, B. (1995). *Judgments of responsibility: A foundation for a theory of social conduct.* New York: Guilford.

Weiner, B., Amirkhan, J., Folkes, V. S., & Verette, J. A. (1987). An attributional analysis of excuse giving: Studies of a naive theory of emotion. *Journal of Personality and Social Psychology, 52,* 316–324.

Weinstein, N. D., Lyon, J. E., Rothman, A. J., & Cuite, C. L. (2000). Changes in perceived vulnerability following natural disaster. *Journal of Social and Clinical Psychology, 19,* 372–395.

Weis, D. L. (1983). Affective reactions of women to their initial experience of coitus. *Journal of Sex Research, 19,* 209–237.

Weisberg, J. (1990, October 1). Fighting words. *The New Republic,* 42.

Weiss, H. M., & Cropanzano, R. (1996). Affective events theory: A theoretical discussion of the structure, causes, and consequences of affective experiences at work. *Research in Organizational Behavior, 18,* 1–74.

Weissenberg, P., & Kavanagh, M. H. (1972). The independence of initiating structure and consideration: A review of the evidence. *Personnel Psychology, 25,* 119–130.

Weldon, E., & Mustari, L. (1988). Felt dispensability in groups of coactors: The effects of shared responsibility and explicit anonymity on cognitive effort. *Organizational Behavior and Human Decision Processes, 41,* 330–351.

Wells, G. L. (1984). The psychology of lineup identification. *Journal of Applied Social Psychology, 14,* 89–103.

Wells, G. L. (1993). What do we know about eyewitness identification? *American Psychologist, 48,* 553–571.

Wells, G. L., & Bradfield, A. L. (1999). Distortions in eyewitnesses' recollections: Can the postidentification-feedback effect be moderated? *Psychological Science, 10,* 138–144.

Wells, G. L., & Luus, C. A. E. (1990). Police lineups as experiments: Social methodology as a framework for properly conducted lineups. *Personality and Social Psychology Bulletin, 16,* 106–117.

Wells, G. L., Luus, C. A. E., & Windschitl, P. D. (1994). Maximizing the utility of eyewitness identification evidence. *Current Directions in Psychological Science, 3,* 194–197.

Wells, G. L., Malpass, R. S., Lindsay, R. C. L., Fisher, R. P., Turtle, J. W., & Fulero, S. M. (2000). From the lab to the police station: A successful application of eyewitness research. *American Psychologist, 55,* 581–598.

Wentura, D., Rothermund, K., & Bak, P. (2000). Automatic vigilance: The attention-grabbing power of approach- and avoidance-related social information. *Journal of Personality and Social Psychology, 78,* 1024–1037.

West, S. G., & Brown, T. J. (1975). Physical attractiveness, the severity of the emergency, and helping: A field experiment and interpersonal simulation. *Journal of Experimental Social Psychology, 11,* 531–538.

Wheeler, L., & Kim, Y. (1997). What is beautiful is culturally good: The physical attractiveness stereotype has different content in collectivistic cultures. *Personality and Social Psychology Bulletin, 23,* 795–800.

Whiffen, V. E., Aube, J. A., Thompson, J. M., & Campbell, T. L. (2000). Attachment beliefs and interpersonal contexts associated with dependency and self-criticism. *Journal of Social and Clinical Psychology, 19,* 184–205.

White, R. K. (1977). Misperception in the Arab-Israeli conflict. *Journal of Social Issues, 33,* 190–221.

Wicker, A. W. (1969). Attitudes versus actions: The relationship of verbal and overt behavioral responses to attitude objects. *Journal of Social Issues, 25,* 41–78.

Wiederman, M. W. (2000). Women's body image self-consciousness during physical intimacy with a partner. *Journal of Sex Research, 37,* 60–68.

Wiederman, M. W., & Allgeier, E. R. (1996). Expectations and attributions regarding extramarital sex among young married individuals. *Journal of Psychology & Human Sexuality, 8,* 21–35.

Wiener, Y., Muczyk, J. P., & Martin, H. J. (1992). Self-esteem and job involvement as moderators of the relationship between work satisfaction and well-being. *Journal of Social Behavior and Personality, 7,* 539–554.

Wieselquist, J., Rusbult, C. E., Agnew, C. R., & Foster, C. A. (1999). Commitment, pro-relationship behavior, and trust in close relationships. *Journal of Personality and Social Psychology, 77,* 942–966.

Williams, D. E., & D'Alessandro, J. D. (1994). A comparison of three measures of androgyny and their relationship to psychological adjustment. *Journal of Social Behavior and Personality, 9,* 469–480.

Williams, G. P., & Kleinke, C. L. (1993). Effects of mutual gaze and touch on attraction, mood, and cardiovascular reactivity. *Journal of Research in Personality, 27,* 170–183.

Williams, K. B., Radefeld, P. A., Binning, J. F., & Suadk, J. R. (1993). When job candidates are "hard-" versus "easy-to-get": Effects of candidate availability on employment decisions. *Journal of Applied Social Psychology, 23,* 169–198.

Williams, K. D., & Karau, S. J. (1991). Social loafing and social compensation: The effects of expectations of co-worker performance. *Journal of Personality and Social Psychology, 61,* 570–581.

Williams, K. D., Cheung, C. K. T., & Choi, W. (2000). Cyberostracism: Effects of being ignored over the Internet. *Journal of Personality and Social Psychology, 79,* 748–762.

Williams, K. D., Harkins, S., & Latané, B. (1981). Identifiability as a deterrent to social loafing: Two cheering experiments. *Journal of Personality and Social Psychology, 40,* 303–311.

Williams, K. J., Suls, J., Alliger, G. M., Learner, S. M., & Wan, C. K. (1992). Multiple role juggling and daily mood states in working mothers: An experience sampling study. *Journal of Applied Psychology, 76,* 633–638.

Williamson, G. M., & Schulz, R. (1995). Caring for a family member with cancer: Past communal behavior and affective reactions. *Journal of Applied Social Psychology, 25,* 93–116.

Williamson, T. M. (1993). From interrogation to investigative interviewing: Strategic trends in police questioning. *Journal of Community and Applied Social Psychology, 3,* 89–99.

Wilson, A. (2000, February 14). Lock 'em up! *Time,* 68.

Wilson, A. E., & Ross, M. (2000). The frequency of temporal-self and social comparisons in people's personal appraisals. *Journal of Personality and Social Psychology, 78,* 928–942.

Wilson, A. E., & Ross, M. (2001). From chump to champ: People's appraisals of their earlier and present selves. *Journal of Personality and Social Psychology, 80,* 572–584.

Wilson, D. W. (1981). Is helping a laughing matter? *Psychology, 18,* 6–9.

Wilson, J. P., & Petruska, R. (1984). Motivation, model attributes, and prosocial behavior. *Journal of Personality and Social Psychology, 46,* 458–468.

Wilson, J. Q. (1993, June 21). Stagestruck. *The New Republic,* 30–33, 36.

Wilson, M., Daly, M., Gordon, S., & Pratt, A. (1996). Sex differences in valuations of the environment. *Population and Environment, 18,* 143–159.

Wilson, T. D. (1990). Self-persuasion via self-reflection. In M. Olson & M. P. Zanna (Eds.), *Self-inference processes: The Ontario Symposium* (Vol. 6, pp. 43–67). Hillsdale, NJ: Erlbaum.

Wilson, T. D., & Brekke, N. (1994). Mental contamination and mental correction: Unwanted influences on judgments and evaluations. *Psychological Bulletin, 116,* 117–142.

Wilson, T. D., & Kraft, D. (1993). Why do I love thee?: Effects of repeated introspections about a dating relationship on attitudes toward the relationship. *Personality and Social Psychology Bulletin, 19,* 409–418.

Wilson, T. D., & Schooler, J. (1991). Thinking too much: Introspection can reduce the quality of preferences and decisions. *Journal of Personality and Social Psychology, 60,* 181–192.

Winett, R. A. (1998). Developing more effective health-behavior programs: Analyzing the epidemiological and biological bases for activity and exercise programs. *Applied & Preventive Psychology, 7,* 209–224.

Winquist, J. R., & Larson, J. R., Jr. (1998). Information pooling: When it impacts group decision making. *Journal of Personality and Social Psychology, 74,* 317–377.

Winstead, B. A., Derlega, V. J., Montgomery, M. J., & Pilkington, C. (1995). The quality of friendships at work and job satisfaction. *Journal of Social and Personal Relationships, 12,* 199–215.

Wiseman, H. (1997). Far away from home: The loneliness experience of overseas students. *Journal of Social and Clinical Psychology, 16,* 277–298.

Wolf, N. (1992). Father figures. *New Republic, 207*(15), 22, 24–25.

Wolf, S., & Bugaj, A. M. (1990). The social impact of courtroom witnesses. *Social Behaviour, 5,* 1–13.

Wolfe, B. M., & Baron, R. A. (1971). Laboratory aggression related to aggression in naturalistic social situation: Effects of an aggressive model on the behavior of college student and prisoner observers. *Psychonomic Science, 24,* 193–194.

Wood, W. (1982). Retrieval of attitude-relevant information from memory: Effects on susceptibility to persuasion on intrinsic motivation. *Journal of Personality and Social Psychology, 42,* 798–810.

Wood, W., Wong, F. Y., & Cachere, J. G. (1991). Effects of media violence on viewers' aggression in unconstrained social interaction. *Psychological Bulletin, 109,* 371–383.

Wood, W., Christensen, P. N., Hebl, M. R., & Rothgerber, H. (1997). Conformity to sex-typed norms, affect, and the self-concept. *Journal of Personality and Social Psychology, 73,* 523–535.

Wood, W., Pool, G. J., Leck, K., & Purvis, D. (1996). Self-definition, defensive processing, and influence: The normative impact of majority and minority groups. *Journal of Personality and Social Psychology, 71,* 1181–1193.

Woodbury, R. (2000, April 17). Bugging a gravestone. *Time,* 68.

Wright, R. (1994, November 28). Feminists, meet Mr. Darwin. *The New Republic,* 34, 36–37, 40, 42, 44–46.

Wright, R. (1995, March 13). The biology of violence. *The New Yorker,* 68–77.

Wright, S. C., Aron, A., McLaughlin-Volpe, T., & Ropp, S. A. (1997). The extended contact effect: Knowledge of cross-group friendships and prejudice. *Journal of Personality and Social Psychology, 73,* 73–90.

Wright, S. S. (2000). Looking at the self in a rose-colored mirror: Unrealistically positive self-views and academic performance. *Journal of Social and Clinical Psychology, 19,* 451–462.

Wuensch, K. L., Castellow, W. A., & Moore, C. H. (1991). Effects of defendant attractiveness and type of crime on juridic judgment. *Journal of Social Behavior and Personality, 6,* 713–724.

Wyer, R. S., Jr., & Srull, T. K. (Eds.). (1994). *Handbook of social cognition* (2nd ed.) (Vol. 1). Hillsdale, NJ: Erlbaum.

Wyer, R. S., Jr., Budesheim, T. L., Lambert, A. J., & Swan, S. (1994). Person memory judgment: Pragmatic influences on impressions formed in a social context. *Journal of Personality and Social Psychology, 66,* 254–267.

Yates, S. (1992). Lay attributions about distress after a natural disaster. *Personality and Social Psychology Bulletin, 18,* 217–222.

Yik, M. S. M., Bond, M. H., & Paulhus, D. L. (1998). Do Chinese self-enhance or self-efface? It's a matter of domain. *Personality and Social Psychology Bulletin, 24,* 399–406.

Yik, M. S. M., Russell, J. A., & Barrett, L. F. (1999). Structure of self-reported current affect: Integration and beyond. *Journal of Personality and Social Psychology, 77,* 600–619.

Yoon, C. K. (1999, June 8). Study exposes craven motive of the brave meerkat sentry. *New York Times,* F3.

Yoshida, T. (1977). Effects of cognitive dissonance on task evaluation and task performance. *Japanese Journal of Psychology, 48,* 216–223.

Youille, J. C., & Cutshall, J. L. (1986). A case study of eyewitness memory of a crime. *Journal of Applied Psychology, 71,* 291–301.

Yovetich, N. A., & Rusbult, C. E. (1994). Accommodative behavior in close relationships: Exploring transformation of motivation. *Journal of Experimental Social Psychology, 30,* 138–164.

Yu, W. (1996, May 12). Many husbands fail to share housework. *Albany Times Union,* pp. A1, A7.

Yukl, G., & Falbe, C. M. (1991). Importance of different power sources in downward and lateral relations. *Journal of Applied Psychology, 76,* 416–423.

Yukl, G. A. (1998). *Leadership in organizations* (4th ed.). Englewood Cliffs, NJ: Prentice-Hall.

Yzerbyt, V. Y., Rogier, A., & Fiske, S. T. (1998). Group entiativity and social attribution: On translating situational constraints into stereotypes. *Personality and Social Psychology Bulletin, 24,* 1089–1103.

Zaccaro, S. J., Foti, R. J., & Kenny, D. A. (1991). Self-monitoring and trait-based variance in leadership: An investigation of leader flexibility across multiple group situations. *Journal of Applied Psychology, 76,* 308–315.

Zajonc, R. B. (1965). Social facilitation. *Science, 149,* 269–274.

Zajonc, R. B. (1968). Attitudinal effects of mere exposure [monograph]. *Journal of Personality and Social Psychology, 9,* 1–27.

Zajonc, R. B., & McIntosh, D. N. (1992). Emotions research: Some promising questions and some questionable promises. *Psychological Science, 3,* 70–74.

Zajonc, R. B., & Sales, S. M. (1966). Social facilitation of dominant and subordinate responses. *Journal of Experimental Social Psychology, 2,* 160–168.

Zajonc, R. B., Heingartner, A., & Herman, E. M. (1969). Social enhancement and impairment of performance in the cockroach. *Journal of Personality and Social Psychology, 13,* 83–92.

Zajonc, R. B., Adelmann, P. K., Murphy, S. T., & Niedenthal, P. M. (1987). Convergence in the physical appearance of spouses. *Motivation and Emotion, 11,* 335–346.

Zammichieli, M. E., Gilroy, F. D., & Sherman, M. F. (1988). Relation between sex-role orientation and marital satisfaction. *Personality and Social Psychology Bulletin, 14,* 747–754.

Zanna, M. P., & Aziza, C. (1976). On the interaction of repression–sensitization and attention in resolving cognitive dissonance. *Journal of Personality and Social Psychology, 44,* 577–593.

Zdaniuk, B., & Levine, J. M. (1996). Anticipated interaction and thought generation: The role of faction size. *British Journal of Social Psychology, 35,* 201–218.

Zebrowitz, L. A. (1997). *Reading faces.* Boulder, CO: Westview Press.

Zebrowitz, L. A., & Collins, M. A. (1997). Accurate social perception at zero acquaintance: The affordances of a Gibsonian approach. *Personality and Social Psychology Review, 1,* 204–223.

Zebrowitz, L. A., Collins, M. A., & Dutta, R. (1998). The relationship between appearance and personality across the life span. *Personality and Social Psychology Bulletin, 24,* 736–749.

Zeitz, G. (1990). Age and work satisfaction in a government agency: A situational perspective. *Human Relations, 43,* 419–438.

Ziller, R. C. (1990). *Photographing the self: Methods for observing personal orientations.* Newbury Park, CA: Sage.

Zillmann, D. (1979). *Hostility and aggression.* Hillsdale, NJ: Erlbaum.

Zillmann, D. (1983). Transfer of excitation in emotional behavior. In J. T. Cacioppo & R. E. Petty (Eds.), *Social psychophysiology: A sourcebook* (pp. 215–240). New York: Guilford Press.

Zillmann, D. (1984). *Connections between sex and aggression.* Hillsdale, NJ: Erlbaum.

Zillmann, D. (1988). Cognition–excitation interdependencies in aggressive behavior. *Aggressive Behavior, 14,* 51–64.

Zillmann, D. (1993). Mental control of angry aggression. In D. M. Wegner & J. W. Pennebaker (Eds.), *Handbook of mental control.* Englewood Cliffs, NJ: Prentice-Hall.

Zillmann, D. (1994). Cognition–excitation interdependencies in the escalation of anger and angry aggression. In M. Potegal & J. F. Knutson (Eds.), *The dynamics of aggression.* Hillsdale, NJ: Erlbaum.

Zillmann, D., Baron, R. A., & Tamborini, R. (1981). The social costs of smoking: Effects of tobacco smoke on hostile behavior. *Journal of Applied Social Psychology, 11,* 548–561.

Zimbardo, P. G. (1977). *Shyness: What it is and what you can do about it.* Reading, MA: Addison-Wesley.

Zoglin, R. (1993). The shock of the blue. *Time, 142*(17), 71–72.

Zusne, L., & Jones, W. H. (1989). *Anomalistic psychology: A study of magical thinking* (2nd ed.). Hillsdale, NJ: Erlbaum.

Name Index

Subject Index

Credits

Chapter 1

Page 6, Photo Researchers, Inc. © USDA/Science Source; 7, © Robert Brenner/PhotoEdit; 11, (left) © Jeff Moore/Pressnet/Topham/The Image Works, (right) The Image Bank/© 1999–2001 GettyImages. All rights reserved; 16, (left) © SuperStock, (right) © Catherine Karnow/Woodfin Camp & Associates; 17, (left) Courtesy of Wallace Nutting, (right) Courtesy of Lincoln Faurer; 19 and 31, Photos courtesy of Robert A. Baron; 33, (left) © Najlan Feanny/Stock Boston, (right) © David Young-Wolff/PhotoEdit

Chapter 2

Pages 41, 42, and 43, Photos courtesy of Robert A. Baron; 48, © FPG International/GettyImages/E. Dygas; 59, (left) © M. Richards/PhotoEdit, (right) © Michael Szulc-Krzyzanowski/The Image Works; 60, (left) © AllSport/GettyImages, (right) © Pascal/Rondeau/AllSport/GettyImages; 64, (left) © Bob Daemmrich Photography, (right) © Tom Prettyman/PhotoEdit; 65, Courtesy of the Archives of the History of Psychology; 73, (left) © Robert Brenner/PhotoEdit, (middle) © Bonnie Kamin, (right) © Billy E. Barnes/PhotoEdit

Chapter 3

Page 81, © Michael Newman/PhotoEdit; 83, © Hulton Archive/GettyImages; 86, (left) © Tom Carter/PhotoEdit, (right) © David J. Sams/Stock Boston; 92, © Michael Dwyer/Stock Boston; 96, © Gary Mortimore/AllSport/GettyImages; 98, © Davies & Starr, Inc./Stone/GettyImages; 101, © J. Shaffer/PhotoEdit; 103, Photo courtesy of Robert A. Baron; 111, © SuperStock; 112, (left) © Mary Kate Denny/PhotoEdit, (middle) © Bonnie Kamin, (right) © SuperStock

Chapter 4

Page 119, Bruce Flynn/Stock Boston; 123, © R. Hutchings/PhotoEdit; 124, Stuart Cohen/The Image Works; 129, Courtesy of the Archives of the History of Psychology; 131, © Bob Daemmrich/Stock Boston; 135, Photo courtesy of Robert A. Baron; 136, © Eric Neurath/Stock Boston; 149, (left) © A. Ramey/PhotoEdit, (right) © R. Brenner/PhotoEdit; 152, (left) © Spencer Grant/PhotoEdit, (middle) © Tony Freeman/PhotoEdit, (right) © M. Neal McVay/Stock Boston; 154, © Nancy Alexander/PhotoEdit; 155, (left) © SuperStock, (middle) © Paul Conklin/PhotoEdit, (right) © M. Richards/PhotoEdit

Chapter 5

Page 163, Photo courtesy of Cognitive Evolution Group, University of Louisiana at Lafayette; 170, © Bob Daemmrich Photography; 177, © Bob Daemmrich Photography; 179, David Karp/AP/Wide World Photos; 181, © Michael Newman/PhotoEdit; 187, © Hulton Getty/GettyImages; 193, PhotoFest/© Lions Gate Films, "American Psycho 2000"; 198, Courtesy of State Farm Mutual Automobile Insurance Company; 203, (left) Photo Researchers, Inc./National Archives, (middle) © David Young-Wolff/PhotoEdit, (right, top) © Bachman/Photo Researchers, Inc., (right, bottom) Sean Dempsey/AP/Wide World Photos

Chapter 6

Page 209, Louis Lanzano/AP/Wide World Photos; 212, © Ricky Rogers/Reuters/GettyImages; 216, Photo by Visual News/GettyImages; 222, (left) Hillery Smith Garrison/AP/Wide World Photos, (right) Jim McKnight/AP/Wide World Photos; 223, © Elliott Erwitt/Magnum Photos; 231, © David Young-Wolff/PhotoEdit; 234, Adam Tanner/The Image Works; 246, Robert Burke/Stone/GettyImages; 248, © Robert Brenner/PhotoEdit; 249, (left) © Jeff Greenbery/PhotoEdit, (middle) David Cannon/Allsport, (right) H. Snitzer/StockBoston

Chapter 7

Page 257, © Tim Barnwen/Stock Boston; 262, (left) © Breni Jones/Stock Boston, (right) Sheila Terry/Science PhotoLibrary/Photo Researchers, Inc.; 272, Nova Stock/PhotoEdit; 275, Photo courtesy of PhotoFest/© 20th Century Fox. All rights reserved; 277, Photos courtesy of Dr. Judith H. Langlois, Charles and Sarah Seay Regents Professor, Dept. of Psychology, University of Texas, Austin. Used with permission; 278, (left) Mitchell Gerber/CORBIS, (right) KOBAL COLLECTION/KISPAL, MAGDALENE/REGENCY ENTERPRISES; 279, (left) © Mike Grey/Online USA/GettyImages, (right) © Rose Prouser/GettyImages; 288, PhotoFest; 292, (left) © Stock Boston, (right) © Bob Daemmrich/Stock Boston; 293, (left) © Bob Daemmrich/Stock Boston, (middle) © Tom McCarthy/PhotoEdit, (right,top) Eric Draper/AP/Wide World Photos, (right,bottom) © Spencer Grant/PhotoEdit

Chapter 8

Page 300, (left) Bob Adelman/Magnum Photos, Inc., (right) © Jean-Paul Ferrero/Auscape; 301, Photos courtesy of Professor

Colwyn Trevarthen, Dept. of Psychology, The University of Edinburgh; 303, Doug Mills/AP/Wide World Photos; 305, © Michael Wickes/The Image Works; 307, Edmee Rodriguez/AP Photos/News-Leader; 313, © Mary Kate Denny/PhotoEdit; 315, © Bob Daemmrich Photography; 319, Colin Paterson/PhotoDisc; 326, © Tom Miner/The Image Works; 328, (left) Ed Bailey/AP/Wide World Photos, (right) © Bob Daemmrich/Stock Boston; 331, © Michael Newman/PhotoEdit; 339, (left) Kenneth Lambert/AP/Wide World Photos, (right) Yun Jai-Hyoung/AP/Wide World Photos; 342, © SuperStock; 343, (left) PhotoFest, (middle) Damian Dovarganes/AP/Wide World Photos, (right) © Myrleen Ferguson/PhotoEdit

Chapter 9

Page 350, Steve Starr/Stock Boston; 351(left) Courtesy of the Archives of the History of Psychology; 353 (top) © Michael Newman/PhotoEdit, (bottom) © Tony Freeman/PhotoEdit; 357, PhotoFest/© Copyright 1952 Universal Pictures Co., Inc. Used with permission; 358, Photo courtesy of Robert A. Baron; 363, (left) James Wilson/Woodfin Camp & Associates, (right) © M. Richards/PhotoEdit; 369, © Tom McCarthy/PhotoEdit; 371, Rhoda Sidney/Stock Boston; 374, © Mary Kate Denny/PhotoEdit; 375, © Bernard Boutrit/Woodfin Camp & Associates; 381, © Paul Mozell 1992/Stock Boston; 383, (left) © Peter Vanderwarker/Stock Boston, (middle, top) © Bill Aron/PhotoEdit, (middle, bottom) © Michael Newman/PhotoEdit, (right, top) © Bachman, (right, bottom) © J. Nourak/PhotoEdit

Chapter 10

Page 400, © Bob Daemmrich/Stock Boston; 402, (left) Shooting Star, (right) Shooting Star/© Fox Broadcasting Co. All rights reserved; 409, © Dion Ogust/The Image Works; 410, PhotoFest; 413, © Mario Tama/Liaison/GettyImages; 418, © Michael Newman/PhotoEdit; 424, Ou Neakiry/AP/Wide World Photos; 427, © D. MacDonald/Animals Animals/Earth Scenes; 429 (left) © Jeff Greenberg/PhotoEdit, (right) © Richard Hutchings/PhotoEdit; 430, PhotoFest/© 1964 © by York-Jerry Lewis Productions and Paramount Pictures Corp. Used with permission.

Chapter 11

Page 435, Staton R. Winter/AP/Wide World Photos; 439, Courtesy of the Archives of the History of Psychology; 440, Photo courtesy of Robert A. Baron; 442, Paul Sancya/AP/Wide World Photos; 452, © Esbin-Anderson/The Image Works; 458, © Michael Newman/PhotoEdit; 463, AP/Wide World Photos; 466, Photo courtesy of Robert A. Baron; 468, (top) © David Young-Wolff/PhotoEdit, (bottom) © Gary Conner/PhotoEdit, 469, © Bonnie Kamin/PhotoEdit

Chapter 12

Page 475, (left) John Coletti/Stock Boston, (right) Don Spiro/Stone/GettyImages; 481, Nick Wass/AP/Wide World Photos; 487, © Michael Newman/PhotoEdit; 498, © Spencer Grant/PhotoEdit; 500, © Michael Newman/PhotoEdit; 513, (clockwise) © Jacksonville Journal Courier/The Image Works/Steve Warmowski; Richard Pasley/Stock Boston; © Bernard Asset/Agence Vandystadt/Photo Researchers, Inc.; © Ulrike Welsch/PhotoEdit

Chapter 13

Page 519, (left) © Bob Daemmrich/Stock Boston, (middle) Photo Researchers/Science Source, (right) © Bob Daemmrich Photography; 526, Charles Krupa/AP/Wide World Photos; 529, Copyright *American Psychological Society.* Blackwell Publishing, Ltd. These images originally appeared in *Psychological Science,* 10, 243–248. They are used with kind permission of Professor A. M. Burton, Dept.of Psychology, University of Glascow; 531, © John Neubauer/PhotoEdit; 553, Photo courtesy of Robert A. Baron; 556, all images Corbis-Bettmann/GettyImages, Abraham Lincoln photograph by Alex Hesler; 564, (left) © John Nordell/The Image Works, (right) Steve Ueckert/AP/Wide World Photos; 565, (left) AP/Agence France Press Pool/Vince Bucci, (right) Philip Kamrass-Albany Times Union/The Image Works